Beyond the Water's Edge

An Introduction to U.S. Foreign Policy

Donald M. Snow
University of Alabama

Eugene Brown
Lebanon Valley College

St. Martin's Press
New York

Sponsoring editor: Beth A. Gillett
Manager, publishing services: Emily Berleth
Senior editor, publishing services: Douglas Bell
Project management and graphics: York Production Services
Production supervisor: Dennis Para
Cover design: Patricia McFadden
Cover art: Nicholas Wilton/Studio Zocolo

Library of Congress Catalog Card Number: 95-73202

Manufactured in the United States of America.

1 0 9 8 7
f e d c b a

For information write:
St. Martin's Press, Inc.
175 Fifth Avenue
New York, NY 10010

ISBN: 0-312-13298-0 (paperback)
        0-312-16385-1 (hardcover)

Acknowledgments

Page 67:   Mikhail S. Gorbachev, *Perestroika: New Thinking for Our Country and the World.* New York: Harper & Row, 1987. Reprinted with permission.

Table 3.2:   Project Ploughshares, *Armed Conflict Report: Causes, Conflicting Parties, Negotiations, 1993.* Waterloo, Ontario: Institute of Peace and Conflict Studies, 1994. Reprinted with permission.

Page 236:   Raymond Bonner, "Trying to Document Rights Abuses," *New York Times* (national edition), July 26, 1995, p. A4. Reprinted with the permission of The New York Times.

Page 320:   "A Global 'No' to Clinton's Car War," *World Press Review,* July 1995, pp. 4–5. Reprinted with permission.

Contents

Features

Preface

Beyond the Water's Edge represents the second stage of a collaboration between the authors that began when we were visiting professors and office mates at the U.S. Army War College at Carlisle Barracks, Pennsylvania, between 1989 and 1991. The first stage of our collaboration produced a supplementary textbook on U.S. foreign and defense policy-making titled *Puzzle Palaces and Foggy Bottom*. The basic underlying premise of the book is that foreign policy process and substance are reciprocally related and a changing post–Cold War environment would likely witness changes in how foreign and defense policy were made as well. By and large, our premise has proven correct.

Encouraged by the reception the original book received, we began to consider enlarging it into a full-service foreign policy text. This text began with the original text as its core but we expanded it to include more historical material on the post–World War II evolution of policy and contemporary policy issues and to relate those issues to the policy process. We were encouraged to think along those lines by our former editor at St. Martin's Press, Don Reisman, a commitment continued and expanded by our current editor, Beth Gillett, both of whom counseled us on the perceived need for a fresh, explicitly post–Cold War text written at the level and tone (undergraduate) of *Puzzle Palaces*.

The result is *Beyond the Water's Edge*. As the first pages reveal, the title was chosen purposely to indicate that the environment in which foreign policy is made has changed. Prior to World War II, the nonpartisan, virtually nonpolitical nature of foreign policy was captured in the idea that "politics ends at the water's edge." Clearly, this is no longer the case: politics extends well beyond the water's edge.

Highlights

To develop this notion of change, we have added several chapters and significantly revised others. The introductory and concluding chapters have been extensively revised to reflect the broader purpose of the book. Chapters 2 and 3 are completely new, providing historical material on the Cold War and the residues of that period which affect the present and future. Likewise, Chapters 10, 11, and 12 have been added to describe current functional problems that face U.S. foreign policy (security, economics, and other, including transstate, issues). The core chapters from *Puzzle Palaces* have been updated and revised as needed.

We hope the text fulfills a need in the U.S. foreign policy market. The book is designed to be readable, factual, and accessible to students (especially these approaching the subject for the first time). We have attempted, as we did in *Puzzle Palaces*, to engage the student through the use of factual materials and anecdotes about real policy. These are contained both in the main text and the boxes, which are an added feature of the new book. To facilitate the learning process, we have consciously minimized the amount of political science jargon and theoretical material included. We hope the result will be a text from which students can gain a solid body of knowledge presented in a manner that will engage their attention as well as instruct.

Clearly, a work of this magnitude could not be undertaken or successfully concluded without the considerable assistance of many others. The editorial and production staffs of St. Martin's Press have labored long and hard in the book's behalf. In addition, the book has been extensively read and reviewed by colleagues who corrected our mistakes and broadened our perspectives, and we wish to thank them for their constructive help. They are: William H. Baugh III, University of Oregon; Goodwin Cooke, Syracuse University; Maryann K. Cusimano, The Catholic University of America; Ralph B.A. DiMuccio, University of Florida; Paula Fleming, California State University, Los Angeles; John H. Gilbert, North Carolina State University; Silvana Rubino Hallman, Syracuse University; Roger Hamburg, Indiana University of South Bend; E. James Holland, Angelo State University; W. Ben Hunt, New York University; Kofi Johnson, North Carolina Central University; Joseph Lepgold, Georgetown University; Robert McCalla, University of Wisconsin; William Newmann, Virginia Commonwealth University; Chau T. Phan, Rider College; George R. Quester, University of Maryland; Timothy J. Schorn, University of South Dakota; Philip Schrodt, University of Kansas; Douglas Simon, Drew University; Louis M. Terrell, San Diego State University; Elizabeth Van Wie Davis, Illinois State University; and James J. Zaffiro, Central College.

Finally, we would like to thank our families and our home institutions, the University of Alabama and Lebanon Valley College, for their considerable support.

About the Authors

Donald M. Snow is professor of political science at the University of Alabama and has held visiting faculty positions at the U.S. Air Command and Staff College, the U.S. Naval War College (where he was the first Secretary of the Navy Senior Research Fellow), and the U.S. Army War College. He is currently a visiting professor at the U.S. Air War College. His most recent books include *Distant Thunder: Third World Conflict and the New International Order* (St. Martin's Press, 1993); *From Lexington to Desert Storm: War and Politics in the American Experience,* with Dennis Drew (M. E. Sharpe, 1994); *National Security: Defense Policy for a New International Order,* 3rd edition (St. Martin's Press, 1995); *The Shape of the Future: The Post–Cold War World* 2nd edition (M. E. Sharpe, 1995) and *Uncivil Wars: International Security and the New Internal Conflicts* (Lynne Ritnner, 1996). He holds the B.A. and M.A. degrees from the University of Colorado and the Ph.D. from Indiana University.

Eugene Brown is professor of political science at Lebanon Valley College in Annville, Pennsylvania, and has held visiting faculty positions at the U.S. Army War College and Nanjing University in China. He is the author of *J. William Fulbright: Advice and Dissent* (University of Iowa Press, 1985) as well as a number of papers, articles, monographs, and book chapters on Japanese foreign policy. A former Army intelligence analyst in Japan and Vietnam, he received his Ph.D. from the State University of New York at Binghamton.

Together, Snow and Brown are the authors of *Puzzle Palaces and Foggy Bottom: U.S. Foreign and Defense Policy-Making in the 1990s* (St. Martin's Press, 1994), and *The Contours of Power: An Introduction to Contemporary International Relations* (St. Martin's Press, 1996).

CHAPTER 1

The Concept and Changing Environment of Foreign Policy

It used to be an axiom of American politics that "politics ends at the water's edge." The "water's edge" was a symbolic way of describing the state's boundaries; when matters of foreign policy were being decided, normal partisan politics were supposed to be suspended. In dealing with foreign policy, the country would unite behind policy rather than haggle and disagree, as was the case in internal politics.

This depiction which guided perceptions about the conduct of foreign policy until at least the end of World War II, rested on a couple of assumptions, one explicit and the other implicit. The explicit assumption was that the government must present a united front to the world. Speaking with several voices could only undercut the appearance of unity and hence weaken the ability of the United States to succeed in the world. The implicit assumption was that foreign policy actions had few direct domestic consequences, and certainly did not affect American citizens the way the outcomes of domestic policy issues did. Moreover, foreign policy issues were a relatively minor part of the internal political process and debate.

Clearly, both assumptions are less valid today. As even a casual scanning of the evening newspaper or television newscast reveals, foreign policy is now a prominent part of American life. Domestic and foreign policy are intimately related to one another. Many domestic policy outcomes affect other countries and their governments, and many foreign policy issues have direct domestic impacts. Moreover, the explicit need for a united front on foreign issues has been dashed in partisan debates over controversial issues like Vietnam, and, more recently, U.S. troop deployments to Bosnia.

Consider these examples. When the U.S. government decides to adopt new standards on automobile emissions or redefines how many of the parts of an automobile must be made in the United States for a car to be classified as American, automakers in Europe and Japan are affected. To the extent regulations affect sales of foreign cars in the United States, foreign governments are concerned as well. Similarly, American citizens are often differentially affected by foreign affairs. The implementation of the North American Free Trade Agreement (NAFTA) will benefit some American industries (and hence geographic regions) and hurt others. The electronics industry, for instance, is supposed to benefit by gaining preferential access to Mexican markets; the textile industry will likely suffer. At a more local level, the decision of Mercedes Benz in 1994 to build its first plant outside Germany in Alabama (the product of a fierce competition in terms of incentives packages by a number of American states) rather than somewhere else will have a substantial impact on the communities surrounding it.

This intermixture of domestic and foreign policy means that the two areas can no longer be thought of as discrete realms but rather as an increasingly single, unified process. Indeed, politics now extends well "beyond the water's edge," and if the global economy and political system continue to develop as they have in recent years, it will almost certainly do so even more in the future.

In the days when politics ended at the water's edge, the overwhelming proportion of foreign policy dealt exclusively with the formal relations between governments; except in times of crises, those interactions were relatively minor. Today, of course, foreign policy deals not only with the governments of sovereign states, but also extends to groups within states (what are known as subnational actors) and groups transcending state borders (known as supranational actors). A local labor union or an interest group like the Sierra Club is an example of a subnational actor, and an international organization like the United Nations is an example of a supranational actor.

The nature of foreign policy is complex and evolving in a rapidly changing world. This book develops three central themes about policy and the policy process. The first theme, already introduced, is that the distinction between foreign and domestic politics has virtually disappeared and will continue to do so. The second theme is that the substance of policy (foreign policies) and the way policy is made (foreign policy processes) are clearly related to one another and that processes are undergoing change to adapt to new and dynamic policy requirements. The third theme is that change in both substance and process is substantially driven by the intense dynamism of the global environment. That environment is probably best exemplified in the economic realm and symbolized in the increasingly globalizing economy.

These themes are clearly interactive. The changing environment is blurring the line between domestic and foreign policy. As foreign policy issues increasingly appear on the domestic agenda, there is a need for both policy and policy process adjustments. In turn, the government adopts policies that help shape the nature of change in the system.

We begin to explore these matters by looking at the international system that serves as a major part of the context within which states carry out their foreign policies. We then discuss the nature of the foreign policy process and how it is conducted, specifically in the American context. Finally, we examine factors that have contributed to the way the United States conducts its foreign policy and how the United States was forced to alter both its process for conducting foreign policy and the substance of that policy.

The International System

The contemporary international system is basically the product of a series of agreements that ended the Thirty Years' War in 1648. That war had engulfed most of Europe, and central to its purpose was the question of the relations between political units and where ultimate authority lay within the system (largely a contest between the secular monarchs of northern Europe and the papacy). The agreements are known collectively as the Peace of Westphalia, and the system it created is often called the Westphalian system. The building blocks of that system are a series of *sovereign states* (states possessing supreme authority in the system) that are designated as the principal political entities in the world. This highlighted term introduces two separate concepts, each of which is critical to understanding international relations and thus foreign policy.

The first concept is *sovereignty,* which we define as supreme authority. The entity that possesses sovereignty, whether it be a government or the individual (a matter of some controversy), has no higher authority that can order or control its political fate. In the early days of the modern international system, sovereignty was thought to reside in the monarch and was used to justify monarchical rule within states (hence the interchangeable use of the terms *monarch* and *sovereign*). Somewhat later, the basis of sovereignty came to be viewed as residing in the state and its government, or even in individuals (who delegate part of their sovereignty to the state as part of the social contract with the state).

The result has been that sovereignty is considered an attribute of states, and more precisely, the governments of states. Once again, we have introduced a new term, *state*. The term is legal and political in character and refers to exclusive jurisdiction over a piece of territory. The boundaries of a political map are state boundaries, and exclusive jurisdiction is the operational definition of sovereignty: states legally possess sovereignty.

Occasionally, the terms *nation* and *nation-state* are used as synonyms for the state. We do not do so here because these terms have different meanings. *Nation* is an anthropological term that refers to group loyalties. The characteristics that usually define nationality include ethnicity, common language and historical experience, religion, or even the simple feeling of belonging. The expression of loyalty to a nation is known as *nationalism*; in its most strident form, nationalism is at the root of many problems in the contemporary system (a major foreign policy problem for the United States and other countries we discuss later). *Nation-state* is a compound word and idea that refers to an ideal condition whereby membership in a national group is coterminous with the boundaries of the state. In a pure nation-state, all members of a nation live in a single state and no other nationalities inhabit that state. The desire to create such nationally pure states through so-called ethnic cleansing and other forms of national self-determination are major sources of instability in the post–Cold War system.

The principle of state sovereignty has stood at the base of international politics and is expressed as the right of each state to maintain total and absolute jurisdiction over its sovereign territory and those who live within that territory. This principle has come under some criticism in the contemporary world by people such as U.N. secretary-general Boutros Boutros-Ghali because of very public abuses of citizens by their governments in places like former Yugoslavia, Iraq, and Rwanda.

The application of sovereignty has quite opposite consequences within and between states. Internally, sovereignty creates authority (the power to make and enforce decisions about how relations among people and between the people and the government will be regulated), which was the original purpose of the concept in the writings of its earliest proponents like Jean Bodin and Niccolò Machiavelli. Authority and jurisdiction are closely related, and the result is normally some semblance of physical order. In most Western systems, that authority is not imposed but is the result of the system's *legitimacy,* the right to govern which the populace gives freely to the government. In other systems, authority is enforced by coercion or by tradition (as in monarchies). When no government can successfully enforce sovereign control within the state, as was the case in Somalia that caused American and other intervention starting in 1992, the result can be chaos.

The consequences for the international system are quite the opposite. The same sovereignty that permits a government to govern within its own territory prevents it from imposing its rules on other governments, since they possess sovereignty over their own territory as well. The result is the absence of authority in the relations between states. International politics is thus formally a state of anarchy, or the absence of government.

In a situation of anarchy, international relations must operate very differently than domestic politics. The absence of government means the absence of enforceable rules to regulate how the state actors operate. As a result, international politics are inherently *power politics,* where states try to use their power (defined as the ability — or resources — to get someone to do something he or she would not otherwise do) to influence the behavior of other states but where they lack the authority to impose solutions in a legal sense.

Foreign policy deals with how states pursue their interests in a world where those states lack authority over the actions of other states. The need for foreign policy arises because all states have *interests,* conditions that are important to their well-being or, in some cases, even their existence, and because the interests of different states sometimes come into conflict. When conflicts of interest arise (situations where two or more states cannot simultaneously pursue their interests), then foreign policy attempts to resolve those disagreements.

At the top of the hierarchy of interests are *vital interests,* conditions and situations so important to the state that it will not voluntarily forfeit the desired condition. Three comments should be made here. First, vital interests are properties of states alone, and it is a primary difference between domestic and international politics that vital interests exist. Domestically, the state's possession of vital interests means the interests of individuals and groups are ultimately subordinate to those of the state.

Internationally, such interests are too important to be subordinated to an authority, which is why states prefer a legal anarchy. Second, the word *voluntarily* means that although states will not willingly forfeit vital interests, in some cases they can be compelled to do so by more powerful states. Third, it is conventional to describe vital interests as those over which a state would go to war.

An example may be helpful. In his 1980 State of the Union address, President Jimmy Carter declared the free flow of oil from the Persian Gulf to be a vital American interest. Clearly, the United States has no authority to compel states of the Persian Gulf littoral to supply that free flow, since they have sovereignty over the oil fields within their own territory. That means the United States guarantees continued access—if it is threatened—by the application of power (which, we see later, is a prime way that states conduct their foreign policies). When Iraq invaded and conquered Kuwait in 1990 and threatened to interrupt that flow of oil, the United States and a coalition of other states (some of which were motivated by a desire to punish Saddam Hussein for his violation of sovereign Kuwaiti territory) employed military force to reverse the situation.

When vital interests and possible military action are involved, as they were in the Persian Gulf, foreign policy merges with *national security policy,* where the national security is defined in military terms. Foreign and national security policy were often used synonymously during the Cold War because many East-West questions were military in nature. Technically, however, national security policy is a subset of foreign policy, which refers to all contacts between states.

The Westphalian system is under at least mild assault in the post–Cold War world. Three examples, each of which we will address in subsequent chapters, stand out. One is the emergence of problems that transcend state boundaries in ways over which states have little control and that cannot be solved by individual state action alone. These *transstate issues* are the subject of Chapter 12. Another is the emergence of a *global economy,* a condition of international economic activity over which the governments of states have decreasing effective authority, a problem we address in Chapter 11. The third is the assertion that, at least in some cases, *the rights of individuals and groups* may transcend the sovereignty of states in situations of great atrocity, such as occurred in Somalia in 1992 and in Rwanda in 1994. The debate over that proposition is part of the security debate discussed in Chapter 10.

The Conduct of Foreign Policy

Foreign policy interactions occur within the changing contours of the international system. Considerable change in that environment affects both the substance of policy and ultimately the processes by which that policy is determined, which is central to our thesis. Here we introduce some basic ideas about the substance and processes, which we elaborate on in subsequent chapters.

The conduct of American foreign policy today would be quite unfamiliar to historical practitioners. As late as the end of World War II, foreign policy was a secondary concern of the government, consisting for the most part of the formal diplomatic interactions of the State Department and its system of embassies in foreign countries. Foreign policy and diplomacy were more or less synonymous, and the popular image was of cutaway tuxedos and top hats. Foreign policy was dull, dry, and not very important to the average American. The exceptions to this typification, of course, were American participation in the two world wars of this century, where the United States was forced by circumstance to act as a major—even *the* major—international actor.

That image clearly does not hold true any longer. The interactions between the government of the United States and the governments of foreign countries and other foreign entities are very extensive, those relations command a large part of the media coverage of the government, and many agencies of the federal government are involved in the action. There is wide and growing recognition that foreign policy issues have a major impact on the lives of all Americans.

As we already suggested, the study of foreign policy requires looking at its two interactive dimensions, the *content of policy* and the *policy process*. Each has changed, and has caused the need for change in the other.

The changing content of foreign policy in response to a changed environment, which in turn required changes in the process, is the most obvious case in point. Prior to World War II, the United States consciously minimized its political (although not economic) relations with the rest of the world. The United States preferred a condition of "splendid isolation" from what it considered a tarnished, even corrupted international system, and believed, largely wrongly, that it could enforce that isolation through the application of judicious diplomacy by the elite establishment in the State Department.

American participation in World War II and the Cold War that it spawned changed both policy and process. The worsening of relations between the United States and the Soviet Union that largely defined the Cold War international system meant at least two things for the country. First, the United States could not detach itself from the international system as it had done after World War I, for fear the Soviets would expand and control those places, such as Western Europe and Japan, that Americans would in the process have abandoned. A return to isolationism was simply an unaffordable luxury. Second, the Soviet-American competition was largely a military confrontation. The prospect of war between the communist and noncommunist worlds was a constant possibility for which preparation was necessary; the language of *deterrence* (convincing the Soviet opponent that it was not in its interest to start a war with the United States) became a standard part of foreign policy discussion. In the process, national security concerns were added to and even dominated more traditional foreign policy matters; for many purposes, foreign and national security policy became the same thing.

As the Cold War evolved, and especially since it has collapsed, the agenda of foreign policy has changed as well. At least within the relations among the most prosperous countries of what we call the First Tier (the most prosperous market-based democracies), international economic concerns began to become prominent. With the receding nature of security concerns on the post–Cold War foreign policy agenda, economic issues have risen arguably to the top of the agenda. In 1993, the Congress approved the North American Free Trade Agreement (NAFTA) that will create a free trade area (one in which all restrictions on trade such as tariffs are removed) between the United States, Canada, and Mexico over a 15-year period of implementation (Chile was approved as the fourth member in 1994). In late 1994, President Clinton and the elected presidents of all the Latin American states except Cuba met in Miami and agreed in principle to extend NAFTA throughout the Western Hemisphere in the guise of the Free Trade Area of the Americas. A month earlier, the United States entered into a similar agreement in principle with 17 other countries of the Pacific Rim within the context of the Asia-Pacific Economic Cooperation meeting. Also in 1994, the General Agreement on Tariffs and Trade (GATT) Uruguay Round were approved and entered into force. (We discuss these initiatives and their significance in detail in Chapter 11.)

The agenda has changed in other areas as well, notably the transstate and related issues we alluded to earlier. Global environmental concerns became visible to all at the so-called Earth Summit in Rio de Janeiro in 1992. Population concerns and the rights of women dominated the Cairo population summit of 1994 sponsored by a U.N. agency. Drugs have been an ongoing concern, and the outbreak of domestic terrorism at Oklahoma City has made the topic of terror a major part of the agenda.

This changing content has been reflected in corresponding alterations in the way policy is made. Prior to World War II, as we noted, foreign policy was the virtual sole preserve of the State Department. The nature of diplomacy was low key, even invisible, and the State Department went about its business largely unobserved and with only token supervision by the foreign relations committees of the Congress.

The emergence of the Cold War changed that. At a minimum, the military content of the Cold War meant the defense establishment had to be integrated into the process. The vehicle for doing so was the National Security Act of 1947. Among other things, the act unified the armed services into a single cabinet-level Department of Defense. It also created the National Security Council (NSC) as the penultimate decision body in the foreign policy area. Of great symbolic importance, the secretaries of state and defense (in addition to the president and vice president) are the statutory members of the NSC; the secretary of defense, in effect, became virtually equal in importance to the once omnipotent Department of State in foreign policy matters. Over time, the NSC evolved a layered bureaucracy of working groups to deal with various foreign policy problems that became the centerpiece of foreign policy decision making in the 1980s and remains at the heart of the process within the executive branch of the government.

The redefinition of the foreign policy agenda had another major structural effect: the rise of congressional interest and activism in foreign policy. Before the Cold War, foreign policy was viewed as a nonpartisan, patriotic effort whose purpose was to present a monolithic front to the rest of the world. (Woodrow Wilson's partisan fight for American participation in the League of Nations at the end of World War I was an exception to that rule.) Several things have changed that view, including the extension of foreign policy concerns (for instance, in the economic realm) to the point where they directly affect American citizens and thus become matters of attention for their elected representatives in Congress. At the same time, influences like global television mean that a larger portion of the voting public is exposed to foreign policy issues. Much of this activism derives from the perception of presidential misstepping on major issues (the most notable being Vietnam) that require greater scrutiny by Congress. The result has been a much more assertive Congress (see Chapters 5 and 6).

The American View of Foreign Policy

All states view the world and their role in it through the lens of their national experience and the way that experience molds their perceptions about foreign policy. A number of political scientists developed the idea of *political culture* to describe the general political characteristics of different states, and national security analysts sometimes refer to a *strategic culture* to describe how different states relate to war and its conduct.

In a manner similar to that of strategic culture, we can define a set of influences we call the *foreign policy culture,* which contributes to both the style and content of different states' views of foreign policy. Recognizing that no such list of influences will be entirely encompassing or equally acceptable to all observers and analysts, we next delineate some of the characteristics that help explain why Americans tend to look at foreign policy concerns the way they do. The factual content of the assorted components varies considerably.

The first, and perhaps most important, characteristic is the American belief that the United States is a *special state with a special destiny*. This sense of specialness has much to do with the founding of the Republic. The early American immigrants fled from what they perceived as the tyranny of their European homelands, determined to start a new life in the vast reaches of the New World. Feeling the Old World was tainted by its experience, America offered the chance for rejuvenation in the unspoiled majesty of its vast landmass.

The fact that the early Americans fought and succeeded against great odds to form the modern state system's first practicing democracy only added to the sense of being special. The United States was set aside from other states by the political freedom it attained, and this sense of attraction remains to this day, creating what Harvard political scientist Joseph S. Nye, Jr., refers to as the "soft power" of the United

States—the attractiveness of the institutions and ideas that compose the American system.

The second, and closely related, characteristic of the American approach is the idea that the United States is a *role model for the world,* what former president Ronald W. Reagan was fond of calling the "shining house on the hill." The idea behind this assertion is that the American set of ideals is universal and should be emulated as a universal virtue. In its more strident and xenophobic representation, this creates a crusading zeal, what in the nineteenth century came to be known as a "manifest destiny" to spread the boundaries of the American republic from the Atlantic to the Pacific Oceans. Enthusiasm for the emulation of the American system in the wake of the end of the Cold War (and the fact the American system "won" the Cold War) can be seen as further evidence of this tendency.

The depiction of the house "on the hill" symbolizes a third, and contradictory, impulse: *isolationism.* Because so many Americans fled some form of tyranny, there is a corresponding desire to be aloof from the taint of the old system. The symbolism of the house being on top of the hill is that it is somehow separate from the rest and that separation is good.

The desire to be somehow apart was reinforced by accidents of geography and history to create a mythology about American separation from the rest of the world. The United States is effectively an island state, with the Atlantic and Pacific Oceans providing a buffer against any other state that might wish the United States harm. When combined with the fact of relatively weak and usually benign bordering neighbors, it has meant the United States had very few security problems with which to grapple through most of its history. Aside from raids by Pancho Villa into southern Arizona and New Mexico in the 1910s, Americans themselves are the only ones who brought war to the country's territory (the Civil War) after Great Britain was expelled during the War of 1812.

Geography reinforced the sense of preferred independence that lies at the heart of isolationism in another way. Until the post–World War II period, the United States was largely self-sufficient economically. The country is blessed by large amounts of arable land (for instance, the savannah grasslands of the Middle West), so there has never been a need to import food. Moreover, the United States was blessed with all the natural resources necessary for the first industrial revolution's emphasis on heavy industrialization: iron ore, coal, and petroleum, to name three. The need to rely on outside sources of materials to enhance American well-being has been relatively recent, the product of the exhaustion of readily available and economically extractable resources (petroleum) or the emergence of the need for relatively exotic materials that are not part of the American natural endowment (titanium for jet engines, for instance).

There is also an historic element to the predisposition toward isolation. During much of the formative period of the American republic, and especially during the nineteenth century, political aloofness from Europe was not only a preference, but it was perceived to be a policy the United States could enforce: although the perception was largely untrue, many believed the United States remained separated from Europe primarily because that was what the United States wanted.

The roots of the isolationist desire go back to the founding of the country. One of the present authors has argued, for instance, that the British military "occupation" of much of New England was a prime cause of the political movement that ended in the American Revolution (see *From Lexington to Desert Storm,* listed in the suggested readings at the end of this chapter). The isolationist theme was sounded by President George Washington in his farewell address on September 17, 1796, when he said, "Tis our true policy to steer clear of permanent alliances, with any portion of the foreign world." As a guideline for foreign policy, the most eloquent and forceful articulation came from President Thomas Jefferson in his inaugural address on March 4, 1801: "peace, commerce, and honest friendship with all nations, entangling alliances with none."

An important, if incongruous, principle is articulated in these two statements that resonate through the history of American foreign policy and are not totally laid to rest until the aftermath of World War II (in fact, some would argue they have not totally gone away yet). That principle is the distinction between economic and political relations between the United States and the rest of the world. The distinction recognizes that the United States is economically related to the rest of the world and this condition is desirable; what it denies is the desire for any political relationships, and especially those that might have a military aspect (entangling alliances). The incongruity is that, in fact, economics and politics are inextricably related to one another. That was certainly true in the mercantilist eighteenth century when governments routinely promoted industries that could contribute to national power, and it is equally true today.

The historical myth was the notion that the United States could somehow enforce its preferred political isolation. The major evidence for the enforcement of isolation was the fact that the United States was able to steer a clear course from entanglement in European conflicts for 100 years—the end of our theater of the Napoleonic wars, the War of 1812, and World War I. The myth is flawed in at least two ways.

The first flaw is that during the period, there were no major European wars general enough or serious enough to involve a United States which was, until the end of the nineteenth century, too weak to be of consequence anyway. The nineteenth century was, generally speaking, an introverted experience in Europe where political and economic adjustments within European states (including the formation of important states like Italy and Germany) were more important than international relations and where foreign adventures were largely concentrated on completing the colonization of Africa and Asia.

The second flaw is that whenever there was general upheaval in Europe, the United States was dragged into it anyway, largely for economic reasons that cannot be separated from political concerns. The major upheavals, of course, were at each end of the 100 years; the roots of the War of 1812 are largely found in the American desire to trade with both sides (a practice opposed by both sides, each of which wanted exclusive rights to the American trade). Similarly, the depiction of America's entrance into World War I as a moral crusade (Woodrow Wilson's entreaty that "the world must be made safe for democracy") obscures the fact that American industry might well be excluded from the European trade by a victorious Germany, particularly if Germany gained dominance over the north Atlantic Ocean in the process.

Myths, however, die hard. The desire to return to aloofness resulted in "splendid isolationism" between the world wars that arguably made the Second World War inevitable. While the Cold War made isolationism impractical, the innate desire to be as removed as possible from the world remains a strand in the ongoing debate about foreign policy in the form of so-called neoisolationism.

The fourth characteristic of the American foreign policy culture is American *ahistoricism*. On the one hand, Americans have a relatively short history, particularly in comparison to Europe and the major civilizations of Asia, Latin America, and Africa. America's history as an independent state is a little over 200 years old, compared to a Chinese or Egyptian history that measures in the thousands of years. On the other hand, the sweep of American history is not shared by a large proportion of the population. As a land of immigrants, Americans have been in the country for varying periods of time; that no Vietnamese-Americans are eligible for membership in the Daughters of the American Revolution (DAR) is an example of this fact.

This lack of shared experience arising from ahistoricism has a number of consequences for the way Americans look at the world. For one thing, the United States is a polyglot of cultures, religions, and languages that commonly define national identities (nationalism). The United States, for instance, lacks a shared sense of enmity for foreign countries, both because of geography and because Americans have no equivalent of the cultural abyss between, say, the Persians of Iran and the Arabs of Iraq, whose cultural rivalry dates back to biblical times (Persia and Mesopotamia), or Franco-German rivalry. It was one of the striking features of the Cold War that it was contested between two culturally highly diverse states between which there was absolutely no historical basis for animosity: average Americans did not dislike average Russians, and vice versa.

This lack of historical animosity is also evidenced by the American sense of uncertainty and ambivalence about support for national security measures. The United States has not been physically at risk (other than by Soviet nuclear missiles) for most of its existence and has generally maintained a small and isolated armed force during peacetime, mobilizing when war came and demobilizing quickly after it was over. The long Cold War experience is a single exception to the historical American experience in this regard; in the less threatening environment of the post–Cold War, it is possible that a reversion will occur.

This attitude about national security reflects another consequence of ahistoricism, a generally optimistic view of America and its place in the world derived from a perception of a successful history. Until the Vietnam War, the general experience of the United States was one of success: the first prodemocratic, anticolonial war, a series of westward expansions that encompassed the North American continent, the two successful world wars.

This attitude toward the American experience helped make Vietnam as traumatizing as it was. The great perception about the war in Southeast Asia is that it was the first time in American history the country had lost a war. Such a view is, of course, only sustainable through a decidedly cursory view of the overall American experience at war. It is difficult to describe the War of 1812 as anything other than a defeat. The United States won precisely two battles in the war: a naval battle on the Great Lakes where the British were outnumbered two to one, and the Battle of New Orleans, fought more than two weeks after the armistice ended the war. Moreover, the United States did not achieve any of its political goals: Canada was certainly not annexed (an objective abandoned within a year of the war's beginning), and the British had agreed to end the impressment of American sailors (most of whom were British deserters) before war was declared. Similarly, American prowess in unconventional war was belied by the historical record: the campaign in Florida against the Seminoles in the 1820s, the Philippine insurgency at the turn of the twentieth century, and the campaign against Pancho Villa were hardly high points for the American military.

Finally, although the lack of a common historical perspective may mean that Americans lack the national bond of a people with a common historical experience, it also means they largely lack the kind of historical rivalries that polarize the population and result in the poisonous, even atrocious events that are plaguing so much of the post–Cold War world. American nationalism has been, by and large, *inclusionary,* embracing new and different nationalities (admittedly with greater or lesser enthusiasm for some nationalities at different times). The darker side of nationalism, so evident in the Balkans, parts of the former Soviet Union, and in Africa, is *exclusionary,* seeking to create nationally pure communities and willing to engage in bloody atrocity to achieve those ends.

The fifth characteristic of the American foreign policy culture that authors often cite is the American *disdain for power politics.* This is largely a historical matter, reflecting the way the United States was populated, as we mentioned earlier. People had fled the corruption first of Europe and later other parts of the globe, seeking refuge from the injustice of flawed political systems. The United States represented a sanctuary from those old worlds, a place above the fray of common power politics. To involve the United States in the power politics of the international order was thus to risk being dragged down to its level.

This disdain is, of course, all part of the American self-perception of its specialness and the consequent mandate to remain the exemplar in an otherwise corrupt world. The large consequence has been to reinforce the desire toward isolationism, but it has also given rise to another strand in policy, an idealism that occasionally becomes schizophrenic. On the one hand, it seeks to maintain the purity of the American experience by staying aloof from power politics; at the same time, it sometimes gives way to a crusading zeal that wants to "save" the world from itself in the name and image of the American dream.

As we see in the next section, idealism is one of the great traditions in the debate over American foreign policy. Idealists, broadly speaking, want to improve the global condition, corrupted by the influence of the power politics that marks the creed of their ideological opponents, the realists. Occasionally, this American sense of idealism becomes activated and forms the basis for American crusades to save the world from itself.

The consequences of this tendency are seen most strongly in military affairs, as the power politics of war become transformed into questions of good and evil, the latter to be expunged. The classic example was American entrance into World War I. Both sides in the Great War sought either American involvement on their side (especially Britain and France) or, failing in that, American neutrality (especially Germany). The isolationist strand in the American tradition concluded that involvement was not in the American interest, which was better served by commerce with both sides (as was the case 100 years earlier in what became the War of 1812). An objective analysis would probably have concluded that American involvement was unnecessary if the Western allies prevailed or the war continued inconclusively, but that involvement to prevent a German victory was probably in American self-interest.

The British, especially, and the French, understood both the need for American intervention and that the way to appeal to the United States was emotionally. British propagandists mounted a campaign that sought simultaneously to paint the war as a contest between democracy and authoritarianism and as a consequent matter of good versus evil (depicting the Germans as the Huns, for instance).

This campaign ultimately worked. Although there were competing arguments for and against American entrance into the war, the proximate trigger was the economic and emotional issue of Germany's practice of unrestricted submarine warfare against shipping (including American) suspected of providing supplies to the Western allies. It was economic because it reflected the commercial desire to profit from the war; it was emotional because the sinking of vessels by submarines had been ruled unlawful by the Geneva rules of war (see Amplification box "Unrestricted Submarine Warfare") earlier in the century and had resulted in numerous noncombatant deaths (the Germans rescinded the practice before the United States declared war on April 6, 1917—an action parallel to Britain suspending impressment prior to the declaration of the War of 1812). Moreover, the highly convoluted debate over the policy demonstrated the highly emotional spirit of the times.

Prior to the American declaration of war in World War I, it had been the intention of the American government and especially President Woodrow Wilson to negotiate an end to the fighting where neither side prevailed: "peace without victory" was

AMPLIFICATION

Unrestricted Submarine Warfare

The issue of German submarine attacks on Allied shipping, especially on ships carrying American passengers (for instance, the *Lusitania*) became the most volatile issue between the United States and Germany. The irony of the issue involves the restrictions that were supposed to be placed on submarines in war by the Hague Convention and the fact that Germany stressed surface ships rather than submarines thanks to the influence of an American naval strategist, Alfred Thayer Mahan.

Anticipating the introduction of the submarine at the turn of the twentieth century, those charged with crafting rules of war at the Hague placed two notable restrictions on submarines, which, if adhered to, left the vessels utterly useless. A submarine had to surface and give warning of an impending attack before firing, and it must make provision to take aboard any survivors. The first restriction was implausible because a surfaced submarine loses the crucial element of surprise and when on the surface is highly vulnerable to being sunk. The second was impractical because the submarines of the era were quite small and incapable of taking on more than a few survivors. The Germans could thus obey the law and render their fleet ineffective, or break the law and employ their force to effect.

To make matters worse, the Germans had underinvested in submarines, which were the only effective part of their navy. Kaiser Wilhelm was an avid fan of the American naval strategist Mahan. The latter had argued in his famous book *The Influence of Seapower upon History* that navies should rely on heavy capital ships (which the Germans could never get out into the North Atlantic in numbers) rather than "commerce raiders," of which the submarine was a prime example.

---

the key catchphrase. That changed when war was to be undertaken. The American purpose became "to make the world safe for democracy," which required an emotional American involvement. The crusading spirit was well captured in Wilson's address to the Congress proposing a formal declaration of war: "The day has come when America is privileged to spend her blood and her might for the principles that gave her birth and happiness. God helping her, she can do no other."

This crusading impulse also manifests itself in a historical American preference for total wars—wars whose purpose was to cause the total submission of the opponent, up to and including the overthrow of the enemy government. The key phrase here is "unconditional surrender," a concept originally articulated by Ulysses S. Grant as he demanded the surrender of Fort Donelson, Kentucky, during the American Civil War and later stated as the U.S. objective against the Axis powers in World War II. This preference faded during the Cold War, since the only total war available to the United States was a nuclear World War III with the Soviet Union that would likely have resulted in the utter destruction of both sides.

All of these characteristics of the American foreign policy culture influence, directly or indirectly, how the United States views its place in the world. Most are historically derived, and one can debate the extent to which they apply with equal vigor to the present as they may have to the past. What is clear is that they all bear on the debate about American foreign policy in the post–Cold War world.

The Debate over Future American Policy

We can think of American foreign policy across time as having gone through two great phases, each punctuated by a period of transition. The first phase, which lasted from the American Revolution up to World War I, was an inactive period in which foreign policy played a relatively minor role in a United States more intent on internal development and where the notion of isolationism was supreme. World War I punctured the myth of isolationism and was superceded by a period of transition between the world wars. Although the country returned to isolationism, by the time the clouds of World War II were mounting, many had come seriously to question the continuing viability and even possibility of American aloofness from the world. The war effectively shattered the paradigm of the nineteenth century and led to the second phase.

The second phase, of course, was the Cold War that gradually developed in the years immediately after the end of World War II and ended with the implosion of communism between 1989 and 1991. That phase was marked by the global competition between the communist and noncommunist worlds, a period in which the United States abandoned its isolationist past and became the activist leader of the Western world in its competition with the Soviet-led communist world.

The effective end of the Cold War has left the United States in another period of transition, the exact outcome of which remains uncertain. The result is an ongoing debate about the future of American foreign policy. The two great intellectual positions, realism and idealism, remain at the core of that debate, although, in practice, they sometimes find themselves in reversed roles. In turn, the substance of the debate can be captured in terms of a series of concerns: the proper level of American involvement in the world; the American standing in the world; proper American priorities; American interests and responsibilities in the world; and the efficacy of American power. Politically, the debate occurs within the context of the first truly post–Cold War administration.

The Worldviews: Realism and Idealism

The distinction between these two most basic schools of thought applies, in somewhat different ways, both to how people view the world (the concern of international relations) and what the American position in that world should be (the concern of American foreign policy). They start from distinct views of the basic nature of the international system that is the environment of foreign policy and hence draw different conclusions both about system dynamics and America's role in international politics.

Both traditions have long historical roots, although their more contemporary salience has been their application to the twentieth century. Many scholars trace realism back as far as Thucydides' *A History of the Peloponnesian War,* an account of a conflict between Athens and Sparta in the fifth century B.C., or to Niccolò Machiavelli's *The Prince,* a manual for Italian rulers written in the sixteenth century, or even to Thomas Hobbes's *Leviathan,* a philosphical tract written in seventeenth-century England. Similarly, the roots of idealism can be traced back to writers such as Jean Bodin, the chief champion of the concept of sovereignty in the sixteenth century, or Hugo Grotius, the father of modern international law, who wrote in the seventeenth century, among others.

The principal difference between realism and idealism is their analyses of the role of power in international relations. To the realist, the basis of international relations in an anarchic, state-centered system (the direct consequence of state sovereignty) is the exercise of power. States are the central actors, and they fail or succeed to the extent that they accumulate and exercise power in their relations with other states. Among the forms that power takes is military force, and in a system of sovereign states, the recourse to force is a natural aspect of international relations. To many early realists (Hobbes, for instance), this emphasis on power and its violent exercise was the result of the "bestial" side of human nature; many modern realists (variously referred to as structural realists or neorealists) accept the classic realist description of the international system, but divorce that observation from any assumptions about the nature of humankind. At any rate, basic to the realist paradigm is that states act out of a concern for their vital interests, most basic of which are the maintenance of their power and sovereign authority, and that war is a natural, even inevitable, consequence of an anarchic world.

Idealists view the historical record differently, arguing that its principal dynamic is the existence of peace periodically interrupted by costly, unnecessary, and avoidable wars. If realists see war as a normal and necessary aspect of international life when vital interests are at risk, idealists generally view the recourse to war as a defect in the system, the causes of which should be alleviated. The traditional idealists, in other words, were dedicated to making the world a more peaceful place by reducing or eliminating the recourse of states to war by structural reform, including the collective use of force against those states that threatened to or actually breached the peace (the concept of collective security).

Both realism and idealism have been dominant paradigms in the twentieth century. In the transitional period between the two world wars, the scholarly — and much of the policy community — was so reviled at the enormous carnage of World War I, there was a powerful movement to change the system so another war like it would not occur. Grounded in the Wilsonian principles of freedom and national self-determination (concepts which, as we see later, are now often contradictory in application in the contemporary world but were not so viewed at the time), the anchor of postwar idealism was support for the League of Nations, and especially its collective security provisions. Much research was focused on strengthening international law and organization for the purpose of making the League more vital.

Although the attribution is not entirely fair, idealism was partially blamed for the spiral to World War II. The reaction to the failure of the League, and the idealist thought that underlay (or at least was associated with) it, was the revival of twentieth-century realism. The father of that revivial was E. H. Carr, who published *The Twenty-Years' Crisis, 1919–1939: An Introduction to the Study of International Relations* in 1939. The book describes the downward spiral of political events from the peace treaty settling the First World War and blames the idealists because, he alleges, they concentrated on the way they thought the world ought to be, rather than the way the world really was, thereby missing the central dynamics that led to war once again.

As the Cold War emerged, realism was clearly the dominant position. A world of military competition lent itself to a political philosophy that described the world in terms of power and the need to think primarily in terms of a national security state and military force. The idea of reform leading to the reduction of military power and the elimination of war seemed Pollyannaish to most serious observers during the Cold War. Moreover, the mind-set of realism is inherently conservative, prone to believing that, particularly in military matters, the clash of power meant one should err on the side of too much, rather than too little, military power.

The Foreign Policy Debate

The end of the Cold War and the consequent end of a system in which great power military threats and confrontations are the dominant features of international relations reopens the debate between the idealists and the realists, although often casting them in opposite roles. The clear need for the realist perspective of the Cold War is made questionable by the absence of distinct threats; strict adherence to the realist paradigm probably would result in a much more restrained foreign policy because important interests are less threatened than they previously were. At the same time, the spate of atrocities in the old Third World (places like Somalia and Rwanda) suggests the need for international reform, the province of a newly energized idealist strain.

Before looking at the future of foreign policy directly through the lens of the American foreign policy debate, an example of this confusion of roles, really the reversal of activism, may help. Our example revolves around the notion of sovereignty and its application and importance in the contemporary system.

Two different distinctions are made about the nature of sovereignty, each of which flows from the other. One is about the extent of control attached to the sovereign entity. Its polar opposites are *absolute sovereignty,* which asserts the holder of sovereignty has complete domain over what occurs within sovereign territory, and *popular sovereignty,* which asserts that sovereignty ultimately resides in the citizenry, which delegates some of its sovereignty to the authorities in order to maintain order. The other conception of sovereignty has to do with its locus. One side argues for *state sovereignty (the rights of states),* that all sovereignty resides in the state; the other argues that sovereignty resides with citizens *(the rights of individuals and groups).*

Clearly, these are related. Absolute sovereignty asserts the supremacy of the rights of states and is a basic position within realism. According to this position, states have no right to intervene in the affairs of one another, except in special circumstances such as invitation. Popular sovereignty suggests that the rights of individuals and groups may occasionally override those of states.

Here realism and idealism reverse roles. During the Cold War, the need for military force was generally supported by realists on the grounds of protecting vital state interests, and realists argue that force should only be used in defense of vital interests (which also meant that many realists opposed the use of force when they felt vital interests were not involved, as, for instance, George Kennan maintained about Vietnam). Idealists, on the other hand, maintain that, since the rights of individuals and groups are sometimes more important than those of states, there is a right and even obligation to interfere in the affairs within states when gross violations of human rights occur and even if traditional vital interests are not involved.

The reversal becomes evident in a place like Somalia. In this case, most realists opposed intervention on the grounds that no important interests were involved: those who did not oppose the use of force there (such as Colin Powell) felt there was little risk to Americans. Many idealists, on the other hand, supported the intervention on the assertion of what some (notably U.N. secretary-general Boutros Boutros-Ghali) called *humanitarian* human rights; those who normally oppose force supported it in this kind of situation. Many Cold War hawks (the realists) thus become the post–Cold War doves, and the Cold War doves (the idealists) emerge as the post–Cold War hawks.

If all this seems confusing, it is because of the transitional nature of the international system and uncertainty over how the United States fits into the new international order. The debate over America's role, far from over, can be organized around five concerns. Each is represented by polar opposite positions, and most are consistent with one another. These are captured in summary form in the box "The American Foreign Policy Debate."

Summary: The American Foreign Policy Debate

Concern	Positions
1. Approach to Foreign Policy (Levels of Involvement)	Internationalism vs. Neoisolationism
2. Standing in World	Optimism vs. Declinism
3. National Priorities	Foreign vs. Domestic
4. Interests and Responsibilities	Expanded vs. Traditional
5. Efficacy of Power	Necessary vs. Narrow

Because they help make some sense of the ongoing debate, we discuss each concern individually.

Approach to Foreign Policy (Levels of Involvement)   The extent to which the United States should actively involve itself in international politics has been a subject of disagreement throughout American history. As we discussed earlier, the early days of the Republic were dominated by the isolationist preference—seeking to limit American involvement in the politics, if not the economics, of the world. This preference is reflected in a number of the characteristics of the American foreign policy culture.

Isolationism was never entirely unopposed. The internationalist position, which argues for an active involvement in international affairs, was for a long time the preserve of what is known as the Eastern liberal establishment—a group of intellectuals and businesspeople who were oriented toward Europe and felt America's destiny was inextricably tied to the affairs of Europe—which were, of course, effectively world affairs for most of the nineteenth century.

The end of World War II and the outbreak of the Cold War made isolationism both impractical and unfashionable. Clearly, the United States was the only country left in the world physically capable of leading the fight against what was perceived as an expansionist Soviet communism, and the potential vulnerability of the United States itself to the communist onslaught added to the impracticality. Moreover, a sizable body of thought, much of it concentrated in the government and academia, believed both that World War II would not have occurred had a robust, activist United States been engaged in interwar international politics and that consequently American presence was necessary to guarantee the peace after World War II.

The end of the Cold War permits the debate to be reengaged, although within limits. Global interdependence at the economic and political levels make isolationism as it was advocated before World War II impossible to sustain. Real limits on American power make total internationalism equally impractical. Within these broad boundaries, however, a debate has reemerged.

The neoisolationist position is probably most closely associated with political columnist and frequent Republican presidential candidate Patrick Buchanan. At the heart of the neoisolationist position is the idea that the United States can and should scale back its international obligations. Several reasons are cited in support of this proposition. In the first place, in the current environment American interests are less threatened than they were previously, meaning the United States has the luxury of scaling back involvement now that there is no communist threat. Secondly, although it may be true that the collapse of the Soviet Union leaves the United States as the sole remaining superpower, its relative power is not that much greater than other states like Germany and Japan, which can be encouraged to share more of the load. This burden sharing would allow the United States to redirect resources to other, more important domestic priorities that were ignored during the Cold War.

Internationalists find this position needlessly gloomy. They argue that a retreat from global leadership is both irresponsible and impractical. It is irresponsible because the United States is the only country with the resources and reach to provide global leadership, which the world expects of it. A prime example is the role of the United States in brokering and legitimating the progress toward a permanent peace between Israel and its Islamic neighbors and in Northern Ireland, a progress the internationalists argue would have been quite unlikely without American stewardship. A retreat is impractical because of the degree of interdependence among members of the First Tier (the major market democracies) and the need to develop policies toward the Second Tier of states. Any noticeable American retreat from global leadership would simply multiply the sense of international disorderliness that many argue is the central problem of the contemporary, post–Cold War international system.

The question of level of involvement reflects the reversal of positions among realists and idealists. During the Cold War, realists were necessarily internationalists, at least in the area of national security. The realist position on military matters becomes nearly neoisolationist on security concerns in the post–Cold War environment where vital interests are relatively unthreatened. Idealists, on the other hand, find themselves more assertive and internationalist on the same security grounds.

America's Standing in the World   Whether the United States is an ascending or descending force on the global stage is a question raised most dramatically onto the foreign policy agenda by Yale historian Paul Kennedy in his 1987 book *The Rise and Fall of the Great Powers: Economic Change and Military Change from 1500 to 2000*. The thesis of what became known as declinism is that the great states, among them Great Britain and Russia, have historically overextended themselves militarily, and the result has been such a strain on their national economies that they eventually declined as great powers. Viewing the United States in the mid-1980s, Kennedy mused that the United States might be the next victim of this "imperial overreach."

Within the context of the 1980s, there seemed to be support for the declinist thesis. American scientific, technological, and especially manufacturing prowess was being seriously challenged by Japan and the European Community (European Union since 1994), and American competitiveness in the world marketplace was widely being challenged. American decline could be shown in areas as diverse as share of world production to scores on standardized mathematics and science tests. All of this was occurring within the context of the Reagan defense buildup, the most costly in American peacetime history.

The declinist thesis did not go unchallenged at the time, and it has itself been in decline as the American economy underwent a resurgence in the early 1990s compared to its leading competitors. Joseph Nye was among those leading the optimist retort in books such as *Bound to Lead*. Nye and others accused the declinists of essentially "cooking the books" on elements of American decline. Although it was true, for instance, that the American portion of global productivity had declined from an artificially high level of around 40 percent immediately after World War II to slightly over 20 percent, that share had stabilized in the mid-1970s and, if anything, was once again on the incline. The resurgence of American technology and industry in areas like automobiles and consumer electronics in the early 1990s has laid much of the declinist argument to rest.

Whether the United States is in decline as a world power or not is obviously relevant to the extent of the American role in the world. Optimists suggest that acting on the declinist thesis, which calls for drawing back from world affairs in ways largely prescribed by the neoisolationists, would create a self-fulfilling prophecy where American preeminence shrinks because we act as if it has shrunk. Rather, the optimists contend, an active American leadership role in an increasingly interdependent global economy and international system is necessary if the twenty-first century is to resemble the twentieth as an "American century."

American Priorities   The 1992 presidential campaign brought into the spotlight the question of where the United States should concentrate its energies and resources now that the Soviet threat had evaporated. During the Republican nominating process, Buchanan argued for a redirection toward domestic concerns; incumbent president Bush preferred to emphasize foreign achievements such as the Gulf War. Candidate Bill Clinton chose to focus on a domestic revival to help bolster American competitiveness in the global economy.

The debate has shifted subtly since then, as the 1996 election campaign emerged. The most resource-intensive aspect of involvement in the international system is military spending, which has declined by as much as one-third in real buying terms during the Clinton presidency and will soon dip behind service on the national debt to be the third largest category of government expenditures (entitlement programs are by far the largest category). At that, the American decline has been part of a global phenomenon in defense spending, so the United States still spends far more than any other state on defense. The question is how much decline in defense budgets and reallocation to domestic needs is possible given American global commitments and its leadership role, a consideration clearly related to the other aspects of the overall debate.

Neither side in the debate argues whether a greater emphasis on domestic priorities is necessary and desirable; what they disagree about is where and how to make changes. The Republican leadership of Congress advocates reallocations across the board to reduce deficits leading to a balanced budget; some Republicans go a step further to include tax reductions. The Clinton administration also favors deficit reductions, but believes that certain government programs, and specifically programs that enhance American competitiveness in the global economy are of prime importance.

Positions become confused. Those who want to reduce American financial commitments to allow reallocations often favor military spending and want to find cuts elsewhere. A particular chestnut is the regular assault on foreign economic assistance currently led by Senate Foreign Relations Committee (SFRC) chair Jesse Helms, who wants to do away with foreign aid to help the deficit. Since the entire foreign aid budget is about $13 billion a year (less than *1 percent* of the federal budget), it is difficult to describe such a reduction as meaningful. At the same time, the administration seems more willing to cut defense than nondefense foreign budget items.

American Interests and Responsibilities   Basic to the continuing American role in the world is both the ongoing nature of American interests and also the extent to which the United States continues or inherits unique responsibility in a changed environment. American interests are not greatly changed in the contemporary system, although the threats to them are clearly different. America's responsibilities raise a greater question, which has at least two distinct if related aspects.

The first is the American role as the sole remaining superpower. What exactly does that mean? Clearly, the United States does not have hegemonic power in the system in the sense of being a supreme power capable of ordering the world as it likes. At the same time, what sets the United States apart from other major powers is that it possesses the full range of so-called instruments of power available to pursue its interests, something no other state can claim. The major instruments are economic power, military power, and diplomatic/political power. The United States still has the world's largest economy, the world's most powerful military forces (the only state capable of projecting military power globally), and enough of Nye's soft power to give it diplomatic persuasiveness. Other states may possess significant power in one or another of these categories (Japanese economic power, Russian military power), but no other state has the entire array.

What this means in practical terms is that regardless of what the international problem area, the American position is of direct consequence. If, for instance, the members of the United Nations decide they want to send peacekeeping forces into some part of the Second Tier (basically the old Third World), they need American logistical support to move large numbers of people and supplies in the most timely manner. In negotiating trading pacts, the effect of American support or opposition can be critical in areas such as the proposed expansion of the North American Free Trade Agreement (NAFTA) into the Western Hemisphere–wide Free Trade Area of the Americas put forward in Miami in December 1994. Arguably, this creates a responsibility for the United States to undertake a leadership role across the board. American leadership in solving the world's problems has become expected.

The debate is really over how much of a direct burden the United States should shoulder in individual matters, leading to the second aspect of the question of responsibilities, the debate over so-called burden sharing. If the United States is to lead but not spend itself into decline, the argument goes, then others who are also capable of providing resources to deal with the world's ills should foot part of the bill as well.

The problem is most pointed when it comes to international military affairs, which can be quite costly. Two examples help show this. The first is the funding of the Gulf War of 1990–1991. Clearly, the United States took the lead military role, as the case study in Chapter 12 elaborates. The United States organized the coalition that would face Iraq in the Kuwaiti desert, provided logistical support and equipment for a number of participating states, and contributed the majority of the military forces (over 465,000 personnel out of a coalition total of about 695,000).

The problem was who was going to pay for the effort. Clearly, more states benefited from the American-led effort than the United States alone. Kuwait and neighboring (and threatened) Saudi Arabia certainly benefited and contributed forces to the extent they had them. But others were served as well from the effort; any state that received petroleum from the Persian Gulf area would profit from the normalization of relations in the region. The question was whether those who benefited but sent no troops should be allowed to be "free riders" or whether they should contribute in some other way.

The controversy centered on Japan and Germany. Both were prohibited by constitutional provision from sending troops overseas (Germany has since modified its Basic Law to allow contributions of troops to U.N.-sponsored peacekeeping operations), but both received considerable Persian Gulf petroleum. As part of the coalition arrangement, the United States solicited financial contributions from those who most benefited in the form of cash or guarantees to buy American military equipment. In the end, the effort was so successful that more funds were pledged than the actual cost of the operation.

Contributions to U.N. peacekeeping operations represents the second, and highly topical, example. Because the U.N. operating budget is so modest (about $2.5 billion in 1995), such operations must be financed on the basis of member contributions from special assessments. According to a formula devised when the U.S. economy was more predominant than it is today, the current American assessment is 31 percent of the total, and many others, notably Germany and Japan once again, are charged well below their ability to contribute, making them virtual free riders in this area as well.

To share the burden more equitably, two proposals are currently circulating. The Clinton administration as part of Presidential Decision Directive 25 on peacekeeping proposed in 1994 that the American contribution be reduced to 25 percent, a proposal that has subsequently been enacted into American law. The second proposal has been to expand the permanent membership on the U.N. Security Council to include Japan and Germany (and maybe others) to increase the justification for increased contribution.

Efficacy of American Power   A final area of debate is the effectiveness of American power in bringing compliance with American interests around the world. The concern arises in some measure out of the restructuring of the post–Cold War international system; it is clear that some of the traditional ways of gaining compliance with demands are no longer effective. The problem has both economic and military aspects.

The economic aspect primarily affects the relations among the most wealthy countries of the world, the series of countries we call the First Tier and that President Clinton refers to as "the circle of market democracies." Because of the enormous degree of interpenetration of the economies of all these states by the private sector (the actions of the multilateral corporations, for instance), controlling national economies has virtually become a thing of the past, and there are very real questions about whether a state can in fact control its own "national" economy well enough to bring the economic instrument to bear. Instead, states are limited to tactics like punitive trade practices, such as the Clinton administration's imposition of high tariffs on Japanese luxury automobiles in May 1995 because of the alleged Japanese refusal to allow American automobile and parts firms to compete fairly in Japan. Even that kind of action was circumscribed by American membership in the World Trade Organization (see Chapter 11).

The military dimension has to do primarily with the application of American force in the countries of the old Third World (Second Tier), and especially in the spate of vicious, often ethnically based internal wars that have broken out in places like Somalia, Liberia, and Rwanda since the end of the Cold War.

These conflicts are discussed in detail in Chapter 10. What is important here is whether the United States should involve itself actively to try to alleviate the suffering that accompanies these outbreaks of violence. Realists and idealists disagree on this question at two levels. The first level is *whether* the United States should become involved: most realists argue that Americans have no interests in these places and should not commit forces; some idealists argue for some form of activism based on humanitarian grounds. The second level is whether the United States can intervene *successfully*. Can American intervention solve the problems, especially since the underlying causes are normally the failure of the states to govern themselves? State building, in turn, is a task for which military forces are less than ideally suited. The Somali experience seemed to tilt this debate in favor of the realists; if Haiti remains reasonably tranquil for some time after American withdrawal, the pendulum could tilt back toward the idealists. The Bosnian experience could prove the ultimate determinant of future policy.

Conclusions

American foreign policy is in a state of considerable flux and change. The vast majority of change has been forced on the United States by an altered environment in which policy is made; the catalyst has been the end of the Cold War and the consequent process of transition that has ensued because of the trauma.

The result is an ongoing debate about how the United States should confront this new, and in many ways bewildering environment. The debate does not occur in a vacuum, of course, but is bounded both by factors from the American foreign policy culture that help define how Americans look at foreign affairs and by ongoing debates that have long-standing intellectual bases, such as that between the idealists and the realists, the internationalists and the isolationists.

The debate is also defined by people and processes. The end of the Cold War not only witnesssed a visible change in international relationships, it also coincided with the emergence of a whole new generation of political leaders, most of whom had a much less intimate experience with the Cold War and the intellectual baggage it entailed.

The election of Bill Clinton in 1992 symbolized the ascent of this new generation. Clinton was the first post–World War II president who had no military service (one can argue that George Bush may have been the *last* postwar president who did have military service for the foreseeable future) and hence no intimate personal relationship with the national security state structure that was the result of Cold War dictates. Rather, Clinton and Vice President Al Gore are much more products of the technological age that is producing the global economy; that their foreign policy activism was in the economic area is not surprising given their perspective. At the same time, those whose orientations and worldviews were largely formed during the Cold War remain potent forces, as the 1996 election campaign demonstrated.

The processes of change have sizable impacts on the structures within which foreign policy is made. The executive branch, and agencies within that branch, have adapted structurally and behaviorally to new forces set forth by change (the Department of Defense, for instance, now has a major organizational effort in the area of humanitarian relief). Congress and the administration clash more stridently, particularly in the wake of the election of a Republican Congress in 1994. How changes in the environment affect the way policy is made is a major and recurring theme of the pages that follow.

The past, of course, is the context within which the present and future are shaped. Although the Cold War is a memory for many, the experiences it created remain an important part of the backdrop of current policy; it is impossible fully to understand the current debates without understanding those contexts. For that reason, Chapter 2 is devoted to an historical overview of American foreign policy, with particular attention to the Cold War period.

SUGGESTED READINGS

Brown, Seyom. *New Forces, Old Forces and the Future of World Politics: Post–Cold War Edition.* New York: HarperCollins, 1995.

Carr, E. H. *The Twenty-Years' Crisis: 1919–1939.* London: Macmillan, 1939.

Deese, David A. (ed.), *The New Politics of American Foreign Policy.* New York: St. Martin's Press, 1994.

Fromkin, David. *The Independence of Nations.* New York: Praeger Special Studies, 1981.

Johnson, Loch. *America as a World Power: Foreign Policy in a Constitutional Framework.* New York: McGraw-Hill, 1991.

Kennedy, Paul. *The Rise and Fall of the Great Powers: Economic and Military Change from 1500 to 2000.* New York: Random House, 1987.

Kissinger, Henry. *A World Restored.* Boston: Houghton Mifflin, 1973.

Machiavelli, Niccolò. *The Prince.* Irving, TX: University of Dallas Press, 1984. (Original work published 1513)

Nye, Jr., Joseph S., *Bound to Lead: The Changing Nature of American Power.* New York: Basic Books, 1990.

Singer, Max, and Aaron Wildawsky, *The Real World Order: Zones of Peace, Zones of Turmoil.* Chatham, NJ: Chatham House, 1993.

Snow, Donald M., and Dennis M. Drew, *From Lexington to Desert Storm: War and Politics in the American Experience.* Armonk, NY: M. E. Sharpe, 1994.

Thucydides, *The History of the Peloponnesian Wars.* New York: Penguin Books, 1954.

CHAPTER 2

The Context of Foreign Policy:
The Cold War

American foreign policy did not begin with the end of World War II, and a complete history of American foreign relations would have to go back to the Founding Fathers and bring the chronology forward to the present. Doing so would go beyond present purposes because our primary concern is with contemporary foreign policy issues and processes, and the most important of these have their roots in the period since 1945.

This is not to argue that the pre–World War II experience is inconsequential and unworthy of consideration. Clearly, most of the roots of what we identified as the American foreign policy culture go back to the earliest days of the American republic, and their influence remains a part of the heritage and framework within which foreign policy is carried out. Equally clearly, the constitutional basis of foreign policy responsibilities comes from the formative period of the Republic, and some of the constitutive rules (or their absence) only gain meaning within the historical context in which they were devised. Similarly, basic American orientations toward different parts of the world have their origins far before the end of the Second World War.

Having noted those historical roots, beginning our review of American foreign policy at the end of World War II is justifiable on several grounds. The most obvious, if the analysis in Chapter 1 was accurate, is that the end of World War II provided the decisive event in the transformation of American policy from its first long period to its second, the Cold War. As already noted, foreign policy was not a major part of the concern of Americans or their government for much of the first 150 or so years of American history; the postwar world ended U.S. disengagement with the world and thrust Americans into the limelight, whether they wanted that prominence or not.

The period since World War II has also been the most furtive period in terms of policy and procedural development. The United States became a conscious world power with accepted responsibilities after World War II simply because no one else was physically capable of accepting the role. That fact alone caused the United States to enter a period of policy development unprecedented in American diplomatic history. As we see presently, this development was especially active during the years immediately after 1945 as a number of actions and reactions to Soviet actions created the framework for the Cold War that Americans are now in the process of refashioning.

Finally, the Cold War period is the explicit context within which the transition to a post–Cold War world is occurring. The influence was pervasive and remains, for many adult Americans, a reference point difficult to abandon, especially in the clear absence of an alternative organizing device. The agony of reconstituting a post–Cold War world is made all the more difficult by the pervasiveness of the Cold War experience (and it may be symbolic that five years after the end of the Cold War we still do not have a name for the new system that does not include the words *cold war* in it).

The Cold War should not be conceptualized as a monolithic, unchanging experience. First, the major issues and themes that defined the Cold War changed across time. If the Cold War began as a competition between a Soviet-controlled communist bloc and an American-led anticommunist bloc where both leading states could maintain considerable control over their allied states (a condition known as *tight bipolarity*), gradually states in both blocs were able to exercise more and more discretion from the superpowers. The problem of dealing with a decolonizing Third World was not a part of the menu of issues in 1945, but by the 1950s and 1960s it not only became an important consideration for policy but a major forum of East-West competition. Moreover, as time went by a whole new set of issue areas, from neutralism to nationalism to economic interdependence to transnational issues like narcotics, terrorism, and the environment arose to compete with the central Soviet-American geopolitical focus of the Cold War.

Second, the Soviet-American relationship that was the centerpiece of the Cold War evolved over time. The "protracted conflict," as the late Yugoslav dissident Milovan Djilas described the competition, evolved across time, influenced by events and changes. One way to organize that evolution, which forms the organizational device for the rest of this chapter and the beginning of the next, is depicted in the Summary box "Evolution of the Cold War."

Summary: Evolution of the Cold War

Engagement of the Cold War, 1945–1950

Height of the Cold War, 1950–1962

Thawing the Cold War, 1962–1969

Redefinition of the Cold War, 1969–1977

Last Gasp of the Cold War, 1977–1985

Gorbachev and the End of the Cold War, 1985–1989

These divisions are, of course, somewhat arbitrary, and one can take issue with them or propose alternatives. Each division is based on an important occasion that served to alter the way the Cold War was fought. The outbreak of the Korean War in 1950 effectively ended any speculation about the relationship between the communist and non-communist world, for instance, and ushered in a period of unrequited confrontation that was only mitigated by the sober reflection of a nuclear war that might have been in the Cuban missile crisis of 1962. The divisions also suggest a kind of uneven evolutionary flow in the Cold War as the two sides came to see one another differently as time went by. As we see later, the potential deadliness of their relationship, like two scorpions in a bottle in one popular analogy, forced them to learn to live with one another.

Engagement of the Cold War, 1945–1950

The context of the Cold War was World War II, the most physically destructive war in history. Although official estimates are, in a number of cases, highly suspect, more than 80 million people, combatants and citizens, died in the war; of those upward of 30 million were citizens of the Soviet Union, which bore the heaviest physical brunt of the war (including the execution of many Soviet citizens by Soviet authorities in retribution for collaboration with the Germans).

The war was the epitome of what had been a near century of total war. Beginning with the American Civil War and including World War I, the trend for unconditional surrender of vanquished foes and total societal mobilization for war reached its zenith in the United States (as "the arsenal for democracy") and elsewhere. In a sense, the war ended the simplicity of conducting war wherein there was no ambiguity about enemies or purposes; for Americans, William T. Sherman's promise to bring "the hard hand of war" to the South in 1864 was a comfortable way to think about the Axis powers.

The central legacy of the war was the failure of the international system to avoid its occurrence. For the victorious Allies who would be responsible for reconstituting the new order, the central reality was a fundamental change in the the global balance of power. Their problem was to reconstitute the international system, hopefully in a manner that would avoid the mistakes of the interwar period that had resulted in the second world conflagration. The major variables in determining how the new system would be shaped were the continuing nature of Soviet-American relations after the war and the existence and role of the novel weaponry produced in the war, nuclear weapons. Each of these variables would shape the nature of the Cold War, its evolution, and ultimately its end.

Changed Balance of Power

The outcome of World War II moved effective power and control of the European-centered international system from the heart of Europe to its periphery, a process begun by World War I, as shown in the Summary box "Major Powers by Era."

Summary: Major Powers by Era

Pre–World War I	Interwar Period	Postwar
Britain	Britain	United States
France	France	Soviet Union
Russia	Germany	
Germany	Soviet Union	
Austria-Hungary	Japan	
	Italy	

The major transformation was the physical defeat of three members of the interwar period (Italy, Germany, and Japan) and the virtual exhaustion of two "victors" (Great Britain and France), which would be reduced to the status of regional powers due to their physical and financial debilities incurred in the war.

That left only two powers with enough residual power at the end of the war to restructure the system. Both the United States and the Soviet Union were physically on the periphery of the two systems and were inexperienced in international relations, the United States by self-exclusion and the Soviets because they had been excluded as pariahs until their help was needed to vanquish fascism.

In this circumstance, power was bipolar: only the United States and the Soviet Union had significant power, and other states congregated around them and could be influenced by them. The sources of their power were very different. The United States emerged from the war as the economic superpower of the world, with virtually the globe's only thriving economy. American goods were the standard of the world, and only the United States had the financial resources to underwrite the reconstruction of the ravages of war. Moreover, until 1949 the United States maintained a monopoly on the possession of nuclear weapons, which formed the basis of its military might. Soviet power, on the other hand, was based almost exclusively in the retention of a huge Red Army that occupied most of Eastern and Central Europe and which could and would be used to enforce Soviet policy preferences.

If power was bipolar, it was also asymmetrical. Certainly in 1945, the United States was far more powerful than the Soviet Union; arguably, the United States had a power advantage over the Soviets greater than at any time until the post–Cold War period. Even though the United States rapidly demobilized at the war's end (an armed force of 12 million at the war's peak had been reduced to about 1 million by the end of 1946), the war had actually strengthened the American economy by turning the depressed economy into the "arsenal for democracy," and only the United States had the nuclear weapons that had been so important in ending the Pacific theater of the war. By contrast, the Soviet Union had been physically devastated by the war; it is estimated, for instance, that upward of two-thirds of Soviet industry was destroyed, as were whole towns and villages in addition to the enormous loss of lives. The Soviets' chief asset was retention of a large army.

Reconstituting the World Order

Planning for the postwar order did not, of course, wait for the end of the war. Rather, considerable work was done, especially within the U.S. Department of State, to produce a new and superior structure of peace than that it replaced.

The first question confronting the planners was what had gone wrong in the interwar period and that henceforth needed to be changed to produce a more stable international order. The peace between the world wars had been structurally entrusted to the League of Nations and the system of collective security that it created to keep the peace. Major responsibility for organizing the peace after the war would fall on the newly created United Nations. How could the United Nations be made better than the League?

The answer to that question required beginning with the failed dynamics of the League collective security system favored by many idealists after World War I. In theory a collective security system deters aggression by members of the system by presenting potential aggressors with the certain prospect that their aggression will be opposed and certainly defeated, making the aggression futile and dissuading the potential aggressor from acting.

For a collective security system to operate, it must meet three requirements. First, the preponderance of force in the international system must be available to the collective security mechanism. As a practical matter, this means that all the most important states, such as those listed in the Summary box "Major Powers by Era," should be members. Second, the members of the system must be committed to the dual, if related, propositions that the status quo is basically just and supportable and only peaceful changes in the status quo will be permitted. This translates into the requirement that all the major members of the system need to have similar worldviews, at least in general support of the structure of the system and the prohibition on changing that system through war. Third, there must be sufficient commitment on the part of the members of the system so peace will be enforced and threats or breaches of the peace will be dealt with effectively. A potential transgressor of the peace, in other words, must be convinced that its breach of the peace will be put down, thereby making such an act futile and deterring the action.

None of these conditions were met within the League of Nations setting. At no time were all the most powerful states members of the League. The United States was never a member because the U.S. Senate refused to ratify the peace treaty ending World War I, of which the League covenant was a prominent part. Following the Bolshevik Revolution, the new Soviet Union was refused admission, in the odd hope that if this new communist state was somehow isolated from the rest of the system, the quarantine would allow the "patient" either to recuperate or succumb to the disease of Marxism. In the middle mid-1930s, the Axis states (Germany, Japan, and Italy) resigned, at which point the Soviets were allowed to join, thereby effectively recreating the Triple Entente alliance of Great Britain, France, and Russia that had fought World War I together.

Clearly, the situation was also not conducive to universal support of the status quo or a commitment only to permit peaceful change to the status quo. All of the countries that would form the Axis had grievances arising from the Versailles peace process. Germany was stripped of its empire, required to accept total blame for starting the war, and saddled with huge monetary reparations. Italy was denied strategic territory that it coveted (notably Trieste), and the Japanese saw islands in the western Pacific given in trusteeship to the United States rather than Japan (which it deemed unjust due to its contributions during the war and because these islands were to be parts of the growing Japanese empire). Since none of these states supported the territorial status quo created at Versailles, they could hardly be expected to be its ardent champions. Ultimately, of course, each would reject the entreaty for peaceful change.

There was also insufficient commitment to enforcement of the collective security system. Procedurally, the League could not compel its members to enforce sanctions against those who might breach the peace. Rather, the League Council could pass resolutions that included sanctions (up to and including the use of force), but enforcement required that individual members volunteer to take the requisite actions to enforce the sanctions, which they did not always do. Instead, lacking the will to enforce the status quo, the permanent members stood aside while each member of the Axis committed acts of unopposed aggression: the Japanese invasion of Manchuria in 1931, the Italian invasion of Ethiopia in 1935, and the German remilitarization of the Rhineland in 1936.

The failure of the League was not lost on the framers of its post–World War II successor, the United Nations. The lessons seemed clear. First, all major members of the system, and especially the United States, must be full participating members. (Rightly or wrongly, many concluded that had the United States been a member of the League willing to oppose fascist expansion, World War II might have been averted.) Second, there had to be agreement on the nature of the status quo among the major states so they would be willing to defend against violent breaches. Third, there had to be a better mechanism for enforcing U.N. sanctions than was available within the "hue and cry" (raising a concern and calling for volunteers) system of the League if U.N. resolutions were to have weight.

Importantly, there was not agreement on whether these conditions would all be met. As we see in the next section, it was not at all clear that the wartime collaboration between the United States and the Soviet Union could continue in the new environment because of different visions of the world (contrasting visions of a preferred status quo). At the same time, agreement on and the willingness to commit appropriate forces to oppose breaches of the peace remained a problem well into 1995, as members bickered about what kinds of force were appropriate to deploy in Bosnia and recalcitrant Bosnian Serbs displayed their "awe" for U.N. forces by kidnapping peacekeepers and chaining them to potential targets of Allied bombers.

Within that context, the framers of the U.N. Charter created a system that would encompass collective security but also provide some organizational basis in case collective security proved impossible. The collective security system is established in Article 2 (4), which states, "All members shall refrain . . . from the threat or use of force." At the operational level, Chapters VI and VII of the charter provide for a series of actions that can be taken against those who threaten to breach or actually breach the peace, up to and including the use of force (procedures used most publicly against Iraq in the Gulf War of 1990–1991, as described in the case study in Chapter 12). Chapter VII also authorizes a permanent standing armed force under U.N. auspices for enforcing U.N. Security Council Resolutions.

At the same time, the charter provides for a world wherein collective security is inoperative. Article 51 of the charter, the so-called collective defense article, provides that "nothing in the present charter shall impair the inherent right of individual or collective self-defense." In other words, if collective security does not work, then the members can form alliances, as they did.

The framers of the charter are often criticized for having been naive in crafting the collective security provisions of the United Nations, but the criticism misses an important point. Those academics working in the State Department during the war who drafted much of the charter did not start from any naive, Pollyannaish visions of Soviet-American cooperation after the war; most felt continued collaboration was unlikely. What they did was to craft a document that could provide for an effective collective security system *if the conditions for such a system could be met*. During the Cold War, those conditions did not exist, and U.N. collective security was disengaged; now that the Cold War is over, the viability of the concept is being revisited.

Defining the Variables

How the international system would be reconfigured after World War II depended critically on two uncertain bases, the nature of Soviet-American relations and the systemic role of nuclear weapons. While the direction and substance of those variables seems obvious in retrospect, it was not so clear in 1945.

As the remaining functioning powers in the world, whether the United States and the Soviet Union could sustain the wartime collaboration or whether that relationship would deteriorate was crucial. On the positive side, the two states had no history of enmity—Russians did not hate Americans on historic grounds or vice versa—and they had cooperated well during the final stages of the campaign against Germany (a comraderie well remembered in reunions marking the 50th anniversary of the war's end in 1995). At the same time, the two systems could hardly have been more different politically and economically, both had their evangelical aspects, and it was hard to imagine that both states could find a common status quo each could defend with equal enthusiasm.

The prevailing attitude in 1945 combined general pessimism with some residual hope that collaboration could continue. The continuation of cooperation could mean a tranquil international environment wherein U.N. collective security would organize and enforce the peace. The outbreak of discord, on the other hand, provided a much more uncertain set of prospects.

The period between 1945 and 1950 can be seen as a process of gradual realizations that collaboration and cooperation could not be sustained. A series of events occurred which, individually and certainly cumulatively, defined an increasingly acrimonious, confrontational relationship that came to be institutionalized as the Cold War. In turn, the United States responded to events with a series of policies that collectively defined the overall American foreign policy of the Cold War, the policy of containment.

The storm clouds did not take long to begin gathering, and while it goes well beyond our purposes to chronicle all the critical events, some stand out. During the months of 1945 before and after the war ended, the Red Army occupied Poland, Romania, Bulgaria, Hungary, and Czechoslovakia, making some wary if the rights to self-determination agreed to at the Yalta Conference would be honored. In early 1946, the Soviets refused to end their occupation of the Iranian province of Azerbaijan (adjacent to the then Soviet republic of Azerbaijan), forcing the United States to position naval forces in the eastern Mediterranean Sea to force the withdrawal. At the same time, communist forces were engaging in civil war in Greece with apparent Soviet backing that violated wartime spheres of influence agreements (in fact, the Soviets did not back the communist rebels). In Fulton, Missouri, Winston Churchill rumbled ominously that "from Stettin in the Baltic to Trieste in the Adriatic an iron curtain has descended across the Continent."

During 1947, the United States responded to Soviet provocations with a series of policies that arguably added fuel to the fire of disagreement. In 1948, matters heated up in ominous ways. First, a communist government replaced the democratically elected government of Jan Masaryk in Czechoslovakia after he allegedly jumped from a window in the presidential palace and committed suicide (it has been alleged that Masaryk was in fact pushed). Shortly thereafter, the Soviets suspended all ground access to Berlin over the issue of currency reform in the jointly administered occupation zones of Germany, prompting the Berlin airlift that continued until the Soviets lifted the blockade in 1949. In France, the slow pace of recovery from the war had made the Communist Party the largest electoral party in the country (at about 25 percent of the popular vote), and the war in Indochina was not going well as France sought to reimpose its colonial will over communist Viet Minh rebels led by Ho Chi Minh. In 1949, the nationalist Chinese government fell to Mao Tse-tung's communist forces. The map of the world was rapidly turning red; the trend lines appeared ominous.

This period of deteriorating relations produced a whole series of policy responses by the United States. The tone was set in 1946 within the government when George F. Kennan, the leading expert on the Soviet Union in the State Department, sent what became known as the "long telegram" from the embassy in Moscow. That document, released the following year in the journal *Foreign Affairs* under the title "The Sources of Soviet Conduct" (Kennan was identified simply as "X"), laid out in stark terms the nature of the Soviet system, its implacable hostility to the Western system of democracy and capitalism, and a strategy to confront the Soviet menace. That strategy was one of "long-term, patient, but firm and vigilant, containment."

The Kennan strategy became known as the policy of containment, which in turn was implemented by a series of foreign policy and security actions. The first in 1947 was the *Truman Doctrine,* by which the United States agreed to replace a financially disabled Great Britain as the supplier of military assistance to the Greek and Turkish governments in their struggles against communist insurgents; this became the precedent for the provision of military assistance to governments besieged by communist insurgencies around the globe. Later that same year, Secretary of State George C. Marshall provided a blueprint for economic recovery in Europe that became known as the *Marshall Plan.* Originally extended to countries on both sides of the Iron Curtain, it was rejected by the communist governments of Eastern Europe and the Soviet Union (the tentative acceptance of an invitation to the initial meeting by President Masaryk was presumably linked to his untimely demise). The plan called for a pool of funds to be provided by the United States but administered by the Europeans themselves to effect economic recovery; it became the basis for extending developmental assistance to anticommunist governments elsewhere.

The other major efforts had large national security contents. The *National Security Act* of 1947 created the framework for the national security state as well as encouraging (not very successfully) military reform and the consolidation of the American defense effort. In terms of defining the structure of the Cold War system, the negotiation of the *North Atlantic Treaty Organization (NATO)* in 1949 was of particular salience. NATO directly ties the United States to the defense of Western Europe, pretensively in the face of a possible Soviet invasion (nowhere in the treaty was the Soviet Union identified by name). Operationally, in the event of an aggression against any member, all members are to consider such aggression as an act against them individually and to respond according to their constitutional processes. (This latter provision was included to get the treaty through the U.S. Senate, because it preserves the Congress's authority to declare war.)

If there was any question about the evolving nature of the U.S.-Soviet relationship, it was laid to rest on June 25, 1950, when troops of the Democratic People's

Republic of Korea (North Korea) invaded the Republic of Korea (South Korea). Since the Soviet Union was the patron of the North Koreans, it was assumed they had authorized the invasion and hence made the Cold War turn hot (archival information is beginning to be released on the actual Soviet role). The attack was widely placed in the context of the communization of China the year before and the French struggle against the communists in French Indochina (Vietnam). In that light, the competition became military and earnest.

The shape of the military relationship was, in turn, vitally influenced by the other variable, the role of nuclear weapons. Advances that would culminate in successful nuclear fission and eventually the explosion of the first nuclear device over White Sands, New Mexico, on July 16, 1945, had their birth in the years between the world wars, where parallel efforts were ongoing among American, British, German, French, Italian, and Soviet scientists, and where collaboration was widespread.

The growing clouds of war changed this scientific effort. First, collaboration among potential enemies decreased greatly, and many of the German nuclear scientists fled the Nazi regime because they were Jewish. Second, efforts moved from purely scientific inquiry to their weapons prospects. In 1939 (largely at the urging of Albert Einstein), the United States initiated a weapons program, the Manhattan Project, as a hedge against a possible German breakthrough, and that program continued even after it was learned that Germany had abandoned its program.

The atomic bomb was used against the Japanese cities of Hiroshima and Nagasaki on August 6 and 9, 1945, as a way to hasten Japanese capitulation and to avoid the necessity of an opposed invasion of the Japanese home islands (which, it was estimated, could cost a million American casualties). After the second attack, the world returned temporarily to a state of nuclear disarmament (the United States had no other fabricated bombs), a condition that would not last long.

The question was, what difference do nuclear weapons make? Gen. Lesley Groves, commander of the Manhattan Project, had said prophetically after watching the Trinity test in New Mexico, "This is the end of traditional warfare." Or was it? From 1945 until 1949, the question was abstract, since only the United States possessed atomic weapons. After the Soviets detonated a bomb in 1949 and followed that by successfully testing a hydrogen (or thermonuclear) device in 1953, less than a year after the United States had done so, their inability to deliver nuclear weapons to American soil (the Soviets never developed a truly intercontinental bomber force) still left the problem manageable.

The launching first of an intercontinental ballistic missile (ICBM) and the *Sputnik* space vehicle changed all that. Soviet possession of ICBMs meant they could indeed attack American soil, putting American territory at physical risk for the first time since the War of 1812. Moreover, since there were no known defenses against these weapons, there was no way to protect the United States from the physical devastation of a nuclear attack. Nuclear weapons thus became a vital foreign and national security concern. Deterrence—the avoidance of nuclear war—became the key concept.

From the beginning of the nuclear age, there had always been two contradictory schools of thought. One side argued that, while nuclear weapons were certainly quantitatively different than conventional munitions, they were just another form of weaponry that could and would be used in war. The other side argued that nuclear weapons provided a qualitative change in the nature of warfare, which would change how we have to think about war generally.

Those who argued that nuclear weapons represented another step—if indeed a large one—in the evolution of warfare had at least one strand of twentieth-century military history on their side. The period beginning with the American Civil War and culminating in World War II had indeed witnessed an important transition in warfare. War had become more total in both the purposes for which it was fought and in the extent to which entire societies were mobilized to aid in its conduct. World War II epitomized this trend: the total capitulation and overthrow of opponent governments provided the purpose for combat, and the war became a contest of national productive capabilities to see which societies could militarily outperform the others.

This shift changed the nature of warfare, probably forever. In previous eras, war could only be waged against other combatants (armies and navies), not against civilian populations. To attack civilians purposely was not only considered cowardly but also a violation of the rules of war. However, if civilians produced the wherewithal that allowed for states to conduct war, then they became militarized and hence an appropriate target in war. The idea, captured in the theory of strategic bombardment (see Amplification box "The Theory and Practice of Strategic Bombardment"), was that if you could destroy an opponent's ability to sustain the war effort, then you could defeat the state in war.

The problem with implementing strategic bombardment campaigns was the relative crudity and inefficiency of the munitions available to the bombadiers; the destruction of a key steel mill or ammunitions dump could take literally hundreds or even thousands of dangerous sorties by Allied bombers, resulting in considerable damage to the areas surrounding the targets and the loss of considerable numbers of attacking airplanes and their crews to antiaircraft defenses.

If one thought along these lines, what was needed was a more adequate munition for the strategic bombardier, and the atomic bomb could provide the answer. Instead of expending a large number of missions against a target (as, for instance, in the fire-bombing of Dresden, Germany, or Tokyo), the attacks on Hiroshima and Nagasaki had demonstrated what a single atomic sortie could accomplish.

The first study suggesting the continuity of nuclear weapons was a little known book by William Liscum Borden, an international lawyer who would gain notoriety for his involvement in pursuing atomic scientist Robert Oppenheimer because of alleged communist connections. In 1946, Borden published *There Will Be No Time,* whose central thesis claimed that because nuclear weapons existed, surely they would eventually be used. He argued, however, that they would only be employed against military (what have come to be called counterforce) targets.

AMPLIFICATION

The Theory and Practice of Strategic Bombardment

The idea of strategic bombardment as the crucial feature in modern warfare appeared between the world wars, springing principally from the work of aviators like Italy's Guilio Douhet, England's Sir Hugh Trenchard, and America's William "Billy" Mitchell. From an American viewpoint, the theory was most fully elaborated by a group of officers at the Air Corps Tactical School at Maxwell Field in Montgomery, Alabama.

The heart of the theory was that evolving aviation would make other forms of warfare obsolete because of the ability of the bomber to bypass the land and sea by flying over it. This was crucial because it would allow the bomber fleet to attack directly what was known as the "vital centers" of the enemy, those targets that produced the wherewithal necessary to conduct military operations. Thus, the idea was to identify the most important targets, such as fuel refineries or critical factories, that composed the "industrial web" on which the other aspects of the war effort counted.

The theory has been controversial in at least two ways. First, many argue it has never been proven, that airpower has never been crucial to success in a war, as the aviators claimed it would be. Some maintain that the bombardiers were finally vindicated in the successful Allied campaign against Iraq in the Persian Gulf War in 1991. Second, attacks against the industrial web involved what were previously considered civilian targets beyond the legitimate objects of war. Even if civilians were not directly targeted, stray bombs (so-called collateral damage) meant civilians would be the inevitable victims of modern attacks.

A much larger group of analysts saw nuclear weapons as something far more ominous. Rather than representing a quantitative extension of warfare as it had been known, these individuals argued that nuclear weapons represented such a qualitative change in weaponry that they required a rethinking of warfare. The chief representative of this line of argumentation was Bernard Brodie, who argued in a widely read book in 1946 titled *The Absolute Weapon* (of which he was editor and contributor) that nuclear weapons transformed traditional notions about war and in the future, the purpose of military force would be reduced to deterrence, the avoidance of war, rather than open warfare. Moreover, since any conflict in the future had the potential to become a nuclear war, conventional war had to be avoided as well. Deterrence became the overwhelming value.

The outcome of these debates seems very clear today, but they were not in 1945. Americans could still hope for Soviet-American cooperation in 1945, even if it was increasingly hard to conjure. The nuclear monopoly made the impact of nuclear weapons problematical, and the ideas spawned in 1946 went into virtual intellectual hibernation, only to be revived in the mid-1950s when the hydrogen bomb and ICBM made the possibility and consequences of nuclear weapons a real problem for everyone.

If these ideas also seem a bit archaic, they should not. The entreaties of General Groves and Dr. Brodie have salience in understanding how and why the Cold War ended. In essence, the thermonuclear balance that existed by the mid-1980s made the possibility of nuclear exchange so absolutely unimaginable that the fuel for that possibility, continuing antagonism between the superpowers, became an unaffordable luxury that had to be jettisoned in the interest of survival. None of that, however, was evident in 1950.

The Height of the Cold War, 1950–1962

Ushered in by key events like the fall of China to communism, the ongoing war in Indochina, and finally the North Korean attack on South Korea, the period between the onset of the Korean conflict and the Cuban missile crisis of 1962 witnessed the Cold War at its most intense, furtive, and confrontational. A hostile international environment was buttressed by a wave of domestic anticommunism that crested with the strident attacks by Sen. Joseph ("Tail Gunner Joe") McCarthy on alleged communists in major governmental departments; only when he impugned the loyalty of members of the U.S. Army (accusing them of "coddling communists") in 1954 did the public turn against his crusade.

The major theme of the period was the intractibility and irreconcilability in the relations between the "free" countries of the West (roughly any country that espoused anticommunism) and the so-called international communist conspiracy orchestrated and controlled by the Kremlin. The nature of the confrontation was pervasive, spanning all aspects of the relationship between the two sides. Moreover, the conflict was a zero-sum game, in which the gains of one side were the losses of the other and there was no room for possibly constructive compromise.

These themes promoted an interesting mind-set composed partly of fact and partly of mythology. One manifestation was a thoroughly pessimistic, even fatalistic popular culture that believed the competition could only be reconciled by a fiery war that was potentially a nuclear Armageddon by the mid- to late 1950s. Many people did not ask so much *whether* there would be war with the communists, but rather *when* that war would occur. Schoolchildren ducked their heads under their desks in a nuclear fire drill; people debated heatedly "better red than dead" or "better dead than red." Movies like the apocalyptical *On the Beach* (based on Nevil Shute's best-selling novel depicting the nuclear radiation cloud approaching the last world survivors in Australia) reflected the popular mood.

Anticommunism became the basis of national loyalty, whether reasoned and intellectual or not. Students were not permitted to read original communist works like *Das Kapital* and *The Communist Manifesto* on the curious premise that they would somehow be infected and seduced by their poisonous content; those who dared to anyway were censored and vilified. *I Led Three Lives,* a potboiler in which the hero was simultaneously an insurance salesman, member of the Communist Party, and informant for the Federal Bureau of Investigation, was the number-one show on television, as Herb Philbrick regularly exposed the weekly communist cell in the last reel and snuck out the back door as the FBI burst in and apprehended the "commies."

The perception of the international scene was dominated by a belief in the communist conspiracy. The politically active asserted that all communist activity occurring anywhere in the world had to be the work and inspiration of the occupants of the "bowels" of the Kremlin and that hence the secret to suppressing the communist menace anywhere in the world required somehow dissuading the Soviets from issuing the mischievous orders to foment mayhem.

The major events reflected this confrontational, zero-sum mentality. The Korean conflict ended in 1953 as a stalemate along the same boundary where it began in 1950; the fact that North Korea had not been liberated was viewed by many as a sign of failure. In 1954, the Indochinese war ended with the triumph of the communist Viet Minh and a humiliating French withdrawal. An American-negotiated settlement divided the country into two de facto states until unifying elections (which many believed would never occur) could be held. The fact that half the country "fell" to communism was viewed as a sufficient loss that the Eisenhower administration refused to sign the Geneva Accord it had proposed.

West German rearmament in 1955 created a similar stir. The premise of rearming the Germans was that they should share in their own defense; the prospects of Germans in uniform was sufficiently appalling in Eastern Europe that the Soviet bloc countered by forming the Warsaw Treaty Organization (WTO or Warsaw Pact) in 1955. During this period, the military aspect of the Cold War formally extended to China, as the American Seventh Fleet was twice interposed between the mainland and the tiny islands of Quemoy and Matsu, possessions of the exiled Chinese nationalist regime on Taiwan. In 1961, the Soviets erected the Berlin Wall to staunch the flow of intellectuals out of East Germany. The West was appalled but did not act. The period ended with the trauma associated with the Cuban crisis.

While the major events were confrontational, there were also isolated undertones of cooperation. In 1955, the first summit conference between an American head of state and his Soviet counterpart occurred as the United States, Great Britain, France, and the Soviet Union met in Geneva, Switzerland. The resulting "spirit of Geneva" extended to a series of summit conferences, such as Nikita Khrushchev's visit to the United States (which ended when he slammed his shoe against the tabletop of the U.N. Security Council chambers in New York) and Vice President Richard M. Nixon's heated "kitchen debate" with Khrushchev in Moscow over which side could produce superior goods.

By 1950, the power balance was well established in the two zones. NATO was a reality, and the Marshall Plan provided both necessary financing to fuel Western European economic recovery and to provide the United States considerable leverage. In the Soviet bloc, communist governments were in place in all of Eastern Europe, and the formal military ties among the major communist states (the Soviet Union, Poland, Hungary, Czechoslovakia, East Germany, Romania, and Bulgaria) were cemented with the signing of the Warsaw Pact.

The period saw considerable evolution in the dynamics of bipolarity. During the early phase of the height of the Cold War, tight bipolarity reigned: the Soviets and the Americans clearly were predominant and could largely control events within their blocs. That changed as the period progressed; 1956 is a convenient year to establish a watershed between tight bipolar control and a situation of influence where bloc members could exercise increased discretion and independence. This change was partially the result of the emergence of the Third World of newly independent states; it was also the result of two significant events, each of which had the long-term effect of loosening superpower domain over the states within its sphere of influence.

The first event, which weakened American control over the Western bloc, was the *Suez Crisis* (see Background box "The Suez Crisis" for the chronology). It became an issue because none of the three countries involved in the invasion consulted with the United States before occupying the Suez Canal Zone and Sinai Peninsula; it left the United States, at least officially, in a very untenuous position.

BACKGROUND

The Suez Crisis

The roots go back to July 1956, when Western investors (including the United States, Britain, and the World Bank) withdrew financial support for the Aswan High Dam on Egypt's Nile River. The Egyptian president, Gamal Abdel Nasser, responded by nationalizing the British- and French-owned Suez Canal as a means to provide revenue for the dam. He brought in the Soviets to help complete the project.

Fearful they would not be compensated for their investment, the British and the French conspired with Israel to capture the Canal Zone and the Sinai Peninsula, a goal they accomplished through a joint military exercise beginning on October 29, 1956, when Israeli commandos occupied Sinai; on October 31, British and French forces were air-dropped into the canal zone. On November 6, 1956, a U.N. cease-fire took hold, and debate began about how to treat the incident.

The event immediately became an American foreign policy problem that ended by driving a wedge between the United States and its two principal allies, especially France. American secretary of state John Foster Dulles, a deeply moralistic man, had been instrumental in withdrawing support for the Aswan High Dam project because of Egyptian dealings with the Soviets (Dulles believed that if you do not oppose evil, you condone it, which the Egyptians were apparently doing). After the invasion occurred, Nasser portrayed Egypt as a kind of David beset by the Goliath of Israel, Britain, and France. What was the United States to do in this circumstance?

The United States had two contradictory options. The Third World was just beginning to emerge from colonialism, and the Americans and Soviets were embroiled in a competition for influence in this part of the world. Most Third World states supported the Egyptian demand for withdrawal by the invaders. The British and the French, however, saw American support for their action as an indicator of the constancy of the United States toward its closest allies.

The United States was thus left with a devil's choice. It could back the British and French in the Security Council, joining in their veto of the resolution demanding their withdrawal; the cost would be considerable goodwill and influence in the Third World. Or, it could join the Soviet Union in sponsoring the withdrawal resolution; the result would be to avoid embarrassment in the Third World but invite the wrath of Britain and France.

Ultimately, the United States joined the Soviets in the condemnation, but doing so came with a price: unity within the North Atlantic alliance. The French, and particularly their suspicious and independent leader Charles de Gaulle, never trusted the United States again and began to act more independently. The British, more reliant on the Americans than were the French, were quieter in their disappointment, but were unhappy nonetheless.

The Soviet ability to enjoy this crisis within the Western alliance was sharply circumscribed by its simultaneous involvement in crushing the *Hungarian Revolution,* the second major event of 1956 (see Background box "The Hungarian Revolution"). Although the intent was to show the strength of Soviet control over its empire, in the end the result weakened their domain.

Because the Soviets successfully ended the rebellion and were able to impose a harsh regime under Janos Kadar in its place, the initial reaction was to treat the episode as evidence of the continuing Soviet sway over its bloc. Such a conclusion is, however, misleading.

A major consequence of crushing the Hungarian revolt was to give the Soviet Union an enormous black eye in the Third World. In that competition for influence, the Soviet Union had been portraying itself as the peace-loving champion of freedom and independence, a difficult position to sustain in the face of a seemingly ceaseless flood of pictures of the carnage being supplied globally by the U.S. Information Agency. The Soviets learned from the propaganda legacy of Hungary that such an episode could be repeated only at the cost of considerable goodwill in the Third World.

BACKGROUND

The Hungarian Revolution

The Hungarian Revolution has its roots in 1953, when Imre Nagy became premier of Hungary without the authorization of the Soviet Communist Party. He instituted a program of reform within the country, including the extension of civil liberties and even suggesting that the future of Hungary might lie in neutrality, as declared in 1955 in Austria (Austria and Hungary had been members of the Austrian, and later Austro-Hungarian, Empires). His policies were incompatible with those of hard-line communists within Hungary, including Hungarian Communist Party head Matthias Rakosi, who had the popular Nagy removed in 1955.

During 1956, Rakosi himself stepped down, but repressive policies reversing most of the Nagy reforms continued under those who replaced him. As a result, a protest movement dominated by students and intellectuals took to the streets, where they confronted and battled with police and the army. When the Hungarian communists proved unable to quell the spreading rebellion, the Soviets intervened with physical force, crushing the rebellion. In the end, many Hungarians were killed or jailed, and about 200,000 fled the country. The world's lasting image of the event was Soviet tanks pushing through crowds of unarmed protesters.

This caution was eventually not lost on the regimes of Eastern Europe, and especially Hungary itself. The Hungarians learned the real lesson of the revolt: the Soviets will have to grant you considerable autonomy in the future for fear of another public relations disaster as long as you do not appear to threaten Soviet security (some of Nagy's supporters had suggested nonparticipation in the new Warsaw Treaty Organization). As a result, by the early 1960s, Kadar had instituted a series of economic reforms (the New Economic Mechanism) that included the introduction of some aspects of a free market economy into the socialist command economy, without Soviet approval (this groundwork helps explain why Hungary was better positioned to begin economic reform than other Eastern European states in 1989).

Other dynamics were involved during the period as well. One additional factor was the emergence of the Third World from the colonial domain of the European powers. The process began in the latter 1940s, principally in Asia (India, Pakistan, and Indonesia, for instance), intensified and spread to Africa in the 1950s, and became a full-blown phenomenon by the 1960s. The growth of the number of independent states from around 60 at the end of World War II to the current number of almost 200 had both international and foreign policy ramifications during the height of the Cold War.

In terms of the international system, the new states introduced the idea of *non-alignment,* the belief that allegiance to one side or another in the Cold War did not serve their interests. This meant that relations between the new states and the major powers would have to be courted, not assumed on ideological grounds. Thus neither superpower could control events in these new countries, thereby further loosening bipolarity and even making it increasingly irrelevant as a way of describing the international system in the Third World.

The emergence of the Third World also added to the foreign policy competition between the superpowers. From a Western viewpoint, the shocking spread of communism into eastern Asia had to be avoided in the new emerging countries. This goal formed the basis and rationale for policy instruments such as military and economic assistance extending from the precedent of the Truman Doctrine. Thus, in regional balances, the United States was likely to become the principal sponsor of one state and the Soviet Union the patron of its competitor. This dynamic even extended to sponsorship of competing factions within countries.

Another major factor was the evolving nuclear balance between the superpowers. In 1950, both the Soviets and Americans had an atomic bomb, and in 1952 the United States successfully tested the first hydrogen, or thermonuclear device, a feat matched by the Soviets in 1953. Until 1957, however, the United States maintained an effective monopoly on delivery capability, since it was the only state with an intercontinental bomber force; the ICBM changed that kind of thinking and also American national security policy about nuclear weapons.

Delivery vehicles against which there were no defenses (ballistic missiles) changed the calculus of war in favor of Brodie's position (rethinking of warfare). In a world where the only way to avoid being killed in a nuclear war was to avoid that war entirely, the idea of deterrence became supreme, and the hallmark of policy (and strategy and forces) was the extent to which they contributed to deterrence. The ICBM stimulated an in-depth consideration of the concept of deterrence and a golden age of writing on the subject (see Suggested Readings). It also raised national security policy into question.

Prior to the Korean conflict, it is probably overblown to suggest the United States had ever had a comprehensive national security policy, for the simple fact that such a policy was unnecessary. In early 1950, a Defense Department task force under the leadership of Paul Nitze produced a talking paper known as NSC-68, which assessed the threat facing the United States as a basis for forming a national security policy. The North Korean attack diverted attention from that document. It was not until 1953, when the Korean War ended and Dwight D. Eisenhower, who was himself a military hero, became president that such a policy was adopted.

The Eisenhower policy was known as the New Look. It was premised on the bases that defense spending must be bounded ("Ike" believed a balanced budget was the key to national security), the United States should avoid another ground war in Asia (a "lesson" periodically learned and unlearned), and the international communist conspiracy was indeed the source of most of the mischief in the international system.

The heart of the New Look was the nuclear doctrine of *massive retaliation*. Announced by Secretary of State Dulles, its key provision was the threat to use nuclear weapons "at times and in places" of American choosing in response to any provocation the United States deemed sufficient to warrant the attack.

Although it may seem strange today, the doctrine had considerable appeal within the context of 1953. First, its implementation—in terms of building nuclear bombs and bomber aircraft—was relatively inexpensive, certainly in comparison to maintaining a large standing armed force. Nuclear weapons, in the words of Eisenhower's secretary of defense Charles ("Engine Charlie") Wilson produced "more bang for the buck" than other forms of weaponry. Second, the threat was aimed directly at the Soviets, who were the cause of the problem and quite unable either to deflect or retaliate against such an attack, presuming the United States decided to launch it. Moreover, the threat was sufficiently vague that the Soviets hopefully would be dissuaded from *any* action that might trigger the response.

Massive retaliation always had critics. During the early days, the major objection held that a cataclysmic nuclear attack on the Soviet Union was hardly warranted by minor Soviet incursions along the containment line (which had been extended, over Kennan's objections, all along the Sino-Soviet periphery) and hence was not credible. Partly to make the threat more believable, the United States negotiated a number of bilateral and multilateral mutual defense treaties with Third World countries to give the appearance of enough of a stake to enliven the threat (the process was known as "pactomania" among critics).

The policy was effectively undermined by the ICBM and hence the ability of the Soviet Union to retaliate. Critics argued that the United States could no longer consider employing nuclear weapons against all provocations (the so-called spectrum of risk). The threat would have to be restricted to defense of America's most vital interests. To deal with lesser concerns, there was revived interest in conventional forces and, after his election in 1960, so-called unconventional forces, by President John F. Kennedy.

The height of the Cold War ended with the Cuban missile crisis. For reasons that continue to be debated, Soviet leader Nikita Khrushchev authorized the emplacement of intermediary range ballistic missiles on the island of Cuba which, if activated, could have threatened the American Southeast and most of the East Coast. The Soviets had gotten as far as constructing concrete launchers when the United States revealed the activity and demanded their removal, thereby provoking the crisis.

There are many excellent accounts of the crisis, including Graham T. Allison's *Essence of a Decision* and Robert F. Kennedy's *Thirteen Days* (see Suggested Readings). The importance of the crisis, however, was its apparent effect on the Cold War and the Soviet-American relationship. In retrospect, most observers believe the crisis was the closest the Americans and Soviets ever came to nuclear war (although we can never know exactly how close they came) and that the experience frightened the leadership in both countries. From that reaction came the explicit realization that the two sides had at least one common interest: their mutual survival through the avoidance of nuclear war. From that recognition came a change in the tenor of foreign policy between the two.

Thawing the Cold War, 1962–1969

The reaction to the Cuban missile crisis ushered in a period of improved relations between the United States and the Soviet Union at the same time that fissures within the two blocs which had their roots in the previous period became more evident. The period beginning with the crisis in Cuba and roughly ending with the beginning of the Nixon administration in January 1969 was one of growing recognition of a shared interest in avoiding nuclear war that transcended even traumatic events involving both countries, notably the American involvement in Vietnam and the Soviet invasion of Czechoslovakia.

Arms Control

The centerpiece—some would argue essentially the entirety—of Soviet-American accord was the mutual effort to lessen the likelihood of nuclear war through arms control. Prior to the missile crisis, a number of major arms control proposals had been put forward unsuccessfully (the exception was the Antarctic Treaty of 1959 that banned militarization of Antarctica). In addition to the recognition of shared interest that resulted from Cuba, two other factors played into the change that occurred.

The first was a growing clamor in the United States and in eastern Asia—notably Japan—for control of nuclear testing. The other factor was the advent of reconnaissance satellites—the "spies in the skies"—that could monitor from earth orbit the extent to which either party was obeying the provisions of any agreement they might make. This monitoring ability was critical: neither side trusted the other not to cheat in the absence of some way of verifying compliance, and neither was anxious to have on-site inspections by potential spies or to allow violation of sovereign air space by aircraft overflight. The satellite rendered that problem moot.

The result was a flood of arms control agreements with the dual purposes of making war between the superpowers less likely and of restricting the spread of nuclear weapons to current nonpossessors. The first, signed in 1963, was the *Limited Test Ban Treaty (LTBT)*. This agreement among the United States, the Soviet Union, and Great Britain banned all nuclear testing in the atmosphere and demonstrates both the dual motivations of the parties and the characteristics of successful arms control. All parties could agree to the treaty without giving up much because all had already learned what they needed to about the dynamics of atmospheric explosions. So little was sacrificed by the ban, and hence there was little opposition within governments. The agreement thus opened the door to future cooperation (thereby contributing to lowering the likelihood of war), but it also could be an inhibitor in the area of proliferation of weapons to other states because no state at that time would have sufficient faith in the design of a bomb if it could not explode a prototype in the atmosphere.

These reasons help explain why the LTBT was successful. It served the dual purposes of the signatories without arousing significant opposition in any of their governments. Moreover, it responded to criticisms in the United States and Japan that the nuclear radiation of American and Soviet tests was drifting across the United States from Nevada test sites and from the Soviet Union to Japan, causing health problems.

This process continued through the balance of the period as additional test bans were negotiated covering outer space and the seabed, and a hot line agreement between the superpowers allowed instant communications in the event of crisis. It culminated in 1968: the *Nuclear Nonproliferation Treaty (NPT)*, extended in force in 1995, was concluded (see Chapter 10), and negotiations began on the first treaty to stabilize the arsenal sizes and characteristics of the two superpowers, the *Strategic Arms Limitation Talks (SALT)*.

This remarkable process continued alongside conflicting events involving the two superpowers (Vietnam and Czechoslovakia) and in the face of fundamental changes in the international system.

Vietnam and Czechoslovakia

The American involvement in Vietnam with active combat forces from 1965 to 1973 was the most traumatic experience in American military history. First, it was the longest U.S. war: active combat occurred over an eight-year span, and American involvement in a support role went back to 1950. By contrast, America's second longest war was the American Revolution at six years (from Lexington and Concord to Yorktown). It is axiomatic that political democracies dislike long wars, thus creating one basis for unpopularity.

Second, Vietnam was America's most complex war. There is clear evidence that those making the decisions to go to war did not fully understand the nature of the war (a central theme of Secretary of Defense McNamara's mea culpa in his memoir of the event) or how to conduct it. The question of attainable objectives was never satisfactorily answered, and the decision process to escalate involvement was convoluted and outside the public eye (see Amplification box "Bumbling into Vietnam.") As a result, the American public was never given a real opportunity to voice support or opposition to the war. One of the clear messages to the American military after the war was the intolerability of this condition, which meant effectively that the armed forces lacked the total support needed to conduct the war.

AMPLIFICATION

Bumbling into Vietnam

One of the ongoing criticisms of Vietnam was the way the United States became involved. There was never anything resembling a declaration of war, nor even a calling up of reserves that would force the American population to voice its support or opposition to the war.

American involvement was gradual. Until the move to leave in 1969 (Vietnamization), decisions were uniformly for an incremental increase in the U.S. commitment, not because anyone thought such a course would solve the problem, but because it was the most politically expedient.

When decisions had to be made, there were generally four options, each with disadvantages. The United States could decide to *pull out* and leave Vietnam, declaring it a hopeless case (the last time this was seriously suggested was in 1963 after the assassination of South Vietnamese president Ngo Dinh Diem). The problem was the United States would have to relinquish its involvement. A second option was to retain the *existing policy,* but the need for a new decision suggested the current policy was failing. At the other extreme, the government could decide on a *major escalation;* the problem was that doing so probably required asking the American public for a mandate that might not be forthcoming.

That left *incremental escalation* as the remaining option. The process from the Gulf of Tonkin incident of 1964 to the major introduction of U.S. troops in 1965 illustrates how that worked. In 1964, there were alleged attacks on American destroyers in the Gulf of Tonkin off North Vietnam by North Vietnamese patrol boats. President Lyndon Johnson chose the incremental step of retaliatory raids against North Vietnamese naval facilities (authorized by the Gulf of Tonkin Resolution). Some of these attacks were made by American planes based at airfields in South Vietnam; the North Vietnamese responded by attacks on the airfields that the U.S. Air Force guards were underequipped to repel. Another decision point was reached: in order to protect the air bases, the first American combat troops, 27,000 U.S. Marines, were committed in March 1965 to guard the bases. The United States had entered the ground portion of the war in Vietnam (an action that the lesson of Korea should have taught it to avoid) without any explicit decision to do so.

Source: Donald M. Snow and Dennis M. Drew, *From Lexington to Desert Storm: War and Politics in the American Experience.* Armonk, NY: M. E. Sharpe, 1994, pp. 208–240.

Third, Vietnam was the first war the United States perceived itself to have lost, and it is the indelible memory of failure that most haunts Americans about the war. But what did losing mean? It did not mean the disgrace or defeat of American armed forces; the United States may never have figured out an effective way to defeat the enemy militarily, but neither was it defeated on the battlefield. Moreover, the American armed forces withdrew from Vietnam militarily intact, not a tattered, broken force.

Success at war, however, is measured against achievement of the political objectives for which a state goes to war in the first place. During American involvement, that objective took two forms. The first, while Americans were in the field, was to guarantee an independent Vietnam, and as long as Americans remained, it was accomplished. South Vietnamese independence was erased in 1975, meaning that objective ultimately failed. After 1969 and the Nixon policy of Vietnamization (turning responsibility for conducting the war to the South Vietnamese), the objective changed to providing a reasonable chance South Vietnam would survive. That goal also failed with the fall of Saigon in May 1975. The failure to achieve the objective is the most meaningful depiction of American failure.

The fourth and fifth reasons are related. The Vietnam War was the most media-influenced and most politicized war in U.S. history. It was the first (but by no means the last) American war that underwent ceaseless, daily coverage via the electronic medium of television; as such, it was the first "living room war," a conflict that could only be avoided by not watching television news. The high awareness Americans had of the war added to the political polarization the war induced in the American population. It helped turn them against the war and tear a political gap in the society.

All these things that happened in Vietnam had happened to the United States before; what was different is that they had not all happened in a single American military adventure. The United States had fought long and complex wars before including largely unsuccessful guerilla campaigns against the Seminole Indians in the 1820s in Florida and in the Philippines between 1899 and 1902. The War of 1812 can hardly be described as anything but a failure, the Spanish-American War was—to some extent—an offshoot of the New York newspaper circulation between Joseph Pulitzer and William Randolph Hearst, and the Mexican War's campaigns can only fully be understood in light of President James K. Polk wanting neither of his major commanders, Winfield Scott and Zachary Taylor, to get too many headlines in Washington, since he assumed one of them would oppose him in the 1848 election.

What is amazing, and symptomatic of the change in Soviet-American relations, is that those relations were hardly affected by the war. The Soviets were the major military supplier of North Vietnam (along with China) throughout the war, and North Vietnam was allied to the Soviet Union by a mutual defense treaty. Americans killed Soviet allies and the Soviets supplied those allies with the weapons that killed Americans, yet relations in areas such as arms control continued as if the war did not exist.

The Soviets had an analogous situation in August 1968 when the Soviets crushed the "Prague Spring" reforms of the Alexander Dubcek regime in Czechoslovakia.

The situation was similar to Hungary in 1956. Dubcek had come to power in early 1968 without Soviet authorization, promising sweeping reforms in areas such as free speech, press, assembly, and the like. When that free speech spread to criticism of the Soviets and even whisperings about removing Czechoslovakia from the Warsaw Pact, the Soviets reacted characteristically and brutally replaced Dubcek with a more compliant leader, Gustav Husak.

The consequences of Soviet action were less dramatic than in 1956. Although the West condemned the invasion in predictable places like the United Nations, very little else occurred. The one consequence of note was that President Lyndon B. Johnson, who by this point had withdrawn from the election campaign, reluctantly postponed the beginning of the SALT talks that were to have been the crowning achievement of his presidency, fearing that to allow them to commence as scheduled would appear to reward the invasion.

Changing Power Balances

While all these developments were occurring in Soviet-American relations, the system as a whole was changing as well. The balance of power was moving beyond a strict accounting in military terms to a layer cake of military, economic, and political considerations. At the same time, the nature of relations within and between the blocs and in the relations of the communist and anticommunist worlds and the emerging Third World were changing as well.

The layer cake analogy suggests that different configurations of power were occurring within different forms of foreign policy interaction, as depicted in Figure 2.1. The figure suggests a more differentiated world with different states possessing one kind of power or the other.

The top layer is military power, and it remained largely bipolar as the United States and the Soviet Union even increased their relative advantage in the amount of nuclear power they had compared to the others. The middle layer represents economic power; the emergence of a resurgent Japan and a rapidly expanding European Economic Community (EEC) challenged American preeminence and leadership, creating a condition of economic tripolarity that would increase across time.

The political layer is especially interesting. Within the major blocs, fissures had occurred. By the early 1960s, the Sino-Soviet split that had begun in the 1950s was publicly acknowledged; the days of monolithic communism were over, and the two largest communist states were open rivals. The split within the Western alliance that began in the 1950s continued and even accelerated as Western Europe became more economically independent of the United States. At the same time, the Third World began to emerge as an independent source of political power, with states like India and Egypt seeking to lead the "nonaligned bloc" (put in quotations because it is a fundamental contradiction in terms).

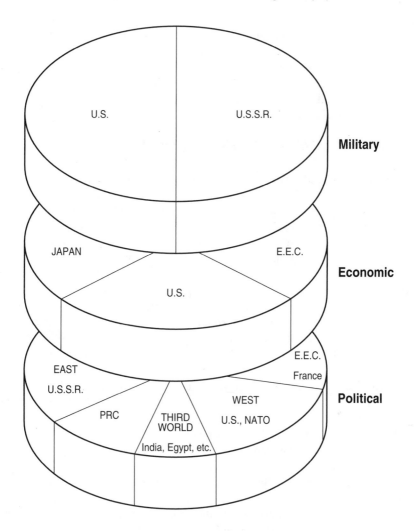

FIGURE 2.1   The Layer Cake

These changes were reflected in the relations within and among the blocs. Within the Western bloc, there was a combination of military cooperation through the NATO alliance (even if the French did not participate in the military command; see Chapter 10) and growing competition between the United States and the EEC. Within the Eastern bloc, the growing rivalry between China and the Soviets was conducted both in terms of gaining influence in other communist countries and in competing courtships of noncommunist states and procommunist movements within noncommunist states.

East-West relations were already largely checkmated by the existence of a large nuclear arsenal whose implications for total destruction were more poignantly recognized after the Cuban crisis than before. Unable to challenge one another directly along the inter-German border dividing East and West Germany, that competition had to move instead to the Third World, where the stakes were lower and failure was of lesser consequence.

Redefinition of the Cold War, 1969–1977

The year 1969 saw the rise to the White House of one of the original cold warriors, Richard Nixon. The Californian had risen to fame in the 1940s for his robust (some would suggest opportunistic) anticommunism, and he had been a vocal anticommunist while vice president under Eisenhower. In this light it is ironic that Nixon would oversee the birth of the concept of détente as a means to contain the Soviets by entangling them with the West, sign the first Strategic Arms Limitation Treaty (SALT I), and provide the leadership in ending 23 years of diplomatic isolation between the United States and the People's Republic of China.

What makes this period distinct from what followed was its emphasis on expanding the nature of the positive relationship between the United States and the Soviet Union under the banner of détente. This change occurred in the midst of conflict elsewhere. In 1969, for instance, Leonid Brezhnev declared that it was the right and duty of the Soviet Union to come to the aid of beleaguered fellow socialist states, a justification for the invasion of Czechoslovakia that became known as the Brezhnev Doctrine. Fighting broke out between China and the Soviet Union along their mutual border, and the United States remained mired in Vietnam. In 1971, the United States renounced the gold standard for its currency, thereby effectively undermining the Bretton Woods system that had underlain the international economic system since the end of World War II.

Within that context, Nixon and his national security adviser (and later secretary of state) Henry Kissinger undertook to change the geopolitics of the Cold War. This took on two forms. Toward the Soviets, the policy of détente became the shibboleth, with the SALT negotiations its central feature. Toward the Chinese, there were intricate manuevers that concluded with Nixon traveling to China in 1972 and beginning limited relations with the PRC (full diplomatic recognition was extended by President Jimmy Carter).

Détente was the master concept. The term itself is French, from the verb *détendre* which, in its literal sense, is an archery term that describes the slight lessening of tension on a fully drawn bow to allow the archer to steady his or her aim before releasing the arrow. It became the covering concept to describe U.S.-Soviet relations, at least by the Americans, and it was used to describe a gradual expansion of cooperation in the overall relationship between the two superpowers. At his most expansive, Kissinger liked to talk about the "spreading glow of détente," implying that it could provide the basis for ending the Cold War rivalry. In context, of course, the purpose of détente as a policy tool was not to bring about a universal reconciliation with the Soviet Union so much as a new way to enforce containment; the way it was sold publicly suggested the idea of expanding cooperation and created expectations that would eventually be frustrated.

Détente was always a somewhat controversial concept. For one thing, it was never clear that the Soviets accepted it as the basis of the evolving relationship. They never used the term themselves, preferring their rough counterpart concept, *peaceful coexistence*. The core of this concept, used repeatedly by Brezhnev and other Soviet leaders, was twofold. First, it asserted that the existence of large thermonuclear arsenals on both sides made war between them unacceptable, and they agreed that cooperation was necessary to avoid such an occurrence. Second, however, the clash of ideologies meant that decisive competition between the two rival systems was inevitable and would continue outside the realm of areas that could lead to nuclear war.

It was also never clear that détente as applied did not distort the original French idea or that it actually described the superpower relationship as well as peaceful coexistence did. As any archer knows, the relaxation of tension to steady the aim is only a *slight* reduction of tension; tension remains, however, or the arrow cannot be propelled very far. This idea of a limited, slight reduction in an environment where considerable tension remained was the essence of peaceful coexistence, which said, in essence, we can cooperate in a bounded area such as arms control that reduces the likelihood of nuclear war, but we will continue to compete elsewhere.

Whether one conceptualized the relationship in terms of American détente or Soviet peaceful coexistence had real consequences. In terms of détente, cooperation could gradually grow into areas beyond arms control; in terms of peaceful coexistence, those prospects were more limited. Similarly, the reasons for cooperation contrasted with one another: from an American viewpoint, the purpose was better overall relations; from the Soviet viewpoint, some cooperation was simply a necessity. At the bottom line, under détente the overall relationship could become cooperative, but peaceful coexistence maintained the relationship would necessarily remain adversarial.

By the end of the Ford presidency that marks the end of this period, it was becoming apparent that the Soviet view (or détente narrowly defined within its French context) more accurately described the relationship, and the failure of détente to spread became part of a generally pessimistic outlook within the body politic that had several different bases.

The first was the winding down of the Vietnam War. Candidate Nixon had promised in 1968 that he had a secret plan (the content of which he never revealed) to end American involvement in Vietnam and bring "peace with honor." The content of this plan, as time revealed, was gradually to turn the war over to the South Vietnamese, training them and equipping them well enough so they stood a reasonable

AMPLIFICATION

The Nixon Doctrine

The policy that became known as the Nixon Doctrine has its roots in the Eisenhower administration, in which Nixon served as vice president. In reaction to public disillusion with the Korean conflict, Eisenhower was intent on limiting future American involvement in Third World conflicts. The method for doing so was a policy (that never gained the embellishment of being called a doctrine) of American intentions in situations where governments friendly to the United States were beseiged.

The core of the Eisenhower policy—and hence the Nixon Doctrine—was the resolve that the United States would not become personally involved in future Third World ground wars. It said that the United States would assist its Third World friends, but American help would be limited to the provision of funds and equipment, including weapons, to aid regimes in their self-defense. Americans would also provide training for indigenous personnel in the operation of American equipment. In special circumstances, the United States might provide air and sea power to help friends, but under no exigency should a beleaguered state expect American ground forces.

chance at success. This policy became known as *Vietnamization,* and was a major application of the Nixon Doctrine, which the president enunciated shortly after entering office (see Amplification box "The Nixon Doctrine"). Unfortunately, the policy only served to raise more public cynicism and disillusionment with the war in the long run.

The policy had two major problems. First, its implementation took a long time: the last American combat troops were not withdrawn until March 1973, almost exactly eight years after they were first introduced into the war and fully four years after the policy was introduced. During this period of time, casualties continued to mount and military morale and effectiveness plummeted precipitously as evidenced by widespread drug use and attacks on American officers by American troops. An increasingly cynical public asked why it was taking so long. A second problem was that it was not clear the policy was bringing *either* peace or honor. Fighting continued throughout the implementation period and for two years thereafter until Saigon fell, belying "peace." The ultimate crushing defeat of the South Vietnamese raised further questions about the "honor" of the policy. Added to public reaction to the Watergate scandal and Nixon's resignation from office to avoid impeachment, Vietnam added to a public disillusionment with government and foreign policy that would form a large part of the public mood when Jimmy Carter became president.

The great American foreign policy victory of the period was the opening of relations with China. Using Pakistan (which the United States had supported during the Bangladesh secession in 1971) as an intermediary, "back door" secret negotiations began in 1971. In a classic case of the diplomatic practice of signaling (making intents known through indirect means known as signals), the Chinese invited the U.S. table tennis team, just completing a competition in South Korea, to visit China for a series of exhibition matches against Chinese opponents. This "Ping-Pong diplomacy" helped propel the process that culminated in Nixon's visit to China in 1972, thereby beginning the process of normalization between the United States and the world's most populous state.

These changes were reflected in the power balance as well. The military layer remained bipolar, but with some changes. The Soviet Union engaged in a significant military buildup throughout the period, especially in the area of nuclear weapons. By some measures of nuclear power, the Soviets attained parity or even passed the United States, and a debate began over whether the emerging Soviet advantage in nuclear arms produced any exploitable advantage for them. American defense efforts were channeled into Vietnam; after the war ended, the legacy of a Vietnam hangover was an American public aversion to any spending on military capabilities. During the period, Soviet military might appeared to incline; American military capability appeared to decline.

The economic layer was also in turmoil. The American renunciation of the gold standard (the promise to redeem American dollars with gold) set off a high degree of competition between the major economic powers (the United States, Japan, and the EEC) that effectively ended American control of the international economic system and presaged the global competition that would ensue in the 1980s and 1990s. The oil shocks of 1973 and 1979, when Middle Eastern members of the Organization of Petroleum Exporting Countries (OPEC) withheld petroleum from the market and drove up prices, added to the competition. Imported oil became so expensive that the only way major states could pay their energy bills was by trying to develop trade surpluses with everyone else.

Another trend, largely unnoticed at the time, also came into play during this period. The economic competition among the major Western powers would ultimately fuel their mutual expansions during the 1980s, largely thanks to the application of high technology to an increasingly globalizing economy (see Chapter 11). At the same time, growth in the Soviet economy ceased. Western analysts did not observe this phenomenon, which Russians now refer to as the "period of stagnation." As a result, the gap in productivity between the socialist and capitalist worlds began to widen to a chasm, creating a further Soviet incentive to call off the Cold War in the 1980s (see Chapter 3).

Politically, the further emergence of the Third World was a major factor. Decolonization was essentially complete by 1975, when Portugal finally granted independence to the remnants of its empire (notably Mozambique and Angola). The developing world states by now outnumbered the developed world, and they were becoming more restive, demanding considerable developmental assistance from the West as compensation for the colonial yoke. The core was the so-called *Group of 77,* a coalition of Third World countries formed in the 1960s that originally had 77 members (which expanded to well over 120). By the mid-1970s, it was demanding a New International Economic Order (NIEO) under which the most developed countries would annually transfer 1 to 3 percent of their GNPs to developing countries. The success of this initiative is indicated by the fact that in 1995 the U.S. government devoted less than 1 percent of the *federal budget* to developmental assistance.

The Last Gasp of the Cold War, 1977–1985

The seeds of a final return to something resembling the aura of the Cold War were planted during the Nixon years, only to blossom into one last gasp during the very different presidencies of Jimmy Carter and Ronald Reagan. The seed that would emerge during the Carter years was Soviet human rights violations against its citizens, and specifically the Soviet policy of denying exit visas to Soviet Jews who wanted to emigrate to Israel. The seed that would influence the Reagan administration, on the other hand, was the unremitting Soviet military buildup which, when combined with a cutback in military spending in the United States after Vietnam, had left the United States in what many Reagan supporters and aides felt was a precarious position that had to be redressed.

Thus, both a liberal Democratic and a conservative Republican president, starting from almost entirely different, and in many respects contradictory, positions about the world and America's place in it reached a similar conclusion about détente and Soviet-American relations. Carter started from a firm belief that human rights should be the cornerstone of foreign policy and ran afoul of a Soviet Union not yet ready to embrace that concept (despite having committed to the protection of human rights by signing the Helsinki Final Accord of 1975). Reagan was less troubled (although not disinterested) about human rights and more concerned about a geopolitical power balance becoming unbalanced because of the actions of an "evil empire." In both cases, the result was to scuttle Kissinger's "spreading glow" of détente. Also, both positions resulted in a debate about the nature of American foreign policy.

The Carter Contribution

Carter's position on human rights was partly political and partly philosophical. Politically, Carter inherited the 1975 Jackson-Vanik amendment to a trade agreement with the Soviets which specified that Soviet most favored nation (MFN) status—

receiving the same trade status on goods and services as the state with the best arrangement—was contingent on its human rights record. The Soviets rejected this arrangement as a clear violation of its sovereignty (which it was), creating a breach in relations between the two that was ongoing when Carter entered office (and which presaged a similar ongoing disagreement between China and the United States in the 1990s). This inability to cooperate on the issue was strange, since the Soviets that same year signed the Helsinki Accords (which accepted the post–World War II boundaries of Eastern Europe in return for communist world acceptance of basic human rights and created the Conference on Security and Cooperation in Europe to oversee compliance). It should be noted here that many believe the old, authoritarian structure of the Soviet Union was doomed by the implications of the Helsinki Accords.

Philosophically, Carter believed the United States could not disregard emphasizing human rights and democracy in its policy without jeopardizing its own ideals. Ignoring human rights violations, especially when committed by so-called friendly states (such as Argentina and Nicaragua at the time) is shortsighted: if American ideals are in fact superior, he reasoned, they will eventually prevail. When they do, those associated with their violation will be rightfully viewed as hypocritical, making the United States a long-term loser.

The human rights emphasis rejoined the realist-idealist debate. The realists, who had predominated throughout the Cold War, argued that the communist threat was so compelling it overrode other concerns—such as human rights—whenever they came into conflict. Anticommunism was the primary criterion for defining friends from foes. Idealists argued instead that the promotion of American values should be the primary emphasis of foreign policy, and friends should be measured by the extent to which they shared and enforced democratic practices. Moreover, they maintained that a United States true to its own values would promote its anticommunist goals more effectively than a country that ignored violations of those values.

This debate and its consequences can be seen in graphic form, as Figure 2.2. The figure portrays the realist emphasis horizontally and the idealist emphasis vertically, and it creates four cells, each of which suggests a possible combination of values a state might adopt on the two value continuums.

The realists and idealists agree on the virtues of two combinations and that one is oxymoronic. Thus, both intellectual persuasions agree that anticommunist democracies (top right cell) are desirable, since they represent the prime values of both groups. Similarly, they agree that antidemocratic communist states (bottom left cell) are undesirable. Finally, they agree that democratic communist states (top left cell) are so unlikely as to be oxymoronic.

The debate, on which Carter made his mark, is over the states that are simultaneously anticommunist and antidemocratic. The realists had argued that the anticommunism of these generally right-wing authoritarian states overrode their lack of democracy. The result was that the United States found itself supporting some fairly

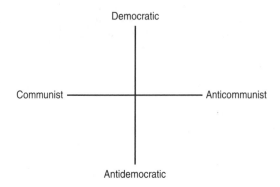

FIGURE 2.2   Anticommunism and Democracy

unsavory regimes in many Latin American states and elsewhere. The idealists believed this kind of regime was profoundly unstable and would eventually fall. If the United States was to end up "on the side of the angels" when democratization inevitably occurred, then it needed to order its priorities to bring about change, which meant rewarding regimes for democratic behavior and punishing those which remained antidemocratic.

In addition to cutting off military and economic aid to places like Argentina and, for a time, Turkey, this policy was applied with particular vengeance to Iran and its leader, Shah Reza Pahlavi. The American administration cajoled the Iranians into reforms that many believe emboldened Shiite reformers who took to the streets and eventually toppled the regime in 1979. Followed closely by the Soviet invasion of Afghanistan over Christmas 1979 (when Carter ill-advisedly admitted that in the two weeks following the invasion, he had learned more about the Soviets than in his three previous years in office), the policy seemed to have unraveled.

Two other events bearing directly or indirectly on Soviet-American relations must be mentioned. The first is the Israeli-Egyptian peace process, topped off by Carter's efforts at the Camp David summit between Egypt's Anwar Sadat and Israel's Menachem Begin in 1978 that resulted in the peace treaty. This event is generally viewed as the high point of the Carter presidency (certainly of his foreign policy). Its Soviet-American tie is that, by the time Sadat went to Jerusalem in 1977 to begin the process, the Soviets had effectively been pushed out of the Middle East; the United States could broker the process and be effective precisely because the protagonists had nowhere else to go but to the Americans for leadership (a situation which arguably continues to the present).

The other event, which greatly worsened American-Soviet relations, was the aftermath of the Soviet invasion of Afghanistan. Although the United States had essentially no interests in the mountainous central Asian state with its long land border and history of relations with the Soviets, the Carter administration roundly condemned this application of the Brezhnev Doctrine and demanded Soviet withdrawal. The Soviets refused, with policy repercussions that left the Cold War looking quite vigorous by the time Carter left office.

In response to Soviet refusal to leave Afghanistan, Carter ordered two acts of punishment. First, he ordered an embargo on grain shipments to the Soviets, which they badly needed as feed for Soviet livestock. Second, he ordered a boycott of the 1980 Olympic Games in Moscow, an event for which the Soviets had long planned as a way to enhance its image as a world-class city (the Soviets, of course, responded by boycotting the 1984 Games in Los Angeles).

The other victim was the SALT II treaty, which proposed actual reductions in the nuclear arsenals of the superpowers. The treaty, a follow-on to the agreement signed by Nixon and Brezhnev in 1972, was controversial from the outset. Opponents, notably Reagan, believed the United States gave up too much under the treaty's provisions and the Soviets were left with a sizable advantage. The result was that a major fight over ratification was looming for the 1980 Senate session. The Soviet invasion of Afghanistan, in a manner similar to their invasion of Czechoslovakia in 1968, meant the treaty was buried: the Soviets, once again, were not to be rewarded for another brutal invasion with an arms control treaty. Carter, like Johnson, was denied his crown jewel of a major arms control agreement.

The Reagan Contribution

Ronald Reagan entered office with a very different agenda. A longtime anticommunist whose political leanings had been honed in the 1950s as president of the Screen Actors Guild, he was deeply suspicious of the Soviet system (the "evil empire," as he put it in a Florida speech in 1983) and its leadership, which he distrusted. Moreover, he believed the only thing the Soviets understood was military strength, which he felt the Carter administration had allowed to deteriorate to a dangerous level (in the campaign, he referred to the "unilateral disarmament" that the Carter administration had practiced).

The two Reagan terms in office are almost totally unlike in their attitudes toward the Soviets and the Cold War. During his first term the mood was intensely hostile, to the point that between his inauguration in 1981 and the middle of the reelection campaign of 1984, there were no face-to-face encounters between the Soviets and the Americans at the level of foreign minister (secretary of state) or above.

Two dynamics dominated Soviet-American relations during the first Reagan term. The first of these was the *massive buildup of American armaments,* a major campaign promise in 1980. Much of this buildup had actually begun in 1979 under Carter, but it was accelerated and publicized to the hilt by Reagan and his secretary of defense, Caspar Weinberger. (The latter, who had earned the nickname "Cap the

Knife" for his budget cutting as secretary of health, education, and welfare under Nixon, became known instead as "Cap the Shovel" for the amount of money he made available for military programs.) Reagan also instituted the Reagan Doctrine, a rationale for the United States to come to the aid of anticommunist movements in communist states. It was used to justify assistance to Nicaraguan and Afghan rebels.

The program included sizable increases across the board for both conventional and strategic nuclear forces. Two programs in particular stood out for symbolic reasons. One was the call for and decision to pursue the "600-ship navy," a building program that would increase the size of the navy by almost 50 percent and present the Soviet navy with a serious, possibly insurmountable naval challenge. The other was the Strategic Defense Initiative (SDI), a high-technology program whose purpose was to design and eventually deploy a space-based missile defense system that could make nuclear weapons "impotent and obsolete," in Reagan's own terms. While the feasibility of the SDI was always questionable, the amount of research and development dollars expended on it (upward of $5 billion per year at its height) was not.

All this provocative behavior, by which its proponents hoped "to spend the Soviets into the ground," occurred in an atmosphere of great suspicion, even hostility, to superpower arms control, the great symbol of détente and cooperation during the 1960s and 1970s. Opponents of arms control in the administration, led by assistant secretary of defense Richard N. Perle, believed that arms control was "bad medicine," in their own phrase. They believed that whenever the Soviets and Americans negotiated an arms control agreement, one of two things happened: either the Soviets negotiated a treaty that favored them; or if not, they simply cheated on its provision. In either case, the United States came out on the short end of the stick. During the first Reagan term, there was no progress on arms control.

The other event was beyond American control or influence, but its outcome transformed the relationship. That event was the *beginning of the Soviet succession process*. It began with the death of longtime Soviet leader Leonid Brezhnev in 1982. He was replaced by the former head of the Committee on State Security (KGB), Yuri Andropov, who was suffering from a disease that would take his life in 1984. In turn, Andropov was replaced by Konstantin Chernenko, the last of the Brezhnev cohort group. None of these changes affected greatly the tone or substance of Soviet-American relations, except to the extent that there was an absence of vigorous leadership at the very top of the Soviet hierarchy. Chernenko died slightly more than a year after ascending to power; within days, he was replaced by a younger and more vigorous leader, Mikhail S. Gorbachev.

In a sense, both Carter and Reagan, each in his own way, contributed both to this last phase of the Cold War and to conditions that would transcend the Cold War. Carter's call for human rights did not make a great dent at the time, but has become a bellwether in a post–Cold War world where the axis of communism-anticommunism (depicted in Figure 2.2) is no longer relevant. Carter's entreaties may simply have been slightly ahead of their times. Reagan's arms buildup was also significant.

By demonstrating to the Soviets how expensive competition with the United States in armaments, and especially military technology (the legacy of SDI), could be, Reagan almost certainly accelerated the decision process that concluded the need to end the Cold War.

Conclusions

The preceding pages have attempted to capture and transmit the character and quality of relations between the major powers that dominated the period between 1945 and 1985. The Cold War dominated international politics and hence American foreign policy throughout this period; the most important thing the United States had to do was to contain Soviet communism and, in the process, to avoid nuclear war with the Soviet Union.

Clearly, the Cold War evolved. What seemed in the 1950s to be an absolutely intractable competition that could only be resolved by war softened in the wake of the Cuban crisis. A greater optimism that the two systems could live together reached a peak during the mid-1970s, only to backslide as the 1970s ended and the 1980s began.

That the year 1985 was indeed a watershed was not recognized at the time, although it is increasingly apparent now. Things changed because the people changed. The rise of Gorbachev to power in the Soviet Union was truly an epochal event, although Americans and most others initially demurred from the idea that he was a truly different kind of Soviet leader. As we now know, Gorbachev was a real reformer although, as we see in Chapter 3, those reforms spun beyond his control and in directions he could not possibly have approved. Once astride the crest of the wave, all he could do was go along for the ride.

What was less apparent then and is still not entirely accepted is that Ronald Reagan changed somewhere between his first and second terms. We explore one explanation of this change—that he truly became convinced of the need to unravel the nuclear showdown because of a series of events in the surrounding years—which resulted in a shift from confrontation to accommodation. The first Reagan administration attempted to "spend the Soviets into the ground"; the second Reagan administration (at Reykjavic, Iceland) came within a hair's breadth of negotiating complete nuclear disarmament. Something must have changed.

SUGGESTED READINGS

Allison, Jr., Graham T., *Essence of Decision: Explaining the Cuban Missile Crisis.* Boston. Little, Brown, 1971.

Ambrose, Stephen. *Rise to Globalism* (4th ed.). New York: Penguin Books, 1985.

Borden, William Liscum. *There Will Be No Time: The Revolution in Strategy.* New York: Macmillan, 1946.

Brodies, Bernard. (ed.), *The Absolute Weapon: Atomic Power and World Order.* New York: Harcourt Brace, 1946.

Clark, Ronald W., *The Greatest Power on Earth: The International Race for Nuclear Supremacy from Earliest Theory to Three Mile Island.* New York: Harper & Row, 1980.

Gaddis, John Lewis. *Strategies of Containment: A Critical Appraisal of Postwar American Foreign Policy.* New York: Oxford University Press, 1982.

Kennan, George F. *American Diplomacy, 1900–1950.* New York: New American Library, 1951.

Lerche, Charles O., Jr., *The Cold War . . . and After.* Englewood Cliffs, NJ: Prentice-Hall, 1965.

Mitrany, David., *Toward a Working Peace System.* London: Royal Institute of International Affairs, 1943.

Snow, Donald M., *Nuclear Strategy in a Dynamic World.* Tuscaloosa: University of Alabama Press, 1981.

Spanier, John, and Steven W. Hook, *American Foreign Policy Since World War II* (13th ed.). Washington, DC: Congressional Quarterly Press, 1995.

CHAPTER 3

Beyond the Cold War

On March 10, 1985, Moscow announced that Konstantin Chernenko had died of lung, heart, and liver disease. The third Soviet leader appointed in less than three years had been in poor health almost since being named general secretary of the Soviet Communist Party on February 13, 1984, and there had been speculation about whether he had in fact been dead for some time before the announcement. While the demise of the leader of any major power (and especially one like the Soviet Union that had no well-established formal means of governmental succession) was a matter of concern, no great significance seemed to attach to the event. Thus, the rise of Gorbachev began a process of seismic importance that was almost totally unrecognized and unidentified at the time.

Mikhail S. Gorbachev was named general secretary the next day, March 11, 1985. Although the putative protégé of Yuri Andropov was known to be a top contender for leadership, not a great deal was known about Gorbachev other than at 51 years old he was the youngest leader of the Soviet Union since Lenin and as a law school graduate of Moscow State University (specializing in criminal defense, an unlikely recipe for success in the Stalinist system), he was the first Soviet leader with a college degree.

Most observers around the world did not expect great change under Gorbachev's leadership, and the earliest actions by his regime seemed to reinforce continuity. On April 26, 1985, for instance, the Warsaw Treaty Organization extended its mutual defense pact for an additional 20 years. On July 2, Andrei Gromyko, Brezhnev's foreign minister who had earned the diplomatic nickname "Dr. No" for his predictable opposition to western initiatives, was named president and chairman of the presidium of the Supreme Soviet in an apparent compromise with the old guard of Brezhnev contemporaries.

The first public hint that Gorbachev might be different than his predecessors emerged on November 19–20, 1985, when the new Soviet leader met with American president Ronald W. Reagan at Geneva, Switzerland. It was Reagan's first summit meeting in his nearly five years in office, signaling the possibility of a shift in his views on dealing with the Soviets. Public attention, however, focused on Gorbachev, dressed in carefully tailored Italian suits, urbane, witty, and outgoing, in vivid contrast to the long line of dour Soviet leaders in their ill-fitting gray gabardine. Earlier in the year, Gorbachev and his stylish wife Raisa had visited London (up to that point, the wives of Soviet leaders were rarely seen in public and were never taken overseas with their husbands), where they charmed British leader Margaret Thatcher. Reagan and Gorbachev quickly hit it off, beginning a warm dialogue that would continue through the remainder of Reagan's second term.

No one in 1985 could have predicted how fundamentally the world would change within ten years, and many of the principals who helped bring about that change would have bridled at the future had they been able to anticipate what it would be like. Foremost among those who led change but who would have resisted its direction was Gorbachev himself.

In retrospect, it is easier to see why change was in the wind. The Cold War was 40 years old and apparently going strong. Record peacetime military budgets were being proposed in the United States, and a Soviet Union whose obstinacy was assumed in the protracted conflict looked little different than it had before.

Change was, however, about to occur, and it is necessary to analyze it in order to understand why Russia has evolved as it has and what impact that change has had on American foreign policy. Thus, in the next section, we look at why Gorbachev and those around him concluded that domestic reform was necessary and why the Cold War needed to be terminated. Next, we describe the turbulent events between 1989 and 1991 that resulted in the effective demise of the communist world, including the peaceful dissolution of America's primary adversary, the Soviet Union. The disappearance of the Cold War left behind it some residual problems to which we also turn our attention. We conclude the chapter by looking at the emerging international system, the post–Cold War world, in terms of a world of tiers.

Gorbachev and the End of the Cold War, 1985–1989

When Gorbachev came to power in 1985, he inherited a series of societal problems that were not apparent, either individually or collectively, to observers in the West more accustomed to describing Soviet strengths than in observing Soviet weaknesses. The greatest internal problem was an economy that had stagnated during the 1970s, as we noted in Chapter 2. That stagnation had both domestic and international repercussions. Domestically, it meant goods and services were in short supply to a point beyond the tolerance of even the most silently suffering Soviet citizen. Internationally, the Soviet economy and the technological base underpinning it were falling progressively behind the West, which was experiencing unprecedented growth and expansion driven by the very technologies in which the Soviets were lagging.

Even a partial list of Soviet agonies expresses the enormous difficulties the new Soviet leadership faced. The economy was in shambles: since the early 1970s the only industry that was expanding was the production of vodka. Otherwise, overall economic production was slightly down from its 1970s levels. This decline was felt particularly in the area of high technology, and especially the computing and telecommunications bases of technology. The goods that were available were often of shoddy quality; patients injured by exploding television sets, for instance, were common in Moscow hospitals. Reinforcing this decline was domestic political inertia. The government and the Communist Party of the Soviet Union (CPSU) were controlled by cronies of the late Brezhnev, and these *nomenklatura* were the managers of an incredibly inefficient state-owned production system in need of fundamental reform. All of this manifested itself in growing social discontent among the Soviet people.

These problems had clear military and foreign policy implications for the Soviet leadership. The technology gap was beginning to be evidenced in a growing military technology gap that worried the top echelons of the Soviet armed forces (a concern later reinforced by the ease with which the United States in 1991 dispatched a Soviet-equipped Iraqi armed force largely due to technological superiority). Attempting to compete with the Reagan military buildup was becoming a progressive burden, eating into scarce resources needed for domestic problems. At the same time, subsidizing its allies in Eastern Europe with benefits like cheap energy and maintaining expensive overseas commitments in places like Cuba, Afghanistan, Nicaragua, and Mozambique were becoming unaffordable luxuries. Internal problems like the Chernobyl nuclear plant disaster of 1986 (which the Soviets initially tried to suppress despite the radiation dangers to a number of European states) and an earthquake in Armenia in 1988 that killed 25,000 (largely due to inferior construction standards that caused buildings to collapse) only added to the panoply of troubles.

Very little of this was known in the West at the time because the Soviet leadership had created a facade of strength and prosperity that obscured the internal rot. But the problems were known to a group of Soviet intelligentsia, and especially academic economists, who had been monitoring their country's economic woes for over a decade and had even been communicating the state of the economy via Soviet academic journals. This group adopted Gorbachev as their standard-bearer, probably in part because Raisa Gorbachev was a colleague at Moscow State University, where she taught the Soviet equivalent of sociology, thus providing them access to the rising communist leader. When Gorbachev gained power, an underground of reformers were ready to begin the process of change.

That process, however, must be understood within the context of Gorbachev as its symbol, because the character of Gorbachev so profoundly, and in many cases perversely, affected the way change was approached. At the core, Gorbachev was a loyal, believing Marxist and member of the CPSU. Because of his deeply ingrained belief in Marxist tenets, he was always more reluctant than the outside world — and sometimes his own supporters — wanted him to be in making the switch from Soviet communism to a more Western system.

Gorbachev's Odyssey

Gorbachev was faced with a series of options for dealing with the internal and external malaise that he inherited. In terms of dealing with the Soviet domestic system, he had essentially four choices. The first was simply to continue the structure as it had evolved under Brezhnev. This was certainly the path of least resistance, but it was also the path that had created the problem in the first place.

The second option was incremental reform, a gradual process of fine-tuning the system to bring its operation onto a more competitive level. This was initially the most appealing strategy because it began from a first premise about the society that said its bases were fundamentally sound and the problems could be solved without questioning or dismantling the Marxist-based edifice already in place. This initial emphasis, formalized in the book by the same name that Gorbachev published in 1987, was *Perestroika,* described in the Amplification box "The Gorbachev Reforms."

The third option was gradually expanding reform to include both some level of capitalist economics and political democratization within a socialist framework. This was an option that Gorbachev repeatedly referred to as "humane, democratic socialism," or what others refer to as "soft (because it incorporates political freedom) communism" in contrast to old-fashioned authoritarian socialism (hard communism). At the core of this option, however, was that communism remained the core of the system.

The fourth option was radical reform, the abandonment of the socialist economic system and the monopoly of power by the CPSU. The system would be encouraged to make as rapid a transformation as possible as the only effective way to make the system competitive.

Gorbachev's personal odyssey moved through the middle two options. He preferred the second option initially because it left the structural system and especially the CPSU, whose leadership he sought to enhance, in place. Moreover, if this option worked, then it would vindicate his belief in the political and economic correctness of Marxism.

The problem with the second option is that either it did not work at all or certainly could not achieve its goals rapidly enough; as a result, Gorbachev was forced to move toward the third option, eventually concluding that the CPSU was in fact a major part of the problem. He eventually moved to dismantle the CPSU's monopoly of power within the government and to allow rival political groups to compete.

The one step that Gorbachev was personally and philosophically unable to accept was the idea of radical reform, of a concerted movement toward capitalism that involved renouncing principles and beliefs he had held all his life. Because of this, he appeared increasingly to vacillate and hesitate, particularly as his aides clamored for the fourth option. In the end, Gorbachev found himself isolated in the middle of a political spectrum turned on its head: he was opposed by "conservative" communists on his political right for dismantling their dominance and by "liberal" capitalists on his left for being too resistant to "radical" change.

AMPLIFICATION

The Gorbachev Reforms

The initial Gorbachev reform program was based on four organizing principles, three domestic and one primarily international:

1. *Uskeronie.* This term translates as "acceleration." The idea was that immediate improvements could be made in the system if people were encouraged simply to work harder and more productively, since the inefficiency, even laziness, of Soviet workers was a poorly hidden scandal. One major example of this emphasis was a restriction on the availability and accessibility of vodka, on the premise that if workers were encouraged to show up on the job sober, they would work more effectively.

2. *Perestroika.* This term translates roughly as "restructuring." It refers primarily to economic reforms designed to remove impediments to productivity. Gorbachev hoped such fine tuning would be enough to solve the country's economic problems. Among the chief targets in need of *perestroika* were the *nomenklatura,* who benefited from the existing system and were a major source of opposition to change.

3. *Glasnost.* This term is usually translated as "openness" or "criticism," although its literal meaning is "speaking up." Recognizing that barriers to change were deeply imbedded in the system, the objective was to allow the Soviet citizenry the independence to criticize those parts of the society that were causing the economic miseries being challenged. An intended target of that criticism was, once again, the *nomenklatura.*

4. *New Political Thinking.* This was the foreign policy dimension of the policy. Gorbachev proclaimed a new Soviet worldview that emphasized the equality of states, the need to live together in peace and harmony, renunciation of the Brezhnev Doctrine, and other measures whose purpose was to end Soviet isolation from much of the world and to portray the Soviet Union as a "normal" state deserving of access to Western technology and assistance.

Source: Mikhail S. Gorbachev, *Perestroika: New Thinking for Our Country and the World.* New York: Harper & Row, 1987.

The U.S. government remained ambivalent, even slightly skeptical, throughout this period. On the one hand, the government and the public were positively struck by the Gorbachevs, to the point that Gorbachev was named "Man of the Year" by *Time* magazine. At the same time, 40-plus years of Cold War had left the American people wary of any positive change within the Soviet system. Many conservative Americans, including many within the Reagan administration, urged caution in embracing these "new" Soviets, on the premise that the whole reform movement might be an act of disinformation intended to lull an unsuspecting West into complacency from which the Soviets would gain.

The Decision to End the Cold War

The Soviet leadership understood better than its Western counterparts the necessity of fundamental change both within their country and in the international system. Gorbachev and those around him realized they were holding a losing hand in the global competition that was bound to become obvious to the rest of the world. This assessment was based on two realizations that, in combination, militated to calling off the game—ending the Cold War.

The first realization was that *the economic and technological gap between East and West was growing* at an alarming rate that would, if not corrected, leave the Soviet Union a virtual Third World country in the not so distant future. The widening economic gap was, as we noted, the result of stagnation in Soviet growth that coincided with a burgeoning prosperity throughout the most developed states in which all were sharing and from which the Soviets were both excluded and had excluded themselves. The great symbol of Western economic domain after 1985 was the series of economic meetings among the Group of Seven (or G-7) states (the United States, Canada, Germany, Great Britain, France, Italy, and Japan), a group that conspicuously did not include the Soviets. (In his last years in office, Gorbachev did get a kind of guest invitation to the meetings, which were informally renamed the Group of 7 1/2 when he was present.)

The economic gap had both ideological and practical consequences. Ideologically, the massive failure of socialism suggested to many the intellectual bankruptcy of the philosophy, particularly in the face of the conscious capitalism of the market democracies. As reform began in the Soviet Union, it became evident that many Soviets, and especially economists, were willing to shed Marxist economics without regret; Boris N. Yeltsin was an early champion of this position, which Gorbachev had difficulty embracing.

At the practical level, the differences in standards of living were becoming increasingly obvious to people within the Soviet bloc countries. West German television beaming into Eastern European countries portrayed a vibrant, prosperous society in sharp relief to that at home. Under *glasnost*, even Soviets became aware of the glaring contrasts. Support for the old system waned rapidly, except among the elderly (fearful that change would undercut the social security they expected as one of the few benefits of communism) and some in the military (conservatives who opposed capitalist change).

The technological side of the imbalance was, in some ways, even more troubling because modern technology both underlay the expanding economies of the West and provided the advanced capabilities for the military system. The inability to compete technologically would, as Gorbachev repeated frequently, relegate the Soviet Union to second-class status.

At the heart of the technology gap were computing and telecommunications, areas in which the Soviets had lagged for years. The critical decision on computers occurred in the early 1960s, when the Soviet Academy of Sciences disbanded its computing division, assigning the scientists to more practical endeavors, such as weapons design. (Andrei Sakharov complained at the time of the deleterious effect this would have—he was right—which won him internal exile until he was rehabilitated by Gorbachev.) By the mid-1980s, the Soviet Union was a full two generations of computers behind the West and falling further behind.

To get some idea of this gap, the leading microcomputer in the mid-1980s was a machine called the Agat. Sold in a bright red cabinet, it was roughly the equivalent of an Apple II, although its computing speed was about 30 percent slower than that obsolete Apple. The cost of an Agat, however, was the equivalent of about $17,000. The Soviets at one point obtained an IBM 360/50 computer, which they reverse designed (tearing it apart and putting it back together to see how to manufacture it). This process took the Soviets longer than had the original design of the 360/50. In his book *Perestroika,* Gorbachev vowed to end this "import scourge."

The related area of telecommunications was no better. Except for military satellites, the Soviets lagged behind the West in virtually all telecommunications technologies. As the West was building fiber-optic networks to allow the transmission of greatly enhanced quantities of data worldwide instantaneously, it was (and is to this day) impossible to transmit digitized information *across Moscow* because of the poor quality of telephone transmission lines.

All this differentiation was concentrated in the emergence of a truly global economy among the leading market democracies (see Chapter 11). The problem for Gorbachev was Soviet exclusion from the process. In part, the Soviet economy had self-excluded itself from the world economy with its noncontrovertible currency and its system of highly artificial subsidies that could not withstand exposure to the market (bread, for instance, was artificially priced at around 10 cents a loaf). At the same time, the countries of the West would not share large parts of their prosperity, especially technology, because so much of the technology was dual use, meaning it had both civilian and military applications. Would you, for instance, sell your most advanced computers to a country that might use them to develop weapons with which to make war on you?

In *Perestroika,* Gorbachev set the attainment of "world technological standards" as a major goal of the system (ironically, in the Soviets' twelfth Five-Year Plan, a process that was at the heart of the malaise). The problem was how to achieve those goals. It became evident to Gorbachev and those around him that they would have to gain access to the technology and capital of the West or face an impoverished future. It left the Soviet leader with a devil's choice: the Soviet Union could remain Marxist but sink into economic oblivion; or it could jettison Marxism, join the West, and have at least some chance of remaining a superpower. The question was whether the West would let the Soviets join.

The other realization was the *military stalemate* between the two contending blocs, a situation that was rendering the military competition increasingly meaningless and ritualistic. The more the pursuit of the arms competition increasingly expended resources that could better be put into economic development, the less acceptable the expense became. Moreover, the military competition was the chief barrier to improved relations between the two countries. As Gorbachev himself argued in the 1987 *Perestroika,*

> Pondering the question of what stands in the way of good Soviet-American relations, one arrives at the conclusion that, for the most part, it is the arms race . . . on a level that is really frightening. Both the Soviet Union and the United States now have the capacity to destroy each other many times over. (p. 218)

This quotation both captures the problem and the contribution that the military stalemate, and especially the thermonuclear balance, would have on ending the Cold War. The basic argument is that the nuclear balance created a situation of "necessary peace" between the superpowers: a stabilization in the military competition caused by their mutual fear of nuclear war. There was broad agreement that neither side could win such a war and thus it had to be avoided. The unique addition of the 1980s was that, since *any war* in which the United States and the Soviet Union participated was a potential nuclear war, no war could be fought between them. Thus, vast wealth and energy were being expended preparing and practicing for a war that both were absolutely committed to avoiding.

This was not a widely accepted dynamic in 1985. When Gorbachev proposed nuclear disarmament by the year 2000 in a full-page advertisement in the *New York Times* in January 1986 (the transcript of a speech that apparently was not deemed newsworthy enough to cover), it was dismissed as pure propaganda. When in *Perestroika* he suggested the desirability of ending the arms race, it was similarly discounted, and analysts reminded the citizenry that Gorbachev was the protégé of the father of Soviet disinformation, Andropov.

Soviet words were clearly not enough to bring about change in the military balance, and especially in controlling or eliminating nuclear weapons. Gorbachev's major ally in the West on the question of nuclear disarmament, it turns out somewhat ironically, was President Reagan. Most serious analysts agreed that the Soviets simply could not be trusted and only the most naive observer would take Gorbachev at his word. It would take the fall of the Berlin Wall to get the attention of many in the West that change was in the air.

The two problem areas were interactive and mutually reinforced the desirability of ending the Cold War. If the Soviet Union was to gain access to Western technology and capital to aid in its economic transformation, it clearly had to remove American suspicions that blocked the transfer of technology to the Soviet Union. At the same time, even the Soviet military recognized that its underlying strength was related to the Soviet system as a whole. This, once again, was particularly true in the area of technological development; one reason the Soviet military acquiesced in the reform process was the hope that a revitalized economy would benefit them as well. With these dynamics and incentives in place, the stage was set for the events of 1989 that would transform the system.

U.S. Policy toward the Soviets

Foreign policy toward the Soviet Union did an about-face in the second Reagan term. Between 1981 and 1985, the tone had been belligerent and antagonistic (the "evil empire" approach) with no high-level contact. Beginning in 1985, that all changed. The initial focus of an improved relationship was, predictably enough, in arms control; the first Reagan administration had brushed aside arms control as "bad medicine"; the second Reagan administration embraced the concept wholeheartedly.

One arms control issue illustrates this change of direction better than any other: the problem of *intermediate nuclear forces (INF)*. The term refers to nuclear-tipped missiles with ranges from 300 to 3,000 miles intended for battlefield or theater use, primarily in Europe where both sides had literally thousands of them in place (the Soviet Union also had a number of these systems along its border with China). Because these weapons might well be used early in any war between NATO and the Warsaw Pact, thus increasingly the likelihood of nuclear escalation, they were a prime candidate for controlling or elimination.

Eliminating them was first proposed by the United States during the first Reagan term (1982). The heart of the proposal was the so-called zero-zero option, by which both sides would have had to dismantle all existing INF weapons as well as renouncing plans to build any more. The proposal was particularly disadvantageous to the Soviets, who had just completed a major deployment of mobile missiles and still had to worry about China. As a result, the Soviets rejected the plan out of hand, effectively ending arms control talks between the two sides for the remainder of Reagan's term.

What is significant about this episode is that *Soviet rejection of the zero-zero option was precisely why the proposal was made.* Led by Richard Perle, the administration realized it needed to appear to engage in arms control because the public favored arms control negotiations. The only way to appear to be engaging in arms control without the bad medicine of an actual agreement was to make a proposal that the administration knew would be so unacceptable as to guarantee its rejection. Not only was an agreement avoided, but Soviet intransigence could be blamed for the failure.

The tables turned in 1987, when the Soviets put the zero-zero option back on the table as their own. The mood had changed within the administration, which quickly adopted the idea and entered negotiations that ended in the signing of the INF Treaty and its ratification by the U.S. Senate in 1988. The terms were essentially identical to those proposed in the first term.

What had changed between Reagan terms? The clearest factor was the emergence of Gorbachev as a world leader, although most Americans (and especially many of the conservative Republicans surrounding Reagan) were initially suspicious of Gorbachev and his apparent differences from previous leaders. As he remained in power, and especially as changes actually began in the Soviet Union, the American public became increasingly enchanted with Gorbachev; unlike previous Soviet leaders, Gorbachev was a person Americans wanted to trust.

Among those apparently most taken by Gorbachev was Reagan. The two men first met at the November 1985 summit in Geneva, and by all accounts, the 51-year-old former communist lawyer and the 73-year-old former actor hit it off well, triggering a whole string of meetings between the two.

Although the two men could hardly have been more unlike as people and as politicians, they apparently did find common ground on one issue: nuclear disarmament. Ronald Reagan's hatred of nuclear weapons was long standing, going back at least to his time as governor of California in the 1960s. Moreover, the real basis of the SDI program to make nuclear weapons "impotent and obsolete" was to create the precondition for their elimination. When Gorbachev expressed a similar interest, there was common ground between the two.

The rise of Gorbachev thus may have activated an impulse in Reagan that had remained fallow during his first term. In addition, events during the period leading to the second term may have come into play. In 1983, for instance, the downing of Korean Air Lines (KAL) flight 007 by the Soviets revealed deep flaws in Soviet command and control. Two months later, the Soviet command apparently badly overreacted to a NATO exercise known as Able Archer, placing forces on a perilously high level of alert that may have shaken Reagan's complacency about lowering the prospects of war. Although he did not refer specifically to Able Archer, Reagan wrote in his memoir *An American Life* that "many Soviet officials know us not only as adversaries but as potential aggressors," and he commented, "I was even more anxious to get a top Soviet leader in a room alone and try to convince him we had no designs on the Soviet Union" (p. 450).

For whatever reasons, the second Reagan term was almost entirely the opposite of the first in terms of its relations with the Soviets. Much of the difference was the cordial interaction between the two world leaders and their apparently genuine interest in nuclear disarmament, an idea not taken seriously within the "defense intellectual" community and within the government generally. That change in relationship helped create the context within which the truly remarkable events of 1989 to 1991 occurred.

Dismantling the Cold War, 1989–1991

When Gorbachev began the process of reform in the Soviet Union, he had little or no idea how much change would occur. He ended up getting much more than he bargained for, including the fall from power of the political party to which he had devoted his adult life and the dissolution of the country he had sought to save. It is almost certain that, had he been able in 1985 to see what his world would be like on January 1, 1992 (the day after the Soviet Union disbanded), he would have tried to stop reform, or certainly would have approached it differently.

In light of the factors just discussed, however, Gorbachev had little real choice other than the course he took. Had another caretaker from the Brezhnev era succeeded Chernenko rather than Gorbachev, the process might have been delayed, but particularly the economic deficit with the world would only have worsened, making the transition even more difficult.

The evidence suggests that Gorbachev began the process of reform without any great plan. In *Perestroika,* he blamed much of the country's ills on the lack of democratization in the country (democratic socialism), but with the firm belief that soft communism was the solution to the problem. As he put it, "we aim to strengthen socialism, not replace it with a different system."

By 1989, significant change had already begun to occur domestically within the Soviet Union and in the Soviets' dealings with the rest of the world. Various aspects of *perestroika* were being put in place, and Gorbachev, frustrated by resistance to change emanating from within the *nomenklatura* of the CPSU, had effectively moved his political base from the party to the Soviet government. He accomplished these internal reforms by getting himself elected president, creating an alternative legislative body to the Supreme Soviet and its praesidium (which were effectively organs of the CPSU) in the form of the Congress of People's Deputies, renouncing Article VI of the Soviet constitution that guaranteed a monopoly on power for the CPSU, renouncing the socialist monopoly on the economy in favor of what he called "controlled private enterprise," and formally transferring power from the party to the presidency and the government.

Internationally, he was acting in harmony with the new political thinking as well. In *Perestroika,* he offered his assessment of the world situation: "We started perestroika in a situation of growing international tension. The *détente* of the 1970s was, in effect, curtailed. Our calls for peace found no response in the ruling quarters of the West. . . . The arms race was spiralling anew. The war threat was increasing" (p. 135).

His vision of the tenor of East-West relations carefully shaded Kissingerian détente and peaceful coexistence: "Economic, political, and ideological competition between capitalist and socialist countries is inevitable. However, it can and must be kept within a framework of peaceful competition which necessarily envisages cooperation" (p. 149). As if to demonstrate the sincerity of his adherence to these principles, the Soviet Union completed its withdrawal from Afghanistan after an eight-year intervention justified under the Brezhnev Doctrine (which Gorbachev had formally renounced).

These words and deeds were inadequate to convince the leaderships of the Western alliance that there were fundamental changes going on in the Soviet Union that could lead to an embrace between West and East. Although change was obvious, the old edifices of the Cold War—the barbed wire that constituted the Iron Curtain, the armed forces of the two alliances eyeing one another across that barbed wire, and most infamously the Berlin Wall—remained.

Although the evidence is less than ironclad, Gorbachev and those around him apparently concluded at the end of 1988 or the beginning of 1989 that relations between Eastern Europe and the Soviet Union were going to have to change. Partly, the Soviets needed to get out from under the drain on the economy that subsidizing Eastern Europe represented. At the same time, the leader in most of the Warsaw Pact countries were openly corrupt, out of step with their populations, and rigidly Stalinist. Gorbachev could, and probably did, envisage a process of reform that would sweep away the old order as he was attempting to do and result in the accession of younger, more vital, and reform-minded communist leaders (in other words, people like him) throughout the bloc.

All this is somewhat speculative, but the results are not. During the summer of 1989, Gorbachev and his foreign secretary Eduoard Shevardnadze (now president of the Republic of Georgia) informed the leaders of the Warsaw Pact countries that it was time to make peace with their own people and if they could not, Red Army tanks would not be available to protect them.

The breakup of the communist world began in late August 1989. On August 19, the Polish regime elected Tadeusz Mazowiecki, a member of the reform movement Solidarity, as Poland's first noncommunist prime minister since 1945; Communist rule ended on August 24. It was to prove the first step in dismantling communist authority in Eastern Europe. On August 23, upward of 1 million citizens of Latvia, Lithuania, and Estonia gathered for a peaceful protest of the 50th anniversary of Soviet rule of their countries, without repression. The beginning of the end had begun for the Soviet Union itself.

Events in Eastern Europe quickened to a torrent of anticommunist activity. Emboldened by the Polish action (Mazowiecki presented his cabinet on September 12 and declared the country would become a "normal market economy" with fully democratic institutions) and the absence of Soviet suppression, others followed. On September 10, Hungary opened its border with Austria, allowing more than 24,000 East Germans to go to the West. The Czech government followed suit on September 30, allowing 7,000 East Germans to go to West Germany.

The political beat continued and accelerated in October and November. On October 7, the Hungarian Communist Party voted itself out of existence (becoming the Hungarian *Socialist* Party), and on October 18, that country's parliament declared Hungary a multiparty democracy. That same day, Erich Honecker, the Communist Party boss of East Germany, resigned in the midst of a scandal that would bring down his government.

The pace certainly did not slow in November. On November 7, the East German government resigned amid massive demonstrations. Two days later, the East German government opened the Berlin Wall, and gleeful Germans tore it down with abandon. On November 10, Bulgaria's communist leader, Todor Zhivkov, resigned, the first step toward the renunciation of communist rule in 1990. On November 24, the same thing happened in Czechoslovakia. On November 15, Solidarity leader Lech Walesa addressed a joint session of the U.S. Congress.

The year closed with a flourish. On December 3, the entire East German government resigned, replaced by a noncommunist leadership on December 6. In Czechoslovakia, the process of reform continued, culminated by the election of dissident playwright Václav Havel as president on December 29. On December 22, Romanians overthrew Nicholai Ceaucescu, and three days later, executed him and his wife.

This remarkable chain of events continued into the new year. On January 22, 1990, the Albanian Communist Party voted for limited reforms, beginning a process by which Albania ceased being the last communist state in Eastern Europe in 1993. On April 3, the Bulgarian parliament voted itself a multiparty democratic state. On May 18, officials from East and West Germany signed the treaty leading to German reunification, which took place in July. By the end of the year, the only member of the Warsaw Pact that still had a communist government was the Soviet Union. And even that was about to change.

The Soviet Union and the last vestiges of the Eastern bloc imploded in 1991. On July 1, the members of the Warsaw Pact, meeting in Prague, Czechoslovakia, agreed unanimously to dissolve the alliance, thereby removing the formal structure opposing NATO. In parallel discussions, the Soviets began negotiating the terms and conditions for removing Soviet forces from the territories of the former members.

The most shocking and consequential process was, of course, the physical dismemberment of the Soviet Union itself. Leading the way were the Baltic states, which had forcibly been annexed by the Soviet Union in 1939 as it prepared for World War II. By the middle of 1991, the movement toward secession had spread more widely, coming to a head in August. First, a group of communist leaders calling themselves the State Committee for the State of Emergency and headed by Soviet vice president Gennadi Yaneyev staged an apparent coup against Gorbachev on August 19. Gorbachev was vacationing at his dacha in the Crimea and was placed under house arrest, and the coup leaders apparently hoped to reverse the disintegration of the Soviet Union by their actions.

The coup turned out to be a comedy of errors that demonstrated clearly the ineptitude of those members of the CPSU whose interests the plotters purported to represent. Supporters of the coup clashed with forces loyal to Russian president Boris Yeltsin, who became a worldwide celebrity by posing defiantly on a Russian tank. The coup leaders called a televised press conference the day after their action to explain that they had not really staged a coup at all but were simply assuming authority while Gorbachev convalesced from a mysterious illness. By August 21, the coup had fallen apart, the leaders were arrested, and Gorbachev returned to Moscow.

In the midst of this confusion, the Soviet Union began to unravel. On August 20, Estonia declared independence from the Soviet Union; the next day Latvia followed suit and Lithuania reaffirmed its 1990 resolve to leave the union. The Ukraine declared its independence on August 25, followed by Moldavia (now Moldava) two days later. By September 9, they had been joined by Azerbaijan, Uzbekistan, Kirghizia, and Tajikistan. On September 2, the Congress of People's Deputies approved a plan for confederation of the formerly Soviet states that would become the Commonwealth of Independent States on December 21.

On December 8, Russian, Ukrainian, and Byelorussian leaders declared the Soviet Union had ceased to exist, and on December 17, Gorbachev announced that all central Soviet governmental structures would stop operating at the end of the year. On December 31, the flag of the Soviet Union flew over the Kremlin for the last time. The next morning, it was replaced by the national flag of Russia. The Soviet Union was gone. And the Cold War was formally history.

This process was historically unprecedented, and it was almost totally unanticipated in the West. As late as early 1989, debates about upgrading NATO military capabilities were as vital as they had been in 1969. Although relations between the superpowers had improved under Gorbachev, there was still the firm belief in the vitality of the Soviet adversary and the need to remain vigilant in the face of the Soviet threat. As the new Bush administration took office, anyone who might have predicted such an outcome would have been regarded as a lunatic.

The failure to anticipate the end of the Cold War was, in large measure, the result of the collective inability of the expert community in and out of government to imagine change on the scale that occurred. Because Soviet overall power had been measured almost exclusively in military terms throughout the Cold War, the depth and intensity of the economic problem that triggered its unraveling was largely unnoticed or ignored. Certainly, people realized there was little popular support for the communist regimes in Eastern Europe and even the Soviet Union itself, but that hardly seemed to matter in societies with the monopoly of force to enforce authority. When the critical element of Soviet force was removed from the governmental equation, the bankruptcy and hollowness of the regimes became manifest. Lacking legitimacy and riddled with corruption, these regimes, which had been imposed on Eastern Europe by communist quislings after World War II, were simply swept aside. The lingering memory one carries from the time was the looks of disbelief on the faces of ousted communist leaders as their citizens discarded them.

The peaceful, unopposed dissolution of the Soviet Union itself was so unprecedented in modern history that it was not seriously considered until it happened. States had come into and gone out of existence before as the result of catastrophic events such as major wars, but the idea of a state of the consequence of the Soviet Union allowing itself to dismember without resistance (and it is remarkable how little attempt *anyone* made to salvage the Soviet state as it spun apart) was virtually inconceivable. Certainly it challenged the commonly accepted view that communist dictatorships would not reform peacefully.

But it happened as an incredulous world watched stupefied. Gorbachev, the world's second most powerful man (after the president of the United States), found himself unemployed as of January 1, 1992, the president of a nonexisting political entity. Most of the residual vestiges of the Soviet state fell to Yeltsin and Russia. Gorbachev would have to form his own Russian equivalent of an American think tank, the Gorbachev Institute, to remain a commentator on the world scene.

Gorbachev clearly did not envisage what would happen when he began his odyssey to reform the Soviet Union and create create socialism with a human face. As suggested, he would have recoiled from the future over which he presided had he any idea what would occur. It was Gorbachev's genius and legacy that he foresaw the need for change and had the tenacity to sit astride it. He oversaw the destruction of the two institutions to which he had the greatest loyalty and that he had sought to reinforce: the Soviet Union and the Communist Party.

More than the destruction of the socialist bloc, the events of 1989 to 1991 also produced the effective discrediting of the idea that underlay them, Marxism as modified by Lenin and codified by Stalin. The socialism at the heart of Marxist economics turned out to be an uncompetitive philosophy in the 1980s and one now being rapidly abandoned by peoples around the world. The authoritarian rule perfected by Stalin turned out to be necessary to enforce socialism, but it failed to convert citizenries to its political or economic credo because, as Joshua Muravchik argued in a 1990 *New Republic* article, "The problem is not, as some claim, that the two concepts, democracy and socialism, are intrinsically incompatible. The problem is that where the people are sovereign, they never choose socialism . . . they never opt against economic freedom, that is, capitalism." Democratic socialism, in other words, does not work.

This collapse has fundamentally changed the international environment in ways to which policymakers are still adjusting. Communism has all but disappeared as an operating political enterprise. The Communist Party remains in power and enforces authoritarian politics in the world's most populous country, China, but its leadership actively denigrates socialism and points with pride to its capitalist "special economic zones." Similarly, the communists remain in power in Vietnam, but are among the world's most aggressive pursuers of outside capitalist investment. Only North Korea and Cuba remain within the communist fold among the world's states of note, and it appears only a matter of time until that changes as well.

The result is a virtual void in looking at and forming policy toward the outside world. The Cold War may have been perilous and ultimately very dangerous, but it was also orderly: the United States knew who the enemy was, what the nature of the competition was, and hence what had to be done to ensure that U.S. interests were best served. In the contemporary environment, such clarity is missing. Enemies are diffuse and changing, and interests and threats to those interests often have little if anything to do with one another. In this situation, a new set of patterns is emerging, which we turn to later after looking at residual problems in the system.

Unfinished Cold War Business

The vestiges of the Cold War did not vanish without a trace. Although the Cold War extended globally in terms of the competition for influence and even converts, its heart focused on Europe, which is where the unresolved residues are concentrated. One problem area deals with the center of Europe and has implications both for European security and the inclusion of the formerly communist countries into the general European economic prosperity. Another problem deals with relations with the successor states to the Soviet Union, and especially Russia.

European Security and Economic Integration

We can think about the effects of ending the Cold War in Europe in terms of two dynamics: the evaporation of half of its security system, leaving a vacuum into which something must be drawn; and a formerly communist world that abandoned socialism to join the capitalist prosperity of the West and anxiously looks for ways to fulfill its desired affiliation. The first problem centers on NATO, the second on the European Union (EU).

The problem of European security has come to focus on what is awkwardly referred to as a successor "security architecture" to the Cold War that can encompass and provide a reasonable sense of security for all of Europe. In a sense, such an institution already exists for the 16 states who are members of NATO, although it is not entirely clear from whom they are secured by an institution that has no visible adversaries. The initial concern was on the former members of the Warsaw Pact and especially its most prominent member, Russia. The ongoing war in the Balkans and the miserable inability of existing institutions to deal effectively with it suggests the need for a Europeanwide security system that can, among other things, provide security for Europeans from themselves.

There are two basic aspects to the security problem. One is membership: who will or must be members of a successor organization for it to be effective? The other is organizational form: can one or another existing European organization be adapted more easily to the task of incorporating new members?

The membership question focuses on the two behemoths at either periphery of Europe, the United States and Russia. Almost all observers agree that the central membership problem is how to draw the formerly communist states under a single security umbrella with the democratic states of Western Europe. A minority of Europeans would like to see the United States outside this architecture—basing the security arrangement around something like the EU—although this is a decidedly minority view. Most Europeans agree that a security organization cannot be effective without American participation and leadership, although they grouse publicly and in private about the constancy and quality of American leadership (for instance, in the matter of how to deal with the Bosnian war). At the same time, there is concern about the nature of Russian affiliation. Russia feels that its size and stature means it should not be treated like "just another state," and advocates of various alternatives are sensitive to Russian concern that the former members of the Warsaw Pact be incorporated into an organization hostile to Russia.

The question of organizational form centers around the two major candidates for successor architecture, the Organization on Security and Cooperation in Europe (OSCE) and NATO. Advocates of the OSCE point out that there is no membership problem with that organization, since it includes all states in Europe as well as the United States and Canada (Yugoslavia's membership was suspended in 1992). Its detractors point out that all OSCE actions must be authorized unanimously (everyone has a veto), it has only a small and relatively new bureaucratic structure in Prague, and it has absolutely no experience in dealing with military matters.

That leaves NATO as the major alternative, and it is likely that some form of expanded NATO will become the basis for the future. NATO exists, it has the bureaucratic structure that OSCE lacks, it has military plans and contingencies, and its major members have performed militarily together (for instance, Anglo-French and American cooperation during the Persian Gulf War of 1991, in which NATO war plans were the basis for the successful campaign).

Support for NATO ebbs and flows. Immediately after the implosion of the Cold War, there was widespread skepticism about the future of an organization specifically designed to deal with a problem that no longer exists. Moreover, the interests of the major powers within the alliance are only occasionally identical when dealing with crises outside of Europe (the so-called out-of-area problem), and the inability to formulate and implement an effective policy toward Bosnia is offered as evidence of its lack of viability.

Having said that, NATO does exist and has begun taking steps to incorporate Eastern European states into the organization. The major vehicle for doing so, announced by President Clinton in January 1994, is the Partnership for Peace (P4P or PfP). The idea of P4P is to provide a way for nonmembers of NATO to be affiliated with the organization in a manner short of full membership. It is a compromise, interim solution to the political problem of European security. On one side, many of the states of Eastern Europe (Poland, Hungary, the Czech Republic, Slovakia, Bulgaria, Romania, Estonia, Latvia, and Lithuania as of June 1995) have applied for full membership, and should they be admitted, the floodgates would be open. This presents a twofold political problem that P4P status seeks to ameliorate. On the one hand, if Eastern European states are given full membership, then existing members will be fully committed to their defense, and it is not at all clear that either European or American public opinion would rise to the military defense of many of these countries. On the other hand, the extension of membership to countries that border on the former Soviet Union means Russia must be reconciled to the system, and it is not clear that the current Russian leadership or public has resolved its future on the security issue, for reasons discussed later.

P4P defers these decisions and political problems by providing partial membership through an affiliation that has virtually no written conditions or stated commitments, and which has no timetable or firm commitment to full membership at any particular time in the future. Most of the non-NATO states of Europe, including a number of the Soviet successor states, have signed on (a total of 23 in spring 1995). Russia has vacillated on its own form of participation, finally acceding to a vaguely defined form of affiliation in May 1995. Those states demanding full membership are forced to accept this "half a loaf" solution and grumble for an accelerated timetable for full NATO membership.

The United States has demonstrated a certain level of ambivalence on the NATO membership question. On one hand, Americans very much want to tie the militaries of the Eastern European countries to their own, as a way to ensure that they become and remain a democratizing factor in their countries (the United States already sponsors a considerable number of exchanges and the like with Eastern European officers). On the other hand, the United States is one of those countries where the support for defending formerly communist countries is suspect, and Americans are particularly sensitive to how the Russians feel about expanding the alliance.

The other European problem has to do with how or whether to extend the economic prosperity enjoyed by Western Europe to the formerly communist countries. No one opposes the general proposition that the conversion of the formerly communist societies into market democracies is desirable for the tranquillity and well-being of Europe. The questions have to do with the feasibility and timetable for conversion, and the cost of the effort for the rest of Europe.

The economic issue focuses on the European Union and whether or how to incorporate the formerly communist countries into the EU. This in turn raises at least three separate concerns: what, if any, preference should be given to these states over other applicants; whether the states of Eastern Europe can successfully meet the criteria applied to past applicants; and what effect adding these states would have on the nature of the union.

The EU has expanded in the past, and will continue to do so in the future. Membership originally stood at six states, and with the addition of Austria, Sweden, and Finland in 1995 now stands at 15 (Norway has the distinction of being the only country to date to vote down membership in a 1994 referendum). Several members of the old European Free Trade Area stand outside the union and would seem reasonable candidates for association.

Politically, the real sticking point in allowing Eastern European states into the union before others are considered centers on the application of Turkey. Turkish interest in joining the EU is manifest, but the union has not acted favorably on the application, citing the fragility of Turkish democracy, an economy not at the same level as the existing membership, and the ongoing suppression of Turkish Kurds in eastern Turkey by the armed forces. These same criticisms can be made about near-ly all the formerly communist states, and to act favorably on the applications of coun-tries like Poland and Hungary (both of which have made formal applications for membership) before Turkey would reinforce the widespread Turkish perception that the real reason for their exclusion is that Turkey is an Islamic state.

This leads to the question of criteria for membership. The original members were all homogenous states with market-based economies and stable political democracies. That future member states would have to meet those dual tests was first demonstrated when Spain and Portugal applied in the 1970s. In both cases, they had only recently replaced authoritarian regimes with democratic rule, and their economies were considerably less developed than those of the then current member-ship. As a result, Spain and Portugal were not admitted instantly, but instead served what amounted to a probationary period during which they could engage in EU-assisted development and demonstrate the firmness of their commitment to political democracy.

This "Spain and Portugal rule" has been applied to all subsequent applicants, and will certainly be applied to the formerly communist states as well. Doing so will dis-qualify all of them in the short run on both economic and political grounds, although a few (Poland, Hungary, the Czech Republic, Slovenia, for example) are closer on economic grounds than others. None, it should be added, is closer to meeting the cri-teria than Turkey.

Whether to waive or moderate these criteria is largely a question of what kind of union Europeans want, and there is disagreement on that count which has implica-tions for new members. One group of states, led by France, wants to emphasize "deepening" of the union by concentrating on efforts to integrate the economic and political relationships among existing members more fully rather than adding new states to the organization.

Other states, notably Great Britain, prefer increasing membership as a way to tie the formerly communist states to the European system and to make sure those states do not backslide into new authoritarian forms. The motivation of these "wideners" is not entirely pristine; the British, for instance, have misgivings about the amount of integration that has already occurred and see broadening the membership base as a way to avoid further unwanted integration.

In addition, there is concern about the economic effects of extending member-ship to less developed states. The union learned from integrating Spain and Portugal (as well as Greece) that bringing new members up to the standards of the existing membership, which is necessary if the quality of the union is not to be diluted, is terribly expensive, time consuming, and uncertain. Any Europeans who have forgotten those problems have only to look at the painful experience Germany is having bringing formerly communist East Germany up to the standards of the rest of the republic. The expense would be further accentuated because of the need for enormous environmental cleanup in several formerly communist states.

American policy on this matter is straightforward: it supports the wideners. American standards of living will not be affected by efforts to develop the economies of the aspirants to membership, and their accession to EU status would ease somewhat the fervor of their desires to join NATO, thereby easing that problem with the Russians.

Russia and the Successor States

Where once there was a single Soviet Union, now there are 15 fiercely independent states; the uprising in Chechnya demonstrates that even splintered as Russia is, there are still peoples within those successor states that would like to further alter those political boundaries. Twelve of the states (all except the three Baltic republics) are loosely affiliated with one another through the Commonwealth of Independent States, which provides very little unifying effect.

At the center of this disunion stands Russia. Possessing roughly three-quarters of the landmass of the old Soviet Union, Russia is still the largest country of the world in physical area, has a population of around 150 million, and retains control of the former Soviet nuclear arsenal. For all these reasons, what happens to Russia is important to American foreign policy, as it is to the rest of the world.

Russia has sizable problems, all associated with the disintegration of the Soviet Union. Economically, it is dogged by two major, interrelated difficulties. On the one hand, conversion from a command to a market economy has proven extremely difficult for a society very poorly prepared for the transition. Regulating the economy of a country that had no central bank is an economic problem for which there are not easy solutions, and moving toward private enterprise in a system that has no laws covering private ownership of property is a difficult proposition, to cite two examples. The criminalization of much economic activity is another. The result is shaky support for the economy and the regime. On the other hand, breaking up the union also disrupted the flow of goods and services between what was an integrated economic system that is now a series of sovereign states. Setting the price of Ukrainian wheat in Russia or of Russian energy in Ukraine are also proving to be difficult tasks. The ramifications of economic success or failure in Russia and elsewhere in the successor states will have an impact on political stability as well.

There are deep-seated instabilities, some of them violent, both within and between some of these states. The Chechens' attempt to gain independence has been well documented and reported, but separatists abound within the successor states—Abkhazian secessionists in Georgia and radical Muslims in Tadjikistan, to name two. The successor states of Christian Armenia and Islamic Azerbaijan have been fighting for over three years over the enclaves of Nagorno-Karabakh and Nakichevan (a matter that gains outside interest as Azeri-controlled oil and gas fields in the Caspian Sea near production).

There is also the minorities problem. Approximately 65 million citizens of the former Soviet Union live outside their native republics. Of these, about 25 million are ethnic Russians living in the successor states. The Russians worry openly about the fate of these people. A major goal of their defense effort is the promise to come to the rescue of ethnic Russians in the "near abroad" (the way the Russians refer to the successor states).

The problem of protecting Russians outside of Russia is part of a broader security problem that has at least two other aspects. One is the physical security of Russia from its enemies. Although the Russians now have effective control of the old Soviet strategic nuclear arsenal, the overall capabilities of the Russian armed forces have shrunk to about one-quarter of their Cold War levels, with very real concerns about their quality, as shown in the way they have acted to attempt to break the attempted secession of Chechnya.

This diminution of military power is very painful for Russia, whose claim to major power status is now limited to its nuclear arsenal. Russia does not lack enemies, many of them now in the successor states, and many Russians see the expansion of NATO into Eastern Europe as a development that could pose a potential threat. The anguished debate over Russian participation in P4P will undoubtedly be replayed when the demands for full membership can no longer be suppressed.

The other aspect of the security question is how to deal with present and future instability in the successor states. The kinds of situations that have engaged the international community in places like Somalia are present in the southern tier of states between Russia and the Middle East, and it is not at all clear that the principals involved are capable of containing or resolving these difficulties themselves. It is even less clear what outsiders have enough interests in places like Kazakhstan or Kirghizia to participate in peacekeeping or peace enforcement actions in the successor states. The only exception is Russia itself, but Russian intervention, as it did to save the Shevardnadze regime in Georgia in 1993, will almost always be viewed suspiciously as part of Russian imperial reassertion.

These problems are all direct consequences both of the end of the Cold War and the disintegration of the Soviet Union. American interest is in spreading the general prosperity and tranquillity of the major market democracies to the formerly communist world, as well as the countries of the old Third World. To understand the dynamics and problems associated with this expansion, we must now turn to a description of the emerging patterns of the international system and what problems and opportunities they provide.

A World of Tiers

During the 1950s, a French economist devised a way to describe different groups of states by dividing them into "worlds." There was a First World that consisted of the most advanced states of the world—the industrial democracies; a Second World that included the socialist or communist states; and a Third World made up of the emerging countries of Africa, Asia, and Latin America (some analysts added a Fourth World to depict the very poorest emerging countries, those which had little realistic short- or medium-term prospect of economic development).

The disappearance of the Second World—mostly into the Third World using the old designations—makes this classification scheme obsolete and asymmetrical. What we suggest is that the world can now be better understood as being divided into two distinct "tiers" (for an introduction, see Snow and Brown, *The Contours of Power,* listed in the Suggested Readings). Our scheme closely parallels that of several other analysts, including Singer and Wildavsky in *The New World Order,* in its depiction both of divisions in the system and the dynamics within and between groups of states.

The First and Second Tiers

We divide the world into two tiers. The core of the system is the First Tier: the leading market-based democracies of the world that was also the basis of the First World category. Consisting of the countries of North America, the European Economic Area (the EU and EFTA), Japan, and the Antipodes (Australia and New Zealand), these are the countries most clearly a part of the emerging global economy. They all possess political democracies and market-based economies (making them what President Clinton refers to as the "circle of market democracies"). These are the countries that have entered the Third Industrial Revolution (the information-based revolution in computing and telecommunications), are producers rather than consumers of high technology, and have increasingly intertwined economies and convergent political philosophies. They also are the key countries in the evolving regionalization of trade through bodies such as the EU, the North American Free Trade Area (NAFTA), and the Asia-Pacific Economic Cooperation (APEC). Their group identity in the economic sphere is through the G-7 summit of the most economically powerful members.

The rest of the world is composed of the Second Tier, a grouping that encompasses almost all the Second World and all the old Third and Fourth Worlds. Whereas the countries of the First Tier share great similarities, the Second Tier is a very diverse array, from near–First Tier states in economic and political terms (for instance, some Pacific Rim states like South Korea and Taiwan) to the extremely poor states that are concentrated in Africa and parts of southern Asia.

Because of this diversity, we have subdivided the Second Tier into four subtiers, as noted and defined in the Summary box "Second Tier Subtiers."

Summary: Second Tier Subtiers

Developed: Countries with highly developed economies and normally fragile (new) democracies or systems with democratic aspects. Economies have concentrations in Second Industrial (consumer goods, services, licensure) and Third (information) Revolution industries.

Partially Developed: Countries that have undergone qualitative development, with sizable concentrations on heavy industry and basic consumer goods. Often development is uneven across regions within a country.

Developable: Countries with varying developmental prospects, with concentrations of economic activity in subsistence agriculture, mineral extraction, or cottage industry.

Resource Rich: Rich, normally nondemocratic countries with little developmental infrastructure (other than a financial sector); an anomaly in a developmental sense, most would revert to lower subtiers without extraction.

Although the definitions are reasonably self-explanatory, some elaboration may be helpful. The first three subtiers are sequential in terms of levels of development and hence approximation to the First Tier. To classify individual states within these subtiers, we used two sets of criteria: level of economic development that used dominant forms of activity and income as guides; and political development as a secondary measure (with levels of democratization as the benchmark). Thus, developed countries—which are those most likely to join the First Tier—have probably entered the Second or even Third Industrial Revolution by possessing a sizable service industry, and have at least fragile democracies (democratic governments that are not long standing). South Africa and Chile are examples. What distinguishes them from First Tier states is the stability of their systems and hence their achievement of what Singer and Wildavsky call "quality economies"—where politically free people do work of their own choosing and are thus highly motivated and productive.

At the other end of the scale are the developable countries. All three categories represent continua, and this subtier is no exception. Countries in the developable subtier range from those in the process of moving from a subsistence agricultural-based economy to an industrial economy (thus nearing the partially developed subtier) to extremely poor countries where almost all the population is engaged in subsistence farming.

TABLE 3.1
Second Tier States by Region

	Developed	Partially Developed	Developable	Resource Rich
Asia, Pacific	4	8	17	1
Middle East	2	6	2	7
Latin America	5	19	8	1
Former Communist	1	8	19	0
Africa	1	11	36	4
Totals	13	52	82	13

The resource-rich countries are an anomaly, made up primarily of those countries for which the production of petroleum is the major economic activity but that provides a high standard of living associated with First Tier or near–First Tier states. The difference between the resource rich and the First Tier is structural: if petroleum wealth is removed, almost all the resource rich would fall into the partially developed subtier, and most (Trinidad and Tobago are the obvious exception) do not have democratic governments.

Countries of the various subtiers are distributed across the globe, as summarized in Table 3.1 (a detailed listing of countries by region and subtier is provided in the appendix). There are several notable points about this distribution. Over half of the states (82 of 160) are in the lowest developmental category, giving some indication of the enormity of any developmental process one might devise. Moreover, those states in the developable category tend to be concentrated in three areas: Asia and the Pacific (South and Southeast Asia, a few Pacific islands); the formerly communist world (the southern tier of Soviet successor states, the Balkans); and Africa (sub-Saharan Africa), where 36 of the continent's countries fall in this category. At the same time, the smallest category within those subtiers in the developmental ladder are the developed states, meaning the number of candidates for movement upward into the First Tier is limited.

Implications for Policy

Conceptualizing the world as one of two tiers has utility in dealing with the post–Cold War world in two ways. First, it provides a vehicle for describing how the world is different than it was during the Cold War. Second, it also helps to define the broad foreign policy problems and challenges the United States faces in the years to come.

Thinking in terms of a world of tiers reveals three different ways in which the world has changed: the distribution of power in the system, the changing nature of power, and the dynamics of the international political system. We examine each in the final section of the book but introduce the ideas here.

The changed distribution of power is the most glaring difference between the Cold War and now. Most obviously, there is only one "bloc" left, the market democracies that compose the First Tier. Within that single bloc is a single remaining superpower, the United States. Each of these characteristics is important.

The fact that all the world's most important states—in an economic and political sense—are in the First Tier and that they share an overarching commitment to the same worldview means there is a tranquillity among the most important states that has not existed since the eighteenth century; it is not too strong a statement to make that, at the extreme, there are no meaningful prospects that any First Tier state or states will go to war with any other like states. The only global states outside the First Tier are Russia and China, and while they could disrupt the system, there is little reason for them to do so. As a result, the system does not need to worry anymore about a system-threatening war such as a Soviet-American nuclear war. And that is one way in which the system is decidedly improved.

The United States is *the* remaining superpower within the new system. This does not mean the United States has hegemonic power that allows it to dictate world events; but it does mean that the United States is the only country that has both significant military and economic power available. That translates into political power, as the United States alone has major interests globally.

The nature of power within and between the tiers has changed as well. Generally speaking, military power is of less importance, especially for First Tier states: military threats and the like are meaningless among First Tier states; the interest-threat mismatch means there are many situations in the Second Tier (the locus of instability and violence in the system) where First Tier force might be used but could hardly be justified by public opinion; and there are situations, like those in Rwanda and Somalia, where it is not clear that First Tier military forces would be appropriate to the situation. The threat and use of violence, especially within countries, remains an apparently viable tool, but the violent conflicts that exist do not threaten the system more generally.

In the emerging system, economic activity looms as increasingly important, especially among the countries of the First Tier. The global economy, where economic activity flows freely across state boundaries with little governmental ability to regulate factors like investment, has become increasingly common, and states are now able to interfere and regulate economic actions (where they want to) only at the margins, such as trade policies and investment incentives. Large well-publicized incidents such as the Japanese-American fight over exclusion of American automobiles and parts in 1995 obscure the basic seamlessness of global economic activity. Virtually all the countries outside the First Tier clamor to become part of the general prosperity, and it is a policy question how much of a helping hand to extend.

This has affected the dynamics of the international system itself. The absence of any prospects for a system-threatening war has caused military reductions throughout the First Tier and given life to a debate within the United States about how many and what kinds of military forces for what reasons the United States should retain in the future. What political scientist Samuel P. Huntington calls the "third wave of democracy" unleashed by the events of 1989 raises questions about how far the tranquillity of the First Tier can be pushed and at what costs. The isolation of most instability and violence within the Second Tier similarly raises questions about the extent to which there is a systemic commitment to limiting violence.

These changes have direct implications for American foreign policy and are all part of the ongoing debate about the shape of that policy. Areas for policy development that can be understood in the context of the world of tiers include dealing with Russia and China, the broader question of the priority assigned to bringing Second Tier states toward or into the First Tier, the locus of conflict management (especially in intertier relations), and finally, the American responsibility to provide leadership in the new international order.

Clearly, Russia and China stand outside the prosperity and tranquillity of the First Tier, and both would like to enjoy at least its economic benefits. If either or both could somehow be brought into and accept the values of First Tier states, the system would be more stable than it currently is. Two policy questions arise: what are the barriers to First Tier status? and are those barriers surmountable by First Tier action? The answers would appear to vary by country.

The problems of Russia are overwhelmingly economic. By almost all standards, Russia is a partially developed state economically. Its industry is overwhelmingly First Industrial Revolution heavy industry with some consumer emphasis, whereas much economic activity remains in mineral and energy extraction and agriculture. The old Soviet system did not provide the framework for institutional change to a market economy, and support for the fragile democratic system of Russia is jeopardized by citizen discontent with the economy.

Solving these problems is made daunting both by the size of the task, the enormous amount of resources necessary for upgrading the Russian economy, the limited ability of the Russian economy to absorb outside resources, and the absence of a clear set of guidelines about how to convert a command to a market economy. These difficulties combine to make short-term prospects dismal; given the assaults on foreign assistance in the United States, probably the most Americans can do is to provide expert assistance, for instance in public safety and the containment of organized crime, hoping that Russian democracy will not drown amid the wailings over economic misery.

The Chinese problem is different. The heart of the Chinese economic system is sound and growing, thanks to their experience with the Special Economic Zones (SEZs). Unfortunately, that development is not geographically universal: southeastern China is virtually a First Tier state, but much of the northern and western parts of the country are closer to the developable category. Until the market permeates all of China (or China is reconfigured as a country), First Tier status will be elusive.

The Chinese also have a political problem of transition both of the succession after Deng Xiao Peng dies and in the longer term movement toward some form of democracy. The country remains firmly in the grip of the Chinese Communist Party, which argues for its monopoly of power not on ideological grounds, but to avoid a

Soviet-style disintegration of the state. This creates a dilemma. China will not achieve First Tier status until it democratizes (which many in the SEZs already demand), but democratization will almost certainly result in its dismemberment. One scenario heard in the West but rarely voiced in China itself would have the prosperous southeast of China forming a democratic country that includes Hong Kong, Macao, and Taiwan and races toward the First Tier, while the rest of the country further splinters and parts fall into different Second Tier subtiers.

The cases of Russia and China are actually examples of the broader question of what the First Tier can or should do to promote movement through the developmental sequence of the Second Tier. The problem is more difficult the further one goes down the development ladder: assisting the movement of developed subtier states into the First Tier is a good bit less difficult (the recent economic crisis in Mexico demonstrates it will not be easy) than moving the poorest developable states out of their morass. Economic and political development make sense in that they would produce a more tranquil world and enlarge global markets. The question of will and available resources to try to bring such change about is not yet evident.

The problem of violence and instability is also different in a world of tiers. In the contemporary system, violence is almost exclusively located in the poorer parts of the Second Tier, and much of it is in the form of internal wars. The distribution of conflicts in 1993 by area and subtier is included in Table 3.2.

The composition is illuminating and fits the earlier observation. Most of these wars occur in the developable subtier (two-thirds of the conflicts, whereas the subtier is slightly over one-half of the Second Tier). Moreover, they are concentrated in the areas identified: Africa (almost one-third of the total), south and southeastern Asia (over one-fourth), and the successor states and Balkans (almost one-sixth).

The question is who will regulate these outbreaks of violence, if anyone does. The Second Tier itself lacks the necessary resources, leaving the First Tier. But does the First Tier have the will or interests to become involved in, say, central Africa?

TABLE 3.2
Violent Conflicts[1] by Area and Subtier

	Developed	Partially Developed	Developable	Resource Rich
Asia and Pacific	0	2	8	0
Middle East	1	2	0	3
Latin America	0	2	2	0
Formerly Communist	0	1	5	0
Africa	1	1	10	0
Totals	2	8	25	3

[1]Armed conflicts are those that have produced 1,000 or more casualties over their duration.

Source: Project Ploughshares, *Armed Conflict Report: Causes, Conflicting Parties, Negotiations, 1993.* Waterloo, Ontario: Institute of Peace and Conflict Studies, 1994.

The pattern of violence seems tailor-made toward organizing systemic response around the original conception of the U.N. collective security provisions, but the record to date has been inconsistent at best, ineffective at worst.

Adjusting to a system in which the interactions of the tiers represents the major policy challenges means the First Tier needs to come to grips with how it wants to deal with these problems. That will require leadership from the most important First Tier states, which in turn means the United States, as the remaining superpower, will have to adopt a leadership position. The content of that leadership position, in turn, is the major foreign policy question posed by the new order.

Conclusions

The world of the mid-1990s bears little resemblance to the international system of 1989, and certainly to the Cold War system that came tumbling down beginning in 1989. That hardly anyone foresaw the nature, extent, and consequences of the changes that occurred between 1989 and the end of 1991 made them all the more shocking and difficult to adjust to. During World War II, people knew the war would end, so they could plan for the postwar world. Since there was so much less anticipation of the Cold War ending, Americans lacked the lead time to prepare for a post–Cold War world few had envisaged or even thought about.

The change has been seismic. The global competition between communism and anticommunism has been swept away, and what remains is the more amorphous world of tiers, where states are differentiated by their levels of adherence to political democracy and levels of commitment to and robustness of market economies. Americans no longer go to bed worrying about whether there will be a nuclear war when they awake (to borrow from President Bush); people *do* go to bed wondering how much a Lexus may cost tomorrow.

The substance of foreign policy must change in order to deal with changing challenges emerging from the environment, but that is not all. The structures of government through which foreign policy is made also must undergo change because they were, by and large, crafted to deal with the Cold War problem. How the government organizes to deal with foreign policy and how that organization is changing to meet a new foreign policy environment is the subject of Part II.

SUGGESTED READINGS

Crotty, William. (ed.). *Post–Cold War Policy: The International Context*. Chicago: Nelson Hall, 1995.

Gaddis, John Lewis. *The United States and the End of the Cold War: Implications, Reconsiderations, Provocations*. New York: Oxford University Press, 1992.

Gorbachev, Mikhail. *Perestroika: New Thinking for Our Country and the World*. New York: Harper & Row, 1987.

Huntington, Samuel P. *The Third Wave: Democratization in the Late Twentieth Century*. Norman: University of Oklahoma Press, 1991.

Laqueur, Walter. *The Long Road to Freedom: Russia and Glasnost*. New York: Scribner's, 1989.

Muravchik, Joshua. "Gorbachev's Intellectual Odyssey." *New Republic* 920, 3 (March 5, 1990), 20–25.

Oberdorfer, Don. *The Turn: From Cold War to a New Era*. New York: Poseidon, 1991.

Rubinstein, Alvin. (ed.). *America's National Interest in a Post–Cold War World: Issues and Dilemmas*. New York: McGraw-Hill, 1994.

Snow, Donald M. *The Necessary Peace: Nuclear Weapons and Superpower Relations*. Lexington, MA: Lexington Books, 1987.

Snow, Donald M., and Eugene Brown. *The Contours of Power: An Introduction to Contemporary International Relations*. New York: St. Martin's Press, 1996.

CHAPTER 4

The President

Arriving in a foreign capital aboard *Air Force One*—a massive Boeing 747 emblazoned with the seal of his office—the president of the United States is greeted by the pomp and ceremony once reserved for monarchs. The outward symbols of great power are all there: swarms of security guards, a small army of aides and advisers, a doting band of news reporters, technicians who keep him in instantaneous communication with the White House, and a fleet of presidential limousines and helicopters that were flown in ahead of the president's arrival. These ornate trappings of power are merely the visible manifestations of the overriding fact of international life during the past half century: the United States is the world's greatest superpower, and the president of the United States is its most powerful foreign policymaker and a world leader.

It is a reality that would have startled the country's Founding Fathers. In their deliberations over the new republic's constitution at the Philadelphia convention in 1787, the 55 delegates were all too aware of the dangers of excessive concentration of power—especially power over foreign affairs—in the hands of the executive. Their eighteenth-century world was filled with the object lessons of unaccountable European monarchs treating war and international intrigue as a personal amusement.

The resulting American Constitution, little altered for two centuries now, carefully divides formal policy-making authority between the executive and legislative branches. In the memorable words of the late Edward S. Corwin, "The Constitution . . . is an invitation to struggle for the privilege of directing American foreign policy." Each branch was given its own independent sources of authority, but the powers of each were carefully checked and balanced by countervailing powers given to the other. In the making of public policy, then, including foreign policy, the Founding Fathers believed in *codetermination* by the two coequal elected branches, with neither branch dominant over or subordinate to the other. One of the most widely held myths about the American constitutional system is the notion that the Founding Fathers intended foreign policy to be the province of presidents, with Congress relegated to a decidedly secondary role. The point is of such fundamental importance that it bears repeating: what the Founding Fathers contemplated was a vigorous executive branch *and* a vigorous legislative branch whose separate views and powers would together set the country's course in international affairs. Those who find a constitutional intent for presidential primacy or congressional primacy misread the country's fundamental political charter.

The practice of the past two centuries, however, shows that the carefully calibrated balance envisioned by the Constitution's authors is difficult to maintain. The result has been a recurring swing of the pendulum between periods of presidential dominance of foreign policy and periods of congressional reassertiveness. The modern era of U.S. foreign policy, the period since World War II, has been one of presidential dominance, but that dominance has been challenged by the most recent phase of congressional assertiveness, which began in the 1970s.

Despite the Founding Fathers' vision of equal policy codetermination between the two elected branches, then, presidents are often able to dominate the foreign policy-making process. To understand why this is so, we need first to look at the formal powers granted to presidents and then to consider the informal powers and international circumstances that greatly enhance the president's formal authority.

Formal Powers of the Presidency

The Constitution confers on presidents six formal roles and powers that together give him considerable, although hardly overwhelming, authority in foreign affairs. First, we simply list them, and then we turn to a brief discussion of each. Constitutionally the president is the (1) chief executive, (2) chief of state, and (3) commander in chief of the United States; he is also granted enumerated powers in regard to (4) treaty making, (5) appointment of key personnel, and (6) the recognition of foreign regimes.

Chief Executive

Article II, Section 1, makes the president the nation's chief executive. In this capacity, he presides over the vast array of federal agencies that carry out the business of government. Although few presidents devote much time or energy to the actual supervision of the sprawling federal bureaucracy, the fact that the president is chief executive means all the agencies which possess the kind of specialized information and expertise essential to foreign policy-making report to the White House. Agencies such as the State Department, the Pentagon, the CIA, and the Office of the U.S. Trade Representative have incomparable resources, the most important of which is the large number of experienced and well-informed experts with unrivaled access to vital information. Although in recent years the Congress has strengthened its own institutional capabilities for independent analysis and foreign policy development, its staff cannot begin to compare to the rich lode of seasoned expertise residing throughout the sprawling executive establishment.

One challenge a president must meet is to develop a management and decision-making style that will ensure the mobilization of the executive agencies around presidential objectives rather than their pursuit of their own institutional interests. Presidents who successfully meet this challenge begin the foreign policy-making process with an advantage over Congress, which cannot match the analytic capabilities, specialized knowledge, and subject-matter expertise found in the foreign affairs bureaucracies. On the other hand, the growing proliferation of bureaucratic players in foreign policy-making, coupled with the fact that executive agencies often work against one another in seeking to influence foreign policy, somewhat lessens the older image of a president sitting securely atop an executive establishment reliably harnessed to his policy objectives.

Chief of State

When acting in his capacity as chief of state, the president is the symbolic personification of the American state. Although some writers sometimes dismiss this role as merely a ceremonial function, skillful presidents know how to use its powerful theatrical potential to enhance their political clout in the continual interbranch wrangling over defining U.S. foreign policy. Because he is a living symbol of the state—just as the American flag or the national anthem symbolizes the shared legacy and ideals of the country—the president is treated with extraordinary deference. His legal authority may indeed be comparable to that of Congress, but through his stature as national icon he is elevated to an entirely different plane than any member of Congress could ever enjoy. Both symbolically and emotionally, the public regards the president as the country's leader, and not merely as the head of one branch of the federal government. Because of his exalted symbolic stature, he is the one political leader everybody knows. He flies on his own airplane, he is chauffered in his own limousine, he resides in his own mansion, and he even has his own song, "Hail to the Chief."

Presidents who take the ceremonial role of chief of state lightly do so at their own peril. Jimmy Carter, for example, took office determined to get rid of the trappings of the "imperial presidency" of Richard Nixon, and so he made it a point to ride in ordinary sedans, wear cardigan sweaters while giving televised speeches from the Oval Office, and carry his own luggage when traveling. While initially refreshing, Carter's "plain folks" behavior eventually proved unsettling to the American people, who want leaders who are in many ways not like them but rather convey a certain theatrical sense of majesty. Carter's successor, Ronald Reagan, understood this desire perfectly well. He had, after all, been an actor, and he thoroughly enjoyed his new duties as ceremonial representative of the American state embodied in the role of chief of state. Reagan's skill at playing the part of chief of state was an advantage when he turned to the more prosaic political tasks of dealing with Congress over the conduct of U.S. foreign policy.

Commander in Chief

Article II, Section 2, makes the president the commander in chief of the country's armed forces. While the constitutional language conferring this power to the president is clear enough, its deeper meaning is not. Two centuries of practice and precedent have established a presidential role that goes far beyond the merely ceremonial concept of civilian command. Successive presidents have sought to expand the concept to give the White House a policy-making authority to determine when, where, and for what purpose U.S. armed forces are committed abroad. While the Constitution clearly reserves to Congress the formal authority to declare war, modern presidents have asserted a decidedly expansive interpretation of their prerogatives to embark on armed hostilities without a formal declaration of war. Indeed, about 200 presidentially ordered conflicts in U.S. history were not accompanied by a declaration of war. Truman's commitment of large-scale forces to resist communist aggression in Korea in 1950, Johnson's invasion of the Dominican Republic in 1965, Reagan's invasion of Grenada in 1983, and Bush's invasion of Panama in 1989 are all examples of presidents relying on their capacious definition of their powers as commander in chief to commit the country's armed forces to combat operations abroad. Although he informally sought congressional blessing for deploying troops to Bosnia, President Clinton also operated on this principle.

Given the recent presidents' expanding interpretation of their independent authority to act in their capacity of commander in chief, Congress sought to reinstate the Constitution's intent and curb the president's independent ability to commit the country to war. In 1973, Congress passed the War Powers Resolution over presidential veto. This legislation attempts to strike a balance between the need for presidents to respond to emergencies, on the one hand, and the constitutional design of joint executive-legislative codetermination of this most fateful foreign policy power, on the other. As we see in Chapter 7, this act has been only partially successful in dissuading strong-minded presidents from adopting a highly permissive interpretation of their authority as commander in chief.

Treaty Negotiator

The authority to commit the country to legally binding international commitments is a major source of the president's power. It is significant, therefore, that the Constitution (Article II, Section 2) carefully divides this power between the president and the Senate in the well-known formulation that the president "shall have Power, by and with the Advice and Consent of the Senate, to make Treaties, provided two-thirds of the Senators present concur." While the president and his agents may thus have the initiative in negotiating treaties, they must be mindful of the ultimate need to win approval of two-thirds of the Senate.

President Woodrow Wilson's inability to win Senate approval of the Versailles Treaty and, with it, American participation in the League of Nations left a bitter after-taste among successive presidents regarding the entire treaty-making process. Hence, the twentieth century has seen the growing presidential practice of relying on *executive agreements* to codify international agreements. Unlike treaties, executive agreements do not require congressional approval. The problem with executive agreements is that they are nowhere mentioned or legitimized in the Constitution. Their use evolved gradually, but until recently they represented a relatively noncontroversial means of handling routine aspects of international dealings. Recent presidents, however, have increasingly used executive agreements to make major international commitments on behalf of the state. This constitutes a sharp departure from the constitutional design that presidents should not be able unilaterally to determine U.S. foreign policy.

Today, executive agreements outnumber treaties by a ratio of nearly 20 to 1. Understandably, presidents want to have as free a hand as possible in what they have come to regard as their personal domain of foreign affairs. The danger is that both modern presidents and the American people appear to have forgotten the Constitution's clear intent and to have persuaded themselves instead that it is somehow a presidential right to determine the country's international course.

Nominator of Key Personnel

Article II, Section 2, of the Constitution authorizes the president to name senior executive officials and ambassadors "by and with the Advice and Consent of the Senate." Thus, his control over key foreign policy personnel is limited by the necessity to win Senate approval for his selections. Ordinarily, the Senate gives the president broad latitude in selecting his foreign policy team. Sometimes it swallows hard and confirms diplomatic appointees of dubious suitability. In recent decades about one-third of U.S. ambassadors have been political appointees (that is, they are not career diplomats). Of these, some are individuals with distinguished records of achievement in academic life (as was the late Edwin 0. Reischauer, the foremost U.S. Japan scholar who was named ambassador to Tokyo by President Kennedy) or political life (as was Robert Strauss, former Democratic Party leader named by President Bush to head up the Moscow embassy). But others are wealthy campaign contributors who possess no apparent credentials for the challenging world of diplomacy. President Reagan's nominee for ambassador to Botswana, St. Louis businessman Theodore Maino, told the Senate Foreign Relations Committee that he was qualified for the job because he had a "commitment to public service, having a lifetime association with the Boy Scouts of America." The senators gulped hard but voted to confirm Maino anyway.

Occasionally, however, the confirmation requirement becomes the occasion for intense executive-legislative conflict. In 1981, for example, the Senate rejected

President Reagan's first choice to be assistant secretary of state for human rights, Ernest W. Lefever. In part, the vote against Lefever reflected serious doubts about the nominee's suitability, but more fundamentally it registered the Senate's concern that the Reagan administration seemed insufficiently committed to the human rights agenda. President Bush's 1989 nomination of former senator John Tower as secretary of defense triggered a pitched battle between the president and the Senate. Tower's rejection meant that Bush would have to name a secretary who enjoyed the confidence of members of Congress. The easy confirmation of Dick Cheney, an affable, well-liked congressman from Wyoming, showed once again that presidents are generally granted broad latitude in selecting key executive officials, as long as those officials have earned the respect of Congress. Occasionally, Congress will use the power to deny confirmation to settle old political scores by denying positions to highly qualified old enemies, as in the case of Clinton's nominee for assistant secretary of defense, Morton Halperin.

Recognizer of Foreign Governments

Derived from the constitutional grant, in Article II, Section 3, that "he shall receive Ambassadors and other Public Ministers," this power has been interpreted as enabling presidents to commence or terminate diplomatic relations with other states by refusing either to receive their ambassador or appoint an American ambassador to their capital. Today it is difficult to recall the bitterly poisoned relations that existed between the United States and the communist regime that came to power in China in 1949. Chinese leaders denounced American "imperialism" and proclaimed their intention to encircle and defeat the United States by sponsoring anti-American revolutions throughout the Third World. The United States, embittered by China's entry into the Korean War and racked by hysterical anticommunism at home, refused to recognize the Beijing regime for a quarter of a century, insisting instead that the defeated Chinese Nationalists on the island of Taiwan "represented" China. By the mid-1960s sentiment was growing in Congress and elsewhere for the U.S. government to acknowledge the reality that the Chinese communists did indeed govern China and should therefore be dealt with on a government-to-government level. The decision to alter U.S. policy, however, belonged entirely to the president. Not until Richard Nixon's historic trip to China in 1972 did the United States reverse its policy of isolating China diplomatically and begin the process of normalizing relations between the two nations. Similarly, the centrifugal forces of religion and ethnicity are today tearing apart many of the former communist nations of Europe and a number of multiethnic African countries. The decision to recognize new claimants to the mantle of statehood is an important question in U.S. foreign policy. Again, it is the president who alone determines if and when the United States will extend to them the legitimacy conferred by diplomatic recognition.

These six roles and powers comprise the formal powers available to any president in the shaping of U.S. foreign policy. Yet, as we noted earlier, this is hardly an overwhelming cluster of constitutionally sanctioned authority. As we see in Chapter 6, the Congress can point to an equally impressive array of constitutional powers in foreign policy-making. Indeed, American history displays about as many eras marked by congressional dominance in directing foreign policy as it does periods of presidential dominance. Given all these considerations, how are we to account for the fact that modern presidents are ordinarily able to dominate the foreign policy-making process? The answer lies in an assortment of informal sources of presidential influence. Theoretically available to any White House incumbent, they have been mastered by only a handful. Those who do master them, however, can transform the relatively modest formal authority of the presidency into a capacity to lead the country in its dealings with the outside world.

Informal Powers of the Presidency

Presidential Singularity

The president's greatest advantage over the Congress is the fact that he is a single, universally known leader, whereas the Congress is inherently a rather faceless corporate body comprised of 535 members. Members of Congress do not make it to Mount Rushmore; only presidents do. It is this presidential singularity, coupled with his designation as the country's symbolic chief of state, that has so enhanced the modern presidency beyond its rather sparse constitutional foundations. In moments of crisis, the country instinctively looks to the president for strength and reassurance about the future. His informal designation as the national "leader"—in ways that transcend his rather austere constitutional position—gives the president a built-in advantage over Congress in the ongoing institutional competition over who will define the country's foreign stance. There are three other informal sources of presidential power—his role in molding public opinion, his dealings with foreign leaders, and his proclamation of presidential doctrines—in the foreign policy-making process, but note that all three flow from the basic fact that the presidency ultimately comes down to a single figure.

Shaping Public Opinion

In his capacity to shape public opinion, again, the president enjoys the inherent advantage of being the people's focal point for leadership in a way that the "faceless" Congress is not. A president's ability to mobilize the public around White House policies is defined by his approval ratings and skill in using the media. With regard to the president's popularity at the moment, the public is always fickle. (Harry Truman underwent the widest swing in the opinion polls, receiving a record-high 87 percent approval rating at the beginning of his term and seeing that figure descend to a low of 23 percent.) Nonetheless, public support is a resource much prized by political leaders. Certainly, presidents who see their approval ratings drop sharply during their terms (both Johnson and Reagan bottomed out at 35 percent approval, Nixon hit a then-record low of 24 percent, and the hapless Carter plummeted to a dismal 21 percent approval) are less persuasive in rallying an already disapproving public around presidential objectives than are presidents who find themselves riding the crest of public affection. Truman, Kennedy, Johnson, and Bush all recorded approval ratings in excess of 80 percent; in each instance, however, the public's backing accompanied a grave international crisis and proved to be ephemeral.

Enhancing or inhibiting a president's ability to rally public support for his foreign policy objectives is his skill in using the media to reach the people, define the policy agenda, and arouse the public to back him. The modern master at communicating directly to the people through the electronic media was Franklin D. Roosevelt, whose pretelevision fireside chats via radio created an unusually close bond between the public and its president and have been recreated by Bill Clinton with parallel intent. Similarly, John F. Kennedy and Ronald Reagan employed their natural eloquence and charm to great advantage in appealing directly to the people for support of their foreign policy objectives. Although much less graced by personal warmth, Richard Nixon often used prime-time televised addresses to go over the heads of Congress and the country's opinion leaders in an effort to shore up public support for his foreign policies. Skillful presidents, then, are able to use their personal popularity and unrivaled access to the national media to generate popular support for their foreign policy preferences.

International Diplomacy

Most modern presidents have developed a keen personal interest in the glamorous arena of international diplomacy and have devoted a great deal of their time and the prestige of their office to meetings with foreign leaders. During the domestic budget summit in 1990, President Bush made an unusually candid admission of his own preference for foreign policy over domestic policy: "When you get a problem with the complexities that the Middle East has now . . . I enjoy trying to put the coalition together and . . . seeing that this aggression doesn't succeed. I can't say I just rejoice every time I go up and talk to [former Congressman] Danny Rostenkowski . . . about what he's going to do on taxes." Presidents can claim credit for dramatic foreign policy successes, whereas domestic problems seldom lead to clear-cut victories and, when they do, presidents can less plausibly claim credit for themselves.

Televised images of U.S. presidents traveling abroad enhance the notion that it is natural for presidents to determine the country's external posture, while comparable efforts by members of Congress are dismissed as mere meddling. Certainly, all recent presidents have devoted a large proportion of their time and energies to foreign affairs and are commonly associated with their international adventures: Franklin D. Roosevelt at Yalta, Eisenhower escorting Nikita Khrushchev on his historic visit to the United States, Kennedy meeting Khrushchev in Vienna and later electrifying the people of Berlin, Johnson visiting American soldiers in Vietnam, Nixon on his historic 1972 visits to Beijing and Moscow, Ford's arms control mission to Vladivostok, Carter's Middle East peacemaking at Camp David, Reagan's Berlin exhortation, "Mr. Gorbachev, tear down this wall!," George Bush's visit to American troops in Saudi Arabia during Operation Desert Shield/Desert Storm, and Bill Clinton's meeting with Russian president Boris Yeltsin in Moscow in 1995. These settings allow presidents to feel most in control of the national interest and to bask in international acclaim for policy triumphs associated with them.

Presidential Doctrines

The fourth informal source of presidential power is the president's ability to put his distinctive stamp on policy by unilaterally proclaiming doctrines bearing his name. Although not, strictly speaking, binding on the country, presidential doctrines carry great weight, both at home and abroad. Domestically, they constitute the framework within which the policy debate occurs and are typically accepted—with varying degrees of enthusiasm—by the public and policy elites because to repudiate them would be to present an image of national disarray to the rest of the world. Abroad, presidential doctrines are carefully noted in official circles and treated as authoritative pronouncements of U.S. policy.

Hearkening back to the historic Monroe Doctrine, the names of five recent presidents have been attached to foreign policy doctrines. The Truman Doctrine, unveiled in a speech to Congress in 1947, set the tone of ideological anticommunism in postwar U.S. foreign policy. The Eisenhower and Carter doctrines asserted U.S. vital interests in the Middle East. The Nixon Doctrine, introduced in a rambling chat with reporters on Guam Island during a refueling stop in 1969, announced U.S. unwillingness to become mired in protracted Third World wars, as it had done in Vietnam. Finally, the Reagan Doctrine, a term coined by a journalist in 1986, captured Reagan's determination to go beyond the containment of communism and instead seek its undoing in Third World outposts such as Nicaragua and Afghanistan. In each instance, the president seized the policy-making initiative and defined the essential direction of the country's foreign policy through his capacity to command wide attention, speak with a single voice, and conduct himself as the broadly defined national leader that so many now expect American presidents to be. Next we examine how recent presidents have approached the formidable task of directing the foreign policy bureaucracy and making decisions about the actual content of U.S. foreign policy.

Styles of Presidential Decision Making

Bill Clinton is the 41st American president (although his presidency is the 42nd, a function of Grover Cleveland's two terms—the 22nd and 24th presidencies—being interspersed with that of Benjamin Harrison). Like all his predecessors, Clinton wears the hat of chief executive, and in this role, he sits at the pinnacle of the executive branch. His formal authority over executive agencies is assured him by the same constitutional language that made George Washington the first chief executive.

Even though the Constitution has changed little during the past two centuries, the realities of the federal establishment have been altered beyond recognition since the early days of the Republic. The executive branch has grown so vast and complex that it inherently resists central direction. The sheer scale of the president's job of running the executive branch is nearly overwhelming, whether measured by employees (over 4 million civilians and members of the armed forces) or budget (in excess of $1 trillion annually) or administrative structure (14 cabinet departments and 60 noncabinet-executive agencies). Sixty years ago President Hoover could direct his executive domain with a White House staff of 3 secretaries, 2 military aides, and 20 clerks; Bush's White House staff of 500 seemed as swollen as the executive apparatus it sought to direct; President Clinton promised to reduce staff by 25 percent, still leaving a sizable number.

Given the elephantine dimensions of the federal bureaucracy, it is difficult for any president to get a handle on it. The kind of specialized information, policy expertise, and analytical skills necessary for policy formulation are broadly dispersed throughout the executive branch. So the president needs to attain command over his branch so that talent and information will be mobilized around presidential purposes. Thus, each president needs to select and institute a management system that will get the executive establishment to serve *his* ends of presidential decision making rather than degenerating into an array of competing and unelected fiefdoms.

There is, of course, no one best way for a president to manage the bureaucracy. Rather, each president must set in place a decision-making management system that best fits his own experience and personality. So we begin here by focusing on the personality characteristics and idiosyncrasies of recent presidents. They do make a difference.

To start us thinking about the considerable variance among presidents in terms of traits like intellectual capacity, how they relate to other people, their sense of themselves, and the like, in the Amplification box "The President Speaks," are eight quotations from post–World War II presidents. See if you can match the presidents—Truman, Nixon, Ford, Reagan, and Bush—with the quotations (answers are on page 129 at the end of the chapter), and as you do so, try to specify the personality traits that you think are most important in shaping the way presidents approach the task of foreign policy decision making.

AMPLIFICATION

The President Speaks

1. "I'm afraid that I let myself be influenced by other's recollections, not my own. . . . The only honest answer is to state that try as I might, I cannot recall anything whatsoever about whether I approved an Israeli sale in advance or whether I approved replenishment of Israeli stocks around August of 1985. My answer therefore and the simple truth is, 'I don't remember, period.'"

2. "I don't pretend to be a philosopher. I'm just a politician from Missouri and proud of it."

3. "There is no Soviet domination of Eastern Europe and there never will be any under (my) administration."

4. "I guess it just proves that in America anyone can be president."

5. "Now, like, I'm president. It would be pretty hard for some drug guy to come into the White House and start offering it up, you know? . . . I bet if they did, I hope I would say, 'Hey, get lost. We don't want any of that.'"

6. "When the president does it, that means it is not illegal."

7. "Once a decision was made, I did not worry about it afterward."

8. "I have often thought that if there had been a good rap group around in those days I might have chosen a career in music instead of politics."

Typology of the Presidential Personality

In order to help us move beyond the merely quirky aspects of presidential personality and begin to get an analytical grasp of how personality affects foreign policy decision making, we need to establish a conceptual framework that reveals what the important factors are and how those factors can help or hinder presidents as they seek to manage the immense resources available in the federal agencies. Probably the best work done on this subject is that of Professor Alexander George of Stanford University. In his writings, George alerts us to the importance of three key personality variables that affect the ways presidents approach the tasks of management and decision making. In the exercise, perhaps you came up with a different set of personality traits that you regard as prime movers in presidential decision making. If so, see if you agree with George or if you feel his framework omits some important factors. In any case, we use George's typology here as a way of stimulating thought on this important topic.

The first variable is what Professor George calls a president's cognitive style. It refers to how a president processes information, how he defines his information needs, and how he gets the information he wants. Some presidents are information minimalists. A good example is Ronald Reagan, who seldom read serious material, displayed minimal intellectual curiosity about the details of the policy issues he was deciding, and had a limited attention span that required his aides to keep their briefings truly brief lest he nod off in midpresentation. Other presidents like to receive as much information as possible on policy issues. Kennedy, for example, immersed himself in the intricacies of policy questions, as Nixon did and Clinton does. All three were voracious readers with remarkable memories. Similarly, Jimmy Carter tried to master the most minute detail, even going so far as supervising the scheduling of the White House tennis court.

The concept of cognitive style also alerts us to the ways presidents prefer to get their information. Some (e.g., Nixon) are more comfortable with the written word; others (e.g., Bush) prefer the interactions of oral briefings and discussions with senior aides and subject-matter specialists.

The second key personality variable is a president's personal sense of efficacy and competence. This trait simply refers to what the president himself feels he is good at and what he regards himself as less competent in doing. Ronald Reagan, for example, knew his limits as a thinker and a hands-on manager, but he thoroughly enjoyed the ceremonial role of chief of state. He was unusually effective in the symbolic uses of the presidency to reach out and communicate to the country. Jimmy Carter, by contrast, was not an uplifting orator but was much more at home immersed in the details of policy issues. Both Bill Clinton and George Bush are renowned for their interpersonal skills, which have enabled them to work amicably with political supporters and opponents alike. Richard Nixon, perhaps America's most complex and troubled president, was most comfortable grappling with complex foreign policy issues that required the mastery of a great deal of information and strong analytical abilities. However, he was chronically uncomfortable around other people, especially in unstructured settings. He was awkward and ill at ease, and had almost no knack for making small talk. Standing atop China's Great Wall in 1972, during his historic trip that restored U.S. relations with that gigantic nation, Nixon could only remark,

"This sure is a great wall." So presidents, like the rest of us, are well suited by their particular skills and temperament to do some aspects of their job and feel much less at home performing other parts of their complex job.

The third key personality variable is the individual president's orientation toward political conflict. The conflict of competing ideas and interests is, of course, the essence of political life, but political leaders vary enormously in how they react to conflict. Some, like Franklin Roosevelt, thrive on it. Roosevelt never saw politics as dirty or unsavory, but instead viewed it as the untidy reality of democratic life. Other presidents dislike disagreements, debate, and conflict, and so try to avoid them. Nixon, despite his aggressive and contentious political oratory, was uncomfortable when personally facing conflict. He did not enjoy hearing his advisers debate one another, nor did he like being in situations where he could be contradicted. Therefore, as president, Nixon would often withdraw into private solitude where he could mull over his own ideas without the tensions of interpersonal disagreement. Nixon relied on a handful of powerful White House assistants to filter out face-to-face dealings wherever possible.

These three personality traits—cognitive style, sense of personal efficacy, and orientation toward political conflict—influence presidents as they attempt to create a decision-making management structure that will best suit them and help them master the vast federal bureaucracy and assure presidential dominance of the foreign policy-making process. As Richard Johnson (in his book, *Managing the White House*) has shown, each president's personality then leads him, whether self-consciously or intuitively, to select one of three alternative management and decision-making styles. Here we briefly describe the three models and then illustrate each with case studies of recent presidencies.

The first is the *competitive model*. This management style places great stress on the free and open expression of diverse advice and analysis within the executive branch. Individuals, departments, and agencies openly compete with one another to influence presidential policy-making. The competition of personalities and agencies is inherent in any bureaucracy, but this decision-making style both tolerates and encourages it. Presidents who employ this style want to ensure that as many options as possible reach them and as few decisions as possible are resolved through bureaucratic bargaining at lower levels. In practice, this model is anything but tidy. Multiple channels of communication to and from the president are tolerated, and a good deal of overlap in agency jurisdiction occurs.

The second style is the *formalistic model*. Presidents who opt for this approach emphasize an orderly decision-making system, one with structured procedures and formal, hierarchical lines of reporting. Presidents who choose this style prefer the orderly adherence to well-defined procedures and formal organizational structure to the open conflict and bureaucratic bargaining inherent in the competitive model.

The third style, the *collegial model,* seeks to retain the advantages of the other two models while avoiding their drawbacks. Presidents using this model try to bring together a team of key aides, advisers, and cabinet officers who will truly function as the president's team. Ideally, this model encourages a diversity of outlook, competition among policy alternatives, and group problem solving within the presidential team. Department and agency heads are expected to regard themselves more as members of the president's team than as spokespersons for their organization's perspective, but by stressing the collegial character of decision making, the extreme bureaucratic infighting associated with the competitive model is avoided.

Now that we have identified the three key personality variables associated with presidents and the three alternative presidential management styles, we present a brief survey of the foreign policy decision-making styles of recent presidents. We begin with Franklin D. Roosevelt, who presided over the gravest U.S. crisis in World War II and move chronologically to the Clinton administration. This sample of 11 presidents will give us some insight into which management styles have led to good foreign policy-making and which have spawned policy failures.

Franklin D. Roosevelt

Franklin D. Roosevelt (1933–April 1945) offers the only successful example of the competitive model of presidential decision-making management. Roosevelt's choice of this style was rooted squarely in his personality. Supremely self-confident and entirely at home as president, Roosevelt delighted in the game of politics and viewed it as a means of achieving beneficial policies for the country. In terms of cognitive style, he had an insatiable appetite for detail and preferred to learn in face-to-face encounters. His sense of efficacy and competence was exceptionally strong, for he believed himself to be uniquely qualified to lead the country through the twin crises of the Great Depression and World War II. Finally, Roosevelt was comfortable in the presence of political conflict, which he viewed as a necessary, inevitable side effect of democratic life.

Given his personality, the competitive model made sense for Roosevelt. As president, he deliberately stirred up competition and conflict among the various executive agencies and cabinet officers. This was his way of ensuring that the important issues wound up in his own hands. Roosevelt would often bypass cabinet heads and deal directly with lower level officials in order to get the information he needed. Sometimes he would assign several departments the same task of developing alternative policy options, thus assuring that the bureaucracy would not settle issues itself and present the president with only bland proposals representing the lowest common denominator of bureaucratic bargaining.

The unorthodoxy of Roosevelt's style looked chaotic to outsiders and to management specialists, but it generally worked for him because of his unique combination of personality traits, not the least of which was his extraordinary self-confidence. A clear danger of the competitive management style is that the president can become overloaded with information and by the need to make decisions that would ordinarily be resolved at lower levels. Roosevelt usually avoided this pitfall by using the competitive approach selectively; in a number of issue areas, he insisted that the pertinent agencies and his subordinates resolve policy disputes among themselves.

Harry Truman

Harry Truman (April 1945–January 1953) was in many ways an improbable man to become the country's chief executive. A plain man of modest background, little about him suggested a capacity for exceptional leadership, but historians today give him high marks for his courage and steadfastness in making exceedingly difficult decisions. It fell to Truman, for example, to decide whether or not to use the secret new atomic bomb against Japan to end World War II. The historic U.S. response to the Soviet challenge in the aftermath of the war was also the result of Truman's unblinking resoluteness. It was Truman, too, who negotiated the Marshall Plan, who presided over the formation of NATO, and who committed U.S. forces to counter communist aggression in Korea.

Determined to carry on Roosevelt's legacy of internationalism, Truman was equally resolved to rein in the turbulent bureaucratic politics that Roosevelt so thoroughly relished. Truman did this by instituting a formalistic management and decision-making system. Under Truman, the authority of department heads within their respective policy domains was strengthened and a more traditional, hierarchical chain of reporting and command was instituted. The president would no longer dilute the authority of cabinet officers by dealing directly with their subordinates, nor could those subordinates kick over the traces of formal authority and gain easy access to the president.

Although personally modest and unassuming, Truman had an acute sense of the dignity of the office he inhabited and was adamant that presidential authority be respected within his administration. Accordingly, his approach was to delegate heavily to his agency heads on routine issues while insisting that the president alone must make the major decisions. Truman did not particularly welcome the National Security Council system established in 1947, viewing it as a potential intrusion on presidential prerogatives. He therefore kept the NSC machinery at arm's length, and for advice, he relied heavily on his secretary of state, Dean Acheson. In the end, however, it was Truman himself who charted the U.S. course during the turbulent, formative years of the Cold War.

Dwight D. Eisenhower

Dwight D. Eisenhower (January 1953–January 1961) brought to the presidency the long-standing assumptions and practices he had acquired during his distinguished military career. Accustomed to clearly delineated lines of authority and solid staff work, it is not surprising that Eisenhower, like Truman, opted for the formalistic management model. His well-known insistence that aides distill issues requiring presidential decision into one-page memos has led to some misunderstanding of Eisenhower's cognitive style. He was, in fact, uncommonly well informed on international affairs but preferred to receive much of his information through staff briefings. In terms of sense of efficacy, Eisenhower's command of Allied forces in Europe during World War II left him self-confident about his abilities to deal with complex organizations and strong-willed figures. He was less at home in the rough-and-tumble world of political conflict than presidents who have risen through the political ranks, however, and so the formalistic model was well suited to his personality, experience, and leadership style.

Eisenhower's policy-making style differed from Truman's principally in Eisenhower's greater reliance on centralized staffing to channel the flow of information, options analyses, and the like. Where Truman had made minimal use of the NSC machinery, Eisenhower more eagerly embraced it as a way of routinizing policy analysis and debating policy options. It was Eisenhower who first created the position of assistant to the president for national security affairs. The first person to hold the job was Robert Cutler, a Boston investment banker, who both coordinated the activities of the NSC and, when asked, advised Eisenhower on foreign policy issues.

Although many historians have depicted John Foster Dulles, Eisenhower's secretary of state, as an exceptionally influential figure in the shaping of Eisenhower's foreign policy, more recent interpretations find Dulles's role to have been much exaggerated. As the newer revisionist accounts argue, it was Eisenhower who orchestrated his administration's policy stance, albeit often through indirect, hidden-hand methods.

John F. Kennedy

John F. Kennedy (January 1961–November 1963) brought to the White House a youthful vitality, a commitment to foreign policy activism, and a determination to be more personally involved in the details of policy-making than he (perhaps erroneously) believed Eisenhower to have been. This determination was intensified early in his administration by the humiliating failure of the U.S.-sponsored effort to topple Cuba's Fidel Castro in the Bay of Pigs fiasco. In his own postmortem of the disaster, Kennedy concluded that the operation's poor planning and execution were due in large part to faulty assumptions embedded in the executive agencies, especially the CIA, which had gone largely unchallenged. Henceforth, Kennedy concluded, foreign policy would be closely directed from the White House. That, in turn, required a team of policymakers who were more loyal to the president than to their agencies' parochial outlooks. The result was a collegial style of policy-making, which placed Kennedy at the hub of a team that included Secretary of State Dean Rusk, Secretary of Defense Robert McNamara, and National Security Adviser McGeorge Bundy.

The collegial style, with its freewheeling give-and-take among a close-knit team in which the president is first among equals, was a good match for Kennedy's personality. He had an unquenchable appetite for information. In terms of sense of efficacy and competence, he had displayed a serene self-confidence throughout his life. Finally, he was a thoroughly political creature who delighted in spirited political discourse. His personality, then, combined with his determination to be intimately involved in the details of foreign policy-making, made the collegial model a good choice for him.

Kennedy's crowning achievement in foreign affairs was his skillful and successful direction of the Cuban missile crisis of October 1962. A number of writings have chronicled the close teamwork and thoughtful debating of policy options among Kennedy's foreign policy circle. When Soviet leader Khrushchev backed down and agreed to withdraw Soviet missiles from Cuba, it marked a signal victory for U.S. policy. Nuclear war had been averted, and Kennedy's collegial decision-making management style had been vindicated.

Lyndon B. Johnson

Kennedy's assassination in November 1963 elevated Lyndon B. Johnson to the presidency, which he occupied until January 1969. Johnson idolized Franklin D. Roosevelt ("He was like a daddy to me," he would often note) and sought to emulate both his philosophy of governmental activism and his competitive management style. Like FDR, Johnson did possess a great ability to persuade and manipulate other leaders in one-on-one dealings, a skill he had employed masterfully as Senate majority leader during the Eisenhower years.

But Johnson differed from Roosevelt in two crucial ways that would ultimately doom his presidency. First, where Roosevelt had been supremely self-assured, Johnson was a deeply insecure man. He often masked his insecurity with an outward show of forcefulness and dominance, but he was remarkably thin-skinned, easily wounded by real or imagined slights, and constantly seeking to win the approval of others through his immense political gifts. One biographer traces Johnson's relentless drive to achieve greatness to his chronic need to shore up a congenitally fragile self-esteem. Second, where Roosevelt was a committed internationalist, Johnson remained unusually parochial for a national leader. His deep ignorance of international issues, coupled with his unrequited craving for the approval of Kennedy's elegant loyalists, left him exceptionally dependent on the foreign policy team he had inherited from the slain Kennedy.

For a time, Johnson's presidency worked wonderfully well. His promise of a golden age for the United States, captured in the soaring rhetoric of a "great society," led to a landslide victory over conservative Republican challenger Barry Goldwater in 1964. After 1965, however, Johnson became ever more deeply mired in the nightmare of Vietnam. Warmly expansive when his relentless activism won him public praise, Johnson reacted with petty defensiveness as his war policies came under increasing attack in Congress, on college campuses, in the media, and among the general public.

By the late 1960s Johnson was a besieged president. Reviled by antiwar protesters ("Hey, hey, LBJ, how many kids did you kill today?" went one of their more printable chants), abandoned by his fellow liberal Democrats, scorned by the media, backed by a shrinking constituency, and criticized even within his own executive branch by figures such as George Ball, Roger Hilsman, and Townsend Hoopes, Johnson endured a firestorm of criticism over his failed militarization of the conflict in Vietnam. Denied the public approval he craved, Johnson increasingly retreated into a closed circle of trusted loyalists. As he did so, he abandoned the competitive model of decision making in favor of a variant of the collegial model in which he was shielded from face-to-face dealings with his critics.

As early as 1966 Johnson was relying on a foreign policy coordinating mechanism known as the "Tuesday lunch," in which he met regularly with Secretary of State Rusk, Secretary of Defense McNamara (and, in 1968, his successor, Clark Clifford), Richard Helms of the CIA, and National Security Adviser Walt Rostow. By confining discussion of Vietnam policy to this tight band of loyalists, Johnson was somewhat able to seal himself off from conflicting views and from the painful reality that his policies were not working. By 1968 Johnson was so thoroughly unpopular that he could safely make public appearances only at military bases. After an embarrassing near defeat in the New Hampshire primary, Johnson took himself out of the race for reelection and withdrew to his Texas ranch, a tragic figure brought down by a disastrous foreign policy in a peripheral land.

Richard M. Nixon

Johnson's political disgrace, as well as a broad public revulsion against the excesses of the 1960s, made possible the improbable political comeback of Richard M. Nixon, who had narrowly lost to John F. Kennedy in 1960 and was written off as a national figure after his humiliating defeat in the 1962 California gubernatorial race. Nixon, who would occupy the Oval Office from January 1969 until his resignation under the cloud of Watergate in August 1974, brought to the presidency an extraordinarily complex personality. Throughout his political career, he seemed to remain an oddly private person in the most public of professions. Driven by deep-seated insecurities and inordinately sensitive to criticism, Nixon appeared to form few lasting friendships. Given his difficulties in interpersonal relationships, both the competitive and collegial models were ruled out.

At the same time, Nixon came to office determined to dominate the foreign policy-making process. Caring little about domestic issues, Nixon had a passionate interest in foreign affairs and regarded himself as an expert on the subject. However, he also harbored a deep distrust of the very foreign policy bureaucracy he now headed. His deepest contempt was reserved for the State Department, which he viewed as a hotbed of liberal Democrats likely to be hostile both to him personally and to his policies.

The upshot of this peculiar mix of personal vulnerability and political will was a decision-making management system unlike anything seen before or since. Creating his own variant of the formalistic system, Nixon sought to centralize White House control over foreign policy by vastly expanding the role and stature of the National Security Council staff, whose loyalty to the president was more certain. Pivotal to the new system was the head of the NSC staff, the national security adviser. For this position Nixon selected Harvard political scientist Henry Kissinger, even though the two had not met prior to Nixon's election. The trend toward a strengthened role for the national security adviser had begun under Kennedy, who had similarly turned to Harvard, selecting McGeorge Bundy for the job. But whereas Bundy had a staff of 12, Kissinger would create a formidable White House operation with a staff of 100.

Despite their differences in background (Nixon was raised a Quaker and had spent his adult life in the tumultuous world of national politics, whereas Kissinger was a Jewish refugee from Hitler's Germany and had spent his adult life in the elite environs of Harvard), the two men shared a number of key traits and assumptions. Kissinger reinforced Nixon's disdain for the bureaucracy, which both regarded as typically stodgy, mediocre, incapable of creativity, and unable to rise above narrow agency perspectives. Like Nixon, Kissinger was a believer in unsentimental Realpolitik grounded in an impersonal calculus of national interest and the balance of power. Finally, the two men shared a penchant for secrecy and dramatic surprise.

Academic treatments of the Nixon years often give Kissinger credit for the administration's shrewd diplomacy and blame Nixon himself for the era's political and diplomatic reversals. A better reading of the available evidence suggests that Nixon deserves at least as much credit as Kissinger for such strategic innovations as the opening to China and the relaxation of tensions with the Soviet Union. Despite Kissinger's stature as a media celebrity, there is no reason to doubt that Richard Nixon was fully in control of his own administration's inventive foreign policy.

It was entirely Nixon's idea to create the most centralized and structured White House foreign policy apparatus ever. The essence of his creation was the well-known system of six interagency committees, each of which was chaired by Kissinger and so was attuned to presidential perspectives. They were (1) the Vietnam Special Studies Group, which dealt with the most pressing policy issue of the day; (2) the Washington Special Actions Group, which was concerned with international crises; (3) the Defense Programs Review Committee, which added a White House layer to the executive branch's development of military and security policy; (4) the Verification Panel, which dominated administration policy-making on strategic arms control; (5) the so-called 40 Committee, which imposed White House control over covert operations abroad; and (6) the Senior Review Group, which treated policy development on all other issues. These six committees were clearly the locus of foreign policy-making within the executive branch, thus ensuring that lower level officials in the various agencies would either strive to have their voices heard within the White House system or would be frozen out of the policy-making action. In addition, the committees could reach down into agencies such as State, DOD, and the CIA, absorbing key personnel and defining the parameters of policy discussion. Keeping the career foreign policy bureaucrats constantly off balance, in the dark, and out of the policy-making loop was most definitely an intentional by-product of the Nixon-designed operation so skillfully implemented by Henry Kissinger.

To further ensure that the White House would encounter minimal resistance from the entrenched foreign affairs bureaucracy, Nixon named his former law partner, William Rogers, to be secretary of state during his first term. Nixon had cunningly calculated that Rogers's lack of foreign policy expertise or stature would render him a weak advocate of State's institutional perspective, thus enhancing Nixon's strategy of maintaining tight White House dominance of the foreign policy process.

By ensuring that all information, analysis, and policy advocacy went through Kissinger, Nixon thereby assured his own primacy in foreign policy-making. Discussions of whether or not Kissinger was a too-powerful figure miss the point that he was only as powerful as Nixon determined would serve his own presidential interests. It is true that Kissinger understood all too well Nixon's craving for secrecy and seclusion and that Nixon typically made major decisions in lonely isolation using the cogent options analyses prepared by Kissinger. But descriptions of Nixon as an unwitting captive of Kissinger's dominating intellect are generally mistaken. In essence, Nixon used Kissinger, not the other way around.

The dangers of Nixon's extreme policy-making centralization are readily apparent. In the first place, however cautious and unimaginative the State Department and other agencies may be, they are the repository of valuable subject-matter expertise and diverse points of view. Little is gained by deliberately ignoring their assessments, and a great deal of expert opinion is wasted in demoralizing schemes to bypass conventional channels. Second, Nixon's utilization of Kissinger for operational missions (as in his secret 1971 trip to China and his role as presidential emissary to the Vietnam peace talks held in Paris) altered the role of national security adviser from that of policy analyst and presidential counselor to that of foreign policy executor, a precedent that would return with alarming consequences in the Iran-contra affair during the Reagan administration. Since the national security adviser is neither confirmed by Congress nor compelled under ordinary circumstances to report to Congress, his involvement in the actual conduct of foreign policy raises serious questions regarding accountability and the constitutional prescription of checks and balances. Finally, there is some merit to the argument that in isolating himself from his own executive establishment, Nixon was dependent not only on the information and analysis provided by Kissinger, but also on Kissinger's forceful advocacy of specific policy options. Nixon's very success in keeping the foreign affairs bureaucracy at arm's length meant there was seldom a serious counterweight to Kissinger in urging the president to adopt one policy initiative over another.

In light of Nixon's unusual personality as well as his determination to personally dominate U.S. foreign policy-making, his White House–centered decision management system was perhaps the model most appropriate for him. Whatever the ultimate verdict of historians regarding his character and leadership, most observers credit Nixon with achieving remarkable breakthroughs in relations with the then-menacing communist giants, China and the Soviet Union. But the very contempt for established institutions and penchant for secrecy that served him so well in international affairs had also spawned a White House culture of deceit, evasion, and criminality that made Watergate an ever-present possibility. As Nixon became ever more hopelessly ensnared in an illegal cover-up of his own making, his political legitimacy was so eroded that, in the end, he had little choice but to resign the presidency he had fought to attain all his life.

Gerald R. Ford

Nixon's successor, Gerald R. Ford (August 1974–January 1977), can be dealt with quickly because of the brevity of his tenure. Sharing Harry Truman's unpretentious modesty but not his capacity for transcendent greatness, the hapless Ford presided over a demoralized country and is best remembered for helping restore American faith in the elemental decency of its president. In the wake of Watergate and the definitive failure of U.S. policy in Vietnam in 1975, the American people were broadly suspicious of political leaders and wished to turn away from strenuous exertions in foreign affairs. Faced with such strong public sentiments and acknowledging his own limitations as an international statesman, President Ford essentially retained the Nixon foreign policy team and continued Nixon's policies, but he rejected Nixon's obsessive secrecy and insistence on exclusive White House control of the policy process.

Ford's formalistic management system was closer to the Truman and Eisenhower model than to Nixon's. Matters were made easier by the fact that Henry Kissinger had become secretary of state in 1973 and had, unsurprisingly, "discovered" the merits of the department's professional corps. In his place as national security adviser was Air Force lieutenant general Brent Scowcroft, himself a Kissinger protégé but nonetheless very much his own man. In Scowcroft's hands, the NSC staff reverted to its traditional role of coordinating the flow of information and analysis of competing policy options, but its operational mission was virtually eliminated. Unlike Kissinger, Scowcroft was a self-effacing man who was more interested in assuring that the president was apprised of pertinent information and aware of diverse points of view than in using his position to press his own preferred policies.

From the mid-1960s to the mid-1970s, the country was convulsed by the twin disasters of Vietnam and Watergate. Taken together, they left a deeply demoralized public shorn of its earlier innocence and faith in its political leaders. Although ideological and partisan opposites, Johnson and Nixon shared a dangerous combination of deep personal insecurity and overwhelming political ambition. Their combined political legacy was poisonous to the body politic, corroding the moral legitimacy of government and the bond of trust between leaders and the led that is essential in a democracy. Thus, in the presidential election of 1976 the American public vented its anger against Washington politicians by turning to an outsider, a former Georgia governor who emphasized his personal integrity and made his lack of Washington experience seem like a virtue.

Jimmy Carter

Jimmy Carter (January 1977–January 1981) arrived in Washington as head of the political establishment he had successfully run against. He brought to the task an array of personal traits so attractive that they make the disappointments of his term all the more keenly felt. Nearly everyone admired Carter for his strength of character, high intelligence, abiding decency, personal discipline, exceptional work ethic, and extraordinary appetite for detailed mastery of complex issues. To compensate for his lack of experience in foreign affairs, as president he further intensified his long established workaholism, immersing himself in endless books, documents, and reports on the intricacies of international matters.

Carter's voracious capacity for detail and his insistence on being involved during the early stages of policy development—rather than reviewing options presented to him by the bureaucracy and NSC staff—accounts for a great deal of his foreign policy decision-making style. Moreover, his robust self-confidence and personal comfort in the give-and-take of policy debate meant the formalistic model would not suit him particularly well. Aware that perhaps no one besides Franklin Roosevelt could juggle the burdens of the competitive model, Carter settled on the collegial model as his typical approach to foreign policy decision making.

Carter was critical of the extreme centralization of power in the White House under Nixon. He believed that it had too often left Nixon isolated from diverse points of view. The collegial model, he felt, would avert a similar isolation in his own administration by regularly exposing him to policy debate with the members of his foreign policy team. At the same time, he wanted to make greater use of the formalized capabilities of the NSC staff than Kennedy had done and to restore the authority and stature of cabinet heads. Thus, Carter's version of the collegial model also contained some ingredients of the formalistic model.

Given Jimmy Carter's ambitious cognitive style, his high sense of personal efficacy and competence as a decision maker, and his comfort amid the tumult of political conflict, the collegial model best suited his personality and policy-making style. Unfortunately, the reverse was not true: Carter was not the best person to attempt the collegial system. In order to understand why this is so, we need to examine more closely the preconditions for successfully utilizing this model.

If decision-making collegiality is to work, at least one of two conditions must be present. First, while remaining receptive to diverse points of view, the president must be a commanding figure who articulates a clear sense of vision from which the collegial deliberation of policy specifics takes its bearings. Without that condition, the second prerequisite for successful collegiality is an essential commonality of outlook among the key players. A shared worldview, then, whether imposed by the president or arising voluntarily among the chief actors, is the essential glue that holds collegial deliberations together and permits the development of policy coherence. In time it would become painfully apparent that neither of these conditions was present in the Carter White House.

Trained as an engineer at the U.S. Naval Academy and later displaying a talent for the pragmatics of business, Carter was most at home dealing with the nuts and bolts of problem solving. His career in Georgia state politics was characterized by high personal integrity and diligent attention to the details of day-to-day problems. Never much of a conceptualizer, and almost entirely without foreign policy credentials, Carter found it difficult to articulate a coherent foreign policy strategy that went beyond earnest platitudes. Apart from his laudable insistence that concern for human rights must be one of the U.S. international objectives, Carter's foreign policy vision seldom amounted to more than well-intended bromides. So there would be no top-down grand design to shape the efforts of Carter's collegial decision-making team.

At the same time, the very composition of that team ensured the lack of a spontaneous commonality of worldview among the men charged with clarifying policy for the nation. Besides Carter, the major players were Secretary of State Cyrus Vance, Secretary of Defense Harold Brown, and National Security Adviser Zbigniew Brzezinski. Brown, like Carter, was a talented pragmatist who neither created nor obstructed the kind of overarching sense of purpose and vision necessary for policy coherence. Vance and Brzezinski, on the other hand, held deep convictions about the overall strategic design the United States should be pursuing in the post-Vietnam era. Those convictions, however, were fundamentally incompatible. In essence, Jimmy Carter's foreign policy foundered on his own inability to embrace definitively either the worldview articulated by Cyrus Vance or that of Zbigniew Brzezinski.

Vance had held Pentagon positions during the Johnson administration and became personally haunted by what he came to regard as the senseless militarization and violence of America's tragic involvement in Vietnam. By the time he became secretary of state in 1977, he was a committed dove, advocating a diplomacy of humane globalism. Vance believed that the Cold War standoff with the Soviet Union had lost its vitality and could be virtually ended through conciliatory U.S. efforts. To Vance, it was in the best interest of the United States to reduce Cold War tensions, press for further arms control agreements, and place a new emphasis on Third World development and on the enhancement of universal human rights.

Brzezinski, by contrast, proceeded from a worldview that emphasized the necessity of remaining firm against what he regarded as a Soviet Union still committed to expanding its sphere of global influence and propagating totalitarian communism in Third World states. To a hawk like Brzezinski, strategic arms limitations agreements were more key to Soviet interests than American ones. The United States could afford the stiff costs of a prolonged arms race, he reasoned, whereas the Soviets could not. Therefore, Brzezinski argued, the United States should take a hard line against Soviet adventurism in such Third World locales as Angola, Ethiopia, and Afghanistan. He advocated a policy known as "linkage," whereby progress on arms control and other aspects of East-West détente would be linked to Soviet restraint abroad, particularly in the Third World.

Given the fundamental incompatibility of his two most important foreign policy advisers, and lacking a clear strategic vision of his own, President Carter practiced the politics of equivocation. Unwilling—and perhaps unable—to choose between the worldviews of Vance and Brzezinski, he tried to resolve the split in his foreign policy team by embracing elements of both positions. On one memorable occasion in 1978, Carter asked Brzezinski and Vance each to prepare recommendations for a major speech he was scheduled to give on Soviet-American relations. As expected, the two memos contained contrasting and incompatible views. In essence, Carter simply stapled the two papers together and gave a speech filled with embarrassing contradictions and mixed messages about the true U.S. stance.

Two events in late 1979—the Iranian hostage crisis and the Soviet invasion of Afghanistan—swung Carter decisively toward Brzezinski's hard-line stance. Vance's resignation in the spring of 1980 meant that, at long last, Carter's collegial foreign policy-making system could proceed from the unity of outlook essential for it to function. But for Carter, foreign policy coherence came too late. Disillusioned by his stewardship both at home and abroad, the people rejected Carter in the 1980 election in favor of his Republican challenger.

Ronald Reagan

As Ronald Reagan began his two terms (January 1981—January 1989), he was, at age 69, the oldest man ever inaugurated as president. But his advanced age was only one of the characteristics that made him seem an unlikely occupant of the White House. He had spent most of his adult life as an entertainer, beginning in radio and advancing to the movies and to television roles. Foreign observers were perplexed and bemused to find that a man who had once costarred in a movie with a chimpanzee (in *Bedtime for Bonzo*) was now the leader of the free world. Even more troubling than his advanced age and his unusual background were his casual work habits. During his two terms as governor of California, Reagan had displayed the intellectual and management traits that he would bring to his new role in Washington: (1) a near absence of intellectual curiosity and a disinclination to grapple with the complexities of policy matters, and (2) a casual, nine-to-five management style that required delegating extensive authority to subordinates.

Reagan's cognitive style was that of a minimalist. He rarely read works of non-fiction, preferring to acquire information through short briefings from his aides on the essentials of policy issues. Reagan's command of the complexities of substantive matters was so uncertain, and his memory so unreliable, that his aides regularly equipped him with prepared remarks on 3×5 cards for use in "conversations" with foreign leaders.

In terms of personal sense of efficacy and competence, Reagan cared little about the rigors of hands-on management of the executive establishment, nor was he particularly at home engaging in freewheeling debate over alternative policy proposals. Rather, he enjoyed the symbolic uses of the presidency to communicate with the country in carefully staged events. Dubbed the Great Communicator, Reagan was well served by an uncommonly smooth and effective delivery style he had honed during his many years as an actor and as a corporate spokesperson for General Electric. Perhaps his greatest leadership strength was his exceptional knack for connecting emotionally with the mass public through televised addresses prepared by his talented team of speechwriters.

His often powerful speeches were not merely a case of a trained actor effectively delivering his lines. In Reagan's case, two factors made his rhetoric an uncommonly powerful instrument in rallying public support around presidential objectives. The first was his apparent sincerity. Although intellectually uncomplicated, Reagan was genuinely committed to a core set of conservative principles. He believed ardently that by reducing governmental regulation of business and reducing taxes, "the miracle of the market" would produce expanded economic growth and opportunity at home. Internationally, he believed the United States should aggressively confront totalitarian communism and seek to defeat it, not accommodate it. He believed the United States had retreated from international leadership in a wave of post-Vietnam self-doubt. To reassert its rightful role, the United States would need to enhance its military capability and, more importantly, to assert its values forcefully and confidently, whether that meant condemning the Soviet Union as an "evil empire" or standing up to leftist Third World autocrats. U.S. reassertiveness, then, was Reagan's irreducible foreign policy principle.

The second trait that made Reagan more than a mere orator was his genuinely warm and serene disposition. If he did not possess the furious energy of Lyndon Johnson or the intellectual prowess of Richard Nixon, neither was he possessed of the inner demons that haunted both men. His sunny outlook and personal warmth made it difficult for anyone actually to dislike Reagan. Even his harshest political critics shared in the pervasive aura of good feelings that surrounded the genial Californian. Reagan's generally high approval ratings in opinion surveys helped strengthen his hand in dealing with the Congress and with foreign leaders.

Given his blend of deeply held core values, lack of personal expertise on international matters, and a disengaged executive style, it is not surprising that Reagan adopted a formalistic decision-making management style. Reagan intended that his administration would derive its foreign policy bearings from his own clearly stated principles. For developing concrete policy stances and overseeing the actual conduct of U.S. diplomacy, Reagan intended to (1) delegate broad authority to cabinet officers, and (2) count on his national security adviser and the NSC staff to ensure overall coordination.

This last-named intention continually bedeviled the Reagan presidency. In seeking to restore the authority of cabinet officers, Reagan permitted the pendulum to swing too far away from the Kissinger-Brzezinski model of strong presidential assistants. During his eight years as president, Reagan went through a record six national security advisers. Of the six, the first four were arguably out of their element. The first, Richard Allen, was a rather peripheral figure in foreign policy circles. Reagan had so thoroughly downgraded the NSA's role that Allen did not even have direct access to the Oval Office but reported instead through the White House chief of staff, Edwin Meese.

In 1982 Allen was replaced by William Clark, a former California rancher and state judge who had no foreign policy credentials whatever, admitting in his confirmation hearings that his total foreign policy experience consisted of a 72-hour business trip to Chile. Reagan selected him for the sensitive position because the two men were old friends and because Reagan trusted Clark and felt comfortable in his presence. From late 1983 to 1985 the NSA chief was Robert "Bud" McFarlane. A marine colonel and protégé of Henry Kissinger, McFarlane was a decided improvement over his two predecessors and performed generally well except for presiding over the Iran-contra fiasco (which was a rather significant problem). In 1985 McFarlane was succeeded by John Poindexter, a navy admiral of substantial technical skills but almost wholly lacking in foreign policy or political competence.

By 1985 and 1986 the NSC staff occupied the worst of two bureaucratic worlds: on the one hand, its downgraded leadership was a pale imitation of the policy-making role exercised by Kissinger and Brzezinski; on the other hand, Reagan's hands-off managerial style delegated so much autonomy to the NSC staff that the excesses of Oliver North were given free play. The resulting Iran-contra scandal was a foreign policy disaster for the country and a severe blow to Ronald Reagan's reputation.

Not until late 1986, with the naming of Frank Carlucci, did Reagan have a national security adviser of adequate knowledge and competence. When Carlucci was shortly thereafter named as secretary of defense, he was replaced at the NSC by the equally intelligent and pragmatic Colin Powell, an army general. Unfortunately for them and for Reagan, too, they arrived at their posts in the autumn of the Reagan presidency, well beyond the point when the administration's essential identity was formed.

Thus, Reagan's original wish to establish a smoothly functioning formalistic decision-making system, one that would fill in the policy specifics outlined by his broad-brush core convictions, was severely undercut by the constant personnel changes, incompetence, and—in the case of the Iran-contra scandal—illegal conduct within the NSC staff. And yet it would be a mistake to conclude that the Reagan administration was unable to attain coherence in its foreign policy-making. However one judges the merits of his foreign policy, it was indeed more often than not reasonably coherent. We thus confront the irony that Jimmy Carter, for all his high intelligence and personal attention to substantive detail, seldom obtained foreign policy coherence; his nemesis, Ronald Reagan, for all his vagueness and disengaged leadership style, frequently did.

How can this seeming paradox be explained? The answer lies largely in other aspects of Reagan's formalistic policy-making system that we have not yet discussed. In order to achieve foreign policy coherence in a formalistic decision-making system, at least one of three conditions must be met. The first is firm, hands-on policy-making management at the top, as was the case with Truman and Nixon. As we have seen, this condition was most assuredly not present in the somnolent Reagan presidency. Second, coherence can be enhanced through strong coordinating leadership from the national security adviser. As we have seen, four out of Reagan's six NSAs were of dubious competence. The third and final possibility is a policy coherence that arises naturally from an essentially common worldview among the key policymakers. This, precisely, was the strength of the Reagan team.

Although differences occurred, they were seldom of a fundamental nature as were the irreconcilable differences between Secretary of State Vance and National Security Adviser Brzezinski during the Carter years. Under Reagan, the differences among the major policymakers were matters of style (seen in the short-lived tenure of the abrasive Alexander Haig, Reagan's first secretary of state) or involved secondary matters. The principal members of Reagan's formalistic policy-making team were Secretary of State George Shultz, Secretary of Defense Caspar Weinberger, and CIA director William Casey. Shultz and Weinberger were old friends; both had held important positions in the Nixon administration and had worked together as senior officers in the Bechtel Corporation. Both shared the essentials of Reagan's conservative outlook, although neither was as ideologically driven as their chief. On most major issues, the two men saw eye to eye, the significant exception being Shultz's advocacy of the use of force to counter terrorism in the Middle East and Weinberger's opposition to it. By presenting Reagan with agreed upon policy recommendations on specific issues, the Shultz-Weinberger-Casey team made it possible for Ronald Reagan to preside over a reasonably coherent foreign policy. To the extent that his formalistic decision-making system worked, it is due to the shared worldview among his principal agency heads.

George Bush

Reagan was succeeded by his vice president, George Bush (January 1989–January 1993). Bush's election was greeted with the expectation that he would devote himself heavily to his favorite subject, foreign affairs. Unlike Reagan, Bush had had extensive foreign policy experience prior to becoming president. He had represented the United States in China and at the United Nations and had served as head of the

CIA. Where Reagan was heavily ideological but intellectually casual, Bush was more pragmatic and exceptionally well informed on complex international issues. In contrast to Reagan's disengaged policy-making style and extensive delegation to subordinates, the energetic Bush relished a hands-on management style and personal immersion in the details of foreign policy-making.

Given his deep interest in international affairs, his self-confidence in dealing with other people, and his extensive experience in the policy-making process, the collegial model represented a natural decision-making style for Bush. Like Kennedy and Carter, the two prior practitioners of collegial decision making, Bush was thoroughly engaged, hard working, energetic, and intelligent. He came to office much more steeped in world issues than Carter, a one-term Georgia governor. In addition, Bush had held a variety of positions in the foreign policy agencies, unlike Kennedy, whose prior experience had been as a congressman and senator. In terms of personality traits and prior experience, then, Bush seemed the ideal president to make successful use of the collegial decision-making system.

The makeup of the collegial team President Bush assembled was also encouraging. James Baker, the secretary of state, had been a close personal friend of the president for 30 years. He had served in the Reagan administration as White House chief of staff and as secretary of the treasury. His intelligence, political shrewdness, and close relationship with the president ensured that he would be both a strong secretary of state and a team player within the administration. For secretary of defense, Bush turned to Dick Cheney, a former White House chief of staff under Gerald Ford and later congressman from Wyoming. One of Washington's most respected and well-liked figures, Cheney—like Baker—promised to be both a strong head of his agency and an effective player within the White House team. Finally, as national security adviser, Bush turned to Brent Scowcroft, who had previously held the position in the Ford administration. Widely admired for his scholarly grasp of international issues (he holds a Ph.D. in Russian history) and his unpretentious demeanor, Scowcroft looked like an ideal NSA: more competent than most of Reagan's men had been, yet less abrasive and self-serving than Kissinger and Brzezinski had been.

A number of factors made this an unusually cohesive collegial team. All had held positions in the Ford administration, all shared a worldview of pragmatic, moderate conservatism, and all were congenial personalities who gave little evidence of undue egoism or arrogance.

In more stable times, the Bush policy-making team almost certainly would have been a striking success. Their ability to work well with one another was a decided plus, as was their undeniable intellectual command of Cold War international politics. Their problem was that the world they all knew so well was collapsing around them, and, as it did so, the Bush team too often seemed to be a half step behind the march of history. For 45 years, the Cold War had provided the fixed compass points of world affairs. It defined the givens within which American policymakers were forced to operate. The bipolar schism between two ideologically incompatible superpowers, each heavily armed and each presiding over its subordinate bloc of allies—this had been the foreign policy playing field that George Bush and his talented colleagues had known so well. But in the very year he took the presidential oath of office, the Cold War edifice collapsed amid the ruins of communism.

It was thus George Bush's fate to reach the presidency with his instinctive caution, pragmatism, and considerable talent for problem solving at the precise historical moment when revolutionary upheavals were rendering those traits less useful. Certainly, his presidency was an eventful one: 1989 saw the brutal crackdown on student protesters in China, the collapse of communism in Central Europe, and the U.S. invasion of Panama. The years 1990 and 1991 were dominated by the U.S.-led effort to expel Saddam Hussein from Kuwait and the definitive failure of communist rule in the Soviet Union. The year 1992 saw the eruption of ancient ethnic hatreds in the formerly communist-controlled republics that had comprised the Soviet Union and Yugoslavia, as well as the promise of a single North American trade bloc and a new global emphasis on the environment.

In fairness, perhaps no president, and no decision-making model, could have performed any better amid the dizzying pace of events of Bush's term. In addition, the revolutionary changes confronting Bush were the result of an historic triumph of U.S. Cold War foreign policy. Containment of the Soviet Union and of communism, waged for so many years and at such high cost to the American people, had worked; communism, the twentieth century's boldest social experiment, had failed spectacularly. In a very real sense, then, whatever problems the Bush presidency encountered in developing a foreign policy appropriate to the times were the most welcome problems of the country having succeeded in its central foreign policy objectives of the past 45 years.

And yet there was an inescapable sense that Bush's foreign policy-making team constituted the right group of players assembled for the wrong game. Three of their best known decisions capture both their very real strengths and the vulnerabilities of Bush's collegial foreign policy-making approach. The first was his dramatic proposal for conventional force reductions in Europe unveiled at the Brussels NATO summit in May 1989. Frustrated by the blandness of an early interagency study of the best approach to use with the Soviet Union, and piqued that Mikhail Gorbachev was widely hailed in the West for his bold measures aimed at ending the Cold War, President Bush retreated to his Kennebunkport, Maine, vacation home with his foreign policy inner circle and tasked the group to help him develop a dramatic gesture that would take the spotlight off Gorbachev. The result was a sweeping proposal for deep, asymmetrical cuts in conventional troops and equipment stationed in Europe. Bush made it a point to exclude the regular foreign policy bureaucracy in his Kennebunkport discussions, deeming such departments and agencies as State, DOD, and the Arms Control and Disarmament Agency too cautious for the sort of dramatic surprise he wished to spring. In the end, Bush's proposal achieved its short-term public relations objective and its medium-term arms control objectives, serving as the basis for the 1990 Conventional Forces in Europe (CFE) arms reduction agreement. But its very preoccupation with the mesmerizing figure of Mikhail Gorbachev was symptomatic of Bush's slowness in grasping the profoundly centrifugal forces at work in the Soviet Union that would ultimately make Gorbachev irrelevant. As late as 1991, Bush and his collegial policy-making team were preoccupied with how to cope with Gorbachev and the Soviet Union and were surprisingly late in acknowledging that the future lay with Boris Yeltsin and the other heads of a post-Soviet, noncommunist assortment of republics, not with Gorbachev and a centralized state known as the Soviet Union.

Similarly, Bush and his foreign policy inner circle won wide praise for their skillful response to Saddam Hussein's invasion of Kuwait in August 1990. In his handling of Operation Desert Shield/Desert Storm in 1990 and 1991, Bush went to great lengths to confine critical information and the consideration of policy options within his tight collegial circle of Baker, Cheney, Scowcroft, and Gen. Colin Powell, now chairman of the Joint Chiefs of Staff. In the war's aftermath, however, serious questions were raised about the Bush administration's indulgent attitude toward the Iraqi dictator prior to his fateful invasion and annexation of Kuwait. However brilliant the campaign to eject Saddam from Kuwait had been, it became apparent that earlier U.S. policy itself had sent Saddam Hussein the wrong signals regarding U.S. intentions.

Finally, at the Earth Summit held in Brazil in the summer of 1992, the Bush administration staked out an American position on environmental issues that was seriously at odds with the overwhelming sentiment among the assembled states of the world. Particularly controversial was the U.S. decision not to sign a treaty aimed at protecting the earth's biodiversity. Once again, Bush had arrived at his policy within the collegial confines of his foreign policy-making team. In doing so, however, he had excluded important voices within his own administration—including William Reilly, director of the Environmental Protection Agency—who was advocating U.S. support for the biodiversity treaty and other international environmental measures.

Each of these decisions (1) was made within a closed circle comprised of Bush's foreign hand-picked policy-making team, and (2) was essentially reactive in character rather than arising from a coherent vision of how the United States intended to lead the post–Cold War world. A good case can be made that in attempting to address such newly important issues as international environmental protection, the closed-circle nature of Bush's foreign policy-making style left him vulnerable to the syndrome of *groupthink*. This term, coined by the Yale psychologist Irving Janis, refers to the tendency within small groups to minimize conflict and screen out ideas that threaten the cohesiveness of the group. A more fundamental problem for George Bush, however, was his congenital inability to think through, articulate, and act on a coherent vision of the larger purpose behind his frenetic activity. "The vision thing," as he once called it, would have been less of a problem in an era of stability that prized pragmatic problem solving. But amid the revolutionary pace of global events during his administration, Bush's lack of a clear sense of overarching purpose too often left him and his admirable team of foreign policy associates adrift without a conceptual compass.

Bill Clinton

The election of Bill Clinton in 1992 reflected a pervasive national yearning for change. Polls routinely revealed a deep public anxiety that the United States had in some fundamental sense lost its way and that the incumbent George Bush and his fellow Republicans had all too little sense of how to get the country back on track. Although all new presidencies send the country's pundits into predictable declarations that "historic change" is at hand, the elevation of Bill Clinton did indeed seem to betoken a genuine turning point in American life. This was due largely to the restoration of Democratic control of both elected branches of the federal government and the presumed end of the paralytic syndrome known as "gridlock"; Clinton's youth and the related phenomenon of generational change; and the widely held—if naive—belief that the end of the Cold War would permit America a respite from international exertions and allow a less distracted focus on a host of domestic needs, ranging from education to race relations to health care to the rebuilding of the country's industrial prowess.

The end of governmental gridlock, it soon became apparent, had relatively little to do with Congress and the presidency being in the hands of different political parties. (The Republican Eisenhower had enjoyed cordial relations with the Democratic Congress; the Democrat Carter had a turbulent relationship with an even more Democratic Congress.) Rather, what was needed was a new degree of common purpose among the American people and a president who frankly relished the give-and-take that is the essence of political life. On both counts, the Clinton years promised a noticeable reduction—although most assuredly not the end—of policy gridlock. The 1992 campaign had reflected a new seriousness within the electorate that the country's frayed social fabric must be repaired, and the elected leadership in both branches mirrored the new sobriety concerning matters such as education, global competitiveness, and the runaway national deficit. Moreover, Clinton's much advertised political skills initially assisted him in working with a Congress that had grown overly adversarial toward the executive branch. When an equally energetic but politically conservative Republican majority assumed control of Congress, and especially the House, in the 1994 election, Clinton lost ground.

The second harbinger of change was the theme of youth and generational succession. At age 46, Clinton was the second youngest elected president. John Kennedy had been elected at age 43, but Kennedy's celebrated rhetoric of change was essentially a summons for an intensification of the Cold War, not a call for a drastic change of national purpose. Clinton was the first president born after World War II, and his ascendancy to the country's top job cast into bold relief how little he and his fellow baby boomers had in common with the life experiences and shared worldview of the generation of Cold War leaders.

Despite the great range of their ages at the time they were inaugurated (Kennedy was 43, Reagan was 69), all the post–World War II presidents prior to Clinton had shared two traits. First, all had been preoccupied with the central struggles against totalitarianism in World War II and the protracted Cold War and, second, all had served in the country's armed forces. Truman had served in Europe in World War I, Eisenhower, Kennedy, Johnson, Nixon, Ford, Reagan, and Bush had served in World War II, while the Annapolis-trained Carter alone wore the uniform during peacetime. Clinton's much discussed avoidance of the draft during Vietnam—and his difficulty in presenting a consistent and straightforward account of the circumstances surrounding his evasion of military service—meant that the new commander in chief would be watched closely for any signs of undue softness in military matters or, perhaps more dangerously, of a tendency to resort too readily to force to dispel the lingering doubts that wartime draft evasion inevitably create.

More fundamentally, however, Clinton's would be the first truly post–Cold War presidency. While the protracted conflict had ended during the Bush years, the essential character of the Bush foreign policy was grounded in the 40-year political, ideological, and military struggle against the Soviet-led coalition. Even with the Cold War won, Bush's difficulties in adapting both the country's institutions and its policy premises to a post–Cold War environment were all too apparent. Clinton, by contrast, had been little affected personally by the country's geostrategic exertions and would take office unencumbered by Cold War imperatives. In addition, Clinton liked to surround himself with fellow fortysomething boomers. To this age cohort, the Great Depression, Hitler, and Stalin were the stuff of history lessons. Their common defining experiences were the youthful charms and terrors of the 1960s, including a broad opposition to U.S. policy in Vietnam, obligatory experimentation with hallucinogenic drugs (whether or not one inhaled), a heightened sensitivity to racial and gender discrimination, and—following the disillusionment with the liberal Lyndon Johnson and the conservative Richard Nixon—an early loss of political innocence and the near absence of credible heroes. Shorn of the heroic foreign crusades of their parents' generation and skeptical of the perceived verities of their society, Bill Clinton and his youthful colleagues did indeed represent a departure from the generation that had endured the Great Depression, defeated the Axis powers in World War II, and maintained a firm and, ultimately, successful containment against totalitarian communism.

Another source of the broad expectation that the Clinton era would mark a genuine turning point was the hope—shared by Clinton and the public alike—that the demise of the Cold War would permit a sharp downgrading of foreign affairs and a corresponding renewal of attention to the country's domestic requirements. To Clinton, the hoped for respite from international matters was a product of both experience and conviction. In terms of experience, Clinton assumed the presidency almost wholly lacking in foreign policy credentials. A career politician, he had served an unprecedented five terms as governor of Arkansas, a small, poor, southern state. Aside from participating in three foreign trade expeditions, Clinton had devoted virtually none of his professional life to international matters. In terms of personal conviction, Clinton ardently believed that the nation's most pressing needs involved domestic policy. His 1992 campaign manager, James Carville, had posted a hand-lettered sign in the Little Rock campaign headquarters that was meant as a daily reminder to the campaign staff of their central issue. "It's the economy, stupid," it read, but it could as easily have served as a concise summation of Clinton's abiding passion. He deeply believed that the most fundamental prerequisite to great power status was a healthy economy at home, and he was equally persuaded that the debt-riddled U.S. economy of the early 1990s would slowly erode the country's capacity both to offer its own people a better future and enable the United States to continue to function as a world leader. Both by background and intellectual conviction, then, Clinton took office hoping to be able to concentrate on the country's economic and social ills.

Whatever his hopes, it was soon apparent that the post–Cold War world would not be a tidy place from which the United States could disengage. Economic interdependence, ethnic conflicts, the collapse of state authority in much of the former communist world, the proliferation of weapons of mass destruction and missile technology, and the challenge to order posed by regional aggression all meant that Clinton would be denied the foreign policy breather he had hoped for.

Despite Clinton's lack of foreign policy credentials, and despite the fact that the world confronting him was one in which the familiar signposts of the Cold War were now entirely gone, thus requiring uncommon astuteness in analyzing global currents, it was clear from the beginning that Bill Clinton would be the hands-on manager and architect of his administration's foreign policy. In order to understand why this is so, let's review the three critical personality variables identified by Professor George and note Clinton's characteristics on each.

In terms of cognitive style, Clinton himself has accepted the label of "policy wonk," reflecting his superb intellect and his insatiable appetite for policy-relevant details. Raised in rural Arkansas, never personally far from the state's pervasive poverty, Clinton experienced a meteoric rise that was a classic demonstration of merit fueled by ambition. Following undergraduate work at Georgetown University, he studied at Oxford on a coveted Rhodes Scholarship and capped his formal training by earning a law degree at Yale University. A quick study with a prodigious memory, Clinton relished the most arcane aspects of public policy matters. So, despite his lack of formal experience in world affairs, Clinton assumed the American presidency confident that his customary diligence and intelligence would permit him quickly to come up to speed on the intricacies of global politics.

Similarly, Clinton brought to the presidency an exceptional sense of his own political efficacy. An inveterate people person, he had nurtured a gift for persuasion and coalition building during his long political ascent. Supremely self-assured in face-to-face dealings and blessed with perhaps the most thoroughly honed political skills of any U.S. president since Franklin Roosevelt, Clinton bore the can-do air of

a man who is convinced that with enough effort and persuasion he can bring together political adversaries in support of sound policy objectives.

It is the third personality variable—orientation toward political conflict—that
is most problematic in Clinton's case. Justly celebrated for his skill in finding common ground between widely divergent positions, Clinton is a genuine people pleas-
er who goes to great lengths to avoid or minimize political conflict. While psycho-
logical interpretations of political behavior can easily be overdone, Clinton himself
has acknowledged that growing up in a household dominated by an abusive alco-
holic stepfather left its mark on him in the eagerness to please that is often the common lot of children of alcoholics. Clinton's relentless efforts to act as a peacemaker and an uncommon knack for finding common ground between political enemies
can be a source of strength as the United States attempts to dampen the bloody ethnic and national hatreds of the post–Cold War world in places as diverse as Bosnia
and Northern Ireland. It is also true, however, that his reluctance to take a firm
stand and alienate others (i.e., standing up to domestic interest groups on trade
issues) may lead to a dangerous policy drift in a chaotic world requiring decisive
leadership.

Clinton's confidence in his own political skills and intellect meant that he would
place himself at the center of a collegial foreign policy-making team. Joining Clinton's inner circle are Secretary of State Warren Christopher, Secretary of Defense
William Perry (who replaced the late Les Aspin), and National Security Adviser
Anthony Lake. Sixty-seven years old at the time he took office, Christopher was a
link to the generation of American leaders that Clinton and his fellow baby boomers
were supplanting. A Los Angeles lawyer by profession, Christopher had served as
deputy attorney general in the Johnson administration and as deputy secretary of state
in the Carter administration. In both his public service and his private practice,
Christopher was broadly admired for his intelligence, his meticulous grasp of precise
details, his skill as a quietly effective negotiator, and his determinedly noncharis-
matic discretion and loyalty. While these traits serve him well as a tactician and as a
trusted presidential confidant, great secretaries of state have demonstrated two additional traits: a capacity to conceptualize and to communicate. Christopher's preferred
world is that of mastering detail, not the development of overarching vision. And
while his private communication reflects lawyerly precision, he is notably not a commanding public orator. His loyalty as a team player and his keen intelligence make
him a valuable member of Clinton's collegial team. By 1995, his quiet, dogged style
appeared to be finding success as he served as administration intermediary in troubled global hot spots such as the Middle East.

Clinton's original secretary of defense, Les Aspin, demonstrated the early problems the administration experienced in the foreign policy area. He matched Clinton's
own academic accomplishments, with degrees from Yale, Oxford, and MIT. A former Pentagon analyst, Aspin emerged as the House of Representatives' leading
defense intellectual during his two decades in Congress. Renowned both for his ana-

lytical flair and for his knack for generating publicity, Aspin helped move the Democrats away from their reflexive post-Vietnam opposition to a strong national defense and the use of force. Unfortunately, those intellectual traits that made Aspin effective in a legislative setting made him an uncertain administrator, often appearing to equivocate when decisive action was needed, a characteristic for which the administration more generally has been criticized.

Clinton's second secretary of defense, William Perry, is also a low-key administrator who seemingly specializes in giving offense to as few people as possible. His Pentagon bureaucratic background is in the decidedly unromantic area of acquisition reform. He has gained growing respect from the military (a commodity in short supply for the Clinton administration) in two ways. For one thing, he is a much more able administrator than Aspin, thereby recreating some semblance of order in the Pentagon. For another, he is gaining acclaim for his efforts to create military-to-military diplomacy, encouraging direct contact between former conflicting militaries.

Anthony Lake, Clinton's national security adviser, entered the Foreign Service following schooling at Harvard, Cambridge, and Princeton. He rose quickly to become Henry Kissinger's principal assistant for Vietnam during the Nixon years and later directed the State Department's policy planning during the Carter administration. Unlike such predecessors as Brent Scowcroft, Colin Powell, Robert McFarlane, and John Poindexter, Lake has little firsthand experience in military matters. And unlike Kissinger or Brzezinski, Lake is not a prominent academician with well-developed policy prescriptions spelled out in numerous books and articles. But in a book he coauthored in 1984, Lake argued that the proliferation of foreign policy players and the erosion of consensus over what American policy should be severely hampered the country's ability to forge a coherent and effective foreign policy. He has been an especially forceful advocate for placing greater weight on the expertise and views of career Foreign Service officers.

To Lake, the end of the Cold War renders the old debate between interventionist hawks and conciliatory doves meaningless. Rather, he believes the principal policy schism within the United States is between traditionalists who believe the country's interests are protected by the maintenance of a balance of power and modernists, like himself and President Clinton, who believe U.S. interests are best protected by using the country's overwhelming power to promote democracy around the world, and that this end is best served by an active American policy of engagement and enlargement of free markets and free societies where possible. Lake's grasp of the intricacies of world affairs exceeds that of the other members of Clinton's foreign policy inner circle, with the possible exception of U.N. ambassador Madeleine Albright, who has emerged as a central foreign policy player.

The relative lack of conceptual flair among Clinton's team assures that Clinton himself will remain at the center of his administration's foreign policy development. This presents three potential dangers. First, as with Jimmy Carter, Clinton's lack of foreign policy experience and absorption with the details of domestic policy issues could leave him overburdened and paralyzed by the enormity of presidential decision making. Second, Clinton's collegial team might fail to cohere either personally or in terms of developing a consensual worldview. Recall that for collegial decision making to work well, at least one of two conditions must be present: (1) a commanding president who articulates a clear strategic vision from which the collegial deliberation of policy specifics takes its bearings, or (2) an essential commonality of outlook among the principal players. Clearly, Bill Clinton is trusting that the intelligence and diligence which won him the presidency will serve him well as he orchestrates the U.S. approach to the uncharted international waters of the 1990s. The third problem is gaining and maintaining presidential interest and hence constancy in leadership. In other than foreign economic policy, the president has not shown consistent leadership, and this has been reflected in policy inconstancy.

Conclusions

From this survey of the foreign policy decision-making styles of the 11 most recent U.S. presidents, three conclusions emerge. First, the competitive decision-making model is the most problematic of the three, having been used successfully only once (by Roosevelt) and attempted unsuccessfully by one other president (the early phase of Johnson's term). Given the overwhelming complexity of contemporary government and the enormous demands on a president's time and attention, the challenges of the competitive model are simply too daunting to make it a recommended presidential practice.

Second, the collegial model has worked well under optimal circumstances (Kennedy's), but in the absence of a coherent presidential vision (as in the cases of Carter and Bush) or presidential expertise in foreign affairs (as in the case of the late Johnson administration), collegial White House decision-making runs the risk of excluding outside views and miring the president in the "trees" of specific issues without providing an overall map of the foreign policy forest he intends to nurture.

Finally, the formalistic model is the favorite among recent presidents, with five of our most recent presidents opting for it (Truman, Eisenhower, Nixon, Ford, and Reagan). Not only has it been used most frequently, but it has often been associated with successful presidential leadership, as in Truman's visionary policies at the inception of the Cold War, Eisenhower's avoidance of major war during the tense crises of the 1950s, and Nixon's celebrated opening to China and policy of détente with the Soviet Union. While the choice of decision-making management system is up to the individual president, and naturally reflects his long-established personal traits and style, the formalistic model is the one that has most reliably led to successful policy-making during the past 50 years.

ANSWERS TO PRESIDENTIAL TRIVIA QUIZ, PAGE 103

1. Ronald Reagan, Letter to Tower Commission, February 20, 1987.

2. Harry Truman, *Quote Magazine,* October 23, 1955.

3. Gerald Ford, in second Ford-Carter debate, October 6, 1976.

4. Gerald Ford, cited in Richard Reeves, *A Ford Not a Lincoln.*

5. George Bush, to schoolchildren in Amish country, 1989.

6. Richard Nixon, TV interview with David Frost, May 20, 1977.

7. Harry Truman, *Memoirs,* Vol. II, Ch. 1.

8. Richard Nixon, quotation cited in *Newsweek, 1990.*

SUGGESTED READINGS

Barilleaux, Ryan J. *The President as World Leader.* New York: St. Martin's Press, 1991.

Clark, Keith C., and Laurence J. Legere, eds. *The President and the Management of National Security.* New York: Praeger, 1983.

Corwin, Edward Samuel. *The President's Control of Foreign Relations.* Princeton NJ: Princeton University Press, 1917.

Falkowski, Lawrence S. *Presidents, Secretaries of State, and Crises in U.S. Foreign Relations: A Model and Predictive Analysis.* Boulder, Colo.: Westview Press, 1978.

George, Alexander L. *Presidential Decisionmaking in Foreign Policy. The Effective Use of Information and Advice.* Boulder, CO: Westview Press, 1980.

Hilsman, Roger. *The Politics of Policy Making in Defense and Foreign Affairs. Conceptual Models and Bureaucratic Politics* (2nd ed.). Englewood Cliffs, NJ: Prentice Hall, 1990.

Hoxie, R. Gordon. *Command Decision and the Presidency. A Study in National Security Policy and Organization.* New York: Reader's Digest Press, 1977.

Johnson, Richard T. *Managing the White House.* New York: Harper & Row, 1974.

Kellerman, Barbara. *The President as World Leader.* New York: St. Martin's Press, 1991.

Mosher, Frederick W., David Clinton, and Daniel G. Lang. *Presidential Transitions and Foreign Affairs.* Baton Rouge: Louisiana State University Press, 1987.

Neustadt, Richard E. *Presidential Power and the Modern Presidents: The Politics of Leadership from Roosevelt to Reagan.* New York: Free Press, 1990.

Nuechterlein, Donald Edwin. *National Interests and Presidential Leadership: The Setting of Priorities.* Boulder, CO: Westview Press, 1978.

Rubin, Barry. *Secrets of State: The State Department and the Struggle over U.S. Foreign Policy.* New York: Oxford University Press, 1985.

CHAPTER 5

The Role of Executive Agencies

The personal style and priorities that the Clinton administration brought with it to the presidency have affected the relative importance and use of the executive branch agencies that recommend and implement presidential foreign policy decisions. The end of the Cold War and the subsequent changes in the international environment would have caused institutional change even if Bush had taken the presidential oath of office on January 21, 1993. A new president with a different background and set of priorities accelerated that change.

It has become commonplace to describe the Clinton administration as the first post–Cold War presidency. But what does that phrase really mean? In a literal and chronological sense, the 1992 election was the first presidential election since the revolutions of 1989 began to tear down the Cold War structure. If that were the sum total of what the concept of a post–Cold War presidency meant, it would not tell us very much. However, it means a lot more.

The election of Bill Clinton and Al Gore was important for two other reasons that have contributed to change. First, the change was generational: the Bush administration, from the president down through his closest advisers, was dominated by people in their fifties and sixties whose intellectual roots were in the Cold War international system. Clinton and Gore belong to the baby boomer generation that first confronted foreign and defense matters through the distorting eye of Vietnam. The deep Cold War experience of the 1940s (the fall of Eastern Europe, the Berlin blockade, the communization of China), the 1950s (Korea, Hungary, Quemoy and Matsu), and the early 1960s (the Cuban missile crisis) forged the worldviews of most of the Bush team; they were history lessons to the new leaders. A change in the White House in January 1997 could have reversed that effect.

Second, the change of administrations brought the presidency back to the Democratic Party for the first time since 1981. Although too much can be made about how Democrats and Republicans differ in their approaches to policy generally or to foreign and defense policy, we can make two observations with some surety. On one hand, Democratic activists tend to be somewhat younger than their Republican counterparts; the generation of political appointees who filled positions in the Clinton administration was contemporary to or younger than the president and thus their orientations will also be post–Cold War (many of them were, for instance, contemporaries who share the Christmas Renaissance Weekend experience with the president at Hilton Head, South Carolina). On the other hand, the people who came into the government had been on the outside of government power for 12 years and had spent some of that time concocting different solutions to problems than those to which Americans have become accustomed.

The changes have been both procedural and institutional as well as substantive, and in many cases they have been closely related. The first institutional change that Clinton announced during the transition was his intent to form a National Economic Council parallel in function to the National Security Council which would facilitate a substantive change toward a more prominent, activist position in the economic area. Although that formal proposal did not bear fruit, the emphasis on economics has.

The remainder of this chapter discusses the most prominent executive branch departments and agencies that serve the president in the general area of defense and foreign policy. In each case, we begin by describing the traditional role of the agency and how it has been organized to fulfill that role. We then examine how that role is likely to change and how change is likely to be reflected institutionally.

We begin by discussing the two agencies whose functions continue to undergo the greatest change—the Department of Defense (DOD) and the intelligence agencies. The DOD has been an obvious candidate for change and contraction because it is a unique artifact of the Cold War. Nonetheless, early indications suggested a revived role for the agency in the area of peacekeeping and peace enforcement. The intelligence community, too, as a product of the Cold War, has also been a prime candidate for restructuring and contraction.

Our discussion then moves to the Department of State. Traditionally, State was the preeminent and virtually the only actor in foreign policy, but the national security tenor of the Cold War eroded its dominance. Its role now that the Cold War is over is a matter of great interest. Finally, an emerging concern is the complex of institutions that attempt to influence both domestic and international economic policy, two areas that are increasingly difficult to separate. Using the National Economic Council structure as an organizing device, we examine how the administration is planning to deal with this obvious priority.

The Defense Department (DOD)

Across the Potomac River from Washington sits the five-sided building housing the Department of Defense. Those who work there have given its headquarters, descriptively called the Pentagon, many nicknames. To some critics, it joins the National Security Agency in being called the puzzle palace; to most, and especially the uniformed officers who bustle about in its stark hallways, it is simply "the Building."

Physically, DOD's most notable characteristic is its size. The Pentagon, its main headquarters, is the largest office building in the world. Size, however, is also measured in terms of the number of people who work for the department and the share of national resources that Defense commands. In terms of employees, the Department of Defense is the largest single agency of the federal government. Before downsizing of the force began in 1990, DOD employed roughly 3 million people, 2 million in uniform and 1 million civilians in a variety of roles. Cuts in the defense area made possible by the end of the Cold War have reduced those numbers by over 25 percent and will reach nearly one-third when all Clinton-mandated reductions are implemented. Within the armed services themselves, these cuts will be somewhat differential: the army, for instance, will lose the most personnel; the marines will lose the least. At issue for the Clinton or a successor administration is how many more cuts can be made without undercutting the national defense.

The other dimension of size, which creates great leverage for DOD, is the extent of its claim on budgetary resources. Before the end of the Cold War, DOD's budget was the second largest (behind entitlement programs such as Social Security and Medicare) within the federal budget, claiming upward of one-quarter of all appropriated dollars. Moreover, two-thirds of the budget is controllable, which means it must be appropriated annually by Congress. The other category, the uncontrollable budget, consists of items that are automatically appropriated in the absence of interfering legislation; Social Security and interest payments on the national debt are examples. This controllable portion of the DOD budget is by far the largest single discretionary element in the overall federal budget, making defense dollars potentially vulnerable to those seeking new policy priorities for which dollars are not currently available.

The defense budget, like personnel levels, is scheduled to decline gradually; in fact, by 1996 defense will command less than 20 percent of the budget and will have been replaced by debt service as the second largest budget item. This cut is causing some controversy, however. Many defense dollars are spent in local communities: support services for military bases, orders for military equipment, for example. Cutting those dollars can be politically difficult as cuts may economically depress communities or sectors of the economy, as the 1993 and 1995 fights over base closings highlighted. At the same time, the absence of an overwhelming threat has led many observers to recommend that those controllable defense dollars be redirected toward other priorities. Early indications suggest an additional reduction of about 5 percent and a reorientation of research and development monies to projects with both military and civilian applications.

DOD had the paramount historical role in the military dimension of the Cold War and was created specifically to deal with the prospect of a World War III, in which the United States was projected to lead one coalition and the Soviet Union the other. When the threat was lively and the confrontation serious, these projections were matters of potential national life and death. Accordingly, the national security establishment had a very high priority within the government; the simple appeal to national security was enough to guarantee whatever the Defense Department wanted.

The end of the Cold War has changed that elevated position. Although both the United States and the Russian Republic maintain large nuclear arsenals with which they could still incinerate one another, the motive to employ them has vanished. In former President Bush's 1992 campaign phrase, we no longer "go to bed worried about nuclear war." The post–Cold War world offers no apparent equivalent of the Soviet menace, and, as a result, the Defense Department has lost some of its special status within the government.

To think of DOD as a monolith representing defense interests with a single, uniform vantage point would do disservice to our understanding of the department. Like the government more generally, the Pentagon has instigated a series of informal checks and balances representing competing interests and perspectives and assuring the representation of differing viewpoints before decisions are made. To understand how this informal check and balance works requires a brief look at how DOD is organized and the dynamics of interaction within "the Building."

Organization

The basic operating principle underlying the entire defense establishment is civilian control of the military. Beginning with the American Revolution, the people expressed the fear that a standing military might pose a threat to civilian institutions. In the eighteenth century, this fear was so great and produced such tight control over the military that Gen. George Washington, during a particularly unpleasant interchange with the Continental Congress, once decried that he could understand why the Congress opposed an army in peacetime, but that he could not understand why they opposed an army during war.

Through most of U.S. history, the peacetime military was very small. In fact, only since World War II and the onset of Cold War has the United States maintained large numbers of active-duty military personnel. The principle of civilian control means that every military person, regardless of role, reports and is accountable to a civilian official: the chairman of the Joint Chiefs of Staff to the president, the chief of staff of the army to the secretary of the army, and so on. This arrangement often creates some friction—specifically, military personnel often feel civilians are incompetent to review and reverse sheerly military judgments, for instance—but it does assure tight civilian control over the military.

Any depiction of an organization as vast as DOD requires a simplification that is somewhat distorting. For present purposes, we can think of that organization in four parts. At the pinnacle is the secretary of defense, the cabinet official who reports directly to the president and is responsible for the overall operation of the DOD. The second part is the Office of the secretary of defense, which consists of a number of subcabinet-level functions that cut across military services. The third part is made up of the services themselves, each with its separate bureaucracy and set of interests. The fourth is the Joint Chiefs of Staff, which has the presumptive role of coordinating the military activities of the various services.

Secretary of Defense   The secretary of defense, or the SECDEF, as the individual is known within the Pentagon, is the chief adviser to the president on defense matters. (The chairman of the Joint Chiefs of Staff is, by law, the chief military adviser to the president.) As such, it is his or her responsibility to advise the president on defense matters. For example, should we use force in a given situation? What kinds of weapons and levels of personnel do we need? In addition, the SECDEF is a policy implementer, being responsible both for carrying out the policies mandated by the chief executive and the Congress and for managing the department's internal affairs.

Office of the Secretary of Defense   In carrying out his or her tasks, the SECDEF is assisted by the group of agencies known as the Office of the Secretary of Defense (OSD). Normally headed by an undersecretary or an assistant secretary, OSD agencies are broadly functional in their responsibilities, not unlike functional bureaus within the State Department.

The department has undergone two reorganizations during the Clinton administration. When Clinton's first SECDEF, the late Les Aspin, took office, he sought to revamp the structure he inherited from his predecessor, Richard Cheney. Previously, over two dozen undersecretaries and assistant secretaries reported directly to the SECDEF. The new organization changed the pattern in two ways. First, it reduces the number of people reporting to the secretary to four undersecretaries (USDs) and six assistant secretaries (ASDs). Second, it altered the titles and functions from previous organizations.

In reorganizing the pattern, Aspin sought to accomplish three apparent goals. The first, achieved through the USD designations, was to pull some DOD-wide functions directly into OSD, thereby strengthening the SECDEF's hand and weakening the hands of the services. This is particularly true in the area of personnel and readiness and the area of technology and hardware, which deals with equipment and weaponry. Second, he realigned the ASD level so it more closely parallels the State Department, presaging an oversight and competition between the two agencies. In the process, he created functional areas that would have been quite unthinkable during the Cold War—ASDs for economic and environmental security, regional security, and democratic security, for instance. Third, the reorganization wipes out a number of historically important offices within OSD. Initially eliminated, for instance, were the positions of ASD for international security affairs and international security policy, two of the historically most powerful ASD positions, although Secretary Perry reinstated the latter.

When William Perry, a longtime Pentagon insider, replaced Aspin (who was forced to resign and later died), he made further changes. Fewer offices report directly to Secretary Perry. At the same time, many of the most visible areas (special operations and low-intensity conflict, for instance) from the Cold War era now report indirectly to the SECDEF through the undersecretary for policy. Also, the under secretary for acquisition, a position mandated by the Goldwater-Nichols Reorgnization Act of 1986 (discussed in Chapter 7), becomes more prominent, reflecting Perry's penchant for fiscal management and the dictates of budget reductions.

Service Departments   The third layer of agencies that help the SECDEF consists of the service departments. Each military service has its own individual department within the Pentagon that attends to the interests of and administers the individual services. At the top of each of these bureaucracies is a service secretary (the secretaries of the army, navy, and air force), who is assisted by the chief of staff of each service. The service chief (chief of staff of the army and the air force, chief of naval operations) is responsible for the internal operation of his service and acts as his service's representative to the Joint Chiefs of Staff (JCS).

The Defense Department was created largely to bring all the services under one umbrella and thereby reduce interservice bickering and rivalry over such matters as budgetary allocations. (Prior to the National Security Act of 1947, each service independently argued for its budget before Congress.) The individual services remain extremely powerful, however, and the locus of primary loyalty for their members. As a result, to outside observers of the process, service considerations often appear more important than broader national objectives. Moreover, the services have strongly resisted attempts at reform that would reduce their independence (see Amplification box "Attempting to Reform the Military Establishment").

Joint Chiefs of Staff   Overcoming service rivalries and facilitating interservice cooperation was a major purpose of creating the Joint Chiefs of Staff. The original idea was to provide, through the service chiefs and a modest Joint Staff, a vehicle for interchange and coordination. Because loyalties and rewards such as performance evaluations and promotions remained the province of the services, joint staff assignment has historically been considered odious duty for service members. At best, being a "purple suiter," as joint staffers are known (the analogy is that if one combined the colors of the uniforms of the services, the resulting color would be purple), was considered an interruption in useful service; at worst it was considered an absolute hindrance to one's career.

In 1986 Congress passed the Goldwater-Nichols Defense Reorganization Act in part to strengthen the chairman of the JCS and the Joint Staff. The legislation was motivated by the belief that the absence of coordination and cooperation had hindered military efficiency in a number of recent operations (the Desert One hostage rescue attempt in Iran in 1980 and the invasion of Grenada in 1983, for example), the

AMPLIFICATION

Attempting to Reform the Military Establishment

Periodically, an attempt is made to reform the structure of the armed forces somehow to make that structure more rational and efficient. The first major effort came out of World War II and was the result of perceptions that a single defense department could contain rivalry between the services and rationalize military roles and missions. The first goal was addressed in the National Security Act, which created the Defense Department. In 1948, the services, at the direction of SECDEF James Forrestal (a retired admiral), met at Key West, Florida, to hammer out an agreement among them on which services would carry out what military roles and missions. The result was virtually no change.

This process is repeated periodically. Most recently, in July 1995, a commission mandated by the Goldwater-Nichols Act completed a similar review of roles and missions, the putative purpose of which was to reduce redundancy in the military. One of the most controversial areas it had to confront was the so-called four air forces problem: the fact that the air force, navy, marines, and army all have independent air assets that operate essentially independently of one another. Each service jealously guards its claim to air resources, and the White Commission (named after its chairman, Dr. John White, who was at the time the designated undersecretary of defense for policy), meekly complied with the services' demands not to lose their air arms. Within a historical context, the result was not surprising at all.

nature of modern warfare required much closer coordination of military elements, and strengthening the JCS and thereby weakening the power of the services was the best way to accomplish that coordination.

Rivalries within the DOD

No one has ever accused the defense structure of excessive efficiency. This huge, complex organization houses multiple interests and rivalries that individually and cumulatively may hinder efficiency, but at the same time promote the kinds of informal checks and balances which may ultimately contribute to the department's effectiveness.

Rivalries exist at several levels, one of the most obvious being between the civilian and military personnel who work for DOD. Career military people tend to be suspicious of the competence of their civilian counterparts (unless the civilians are retired military officers, or so-called phony civilians). This is especially true of political appointees at the middle and upper ranks of the department (e.g., deputy assistant secretaries and above), who typically arrive from outside the establishment with a new administration and return to private life when that administration leaves. This level of rivalry institutionally focuses on the services, which are more closely controlled by the uniformed personnel and OSD, which is more the preserve of the civilians.

Rivalry also exists between the services themselves and between the services and the JCS. Interservice rivalry arises primarily over mission assignments and budgetary allocations, two matters that are, of course, related. When the extremely long and complex budget cycle is being conducted (which is a full-time, year-round exercise), there are no more critical reviewers of the service budgets than the other services. An extra dollar appropriated for the army, for instance, is a dollar unavailable to the navy.

At the same time, the issue of control of operations and the unified and specified commands between the JCS and the services forms another layer of competition. Each of the commands, which contains military elements from all the services, is administratively assigned to an individual service. Hence, the European Command is assigned to the army, which would have the primary operational responsibilities in a war there, the Pacific Command is commanded by a navy admiral, and the Space Command is assigned to the air force. Historically, however, funding for each command came through the individual service budgets, and services tended to be more generous to those commands they controlled than to those they did not. Part of the 1986 legislation was intended to allow the individual commanders in chief (CINCs) to appeal directly for funding, bypassing and weakening the budgetary control of the individual services. Once again, the services resist turning over more power to the CINCs. They largely succeeded in resisting this form of reform in the White Commission report that examined roles and missions in the post–Cold War world.

Congressional review and oversight is particularly important in the defense area as well. The reason is simple enough: the defense budget is so large and affects so many congressional districts so intimately that members of Congress want to be apprised of anything going on in "the Building" that might affect them. This interest is often the source of considerable friction as Pentagon officials (civilian and uniformed) are dragged before Congress for what appear to be endless congressional hearings or are forced to answer detailed inquiries from congressional staffers who are often considerably junior in age and experience to those on whose time they are intruding. At its worst, this process is derisively known within the Pentagon as congressional "micromanagement."

Effects of Change

How has the Defense Department been affected by the twin impacts of the end of the Cold War and the existence of a Democratic administration? The question is particularly important in the context of the decade of the 1980s. That was a time of considerable prosperity and growth for the Defense Department, particularly in the early part of the decade when the Reagan buildup—the largest increase in peacetime defense spending in the country's history—was occurring.

Three obvious sources of change are evident, each of which has both substantive and organizational ramifications. The first is size, structure, and roles in a post–Cold War environment. The entire structure of the defense establishment was designed to meet the military threat posed by a military adversary that simply no longer exists (remaining concern is consigned to the Office of Soviet Union/Nuclear Affairs, which reports to the ASD for International Security Policy, a position eliminated by Aspin and resuscitated by Perry). By some accounting schemes, fully 60 percent of defense spending (personnel, equipment, weapons, planning) in the Cold War was devoted to the problem of massive ground and air war in Europe. Some of that equipment proved useful in Operation Desert Storm. Such a force structure, size, and preparation seem appropriate for few (if any) other foreseeable contingencies.

As a result, a major concern continues to be how much cutting and restructuring can occur. Not all possible needs and problems can be confidently predicted in advance. Who, for instance, would have predicted a major U.S. expedition to the Persian Gulf in the first half of 1990? As a result, a naturally conservative, cautious military will always be reluctant to cut back, given the uncertainties about the future. This, in essence, was the rationale for General Powell's "base force," a military capability approximately three-quarters the size of the Cold War force. Powell contended that a more drastic cut in the force would cause it to lose effectiveness and the ability to meet different problems.

The second area of concern arises from the breakdown of the old international system and the military's role in it. The Cold War possessed a symmetry and predictability that the post–Cold War world lacks. With a clearly defined adversary, it was possible to design forces, doctrines, and arrangements to meet these known problems. Unfortunately, those constructs no longer clearly apply in the much less structured, more fluid environment that developed after 1989. Since then, the military establishment has been called on to undertake activities for which the Cold War preparation was irrelevant.

As an example of this change, let us look at the active uses of American force since 1989. In December 1989, a total of 22,500 U.S. troops were dropped into Panama (Operation Just Cause) to capture and bring to justice Manuel Noriega, interrupt the rampant drug trade through the country, and reinstitute political democracy by restoring the elected president to power. In August 1990, Operation Desert Shield landed in the Saudi desert and transformed itself into a Desert Storm force numbering 475,000 U.S. forces in 1991. Desert Storm then spawned the relief effort to save the Kurds, which ultimately produced an "exclusion zone" for the Kurds in northern Iraq from which Iraqi authorities are excluded from operating by U.S. forces (Operation Provide Comfort). Also in 1991, U.S. forces flew relief supplies into flood-ravaged Bangladesh (Operation Sea Angel), followed in 1992 by expansion of the exclusion zone idea to protect Shiites in southern Iraq (Operation Southern Watch) and by mounting the massive relief effort to stop Somali starvation (Operation Restore Hope) that lasted from December 1992 until spring 1994. Later in 1994, American forces entered Haiti unopposed to help reinstate the elected government of Jean-Bertrand Aristide, withdrawing in spring 1995. In December 1995, American troops entered Bosnia as part of the Implementation Force (IFOR) to monitor the peace treaty there.

With the exception of the Persian Gulf War, these are unconventional defense missions, raising the third concern: new missions and new conditions for military application. If the aforementioned list of activities has a common thread, it is the use of force within states by multilateral contingents to ameliorate internal disorder. One institution that the end of the Cold War clearly helped revive is the United Nations, which has become the legitimating body for peacekeeping and peace enforcement operations. The U.S. defense establishment has never given such actions high priority, nor has it been structured to cooperate with international authorities.

How does the Defense Department respond to changing circumstances? If "humanitarian intervention" of the Somali variety is to be a staple in the future, is the U.S. Army the appropriate vehicle? How does the decision process adapt to such contingencies? Does DOD now need to place greater emphasis on the director for peace-keeping/peace enforcement position under the ASD for international security policy to deal with the Somalias and Bosnias of the world, possibly complete with a new command that augments traditional forces with peacekeepers and dispensers of humanitarian aid? Do doctrine and practice have to be modified to take part in U.N.-sponsored actions? Or can Americans continue to finesse the situation by mounting a U.S. operation under the guise of the United Nations and then turn it over to the United Nations when they leave, as they have done in Somalia?

These questions of role and missions will continue to be important concerns, partly because the structure of the post–Cold War international system is still evolving, and the problems of the new order are different and less predictable than they were in the past. At the same time, the way the United States reacts to each new problem can be precedent setting, predisposing Americans either to do or not to do things in the future based on their current experience. Thus, the DOD will have to deal with the changing shape of the national security architecture in creative ways that will require changes in both structure and policy.

The Intelligence Community

Many of the comments that have been made about the defense establishment apply to the intelligence community as well. Like the DOD, the complex of agencies that collectively comprise the intelligence capability of the United States came into being to deal with the Cold War competition. Because the Soviet threat activated the intelligence community, it developed in a manner that would be most attuned to that problem. As a result, the evaporation of the Soviet threat leaves an intelligence structure and capability that is not obviously fitted to the problems of the new order.

The development of the U.S. intelligence community owes much to its competition with its Soviet counterpart, the Committee on State Security (KGB). The Soviet organization was highly clandestine, paramilitary in structure and practices (its officers had military rank), and protective of information in a closed, hostile society. The one organization sought to gain politically useful information from and about the other from generally secret, protected sources. The KGB attempted, through various means, to obtain secret American information; U.S. intelligence sought to prevent that, and vice versa. Inevitably, U.S. intelligence agencies came to share some unfortunate aspects of the Soviet agency, such as excessive secretiveness.

With the end of the Cold War, the appropriateness of an intelligence structure designed to counter an agency like the USSR and the KGB (which no longer exists as such) has come into question. Certainly, clandestinely organized intelligence agencies continue to exist in other countries, and the United States still requires information about other governments that is not always publicly available. The important question is whether Americans need a system designed for the Cold War to carry out current and future tasks.

Beyond questions of its possible dysfunction, the intelligence community has further been rocked by public disclosure of scandals, notably within the CIA. In 1993, it was revealed that the agency had failed for over five years to detect the presence of a Soviet mole in its ranks, Aldrich Ames, despite behavior on his part that was highly suspicious. In addition, tainted information appears to have been sent on to intelligence consumers. In 1995, covert support for Guatemalan human rights violations (including assassinations) by CIA case officers (who apparently did not report their activities to their superiors) further added to demands for reform.

The current intelligence community is a large, complex set of organizations within the federal government that can be grouped into three categories by bureaucratic sponsor: the Central Intelligence Agency, defense-related agencies, and cabinet-level agencies.

The Central Intelligence Agency (CIA)

The most visible component is the Central Intelligence Agency (CIA), which for many Americans *is* the intelligence community. Created as part of the National Security Act of 1947, the CIA was the nation's first peacetime civilian intelligence-gathering agency. It is an independent agency and is attached to no other cabinet-level agency. It is led by the director of central intelligence (DCI) who, by law, has the additional responsibility of coordinating all government intelligence activities.

Defense-Controlled Agencies

The largest category in terms both of agencies and employees are those intelligence agencies controlled by the Department of Defense. There are six such agencies, four of which are associated with the individual services (army, air force, navy, and marines) and have intelligence responsibilities relevant to their individual service missions. Although some observers have suggested that the term *military intelligence* is oxymoronic, for instance, air force intelligence has for years conducted extensive aerial satellite reconnaissance through photography of Soviet nuclear missile capabilities.

The other two defense-controlled agencies also have specified tasks. One of them, the National Security Agency (NSA), is the most clandestine and technical. It was created in 1952 by secret presidential directive, and its major responsibility is to intercept foreign electronic communications and prevent other states (notably the former Soviets) from intercepting U.S. government communications. This activity is known as signal intelligence (SIGINT) and is highly technical and convoluted in action, earning its headquarters the nickname "puzzle palace."

The final defense-controlled agency is the Defense Intelligence Agency (DIA), a body created in 1961 to consolidate the information gathered by the various service intelligence agencies. In this way, it provides the secretary of defense with an independent source of information relevant to defense. At the time it was created, the DIA was expected eventually to absorb some of the duties of the service agencies, thereby causing them to shrink. Each service, however, has proven jealous and protective of its intelligence operation, a problem we see presently in the overall intelligence community.

Cabinet-Level Agencies

Cabinet-level agencies other than the Defense Department also have intelligence capabilities. For the most part, these are relatively small and specialized efforts. The Department of Energy monitors nuclear weapons programs internationally. The Treasury Department collects information on foreign economic activity, as well as violations of the alcohol, tobacco, and firearms laws. The Federal Bureau of Investigation is not directly involved in foreign intelligence collection, but it works with other federal agencies to assist in its investigation of treason and other forms of security violations by U.S. or foreign nationals. Finally, the State Department operates the Bureau of Intelligence and Research (INR). Although this agency does not engage in systematic intelligence collection (beyond analyzing routine cable traffic), it does interpret raw intelligence from other agencies from the bureaucratic vantage point of the State Department.

This multiplicity of agencies is supposedly coordinated by the director of central intelligence (DCI) and the intelligence community staff. The DCI is essentially "dual hatted" in that he not only runs one of the competing agencies, but he also coordinates overall community activity. This makes perfect sense in all but a bureaucratic setting: it should avoid unnecessary duplication in effort, including the prospect that two or more agencies might be competing for a given bit of intelligence. In principle, no one disagrees that coordination is desirable.

In practice, however, attaining cooperation in the intelligence field has been rather elusive. Cabinet secretaries who have their own intelligence agencies (like the Defense Department) become protective of them and their control. Since the CIA is one of the competing players, the DCI's objectivity in parsing out cooperative tasks is suspect. Moreover, the heads of the various intelligence agencies report to and are rewarded by their secretaries, not the DCI. Given contradictory instructions by the DCI and the SECDEF, it is not at all difficult for the director of the NSA to decide whose orders to carry out. These kinds of dynamics make reforms aimed at streamlining and coordinating the actions of the intelligence community bureaucratically easier said than done.

Intelligence and Operations

The intelligence community's activities, especially those of the CIA, are also the cause of some controversy that dates back to the agency's first days. Intelligence organizations can have two basic duties, intelligence and operations, and in different countries some have both, while others have one or the other. *Intelligence* refers to the gathering, by public or clandestine means, and analysis of information. As such, intelligence is akin to academic research, except that some of the information is secret and is sometimes collected by so-called extracurricular means. *Operations,* on the other hand, refers to actions taken clandestinely to affect politics in foreign countries. The most obvious form of operations is covert action, activities undertaken by the U.S. government secretly to affect foreign governments, but in such a way that the target does not recognize American action and the U.S. government can deny culpability (what is known as "plausible denial").

Operations is far more controversial than intelligence because it is done in secret and is obscured not only from the target but also from the American public, thereby stretching standards of accountability. Secrecy is often taken to its extremes. One report (naturally neither confirmed nor denied) has it that during a fire alarm at CIA headquarters (the so-called campus), a number of operations personnel actually wore bags over their heads to obscure their identities from other CIA personnel.

Many of operations' actions are also illegal, both within the United States and the target countries where they occur. Operations can involve activities such as making illegal payments to political groups or individuals, arranging sexual liaisons for foreign government officials and then bribing them by threatening to reveal the actions, and the like.

Operations thus raises some difficult moral dilemmas that have caused many people to conclude that the United States should not engage in covert actions or that at least they should be severely limited. Currently, covert actions are governed by the Intelligence Oversight Act of 1980, which requires a presidential "finding" (a written statement by the president authorizing the activity and justifying it on national security grounds) before covert action can be carried out.

When the CIA was originally formed, the prevailing sentiment was that it would be strictly an intelligence, and not an operational, agency. The vagaries of the developing Cold War quickly intruded on the CIA's purity of mission, however, so that by the end of the 1940s, the CIA was engaged both in intelligence and operations. The most important directorates (administrative subdivisions) of the CIA remain the Directorate of Intelligence and the Directorate of Operations. Although these are distinct administrative entities, they retain some overlap, since some intelligence is gathered by what are called extralegal, covert means.

The operations mission has come under assault because with the Cold War ended, many now question the continuing need for such a capability. A major rationale for such a capacity has always been that the other side engaged in covert action and the United States would be figuratively competing "with one hand tied behind its back" if it lacked a similar capability. Moreover, the geopolitical importance of winning the Cold War meant acting in ways that Americans would not have otherwise. Effectively, "the devil (the Soviet Union) made us (the Americans) do it."

With the Soviet threat gone, the geopolitical rationale has largely disappeared as well, which strengthens another argument against the operations mission: covert actions can and often do lead to some very bad policy that, if or when revealed, is very embarrassing to the U.S. government. The prime lingering example is the Iran-contra scandal of the early 1980s.

The series of activities that became known as the Iran-contra scandal was not so much an intelligence as a covert action disaster. The CIA was implicated in the operation to trade weapons for the release of hostages and to divert the profits from weapons sales to the Nicaraguan contras only indirectly. There is widespread if not conclusive evidence that DCI William Casey was involved in some of the planning and encouraged Lt. Col. Oliver North, around whom the operation centered. The exact nature and extent of that alleged involvement went to Casey's grave with him when he died during the investigation.

Iran-contra was notable because it was a covert action that violated the basic rules of reporting such actions. Proper procedures were not followed in rendering a finding for the operation, and the White House operatives took great liberties with congressional bans on contra aid and obstructed congressional attempts to investigate Iran-contra–related activities. Moreover, as the scandal unraveled, many observers judged it to have been such a harebrained scheme that it would have been stopped instantly had it been subjected to normal and proper scrutiny.

Proposed Changes in the Intelligence Community

Because of questions about its continuing role and the scandals dogging it, the intelligence community has seemed a prime candidate for reform, and especially for consolidation and shrinkage. While the Democrats were still in a majority between 1993 and January 1995, it appeared that a reform bill, the Boren-McCurdy Reorganization Act (named after the then-chairs of the House and Senate Intelligence Committees and patterned roughly after the Goldwater-Nichols Defense Reorganization Act) would accomplish that purpose. To date, it has not.

This lack of sustained momentum had at least two political causes. At the most obvious level, the resignation of Senator Boren (to become president of the University of Oklahoma) and the defeat of Representative McCurdy in 1994 meant that the bill's prime champions were in no position to continue their advocacy. At the same time, the Republican majority elected in both houses of Congress in 1994 has shown relatively little enthusiasm for reforming the intelligence area. Although President Clinton appointed a reform-minded DCI in John Deutsch, he has displayed relatively little personal interest in the field. A blue-ribbon panel appointed in 1995 issued a report calling for reform in 1996; how many of its recommendations will be implemented remains to be seen.

Despite being sidetracked for the time being, change in the intelligence area, and especially the CIA as the visible centerpiece of intelligence, is inevitable. That change is likely to take on three related forms.

The first and most obvious kind of change will be a reduction in the overall size of the intelligence community. For the same reasons that it is less necessary to maintain as large a standing military force as was needed for the Cold War, there are also somewhat fewer reasons and objects on which the United States needs to collect intelligence information. Critics of reform, it might be added, retort that the unpredictability of events in this less orderly post–Cold War world require more intelligence collection, not less, given the new problems we face.

The second change is in the weighting of expertise within the intelligence community. By most estimates and public pronouncements from the CIA itself, almost half of the intelligence experts within the agency have their principal expertise in the Soviet Union and Eastern Europe. While such a weighting was appropriate for Cold War purposes, it is unjustifiable in the current circumstances. At the same time, the CIA is deficient in analytical power (including language proficiency) in areas such as the Middle East and Africa, which are the loci of so much of the violence and instability currently troubling the world.

The third area of change is likely to be in the area of operations. The conduct of secret operations (at least beyond gaining information clandestinely) has always been controversial if for no other reason than it often involves activities that would be criminal within the United States. The old argument that the United States had to have and exercise such a capability because its opponents did does not carry the same weight as it once did. As a result, the Directorate of Operations is likely to remain vulnerable to additional reductions in the future.

The State Department

It is one of Washington's most predictable rituals: an incoming president proclaims that he will look to the State Department to play the lead role in his administration's foreign policy-making and execution, followed, usually in a matter of mere months, by expressions of presidential disillusionment with the department's weak leadership of the foreign affairs machinery. The proud institution first headed by Thomas Jefferson has been scorned by recent presidents as being both insufficiently responsive to presidential perspectives (Jimmy Carter thought it too conservative; Richard Nixon and Ronald Reagan felt it was much too liberal) and simply not sufficiently aggressive in interagency tussles to take the lead role (John Kennedy dismissed the State Department bureaucracy as "a bowl of jello"). Virtually every recent president has shared the conclusion that State is too sluggish, unimaginative, and bureaucratically timid to truly "take charge" of U.S. foreign policy-making, but none has described it as colorfully as did Franklin Roosevelt. "Dealing with the State Department," he once said, "is like watching an elephant become pregnant; everything is done on a very high level, there's a lot of commotion, and it takes twenty-two months for anything to happen."

It was not always so. Prior to the U.S. emergence as a world power, the State Department was at the center of both determining and carrying out the country's limited international role. Even during the first half of the twentieth century, when the United States had attained the rank of major power, but prior to the protracted struggle of the Cold War, State retained its pride of place as the preeminent cabinet agency and the hub of foreign policy-making. The post–World War II erosion of its influence, at least in relative terms, and the State bashing that routinely occurs among students and practitioners of U.S. foreign policy reflect important changes in the country's policy-making process. However, since much of State's diminished stature is due to the way the institution conducts itself, first we need to explore some fundamental matters of organizational structure, behavior, and institutional culture. Then we attempt the more ambitious task of accounting for the diminished role of today's State Department in the foreign policy-making process.

Organization

Like the rest of the federal government, the State Department has grown exponentially over the years. The first secretary of state presided over a "bureaucracy" consisting of five clerks, one translator, two messengers, and two overseas diplomatic missions, then called legations. In contrast, today's State Department is housed in a ponderous eight-story building that sprawls across 12 acres in northwest Washington's Foggy Bottom, named for the area's once swampy topography. Whether measured by budget (in excess of $1.5 billion), employees (over 24,000), or overseas embassies, consulates, and missions (historically nearly 300, but recently reduced in number), the State Department of the 1990s bears no resemblance to the department that Jefferson presided over in the 1790s. In some ways, however, these numbers are misleading. Today's State Department may spend more money hiring more people to do more things than ever before, but it remains the *smallest* of all the cabinet-level agencies. Its budget amounts to only 6 percent of the Pentagon's, and its employees number fewer than 1 percent of the Pentagon's.

Secretary of State   Organizationally, the State Department is a conventional hierarchy built atop an array of geographic and functional bureaus. At the head of the organizational pyramid is the secretary of state. As a presidential appointee, the secretary often finds himself caught between the competing pressures of his loyalty to the president and of his role as advocate of the department's institutional perspective within administration councils. Although the two roles are not always mutually exclusive, they frequently are. Secretaries who become too closely identified with their agency's outlook run the risk of becoming suspect as a member of the president's inner circle. This is a particular danger to secretaries who serve in administrations committed to the collegial style of decision making, as was the case with Kennedy, Carter, and now Clinton. Alternatively, secretaries who are seen as too closely identified with White House perspectives run the risk of eroding the morale and authority of the State Department's career professionals, thus weakening the very organization they were appointed to lead.

Alexander Haig, Ronald Reagan's first secretary of state, exemplifies the pitfalls of the first approach. Despite his gruff public demeanor, Haig was a strong advocate within the administration for the moderate, pragmatic policies typically favored by career diplomats on issues such as how to deal with the Soviets and how to respond to leftist pressures in Central America. He developed working relationships with State's career professionals and served as a vigorous protagonist of his agency's perspectives. His relative moderation put him at odds with the more devoutly conservative ideologues surrounding Reagan, however. This stance, coupled with Haig's insistence on his own and his department's position as first among equals in the policy-making process, assured the briefness of his tenure as secretary of state: it lasted a mere 18 months.

The second approach, stressing the secretary's personal role as a member of the presidential team to the detriment of his leadership of the department's bureaucracy, was exemplified by John Foster Dulles in the Eisenhower years, Dean Rusk during the Kennedy-Johnson years, and Henry Kissinger in Nixon's aborted second term and Ford's brief presidency. In each instance, the secretary of state, as an individual, exerted considerable influence in molding presidential decision making on international matters. However, each also remained aloof from the professional corps of career diplomats who comprise the State Department's greatest resource. Instead, they preferred to rely on a small circle of aides whose careers revolved around their personal loyalty to the secretary rather than to the institutional perspective of the State Department. A strong secretary of state, then, does not necessarily mean a strengthened role for the Department of State. As often as not, it leads to precisely the opposite: a leaderless, ignored, and demoralized institution.

Immediately below the secretary is the deputy secretary, who ordinarily functions as the department's principal day-to-day manager. The two most recent secretaries of state—Lawrence Eagleburger in the waning months of the Bush administration and Warren Christopher in the Clinton administration—previously served as deputy secretary and thus assumed the top job with an intimate familiarity of the State Department machinery. At the third tier are five undersecretaries of state: one each for political affairs; global affairs; economics, business, and agricultural affairs; international security affairs and arms control; and management. At a comparable rank is the counselor, who serves as the department's principal legal adviser.

Next in rank are the assistant secretaries, and they numbered 22 in the Bush administration. Sometimes wielding considerable influence in the policy process, each assistant secretary directs the department's principal administrative units: its bureaus.

The Bureaus   Of the 22 bureaus, 16 are referred to as functional; that is, they concentrate on a particular function rather than a specific part of the world. Among the more prominent functional bureaus in the policy process are the Bureau of Human Rights and Humanitarian Affairs, which prepares an influential annual report to Congress assessing human rights practices around the world; the Bureau of Intelligence and Research (INR), which analyzes intelligence collected by other agencies, thus giving State some in-house capacity for independent intelligence analysis; the Bureau of Legislative Affairs, which is State's liaison with a Congress that is more involved in foreign policy-making than ever before; and the Bureau of Public Affairs, which reflects the department's belated recognition that as foreign policy has become increasingly politicized and democratized, the State Department must maintain a constant public relations effort to help its views receive public attention comparable to that given more aggressive bureaucratic rivals and private interest groups.

Of greater influence in policy-making, however, are the geographic bureaus (Europe and Canada, East Asia and the Pacific, South Asia, the Near East, the Americas, and Africa). The regional assistant secretaries frequently attain public visibility rivaling that of the secretary himself and often exert considerable influence in formulating U.S. foreign policy toward their area. During the Reagan administration, for example, two assistant secretaries virtually dominated executive branch policy-making in their regions of expertise: Elliot Abrams, who was the principal architect of a new hard-line policy against leftist movements in Central America and the Caribbean, and Chester Crocker, assistant secretary for African affairs, who was responsible for the controversial policy of "constructive engagement" with the white-minority regime of South Africa.

Within the geographic bureaus are the true custodians of State Department expertise: the numerous desk officers and country directors who both manage the day-to-day relations between the United States and their country of specialty and possess the specialized knowledge and analytical insights on which sound policy-making depends. While the assistant secretaries and the officers above them are presidential appointees, and hence are drawn from a variety of professions as well as from the ranks of State's career professionals, the desk officers within the regional bureaus are nearly always Foreign Service officers (FSOs), the country's much criticized and underutilized corps of professional diplomats. Shortly, we look at the problematic character of the distinct Foreign Service culture, which has been routinely denounced in a steady stream of academic and government studies. Here, however, we simply note that the talented men and women of the Foreign Service conduct the routine tasks of diplomacy and sometimes play a role in molding U.S. foreign policy.

Warren Christopher's first act as secretary of state was to reorganize and simplify the structure of the State Department. In an undated "Message for All State Department Employees" issued as he took his oath of office, Christopher moved to realign the department. Five undersecretaries—for political affairs; economics, business, and agriculture; arms control and international security; global affairs; and management—would become his "principal advisers." Positions would be rearranged to create "new focal points," eliminate "redundancies," and reduce "excessive layering to streamline information flow and decisionmaking."

The reorganization parallels that done by Aspin and does result in two agencies with similar structures. The major innovation is the establishment of an undersecretary for global affairs, under whose auspices a whole series of activities associated with the post–Cold War world will be housed—human rights, refugees and migration, and environment, for instance. This impressive array explains why a former U.S. senator, Tim Wirth of Colorado, would be attracted to an undersecretary-level position. Another innovation is the undersecretary for economics, business, and agriculture, reflecting the Clinton administration's emphasis on global economic competitiveness.

Embassies, Consulates, and Missions   Before leaving the topic of organizational structure, we need to mention the nearly 300 embassies, consulates, and missions the United States maintains abroad. U.S. embassies are the principal locus of conducting U.S. foreign policy overseas. Each is headed by an ambassador named by the president. Ordinarily, about two-thirds of all ambassadors are selected from the ranks of FSOs. The rest are political appointees, who range in quality from the distinguished to the unqualified, and are usually—and not coincidentally—wealthy campaign donors. In July 1990, President Bush strengthened the authority of ambassadors overseas, so that today they are, in theory, in charge of all executive branch U.S. offices and personnel in the country to which they are accredited, except for military personnel. The rise of instantaneous communications and jet travel may have diminished the significance of ambassadors, but they remain important both as symbolic representatives abroad and as head of the U.S. "country team." Their information gathering, analysis, and reporting of local trends and thinking are indispensable inputs into Washington's policy-making process. At the same time, use of informal negotiators, as discussed in the Amplification box: "Jimmy Carter, the Informal Envoy," can erode ambassador's roles.

Foreign Policy Role

The much noted erosion of the State Department's role in the foreign policy-making process is a phenomenon that some applaud and others lament, but one that

---

AMPLIFICATION

Jimmy Carter, the Informal Envoy

Although he is hardly the first person to act as a personal negotiator outside the formal mechanisms of the government, former president Jimmy Carter has emerged as a very prominent, and apparently useful individual for the government to employ in difficult diplomatic situations. The former president's primary attributes seem to be his unquestioned integrity and his sincere commitment to peace, which his followers say adds to his credibility (his detractors argue those characteristics add to his naïveté and the ability of opponents to cut an unfair deal with him).

Carter has become prominent in at least three different negotiations. He led the international delegation that monitored the Nicaraguan elections of February 1990 which saw the defeat of the Sandinistas and the rise to power of anticommunist Violetta Chamorro. In June 1993, Carter traveled to North Korea as President Clinton's envoy to negotiate a solution to the crisis between the United States and North Korea over inspection of that country's nuclear facilities. In 1994, he was the personal liaison between the Haitian military junta and the American government, arranging terms for the junta to leave the country, for President Aristide to return, and for American armed forces to land in Haiti without opposition to help in the restoration of order to that country.

few deny. Like an ailing patient, the State Department is constantly probed and examined by a legion of scholars and journalists, all hoping to uncover the malaise that has allegedly drained the grand old institution of its vigor and left it a limp and fragile player in the rough-and-tumble game of Washington policy-making. Three factors may explain State's loss of primacy in foreign policy-making: (1) the rise of security, economic, humanitarian, and environmental issues that have joined State's traditional preoccupation with diplomacy as central components of foreign policy, and the related rise of institutional players with special expertise in these policy domains; (2) the trend toward personal presidential dominance of foreign policy-making and conduct, and the related centralization of policy-making in the White House–based National Security Council (NSC) staff; and (3) some deeply ingrained features of the Foreign Service's culture that tend to isolate FSOs from other bureaucratic players and limit their influence in interagency dealings.

First, as we saw in Chapter 1, our concept of foreign policy has been stretched beyond its traditional preoccupation with state-to-state diplomacy. A host of issues that used to be regarded as purely domestic in character are now properly understood to include an international dimension. The drug problem, for example, requires both domestic efforts to reduce demand and international efforts to reduce supply. Similarly, environmental protection is increasingly recognized as a problem that transcends state boundaries and demands international coordination. Furthermore, it is now a commonplace to note that U.S. economic well-being is closely bound up with international factors such as reducing trade barriers, coordinating monetary policies among the leading industrial nations, and providing a measure of hope and stability to the peoples of the Third World where much of the planet's natural resources are located.

As these and other "intermestic" (partly international, partly domestic) issues have joined the traditional diplomatic concerns of the State Department, they have brought in their wake a proliferating roster of executive agencies with special expertise and institutional stakes in the shaping of policy affecting "their" policy domains. The Commerce Department, for example, is now much more involved in promoting U.S. economic interests than was the case when the United States was less dependent on international trade and capital flows. Similarly, agencies as diverse as the Energy Department, the Department of Agriculture, the Treasury, the Drug Enforcement Agency, and the Environmental Protection Agency insist that they be included in the foreign policy-making process whenever their policy domains are under discussion. Clearly, the biggest institutional challenger to State Department primacy in foreign policy-making is the Department of Defense. As we noted earlier in the chapter, the rise of the protracted Cold War struggle brought to the fore a new emphasis on national security policy, which in turn opened the door for aggressive Pentagon planners to quickly catch up to—and in some ways surpass—the influence of the State Department.

Despite the vast changes we will hardly return to a simpler world that permits a tidy distinction between domestic and international issues. Therefore, it follows that the State Department seems destined to accept a policy-making climate in which it is just one of many bureaucratic players. Many of these players have demonstrated an aggressiveness and political adroitness that leaves Foggy Bottom traditionalists nostalgic for the good old days when everyone just knew that *real* foreign policy was the province of the State Department.

Second, with the rise of the United States as a world power, presidents have increasingly sought to establish their personal dominance of foreign policy-making. The reasons for this trend range from the personal and petty (international statecraft is dramatic and exciting in a way that, say, determining price-support levels for agricultural commodities is not) to the high-minded. (In the post–Cold War age, the stakes of international politics are so great that presidents feel a heightened sense of responsibility to assume greater personal direction of the country's foreign policy.) The creation of the National Security Council (NSC) in 1947 greatly strengthened White House dominance of the overall policy-making process, permitting presidents to integrate more coherently the views and expertise of the various agencies and, in the course of doing so, supplant State's traditional role as the chief foreign policy-making institution in the executive branch.

Third, a peculiar culture permeates the world of the Foreign Service. Without doubt, the 9,000 men and women who comprise the Foreign Service are a remarkably talented elite. Since the passage of the Rogers Act in 1924, the State Department has developed a world-class corps of professional diplomats who are hired and promoted on the basis of merit. Entry into the Foreign Service is gained through an intensely competitive process. (In a recent year, 17,000 people took the rigorous written examination, of whom only 2,500 passed. Through a grueling day-long series of oral examinations and participation in group simulations, the pool of candidates was winnowed down to 600, of whom 200 were granted entry into the exclusive ranks of the Foreign Service.) In addition, the department's "up or out" personnel system requires that FSOs earn promotion to successively higher ranks within a limited period of time or be "selected out" of the service. Individual FSOs are among the most intelligent, articulate, and analytically sophisticated members of the foreign policy community. Collectively, however, they manage the remarkable feat of adding up to less than the sum of their parts. As a group, their influence in formulating policy is typically well below what one would expect in light of their individual excellence. To understand why this is so, we need to delve into the much studied phenomenon of the FSO culture.

The Foreign Service   Once admitted to the elite circle of the Foreign Service, its members are surrounded and conditioned by an ingrained set of institutional values and attitudes. These values and attitudes strengthen the internal cohesion within the Foreign Service, but, at the same time, they also erect a psychic distance between FSOs and other participants in the policy-making process. The very elitism of the Foreign Service gives rise to an unusually high degree of resistance—even disdain—

toward the views of outsiders. Foreign affairs specialists who are not members of the FSO's exclusive club (academics would be an example) often find that not only are their insights not welcomed by FSOs but also that their very presence in State Department circles (for example, as members of the Policy Planning Staff) is opposed.

While many professions inculcate a strong sense of identification with the group and a heightened sense of separateness from those outside the group, this tendency appears to be especially pronounced in the insular and exclusionary culture of the Foreign Service. FSOs have also been long noted for their tendency to remain generalists. Similarly, they are disinclined to embrace the more rigorous and formal methods of social science analysis that have been widely adopted within the intelligence community and the DOD. Fully aware of their unusually high intellectual capabilities, FSOs retain an exaggerated confidence that a broadly educated generalist can do just about any foreign affairs job. This institutional resistance to subject-matter specialization and the more advanced forms of social science analysis account for the broad perception that, despite the impressive gifts of individual FSOs, the State Department's analyses of world affairs are typically less sophisticated and rigorous than those of rival agencies, especially the Pentagon and the CIA.

The FSO culture stresses caution, an aversion to confrontation, and the appearance, at least, of undue timidity in advancing controversial policy proposals. Playing down differences, seeking common ground, and avoiding open confrontation are simply inherent in the diplomatic enterprise. The kind of personal subtlety and tendency to compromise that often facilitate international conciliation can prove to be a liability in the elbows-out world of interagency Washington struggles to define U.S. foreign policy. Moreover, the State Department is one of the few cabinet-level agencies that lacks a domestic political constituency. Thus, it is an easy target for the scapegoating bullying of demagogues such as the late senator Joseph McCarthy (R-Wis.), who in the early 1950s ruined the careers of numerous loyal FSOs and intimidated countless others through his sensational and utterly unfounded accusations of procommunist treason within the Foreign Service. Long after McCarthy's death, his legacy remained in the form of an extraordinary degree of caution and a tangled system of cross-clearances. As a result, new ideas from the Foreign Service rank and file emerge at a glacial pace. Finally, the intensely competitive nature of advancement within the service leaves many FSOs exceedingly cautious about making waves or advocating unorthodox views for fear that doing so will harm their all-important performance evaluations. Conformity, caution, and a disinclination to speak out on behalf of new or unpopular ideas are thus innate characteristics of the FSO culture.

Another factor that holds the FSOs back is the perception that they are haughty and arrogant. Not all, and probably not even most, FSOs could fairly be described this way, but the tendency to project a sense of social and intellectual superiority is sufficiently ingrained among them that many of the more down-to-earth participants in foreign policy simply dislike them.

Taken together, these four traits — resistance to outsiders, preference for generalists and for intuitive analysis, inordinate caution, and too frequent imagery of snobbery — define much of the institutional culture that influences the thinking and behavior of FSOs. Most outside observers agree that these norms and values are simply self-defeating. But while organizational change can be effected through simple edict, cultural change occurs slowly. Until the Foreign Service takes independent steps to cast off its outdated and self-defeating culture, it will remain a remarkably talented corps of men and women with diminished actual influence on policy-making. President Clinton's national security adviser, Anthony Lake, is an ex-FSO who has long argued that the views and expertise of the Foreign Service should play a greater role in shaping policy than it has in the post–World War II era. While influential friends like Lake can help the State Department recapture its former pride of place as the central institution in U.S. dealings with the world, State's career diplomats can still best help themselves by aggressively reforming their own peculiar institutional culture.

The Economic Agencies

Improving the U.S. economy was the core of the 1992 Clinton presidential campaign. Indeed, in the transition period between the election and his inauguration, economic matters dominated the visible aspects of Clinton's actions. The cluster of economic appointments, centering around a new National Economic Council, were his first appointments, and the two-day December 1992 economic summit in Little Rock was likened to a graduate seminar in economics.

While Clinton's primary concern is the domestic economy, international economic matters have become the cornerstone of his overall foreign policy because, first, economic issues are among the most intermestic of all foreign policy areas. It is hard to imagine a major domestic economic decision that does not have international ramifications, and vice versa.

Second, the health of the American economy depends largely on the state of the world economy. The recession that created the conditions which helped elect Clinton was global, and the U.S. recession was just one case of that global slump. Any recovery of the U.S. economy requires recovery among the Group of Seven (G-7) states. This leads to a third reason: for the recovery to be complete, these countries (the United States, Canada, Japan, Great Britain, France, Germany, and Italy) must become primary markets for U.S. goods and services.

New Economic Themes

The themes sounded at the Little Rock seminar suggested a heavy emphasis on economic themes that have an acknowledged heavily intermestic content and have become bellwethers of Clinton economic policy. The group assembled, which was hardly representative of the spectrum of economic policy opinion, sounded several themes that are often elucidated by those who favor a more active United States, including federal intrusion into international economic affairs. The bellwether of these themes was secretary of labor Robert Reich, who has been a prominent spokesman for these themes in the past. Three of the most important themes—competitiveness, emphasis on high technology, and industrial policy—are interrelated and all lead toward the global economy that is the major topic of Chapter 11.

Economic Competitiveness   Economic competitiveness is an inherently international economic concept. Underlying this theme is the notion that U.S. prosperity requires greater competitiveness against other national economies. Advocates point out that the United States had systematically lost the competitive edge in a number of productive areas, from consumer electronics to automobiles and conceivably to aeronautics, biotechnical products, and mainframe computers during the 1970s and 1980s.

The issues surrounding competitiveness are complex and contentious. They also combine domestic and international policy responses if the United States is to reestablish its competitive edge. Among domestic policy priorities is a revival of U.S. education, especially in the areas of science, mathematics, and engineering. In these subject areas, among the student populations of the most developed countries, American students now rank among the lowest in standardized tests. Another domestic policy area, which is also part of industrial policy, involves tax breaks (subsidies, deductions) provided for engaging in research and development or for collaboration between industry and education.

Internationally, it is necessary to protect U.S. "intellectual capital." Specifically, care must be taken that scientific discoveries and the like do not find their way into foreign manufacture before they are commercialized in the United States. This capital has sometimes been lost because of the absence of restrictions on the international transportation of ideas. In other situations, the United States has simply given away technologies. For instance, the Sony Walkman was originally designed by a U.S. firm that discarded the idea because it did not believe Americans would buy small radios with tinny sound systems. Sony reasoned differently; the rest is history.

Emphasis on High Technology   The high-technology or Third Industrial Revolution is the result of remarkable progress in three related areas: knowledge generation, knowledge dissemination, and derivative technologies. Progress in knowledge generation is the product of advances in computing which allows greater and greater amounts of information to be processed with increasing speed, thereby accelerating exponentially the amount of knowledge that can be generated.

Progress in dissemination is the result of the telecommunications revolution in areas such as satellite transmission and fiber optics, which allow enormous amounts of data to be shared worldwide, thereby increasing communications and commercial and scientific interactions. Finally, the first two areas have helped spin off and accelerate a number of derivative technologies in areas as diverse as fiber optics, materials science, biotechnology, avionics, and computer-aided design/computer-aided manufacturing (CAD/CAM).

Moreover, all three of these areas are interactive. Advances in computing facilitate better designs of satellites and progress in materials that are incorporated into the next generation of computers.

Advances in telecommunications promote the interchange of scientific information between scientists and engineers at remote locations, thereby speeding up scientific progress. Fiber optics, a major derivative technology, speeds the transmission of accurate information, including the use of fiber-optics networks transmitting multiple television programs (making the telephone company a competitor of cable television systems).

High technological proficiency (or its absence) is crucial to international economic competitiveness. The key aspect is commercialization of high technology. In other words, in order to maximize its position in the world economy, the United States must not only lead in the high technological areas tied to basic research and science, but it must also be at the forefront of realizing the market potential of discovery and getting those technologies to market. This has become an area of American disadvantage that has caused invidious comparisons between the United States and Japan: the United States leads in scientific breakthroughs, but the Japanese are first at discovering and exploiting the commercial potentials of those technologies.

Restoring the commercial edge in areas of American scientific advantage is crucial to U.S. competitiveness, at least partially because high technological advantage and its commercial applications mark the cutting edge of knowledge and production in the future and the key element in First Tier status. The Clinton administration, through apostles such as Reich, seems to recognize this fact; their vehicle for doing so is industrial policy.

Industrial Policy   Industrial policy calls for the government, through incentives and disincentives, to create public policy that will move private entrepreneurial activity in directions that will maximize competitiveness and profitability. The idea is controversial. Republicans (especially the conservatives) oppose government involvement in the private sector, arguing that such intervention is harmful because private entrepreneurs will make better business decisions than government functionaries. As a result, there was no industrial policy during the Reagan and Bush presidencies. Industrial policy advocates (once again led by Reich) retaliate that the United States is the only major industrialized country without such a policy.

The Clinton administration has attacked this area through two strategies, one primarily domestic, and the other more international. The first strategy is to urge collaboration in areas specified for emphasis. Part of this collaboration is among firms operating in the same areas, relaxing antitrust regulations and encouraging a pooling of resources in areas such as electronics. Another part of this collaboration is to encourage more advanced cooperation between corporations and research scientists largely located in colleges and universities. Here the government's role is to serve as facilitating agent through stratagems such as tax incentives and funding for research in designated areas where commercial applications seem promising and where U.S. preeminence can be established.

This leads to the second strategy, the targeting of specific areas where U.S. commercial advantage can be extrapolated from basic scientific advantage. In its earliest statements, the Clinton-Gore administration promoted environmental engineering, which would prepare U.S. firms to be at the forefront in producing and operating systems designed for environmental cleanup. To this end, it announced its intention to share research findings sponsored by the Department of Energy and Environmental Protection Agency with firms designing commercial cleanup systems and to create tax incentives for firms entering the field.

Another announced application is in the area of defense-related research, whereby systems with both military and commercial applications would be favored over those with only military outcomes. Funding aerospace and nautical research that can lead to better airlift and sea-lift capability (a Clinton defense priority) and commercial airplanes and ships is an example.

In order to implement these changes, Clinton pledged institutional change. Having campaigned on the promise of forming an "economic security council" to parallel the National Security Council, he moved quickly during the transition to form a strong economic team and to create the position of economic adviser, which he filled with Robert Rubin. The purpose is clear: to bring order and coherence to economic policy in both its domestic and international dimensions. One might well ask why greater coordination has become necessary, given the obvious importance of economic matters to the national well-being. Several overlapping reasons appear to have contributed.

First and foremost, for most of the Cold War period, the problem did not seem pressing. The U.S. position was preeminent until the mid-1970s, and deterioration was so gradual that it was not widely recognized until the mid-1980s, when the competitiveness issue began to appear widely in professional economic discussions. Second, administrations tended to be more fixated on national security concerns phrased in military and geopolitical terms. When the Soviet threat was present, this approach was appropriate. As the Soviets began to falter, however, definitions of national security began to expand to include economic issues as well.

Third, the bureaucratic nature of the problem stunted coordination. The primary cabinet-level actors, the Departments of Treasury, Commerce, and Agriculture, were all more clearly focused on the domestic aspects of their responsibilities. International economic matters were relegated to subcabinet officials within each. Until the Omnibus Trade and Competitiveness Act of 1988 specified the U.S. trade representative (USTR) as the official responsible for trade policy formulation and implementation, there was no clear symbol within the government. Moreover, the USTR did not have cabinet rank; rather, she or he served as the equivalent of an ambassador with a relatively small staff.

Fourth, during their 12-year ascendancy, the Republican administrations were reluctant to enter this field forcefully. This attitude was an extension of the general conservative reluctance to involve the government in the economy. President Reagan did propose a Department of International Trade and Industry (DITI) in 1983, but this clone of the Japanese Ministry of International Trade and Industry (MITI) proved to be stillborn in Republican circles and was quietly dropped. The Clinton administration is more focused on economic policy in all its aspects. The great symbol of this commitment—the 1992 campaign office reminder "It's the economy, stupid"—reflects these priorities.

Conclusions

International economic policy joins other areas of institutional and policy change as highlighted in the post–Cold War world. It has proven to be the focal point of policy and structural innovation during the Clinton presidency. Clinton brings a level of interest, enthusiasm, and expertise to the economic area that is unique among recent presidents. His direction and success are not entirely within his grasp, however. As an integral part of the international economy, U.S. progress cannot be achieved unilaterally. Therefore, his success in his dealings with the G7 has been critical. At the same time, structural economic problems such as the deficit, health care, and the nation's infrastructure are long-term, intractable problems that cannot be dismissed easily, a point he has made repeatedly. Finally, the philosophy he brings to economic matters is not universally accepted. If the economy does not respond to his medicine, conservative opponents of areas such as industrial policy will be quick to attack his policy and structural innovations.

SUGGESTED READINGS

Carnegie Endowment for International Peace-Institute for International Economics. *Special Report: Policymaking for a New Era*. Washington, DC: Carnegie Endowment, 1992.

Clark, Duncan. *American Defense and Foreign Policy Institutions: Toward a Solid Foundation*. New York: Harper & Row, 1989.

Cohen, Stephen D. *The Making of United States International Economic Policy* (3rd ed.). New York: Praeger, 1988.

Gilpin, Robert. *The Political Economy of International Relations*. Princeton, NJ: Princeton University Press, 1987.

Johnson, Loch K. *America's Secret Power. The CIA in a Democratic Society.* New York: Oxford University Press, 1989.

Lairson, Thomas D., and David Skidmore. *International Political Economy: The Struggle for Power and Wealth.* New York: Harcourt Brace Jovanovich, 1993.

Richelson, Jeffrey T. *The U.S. Intelligence Community.* (2nd ed.). Cambridge, MA: Ballinger Books, 1989.

Rosati, Jerel A. *The Politics of United States Foreign Policy.* New York: Harcourt Brace Jovanovich, 1993.

Rosecrance, Richard. *The Rise of the Trading State: Commerce and Conquest in the Modern World.* New York: Basic Books, 1986.

Rubin, Barry. *Secrets of State: The State Department and the Struggle over U.S. Foreign Policy.* New York: Oxford University Press, 1985.

Smith, Hedrick. *The Power Game: How Washington Works.* New York: Ballantine Books, 1988.

Turner, Stansfield. *Secrecy and Diplomacy: The CIA in Transition.* Boston: Houghton Mifflin, 1985.

CHAPTER 6

The Congress

The second branch of the federal government with major foreign and defense responsibilities, the U.S. Congress, is unique among the world's legislative bodies. Congress has broad policy-making powers and a constantly changing relationship with the executive branch.

No other legislative assembly on earth quite compares with the U.S. Congress. Nearly all other democracies have opted for the British-style parliamentary model, under which executive leaders are chosen by the legislature and are accountable to it. Although theoretically enjoying legislative supremacy, parliaments in fact are typically dominated by the strong executives who arise within their ranks.

In contrast, the United States is one of the few democracies to have adopted a separation of powers system. Under this system, the powers of government are first split apart and then constitutionally distributed among the three branches of the federal government. Originally conceived as a means of warding off the potential tyranny that could result if any one leader or group of leaders consolidated the coercive capabilities available to modern governments, the separation of powers system has two principal consequences for U.S. foreign policy-making today.

First, it creates a legislature with an extraordinary amount of independent policy-making authority. No other legislature plays such a crucial role in determining foreign policy. Some constitutional scholars believe that the Founding Fathers actually intended Congress to be the dominant policy-making organ. Congress, after all, was the first branch treated in the Constitution (in Article I), and considerably more detail is given to enumerating its powers than is given to the executive branch (in Article II). Other scholars doubt that the Founding Fathers necessarily intended to *elevate* the legislature above the executive. However, no one doubts that they set about to establish a vigorous legislative body that would enjoy comparable status to the president in determining the country's international stance.

Second, that fragmentation of authority between the two elected branches can produce the phenomenon known as *gridlock,* which is the result of policy disagreements between Congress and the president. When the two branches are unable to achieve a working agreement on the country's proper international role and interests, the separation of powers system makes governmental stalemate and policy paralysis an ever-present possibility. Gridlock is especially likely to occur when partisan divisions intensify the institutional rivalry inherent in a separation of powers structure. This problem has been acute in recent decades, which have seen the White House in Republican hands for the past quarter century (except for Jimmy Carter's single term), while the Democrats have controlled the House of Representatives continually since 1954 and, with exceptions such as a six-year stint in the early 1980s, have dominated the Senate as well. The election of Bill Clinton, a Democrat, in 1992 augured well for a sharp diminution of interbranch gridlock, since both legislative chambers were in Democratic hands, but in 1994 the Republicans captured both houses of Congress, thus returning the country to structural gridlock.

Although Congress is constitutionally empowered to wield vigorous authority in making foreign policy, it has not always done so. American history has witnessed repeated oscillations between periods of executive and congressional dominance of the policy process. As a broad generalization, from the 1930s to the 1970s, Congress often deferred to presidential leadership in dealing with the crises of the Great Depression, World War II, and the Cold War. During the first quarter century of the Cold War, Congress was generally content to follow the foreign policy course set by the president in the belief that the nation could not afford to appear divided and irresolute in the face of a protracted global crisis. Indeed, it was a member of Congress, Sen. J. William Fulbright (D-Ark.), who in 1961 wrote,

> I wonder whether the time has not arrived, or indeed already has passed, when we must give the Executive a measure of power in the conduct of world affairs that we have hitherto jealously withheld. . . . It is my contention that for the existing requirements of American foreign policy we have hobbled the President by too niggardly a grant of power.

Just 13 years later, however, the same Senator Fulbright was voicing a vastly different message:

> I believe that the Presidency has become a dangerously powerful office, more urgently in need of reform than any other institution in American government. . . .Whatever may be said against Congress—that it is slow, obstreperous, inefficient or behind the times—there is one thing to be said for it: It poses no threat to the liberties of the American people. (Quoted in Brown, 1985.)

Fulbright's pronounced change of heart captures in microcosm the sea change of opinion that had washed over Congress in the late 1960s and early 1970s. What caused this sudden congressional reassertion of its place in the constitutional order? We have already seen the principal reason in Chapter 4. The decade bounded by Lyndon Johnson's escalation of the war in Vietnam in 1965 and Richard Nixon's resignation in disgrace in 1974 was a time of torment and bitterness for the American people. The protracted agony of Vietnam coupled with the White House criminality of Watergate gave the country back-to-back disasters that eroded the moral legitimacy of the presidency. Long after Johnson and Nixon had left Washington, their legacy of presidential failure lingered, puncturing the myth of superior presidential wisdom. From that bitter decade came a broadly renewed rediscovery of and respect for the constitutional design of policy codetermination by the two coequal elected branches.

Added to the diminished luster of the presidency were other developments which, taken together, produced a much more assertive Congress in the foreign policy-making process. These developments included a large infusion of young congressional representatives and senators in the mid-1970s, the weakening of party discipline, the erosion of the seniority system, the proliferation and expanded authority of subcommittees, and the growth in congressional staff. All these changes culminated in the reality we confront today: a Congress unwilling to submit meekly to the president's lead in defining U.S. foreign policy. It is a reality that some applaud and many curse, but it is a reality not likely to change anytime soon.

Congressional Procedures and Committees

Although we speak of Congress in the singular, it is a bicameral body consisting of a House of Representatives, comprising 435 members who represent comparably sized districts and serve two-year terms, and a Senate, consisting of two senators from each state serving six-year terms. As a result of their size as well as the wave of internal democratization that swept Congress in the mid-1970s, both chambers are highly decentralized bodies. While most students of U.S. policy-making are familiar with the decentralization of congressional authority over the past two decades, it should be noted that the House of Representatives has recently adopted new rules that greatly strengthen the Speaker's authority over committee chairpersons. The first public demonstration of the Speaker's enhanced position occurred early in 1993, when Speaker Tom Foley (D-Wash.) removed Congressman Dave McCurdy (D-Okla.) as chairman of the House Intelligence Committee because of McCurdy's unseemly efforts to undercut his fellow Democrats in a futile attempt to be named President Clinton's secretary of defense. But the McCurdy case is the exception that underscores the general rule of congressional decentralization.

The fragmentation of authority in Congress expands the opportunities for individual legislators to affect foreign policy issues and opens the body to a wide spectrum of opinion, but it also creates additional obstacles in forging coalitions large enough to pass legislation. Whereas 20 years ago, power in Congress was concentrated in the hands of a small number of powerful committee chairpersons chosen through seniority, today's chairs are less able to crack the whip and demand compliance by their more junior colleagues (this is particularly true of the 73 new Republican members of the House elected in 1994). The resulting opening up of the legislative process means that all views will be heard, but it also indicates that majorities may be even harder to forge. When we add to that the fact that, in order to enact a law, both the House and the Senate must adopt identical measures, the legislative process can seem distressingly unwieldy.

Despite their caricature as corrupt and out of touch, most members of Congress are intelligent, hard-working, honest, and well informed of the views of their constitutents. The very diversity of those constituent views, however, can make legislative agreement elusive. Unsurprisingly, a representative from Pittsburgh will be more likely to seek protectionist relief for the country's (and his or her district's) troubled steel industry, whereas a representative from rural Iowa will argue against trade protectionism, in part because his or her district depends heavily on export markets for its agricultural products. The constant turbulence of competing outlooks is the essence of legislative life. It is not neat, it sometimes leads to deadlock, but it captures the inherent tugging and pushing among diverse points of view that is the essence of democratic life.

Organizing Mechanisms

A measure of order and coherence is imposed on these inherently fractious bodies through the organizing mechanisms of political parties and legislative committees. The majority in each chamber chooses its majority leader and an array of lieutenants to oversee the flow of legislation and attempt to unite party members behind major bills. The minority does the same. Although the formal discipline of U.S. political parties has eroded over the years, each party has become more internally homogeneous and readily identified with certain policies. Twenty years ago both parties were divided between their own liberal and more conservative wings. Today, the Democratic Party is more consistently the home of political liberals and moderates; the Republicans are overwhelmingly conservative to moderate. This growth in programmatic coherence within each party gives form and substance to an otherwise fragmented Congress.

Another organizing mechanism in the House and Senate is the system of committees that are organized by subject matter and ordinarily have the most important influence in determining the fate of legislative proposals. About 10,000 bills and resolutions are submitted to Congress each year. Of these, fewer than 10 percent clear all the legislative hurdles to become law. The committee system makes Congress's workload possible. By dividing the vast number of proposals among its standing committees (18 in the House and 18 in the Senate), bills are given closer attention and members are able to develop a degree of policy expertise that comes with specialization. Since the early 1970s the work once performed by full committees is increasingly being done by the proliferating number of subcommittees. This development was necessitated by the growing complexity of policy proposals and the demand of junior members to expand the policy-making opportunities within Congress. Today, about 90 percent of legislative hearings occur before subcommittees. Similarly, it is subcommittees that, by developing expertise on the proposals before them, very nearly hold life and death power over bills. An unfavorable vote in subcommittee makes it unlikely that the bill will even be considered by the full committee, let alone the full House or Senate.

In the Senate, the most important foreign policy committees are Foreign Relations, Armed Services, Appropriations, and the Select Committee on Intelligence. Given the Senate's special prerogatives in approving presidential appointments and ratifying treaties, its Foreign Relations Committee has long been among the most august in Congress. Reaching the modern peak of its influence under the long-running chairmanship of J. William Fulbright, the committee has seen a gradual erosion of its authority owing both to the diminished status of committees in general and the succession of less influential leaders who succeeded Fulbright as committee chair.

In the House, the key foreign policy committees are International Relations, National Security, Appropriations, and the Select Committee on Intelligence. Traditionally considered the poor cousin of its prestigious Senate counterpart, the House International Relations Committee has recently acquired a new stature, as a result of a growing interest in foreign policy issues in the House and the aggressive role in policymaking played by younger committee members and some veterans, as the Case in Point box "The Chair" illustrates.

CASE IN POINT

The Chair

The Republican electoral tidal wave of 1994 brought to new prominence an unlikely figure: Rep. Benjamin A. Gilman of New York. At age 72, Congressman Gilman had spent 24 years in the House prior to his elevation to chair of the International Relations Committee. Before assuming the committee's chair, it does not impugn his legislative skills to say he was one of the most obscure members of the House. But during this time, the Congressman was developing some clear ideas about post–Cold War American foreign policy. Gilman had been a critic of President Clinton, albeit a low-key one. As chair, however, he felt freer to speak out. His central issues are human rights, drugs, Middle East peace, and the need for the administration to consult more with Congress. Gilman is particularly adamant on this latter point, questioning why President Clinton commits U.S. forces abroad without consulting Congress. He criticized the dispatch of 25,000 American troops to Haiti in 1994, the promise to send troops to Bosnia in 1995, and the policy of favoring Russia over the other Soviet successor republics, to cite three examples.

Congressional Powers

Determined to prevent too much power from being concentrated in the hands of the executive, the Founding Fathers bestowed generous grants of constitutional authority on the Congress. Constitutionally, the Congress is able to affect American foreign policy through its (1) lawmaking power, (2) power of the purse, (3) confirmation power, (4) oversight power, (5) war power, and (6) treaty power. All six of these formal powers are either specifically enumerated in the Constitution or are logical derivatives of explicit constitutional grants.

Lawmaking Power

In a sense the preeminent power in any government, the lawmaking power is the capacity to create legal authority for certain actions and to forbid others altogether. The person or agency that possesses the lawmaking power is thus a matter of fundamental importance. The Founding Fathers settled this crucial issue in the very first section of the first article of the Constitution, which reads in its entirety: "All legislative Powers herein granted shall be vested in a Congress of the United States, which shall consist of a Senate and House of Representatives." While ordinary legislative enactments are subject to presidential veto, vetoes can be overridden by two-thirds of the House and Senate, thus giving Congress the last word on defining what is legal and what is illegal.

In the field of international affairs, Congress uses its lawmaking power to shape policy in several ways. It can adopt legislation that directly defines U.S. policy. For example, whether or not China continues to be granted Most Favored Nation (MFN) trading status is subject to the lawmaking authority of Congress. Through its lawmaking power Congress can also delegate certain tasks and powers to the president. For example, in 1974 Congress initiated the fast-track authority on trade matters, which President Bush used to enter into negotiations with Canada and Mexico over creation of a North American Free Trade Area (NAFTA). Under fast-track procedures, presidents submit trade agreements to a prompt up or down vote with no floor amendments allowed. Congress can also influence foreign policy indirectly by structuring the executive branch and stipulating its budgetary resources and legal authority. Examples would be charging the Commerce Department with supervising exports of sensitive products or establishing a trade representative with cabinet-level status.

The 1986 South Africa sanctions bill illustrates the congressional use of lawmaking authority to shape foreign policy. Since its independence in 1910, South Africa had been ruled by its white minority. That rule became especially odious in 1948 when the right-wing National Party instituted a thoroughgoing policy of apartheid, or racial separation. The nation's black majority was systematically oppressed through forced segregation, inferior education and jobs, and the denial of basic liberties. By the 1980s South Africa's 25 million blacks increasingly challenged a system that denied them any political voice, while the country's 5 million whites dominated a three-chambered Parliament that included segregated chambers for the nation's 3 million people of mixed race and 1 million Indians.

The Reagan administration agreed with Congress that the United States had a moral obligation to help end apartheid but insisted that its policy of constructive engagement offered the best hope of a political solution. The brainchild of assistant secretary of state for African affairs Chester A. Crocker, constructive engagement assumed that through quiet diplomacy the United States could encourage the south African regime to dismantle apartheid and achieve regional settlements in southern Africa. Thus, the Reagan administration strongly opposed stringent economic sanctions against the white supremacist regime. In 1985, in an effort to head off mounting congressional sentiment for tough sanctions, Reagan issued an executive order that imposed on Pretoria some of the milder penalties then being discussed on Capitol Hill.

By the summer of 1986, however, it was apparent that Reagan was out of step with many of his fellow Republicans on this issue as momentum built in Congress for a tough sanctions bill. In June of that year the Republican-controlled Senate passed a strong measure that barred new U.S. investments in South Africa (although existing investments were left untouched) and also prohibited imports of crucial South African commodities such as coal, uranium, steel, iron, agricultural products, and textiles. The measure cleared the Senate by a wide margin of 84 to 14. In September, the House adopted the bill by a similarly lopsided vote of 308 to 77.

On September 26, 1986, President Reagan vetoed the measure, calling economic sanctions "the wrong course to follow." His veto pitted him not only against congressional Democrats, but also against some of the leading Republicans in Congress. Indiana Republican Richard Lugar, then chairman of the Senate Foreign Relations Committee, announced that he would lead Senate efforts to override Reagan's veto. On September 29, the Democratic-controlled House voted 313 to 83 to override the veto, well over the two-thirds majority required. In the floor debate on the issue, Rep. William Gray, a Pennsylvania Democrat, declared, "this bill will send a moral and diplomatic wake-up call to a President who doesn't understand the issue." Two days later the Senate, by a comfortable margin of 78 to 21, dealt Reagan a decisive defeat by repassing the sanctions bill, thus enacting the measure over determined executive opposition.

The stringent U.S. economic sanctions proved to be instrumental in the decision of South African president de Klerk to begin dismantling apartheid in 1990. One by one, the symbols and instruments of South Africa's racial oppression have fallen: the state of emergency that gave Pretoria extraordinary police powers was lifted; the notorious Population Registration Act and Group Areas Act were repealed; democratic political parties were legalized; and negotiations were begun with black leaders to establish a democratic system. The election of Nelson Mandela holds out great hope for long-term democratization.

As vice president in 1986, George Bush had opposed the sanctions bill, but in 1991 President Bush tacitly acknowledged the bill's role by proclaiming apartheid's end "irreversible." He announced that sufficient progress had been made in South Africa that he was lifting some of the most severe sanctions, as the bill permitted him to do. Hence the Congress, in following its own judgment, set U.S. foreign policy on a course that led to the dismantling of one of the world's most loathsome political systems. This example shows the kind of influence Congress can wield through its power to decide what is legal and what is illegal for American citizens and their government.

Power of the Purse

The power of the purse is really two powers in one: legislative control over revenue raised by the federal government and congressional control over how that money is spent. On this point the Constitution is crystal clear: Article II, Section 9, states,

---

CASE IN POINT

Congress and the Fast Transport

Sometimes congressional authority over how federal dollars are spent is undermined by the way executive officials carry out—or fail to carry out—appropriations decisions. A telling illustration is the case of the transport ships that the Pentagon refused to buy. For some time defense-oriented legislators had worried about the military's ability to deploy rapidly large numbers of troops and their equipment in the event of a serious regional crisis. (The Middle East was widely considered to be the most likely occurrence.) Transporting a single mechanized division from the United States to the Middle East requires eight fast sea-lift ships and entails a two-week voyage from East Coast ports. (Regular freighters need twice that time.)

Since the Defense Department had only eight of those fast sea-lift ships, in 1989 Congress appropriated $600 million to be used to purchase four more such vessels. The navy, however, has traditionally had little interest in transport ships, which it tends to view as unglamorous utility craft of use principally to the army. Navy leaders are much more interested in warships such as aircraft carriers, destroyers, and submarines.

Deferring to the navy, Defense Secretary Cheney approved the diversion of some of the $600 million appropriation for other programs of interest to the Pentagon and simply refused to spend the rest. In other words, the Pentagon "no money shall be drawn from the Treasury, but in Consequences of Appropriations made by Law." Since the lawmaking power belongs to Congress, it follows that the all-important power to determine "Appropriations made by Law" is also a congressional prerogative.

If, as some have argued, *policy is what gets funded,* then the power to decide what gets funded is a very great power indeed. The power to resolve perennial issues such as the size and composition of the defense budget and the U.S. contribution to the U.N. budget indicate the kind of policy influence Congress has through its control of the nation's purse strings. See, however, Case in Point box "Congress and the Fast Transport" for an example of how congressional authority can be undermined.

The annual debate over foreign aid offers a useful look at how Congress wields its financial authority to shape U.S. foreign policy. Beginning with the hugely successful Marshall Plan that helped rebuild Europe after World War II, the United States has utilized economic assistance as one of its foreign policy tools. In 1961, Congress passed the landmark Foreign Aid Authorization Act, which created the Agency for

---

effectively overrode the express will of Congress, believing its judgment was superior to that of Congress and arrogating to itself the right to ignore a clear congressional mandate.

After Saddam Hussein invaded Kuwait in August 1990, however, the Pentagon was confronted with the extraordinary logistical challenge of moving huge quantities of troops and equipment 12,000 sea miles (8,000 miles by air) from the continental United States to Saudi Arabia. The navy was so lacking in rapid sea-lift capability that it was forced to activate older and slower freighters from its ready-reserve fleet to transport heavy armored equipment such as tanks and personnel carriers.

It was sheer good fortune for the United States that Saddam Hussein failed to continue his military drive into Saudi Arabia as had been widely feared. Instead, Iraqi forces held their lines of conquest at the Kuwait-Saudi border, thus allowing U.S. forces the fortuitous luxury of time to carry out their enormous deployment of troops and equipment to the Persian Gulf. The next time a similar crisis occurs, however, the Pentagon might not be so lucky. Unglamorous although it may be, adequate military transportation is essential to ensure the nation's rapid response to sudden regional contingencies.

Congress was clearly right in this case. Had its 1989 appropriations been carried out by the Defense Department as Congress intended, the United States would today be better prepared for the kind of sudden regional contingency encountered in the Persian Gulf in 1990–1991.

International Development (AID) to administer general development assistance, and established the policy framework that has guided American aid efforts ever since. Although foreign aid always had its critics on Capitol Hill, working majorities in support of annual aid appropriations could reliably be forged from an unlikely alliance of Cold War hawks and liberal do-gooders, each of whom saw foreign economic assistance as advancing its objectives. Recent foreign aid budgets have been about $16 billion annually, a figure that includes activities as diverse as direct bilateral economic development grants, food donations, military assistance, contributions to multilateral agencies such as the World Bank, and international environmental projects. Wielding its constitutional prerogatives, Congress has regularly earmarked foreign aid monies for a few favored countries. Nearly two-thirds of recent U.S. aid has gone to four countries: Israel, Egypt, Greece, and Turkey. Today the United States remains a large foreign aid donor, although as a percentage of gross national product its contributions rank it only 25th among the aid-giving industrial states.

In recent years, congressional support of foreign aid has declined sharply. A primary reason is the end of the Cold War, which left much of the program without an overarching strategic rationale. Propping up anticommunist clients in remote locales is no longer a politically salable rationale for giving away American taxpayers' money. Moreover, the combination of unmet social needs, together with the enormous federal budget deficits, means that many lawmakers no longer see the United States as a state with an abundance of money to give away to foreigners. Finally, empirical evidence shows a great gap between the idealistic aspirations of the early foreign aid programs and the actual results in Third World countries. In Africa, for example, a disproportionate share of U.S. assistance has gone to five states which, at various times, figured prominently in Washington's strategic objectives. Those five countries—Zaire, Sudan, Ethiopia, Liberia, and Somalia—actually posted *lower* economic growth rates than the rest of Africa from the 1960s to the 1980s. Similar disappointments in the outcomes of American assistance add to calls by some members of Congress who want to do away with the U.S. Agency for International Development (USAID) and other foreign aid programs. The prospects for the U.S. historic foreign aid program are frankly rather bleak.

Confirmation Power

Unlike the previous two powers, the confirmation power is exercised only by the Senate. Its constitutional basis is found in Article II, Section 2, which stipulates that the president "shall appoint ambassadors, other public ministers and consuls, . . . and all other officers of the United States" *subject to* "the advice and consent of the Senate." Thus, foreign policymakers such as the secretary of state and secretary of defense must win Senate approval before they can take up their duties. In the normal course of events, presidential nominees ordinarily win Senate approval; indeed, failure to confirm the president's choice is regarded as a major setback for the White

House. Rather than risk the embarrassment of Senate rejection, presidents sometimes choose to withdraw their more problematic nominees.

Early in his term, for example, George Bush nominated a number of his more generous campaign contributors for senior executive positions, including ambassadorships. Among the most egregious cases was his selection of Joy A. Silverman to be U.S. ambassador to Barbados. Silverman had no discernible foreign policy credentials and, for that matter, had had virtually no paid employment in her life. In explaining why she felt she was qualified for the rank of ambassador, Silverman wrote that she had "assisted husband . . . by planning and hosting corporate functions." Apparently her real credential, in the Bush administration's eyes, was the nearly $300,000 she had donated to the Republican Party between 1987 and 1989. However, faced with a determined Senate opposition led by Maryland Democrat Paul Sarbanes, the Bush administration quietly withdrew the nomination in favor of a qualified diplomat.

The confirmation power permits the Senate to influence the policy process. Specifically, confirmation hearings are sometimes used as highly public forums for airing substantive policy controversies and, in the course of doing so, altering executive positions on important issues. This was the case in 1989, for example, when a number of senators developed serious doubts about the agreement already negotiated with Japan for joint U.S.-Japanese codevelopment of an advanced jet fighter, the FSX (see Chapter 13). The senators seized the opportunity afforded by secretary of state designate James Baker's confirmation hearings to get Baker to agree to an interagency review of the deal.

Baker was confirmed in due course, but the subsequent review of the FSX agreement opened up an interagency brawl between the project's defenders (centered principally in the Departments of State and Defense) and its critics (mostly found in the Department of Commerce, Office of the Trade Representative, and Department of Labor). The review led to new negotiations with Japan, which thought it had a final agreement with the United States and deeply resented what it regarded as high-handed treatment from the Americans.

A more dramatic way the Senate can use its confirmation power to affect the policy process is through outright rejection of presidential appointees to high office. An illustration was the bitter battle over President Bush's first choice to be secretary of defense, former senator John Tower of Texas. A 24-year Senate veteran and former chairman of the Armed Services Committee, Tower was by all accounts well versed in the substance of defense policy. His nomination by President-elect Bush in December 1988 to head the Department of Defense, however, quickly ran into trouble among his former colleagues on Capitol Hill.

Opposition to Tower came from three fronts. First, some conservative activists, including the lobbying group Americans for the High Frontier, which was ardently committed to space-based missile defenses, opposed Tower because he did not fully support the Star Wars missile shield envisioned by Ronald Reagan. Second, although few would say so publicly, most senators had little regard for Tower personally. His four terms in their midst had won him few friends but had left instead a reputation for aloofness and arrogance in an institution that prizes smooth collegiality. Finally, and most importantly, the twice-divorced Tower was dogged by persistent rumors of hard drinking and womanizing. Although the Senate's eventual vote against confirming Tower closely followed party lines, the first public allegations of the diminutive Texan's drunkenness and philandering were made by a conservative Republican activist, Paul M. Weyrich. Despite a thorough FBI investigation of the charges surrounding Tower, the issue of his character remained inconclusive. But it is no doubt true that the deluge of rumors, including a particularly colorful account of an alleged drunken dalliance with a Russian woman, created a political climate of doubt that simply could not be dispelled.

Although President Bush's Republican supporters argued that the Senate should not block his choices for cabinet heads, most Senate Democrats, including the respected chairman of the Armed Services Committee, Sam Nunn, asserted that the Senate had a constitutional responsibility to decline a nominee whose character and judgment were so surrounded by doubt. After Tower's defeat in March 1989, President Bush nominated in his place former congressman Dick Cheney of Wyoming. Cheney's affable relations with the Hill and unblemished personal record won him easy confirmation as secretary of defense.

Oversight Power

Although not specifically enumerated in the Constitution, the power to review how the laws it passes are being implemented by the executive branch and the actual effects of the policies it creates follows logically from the constitutional grant of lawmaking authority. In the course of exercising its oversight prerogatives and responsibilities, Congress engages in an ongoing round of studies, hearings, and investigations. Those activities, in turn, require a substantial amount of time and effort from executive branch officials, who are called on to prepare reports ordered by Congress and provide testimony to congressional committees engaged in oversight activities.

It is useful to distinguish routine congressional oversight from the more dramatic investigations it sometimes undertakes. A good example of routine oversight is congressional monitoring of CIA activities. Until its burst of institutional reassertiveness in the mid-1970s, Congress often had little awareness of U.S. intelligence operations and lacked a systematic means of acquiring information about them. In 1975, however, the Senate established a select committee to investigate allegations of CIA involvement in covert activities such as destabilizing the leftist regime of Chilean president Allende, orchestrating a secret war in Laos, and intervening in factional warfare in Angola. Chaired by then senator Frank Church of Idaho, the committee uncovered evidence of covert intelligence operations that bore the imprint of U.S. policy but about which the Congress had virtually no knowledge. Determined to routinize its oversight of intelligence activities, Congress established new intelligence Committees in both houses and adopted legislation that required the president to both authorize any covert operations and report those operations to the House and Senate Intelligence committees. The purpose of the legislation was to strengthen democratic accountability over secret CIA operations. By requiring both presidential clearance and congressional notification, the two elected branches of government are now more firmly in control of and responsible for covert operations.

A much more dramatic form of congressional oversight occurs when Congress conducts special investigations into especially troubling policy issues. In a number of instances, especially during the Vietnam years, the country's foreign policy climate was altered by congressional hearings. Throughout the 1960s, as the war in Southeast Asia escalated in scope, costs, and casualties, so too did doubts about its wisdom begin to grow. Those doubts were given a prominent and respectable showcase in a series of highly publicized Senate hearings presided over by the chairman of the Foreign Relations Committee, Sen. J. William Fulbright. A former Rhodes scholar and university president, the bookish Fulbright was an articulate internationalist who had been an early supporter of the Kennedy-Johnson escalation of American commitment. By 1965, however, Fulbright was having second thoughts, and in early 1966, well in advance of most of his contemporaries, he reversed course and broke with his longtime friend Lyndon Johnson over the wisdom of the U.S. Vietnam policy.

Fulbright then exercised his prerogative as committee chairman by conducting a series of televised hearings on the war. The first, held in January and February 1966, created a national sensation. Lavish media coverage served to focus the country's attention on a wide-ranging discussion of U.S. interests in Vietnam, the nature of the threats to those interests, and the best means of countering those threats. Viewers around the country were exposed to the reasoned, articulate criticism of U.S. policy from such men as the diplomat-scholar George F. Kennan and Lt. Gen. James Gavin. Their stature, in turn, helped dispel the notion that foreign policy dissent was merely the unpatriotic chanting of a few student radicals. Their cogent analysis and critique of the Johnson administration's policies served to crystallize doubts that many Americans had begun to feel.

More recently, the country's foreign policy climate was influenced by televised congressional hearings on the Iran-contra scandal. During the summer of 1987 U.S. television viewers were alternately fascinated and appalled by gripping insider testimony provided by dozens of witnesses, including, most famously, marine lieutenant colonel Oliver North, the National Security Council staffer who orchestrated much of the ill-conceived policy. By the time the joint House-Senate investigating committee concluded its public inquiry, the American people had received a memorable lesson in the perils of secret and sometimes illegal covert actions carried out by amateurs acting in the name of an intellectually disengaged president. The hearings made it clear for all to see that federal laws had been broken by executive officers, democratic accountability was undermined, and the country suffered a needless international embarrassment.

As its hyphenated name suggests, the scandal was really two separate misadventures. The "Iran" half of the scandal arose from a series of arms sales to the Muslim fundamentalist regime that had seized power in Iran in 1979 and had supported terrorist violence against the United States and its citizens ever since. During the summer and fall of 1985, President Reagan, reacting emotionally to pleas by the families of American hostages held in Lebanon by Iranian-backed groups, authorized the sale to Iran of 504 TOW antitank missiles and 120 HAWK antiaircraft missiles. Reagan was apparently convinced that selling advanced weaponry to a terrorist-sponsoring, anti-American regime would be a good way both to get the hostages back and improve U.S. relations with Iran.

Secretary of State George Shultz and Secretary of Defense Caspar Weinberger advised Reagan against the weapons sales, arguing that the policy was both politically misguided and of dubious legality. Reagan, however, was determined to proceed with the missile sale and so turned to an odd assortment of private citizens and National Security Council (NSC) staffers to carry out the operation.

The "contra" half of the scandal's name refers to White House efforts to engage in secret fund-raising for the rebels in Nicaragua (the contras) who were attempting to overthrow a leftist regime that had come to power in 1979. Congress had ordered a cutoff of U.S. aid to the contras in fiscal year 1983 and again in 1985 (the Boland amendments). Thus thwarted, Reagan's operatives on the NSC staff sought to evade the law through an elaborate covert program of contra assistance funded by contributions from private sources and foreign governments. The two operations became linked when profits from the arms sales to Iran were diverted to the secret contra fund.

When this clandestine White House foreign policy was exposed in late 1986, leaders of the House and Senate agreed to conduct a joint inquiry through a special House-Senate investigating committee. The sheer scope of its investigation was remarkable: 311 subpoenas were issued, over 200,000 documents were examined, and witnesses presented about 250 hours of public testimony during 40 days of open hearings.

Television viewers were treated to memorable testimony, such as Fawn Hall, Colonel North's secretary, setting out her novel legal theory that "sometimes you have to go above the written law." Similar confusion emanated from Adm. John Poindexter, former national security adviser to the president, who asserted that "the buck stops here with me." Observers were quick to point out that, as Harry Truman never forgot, the buck of responsibility rightly stops with the president, not his underlings. Some administration witnesses detailed their strong objections to the secret misadventure. Secretary of Defense Weinberger, for example, believed there were no "moderates" in Iran and that the regime then in power could not be made more pro-U.S. by selling it arms. Other officials made clear their willful ignorance of the operation's more sordid aspects. Assistant Secretary of State Elliot Abrams admitted that "I was careful not to ask Colonel North questions I did not need to know the answers to."

Through the 1987 hearings, Congress informed both itself and the public of foreign policy activities that were illegal, counterproductive, and undemocratic. The pattern of *illegal* action included (1) deliberate violation of the statutory requirement that Congress be notified of all covert actions in a "timely fashion" (Poindexter said he kept Congress in the dark because he didn't want "outside interference" in the foreign policy process); (2) North's admission that he and other officials repeatedly lied to Congress about the two covert actions and that he had destroyed or altered official documents; and (3) the illegal diversion of U.S. government proceeds from the Iran arms sale to the Nicaraguan contras in clear violation of the Boland amendment prohibiting U.S. assistance to the contras.

The policies were *counterproductive* because they undermined U.S. credibility with allies by secretly selling arms to Iran while publicly urging other states to refrain from just such sales. The number of American hostages was not reduced, nor was a better relationship achieved with the hostile regime in Teheran. Hence, the Iran-contra shenanigans dealt a serious blow to the U.S. international reputation for prudent diplomacy.

Finally, the episode revealed much that was *undemocratic* in the worldview and behavior of key Reagan administration officials. Numerous officials, including North, Poindexter, and Abrams, lied to, misled, or withheld information from Congress. The hearings reflected a profound hostility toward Congress as an institution and a contempt for the constitutional design of separation of powers and checks and balances. From Poindexter's belief that Congress should be kept in the dark regarding covert action on behalf of the contras because "I simply did not want any outside interference" to North's admission that "I didn't want to tell Congress anything" about his covert activities, a deep strain of executive branch disdain for both the Constitution and the Congress was evident.

In addition, within the executive branch, certain important officials were often shut out of critical decisions, thus lessening accountability. President Reagan himself said he knew nothing of North's covert actions to help the contras and was not told of the diversion of arms sale funds for that adventure. The secretary of state, who deals with foreign governments, was not told of North's solicitation of millions of dollars from those governments to funnel to the contras.

What the Iran-contra hearings of 1987 revealed was disturbing. In the end, however, the system of checks and balances was vindicated. Vigorous congressional efforts to get at the truth of what had happened and to educate the public on what had gone wrong reflected the Founding Fathers' intent when they created a separate legislative branch and endowed it with a robust array of independent powers.

War Power

In Article I, Section 8, of the Constitution, the Founding Fathers established that "The Congress shall have Power . . . to declare War." Records of the Constitutional Convention show broad agreement that the executive must not be enabled to commit the country to a course of war on his own authority. While bestowing on the president the role of commander in chief of the armed forces and acknowledging that he would have inherent authority to use force to repel sudden attacks, the Constitution's framers were nonetheless clear in their insistence that the fateful decision to initiate war must await formal declaration by Congress.

The practice of the past two centuries, however, has borne little resemblance to the Founding Fathers' carefully constructed design. As the United States rose from isolation to the leading rank of the world's states and as the technology of modern aircraft and intercontinental missiles created the requirement for rapid response to international crises, the actual power to initiate and carry out wars tilted from the interbranch balance of the Constitution to a pronounced strengthening of the president's role. Of the more than 200 instances in which U.S. armed forces have been used abroad, only five have been sanctioned by formal declarations of war.

By the middle of this century, some authorities believed that the whole concept of declaring war was obsolete. So too, some argued, was the constitutional concept of joint war making by the president and the Congress. The trauma of the protracted, failed, and undeclared war in Vietnam stimulated Congress to set out to recapture its war powers that had gradually atrophied through disuse. The resulting War Powers Resolution of 1973 represents an historic and controversial effort by Congress to restore the interbranch balance to something more closely approximating the code-termination envisioned by the writers of the Constitution. In Chapter 7, we examine the whole question of war powers and the effects of the 1973 legislation in detail.

Treaty Power

The treaty power is spelled out in Article II, Section 2, of the Constitution, which states that presidents may make treaties with foreign governments "by and with the Advice and Consent of the Senate . . . provided two thirds of the Senators present concur." Here it should be noted that, like the confirmation power, the congressional treaty power is assigned to the Senate alone. Its possession of these two constitutional prerogatives gives the Senate greater stature than the House of Representatives in the foreign policy process.

We should also note the requirement for an extraordinary majority. Simple majorities are difficult enough to attain in fractious legislative assemblies; getting two-thirds of the Senate's members to agree on anything presents a formidable challenge. Why, then, would the Founding Fathers have designed a process that made treaties so difficult to attain? The question nearly answers itself. Deeply isolationist and profoundly suspicious of the monarchies then ruling Europe, the framers of the Constitution deliberately made it quite difficult for the new country's leaders to enter into formal "entanglements" with foreign governments. Recall that George Washington's famous farewell address warned against the pernicious lure of "permanent alliances." Washington faithfully mirrored the American outlook of his day.

Occasionally, Congress and the president become so deeply opposed on fundamental issues that they are unable to work out their differences and find a compromise formula for a treaty. This difficulty was classically illustrated in the aftermath of World War I when President Woodrow Wilson was unable to secure Senate approval of the Treaty of Versailles in the form in which he had negotiated it. U.S. membership in the newly created League of Nations was one of the treaty's chief provisions. The fact that the United States did not join the League seriously weakened it as a credible international body, and it was an emasculated League of Nations that was shortly confronted with armed aggression by the fascist regimes of Germany, Italy, and Japan. Many textbooks blame World War II on the League of Nations' failure to stop the Axis powers' aggression at an early stage. It was unable to do so, they argue, because the United States failed to join it. That failure, in turn, is often laid at the feet of Congress, which allegedly was a hotbed of isolationist sentiment.

Critics of congressional influence in foreign affairs often point to this episode as a cautionary tale against the alleged isolationism and parochialism of Congress in contrast with the progressive internationalism of the executive. In actual fact, however, the U.S. failure to join the League of Nations was at least as much the fault of President Wilson as it was the Senate. Wilson, a rigid idealist, had refused to include congressional representatives in the U.S. delegation at the Versailles Peace Conference and later presented the Treaty of Versailles to the Senate with the demand that it ratify *his* treaty as is. When the Senate leader, Henry Cabot Lodge (R-Mass.), persuaded the Senate to adopt a series of rather innocuous reservations to the treaty, Wilson stiffly refused to compromise. In a titanic struggle of wills, Wilson would not budge an inch. In the end, he had so thoroughly alienated enough senators by his rigidity that the Senate dealt him a defeat and rejected the treaty that Wilson regarded as his crowning achievement. Solid majorities of the "isolationist" Senate favored the Treaty and with it U.S. participation in the League.

Mindful of Wilson's historic miscalculation, modern presidents ordinarily attempt to ensure congressional involvement in the treaty-making process in hopes of improving the chances that the negotiated document will be ratified. Sometimes, however, even this strategy is not enough. In the recent history of strategic arms control agreements, for example, President Jimmy Carter went to great lengths to keep legislators fully apprised of the progress of negotiations on the second strategic arms limitation talks (SALT II). But by the time the draft treaty was ready for Senate consideration in 1980, the political climate between the United States and the then Soviet Union had markedly worsened. The Soviet invasion of Afghanistan in December 1979 was the final straw. Aware that he did not have the votes to ratify the SALT II Treaty and moving toward a more hard-line position himself, Carter withdrew the treaty from Senate consideration.

This section should dispel the myth that the Founding Fathers intended the Congress to play second fiddle to the president in charting the nation's international course. Its impressive array of constitutional powers—to pass laws, fund programs, confirm executive appointments, oversee executive conduct, declare war, and ratify treaties—give it a strong repertoire of formal authority to share coequally with presidents in the foreign policy-making process. We now turn to an examination of how Congress wields its considerable policy-making powers in a previously neglected policy domain that promises to be a national issue throughout the 1990s: the politics of trade.

Congress and the Politics of Trade

Just as the Cold War dominated American life from the late 1940s to the fall of the Soviet Union in 1991, so too will the struggle to reinvigorate its economy likely be the country's greatest preoccupation in the 1990s. The Cold War primacy of the United States was undergirded by its unquestioned economic supremacy. In the aftermath of World War II, the United States accounted for nearly half of the world's economic productivity. As expected, the country's position has gradually eroded in relative terms. It now accounts for about one-fifth of global productivity, a decline due in large part to the very success of postwar U.S. efforts to rebuild Europe and Japan and stimulate international economic activity. More alarmingly, however, it has by some measures declined in absolute terms as well, as evidenced in particular by the fourfold growth of the national debt since 1980.

The prospect of handing the next generation a less abundant society than the one they inherited has aroused ordinary Americans in the same way that the specter of communism galvanized public opinion in the 1950s. Voters in the 1992 presidential election were more concerned about the country's future economic health than about any other issue, foreign or domestic. Their selection of Bill Clinton, whose campaign focused on the theme of economic renewal, was widely seen as a mandate to the country's elites to pay more attention to the economic well-being of the ordinary American citizen who had borne the burdens of defeating international totalitarianism for the past half century. While the country's economists and political leaders remain deeply divided over how best to attain the shared goal of economic renewal, they all agree that U.S. economic well-being is inseparably linked to the increasingly interdependent global economy.

This was not always the case. Blessed with a large domestic market and abundant resources, the United States has traditionally been less intertwined with economic forces beyond its borders than have most industrial states. As recently as 1960, trade accounted for only about one-tenth of the country's gross national product (GNP).

Today, however, the U.S. economy and the global economy are irreparably joined at the hip. The United States is as heavily dependent on trade as are Japan and the European Union (EU). About one-fourth of U.S. GNP comes from imports and exports of goods and services. The proportion of the economy accounted for by trade has increased 2.5 times since 1960. Most people know that the United States is the world's largest importer, but fewer noticed that in 1991 it passed Germany to become the world's largest exporter as well. About half of its economic growth during the early 1990s was due to its strength in exports.

Members of Congress, acutely sensitive to issues affecting jobs and prosperity in their home states and districts, have responded to the country's growing economic interdependence by elevating trade policy to the top of the political agenda. The increasing politicization of trade issues both reflects growing interest among political leaders and, in turn, serves to stimulate further political attention to the domestic consequences of trade policy. As now former congressman Dan Rostenkowski (D-Ill.) put it, "Trade is becoming very, very parochial. It's employment, it's our jobs." As Congress devotes more time and attention to a multitude of trade issues, its approach will be shaped by the fragmentation of authority within Congress; the country's philosophical division between free traders and protectionists; and the influence of partisan and constituent interests.

Fragmentation of Authority

Neither chamber of Congress has a standing committee devoted principally to trade policy. The result is a balkanization of committee jurisdictions that results in delays and duplication of hearings and deliberation, multiplies the access points for interest group lobbying, and greatly complicates the inherent task of forging coherent legislation.

In the Senate, the Finance Committee—and within it, the International Trade Subcommittee—exercises primary authority over trade legislation, but at least a half dozen other committees typically view some aspects of trade issues as falling within their sphere of authority. They include the Agriculture Committee (through its Domestic and Foreign Marketing and Product Promotion Subcommittee); the Commerce, Science, and Transportation Committee (Subcommittee on Foreign Commerce and Tourism); Committee on Foreign Relations (Subcommittee on International Economic Policy, Trade, Oceans, and Environment); Judiciary Committee (Subcommittee on Patents, Copyrights, and Trademarks); and the Small Business Committee (Subcommittee on Export Expansion).

In the House there is a similar lack of clarity of committee jurisdiction. As a result, the new attention to trade issues invites a swarm of committees and subcommittees, each jostling with the other in attempting to put its stamp on legislative proposals. A partial listing of the most important House committees (and their pertinent subcommittees noted in parentheses) involved in trade matters would include Agriculture (Subcommittee on Department Operations, Research, and Foreign Agriculture); Banking, Finance, and Urban Affairs (Subcommittee on International Development, Finance, Trade, and Monetary Policy); International Relations (Subcommittee on International

Economic Policy and Trade); Small Business (Subcommittee on Exports, Tax Policy, and Special Problems); and Ways and Means (Subcommittee on Trade).

Trade issues inherently touch on both international and domestic matters. As mentioned earlier, some writers use the term *intermestic* to refer to this blurring of traditional distinctions between internal and external affairs. For Congress to be able to deal coherently with all the diverse aspects of trade matters, then, it should establish new committees in each chamber to deal specifically with trade legislation.

Free Traders versus Protectionists

Today's advocates of free trade are the doctrinal heirs of Adam Smith and David Ricardo. Smith, an eighteenth-century Scottish writer, codified the principles of free market economics in his classic work *The Wealth of Nations,* published in 1776. Essentially the bible of modern capitalism, Smith's tract set out to show the advantages of minimal governmental control of economic activities. According to Smith, the free market, driven by the laws of supply and demand, will stimulate productivity, enhance individual freedom, raise living standards, reward effort and talent, and ensure an abundant flow of desired products at optimal prices. The force of competition, Smith believed, would act as a sort of "hidden hand," assuring fairness, quality, and responsiveness to consumer tastes—all without the heavy hand of governmental control.

Smith's principles were extended into the realm of international economics by the theorist David Ricardo, who argued in 1817 that states should concentrate their capital and labor on those things they do best and depend on other countries to provide them with the things they cannot do themselves. States with lower labor costs, for example, can produce labor-intensive goods at lower cost, thus benefiting consumers in high-wage societies. Countries with large numbers of highly educated (and expensive) workers could be expected to focus on high-technology manufacturing, thus spurring the pace of technological advance and product development. The concept of *comparative advantage,* Ricardo argued, points in the direction of free trade, whereby all states stand to gain by doing what they do best and receiving the benefits of what other states do best. According to free trade theory, restraints on trade such as tariffs (which make foreign products less competitive by raising their cost) or quotas (which limit the amount of foreign goods that can be imported) reduce the beneficial effects of competition among producers and diminish incentives for manufacturers to lower costs and improve quality.

The free trade doctrine has been dominant in U.S. policy-making circles since the 1930s. There has been a broad consensus that the anti–free trade protectionism manifested in the notorious Smoot-Hawley Tariff Act of 1930 served to contract the volume of world trade and make the Great Depression even more devastating to the country's workers and businesspeople. The United States used its towering dominance of the international system in the years after World War II to set in place multilateral treaties and institutions that would encourage free trade and global economic liberalization. The most important treaty regarding trade was the 1947 General Agreement on Tariffs and Trade (GATT). Originally a club of the industrialized countries, GATT today has over 130 signatories who work to harmonize their trading practices and promote open markets. In 1995, the World Trade Organization (WTO) institutionalized the GATT process.

Although it remains a more open market than most major traders, including the Japanese and the Europeans, the United States is by no means the wide-open trading mecca that many Americans seem to believe it is. The United States maintains quotas on 3,600 products ranging from wool suits to peanuts, and tariffs on nearly every imported good from coffee to computers. The sugar industry provides a classic case of domestic producers banding together to persuade legislators to enact steep tariffs and quotas on imported sugar. The result is that American consumers pay the difference between the 8.5 cents per pound that sugar costs on the world market and the 21.5 cents a pound in tariffs on imported sugar. On balance, however, the U.S. economy is still among the most free and open to international trade of the world's major economies.

While free trade doctrine has generally prevailed among U.S. economists, recently a school of thought has emerged that challenges the country's attachment to classical laissez-faire ideals. Although most analysts would resist the label "protectionist" as pejorative, their calls for a national industrial policy and emphasis on preserving certain key industries lends them a broadly protectionist quality. One of their most prominent spokespeople is Clyde Prestowitz, now president of the Economic Strategy Institute in Washington, D.C. Prestowitz is a former Commerce Department official with long experience in U.S.-Japan trade issues. His observations of the deep differences between U.S. free trade practices and Japan's government-orchestrated export strategy led him to conclude that free trade works only when all the major players are playing by the same rules. In Japan's case, he concluded, the rules were to relentlessly expand its global market share by undermining foreign producers while systematically denying them equal access to Japan's home market.

To Prestowitz and other advocates of so-called managed trade, the United States must take necessary steps to ensure the survival of critical manufacturing industries. As Prestowitz is fond of pointing out, the ability to make potato chips is quite different from the ability to make computer chips. Simply leaving the fate of critical industries to the laws of the market risks making the United States dangerously dependent on foreign firms whose governments have refused to permit the decline of their industrial base in the name of comparative advantage.

Partisan and Constituent Influence

This debate among economists is repeated daily among members of Congress, but congressional debate is seldom a pure exercise in academic theorizing because of partisan and constituent influence. Since any trade policy will produce winners and losers, it is not surprising that members of Congress are heavily influenced by the economic characteristics of the districts and states they represent and the extent to which their constituents are helped or harmed by trade. Among the winners of liberalized trade policies are most sectors of agriculture, aircraft manufacturers, machine tools, pharmaceuticals, telecommunications, and mainframe computers. Sectors that have fared less well amid global competition include textiles, steel, and automobiles.

Members of Congress who represent these less competitive, high-wage manufacturing industries will naturally be less inclined to support free trade policy than members who represent, say, export-dependent wheat-growing areas. As a broad generalization, the heavily unionized, traditional manufacturing areas of the Rust Belt—an area that extends across the Great Lakes states from Michigan to New York—tend to be strongholds of the Democratic Party; the agricultural west and service-oriented Sun Belt have become more heavily Republican. Thus, as one would expect, a Democratic congressman from Michigan who represents a large number of autoworkers is more likely to be a protectionist on trade issues than would be a Republican congresswoman from Kansas who represents corn growers dependent on foreign markets for their produce.

Let us now turn to three recent and current disputes involving trade policy to which Congress has devoted a great deal of time and attention: (1) the issue of Japan and the battle over a policy tool known as Super 301, (2) the debate over how best to influence China's human rights practices and the conflict over Most Favored Nation (MFN) trading status, and (3) controversy over the North America Free Trade Area (NAFTA) and the related issue of fast-track negotiating authority.

Japan's "Unfair Trade" and the Battle over Super 301

Japan is the greatest trading rival of the United States. The extraordinary Japanese economic renaissance since World War II can be ascribed to a combination of admirable qualities at home—including a strong work ethic, an emphasis on high educational achievement for all students, a high savings rate, cooperative labor-management relations, and a commitment to quality goods—and fortuitous external circumstances, especially the liberalized international economic order created largely by the United States. During most of its postwar history, the Japanese government (particularly its Ministry of International Trade and Industry, known as MITI) has pursued an aggressive industrial policy, bringing financiers and industrialists together, identifying emerging manufacturing opportunities, targeting likely export markets, and erecting protectionist barriers against imports. The United States, with its traditional free market laissez-faire philosophy, typically left economic outcomes to the play of market forces and, compared to Japan, allowed much greater import access to foreign producers.

By the mid-1980s it was becoming apparent that the two economies were not interacting as classical market economics would suggest. Instead, Japan's single-minded drive for exports, coupled with its broadly protectionist policies against manufactured imports, was producing extraordinarily high trading imbalances in Japan's favor. In 1987, the U.S. trade deficit with Japan reached a stunning $56 billion out of a worldwide U.S. deficit of $160 billion. Clearly, such an extraordinary outflow of the country's wealth, and with it the loss of U.S. manufacturing jobs, was politically untenable.

In 1988, Congress, frustrated by Japanese foot-dragging on trade talks and aroused by constituent anger over perceived Japanese "unfairness," adopted the Super 301 provision contained in that year's trade bill. Super 301, named for Section 301 of the 1974 trade act, was an unusually strong effort by Congress to direct the executive branch's handling of trade disputes. Opposed by the Reagan and Bush administrations, Super 301 was assailed by free traders and by foreign governments for its unilateralism and as a possible violation of GATT rules. Under its provisions, the U.S. trade representative was required to identify countries whose trade practices were systematically unfair to U.S. exporters, attempt to alter those practices through negotiations, and, as a last resort, impose retaliatory penalties on the offending states. It was readily apparent that the law was written with Japan foremost in the legislators' minds.

Implementation of Super 301 was in the hands of the executive branch. As proof of its seriousness, however, Congress kept a close eye on the Bush administration's approach to determining which countries to list as trade offenders. In May 1989, when it appeared that the administration might elect not to list Japan for fear of undermining the overall political and strategic relationship, a number of influential senators—among them Lloyd Bentsen of Texas (Clinton's first secretary of the treasury), John Danforth of Missouri, and Robert Byrd of West Virginia—met with trade representative Carla Hills to warn of the certain eruption of congressional anger that the administration would confront if it did not cite Japan. In order to placate Congress, the administration in late May 1989 cited Japan for discriminatory trade practices in communication satellites, supercomputers, and wood products. Partly to avoid the impression that Japan was being singled out, Brazil and India were also listed as unfair trading partners.

Japan escaped the stiff retaliatory penalties provided for in Super 301, largely by agreeing to enter into comprehensive discussions over how to harmonize economic relations with the United States—the Structural Impediments Initiative (SII) talks. To a number of legislators, however, the SII talks looked like an elaborate evasion of Congress's clear intention for the United States to get tough with Japan once and for all. Sen. Lloyd Bentsen (D-Tex.), who at the time was chairman of the Senate Finance Committee, was speaking for many of his colleagues when he said, "I've never had a lot of faith in the idea of those talks." Meanwhile, Super 301 expired in 1990.

The next congressional round with Japan would be the comprehensive debate scheduled for 1992. Anticipating that debate, House majority leader Richard Gephardt (D-Mo.), a leading congressional advocate of protectionism and trade retaliation, unveiled his own tough proposal late in 1991. Assailing the Bush administration for a "failed" trade policy, Gephardt proposed not only reauthorizing Super 301 but also rewriting it to require the administration to (1) target any country that accounted for 15 percent of the U.S. trade deficit, and (2) take action against all states so targeted.

Gephardt's plan was too protectionist even for his Democratic House colleagues. Instead, they closed ranks behind a bill crafted by Dan Rostenkowski (D-Ill.), the then influential chairman of the Ways and Means Committee and ordinarily a voice for free trade among House Democrats. In an effort to paper over differences among Democrats, the Rostenkowski plan, endorsed by Gephardt, dropped Gephardt's earlier insistence that any country that maintains a substantial trade surplus with the United States would be subject to retaliation. It captured the essential concerns of the Gephardt-led "trade hawks," however, by reauthorizing for five years the controversial Super 301 provision. In an effort to ward off even more protectionist amendments from other House Democrats, Rostenkowski's bill also included tough language on limiting Japanese automobile imports. Thus, there was little doubt that the main target of the bill was Japan. As Congressman Sander Levin (D-Mich.) put it, "When you've got this persistent trade deficit on the part of the Japanese, you just can't keep going the way we're going."

The Rostenkowski bill passed the House Ways and Means Committee in June 1992 and was adopted by the entire House on July 8. In order to become law, however, it would have to overcome three formidable obstacles. First, the U.S. surge in exports in the early 1990s seriously undercut the political appeal of trade legislation that risked provoking retaliatory action from other states. The unilateral character of the Super 301 procedure was widely criticized by other countries, who threatened similar national action against what they regarded as U.S. protectionist practices. Second, the Senate is a less protectionist-oriented chamber than the House and was unwilling to go along with the Rostenkowski plan. In the end, the Senate simply failed to act on the House-passed measure. Finally, the Bush administration threatened to veto the House bill if it was adopted by Congress. The arithmetic was plain to all: the House had adopted the Rostenkowski bill on a 280 to 145 vote, not enough to override a veto. Taken together, these three obstacles proved too great for the House's trade hawks to overcome.

The failure of Congress to renew Super 301 means that the executive branch retains more latitude in conducting ongoing trade talks with Japan and other trading partners than it would otherwise have had. For the time being the political appeal of trade protectionism has waned and, with it, congressional support for tough retaliatory policies such as Super 301. Should the encouraging surge in American exports falter, however, and the U.S. trade deficit once again begin to climb to the extraordinarily high levels of the late 1980s, Congress's trade hawks will most certainly renew their drive for tough legislation that will require the Clinton administration to take retaliatory steps against the Japanese and other states seen on Capitol Hill as unfair trade partners. President Clinton's threatened tariff on Japanese luxury cars in May 1995 is evidence that the problem persists.

China and the Battle over MFN

One of the most emotionally charged trade issues of the 1990s is, in fact, only secondarily concerned with trade per se. More fundamentally, it reflects a deep split between Democrats and Republicans over the U.S. stance toward China. Given the fact that the Democrats controlled Congress while, prior to Clinton's 1992 triumph, the Republicans have dominated recent presidential elections, the issue has also reflected an interbranch rivalry. The immediate issue is under what conditions the United States should extend Most Favored Nation (MFN) trading status to the communist-controlled government of China. The United States grants MFN status to virtually every country in the world. The concept simply means that imports from states enjoying MFN status will be permitted to enter U.S. markets at the lowest tariff rates. The 130 members of GATT routinely grant MFN status to one another's exports.

The Jackson-Vanik amendment to the 1974 Trade Act sharply curbed the president's ability to extend MFN to communist countries, however. To do so, the president must (1) negotiate a commercial trade agreement, which would be subject to congressional approval, and (2) either certify that the country was allowing free emigration or waive this requirement on the grounds that the country was improving its emigration policies. If he opted for the waiver, he would have to renew it annually.

In 1980, China first received MFN status from the United States as part of a commercial trade agreement that is renewable every three years. Since then, presidents have annually renewed the waiver to the Jackson-Vanik emigration provision.

Following Beijing's brutal crackdown on student protesters in the Tiananmen Square slaughter of June 3–4, 1989, a deep policy split developed between congressional Democrats and the Republican president and legislators over how to deal with the Chinese regime. Broadly speaking, Republicans—including, most notably, President Bush—argued that the United States can encourage the progressive, modernizing elements in China by retaining active trade ties. In 1990, Bush argued, "The people in China who trade with us are the engine of reform, an opening to the outside world." A year later, in a May 1991 address at Yale, he returned to the same theme: "If we withdraw MFN or imposed conditions that would make trade impossible, we would punish South China . . . the very region where free-market reforms and the challenge to central authority are the strongest."

Congressional Democrats, on the other hand, sought to use trade as an instrument to influence the hard-line rulers of China. As Congressman Don Pease (D-Ohio) argued in 1990, "Our aim as a nation should not be to cut off MFN but to use the leverage of annual renewal to make progress." Similarly, Sen. George Mitchell (D-Me.), the Senate's majority leader, argued in 1991 that "Clearly, the Bush administration's China policy has failed. It hasn't produced improved human rights conditions in China." The result has been a continuing effort by congressional Democrats to enact legislation that would make China's continued eligibility for MFN status dependent on a number of conditions that the Beijing regime would have to meet.

Their reasoning is that trade is an ideal vehicle for U.S. policy because (1) it is a peaceful, noncoercive policy instrument, (2) China's growing trade surplus with the United States—second only to Japan's—makes continued access to U.S. markets a major interest to China's rulers, and (3) the fact that loss of MFN would raise U.S. tariffs on Chinese imports from an average of about 8 percent to nearly 48 percent means that China's sales in the lucrative U.S. market would plummet. To many congressional Democrats, then, legislating MFN conditionality seemed an ideal way of influencing the repressive regime in China. As in the case of the effort to enact tough trade legislation aimed at Japan, the House of Representatives has been in the vanguard of attempts to legislate MFN conditionality for China. The Senate has been slower to act, and, when it has acted, it has adopted milder measures than the House.

The first round in the ongoing skirmish between Congress and the president occurred in 1990. In October of that year the House adopted, by an overwhelming 384 to 30 margin, HR 4939. Sponsored by Ohio congressman Don Pease, the bill required the Chinese government to take a number of steps to correct human rights abuses in order to be eligible for MFN renewal in 1991. Among the required steps would be releasing political prisoners, lifting martial law, accounting for all those arrested since the 1989 Tiananmen Square massacre, and ending restrictions on the news media. The Bush administration strongly opposed the measure, but even a number of House Republicans departed from their president to join Democratic colleagues when the measure came to a vote. The Senate, however, neither took up the House-passed bill nor adopted a measure of its own. For 1990, therefore, the president would have no congressional mandate regarding trade policy with China.

In 1991 and early 1992, however, both houses of Congress adopted tough legislation tying China's continued eligibility for MFN not only to progress on human rights practices, but also to changes in its trade policy (especially its protectionism and violation of U.S. copyright and patent protections) and limits on its sales of nuclear, biological, and chemical weapons. Although both chambers adopted the measure (HR 2212) by solid margins (409 to 21 in the House's November 26, 1991, vote and 59 to 39 in the Senate vote of February 25, 1992), Senate support was not sufficient to withstand President Bush's veto on March 2, 1992. The House voted to override Bush's veto by an overwhelming 357 to 61, but the Senate's March 18 vote of 60 to 38 fell six votes short of the two-thirds necessary to override.

In 1992, the commercial trade agreement with China was up for another three-year renewal. The year found congressional Democrats more determined than ever to punish China for its gross violations of human rights, which were seen most vividly in the 1989 massacre of student protesters. President Bush continued to insist that Congress should not attach conditions to China's continued MFN status, arguing that the result would be a more sullenly isolated China, not a more reform-minded one. His arguments failed to persuade House and Senate Democrats, however, who once again attempted to craft a legislative vehicle that could win solid enough majorities in both chambers to render it veto proof.

Once again, the principal push came from the House, whose bill was cosponsored by representatives Don Pease (D-Ohio) and Nancy Pelosi (D-Calif.). Whereas previous bills threatened MFN status for all Chinese exports, the Pease-Pelosi bill (HR 5318) targeted only China's state-owned industries. This bill was an attempt to win additional backing by undercutting the Bush administration's argument that threatening China's MFN status was tantamount to threatening the emergence of China's growing ranks of reform-minded entrepreneurs. The Pease-Pelosi bill would authorize renewal of MFN for 1993, provided China made "overall significant progress" in human rights, trade practices, and weapons proliferation. If it failed to do so, the measure would obligate the administration to impose steep tariffs on imports from Chinese state-owned industries. Passed by the Ways and Means Committee on July 2 and adopted by the entire House by an overwhelming 339 to 62 vote later that month, the Pease-Pelosi measure once again identified the House of Representatives as the more activist and aggressive chamber within Congress. As in past years, the Senate was in a largely reactive mode, moving slowly and allowing House activists to define the parameters of its own deliberations. While the Senate did pass the House measure by voice vote in September 1992, unlike the House of Representatives, it was unable to muster the requisite two-thirds needed to override President Bush's September 28, 1992, veto of the bill.

Bill Clinton's campaign rhetoric suggested that he would take a drastically different approach than Bush toward China's aging dictators. In October 1992, he charged that Bush was too eager to befriend "potentates and dictators," and he said that if elected he would be more willing than Bush to use trade sanctions to promote human rights. Less than three weeks after his election, however, Clinton struck a sharply different tone, publicly praising China's "progress" on human rights and trade violations under Bush's policies. While Clinton had considered the views of his fellow Democrats in Congress, including Senate majority leader George Mitchell (D-Me.) who described the Bush policy toward China as "immoral" and called for a revocation of MFN status to compel China to relax its human rights policies, it seems unlikely that Clinton will lead the charge for such legislation. Without a clear summons from a fellow Democrat, it is equally unlikely that Congress will undercut Clinton by adopting a revocation of China's MFN status over Clinton's objection.

NAFTA and the Fast-Track Negotiating Authority

Our final case study of congressional efforts to mold U.S. trade policy concerns the historic effort to create a North America Free Trade Area (NAFTA). When fully implemented, a preliminary agreement announced on August 12, 1992, will—over a 15-year period—join the United States, Canada, and Mexico in the world's largest free trade zone. The eventual elimination of tariffs and other trade barriers among the three states (and others, like Chile, that may join) would permit goods produced anywhere in North America to be traded freely throughout the continent. With a population of about 385 million in 1995 and a combined economic production exceeding $6 trillion per year, NAFTA would represent a greater duty-free market than the European Union (EU), which served as its model.

The United States and Canada had previously established a free trade agreement that went into effect on January 1, 1989. When President Bush and Mexico's president Carlos Salinas agreed in June 1990 to negotiate a U.S.-Mexican free trade agreement, Canada joined the talks in the shared hope that a true continental customs union would result.

The accord announced in August 1992 has been ratified by the three signatory states, and its provisions are gradually being implemented. In the case of the United States, congressional influence was wielded in two ways: (1) in legislating the procedures under which the trade agreement negotiated by the executive is treated in Congress, and (2) in exercising its authority to accept, modify, or reject the NAFTA agreement altogether.

Congress alone determines the rules that will govern its own handling of trade issues. Acutely aware that trade bills, with their intricate domestic implications, can all too easily become "Christmas trees" on which all sorts of specialized amendments are hung, Congress in 1974 first established what is known as fast-track legislative procedures for trade measures. Under fast track, Congress gives itself 60 days from the time a trade agreement is presented to it to vote the measure cleanly up or down; no amendments are permitted under fast track. In many ways a statesmanlike move by Congress, the adoption of fast-track procedures involved a frank acknowledgment of its vulnerability to special pleading by constituents and organized interests. Its achievement was to make clear Congress's determination to overcome the morass of conflicting parochial interests and vote directly and expeditiously on major trade matters. Specifically, fast track requires that (1) committees cannot amend trade bills and must approve or disapprove them within 45 days, (2) both the House and the Senate have to vote on the bill within 15 days after committee action, and (3) floor debate in each chamber is limited to 20 hours and no amendments are permitted. In 1988, Congress reauthorized the fast-track procedure until 1991. Included in the reauthorization was provision for an additional two-year extension to 1993 *unless* either chamber objected. This short window was specified in hopes that it would encourage successful completion of the Uruguay Round of GATT talks, which deals heavily with agricultural matters. By 1991, however, the politics of permitting fast track to extend until 1993 were inseparably bound up with the free trade talks then underway with Mexico.

Hence, 1991 saw efforts by the more protectionist wing of the Democratic Party to block the two-year extension of fast-track authority as a surrogate way of expressing disapproval of the forthcoming trade agreement with Mexico. Hoping to head off legislative attempts to terminate fast track—which would surely spell trouble for the NAFTA agreement then being negotiated—the Bush administration issued an action plan on May 1, 1991. Contained in the document were administration pledges to address the principal concerns voiced relative to the proposed free trade agreement with Mexico, including promises regarding environmental protection, retraining of workers adversely affected by the agreement, and help for affected industries in the form of protracted transition periods. With its action plan in place, the Bush administration hoped to be able to paint congressional opponents of free trade—and of its 1991 surrogate, fast track—as retrograde protectionists who were working against the nation's long-term economic interests.

Most congressional Democratic leaders gave lukewarm support to Bush's plans for NAFTA and, with it, extending fast track through 1993. House speaker Tom Foley expressed cautious support, as did the then chairman of the Senate Finance Committee, Lloyd Bentsen, and the then chairman of the House Ways and Means Committee, Dan Rostenkowski. But all of these key Democratic leaders voiced concern that the final NAFTA agreement might prove too costly to American workers and might not contain adequate environmental safeguards. As Rostenkowski put it, "My inclination is to be supportive, but I see the storm brewing out there."

Powerful interest groups lobbied hard to defeat fast-track extension and, with it, to make ratification of a NAFTA agreement extremely unlikely. The AFL-CIO argued that free trade with Mexico would come at the price of lost American jobs; environmental groups such as Friends of the Earth argued that Mexico's lax pollution standards would generate pressure to relax U.S. air quality standards in order to keep manufacturers from relocating to Mexico. Both groups made defeat of fast track a top lobbying priority for 1991.

Although Chairman Rostenkowski favored extending fast track through 1993, he agreed to bring a bill to terminate it, sponsored by Congressman Byron Dorgan (D-N. Dak.) to a vote in his Ways and Means Committee and then before the whole House. The committee voted against Dorgan's bill by a vote of 9 to 27 on May 14, and on May 23 the House similarly defeated the Dorgan measure by 192 to 231. As a sop to the Democrats' more protectionist wing, however, Rostenkowski and Richard Gephardt cosponsored a nonbinding resolution pledging that Congress would terminate fast track if the administration failed to keep its promise to protect the environment and U.S. workers in the forthcoming agreement with Mexico. On the same day that it defeated Dorgan's bill to suspend fast track, the House also adopted the nonbinding Rostenkowski-Gephardt resolution by an overwhelming 329 to 85 vote.

Meanwhile, the Senate was presented with a similar measure to kill fast track, sponsored by Ernest Hollings (D-S.C.). Senator Bentsen's Finance Committee voted against the measure 15 to 3 on May 14, and 10 days later the Senate as a whole also rejected Hollings's proposal on a 36 to 59 vote.

On June 1, 1991, therefore, the two-year extension of fast track went into effect. This meant that the new Clinton administration would have until June 1993 to ensure expeditious handling of the NAFTA agreement. Moving swiftly prior to his inauguration in January 1993, Clinton emerged from a meeting with President Salinas of

Mexico to proclaim that his administration would press for speedy congressional approval of the North American Free Trade Agreement *providing* Mexico agreed to specific understandings protecting U.S. workers and the environment. As a Democratic president, and hence the leader of a political party more beholden to powerful domestic labor and environmental interests, it was an act of considerable courage on Clinton's part to embrace NAFTA—and attempt to ensure its approval in Congress during the remaining five-month window of assured fast-track processes—in the face of considerable opposition to the treaty within his own party.

As these three cases show, Congress is increasingly involved in the intermestic details of contemporary trade issues. But Congress is not optimally organized to deal with trade matters, with numerous committees claiming jurisdiction over its various facets. The House and Senate are also split philosophically between devotees of free trade doctrine and advocates of a more retaliatory and protectionist stance. Further divisions grounded in partisan and constituent interests are also evident in congressional proceedings. Yet, as in the case of its adoption of fast-track procedures, Congress has shown both a desire and a willingness to rise above these limiting divisions and to treat complex trade matters as serious issues affecting the country's future. Whether Americans agree or disagree with the positions Congress adopted in the cases we have examined, clearly the congressional approach to trade issues has been governed by a seriousness and concern for the country's economic future.

Congressional Activism in Foreign Policy-Making

The contemporary pattern of congressional assertiveness in U.S. foreign policy is nothing if not controversial. Here we look at three arguments often leveled against congressional activism and assess the merits of those arguments.

Need to Present a United Front

Some observers argue that, if Congress does not willingly accept second billing to the president, the United States will present an inconsistent face to the outside world. Without clearly accepted presidential leadership, it is stated, other governments will be confused as to who is speaking for the United States and what the country's policy actually is. Whereas the executive branch is headed by a single chief executive and thus can speak with one voice, the decentralized Congress sometimes threatens to act like "535 secretaries of state," the critics say.

This is indeed sometimes a problem, particularly if individual legislators overstep the bounds of shaping foreign policy and begin to involve themselves in its actual conduct. In 1987, for example, then Speaker of the House Jim Wright (D-Tex.) injected himself in the struggle between Nicaragua's leftist Sandinista regime and the contra rebels seeking to overthrow it. President Reagan had refused to meet with the Sandinista leader, Daniel Ortega, but Congressman Wright held his own talks with Ortega. Understandably, some foreign observers did not know whether official U.S. policy was to back the contras' effort to bring down the Sandinistas or to act as a conciliator between them. Similarly, former congressman George Hansen (R-Idaho) set out for Iran in 1980 on his own (unsuccessful) effort to secure the release of U.S. hostages.

These and similar actions can indeed distort the U.S. position on international issues, and it is reasonable to expect responsible legislators to refrain from grandstanding acts that might undermine U.S. foreign policy. At the same time, however, it is also true that rival factions and agencies within the executive branch frequently pursue different and incompatible foreign policy agendas. Their incessant maneuvering to prevail within the executive branch and win support in Congress and with the public sometimes sends contradictory signals abroad and undercuts the coherence of U.S. policy. In the increasingly important bilateral relationship with Japan, for example, the Pentagon and State Department often appear to have a de facto bureaucratic alliance based on their shared institutional perspective. That perspective stresses the strategic and political sides of the relationship and takes pains to play down "secondary" economic frictions that could destroy a pivotal link in the architecture of world order. Other agencies, including most notably the Office of the U.S. Trade Representative, Department of Commerce, and Department of Labor, pay much more attention to the economic aspects of the U.S.-Japan connection and are not at all comfortable with what they see. These agencies often press for a more aggressive U.S. stance toward Japan's challenge to U.S. economic interests and believe that the Pentagon and State Department needlessly coddle the Japanese.

Thus, although an activist Congress adds to the inherent challenge of defining and implementing a clear and consistent foreign policy, congressional passivity would not thereby produce it. Interbranch politics would merely be replaced by intrabranch politics.

Lack of Foreign Policy Expertise

Many observers contend that few members of Congress are true foreign policy experts. Therefore, the argument goes, a policy shaped by Congress is bound to be a policy of amateurism, hardly the kind of thoughtful approach that befits a great power. It is indeed a fact of legislative life that members of Congress must deal with the whole spectrum of policy issues confronting the country. In any given legislative session, members will have to make more or less informed voting choices on issues ranging from farm price-support subsidies to Alaskan wildlife preservation to school voucher programs to the problems of urban decay. For most members, the pressures to be reasonably adept generalists make it difficult, if not impossible, for them to attain the depth of knowledge they need to become true foreign affairs specialists. It is thus unrealistic to expect all of them to be fully informed on the nuances of the dozens of foreign policy issues.

It does not follow, however, that Congress is inherently incapable of acting wisely on foreign affairs. Presidents, no less than legislators, are faced with similar demands to be more or less conversant with the whole spectrum of policy issues facing the country, no matter how much they might wish to focus on foreign affairs. Yet no one argues that as a consequence, the president is unable to handle the foreign affairs aspects of his job.

To the extent that Congress is able to act knowledgeably on foreign policy issues, this ability is attributed mainly to the growth in congressional staff and the expertise of the Congressional Research Service and the Office of Technology Assessment. Through the much noted explosion in congressional staff over the past two decades, legislators now have the support of subject-matter experts who do not owe their livelihood to the executive branch and so are not beholden to its policies. The same critics who want Congress to submit meekly to presidential leadership also berate it for hiring more staffers, but it is that very strengthening of its own institutional capability that helps Congress discharge the independent policy-making role envisioned by the Constitution. In addition, the less noted but no less important repository of policy expertise found in the Congressional Research Service and the Office of Technology Assessment gives Congress additional "bench strength" in analyzing international currents and evaluating the pros and cons of alternative foreign policy proposals.

Today Capitol Hill is well populated by foreign policy congressional staffers with impressive credentials. Many hold advanced degrees in the field, some are former Foreign Service officers, and most bring to their jobs considerable intelligence and solid analytical abilities. Those skills are being used in researching issues and developing legislative initiatives for individual members or for the committees employing them.

A good example of the caliber of congressional staffers is Larry K. Smith. A defense intellectual who has taught at Dartmouth College and Harvard's John F. Kennedy School of Government, Smith is well respected in academia, the think tank community, and the government. He was hired by then House Armed Services Committee chairman Les Aspin (D-Wis.) to help reformulate the country's defense policy for the post–Cold War era. Smith's mastery of security policy issues combined with his pragmatic political skills have won him praise from both sides of the political aisle. As Alton Frye of the prestigious Council on Foreign Relations said of Smith, "Linking national security issues with the practical politics of getting things done: That's where his brilliance lies." Smith is not the only such expert on Capitol Hill. Equally impressive foreign policy experts are found on the staffs of individual members as well as the appropriate House and Senate committees. Therefore, while not all members of Congress are able to immerse themselves thoroughly in the intricacies of international issues, they have available to them the considerable talents of their staff assistants to aid them in staying abreast of world events. Also strengthening Congress's overall sophistication on foreign policy matters is the fact that some of its members do manage to develop genuine expertise on world affairs.

The Politicization of Congress

A third charge often leveled against congressional activism in foreign policy-making is that Congress is so deeply politicized, split by partisan and ideological divisions, and vulnerable to the special pleadings of powerful interest groups that it is incapable of transcending political parochialism and acting on an elevated conception of the long-term national interest. Of course, Congress is an inherently political institution, and politics in the negative sense of the term does sometimes intrude on the policy-making process. However, it is generally unfair to conclude that members of Congress are unable to think and act in terms of the higher national good. It was Congress, after all, that transcended the instinctive isolationism of its constituents and courageously enacted the critical legislation establishing early Cold War policy. The Marshall Plan, aid to Greece and Turkey, and U.S. participation in NATO were all made possible by congressional action. More recently, as we have seen, it was Congress who insisted on a policy of strong U.S. economic sanctions to help bring down South African apartheid. Finally, Congress itself took the unusual step of tacitly acknowledging the dangers of politicized parochialism when it adopted the fast-track procedure for handling complex trade legislation.

Conclusions

For all its very real shortcomings, then, Congress remains essentially what the Founding Fathers intended it to be: a constitutionally independent, coequal, and democratically rooted voice in shaping U.S. foreign policy. While there is every reason to believe that Congress bashing will remain a national pastime rivaling baseball in its mass appeal, a better reading of the evidence suggests that the U.S. Congress faithfully mirrors, more often than not, both the ideals and the anxieties of the American people.

SUGGESTED READINGS

Barnhart, Michael (ed.). *Congress and United States Foreign Policy*. Albany: State University of New York Press, 1987.

Blechman, Barry M. *The Politics of National Security: Congress and U.S. Defense Policy*. New York: Oxford University Press, 1990.

Brown, Eugene. *J. William Fulbright: Advice and Dissent*. Iowa City: University of Iowa Press, 1985.

Dahl, Robert A. *Congress and Foreign Policy*. New York: Harcourt, Brace, 1950.

Feld, Werner J. *Congress and National Defense. The Politics of the Unthinkable*. New York: Praeger, 1985.

Franck, Thomas M., and Edward Weisband. *Foreign Policy by Congress*. New York: Oxford University Press, 1979.

Grassmuck, George. *Sectional Biases in Congress on Foreign Policy*. Baltimore: Johns Hopkins University Press, 1951.

Lindsay, James M. *Congress and Nuclear Weapons*. Baltimore: Johns Hopkins University Press, 1991.

Pastor, Robert A. *Congress and the Politics of U.S. Foreign Economic Policy, 1929–1976*. Berkeley: University of California Press, 1980.

Robinson, James Arthur. *Congress and Foreign Policy-Making: A Study in Legislative Influence and Initiative*. Homewood, IL: Dorsey Press, 1967.

Rourke, John. *Congress and the Presidency in U.S. Foreign Policymaking: A Study of Interaction and Influence*. Boulder, CO: Westview Press, 1983.

Stennis, John Cornelius. *The Role of Congress in Foreign Policy*. Washington, DC: American Enterprise Institute for Public Policy Research, 1971.

Whalen, Charles W. *The House and Foreign Policy: The Irony of Congressional Reform*. Chapel Hill: University of North Carolina Press, 1982.

CHAPTER 7

Coordinating the Players

Before the United States became a major actor on the world stage, Americans widely believed that foreign policy, unlike domestic policy, was essentially apolitical—that politics indeed ended at the water's edge. The United States was hardly threatened by anyone physically, foreign and security matters were relatively infrequent and tangential to most people, and the few dealings Americans had with foreign affairs were tainted by association with what many viewed as a corrupt European-based international system. According to this mind-set, foreign relations was minimal and consisted mostly of diplomatic relations conducted by a small corps of professional diplomats.

This depiction fairly accurately reflected the American circumstance until the Second World War forced a permanent participation in global affairs. In the Cold War system that evolved, almost anything that happened anywhere came to be viewed as consequential to some Americans and some interests. Foreign and defense policy, in a word, mattered.

The Politicization of U.S. Foreign Policy

As foreign and defense concerns occupied a growing part of the national agenda, they would inevitably become political. First, as the agenda broadened, so also would disagreement about the place of the United States in the world. At the philosophical level some disagreement occurred as to the degree to which America should be engaged; in more specific areas, the U.S. position and role with individual countries and in different situations became contentious. Since opposing policy preferences cannot simultaneously be official policy, political processes had to be engaged to decide what the U.S. policy toward the world would be.

Foreign and defense policy and its implementation became an increasing part of the competition for scarce governmental resources. In 1955, for instance, the Department of Defense budget accounted for fully half the overall federal budget; it still makes up over one-fifth of federal expenditures, although that proportion is declining. At the same time, any dollars spent on foreign economic assistance (as in proposals to help underwrite economic reform in Russia) compete with domestic priorities, from the development of infrastructure to education. Policy is what gets funded. In a condition of scarce resources where there is not enough money to fulfill all needs, the policy process must find ways to decide who gets what.

The relative priority of foreign and defense matters, as well as policy options in general and specific situations, cover the spectrum of opinion, and there are politicians, interest groups, and think tanks to articulate them all. With the increasing prevalence of foreign policy influences on the daily lives of Americans, inevitably the political aspects of foreign policy are increasingly a part of, and even dominate, the political process. The content may decreasingly be military/national security, as it was in the Cold War, but economic issues have certainly come to the fore, especially in the Clinton administration.

Deciding on policies is what the policy process is for and about. In the U.S. system as described in previous chapters, the foreign and defense policy process consists of (1) policy-making within the executive branch of government, and (2) the executive-legislative interaction power.

Policy-Making within the Executive Branch

The various agencies that propose and execute policy interact to choose among policy alternatives which the executive branch will implement or, if necessary, submit to the legislative branch for its approval. Generally, administrations have sought to involve Congress in foreign policy matters as little as possible. Presidents and their advisers often come to think of foreign and security policy as their own preserves, matters they should be allowed to handle with minimum interference, especially when sensitive or classified information is involved. At times in U.S. history, Congress acceded to this attitude, but in recent decades that has clearly been less the case. When presidents ignore Congress, fail to consult it adequately (as defined by Congress), or engage in foreign policy misdeeds or misguided policies, the battle is joined, and this is especially true when one party occupies the White House and the other controls one or both houses of Congress.

During the 1980s the executive branch's approach to resolving policy questions came to be known as the *interagency process*. Fashioned as it was during the Cold War, the centerpiece of this system was the National Security Council. Presidents have relied on this mechanism to varying degrees across time. President Eisenhower hardly ever used it at all, whereas it was very important to President Kennedy. During the Reagan-Bush years, however, it came to involve an elaborate set of multilevel deliberative bodies that debated policy from various institutional perspectives. The Clinton administration has continued to employ the process, although in a more low-key way (reflecting the international environment) and with greater emphasis on economic issues.

Executive-Legislative Interaction

Interaction between the branches is constitutionally mandated. Congress is responsible for enacting laws, and most foreign dealings have legal implications within the United States. In addition, the power of the purse means that when foreign policies require the expenditure of governmental funds—and they nearly always do—then the Congress must be involved.

The dominant theme of executive-legislative interaction has been the rise of congressional activism. When Congress feels it has either been excluded or that the executive branch has acted wrongly or unwisely, Congress reacts. It may cut off funding for foreign and defense policies. The Church amendment to the appropriations bill of 1973 cut off U.S. government support for the republic of Vietnam, for instance, and the various Boland amendments between 1982 and 1986 (named after Rep. Edward Boland, D-Mass.) sought to prevent federal funds from being provided to the contras in Nicaragua.

When the president, in the absence of legal restriction, acts in ways that Congress disapproves of, it may pass legislation that restricts or guides the executive's actions. We examine three such acts, the War Powers Resolution, the Goldwater-Nichols Defense Reorganization Act, and the Cohen-Nunn Act, later in this chapter to demonstrate this form of congressional activism.

The Interagency Process

Even the relatively like-minded people who surround the president will disagree on different policy options. Therefore, a need has arisen for a set of mechanisms whereby the options can be debated and, hopefully, resolved. Moreover, since the executive branch is the repository of most government expertise within the bureaucracies of the executive agencies, there is a need to bring that information and expertise to bear on policy problems.

Within the Reagan and Bush administrations, the mechanism for dealing with foreign policy problems became known as the interagency process. It was centered around the National Security Council, thereby bringing it fully under the control of the White House and the chief executive's closest advisers. An examination of the structure reveals both how it was designed to deal with foreign policy problems and what areas of change the Clinton administration has addressed.

Structure of the Interagency Process

The National Security Council At the top of the hierarchy of working groups responsible for resolving policy divisions within the executive branch is the National Security Council itself. The role of the NSC is to advise and assist the president in integrating all aspects of national security policy as it affects the United States, including domestic, foreign, military, intelligence, and economic considerations. The Bush administration, in one of its first actions upon coming to office, stipulated in National Security Directive (NSD)-1 that the NSC was the principal forum for considering national security policy issues that require presidential determination. President Clinton has continued this practice.

As stated earlier, the NSC has four statutory members (the president, vice president, secretary of state, and secretary of defense), two statutory advisers (the director of central intelligence, or DCI, and the chairman of the Joint Chiefs of Staff, or CJCS), two special advisers (the director of the Arms Control and Disarmament Agency, or ACDA, and the director of the United States Information Agency, or USIA), and anyone else the president may dictate, always including the national security adviser (NSA) and the White House chief of staff. When convened, their role is to offer advice to the president but not to take binding votes on policy issue outcomes. In Clinton administration NSC meetings, treasury secretary Robert Rubin and U.S. ambassador to the United Nations Madeleine Albright are often included.

The Bush administration probably made more use of this group than any previous administration in history. One reason may be that Bush himself was part of this process in two previous positions he held: as vice president and as director of central intelligence. Another reason may be the close symbiotic relationship that existed between Bush and those he appointed to formal positions in the process. In addition to his closest friend, Secretary of State James Baker, his relationship to Secretary of Defense Richard Cheney, NSA's Brent Scowcroft, and CJCS's Colin Powell goes back to their mutual service in the Gerald Ford administration in 1975. The result was an extremely homogeneous working (and some have argued too congenial) group. The Clinton team in 1995—SECDEF William Perry, Secretary of State Warren Christopher, DCI John Deutsch, NSA Anthony Lake, and CJCS John Shalikashvili—is more diverse in background and was not previously close on a personal level. Whether this difference will mean they work less well together or will air more different points of view remains to be seen. Clinton has maintained that the criteria for selecting these officials included the ability to work as a team. As the accompanying Case in Point box "Presidents and Their Advisory Teams," indicates, different presidents have handled the situation differently.

The Principals Committee   Below the NSC itself are three layers of organization. The first layer, the Principals Committee (NSC/PC), is chaired by the national security adviser and is composed of the secretaries of state and defense, DCI, CJCS, the White House chief of staff, and any other officials who may be deemed helpful in a given policy matter. As the senior interagency forum for considering policy issues affecting national security, the Principals Committee's function is to review, coordinate, monitor, and implement basic national security policies that do not require direct and personal presidential involvement. The committee is convened when the president cannot or feels he does not need to be present.

CASE IN POINT

Presidents and Their Advisory Teams

The kinds of foreign and national security advisory teams that a president assembles can go a long way toward explaining personality factors discussed in Chapter 4 and also how active and visible a president wants to be in the foreign policy area. If we go back as far as the Nixon presidency, we can see this in action. President Nixon's deep animosity toward the State Department and personal conviction that he was best capable of making foreign policy caused him to place a bland, weak secretary of state in place, William Rogers, and a strong, flamboyant person, Dr. Henry Kissinger, as national security adviser (Kissinger became secretary of state in the waning months of Nixon's shortened second term). President Gerald Ford, Nixon's successor, had little interest or expertise in foreign policy and thus returned power to Kissinger at the State Department.

The Carter administration, almost predictably, presented a mixed message. It was never clear where the seat of effective decisions was, in State under the phlegmatic Cyrus Vance, or within the NSA under Zbigniew Brzezinski. In fact, confusion over who was the chief spokesman caused Vance to resign in 1980.

President Reagan, like Ford, had little personal interest in the day-to-day conduct of foreign policy. The NSA position was effectively downgraded (six people held the position during Reagan's eight-year term), and effective competition occurred between Secretary of State George Shultz and Secretary of Defense Caspar Weinberger.

Thus, it is little surprise that Bush and Clinton should fashion their own, distinct teams. As the discussion in the body of the chapter suggests, the key element in the Bush team was collegiality and the shared belief in the team's competence. Under Clinton, the assembled group has left the impression of bland competence, with a clear reluctance to try to steal any of the spotlight from the gregarious president and vice president.

Although it was not called the PC at the time, President Kennedy made use of the NSC in this manner during the Cuban missile crisis. He ordered that the NSC meet without him (which is essentially the composition of the PC) to discuss options during the crisis. His rationale was that the members would have franker discussions if he was absent and would not have to worry about what he might think of their ideas.

The NSC and the Principals Committee are assisted by two working-level groups, the Deputies Committee and the Policy Coordinating Committees. These bodies are responsible for doing much of the staff work necessary to flesh out decisions made at the top levels as well as to lay out policy options.

The Deputies Committee　The Deputies Committee (NSC/DC) is directly beneath the Principals Committee. As the name suggests, this committee is composed of the chief assistants of the members of the Principals Committee. Chaired by the deputy NSA, its members are the undersecretary of state for political affairs, the undersecretary of defense for policy, the deputy DCI, and the vice chairman of the JCS. Equivalent-level officials from other agencies meet with the deputies when necessary.

The Deputies Committee is intended as a prime working group. Officially, it serves as the senior subcabinet forum for considering policy issues affecting national security, by reviewing and monitoring the work of higher levels of the process, and as a forum to propose and consider recommendations concerning ways to develop and implement policy. For example, one function of the deputies is to formulate a complete set of contingency plans for U.S. responses to conceivable crises worldwide.

The Policy Coordinating Committees　These committees (NSC/PCC) are a series of working groups that draw from the major geographic and functional areas of foreign and defense policy. Geographically, Policy Coordinating Committees (PCCS) have been established for Europe, East Asia, the former Soviet Union, Africa, Latin America, and the Near East and South Asia. The job of these groups, at yet a more detailed level of specificity than the higher groups, is both to monitor and propose policies regarding national security policies in their respective areas. Functionally, PCCs have been set up for defense, intelligence, arms control, and international economics. (This is the highest level at which economic concerns are a formal part of the interagency process.)

The PCCs are made up of officials at the assistant secretary level. Chairs are appointed by different individual executive agencies depending on the area of concern. All the regional chairs are appointed by the secretary of state. Thus, the chairs are the assistant secretaries of state for each region. The defense PCC is appointed by the secretary of defense, the international economics PCC by the secretary of the treasury, the intelligence PCC by the DCI, and the Arms Control PCC by the NSA.

PCCs are the level at which detailed positions are reached and where staff position papers are devised and debated for transmission to higher levels in the process. The PCC for Near East and South Asia, for instance, is the appropriate venue for discussing and devising policy positions to deal with Saddam Hussein. This is presumably where the original options were worked out for defining U.S. political objectives in Operation Desert Storm.

The agencies represented at each level in this process are the same—State, Defense, Central Intelligence—and can be considered the core actors within the executive branch. Organized as they are within the context of the NSC system, the PCCs were clearly devised to deal with foreign and national security policy within the context of the Cold War where foreign and national security policy were viewed as essentially synonymous. Hence, the highest ranking official representing concerns about international economic policy is an assistant secretary of the treasury in the PCC. Nowhere is there a permanent representative of environmental issues or other nontraditional concerns (population or narcotics, for instance). With the parallel Council of Economic Advisers and a much heightened concern for environmental issues symbolized by Vice President Gore, both areas are being elevated in importance in the Clinton administration.

Concerns about the Interagency Process

When the Clinton administration took office, one question it was almost immediately forced to confront was the continuing adequacy and relevance of the interagency process that it inherited. Because of the new president's relative inexperience in the foreign and defense areas, the quantity and quality of advice he received from this process was critical to his early success or failure in the foreign and defense area. In deciding how to deal with the problem, the following four legacies of the Bush interagency process came under scrutiny as different variations of the Clinton administration's version of the interagency process were fashioned.

Utilization of the Entire Process

During the Bush administration, decision making tended to be concentrated at the top, among the president and that group of advisers who formed the NSC and the Principals Committee, with relatively little influence from the Deputies and Policy Coordination Committee levels. The decision-making style, in terms of organization theory, appeared to be top down (instructions flowing from the top echelons downward for implementation, with little input on framing decisions rising through the ranks), as opposed to bottom up, where options and opinions are sought from lower levels in the actual formulating stages. Two examples of this style are the now familiar case of Desert Storm and Yugoslavia.

With regard to Desert Storm, many observers (including the authors here) presumed that once the invasion occurred, formulations of various possible outcomes, including the enumeration of costs, as well as benefits and second- and third-order effects of different courses of action, would be consigned to the Deputies Committee. It was thought that their counsel, in the form of staff reports and recommendations, would define the debate within the White House and how the options would be presented to the public. If sources such as Bob Woodward's book *The Commanders* are reasonably accurate, this approach was not adopted. Decision making was so tightly controlled that CJCS Powell relates that he learned of the decision to go to war only as he watched the presidential news conference at which Mr. Bush said of the occupation of Kuwait, "This shall not stand."

With regard to the Bush administration's handling of the unraveling of Yugoslavia, including the brutalization of Bosnia and Herzegovina, the breakup of Yugoslavia came as no surprise to the expert community. It had been predicted since the 1970s, when the consequences of the death of President Josip Broz Tito (the overarching symbol of the Yugoslav state) began to be discussed in academic and governmental circles. Examining that situation, its likely directions, and possible U.S. responses was the kind of task for which the PCC is ideally suited, with the DC acting to sharpen options as events progressed. Tragically enough, most of the experts' predictions came true. Yet, in the face of contingencies that its open process should have made it aware of in advance, the administration seemed paralyzed and indecisive during the summer of 1992.

Like-Mindedness When President Bush first assembled his group of closest advisers (Baker, Scowcroft, Cheney, Powell, Quayle), many analysts heralded the assemblage because the men involved knew one another so well and shared such similar views that the system could be much more decisive than would have been the case if a less compatible team was assembled. The negative side of this grouping was that their similarities in background and worldview were so great that the principle of informal checks and balances could not operate.

This like-mindedness was reinforced by the top-down style of the administration and the dominant role Bush assigned to members of the NSC staff throughout the process. All members of the NSC staff are personal appointees of the president, unconfirmed by the Senate, and thus serve as the president's highly personal staff. Each of the 30 or so professional members of the staff serves strictly at the president's pleasure and can be removed when he sees fit. Among these members are professionals borrowed from other agencies who bring with them their agency perspectives. Most of the staff recruited is likely to be ideologically very compatible with the president and much more sensitive to carrying out the president's wishes than, say, a Foreign Service officer working in the State Department who is protected from dismissal by Civil Service protections. That sensitivity is also likely to produce less dissent and to inject fewer ideas presumed to be heretical by the chief executive.

Structural Inclusiveness Because it was set up within the confines of the National Security Act, the Bush interagency process reflected a national security structural bias. International economic concerns were not directly represented above the PCC, and other concerns, such as the environment, were not directly represented at all on a permanent basis.

That this structure may act perversely on occasion was apparently the case at the so-called Earth Summit in Rio de Janeiro in 1992. That meeting was called to try to devise global solutions to the problem of environmental degradation. This tricky agenda became quickly enmeshed in side issues such as Third World development. (Third World countries in essence demanded developmental assistance in return for ending environmentally destructive but economically productive practices such as cutting down rain forests.)

The U.S. position at the event was confused and ultimately highly criticized. The chief U.S. delegate was the director of the Environmental Protection Agency (EPA), William Reilly, who generally supported the goals and resolutions being proposed. At the core was a proposal for a convention protecting endangered life species that was universally supported—except by the Bush administration, which argued that its provisions would be economically deflating by restricting scientific investigation on some species that may yield natural products with pharmaceutical applications. When President Bush announced this extremely unpopular position in his speech before the summit, it was widely condemned both domestically and abroad. The condemnation was all the harsher because the president's speech contradicted parts of the positions being advocated by the American delegation. With Vice President Gore spearheading environmental policy, a repeat of the Earth Summit disaster is unlikely.

Congressional Intrusion In light of questionable practices and policies deemed inappropriate by Congress, numerous lawmakers contend that the system needs modification—possibly through legislation. A major part of the criticism is the exclusionary, closed nature of the system, which does not always respond to policy initiatives from Congress. In this case, one reaction is congressionally mandated change. For instance, when Lt. Col. North's central role in the Iran-contra scandal of the mid-1980s was revealed, Congress voiced considerable sentiment favoring legislatively passed limits on the NSC, including congressional confirmation of the NSA. This sentiment was not, however, translated into law.

As we see in the following section on congressional activism, historically such intrusion has not been welcomed, primarily because it intrudes on the one area of broad presidential discretion, the White House Office, of which the NSC staff is a part. Signs of friction began to become evident shortly after the election of a Republican Congress in 1994 and sharpened as the 1996 election campaign began to take shape in highly partisan terms.

Congressional Activism

At its best, congressional interaction with the chief executive on matters of foreign and defense policy is marked by cooperation and compromise. The president consults formally or informally with congressional leaders, weighs their advice, and takes actions which reflect that consultation. In the process, interbranch dynamics create policy around which a consensus can be forged so that Congress can support the president's positions, and vice versa.

Unhappily, this is seldom the case. As foreign and defense matters have become both more complex and more consequential, positions have divided over them, and increasingly along partisan lines. Exacerbating the problem is the fact that, in 26 of the 40 years preceding the 1992 election, and again since the 1994 off-year election, different parties occupied the White House and controlled the Congress. From 1981 to 1993, a Republican president faced a Democratic Congress (the partial exception being Republican control of the Senate from 1985 to 1987). Now, a Democratic president faces a GOP-controlled Congress. As a result, foreign and national security questions have been part of the partisan debate.

The partisan wrangle becomes most pronounced when Congress, acting both from philosophical differences with an incumbent president or out of perceptions of excesses by the executive branch, enacts legislation in an attempt to curb executive power and discretion. At these times, interbranch rivalry is at its greatest, and the issues that can divide the branches are at their starkest and most dramatic. For that reason, we have chosen three particularly dramatic examples to view in some depth. They are important because their outcomes have helped frame the ongoing relationships between the branches and they illustrate in very clear terms what causes such interactions. The first of these instances, the War Powers Resolution, pitted a Republican president, Richard M. Nixon, against a Democratic Congress reacting to the Vietnam War. The other two found President Ronald W. Reagan facing a divided Congress in 1986 over the issue of defense reorganization, in light of a number of instances in which the U.S. military had performed at questionable levels.

Key Legislation Curbing Executive Powers

The extent and nature of disagreement between the executive and legislative branches of the government has become increasingly frequent and formalized over the past 20 years or so. The watershed event was the Vietnam War with its generally corrosive effects on both public and, by reflection, congressional satisfaction with foreign policy-making. Until nearly the end of the U.S. involvement in Vietnam (U.S. withdrawal from which was ultimately mandated by Congress), Congress felt it had been effectively excluded from the important decisions that had defined American commitment there. With the public foreign policy consensus broken by the war and support for the government generally shaken by the Watergate scandal, the opportunity for congressional reassertion was ripe.

No president has been immune from congressional wrath in the foreign and national security policy arena. Although disagreement is undoubtedly more likely and more frequent when the presidency and the Congress are controlled by different parties, this has not always been the case. Democratic president Jimmy Carter, for instance, had Democratic majorities in both houses of Congress throughout his term in office, but that advantage did not automatically translate into cooperative relations between the branches. Carter faced tough bipartisan opposition before the Senate ratified the Panama Canal Treaty in 1977, and in 1980 he was forced to withdraw the second Strategic Arms Limitation Treaty (SALT II) because of opposition arising from the Soviet invasion of Afghanistan in December 1979.

At least three themes recur when the branches come into direct conflict in the foreign policy arena. First, when members of Congress perceive that their constituencies are directly and adversely affected by foreign or national security matters, Congress becomes active and will oppose the executive.

This involvement is obvious in both the economic and security areas that we have been emphasizing. In the economic sphere, for instance, the status of Japanese-American trade negotiations directly affects American workers, especially farmers. The amount of citrus fruit Japan buys from the United States has a direct bearing on the prosperity of citrus growers in Florida, Texas, Arizona, and California. Not surprisingly, the congressional delegations from those states take a very proprietary interest in those negotiations. In matters of defense, the debate over national security strategy in a post–Cold War world has equally direct consequences in areas that have traditionally relied heavily on defense procurement (e.g., the aerospace industry of southern California) or in the number and size of reserve units and armories in different states.

A second theme involves executive overreach—the so-called imperial presidency. Because of his constitutional designation as the head of state, the president is most prominent in his dealings with foreign policy and foreign dignitaries. Depending on the individual and how he includes the Congress in foreign dealings, the appearance of haughtiness, even disdain, can creep into the relationship. This was especially a problem during the Nixon presidency. Nixon considered himself and National Security Adviser Henry Kissinger so well qualified in foreign policy that they did not seek much congressional advice. The symbol of the imperial presidency was particularly caught in Nixon's directive that the White House guards be clothed in highly militaristic uniforms that appeared to be a cross between nineteenth-century Prussian uniforms and Gilbert and Sullivan operetta costumes. These uniforms engendered such ridicule that they were discarded.

Third, Congress becomes activist when it believes the executive is mishandling foreign affairs. Sometimes, the motivation is partisan and political, as, for instance, in criticism of the Bush administration's approach to the Earth Summit in 1992. At other times, the motivation can arise from a genuine belief that executive action is both wrong politically and has potentially erosive effects on the political system. The political wrongheadedness of the policy and the evasion of statutory checks and balances in the Iran-contra affair illustrate both concerns. An example of this dynamic is provided by the Case Study box "The Partisan Nature of the Foreign Policy Process."

CASE STUDY

The Partisan Nature of the Foreign Policy Process

When different parties gain control of the executive and legislative branches of government, the effect is to increase the partisan nature of the foreign policy process. When the Republicans gained control of the Senate in 1994, one consequence was that Jesse Helms, senior Republican senator from North Carolina, became chair of the Senate Foreign Relations Committee (SFRC). Helms, a fiery conservative with some very strong, if unorthodox, views on foreign policy issues, almost immediately came into sharp conflict with the White House on a variety of issues.

Policy toward the United Nations provided a lightning rod. In 1993, the Clinton administration was a champion of the world body and its growing role in world affairs, notably dealing with internal violence and instability. As a number of U.N. missions failed to meet expectations (Somalia and Bosnia, as the two most obvious examples), that relationship cooled. In a September 1993 speech at U.N. headquarters in New York, Clinton argued that for the United States to say "yes" to U.N.-sponsored actions, the world body would have to learn to say "no" to some proposed actions. Sensing public opposition to a broader U.N. role in the world, Clinton further proposed a reduction in American assessments for U.N. peacekeeping missions from 31 percent to 25 percent, which has been enacted into law.

This adversarial relationship has also extended to reorganization of the State Department and the confirmation of diplomatic personnel. Ostensibly to save money, Helms has insisted on reorganization of the State Department, notably folding the United States Information Agency and the Arms Control and Disarmament Agency into the department, an action the administration considered inconsequential and refused to consider. In retaliation, Helms refused to hold confirmation hearings on a number of ambassadorial nominees, including that of Walter Mondale to Japan. At the end of 1995, those appointments remained locked in the SFRC.

The War Powers Resolution

Of the many powers wielded by modern governments, none has as fateful consequences or is so surrounded by emotion as the power to commit the state to war. Social, environmental, educational, and economic policies all affect, for better or worse, the quality of the country's life. Given the profundity of the decision for war or peace, the legal power to make that decision is among the most fundamental issues in American democracy.

Context for Passing the War Powers Resolution   Enactment of the War Powers Resolution in October 1973 represented a dramatic milestone in the reassertion of congressional prerogatives in international affairs. The momentum to do so had been building since the late 1960s. The resolution was most definitely not the product of a sudden surge of legislative hormones. Rather, it was the final product of a long-brewing debate among constitutional scholars and policymakers in the two elected branches to the question: "Whose power is the war power?"

Why did so many leaders think it was necessary to pass legislation to clarify this most fundamental issue? And why was that controversial legislation politically attainable in the early 1970s? The answers to both questions are found in four factors: inherent constitutional ambiguity, a long-term trend toward executive dominance on matters of war and peace, the bitter legacy of Vietnam, and the shifting political balance of power between a Democratic-controlled Congress and the Republican administration of Richard M. Nixon.

Constitutional Ambiguity   In their deliberations at Philadelphia, the Constitution's framers wanted to ensure that the new republic they were creating would be free of what they regarded as the ultimate vice of the European monarchies of the day: the easy resort to war by an unaccountable and unresponsive executive. As we have seen in previous chapters, the Founding Fathers were reflexively suspicious of any concentration of unchecked executive power. This suspicion was compounded in matters involving war and peace.

It is true that the extreme dilution of executive authority of the Articles of Confederation had brought them to Philadelphia in the first place. If eighteenth-century Europe embodied all that was wrong with unaccountable executive privilege, then the manifest weakness of the Articles of Confederation showed the paralysis of a too weak executive. Somewhere between these extremes lay a balance between the capacity for decisive action characteristic of strong executives and an inclination toward deliberateness and accountability characteristic of elected legislative assemblies. The Founding Fathers were attempting to strike such a balance as they set about to create the new state's most basic legal charter.

Records of the Constitutional Convention's debates reflect surprisingly little discussion on allocating the power to commit the country to war. This reflects a broad consensus among the convention's delegates, nearly all of whom agreed that the executive must not have the power unilaterally to take the country into war. This consensus was mirrored in the Constitution's working draft, which gave Congress sole power to "make war." At the suggestion of delegates James Madison and Elbridge Gerry, however, this language was modified—to create the now famous congressional power to "declare war." As Madison's notes make clear, this slight change was intended to give presidents the ability to respond to sudden, unexpected attacks. It was most definitely not intended to alter the Founding Fathers' determination to assign to the legislative branch the supreme power to determine if and when the country should initiate hostilities against another country.

In light of these considerations, why do we so often speak of constitutional ambiguity with regard to the war power? There are two reasons. First, the Constitution named the president as commander in chief of the armed forces in order to establish the important principle of civilian supremacy over the country's armed forces. But the role itself contains the seeds of ambiguity. Ambitious presidents eager to maximize their powers have advanced exceedingly expansive interpretations of what it means to be commander in chief. Some even insist that it permits the president to commit U.S. armed forces with or without explicit congressional authorization.

Another source of constitutional ambiguity is the later disagreement among the men who wrote the Constitution over the meaning of what they had written. By 1793 James Madison and Alexander Hamilton, both prominent delegates at Philadelphia, were promoting opposite interpretations of the Constitution's war powers provisions. Hamilton argued the war power was an inherently executive function, subject to a few legislative checks but not thereby denied to U.S. presidents. In contrast, Madison insisted that the Constitution had clearly made the war power a legislative power, leaving the execution of legislative decisions to the president in his capacity as commander in chief.

If Hamilton and Madison wound up with diametrically opposite interpretations of what the document intended, it is no wonder that later generations have struggled to make sense of the ambiguous intentions of the Founding Fathers. The result is what former Supreme Court justice Robert Jackson once spoke of as "a zone of twilight" that lay between the powers of the Congress and the president on matters of war and peace. It is in that "twilight zone" that presidents and legislators have found themselves for the past two centuries.

Executive Dominance on Matters of War and Peace   As noted, U.S. armed forces have been used abroad over 200 times since the founding of the Republic. How many of these instances have been accompanied by a congressional declaration of war as contemplated by the Constitution? The answer is precisely five: the War of 1812, the Mexican War, the Spanish-American War, World War I, and World War II. While other conflicts, such as Operation Desert Storm in 1991, were authorized by congressional action short of formal declarations of war, the fact remains that 98 percent of these foreign conflicts were undertaken by presidents whose interpretation of their prerogatives as commander in chief would be virtually unrecognizable to James Madison.

Those presidents' broad view of their powers has been buttressed by a long succession of executive branch apologists of presidential supremacy. For example, President Truman dispatched U.S. troops to Korea in the summer of 1950, leading the country into a major conflict that lasted for three years with neither congressional approval of his actions nor a formal declaration of war against North Korea. He believed that he was empowered to undertake such a step on his own authority, a position buttressed by a State Department memorandum prepared within days of the troop dispatch. The memorandum asserted that a president's power as commander in chief is virtually unlimited and the president can order troops into combat without congressional authorization owing to his inherent foreign affairs powers. In a similar vein, a former State Department legal adviser, Abram Chayes, has asserted that the declaration of war is now little more than an obsolete formality!

By the late 1960s and early 1970s, this mounting record of presidentially initiated hostilities, coupled with broad dissemination of intellectual rationalizations on behalf of executive dominance, persuaded a growing number of legislators of the need to restore the balance between the two elected branches to a level that more closely approximated the Founding Fathers' intentions.

The Traumatic U.S. Experience in Vietnam   The war began in the early 1960s as a limited U.S. undertaking aimed at thwarting Nikita Khrushchev's announced intention of expanding the communist orbit by fomenting so-called wars of national liberation in the Third World. U.S. policy makers, opinion elites, and the mass public generally regarded President Kennedy's expansion of the role of U.S. advisers to South Vietnamese forces as a necessary commitment during a particularly dangerous phase of the Cold War.

When President Johnson sharply increased the level of U.S. forces in Vietnam and expanded their mission to one of offensive combat operations during 1964 and 1965, he did so with broad support from both the American public and Congress. The most vivid and controversial expression of congressional support for Johnson's war policy was the famous Gulf of Tonkin Resolution adopted in August 1964. Passed after only token debate, the measure was unanimously endorsed by the House of Representatives and met with only two dissenting votes in the Senate. (Interestingly, both opponents—senators Wayne Morse of Oregon and Ernest Gruening of Alaska—were subsequently defeated in their bids for reelection.)

In its haste to demonstrate a unified U.S. front to the Vietnamese communists, Congress enacted exceedingly sweeping language in support of the president. The heart of the resolution declared that "the Congress approves and supports the determination of the President, as Commander in Chief, to take all necessary measures to repel any armed attack against the forces of the United States and to prevent further aggression." A bit later, in Section 2, it asserts that "the United States is . . . prepared as the President determines, to take all necessary steps, including the use of armed force."

The resolution was couched in strikingly permissive language. Congress announced ahead of time that it would "approve and support" "all necessary steps" that the *president* might decide to undertake in Vietnam. Years later, as the national consensus that spawned the Gulf of Tonkin Resolution dissolved in a monsoon of failure in Southeast Asia, members of Congress would look back on their fateful votes of August 1964 with grief and bitterness.

By the early 1970s, with the magnitude of the Vietnam disaster clear for all to see, even the most passive lawmakers knew that something had to be done. Never again, they vowed, should the Congress so promiscuously hand over its constitutional prerogatives to the president. Their determination to reclaim legislative war-making powers was strengthened in 1971 when Congress repealed the Gulf of Tonkin Resolution, only to find the Nixon administration now claiming an inherent executive right to prosecute the Vietnam War, with or without explicit congressional authorization.

The Political Character of Policy-Making   By 1973 the Democratic Party had held firm majorities in both houses of Congress for nearly two decades; the White House, however, had been captured by the Democrats in only two of the last six presidential elections. The force of partisanship, then, was joined with the built-in tensions for political supremacy created by a separation of powers system of government. Either force can make political cooperation difficult; added together, they too often produce interbranch gridlock.

In addition to these two political forces, two others made legislative-executive relations particularly volatile in the early 1970s: the rising tide of reassertionist sentiment taking root in Congress; and the declining prestige of the presidency caused by the Vietnam fiasco and the Watergate scandal. These two factors are closely related. If during most of the Cold War Congress had frequently deferred to presidential leadership on foreign policy issues, it was due in large part to the belief that U.S. presidents were generally honest and prudent custodians of the national interest. But the back-to-back disasters of President Johnson's Vietnam policy and the Nixon administration's dishonesty and criminality combined to rock the foundations of presidential dignity and respect. By 1973, with Nixon ever more grimly impaled on the stake of Watergate, his political opponents—mostly liberal, mostly Democrats, and mostly members of Congress—were only too eager to seize on his weakened position in order to reclaim and reassert legislative foreign policy powers that had generally atrophied during the Cold War.

Taken together, then, inherent constitutional ambiguity, a long-term trend toward presidential dominance on matters of war and peace, the bitter experience of Vietnam, and the partisan political struggles between a newly assertive Congress and a presidency weakened by scandal—all converged to set the stage for the enactment, over Nixon's veto, of the landmark War Powers Resolution of 1973.

The War Powers Resolution   As finally adopted, the resolution contains three principal provisions. They specify when the president must *consult* with Congress, when he must *report* to Congress, and when he must *terminate* hostilities and withdraw U.S. armed forces. A brief look at each of these provisions will clarify what the Congress intended through this legislation. It will also help us appreciate the difficulties of translating general legislative intent into precise, unambiguous statutory language.

The requirement that presidents consult with Congress before committing armed forces to hostilities is spelled out in Section 3 of the resolution. The key language states that "the President in every possible instance shall consult with Congress before introducing United States Armed Forces into hostilities or into situations where imminent involvement in hostilities is clearly indicated by the circumstances." Although the section's general intent is clear enough, translating congressional intention into executive conduct presents several problems. It is not entirely clear what presidents would have to do to satisfy the requirement that they "consult with Congress." Do they need to acquire congressional approval prior to acting? Section 3 does not seem to go quite that far, but it appears to suggest a good bit more than mere presidential notification of impending moves.

If the precise meaning of consultation is not entirely clear, neither is the precise identity of who it is that the president must consult with. It is obviously unrealistic to expect presidents to hold discussions with all 535 members of Congress before undertaking critical national security operations, but nowhere can one look up the answer to the question of who and how many members of Congress must be consulted in order to fulfill the spirit of Section 3.

Finally, as the resolution's language concedes, the president must consult with Congress "in every possible instance," implying that in some instances, prior consultations are impractical. For example, at the time of the *Mayaguez* incident in 1975, four key congressional leaders were in Greece, four others were in China, and others were scattered in their states and districts. Clearly, presidential consultations with Congress were not feasible under these circumstances.

The resolution's second key provision is the reporting requirement contained in Section 4. This requirement obligates the president to report to Congress within 48 hours any time U.S. armed forces are dispatched (1) "into hostilities or into situations where imminent involvement in hostilities is clearly indicated by the circumstances," (2) into foreign territory while "equipped for combat," or (3) "in numbers which substantially enlarge United States Armed Forces equipped for combat already located in a foreign nation." The president's report to Congress must specify (1) the circumstances necessitating the introduction of U.S. armed forces, (2) the constitutional and legislative authority under which such an introduction took place, and (3) the estimated scope and duration of the hostilities or involvement.

The third and final key provision of the War Powers Resolution is Section 5, which deals with the termination of hostilities and the withdrawal of U.S. forces. Intent on reversing the trend toward presidentially instigated wars that could drag on unless Congress took overt action to end them, the drafters of the War Powers Resolution rewrote the ground rules so that any protracted hostilities by U.S. forces would require explicit legislative approval. Congress, it is said, will now share the controls of foreign policy takeoffs, not just the crash landings.

How is this congressional codetermination to be achieved? Section 5 spells out two means of doing so. First, once the president has reported to Congress that U.S. forces are being introduced into hostilities or into circumstances indicating imminent hostilities as specified in Section 4, the so-called 60-day clock begins. Thus, the president will be without legal authority to continue conducting hostilities unless Congress acts within 60 days to (1) declare war, (2) adopt a specific authorization such as the Gulf of Tonkin Resolution of 1964, or (3) extend the president's war-making authority beyond 60 days. If the Congress takes no action at all, then the president is legally bound to terminate hostilities 60 days after his initial report to Congress. (An additional 30 days are authorized if needed for the safe withdrawal of troops, for a total of no more than 90 days maximum unless Congress specifically provides otherwise.)

Section 5's second congressional tool for terminating hostilities provides that the Congress can order a cessation of U.S. involvement in hostilities at any point simply by adopting a concurrent resolution. The crucial point here is that a concurrent resolution, adopted by simple majorities of the House and Senate, does not require the president's signature to take effect and thus is not subject to presidential veto. This passage is now constitutionally suspect in light of a 1983 Supreme Court ruling (*INS v. Chadha*) that struck down so-called legislative vetoes. Some observers contend that the Court's ruling invalidates the way concurrent resolutions are used in the War Powers Resolution. In the absence of a definitive ruling, however, Section 5, along with the rest of the Resolution, still stands as the law of the land.

Effects of the War Powers Resolution   In some respects, a substantial gap remains between the resolution's intent and actual accomplishment. This situation partly reflects the inherent difficulties in seeking legislative solutions to fundamental philosophical, constitutional, and political matters. But the most important reason is the executive's consistent pattern of hostility to it.

The announced purpose of the War Powers Resolution was to "insure that the collective judgment of both the Congress and the President will apply to the introduction of United States Armed Forces into hostilities." It was Congress who embraced this "doctrine of policy codetermination;" presidents have viewed the matter quite differently. The tone was set by Nixon, who tried unsuccessfully to kill the measure by vetoing it. All of his successors—Ford, Carter, Reagan, Bush, and Clinton—have consistently objected to the resolution as an unnecessary and perhaps even unconstitutional infringement on their powers. Such attitudes cannot simply be legislated away. Presidential hostility toward the resolution has been especially evident with regard to the resolution's consultation and reporting requirements.

Set against Section 3's requirement that "the President in every possible instance shall consult with Congress before introducing United States Armed Forces into hostilities or into situations where imminent involvement in hostilities is clearly indicated by the circumstances," the record of the past two decades is one of repeated presidential violation of both the letter and spirit of the law. For example, the Reagan administration's planning for the 1983 invasion of Grenada was completed and set in motion without any effort to "consult" with the Congress. Reagan issued the order for U.S. forces to commence the invasion at 6:00 P.m. EST on October 24, 1983. Only several hours later was a small group of congressional leaders brought to the White House and informed of the impending invasion. Their advice was not sought.

A similar circumvention occurred in March 1986, when the Reagan administration launched Operation Prairie Fire. Aimed at challenging Libyan leader Muammar el-Qaddafi's claim of sovereignty over 150,000 square miles of the Gulf of Sidra, the operation involved a large U.S. naval task force of 30 ships, 25,000 troops, and armed aircraft probes across Qaddafi's proclaimed maritime boundary, nicknamed the "Line of Death." The resulting confrontation left 40 Libyan sailors killed, two of their patrol boats destroyed, and an antiaircraft missile installation crippled. The U.S. administration pointedly informed the Soviet Union of its operational plans in advance but did not similarly inform, much less consult, the U.S. Congress. As Michael Rubner has noted, "it thus appears that in the administration's curious judgment, the Kremlin could, and Congress could not be entrusted with highly sensitive details about American military moves against Libya."

A final example of presidential avoidance of the consultation requirement is the Reagan administration's handling of the April 1986 bombing of Libya in retaliation against Qaddafi's support of international terrorism. At 4 P.M. Washington time on Monday, April 14, 1986, a congressional delegation was brought to the White House. At that very moment, 13 F-111 fighter bombers were already four hours into a seven-hour flight from their British base to their targets in Libya. According to the legislators present, the "consultation" consisted of briefings by President Reagan (who read from typewritten notes), Secretary of State George Shultz, and National Security Adviser Admiral Poindexter. The general congressional sense of having been manipulated by executive officials was best captured by Republican congressman Robert Michel, who wondered aloud: "if I had some serious objection, how could I make it now?"

Although the resolution's wording requiring consultation "in every possible instance" permits presidents some flexibility regarding consultation with Congress, in these and numerous other cases congressional leaders were readily available in Washington for meetings with the president and his aides. In addition, each case permitted plenty of time for those consultations to occur. In no instance was the president required to repel a sudden assault on U.S. territory or personnel.

In most instances, presidents have chosen to violate both the letter and the spirit of Section 3 because there was little if any penalty for doing so. The executive view has typically equated notification and consultation. The House Foreign Affairs Committee emphatically rejected that view during the 1973 debate over adopting the resolution, stressing in its report that "consultation in this provision means that a decision is pending on a problem and that members of Congress are being asked by the President for their advice and opinions."

A similar presidential attitude has shaped compliance with the important requirement in Section 4 that Congress be notified anytime American armed forces are introduced into hostilities or where hostilities seem imminent. While presidents generally do report to Congress, they do so in a way that skirts the clear requirements of the War Powers Resolution.

Since 1973 about 25 instances have arguably required presidential reporting under Section 4. In two-thirds of those cases, presidential reports have indeed been submitted to Congress, but the pattern has been to report "consistent with" the resolution rather than "pursuant to" the resolution. Only once, in the *Mayaguez* incident of 1975, was the president's report specifically "pursuant to" the War Powers Resolution.

This distinction is important because Section 5 states that the use of U.S. armed forces will be terminated "within 60 days after a report is submitted . . . pursuant to Section 4 (a) (1)." The 60-day clock does not start automatically when troops leave the United States, but is started only by a presidential report notifying Congress of the initiation of hostilities as specified in Section 4 (language which presidents never use, since they do not want the clock to start ticking). The point may seem obscure to laypeople, but the now common presidential practice of providing information to Congress without specifically acknowledging the obligatory character of the War Powers Resolution renders its most important legal provision effectively inoperable. Of course, Congress could also start the 60-day clock by passing a bill saying the War Powers Resolution has been invoked in a particular case, but this is difficult to do in practice. The 20-year record of presidential compliance with this critical provision of the resolution thus reflects a calculated White House strategy of performing the minimum political obligation, but doing so in such a way as to neutralize the legal heart of the resolution.

It would be a mistake to conclude that the War Powers Resolution has been a total failure. Its mere existence reminds presidents of the importance of congressional views. The need to develop a working consensus between the two branches—which was, after all, the resolution's principal objective—was one of the Bush administration's prime concerns in the months leading up to Operation Desert Storm in 1991. Clearly, a few amendments are now needed to (1) clarify who must be consulted and what would constitute adequate consultation, (2) specify more precisely the reporting requirements, and (3) define hostilities more precisely. At bottom, however, it has been the lack of congressional will that has permitted presidents to avoid full compliance with the resolution. As long as Congress is unwilling to invoke the War Powers Resolution and demand full compliance with it, presidents will continue to maximize their own prerogatives by minimizing their adherence to it.

This unwillingness is particularly likely in the dispatch of U.S. forces for nontraditional missions. In December 1992, for example, President Bush ordered 20,000 members of the armed forces to Somalia to establish secure food distribution to the starving people in that area. Few in Congress voiced opposition to Operation Restore Hope, as it was dubbed. A few, however, including Sen. Paul Wellstone (D-Minn.), argued that Congress "should be accountable" by invoking the War Powers Resolution. Wellstone's view was a decidedly minority one, however, and Congress essentially relegated itself to the role of sideline supporter of a major—albeit humanitarian—overseas deployment of U.S. armed forces.

Context of Goldwater-Nichols and Cohen-Nunn Acts of 1986

The effort by Congress to change the structure and direction of U.S. national security policy reached a crescendo in 1986 when Congress initiated, passed, and imposed on the executive branch two laws in the space of one month. The first and more famous, the Goldwater-Nichols Defense Reorganization Act, Public Law (PL) 99–433, passed in October and dictated fundamental changes in the organizational priorities of the DOD. The Cohen-Nunn Act (PL 99–661), which passed in November, dealt more specifically with the issue of special forces and their place in defense priorities.

Both pieces of legislation were responses to perceptions that the Pentagon was simply not doing its job effectively, that it was apparently unable or unwilling to correct those policies and procedures which were impeding its efficient conduct of its job, and that only outside—namely, congressional—intervention would solve the problem. Spearheading the inclination to reform was a bipartisan group of over 100 members of Congress who had organized in the early 1980s as the Military Reform Caucus.

A number of issues and perceptions emerged from the caucus deliberations to set the agenda for change. Although the public had been galvanized by certain aspects of what was wrong, the impetus for change came from within Congress—from elected members, their staffs, and retired military personnel who were frustrated by their prior experience and who counseled the Congress. The effort was clearly bipartisan, for both acts bore the sponsorship of members of President Reagan's own party: Sen. Barry Goldwater, chair of the Senate Armed Services Committee (SASC) and GOP presidential standard-bearer in 1964, Rep. William Nichols of Alabama, and Sen. William Cohen of Maine. The lone Democrat, Sen. Sam Nunn of Georgia, shared a generally conservative, prodefense reputation with his Republican colleagues as ranking Democrat on SASC.

Any list of factors leading to setting the agenda for reform will suffer the risk of omitting some crucial influence, but at least six interrelated reasons can be cited: a general discontent with the performance of the All-Volunteer Force (AVF) concept; a perceived negative record of U.S. forces; the military's preparation for war; organizational flaws within the Pentagon; waste, fraud, and abuse; and Defense's indifferent record despite budget increases.

Performance of the AVF Concept   Discontent with the AVF had been in place since the end of 1972. In reaction to the popular discontent with the Vietnam War, the Nixon administration had ended conscription at the end of 1972. In the wake of U.S. extrication from its most unpopular and unsuccessful military experience, the armed services had vast difficulty competing successfully for quality young men and women for the rest of the 1970s. Very few young people with other options chose military service for a variety of reasons, from disgust with the military to an economy that was providing better civilian job opportunities.

The Reagan presidency was supposed to solve that particular problem. Draped in patriotism and lubricated with generous amounts of new resources (money), the result was supposed to be a renaissance of military prowess that would rekindle U.S. preeminence. Many were not convinced it had succeeded, at least to that point.

The Negative Military Record   The problem, and hence the second cause of concern, was a perceived negative record of U.S. forces since Vietnam. The perception arose from a series of incidents in which a U.S. military force was applied with uniformly negative outcomes, representing almost a caricature of the successful application of military power.

The first incident occurred in 1975, when President Ford ordered an expedition to free the crew of the *Mayaguez,* an American freighter that had been captured by Cambodian pirates in the Gulf of Thailand. Through faulty intelligence, the ensuing assault, in which 38 American servicemen perished in a helicopter crash, was directed at an island abandoned by the pirates and after the abductors had released the ship and its crew. Ford's attempt to demonstrate that the post-Vietnam United States was not a "pitiful giant" clearly backfired.

The situation did not improve materially under President Jimmy Carter. The most notorious incident of military ineptitude during his administration was the abortive attempt to rescue the 53 Americans held hostage in the U.S. Embassy in Teheran, Iran. Known as Desert One (for the designation of the landing site in the desolate Dasht-e-Kavir area of Iran), the mission ended in tragedy. Not enough of the helicopters (which were designed to operate at sea) could brave an unanticipated sandstorm to arrive at the site, and eight American servicemen died when an army RH-53 helicopter and an air force EC-130 collided during takeoff as they tried to leave the scene. Because they were most prominent in the operation, Desert One particularly stained American Special Forces. In addition to adding to the perception of the military's general ineptitude, it served as an impetus to Cohen-Nunn.

This general pattern appeared to continue under President Ronald Reagan. In 1983 U.S. marines were inserted (for a second time) into Beirut, Lebanon, with the vague mission of helping to stabilize the religious violence that had resulted in a bloody Christian militia assault on a Palestinian refugee camp and the assassination of the Christian president of Lebanon, Bashir Gemayel. The marines, an elite assault force curiously inappropriate for the garrison duty of guarding the Beirut International Airport (the task to which they were assigned), saw their mission end tragically as a truck loaded with bombs penetrated security and exploded at a dormitory in which marines were sleeping, killing 241.

The final major negative episode occurred later in 1983 when U.S. forces were inserted into Grenada, a tiny Caribbean island, to rescue American medical students who were under siege as a result of the internal unrest accompanying the ascendancy of a supposed Castroite to power. Although the mission accomplished its basic purpose, it was marred by logistical and communications problems that resulted in unnecessary delays and casualties. The chief culprit was interservice rivalry that made communication between the services impossible. In the most celebrated example, the lack of common frequencies between army and navy radios for transmission and reception of messages necessitated that an army officer use his personal long-distance telephone credit card to call his home base at Fort Bragg, North Carolina, so that DOD could relay instructions to a navy vessel off the coast.

The U.S. Military's Preparedness   The cumulative effect of these incidents was to raise a third concern: was the U.S. military system adequately preparing the country to go to war? Each of the incidents just described involved the fairly minor application of force in specific, limited ways, and yet the military proved incapable of even such small tasks. That being the case, critics reasoned, what would occur if the United States had to go to war in the most serious fashion, as in an East-West confrontation in Europe which had been the focal point of planning virtually since the end of World War II?

For some, the answer was not reassuring. A common theme that seemed to run through the U.S. forces' combat experience since Vietnam was the inability of the services to cooperate with one another in military operations. As we see, this chronic inability had structural as well as interservice rivalry underpinnings, but the common perception was that in the puzzle palace, Pogo's dictum held: "We have met the enemy, and he is us." From this perception, the emphasis on "jointness" (interservice cooperation and joint action) that is so prominent in Goldwater-Nichols was born.

The Pentagon's Organizational Flaws   It was generally perceived that organizational flaws within the Pentagon contributed to poor performance by the defense establishment. The most basic aspect of this concern was organizational structure. Prior to reform, the basic focus of organization was the individual services, which controlled the funding and effectively the career destinies of career military personnel. The alternative form of organization was to focus on the Joint Chiefs of Staff and the unified and specified commands, those units assigned operational responsibility for different theaters of operation (e.g., the Pacific) or missions.

In the prereform system, the services prevailed. Thus, key elements of core activities such as budgets were funneled from the operational commands through the various service bureaucracies rather than the other way around. Even though the CINPAC (commander in chief, Pacific), a navy admiral, had as part of his operational responsibility air force and army assets, his requests for funds and resources for those other service elements were funneled through the departments of the army and air force, where they had to compete with other internal service priorities.

Moreover, the system tended to downplay the role and importance of the Joint Chiefs of Staff and especially the chairman of the JCS. The idea behind the JCS was to create an entity within the military chain that could coordinate interservice planning and actions. It did not work that way, for several reasons.

With power concentrated in the services, time spent on the Joint Staff was viewed as detrimental to an officer's career. During the time officers served on the Joint Staff, for instance, their annual performance evaluations continued to be made by their individual service and not by the Joint Staff. Since the services viewed the JCS as a rival, members of the staff quickly realized that they would be rewarded for how well they protected their service's interests, not for the degree of interservice cooperation they displayed. This dynamic extended all the way up to the various service chiefs who composed the JCS. At the same time, the CJCS, who was supposed to epitomize the interservice process, was given essentially no power. He had no operational command of forces, he was only one of the president's military advisers, and he had a tiny staff of five professionals and no full-time vice chairman.

In the eyes of the reformers, this lack of interservice cooperation hindered the U.S. military effort in an increasingly complex world where military problems more and more required the application of different kinds of force housed in the different services. This lack of coordination helped explain why the navy and the army operated radio equipment on different and incompatible frequencies (the telephone credit card case at Grenada). It also led to the generalized perception that U.S. military performance would not improve markedly until real jointness became part of the system.

The problem was that the DOD itself opposed change. The service bureaucracies, including both members of the uniformed services and the large civilian bureaucracies that had developed during the Cold War, were comfortable with the system as it was. This opposition extended all the way to the secretary of defense, Caspar Weinberger, who viewed congressional reform initiatives as unnecessarily meddling into his business and as examples of congressional "micromanagement" of the Defense Department.

Waste, Fraud, and Abuse   One of the more common criticisms of Pentagon performance was in the way the Pentagon spent public monies: the issue of waste, fraud, and abuse. During the early 1980s, defense budgets escalated as a result of Ronald Reagan's drive to reverse the decline in defense spending instituted by his predecessor, Jimmy Carter. Reagan claimed in the 1980 campaign that Carter had presided over the unilateral disarmament of the United States. As spending levels increased, however, so did well-publicized instances of apparent malfeasance: $600 toilet seats for a new air force plane, $500 hammers, and the like. At the forefront of this criticism was the maverick Democratic senator from Wisconsin, William Proxmire, who annually awarded his "Golden Fleece Awards" for what he viewed as especially egregious abuses of public funds.

Whether the instances of waste were aberrations or symptomatic of a general malaise within DOD was never established. In many cases, however, the defense officials' reactions only served to worsen public perceptions that something was wrong that required fixing, such as instances of stonewalling by accused contractors.

Lackluster Performance   The sixth and final factor, exacerbating the rest, was that performance was not improving despite large budget increases for defense in the first half of the 1980s. During the first Reagan term in particular, increases in real spending power (additions beyond adjustments for inflation) occurred regularly. Many members of Congress believed the Reagan administration thought the role of Congress was simply to ratify the administration's request without amendment.

Secretary Weinberger epitomized this attitude. In the Nixon administration, he had been secretary of the then Department of Health, Education, and Welfare, where his money-pinching ways had earned him the nickname "Cap the Knife" (a sobriquet he had originally earned while working in California state government) for his attempts to cut his departmental budget. As secretary of defense, that changed. Annually, he would go to the Congress with ever increasing requests on which he obdurately refused to compromise, suggesting that any decreases would gravely compromise the country's security. He became known as "Cap the Shovel" for his apparent belief that all defense problems could be solved with the application of more dollars. As greater questions of performance and fiscal abuse mounted, Congress's generosity came to be part of the problem.

All these influences came together to produce the impetus for Congress to take the lead and to force reform on the defense establishment, despite the opposition of the president and the hierarchy of DOD itself. The two pieces of legislation, Goldwater-Nichols and Cohen-Nunn, must be seen in tandem and in decreasing order of magnitude. The Goldwater-Nichols Defense Reorganization Act of 1986 was both chronologically first in terms of enactment and in scope of reform. The problem addressed by Cohen-Nunn, special operations forces, is mentioned almost as an afterthought in the larger bill. The DOD's negative reaction to Goldwater-Nichols helped goad the Congress into speedy enactment of Cohen-Nunn.

The Goldwater-Nichols Act

Although it has several separate, important provisions, the heart of the Defense Reorganization Act was to change the effective power structure within the Pentagon. The means of doing so was by reducing the power of the individual services and transferring that power to those organs of the Pentagon with a more interservice orientation—the commanders in chief (CINC) of the unified and specified commands, whose commands by definition contained elements from more than one service; and the JCS, particularly the CJCS. The legislation accomplishes this task through three significant changes.

The first thrust strengthened the JCS and its chairman within the military hierarchy. To clarify and elevate the CJCS, he was designated as the principal and only military adviser to the president, the National Security Council, and the secretary of defense. Depending on the administration, the service chiefs had previously had direct access to the top leadership, bypassing the chief; under Goldwater-Nichols they had to go through him.

The entire Joint Staff was also placed under the "authority, direction, and control" of the CJCS rather than the JCS as a whole. Previously, the CJCS had only a very small personal staff reporting to him, while the bulk of the Joint Staff reported to the JCS as a whole, which meant that officers remained the effective "property" of their parent services. To further move away from the parochialism of service loyalty, the act created a promotion review of joint officers under the supervision of the CJCS. This review applies to former as well as currently serving Joint Staff members. Finally, the position of vice chief of the JCS (VCJCS) was created, thereby adding to the flexibility of the chief.

The act also encouraged jointness by creating a specific joint officer specialty within the services. To guarantee that the designation had clout and would attract officers, the act requires that at least 50 percent of the slots at the major/lieutenant commander (0–4) level, where much of the staff resides, would have to be officers with a Joint Staff specialty. To add further clout to the "purple suiters," it was further stipulated that no officer could be promoted to flag rank (general or equivalent) without joint service on his or her record unless an explicit exception was made.

Another provision aimed at reforming the effective power base dealt with increasing the importance of the eight commanders in chief of the unified commands. Five of these commands have geographic responsibilities (Atlantic Command, Central Command, European Command, Pacific Command, and Southern Command), and three have functional responsibilities (Space Command, Special Operations Command, and Transportation Command). By definition, all have interservice responsibilities, and units from different services are assigned to them. Earlier, the problem was that the CINCs had neither budgetary nor total operational control over forces from services other than their own. Goldwater-Nichols remedied those problems in two ways.

On the one hand, the act designates that the CINC has direct and total control over all forces under his command. This concept was first successfully applied by Gen. Norman Schwarzkopf, CINC of Central Command, in Operation Desert Storm. On the other hand, the CINC now makes budget requests directly to the secretary of defense without having to go through the various service departments. This provision has been somewhat controversial. Proponents argue that it assures each command has adequate supplies and the like to conduct its mission, since the CINC's focus is on operations. The other side of the coin is that the CINCs will slight long-term investment in areas such as research and development for new advanced weapons. It has even been argued that if CINC-controlled budgeting had been in force five years earlier than it was, U.S. forces would not have had many of the high-technology weapons used to such great effect against Iraq.

The act accomplished three other noteworthy effects. First, in response to "waste, fraud, and abuse" charges in procurement, the bill created an assistant secretary of defense position, designated as the number-three person in the DOD, to coordinate and approve all Pentagon buying. Instantly nicknamed the "procurement czar," this position has never matured with the power envisioned by the act's drafters.

Second, the act mandated that the president provide an annual national security strategy of the United States and submit it to the Congress. This requirement was necessary because the administration probably lacked a clear strategy and thus needed to develop one, and because of a belief that such a strategy should be subject to public scrutiny and debate. These convictions were widely held in the defense community but were opposed by the Reagan and Bush administrations as an unnecessary annoyance. As a result, only four of the documents had been produced as of the end of 1992, and they have all been written, in fact, by middle-level officials within the DOD. The Clinton administration has produced the document every year as required.

Finally, the act called for a review of the need for "creation of a unified combatant command for special operations missions." Before that review could be undertaken, Congress had already passed the Cohen-Nunn Act.

The Cohen-Nunn Act

As was true of the broader Defense Reorganization Act, the impetus to pass legislation creating a congressionally mandated institution to deal with special operations and the lower end of the conflict spectrum came from executive-legislative disagreement and distrust.

The disagreement was about the relative weight that should be given within the Pentagon to special operations and low-intensity conflict (SOLIC). The executive branch, heavily influenced by the armed service bureaucracies, tended to emphasize the traditional Cold War confrontation and the forces and strategies deriving from the East-West conflict. Those in Congress who supported the bill, on the other hand, looked at the recent record and saw in special operations such as Desert One, Grenada, and Beirut the kinds of situations the U.S. military would increasingly face in the future, but for which experience had shown them to be badly underprepared.

There was the added perception that the United States had not fared very well in the past when dealing in special operations. As Sen. William Cohen, the bill's cosponsor, said in his opening remarks when the bill was introduced as an amendment to the fiscal year (FY) 1987 Defense Authorization Act (Senate Bill S2567) on August 6, 1986, "I do not believe this [negative] record is attributable to persistent bad luck or an inadequate caliber of men in the armed services. In my view, we have not been effectively organized to fight the most likely battles of the present or the future."

Distrust came from the armed services' and the Pentagon's general attitude toward SOLIC. Because the defense bureaucracy both disliked and was not very adept at SOLIC (dislike and skill are two phenomena reciprocally related to one another), they could be expected to footdrag or subvert efforts to impose this mission on them, as they had in the past. The late Rep. Dan Daniels (D-Va.), who sponsored the legislation in the House of Representatives, summarized this position in the August 1985 issue of *Armed Forces Journal International:* "No amount of directive authority — budgetary or otherwise — will overcome the capacity of Service Chiefs to commit mischief should that be their bent. And, as long as special operations forces remain outside the services' philosophical core, the temptation to do so will be near irresistible."

This distrust meant that the only way to force the executive branch to take SOLIC seriously was through a law specifically requiring them to do so. Originally, Senator Cohen had considered putting forward the SOLIC case as a nonbinding "sense of the Congress" for the Pentagon to consider. Initial grumbling and objections to Goldwater-Nichols convinced the sponsors of Cohen-Nunn that the Pentagon would ignore or push a sense of Congress to the back burner. The result was a full-fledged law.

The Cohen-Nunn Act contains four major provisions. The first provision created an institutional focus by designating a unified command, the United States Special Operations Command (USSOCOM). Eventually based at McDill Air Force Base in Florida, it has the distinction of being the first unified command designated by law. (All the others were created administratively by the executive branch.) The reason was straightforward: DOD would never have created USSOCOM on its own.

Second, the act created within the DOD the position of assistant secretary of defense for special operations and low-intensity conflict (ASD/SOLIC). Secretary Weinberger bitterly opposed this provision as an intrusion on his administrative prerogatives, as did other assistant secretaries fearful they would lose those parts of their responsibilities that touched on SOLIC. Thus, DOD waited several months before it submitted a nominee to the Senate. When it did, the name it produced was Kenneth Bergquist, a gentleman most distinguished for his vocal opposition to the legislation.

An executive-legislative branch feud ensued. The Senate promptly rejected Bergquist, and the DOD replaced him on an interim basis with Larry Ropka, an assistant to Richard Armitage, assistant secretary of defense for international security affairs (ASD/ISA) and also a vocal opponent of the bill. Convinced that the Ropka appointment was akin to "the fox guarding the hen house," a frustrated Congress responded in December 1987 by passing another law (PL 100–180), which required that the secretary of the army, John O. Marsh, assume the duties of the ASD/SOLIC until a confirmable nominee was presented and confirmed.

That process took nine months, when DOD nominated retired ambassador Charles Whitehead, who was confirmed nearly 18 months after the legislation was passed. He was subsequently replaced by Jim Locher who, as an aide to Senator Nunn, had primary responsibility for drafting the legislation in the first place.

The ASD/SOLIC position was neither the only new position created by Cohen-Nunn nor the only one that spawned interbranch conflict. A third provision of the act was to mandate a deputy assistant to the president for national security affairs for low-intensity conflict. Designating this high-level staff position had a direct impact on the prerogatives of the president and thus created resistance within the more general foreign policy bureaucracy.

The problem in principle arises from the nature of the NSC staff. As mentioned earlier, those who serve on the NSC staff are considered the personal staff of the president; he decides who they are, what their individual assignments and titles are, and the size of the staff. As such, the NSC staff, up to and including the national security adviser, is subject neither to Senate confirmation nor to congressional oversight. (Members of the staff, for instance, cannot be compelled to testify before Congress.) Moreover, none of their positions (including the NSA) are specified by law.

Cohen-Nunn anticipated that the person who filled this position would have two major responsibilities: to coordinate NSC activity in the SOLIC area on a full-time and primary basis; and to convene a low-intensity conflict board within the NSC staff.

The special assistant's position has never been filled with a full-time person. Leading opposition to it in the Bush administration was Brent Scowcroft, the NSA, who felt the position was a Trojan horse that would set a precedent for broad-scale congressional specification of positions within the NSC, including his own. As a result, the duties have been assigned as a part-time responsibility to the assistant national security adviser for international programs. Congress and the administration continue to disagree about the adequacy of the arrangement.

Fourth and finally, the legislation created the so-called LIC Board within the NSC. The idea behind this provision was to create a vehicle for interagency discussion of the LIC mission and to develop a series of scenarios and American response options to various LIC contingencies that might arise in different Third World countries.

The LIC Board provision has also languished. The Reagan administration appointed a board but never convened it. The Bush administration also appointed a board, but as of December 1990 it had met precisely twice and had not yet adopted a commonly acceptable definition of a low-intensity conflict.

Conclusions

Intrabranch and interbranch rivalry and disagreement are at the core of foreign and national decision making. That different individuals and groups within the executive branch and the Congress would disagree on elements of policy, and even on how policy is made, reflects both the importance and contentiousness of the foreign policy enterprise. If foreign and defense policy were peripheral and inconsequential, there would be no need for an interagency process, an ongoing interbranch wrangle over the power to commit troops to conflict, or a reform process to reshape the national security community.

The disagreements are not limited to the halls of government. Indeed, outside the formal lines of authority, there is a series of groups whose purpose it is to influence how and what government does. The next two chapters will examine the activities of two pairs of these outside influences, interest groups and think tanks, and public opinion and the media.

SUGGESTED READINGS

Bacchus, William I. *Foreign Policy and the Bureaucratic Process*. Princeton, NJ: Princeton University Press, 1974.

Davis, David Howard. *How the Bureaucracy Makes Foreign Policy*. Lexington, MA: Lexington Books, 1972.

Destler, I. M. *Presidents, Bureaucrats, and Foreign Policy: The Politics of Organizational Reform*. Princeton, NJ: Princeton University Press, 1974.

Elder, Robert Ellsworth. *The Policy Machine. The Department of State and American Foreign Policy*. Syracuse, NY: Syracuse University Press, 1960.

Franklin, Daniel Paul. "War Powers in the Modern Context." *Congress and the Presidency,* Spring 1987, pp. 77–92.

Glennon, Michael J. "The War Powers Resolution Ten Years Later: More Politics Than Law." *American Journal of International Law,* July 1984, pp. 571–581.

Halperin, Morton H. *Bureaucratic Politics and Foreign Policy*. Washington, DC: Brookings Institution, 1974.

Leacacos, John P. *Fires in the In-Basket: The ABCs of the State Department*. Cleveland, OH: World Publishing, 1968.

Lindbloom, Charles E. *The Policy Making Process*. Englewood Cliffs, NJ: Prentice-Hall, 1968.

Rubner, Michael. "The Reagan Administration, The 1973 War Powers Resolution, and the Invasion of Grenada." *Political Science Quarterly,* Winter 1985–1986, pp. 627–647.

Smyrl, Marc E. *Conflict or Codetermination? Congress, the President, and the Power to Make War*. Cambridge, MA: Ballinger, 1988.

Turner, Robert F. *The War Powers Resolution: Its Implementation in Theory and Practice*. Philadelphia: Foreign Policy Research Institute, 1983.

Warburg, Gerald F. *The Struggle Between Congress and the President over Foreign Policymaking*. New York: Harper & Row, 1989.

Woodward, Bob. *The Commanders*. New York: Simon & Schuster, 1991.

CHAPTER 8

Outside Influences I:
Interest Groups and Think Tanks

Not everyone who has a voice in the policy process seeks to govern or formally to enact legislation. In addition to those elected and appointed officials who compose the federal government is a large and diverse, often amorphous, conglomeration of individuals and groups who are not a formal part of the governmental structure but who seek to influence government policies.

The largest concentration of these individuals and groups lives and works in the Washington, D.C., area. They are known as the "inside the beltway" group because they work and live either within or near the Interstate 95 beltway that encircles the District of Columbia. In fact, so many people are engaged in this capacity that it is regularly asserted that Washington has more people employed to influence the government than there are employees of the government itself.

Historically, most of these actors performed outside the public spotlight, lobbying individual members of Congress to adopt positions they espoused, interacting with governmental officials informally at Washington cocktail parties, or sharing with interested individuals access to the most hotly pursued status symbol in the capital, tickets to Washington Redskins football games. In addition, this "invisible government," as it is also occasionally known, provided a revolving door for individuals, coming and going into and out of government to organizations and positions seeking to influence what government does. As the Bush administration prepared to leave and the highly visible Clinton transition began, so did the shuffling of personnel into and out of government.

The result is to add opaqueness to the public's understanding of what really transpires in government, particularly with respect to foreign and defense policy. In the area of foreign policy, general public ignorance and lack of interest has meant that influencing government policy was the preserve of elite groups with special expertise. Thus, an organization such as the Council on Foreign Relations, a Brahmin-like institution with elegant headquarters at the corner of 68th Street and Park Avenue in New York, had great influence over both who and what made U.S. foreign policy. In the defense area, the highly technical and usually classified nature of many defense issues has meant that related organizations hired retired military officers to influence decisions in the same areas in which they had formerly labored.

The traditional roles of those who seek to influence the government have also bred orthodox ways of categorizing and looking at what they do. As we see, some of these roles are changing and will continue to do so as the post–Cold War world progresses. In anticipation of more detailed consideration of each category, however, let's review briefly how two kinds of institutions that stand at the boundary between the population and the government operate.

The first and historically most important traditional outside influences have been the interest groups, organizations that represent some group of people or institutions with common interests that they want to see promoted and protected. These organizations have traditionally been regarded as the gatekeepers between the public and the formal government itself. This gatekeeping function entails funneling to government the public's feelings and positions toward public policy. Interest groups collect what their followers feel, and they represent those interests to appropriate executive and legislative constituencies via such activities as *lobbying* (seeking to convince individual members of Congress or executive agency officials to support their groups' positions), *education* (writing articles and the like, testifying before congressional committees, etc.), and *pressure* (convincing officials that they will suffer if they defy the groups' will).

In recent years, the activities of interest groups have come under some public suspicion. Those in the field like to think of themselves as engaging in "Washington representation," a value-neutral term. Many in the public, however, including many aspiring to public office and trust, view them in a less favorable light. Tough legislation on interest group registration and disclosure of activities enacted in 1995 reflects suspicion of interest groups.

Suspicion of the traditional interest group role closely parallels the American people's general suspicion of the government. The term *Washington insider* has become a pejorative, encompassing those "professional Washington politicians" that candidates regularly defile and of which traditional Washington representatives are often the consummate examples.

At the same time, the aura of favoritism and gratuities surrounding many of the traditional methods of influence (e.g., throwing cocktail parties for officials who can help one's cause, contributing to campaign funds or a politician's pet charity) offend public sensibilities in an ethics-conscious era. This sensitivity was highlighted during the Clinton transition as the new president announced an executive order banning any official in his administration from lobbying the government for five years after leaving government service (a method ex-officials have traditionally used to capitalize on their government service).

In addition, interest groups often wield what some think is disproportionate power because of the resources they have at their disposal. Here a principal target has been the *political action committee* (PAC), interest group–controlled funds that funnel campaign monies to officials who support the group and also to opponents of those who oppose them.

The defense and foreign policy-making process is not immune from these kinds of activities and suspicions. One of the first and most widely publicized examples of possibly nefarious relationships between interest groups and the government was cited in President Dwight D. Eisenhower's farewell address, when he referred to the military-industrial complex and its potential erosive and corrupting influence on the American system. The military-industrial complex idea is discussed in the Expanded Horizons box "Is There a Military-Industrialized Complex?"

The military-industrial complex is but one, if a very important, example of a common concept in the U.S. political system, the *iron triangle*. Iron triangles are formed when those agencies or programs of the federal government that administer a given area find common cause with the congressional committee overseeing that activity and the interest group promoting the area. The iron triangle as it relates to the military-industrial complex can be seen in Figure 8.1.

The iron triangle here consists of the defense industry that contracts with elements of the armed services, the armed services who write contracts for different military hardware produced by the industry, and the appropriations subcommittees of the two houses of Congress that approve expenditures for various weapons.

There is nothing unnatural or necessarily wrong about such relationships, nor are they limited to the defense area. The air force, for instance, wants the best possible military aircraft and shares with the manufacturer the desire to produce aircraft. At the same time, all three sides of the triangle share expertise and common interests in military aircraft. (A member of Congress with no personal or constituency interests in military procurement is unlikely to volunteer for those committees.)

The relationship becomes a problem when it becomes incestuous and interests become *vested*. This term refers to the revolving door phenomenon depicted by the arrows in Figure 8.1. When, for example, a prime retirement job prospect for an air force officer is a senior position with the aerospace company whose contracts he is monitoring, is there room for compromise? The same is true of an aerospace executive

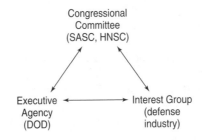

FIGURE 8.1   Military Iron Triangle

EXPANDED HORIZONS

Is There a Military-Industrial Complex?

The notion of a military-industrial complex that may perversely affect government decision making on defense procurement has been a part of the foreign policy scene since President Dwight D. Eisenhower alerted the public to it during his farewell address on January 17, 1961. While the idea of an iron triangle captures the heart of the idea, it also partially oversimplifies what is, and is not, involved.

There is disagreement about what constitutes the military-industrial complex and, indeed, if it even exists. For instance, in addition to the iron triangle of congressional committees, DOD, and the defense industry, many would add other components, such as labor unions whose members are employed in the defense industry, local communities where defense contracts are let, and even individual members of Congress whose districts may benefit from defense contracting. Clearly, this widens the circle of competing elements and detracts from the impression of a monolithic structure.

Others maintain that there really is not a single military-industrial complex at all, but rather a series of competing subcomplexes. At a minimum, each of the services has its own set of supporters, each seeking to maximize its share of the defense procurement budget and thus wary of claims of the other services. In this sense, the various services act as an informal check and balance on one another, a means to ensure adequate scrutiny of defense requests.

who takes a position in the civilian air force bureaucracy or a congressional staffer who moves to industry or the Pentagon. Abuses have spawned a number of laws intended to regulate these movements back and forth from government to industry as a means of restricting the development of vested interests.

A comparatively new group of outside influencers is exemplified by the think tanks, scholarly and research-based organizations that offer expert advice to various government organs. Sometimes, these organizations act as scholarly outlets, providing academic analyses on different problems. Much of the prestige of individual think tanks derives from their reputations for scholarly integrity and impartiality. At the same time, many of them engage in activities more generally associated with interest groups, and they are also part of the revolving door phenomenon moving into and out of the formal governmental structure.

In the remainder of this chapter, we go beyond the common analysis of these outside influences by introducing dynamics that may be changing their roles and places on the public agenda. We introduce five factors that constitute potential change agents, realizing they reflect changes that, in most cases, we have already described in earlier chapters.

The first factor is the *convergence of foreign and domestic issues.* The old distinctions between a foreign and domestic issue have largely disappeared into the realm of intermestic policies, especially in the changing world economy. Although that confluence affects the way the government itself is organized, it also has an effect on how the public views what government does. The end of the Cold War means the public will no longer automatically embrace defense spending, nor will the public permit government to be elusive about international economic matters. As foreign and national security policy get closer to the pocketbooks of the average citizen, the salience of those issues increases. The ongoing debate over whether public aid should be given to the new Russian Republic provides an example.

Public awareness and access is made easier by the *increased transparency of international events.* The global telecommunications revolution is at the heart of the public's greater access to foreign affairs at a time when those events are more immediate to them. Moreover, through global television outlets such as CNN, the initial information on breaking international affairs available to the public is precisely the same information available to decision makers: the president and his advisers, as well as members of the public, see the same reportage on CNN. At a minimum, the government's treatment of the media and concern for initial public opinion must be greater than in the past. At a maximum, it may mean more detailed scrutiny of public decisions by all those outside government who seek to influence government actions.

This factor relates to a third phenomenon: the greater analytical capability that accompanies global television's ability to cover worldwide news *increasingly makes the global media an actor and influence in that process.* Global television—CNN and the British-based Independent Television Network (ITN)—has clearly been the leader in this regard and is the first source of information to the public and, in many cases, governmental officials. More than that, the modern news conglomerate also provides considerable interpretation of events to a public that largely lacks the knowledge and perspective to interpret those events itself. With 24 hours a day of airtime to fill and not enough hard news to fill it, it becomes necessary to augment the bare facts with some notion of what the events may portend.

The fourth source of change is the *rise of so-called electronic experts,* those people with acknowledged expertise who are used by all the networks to provide legitimacy to the interpretation of currently breaking events. These individuals, most visibly seen during the Persian Gulf War, are especially important in the defense and foreign policy arena because much of that material is relatively technical and the public is unfamiliar with it. In the Persian Gulf War, all the networks featured both military and political experts who were drawn from outside their regular payrolls. They explained everything from the logistics of ground attack to the operation of precision-guided munitions.

These experts are generally unpaid guests and tend to come from the military, think tanks, and academia. Many are retired military officers (mostly colonels and generals or equivalent), who have experience, knowledge, and contacts within the Pentagon that give them superior access to information than that available to regular reporters, who are generally distrusted by military people. Retired air force lieutenant general Perry Smith, who provided analysis of the air campaign for CNN, is an example, and retired army colonel Harry Summers is another.

Another source for experts are the think tanks, especially those located in and around network headquarters in New York and Washington. For instance, coverage of Operation Desert Storm gave the Washington-based Center for Strategic and International Studies (CSIS) wide exposure.

Finally, experts found in academia, particularly international relations experts from around New York and Washington, frequently appear in the media. In the unraveling of the former Soviet Union, for example, Columbia University's Robert Legvold and Princeton University's Stephen Cohen were prominent analysts.

The fifth and final source of change is *growing public disaffection with the competency of the political leadership*. Running against Washington and the insiders first became a prominent strategy in Jimmy Carter's successful assault on the White House. It was a theme in Ronald Reagan's first campaign and became virtually an art form in the H. Ross Perot campaign of 1992. Dissatisfaction with how the system works has become broader than that evident just at the level of presidential election politics, however. Witness the number of U.S. representatives and senators who retired in 1992 (although the reason was partly because 1992 was the last year that a member of Congress could keep excess campaign contributions beyond campaign expenses) and the number who were defeated for reelection in 1994. Part of this dissatisfaction is undoubtedly fueled by the greater access to information that is a legacy of the electronic revolution.

This discussion provides the basis for examining how interest groups and think tanks operate outside the government's formal structure and some of the forces that are changing how they operate. We emphasize how they relate specifically to foreign and national security matters.

Interest Groups

In political terms, an interest group can be defined simply as any organized group of people who share common interests distinct from those of others and who attempt to influence public policy in the direction of that interest. As such, interest groups share some common interest, whether it be maintenance of a strong national defense, the preservation of the environment, or the protection of the right to bear firearms. They have come together into some formal organization of like-minded individuals, and they seek to represent their common interest to the political system and to influence public policy in the direction of their interest.

Characteristics

The characteristics of interest groups are progressive. For instance, many people have common interests, but they do not as a result organize; although organizations in fact exist, not many left-handed people belong to organizations of lefties. At the same time, not all organized groups seek to influence the political system. Left-handed people may meet to commiserate about the tyrannies of a right-handed world, but they do not pressure the government to provide left-handed-only parking spaces at supermarkets.

Interest groups stand as gatekeepers between the public and the government. The organizations collect the interests that people share, distilling public feelings into a more manageable set of interests that they represent and can relate to the government.

The function performed by interest groups is provided for in the First Amendment to the Constitution, which guarantees the right to "petition the Government for a redress of grievances." The basic idea underlying this right was discussed in the *Federalist Papers* from which the Constitution was derived. It finds its modern expression in the idea of pluralism, the notion that all interests should be freely able to compete for influence within the government.

Theoretically, the ability to form interest groups and to compete in the arena includes the entire population and is an option available to all Americans. In fact, however, that is generally not the case. Numerous studies have shown that the upper strata of society, as measured by yardsticks such as wealth and education, are over-represented in interest group activity. In one sense, this stands to reason, for interest group activities, like almost everything else, cost money. Hence, those who possess resources will have first access. Similarly, educational attainment and political activity are positively related.

To understand the role of interest groups, we need to examine what interest groups do in order to represent and promote their interests. We also look at the kinds of interest groups that are active in the foreign and defense policy arena.

What Interest Groups Do

Different observers categorize the activities of interest groups differently, and no set of categories will satisfy all of them. For our purposes, however, we divide those activities into three categories: lobbying, education, and pressure. Each function entails distinct actions, although most interest groups use some combination of them all.

Lobbying   Interest groups are most closely associated with *lobbying*. The term itself goes back to the 1870s. Although the First Amendment to the Constitution provides for the right of petition, it prohibits the presentation of petitions on the floors of the houses of Congress. As a result, those seeking influence were forced to make their representations outside the chambers, especially in the corridors and lobbies of the Capitol Building. Hence, the term *lobbying* was born.

The purpose of lobbying, like all other interest group activity, is to persuade those with the ability to make decisions—in the Congress or the executive branch—that their interests should be reflected in public policy. Lobbying connotes the personal representations of positions to individual members of Congress or executive branch agents in the effort to convince them of the virtue of their positions. Although some lobbying occurs within the executive branch, more of it occurs in the interactions between interest groups and members of Congress.

The cornerstones of lobbying are the Washington-based offices of various interest groups and lobbyists. Although precise figures are hard to obtain, it is estimated that over 40,000 people work in the Washington offices of the nearly 1,800 associations represented there. In addition, over 2,000 individuals are registered with the government as lobbyists.

Lobbyists come in several varieties. Some are amateurs, members of interest groups who are sent to Washington for the specific task of influencing a piece of legislation, for instance, by attempting to persuade their own congressional member or state delegation to vote for the bill. In the foreign and defense policy area, organizations such as the American Legion often reward rank-and-file members by sending them to Washington in this capacity.

A second kind of lobbyist is the professional, usually someone with considerable government service who has developed expertise and extensive contacts within some policy area that he or she is willing to share with clients for a price. (Professional lobbyists typically work for several clients rather than a single one.) Many of these individuals are lawyers who have developed expertise in specific areas of the law, such as food and drug law; hence, they are attractive representatives for clients such as the pharmaceutical industry. In the foreign policy area, Henry Kissinger Associates is probably the most famous and powerful example of a professional lobbying organization.

Yet another type of lobbyist is the staff lobbyist. Unlike the professional lobbyist, the staff lobbyist works full time for the Washington office of an organization that seeks to influence the policy process. In addition to formal lobbying, staff lobbyists typically perform other administrative duties as well. All organizations with large operations in Washington employ some staff lobbyists. The aerospace industries represent an example in the defense area.

The purpose of all lobbying efforts is to gain access to decision makers and to persuade them of the efficacy of the interest the lobbyist represents. Highly successful lobbyists make themselves so invaluable to people within the process that they virtually become a part of it—for instance, having such great knowledge of a policy area that they are consulted on language for a piece of legislation. This quality of access is attained in part through the second form of interest group activity, education.

Education   Interest groups seek to influence the political system by providing expert information in an issue area that can be used to educate both those in power and the public at large of the desirability of their positions.

When educational efforts are directed at the general public, they usually take one of several forms. One obvious form is the advertising campaign, which increasingly uses professional television spots to galvanize public opinion on a subject. The ad campaigns on both sides of the abortion issue are a particularly vivid example. Sometimes these campaigns are directed at the general public, and other times at specialized segments of the population. An example of the latter was a series of advertisements in the *New York Times* placed by pro-Serbian groups in June 1992 seeking to convince readers that the situation in Bosnia and Herzegovina was not a Serbian act of aggression and atrocity, but instead the continuation of Serbian resistance to Croatian fascism with roots in World War II. (Such tactics do not always work, as they did not in this case.) Another educational effort may be to provide speakers' bureaus to speak to groups or to be available for newspaper and television interviews. At the same time, groups often provide news releases to newspapers in the hope that they will be printed in local papers.

More commonly, educational efforts are directed toward members of Congress or their staffs. Interest groups collect and make available information about their particular policy area, which, although self-interested, provides a useful supplement to the member's ability to gain information through his or her staff. This information may be provided in the form of position papers, fact books, reference services to which a member has access, or even expert testimony to congressional committees and subcommittees.

Members and their staffs greatly appreciate this form of activity, if provided honestly rather than as obviously biased propaganda. Despite the great expansion of staffs described in Chapter 6, Congress is still at a disadvantage in its competition for information with the executive branch. An interest group that provides honest, valuable information thus extends Congress's capabilities. A few try to mislead Congress, but such a tactic is shortsighted and almost invariably exposed, thereby compromising the interest group in the future. When competing interest groups present conflicting information or interpretations, the member can make a comparative assessment of the various positions.

A good example of an interest group that uses educational programs as a primary tool is the Arms Control Association (ACA). It publishes its own journal, *Arms Control Today,* which it distributes to libraries and interested citizens. It features a speakers' bureau for places such as college campuses, and its leading staff members are regularly available for interviews. Congressional members receive the journal, and ACA provides both expert witnesses for testimony before congressional committees and a resource for information on weapons levels, characteristics, and the like. As a further means of endearment, *Arms Control Today* frequently publishes articles and speeches by sympathetic members of Congress.

Pressure   Interest groups also seek to influence the system through pressure, a form of influence peddling that represents the most negative side of interest group activities. Pressure activities comprise actions that are designed not so much to persuade officials of the virtue of the group's position as to convince the official of the negative consequences of opposing the interest or the positive benefits of support.

In the last 20 years or so, the negative side of pressure has come to be associated with the emergence of political action committees (PACs). The basic purpose and tactic of PACs is to influence elections by collecting money from their membership and using it to support candidates sympathetic to their causes and to oppose their opponents. This is sometimes done by the PAC making direct contributions to campaigns; limits on the amount that can be given to any candidate by an organization also necessitate a second tactic, which is for the PAC to encourage members of the group also to contribute.

The cost of modern campaigns, largely inflated by the expense of television advertising, makes the PACs more and more powerful and the increasing target of regulation, as promised by candidate Clinton during the 1992 campaign and reiterated—without follow-up—by Clinton and house speaker Newt Gingrich in 1996 in the form of election reform legislation. They are big business and growing in number and influence. The Federal Election Commission (FEC), for instance, identified 608 PACs at the end of 1974; by the end of 1987 that number had risen to 4,165. The largest number of these—1,775—were PACs with corporate affiliations. The amount of money that PACs spend has also escalated. The FEC estimated PAC contributions to campaigns for 1977–1978 at just less than $78 million; by 1987–1988 that figure was over $364 million.

PAC activities are more closely associated with domestic than foreign and defense issues. Thus, two of the largest and most influential PACs are those connected with the American Medical Association and the National Rifle Association. There are, however, corporate PACs that seek to influence the size and direction of defense procurement; the aerospace industry is particularly active in this regard.

Pressure can take other forms. Lobbyists, for instance, can offer favors to sympathetic members of Congress. Historically, for instance, interest groups would offer speaking engagements, complete with speakers' fees (honoraria) and expenses; abuses of this practice have resulted in reform legislation that virtually prohibits the practice for any federal employee and eliminated the acceptance of gifts by members of Congress.

The size of the stakes involved inevitably leads to abuses and most commonly *bribery,* the offer and acceptance of illegal funds by some official from an interest group. Instances of bribery are rather infrequent, but when they do occur, they are spectacular. One large-scale bribery case involved banking magnate Charles Keating and his defrauding of the federal government in the savings and loan association scandal. The corruption touched five U.S. senators, the Keating Five (Alan Cranston of California, John Glenn of Ohio, Dennis DeConcini of Arizona, John McCain of Arizona, and Donald Reigle of Michigan).

In the foreign and defense area, one of the most famous cases involved a foreign lobbyist, Tong Sun Park of the Republic of Korea. Park, a flashy, well-liked figure, induced support for his government through lavish social occasions for governmental officials, including gifts for congressional members and spouses. The gifts ultimately got him in trouble because they exceeded allowable limits. One of the people who was forced to resign his position because of this scandal was Ronald Reagan's first national-al security adviser, Richard V. Allen, who accepted two watches from Park.

Types of Interest Groups

There are as many interest groups in the country as there are interests that people hold. Most concentrate on influencing the domestic agenda. As such, their activities go beyond our scope, but we should recognize that the blurring of domestic and foreign policy means that almost all interests are affected by international events some of the time. With that rejoinder in mind, we can explore the kinds of groups that seek to influence foreign and defense policy by looking at five overlapping distinctions about kinds of interest groups.

General and Specific   General interest groups are those whose interests span the spectrum of policy areas, including but not specifically emphasizing foreign policy. These groups—two examples of which are the American Federation of Labor-Congress of Industrial Organizations (AFL-CIO) and the American Association of Retired Persons (AARP)—take an interest in foreign or defense policy when it may directly affect their constituents. If defense spending proposals were to impinge on retirement entitlements, for instance, AARP would become involved. These comprehensive interest groups are often large and have considerable general influence, but they frequently lack great expertise in the specific area of defense and foreign policy.

Other interest groups concentrate on foreign and defense policy or some part of it exclusively. Although it also has some of the characteristics of a think tank, the powerful Council on Foreign Relations is an example of an organization that focuses solely on foreign affairs. Its roughly 3,000 elected members represent the Eastern establishment foreign policy elite and thus bring both great expertise and prestige to the policy process, especially because many members are also former high-ranking officials of government.

One organization that concentrates on a specific aspect of the foreign policy process is Amnesty International (AI). Although it considers itself more of a think tank because of the academic impartiality of its inquiry, AI is dedicated to the protection of

AMPLIFICATION

Amnesty International and the Travails of Success

Created in 1961 to promote freedom of expression and the release of political prisoners, Amnesty International has grown to become the world's most famous human rights advocate, with chapters in a number of leading states. But in a post–Cold War world with a voracious appetite for news to cover, it may have become a victim of its own success.

Because human rights abuses have become so widespread and received so much publicity on global television, the media, notably CNN, regularly attempts to create or substantiate news by contacting AI. The volume of requests has become so great that it has taxed the ability of the organization to carry out the on-the-spot, meticulous research by which it gained its reputation for fairness. This creates a dilemma for the organization. As Pierre Sane, AI's secretary general, puts it, what the organization prefers is "a nice piece of research that is verified to death. But if that corners you into inaction, then what's the point? Amnesty is a campaigning organization."

A politically activist AI offends many of its supporters and foreign chapters. In the United States, AI now competes for support with Human Rights Watch, a parallel organization that often gets more headlines than AI and hence attracts more funding. The result, according to some disgruntled AI researchers (some of whom have resigned as a result), is pressure "to get it out fast" rather than "to get it right." The executive director of the Dutch chapter of AI fears that the movement is subtly being changed for the worse: "We don't want to be a political movement that influences everything. We want to do what we do well."

Source: Raymond Bonner, "Trying to Document Rights Abuses," *New York Times* (national edition), July 26, 1995, p. A4.

human rights globally, and investigates and publicizes instances of human rights abuses. AI often comes into direct conflict with the State Department, which has the statutory mandate to produce a list of countries that are human rights abusers. Its list, partially constructed with geopolitical considerations in mind (how important a country is to the United States regardless of its human rights record), is almost always shorter than the AI list. The AI list of abusers thus serves as a club that members of Congress can use against the State Department, a part of the system of informal checks and balances of the government. AI is the subject of the accompanying Amplification box "Amnesty International and the Travails of Success."

Permanent and Ad Hoc   Permanent groups have been in existence for an extensive period of time and expect to continue for the indefinite future. They must therefore rely on long-term stable relationships both with their constituencies and with those inside the government they seek to influence. This in turn affects the ways they operate: they are naturally prone to more low-key activities that nurture long associations.

Examples of permanent interest groups in the foreign and defense area include the various groups that support the services: the Association of the United States Army (AUSA), the Air Force Association (AFA), and the Navy League. In addition to providing some contact with the services for retired personnel, each of these associations seeks to influence the government about their services and toward general veterans' issues.

Ad hoc interest groups, in contrast, are part of the broader phenomenon of the single-interest interest group, an organization that comes together just to affect the outcome of a particular issue but ceases to operate when the particular issue is resolved. The original ad hoc groups date back to the 1960s, and a prototype of sorts revolved around a national security issue, the Vietnam War. The entire loose, sprawling anti–Vietnam War movement was spawned on American college campuses shortly after U.S. active combat involvement in the war began. (The actual genesis came before the United States intervened in terms of teach-ins at major campuses in 1964, notably the University of California at Berkeley.) The movement widened to encompass a broad spectrum from counterculture youth to the Vietnam Veterans Against the War that shared a common, but single, interest in ending the war. Once that purpose was accomplished, the movement splintered and ultimately disappeared. In the current nonforeign policy context, the various abortion-antiabortion phenomena provide a parallel.

Groups with Continuous or Occasional Interests   Interest groups with a continuous interest in foreign and defense affairs tend to be comprehensive in their approaches to what interests them and what they seek to influence. The continuity of interest helps create expertise, which makes the group's counsel more sought after than would otherwise be the case. In turn, the reputation for expertise makes the group's recruitment of experts easier. Examples of this kind of group are the Council on Foreign Relations and the Foreign Policy Association.

By definition, groups with occasional interest in foreign policy are selective in the foreign and defense issues they seek to influence. Normally with a primary focus in some other policy area, these groups intrude into the foreign policy area only when a specific issue directly affects them and then only for as long as their interests are engaged.

An example might be the American Farm Bureau Federation, whose primary focus is on agricultural policy. But when issues such as grain sales overseas arise, they become engaged in the foreign policy process. The group might be expected, for example, to take an active position on probable legislation limiting the diversion of agricultural credits to foreign governments to other purposes (for example, Iraq's use of credit to buy military, including nuclear, hardware). Similarly, the AFL-CIO has a lively interest in the North American Free Trade Agreement, and the National Association of Manufacturers has a strong concern about those parts of the Treaty of Maastricht that might exclude U.S. goods from the states that comprise the European Union.

Private and Public   The largest number of private interest groups are those representing individual corporations that do business with the government (contractors such as the aircraft industries or defense suppliers generally) or are regulated by the government (for instance, the pharmaceutical companies regulated by the Food and Drug Administration) and associations of corporate institutions (such as the National Association of Manufacturers). In the foreign and defense policy area, the majority of private interest groups have historically been attached to defense, especially defense procurement. As international economic issues become more important in foreign policy generally, we can expect interest groups that have historically focused on domestic politics to conduct more foreign policy efforts.

Public interest groups, on the other hand, purport to represent the body politic as a whole, especially those citizens whose interests are underrepresented otherwise. Largely a product of the 1960s, these groups typically are financed by large numbers of small donations and maintain an air of impartiality (whether deserved or not). Common Cause is the prototype of this kind of interest group.

National and International   We think of American interest groups seeking to influence the U.S. political system as the norm, as the kind of activity sanctioned by the First Amendment. For most purposes and most of the time this is the case; to this point the discussion has focused exclusively on this kind of interest group action. Americans are not, however, the only people interested in influencing U.S. policy, especially its defense and foreign policy. Foreigners, notably foreign governments, also share a lively interest in trying to affect U.S. government actions toward themselves and others, and they do so in a number of ways. Sometimes they use their own citizens, such as a particularly attractive ambassador, as an informal lobbyist with the government. Prince Bandar bin Sultan, the Saudi ambassador to the United States, has been especially successful in this role, particularly when opposition to selling weapons to the Saudi kingdom has arisen and especially during the Persian Gulf War.

Foreign governments also get their interests represented by hiring Americans, quite often former government officials, to represent them. People who represent foreign governments must register as foreign agents, and quite often their value derives from their ability to gain access to officials for their foreign clients. Henry Kissinger Associates is an example. Yet another way for foreign governments to influence U.S. policy is to nurture Americans whose origins are the same as the nation seeking the influence. "Hyphenated Americans" (Italian-Americans, Irish-Americans, etc.) can be quite effective if these organizations can plausibly be argued to represent vital segments of the American public. Probably the largest and most successful of these is the Israel lobby and its action arm, the American-Israeli Political Action Committee.

Interest groups and the activities they engage in are a long-standing, integral part of the U.S. political system. In a sense, although they are outside the halls of formal government, they reflect the same kind of system of checks and balances created inside government: almost all possible interests on most subjects have an organization representing that interest. Thus, the right to petition is available. If there is a limit or shortcoming, it is the attachment between interests and money; the public interest groups notwithstanding, those who have the money can afford to hire those who represent their interests. Occasionally, the result will be some perversion or corruption of the system.

Policy Elites and Think Tanks

A relatively new and burgeoning phenomenon is the emergence of a sizable community of individuals with expertise on public policy matters (the policy elite), which attempts to use its knowledge to affect public policy. In most cases, these individuals are aggregated in not-for-profit, nonpartisan research institutes and organizations that conduct research on policy matters and share that knowledge with policymakers. In the jargon of Washington, these organizations have been known as think tanks since the presidency of John F. Kennedy (whose administration witnessed a proliferation of them). Before that metaphor took root, synonyms included "brain banks," "think factories," and "egghead rows." (A number of the early ones were located in a row on Massachusetts Avenue in Washington, D.C.)

Think tanks and interest groups share two apparent similarities: some of their activities coincide, and they both operate at the boundary between the government and the populace. But they differ in emphasis, membership, and the range of activities they undertake.

The basic purpose of both think tanks and interest groups is citizen education, although for different reasons. Interest groups view education instrumentally, as a device to cause conversion to their interest. In contrast, traditional think tanks have sought knowledge and its educational application more abstractly, as a way to improve government, although some newer think tanks are edging toward the instrumental purpose. Both types of organization also operate at the boundary between government and the public, although it is a different boundary. For interest groups, it is the line between the formal system and organized citizens with particular interests; for think tanks, it is normally the line between government and the policy-active intellectual community.

The two entities also differ in significant ways. The emphasis of interest groups is overtly political: they generally seek to move policy in self-interested directions.

Think tanks, though often ideologically identifiable, adopt a more detached, scholarly view of policy. Similarly, most of those associated with the think tanks are academics in one sense or another, or people with experience-based expertise (retired military officers, ex-government officials), whereas traditional politicians are more often associated with interest group activity.

They are also distinct in their range of activities. Because of their heritage based in academia, think tanks rarely engage in gross advocacy of particular policy issues, whereas lobbying and pressuring in favor of specific legislation is the raison d'être of interest groups.

The think tank phenomenon is not well understood generally. Much of it occurs inside the beltway in a low-key manner. The activities of the think tanks are particularly important in the areas of foreign and defense policy because these issues are at least part of the agendas of most prominent think tanks. Examining the characteristics of these organizations and their activities is important to understanding how the process works.

Characteristics

The movement that evolved into the modern think tanks took place around the turn of the twentieth century. Its impetus came from a group of scholars, principally from the social sciences, who believed that public policy and process could be improved by applying social scientific means and research.

The first identifiable think tank, the Russell Sage Foundation, was chartered in 1907 and was followed fairly quickly by the Twentieth Century Fund and a handful of others. All of these early efforts viewed themselves as citadels in which disinterested research (research not associated with personal or institutional gain) could be pursued and the results applied to societal problems dispassionately. These research interests remained peripheral to the foreign policy process until the activism in politics associated with the 1960s. Until then there were relatively few think tanks in existence, what they did was largely academic, and they generally did not engage in much self-promotion.

All that has changed. According to a major study of the subject, James Allen Smith's 1991 book, *The Idea Brokers* (see Suggested Readings), about two-thirds of the think tanks operating in the Washington area today have come into existence since 1970. At the same time and led by the example of the conservative Heritage Foundation, many have become more activist, openly gearing their research to promoting particular political ideas and causes.

The think tanks are important to the understanding of foreign policy because foreign and defense policy are important to them. In the appendix to his book, Smith provides what he calls a sampler of 30 of the most prominent think tanks. Table 8.1 depicts those institutions in terms of the foreign and defense nature of their activities.

TABLE 8.1
The Foreign Policy Activity of the Leading Think Tanks

Exclusively Foreign Policy
Carnegie Endowment for International Peace
Center for Defense Information
Center for Strategic and International Studies
Institute for International Economics
Overseas Development Council
World Policy Institute
World Resources Institute
Worldwatch Institute
Total: 8

Partly Foreign Policy
American Enterprise Institute
Brookings Institution
Cato Institute
Center for Budget and Policy Priorities
Center for National Policy
Ethics and Public Policy Center
Heritage Foundation
Hoover Institution
Hudson Institute
Institute for Contemporary Studies
Institute for Policy Studies
Joint Center for Political and Economic Studies
Progressive Policy Institute
RAND Corporation
Twentieth Century Fund
Total: 15

No Foreign Policy
Committee for Economic Development
Economic Policy Institute
Manhattan Institute for Policy Research
Resources for the Future
Rockford Institute
Russell Sage Foundation
Urban Institute
Total: 7

Of the 30 organizations listed in the table, 23 (or 77 percent) concern themselves at least part of the time with foreign and defense concerns. Among the larger institutes, it is not unusual for their research activities to be divided into three program areas: foreign and/or security affairs, economic studies, and domestic or governmental studies. This is the pattern, for instance, of the prestigious Brookings Institution.

Of those with no current programmatic concern for foreign affairs, the increasing internationalization of the economy is likely to impel organizations such as the Committee for Economic Development and the Economic Policy Institute, both of which concentrate on domestic economic issues, to broaden their concerns.

The research institutes are also defined by the people who work for them. Especially among those with a foreign and defense policy emphasis, they tend to come from one of three backgrounds: academia, the military, or the government. Academics are usually individuals with doctoral degrees in political science, economics, history, or international relations who are more interested in applied research (studying and influencing concrete public policy) than in abstract, theoretical academic research. Some of the abstract research can be found in institutes and centers affiliated with universities, but the typification holds for most nonuniversity academics working in the think tanks.

Even a partial list of academics is impressive. It would include John Steinbrunner, Dimitri Simes, Lester Thurow, Stanley Hoffmann, Edward N. Luttwak, Walter Laqueur, Ernest Lefever, Milton Friedman, Seymour Martin Lipset, the late Herman Kahn, and Fred Bergsten, all of whom are or have been associated with research associations at one time or another. Until her appointment as U.N. ambassador by President Clinton, Madeleine K. Albright (who was president of the Center for National Policy at the time of her appointment) could have been on the list along with Robert Reich, now secretary of labor, and Gordon Adams, now deputy director of the Office of Management and Budget. Not all are household names, but a quick bibliographical check at the library or look at the identifying credits when experts are voicing opinions during foreign policy crises on television reveals how impressive they are.

As one might expect, retired military officers tend to be concentrated in think tanks primarily studying security rather than foreign policy problems as more broadly defined. Many who have retired below the rank of flag officer (general or admiral) are located in organizations that do contract work for the government or in institutes run in-house by the services. In addition, a number of the Ph.D.s who work in the think tanks have military backgrounds, probably reflecting a greater action orientation than is normally associated with academic life. Prominent examples of retired military in the research institutes include retired rear admiral Gene LaRoque, head of the Center for Defense Information, and retired army colonel William J. Taylor, an executive at the Center for Strategic and International Studies (CSIS).

Among the former governmental officials, one group includes those whose positions provided them with considerable insight and expertise that is a valuable addition to the expert and prestige base of the institutes they join. Lawrence J. Korb (Brookings Institution) and Richard N. Perle (American Enterprise Institute, or AEI), both assistant secretaries of defense in the Reagan administration, and Jeane Kirkpatrick (AEI), former ambassador to the United Nations, are examples.

Another group are high-ranking officials who, out of ideological or political conviction, lend their names to institutes by serving as chairs, members of the board, or the like. This category includes the late former secretary of state Edmund Muskie, former secretaries of defense Donald Rumsfeld and Caspar Weinberger, and former White House counsel Edwin Meese.

Sources of Funding   The research institutes are also defined by the sources of their funding. They vary tremendously in size of staff and extensiveness of program, and thus in the need for and size of funding base. For most organizations, however, funding comes from a combination of six sources: foundations, corporate sponsorship, bequests and large contributions, individual contributions, sales of books and periodicals, and government-sponsored research.

The first source, large foundations with considerable resources, such as the Ford or Kettering Foundations, provide funds to support research, including that conducted by the think tanks. Foundation support is most likely to be associated with research institutes that do not have an activist political agenda.

With regard to corporate sponsorship, as long as the funds are not attached to a political agenda (hence qualifying as interest activity), corporations can and do provide funds for institutes. Moreover, through bequests and large contributions, a number of institutes have endowments that produce revenue to support their activities. The amounts vary. The Brookings Institution, for instance, has an endowment of about $100 million, whereas CSIS has about $9 million in endowed funds.

A fourth source of operating funds is individual contributions. Among the major think tanks, the Heritage Foundation, which lists 43 percent of its income from this source, probably leads the way. Another source is sales of books and journals or magazines. Most research institutes publish their research, normally for a price, and this feeds into the budget. Finally, some institutes receive funding from government-sponsored research. The bellwether in this category is the RAND Corporation, which was created in 1948 largely to serve as a think tank for the newly independent U.S. Air Force and still conducts much of its research for the air force and the army.

Ideological Leanings   Another characteristic sometimes applied to research institutes is their general ideological or political persuasions. A number of institutes created in the 1970s were established out of the conservatives' belief that they needed a formal articulated agenda that could be used to appeal to the public or to provide a program for aspiring conservative candidates. The most prominent case in point of this phenomenon is the Heritage Foundation.

Think tanks run the political gamut. During the latter 1970s and early 1980s, for instance, the American Enterprise Institute became associated with the moderate wing of the Republican Party. (A number of people associated with the Ford administration affiliated with it after Ford's loss to Jimmy Carter in 1976.) The Brookings Institution, on the other hand, has always been identified with more liberal positions and has sometimes been referred to as the Democratic think tank, as has the Center for National Policy.

Affiliations   Think tanks may also be categorized in terms of three basic forms of association in the foreign and defense policy area.

The first and dominant pattern includes the private, freestanding research institutes, which represent the original pattern that was established. When many people talk about the think tanks, they are talking about these. All the institutes identified in Table 8.1 belong to this type.

Some institutes are also associated with universities. The number is growing as universities, facing diminishing traditional federal sources of research funds, have adopted entrepreneurial strategies to attract funding by establishing centers, institutes, and the like. Among the most prestigious and best established entities are the Center for Science and International Affairs (a cooperative enterprise of the Massachusetts Institute of Technology and Harvard University); the Foreign Policy Research Institute (affiliated with the University of Pennsylvania); the Institute for Foreign Policy Analysis (associated with the Fletcher School of Tufts University); and the Hoover Institution (formally private but with a working relationship with Stanford University).

Yet another form of affiliation is with a governmental organization. Each of the military services, for instance, maintains its own in-house think tank. These are generally associated with the war colleges. Thus, the army maintains its Strategic Studies Institute (SSI) at the U.S. Army War College in Carlisle Barracks, Pennsylvania; the navy its Center for Naval Warfare Studies (CNWS) at the U.S. Naval War College in Newport, Rhode Island; and the air force its Aerospace Research Institute (ARI) at the Air University in Montgomery, Alabama. There are also instances of joint service activities, such as the Army-Air Force Center for Low-Intensity Conflict. The State Department also maintains the same kind of capability in its Center for the Study of Foreign Affairs.

Thus, the evolution of the think tank phenomenon has been an eclectic affair. There are just about as many different kinds of think tanks as ways to categorize them. The pattern is continuing to evolve, particularly in the funding-tight 1990s, when the research institutes are being forced to compete with one another and with other institutions such as universities for dwindling resources.

Patterns of Function and Activity

The research institutes and the policy intellectuals that staff them engage in a variety of different activities. Some organizations, of course, place greater emphasis on certain functions than on others, and the pattern is evolving, as are the organizations themselves. Some of these activities are shared with interest groups; some are distinct.

The activities and functions can be divided into six groups: research, publications, expert advice, talent bank, a focal point for like-minded individuals, and the media connection. The first and most fundamental category, naturally, is *research*. Much of the prestige and early influence of the original research institutes was the result of their adherence to objective, scholarly pursuit of knowledge based in social scientific methods of inquiry.

The research emphasis, which produces and disseminates knowledge applicable to dealing with societal problems, distinguishes the think tanks, giving them their character and identity. Moreover, the analyses they perform are the basic product they have to sell to the system; it is the way they help set the political agenda and influence the public debate. In the absence of a research base, think tanks would be little more than interest groups representing the policy intellectual community.

The concern about the continuing purity of research efforts coming from the institutes arises from two bases. The first is the emergence of the activist, openly political think tank. The Heritage Foundation is the prototype. The organization openly admits that it engages in inquiry for the purpose of promoting the conservative agenda, and it publicizes only those research findings which support its point of view. The fear is that this emphasis will undercut the reputation for scientific integrity that has been important to think tank influence in the past.

The second source of concern is financial. In the 1990s the sources of funds needed to support the research institutes contracted at the same time that other funding sources, such as government grants, also became more scarce. As a result, the think tanks must compete with one another. Often the things that most successfully sell contributors relate to overt political influence, once again with the potential consequence of compromising the organization's scientific purity.

The research institutes promote their research through *publications,* which may take several forms. One is the commissioning and publishing of books on topics of public interest. One fairly common pattern is for the think tank to employ a visiting scholar for a period of time (a year or two) with the express purpose of producing a book. Ideally, these books attract broad public readership, or at least the attention of policymakers. The results can be added prestige for the think tank, influence on the policy process, and, not least importantly, revenue to support the institute. The Brookings Institution has always supported a vigorous book list, as has CSIS through its *Washington Papers* series, and the Council on Foreign Relations through its own press.

Another form of publication is technical reports. The RAND Corporation disseminates short technical reports that are available to policymakers and the general public. Staff members also write articles for the opinion and editorial pages of leading national newspapers, such as the *New York Times, Washington Post,* and the *Christian Science Monitor.* In addition, a number of think tanks produce journals that are used as research sources by scholars and others conducting policy relevant research. A representative list with foreign and defense policy relevance includes the *Brookings Review* (Brookings Institution), *Cato Journal* (Cato Institute), *Foreign*

Policy (Carnegie Endowment), *Defense Monitor* (Center for Defense Information), *Washington Quarterly* (CSIS), *Policy Review* (Heritage), *World Policy Journal* (World Policy Institute), and *World Watch* (Worldwatch Institute).

Many research institutes provide *expert advice* to the government in a number of ways. Some organizations, for instance, contract with the government to provide specific expertise on technical matters. This activity is more often associated with consultants (sometimes known as beltway bandits because of their locations along the Washington beltway and the alleged quality of their work) but is occasionally done by think tanks as well.

More commonly, however, the research institutes act in more subtle ways. A staff member who has just completed a major study may be asked to provide expert testimony to a congressional committee or to serve on a presidential commission investigating an area in which the organization has expertise. At the same time, that expertise can also be applied to watchdogging governmental activities. The Defense Budget Project, directed by Gordon Adams and sponsored by the Center on Budget and Policy Priorities before his OMB appointment, critically analyzes the defense budget proposal produced by the Defense Department and publishes and circulates that critique throughout the government.

In addition, think tanks provide a *talent bank* (the term used by the Nixon administration) for the government. This process works in two directions. On the one hand, when an administration leaves office and is replaced by another, some personnel dislocation always occurs among the several thousand officials who hold political appointments and find their services are no longer required as a new president forms his own distinctive team. Many officials so removed do not want to leave the Washington scene altogether and even have aspirations of returning to senior government service in the future.

For such people, appointment to a position in one of the research institutes can provide an attractive option that serves both the individual and the organization. From the individual's viewpoint, a think tank appointment can serve as a safe haven, a sanctuary between periods of government service wherein the person can remain abreast of what is happening in Washington. From the organizational vantage point, the association of important former governmental officials can enhance both the prestige and expertise of the organization.

In the other direction, the staffs of the research institutes provide a ready talent pool for filling governmental positions. It has been argued, for instance, that the Brookings Institution, as well as the John F. Kennedy School of Government at Harvard University, provides a kind of "government in waiting" for any new Democratic president just as the Heritage Foundation provided a source of policy inspiration and personnel availability for the Reagan administration. The Clinton administration has continued this practice.

The think tanks are a *focal point for like-minded individuals*. This function formed one of the major purposes of formalizing the conservative movement through

Heritage and other organizations following Barry Goldwater's crushing defeat by Lyndon Johnson in the 1964 election. The feeling was that conservatives had failed to develop and articulate a politically attractive agenda because they had no mechanism around which those of like persuasion could rally. A research institute with an active research and publication program can fill this bill. Research leading to the articulation of policy positions can help clarify the policy agenda for any group. A publications program utilizing books, technical reports, talking papers, or articles in a house-sponsored journal can help circulate ideas and establish networks of like-minded scholar-policy analysts.

A newly emerging function of think tanks is the *media connection,* and more specifically, the role of the *electronic expert.* This phenomenon is the result of the media's burgeoning need for information and expertise, combined with the opportunities for organizational and self-promotion that the electronic expert's role provides for the think tanks.

The media's needs date back to the Vietnam period. Events, and especially their analysis and understanding, often went beyond the expertise of the television networks and print media who, for instance, did not possess staff experts on Southeast Asian history and politics or the principles of mobile-guerrilla warfare (the style of war employed by the North Vietnamese and their Viet Cong allies). Those media, with headquarters and major bureaus in the same locales as the major think tanks (which *did* have staff with expertise in those very areas), created an obvious marriage of convenience. The media's need was for experts who exuded authority, whereas the think tanks sought the exposure that having members of their staffs appearing on the evening news could provide.

This role has been expanding as a result of trends in electronic mediation. Once again, CNN is the trendsetter. CNN by necessity engages in a great deal of news analysis in addition to reporting. To analyze the news requires expert authorities, and the think tanks are a fertile ground. But that is not all. In addition, CNN has also changed the extent and depth by which breaking news events, and especially foreign events, are covered. Knowing that CNN will produce very detailed coverage of an international crisis forces the other news organizations (wire services, leading papers, television networks) to cover events in more detail than ever before. The alternative is to concede news coverage supremacy to CNN. Unwilling to do that, the need for experts proliferates. The Amplification box "Amnesty International and the Travails of Success" illustrates the stresses media demands can create.

This new phenomenon reached an apex during the Persian Gulf War and the preparations for it. Each television network recruited its own complement of experts to appear daily to explain what had happened, as well as periodic appearances by others. Members of the staffs of the more aggressive research institutes (CSIS was among the most prominent) were among the most often seen. Unless there is a trend reversing the expansion of news coverage (which hardly seems likely), this trend is likely to continue and expand in the future.

Conclusions

Both think tanks and interest groups can be seen in the context of the system of informal checks and balances on which the political system operates. Nearly every interest has a group to represent it and make sure its voice is heard; the think tanks span the range of intellectual points of view. In the overall context of the U.S. government, interest groups are a more important phenomenon than the think tanks. They are larger, more numerous, more visible, richer, and hence more powerful. The think tanks, on the other hand, are probably more represented and effective in influencing foreign and defense policy than in other areas because international relations is an important area of social science inquiry. Were our focus not on foreign affairs, there would have been less reason to examine the think tanks in any detail.

The two kinds of institutions share similarities and differences. Both, for instance, seek to influence rather than to govern (although some think tank staffers move in and out of government), but they do so differently and for different reasons. Interest groups act self-interestedly: they attempt to move public policy so it will favor those they represent. The early think tanks in particular sought to improve government not out of self-interest but out of an academically driven sense of improving the government.

The purposes are reflected in the means used. Although both institutions seek to educate the public and those who govern, their methods differ. The tools of interest groups are persuasion (lobbying), education, and pressure. The extreme form of their actions are found in PAC activities. This is the natural result of acting out of self-interest: specific outcomes are highly personalized. Because they presumably act disinterestedly, the think tanks use persuasion based in expertise and objective knowledge as their major tool.

Some of these distinctions may be vanishing as some think tanks begin to operate more and more like interest groups. The politically activist, and especially conservative, movement within the research institute community during the 1980s has produced a hybrid—the think tank with a specific political agenda. The tools may remain educational in the broad sense, but they result from directed research. This research is aimed not at increasing the general pool of knowledge, but at providing knowledge that reinforces political predilections. Once again, the Heritage Foundation stands at the forefront of this variant.

Finally, the two institutions form a bridge between government and the broader society that is the subject of Chapter 9. In broad terms, interest groups aggregate, articulate, and seek to influence the public at large. At the same time, the media are the object of some educational elements by both groups, and the growing phenomenon of the electronic expert provides a new linkage between the media and the think tanks.

SUGGESTED READINGS

Bayes, Jane H. *Ideologies and Interest Group Politics. The United States as a Special Interest State in the Global Economy.* Novato, CA: Chandler & Sharp, 1982.

Chittick, William O. *State Department, Press, and Pressure Groups. A Role Analysis.* New York: Wiley-Interscience, 1970.

Miller, Stephen. *Special Interest. Groups in American Politics.* New Brunswick, NJ: Transaction Books, 1983.

Ornstein, Norman J. *Interest Groups, Lobbying, and Policymaking.* Washington, DC: Congressional Quarterly Press, 1978.

Smith, James Allen. *The Idea Brokers. Think Tanks and the Rise of the New Policy Elite.* New York: Free Press, 1991.

Watson, Bruce W., and Peter M. Dunn (eds.). *Military Intelligence and the Universities. A Study of an Ambivalent Relationship.* Boulder, CO: Westview Press, 1984.

Weiss, Carol H. *Organizations for Policy Analysis: Helping Government Think.* Newbury Park, CA: Sage, 1992.

Zeigler, L. Harmon. *Interest Groups in American Society.* Englewood Cliffs, NJ: Prentice-Hall, 1964.

CHAPTER 9

Outside Influences II:
The Public and the Media

Within the philosophy underpinning the U.S. political system, sovereignty ultimately resides with individual citizens, who in turn delegate part of that sovereignty to government. Governmental authority to carry on the duties of the state, including the authority to conduct foreign and national security policy, flows from and is limited by the amount of sovereignty that has been ceded by the people.

Those who govern pay a price for being given the sovereign authority to govern in the form of the principle of *accountability*. According to this principle, the people reserve the right to inspect what their government does in carrying out the public trust and hence to decide whether or not it is doing the job correctly. On the basis of public assessment, those who govern can be deemed adequate and retained or removed from office.

The media, as provided for and protected by the First Amendment guarantee of a free and unrestrained press, assist the public in rendering its judgments by investigating and publicizing the performance of those who govern. Because a large part of the media's job is to act as a watchdog against incompetent or corrupt governmental action, a natural adversarial relationship exists between the *fourth estate* (a term for the press, first used in the nineteenth century to contrast it with the three classes of citizens of England) and those in government.

Difficulties in Applying Accountability

The relationship between the media and government is neither as simple nor as straightforward as it sounds, especially in the areas of foreign and defense policy. In order to begin to see the complication of the notions of authority and accountability between the government and the people, we look at three sources of difficulty: control of the foreign policy agenda, secrecy, and public ignorance of foreign policy.

Control of the Agenda

In the realm of foreign policy, unlike many domestic policy areas, Americans in or out of government do not always determine what kinds of problems they will deal with. Instead, in a great deal of foreign policy the agenda setters are foreign governments or elements within foreign countries who create situations to which the United States has to respond. Thus, the U.S. government had no control over whether or not the former state of Yugoslavia would dissolve in 1992. In fact, Secretary of State James Baker publicly hoped it would stay together as it was falling apart. The extraordinarily explosive and violent circumstances that arose as a result of that dissolution created the need to try to fashion an effective policy response that the government would have preferred not to have made, a process that continues amid partisan debate and even acrimony somewhat attenuated by the deployment of American troops to Bosnia.

The inability to control the agenda makes it more difficult to apply the principle of accountability. Foreign governments do at times act to make the U.S. government look better or worse, depending on whether a particular government likes or dislikes the administration in office or a policy being pursued. Officials in the former Soviet Union, for instance, regularly acted during presidential election years to put the incumbent in a better or worse light, depending on whether they felt reelection was in *their* best interest.

This problem of agenda control is likely to expand as the blurring between domestic and international politics continues. Decisions made in Tokyo or Berlin can have a real impact on the status and well-being of American citizens, from determining who will have jobs to what will be the cost of interest on automobile loans. Assessing whether or not government has performed admirably is very difficult under these circumstances.

Secrecy

A reasonable proportion of foreign policy, and especially national security policy, is conducted with at least some adversarial content. The ability to conceal what one knows and how one knows it often provides some advantage in dealing with other states. The problem is that the inability to know everything the policymaker does comes at the expense of the full ability to account for action. There is some trade-off between democratic accountability and security. The debate, especially in a post–Cold War world, is how much compromise of democratic ideals remains necessary.

The need to conceal has both legitimate and illegitimate bases. On the positive side, it is sometimes necessary to conceal information that provides the basis for making a decision because to reveal that basis would compromise the source from which it came. This is known as source sensitivity and provides much of the rationale for classifying (restricting access to) information within the intelligence community and the government more generally.

The conduct of diplomacy provides another legitimate example. When negotiating with another country, the negotiator is trying to obtain concessions that will move a situation as close to the national interest as possible. The nature of negotiation is give-and-take, in which each side is willing to compromise in order to get what it wants. One never, however, admits in advance how much one is willing to give away, because once that is revealed, there is nothing left to bargain about.

With even legitimate instances of secrecy, public assessment of performance begins with only a partial record of what happened. How can we know if a source has to be protected from exposure or recrimination? If we do not know the bargaining position our negotiators bargained from, how can we know if the deal they got was the best one possible? The answer, of course, is that accountability is left imperfect.

The negative side of secrecy is that it may be imposed for the wrong reasons, such as to obscure the government's incompetent or illegal actions. In the Iran-contra scandal, for instance, the facts of selling arms to Iran in exchange for assistance in gaining the release of hostages held in Lebanon and the diversion of arms-derived funds to the Nicaraguan contras were kept secret from the American people and Congress. At least part of the reason was that the people would not have approved of the actions, either on the grounds that it was ill-considered policy or that it violated policy and even law.

General Public Ignorance of Foreign Policy

Most analyses of what the public can and should do to affect and judge foreign and defense policy have concluded that the role has been and continues to be very limited, mostly in the form of passive reaction to initiatives made by the political executive.

The reason traditionally cited for the public's historical ineffectiveness in influencing the foreign policy process is their legendary ignorance of international affairs. A very small percentage of the population keeps abreast of foreign events, has traveled abroad, speaks a foreign language, or has taken formal courses at any level dealing with foreign cultures, history, or international relations. This ignorance, combined with widespread perceptions that foreign affairs are so intricate and involved as to be beyond the comprehension of the average citizen, reinforces the people's general ineffectiveness in influencing how government conducts foreign and national security affairs.

One of the central roles of the media is to try to reduce citizen ignorance. As a foreign policy actor, the media's relationship to the process contains several aspects. One of these aspects is whether the media are agenda setters, impelling consideration of policy activity by virtue of those events they cover, or whether they reflect the agenda presented by events and other policy actors. This question is of mounting importance because of global television's increasing proficiency at covering graphically the instability and violence that is sundering a number of newly formerly communist and other Second Tier states. In other words, would the international system have been forced to take any action in Bosnia and Herzegovina had the slaughter of civilians in Sarajevo not been an undeniable and unavoidable fixture of the nightly news? Television brought Somali starvation into American living rooms; similar privation in such places as neighboring Sudan go unreported and hence unnoticed by the public or policymakers. Does television make a difference?

The relationship between the media and those in authority is also relevant. As part of the scheme of things, this relationship is and should be a partly adversarial one, because part of the press's role is to expose governmental misdeeds and the attempts of officials to gain excessive power (the real concern of the Constitution's framers). The problem has become greater in recent years. On the one hand, Americans now have more media coverage of everything, including foreign and national security policy. On the other hand, the Vietnam and Watergate episodes greatly worsened relations between government and the media. In Vietnam, for instance, the media believed they had been duped into falsely reporting progress by the military before the Tet offensive of 1968 (an attack by the North Vietnamese that, if reported casualty figures had been truthful, they would not have had adequate personnel to stage). The media have been suspicious of military pronouncements ever since. For its part, many members of the military believed that the media's negative reporting of the war after Tet contributed to the American loss of the war. The most recent instance of this ongoing distrust was seen in military restrictions on press access to the battlefield in Operation Desert Storm.

The media's place can be viewed as triangular (although not as an iron triangle) as depicted in Figure 9.1. On one side of the triangle is the relationship between the public and the media. The main points of contention in that relationship include the degree to which the media provide the public with adequate and accurate foreign and defense policy information, the degree to which the public takes advantage of the information provided, and whether the media serve to lead or reflect public opinion (or both). The key new variable in the public–media relationship is the emergence in the last decade of the global electronic media and how this changes both the public's access to and awareness of foreign policy events and issues.

The second side of the triangle focuses on the relationship between the media and the government. The relationship is especially strained in the foreign and defense policy area because of the issue of secret (or classified) information. From the media's vantage point, very little information should be restricted, and entirely too much information is classified. The media have the further suspicion that restriction is too often not based on legitimate need but to cover up misdeeds. Moreover, the only people legally bound to maintain the secrecy of classified information are those who have voluntarily done so as a term of employment with the government. Members of the media do not fall under that restriction, which is a source of discomfort to those charged with maintaining the confidentiality of information.

The third side of the triangle is the relationship between government and the people. The media serve as a conduit in this regard, since most of what people know

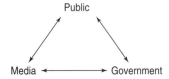

FIGURE 9.1   Public–Media–Government Relationships

about international affairs and the government's reaction to those events comes from the media. The major question is how well the media dispatch this role.

This brief introduction forms the basis of an inspection of both the public's and the media's role in the policy process. As stated at the outset, there is a conventional view of both, and especially of the public. Although we reiterate the basic elements of the conventional wisdom about each, we also explain how roles may be changing in the new international order.

The Public

For most of U.S. history, and certainly before World War II, the public played a minor role in the country's foreign policy. The major reason, of course, was that the public was only rarely affected by foreign policy occasions and hence had very little need or desire to be involved.

The permanent ascendance of the United States to a position of world leadership after World War II began the process of changing that attitude. As the leader of the Western coalition facing an apparently implacable Soviet enemy with whom war could come at any time, there was a need to convince the public that what the United States did in the world was morally right and necessary.

The question was the level and quality of public participation. At one extremity in the debate were the foreign policy professionals, who wanted the role to be as minimal as possible. Their most articulate spokesperson was George F. Kennan. He and others argued that the public role should be simply to accept and ratify the wisdom of the professionals. At the other extreme were more egalitarian voices who maintained that since it was the public that had to bear the burden of foreign policy decisions, it must be involved. The debate has never been resolved in a way that is acceptable to everyone.

One way to look at the traditional role of the public is as a parameter setter. Because the public does not possess great expertise in foreign affairs, it cannot set the agenda, nor is it likely to provide detailed guidance to policymakers. What the public can and does do, however, is to set broad outer boundaries (parameters) of policy that it will accept. Within those boundaries, policymakers have a reasonable discretion to act. When government exceeds those limits, its policy is in trouble. Government must therefore determine whether support will be forthcoming before it acts, especially if its actions will have a direct bearing on the citizenry. The U.S. government learned this lesson the hard way in the Vietnam War, where public opposition ultimately forced the United States to abandon the effort.

Interestingly enough, this relationship was stated in its most articulate form by a Prussian general staff officer over 150 years ago. In his seminal work, *On War,* Carl von Clausewitz identified a "holy trinity" without whose support governmental effort (in his case the conduct of war) could not be sustained successfully. The elements of the trinity are the people, the army, and the government. Clausewitz maintained that the active support of each segment was critical to success.

In retrospect, many observers, especially in the military, think the flaw in the Vietnam debacle was in ignoring the trinity. More specifically, the failure to activate public support (or opposition) before American intervention eventually led the public to turn on the war and the effort, as Clausewitz would have predicted, to collapse. That the military learned its lesson from Clausewitz and Vietnam was seen most forcefully in the Kuwaiti desert: the United States should never become involved in a major military effort again without an active show of support by the government and the people in the form either of a formal declaration of war or at least a mobilization of the body politic in the form of calling up the reserves.

This relationship between public and government was established in two ways. First, after Vietnam the armed forces were scaled down and restructured. Gen. Creighton Abrams restructured roles and missions of the active and reserve compo-

AMPLIFICATION

Political Democracies and Support for War

In all states, but especially in political democracies where the regime's ability to govern rests critically on the support of the population for its policies, public support for the decision to go to war is absolutely critical to a sustained military endeavor. In a work coauthored by one of the current authors (see box source), the basis for popular support was examined through the sweep of American history. The purpose was to determine what kinds of military adventures are and are not likely to achieve support.

The Clausewitzian dictum ("War is politics conducted by other means") captures the essence of why states (or groups within states) go to war: to attain some political objective they could not attain in another way. Thus, public support for war depends critically on articulating a political objective for fighting that the public will support. Looking at the American experience, four criteria for a good objective stand out. The first criterion is that the objective be simple,

nents of the army, so that critical roles were assigned mostly or entirely to the reserves. Thus, no major action could be undertaken without them. The effect was to ensure involvement at the grassroots level of society. If the American people did not want to send their friends and neighbors to war, they could let the system know before action was taken—by objecting to the mobilization.

Second, the Weinberger Doctrine, announced by Caspar Weinberger, President Reagan's secretary of defense, stated as Pentagon policy what Abrams had done operationally by laying out a set of criteria that had to be met before force should be employed. One of the major criteria was the assurance of broad and sustained public support.

Operation Desert Storm was the first application of this new understanding about the relationship between public and government. A first act in forming the force that would be dispatched to the Persian Gulf was a large-scale activation of reserve units. This was the first time the reserves had been called to overseas duty since the Korean War 40 years before. The reserves and the public acted favorably, thus giving the military the kind of assurance it sought.

Is the relationship between the government and the people on important foreign and defense policy concerns established in Desert Storm a precedent for the future or an aberration? Certainly, it met the criteria for a popular war discussed in the Amplification box "Political Democracies and Support for War." To assess that question, we need first to look at the traditional view of the public's role and then to show how that role is changing.

---

straightforward, and unambiguous: Americans must easily be able to understand why they are being asked to make the potential sacrifices war entails. Second, the objective should be morally and politically lofty: the proposed action must be for a cause construed as "good." Third, the objective must be seen as vital to the United States: the criterion here is importance. Finally, and overlapping the third, the objective must be seen to be in the interests of most Americans: the criterion of relevance.

To the degree these criteria are met, the result is likely to be public support. To the extent they are violated, the result is likely unpopularity. One other point should be added; the importance of the criteria relate directly to the length and degree of sacrifice an involvement entails. Generally speaking, the political democracies dislike long and bloody wars, and their support for them is directly tied to their importance as articulated by the four criteria for a good objective.

Source: Donald M. Snow and Dennis M. Drew, *From Lexington to Desert Storm: War and Politics in the American Experience.* Armonk, NY: M. E. Sharpe, 1994, pp. 14–16, 332–337.

The Traditional Role: Multiple "Publics"

Much of the traditional literature on the public and foreign policy has stressed not what the public can and should do, but the limitations on that role. The source of that limitation is the historically high degree of general citizen disinterest and ignorance of the subject matter, which some argue makes their meaningful participation impossible.

Citizen limitation is normally depicted by dividing the electorate into a series of segments, often visualized as a set of concentric circles, as shown in Figure 9.2. The diagram divides the population in terms of its level of interest and expertise, with levels increasing as one moves inward toward the center of the circle.

The Uninformed Public At the outer band of the circle is the uninformed (or inattentive) public. It is by far the largest portion of the population, encompassing 75 to 80 percent of the total. The uninformed public is defined as that portion of the population which does not regularly seek out information about international affairs. Operationally, this part of the public does not read stories about foreign affairs in newspapers or newsmagazines (if it reads these at all), does not read books on the subject, and avoids those parts of news broadcasts dealing with foreign policy.

Because of its lack of information, the uninformed public tends to become aware of or involved in foreign policy issues only under three circumstances. The first occurs when a foreign policy event has a direct bearing on people personally. Almost

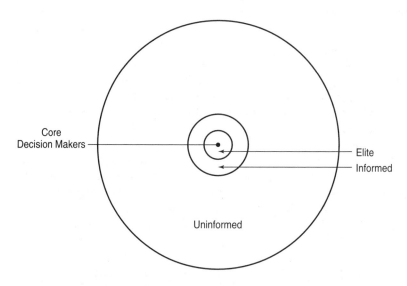

FIGURE 9.2   Foreign Policy "Publics"

30 years ago, conscription for the Vietnam War was of this nature, as was the boycott of the 1980 Moscow Olympics and, more recently, the mobilization of the reserves for Operation Desert Storm and Operation Joint Endeavor in Bosnia.

A second circumstance occurs when broad publicity is given to international events. Publicizing the plight of Kurdish refugees fleeing Saddam Hussein's forces in the wake of Desert Storm created a public awareness that would have otherwise been lost on all but the most dedicated student of foreign policy. The unrelenting daily barrage of reportage about the American hostages held in Teheran at the beginning of the 1980s was also impossible to ignore. Suffering in the Balkans presents a similar situation.

In the third circumstance, conscious efforts are made to mobilize public opinion by the government or others. This ploy is used in particular by incumbent presidents: it is usually true that the public is less critical of foreign policy actions than domestic actions and will generally rally behind the president in foreign policy matters. As a result, the president can often build a consensus behind his position that would be more difficult to build around a domestic policy. Richard Nixon's trip to Egypt in 1974 to divert attention from the Watergate scandal, which would shortly force his resignation from the presidency, is a particularly strong example. (His approval ratings in the polls temporarily rose over 20 points during the visit.) President Clinton's very vocal support for the North American Free Trade Agreement made it more difficult for opponents to rally support against it.

These efforts do not always work. During the heat of the presidential campaign in late June 1992, a beleaguered President Bush complained to a group of reporters that his foreign policy accomplishments appeared unappreciated by the public. Specifically, he commented, "We had [Russian President Boris] Yeltsin here in the Rose Garden, and we entered into a deal to eliminate the biggest and most threatening intercontinental ballistic missiles—the SS-11s of the Soviet Union—and it was almost 'Ho-hum, what have you done for me recently?'" (*New York Times*, July 1, 1992, p. A10). The point is that in a post–Cold War world, nuclear arms reductions probably do not qualify under any of the circumstances that activate the interest of the vast majority of the population.

The attention of the unattentive public is thus difficult to capture and tends to emerge only over large, highly visible events. For the most part, the attention provided by this group is sporadic, short term, and highly malleable. On the majority of foreign policy issues, members of this group simply have no coherent, elaborated opinions. Rather than being agenda setters in any sense of the term, they are much more likely to have their opinions shaped by others. Moreover, this group tends to be demographically distinct: lower educational and occupational attainment, geographic isolation from the major policy centers, and the like.

This grim depiction of the vast majority of the population's orientation toward foreign and defense policy forms the base for much of the elite critique of democratic participation in the foreign policy process. Indeed, as long as most of the population remains uninterested and unknowledgeable in this field, it is difficult to make a case for their inclusion as more than broad boundary setters. If one finds this situation both regrettable and unacceptable in a rapidly internationalizing community where foreign policy has direct and continuing relevance to all Americans, then we can raise the question—explored in the next section—of whether there are viable strategies for change.

The Informed Public   The second concentric circle in Figure 9.2 represents the informed (or attentive) public. As the diagram indicates, this is the second largest population segment, including 10 to 20 percent of the population. As the juxtaposition of titles suggests, the definition of the informed public is virtually the opposite of that of the inattentive public; members of the informed public do regularly seek out information on international affairs. They do so by reading foreign policy stories in newspapers and magazines and watching television coverage of international events.

Several groups of people typically fall into the ranks of the informed public. Local civic leaders who influence the opinions of their communities are one group, as are local journalists, clergy, and others to whom the public at large turns to help them form opinions.

For most members of the informed public, their contact with foreign policy events is indirect rather than direct. Generally, they have relatively few, if any, direct contacts with the process, although that is changing as more and more localities come into direct relationships with foreign investors or because a defense installation or defense contractor does business in their area. With some exceptions, however, this means that informed public members achieve their understanding of foreign and defense policy issues at second hand and vicariously rather than through personal self-action or self-interest.

This relationship to foreign and defense policy affects the informed public's quality and depth of understanding on these issues. With the exception of a foreign or defense policy that directly affects their lives (e.g., a foreign automobile manufacturer building a plant in their vicinity or a military base closing), members of the attentive public are likely to have general rather than detailed knowledge. A member of the clergy, for instance, may be aware of black on black violence as an historical inhibitor to change in South Africa; he or she is unlikely to associate the tribal roots of the two leading black movements in the country (the Xhosa-dominated African National Congress and the Zulu-based Inkthata Party).

The informed public does play a role in the foreign policy process. It does not set the agenda but is instead reactive: it learns generally of issues and expresses a general reaction that helps form the parameters within which policy can be crafted. At the same time, the status of members of the attentive public within their communities means that they inform other members of their community with less interest in issues and interpretations of those issues. As such, their role is to convey information and opinion.

The Effective Public   The third group is the effective (or elite) public. Defined as that part of the public which actively seeks to influence the foreign and defense policy process, this group consists of a relatively small number, generally considered as less than 5 percent of the overall population.

Frequently associated with the elite public are policymakers, national opinion leaders, and foreign policy experts. Policymakers, actual members of government at the national and, to a somewhat lesser degree, state levels are active in foreign policy matters but are not primarily foreign and defense policy experts (see the discussion of core decision makers later). Thus, for instance, a member of Congress from the upper Middle West will not necessarily be an expert on defense matters, but he or she does have a lively concern about European Union policies that effectively exclude American wheat from the European market. Similarly, the governor of a Sun Belt state has a multitude of domestic concerns that consume most of his or her energies, but textile imports and sales of citrus fruits to Japan also create a foreign policy interest.

The national opinion leaders are people whose positions and expertise make them molders of opinion and setters of agendas. Examples include members of the national media whose jobs bring them into direct contact with foreign and defense issues and personalities, or former government officials with recognized expertise — people such as Kissinger and Brzezinski.

Finally, the foreign policy expert community is made up of people who by training and experience have detailed knowledge but who do not happen to be in government. This group consists of scholars in relevant disciplines (international relations or economics, foreign or defense policy, contemporary diplomatic history), leaders of large interest groups with a direct foreign or defense interest, and experts in the research organizations or think tanks.

Distinguishing the effective public from the informed public is both their depth of knowledge and the centrality of foreign and defense matters to their personal and professional lives. Members of the elite public not only read national newspapers (e.g., the *New York Times,* the *Washington Post,* or the *Los Angeles Times*) and newsmagazines (*Newsweek, Time,* or *U.S. News and World Report*), but they also read (and write) articles in specialized journals (e.g., *Foreign Affairs, Survival*) and books on relevant subjects.

In addition, the professions in which the elite public involves itself lead to a certain level of activism and policy advocacy, for example, criticism of government policy and advocacy of alternative policies. This activity is often associated with being part of the "shadow government in waiting," those Democrats who are not in governmental positions during Republican administrations and vice versa. As such, individuals in this group can be the elite public part of the time and core decision makers at other times.

Given the need for access to information and the policy process, members of the elite public have historically been physically concentrated as well, especially on the

Eastern seaboard, notably Washington, D.C., and New York City, the nation's political and economic capitals, respectively. Journals like *Foreign Affairs* are regularly displayed on the newsstands of downtown Washington, for instance, and the Washington bureaus of the news networks provide excellent opportunities for exposure and influence for people such as the electronic experts we discussed in Chapter 8.

Core Decision Makers   The final group at the center of the series of concentric circles in Figure 9.2 are the core decision makers. Although they may not be a part of the general population per se, this group encompasses individuals responsible for actually formulating and executing foreign and defense policy. This group is also the smallest, numbering several hundred people within the government, because of the requirement of formulating policy. While almost every professional in the Department of Defense or State could be said to be involved in implementing policy at some level, the role of most of them is quite restricted. They essentially apply (implement) policy made by others (although they may have some input into the decisions made) rather than decide on basic policy. Those who actually make policy occupy key roles in both the executive and legislative branches. Within the executive, the most numerous are found at the levels of assistant secretary and above in the State and Defense Departments, the international divisions of other cabinet-level agencies, and the National Security Council staff. Within the legislative branch, the most prominent examples are the chairs and ranking minority members of the most important congressional committees and their senior staffs. Thus, the chairs and ranking opposition members of the Foreign Relations (International Relations in the House), Armed Services (National Security in the House), and Select Committees on intelligence, and the chairs of the appropriations subcommittees on defense and foreign policy matters are obvious examples.

The distinctions between core decision makers and elite public are also imprecise. Some individuals move back and forth between the two designations as their status changes and some people are not clearly and unambiguously in one or the other. The assistant secretary of defense for policy, the assistant secretary of state for Far Eastern affairs, or the chairs of the Foreign Relations or Armed Services committees clearly are part of the core by virtue of their positions. On the other hand, individuals with an interest and some expertise in the area are more difficult to locate. Before he became president, Bill Clinton was probably on the boundary between the elite and the informed public on foreign and defense matters, and Vice President Albert Gore was somewhere around the boundary between the elite public and the core decision makers.

This conventional analysis of the public's role is pessimistic and negative. It essentially argues that the vast majority of the population is uncaring and ignorant about foreign and defense policy issues to the point that their opinions can be largely ignored or easily molded to fit the policymaker's agenda. In this view, only those in the two inner circles—the elite public and the core—have the experience and expertise to make intelligent decisions on these issues. The view thus supports the elitist school of thought about the public role.

This is an unsatisfying situation in a rapidly changing world in which international affairs increasingly influence the public agenda and individual lives. A question that may reasonably be asked is whether this situation is acceptable in the world of the future and what, if any, signs of change may be on the horizon.

Sources of Change

The traditional absence of interest in foreign and national security policy among many Americans is grounded in their lack of knowledge of foreign affairs and their perception that this area of policy has no particular relevance for them. These two bases are, of course, linked: people do not learn about foreign affairs because of its seeming unimportance, and they do not know enough about foreign relations to realize its salience.

What can change these traditional attitudes? Is it possible for more uninformed Americans to become the informed public and for the informed public to move onto higher levels of involvement and understanding? While this matter is admittedly speculative, we can point to at least four forces that could make a dent in the ignorance/disinterest syndrome that has limited public effectiveness in the foreign policy arena: greater availability of information, educational reform, increased public awareness of the relevance of foreign policy, and attempts to mobilize public opinion.

Greater Access to Information   This factor is largely the product of the telecommunications revolution that is both intertwining the global economy and politics and producing a cascade of greater information about foreign and defense policy problems. President Clinton, as "seminar leader," has expanded his televised economics seminar to foreign policy more generally.

The key element here is global television, especially television operations such as CNN and the Independent Television Network (ITN), which both collect and disseminate the news worldwide. Moreover, a variety of related technologies including the video camcorder, satellite linkages, and fiber optics give television the ability to provide instantaneous coverage and transmission of events as they happen, thereby adding to the drama of breaking events.

The impact of all these changes on how both Americans and citizens of other countries are affected in terms of their attitudes to foreign affairs remains speculative. Moreover, we do not yet have a perspective on this technological revolution. CNN, for instance, did not exist 20 years ago, and the ability to provide instantaneous coverage over thousands of miles is even newer than that. The early derision of CNN has been quite overturned. When dramatic events occur around the globe, people turn in large numbers to CNN, as they did during the Persian Gulf War. As a result, many citizens have become more aware of events they previously had ignored.

Without Bernard Shaw's unrelenting coverage, for instance, would we have learned very much about the Chinese government's suppression of the "democracy movement" in Tiananmen Square in 1989? Of the plight of the Kurds in the wake of the Persian Gulf War in 1991? Of Serbian barbarity against the citizens of Bosnia and Herzegovina in 1992? At the same time, how much does selectivity of coverage (the slaughter in Mozambique, for instance, was not covered by the media and was ignored by governments) affect the foreign policy agenda? Global television cannot give the citizenry a sophisticated understanding of problems and policy, but it can whet people's appetites for knowledge and make ignorance less sustainable. To move greater numbers outside the ranks of the uninformed requires a second force: educational reform with an emphasis on international affairs.

Educational Reform   The need for educational reform has become a popular shibboleth of the 1990s, with President Clinton a leading standard-bearer. Spurred on by the dismal rankings of American children in science and mathematics compared to children in other countries, there is a clear mandate, if not funding base, to improve the educational system.

One area in which education has failed most emphatically is in giving the school-age population wide exposure to global problems. The litany is disturbingly familiar: less than 5 percent of American students study a foreign language (and far fewer become proficient), most students lack even basic geographical knowledge, and even among college students, less than 3 percent ever take a course in foreign affairs, international relations, or foreign culture.

That picture is changing, albeit slowly. At the collegiate level, increasing numbers of colleges and universities are adding an international education requirement to basic graduation requirements. Organizations such as the American Geographic Society are spearheading efforts to increase the international content of curricula at the high school level and earlier. For these efforts to be maximized, increased funding for education will be needed; funding has proven a major barrier in most states in the past several years.

Increased Relevance of Foreign Policy   The changing nature of the national security problem caused and stimulated by the collapse of communism has more than an abstract importance to U.S. citizens. In the absence of a Soviet enemy to confront, the United States needs less military personnel and hence less military equipment and support services, all of which have provided many jobs for Americans in the past. At a more specific level, the announcement in July 1992 that the United States would no longer produce the enhanced weapons-grade plutonium from which nuclear weapons are fabricated has direct implications for people in Rocky Flats, Colorado, and Oak Ridge, Tennessee, areas where those activities have traditionally been performed.

The globalization of economic activity has created the need for a more sophisticated understanding of international dynamics. Indeed, those who learn to take advantage of the emerging system will prosper and those who do not will suffer. The very public nature of Clinton's commitment to the economy will almost certainly lead to greater appreciation of the dimensions of the problem.

For this kind of emphasis, the state of South Carolina may provide a model. Over two decades ago South Carolina accelerated its involvement in international affairs using the James F. Byrnes Center at the University of South Carolina as a catalyst. The state has been highly successful in arranging trading relationships with foreign countries and in attracting desirable foreign investment in the state. When the first BMW automobile rolled off the Spartanburg, South Carolina, assembly line, it was a testimony to the power of international knowledge.

Mobilizing Public Opinion In the past national leaders appealed for overt mass public support only when the most dramatic and personal events occurred such as those involving peace and war. That situation will almost certainly change. Not only are international events more directly relevant and more visible to more Americans than before, but also the blurring of domestic and foreign policy means that more support will have to be generated to back those policies that could affect domestic priorities. The emergence of so-called humanitarian vital interests, with a heavy moral overtone that tugs at the public heart, represents an additional stimulus with which the Clinton administration has had to come to grips.

The case of assistance for Boris Yeltsin and the Russian Republic provides an example. Historically, a foreign state's request for aid would have been a routine matter and would not have generated much controversy. In a period of fiscal stringency in which domestic policy priorities were being neglected, however, aid to Russia has been juxtaposed with domestic needs. As some critics asked loudly and publicly, should the United States be underwriting change in the Russian economy when it cannot feed and house the homeless? Hardly anyone could argue that assisting Russia was a bad idea or not in the national interest, but enough were able to question the priority of the effort that Yeltsin was sent back to Russia in 1992 largely empty-handed.

If public awareness and participation in foreign and defense policy-making is to increase, then obviously the cycle of ignorance and disinterest will have to be broken. And if that is to happen, greater publicity will have to be given to foreign events, and more effective explanation of the salience of those events to people's lives will have to be presented. The media must play a leading role in that process.

The Media

Media is a shorthand term used to describe those individuals and organizations who collect and disseminate information (news) about what is happening in the world. The media are divided into the print media, consisting of newspapers and newsmagazines, and the electronic media, consisting of radio and television.

The Print Media

Of course, the print media are older than the electronic. Their independence to observe and report on the operation of government is included in the First Amendment of the Constitution, and it was justified as a way to prevent the undue accumulation of power by individuals or governmental institutions. Their independence is assured because all the print media are independently owned by individuals outside government and are unregulated by governmental agencies. The operative principle to ensure continued independence is the doctrine of "no prior constraint" on publication. This doctrine, first articulated in a 1931 Supreme Court case (*Near v. Minnesota*), states that there can be no prior censorship by government of reportage. (A practical exception is reportage of ongoing military campaigns that might provide information to the enemy.)

The print media cover foreign and defense policy through the flagship newspapers, newsmagazines, and the wire services. Probably the most influential are the flagship newspapers such as the *New York Times* and *Washington Post,* which have the time and resources to assign reporters and bureaus full time to coverage of foreign and international events, and the national newspapers, publications that do not have a specific geographical locale (*USA Today,* the *Wall Street Journal,* and the *Christian Science Monitor*). These are the newspapers read by people in the policy process, the elite public, and the better informed members of the attentive public. The function of the major newsmagazines is to provide depth and interpretation to events initially reported by the newspapers. Finally, the wire services, such as the Associated Press or Reuters, provide foreign and defense policy news to local newspapers that do not have the ability to collect and report on foreign affairs on their own.

The Electronic Media

The electronic media, unlike the print media, are subject to at least cursory regulation through the licensing process by the Federal Communications Commission (FCC). FCC regulations basically ensure that radio and television stations do not use transmission bands that interfere with one another's signals; less formally, in their reportage they are expected to honor the principles of equal time to political candidates, the right of rebuttal, and the fairness doctrine in reporting.

The electronic media cover foreign and defense policy issues through the major television and, to a lesser extent radio, networks and report the news to their affiliates. In addition, the emergence of CNN and ITN and other news-based networks has created more or less the equivalent of the national newspapers in the form of a television station devoted solely to the news. Finally, local television and radio stations rely on sources such as the newspaper wire services and television feeds to report foreign and defense news.

Role of the Media

The media's function in the area of defense and foreign policy, although still evolving, has been controversial. To understand how the media stand between the people and the government, we first look at the traditional functions the media performs, noting how they are influenced by the nature of international affairs. We then discuss how technological change, principally in the electronic media, is changing and expanding those functions.

Traditional View of the Media

The media basically observe and report the activities of government and the actions and thoughts of individual political figures. In this role, they are sometimes actively sympathetic and cooperative with those they report on, and sometimes they are not. The media also serve as watchdogs of the public interest, particularly in areas where they perceive the possibility of breaches of the public trust. In this role, the government and the media are almost always adversaries.

In reportage generally, but especially in the area of foreign and defense policy, the media do not communicate evenly with the entire public or even really attempt to do so. This is largely the result of the general public's lack of interest and the kinds of media that cover the area. Readership of the flagship newspapers, for instance, is demographically defined in terms of educational level, wealth, and means of livelihood, as is viewership of outlets such as CNN. In other words, the foreign and defense policy-reporting mechanism is directed at the relatively well educated and affluent, and it is transmitted through those channels that the educated and affluent read and watch.

Any attempt to harness the media to the task of broadening citizen awareness and participation in the foreign and defense policy process must begin with this awareness. Either broader segments of the public must be drawn to the national media, or foreign and defense reportage must be expanded in those channels from which the masses receive their information—local newspapers, local television, and local radio. Media activity in the foreign and defense policy area can be thought of in terms of five different functions.

Collection and Reportage of the News   Through this function, the media observe what the government (and the broader world) is doing and inform the public of those actions. Collection and reportage of the news is also presumably the most objective and least controversial, but the nature of foreign and defense occurrences complicates the straightforward reportage in several ways.

Specifically, too many events are happening worldwide for the media to cover simultaneously. Thus, the media are necessarily selective in what they cover and report, and some people inevitably conclude that not all the worthiest items are being covered. People in the Second Tier, in particular, complain that they receive media attention only in times of wars, natural disasters, and other cataclysmic events. The wide range of events that occurs worldwide does, however, stretch the resources of any news-gathering outlet to cover everything. Corporate buyouts and downsizing of network news (especially foreign news) divisions and the failure or buyout of many newspapers means that fewer reporters are available to cover foreign news stories, leaving the media increasingly reliant on foreign news organizations. Moreover, foreign events are often idiosyncratic and unpredictable, making orderly planning problematic. Another problem in coverage occurs because governments often seek to hide or obscure events that are unfavorable to them. The telecommunications revolution is making obscuring unpleasantries more difficult, however.

Investigation or Watchdogging   At the simple level of reportage, print or electronic journalists may do little more than reiterate what public officials tell them. By self-appointment, however, reporters feel the need to determine the veracity of public pronouncements and to report instances in which they believe the public trust has not been well served. This function, which has increased dramatically in the last quarter century, often places government officials and the media at loggerheads.

The event that more than any other triggered an adversarial and untrusting relationship between government and the media was the Vietnam War. In the early stages of the war (roughly 1965 through 1967), reportage of the war was largely favorable to the military; the press corps dutifully reported progress in the war based on briefings at Military Assistance Command Vietnam (MACV) in Saigon known as the "five o'clock follies." According to the progress reported to the media and transmitted to the American people, the enemy's forces were being rapidly depleted to the point that when U.S. commanding general William Westmoreland reported late in 1967 that he saw "the light at the end of the tunnel," the assertion was not widely disputed.

The Tet offensive of early 1968 broke the bond between the media and the government. When CBS anchor Walter Cronkite saw the first film footage of the Viet Cong in the American Embassy compound, he is reported to have said, "What the hell is going on here?" What was going on was the end of media trust in the government's conduct of defense and foreign policy. That relationship, and the media's consequent perceived need not to take the government at its word, was reinforced by events such as the Watergate scandal, the Iran-contra scandal, and the exclusion of the press from the U.S. invasion of Grenada in 1983 (the first reports of which were received in the United States over Radio Havana).

Interpretation   Because of the general public's ignorance of international affairs, explaining the flow of events is a particularly important function. Many people simply do not have the knowledge base to put foreign and defense policy questions in focus and perspective. In the absence of media interpretation, they would have only government officials, whose explanations are often motivated by self-interest, to provide context.

This function, although valuable, is also controversial because of the media's alleged ignorance of the subtleties and nuances of many foreign and defense issues. Most print and electronic journalists are not trained in foreign affairs any more than the average citizen is. The problem is even more severe in the defense policy area. Since the draft was rescinded at the end of 1972, most young Americans—including the vast majority of reporters—have had no military experience on which to base expertise. The media at least partially understand this deficiency, which helps explain why so many of the electronic experts covering the Persian Gulf War were retired military officers.

The national press, both print and electronic, is also alleged to have a liberal bias. Part of the basis for this claim is geographical: the national press is concentrated in New York and Washington, D.C., which are generally more liberal than much of the rest of the country. It is also partly the result of the fact that more liberal, reformist young men and women tend to be drawn to the media. Many members of the defense establishment believe this liberal bias is also antimilitary, thereby adding to the strained relationship between the media and the military.

Another consideration is that foreign and defense policy interpretation must occur largely in close proximity to events, when their full meaning cannot be known and when some or all of the parties involved may be directed to keep certain facts secret. The danger of the media's "instant analysis" is that when false interpretations of events are offered and accepted, they may continue to affect perceptions even after corrections have been made. When the government itself takes actions to withhold information from the media, thereby crippling its ability to interpret—as often occurs in military operations—the potential for friction between officials and the media is magnified.

Influencing Public Opinion on Issues   Like all the other functions, influencing public opinion is tinged in controversy. Whether the media do in fact influence opinion or whether they simply reflect the opinions that they believe the public already holds is a matter for some debate, as discussed in the accompanying Case in Point box "Electronic Media and the 'Do Something Syndrome.'" The overt expression of opinions occurs primarily on the editorial pages of newspapers, but how many people read or are influenced by editorial positions? Journalists claim that the influence is minimal or even nonexistent, but those in government believe that the editorial power of the national flagship newspapers or the television networks is very great.

Some of the media's critics also point out that the press has power to influence and does not have to bear responsibility for the consequences of advocacy. In this argument, political leaders' statements of opinion have personal consequences; if poor policies are advocated, the voters can demand retribution. However, when

---

CASE IN POINT

Electronic Media and the "Do Something Syndrome"

In the early post–Cold War period, television coverage of a series of instances of great human suffering, even atrocities, in places like the Kurdish areas of Iraq and Turkey, Somalia, and Bosnia, seemed to created a phenomenon that can be called the "do something syndrome." The structure of the situation and the will to respond was similar in each case.

Whether the visible problem was Kurds dying on Turkish mountainsides, starving Somalis, or Serbian detention camps, the revealing of great suffering created an overwhelming urge to alleviate the situation. Thus, troops were sent to Turkey and eventually moved the Kurds back into Iraq under allied (American, British, and French) protection, and the United States and others intervened in Somalia. Only in Bosnia was effective action not taken until late 1995.

The problem with doing something was that while it might relieve the symptoms of underlying malaise, it could not treat the more complex underlying causes: the ongoing civil war between the Kurds (with their dreams of autonomy) and the government in Baghdad, or the virtual anarchy in Somalia. Unable to attend to those underlying conditions, the United States has backed away from these kinds of operations, recognizing their intractable nature. In the process, the "do something" syndrome has been replaced with the "let's appear to be doing something" syndrome where great concern, but little action, is taken.

William Randolph Hearst created the bandwagon that forced President William McKinley to declare war on Spain, McKinley, not Hearst, would have been forced to bear the consequences had the action proven unsuccessful. Of course, the extent of this problem relates directly to the extent of power the media are believed to have.

In this connection, there is the question of how the media seek to influence opinion. In the traditional sense, the editorial page of the newspaper or clearly identified electronic media editorials have been considered legitimate, provided fairness and access by other opinions are available. The controversy emerges when editorial bias sneaks into the objective "news hole" in the form of biased selection of stories and reportage, and the like. The question that arises then is whether the media are serving the function of informing or whether they are propagandizing. This same criticism is also directed at television news analysis shows such as *60 Minutes* and *20/20*.

Agenda Setting   The media try to influence what important issues become part of the public agenda, how the public should perceive these agenda items, and what policy outcomes are desirable. The problem enters in when media attempts to frame issues collide with government efforts to frame the agenda.

Instances of this collision in the foreign and defense arena are legend and are often most heartfelt. The modern prototype was Vietnam, especially after the Tet offensive of 1968. Beyond the simple disillusionment with the military's truthfulness on that occasion, many members of the media came to believe that the war was unwinnable and U.S. withdrawal was the proper course. This conclusion was openly expressed and was reflected in the kind of stories chosen and in the way those stories were presented. The media can also change its minds quickly, altering its projected images of events. Despite coverage that bordered on cheerleading in support of intervention in Somalia, within days of its authorization leading columnists and the editorial page of the *New York Times* were already questioning the attainability of the political objective.

This problem, which often manifests itself in the media's alleged distortions of complex realities, is especially serious for television, particularly at the national level. Foreign and defense issues are normally complex and controversial, requiring considerable sharing of information with a public that is unequipped to make its own judgments. Television, on the other hand, is the medium of the short, pithy explanation; the 45-second sound bite with a vivid optical imprint, the specialty of television, is quite unlike the leisurely analysis provided by a *New York Times* or *Newsweek* feature. Network news stories are rarely more than a minute and a half long, and that may not be long enough to form other than cursory impressions.

Although brief, the impressions created by the visual media can be very strong and influential, especially when violence and suffering are depicted. A 30-second film clip of Bosnians being attacked on the streets of Sarajevo can create an enormously strong anti-Serbian reaction that may or may not be justified. It can also impel governments into action and lead to strong public appeals to force government actions, as occurred when CNN showed pictures of the Kurds in southern Turkey as Saddam Hussein's forces reacted to their uprising following the end of the Persian Gulf War. U.N. secretary Boutros-Ghali, in a 1993 interview, argued such reporting piqued the public conscience and forced leaders to react.

These examples of media activity and its impact are traditional, the stuff of journalism textbooks. A whole new area of possible activity is being created by the fruits of the high-technology revolution manifested in the telecommunications revolution.

Impact of the Telecommunications Revolution

As noted earlier, a series of technologies associated with the enormous growth in knowledge generation, dissemination, and assorted derivative technologies is transforming the modern world of production, economics, and communications. This high-technology revolution is being aided by advances in telecommunications and substantially enhancing the ability to acquire and disseminate information, which is the heart of the media's role.

The electronic media are the major beneficiaries of this process. In subtle ways that neither practitioners nor theoreticians yet understand, these advances are changing the international affairs that are the substance of foreign and defense policy, as well as the way policy is made.

Because we currently lack a theoretical understanding of this phenomenon during the 1980s and 1990s, we can only view the impact impressionistically, using examples. To that end, we now explore how the telecommunications revolution is transforming foreign and defense policy by strengthening the role of the media or downgrading the importance of more traditional policy mechanisms.

Increased Ability to Influence Events   Global television represented by outlets such as CNN is a prime factor in this increased influence. Telecommunications advances have made the world increasingly transparent to media coverage and reportage. When we combine the ability to reach out almost everywhere with technologies such as the video camcorder, there is very little which happens in the world that the media miss. That fact in and of itself affects what and how governments do their business.

Possibly the most dramatic instance of this transparency occurred in the summer of 1991 in Moscow, where a group of conspirators launched a temporarily successful coup against then Soviet president Mikhail S. Gorbachev. In earlier days, when the media could be and were excluded from the inner workings of the former Soviet government, this event might have proceeded quietly, and countercoup activities such as Russian president Boris Yeltsin's very public resistance might have been brutally suppressed.

But this time worldwide television was there, and the coup leaders did not know what to do about it. Reporters covered and transmitted live visual images everywhere, and the coup leaders flinched. The day after the coup took place, the collective leadership felt obliged to hold a televised live news conference explaining that there really had not been a coup and promising to restore Gorbachev after he recovered from his supposed illness. At that point the coup was doomed. Conversely, television coverage of Russia's brutal (if inept) suppression of the Chechen Republic's attempted secession in 1994–1996 embarrassed Yeltsin and limited his policy options.

That is not the only example. Although we may not know for certain for a long time, the Eastern Europeans' complete rejection of communist leaderships in 1989 and 1990 must in part be attributed to their access to Western European television and the glaring disparities it revealed in the standard of living in the East. The only leader who lied and denied the disparities was Romania's Nicolai Ceausescu; he was also the only leader executed by his own people. One clear outcome of the telecommunications revolution is that it will be increasingly more difficult for governments to suppress information—to lie—which has always been a major tool of authoritarian governments.

Impact on the Policy Process   One way in which the impact on the policy process occurs most strongly is through a phenomenon known as media diplomacy, whereby governments conduct some of their relationships with other governments by sending information back and forth about positions and the like through interviews with CNN and other outlets. The media also intrude through the extensive coverage of diplomatic negotiations that until very recently were always held in heavily guarded secrecy.

Relations between the United States and the former Soviet Union illustrate the use of the media as a conduit for information between governments. For example, in 1991, on the eve of Gorbachev's visit to the United States to conclude negotiations on strategic arms reductions (START), the Soviet government apparently had a last-minute change of position on one of the important issues to be discussed. The problem the Soviets now faced was to relay this change to the highest levels of the U.S. government in the most efficient way possible. The traditional method would have been to call in the U.S. ambassador and ask him to transmit the message back to Washington. Feeling this method would be too slow, the Soviets instead called the CNN Moscow bureau chief, who reported the story quickly on the network. The Soviets doubtless sought out CNN because they knew President Bush was an avid CNN watcher. In a similar vein, President Bush used global television to voice his displeasure with the attempted coup against Gorbachev.

The extensive coverage of diplomatic events also represents change. It has always been a canon of diplomacy that it should be as quiet and confidential as possible, thereby creating an atmosphere of candor and flexibility in which compromises can be reached. (If positions are publicly known, compromise becomes more difficult because then it becomes necessary to back away from original positions, thus giving the appearance of losing ground.) Massive media coverage has changed that. It is not unusual for negotiators to end their sessions with a press conference to discuss what happened in the meeting, a heretofore unthinkable idea. Events such as the Earth Summit in the summer of 1992 were as much media events as anything else.

Public figures are still in the learning stages of being television actors. When Saddam Hussein held the British children—his effective hostages—on his lap during the early stages of Desert Shield, he probably thought he was being reassuring, but it did not come off that way. By contrast, as president-elect, Clinton skillfully used his conduct of the Little Rock seminar to demonstrate to the public and to Wall Street, too, his seriousness, maturity, and grasp of complex economic issues.

The Media as Part of the Process   At one level, the way the media cover events influences public perceptions and thus helps structure the responses that government can make. At the same time, media figures such as ABC's Ted Koppel, through the *Nightline* program, actually become active parts of the process. Koppel has held teleconferences with participants in disputes on late-night television that have earned him the nickname of "television's secretary of state."

The impact of such activity is not well established, but it is undoubtedly substantial. Certainly, media coverage of natural or human-made disasters creates a vividness of perception, as well as a common view of events, that would not be possible in the absence of those images. Our picture of the Balkan disaster in Bosnia and Herzegovina, for instance, would have been much more clouded had it occurred 30 years ago, or especially nearly 80 years ago, when the result was World War I.

The Media as Publicist, Interpreter, and Agenda Setter   As a result of the global reach of the electronic media, the volume of material to which the public and policymakers are potentially exposed will continue to expand exponentially. Through their choices of what to publicize among a volume of events and issues beyond their ability to broadcast and the public's capacity to absorb, the media will help define the public agenda. This same increased volume and diversity of coverage will also mean that the public will be exposed to more and more unfamiliar situations for which they will require interpretation. The media are logical candidates for at least part of that role.

The emergence of 24-hour-a-day news broadcasting outlets such as CNN and its clones will create a much larger news hole for the media to fill. Thus, coverage will have to be expanded to areas that have not heretofore received very much coverage. On a global level, the ripe candidate will be the Second Tier (much of Asia, Africa, Latin America), which has been demanding greater exposure of its problems and will almost certainly get it. Once again, the problem lies in the shortage of expertise in the public that requires the media to explain what television is covering.

A beneficiary of this factor is almost certainly going to be the electronic experts, those academics from the universities and think tanks, former government officials, and retired military officers who possess knowledge of global issues that the media staffs frequently do not have. This factor is almost sure to become more prominent as the media expand their coverage to ever more distant corners of the globe.

These are only a few suggestions of how the media will become more important in the future. How its role will evolve is difficult to predict: the pace of technological, economic, and political change is so rapid that establishing a sense of direction is almost impossible—and precise prediction is fool's work. For example, if someone had predicted five years ago that a coup against a democratizing government in the Soviet Union would be foiled at least in part because of the Western news media's live coverage of the event, who would have believed it?

Conclusions

The roles of both the public and the media in the foreign and defense policymaking process are changing. In the past the traditional roles of both were relatively modest. The general public was basically compliant and reactive, allowing the elite to craft policy unless it went beyond public tolerance written in the most general terms. As for the media, it always focused more on the domestic agenda because it lacked the physical and technological ability to report extensively and in a timely fashion on all but a thin slice of international reality.

Both circumstances have changed. As the boundary between domestic and foreign policy has blurred and the direct, personal impact of foreign policy has increased, so has the public interest. In the days of the Cold War, the content of what the public was exposed to was more heavily oriented toward national security. With the Cold War over, international economic foreign policy factors are more important, as are glaring abuses of the human condition. These are less abstract and more personal: they affect jobs and livelihoods and hence have greater salience than, say, the deterrent effect of a particular ballistic missile.

From this change may come greater public interest in foreign and defense policy, gradually widening the population that forms the attentive public. Academics and others have been calling for such interest in the past with little effect; direct personal self-interest may provide a more effective lever.

The telecommunications revolution has been more important in expanding the media's role in the foreign and defense policy area than in domestic politics. All its advances are enhancing the ability to cover the domestic scene, but that ability was already present in abundance. The capacity to cover and interpret foreign policy events was always more circumspect, bounded by the speed with which oral descriptions and pictures could be transmitted from the far-flung corners of the globe. Technology has now made it as physically possible for news organizations based in New York or Washington to air news about events in Africa as it is to cover occurrences in Ohio.

The media's coverage of the 1992 election marked the beginning of a new relationship between politicians and the media. The extensive use of free guest appearances on shows like *Larry King Live* by Bill Clinton and H. Ross Perot showed that politicians had attained a new awareness of how to coopt the media, a phenomenon that will be even more prominent in the 1996 campaign. In effect, they turned a campaign into entertainment. The success of the Perot infomercial suggests a format that Clinton and future presidents may want to use to educate and influence the public on complex foreign and defense issues.

The public and the media share more than an individually enhanced role in the foreign and defense policy-making process. Their roles are also intertwined. A basic limitation on the public's ability to receive and interpret information in the past was access to information in a timely way. Ten years ago, for instance, it was not technologically possible to buy today's *New York Times* in almost any community and CNN was a struggling infant considered primarily an oddity. Today, one dollar will buy today's *Times* nearly everywhere, and over 50 million American homes receive CNN. In other words, the availability of timely information has exploded.

Neither the public nor the media will likely dominate the foreign and defense policy-making process anytime soon, if ever. Although the greater public knowledge of issues provided by the media is not a threat to the roles of formal governmental institutions and experts, the government must be more aware and sensitive than before, which is what democratic government is about.

SUGGESTED READINGS

Almond, Gabriel. *The American People and Foreign Policy*. New York: Harcourt, Brace & World, 1950.

Bailey, Thomas A. *The Man in the Street: The Impact of Public Opinion on Foreign Policy*. New York: Macmillan, 1948.

Brody, Richard A. *Assessing the President: The Media, Elite Opinion, and Public Support*. Stanford, CA: Stanford University Press, 1991.

Cohen, Bernard C. *The Press and Foreign Policy*. Princeton, NJ: Princeton University Press, 1963.

Cohen, Bernard C. *The Public's Impact on Foreign Policy*. Boston: Little, Brown, 1973.

Graber, Doris A. *Public Opinion, the President and Foreign Policy*. New York: Holt, Rinehart & Winston, 1968.

Landecker, Manfred. *The President and Public Opinion: Leadership in Foreign Affairs*. Washington, DC: Public Affairs Press, 1968.

Rosenau, James N. *Public Opinion and Foreign Policy: An Operational Formulation*. New York: Random House, 1961.

Rosenau, James N. *National Leadership and Foreign Policy: A Case Study in the Mobilization of Public Support*. Princeton, NJ: Princeton University Press, 1963.

Smith, Perry M. *How CNN Fought the War. A View from the Inside*. New York: Carol, 1991.

Spragens, William C. *The Presidency and the Mass Media in the Age of Television*. Washington, DC: University Press of America, 1979.

Wittkopf, Eugene R. *Faces of Internationalism: Public Opinion and American Foreign Policy*. Durham, NC: Duke University Press, 1990.

CHAPTER 10

Security in a Changed World

During the Cold War, as we noted in Chapter 1, *foreign policy* and *national security policy* were virtually synonymous and, in fact, the two terms were often used almost interchangeably by scholars and practitioners. The reason was obvious: the most important foreign policy problem facing the United States was its relationship with the Soviet Union; that relationship was, for most of the Cold War, defined primarily in security terms; and the failure of that policy had potentially catastrophic consequences. As a result, the lens of national security was the screening device for measuring policy across the policy spectrum.

Because of this preoccupation, security concerns have been the most unsettled in the wake of the end of the Cold War. Structural effects have extended to the organization and staffing of major governmental agencies like the Defense Department and the CIA and in the renaming and partial reorientation of relevant parts of the congressional committee structure (notably in the House of Representatives). Those outside the formal structure of government increasingly ponder new foreign policy agendas and policy emphases, without evident consensus.

The process of flux is ongoing, and to this point no new consensus has emerged about the national security component of American foreign policy. At least in part, the reason for this is the lack of agreement about what the new world looks like. During the Cold War, the environment may have been hostile, but it was also orderly and relatively unchanging. A new crisis might emerge occasionally that would require some policy adaptation, but in the main, the enemy was clear, the threat was evident, and the policy response flowed from an accepted vision of the environment.

The absence of such orderliness has left many, like political scientist John Mearsheimer, to ponder in a 1990 *Atlantic Monthly* article titled "Why We Shall Miss the Cold War." The new system lacks the clear organizational structure of what it supercedes; events and threats seem almost random, and wars pop up like summer thundershowers in unpredicted places, many of which Americans are unfamiliar with. The new rules of conduct have not clearly been defined in an environment where old animosities subdued by the old system spring forward in gruesome vividness. The confusion is captured by the lack of an agreed on descriptive term to label the new system: calling it the post–Cold War world only tells us what it is not, not what it is.

No part of the foreign policy process and substantive policy has been more affected by change than the national security establishment. It was absolutely focused on the Cold War to the exclusion of other concerns, all of which were considered (probably rightly) as subservient. Thus, the CIA is faced with a great glut of Soviet and East European analysts and hardly anyone who understands central African violence.

Because change has hit them hardest, both those who make and those who implement national security policy have been especially vulnerable. The national security policy complex is inherently conservative, since its failure can have the direst of consequences. This caution is particularly evident among those who implement that policy, those within the armed services themselves. Their missions had been well defined, they had prepared well and diligently to carry them out, and suddenly their raison d'être has evaporated before their very eyes. Everyone agrees there has been great change in the system, but not what change means for the warriors. Unfortunately, so many of those who make and implement policy are themselves "cold warriors" (people whose intellectual foundations were formed during the Cold War) that they have a difficult time making the necessary adjustments.

This chapter identifies and explores the national security policy problem in the post–Cold War world. We begin by looking at the new world of tiers through the clarifying lens of American interests and threats to those interests. Have U.S. interests changed significantly now that the Cold War is over, or is it the threats that have changed? Can or should the United States expand those situations with national security implications in which Americans take an active interest?

The discussion then moves on to some national security concerns left over from the Cold War. As we noted in Chapter 3, NATO and the security of Europe and Russia remain concerns, if at a lower level of urgency than when they were the major focus of policy. At the same time, nuclear weapons and their control remain viable matters, especially the potential spread of weapons of mass destruction to often volatile current nonpossessors. Regional conflicts that pitted old rivals have receded somewhat now that the United States and the Soviet Union are no longer available to act as opposing sponsors, but some, notably the Persian Gulf and the Korean peninsula, have residual interest.

Next, we look at the new pattern of violence since the end of the Cold War. With the withdrawal of the Cold War rivalry from much of the Second Tier and the end of communist control in the Soviet Union and elsewhere, a new pattern of primarily internal wars has emerged. Unlike the classic revolutionary wars employing some variations of the Maoist mobile-guerrilla warfare strategy, these wars are more chaotic, more merciless and bloody, and often more senseless than those before. If one was to try to draw a Cold War analogy, it would be the Khmer Rouge orgy of murder in Cambodia, but even that does not capture the blood lust of Rwanda or the politically vacant movements of so-called revolutionary armies like the "Lord's Army" of

Uganda, whose sole purpose is to destabilize the east African country, presumably to promote the rise of Islamic fundamentalism. The major question for the United States is the degree to which it wants to engage in a broader international effort to deal with these kinds of situations, if it wants to become involved at all. Although the reputation of the United Nations and the concepts of peacekeeping and peace enforcement have become somewhat tarnished due to the bumbling conceptual and physical performance of the world body in Bosnia, both the United Nations and U.N.-sponsored or sanctioned actions remain part of that decision complex.

This examination of the environment does not produce a clear photograph of its contours, but rather resembles a patchwork quilt of contrasting colors and patterns. Our final concern in this chapter is to try to organize this untidy reality into some form of order with which national security policy can deal. What replaces the foreign policy of containment as a guiding hand? If the military strategy of maintaining Soviet force within its existing boundaries produced the heart of Cold War grand and military strategy, what principles guide that strategy now? Strategy, in turn, is supposed to provide guidance for military roles and missions: what may armed forces be expected to do in the future? It is not clear. In turn, those roles and missions provide the "walking orders" for sizing and preparing military forces. For what actions should Americans be prepared in the future?

The Altered Setting of National Security Policy

The Cold War had a deductive orderliness and symmetry of interest and threat that is totally missing in the current milieu. As a result, the entire process was orderly and determinant, virtually down to the last soldier. We knew the problem, we prepared for it, we practiced, and we even depicted it in film (*The Day After* dealt with a nuclear attack on Lawrence, Kansas) and in print (Sir John Hackett's 1978 *The Third World War,* for instance).

We are back to square one conceptually. Instead of the situation where the most important U.S. interests were those most threatened, the opposite is true. Moreover, up to now public and policy elites agreed on this importance. Hence, national security policy rested on a reasonable consensus that went beyond partisan concerns and debates about it, to a great extent, ended at the water's edge.

To see what has changed, we must begin by defining terms. A *national interest* is a situation or condition important to the state (a condition in which it has an interest). The state is not, however, equally interested in all conditions everywhere in the world, and thus establishes priorities that help define the amount and kind of effort it will expend to realize those interests. Donald Neuchterlein (see Suggested Readings) suggests a hierarchy based on two axes: content of the interest (defense of homeland, economic well-being, promotion of national values, and favorable world order), and the intensity of the interest (survival, vital, major, and peripheral).

The meanings of the content differentiations are intuitive: defense of homeland refers to protecting national territory from outside attack (clearly the most important interest without which others pale by comparison), economic well-being refers to the ability to promote the economic good, and so on. The intensity distinctions, especially when combined with the content variables, are both more basic and less intuitively obvious, in fact helping to define the debate over national security.

Physical survival refers to the ability to guarantee that the state persists as an independent entity, and it clearly relates to the defense of the homeland. The next level of intensity, vital interests, is the most important in a national security sense. A vital interest is a situation or condition that is so important, a state will not *willingly* compromise on it and will take all necessary action, up to and including the use of military force, to realize the interest. The term *willingly* is highlighted because there may be circumstances where a condition is intolerable but must be accepted because a state lacks the relevant power to realize its interest. (In fact, some analysts simply define a vital interest as a situation or condition worth going to war for. We do not employ that definition because of its implied circularity: a vital interest is one worth fighting over; if we are fighting, whatever it is we are fighting about must be vital.) Major intensity refers to situations or conditions that, if not realized, would be harmful but tolerable; peripheral interests would inconvenience the state or its citizens but little more.

These distinctions, rooted deeply in the realist paradigm of the world, are critical to understanding national security and to our previous observation that in the post–Cold War world the realists have often become doves (opponents of using force) and the idealists are often hawks (proponents of force).

The key question in national security policy is the location of the line dividing situations important enough or not to employ armed force to guarantee their realization. Clearly, all but the most devout pacificists would include the physical survival of the state as meeting the test of vitality and would hence justify the use of armed force. With that circumstance established, the debate becomes over what other conditions may warrant the use of force to secure. For most Americans during the Cold War, an independent Western Europe was considered vital to the United States for political, economic, and cultural reasons, and the same is true about northeastern Asia (Japan and South Korea). President Carter added access to Persian Gulf oil to the list of vital interests in 1990 (the Carter Doctrine).

Are there other areas of the world wherein particular sets of conditions are important enough to justify, even compel, the United States to threaten or use military force to protect its interests? This is the basic security question, and it is one on which people legitimately disagree. In fact, one way to think about the debate over national security is to conceptualize it as a disagreement about where to draw the line between vital and major interests (in Neuchterlein's terms), which is not so much a line but a confidence interval within the boundaries of which the debate proceeds.

An example may help clarify the debate over locating the line. Almost everyone would agree that it is in U.S. best interests for there to be peace and stability throughout the Western Hemisphere for security and economic reasons. But just *how* important is that condition? Clearly, it depends to some extent on which states one is talking about, since some are closer physically and economically to the United States than others.

The issue moved beyond the abstract during the early and mid-1980s over the issue of the Marxist Sandinista government in Nicaragua. One clear way to define conditions the United States found desirable and undesirable in Latin America was the existence of Marxist, and especially communist, governments in the hemisphere. Already stuck with a full-blown communist state 90 miles from the Florida coast in Cuba that was providing support for the Sandinistas, the questions were, how intolerable is another Marxist state in the hemisphere, and what was the United States willing to do to secure U.S. interest in a noncommunist hemisphere? Was the existence of a Marxist (and potentially full-blown communist) regime a major or vital concern to the United States?

There was partisan disagreement on the issue. The Reagan administration, including the president himself, apparently decided the situation was important enough to commit the United States to the overthrow of the Sandinistas. To this end, it created, recruited, trained, and equipped an armed opposition movement, the contras, to attempt a military toppling of the Sandinista regime (thereby implicitly defining the interest as vital). Others, notably a number of congressional Democrats, disagreed, arguing that the Sandinistas were no more than an annoyance, there was no domino effect by which the fall of Nicaragua to communism would be followed by other communist triumphs in Central America (as some in the administration argued), and the risk of becoming involved with American forces directly outweighed the benefits of being rid of the Sandinistas. Based on this conviction that the problem was at most major in intensity, the Congress passed a series of resolutions (the Boland amendments to the appropriations bill) forbidding the physical support for the contras by the government. Covert evasions of those provisions became the basis for the Iran-contra controversy.

Another example of a debate that can be framed in these terms is the question of granting full membership to Eastern European countries within NATO. To do so would mean extending the security umbrella and, with it, the tacit commitment to defend these countries against attack. The result would be an expansion of American vital interests. Whether the American public will support this change in the structure of U.S. interests will be seen when NATO finally considers their applications for membership.

The potential expansion of NATO notwithstanding, one of the major characteristics of interests — at almost any level of intensity but especially vital interests — is that they are relatively unchanging. Access to the market democracies of Western Europe and northeastern Asia was vital to the United States throughout the Cold War (and before, certainly in the case of Western Europe), and it remains so today. The only acknowledged vital interest the United States has added since 1950 is the Persian Gulf, whose promotion was a combination of growing dependency on petroleum as an energy source and gradual exhaustion of economically viable U.S. reserves.

What *has* changed is the structure of threats to American interests. Here we reintroduce a concept raised in passing earlier: the *interest-threat mismatch*. Unlike the situation of Cold War symmetry described earlier, the United States is faced with the mismatch: the most important U.S. interests are hardly threatened; and the threats that exist are hardly interesting. What does this mean? If we look at the traditional areas of American interest, they are all part of the First Tier, which is the most peaceful part of the world. The places where the United States would be most willing to use armed force are the places it is least likely to be called on to use force. The exception, of course, is the Persian Gulf, where the prospect of renewed hostilities is at least high enough to create some symmetry between interests and threats. (We consider the other possible overlap, Korea, in the next section.)

The threats within the system, conversely, come in places and within situations outside the traditional range of important American interests. As we noted earlier, most of these are internal wars where various groups vie for political control and the United States has few, if any, geopolitical or economic stakes in the outcome. Who (if anyone) finally prevails and gains control and establishes a government in Somalia will not affect many Americans very much, and the same is true of ongoing violence in most of central Africa and the southern successor states of the Soviet Union. Where there are threats, there are no interests worth committing forces.

This change in affairs has created a new debate that has contributed to the inversion of positions within the realist-idealist disagreement. From a strictly realist viewpoint, the only times in which American armed force should be considered for involvement is when American vital interests are at stake. During the Cold War, this position was associated closely with a promilitary, prodefense stance, since the threats to American interests were generally all to vital interests. This situation was usually defined in communist-anticommunist terms, which occasionally, as in Vietnam, got the United States into situations of questionable interest. Nonetheless, it provided a set of guidelines that made the position of the realists hawkish (highly supportive of military force).

The realist position on the use of force has not changed; the situation has changed. The same realists who were military activists during the Cold War now counsel caution in the use of force, for the same reasons they employed before. The difference is that there are few vital interests threatened and, in agreement with the realist position, they urge caution before putting American forces in harm's way when the United States has little to gain. Opposition to American military involvement in the tragedy of Bosnia is a good example.

The situation is virtually reversed for idealists. During the Cold War, idealists rejected the realist analysis claiming it tended to perpetuate a status quo in an international system in need of improvement, it promoted military solutions to problems with potentially devastating consequences (like World War III between the superpowers), and it hence deemphasized cooperative international solutions to problems.

The changed structure of threat creates a different set of consequences for the idealists. Although acknowledging the realist assessment of traditional threats, idealists—with their penchant for reform—see conditions and situations in the new environment that cry out for change and where attempts at reform are now feasible. Foremost among these new circumstances are the enormous violations of basic human rights that have surrounded many of the internal wars in the Second Tier and the opportunity to help end the suffering of people in places like Somalia, Rwanda, and Bosnia.

U.N. secretary-general Boutros Boutros-Ghali has been a major champion of this new category of "humanitarian vital interests," conditions of humankind that transcend traditional structures of interest consideration and can only be addressed by international effort, including the issue of international armed force. The idea of war crimes and trying war criminals for acts against humankind has been revived to deal with the aftermath of Rwanda and in Bosnia, for the first time since the war crimes trials at the end of World War II. To the extent that idealists became involved in promoting military action in these kinds of situations, they are expanding the definition of vital interests and are becoming hawkish by advocating the use of force in situations where realists would not.

The Clinton administration's position on these questions has evolved across time, with the Somali experience the primary source of early education. When Clinton entered office, his impulses were to concentrate on domestic rather than foreign policy, as indicated by his hands-off approach on the decision to reinsert American troops into Somalia after the original handoff to the United Nations proved unsuccessful. Rather, it was the military itself, including General Powell, that proposed the large-scale involvement (partly to avoid being sent to Bosnia) and the unsuccessful Ranger raid to capture the late Gen. Mohammed Farah Aidid in a Mogadishu hotel. It ended with the dragging of an American Ranger's corpse through the streets on worldwide television, and Clinton's position began to change toward that of the realists. In May 1994, Presidential Decision Directive (PDD) 25 was issued by the White House (although its provisions were well known and in place earlier). The document contains cautious policy guidelines about the circumstances in which the United States will engage in different kinds of actions to support U.N. peacekeeping. In each case (financial support for U.N. actions of which the United States is not a part, U.S. participation in peacekeeping missions, and U.S. involvement in military actions), the demonstration that an American vital interest will be promoted is a prominent criterion. Defining what constitutes a vital interest in any specific case remains problematical.

Residual National Security Concerns

Although the end of the Cold War removed the most important national security problem from the agenda, it did not do away with all sources of concern. We have already dealt with one of those residual problems, the fate of NATO within a post–Cold War security system for Europe. In this section, we look at two additional ongoing policy areas: the role of nuclear weapons and arms control, especially within the context of the possible proliferation of nuclear and other weapons of mass destruction to Second Tier states; and the ongoing problem of bitter conflicts pitting regional adversaries against one another.

Nuclear Weapons, Arms Control, and Proliferation

The breakup of the Soviet Union ended the nuclear confrontation. The nuclear arsenals of the Cold War superpowers still faced one another, if with less murderous intent, and an accord would have to be reached to deal with that balance. At the same time, the perennial concern over the possible spread of nuclear weapons to nonpossessing states—especially in the volatile Middle East—was of sufficient concern to enliven arms control discussions.

When the Soviet Union dissolved itself, its strategic nuclear weapons (warheads on launch vehicles—rockets—capable of reaching the American homeland) were located in Russia, Kazakhstan, Ukraine, and Belarus (formerly Byelorussia), and the successor governments claimed control of them (although only the Russian government, as the designated successor to the Soviet Union, possessed the launch codes necessary to fire them). The first problem of post–Cold War nuclear balance thus became how to consolidate control of the entire former Soviet arsenal into Russian hands to avoid the likelihood of rogue usage and to facilitate arms control negotiations to reduce arsenal sizes.

The negotiations involved Russia, the other possessors, and the United States. The governments of Kazakhstan, Belarus, and Ukraine understood the desirability of consolidation but did not entirely trust the Russians. As well, the retention of the weapons provided a bargaining chip that the governments could use to gain assurances of Russian intentions toward them and even to gain economic and security assistance with the West. The Clinton administration helped broker agreements between the various sides through bilateral and occasionaly trilateral negotiations; Ukraine became the last member to agree to relinquish control in late 1994.

Progress toward large-scale reductions has been more difficult than originally envisioned before the breakup of the Soviet Union. The two sides had negotiated the first Strategic Arms Reduction Talks agreement (START I), by which the arsenals were reduced to between 7,000 and 9,000 per side aimed at one another, and in 1995 it was announced that both sides had agreed to quit targeting their warheads at one another, instead programming them at remote ocean sites. Nuclear forces have been placed at lower alert levels. There is no longer an American bomber in the air at all times able to deliver a retaliatory attack in the event of a Russian nuclear attack, for instance.

Progress toward ratifying and implementing the already negotiated follow-on START II agreement that would leave arsenal sizes at about 3,000 weapons apiece had not, through mid-1996, made decisive progress. The major obstacle appeared to be the political position of President Boris N. Yeltsin within Russia; with a tenuous hold on power, Yeltsin was reluctant to alienate those members of the Russian Duma (parliament) and military who want to retain a large arsenal as a sign of continued Russian might. The Clinton administration, sensitive to the Yeltsin predicament, was reluctant to press the matter for fear of contributing to a further deterioration in Yeltsin's political position. Shortly after Yeltzen won Russia's 1996 Presidential election, the treaty had been ratified by the Untied States but not by Russia. Few, however, doubted that the START II limits would eventually be imposed.

The breakup of the Soviet Union also contributed to the other problem, the proliferation of nuclear and other weapons of mass destruction (collectively known as nuclear, biological, and chemical, or NBC weapons) to states that heretofore did not possess them. After the Persian Gulf War, this concern centered on the alleged nuclear weapons program of Iraq, especially in light of the ongoing skirmish between Saddam Hussein's government and U.N. nuclear facilities inspectors. In 1994, concern about nuclear proliferation centered on North Korea (especially during the transition after Kim Il Sung died on July 8 and was replaced by his son and designated successor Kim Jong Il), a crisis eventually averted. In 1995, the focus moved to Iran, which was apparently attempting to buy nuclear technology from, among other places, Russia (which set off a sometimes rancorous debate between Russia and the United States).

The Russian connection to this proliferation problem has several aspects. Although the Russian government strongly opposes proliferation—most of the potential proliferators are much closer physically to Russia than to the United States—it finds itself in a double bind. On the one hand, Russia is absolutely desperate for hard foreign currency to underwrite the conversion of its economy and to bring in much needed capital. There is very little the Russians produce for which other states are willing to pay in hard currency. Nuclear equipment and technology represent one notable exception, and it was apparently that incentive which caused the Russians to accept Iranian professions of peaceful intent in 1995, despite American objections. On the other hand, a large number of nuclear scientists and engineers in Russia whose skills and knowledge are no longer needed by their government might sell their services to the highest bidders, most of whom are in the Middle East. One way to blunt the problem has been an American offer to subsidize a number of these experts to make them less susceptible to prurient offers. Further, the Russians fear that theater and tactical weapons not well accounted for could fall into the wrong hands (see Amplification box " 'Loose Nukes': A Russian Nightmare").

The focus of arms control since the end of the Cold War has understandably moved from reducing the likelihood of nuclear war between what are now past adversaries to preventing the spread of nuclear weapons to others (which, as we noted in Chapter 2, was a secondary appeal of superpower arms control in negotiations like the Limited Test Ban Treaty).

AMPLIFICATION

"Loose Nukes": A Russian Nightmare

The problem of accounting for and gaining control of the former Soviet strategic nuclear arsenal was a relatively simple matter, since the sites and weapons were under the fairly tight control of the Committee on State Security (KGB). What is not so widely acknowledged is what has become of the tactical and battlefield weapons of the old Soviet Union that were deployed throughout the country, but especially in the central Asian and Asian republics facing China. The simple answer is that a full accounting has never been completed and, given the quality of management in the old Soviet Union, probably never will be. The Russians are not at all certain that a few (or more) nuclear weapons may not be figuratively lying around.

This raises four potentially horrific scenarios. One, a weapon might fall into the hands of a fanatical group within one of the successor states, who might threaten or use such a weapon against Russians living in the successor state or against Russia itself. Fundamentalist Muslims in Tajikistan are a popular candidate. Two, these weapons might fall into the hands of the *government* of a successor state, which could then threaten either to attack Russia or Russians in the

---

Nuclear proliferation and the safety of the weapons and nuclear materials have been worries since the beginning of the nuclear age, but they were placed down the list of priorities during a Cold War more concerned with the central relationship. Moreover, most potential proliferators shared the dual characteristics of being motivated by fears of being disadvantaged in regional conflicts with ancient enemies and of being more or less aligned with opposite sides in the Cold War. These characteristics had opposite effects, both of which are largely missing in the post–Cold War world.

The possession, or fear of the attempt to gain possession of NBC weapons—and ballistic missile means by which to deliver them—fueled arms races in a number of areas of the world. The most notable was the south Asian subcontinent, where Chinese acquisition of nuclear weaponry spurred on the Indian research effort, which in turn motivated the development of Pakistan's "Islamic bomb." At the same time, the progress of these programs was partly vitiated by superpower influence: as the chief sponsor of Pakistan, the United States tried to suppress the Pakistani nuclear program, and the Soviets did the same with India. The reasons were not, however, pristine: the main motive on both sides was the fear that another India-Pakistan war might turn nuclear, with unpredictable escalatory prospects that might draw the superpowers into a confrontation neither wanted but might not be able to avoid.

republic. Three, someone in a successor state could sell a nuclear weapon or more to some state like Iran, which might, in a future confrontation, threaten or use them against one of the successor states or Russia. Intense arms control efforts between the United States and Russia are said to have reduced significantly the likelihood that a fully assembled weapon could be stolen.

Perhaps more troubling than the possibility of a loose, already assembled nuclear bomb is the fourth scenario, the virtual *certainty* of loose nuclear fissile material. Authorities in Germany, Lithuania, and Switzerland have already confiscated small quantities of bomb-grade materials, apparently smuggled by Russian organized-crime networks out of Russian nuclear laboratories, research facilities, and civilian nuclear power plants, where security and accounting procedures are more lax than at military sites.

These scenarios may seem farfetched to Americans, akin as they are to the central precipitating event in Tom Clancy's *Red Storm Rising* (a fundamentalist Islamic attack on a major Soviet power station), but they are quite real to the Russians. As evidence, the Russians announced in 1993 that as part of their new military doctrine they would not rule out a first nuclear attack against a state they believed was about to attack Russia. Many in the West initially interpreted this as sword waving at former adversaries; reflection reveals it was really aimed at old enemies possibly with new and lethal capabilities.

The post–Cold War world lacks these involvements. Both Russia and the United States have drawn back from the Second Tier in the absence of a competition between them that was their chief motivation for a presence anyway. Efforts continue to avoid future proliferation through extending the Non-Proliferation Treaty and increasing its membership. At the same time, the Missile Technology Control Regime (MTCR, an informal grouping that began as an agency of the G-7 and has expanded to over 20 countries) has tried to persuade potential missile providers to refrain from selling missiles. The Nuclear Supplier's Group, a similar organization, attempts to restrain sales of nuclear materials that might be converted to nuclear weapons.

Regional Conflict

Much concern during the Cold War was directed at regional conflict as it existed in selected parts of the then Third World. The most prominent were the Arab-Israeli conflict between Israel and its surrounding Islamic neighbors, the Indian subcontinent confrontation between India and Pakistan, struggles between North and South Korea, and, after 1979 and the rise of a fundamentalist Shiite regime in Iran, the Persian Gulf conflict focusing on Iran and Iraq but extending beyond that relationship. In addition, there were (or are) a number of lesser conflicts with some potential military significance, such as the rivalry among the states of southeast Asia, notably Vietnam, Cambodia, and Thailand.

Concerns about regional conflicts since the end of the Cold War have been simultaneously more frequent and less compelling than before. They have occurred more often because there are relatively so few other national security problems; the United States is now able to focus on smaller concerns, since there is no overwhelmingly dangerous situation with which to grapple.

Regional conflicts are also less compelling because, in significant degree, they are drying up. The old A-B-C (Argentina-Brazil-Chile) rivalry was a conundrum of what could happen badly in South America that has disappeared via the democratization and proposed economic integration of much—if not all—of the continent. The possible clash of a racist South Africa (with, until recently, nuclear weapons until their destruction was announced by then president F. W. de Klerk) and the black Front Line states has become moot with the advent of multiracial democracy in South Africa.

The larger conflicts have decreased as well. In July 1994, Jordan joined Egypt and the Palestine Liberation Organization (PLO) in declaring an end to the state of war between Jordan and Israel at a White House ceremony overseen by President Clinton. As a result, the only former enemy with whom Israel had not negotiated a formal peace was Syria, and Israeli-Syrian negotiations continued periodically throughout 1996. These were temporarily interrupted by the assassination of Israeli prime minister Yitzak Rabin in November 1995 but were restarted in December 1995 in the Maryland countryside at the urging of the Clinton administration. When completed, they will end the military confrontation between Israel and its neighbors that was, during the Cold War, the most volatile manifestation of regional conflict.

The other regional conflict that has largely become apparently dormant is the direct confrontation between India and Pakistan. They remain divided by religious faith (Islamic Pakistan and largely Hindu India) and substantive territorial claims (most prominently, the states of Jammu and Kashmir, which are legally part of India but contain large Islamic majorities that would prefer either independence or association with Pakistan). Both countries, however, are beset by internal ethnic differences which require the expenditure of energy that might otherwise have been devoted to one another. The last time they came close to blows was in 1991, and both publicly concluded that although they would each prevail, the effort would not be worth the monetary cost. The conflict continues to bear watching, however, because of the volatility of the Kashmir situation and the presumed possession of nuclear weapons by both states.

That leaves only two major regional conflicts with important policy implications for the United States: the Persian Gulf and the Korean peninsula. Both involve vital American interests, witness to which is that the United States has fought wars in defense of its interests in each place. Both, moreover, have been the focus of American national security concern: when the then secretary of defense, the late Les Aspin, unveiled his *Bottom-Up Review* of American defense problems and needs, the most stressful military situation identified was a simultaneous attack by North Korea against the South and a renewed Iraqi invasion against Kuwait. Both are repeats of actions to which the United States has responded in the past. How likely, however, are *either,* much less both of these at the same time, to occur?

Answering the question requires delving into speculation. Each requires an assessment of intentions (why would North Korea attack the South? or Iraq reinvade Kuwait?), capability (could either do so successfully?), and, in the case of a simultaneous action, could they likely coordinate their actions, especially without anyone knowing about it? It is hard to answer these questions in such a way that the likelihood of either, and especially both, will occur except as an act of almost sheer irrationality.

Despite the saber rattling during the summer of 1994, the North Korean invasion scenario is probably unlikely given the political and economic realities of the peninsula. The two economies point more dramatically than in any other specific region of the world to the stark contrast between the market democracies of the First Tier and the intellectual and economic poverty of hard communism: North Korea simply does not work (recent evidence of which was large-scale food shortages in winter 1995–1996 that necessitated relief measures—including food from South Korea); South Korea stands on the brink of full First Tier status.

In this circumstance, what could possibly motivate the North to invade the only place on the globe that has the possibility of bringing prosperity to it, à la the German experiment? Most military assessments conclude the best the North Koreans could do is a draw, but one that would leave the economic miracle of the South in ruins, in no shape to aid northern development. The more real prospect on the peninsula is a gradual movement toward unification. There have already been signs of movement in this direction, such as the brokered deal whereby South Korea agreed in June 1995 to provide badly needed grain to the North.

Will reunification occur soon or easily? The answer is likely no on both counts because elites on both sides of the 38th parallel are uncomfortable with the prospects that such an action, favored by most Koreans, entails. Ironically, the example of Germany is cautionary for both. The North Korean political elite must realize that it faces the fate of the East German communists, the loss of power. The South Koreans, on the other hand, see the prospects of a very costly, long-term rehabilitation of the North, which will interfere with their own prosperity and may have hidden social and political costs, as has been the case of integrating the societies of the two Germanies after nearly a half century of very different experiences. This having been said, communism is dying in North Korea, as elsewhere, and it is only a matter of time until integration occurs.

The situation in the Persian Gulf is somewhat more unsettled. Iraq's Saddam Hussein is buffeted from several directions. A resurgent Iran appears intent on attaining advanced weapons capability, presumably to reassert its domain over the region, lost when the shah was overthrown in 1979. Saudi Arabia and its other oil-producing partners of the Gulf littoral remain suspicious of Iraqi intentions, arming themselves against their Arab brethren and denying the Hussein regime succor in the face of U.N. economic sanctions. At the same time, large parts of northern and southern Iraq are effectively denied to the Iraqis as "protected zones" into which the Iraqis are prohibited to enter by American, French, and British military might (Operation Provide Comfort to protect the Kurds of the north and Operation Southern Watch to protect southern Shiites).

In this circumstance, the Iraqi government certainly has no shortage of hostile motivation, but it probably lacks the physical wherewithal to mount an invigorated attack against any, much less all, of its potential opponents. The economic sanctions (imposed because of Iraqi truculence in allowing inspection of possible nuclear weapons sites) have badly crippled the economy, and certainly have meant that the hard currency necessary to rebuild the Iraqi military losses from the Persian Gulf War is unavailable. Moreover, Iraq is one of the most closely watched countries on the face of the earth, meaning it is very unlikely that Iraq could organize a military effort without observers from outside having a very detailed idea in advance what was going on.

Despite the unlikelihood of either contingency, and especially of a simultaneous outbreak, nothing is impossible, and there will be continued pressures to maintain adequate military muscle for these worst case scenarios. At the same time, a whole series of new contingencies in the Second Tier offer more immediate, if more ambiguous, calls to our attention.

New Security Problems: New Internal War

Certainly nothing is new about wars between groups of people within political units to gain control of the state, to punish or suppress internal enemies, or for a variety of other reasons. Within the Cold War context, these struggles went on in much of the developing world, although generally with a Cold War patina: one side, usually the insurgents, espoused a Marxist ideology and was politically affiliated with either the Soviet Union or China (or both); the other side, usually the government, espoused an anticommunist, presumably democratic ideology and was politically supported by the United States. After he announced what became known as the Reagan Doctrine in the early 1980s—by which the United States vowed to assist anticommunist insurgents in communist-controlled countries—these roles reversed in places like Nicaragua and Afghanistan.

Recovering the expenditures lost in sponsoring far-flung insurgencies was one of the Soviet motivations to end the Cold War because little seemed ever to be gained at high costs. As the Soviets beat a hasty retreat from Third World involvements in the latter 1980s and early 1990s, the United States by and large followed suit, since most of American motivation had been to avoid the Soviets gaining influence as much as any intrinsic interest in the outcomes.

The internal wars of the Cold War were limited both geographically and in their conduct. Internal warfare did not occur in the communist world because authoritarian regimes were able to suppress, if not to ameliorate, old animosities that became manifest when the veil of coercive rule was lifted. Warfare occurred in Africa and southern and southeastern Asia, but generally it was restrained by strategic dictates (the Maoist mobile-guerrilla warfare strategy, for instance) and outside sponsor demands that at least caused the worst forms of atrocity to be avoided. The major exception was Cambodia, where the communist giants, the Soviet Union and China, backed opposing elements and the result was a genocidal campaign between 1976 and 1979 in which the murderous Khmer Rouge executed almost one-third of the population.

Characteristics of the New Internal Wars

A new, frightening, and very bloody form of internal war is emerging in the post–Cold War world. It is a qualitatively different form of warfare (and the term *warfare* does not entirely accurately capture the phenomenon) marked by a level of ferocity and absence of inhibition unfamiliar in the Cold War outside isolated situations like Cambodia. It is also a style that eludes conventional social science theory in terms of the kinds of societies and kinds of situations and people involved. Arguably, finding a systemic response to the new internal war represents the greatest challenge to the foreign policies of the major powers, should the United States and others decide to involve themselves (which, to this point, they have not).

This new category of conflicts is evolving, meaning that we can only generalize about it somewhat hesitantly. With that rejoinder in mind, however, we can identify a few common general traits, political traits, and military characteristics of the new internal war, recognizing that the lists will be more suggestive than exhaustive. These characteristics include a tendency to occur in failed states in geographically identifiable parts of the least prosperous parts of the developable subtier of the Second Tier, a frequent infusion of ethnic and multinational qualities, and an interaction among other characteristics.

In general terms, the first characteristic of new internal wars is that they tend to occur in what have been called the *failed states,* those political entities that have exhibited across time an apparent inability to engage in stable, positive governance. Somalia is certainly an obvious example of this, as are the internal conflicts occurring in a number of other central African states.

This relates to a second shared characteristic, which is that most of these wars occur within the poorer countries of the developable subtier of the Second Tier. As you will recall from Table 3.2, nearly two-thirds of the total internal wars for 1993 were in this subtier, with a particular concentration in Africa. As we noted in describing the tier, there is considerable differentiation among developable subtier countries, and most of the violence is in poorer countries like Rwanda, Burundi, Liberia, and Sierra Leone. (This characteristic, it might be added, contradicts some of the political development literature, which suggests revolution-prone societies are those in the midst of development rather than the very poor.)

Moreover, the pattern is geographically distinct, with the highest concentrations in the three areas of the world most tenuously participating in the globalizing economy: the former Soviet Union (notably the southern republics) and the Balkans, most of Africa, and southern and southeastern Asia. These countries not only are outside the global economy but also the areas of traditional interest to the major powers—a limitation on potential interest in dealing with these situations.

A third general characteristic flows from this description: these wars are often fought in the poorest of societies, where the stakes are particularly small and the human misery index is especially high. There are, for instance, a series of conflicts going on in central and western Africa. Their purpose—from the insurgents' standpoint—is simply to destabilize the political system and the government's ability to maintain order as a means to engage in the systematic ransacking of the countryside for what little profit can be made. Liberia is the prototype for this kind of action, and it has been emulated in equally desperate places like Sierre Leone and Kenya (where stirring up religious animosities is a subsidary purpose).

A fourth general characteristic is the apparently multinational, multiethnic nature of the countries in which these wars are occurring. In the formerly communist countries, there seems to be an outpouring of ethnic and religious animosities previously suppressed but not erased by oppressive rule. In Africa, the animosities have been more openly tribal, as is most African politics.

What is not so clear is whether ethnicity is cause or effect or absent. In Somalia, for instance, ethnicity was not a factor at all, but it certainly is in Rwanda, where Hutu and Tutsi carry out a centuries-old rivalry. Even there, however, it is not clear whether the basis of animosity is tribal hatred or the fanning of latent animosity for political gain. Similarly, Bosnian Serbs and Bosnian Muslims are all Serbs ethnically, but are brought to hate one another for other reasons.

Finally, one cannot help but be struck by the interactiveness and circularity of the other factors. Failed states exist in many instances because they are desperately poor and have few prospects ever of attaining prosperity. Without massive outside assistance, how, for instance, can Haiti provide for Haitians the quality of economic existence that can make for tranquil politics? As long as there is little to fight over but less to do constructively, does this mean the battle over what little there is will be especially furtive? Where this economic and political poverty is overlaid with great depth in ethnic difference and animosity, will the prospect of great bloodshed remain high?

The new internal wars also possess a series of political characteristics that make them much different: an absence of clear political objectives to be attained, an equally obvious absence of a justifying political ideology, the lack of a common center of gravity to moderate conflict, and no sense of reconciliation or positive conversion of the losers and the consequent need to engage in state building, as opposed to rebuilding.

Certainly in a Clausewitzian sense, the purpose of war is to end tyranny and attain political power, a goal normally attached to a set of political ideas that form a philosophical, ideological basis for rule. In the Vietnam War, for instance, the purpose of the North Vietnamese and their followers was to reunite the country by force as preface to ruling by a set of Marxist principles that the leaders—and presumably their followers—felt to be correct. These purposes provided guidance to the military leadership, providing them direction for their efforts: what might contribute to a unified Vietnam should be pursued, what might make unification more difficult after the fighting was to be avoided.

The result was a discipline, even limitation on the conduct of war often apparently missing in the new internal war. In the Somali conflict, the sheer struggle between clans represented a political objective of sorts (which would prevail and be able to impose itself on the rest), but one would look hard for anything resembling a unifying set of principles on the part of any group. Similarly, the retention of power by conservative Hutu may have been the object of those who incited the rampage in that country, but it was hardly a set of political ideas that deserve the name.

Another way to describe the apparent absence of constraint is in terms of the lack of a common center of gravity for which the combatants are competing. In traditional insurgency-counterinsurgency situations, it was always possible to describe a major objective of both (or all) sides as appealing for the political loyalty of the population—what Lyndon Johnson first called the "battle for the hearts and mind of men." Since the population was the same for both sides, the problem was how to attack and defeat the opponent without alienating the same center of gravity for which both competed. Generally, the side which could gain that loyalty was likely to prevail in the long run, making the determination critical.

This battle for loyalty inevitably moderates the conduct of hostilities: both sides come from the same population, and both compete positively as well as militarily for that loyalty. Moreover, at the end of hostilities there will be a peace in which both the victors and vanquished must be reconciled. Both sides, in other words, seek converts both during and after the war. Gratuitous violence that will turn potential converts into enemies or will make postwar conciliation more difficult is to be avoided.

This dynamic seems to be almost totally missing in many of the new internal wars. In Somalia, the purpose of intercepting and withholding food from rival clans was not to convert them, it was to starve them into submission. But that flowed from the purpose, which was to impose power, not to win loyalty. The grotesque savagery of Rwanda would have been almost totally dysfunctional if guided by an attempt to convert and reconcile, but it was not: as Hutu slaughtered Tutsi, the purpose was killing, not the peace that would follow. In Bosnia, the butchering of civilians will make a postwar reconciliation next to impossible, but from the viewpoint of the perpetrators, that is all right, since the objective was to force people apart into ethnically pure enclaves.

Another way of making this distinction is to say that, in terms of their underlying political dynamics, the new internal wars are not civil wars at all, but actually international wars that happen to occur within single states. In wars between states, there is less concern about the political repercussions of military acts because those acts do not seek to convert the enemy population, but to subdue it. Reconciliation (or imposition) after the war is entirely a postwar matter, and that is the case in the new internal wars. The result is military conduct that is often much more savage than one would expect otherwise.

Habitation patterns, notably the intermingling of ethnic groups, exacerbates the process of settling many of these conflicts. Since the Tutsi invaded Rwanda and Burundi 400 years ago, they and the Hutu have lived side by side, intermarried, and become, in any genetic sense, a single people (in fact, the basis of classification of a Rwandan as Hutu or Tutsi was a 1930s census in which tribal identity was assigned on the basis of how many cattle a male owned). Yet neighbor has witnessed the slaughter of neighbor, and reconciliation is made more difficult. The same is certainly true in Marshall Tito's great experiment in racial intermixture, Bosnia and Herzegovina.

Finally, the solution to many of these problems, if it is possible at all, does not entail so much the reconstruction of states as it does their construction. The nature of failed states is that they have consistently proven incapable of stable governance, which is largely why they fall prey to chaotic violence. The *Sendero Luminoso* (Shining Path) of Peru could not have thrived for as long as they did had there been a strong legitimate government and honest constabulary and military in that country. Similarly, the chaos in west African countries like Liberia is in large part testament to the absence of viable governmental structures to combat the forces of anarchy.

One of the striking characteristics of the new internal wars is their extreme brutality whose pattern flows from the political idiosyncrasies we already noted. Lacking clear political objectives, these wars often have no apparent military strategies that they attempt to articulate. The forces are highly irregular and undisciplined to the point that it is difficult to think of them as soldiers so much as armed thugs (the so-called technicals in Somalia, teenagers riding machine-mounted Toyota 4×4s, come to mind). Lacking the limitation of trying to appeal to a common center of gravity, the terrorizing of civilian populations is a matter-of-fact occurrence, as is the ferocity of seemingly mindless violence against the target population (the sniper attacks against innocents in Sarajevo is a prime example).

Thus these conflicts are extremely brutal, chaotic, and unmilitary in any conventional sense of the term. They are *fought* (if that is the proper term to describe the rampaging forces that conduct them) either in almost complete ignorance or disregard for the rules and laws of war. As we noted earlier, it is symbolic that two of the most notable examples, Bosnia and Rwanda, have rekindled war crimes tribunals, a phenomenon hardly seen since the end of World War II.

Policy Responses

If the phenomenon of new internal wars is a growing part of the pattern of post–Cold War international dealings, it has not evoked a uniformity of policy response, and especially any sense of the need for involvement, in the United States and elsewhere in the First Tier. This absence of response can be attributed to several different, yet interrelated sources.

The first and most obvious reason for noninvolvement is a sense that these conflicts occur so far outside the important interests of the United States that there is insufficient reason to involve Americans, and especially to put American forces in harm's way. It was a tragedy that the rampage occurred in Rwanda, but it was also an abstraction going on in a strange place. One could appeal on humanitarian grounds, as was indeed the case, and the United States did rise to the occasion to the extent of providing emergency relief assistance (water purifying equipment, sanitary equipment) to refugees huddled in the Zairean town of Goma, but little more.

This lack of interest flows from a second and related reason: simple nonfamiliarity with most of the affected areas. It is fair to say that the vast majority of Americans had never heard of Chechnya before its population attempted to secede from Russia. Similarly, although many Americans are aware of Liberia, since it was largely settled by returning American slaves, few could find it on a map or knew about the political chaos there. On December 3, 1992 (the day before the intervention), relatively few Americans could spell *Mogadishu* (the capital of Somalia).

The Somali experience has also contributed greatly to American reluctance to become involved in the new internal wars. When the Americans entered Somalia (notably the navy SEALS wading onto the beach in the full glare of waiting television cameras directed to the scene by the military command), there was great enthusiasm for this humanitarian enterprise. Saving starving children captured the public imagination as American soldiers taught Christmas songs to the little Muslim children waiting for the chocolate bars that were their reward. The humanitarian impulse had been activated, and Americans had done something to alleviate suffering.

But that is not the way Somalia is remembered in the popular mind. Rather, the lesson of Somalia, to most of the American public and its leadership, is "no more Somalias" because the United States ultimately found itself mired in a situation that it misunderstood and for which it had no ready solutions. Public ardor for structuring a "new world order" quickly gave way to dark and suspicious cynicism with regard to American involvement. Whether this pessimism will in any appreciable manner be assuaged by the apparently more successful experience in Haiti remains a matter of whether stability continues in that country.

A large part of the reason for pessimism and immobilism in the face of these situations is their intractability. It is so difficult to intervene, straighten out matters, and leave with "hope restored" (an inversion of Operation Restore Hope, the code name of the American enterprise in Somalia) because no simple solutions are available. The violent manifestations that so graphically fill television screens are merely symptoms of deeper underlying causes rooted in the failure of states politically and economically. The actions that the United States took to stop the atrocity, restoring the flow of food in Somalia, for instance, simply did not speak to the broader underlying malaise of that country, which was the absence of any stable political system.

Much of this disillusion has come to center on the United Nations and its failure to solve problems. As the post–Cold War world dawned in 1992, there was great optimism that the United Nations could become the agency of choice for solving the world's more nettlesome problems, and U.N. peacekeeping forces were dispensed around the world, principally in places like Bosnia and Somalia where there was no peace to keep. Conceptually unprepared for frustrating situations of which Bosnia is the prime example, the United Nations fell quickly out of favor; the celebration of its 50th anniversary in June 1995 was a decidedly somber occasion.

The final reason for inaction, deriving from the rest, is the lack of public support in the United States for any involvement in these far-flung conflicts. The American public has turned out to be decidedly pragmatic in its orientation toward the Second Tier's conflicts. The experience in Somalia and the paralysis of effective international action for so long in Bosnia have helped desensitize the public to the grotesque horrors of the new internal wars. The public now insists on a positive answer to

AMPLIFICATION

The Clinton Policy Directive

The Clinton policy position was first articulated in his September 1993 speech at the United Nations, the most memorable quote of which was his admonition that, to paraphrase, if the United States is to say yes to U.N. actions, the United Nations must learn to say no to some. The policy was produced in final form in Presidential Decision Directive 25, issued by the U.S. Department of State in May 1994.

The policy consists of three sets of guidelines for different American levels of involvement. For the United States to support but not to participate in a U.N. operation, the criteria are least stringent: (1) there must be a "real threat to the peace" wherein U.S. interests are served and all alternatives have been considered; (2) the mission must be clearly understood as either peacekeeping or peace enforcement; (3) the duration of the mission must be tied to clear objectives and an identified end point; and (4) appropriate funds and forces must be available for the mission.

whether inserting American forces can in fact improve the situation enough to justify potential American sacrifices, notably American casualties.

The policy evolved by the Clinton administration reflects the ambivalence toward these wars that most states feel. The United States has an effective double veto on global responses to these situations: almost all responses emanate from U.N. Security Council resolutions, over which the United States has a formal veto; at the same time, the United States provides major logistical support (air and sea lift) for almost all missions, and an American refusal to participate can effectively shut down or delay the timely implementation of any resolution.

In addition to the political bases for reluctance to become involved in internal wars are military concerns often based within the military itself. For one thing, there is hardly any American experience in peacekeeping and especially what is called peace enforcement (interjecting forces into a war zone to help bring about a cease-fire) or doctrine to direct efforts. The military has come to realize that the largely passive activity of peacekeeping (monitoring compliance to an established cease-fire that the parties want to maintain) is much easier than establishing a peace *and then* attacking the underlying causes of the war to prevent its recurrence (the political task of state building, at which the military has no particular expertise).

There is also the issue of military expertise in many of the parts of the world where the new internal wars occur. Within the army, for instance, the major source of expertise on foreign countries is the Foreign Area Officers (FAO) program, but it is

For the United States to become personally involved in a U.N. peacekeeping mission, the criteria build on the basic criteria and are more extensive: (1) participation must advance American interests and weigh all risks; (2) personnel, funds, and other resources must be available; (3) U.S. participation must be necessary for mission success; (4) the role of U.S. forces must be tied to clear objectives and an established end point; (5) there must be domestic and congressional support for the mission; and (6) the command and control arrangements for American forces must be acceptable (American forces must be under American command).

Finally, there are additional criteria for involvement in peace enforcement that very heavily reflect the Powell doctrine of overwhelming force: (1) "sufficient forces" must be available to "achieve clearly defined objectives"; (2) there must be "a plan to achieve objectives *decisively*" (emphasis added); and (3) there must be "a commitment to reassess and adjust" the size, composition, and disposition of forces as the need arises.

Source: U.S. Department of State.

small, considered a secondary specialty for those who enter it, and is often thought of as a career dead end. Moreover, it has very few experts in the geographic areas where these wars occur. The one area where there is a reservoir of expertise and that is probably an area of growth is in humanitarian relief operations of the nature of the Rwandan refugee effort, for which military discipline and efficiency has proven useful.

The Clinton policy reflects all these concerns and a recognition of growing disillusionment with the United Nations within parts of the public and the Republican Party. It provides different criteria for different forms of American support, as noted earlier and as detailed in the Amplification box "The Clinton Policy Directive." The criteria are increasingly more difficult to attain and show considerable caution and the need for a high level of likelihood of success. In many important respects, they are outgrowths of the so-called Weinberger Doctrine of the mid-1980s.

Adapting to Change: National Security in a New Setting

Adapting to the security environment of the post–Cold War world has been perhaps the most difficult task facing the makers of foreign and national security policy. Partly, the trauma is as great because so many resources—time, energy, money, and lives—went into the effort; for most of the Cold War period, for instance, the defense effort was either the largest or, after the entitlement programs started under Lyndon Johnson became fully operational, the second largest part of the federal budget. Projections now indicate that service (paying the interest) on the national debt will soon surpass defense spending.

The evidence of this trauma is everywhere. Defense spending is being cut back because the nature of the threats in the environment have been reduced. Every other year, there is a new round of base closings that disrupt local economies; soldiers and sailors are mustered out to meet reduced staffing needs; the search for roles and missions for remaining armed forces is heated.

Roles and Missions in the Cold War

During the Cold War, there was little disagreement on basic policy (containment of communism) or on the military strategies and roles and missions necessary for containment. Although containment had economic and political aspects, its most important core was the problem of dissuading the Soviets from launching an attack against the West (at times, deterring China was also part of the problem).

A survey of the environment revealed three possible contingencies with which the United States had to cope and that remained constant parts of the security equation (although they carried different names at different times). At the top of the list of priorities was deterring strategic nuclear war (sometimes called high-intensity conflict, or HIC) with the Soviet Union. This translated into a strategy of deterrence based in demonstrating to the Soviets that they could never gain from a nuclear attack (which would be punished by a devastating counterattack). It dictated the development of highly survivable weapons that would be available for a counterattack. Although most argued this was the least likely provocation Americans faced, it clearly was the most consequential, since national survival was at stake.

The second planning case was conventional war in Europe, also called middle-intensity conflict (MIC). Given the size and lethality of the forces facing one another in Europe, a MIC was middle intensity only when compared to a HIC, and there was always the prospect that a MIC would escalate to a HIC. Once again, this was an important problem, given that a free Western Europe has always been deemed vital to U.S. interests. It was slightly less important than a HIC if nuclear escalation did not occur (the country would survive) and probably slightly more probable than a HIC.

Finally, there were Third World contingencies (low-intensity conflicts, or LICs), normally communist-inspired and sponsored insurgencies or wars of independence from colonial rule in the developing world meant to expand or leapfrog the containment line, thereby adding to those parts of the world that were communist. These kinds of contest were always the most frequently occurring, but were always subject to the test of whether vital interests were involved in the outcome.

These contingencies were concrete, they were real, and each implied military dictates that could guide the defense establishment from lowliest private to the secretary of defense. But the problem is, what of this trinity survives? Nuclear war with Russia remains a physical possibility as long as the weapons remain, but a contingency for which plausible motivations are elusive. The role of nuclear forces has been reduced to peripheral concerns like avoiding proliferation.

The same is true of the MIC scenario. Nine formerly communist countries had applied for full membership in NATO as of June 1995, and surely more will follow. In time, we can reasonably expect virtually all of the P4P states to be part of NATO one way or another. At that point, the violent potential in Europe (where most of the market democracies of the First Tier are located) will be reduced to policing isolated problems (such as in the Balkans) or in NATO attacking itself.

The only member of the Cold War trinity that survives is LIC, although increasingly in the form of conflicts that meet the altered characteristics of new internal war. In sheerly military terms, the cost of preparations for LIC were, and still are, considerably smaller than for the other contingencies: fewer people are involved, and armaments are generally smaller and less expensive, for example. LICs are also, we might add, considerably less popular within the professional military itself than the other contingencies. LICs have always been the kinds of wars in which an American military trained and indoctrinated for conventional war has been least skilled and interested. There remains a real question about how often and in what specific LICs the United States has sufficient interests to become involved, especially since countering Soviet influence can no longer be used as a justification.

American Force in the Post–Cold War Environment

What the preceding discussion suggests is that it is increasingly difficult to justify the Cold War armed forces in a very changed threat environment, one in which the major rationales have been markedly reduced or have evaporated altogether. As the public clamors for a peace dividend that has so far remained a mirage, the question of forces, roles, and missions goes forward.

The debate boils down to questions of the size, nature, and capability needed in the new environment, and how to reform the force to meet the new needs. No one debates seriously that the force should be smaller. In 1988, the last full year of the Cold War, the active duty American armed forces stood at 2.15 million, with about another million in the various components of the reserves. Planning within the Bush administration had reduced the active component to 1.6 million (what General Powell called the necessary size of the "base force"—the size necessary for major operations), and the Clinton administration reduced that figure to 1.4 million by the end of 1995. In the absence of a major national security crisis, it will almost certainly shrink more.

These cuts, while publicly accepted by the military hierarchy, are painful to them. On one hand, they reduce total size to the point where they wonder if there is enough gravity in the force to face an unpredictable major crisis, and what the smaller numbers mean in terms of how long it would take to reconstitute a major force. Moreover, reductions are likely to come in dealing with the European contingency, which dictated a heavy force (an emphasis on large artillery and main battle tanks, for example) to face a heavy Soviet force, when the United States is now in a situation where there are no other heavy armed forces. Of particular significance is how many aircraft carrier flotillas and the like the U.S. Navy really needs when it is the only fully functioning, global (so-called blue water) navy left in the world.

This ambivalence has spawned at least two contrary approaches to the problem, which are interesting because they illustrate the complexities involved. One, issuing from the Department of Defense, is to move from a "threat-based" to a "capability-based" force for planning and acquisition purposes. During the Cold War, planning was threat based, since there was a clearly definable, concrete force that had to be deterred and, possibly, defeated. The characteristics of the enemy force virtually dictated the roles, missions, and capabilities of the forces.

A threat-based force is much easier to fashion when a threat can be identified. Trying to justify a force against a hypothetical problem leaves planners subject to criticism, even ridicule, about the reality of the hypothetical threat (the Iraq-North Korea joint attacks scenario, for instance). In that case, basing the force on what the United States might want to be able to do based on existing and projected technologies becomes attractive. The problem with this capability basing of the force, however, is that it really only sidesteps the question, against whom does the United States want to be able to do whatever the capability can do?

Reformers outside the Department of Defense see force reductions as the way to eliminate what they perceive as redundancy in the force. This position is most closely associated with Sen. Sam Nunn (D-Ga.), the former ranking minority member of the Senate Armed Services Committee (and former chair when the Democrats were in the majority), who retired in 1996. Nunn believes that much is to be saved where now one service duplicates the capability and mission of other services, and he has even proposed a kind of lottery where services bid for different missions.

The most prominent example used to buttress calls for force rationalization is the "four air forces" case. All four of the services (including the marines, which are administratively part of the Department of the Navy) possess their own air assets: the air force has primary responsibility for strategic bombers and air interceptors; the navy has both a carrier-based and a land-based air force (the latter for conducting operations against adversary forces at sea); the marines have airplanes for close air support of marine operations, including amphibious assaults; and the army has a fleet of helicopters to support land combat and a number of support functions (transporting wounded soldiers from the battlefield, for instance).

The causes and reasons for these redundancies are complex and beyond our present interests, having to do largely with service jealousies and the unwillingness and inability of various Pentagon leaderships to force cooperation that might alleviate redundancy. Reduced resources and a diminished threat would seem to provide an ideal setting for rationalizing the roles and missions of the forces, and the Clinton administration indeed commissioned a reexamination of roles and missions, as mandated by the Goldwater-Nichols Act of 1986. That body, known as the Commission on Roles and Missions of the Armed Forces, issued its report in June 1995 and was remarkably tepid on suggesting change, a victory for the services. On the four air forces debate, for instance, its executive summary included this issue in its section titled " 'Problems' That Are Not Problems," stating, "inefficiencies attributed to the so-called 'four air forces' are found mostly in the infrastructure, not on the battlefield; and more joint training, not fewer services, is needed to ensure effective close air support."

Conclusions

The national security challenges facing the United States in the post–Cold War world are different than before, and most would agree that the threats are greatly diminished. That means there is an opportunity to reshape the armed forces to face an emerging rather than a past threat profile.

The armed forces of the future will almost certainly be smaller than those of the past. They may well be able to compensate partially for their smaller size by enhanced application of advanced technologies to the battlefield (the so-called revolution in military affairs). Nonetheless, it is reasonable to assume that they will not be capable of doing everything the Cold War forces could do.

The question is, so what? The capabilities may well be diminished, but so is the threat: the United States may not be able to do as much, but there also may not be as much it wants to do. The likely candidate for American military involvement is almost exclusively in the Second Tier in internal wars and peacekeeping situations. The only real exception is the possibility of regional conflicts in areas of American interest like Korea and the Persian Gulf. At other places and in other contingencies, it is hard to imagine sufficient U.S. interests to invoke a concerted military effort that would win the sustained support of the American people.

SUGGESTED READINGS

Allison, Graham T., Jr., and Gregory F. Treverton (eds.). *Rethinking America's Security: Beyond Cold War to a New World Order.* New York: Norton, 1992.

Boutros-Ghali, Boutros. *An Agenda for Peace: Preventive Diplomacy, Peacemaking, and Peace-Keeping.* New York: United Nations, 1992.

Brown, Harold. *Thinking about National Security: Defense and Foreign Policy in a Dangerous World.* Boulder, CO: Westview Press, 1983.

Damrosch, Lori Fisler. (ed.). *Enforcing Restraint: Collective Intervention in Internal Conflicts.* New York: Council on Foreign Relations Press, 1993.

Gurr, Ted Robert. *Ethnic Conflict in World Politics.* Boulder, CO: Westview Press, 1994.

Manwaring, Max G. (ed.). *Uncomfortable Wars: Toward a Paradigm of Low-Intensity Conflict.* Boulder, CO: Westview Press, 1991.

Metz, Steven, and James Keivit. *The Revolution in Military Affairs and Conflicts Short of War.* Carlisle Barracks, PA: Strategic Studies Institute, 1993.

Moynihan, Daniel Patrick. *Pandaemonium: Ethnicity in World Politics.* New York: Oxford University Press, 1993.

Neuchterlein, Donald. *American Recommitted—United States National Interests in a Reconstructed World.* Lexington, KY: University of Kentucky Press, 1991.

Paschall, Rod. *LIC 2010: Special Operations and Unconventional Warfare in the Next Century.* Washington, DC: Brassey's (U.S.), 1990.

Pfaff, William. *The Wrath of Nations: Civilization and the Furies of Nationalism.* New York: Simon & Schuster, 1993.

Romm, Joseph J. *Defining National Security: The Nonmilitary Aspects.* New York: Council on Foreign Relations Press, 1993.

Snow, Donald M. *Distant Thunder: Third World Conflict and the New International Order.* New York: St. Martin's Press, 1993.

Snow, Donald M. *National Security: Defense Policy for a New International Order* (3rd ed.). New York: St. Martin's Press, 1995.

Stoessinger, John G. *Why Nations Go to War* (6th ed.). New York: St. Martin's Press, 1993.

CHAPTER 11

America in a Globalizing Economy

As national security concerns have declined in prominence within the United States, international economic matters have become progressively more important. Structural adjustments elevating those agencies involved in international economic power, such as the position of the U.S. trade representative (USTR), have achieved a prominence heretofore reserved for the secretaries of state and defense; under President Clinton, for instance, USTR Mickey Kantor became almost as familiar a public face as secretaries Warren Christopher and William Perry, and his elevation to secretary of commerce after the death of Secretary Ron Brown enhanced his role.

The growing importance of economic issues is both cause and effect of the new international order. As we argued in Chapter 3, the growing economic gap and need for access to Western technology and capital was a major factor in the decision by Mikhail Gorbachev and his advisers to call off the Cold War competition. As seems more apparent in retrospect than it did in prospect, the Cold War military and economic struggle had largely bankrupted the Soviets and held up for all to see the philsophical bankruptcy of socialist economics as well.

The evolving economic system is partly the result of the Cold War and its end also. The roots of the rapid change now occurring in the global economy go back to the early 1980s, when the fruits of the high-technology revolution in information generation, processing, and telecommunications were first beginning to be recognized. The result, which became progressively apparent during the decade, was a rapidly expanding international economy of which the members of the First Tier were the most obvious participants. Their economies were becoming so intertwined that a single global economy comprised of the most advanced countries was emerging. That trend has continued and even accelerated as the end of the Cold War has allowed countries and the industries within them to concentrate more on nondefense concerns.

All this has changed the tone of the international relations of the First Tier and the relationship among the tiers. With no comprehensive alternative political and economic ideology to political democracy and market-based economics, the world's major powers are essentially like-minded philosophically, and their economies are so interrelated in terms such as trade and overseas sales, international ownership by individuals and firms, management and work force, and even product mix that anything important happening to the economy of one affects the economy of them all. Economics and politics, to the extent they could ever be meaningfully separated, no longer can be at the international level.

To understand how economic matters have become so prominent in foreign policy requires examining the international economic system as it emerged after World War II and how it evolved, the Bretton Woods system. With the older system in mind, we then move to a description and consideration of how the contemporary system operates and is evolving. This leads us to a discussion of policy areas and problems that face the United States as the leading power in the international realm.

The Bretton Woods System

Politics and economics are never entirely separable. When the planners gathered during World War II to reconstruct the international system, one of their primary concerns was how the international economic system had contributed to the outbreak of the war. They believed that economic matters had been crucial. The assignment of huge reparations payments for Germany after the First World War had contributed to hyperinflation there, making the Great Depression worse in Germany than elsewhere and contributing to the destabilization of the economy and ultimately the political system. At the same time, much of the world, and especially Europe, responded to the Depression by erecting high tariff barriers against foreign goods to protect their own national industries, thereby stifling trade, creating animosities among states, and thus contributing to the slide toward war. Moreover, a lack of monetary regulation had contributed to large fluctuations in the values of currencies, thereby adding to the economic chaos.

The postwar planners were determined to avoid the economic mistakes of the interwar period. To address the question of how to create a more stable system, 44 states, under the auspices of the United States and Great Britain, met in July 1944 in the small New Hampshire resort town of Bretton Woods to devise a new international economic order.

Based on their perceptions of what had gone wrong before, the first two tasks addressed were how to produce reasonable stability in currencies by providing guarantees of their value and how to promote freer trade than had been the case between the wars. In addition, the conference also recognized the need for large-scale economic recovery of ravaged states after the war.

The conference created three institutions, which collectively became known as the Bretton Woods system, to respond to these needs. The first was the *International Monetary Fund (IMF)*, an intergovernmental organization that was authorized to advance credits to promote trade and to bolster and thus stabilize currencies. The second institution proposed was an *International Trade Organization (ITO)*, whose purpose was to promote free trade and to monitor and investigate alleged violations of free trade agreements. The third institution was the *International Bank for Reconstruction and Development (IBRD or World Bank)*, which, as its name implies, had the dual roles of assisting postwar recovery and later of assisting in economic development.

Two of these institutions came into being initially, the IMF and the World Bank. Because the only place where financing for their missions could be obtained was the United States, their headquarters were established in a common city block in Washington, D.C., and both had weighted voting formulas that assured American control. The proposal for the ITO foundered on American objections about its proposed ability not only to investigate alleged violations of free trade but also to hand out mandatory penalties for violations. A more dilute form of ITO was established in 1947, the *General Agreement on Trade and Tariffs (GATT)*, a periodic set of international meetings whose purpose was to promote freer trade among states. As part of the 1993 Uruguay Round of GATT negotiations (so named because the initial meeting in that particular round of negotiations was held in that country), a *World Trade Organization (WTO)* was approved with virtually the same powers and authority as was proposed for the ITO. The WTO burst into public prominence in June 1995 when Japan threatened to haul the United States before the WTO over the issue of proposed doubled tariffs on Japanese luxury automobiles.

American economic power, and especially the availability of U.S. dollars guaranteed at an exchange rate of one ounce of gold for every $35, provided the basis for the Bretton Woods system. At the end of the war, the United States had by far the largest functioning economy in the world and was responsible for nearly 40 percent of the world's economic activity. The United States was about the only country producing goods and services in global demand; states depended on the Americans or they did without in a large range of items.

The strength and controvertibility of the dollar, which was the world's only truly hard currency (a currency acceptable in international trade), made the United States the global superpower for the first 20 years or so after World War II. The dollar was the linchpin of the Bretton Woods system, but as time went by, other factors emerged that militated toward change.

The underlying erosion of the American-dominated international economic system was the result of the recovery and normalization of other traditional economic powers. Thanks in no small measure to Marshall Plan aid to Europe and bilateral aid to Japan, both were in recovery by the mid-1950s. The signing of the Treaty of Rome in 1957 created the European Common Market, which has evolved into the European Union (EU) as an economic rival to the United States. In the 1960s, Japan as well began to emerge as a rival, with "made in Japan" losing its stigma as meaning of poor quality and beginning the process known widely as the Japanese "economic miracle." As this resurgence occurred, the American relative proportion of global productivity (artificially inflated as it was shortly after the war) gradually receded; some would argue that American complacency also contributed to the relative decline.

A series of events and trends during the 1960s in the United States played a part in the need for change. In the mid-1960s, President Lyndon Johnson made the fateful decision to finance the Vietnam War and the package of social programs cumulatively known as the Great Society without raising taxes. The result was the first sizable budget deficits since World War II and a consequent loss of confidence in the economy. Inflationary policies resulted in a flood of U.S. dollars in the domestic economy and elsewhere and increasingly made the American promise to redeem dollars with gold a hollow one. Moreover, by 1970, the American dollar was so overvalued that it was virtually impossible for American producers to compete with their overseas counterparts (it cost too many units of a foreign currency to buy enough American dollars to buy American goods).

Against this backdrop, the Nixon administration renounced the gold standard in 1971. The United States would no longer promise to redeem dollars with gold and the dollar would no longer have the set value the gold standard specified. Instead, the dollar was allowed to float against other currencies; the dollar's value henceforth was determined by market forces that would decide how much a Japanese yen, for instance, was worth in U.S. dollars, and vice versa.

Although the net effect of the renunciation was to destroy the vital core of the Bretton Woods arrangement, reaction was not immediate. Rather, it reflected an accommodation by the United States to a changed environment in which the United States might be the largest, most powerful economic power but where other states and groups of states could compete globally with the Americans. As a corollary, the renunciation also made currency into a commodity like stocks or oil futures, which could be traded for profit.

What made the system respond more fully, however, was a series of economically traumatic events during the 1970s: the oil shocks beginning in 1973 and continuing through the decade. In 1973, the Arab members of the Organization of Petroleum Exporting Countries (OPEC) withheld their crude oil from the markets of those countries (including the United States) that had supported Israel in the Yom Kippur War of that year. Oil became scarce as lines formed at gasoline stations, and prices soared. Later in the decade, OPEC repeated the maneuver as a way to increase prices for its vital resource; in 1979, the Iranian revolution and accompanying interruption of Iranian oil supplies, added to the problem.

The result was devastating for an international economic system heavily reliant on petroleum for its basic energy source. When Western Europe and Japan were rebuilt, energy grids were tied to the burning of oil because it was assumed (incorrectly) that cheap supplies at the rate of $3 to $5 per barrel of crude oil would be available indefinitely. In the United States, the transportation network was firmly tied to the automobile and its perpetual addiction to gasoline. The shocks also helped stimulate a global recession between 1975 and 1978; economic summits during those years created the precedent and framework for the Group of Seven (G-7), discussed later.

The oil shocks meant that all energy users would have larger bills for energy than in the past, and alternate ways to pay for their energy addiction would have to be devised. Conservation became one alternative; President Carter, for instance, faced television cameras in a cardigan sweater and entreated Americans to lower their winter themostats to 65 degrees or less. The search for alternate energy sources experienced a boomlet of interest as well. Mostly, however, all states had to dig deeper into national wallets to meet their bills. The only way to compensate was to become more competitive in international markets: to create positive balances of trade with the rest of the world that could be transferred to the oil barons. Since markets were inherently zero sum, one country's success was necessarily another country's failure. Economic competition became very serious business.

Road to the Global Economy

The breakdown of the Bretton Woods–guided postwar international economy during the 1970s provides the context for the transition to the truly global economy that has emerged in the 1990s. In economic terms, it was a difficult time for the United States. The U.S. economic advantage seemed to slip across the board to newer, often hungrier competitors, and Americans became negatively introspective for the first time. It is no coincidence that Paul Kennedy's declinist thesis, described in Chapter 1, received popular attention when *The Rise and Fall of the Great Powers* appeared in 1987.

The experts disagree on what caused this apparent decline both in the robustness of the American economy and U.S. faith in it. One widely attributed cause was complacency; the United States had been the preeminent economic power for so long that American firms simply did not make the innovations necessary to adapt to foreign markets. The area most often cited was in automobile competition with Japan. The Japanese routinely conducted extensive research on American preferences and then designed cars to accommodate them; as late as 1995, American automobile manufacturers were just beginning to install right-side drive on automobiles designed for the Japanese market (the Japanese drive on the left side of the road).

The attitude that the world would simply come to the Americans has been difficult to shed, especially by the older, larger corporations and industries at less than the cutting edge technologically. As a result, American industries progressively lost market share across the board to more innovative, aggressive competitors in the Far East and elsewhere.

Conditions and attitudes in the United States did not help. In the wake of Vietnam and Watergate, Americans became more introverted and less interested in public involvement (the so-called me generation). At the same time, test scores in science and mathematics tumbled (especially in comparison with similar scores in other leading industrial states), and fewer and fewer young Americans expressed an interest in careers in science and engineering. These latter failings were particularly galling as it became increasingly apparent that the country was entering a new period in which science and engineering would assume a much greater role in defining the high-technology revolution.

In addition, the American productive system was beginning to look older, with both competitive and demographic consequences. The heart of American postwar predominance had been in heavy industry and the products arising from that indus-try—steel production and automobiles, for instance. These industries, located in the Midwest and eastern United States, formed a kind of "rust bucket" of "sunset indus-tries" that were clearly symbolic of the past. The wave of the future were the "sun-rise industries" associated with high technology. The American economic system during the 1980s would have to adjust to these new realities that would allow it to reassert its strength and vitality in the 1990s.

High Technology and the Genesis of Change

The 1980s was a remarkable decade in terms of its impact on the structure of international economics and politics. Powered by the combined might of a burgeon-ing industry in computing and telecommunications and the deregulation of econom-ic activity in the First Tier, the result has been to transform the economic system in ways that no one would have anticipated as little as a decade ago. The effect of the computing and telecommunications revolutions (which are rapidly becoming essen-tially a single phenomenon) has been to break down national controls on economic activity and to accelerate phenomenally the degree to which knowledge is generated and transmitted across state boundaries, often with governments having no say in the transactions. Politically, this great surge produced and accentuated the enormous economic gap between the Second and Third Worlds that produced the bankruptcy of the Second World and led to the end of the Cold War.

To understand this phenomenon, we proceed by steps. First, we need at least a cursory grasp of the dynamics of high technology, which is the engine of change. Then, we look at how the effects of technology have facilitated a rapidly globalizing economy, at least among the states of the First Tier and those developed Second Tier states with clear aspirations to First Tier status. Included in the discussion is some notion of the truly multinational corporation (MNC) and one of the most important examples of the MNC, global television. We then use this framework to define the world economically in terms of progress through the various industrial revolutions and how the First Tier, if it chooses, might be able to assist the Second Tier in the developmental effort.

Dynamics of High Technology   Although its roots go back to Department of Defense–sponsored research (to develop guidance systems for missiles) that pro-duced the first workable electronic chip and to parallel research in agencies such as NASA as part of the space program, the complex of activities we know as high technology came together during the 1980s, driven by several independent but interrelated phenomena. These included advances in computing power and price (largely the result of digitization), great leaps forward in telecommunications, thanks to conceptualization of the computer as a communications as well as a computing device, and the global wave of privatization and deregulation of economic activity within the countries of the First Tier (which facilitated the global spread and interaction of technologies).

Advances in computing power had been gradual, as one generation of computer provided the impetus to design the next, more powerful and efficient, computer. By the early 1980s, supercomputers (the most capable computer at any point in time) produced by firms such as Cray had entered the fourth generation, featuring advanced parallel processing and adapting to communication of information via advances in digitization (the reduction of all messages to streams of 0–1 or "on-off" codes). At the same time, advances in materials science had reduced the cost of computing, allowing more yet to occur.

The rise in computing power coincided with concerted efforts to maximize the potential of computers as parts of telecommunications networks. The genesis of the realization that computers could do more than conduct complex problem solving goes back to the efforts of a group of California- and Utah-based scientists in the late 1960s who, with the assistance of the Defense Advanced Research Projects Agency (DARPA), designed the prototype system that would eventually become the Internet (see Snow and Brown, *The Contours of Power,* p. 372, for a discussion).

The idea that computers could become the basic element in communications was revolutionary, especially when combined with advances in communications technologies such as fiber optics (allowing an enormous increase in the number, quality, and speed of digitized messages that can be transmitted through any network at any time) and satellites (allowing transmission instantaneously from almost anywhere to almost anywhere else). Most importantly, however, these advances simultaneously allowed the transmission of vast amounts of information and communication across national borders (thereby increasing the prospects of phenomena like international scientific communications and business transactions like the transfer of money) in a way in which governments could not participate or interfere. In the process, the computing and telecommunications industries merged into one huge enterprise with which we are all now familiar but that would have seemed inconceivable 10 or 15 years ago.

This maze of technological activity also took place within a different economic climate in the countries of the First Tier that accelerated both its velocity and its internationalization. Largely led by the United States, the 1980s was also the decade of privatization (turning formerly government-owned economic functions over to private enterprise) and deregulation (removing regulations on economic actions). The result, at least according to the proponents, was to stimulate investment (including investment across borders in foreign firms both by firms and individuals) and innovation.

The high-technology revolution is still ongoing. Its pace over the past decade has been so great and, to most observers, unpredictable, that it is difficult, possibly impossible, to suggest its direction or momentum. What we can see, however, is how high technology has transformed the international environment and helped define the post–Cold War world. The fact that it has occurred parallel in time to the collapse of the Cold War only adds to the dramatic effect.

Effects of High Technology   The impacts of high-technology–derived change are comprehensive, spanning the gamut of activities from military proficiency (the revolution in military affairs) to consumer products. Among the most dramatic effects, and the one increasingly dominating the foreign policy agenda, is the contribution of technological change on the structure of the global economy. It is not unfair to say that the economies of the major powers of the First Tier are becoming so intertwined with one another that one can speak meaningfully of "national" economies in only the most abstract manner.

Change is evident in a number of areas. Possibly the most evident is in the development of the *multinational corporation (MNC)* and especially its hybrid, the *stateless corporation (SC),* and in several cutting-edge production areas, including electronics and automobiles.

The MNC is originally the product of the 1960s, when American-based companies like IBM and General Motors and European-based firms like Nestle and Philips emerged on the scene as international phenomena. These corporations, however, were basically owned and controlled by citizens of a single state, but had agencies or manufacturing facilities in more than one state. Ford manufacturing automobiles in Europe for European markets is an example; International Business Machines' global operations is another.

What distinguished the early MNCs, however, was that they could still meaningfully be identified with a single state and, for most purposes, their activities, including their overseas business, were subject to national regulation. Thus, for instance, when General Foods ignored economic sanctions against Uganda during the latter 1960s (because of the policies of its renegade leader, Idi Amin) and continued to purchase Ugandan coffee, the U.S. government was able to bring pressure on General Foods to halt the practice.

Modern multinationals are different. Increasingly, they are owned by nationals (individuals and corporations) from a number of states, have international management and work forces, and have product mixes that include parts and components from various countries. In the extreme case of the stateless corporation, this international blending becomes so great that it is impossible to associate the firm meaningfully with any single national identity.

This is especially true in the high-visibility automobile industry. For instance, despite loud protestations about fairness in trade and the like (see the next section), American and Japanese automobile manufacturers are highly interrelated. The Big

Three American automakers each own a portion of the Japanese company with whom they are associated (General Motors and Toyota, Ford and Mazda, Chrysler and Mitsubishi). Moreover, they coproduce cars on common assembly lines: a California plant builds both Toyota Corollas and Geo Prisms (they are essentially the same car); and Mitsubishi Galants and Dodge Avengers, which share a common chassis, come off the same line in Illinois. The same kind of relationship is found in Europe: Jaguar is a wholly owned subsidiary of Ford, and General Motors owns half of Saab.

Ownership extends to manufacturing. The United States, for instance, classifies cars as American or foreign, not based on nameplate or place of assembly, but on the percentage of components that are American made (the current standard is 75 percent). This occasionally creates some anomalies: a Toyota Camry made in Japan is Japanese because it contains more than 25 percent non-American parts; the same Camry made in Ohio uses over 75 percent American parts and is thus American, except the total number of Camrys, many still manufactured in Japan, in the aggregate have less than 75 percent American parts, so that Ohio-made Camry becomes a foreign car for governmental accounting purposes. The manufacturer's sticker on new vehicles is required to include a statement about the national composition of parts.

Modern technology has made all this more possible than it was when the first MNCs came into being. Computers, the Internet, and high-speed telecommunications allow far-flung operations of firms to coordinate activities in a way that would have been impossible even to imagine a decade or so ago. It is not difficult to envisage a corporation with directors on each of the world's continents holding a board meeting via teleconferencing; complex goods, especially electronics, are routinely assembled of parts from several different countries (wherever comparative advantage can offer the best component at the best price), often at a neutral site. Predicted advances in aircraft and shipping (a 200 knots per hour cargo ship, for instance) will simply facilitate this movement.

Telecommunications also creates financial opportunities that aid in globalization. Stock transactions can be carried out around the clock because a stock exchange is open somewhere all the time (New York, London, and Tokyo, to name the most prominent). Moreover, electronic transfer of funds permits, even facilitates, the movement of capital across national boundaries with no intermediation by governments at either end of the transaction.

Global television offers a special case of the effects of high technology. Obviously, the same telecommunications facilities that assist business are also available to the electronic news media. When the added technologies of hand-held camcorders and satellite dishes are added to the mix, then the ability to report and even create news is magnified greatly.

The result has been an information explosion that is causing public awareness of a much larger amount of news in real time than was ever possible before. The leading apostles of this explosion, as we noted in Chapter 8, have been the American-based Cable News Network (CNN) and British-based Independent Television Network

(ITN). Originally national organizations covering and reporting news events in several countries (not unlike the original MNCs), these outlets are becoming increasingly international as well. CNN, for instance, announced a contractual relationship in 1995 with a media consortium in India by which CNN International will be made universally available on the Indian subcontinent and Indian media will provide coverage of the subcontinent for the rest of the world. In addition, the CNN/ITN phenomenon has caused major American entertainment-based television networks to produce cloned rivals.

Governments, and the U.S. government in particular, barely penetrate this highly dynamic environment. When they do, their impact is generally peripheral and often negative and reactive. Partly, it is the nature of the relationship between science (of which technology is a part) and public regulation that policy almost always follows scientific progress, since, by definition, it is impossible to predict what scientists will discover. At the same time, the sheer pace of change is such that keeping up with it in any meaningful sense is difficult if not impossible. Moreover, with the exception of some amateur technologists like Vice President Al Gore, the highest levels of elected or appointed government officials have relatively few people expert in this area. (This is especially true of Congress.)

The interaction is generally reactive, often negative. The Congress has passed laws restricting the proportion of strategically important industries (industries which loosely are involved in military matters) that can be owned by foreigners. Trade policy can be manipulated to make the importation of goods and services more or less attractive. More controversially, the government can attempt to use incentives to encourage firms to produce certain kinds of goods and service that it feels will be competitive (a practice known as industrial policy).

Thus the world's business is increasingly conducted outside the bounds of traditional foreign policy channels by individuals and firms for which those channels are irrelevant. National boundaries mean increasingly less to businesspeople. While it is certainly not an insight to suggest that business and political loyalty are often less than coterminus, the irrelevance of political concerns to business opportunities seems to be growing.

An example may help capture this dynamic as well as provide a transition. In recent years, there has been a growing movement to reestablish relations between the United States and Vietnam that were severed with the fall of Saigon in 1975. Part of the motivation has been political: Vietnamese Americans who are returning to Vietnam either to visit or live desire formal relations; some veterans' groups have argued that the Vietnamese government has been increasingly forthcoming on the prisoner of war (POW)-missing in action (MIA) issue with regard to unaccounted American military personnel; and there is even the desire of some American veterans to return to Vietnam as tourists.

The real motivation, however, has been economic. Although Vietnam is putatively still one of the world's last communist states (the Communist Party still rules), the Vietnamese government has become one of Asia's most aggressive at trying to attract foreign, including American, private investors as a way to overcome a highly stagnant economy. Through devices such as full-page (and larger) advertisements in magazines and newspapers like the *New York Times* and the *Wall Street Journal,* the Vietnamese have aimed their appeal directly toward the business community, arguing that Vietnam is an ideal place for private commercial development. That kind of campaign, and favorable corporate response to it, has led the process, producing an administration agreement to normalize fully diplomatic relations between the two countries in late 1995 (the United States reopened its embassy in Ho Chi Minh City, formerly Saigon, early in 1995).

What all this amounts to is the progressive privatization of those elements of international relations and foreign policy with an economic content. Within the First Tier, the simultaneous decline of security concerns and rise in economic interactions has already tipped the scale of importance toward economic concerns, a central element of Clinton foreign policy. The dynamics of what has been called *geo-economics* will increasingly play a part in the relations between the tiers, and particularly in which Second Tier countries will be drawn toward the First Tier.

The Second Tier and the Industrial Revolutions   Much of the Second Tier is effectively removed from the complex of activity we have described as the high-technology revolution, other than the limited availability of worldwide television. Almost half of the Second Tier states are in the lowest developmental category, the developable subtier, and within that category there is a wide variety of accomplishment and prospect for improvement.

A major difference in the pattern of violence and instability in the post–Cold War world is that it is occurring disproportionately in the poorest societies rather than in states undergoing development, as older theories of political and economic development suggested. There no longer seems to be a destabilizing period when development is occurring, but the benefits are perceived as less than acceptable (as developmental theorists suggested in the 1950s and 1960s); now the struggle is over the meager scraps of impoverished lands.

The pattern both of impoverishment and instability tends to be geographically specific as well. The developable subtier has its greatest clusters in three geographic regions. The overwhelmingly largest area is Africa, where 36 of 52 states fall into the developable category and where many of the poorest members of the subtier are found. The formerly communist countries provide a second physical area, where 19 of 28 states fit into the category, with most concentrated in the southern boundary areas of the old Soviet Union and in the Balkans. Finally, Asia and the Pacific has 17 developable countries, mostly in southern Asia and some Pacific islands.

How is this discussion relevant to a chapter on the global economy and America's role in that economy? The answer is that the globalizing economy is an expanding phenomenon, where states can be progressively brought through the developmental process and gradually become members of the global economy. Encouraging that to occur makes good economic sense to a country like the United States which values free trade: a more prosperous Second Tier may provide new and virgin markets for First Tier goods and services and may, in turn, provide the setting for the production of goods, components, and the like, at economically more competitive costs. In turn, if the Second Tier comes to approximate more greatly the First Tier in economic terms, it may also be more likely to come to resemble it politically—more democratic and less war prone.

Arguments for assisting in the economic development of the Second Tier would seem to fall on deaf ears in an era of fiscal conservatism when even a budget category as small as that for foreign assistance ($13 billion in 1995) is under assault. While this is true, the underpinning of the globalizing economy is not public investment, but private sector activity. The question, then, is whether it is possible or worth the effort to engage in private efforts, possibly assisted by governments, to engage the developmental process.

The problem can best be understood by referring to progress through the three industrial revolutions, a major criterion by which we defined the various subtiers and assigned individual states to different subtiers. The basic distinctions are summarized in Table 11.1. The table suggests four levels of development in which various states find themselves, and they are distinguished by the *primary,* most advanced form of economic activity that occurs in each.

A number of states in the developable subtier have not yet entered the industrial revolution process at all: economic activity, in these cases, is overwhelmingly involved in subsistence agriculture, which may occupy 80 percent of the population or more. In some states, this is supplemented by the extraction (or potential extraction) of various forms of (normally) nonrenewable natural resources. Countries with some resource potential tend to be those for which the prospects of improvement are best. They have a source of potential income for infrastructure development, for example, that makes them potentially attractive to private investors.

TABLE 11.1
Industrial Revolutions and Economic Status

Industrial Revolution	Economic Activity	Tier/Subtier
Pre-1st	Subsistence agriculture, resource extraction	Developable
1st	Heavy industry, some consumer goods	Partially developed
2nd	Sophisticated goods, services	Developed
3rd	Information, technology	First Tier

The next stage is the partially developed states, countries that have made their way into the first industrial revolution, with its emphasis on heavy industry and the development of a basic consumer products sector in the economy. A number of states in this category, India and China for instance, also have parts of their economies involved in more sophisticated manufacture and services (attributes of the second industrial revolution), but these are counterbalanced by large segments of the population engaged in subsistence agriculture. India, for instance, has a well-educated middle class that numbers around 100 million; it also has a large rural population for which growing personal food supplies is the norm. As noted earlier, China's special economic zones are quite competitive globally; large parts of the interior of China, however, are pre–first industrial revolution.

At the developmental top of the Second Tier are the developed states. Unfortunately, they are few in number: only 13 of the 160 Second Tier states fall into this category. Nine of the 13 are either in Asia (the four tigers: South Korea, Taiwan, Hong Kong, and Singapore) or Latin America (Argentina, Brazil, Chile, Mexico, and Venezuela). What distinguishes these states is that they have entered the second industrial revolution, where the production of sophisticated consumer goods (including many that are direct results of high technology) and services become important parts of the economy. What distinguishes them from the First Tier, in addition to the strength or fragility of their commitment to political democracy, is that they tend to be consumers rather than producers of high technology.

A cautionary note about these distinctions: although relatively easy to place most individual countries into one category or another, there are arguably borderline cases. It is difficult to operationalize the category boundaries with precision. Even the most sophisticated countries retain small pockets of preindustrial revolutionary activity, as well as vestiges of the other industrial revolutions (heavy industry, for instance). Moreover, each category represents a range: some developed subtier states (Korea, for example) are more developed and thus closer to the First Tier than others (Mexico, for instance).

What framing the categories in this manner does accomplish is to set up a general way in which to think of progress toward the global economy and how technology may contribute to that process. Becoming a part of the global economy means emulating, in large measure, the economic patterns of activity that mark more sophisticated subtiers. A state in the developable subtier needs to court sectors of the economy that will emulate the partially developed subtier; the Chinese special economic zones strategy of stimulating private enterprise may be useful in a number of developable states. Moreover, it may be possible technologically to stimulate growth: applications of the so-called green revolution to turn subsistence agriculture into extensive agriculture, for instance.

In the current atmosphere, much of any change that may occur will have to be conducted largely privately, but the high-technology phenomenon can stimulate that kind of activity. Private enterprises are no longer effectively shackled from far-flung reaches of the globe by limits on their ability to communicate or on accessibility: we can talk to and get to places easily that were once out of reach. As we noted in the introduction to this section, that in itself can prove advantageous to private enterprises like MNCs seeking to expand their global activities. Twenty years ago, for instance, it would have been inconceivable to choose Malaysia (a partially developed country) as a place to build parts for electronic equipment. It was too remote and too hard to get Malaysian products economically to market, in spite of an attractive labor market in the country. Technology has helped solve that problem, and now Malaysia is a major supplier of a variety of parts and components for the world's markets.

We have tried to depict in this section the dynamism of the international economic system. The global economy is quite unlike the economic system that the bankers and governmental officials gathered at Bretton Woods could possibly have envisaged. Global economic problems now dominate the foreign policy agenda to a degree not seen since the economic travails of the interwar period. In that unhappy circumstance, the impact of economics on international politics was largely negative, part of the fuel that ignited World War II. The international economic environment of today is a much more positive place, where the intertwined economies of the major powers reinforce one another's prosperity and where the rest of the world tries to devise strategies that will allow them to enter the general prosperity. At the same time, this new environment creates a set of economic policy questions that form an ever increasing part of the foreign policy agenda.

Policy Problems and Prospects

The great dynamism of the international economy, particularly when juxtaposed with the effective end of the Cold War geopolitical competition, has created a contemporary environment far different than what it supplants. Although levels of development vary greatly, there is a uniformity of economic and even political philosophies probably not matched since eighteenth-century Europe, when political monarchism and economic mercantilism reigned supreme. Certainly not all countries of the world have embraced market-based economies and political democracy, but there is very little open opposition to either. Authoritarian regimes still exist at various places in the world, but hardly anyone extols their virtues convincingly; likewise, the bankruptcy of Marxist economics has left the market-based capitalism of the First Tier without a meaningful economic opponent. We have, at least for the time being, reached Francis Fukuyama's "end of history," where opposing ideologies do not exist.

There are, of course, limited exceptions, the most notable being the Islamic Middle East. Islam is an inherently theocratic system, some of whose sectarian variants view political democratization and its accompanying secularism with suspicion. At the same time, certain ideas associated with capitalist economics, notably the charging of interest, are considered usury within strict Islamic practice. The only Islamic countries that are central players in the new international system are those like Turkey which, under Kemal Ataturk after World War I, consciously secularized their societies.

With these limited exceptions, there is little principled objection to the further development of the emerging globalizing economy. The United States under the Clinton administration has been particularly aggressive in this regard, reflecting the interest of the president and his closest economic advisers that was first discussed at the Little Rock economic summit in December 1992. In fact, until his recent successes in promoting peace in places like Bosnia and Northern Ireland, almost all of President Clinton's foreign policy interests (and successes) were in international economics. In addition to high technology, the Little Rock meeting emphasized American competitiveness and industrial policy, both matters of how the United States could compete more effectively in world markets.

As time has passed, the key policy element that has emerged centers around trade, how states can sell goods and services to one another. Terms bandied about include *free trade* (the removal of artificial barriers to trade such as tariffs, quotas, and the like) and *fair trade* (where a given state's goods and services are not disadvantaged by artificial barriers or practices such as dumping goods into a market at prices lower than are charged within a country's home market).

Under Clinton, the United States has become the leader in the movement toward free trade globally, although this position meets isolated opposition in places and industries, such as textiles, where the United States does not produce competitively and where specific industries can only be maintained through trade barriers. The movement to remove those barriers has come along two lines. The first is intra–First Tier, aiming at the removal of trade barriers among First Tier states. This thrust of policy has been most publicly evident in U.S.-Japan trade relations, but affects America's relations with the European Union as well. The second thread intersects the tiers by approaching the question of integrating parts of the Second Tier into the general economic system through the reduction of trade restrictions. This thread of policy has centered both on global mechanisms such as the GATT and emerging regional entities such as APEC and NAFTA.

All of this activity is relatively recent, aided by the technological possibilities created by the high-technology revolution and the collapse of the global geopolitical confrontation. Because it is so new, its exact contours are hard to describe and even harder to extrapolate with confidence into the future. How, exactly, can intra–First Tier economic relations be improved to the mutual benefit of all? Is there an optimal way to incorporate the countries of the Second Tier into the greater prosperity of the First (including, quite prominently, the old adversaries from the Cold War era)?

Freeing Trade within the First Tier

The heart of the international economic system is the triangle of major economic powers of the First Tier—the United States, Japan, and the European Union. There are other members of the First Tier that do not fall into one or another of these three points to the triangle (Australia and New Zealand, for instance), but nonetheless, the three entities dominate.

The major mechanism by which the major First Tier powers coordinate economic policy is the Group of Seven (or G-7), the semiannual meeting of the heads of state of Canada, France, Germany, Italy, Japan, the United Kingdom, and the United States (as we noted in Chapter 3, Russia is sometimes allowed limited participation as a sort of honorary member). Although they discuss a wide range of topics (including missile proliferation that produced the Missile Technology Control Regime), the heart of their discussions is economic.

The members are overwhelming similar. Each is a well-established political democracy with a market-based economy. Levels of government participation in the economy vary among them, and each has some special economic foibles, but on the most important matters of principle, they are fundamentally in accord. These most influential states in the world are in such agreement, in fact, that it is impossible to imagine any issue provocative enough among them to cause a resort to war.

This fundamental accord does not mean there is not disagreement among them. Their disagreements, which occasionally get rhetorically blown out of proportion, are at the periphery of their overall relationship, which is one of basic political and economic agreement. The disputes tend to center around *terms of trade,* the conditions under which their goods and services enter one another's markets.

All three members of the First Tier economic tripolarity agree rhetorically on the value of free trade—the condition when the international exchange of goods is neither restricted nor encouraged by government-imposed trade barriers, and market forces determine the distribution and level of international trade (see Spero in Suggested Readings). At the same time idiosyncratic factors in each country create barriers to the realization of free trade.

The resulting trade issues center around several areas. The most basic is *protectionism,* the extent to which countries erect barriers to trade to protect industries that could not compete in the absence of restrictions on the importation of outside goods and services. These barriers usually reflect the political power of those industries representing the protected good or service.

Examples are not difficult to find. The textile industry of the Carolinas in the United States cannot compete against the lower wages of clothing manufacturers in other countries, and thus favors raising tariffs against their importation. Due to the relatively small size of available plots of land, Japanese rice growers demand tariffs against American rice, arguing, interestingly enough, that Japanese rice tastes different than American rice. Japanese automobiles face stiff tariffs going into Europe, one reason for assembling cars in the United States for the European market (where the barriers are lower). At the insistence of French farmers, the EU's Common Agricultural Policy (CAP) protects notoriously inefficient French and other farmers from outside competition; angry French farmers' protests against assaults on the CAP are well documented (overturned trucks, roads blocked, for instance).

The basic argument against protectionism is the theory of *collective advantage,* the idea that if those who produce a good or service most efficiently are allowed to dominate a market, then everyone will find what they can produce at comparative advantage, and everyone will ultimately benefit. But the process of adjustment whereby those formerly employed in uncompetitive, protected industries are funneled into areas of comparative advantage can be unsettling and politically unpopular.

Protectionism is also manifested in at least a couple of side issues. One of these is *unfair trade practices,* which have the effect of distorting trading patterns. One example is dumping, as we mentioned earlier; a classic government policy in support of dumping is to offer tax incentives or bonuses for goods and services involved in international trade but not for domestic consumption. Another are TRIMs (trade-related investment measures), governmental policies including component source restrictions (what percentage of American parts make a car American), licensing and inspection requirements (such as the very extensive, and expensive, inspection requirements on cars imported into Japan), and a range of other practices, all of which serve to make it more difficult for foreign goods and services to compete in domestic markets.

A related controversy is over *industrial policy,* the extent to which governments encourage private sector firms to engage in particular economic activities, often with gaining trade advantages in mind. These may include contracting research into particular areas to gain national advantage, economic (such as tax) incentives for certain kinds of activities, and even old-fashioned arm-twisting of industry leaders by government officials. Japan has historically been the leader in this area through the actions of the Ministry of Industry and Trade (MITI), but it has become somewhat less influential given that MITI's leadership led the Japanese television industry to support the wrong technologies for high-definition television (see Snow, *The Shape of the Future,* 2nd ed., for a discussion). Industrial policy has always had very limited appeal in the United States, and especially among business leaders who question the economic acumen of governmental officials.

The recent lightning rod in intra–First Tier trade was the 1995 dispute between the United States and Japan over alleged restrictions against American automobiles and automotive parts going into Japan, in which the United States threatened doubling tariffs on Japanese luxury cars if Japan failed to open its market further to American cars and components. The Japanese replied by threatening to drag the United States before the new World Trade Organization on charges of violating the Uruguay Round of the GATT. This latter threat raised some eyebrows among American conservatives, who were suspicious that the WTO was designed specifically for that kind of intrusion on American sovereignty, which they opposed when the Uruguay Round was ratified.

In the end, both sides backed down the day before the added tariffs were to be put in place, and world opinion, some of which is summarized in the Foreign Views box "Clinton's 'Car Wars,'" varied widely. Many other members of the First Tier decried the action as heavy-handed and bullying. On the other hand, the tactic was popular domestically, where a majority saw it as standing up to an insensitive Japan. At the

FOREIGN VIEWS

Clinton's "Car Wars"

President Bill Clinton's threatened doubling of the tariff on Japanese luxury cars created considerable controversy and criticism in the world press, most of it negative and a good bit of it wondering about the fate of the WTO given the proposed action.

One of the strongest condemnations came from the *Age* of Melbourne: "Everyone—except, it seems, the U.S.—knows American goods no longer compete in quality or price with the Japanese counterparts." Acknowledging that barriers erected by Japan distort the relationship, it adds that "these barriers hardly explain the extent or the perennial nature of America's $60 billion trade deficit with Japan." *El Mercurio* of Santiago, Chile, basically agreed, and accused the United States of hypocrisy because "the U.S., the moving force behind free trade . . . unilaterally adopted punitive measures, without waiting for the WTO's ruling regarding its claim."

A number of commentators commented on the WTO connection. The *Financial Times* of London argued that "Washington is showing its disregard for the new body even before it is properly established." The *Times* of London agreed, saying, "The WTO cannot stand on the sidelines."

Condemnation was not, however, universal. Brazil's *O Estado de S. Paolo* argued that "Japanese protectionism has forced the U.S. to go against the ideals of the WTO." The *Jerusalem Post* agreed, saying, "The Japanese have no one to blame but themselves."

Source: "A Global 'No' to Clinton's Car War," *World Press Review,* July 1995, pp. 4–5.

same time, it presumably sent a message to other states that might be contemplating free trade barriers.

Regional Organizations and Intertier Relations

The movement toward freer trade extends to the relationship between the tiers as well as to intra–First Tier economic relations. The trend is moving along two separate tracks, each of which has the expressed or least implicit effect of drawing parts of the Second Tier into the globalizing economy. On the one hand, the actions of the General Agreement on Tariffs and Trade (GATT), as negotiated by the states of the world and as enforced by the WTO, is a global effort. More recently and possibly more significantly has been the rise of two potentially major free trade areas encompassing the Pacific Ocean littoral: the APEC and NAFTA.

Of the two tracks, the GATT process is by far the older. It was the compromise solution at Bretton Woods, creating an international effort to promote the reduction of trade barriers that had been viewed as a major cause of the Second World War. Because the U.S. Senate was reluctant to endorse the International Trade Organization (ITO) as the mechanism for promotion and regulation (especially the latter) for fear that unfavorable rulings might infringe on American national sovereignty, GATT was instead commissioned as a series of negotiations (known as rounds). The states involved would negotiate (and thus not lose sovereign control over) continuing reductions of tariff barriers and each round would have to be ratified by national legislatures.

This system has always had its drawbacks. One is that not all states have participated. The most recent Uruguay Round completed in 1993 had fewer than 130 states participating; most of the states that were outside were poor Second Tier states whose economies felt threatened by the lowering of tariff and other trade barriers (because they lack comparative advantage in enough items for export to compensate for the competition from foreign goods if barriers are lowered or eliminated). States outside the system cannot profit as much from any benefits the system creates as do those that are a part of the GATT system. A second problem has been the lack of an enforcement mechanism to identify and investigate violations of GATT requirements, a shortcoming presumably remedied by the creation of the World Trade Organization (WTO) as part of the Uruguay Round negotiations.

The impact of the WTO remains conjectural and points to the ambivalence of the United States and other states about free trade and its enforcement. In principle, American policy has been pro free trade, or at least in favor of reducing impediments to trade. President Clinton and the economic advisers around him have been particularly loud champions of free trade (although moderated with some interest in industrial policy). This interest is especially manifested in Clinton's enthusiastic promotion of both GATT and the regional organizations, APEC and NAFTA. The administration's advocacy reflects a genuine belief in the economic advantages of free trade and the conviction that freer trade is simply a part of the globalizing economy. In attacking Republican opposition to ratification of the GATT Uruguay Round, Clinton strongly made the point that the failure to ratify would in effect be an attempt to reverse the movement toward a global economy, a retrogressive move.

The ambivalence manifested itself when the administration threatened to impose prohibitive tariffs on Japanese luxury cars in June 1995. The proposed action was clearly contrary to the professed free trade position of the administration, even if it was in response to the allegation of trade restrictions by the Japanese. At the same time, the action could be interpreted as throwing the gauntlet down in front of the WTO and testing its strength while still in its infancy because both countries threatened to pull the other in front of that body. The true test of the organization's strength and the extent of fealty toward its principles was avoided when the two states agreed to a compromise solution on the last day before the trade sanctions were to have taken effect.

The other track has been the emergence of regional organizations. The two most notable, in addition to the EU (which has been in existence since 1958), have been NAFTA and the APEC. Both had quiet beginnings during the end of the Cold War: the first APEC meeting was held in 1989, and negotiations that resulted in the NAFTA agreement began in the middle of the Bush administration's single term. Both organizations shot into the public eye during the transition between Bush and Clinton and have developed considerable momentum, with Clinton as a primary catalyst.

Two events in late 1994 produced the possibility of a basic alteration of the international economic system that may, if brought to fruition, transform that system as fundamentally as the overturning of the Bretton Woods system did in 1971. At a resort town outside Djakarta, Indonesia, the 18 member states of APEC agreed in principle to a two-step process that would, by the year 2020, create a complete free trade area spanning both sides of the Pacific Ocean. That same month the leaders of 34 Western Hemisphere states (all states of the hemisphere except Cuba, the only state in the region lacking a democratically elected leader) agreed in principle to a similar free trading area tentatively called the Free Trade Area of the Americas (FTAA). Since four states share membership in both organizations (the United States, Canada, Chile, and Mexico), it becomes possible to think about the emergence of an amalgamated trading area encompassing both organizations.

Neither of these agreements have been implemented or even finalized in terms of a written agreement (although the drafting of such agreements has been authorized), and neither may ever come into being. President Clinton has been at the center of both negotiations, and the outcome of the 1996 election may well influence whether or how the process proceeds. Having said that, both projects have developed enough momentum that they will not go away easily, and whoever occupies the Oval Office in 1997 will have to deal with the economic thunderclaps of November 1994.

If either or both of these free trade areas emerge, they have enormous potential to transform the international system both in economic and geopolitical terms that will help define the relationship between the tiers. In economic terms, the major implication is in the potential for such areas to provide a conduit through which countries can be moved through the developmental sequence. This prospect is made possible by the wide diversity of states that are members of each in terms of the tiers and subtiers of the international system.

As Table 11.2 indicates, each organization has members in both the First Tier and each subtier of the Second Tier. As the list suggests, the two organizations are different in developmental terms. The membership of APEC is tilted more strongly toward First Tier and developed Second Tier states (11 of the 18 members), as opposed to FTAA (7 of 34 members). FTAA has the largest number of partially developed states, which might suggest a larger number of states that could be uplifted. The list also contains a number of Caribbean states whose economy is based on tourism and have little other expectation for development.

TABLE 11.2
APEC and FTAA by Tier and Subtier

APEC	FTAA (NAFTA members appear with an asterisk)

First Tier

Australia	Canada*
Canada	United States*
Japan	
New Zealand	
United States	

Second Tier (developed)

Chile	Argentina
Hong Kong	Brazil
Korea (South)	Chile*
Mexico	Mexico*
Singapore	Venezuela
Taiwan	

Second Tier (partially developed)

APEC	FTAA
China	Antigua and Barbuda
Indonesia	Bahamas
Malaysia	Barbados
Thailand	Belize
	Bolivia
	Colombia
	Costa Rica
	Dominica
	Ecuador
	Grenada
	Guatemala
	Jamaica
	Panama
	Paraguay
	St. Kitts-Nevis
	St. Lucia
	St. Vincent
	Suriname
	Uruguay

Second Tier (developable)

APEC	FTAA
Papua New Guinea	Dominican Republic
Philippines	El Salvador
	Guyana
	Haiti
	Honduras
	Nicaragua
	Peru

Second Tier (resource rich)

APEC	FTAA
Brunei	Trinidad and Tobago

Each organization offers tantalizing possibilities both for American foreign policy and the growth of the global economy. Because of its diverse membership, APEC's prospects are particularly intriguing. According to the November 1994 pronouncement, the six First Tier states agree to end all trade barriers by the year 2010, and by 2020 the Second Tier states will be added fully to the free trade area. Besides showing the utility of the First Tier-Second Tier distinction in describing reality, this offers several potential effects that border on the revolutionary and have not been given their fair share of attention.

The first and most striking potential effect would be on the troublesome Japanese-American trading relationship. If the heads of agreement become treaty law, the whole basis of contention based in unfair trade laws, including barriers to trade, will disappear no later than 2010, a sizable accomplishment. Second, the inclusion of China provides leverage to influence the character of Chinese development as well a venue for communication with the Chinese regime. One benefit already achieved is Chinese accession to honor the GATT's provisions on guaranteeing intellectual property rights (essentially honoring patent rights and copyrights). Third, the association guarantees an active economic pipeline between the United States and the extremely dynamic economies of the countries of the western Pacific Rim.

A NAFTA expanded into the Free Trade Area of the Americas offers its own potentials. In the most obvious sense, it would create a degree of hemispheric economic unity on an unprecedented scale. This might actually be most obvious among rival South and Central American states that have historically had high barriers among them (the ABC powers—Argentina, Brazil, and Chile—for instance). Although the benefits would be differential, it would create an enormous trading bloc and hence potential market that could not be ignored internationally. It would also solidify relations between the United States and Latin America.

The most exciting economic prospect, however, lies in the possible conjunction of the two areas. Currently, four states are members of both organizations (Canada, Chile, Mexico, and the United States). If both organizations indeed implement their heads of agreement, these states would seem to create a bridge for de facto integration of the two: a good entering the United States from a NAFTA member outside APEC would also be entering the APEC free trade area, unless specific prohibitive provisions are included in one or both treaties. Should the benefits prove enticing, it is not hard to imagine a merger that would produce a free trade area of enormous power and vitality.

Is all this too optimistic a construction? Certainly it would have seemed so a decade or so ago, but things have changed. The globalizing economy is a technologically driven economic phenomenon that has achieved a momentum of its own and is likely to continue to expand (if not in entirely predictable directions) with or without the intermediation of states in forms such as APEC and NAFTA/FTAA expansion. Moreover, it may well be that the formation of these kinds of organizations is simply a first step toward the GATT goal of universal free trade.

The emergence of regional organizations—EU in addition to APEC and NAFTA—has an apparent geopolitical and security aspect as well. If we divide the world into two categories, those inside the globalizing economy as witnessed by membership in one of the three organizations and those not a part of any of these, there is a marked contrast. The areas outside include the former communist world, all of Africa, and most of southern and southeastern Asia. A quick review of global violence and instability quickly reveals that these are the areas both where most of the internal violence is occurring and where the great concentration of national poverty lies.

This is almost certainly not coincidental, and it may suggest that a way to alleviate global violence and instability (assuming that is an important foreign policy objective) is to spread the boundaries of regional economic organizations. The extension of EU membership is one possible concrete manifestation, and it not difficult to imagine APEC extending to southeast and southern Asian states (Vietnam and India, for instance).

Conclusions

International economic policy is rapidly replacing national security policy as the most dynamic area of foreign policy in the 1990s. The motors of this apparent change are dual: the recession of security concerns from the center stage at the same time that the global economy was beginning to take shape. This latter phenomenon was occurring quite independently of the security confrontation between the communist and noncommunist worlds, since virtually all the participants in the First Tier were part of the Western military arrangement. The revolutions of 1989 and beyond simply enlarged the ring of market democracies. The collapse of communism left the market-based democracies without a coherent or appealing opponent.

We can think of international economics and the policy concerns it represents in terms of three post–World War II periods. The first began with the end of the war and extended to 1971, when the American policy decision to renounce the gold standard effectively ended the Bretton Woods system and hence American hegemony over the international economic system. The second period spans 1971 until the end of the 1980s. It can be thought of as a period both of adjustment and of the roots of structural change. The adjustment was the United States settling into a relationship of greater coequality with the rest of the system, adjusting to a more normal (if great) part of the world economy in which it had rivals and partners rather than supplicants. The structural change was the introduction and maturation of the high-technology (third industrial) revolution in the most advanced states of the First Tier, the disappearance of the Second World of socialist economies, and the gradual emergence of a two-tiered economic system.

The third period is the one into which we are now entering the globalizing economy. Spurred by the merging of informational technology from its roots in computing and telecommunications, and the subsequent application of new technologies to production, distribution, and other aspects of economic activity, the result is a global level of economic interaction that quite transcends and often absolutely ignores state interference or mediation.

It is the policy consequences of this internationalizing of the world economy that will command the attention of policymakers and the policy process in the years to come. At one pole are those who would have government take an essentially passive role, arguing that market forces are far more reliable and desirable than governmental directives at stimulating economic prosperity. At the other pole are those, like President Clinton and his top economic advisers, who see the promotion of global activity as such a positive and realistic venture that it should be aggressively pursued, as in the case of APEC and NAFTA.

How this all will unfold is extremely uncertain. Change has come so rapidly in the economic sphere over the past decade or so, and in ways that were not clearly foreseen except by a few, it is difficult to imagine the precise vectors it will move toward in the future. What is more certain, however, is that economic concerns will occupy an ever increasing part of the foreign policy agenda and that the policy process will have to make adjustments to those changing realities.

SUGGESTED READINGS

Forester, Tom. *High-Tech Society: The Story of the Information Technology Revolution.* Oxford, UK: Basil Blackwell, 1987.

Gilpin, Robert. *The Political Economy of International Relations.* Princeton, NJ: Princeton University Press, 1987.

Isaak, Robert A. *International Political Economy: Managing World Economic Change.* Englewood Cliffs, NJ: Prentice Hall, 1991.

Keohane, Robert O. and Joseph S. Nye, Jr. *Power and Interdependence* (2nd ed.). Glenview, IL: Scott Foresman/Little, Brown, 1989.

Markuson, Ann, Peter Hall, and Amy Glasmeier. *High-Tech America: The What, How, Where and Why of the Sunrise Industries.* Boston: Allen & Unwin, 1986.

Nau, Henry. *The Myth of America's Decline: Leading the World Economy into the 1990s.* Oxford, UK: Oxford University Press, 1990.

Rosecrance, Richard. *The Rise of the Trading State: Commerce and Conquest in the Modern World.* New York: Basic Books, 1985.

Schwartz, Herman M. *States versus Markets: History, Geography, and the Development of the International Political Economy.* New York: St. Martin's Press, 1994.

Snow, Donald M. *The Shape of the Future: The Post-Cold War World* (2nd ed.). Armonk, NY: M. E. Sharpe, 1995.

Spero, Joan Edelman *The Politics of International Economic Relations* (4th ed.). New York: St. Martin's Press, 1990.

Thurow, Lester C. *Head to Head: Coming Economic Battle among Japan, Europe, and America.* New York: William Morrow, 1992.

CHAPTER 12

Emerging Issues in an Interdependent World

In an increasingly interdependent world, the dynamics of the new order have either created or accentuated a growing set of other concerns. Modern advances in technology, transportation, communication, and production, and political and economic liberalization facilitated by the fall of the Soviet Union and the end of the Cold War, have made it easier for goods, information, and ideas to flow across state borders in ways that states cannot easily control, restrict, or even track and monitor. The result is a series of concerns that were either absent or less important during the Cold War than they are today.

These problems are generically often called *transnational issues,* defined as problems caused by the actions of states or other actors that transcend state boundaries in ways over which states have little control and which cannot be solved by the actions of individual states or other actors within states alone. The term, however, is both misleading and incomplete. It is misleading because it contributes to the mistaken equation of the terms *nation* and *state,* as we discussed earlier. A more proper designation would be "transstate" (or even "transsovereign") issues, since it is states around which the problems and their solutions exist. It is incomplete because not all the problems that are important and we discuss in this chapter fit into the definition. Some major issues, such as human rights and democracy (discussed later) are described as transnational/transstate, but only meet part of the criteria in the definition; violations of human rights *can* be solved by the actions of individual states; the problem is that all states, for different reasons, do not enforce the same standards. Similarly, other concerns shared by many governments around the world, such as continuing population growth, are potential transstate issues. For instance, when global resources such as food cannot adequately sustain the population, it will become truly a global problem. Moreover, not all the problems or their solutions result from state action; nongovernmental organizations like crime cartels may cause international problems, whereas other NGOs like Doctors without Borders may contribute to solutions. As a result, this chapter concentrates on a series of major emerging global — not limited to traditional transstate — problems that have achieved and are likely to retain prominence on the foreign policy agenda for some time.

The roster of these global problems covers a broad array of both physical and social conditions on the globe: environmental problems such as ozone depletion and global warming, depletion of ocean fisheries, human rights believed to be universal to humankind but irregularly enforced by different state governments, the increasing problem of refugee flows (usually caused by internal wars), and food supply, to name a few.

There are multiple causes of this emerging set of problems. Possibly the most prominent are those technological developments that have contributed to an increasingly interdependent world among those countries sharing in the general prosperity (the global economy). Acceleration of these technologically based trends has been aided by the virtual collapse of ideological opposition to the values of Western-style democracy and market-based economics. In some cases like environmental degradation, they are the result of direct human actions in some countries that affect others, such as the use of chlorofluorocarbons (CFCs) that attack the ozone layer and expose ever growing parts of the world to the harmful effects of ultraviolet radiation. Drug smuggling is an instance where the actions of individuals and groups within countries create a problem that individual states cannot control. This points to yet another source: the rise of organized private groups within and among states that contribute both to the growth of problems and their solutions. The emergence of a new Russian mafia as part of privatization in that country has impacts in places like Brighton Beach, Brooklyn (where many Russian immigrants live). Private nongovernmental organizations (NGOs) are prominent in identifying problems and the need for solutions, especially in the human rights area.

Also contributing to the rise of many of these emerging global issues is the lifting of the Cold War ideological competition. Many of the human rights issues, for instance, could not be frankly addressed in international forums because the Cold War competitors would (often correctly) maintain that the issue was being raised to embarrass them. Although one can overstate the degree to which the veil has been lifted, the end of the ideological competition has facilitated more frank and honest consideration than was the case previously. Before the 1975 Helsinki Accords were signed, for example, discussions of human rights violations in the Soviet Union and Eastern Europe (as well as China) were viewed by some as merely propaganda. The accords, which, among other stipulations, required all participants, and specifically communist and noncommunist Europe, to honor basic rights, began the opening of the communist world and may have contributed to the process resulting in the fall of communism. Similarly, some of the world's worst industrial pollution has occurred in the formerly communist world, and the fall of communism facilitated a more honest definition of the problems of environmental cleanup, especially in Europe.

In many ways, the transstate and other emerging issues represent the downside, or at least the challenge, to what are otherwise thought of as good, progressive international trends: the rise of democracies and capitalist-based economies and freer trade and other phenomena stimulated by the technological, communications, and transportation revolutions to which we have referred in discussing change more generally. They emerge as problems because the fruits of these advances and the dynamic trends they represent is not universally enjoyed. Economic prosperity and demands for political liberalization, for instance, are closely related and close to universally desired; the movement for universal human rights emerges from the attempt to universalize them.

These issues are also intensely political in at least two ways. First, many are classically intermestic, with both domestic and international dimensions and repercussions. The environment is such an issue; the United States, on the one hand, urges in international forums that rain forests in other countries be preserved to aid in controlling carbon dioxide levels, but at the same time has not reached anything like a consensus on the use of public lands in the American West. At the same time, differential environmental regulations (such as the disposal of toxic waste) between Mexico and the United States have been a continuing point of contention in passing and implementing the North American Free Trade Agreement.

In a more directly international context, many transstate and other emerging issues have become major parts of the First Tier-Second Tier dialogue. The structure of a number of the transnational issues brings the two tiers into at least partial conflict. Some international terrorism, for instance, is organized in Second Tier countries (such as Libya and Iran) and directed at First Tier states, although a good bit is homegrown and aimed at fellow citizens (the Tamil Tigers in Sri Lanka) or at other Second Tier states (Sudanese support for Islamic fundamentalists). In areas like environmental pollution, Second Tier states are asked to forgo certain activities (such as rain forest degradation) for the greater good of environmental protection while First Tier states remain major pollution producers, a continuing bone of intertier contention. Human rights initiatives mostly emanate from the First Tier, and some Second Tier states and regions view them as little more than Western cultural imperialism.

More importantly, these issues have become more pressing security concerns since the end of the Soviet threat. Scarce environmental resources and environmental degradation can lead to conflict (as in the numerous clashes over water in the Middle East and especially the conflict in Somalia); refugee flows can exacerbate or cause strife (as in Burundi); and the example of the fruits of criminal insurgency (civil unrest, the purpose of which is to destabilize political control to facilitate criminal behavior by the "insurgents") in countries like Liberia can spread across borders and infect neighboring countries, such as Sierra Leone.

The United States has an important role in the evolution of these problems and their solutions. The human rights movement is, in many important ways, an extension of the dialogue within the United States on matters such as civil and women's rights; it should have been no surprise that early women's rights champions Bella Abzug and first lady Hillary Rodham Clinton were prominent figures at the women's rights conferences held in Beijing in August 1995, for instance. At the same time, problems plaguing the United States, such as the flood of illegal narcotics entering the country or the increasing presence of international criminal syndicates (the Russian mafia, for instance), are international or transstate in their origins.

What is central and common to these issues is that they defy solutions by single states. In the case of a transstate issue like stopping the flow of drugs, the United States is only in partial control of its fate. Despite efforts to educate the citizenry about the deleterious effects of drug usage and attempts to intercept incoming supplies of illicit materials, the campaign only stands a chance of being successful if there is widespread international cooperation to shut down the sources of drugs and to make their transshipment more difficult. These issues become American foreign policy concerns when they affect the interests of the country or of significant numbers of Americans in ways that demand political attempts to mitigate or eliminate them. How important is it to the United States that rain forest depletion cease? Or that political rights with origins in the U.S. Constitution spread to countries where their application can conceivably be beneficial to the citizens of a particular country?

The rest of the chapter discusses a number of these emerging issues that we chose because of their visibility and importance in the American dialogue. They are abuses of human rights and the promotion of democracy (including women's rights); worldwide population growth (including food supply to support it); and protection of the environment in the face of its degradation. Of these, human rights receives the most attention because it is high on the policy agenda and demonstrates many of the trends that have emerged from the technological revolution and shrinking of the globe due to associated advances. It is not strictly a transstate issue because state action could theoretically solve it. It is an emerging issue because some states reject or resist universal definitions. Population and food supply represents a global issue with the potential to become a full-fledged transstate issue, whereas the environment is a classic transstate issue. All three have received a great deal of exposure and discussion both within the United States and in international forums and are likely to continue to do so.

We begin each discussion by describing the problem and why it is an important issue. We then look at the status of the problem, both progress and barriers to progress. Each discussion concludes with an assessment of U.S. interests and the position—or positions—that the United States has adopted.

Human Rights and Democracy

The central proposition dominating the human rights movement is the idea that all humans have certain basic, inalienable rights and there is a universal obligation to enforce and protect those rights; prominent among those human rights is political freedom, or democracy. The issue is not technically transstatist because individual states could, through their own actions, enforce a uniform code. All states, of course, do not do this; there are widespread differences in the quality of the human condition and even disagreement—sometimes honest and heartfelt, sometimes cynically political—about what compose the conditions to which humans are entitled. Moreover, the expressions and concerns are often gender based, since women in many societies have historically enjoyed far fewer rights than men. At the same time, the treatment of children has recently become a prominent part of the dialogue.

Human rights and democracy are an important part of the international agenda because they are tied to ongoing world change. Interdependence and the growing world economy are creating greater economic prosperity, and as prosperity grows, so do calls for human rights from those newly prosperous. Economic and political democracy, in other words, are the economic and political expressions of freedom, and their connection helps produce what Singer and Wildavsky call a "quality economy" (where free people are highly motivated and thus more productive and innovative than nonfree people).

Demands for uniform human rights tend to come in two varieties, one discussed here, the other touched on later. In the first category are basic civil and political rights (such as freedom of speech, assembly, and religion contained in the U.S. Bill of Rights). This category also includes social rights as fought for in the civil rights and antidiscrimination movements in the United States, such as freedom from discrimination in hiring or in public places. These are sometimes referred to as "negative rights" because they state actions that cannot be taken against people.

In the second category are basic human economic rights, the right, for instance, to an adequate diet or a certain level of education. These are sometimes referred to as "positive rights" because they entail positive conditions to which their advocates maintain people are entitled, minimum quality of life standards.

The assertion of a set of human rights is a relatively recent phenomenon. Historically, the superiority of the sovereign authority of the state has meant that rulers routinely have been able to do with their citizens whatever they were physically capable of doing. The classic, absolute assertion of sovereignty maintains that, within the sovereign domain of the state, the ruler has the right to do whatever he or she might, and there is no right that allows others to challenge such action, even when it entails the suppression and even slaughter of parts of the population.

Although there have been periodic expressions of the notion of human rights, they have been comparatively infrequent. Originally, U.S. democracy provided rights for male citizens, for instance, but did not provide political rights for women, and early U.S. citizens did keep slaves.

The philosophical birthplace of the human rights and democracy movement arguably lie in the seventeenth-century work of John Locke, the British philosopher from whom many of the ideas that underlay the American republic were derived (see Amplification box "John Locke and Human Rights"). Among his contributions, which can be seen in contemporary discussions, are notions of popular sovereignty (the idea that individuals, not the state, are the primary repository of sovereignty) implicit in advocacies of intrusions against governments engaged in human rights violations.

AMPLIFICATION

John Locke and Human Rights

John Locke was a seventeenth-century English philosopher who developed a then radical theory about the role of governments. He thought that governments exist solely to safeguard the rights of individuals. His contemporary, Thomas Hobbes, had also postulated that humans are born into a state of nature with certain innate rights. But the two disagreed on the implications of their ideas.

Hobbes adopted an essentially negative picture of human freedom. He believed that the unfettered exercise of human freedom would lead to an intolerable anarchy, "the war of all against all," as he put it. As a result, individual freedom had to be sacrificed to maintain a social order, which meant the establishment of an all-powerful sovereign who could enforce order. Implicit in his assessment was a thoroughly pessimistic view of humans and their ability to interact peacefully. Humans unconstrained by sovereign authority would result in a condition of "continual fear and danger of violent death" where human life was "solitary, poor, nasty, brutish, and short."

Locke disagreed fundamentally with Hobbes's conclusion. He took a far more optimistic view of people's ability to exercise freedom responsibly and to live and interact in peace without overwhelming coercion. Starting from this assessment, Locke extrapolated his famous idea that natural liberties—which are prior to the establishment of civil government in both the philosophical and chronological senses—serve as the sole legitimate basis for constituting governmental institutions. The people, in order to secure and protect their inherent rights, band together and delegate a limited amount of authority to the government that they themselves create and control.

The implications of Locke's philosophy were not widely accepted during his own time. After all, he was merely a philosopher living in an England where only a handful of members of the nobility had any rights. But his philosophy was instrumental in shaping the beliefs of many of the American Founding Fathers (notably Thomas Jefferson), and they remain vibrant principles very much in keeping with the global spread of freedom and democracy today.

Contemporary advocacies of human rights and democracy by some governments and private groups (NGOs) can be thought of as grounded on two related foci. Where human rights, including the political freedom that defines democracy, is not present in particular countries, advocacies are aimed at providing democratization for all citizens. Since the end of the Cold War, political scientist Samuel P. Huntington argues we have entered a "third wave" of democratization for the twentieth century (the first two waves came immediately after the world wars) that is spreading democracy to regions where it was previously not present or certainly not universal (Central and South America, in particular).

The other focus is less universal, involving the forceful advocacy of human rights for categories of citizens within countries that have been denied rights. The most visible and forceful advocacies have been for *women's rights,* the extension of basic and extended rights to women in societies that have treated women as inferiors. These cover a wide range of physical concerns, from basic political rights of participation and equal standing under the law to more social concerns such as the right to enter into and out of marriage freely, reproductive rights, and even matters such as genital mutilation (female circumcision). This category of rights, which was prominent at the Beijing summits (see Amplification box "Women's Rights and the Beijing Meetings"), has also been extended to the treatment of children. Since most of the inequalities and human rights abuses are alleged to occur in the Second Tier and most (if by no means all) of the major advocates are feminists from the First Tier, this issue is a major flashpoint in the First Tier-Second Tier debate on transnational issues.

Status of the Human Rights Issue

Now that the Cold War competition no longer dominates the foreign policy agenda, the issue of human rights has emerged as a major foreign policy concern for many governments, including that of the United States. In the absence of a major ideological opponent to Western-style democracy, it is not surprising that the issue has largely been framed in Western terms.

In this section, we look at two matters. The first is contemporary forces that have pushed human rights issues into such prominence. Although advocacy of human rights goes back to the founding days of the United Nations in contemporary terms, it has gained considerable momentum since the end of the Cold War. The other emphasis is on the status of the movement, particularly in terms of the formalization of ideas of universal human rights.

The human rights movement has clearly benefited from the end of the Cold War and the emergence of the Western system of political democracy and market-based economics as the nearly universally accepted form of political and economic organization in the First Tier and in parts of the Second Tier. This wave of democratization has been aided by at least three other forces that have acted as proponents and publicists: the modern electronic media, the influence of outstanding individuals, and the activities of nongovernmental organizations.

State brutality has long been reported by the traditional print media, but the advent of the electronic *global village,* to borrow Marshall McLuhan's famous term, has made such reporting much more accessible and vivid. Burgeoning telecommunications capa-

AMPLIFICATION

Women's Rights and the Beijing Meetings

In August and September 1995, two conferences were held in and around the Chinese capital of Beijing to explore and elucidate the issue of women's rights. The first to convene was the nongovernmental organizations' (NGOs) Forum on Women, sanctioned by the United Nations, which began its deliberations on August 30 at Beijing's Olympic Stadium with roughly 25,000 delegates in attendance. The second was the U.N. Fourth World Conference on Women, whose 4,000 delegates representing 185 countries convened at the Great Hall of the People on September 4.

The U.N. conference attracted the most attention and produced the most visible results. Although it was marked by some controversy, such as Vatican objections to proposals concerning abortion and family planning and Islamic objections to provisions for equal inheritance rights for women, the conference was able to reach agreement on the basic platform by adopting two resolutions, the Platform for Action and the Beijing Declaration. The Beijing Declaration

bilities have produced news organizations such as CNN and ITN that can transmit information from any point on the globe to another in real time, virtually as events are happening. The nature of visual reporting creates an evocative atmosphere not possible with the written word: we can see atrocities, for instance, with a shock value the printed word could hardly evoke.

The result is coverage and publicity of events that more than likely would have been neglected only a few years ago. The hand-held camcorder and small satellite dish mean that no place on the globe is too remote or physically inaccessible. Although the savage genocidal war in Sudan provides stark evidence that it is not impossible to keep out the media and hence suppress direct coverage of atrocity, it is becoming increasingly difficult to hide inhumanity even in authoritarian states such as China. Can you imagine, a decade ago, the Chinese government feeling the need to provide an elaborate media event to convince the world that it was not systematically starving children in a state-run orphanage, as it felt compelled to do in January 1996?

Individual leaders have also done much to spur the world's awareness of human rights violations, sometimes running against other foreign policy priorities. During much of the Cold War, for instance, human rights records of countries took a backseat to their levels of anticommunism. Thus, the United States sometimes found itself supporting brutal dictatorships in which human rights were regularly suppressed provided a "Bill of Rights for Women" of sorts, containing provisions calling for equal inheritance rights, equal access to education and medical services, and the right of all women to decide freely concerning matters of sexuality (namely childbearing), to cite a few of the more prominent. The Platform for Action provided a framework for implementing the provisions in the declaration.

The NGO Conference, which moved to the town of Huairou the day after it convened, was a more public forum. In addition to decrying publicly Chinese policy toward women and objecting to Chinese governmental restrictions on the conferees, it featured public appearances by a number of prominent women. Pakistani prime minister Benazir Bhutto, for instance, publicly deplored the Asian preference for male children, which she said led to abortion of female fetuses. First lady Hillary Rodham Clinton also appeared, stating, "It is a violation of human rights when women are denied the right to plan their own families, and that includes being forced to have abortions or being sterilized against their wills." She also condemned female genital mutilation, domestic violence against women, and rape of women during war.

because the regimes were strongly anticommunist. Former American president Jimmy Carter, however, won the admiration of oppressed people throughout the Second Tier for his elevation of human rights to the top of the foreign policy agenda during his single term. Carter stated his position forcefully in his memoir, *Keeping Faith:* "Whenever I met with a leader of a government which had been accused of wronging its own people, the subject of human rights was near the top of my agenda." Carter has continued to be an advocate of human rights, leading missions to places such as Haiti where human rights abuses have been long standing. Another example is Pope John Paul II. In visits to his native Poland in 1979 and 1983, he rallied the people behind his call for religious freedom. His advocacy became a rallying cry for the popular movement that overthrew communist rule in Poland in 1989.

Nongovernmental organizations (NGOs) have also become prominent in the human rights movement. Some serve as monitors of the human rights records of states. As we discussed in Chapter 9, Amnesty International annually produces a list of countries where it alleges human rights abuses occur. Its list is often compared to a similar one prepared by law by the State Department (AI's list is invariably longer), and Congress often requires the State Department to explain discrepancies. A newer and more aggressive counterpart is Human Rights Watch, which burst into the public spotlight when it accused the Chinese government in the orphanage scandal in 1995, where the organization clandestinely videotaped alleged neglect and mistreatment of Chinese children in a supposed model orphanage and then released the tapes, to the embarrassment of the Chinese government.

In addition to the monitors, a growing number of NGOs also seek actively to mediate and assist in situations where human rights are abused—for instance, to tend to refugees in war zones. These organizations provide a variety of services, from the provision of food (Care, for instance) and medical care (the French-based Doctors without Borders, for instance). Their work also serves to publicize the suffering they seek to alleviate.

The human rights movement did not begin with the end of the Cold War, even though that event has certainly accelerated activism on the human rights front. The banner was first raised in the twentieth century by President Woodrow Wilson in his Fourteen Points at the end of World War I, and the issue resurfaced in World War II, where the victorious Allies were not only fighting for their physical survival, but also "in the name of freedom," a phrase coined by American president Franklin Roosevelt and British prime minister Winston Churchill in the Atlantic Charter of 1941, which laid out the Allied goals for the war. A postwar emphasis on human rights was further stimulated by revelations about Hitler's Holocaust, which intensified the broad desire to create a more humane world.

This postwar emphasis was formalized in 1945 when representatives of 51 countries gathered in San Francisco to sign the charter that formed the United Nations. The charter called for the original signatories, and the nearly 140 other states that have since become signatories, to "pledge themselves to observe and to respect human rights."

The United Nations has been the focal point for the global human rights movement since the organization's inception. In addition to sponsoring international conferences such as one of the 1995 Beijing conferences on women's rights, the United Nations has also produced a series of five treaties by which signatories bind themselves to specific observations of human rights. The first two of these were passed in 1948; the other three are products of the 1960s.

The first important document was the Convention on the Prevention and Punishment of the Crime of Genocide. It was adopted by the General Assembly in 1948 as the direct result of international revulsion toward Germany's systematic extermination of the European Jewish population (the Holocaust). The most important legal mechanism contained within the convention creates standards for punishing those guilty of acts "committed with intent to destroy in whole or part a national, ethnic, racial, or religious group." The convention currently is providing the legal precedent for establishing war crimes tribunals for both Bosnia and Rwanda and will probably be invoked in future cases where actions like ethnic cleansing resemble genocide. The United States, interestingly enough, did not ratify the convention until 1988. The official reason was congressional concern that the document's requirement of automatic jurisdiction by the World Court (formally the International Court of Justice) on genocide cases could undermine American sovereignty; a less official reason was the fear that several-Native American tribes and African Americans might sue the U.S. government under the convention's provisions for past treatment.

The General Assembly also adopted the Universal Declaration on Human Rights in 1948. This document provided the most sweeping set of international norms protecting the rights of individuals from their governments (the negative, or political rights noted earlier) and creating standards of living to which people are entitled (the positive, or social rights). The rights declared to be inherent for all individuals are very broad. They include (1) the right to life, to due process of law, and to freedom of thought and worship; (2) the right not to be tortured or enslaved; and (3) "the right to a standard of living adequate for the health and well-being of self and family." Critics argued, sometimes disingenuously, that the declaration was too broad and vague for universal application (often because they did not want to enforce its principles); defenders hailed it as constituting new standards for evaluating the performance of states.

Three human rights documents approved as a series of treaties by the General Assembly during the 1960s sought to give additional substance to these early initiatives: the International Convention on the Elimination of All Forms of Racial Discrimination; the International Covenant on Economic, Social, and Cultural Rights; and the International Covenant of Civil and Political Rights. Of these, the International Covenant of Economic, Social, and Cultural rights, passed in 1966, is considered the most basic.

The attitude of the U.S. government, which did not sign the 1966 covenant until 1977 and did not ratify it until 1992 in the waning months of the Bush administration, examplifies the ambivalence Americans have had about these international standards. On the one hand, the United States has been a major player in drafting almost all the accords; the political rights in the Universal Declaration and subsequent political statements closely parallel the American Bill of Rights (some critics argue they dilute Bill of Rights guarantees, thus making them irrelevant). At the same time, there has been considerable opposition to adopting these treaties in the United States. Why?

There are philosophical and political objections. One is the dilution of sovereignty; if the United States signs an international treaty, that document's provisions become part of U.S. law enforceable in U.S. courts. If a treaty's provisions contradict U.S. law, the treaty's dictates *supercede* the existing statute and take precedent over it. It is because of this feature that the opposition to these treaties on the basis of diluting sovereignty is often argued; it is also why treaties require senatorial action.

This leads to a more practical, political concern, particularly as these treaties assert the positive or social rights of people. The debate over the status of women, minorities, or children, and especially to what conditions they are entitled, has both a domestic and an international aspect. The international assertion of a right to an adequate standard of living for all people, for instance, has an obvious parallel in the domestic debate over welfare, medical care, and a whole host of other entitlements. If one is politically opposed to the provision of certain entitlements to groups of

American citizens, then one will be wary of promoting the same rights internationally, especially if international agreements might pose standards that would have to be enforced within the United States to which some Americans are opposed.

Human Rights and U.S. Policy

Clearly, the issue of human rights has not been satisfactorily resolved. A significant gap remains between the language of international proclamations and the everyday experiences of millions, even billions of people worldwide. The result is a continuing human rights agenda over which the United States, as the remaining superpower, has little choice but to preside or, more modestly, actively to try to influence.

The United States has some ambivalence in this regard, although its difficulties have been reduced with the end of the Cold War. As we discussed in Chapter 2, the Cold War produced a geopolitical tension between evaluating regimes primarily on their adherence to democratic values or their professed anticommunist ideology, a wrenching situation when regimes were both anticommunist and antidemocratic. In those circumstances, the communist-anticommunist dimension often prevailed, and the United States was occasionally forced to favor democracy at some points while siding with opponents of democracy at others. President Carter was the first to try to move to primary concern with democracy, but the Cold War sometimes overwhelmed his emphasis.

The removal of the communist-anticommunist concern has removed that barrier. The United States no longer feels any ambivalence about supporting democracy and opposing its opponents, although the strength with which that opposition is voiced may be influenced by other factors like economics, as in the case of China. Generally, however, economic ties create an interest in promoting human rights and democracy because the United States prefers to trade with partners who are law abiding and where its businesspeople will be safe. At the same time, economic concerns also place a parameter on how far the United States is willing to push human rights issues when it fears adverse economic fallout.

The "third wave" of democracy has been enthusiastically embraced by the Clinton administration and as it applies to the political and other human rights of people around the world. When President Clinton has talked of a policy of "engagement and enlargement" of the democratic realm, he is supporting the spread of democracy to those places where it has a reasonable chance of succeeding and where there is a local base of support. Unlike the Cold War period, there is virtually no resistance to such advocacy. Why is this the case? Four answers, largely framed in traditional geopolitical terms, come to mind.

First, the spread of democracy enhances national security. Democratic states historically have not gone to war with one another; essentially all apparent exceptions occur where (1) democracy is not well established, and (2) disputes predate democratization. The Ecuador-Peru border dispute is an example. Being accountable to their people, democratic governments are disinclined to wage aggressive wars, especially against like-minded free people with whom they have little political reason to fight. This principle is well established in the First Tier; presumably it will spread to a democratizing Second Tier as well.

Second, democratic states are the most reliable bulwark for protecting human rights. Although violations of individual rights occur from time to time even in democratic societies, systematic violations of basic political rights are less likely because they are antithetical to the very concept of democratic self-government. More simply put, democratic governance and human political rights are two sides of the same coin.

Third, democratic regimes are, for the most part, more responsible and law-abiding members of the international community than are dictatorships. After all, political democracies are grounded in the rule of law and the accountability of the governors to the citizenry. On the other hand, democracies are also subject to changes in public opinion that may make today's policy untenable tomorrow. The United States, for instance, is often accused of inconsistency in its foreign policy because of public opinion–driven attitude swings. Such vacillation, however, rarely extends to the most basic forms of relationships with other states or the international community.

Finally, the growth of the global economy is closely related to the combined effects of political democratization and free and open market-based economies. Many argue that the two are related because they represent the political and economic manifestations of the same basic principle, freedom of action. Regardless of philosophical roots, however, it is obvious, as we described in explaining the two tiers, that there is a remarkable coincidence between political democracy and economic achievement.

The problem, and especially its solution, is not so clear and unambiguous with regard to the assertion of positive rights, particularly in a political atmosphere where fiscal concerns (for instance, balancing the budget) may threaten to overwhelm concern with human entitlements. When the U.N. treaties of the 1940s and 1960s were being negotiated and approved, there was less than universal accord within the United States about many of the issues that these agreements addressed: the Convention on Genocide and Universal Declaration, for instance, predated the full blossoming of the civil rights movement; and the documents of the 1960s were developed while Johnson's Great Society of social programs was still being developed. The atmosphere of the 1990s may provide a parallel. The extent to which governments can or should take on an activist role in promoting and protecting the human condition in a social and economic sense is nowhere nearly as universally agreed upon as it is in the realm of political rights.

Our final concern is with unresolved issues on the agenda, which can be capsulized in two categories. The first is the absence of reliable enforcement mechanisms, a problem that human rights standards share with other evolving international norms and largely arises from the struggle over the meaning of sovereignty. The second is a disagreement over whether there is a single, universal standard of human rights, a problem that often pits the First Tier against parts of the Second Tier. The two problems overlap in that where there are states that disagree with presumptive universal rights, they will be reluctant to allow them to be enforced.

The problem of enforcement has bedeviled many international efforts. It is a fundamental characteristic of the international system, deriving from the principle of sovereignty, that no force is superior to that of the state; in other words, no international body has jurisdiction over the territory, including the population, of another country. In the human rights field, this becomes a problem when governments abuse their citizens—especially to the extremity of the systematic slaughter of population segments (genocide). In this case, there may be (and are) appeals to a higher authority in order to right wrongs. States invariably resist such demands, fearing their precedential nature: if someone else's sovereignty can be violated, then who is to say mine might not be sometime in the future?

The absence of legitimate supranational (above the state) mechanisms means that international efforts must be more indirect. For example, when faced with evidence of human rights violations, states, or combinations of states, may threaten to cut off foreign aid until abuses cease, which may be effective if the target relies on such assistance. If the violator does not depend on foreign aid, of course, such a threat is ineffective. Economic sanctions offer another possibility, but the result may be that the population target one seeks to help will bear the burden of the suffering (Haiti is an example). Asylum for political dissidents is another possibility; during the Cold War the United States offered asylum to many Cubans fleeing communism, but not to people fleeing anticommunist dictatorships such as Haiti.

None of the enforcement mechanisms is adequate, largely because of the problem of universality. The simple fact is that there is substantial disagreement among different parts of the world on what constitutes human rights. Many of the most serious are gender related; in much of the world, the rights of women (including female children) are considerably more circumscribed than they are for men. In most cases, these differences are encased in long-held practices and traditions creating advantages for men that they do not want to forfeit. Yet, if rights are to be universal, they must apply equally, regardless of race, sex, age, or whatever other yardstick one may devise.

Both disagreements came to the forefront during the two-week U.N. conference on human rights in Vienna in 1993—the first global meeting on the subject in 25 years. In preparation for the June event, preliminary regional meetings were held in Thailand, Tunisia, and Costa Rica. These meetings produced declarations arguing that the Universal Declaration of Human Rights was a mere cultural expression of Western values that did not apply to non-Western societies, most of which were under colonial bondage in 1948 when the declaration was written.

The most strident expression of this objection was set forth in the Bangkok Declaration signed by 40 Asian governments. The declaration argued that notions of freedom and justice are contingent on "regional peculiarities and various historical, cultural, and religious backgrounds." The assertion of universal standards was, according to the Bangkok signatories, no more than another expression of Western imperialism. At the African meeting, the delegates argued for a focus on the economic and social (positive rights) agenda because many of the poorest people in the world were represented at that conference. This logically led to a reemphasis on the developmental agenda, a frequent diversion in First Tier-Second Tier interactions on transstate issues.

Despite these sources of objection, the Vienna conference was able to adopt a declaration which, if implemented by U.N. bodies, will strengthen human rights. Three provisions of the Vienna conference stand out. First, the conference backed an American proposal for stronger U.N. efforts in rectifying human rights abuses, including a call for establishing a high commissioner on human rights. Second, the conference expanded the definition of human rights by calling for special efforts on behalf of women, children, and minorities. The 1994 Cairo conference on children and the Beijing meetings on women were called to further elaborate on these issues. Finally, the conference strongly endorsed the obligation of all states to protect human rights "regardless of their political, economic, and cultural systems," a provision passed over the noisy objections of a handful of states that had dominated the regional conferences.

Population and Food

The rapid growth of the world's population and the inability of certain regions to produce adequate food to sustain their expanding population represents a second major global issue. To repeat, it does not qualify technically as a transstate issue because theoretically, individual state actions could solve it. It is, however, largely a First Tier-Second Tier issue because almost all of the growth is occurring in the Second Tier; most of the entreaties to retard growth and the efforts to increase food supply emanate from the First Tier.

Moreover, the issue has its geopolitical aspects. Attempts to address population matters, such as the 1994 Cairo conference, often devolve into the familiar debate over developmental assistance from the First Tier to the Second. In some parts of the world, First Tier advocacy of limiting population is actually viewed as a plot to keep developing states weak. In its worst aspects, populations become geopolitical pawns, such as the withholding of food in Somalia to force political submission or the forced migration of beleaguered population segments.

The demographics of population growth are straightforward. In 1945, world population stood at about 1.5 billion. Writing in that year, Frank Notestein, a prominent demographer, predicted that population would double to 3 billion by the year 2000, an estimate considered radical at the time. And Notestein did prove wrong: the population of the world, which took until the year 1800 to reach 1 billion, surpassed

3 billion in 1960. In 1974, it reached 4 billion, and it climbed to 5 billion in 1987. It is estimated that by the millenium, world population will exceed 6 billion.

The distribution and growth of the population is highly differential. Between the years 1980 and 2000, the world's population is estimated to grow from 4.4 billion to 6.2 billion. Of that increase of 1.8 billion, 1.6 billion will occur in the Second Tier (which includes the former Soviet Union, in which there is hardly any growth). In the countries of the First Tier, growth will only reach about 200 million. The current population distribution, according to Singer and Wildavsky in *The Real World Order,* is that only one in seven people lives in the First Tier, and that ratio is increasing.

The numbers are demographically imbalanced. By the year 2000, for instance, there will be 1.2 billion people living in China, and 1.1 billion in India, meaning that 37 percent of the world's population will reside in one or another of those ancient rival states.

The bases of the population growth phenomenon are easy enough to demonstrate. For any country, increases in population size are the result of the population growth rate (PGR), which is the difference between the birthrate (BR) and the death rate (DR), plus or minus the impact of migration. Expressed as a formula, $PGR = BR - DR \pm$ migration. Migration may and often does affect growth in individual countries, but it is not a factor in global projections.

The reason that population is increasing is not so much the result of increases in birthrates as it is decreases in death rates. Due to improvements in basic diet, sanitation, and medical services, people are simply living longer than they used to. In many traditional societies, for instance, parents expected many of their children would die during childbirth or early childhood, which no longer occurs thanks to improvements like vaccination against disease. The dilemma is that there have not been corresponding declines universally in birthrates.

The problem inevitably relates to the developmental agenda. Population growth and its decline are closely related to economic prosperity in the sense that the most developed countries tend to have the lowest population growth. In most of the First Tier, the population surge associated with the introduction of modern medicine and sanitation occurred at a time of underpopulation (the aftermath of the great plagues in Europe) and around the time of the first industrial revolution. As prosperity and the ability to accumulate wealth occur, the desire and incentive to have large families dwindles and the birthrate falls with it.

This sequence has not occurred in the same way in much of the Second Tier. Its growth surge began at a time when populations were at relatively high levels and economic improvement was not creating adequate incentives to limit family size. As a result, declines in death rates have not been accompanied by corresponding declines in birthrates across the board (although a good bit of progress has been made in a number of countries).

A growing number of people places a strain on existing food supplies, creating several problems. Population growth often does not occur in places where expansion of the food supply through additional farming is possible. In fact, in the Sahel region of western Africa, for example, the attempt to farm additional land has upset the local ecology, resulting in accelerated spread of the Sahara Desert (known as desertification) that actually decreases arable land. Another problem is that of *carrying capacity,* the maximum ability for land to be productive without decreasing its potential for the future. Phenomena such as the so-called green revolution seek to increase carrying capacity by making land more sustainably productive, but there are limits to this strategy. Finally, there is often a mismatch between the availability of food and the places it is needed, where distribution and transportation problems are difficult to overcome.

Status of the Population Problem

Attention to the problem of population growth and its attendant strain on the ability of the world to feed itself has ebbed and flowed across time. From the 1950s to the 1970s, the United States, and especially President Richard M. Nixon, was at the forefront of the movement to reduce population growth.

Nixon's leadership was manifested in two concrete ways. First, his administration took the leadership role in creating the first intergovernmental organization devoted specifically to population, the United Nations Fund for Population Activities (UNFPA) in 1969. UNFPA conducts studies, disseminates information, and promotes greater global awareness of the population problem. It is funded by voluntary donations from its members, with the United States its largest contributor.

The second major Nixon initiative was pressing for the first U.N. conference on global population in Bucharest, Romania, in 1974. At this conference, the United States proposed an aggressive agenda to help curb global population growth, including sharp increases in assistance for national birth control programs. These proposals were generally not well received in much of the Third World on the grounds of cultural intrusiveness and, more pointedly, the charge that the most important agenda item should be developmental assistance, which, it was argued, represents the ultimate solution to the population problem.

The concerns raised in the context of these early considerations continue to divide the growing Second Tier and the growth-conscious First Tier. To most population growth opponents, the key is the reduction of fertility rates among women in the Second Tier. This advocacy becomes entwined with women's rights over fertility-limiting strategies such as contraception, abortion, and women's control over their reproductive behavior. As the issues intertwine, they raise multiple objections from antiabortion advocates in the United States and elsewhere (the Vatican, for instance) and groups like fundamentalist Muslims who fear that expansion of women's rights, including reproductive rights, challenges traditional male-dominated bases of their societies. Advocates counter that there is simply no alternative to reduced fertility if population growth is to be checked.

In addition to these objections, many in the Second Tier believe the fundamental issue is not explicit efforts to limit population, but the more general need for development. To many Second Tier leaders, advocacy of population programs is little more than a diversion that allows the most developed states to avoid providing adequate developmental assistance to improve the lot of developing world states. Once development begins to occur, they argue, fertility reduction will follow as a natural consequence to modernization, just as it did in the First Tier.

All of these concerns came to a head at the United Nations Conference on Population and Development held in Cairo, Egypt, during December 1994. Over 20,000 delegates representing 170 states and numerous NGOs attended the nine-day conference. It was a highly politicized event where different groups fought for ascendancy and made deals to accomplish at least part of their goals. The fact that the conference was officially on both population and development was a compromise by most First Tier advocates of population control for developing countries. In addition to this symbolism, the conference accomplished four notable tasks.

The first accomplishment was to include in the language of the 113-page final report an explicit acknowledgment of legalized abortion as part of the population control strategy. An otherwise unlikely coalition of Catholic (notably the Vatican) and Islamic states had to be convinced to overcome their objections on the abortion statement for the success of the overall program of the conference.

The second accomplishment, marking a triumph for the feminists who were very active at the event, was to cast the whole program within feminist language and logic. "Empowering women" became the virtual slogan of the event as multiple speakers argued that the empowerment of women was the key to most population problems.

The third accomplishment was the opportunity to showcase those countries that have taken the lead in population increase reduction. Among those highlighted were Bangladesh (with a 50 percent decrease in growth rate over the past 20 years), Thailand, and Indonesia.

Finally, the conference acknowledged the need for outside financial assistance for Second Tier population control programs. The conferees agreed on the immediate need for about $5 billion in assistance and an additional $17 billion between then and the year 2000. Whether this level of assistance will be forthcoming is problematic due to, among other reasons, the attitude of the United States.

The United States and the Population Problem

U.S. policy toward the global population problem has vacillated across time. The Nixon administration was an early advocate of addressing and trying to find global solutions to the problem. But American leadership lagged during the administrations of Ronald Reagan and George Bush, which shared the common philosophies of being antiabortion and opposing governmental regulation of much activity. Population control returned to the forefront under President Bill Clinton, whose philosophy (and especially that of the first lady) is strongly prochoice and for women's rights.

Vacillation on the population issue reflects very much the internal debate within the United States over population control. Advocacy of public efforts to bring about a reduction in population tends to be a liberal, Democratic effort (although it is clearly not limited to liberal Democrats) that has much the same constituency as does human rights. Opposition, on the other hand, tends to be Republican and conservative, although, once again, the constituencies are not coterminus.

The philosophical differences have already been suggested. The most basic surrounds the moral question of limiting fertility; abortion rights is the lightning rod in this aspect of the debate. Because abortion is part of the basic strategy of those favoring global population limitation, the issue cleaves members of the public.

These divisions became particularly stark with the 1994 election of a Republican Congress, which was especially antiabortion. The rise of Republican majorities in both Houses meant Republicans chaired all the major committees, including those that would have to authorize funding for implementation of the Cairo conference's call for assistance to fund population control.

The Environment

The third major issue we discuss here is environmental degradation, which has proven to be a classic transstate problem: the efforts of individual states are inadequate to solve it. It shares many of the characteristics of the human rights and population control problems. The environment issue generally pits the First and Second Tiers against one another, with the question of development never far from the surface. It is also an area on which the United States is in substantial internal disagreement. Many of the issues of environmental degradation, resource usages, and the like, have their equivalents in the internal American partisan political debate.

Environmental degradation covers a broad range of more specific issues. In many respects, human mastery of nature has created rising affluence, breakthroughs in the treatment of diseases, and previously unimagined opportunities for personal fulfillment to those who are the beneficiaries of scientific progress around the globe. But these benefits have been selectively enjoyed—largely by people in the First Tier—and have had costs in terms of the global ecology that has become the focus of environmental efforts. This depiction also helps frame the First Tier-Second Tier nature of the problem. First Tier states, which *already* have benefited from actions resulting in environmental damage, want to slow or reverse those harmful effects. To do so often requires reversing actions that might benefit Second Tier states which have been deprived of those benefits in the past and are being asked to continue to be deprived in the name of the environment.

The range of specific issues on the environmental agenda is long. Donald T. Wells's text, *Environmental Policy,* for instance, has chapters devoted to air quality, water pollution, chemical dependency and degradation, nuclear waste, solid waste, energy policy, land degradation, and the global ecosystem. Each issue is transstate in that none can be solved unilaterally by individual states; at the same time, each exists as an internal policy issue within the United States that divides Americans and makes it more difficult to develop a uniform posture across time in international forums.

Status of Environmental Problems

We do not attempt here to provide a comprehensive overview of all aspects of the environmental agenda. For present purposes, we look at two related policy areas that are broadly representative of the problem of environmental degradation: global warming and deforestation. Global warming is largely the result of the excessive burning of fossil fuels, which produce carbon dioxide (CO_2) that accumulates and has harmful effects in the atmosphere; other than reduced emissions, the chief natural means of dealing with carbon dioxide is through natural photosynthesis by trees, especially those in the green belt that surrounds the earth's equator.

Global warming, which is the direct consequence of CO_2 emissions, has been a vexing international and domestic policy problem, especially compared to progress in dealing with chlorofluorocarbons (CFCs), on which significant progress was made in the Montreal treaty of 1987 (see Case in Point box "CFCs and the Montreal Treaty").

The physical problem is easy to describe in layperson's terms. When fossil fuels, notably oil and coal, are burned to produce energy, they produce CO_2, most of which enters the atmosphere. When there is too much CO_2 to be absorbed by green plants and transformed into water and sugar (as well as oxygen), it accumulates in the upper atmosphere, where it joins other gases such as methane to trap solar radiation and other heat sources. The result is the *greenhouse effect,* where heat cannot escape into space and thus continues to warm the earth's surface, much as a greenhouse traps heat and moisture.

There is general agreement on the effects of global warming. Carbon dioxide has increased about 25 percent in the world's atmosphere since 1900, with a consequent average temperature rise of 2 to 3 degrees Fahrenheit. Continued accumulation at present rates would result in an increase of between 2 and 9 degrees by the middle of the twenty-first century. This range, in turn, leads to more or less apocryphal estimates of the consequences in terms of ice cap melting and the like.

There is also scientific agreement on the actions needed to stop or reverse the process. One, and possibly the major, solution is to reduce CO_2 production by curtailing the burning of fossil fuels. This will happen eventually anyway because supplies of petroleum are finite and dwindling. In the meantime, it is also true that the vast major-

CASE IN POINT

CFCs and the Montreal Treaty

Although the carbon dioxide emission problem has remained vexatious in policy terms, not all contributors to global warming have proven to be so problematic. The notable exception is the containment and reduction of the emission of chlorofluorocarbons (CFCs), which contribute to depletion of the ozone layer girdling the earth.

Once again, the problem is straightforward. CFCs are a group of chemicals that have been used as aerosol propellents in consumer goods and as refrigerants for air conditioning systems (freon is a good example). When released into the atmosphere, CFCs rise to the upper atmosphere, where they reduce the ozone layer that protects the earth's inhabitants from cancer-causing ultraviolet rays. Its depletion is linked to increases in health problems such as skin cancer.

The concern with CFCs led the United Nations to call a conference in Montreal, which produced a 1987 treaty that has been signed by half the world's countries. The signatories agree to slash CFC use by the end of the century. The evidence indicates that signatories are complying; the United States, for instance, is implementing a ban on CFC-based aerosol containers, and effective with 1996 models, freon (a leading CFC) can no longer be used in new automobile air conditioners.

The Montreal treaty shows the ability of states to arrive at constructive environmental solutions when the scientific evidence of environmental cause and effect is evident, where all can readily see their common stake in adopting sensible solutions, and where there are available substitutes. In contrast to CO_2 emissions, there is virtually no dispute about the adverse effects of CFCs, and the issue does not create a fault line between the tiers, since everyone is affected in the same way by both the problem and its solution.

ity of the world's energy comes from this source, and that energy usage is the best indicator of economic productivity. Moreover, no cheap readily available short-term alternative energy sources capable of substituting for fossil fuel burning at current rates of energy production are available; a number of alternative sources, such as the gasohol (derived from sugarcane) that fuels 40 percent of Brazilian automobiles, are possible, but all cost more to produce. The reduction in CO_2 emissions, in other words, may come at the expense of economic prosperity, and the volatile policy question is at *whose* expense will it come. While developing states typically have less stringent antipollution laws in an attempt to attract foreign business and industry (mostly from First Tier states), many First Tier states (such as the United States) are the world's biggest consumers of fossil fuels.

The other solution is an increased ability to absorb and convert CO_2 through photosynthesis, which leads us to our second issue: deforestation. Although deforestation intensifies global warming, there are many other causes of global warming. As a cause, however, deforestation arises from the supposed economic benefits that states gain from cutting down their trees (and especially their rain forests): profits from timber and alternate land use.

Approximately 7 percent of the world's land area is rain forest, with the largest and most important found in Brazil, Indonesia, and Malaysia. These forests contain half the world's species of flora and fauna and are the sole locus of many of those species. As a result, their retention is vital for the biological diversity of the globe. In addition to providing natural habitat for a number of species whose existence would be endangered in their absence, the rain forests are essential for producing oxygen through photosynthesis and as natural sinks for greenhouse gases, especially carbon dioxide.

The rapid clearing of these forests causes many environmental problems. Not only does deforestation contribute to the greenhouse effect and to endangering many species, but without trees to stabilize and enrich topsoil, many deforested areas are not suitable for farming within a short period of time. Rich topsoil is washed away, denuding land and clogging streams and water tables, which reduces the water supply and further restricts agricultural output. Thus, the irony is that while clear-cutting is often done to increase the availability of farmland, clear-cut land does not remain productive for long, thus leading to pressure to clear-cut more land for farming.

In South America and Southeast Asia, it is estimated that as many as 40 million acres of forest (an area about the size of the state of Washington) are being cut down each year. At one point, the world's rain forests covered an estimated 6 million square miles. Due to inadequate fire control, unsustainable commercial logging, overgrazing, and airborne pollutants, deforestation has already claimed up to one-third of the original forests, and the rates of deforestation are rising.

From a global perspective, arrest or reversal of deforestation of the rain forests is clearly desirable. The problem, however, is that these forests are located within the sovereign territory of individual states whose perceived interests clash with the broader global perception. Sovereign authority and planetary preservation and prosperity thus come into conflict.

International efforts to deal with the affected countries have had varied results. In Brazil, some progress has been made in slowing deforestation of the Amazon Basin through debt-for-nature swaps, where large amounts of Brazil's huge economic debt to First Tier countries is canceled in return for assurances that the forests will be preserved. But where there is little accumulated indebtedness, as in Indonesia and Malaysia, this form of incentive may prove especially ineffective. The Malaysians, in particular, have resisted international appeals, insisting on the principle that all natural resources lying inside its boundaries are to be regarded as under the sole prerogative of the Malaysian government, for which the exploitation of its natural resources are a major part of its developmental strategy.

The United States and the Environment

Like human rights advocacy and population control, environmental degradation is also a domestic issue. As a major industrial power, the United States is a large contributor to the production of carbon dioxide gases. Although the United States has no rain forests to deplete, the use of public lands, including national forests, is an ongoing source of heated discussion. A major protagonist in the internal debate is the Environmental Protection Agency (EPA), which is simultaneously one of the most activist and controversial executive branch agencies.

The tension between domestic and international concerns creates great domestic ambivalence and disagreement on environmental issues. It is also an emotional issue pitting entrepreneurs who want to exploit the environment with environmentalists who seek its maximum protection. The country's position at international forums depends on which group has the ear of the White House at any point in time.

Nothing exemplified this ambivalence better than American performance at the Earth Summit in Rio de Janeiro in June 1992. Sponsored by the United Nations under the formal title of the U.N. Conference on Environment and Development (note that the term *development* finds its way into the title), the meeting drew together over 35,000 participants, including representatives from 172 countries, 110 heads of state, and 15,000 representatives from hundreds of NGOs around the world.

The conference's key product was a 1,000-page document known as Agenda 21, the purpose of which was to lay out actions that would result in "sustainable development," meaning that in the future efforts to develop states of the Second Tier economically into higher subtiers must be done in ways that do not further pollute an already polluted environment.

The agenda for the meeting was very extensive and hence well beyond our present concern. It did, however, touch in major ways on the issues raised here. A number of First Tier states made a concerted effort, for instance, to develop strong restrictive provisions on the use of rain forests. They were motivated by concerns about carbon dioxide and, to a lesser extent, biological diversity. Certain Asian states, including India, but especially Malaysia, objected strenuously to the conference proceedings. The Malaysians argued with special vehemence that the provisions represented a direct assault on national sovereignty. Their position gradually was adopted by enough other Second Tier states that the conference was unable to pass anything stronger than a nonbinding resolution calling on states to refrain from deforestation.

The U.S. stance on the biodiversity treaty, a major product of the conference, exemplifies the ambivalence and political impact of domestic politics on U.S.

environmental policy. The biodiversity treaty attempted to ensure the protection of a maximum number of species of flora and fauna through international agreement. Not unlike the EPA environmental impact statement, the treaty put the onus on governments to protect species when engaging in environment-altering activity. The treaty was supported by almost all states in the world, and the American EPA director William K. Reilly, who was the chief U.S. delegate to the conference, was a principal backer as well (since the effect was to do what his agency did anyway).

The problem was that many American interest groups, including many western cattle and logging interests whose support was deemed important to President George Bush's reelection campaign, vehemently opposed the treaty as an extension of the authority of the hated EPA. When President Bush made an eleventh-hour appearance before the Rio conferees, his speech included a specific denunciation of the biodiversity treaty, thereby reversing the position the American delegation had defended. Subjected to uniform criticism of his position, Bush was reduced to arguing that "I'm president of the U.S., not president of the world. . . . I can't do what everybody else does." President Clinton reversed this position and submitted the treaty for senatorial approval, which was granted.

Conclusions

In the preceding pages, we introduced the dynamics of transnational issues by describing the substance of three of the most highly publicized problems: the interrelated concerns of human rights, population, and the environment. There is no shortage of additional issues that could have been explored: traditional concerns such as fisheries and the depletion of the world's oceans due to overfishing or dealing with worldwide medical crises (the emergence of new viruses completely resistant to antibiotics joins AIDS at the top of the list) to nontraditional problems such as international crime syndicates.

What do these problems share in common, and how do they enter the American foreign policy dialogue? All are political challenges that require the actions of states working in concert to solve or at least to contain them. Unfortunately, the commitment of different states varies considerably.

The Brazilian government plans, allows, and sometimes executes the clear-cutting of the rain forest. The Mexican government owns the oil industry, one of the largest polluters in Mexico. The Panamanian government repealed all its antipollution laws in an attempt to attract foreign industries. These *government actions all directly cause pollution*. West African governments have pocketed funds intended for water treatment plants and water and sewer systems. The U.S. government is one of the largest polluters in the country at the millions of acres of military bases. The high cost of cleaning them up to turn the land over for other uses has been one of the chief obstacles to reducing the number of bases (in addition to local political opposition). The list could go on.

Most of these issues share the further political commonality of having both an international and a domestic side where the two aspects further complicate the formation and implementation of effective policy. The international aspect is typically twofold. At one level, transstate issues are by definition international: they transcend boundaries in ways over which states have little control and that they cannot solve unilaterally. Canada, for instance, cannot solve the problem of acid rain caused by the emission of sulphur dioxide from the smokestacks of U.S. industries.

The other international level is that many of these issues get caught up in the general First Tier-Second Tier dialogue, and especially the debate over development. Many of the problems are endemic or certainly most prevalent in the Second Tier, particularly those touching natural (e.g., desertification, chronic food shortages due to drought or flooding) or human made (e.g., overpopulation) miseries. Remedies, where they are possible, require expending resources, and the question immediately arises on what priorities and in what amounts should resources be allocated. It is by no means a coincidence that the term *development* finds its way into so many U.N. conferences trying to deal with these issues.

The international, and particularly the intertier, politics of transstate issues contributes to the intractability of solving problems. Solutions to what would seem to be common problems founder in cultural disagreements. The general desirability of a smaller global population is relatively noncontroversial, but that does not mean reducing *their* population is acceptable to all groups. What people *do* disagree about are acceptable and unacceptable methods of reducing fertility. Certainly such conflicts occur across cultures and civilizations, but they are often divisive within countries as well.

This domestic element to the transnational issues problem often receives less attention than it deserves. There almost always is a domestic counterpart to the debate over the transstate issues that makes formulating coherent international positions more difficult than would otherwise be the case. In the United States, for instance, there are or have been domestic equivalents to all three of the issues examined in this chapter. The American equivalent of the human rights issue has been the civil rights movement, and until the United States began the process of creating legal equality for all its citizens (an ongoing phenomenon), it was necessarily more reluctant to complain about the human rights abuses of others. The question of population control resonates as the extremely divisive issue of abortion and the antiabortion/prochoice debate. The question of responsible use of the environment has its American equivalent in the debate over the uses of federal land.

The confluence of international and domestic elements complicates the formation of coherent policy. How can the United States, for instance, simultaneously favor human entitlements and not provide for the homeless? In a worldwide population control movement, most of whose advocates maintain that abortion has to be part of the strategy of fertility reduction, how can the American debate be resolved into a single position in global forums? How can the United States simultaneously demand greater environmental responsibility in the Second Tier (the idea of sustainable development was, after all, an American one) and call for relaxation of environmental regulations at home?

This interaction of international and domestic aspects of these emerging issues provides further evidence of the convergence of foreign and domestic policy that has been a recurrent theme of this volume. In the context where one party occupies the White House and the other controls the Congress, as has been true for most of the period between 1968 and 1996, and where the two parties have very different positions on these issues, the result can be the impossibility of forming a negotiating position that can be sustained at international meetings and also on the home front. This is especially the case where funding is involved to support the outcomes of international conferences. To cite the most obvious case, abortion rights that are part of the international regime on population require money to pay doctors to perform them. Given the acrimony of debate over funding of abortions the United States, it is hard to see American monetary participation in international efforts.

The final note to make about the transstate issues is that they are unlikely to go away. As humanity increases its demands on the global carrying capacity, they will, if anything, increase in number and intensity. Moreover, the global reach of the electronic media makes their impact all the more visible and the potential effects of problems generated elsewhere on Americans more possible. Disease, for instance, knows no frontiers (the motto of the World Health Organization), and stemming the global ravages of a disease in a small African village—the outbreak of the deadly Ebola virus in Zaire in May 1995, for example,—may require highly international efforts. Transstate issues, like foreign policy more generally, no longer end at the water's edge.

SUGGESTED READINGS

Brown, Lester. *World Without Borders*. New York: Random House, 1972.

Caldwell, Lynton K. *International Environmental Policy* (2nd ed.). Durham, NC: Duke University Press, 1990.

Carroll, John E. *International Environmental Diplomacy*. New York: Cambridge University Press, 1988.

Cline, William R. *The Economics of Global Warming*. Washington, DC: Institute for International Economics, 1992.

Diamond, Larry, and Marc F. Plattner (eds.). *The Global Resurgence of Democracy*. Baltimore, MD: Johns Hopkins Press, 1993.

Donnelly, Jack. *Human Rights in Theory and Practice*. Ithaca, NY: Cornell University Press, 1989.

Haas, Peter M. Robert Keohane, and Marc A. Levy (eds.). *Institutions for the Earth*. Cambridge, MA: MIT Press, 1993.

Huntington, Samuel P. *The Third Wave: Democratization in the Late Twentieth Century.* Norman: University of Oklahoma Press, 1991.

Korey, William. *The Promises We Keep: Human Rights, the Helsinki Process and American Foreign Policy.* New York: St. Martin's Press, 1993.

Porter, Gareth, and Janet Brown. *Global Environmental Politics.* Boulder, CO: Lynne Rienner, 1991.

Singer, Max, and Aaron Wildavsky. *The Real World Order: Zones of Peace, Zones of Turmoil.* Chatham, NJ: Chatham House, 1993.

Shute, Stephen, and Susan Hurley (eds.). *On Human Rights: The Oxford Amnesty Lectures, 1993.* New York: Basic Books, 1993.

Wells, Donald T. *Environmental Policy: A Global Perspective for the Twenty-First Century.* Upper Saddle River, NJ: Prentice Hall, 1996.

Young, Oran R. and Gail Osherenko. *Polar Politics: Creating International Environmental Regimes.* Ithaca, NY: Cornell University Press, 1993.

CHAPTER 13

Case Studies: FSX and Desert Storm

The dynamics of the policy process are best revealed by the way it deals with concrete foreign and defense problems. To this end, we have selected two cases that show both the complexity and idiosyncrasy of the policy process at work. One case deals with the controversy generated when the Japanese sought to develop a new jet fighter aircraft, the FSX, during the 1980s and a debate arose as to whether or to what extent the United States should provide that aircraft. The other case involves the decision process leading to Operation Desert Storm, the military campaign launched to force Iraq to withdraw its forces from conquered Kuwait, and subsequent developments. Although both cases have their genesis either during the Cold War or its unraveling, they each illustrate the dynamic relationship between foreign policy and domestic policy and process that is a key element of this book.

The two cases are different in many respects, including content and focus. The FSX controversy, as it has evolved, has displayed both strong economic and national security content; the kind of jet fighter the Japanese ultimately develop will have an impact both in the areas of defense and economics. Desert Storm, while having some economic overtones—the United States and the West's continued access to reasonably priced Persian Gulf petroleum—was almost exclusively framed and viewed as a traditional national security problem with a military solution.

The two cases also differ in terms of the urgency of the situations. When Iraq's armed forces smashed across the Kuwaiti frontier and rapidly occupied the entire country, there was an apparent need to respond with alacrity. This need for quick reaction was made all the more important because Iraq apparently had the ability to continue to march further south and occupy the rich Saudi oil fields along the Persian Gulf coast as well. This action would have greatly endangered Western oil access. FSX, on the other hand, was a developmental program that would be years in the making. Begun in the mid-1980s, the first and apparently only prototype FSX aircraft is not scheduled to be completed until 1997.

Another difference lay in the visibility of the two situations. Desert Storm was a highly visible event, occupying center stage in the American consciousness and policy process from the August 2, 1990, invasion of Kuwait until the end of the 100-hour ground offensive that broke the Iraqi occupation and ended ground hostilities at midnight, February 27, 1991. By contrast, the FSX negotiations proceeded almost entirely outside the public eye. They were not launched by any dramatic event that captured public attention; in fact, most of the negotiations were conducted quietly and privately in the traditional manner of diplomacy. The attentive public became aware of the issue only when it became an interbranch battle between the new Bush White House and Congress in January 1989.

Yet another difference was the complexity of the issues involved. Of the two situations, the FSX proved to be by far the more complex and thus the more difficult to resolve. Its intricacy arose from two basic sources. On the one hand, both governments, but especially the United States, experienced some difficulty in deciding whether to treat the problem as a national security or an international economic concern at a time when the lines between the two were becoming increasingly hazy. On the other hand, contentiousness emerged because of infighting within the executive branch itself as well as between the executive and legislative branches.

The decision process in Desert Storm was less complex. This campaign was a classic military response to a geopolitical problem, the kind of situation for which the traditional National Security Council system had been designed, even if the problem lacked the communist-anticommunist context in which the system was devised. As the crisis evolved, the branches of government fought not over whether to respond, but only over how and when. The only complicating factor, which actually served to reinforce the administration's desired course of action, was the participation of a United Nations revitalized by the event.

A difference flowing from the others centered on the actors who were most prominently involved in the two occasions. Both began in the executive branch within the context of the traditional NSC system with the Departments of Defense and State predominating. The political decision making surrounding Desert Storm largely remained within that context, as the president and his closest advisers, Vice President Quayle, Secretary of State Baker, Secretary of Defense Cheney, National Security Adviser Scowcroft and his deputy (and later DCI) Gates, and CJCS Powell—all core members of the system—were tightly in control of the evolving situation. Even congressional input was rarely sought—to the annoyance of many members of Congress.

A wider net of participants was necessarily brought into the decision process surrounding the FSX. Because the deal had potential economic consequences at a time when the U.S.-Japanese economic relationship was coming under scrutiny, the executive agencies that had primary responsibility for international economic policy (e.g., the Commerce Department and the Office of the Trade Representative) were ultimately drawn into an adversarial relationship with the State and Defense Departments.

As we will see, one lesson of this bruising experience may be the need, on matters where jurisdictions overlap, to include coequal agencies with economic responsibilities on the NSC. In the Clinton administration, those elements of his economic circle of advisers with direct responsibility for industrial policy would quickly have been engaged in, or even dominated, the process.

A final dissimilarity between the two cases involves agenda setting. In Operation Desert Storm, the primary agenda setter was Saddam Hussein, whose initial invasion created the policy problem and whose continued intransigence dominated the agenda. Desert Storm is a textbook case in which a foreign policy issue is defined by external forces beyond the control of U.S. policymakers, whose role becomes reactive: how does the United States respond to a situation thrust on it?

The agenda setting is less clear cut in the FSX case. Certainly, the Japanese decision that it needed a new fighter aircraft precipitated the situation, but the Japanese did not wholly control either the agenda or its outcome throughout. Because of the historic relationship between Japan and the United States, Japan's reluctance to appear militaristic, and Japan's traditional deference, the Americans were allowed largely to frame the options. Much of what makes FSX noteworthy is the internal U.S. struggle over which of the options it had framed would ultimately be the option chosen.

There are also points of similarity between the two cases. First, a portion of each involved the adversarial relationship between Congress and the executive that has been a recurring theme in this book. Part of the reason is that both occurred within the context of Republican control of the presidency and Democratic control of the legislative branch. Partisanship was clearly more evident in Desert Storm: almost all the senators and representatives who opposed early authorization of combat operations were Democrats. In both cases, the lack of mutual trust between the two branches was evident; politics did not end at the water's edge.

Second, both cases, especially FSX, suggest the need to consider reform of the system. As we will see, FSX was a picture of bureaucratic confusion and rivalry within the executive branch that arose out of its failure to involve all interested parties early on and thus to produce a unified and acceptable administration position. In the case of Desert Storm, the administration's apparent inability to stick by an articulated long-term political objective to be served by the operation continues to raise the question of whether a relatively small insulated set of actors can adequately deal with the large complex issues of national security. Moreover, this instance of U.S.-U.N. military interaction offers some premonition for present and future operations, as we discussed in Chapter 10.

We view these two crises in ascending order of complexity, in opposite chronological order. Both are long-term situations in that neither has achieved resolution. As yet the only FSX jet fighter is a prototype, and there will be no more for some years unless costs can be reduced, and the continuing controversy with Iraq's Saddam Hussein that dominated the period before, during, and after Desert Storm continues.

Case Study: The United States, Iraq, and Desert Storm

The U.S.-led response to Iraq's invasion, conquest, and annexation of its tiny neighbor, Kuwait, between August 1990 and the end of February 1991 riveted public attention in the United States and, thanks to global television, most of the rest of the world as well. The Persian Gulf War, as it is generically known, was highlighted by the brilliantly conceived and executed U.S. military plan, Desert Shield (the activity before offensive action began) and Desert Storm (the offensive air and ground campaigns). Television galvanized the world's attention; where one was when the bombing of Baghdad began on January 16, 1991, may be as defining a moment for some Americans as John Kennedy's assassination was to an earlier generation.

Our purpose here is not to rehash the military decision-making process surrounding Desert Storm. Rather, we view the episode from the vantage point of Desert Storm as a foreign policy and policy-making problem. In this larger sense of the event, we examine (1) the period before the Iraqi invasion, when the United States was actively engaging the Iraqi leader through a generally low-key campaign within the executive branch that sought to bring him into the international mainstream; (2) the invasion, of Kuwait on August 2, 1990, the raising of forces to oppose the invasion, and, most importantly from the American vantage point, the executive branch's appeal to the Congress, as well as the United Nations, to authorize the use of force; and (3) the period since the end of military hostilities, with some attention to whether the Americans accomplished the goals they set out to achieve in the war and how controversy over the postwar situation became a partisan issue in the 1992 presidential campaign.

The Preinvasion Period: The Courtship of Saddam

The tangled events leading to Desert Storm can be seen adequately only in light of the complex international politics of the Persian Gulf region and U.S. efforts to stabilize those politics in order reasonably to ensure a steady flow of Persian Gulf petroleum to the West. It is a history of changing sides and changing fortunes.

Iran and Iraq are geopolitically the most important states of the region in terms of size, population, and military potential. They are also historic enemies whose conflict dates back at least to the days of Persia and Mesopotamia in biblical times. From the early 1950s until the end of the 1970s, the United States aligned itself closely with Iran and especially Shah Reza Pahlavi, whom the United States supplied with military equipment in return for his guarantee that the oil would flow. During this period, the United States and Iraq were adversaries that did not even recognize each other diplomatically.

That changed when the fundamentalist Iranian revolution overthrew the shah in 1979, the same year Saddam Hussein assumed the presidency of Iraq. To the Ayatollah Ruhollah Khomeini and his supporters, the United States was the "great Satan" to be universally opposed. To that end, the U.S. embassy in Teheran was seized and its personnel made captive on November 4, 1979. Iranians with connections to the Americans were arrested and often executed. The United States had dramatically lost its principal ally in the region.

In September 1980, Iraq declared war on and attacked Iran in a war that would last eight years. Iraq's Saddam Hussein believed he could gain an easy victory over an Iranian military whose leadership ranks had been decimated because of connections with the Americans and endear himself to other Arabs by defeating the hated non-Arab Persians and extinguishing the appeal of the militant Shiite fundamentalism of the Iranian leadership.

In this situation, the United States began to shift toward support of Iraq, first assisting in arming the Iraqis and by 1984 suggesting normalization of relations between the two countries. (U.S. diplomats had been expelled from Iraq in 1958.) Prior to the fall of the shah of Iran, Iraq's Saddam Hussein and the Iraqi Ba'ath regime had been viewed as the major destabilizing force in the region; this perception faded as he was compared with the Iranians. Saddam, however, did not change; it was American perceptions that changed.

When the Iran-Iraq War ended in 1988, Iraq was in trouble. It had won modestly on the battlefield, particularly when it resorted to terrorist missile attacks against Iranian cities and chemical weapons attacks against Iranian forces as well as against its own Kurdish minority in 1988 (facts overlooked by the Bush administration). But it had suffered considerable damage that needed repairing, and it had run up huge debts—upward of $40 billion—mostly with Saudi Arabia and Kuwait.

To assist recovery from the war, as well as to bolster his political position within Iraq—whose citizens had wearied of wartime deprivations—Saddam Hussein proposed that Kuwait and Saudi Arabia show their gratitude for Iraqi opposition to Iran by forgiving the loans and by providing massive new credits to help finance Iraqi recovery. Both the Saudis and Kuwaitis refused to cancel the loans and were circumspect about new loans.

This left Saddam Hussein with a problem: how to raise the money for recovery. He proposed to do so by gaining the support of the Organization of Petroleum Exporting Countries (OPEC) to limit production and thus drive up the price of all oil, including Iraqi, as a source of needed revenues. The Saudis and Kuwaitis refused to cooperate. To make matters worse, the Kuwaitis were in effect poaching Iraqi oil reserves at the Rumalia oil fields by "angle drilling"—that is, starting oil wells on the Kuwaiti side of the border and then angling the pipes under the border and syphoning off oil from its Iraqi sources.

The United States was not sitting idly by through all these activities. Instead, it was engaging in a low-profile program of cooperation with the Iraqis. The United States was providing credits to Iraq (through the Commodity Credit Corporation of the Agriculture Department), ostensibly to allow the Iraqis to buy grain and other foodstuffs. The problem was that the Iraqis found ways to exchange those credits for cash that could be spent on other products, including weapons. Hearings in Congress in July 1990 showed that Iraq owed the U.S. government over $2 billion in loans. Most prominently, Sen. William Cohen (R-Me.), ranking member of the Senate Intelligence Oversight Committee, revealed that some of these monies were spent on triggers for nuclear devices that were nearly delivered illegally to Iraq in the spring before their invasion of Kuwait.

Although middle-level officials of the Agriculture and Commerce Departments apparently suspected and reported these diversions (which have come to be known as Iraqgate), it is not clear how widely senior officials in the White House knew about them. Intent on courting Saddam, at a minimum there was less than vigilant pursuit of any wrongdoing. There have been accusations of wrongdoing and coverup that constituted a potential agenda item for President Clinton, which he declined to pursue.

These actions were first revealed in early 1990 by members of Congress demanding sanctions against Iraq; the sanctions were opposed by the Bush administration. The administration's spokesperson, John Kelly, assistant secretary of state for Near Eastern and South Asian affairs, explained that sanctions would dilute the U.S. "ability to exercise a restraining influence on Iraqi actions."

The administration was also systematically misreading and underestimating Saddam Hussein's intentions as the crisis in the Persian Gulf deepened. When Kuwait refused to accede to Iraqi demands to suspend loan payments, then to support a price hike in petroleum, and finally to cease angle drilling at Rumalia, Saddam issued increasingly bellicose threats. The Kuwaiti royal al-Sabah family, the Saudis, and the Americans at the highest levels ignored the threats. Even as CIA intelligence estimates detailed the massing of Iraqi troops in southern Iraq near the Kuwaiti frontier, U.S. ambassador April Glaspie met on July 25, 1990, with the Iraqi leader, where, according to Iraqi transcripts of the meeting, she stated, "We have no opinion on the Arab-Arab conflicts, like your border disagreement with Kuwait."

The major recurring theme of U.S. relations with Iraq prior to the invasion of Kuwait was one of misperception and underestimation of what Saddam would and would not do. The United States possibly acted solipsistically, assuming that given a situation, Saddam would act the way the United States would. If that was the case, the Americans were wrong; Saddam is not motivated by the same drives as Americans, nor does he view different options in the same way.

The question we must raise, even if we cannot answer it satisfactorily, is why were these mistakes made? One possible answer was the nature of decision making in the Bush White House. As we have already seen, foreign and national security policymaking was concentrated among those very close to the president. None of these men was a Middle Eastern or Iraqi expert, and their primary focus was on the geopolitical balance in the region, which they saw the courtship of Saddam as serving.

In the absence of wider consultation, that group may have seen the situation as they wanted to and may have assumed of Saddam Hussein what they wanted to. Certainly, the expertise at the lower levels of the State and Defense Departments was available to warn of the pitfalls of policy that could have been activated at, say, the Policy Coordinating Committee level. But were these experts consulted? If they were, why were they not heeded? If not, was it fear of being the executed messenger that inhibited responsible opposition? The full value of the episode requires an answer to these questions. At any rate, those who had nurtured Saddam Hussein were proven terribly wrong on August 2, 1990, as Iraq overran Kuwait.

Postinvasion Politics: Organizing and Authorizing the Military Response

The administration's response to the invasion was swift and decisive, showing the Bush national security apparatus at its very best. Neither then nor subsequently did the Bush team dwell on why it had been wrong earlier, beyond Ambassador Glaspie's subsequent testimony to the Senate Foreign Relations Committee that "We didn't think he [Saddam Hussein] was that stupid."

U.S. and world reactions to the invasion were swift. On August 2, President Bush condemned the invasion and announced the imposition of economic sanctions against Iraq. A three-pronged process against the invasion began in hopes of rolling it back. It included gaining international backing through the United Nations; forming a military coalition to carry out such authorizations as the United Nations provided; and convincing the U.S. Congress to authorize the use of U.S. forces to expel Iraq from Kuwait.

Gaining International Backing Turning to the United Nations represented an important precedent as to how to legitimize international action and gain international consensus to oppose the aggression. The United Nations had no choice but to condemn the action because of the precedent involved: Saddam's action against Kuwait was the first time in the history of the world organization that one member state had invaded and conquered another member. If the United Nations had failed to act on that occasion, its continuing international relevance would have been highly suspect. By virtue of its own charter, the United Nations could only legitimately authorize an expulsion of Iraq from Kuwait and restoration of Kuwaiti sovereignty. That was all it was asked to do at the time, and that was the extent of the coalition's mandate as long as it retained U.N. auspices. Whether or not the Bush administration used this limit to minimize the debate on American purposes, it certainly accepted them.

It was the second time that the United Nations had ever been able to invoke the principles of collective security found in its charter (although the action did not exactly conform to charter provisions). The end of the Cold War and the emerging international cooperation between the United States and the Soviet Union, which had not yet dissolved itself, made action possible. Whether intentional or not, it set in motion the widening use of the United Nations to legitimate international responses to military emergencies for a time, setting up yet another foreign policy issue for the future Clinton administration.

U.N. actions took the form of four Security Council resolutions of gradually increasing severity. The first resolution, Security Council Resolution 660, passed on the day of the invasion; it simply condemned the invasion, demanded Iraqi withdrawal, and vowed to take subsequent actions if compliance did not occur. The vote was 14 to 0, with one abstention (Yemen). On August 6, with no withdrawal forthcoming, Security Council Resolution 661 was passed, imposing mandatory economic sanctions against Iraq, by a vote of 13 to 2. (Cuba and Yemen voted against it.) Up to this point, the actions were not truly precedent setting; economic sanctions had been imposed before—against South Africa and former Rhodesia (now Zimbabwe).

Precedent began to be set on August 25, when the council passed Resolution 665 by a vote of 13 to 0, with Yemen and Cuba abstaining. This resolution authorized the use of naval forces to enforce the economic embargo against Iraq, including halting "all inward and outward maritime shipping in order to inspect and verify their cargoes and destinations." A similar resolution was passed against Serbia in December 1992.

This partial authorization of the use of force set the stage for the final authorizing action on November 29, 1990. Resolution 678 authorized member states to "use all necessary means" to remove Iraq from Kuwait if the Iraqis did not withdraw by January 15, 1991. This resolution passed by a vote of 12 to 2 (Yemen and Cuba again in opposition), with one abstention (the People's Republic of China). This was only the second time in its history that the United Nations had authorized the use of force (the other being in Korea in 1950) and the first time the Security Council had been able to take such action. (The General Assembly passed the "Uniting for Peace" resolution in 1950.) The power was used again in December 1992 to authorize the use of force in Somalia.

Forming a Multilateral Military Coalition   Although the vast bulk of the forces mobilized to oppose Saddam were American, Secretary of State James Baker assembled a coalition eventually numbering over 25 different states. The roster of states was assembled after no more than a summary consultation with the congressional leadership. The first state to volunteer forces was Egypt, which was joined by a number of European states (Great Britain, France, and Czechoslovakia), Arab states (Saudi Arabia, Syria, Oman, the United Arab Emirates, Morocco, and others), and other states ranging from Australia, Canada, and Argentina to Sierra Leone, Bangladesh, and Pakistan. These coalition members augmented the eventual U.S. force of 475,000, bringing coalition strength to 695,000.

The countries came for numerous reasons. Britain and France sent significant contingents largely because of their continuing interest in the region; both had been mandatory powers in the region between the world wars. The Egyptians came because Baker arm-twisted them into joining: owing the United States a significant debt and desirous of additional military credits, they could be convinced by promises to fulfill their needs. As for Syria's president Hafez al-Assad, he saw an opportunity to humiliate a hated rival, Saddam Hussein.

The degree of Arab participation surprised many observers at the time, but it probably should not have. Just as Saddam's action had violated a basic principle of the United Nations that virtually demanded a U.N. response, so, too, did he transgress against a basic, if unwritten, rule of the Arab world when he conquered and on August 8 formally annexed Kuwait. That basic principle was that the 1919 boundaries by which the Arab states gained their independence are not to be altered by force. The Arab states had no choice but to respond and restore the status quo.

Convincing the U.S. Congress   The most difficult prong of the strategy involved persuading the U.S. Congress to authorize the use of force against Iraq. When the president initially responded to the invasion by condemning it and sending troops to Saudi Arabia to deter further aggression, no dissent emanated from Congress. Congressional support extended to the resolutions invoking U.N. economic sanctions, the call-up of the reserves announced on August 22, and even to Bush's statement before Congress on September 11 that force might be necessary. Broad bipartisan support continued into November, as Operation Desert Shield grew to a U.S. force of over 200,000.

The events that shattered the consensus and evoked an interbranch partisan disagreement occurred on November 8 and 9. The first action, announced by President Bush, was his intention to increase troop strength by 200,000, to a total force of about 430,000. The second, announced by Secretary of Defense Cheney, was to cancel troop rotations back from the Gulf; those deployed would be there for the duration.

The two announcements had the effect of throwing down the gauntlet to Congress by making early military action likely or even inevitable. On November 11, Senate Armed Service Committee (SASC) Chairman Sam Nunn condemned the action as precluding the probability that the sanctions would be allowed to work. The troops, he argued, could not be expected to sit in the desert without rotation for as long as it took the sanctions to compel the Iraqis into compliance. Senator Nunn called hearings of the committee on November 27–29, at which time he presented a number of expert witnesses, including two former chairmen of the Joint Chiefs of Staff (retired air force general David Jones and retired admiral William Crowe, Jr.) and former secretary of defense James Schlesinger, all of whom counseled caution.

The president's actions brought the issue to a head by forcing Congress and the public seriously to confront an actual shooting war, a possibility that had generally been avoided in the hopes that sanctions would work.

The president and some members of Congress had simply come to believe either that the sanctions would never compel an Iraqi withdrawal or at least would not do so rapidly enough to sustain public support in the United States and elsewhere behind the effort. The other side, led by Nunn, suggested that the sanctions be given more time to see if they would work and asserted that the president's actions on November 8 and 9 precluded the successful application of the sanctions, virtually creating their failure as a self-fulfilling prophecy. It is not coincidental that the second view was being expressed before SASC on the very day that the United Nations passed Resolution 678 authorizing force. The fact that the second prong of policy-making (the United Nations) was proceeding at the same time as the third was engaged only inflamed executive-legislative animosities.

Another schism between the White House and Congress regarded the physical toll the war would take. There was widespread disagreement over likely outcomes. In the debate over authorizing the president to use force, for instance, Sen. Edward Kennedy (D-Mass.) stated one side, suggesting that the war would be "brutal and costly" and could end with "thousands, even tens of thousands, of American casualties." The chairman of the House Armed Services Committee (HASC), Rep. (and later SECDEF) Les Aspin, countered with the belief that the war would be over in weeks, certainly not more than a month, and that casualties would be light. In retrospect, the correct assessment is obvious, but it was not so evident at the time. (Aspin's correct view helped raise his prospects for appointment at Defense by Clinton.)

The debate became dormant as the congressional Christmas recess came and diplomatic efforts continued. When Congress returned in January, however, the January 15, 1991, deadline specified in Resolution 678 was impending, but without U.S. force it was a hollow threat. As a result, the president formally requested a resolution from Congress authorizing his use of force (the resolution being a lesser alternative to a formal declaration of war).

The Congress debated the request until January 12, when both houses voted. The results were highly partisan. In the Senate, the vote was 52 to 47 in favor of the resolution, with 42 Republicans and 10 Democrats voting in favor and 2 Republicans and 45 Democrats voting against. In the House, the resolution passed more easily, by a vote of 250 to 183. Still, the results were partisan: 164 Republicans and 86 Democrats supported the resolution; 3 Republicans, 179 Democrats, and 1 independent opposed it.

Post–Desert Storm Politics: Snatching Defeat from the Jaws of Victory?

The smashing military victory, both the precision air war and the "100-hour ground war," seemed to vindicate the president's policy, despite some misgivings about stopping the ground action before it had destroyed Saddam's armed forces. The president's approval rating reached 90 percent in the polls, the highest ratings for any chief executive since such polls have been taken.

Political controversy, however, became especially intense as the 1992 political campaign took shape. The president sought to portray Desert Storm as his finest foreign and national security hour, justifying his reelection to a second term. Democratic nominee Clinton and his running mate, Albert Gore, however, found significant fault in the aftermath of Desert Storm.

The controversy continues, particularly because of the continuing presence of an obviously combative, unrepentant, and assertive Saddam Hussein as president of Iraq. His removal from office was not a stated U.S. goal when the decision to resist the invasion of Kuwait was made, although Bush publicly encouraged his overthrow by the Iraqi people. At a minimum, participation in his removal would have exceeded the U.N. mandate. At times, however, it appeared that this was the case; to those who believed that total success required a change of leadership in Baghdad, the job was not completed.

Controversy over Saddam's eventual disposition has arisen because of the expectation periodically stated by President Bush that his overthrow was desirable. As Operation Desert Shield built in the Saudi desert during the fall of 1990, the president adopted the rhetorical device of demonizing Saddam, calling him another Hitler. The clear implication was that this Hitler must be removed as the other Hitler had been. When he was not, those unsure of the objective could only wonder if it had been achieved. On February 15, 1991, in the midst of the aerial bombardment campaign, the president went a step further, imploring "the Iraqi military and the Iraqi people to take matters into their own hands and force Saddam, the dictator, to step aside."

This statement, presumably aimed at moderate Sunni elements within Baghdad (most believe that any moderates had either fled the country or been executed) and possibly intended tactically to make the coming ground campaign easier, underscores another source of controversy: the administration's apparent vacillation on removing Saddam. On the one hand, the Arab members of the coalition could not accept this objective. Hence, its formal adoption would have splintered the coalition. On the other hand, the fact that the president kept repeating the desire made it look like an objective. If it was, then the so-called U.S. victory was less complete than advertised. As far as we know, this broader desire was never part of policy and would have been widely opposed for broadening the war. Presumably, President Bush got carried away in his rhetoric (as he periodically did). It suggests, if possible, that presidential pronouncements should strive for greater restraint in the future.

Another lingering controversy surrounds the destruction of Iraq's nuclear, biological, and chemical (NBC) weapons capabilities and its stock of ballistic missiles (Scuds). This was an overt purpose of the bombing campaign that began Desert Storm, but inadequate coalition intelligence capability within Iraq could not identify the location of all Saddam's weapons. The destruction of remaining capabilities was an explicit term of the ceasefire negotiated to end the war, as was U.N. monitoring and inspection of sites within Iraq suspected of hiding either the weapons or the missiles.

Saddam Hussein's very public reluctance to cooperate fully with U.N. inspection teams reached a crescendo in July 1992, when Iraq refused the team access to the Agriculture Ministry, where the inspectors believed records on chemical weapons production were hidden. The impasse dragged on for over two weeks, and the Bush administration even vaguely threatened military action in the form of air strikes if Saddam did not comply. Finally, Saddam relented—having had plenty of time to remove any telltale files—and allowed U.N. inspectors access to the building.

Once again, Saddam appeared to triumph, much to the consternation of the Bush administration. Saddam had complied, but the United Nations came away empty-handed. He defied the United States by not letting U.S. members of the inspection team into the building. Finally, he came away as a hero to his own people, as thousands of cheering Iraqis took to the street hailing his defiance of the United States and the United Nations, all before the television cameras.

Yet another source of contention occurred directly at the end of the war. Although apparently not directed at them, President Bush's call to rebellion on February 15, 1991, was taken by the Kurds of the north of Iraq and the Shiites of the south as an invitation for *them,* as opposed to the Sunnis, to rise and overthrow the dictator. Fearing that the success of such rebellions would cut Iraq into three separate states, none of which would provide a postwar counterweight to Iran, the president actively opposed their success. That opposition, however, was not shared with either group; at the time, a delegation of Kurdish nationalists in Washington was even denied a meeting with the State Department, where the administration's position might have been stated.

The result was a massive, ruthless attack by the remnants of the Iraqi military against both groups. Critics pointed out that had the ground war not stopped when it did, Iraq would not have had the wherewithal to engage in massive atrocities, especially against the Kurds. Large numbers of Kurds, fearing retributory slaughter, fled across the border into neighboring Turkey and Iran. Because CNN cameras covered the resulting orgy of death and despair in roughly improvised refugee camps on Turkish mountainsides, the administration responded with a massive assistance program called Operation Provide Comfort, the subject of the Update box "The Continuing Policy Dilemma of Provide Comfort/Southern Watch." It could be argued that the operation would have been unnecessary had not President Bush appeared to incite the Kurds to rebellion, which triggered the retribution. Moreover, Provide Comfort (widened to include air cover for the Shiites of the south in 1992, as Operation Southern Watch) has major precedential potential that we explore in Chapter 14.

Once again, Saddam Hussein benefited. Because the coalition allowed his forces to retreat intact to Iraq, he had the muscle to smash the rebellions. In the process, he reinforced his own internal political position by suppressing political opponents among the Kurds and Shiites.

The net effect of these lingering controversies has taken some of the glow off the triumph in the desert. It does nothing to detract from the skillful, professional manner in which the military conducted its part of the operation. Within its orders, it succeeded admirably. What these problems do reveal, however, was the apparent failure to sift carefully through all the options and their ramifications, something for which the interagency process is supposedly designed.

UPDATE: THE CONTINUING POLICY DILEMMA OF PROVIDE COMFORT/SOUTHERN WATCH

The United States, Great Britain, and France remain committed to the protection of the Kurds and the Shiites under the umbrella of Operations Provide Comfort and Southern Watch, a commitment of which Americans were generally unaware until two American military helicopters were shot down in April 1994 by American jets over Iraqi territory. This operation remains a thorny problem for American foreign policy.

The commitment came about in the case of the Kurds when they had fled to Turkey to avoid Saddam's wrath. They could not stay on the Turkish mountainsides: conditions were unbearable, and the Turkish government, with a Kurdish rebellion of its own, insisted they leave. But they would not return to their homes for fear of extinction. In that circumstance, the tactical decision was made to escort them home but to create an exclusion zone into which the Iraqi government is forbidden to enter (even though it is part of the sovereign territory of Iraq). This zone, and its counterpart for the Shiites, is enforced by the military forces of the three allies.

The policy dilemma is the open-ended nature of the commitment. Basically stated, the United States and its allies are committed to protecting the Kurds from their own givernment until they are convinced that government poses no threat to them. Should the allies simply decide to leave, the Kurds and Shiites would be at the mercy of what has historically been a terribly unmerciful Saddam Hussein. The only alternative solution is the removal of Saddam Hussein from office and his replacement with a more moderate, tolerant alternative, a prospect that few see as likely. Although there is absolutely no reason to believe the United States was committing itself to a long-term stay when it first declared the exclusion zone, that is exactly what it has gotten.

Case Study: The FSX Wrangle

The FSX controversy marked a sea change in the worldview of U.S. policymakers. At first glance it seemed to be a routine disagreement among friends regarding Japan's next-generation jet fighter, the FSX (an acronym for Fighter Support/ Experimental). But the dispute became a lightning rod for pent-up policy disputes between the United States and Japan and—perhaps more importantly—within the American policymaking community. By the time it was finally resolved in the spring of 1989, the tangled episode had placed new strains on an already inflamed U.S.-Japan relationship, had tarnished reputations in both Washington and Tokyo, and, most importantly, had demolished the intellectual and policy wall that had previously separated security and economic issues in the thinking of U.S. policy elites. Before dissecting this complex tale, we need to establish its context amid the strategic U.S.-Japanese relationship.

Context

After defeating Japan in World War II, the United States quickly transformed it into a Cold War ally. The logic behind the policy shift was simple and compelling: Japan's disciplined and well-educated population gave it an industrial potential that might tilt the global balance of power if Japan ever slipped into the communist orbit. At the same time, the shift of the Cold War's focus to Asia signaled by the 1949 communist triumph in China and the 1950 outbreak of the Korean War gave Japan a new strategic significance as a forward base for U.S. armed forces in northeast Asia. With the codification of the security relationship in 1960 and the evolution of bilateral defense cooperation since the late 1970s, the U.S.-Japanese partnership became a bulwark of regional stability in Asia and the Pacific.

With the United States providing Japan's strategic security shield and a postwar constitution that limited its own military efforts to modest conventional defense of its home islands, Japan was free to channel its prodigious energies into a single-minded drive for economic growth. Japan's sensational postwar economic renaissance both helped and hindered the critical relationship with the United States. On the one hand, Japanese prosperity made it a dramatic Cold War showcase of the superior performance of democratic, market-oriented systems. On the other hand, Japan's aggressive pursuit of export markets increasingly made it an economic rival of its strategic patron.

By the 1980s the competitive aspects of the relationship were receiving new emphasis in U.S. circles, particularly as Tokyo began racking up large and growing trade surpluses with the United States. Among U.S. policy elites and opinion leaders, a darker view of Japan began to take hold. Japan, it was argued, owed much of its success to its obsessive, predatory exploitation of the wide-open U.S. market while systematically denying outsiders fair and equal access to its own market. Exaggerated though it was, this image of a Japan that does not play fair gained broad currency in the United States.

Despite the growing economic frictions between the two countries, policymakers in both Washington and Tokyo clung to the informal doctrine that a policy wall should separate the security and economic agendas. From Tokyo's point of view, this doctrine was an exceedingly good deal, since it meant that no matter how frustrated the Americans became by Japanese economic behavior, the United States was unlikely to end its commitment to defend Japan or diminish its considerable military presence in the region. For Washington's part, the doctrine of separating economics and security reflected the pervasive Cold War conviction, shared for 45 years by Democrats and Republicans alike, that the global struggle against communism and Soviet expansionism was the overriding foreign policy issue to which all other policy agendas would have to be subordinated. Should the Cold War turn against the West, the reasoning went, it would make little difference who was guilty of trade protectionism or other economic sins.

The agreed primacy of the security agenda meant that the executive agency created to deal with that agenda—the Department of Defense—would automatically become a bureaucratic heavyweight in directing the overall U.S.-Japanese relationship. Other agencies, such as the Commerce Department or the Office of the U.S. Trade Representative, would, of course, play some role too, but their policy domains were regarded as second echelon, and even a bit drab when compared to the high-stakes drama of deterrence, espionage, and crisis management. It followed that the policymaking role of these economic agencies would be decidedly inferior to that enjoyed by the Pentagon and the State Department.

Unsurprisingly, when the Defense Department looks at the world, it typically does so with little regard for international economic considerations. Nor do Pentagon policymakers typically proceed from a sophisticated grasp of international economic issues. Instead, their career paths require a diligent focus on practical military matters and geostrategic concerns. Hence, the de facto bureaucratic alliance between the Defense Department and the State Department on the crucial U.S.-Japanese relationship meant that security issues would be kept separate from—and superior to—the mundane world of economics.

America's security-economics dichotomy reflected the deep strain of laissez-faire in the thinking of U.S. policymakers and the mass public. According to this belief, economic outcomes are best left to the unfettered play of the free market system, both at home and abroad. The U.S. easy dominance of the global economy after World War II was widely taken as proof of the superiority of its system of minimal government intrusion in the marketplace and maximum economic freedom for producers and consumers to determine economic outcomes. It was an article of faith that the same free market principles that had produced U.S. economic primacy would, if expanded internationally in the form of liberalized global trade and capital flows, ignite a comparable economic boom abroad. The Japanese and, for that matter, all other countries would surely see the light and become ardent converts to U.S.-style free market capitalism.

The confluence of these geopolitical, intellectual, and bureaucratic factors defined the policy-making environment in which the FSX controversy evolved. As it mushroomed into a major conflict between the United States and its most important Asian ally, it challenged, as few other issues have before or since, the traditional U.S. practice of separating security policy and economic policy.

The Dispute, Part I: Washington versus Tokyo

In the early 1980s, bureaucrats in the Japan Defense Agency began weighing alternatives for replacing their Air Self-Defense Force's aging inventory of F-1 fighters, Japan's first ever domestically developed and produced fighter. (Commonly referred to as JDA, the agency is ordinarily regarded as Tokyo's version of the Pentagon, but it enjoys a much less influential position in Japan's policy-making process than the Pentagon plays in the U.S. process.) The range of options was quickly narrowed to two: purchase of existing foreign aircraft (which, given the alliance relationship, would certainly mean U.S. aircraft) or development of a new indigenous Japanese fighter.

These early discussions among Japanese policy planners showed solid support for the all-Japan option—that is, an ambitious high-technology aircraft program that would be designed, developed, and produced in Japan. This sentiment was especially strong in JDA's Technical Research and Development Institute and its Bureau of Equipment, as well as within the Air Self-Defense Force, defense-oriented industrial circles, and the powerful Ministry of International Trade and Industry (MITI).

Their reasoning was that an all-Japan FSX would be a logical step in the evolution of Japan's technological know-how and manufacturing capability. In addition, doing so would merely repeat the established practice of the U.S. major European allies who had their own national military aircraft programs. Between 1982 and 1985, the all-Japan faction worked diligently to overcome objections to its proposed option within Japan's policy community and among opinion elites. Hence, by 1985 Tokyo was at the brink of proceeding with the indigenous development option and expected little objection from Washington should it do so.

Meanwhile, as U.S. diplomatic and military officials in Tokyo and Washington became aware of evolving Japanese thinking, they began a quiet campaign to try to persuade Japanese policymakers to overrule the indigenous development plan. Chief among them were three working-level figures, all of whom were well versed in Japanese politics: Gregg Rubinstein, a career Foreign Service officer who in the mid-1980s was serving in the Mutual Defense Assistance Office in Tokyo; navy commander James Auer, then the Pentagon's principal officer on Japan policy; and Kevin Kearns, another Foreign Service officer, who replaced Rubinstein at the U.S. embassy in Tokyo in 1986.

One of the arguments presented to the Japanese was that the development and production of a small number of fighters (fewer than 150 were planned) would make the plane's per unit cost extremely high. Given the growing closeness of defense cooperation between the two countries, the Americans argued, Japan's limited defense expenditures could better serve mutual objectives by simply buying U.S. aircraft.

The F-16 would be available immediately and, at $15 million per plane, at a fraction of the cost of an indigenously developed FSX. Not only would it be cheaper, but the F-16 Fighting Falcon was a proven world-class fighter. Less than two minutes after engine start, the F-16 can be traveling at the speed of sound at 30,000 feet. For speed, maneuverability, and cost, the F-16 was far and away the best value available to Japan.

U.S. officials also feared that, in order to pay for the FSX, the Japanese would be tempted to seek overseas customers for it, thus ending that state's long-standing policy against selling arms abroad. Given the immense cost of domestic development, the Americans reasoned, Japan's policy of refusing to sell arms abroad would be harder to sustain. By the 1980s, Japan's inherent right to self-defense was generally conceded, even among its Asian neighbors with bitter memories of Japanese aggression in World War II, but the prospect of an arms-exporting Japan would surely undermine the fragile trust and goodwill that Tokyo had gradually rebuilt since 1945. Finally, the Americans argued, an all-Japan FSX would lack what defense planners call "interoperability," or a smooth fit with U.S. military tactics, forces, and equipment.

Quiet pressure from Rubinstein, Auer, and Kearns was having little impact on JDA bureaucrats determined to proceed with indigenous development. At the same time, the overall U.S.-Japanese relationship was steadily deteriorating. Despite a series of sector-specific trade talks and a deeply devalued dollar, the bilateral trade deficit ballooned in the mid-1980s. In 1987, it reached an eye-popping $56 billion out of a worldwide U.S. trade deficit of $160 billion. Moreover, in March 1987, it was revealed that the Toshiba Machine Corporation had illegally exported machine tools to the Soviet Union which would permit the Soviets to make quieter submarine propeller blades, thus making their submarines harder to detect.

Growing numbers in Congress were venting their constituents' anger at Japan's perceived intransigence on trade and outrage at the cynicism of a prominent Japanese corporation. Why, they wondered, would the Japanese now refuse to buy the cheaper and superior F-16, a move that would help reduce the trade deficit, improve defense cooperation, and soothe a badly strained relationship? In the wake of the Toshiba Machine scandal, the U.S. Senate passed, by a vote of 96 to 0, a sense of the Senate resolution calling on Japan to buy its new fighter from the United States.

Despite the mounting economic and political strains, the Pentagon continued to try to compartmentalize the security and economic agendas. In April 1987, for example, it dispatched the Sullivan mission to Tokyo to make a definitive U.S. assessment of the JDA's case on behalf of an all-Japan FSX. Headed by Assistant Deputy Undersecretary of Defense Gerald Sullivan, the mission consisted of military experts drawn from the Pentagon, but it contained no representatives from other agencies. Notably absent was any representation from the Department of Commerce, which was increasingly the hub of those in the executive branch who viewed Japan as an economic threat to the United States and who believed the United States should take a tougher stand on bilateral issues involving trade, technology, and competitiveness.

To be sure, the Sullivan mission's final report would indeed prove to be instrumental in turning Japan's Ministry of Foreign Affairs and Ministry of Finance against JDA's plan for indigenous development. But the report's arguments were grounded in narrow security policy calculations of cost effectiveness and defense interoperability. Given the makeup of the Sullivan mission, its worldview is scarcely surprising.

Hence, the Pentagon's efforts, although competent from a solely security-oriented perspective, suffered from that very narrowness of outlook. And Pentagon dominance of the U.S. stance toward the FSX meant that non-Pentagon perspectives received scant attention. By treating the FSX largely as a matter of defense policy, the Defense Department left unaddressed a whole host of nonmilitary policy matters raised by the project. Chief among these was the question of Japan's broader intentions regarding the commercial jet aircraft market, an area still dominated by U.S. producers. By viewing the immediate matter in isolation from the emerging agenda of international economic competitiveness, U.S. policymakers were acting without an overall strategic concept of the larger U.S. interests in the issue at hand or the broader objectives which the United States should pursue.

Sensing the political fallout of a Japanese decision for the all-Japan option, Secretary of Defense Caspar Weinberger traveled to Tokyo in June 1987 for talks with his counterpart, Defense Minister Kurihara. Insisting that the controversy over the FSX "went to the heart of the U.S.-Japan relationship," Weinberger pressed Kurihara to embrace a third option: *codevelopment*. Under this scheme, the two nations would jointly develop the FSX, using an existing U.S. fighter as the technological base.

By this point, Pentagon and State Department officials believed (1) Tokyo would never agree to an outright purchase of U.S. aircraft, and (2) the momentum building in Japan for indigenous development threatened the overall bilateral relationship. Hence, codevelopment was seen as a sensible third way through which the United States could claim victory for its goal of strengthening deterrence through enhanced bilateral defense cooperation and interoperability. In addition, the Pentagon and State Department saw codevelopment as a way of shoring up the overall U.S.-Japanese relationship. It promised an economic benefit for the United States through the prospective sale of U.S. equipment and technology to Japan.

In Tokyo, the Foreign Ministry agreed with Weinberger that the FSX threatened the overall partnership with the United States and adroitly muscled aside the Defense Agency to win Prime Minister Nakasone's support for the U.S. codevelopment proposal. On October 12, 1987, Nakasone announced his government's decision to work with the United States in the joint development of the FSX. Later that month, General Dynamics' F-16 was selected as the base on which codevelopment research and production would build.

Before work on the project could proceed, however, the two governments would need to negotiate a Memorandum of Understanding (MOU) that would formally codify the terms of the project. Among the issues requiring precise specification in the MOU were the amount of U.S. technology to be transferred to Japan, the division of work between the two countries in both the development and production phases, and U.S. access to new technologies developed by the Japanese in the course of FSX development.

The Pentagon and the State Department paid remarkably little attention to these important details, leaving their resolution to low-level delegations. Their focus had been on getting Japan to agree to codevelopment based on an existing American aircraft in order to counter the mounting anti-Japanese sentiment brewing in Congress. In this way the security partnership could be protected from the intrusion of economic considerations.

Kevin Kearns, a participant in the talks, began to sense that the United States and Japan were pursuing very different agendas in their new undertaking. The United States continued to stress such aspects as cost effectiveness, rapid introduction of an advanced fighter into Japan's Air Self-Defense Force, and maximum interoperability, all of which would clearly call for minimal modifications of the F-16. Japanese negotiators, however, were insisting on extensive modifications of the F-16, a move that would entail, among other things, a massive transfer of U.S. technology to Japan, a great deal of work for Japanese firms, and the assistance of the U.S. contractor, General Dynamics, in any problems it might encounter.

To Kearns, this showed that the Japanese were simply up to their old tricks, taking advantage of U.S. preoccupation with security issues to reap maximum economic benefits. In 1988, Kearns was able to secure a State Department internship on the staff of the Senate Foreign Relations Committee. Knowing that the MOU would ultimately require congressional approval, Kearns had strategically positioned himself for what he increasingly viewed as a campaign to save U.S. foreign policy from its economic naïveté.

In November 1988, the MOU was completed. Under its terms, U.S. firms would get 40 percent of the projected cost of developing four FSX prototypes. When the project moved to the production phase (120 airplanes would be built, beginning in 1997), a second MOU would be negotiated, but the United States assumed it would get a comparable work share as in the development phase. It was also agreed that derivative technology, that is, new technology derived by the Japanese from U.S. F-16 technology, would be transferred to the United States without charge. The companion licensing agreement between General Dynamics and its Japanese collaborator, Mitsubishi Heavy Industries, was completed in January 1989.

The matter was now ready to go before the Congress, which would have 30 days in which to block it. Unless it did so, the MOU would then be in effect. But note the timing: January 1989 meant that the FSX agreement would be passed into the hands of the new Bush administration and would be subject to the scrutiny of a newly installed Congress. What had until then been a rather technical issue of secondary importance was about to become the first foreign policy crisis of the Bush administration.

The Dispute, Part II: Washington versus Washington

In the early months of 1989, the FSX agreement became a political lightning rod for critics who believed that the United States needed to take a more aggressive stance toward Japan on trade, technology, and competitiveness issues. They had concluded that the Pentagon, with its traditional security policy worldview, had left those issues largely unaddressed in the MOU. The Commerce Department emerged as an unexpectedly feisty player of bureaucratic politics because of (1) the naming of Robert Mosbacher, a close personal friend of President Bush, as the new secretary of commerce; (2) a desire within the Department of Commerce to settle old scores with the Pentagon for the shabby way it had been treated during the FSX negotiations (at one point Karl Jackson, then deputy assistant secretary of defense for East Asia, simply refused to provide his Commerce counterpart, Maureen Smith, with a copy of the MOU; as a Pentagon official put it, "We just told Commerce to buzz off"); and (3) new language in the 1989 Defense Authorization bill that now required the Pentagon to include the Commerce Department in negotiating MOUs. Taken together, these three factors made the Commerce Department a suddenly self-confident challenger of Pentagon and State Department primacy on U.S.-Japanese relations.

The Defense Department was left leaderless at this critical juncture as the nomination of former senator John Tower to be the new secretary of defense ran aground on charges that Tower was a hard-drinking womanizer. By the time Dick Cheney was picked in place of the doomed Tower, critics of the FSX deal had rallied important bureaucratic allies and had seized the momentum.

Finally, Congress began to mobilize against the FSX MOU. The opposition was bipartisan, with Sen. John Danforth, a Missouri Republican, seeing Japan's refusal to purchase U.S. fighters as yet another instance of Japanese protectionism, while to Sen. Jeff Bingaman, a Democrat from New Mexico, the issue was one of preserving the U.S. lead in commercial aircraft technology. To him and others, the FSX would transfer vital U.S. technology to an ally who would simply use it to make its own firms more competitive against the Americans.

The arrival of the State Department's Kevin Kearns on Capitol Hill was important, too, for the Senate Foreign Relations Committee now had on its staff a determined opponent of the FSX deal who was intimately familiar with its terms and who had developed an alarming analysis of its implications. Working principally through North Carolina Republican senator Jesse Helms, Kearns orchestrated a masterful setback for FSX supporters (and, in the process, thoroughly alienated himself from his colleagues at State). On January 18, 1989, using notes prepared by Kearns, Senator Helms seized the confirmation hearings of secretary of state designate James Baker to force the perplexed Baker to agree to a review of the FSX MOU.

FSX supporters in the State Department tried to fudge the issue by hastily conducting their own cursory review, which they forwarded to Baker. But the Kearns-led insurgency would have none of it; they insisted on nothing less than a full-dress interagency review. An interagency review was the one thing that supporters of FSX had feared the most, for it meant the long-muted skeptics at Commerce, Labor, the U.S. trade representative's office, and the White House Office of Science and Technology would now have their say.

Bowing to pressure from Congress and the Commerce Department, President Bush—at the urging of Baker and National Security Adviser Brent Scowcroft—directed the NSC to conduct the review and to make certain that all interested agencies were heard from. The inevitable interagency shootout took place at the February 10, 1989, meeting of the NSC's Policy Coordinating Committee. State and Pentagon representatives repeated the now familiar security policy case for the MOU as it stood, but the meeting was dominated by opponents of the deal from Commerce, the Labor Department, the Office of the U.S. Trade Representative, and the White House Office of Science and Technology.

Startled by the breadth of opposition, Bush ordered that a definitive review be undertaken and a unified interagency report on the FSX be submitted to the NSC by March 10. Significantly, NSC chief Scowcroft yielded to Robert Mosbacher's insistence that the Commerce Department share supervision of the review with the Pentagon. Both as symbol and as substance, this meant the economic agenda had now taken its seat at the foreign policy head table right alongside security policy.

The Pentagon-Commerce study was ready in time for the NSC's March 15 meeting, which Washington insiders knew would be the showdown event on U.S. policy toward the FSX. The 16-page paper included a balanced summation of three areas of disagreement between the security policy community at the Pentagon and State Department and the trade-technology-competitiveness faction centered in the Commerce Department. The disputes involved work share, computer source codes, and derivative technology flow-back to the United States.

As to work share, Commerce insisted that the United States get a formal agreement from Japan that 40 percent of the work in the production phase would go to U.S. firms. The Pentagon argued that this agreement was unnecessary at this stage and could be taken up when the second, production-phase MOU was ready for negotiation. With regard to source codes, Commerce argued against allowing Japan access to the sophisticated computer software that controlled the F-16's flight and weapons systems. The Pentagon countered that much of the weapons-control software could safely be transferred but agreed that the flight-control codes should be withheld. Finally, Commerce urged further clarification of the derivative technology flow-back provision; the Pentagon argued that the MOU was clear enough as it stood.

The March 15 meeting of the NSC gave the FSX opponents one more chance to weigh in with their objections. The Pentagon-State alliance was nearly swamped in a sea of vigorous objections voiced by U.S. Trade Representative Carla Hills, White House Chief of Staff John Sununu, Secretary of Commerce Mosbacher, and Secretary of Energy James Watkins. When the meeting was over, President Bush decided that before proceeding further with the deal, "clarifications" with the Japanese would have to be secured.

Thus, on March 20, Japan's ambassador Matsunaga was summoned to the State Department. There he was presented with the new U.S. demands. Perhaps the most significant aspect of the meeting was the composition of the U.S. delegation: Secretary of State Baker was there, of course, as was the new secretary of defense, Dick Cheney. But joining them was none other than Secretary of Commerce Mosbacher. The meeting merits a footnote in the history of U.S. foreign policy-making because it marked the first time that a commerce secretary took part in defense cooperation talks with a foreign government.

The Dispute, Part III: Washington versus Tokyo (Again)

Japan's policy community watched with dismay as Washington's policy factions and bureaucratic rivals turned the FSX into a political Kabuki-by-the-Potomac. Despite the Americans' insistence that they were merely seeking "clarifications," to the Japanese it appeared that Washington was forcing renegotiation of what Tokyo regarded as a completed agreement. Although their public reactions were couched in typical Japanese politeness, in private Japanese policymakers were fuming. From where they sat, it was the United States who had barged uninvited into what was initially an all-Japanese development project and demanded that the United States participate in a joint effort based on an existing U.S. airplane. Now, to add insult to injury, the United States was in effect calling Japan a technology thief who could not be trusted.

Others in Japan were not at all reluctant to lash out at what they regarded as the new habit of the United States to blame Japan for its own economic ills and its heavy-handed treatment of its most important ally. The conservative nationalist Shintaro Ishihara, for example, wrote, "Development by Japan of a fighter craft Japan built itself with its own advanced technology would give it absolute authority over its own airspace, and this would alter both the meaning and the value of the Japan-U.S. defense alliance. The United States then would be unable to continue patronizing Japan in the area of defense."

Tokyo's policymakers, however, concealed their bitterness and decided to grant the United States the policy clarifications it was demanding. Japan's decision to do so was based on its belief that it was too late to pull out of FSX codevelopment or to begin a new all-Japan fighter development program owing to the looming need to replace the aging F-1s. Japan believed, too, that failure of the FSX development would be a grave setback for defense cooperation between the United States and Japan. Through the FSX project, not only would Japan receive sophisticated aircraft technology from the United States, but also the United States would acquire cutting-edge know-how from Japan. To Tokyo, the strategic benefits of strengthening the intricate web of defense and technological interdependence between Japan and the United States outweighed its immediate anger at Washington's high-handed treatment. Thus, on April 28 the two sides announced that they had successfully clarified the MOU by agreeing to most of the Commerce Department's objections.

The Dispute Resolved and Its Lessons

With the ball back in Washington's court, a now unified executive branch submitted the clarified MOU to Congress for its approval. Kevin Kearns and his allies on Capitol Hill believed the new deal was better than the original but still not a good one for U.S. interests. However, the united front presented by Defense, State, and Commerce was enough to overcome congressional skepticism, although just barely so. On

May 16, 1989, the Senate approved the MOU on a close vote of 52 to 47. Had three votes gone the other way, FSX would have died in Congress.

That it did not meant codevelopment would be pursued. It remains to be seen if the dark fears of FSX critics that the deal will boost Japan's commercial aircraft industry will in fact materialize. It is possible that the United States will gain significant benefits through the derivative technology flow-back provision. Under its terms, the United States will acquire the fruits of Japan's research and development on the aircraft, including the commercially important field of composite materials fabrication. Japan is determined to devise new manufacturing processes for building the FSX wing using co-cured carbon fiber, a sophisticated way of making stronger and lighter aircraft components. Should the Japanese succeed in doing so, the United States will indeed have obtained a handsome economic dividend for its early investment in the FSX.

If the jury remains out on the long-term fruits of the FSX, the verdict is entirely clear on the U.S. policy-making process that produced it. What the FSX saga tells us is that U.S. policy-makers can no longer compartmentalize trade and defense issues. Nor can the United States continue to elevate the traditional geostrategic agenda of security and defense above the emerging agenda of trade, technology, and global competitiveness. The United States can no longer function as a kind of technology convenience store where allied countries can drop in for a quick order of U.S. defense know-how, which can then be used commercially in the competition for global markets.

It follows that the numerous strands of U.S. policy must now be coordinated in ways that were not necessary before. That, in turn, means the proliferating roster of policy players must be coordinated more than ever before. Developing a coherent strategy of assuring the country's physical and economic well-being will place greater burdens on the NSC's interagency machinery. It may even be necessary to replace the NSC structure with a new interagency apparatus that is less grounded in the security imperatives of the Cold War and more attuned to the nontraditional issues of global interdependence coming to the fore in the post–Cold War world.

President Clinton's economic team may be the vehicle for this coordination. The new effort, headed by investment banker turned secretary of the treasury Robert Rubin, has as its mandate the overall coordination of the many strands that together make up domestic and international economic policy. Its charge is to help the president attain a measure of coherence in policy domains as diverse as health care, taxes, monetary policy, investment, and trade issues. But the creation of this new emphasis has not assured that economic issues will necessarily be better integrated into the country's overall international strategy than has been the case in the past. What the FSX case shows is the pressing need to develop policy-making procedures that routinize consideration of the economic component of national security decisions and the security and diplomatic implications of economic decisions.

Conclusions

Both cases discussed in this chapter are representative of the kinds of problems the policy-making process will confront in the future. In addition, in both cases the existing policy process did not perform as well as it might, thus suggesting the desirability of reforming that process.

With regard to the representativeness of the cases for the post–Cold War world, the FSX case had its gestation in the Cold War context, and the agreement apparently resolving it preceded by a matter of months the revolutions of 1989 that signaled the end of the Cold War. At the same time, Cold War security obligations played a part in Japan's professed need for a new fighter aircraft.

What makes the case representative is its economic content and the convergence of sometimes contradictory economic and geopolitical interests in foreign policy. The net result of the FSX process was codevelopment of an aircraft by the United States and Japan, even though burgeoning costs have prevented production beyond the prototype stage. Such arrangements are becoming increasingly frequent in associated industries, such as the automotive and electronic industries, where joint ventures and joint ownership are becoming more and more the norm. Not all of these joint activities become foreign policy issues as the FSX did, but the impact of economic considerations on foreign policy is a major part of the post–Cold War world.

So, too, is the convergence of economic and national security criteria and the need to reconcile the two sets of interests. With the Cold War competition ended and in the absence of a compelling and powerful enemy, the traditional case for national security predominance defined militarily will almost certainly decrease. As a result, the actors representing the Defense and State Departments will have to share the process more with other agencies such as Commerce, as they were grudgingly forced to do in FSX. Moreover, FSX is both an example of an intermestic problem (American aerospace jobs, Japanese defense) and the kind of competitiveness issue that energizes many within the Clinton administration. It is a classic Bill Clinton issue.

The challenge posed by Iraq's invasion and conquest of Kuwait is instructive of the kinds of traditional national security concerns the system will have to deal with in the future. The conflict occurred in the Second Tier, where much of the remaining instability and potential for violence resides. Moreover, ethnic and geopolitical concerns—the Kurdish question in Iraq, Saddam Hussein's assertion that Kuwait was rightly the nineteenth province of Iraq—are the kinds of problems being faced today in the disintegrated communist world in places such as Yugoslavia and parts of the former Soviet Union. Iraq may be a worst case of sorts: there are relatively few other leaders with the combined resources and ambitions that Saddam Hussein has displayed. Nonetheless, these are the kinds of situations that the United States may find itself tempted to engage in in the future. The issue also served to stimulate interest in the United Nations as the legitimating agent of choice for authorizing the use of force in the post–Cold War world.

Another common point between the two cases returns us to a theme that has recurred throughout the book. In both instances studied here, the decision mechanisms for making and executing policy—principally the interagency process—were of dubious adequacy to deal with the problems presented to it.

In the case of FSX, the obvious shortcoming was the failure to involve the Commerce Department and other economic interests early on in the process of developing a U.S. position on the Japanese fighter. The Clinton approach of bringing together clusters of affected parties to policy areas may remedy this problem. When we look back at how the FSX controversy evolved, we see that it almost certainly would have been handled differently within such an institutional arrangement.

The shortcomings of Desert Storm may be more personal than institutional. Here, the failure to anticipate and deal in advance with largely predictable consequences of different actions may well have been the result not of inadequate resources so much as the failure to utilize all available resources. Although the record of how policy was made is not yet public, the glimpses we have through sources such as Bob Woodward's The *Commanders* suggests that the decisions were made by a very small group: mostly the president, vice president, chairman of the JCS, secretaries of state and defense, national security adviser, director of central intelligence, and a few other key assistants such as Paul Wolfowitz at Defense and some members of Vice President Quayle's staff. Little available evidence exists that the extensive network of bodies described as the interagency process in Chapter 7 played an extensive part.

Just how much the context in which foreign and defense policy-making has changed and will change is a matter of looking at the future. It is necessarily a speculative venture, since the future has the disadvantage (from the analyst's point of view) of not having yet happened. Such speculation, and the impact of projected change on the policy process, is the subject of Chapter 14.

SUGGESTED READINGS

Aspin, Les. *The Aspin Papers: Sanctions, Diplomacy, and War in the Persian Gulf Crisis.* Washington, DC: Center for Strategic and International Studies, 1991.

Bulloch, John, and Harvey Morris. *Saddam's War: The Origins of the Kuwait Conflict and the International Response.* Boston: Faber & Faber, 1991.

Carpenter, Ted Galen (ed.). *America Entangled. The Persian Gulf Crisis and Its Consequences.* Washington, DC: Cato Institute, 1991.

Congressional Quarterly. *The Middle East.* 7th ed., revised. Washington, DC: Congressional Quarterly Press, 1991.

Ennis, Peter. "Inside the Pentagon-Commerce Turf War." *Tokyo Business Today,* October 1989, pp. 22–26.

Otsuki, Shinji. "The FSX Controversy Revived." *Japan Quarterly,* October–December 1989, pp. 433–443.

Otsuki, Shinji. "The FSX Problem Resolved?" *Japan Quarterly,* January–March 1990, pp. 70–83.

Prestowitz, Clyde. *Trading Places: How We Are Giving Our Future to Japan and How to Reclaim It.* New York: Basic Books, 1989.

Sifry, Michael L., and Christoph Cerf (eds.). *The Gulf War. History, Documents, Opinions.* New York: Random House, 1991.

Spar, Debora. "Co-developing the FSX Fighter: The Domestic Calculus of International Co-operation." *International Journal,* Spring 1992, pp. 265–292.

CHAPTER 14

Looking toward the Future

Americans, as well as the citizens of many other countries, often find foreign and national security policy frustrating and bewildering. Foreign events are often unfamiliar and even alien: names that are hard to pronounce, places that are difficult to find, events that are hard to comprehend. Although Americans are more bombarded than before via the global media about international events, these complexities remain.

For example, sorting out the war in former Yugoslavia perplexed American and European publics and policymakers for more than three years before the United States, acting in its increasing role as global peacemaker, managed to lure the Bosnian, Serb, and Croatian leaderships to the Dayton talks where a peace settlement was finally hammered out. The same was true of American-led efforts convened in the Maryland countryside in December 1995 to move the Syrians and the Israelis toward peace.

Foreign policy can also be frustrating because it is often so difficult to measure (or even to achieve) success. It is as much process as it is product. The United States does not always have control of the agenda in foreign policy concerns, and thus cannot dictate outcomes that reflect its most preferred outcomes. Forces outside government, such as the media, have an impact on the agenda. Moreover, there is generally disagreement within the government itself about what constitutes success—within and among executive branch agencies and between the executive branch and the legislative branch, for instance. The debate over whether to send troops to Bosnia for how long and with what expectations illustrates the point.

The decision process surrounding the Persian Gulf War exemplifies the difficulty of articulating goals on which there is consensus and then implementing policy. As we noted in Chapter 13, there were two major sources of disagreement. The first was between the Democratic leadership in Congress and the Republican White House on how to proceed: whether to let economic sanctions try to solve the problem (the Democratic alternative) or whether to proceed more quickly to military action (the White House preference). The second was the postwar situation in Iraq and, more specifically, whether it should be a goal of the war to remove Saddam Hussein forcefully from power. Although the administration never advocated publicly nor adopted a policy aimed at his overthrow (other than Bush encouraging the Iraqis themselves to act), there were loud public pressures to that effect. The result of a lack of consensus was that many people were disappointed when Hussein remained in control of Iraq at war's end, a feeling that the mission had not truly been completed as a result.

All of these sources of confusion are reflected in the foreign and national security policy process and changes in it. The first post–Cold War president—Bill Clinton—at times seemed adrift, confused, and even disengaged as he has approached the problems currently facing the United States, but he and those around him are not entirely to blame. Even the Bush administration, which prided itself in its foreign policy expertise, was befuddled by Bosnia, Somalia, and Haiti policy. Certainly, an administration headed by a president with no direct foreign policy experience (at least outside economics, a personal area of interest) and staffed at the political levels mostly by people who have been outside government since the Carter years, took some time to adjust to new realities. At the same time, the administration faced a new set of problems such as the rise of internal wars that were new phenomena. To its credit, the administration (partly because of an increase in the president's personal involvement), began to score successes in moving along the peace process in the Arab-Israeli conflict, as well as Northern Ireland and Bosnia.

These changes have meant a need for procedural change as well, and this process was accelerated by the 1994 election of an aggressive Republican majority in Congress with its Contract with America that included a number of foreign policy elements. At one level, inexperienced White House staff are now matched with equally inexperienced chairs of the most important committees of the Congress. The ascendancies of 92-year-old Strom Thurmond of South Carolina to the chair of the Senate Armed Services Committee and volatile Jesse Helms of North Carolina to the chair of the Senate Foreign Relations Committee have been particularly noteworthy.

It is in this atmosphere of change and turbulence that an assessment of the future must proceed. In the remainder of this chapter, we look at likely and possible directions of policy in the major areas that have been the focus of the rest of the book. The device we use to organize the discussion is one we introduced originally in *The Contours of Power:* the idea of the policy domain.

Likely and Preferred Futures: The Policy Domain

The idea of a policy domain is reasonably simple and straightforward. The concept refers to those aspects of a policy area that one would like to change to suit better his or her interests and the policy preferences that flow from those interests. It is activated by an assessment of what the policy area would look like at some future point, then comparing that situation with what you would like the policy area to be. The gap between your projected and preferred positions is the area where you would like to influence policy away from expectation to preference, the policy domain.

We capture this process diagramatically in Figure 14.1. The important point to be made here is the comparison of expectation (the lower line) and preference. The extrapolation of what the policy area is expected to be like is based on an assessment of how things will likely evolve if the United States does essentially nothing (or nothing other than what it has been doing) to intervene, whereas policy preference is what we would ideally like to see the policy area to be. The gap, which represents a range of outcomes intermediate between the two, are steps toward our favored outcome. The purpose of policy-making is to try to determine what, if anything, can narrow the gap, the extent to which the gap can be narrowed, what the United States must do to try to narrow the gap, and whether the costs of trying to change expected outcomes are politically and otherwise acceptable. Needless to say, all of these calculations take place in a circumstance of uncertainty, imperfect information, domestic disagreement about ends and means, and the possible confounding actions of the object of the policy change, which may or may not favor the changes the United States wants.

This rather abstract formulation can be enlivened with a real example that is part historical, part contemporary. For this purpose, we use the situation in South Africa in the early 1980s. At that time, South Africa still had a white supremacist government—a partially democratic system where only the white population (about 17 percent of the total population) had political rights, and where the segregationist system of fundamental (political) and petty (social) apartheid was still in place. At the same time, South Africa was (and is) by far the most prosperous and economically developed state in Africa, and major Western states, through their multinational corporations, had large-scale investments in the South African economy. Further, the virtually universal assessment of the situation was that there were no real threats to the white minority government in the short or medium term (e.g., the end of the century), but that the assertion of majority rule was inevitable in the long run. The question, then and now, was how to accomplish that transition peacefully.

This sets up the policy domain. The situation at the time was one of a white minority government enforcing apartheid, apparently unwilling to entertain reforms that might undercut its monopoly of power, and quite certain that it could enforce its policy preferences for the foreseeable future. From an American (and other First Tier) vantage point, the policy expectation was for a continuation of current conditions if the United States did nothing or simply continued existing policies.

FIGURE 14.1   The Policy Domain

The policy preference of the United States was quite the opposite of that of the South African government. Americans generally agreed on the general proposition that the transition to multiracial democracy was the preferred outcome—either because they believed the transition was inevitable and hoped it would be peaceful, or because they found South African racial policies reprehensible (or both). They disagreed on whether the U.S. government should take active steps to narrow the policy domain gap (those opposed argued to do so was a violation of South African sovereignty) and on how to try to do so.

The arena of the policy domain was thus established. Among those who wanted the United States to act there were two schools of thought on policy. One group, largely liberal and mostly Democratic, argued for punishing and isolating South Africa until that country met international civil and human rights standards. Their tool was divestiture, urging individual Americans and institutions to cease investing in the South African economy and, where possible, to sell those investments they had. (This latter posture was especially popular on college campuses because a number of prominent universities had sizable investments of which they divested themselves.)

The other group, more conservative and more heavily Republican, preferred what they called "constructive engagement," working with the South Africans and trying gradually to change their policies. A favorite tactic was to allow American corporations to invest in South Africa, but only if they adhered to the Sullivan codes (named after a civil rights activist, Rev. Leon Sullivan of Philadelphia). These codes required corporations to treat all employees equally regardless of race in the workplace in terms of salary and working conditions. The idea was that if enough foreign corporations (and other countries were asked to enforce the Sullivan codes as well) also took part that the codes would become a norm, jobs where the codes were in place would be where the workers would gravitate, and thus South African–owned concerns would eventually have to adopt similar standards in order to attract qualified workers.

The South African case illustrates the limits of policy as well. Although constructive engagement was American policy throughout the 1980s, no one would argue that it was the crucial (or even a crucial) element in F. W. de Klerk's decision to end white supremacy in South Africa. In fact, the idea that the white population would simply come to accept the inevitable was hardly part of the 1980s dialogue. Instead, South Africa made its own transition. Now, the problem of policy is how to keep multiracial democracy on track. As long as Nelson Mandela is at the helm, his moral and political stature can keep the policy on-line. The question is what happens after Mandela retires from the scene; the current policy domain concern is what, if anything, the United States can do to keep the process ongoing.

An assessment of at least the short-term direction of policy can be organized around this idea of the policy domain. To this end, we review the major policy areas we have investigated to this point in that light. We begin with the problem of residues from the Cold War, then move to security and economic policies as well as transnational issues, and then conclude with some implications of these changes for the policy process itself.

Cold War Residues

If the old structure of international relations has crumbled, some of its artifacts are still with us, in a process of transition whose outcomes are still not certain. Two stand out in particular: the structure and stability of the successor states to the Soviet Union, and the prospects for the formerly communist countries of Eastern Europe (of which the Balkans remains the greatest problem).

What is the situation in the countries that used to comprise the Soviet Union, and especially in Russia? Over ten years after the rise of Gorbachev and nearly five years after the dissolution of the Soviet Union, Russia remains intact, clinging to a system resembling a political democracy (with at least aspects of freedom such as free speech remaining and even arguably getting stronger), but with an economy still struggling mightily to make the transition from a command to a market basis. The Chechens continue to demonstrate the centrifugal tendency of parts of the country, but the ability of the government to weather that crisis despite global publicity—including Russian television—of atrocities committed in suppressing the rebellion is some evidence of the resiliency of evolving Russian institutions. Periodic outbreaks of violence, however, equally clearly indicate the problem will not simply go away.

Without any organized outside (including American) assistance, what is the situation likely to become? The worst case scenario is a further spiral into chaos, with democratic institutions crumbling and the society—but especially the economy—increasingly controlled by criminal elements, and the people becoming more and more disillusioned by the system. This picture is the Weimar Republic of Germany revisited, where the people might turn to an authoritarian demagogue like Vladimir Zhironovsky in much the manner that the Germans turned to Hitler in the 1930s. A more likely future shows Russia remaining adrift politically and economically, neither rejecting their freedom nor benefiting greatly from the prosperity of the First Tier. The resurgence of the Russian Communist Party in 1996 was a concern before Yeltzin's reelection.

Clearly, none of these outcomes represents an American preference, which would be one of gradual Russian development economically toward the First Tier, with the continued blossoming of political democracy. In other words, the United States, and the other countries of the First Tier, want to see Russia continue progress toward a state of normalcy, one that can at some time be embraced as part of the global economy.

Bridging the gap between likely and preferred futures for Russia clearly shows the limits of policy possibility. The key to Russian progress toward the general prosperity is economic, and there are very real limits on how much can be done to improve the Russian economy in the short run. Russia is not structurally equipped for a full-blown market economy, for instance, and it must develop rules of law to cover a range of basic matters such as ownership and transfer of property and capital. To absorb foreign investment, a central banking system must be developed. Americans, including the government, can aid such a process, but it will be slow. In the current U.S. fiscal climate, the availability of public funds (foreign aid) for Russia or anywhere else is questionable at best. There is turbulence in other parts of the successor states, notably along the southern borders of the defunct union. Armenia and Azerbaijan continue their bloody duel over Nagorno-Karabakh, fundamentalist Islamic civil war boils over in Tadjikistan, and war threatens in Georgia, to name three.

The United States would prefer peace and stability in these regions, if only to reduce the problems for Russia—the danger of suppression of Russian nationals caught in violence in the successor states, for instance. But that preference does not, at least in traditional calculations on the basis of American national interest, have a very high priority or reflect any particular American concern. One can imagine, for example, the public response to a proposal to send American forces to protect Azerbaijani oil fields. The great likelihood is that if violence cannot be contained in these areas, Russia will be the only state with the interest and ability (even that is questionable given the performance in Chechnya) to quell it; such action would, of course, bring objections about the reimposition of empire.

The lingering problems in formerly communist Eastern and Central Europe are at the same time more promising and more vexing. On the positive side is the progress of some of the Eastern European democracies toward political democracy and market-based economies. The success stories are especially great in the northern tier states (Poland, Hungary, the Czech Republic, Slovakia, Slovenia), and the real question is whether that same condition can be extended to more southerly states like Romania, Bulgaria, and even Albania.

If there is a policy problem area affecting the countries of the old Warsaw Pact (plus some others), it is the question of an encompassing security blanket acceptable to all. The current reality, as discussed in Chapter 3, is the Partnership for Peace (P4P), which has served as an interim device somewhere between no affiliation and full membership in NATO. It is clear that this arrangement will not continue to be acceptable over the long haul: the queue of P4P members petitioning for and increasingly demanding full participation in and protection from the Western military alliance is growing. The P4P structure has, however, provided a useful device for organizing non-NATO participation in Operation Joint Endeavor in Bosnia.

The gap between P4P and an encompassing NATO-based or CSCE-grounded security architecture has not been fully addressed in the United States and elsewhere. At one level, anything that will make the formerly communist countries more secure is desirable. At the same time, two issues must be resolved before the stamp of full membership can be resolved.

The first question is how to make Russia a part of such an arrangement. An expanded NATO without Russia would be perceived as a potentially threatening, anti-Russian alliance, possibly reinforcing classic Russian paranoia about being surrounded by its enemies that is part of the current dialogue within Russia. At the same time, Russia will not accept membership for itself unless it has some kind of special status that reflects its military power. A compromise has to emerge somewhere. The other question is whether the United States or its Western allies is willing to accept the added burden that protecting old enemies entails. The American people have not been asked, for instance, what they think of the possibility of sending their sons and daughters into harm's way to protect Hungary or Bulgaria, or the Ukraine. What their response would be is no better than an open question.

The situation in the Balkans remains the most negative part of the equation. The war in the remaining parts of what used to be Yugoslavia went on for nearly four years before the Paris peace accords were signed in December 1995; whether the host of hatreds revived by the fighting can be extinguished is the remaining question. The level of bloodshed, atrocity, dislocation, and suffering perpetrated by all sides will undoubtedly leave a legacy of bitterness and hatred that only generations can overcome; that is certainly the theme of much of Balkan history. Whether the physical settlement can hope to erase or satisfy the desire for revenge remains to be seen. The Balkans will likely remain unstable for years to come, although there may be hope for places like Slovenia (and possibly Croatia); the hope is that Operation Joint Endeavor will cool passions enough to let the healing begin. We shall see.

The Domain of Security

The domain for formulating policy to ensure the national security is a good bit less focused than it was during the Cold War, and that condition is likely to continue for the foreseeable future. If the core of national security is dealing with those problems for which military force in one guise or another may be the appropriate instrument of national power, then the problem has become decidedly diffuse.

In national security terms, expected and preferred positions are largely couched in terms of threats and the reduction or elimination of those threats. In other words, the expected future is a list of threats to American vital national interests, and the preferred policy future is one where as many of those threats are reduced or eliminated as possible.

During the Cold War the structure of the threat was well known, and its shape at most future times could be reasonably well anticipated. The United States knew how many divisions of Soviet soldiers there were and would likely be, and the same calculation could be made about tanks, fighter aircraft, nuclear-tipped rockets, and other measures of Soviet military might. While that threat could not be eliminated, it could be counteracted in such a way as to dissuade the Soviets from using their weapons against the United States, thereby reducing the threat through deterrence.

As we noted in Chapter 10, the disappearance of the Soviet threat leaves the United States without a monolithic threat against which national security policymakers can plan. Indeed, the absence of a concrete enemy has even led strategists to suggest that forces be organized on the basis of desired capabilities (partly because they are technologically possible).

This is not an entirely happy circumstance for national security planners. They are forced to work against abstract and, in some cases, unlikely planning scenarios like the simultaneous North Korean attack on the South and Iraqi reinvasion of Kuwait. At the same time, the absence of plausible threats to American important interests forces them to plan for strained problems, such as "peace operations" and, even more euphemistically, "operations other than war."

If there are no longer major threats to American security, there are still at least problems with which policymakers must come to grips. A few are residual: what, for instance, to do with the lingering commitment to the Kurds and Shiites of Iraq. At the same time, it is clear that the vast majority of violence and instability will be in the Second Tier, where American interests are least obviously engaged. Are there principles to determine what, if anything, the United States wants to do in these situations, and especially in the phenomenon of the new internal wars that have produced the most gruesome manifestations of violence?

The ongoing American commitment to the Kurds and Shiites represents the residual remnant of the Persian Gulf War. As long as the Iraqi government of Saddam Hussein chooses not to challenge this blatant violation of its sovereignty represented by Operations Provide Comfort and Southern Watch (see Update box in Chapter 13), it remains a low-cost, low-key effort, the only negative impact of which is the connection, however tenuous, of Iraqi and Turkish Kurdish movements for autonomy and even independence within a state of Kurdistan, a desire violently opposed by NATO ally Turkey.

This commitment deserves greater publicity than it has achieved because of the way it occurred. At the time the United States engineered the return of Kurdish refugees to their Iraqi homes, there was no grand design involved, at least as is known on the public record. The decision was apparently entirely tactical and expedient: get them off the mountainsides (and off television) and worry about the consequences later. The effect, however, was to bond the United States (as well as Great Britain and France) to the fate of the Kurds and Kurdistan.

What if Saddam Hussein demands that the exclusion zones be lifted, probably including a promise of amnesty and nonretribution against the Kurds and Shiites? Because it would be Saddam Hussein issuing the demand, there would be a powerful tendency to disbelieve him and ignore the request. But the simple fact is that, in any international legal sense, such a request is entirely reasonable. The United States is, after all, directly violating Iraqi sovereignty in a way Americans would find absolutely unacceptable should a state make a similar declaration against them. Since we assume that lifting the zones would result in a ruthless suppression, the United States has to keep it intact or be prepared to intervene physically to stop the slaughter, an action most Americans would be wary about supporting.

Operations Provide Comfort and Southern Watch are symptomatic of the kinds of potential morasses into which the United States may be tempted to become involved in the Second Tier in the future. Almost all the shooting conflicts are internal affairs in the poorest and often most remote parts of the world, where it is difficult to find even the most tangential American interests. Yet the levels of suffering and deprivation that populations are subjected to are heartrending, and the finer impulse "to do the right thing" (to paraphrase President Clinton's rhetorical defense of the Bosnian deployment) about horrible conditions is present.

The United States is by no means alone in lacking policy toward the violent parts of the Second Tier. The spate of such wars in, among other places, much of sub-Saharan Africa has not elicited anything like a uniform response. In some cases, European powers have made limited efforts in selected places where they have had historic interests, as the French did during the rampage in Rwanda. So far, the entirety of American response has been to provide logistical support for those who have intruded and to mount humanitarian relief efforts, as was done for Rwandan refugees in neighboring Zaire.

It may well be that this is all that can be done, that the absence of a positive policy of involvement is the best one can do. Such a position does, however, relegate those parts of the world even further to the periphery of the emerging international system, the centerpiece of which is the globalizing world economy.

The Economic Domain

American foreign economic policy has been a much brighter aspect of policy. This is partly because the dynamics of the global economy among the countries of the First Tier (discussed in Chapter 11) are ongoing and largely self-perpetuating, essentially beyond the regulation and manipulation of national governments. Governments, including that of the United States, are less in a position to mess up the global economy than they are in other policy areas.

Having said that, successive American administrations have made a positive contribution in the economic sphere. The Reagan administration, prominently backed by Great Britain's Margaret Thatcher, took the lead in the process of privatization and deregulation which many champions of the third industrial revolution argue was pivotal to the success of the globalizing of international economics, a policy continued under George Bush. The Clinton administration brought an increased expertise and commitment to the global economy, bucking its reputation for indecisiveness and vacillation in its steadfast insistence on ratification of both the Uruguay Round of GATT and the NAFTA agreement. President Clinton has clearly emerged as a leader in venues such as NAFTA and APEC.

In what directions would the United States like to see international economic policy go? The dynamism of the international economic system makes projection a particularly perilous venture (especially given the symbiotic relationship between the system's evolution and the high-technology revolution). With that rejoinder in mind, however, the expected future one would prophesize would be a greater integration of the general intertwining and prosperity of the First Tier, including the spreading of effective First Tier status to those states such as Asia's four tigers (Hong Kong, South Korea, Taiwan, Singapore), poised for inclusion. While these relations will not always be entirely harmonious—witness the ongoing U.S.-Japan dialogue about fair trading practices—it will be generally to the benefit of those who are a part of it.

If there is a preferred policy future that is probably not the consequence of current efforts, it is in the aggressive extension of the global economy into the Second

Tier. Even here, there are some prospects that have arisen: the agreements in principle to make free trade areas out of the APEC and NAFTA, expanded to encompass all 34 democratic states in the Western Hemisphere (the Free Trade Area of the Americas). Because both organizations include members from both tiers and from all subtiers of the Second Tier, they could provide a model for gradually uplifting the economic and, hopefully, political status of diverse states. The same kind of process extended toward Eastern Europe and even some of the successor states to the Soviet Union by the European Union would further broaden the scope of the effort.

None of this, however, is yet reality. The idea of a Free Trade Area of the Americas or an APEC-wide free trade area by 2020 are ideas and principles, not negotiated and ratified treaties and statutes. Moreover, they have not been subjected to wide popular or congressional debate, and it is not at all clear what the American people and their elected representatives will have to say about them. Given the partisan difficulties that attached to gaining congressional approval of a NAFTA that pales in its potential to the Free Trade Area of the Americas, there is great difficulty in predicting outcomes.

This difficulty is compounded by the fact that these are decidedly uncharted waters. The APEC free trade area approved in a Djakarta suburb in November 1994 would tie together the economies of over one-third of the world's population and well over half of global economic activity. All barriers to U.S.-Japanese trade would be removed; Japan, the United States, and China would be part of one gigantic trading bloc. The economic barriers to uniting Taiwan, Hong Kong, and China (or at least the developed part of China) into an economic superpower that could dwarf all other world economies could be set in motion. What would these outcomes mean for the Free Trade Area of the Americas (recall that the four members of NAFTA also belong to APEC)? How does the EU fit into this context? What about those countries that are excluded from all these arrangements?

All of these prospects are, of course, speculative, but the groundwork has been laid for them. If coherent policy is to be fashioned (which is not a given), then a great deal more attention than has been forthcoming will be necessary in the economic realm. Given the obvious and compelling daily impact of the international economic system on the lives of increasing numbers of Americans, it is a debate with great importance.

The Domain of Transstate Issues

The globalizing economy is not the only way in which the world is shrinking. Indeed, those problems that transcend state boundaries in ways over which states have little control and which cannot be solved by individual state actions alone—the transstate issues—are becoming an increasingly common part of the foreign policy agenda.

As discussed in Chapter 12, these issues come in two essential categories: those that relate to the human condition through the promotion of certain basic rights to which any person is entitled, and those that relate to the physical environment in which people exist.

Each is important. One of the legacies of the revolutions of 1989 has been a heightened interest in universal human rights; indeed, some maintain that it was a human rights document, the Helsinki Final Accords of 1975, that marked the beginning of the end of communism in the Soviet Union and Eastern Europe (which, among other things, forced the communist countries to enforce basic freedoms). These concerns are contained in documents like the Universal Declaration of Human Rights and the Convention on Genocide, and they are being broadened to incorporate more specific concerns, such as reproductive rights and women's rights.

The success in achieving agreements on human rights and on their enforcement has been spotted. Many of the problems are (or are alleged to be) cultural: most of the rights being propounded are essentially Western, and people from some non-Western societies argue that their literal application in specific non-Western contexts is either culturally offensive or simply inapplicable. Often such objections are mere smoke screens behind which to cloak human rights violations; at the same time, the too forceful advocacy of Western ideals leaves those proposing such standards open to charges of cultural imperialism.

The other category of transstate issues are those dealing with the physical condition of the planet. These efforts include the physical environment (the subject of the Rio Summit of 1992), efforts to limit population and thus avoid testing the carrying capacity of the planet, and issues such as the depletion of certain species of fish due to overharvesting of the world's oceans.

Depoliticizing these issues has been the major obstacle to date in this category. In numerous cases, these issues come to be phrased in First Tier-Second Tier terms, whereby Second Tier states are asked to make developmental sacrifices in the name of, say, environmental integrity, and demand compensation in the form of developmental assistance (which First Tier countries come to regard, in essence, as blackmail).

Within the United States, the transstate issues have not received great public attention. In some cases, such as environmental degradation, these issues mirror internal policy issues, such as clean air and water, the use of public lands, or the protection of endangered species, issues on which there is fundamental political disagreement. At the same time, many of these issues lack the kind of immediate impact on individuals and communities of that economic or security decisions, thus relegating them to a lower position in the political pecking order.

Conclusions

These are clearly dynamic times for those who fashion and implement foreign and national security policies. The precipitous and almost universally unanticipated end of the Cold War destroyed not only the structure of the Cold War international system, but also undercut the ways and means by which policy had developed in the Cold War years. As the dust cleared from this enormous avalanche of change, Americans encountered a whole new set of difficult, complex, and unfamiliar problems with which they now have to cope. National security concerns have given way to economic emphases in a rapidly changing environment. The structure of the international system is changing at an unprecedented rate, and the United States struggles to master the dynamics of change and to find adequate responses to them.

It is a time when the political processes must change and adapt as well. As we suggested earlier, the growing importance of international economics, as the most obvious example, has thrust into the limelight those individuals and institutions responsible for trade policy. The U.S. trade representative has become a highly visible foreign policy player in ways that were clearly not the case a decade ago.

The result is a need for flexibility—institutionally, personally, and substantively—within those parts of the political system responsible for foreign policy. As the old distinctions between domestic and international politics blur, the result is a need to redefine—and continue to be willing and ready to redefine again—the location of the water's edge.

SUGGESTED READINGS

Donnelly, Jack. *Universal Human Rights in Theory and Practice*. Ithaca, NY: Cornell University Press, 1989.

Foreign Relations. *Agenda 96: Critical Issues in Foreign Policy*. New York: Council on Foreign Relations Press, 1996.

Gotlieb, Gidon. *Nation against State: A New Approach to Ethnic Conflict and the Decline of Sovereignty*. New York: Council on Foreign Relations Press, 1993.

Haass, Richard N. *Intervention: The Use of American Military Force in the Post–Cold War World*. Washington, DC: Carnegie Endowment for International Peace, 1994.

Huntington, Samuel P. *The Clash of Civilizations: The Debate*. New York: Council on Foreign Relations Press, 1993.

Kegley, Charles W., Jr., and Gregory A. Raymond. *A Multipolar Peace? Great Power Politics in the Twenty-First Century*. New York: St. Martin's Press, 1994.

Mueller, John. *Quiet Cataclysm: Reflections on the Recent Transformation of World Politics*. New York: HarperCollins, 1995.

Snow, Donald M. *Uncivil Wars: International Security and the New Internal Conflicts*. Boulder, CO: Lynne Rienner, 1996.

Wittkopf, Eugene (ed.). *The Future of American Foreign Policy* (2nd ed.). New York: St. Martin's Press, 1994.

INDEX

Able Archer, 72
abortion issue, 343, 344
Abrams, Creighton, 256–57
Abrams, Elliot, 148–49, 174, 175
The Absolute Weapon (Brodie), 38
Abzug, Bella, 329
Acheson, Dean, 107
Adams, Gordon, 242, 246
ad hoc interest groups, 237
Aerospace Research Institute (ARI), 244
Afghanistan, 58–60, 65, 74, 101, 116, 177, 205, 290
Africa, 10–11, 282
African Americans, 337
Agency for International Development (AID),
   169–70
Agriculture Department, 151, 157, 359–360
Aidid, Mohammed Farah, 283
Air Force Association (AFA), 237
Air Force One, 93
Albania, 75, 386
Albright, Madeleine K., 127, 198, 242
Allen, Richard V., 118, 235
Allende, Salvador, 172
Allison, Graham T., 45
All–Volunteer Force (AVF) concept, 215, 216
American Association of Retired Persons
   (AARP), 235
American Civil War, 9, 15, 29
American Enterprise Institute (AEI), 242, 243
American Farm Bureau, 237–38
American Federation of Labor–Congress of Indus-
   trial Organizations (AFL-CIO), 235, 238
American Geographic Society, 264
American-Israeli Political Action Committee, 239
American Legion, 232
American Medical Association, 234
American Revolution, 10, 15, 47, 134
Ames, Aldrich, 141
Amin, Idi, 310
An American Life (Reagan), 72
Andropov, Yuri, 60, 63
Angola, 55–56, 116, 172
Antarctic Treaty of 1959, 46
anticommunism, 57–58, 334–35, 338
Argentina, 57–58, 315, 324, 362
Aristide, Jean-Bertrand, 140, 150
armed conflicts, 89–90
Armed Forces Journal International, 222
Armenia, 83, 386
Armitage, Richard, 222
arms control, 46–47, 70–73, 121–22, 177, 273
   in post-Cold War period, 259, 284–87
Arms Control and Disarmament Agency (ACDA),
   121, 198, 206

Arms Control Association (ACA), 233–34
Arms Control Today, 233, 234
Army-Air Force Center for Low-Intensity Con-
   flict, 244
Articles of Confederation, 207
Asia, 10–11
Aspin, Les, 126–27, 135, 136, 139, 149, 192, 364
Assad, Hafez al-, 363
Associated Press, 266
Association of the United States Army (AUSA),
   237
Ataturk, Kemal, 316
Atlantic Charter of 1941, 336
Atlantic Monthly, 277
Auer, James, 370, 371
Australia, 84, 317, 362
Austria, 80
Azerbaijan, 34, 76, 83, 386

Baker, James, 120, 122, 171, 198, 202, 252, 356,
   362, 374
Bangladesh, 55, 139, 362
Bay of Pigs fiasco, 108
Bedtime for Bonzo, 116
Begin, Manachem, 58
Beijing conferences, 329, 333, 334–35, 341
Belarus, 76, 284
Bentsen, Lloyd, 183, 189
Bergquist, Kenneth, 222
Bergsten, Fred, 242
Berlin blockade, 131
Berlin Wall, 40, 71, 75
Bhutto, Benazir, 335
Bill of Rights, 331, 337
Bingaman, Jeff, 374
biodiversity treaty, 122, 349–50
Bodin, Jean, 4, 16
Boland, Edward, 197
Bolshevik Revolution, 32
Borden, William Liscum, 38
Boren, David, 145
Boren-McCurdy Reorganization Act, 145
Bosnia
   American intervention in, 1, 25, 33, 79, 96,
      140, 165, 206, 252, 259, 282, 283, 381, 386,
      388
   conflict in, 202, 233, 254, 270, 292, 293, 294
   United Nations and, 279, 296
   war crimes tribunal in, 294, 336
Bottom-Up Review, 289
Bound to Lead (Nye), 21
Boutros-Ghali, Boutros, 4, 18, 271, 283
Brazil, 183, 315, 324, 347
Bretton Woods system, 52, 304–7, 316, 321, 322

Danforth, John, 183, 374
Daniels, Dan, 222
Das Kapital, 40
The Day After, 279
DeConcini, Dennis, 235
Defense, Secretary of (SECDEF), 134, 135–36, 138, 143
Defense Budget Project, 246
Defense Department (DOD), 44, 94, 112, 121
  Bottom-Up Review of, 289
  budget for, 21–22, 133, 136, 195, 196
  core decision makers in, 262
  end of Cold War and, 138–40
  foreign policy role of, 132–40, 151, 153
  FSX issue and, 171, 356, 369, 370, 371–72, 373, 374–75, 376
  intelligence agencies controlled by, 142, 143
  interagency process and, 200–201
  Joint Chiefs of Staff (JCS) and, 134, 135, 136–37, 198, 217, 218, 220
  and National Security Act of 1947, 7
  organization of, 134–37, 217–18, 277
  post-Cold War period planning and, 192, 300–301
  waste, fraud, and abuse in, 218–19, 221
Defense Monitor, 246
deforestation, 348–49
de Klerk, Frederick W., 167, 288, 384
democracy, 57–58, 256–57, 330–41
Deng Xiao Peng, 88
Deputies Committee (DC), 200, 201
Desert One hostage rescue attempt, 136, 216, 221
detente, 52–53, 56, 73–74, 115, 116
Deutsch, John, 145, 198
Director of Central Intelligence (DCI), 141, 142–43
Djilas, Milovan, 28
Doctors without Borders, 327, 336
Dorgan, Byron, 189
Douhet, Guilio, 37
Drug Enforcement Agency, 151
drug smuggling, 328, 329–30
Dubcek, Alexander, 49, 50
Dulles, John Foster, 42, 45, 108, 147

Eagleburger, Lawrence, 148
Earth Summit, 7, 122, 202–3, 205, 273, 349–50, 391
Eastern Europe, 34, 41, 74, 76, 121, 131, 272, 328, 391
East Germany, 40–41, 52, 75, 82
economic agencies, 154–58
Economic Policy Institute, 242
Economic Strategy Institute, 181
Ecuador, 338–39
education, 226, 233–34, 264
Egypt, 11, 41–42, 50, 58, 170, 259, 288, 362, 63
Einstein, Albert, 36
Eisenhower, Dwight D., 101, 109, 123, 124, 147
  Geneva Accord and, 40
  military-industrial complex reference and, 227, 228

  New Look policy of, 44–45
  Nixon and, 52, 54
Eisenhower Doctrine, 101
El Mercurio, 320
embassies, 149–50
Energy Department, 142, 157
environment, 122, 329, 345–50
Environmental Policy (Wells), 346
Environmental Protection Agency (EPA), 122, 151, 157, 203, 349, 350
Essence of a Decision (Allison), 45
Estonia, 74, 75, 76, 79
Ethiopia, 32, 116, 170
Europe
  American isolationism and, 9–10, 176
  auto manufacturing and, 1
  general upheaval in, 10–11
  history of, American history versus, 11
  Marshall Plan and, 35, 41, 169, 305
  security concern of, 278
European Economic Community (EEC), 50, 51, 55
European Free Trade Area (EFTA), 81, 84
European Union (EU), 78, 238, 305, 324–25
  challenge to United States by, 21, 50, 55
  Common Agricultural Policy (CAP) of, 318
  expansion of, 80–82
  First Tier and, 84, 317
  NAFTA versus, 188
  open market and, 181, 261
  removal of trade barriers and, 317
  "Spain and Portugal rule" of, 81
  trade dependency of, 178
executive agencies, 131–59
executive agreements, 97

fast-track negotiating authority, 166, 182, 187–90
federal budget, 56, 133, 136, 195–96
  budget deficit and, 22, 306
Federal Bureau of Investigation (FBI), 142, 172
Federal Communications Commission (FCC), 266
Federal Election Commission (FEC), 234
Federalist Papers, 231
Fighter Support/Experimental (FSX), 171, 355, 356–57, 366–69, 372–75, 376
Financial Times, 320
First Amendment, 231, 238, 251, 266
First Tier
  decline in security concerns and, 313
  defined, 84
  democracy and, 339
  deregulation of economic activity in, 308, 309
  environmental issues and, 345, 348, 349
  freeing trade within, 317–20
  international economic concerns and, 7, 24, 303, 313
  international terrorism directed at, 329
  members of, interdependence among, 20
  policy implications and, 86–90
  population and, 341, 342, 343, 344
  Second Tier and, 84–86
  universal standard of human rights and, 339–40

Foley, Tom, 163, 189
Food and Drug Administration, 238
Ford, Gerald R., 120, 124, 147, 243
  detente and, 53
  international diplomacy and, 101
  Mayaguez incident and, 216
  presidential personality of, 102, 103, 113–14,
    199
  War Powers Resolution and, 212
Foreign Affairs, 35, 261, 262
Foreign Aid Authorization Act of 1961, 169–70
Foreign Area Officers (FAO) program, 297–98
foreign governments, recognizer of, 98–99
foreign policy
  changing environment of, 1–26
  concept of, 1–26
  control of, 252
  debate over, 17–25
  economic policy and, 154–56
  future, 15–25, 381–92
  high technology and, 155–56
  partisan nature of, 206
  policy process and, 6, 273–74
  politicization of, 195–97, 206
  secrecy and, 252–53
Foreign Policy, 245–46
Foreign Policy Association, 237
Foreign Policy Research Institute, 244
Foreign Service, 127, 149, 151, 152–54, 192
Forrestal, James, 137
Forum on Women, 334–35
Fourth World Conference on Women, 334–35
France
  aid to Rwanda from, 389
  Communist Party in, 34
  "deepening" of EU and, 81
  G-7 and, 68, 154, 318
  Indochinese War and, 35, 36, 40
  Operation Desert Storm and, 362
  Operations Provide Comfort and Southern
    Watch and, 366, 367, 388
  Persian Gulf War and, 79
  rivalry of, with Germany, 11
  Suez Crisis and, 41–42
  World War I and, 13
  World War II and, 30
Free Trade Area of the Americas (FTAA), 7, 23,
    317–20, 322–24, 390
Friedman, Milton, 242
From Lexington to Desert Storm (Snow and
    Drew), 10
Frye, Alton, 192
  agreement regarding, 171
Fukuyama, Francis, 316
Fulbright, J. William, 162, 173

G-7 (Group of Seven), 68, 84, 154, 306, 318
  Missile Technology Control Regime (MTCR)
    of, 287, 318
Gates, Robert, 356
Gaulle, Charles de, 42

Gavin, James, 173
Gemayel, Bashir, 216
General Agreement on Tariffs and Trade (GATT),
    181, 183, 317
Geneva Accord, 13, 40
George, Alexander, 103, 125
Georgia, 74, 83
Gephardt, Richard, 183–84, 189
Germany
  auto manufacturing and, 2
  confiscation of nuclear material in, 287
  G-7 and, 68, 154, 318
  Holocaust and, 336
  nuclear weapon development by, 36
  power of, relative to that of United States,
    20
  proposed permanent Security Council member-
    ship for and, 24
  remilitarization of Rhineland and, 32
  reparations and, 304
  reunification of, 75, 82, 289
  U.N. peacekeeping forces and, 23, 24
  unrestricted submarine warfare and, 13, 14
  World War I and, 11, 13, 14, 304
  World War II and, 30, 32, 34, 177
Gerry, Elbridge, 207
Gilman, Benjamin A., 165
Gingrich, Newt, 234
glasnost, 67, 68
Glaspie, April, 360, 361
Glenn, John, 235
global economy
  America in, 303–26
  Bretton Woods system and, 52, 304–7, 316,
    321, 322
  defined, 5
  geo-economics and, 313
  high technology and, 308–16
  policy domain of, 389–90
  policy problems and prospects and, 316–25
  regional organizations and intertier relations
    and, 320–25
global telecommunications, 229, 263–64, 311–12
  electronic global village and, 333–34
  global economy and, 311–12
  impact of, 271–74
global warming, 346–48
Goldwater, Barry, 109, 215, 247
Goldwater-Nichols Defense Reorganization Act
    of 1986, 136–37, 145, 197, 219–21, 222
  Commission on Roles and Missions of the
    Armed Forces report and, 215–19, 301
Gorbachev, Mikhail S.
  arms control and, 70–73
  biographical data on, 63–64
  Brezhnev Doctrine renounced by, 67
  Bush and, 121–22
  coup attempt and, 75–76, 272
  dissolution of Soviet Union and, 75–77, 385
  and end of Cold War, 1985–1989, 64–73, 121,
    303

Gorbachev, Mikhail S. *(continued)*
  Gorbachev Institute and, 77
  named as general secretary, 60, 63
  new political thinking and, 67
  Reagan and, 63, 64, 68, 70, 72–73
  reforms of, 66–68, 73–74
  START I and, 273, 284
Gorbachev, Raisa, 64, 65, 68
Gore, Albert, 131, 156, 201, 203, 262, 312, 365
Grant, Ulysses S., 15
Gray, William, 167
Great Britain
  American Revolution and, 10
  arms control and, 46
  Bretton Woods conference and, 304
  expansion of EU and, 81
  G-7 and, 68, 154, 318
  Operation Desert Storm and, 362
  Operations Provide Comfort and Southern
    Watch and, 366, 367, 388
  Persian Gulf War and, 79
  Suez Crisis and, 41–42
  War of 1812 and, 9, 12, 13
  World War I and, 13
  World War II and, 30
Great Depression, 106, 124, 162, 180, 304
Greece, 35, 82, 170, 193
greenhouse effect, 346, 348
Grenada, American invasion of, 96, 136, 213, 217, 218, 221, 268
gridlock, 161–62
Gromyko, Andrei, 63
Grotius, Hugo, 16
Group of 77, 56
groupthink, 122
Groves, Leslie, 36, 39
Gruening, Ernest, 209
Gulf of Tonkin Resolution, 48, 209–10, 212

Hackett, Sir John, 279
Hague Convention, 14
Haig, Alexander, 119, 147
Haiti, 25, 140, 150, 165, 292, 335, 340
Hall, Fawn, 174
Halperin, Morton, 98
Hamilton, Alexander, 208
Hansen, George, 191
Harrison, Benjamin, 102
Havel, Vaclav, 75
Hearst, William Randolph, 49, 270
Helms, Jesse, 22, 206, 374, 382
Helms, Richard, 110
Helsinki Accords, 56, 57, 328, 391
Henry Kissinger Associates, 232, 238
Heritage Foundation, 240, 243, 245, 246, 247
Herzegovina, 202, 233, 254, 264, 274, 294
high-intensity conflict (HIC), 298–99
high technology, 155–56, 308–16
Hills, Carla, 183, 375
Hiroshima atomic bomb attack, 36, 38

A History of the Peloponnesian War (Thucydides), 16
Hitler, Adolf, 111, 124, 336, 385
Hobbes, Thomas, 16, 332
Ho Chi Minh, 35
Hoffmann, Stanley, 242
Hollings, Ernest, 189
Holocaust, 336
Honecker, Erich, 75
Hong Kong, 89, 315, 389
Hoover, Herbert, 102, 244
House of Representatives, 163
human rights
  anticommunism versus, 334–35, 338
  democracy and, 330–41
  humanitarian, 18, 283
  issue of, status of, 333–38
  John Locke and, 331–32
  U.S. policy and, 338–42
  violation of, 57, 328
Hungary, 34, 41–43, 50, 74–5, 79, 81, 131, 386
Huntington, Samuel P., 87–88, 333
Husak, Gustav, 50
Hussein, Saddam
  American courtship of, 358–61
  American policy positions and, 199
  British children held as hostages by, 273
  domination over Persian Gulf region and, 289–90
  Kuwaiti invasion and, 5, 121, 122, 169, 259, 271, 357
  Operations Provide Comfort and Southern
    Watch and, 366, 367
  postwar Iraq and, 381–82

The Idea Brokers (Smith), 240
I Led Three Lives, 40
Independent Television Network (ITN), 229, 263, 266, 311–12, 334
India, 43, 50, 183, 286–88, 315, 325, 342, 349
Indonesia, 43, 322, 348–49
industrial policy, 156–58, 319
Industrial Revolution(s), 84, 85, 155, 313–16
The Influence of Sea Power upon History (Mahan), 14
INS v. Chadha, 212
intelligence, 142, 143–44
intelligence community, 140–46
  cabinet–level, 142–43
  congressional oversight and, 144, 172–75
  defense-controlled agencies and, 142
  proposed changes in, 145–46
Intelligence Oversight Act of 1980, 144
interagency process, 196, 197–203
interest(s), 4
  interest-threat mismatch and, 282
  vital, 4–5, 101, 280, 281–82, 299
interest groups, 226–28, 230–39
  activities of, 231–35
  bribery and, 234–35
  education and, 226, 233–34

National Rifle Association, 234
National Security Act of 1947, 7, 35, 136, 137, 141, 202
National Security Agency (NSA), 132, 142, 143
National Security Council (NSC), 108, 111, 114, 118, 151, 220, 223
  core decision makers in, 262
  creation of, 7, 107, 152
  Deputies Committee (DC) of, 200, 201, 202
  FSX issue and, 374–75, 377
  interagency process and, 196, 197–201, 203, 377
  Iran-contra affair and, 173–75, 203
  LIC Board and, 223
  National Economic Council and, 132, 157
  Operation Desert Storm and, 356
  Policy Coordinating Committees (PCCs) of, 200–201, 202, 361, 374–75
  Principals Committee (PC) of, 198–200, 201
national security policy
  altered setting of, 279–83, 298–301
  during Cold War, 5, 277
  democracy and, 338–39
  domain of, 387–89
  new internal wars and (*see* new internal wars)
  in post-Cold War world, 277–302
  residual national security concerns and, 283–90
nation-state, 3
NATO (North Atlantic Treaty Organization), 41, 51, 76, 78, 121, 193
  Able Archer and, 72
  expansion of, 79–80, 83, 278, 281, 299
  formation of, 35, 107
  P4P states as members of, 79–80, 299, 386
  Persian Gulf War and, 79
  Warsaw Pact's dissolution and, 75
Near v. Minnesota, 266
Neuchterlein, Donald, 279, 280
New International Economic Order (NIEO), 56
New Look, 44–45
New Republic, 77
Newsweek, 261, 271
New York Times, 70, 233, 245, 261, 266, 271, 313
New Zealand, 84, 317
Ngo Dinh Diem, 48
Nicaragua, 57, 60, 65, 101, 150, 174, 190–91, 197, 253, 281
Nichols, William, 215
Nightline, 273
Nitze, Paul, 44
Nixon, Richard M., 60, 124, 147, 246
  as chief of state, 95
  China and, 52, 55, 98, 101, 104–5, 111, 112, 113
  detente and, 52
  gold standard renounced by, 306
  "kitchen debate" and, 40
  Nixon Doctrine and, 54, 101
  opinion polls and, 100
  population problem and, 343, 344

presidential personality of, 102, 103, 104–5, 110–14, 117, 119, 199, 205
  resignation of, 54, 110, 162
  SALT I signed by, 52, 59
  State Department and, 146, 199
  Vietnam War and, 49, 53–55, 111, 204, 207, 210, 216
  Watergate scandal and, 54, 110, 210, 259
nomenklatura, 65, 67, 73
nongovernmental organizations (NGOs), 328, 332, 335–36, 344, 349
Noriega, Manuel, 139
North, Oliver, 118, 144, 173, 174, 203
Northern Ireland, 20, 126, 382
North Korea, 35–36, 77, 150, 285, 287–89, 300, 387
Notestein, Frank, 341–42
Nuclear Supplier's Group, 287
nuclear weapons
  Department of Energy and, 142
  development of, 36–39, 44
  Hiroshima and Nagasaki attacked with, 36, 38
  intercontinental ballistic missiles (ICBM) as, 36, 44, 45, 259
  intermediate nuclear forces (INF) and, 71
  in post-Cold War period, 284–87
  Soviet Union and, 11, 15, 36, 44, 45, 50, 55, 83, 142, 259
  United States and, 50, 60
Nunn, Sam, 172, 215, 301, 363–64
Nye, Joseph S., Jr., 8–9, 21, 22

O Estado de S. Paolo, 320
Office of Management and Budget (OMB), 242, 246
Office of Science and Technology, 374, 375
Office of Technology Assessment, 192
Oklahoma City bombing, 7
Oman, 362
Omnibus Trade and Competitiveness Act of 1988, 157–58
On The Beach (Shute), 39
On War (Clausewitz), 256
Operation Desert Shield, 101, 122, 139
Operation Desert Storm, 101, 122, 139, 200, 201, 220, 257, 358, 361–66
  case study of, 355–56, 357, 358–67
  congressional action regarding, 208
Operation Joint Endeavor, 386, 387
Operation Just Cause (American invasion of Panama), 96, 121, 139
Operation Provide Comfort, 139, 366, 367, 388
operations, 142–43
Oppenheimer, Robert, 38
Organization of Petroleum Exporting Countries (OPEC), 359
  petroleum withheld from market by, 55, 306–7
Organization on Security and Cooperation in Europe (OSCE), 79
Ortega, Daniel, 191

Somalia *(continued)*
  American public awareness and, 295–96
  atrocities in, 17, 270, 329
  as failed state, 4, 291, 293
  internal war in, 24, 83, 294
  starvation in, 254, 341
  United Nations and, 296
  U.S. aid to, 170
South Africa, 85, 149, 167–69, 193, 362, 383–84
South Korea, 35–36, 84, 280, 287–89, 300, 387
South Vietnam, 53–54
Soviet-American relations, 6, 11, 15, 21, 28, 29,
    45–46, 55, 56–57, 112, 147, 255, 290–91
  American attack on Libya and, 213
  arms control and, 71–73, 177
  detente and, 52–53, 56, 73–74, 115, 116
  intelligence community and, 140–41, 142, 144
  national security policy and, 277
  Soviet invasion of Afghanistan and, 58–59,
    177, 290
Soviet Union
  Afghanistan invasion and, 58–59, 65, 74, 116,
    177, 205, 290
  arms control and, 46–47, 70–73
  beginning of succession process and, 60
  Berlin Wall and, 40
  Bolshevik Revolution and, 32
  Chernobyl nuclear plant disaster and, 65
  Committee on State Security (KGB) of, 141,
    286
  Cuban missile crisis and, 45–46, 109, 131
  Czechoslovakia invaded by, 49–50, 52, 59
  dissolution of, 20, 75–77, 83, 278, 327, 385
  formation of Warsaw Pact and, 40
  high-intensity conflict (HIC) with, 298–99
  human rights violations in, 328
  Hungarian Revolution and, 42–43
  Japanese Toshiba Machine scandal and, 371
  military overextension of, 20–21
  nuclear weapons and, 11, 15, 36, 44, 45, 50,
    55, 83, 142, 259
  occupation of Eastern Europe by, 34, 41
  relations with Third World and, 42, 115, 116,
    209, 290–92
  rivalry with China and, 50, 51–52, 71, 291
  successor states to, 82–83, 282, 385
  World War II and, 34
Spain, 49, 81–82, 208, 270
Spanish-American War, 49, 208, 270
Special Economic Zones (SEZs), 88, 89, 315
Sputnik, 36
Sri Lanka, 329
Stalin, Joseph, 63, 77, 124
state(s), 3, 4, 5, 18, 291
State, Secretary of, 147–48, 198
State Department, 33, 35, 94, 112, 121, 127, 135,
    146–54, 199
  Amnesty International human rights abuse fig-
    ures and, 235–36, 335
  bureaus of, 142, 148–49
  Center for the Study of Foreign Affairs of, 244

core decision makers in, 262
embassies, consulates, missions and, 149–50
foreign policy role of, 132, 150–54
Foreign Service and, 127, 149, 151, 152–54
formal diplomacy and, 6, 7
FSX issue and, 171, 356, 369, 372, 373, 374,
    376
intelligence community and, 142, 148
interagency process and, 200–201
organization of, 146–50, 206
Presidential Decision Directive (PDD) 25 and,
    283, 296–97
Secretary of State and, 147–48, 198
stateless corporation (SC), 310
Steinbrunner, John, 242
Strategic Arms Limitation Talks (SALT), 47, 50
Strategic Arms Limitation Treaty
  I (SALT I), 52
  II (SALT II), 59, 177
Strategic Arms Reduction Talks
  I (START I), 273, 284
  II (START II), 284–85
strategic bombardment, 37, 38
Strategic Defense Initiative (SDI), 60, 61, 72, 171
Strategic Studies Institute (SSI), 244
Strauss, Robert, 97
Structural Impediments Initiative (SII) talks, 183
submarine warfare, unrestricted, 13, 14
Sudan, 170, 254, 329, 334
Suez Crisis, 41–42
Sullivan, Gerald, 371
Sullivan, Leon, 384
Sullivan codes, 384
Summers, Harry, 230
Sununu, John, 375
Survival, 261
Syria, 288, 362–63, 381

Tadjikistan, 76, 86, 286, 386
Taiwan, 40, 84, 89, 98, 315, 389
Taylor, William J., 242
Taylor, Zachary, 49
terrorism, 329
Thailand, 288, 340–41
Thatcher, Margaret, 64, 389
There Will Be No Time (Borden), 38
think tanks, 228, 230, 239–47
Third Industrial Revolution, 84, 85, 155
Third World, 117
  American interest in, 83
  atrocities in, 17
  Chinese relations with, 98
  emergence of, 43, 50, 55–56
  Group of 77 and, 56
  Nixon Doctrine and, 101
  Soviet relations with, 42, 115, 116, 209, 290–92
The Third World War (Hackett), 279
Thirteen Days (Kennedy), 45
Thirty Years' War, 3
Thucydides, 16
Thurmond, Strom, 382

Thurow, Lester, 242
Tiananmen Square massacre, 185, 186, 264
Time, 68, 261
Times, 320
Tito, Josip Broz, 202, 294
Tong Sun Park, 235
Toshiba Machine scandal, 371
Tower, John, 98, 171–72, 374
trade, 178–93, 317–18, 320–25
Trade Act of 1974, Jackson-Vanik amendment to, 56–57, 185
trade-related investment measures (TRIMs), 319
Treasury Department, 142, 151, 157
treaty negotiator, 96–97, 166, 177, 182, 187–90
Treaty of Maastricht, 238
Treaty of Rome, 305
Trenchard, Sir Hugh, 37
Trinidad and Tobago, 86
Truman, Harry, 124, 174
    Korean War and, 96, 107, 208–9
    opinion polls and, 99–100
    presidential personality of, 102, 103, 107, 108, 113, 119
Truman Doctrine, 35, 44, 101
Tunisia, 340, 341
Turkey, 58, 81, 83, 170, 193, 270–71, 316, 366, 388
20/20, 270
The Twenty-Years' Crisis, 1919–1939 (Carr), 17

Uganda, 279, 310
Ukraine, 82, 284
"unconditional surrender," 15, 28
unfair trade practices, 319
uninformed public, 253–55, 258–60
United Arab Emirates, 362
United Nations (U.N.), 2, 242
    American disillusionment with, 298
    Fund of, for Population Activities (UNFPA), 343
    General assembly of, 336, 337
    human rights and, 333, 336, 340–41
    International Convention of, on the Elimination of All Forms of Racial Discrimination, 337
    International Covenant of, 337
    Korean War and, 362
    Montreal Treaty banning chlorofluorocarbons and, 346, 347
    Operation Desert Storm and, 356, 361–62, 364
    peacekeeping and, 23–24, 33, 140, 206, 279, 283, 296, 362
    population problem and, 7, 341, 343, 344
    Security Council of, 297, 362
    as successor to League of Nations, 32
    Universal Declaration of, on Human Rights, 337, 339, 340–41, 391
    women's rights conferences and, 334–35, 341
United Nations Fund for Population Activities (UNFPA), 343
United States
    automobile manufacturing for Japanese market and, 307

Bretton Woods conference and, 304
China and, 52, 55
disdain for power politics and, 12–13
economic challenge of Japan and, 21, 55
entanglement in European conflicts and, 10–11
environment and, 349–50
European economic challenge to, 21, 50, 55
G-7 and, 68, 154
history of, 11
interests and responsibilities of, 22–24
isolationism and, 6, 9–11, 15, 19–20, 176, 177
nuclear weapons and, 50, 60
population problem and, 344–45
priorities of, 21–22
as role model for the world, 9
standing of, in the world, 20–21
United States Agency for International Development (USAID), 170
United States armed forces, 7, 18, 21–22, 133, 142, 215–17
United States Constitution
    Bill of Rights of, 331, 337
    First Amendment to, 231, 238, 251, 266
    foreign policy-making powers under, 93–99, 96, 161–62, 163, 166–78
    Iran-contra affair and, 175
    War Powers Resolution and, 207–8
United States Information Agency (USIA), 42, 198, 206
United States Trade Representative (USTR), 94, 157–58
    FSX issue and, 171, 356, 369, 374, 375
    prominence of, 303
    trade with Japan and, 191
Universal Declaration on Human Rights, 337, 339, 340–41, 391
unrestricted submarine warfare, 13, 14
U.S. News and World Report, 261
USA Today, 266
uskeronie, 67
Uzbekistan, 76

Vance, Cyrus, 115, 116, 119, 199
Vatican, 343, 344
Venezuela, 315
Versailles Treaty, 17, 32, 97, 177
Vietnam
    American reestablishment of relations with, 312
    APEC membership and, 325
    communists retention of power in, 77, 312–13
    Congress and, 8, 173
    foreign policy and, 1, 8, 18, 101
    French opposition to communism in, 35, 36, 40
    POW and MIA issue and, 312
    rivalry of, with Cambodia and Thailand, 288
Vietnamization, 53–54
Vietnam Veterans Against the War, 237
Vietnam War, 12, 47–49, 52, 53–55, 109–10, 111, 113, 115, 124, 131, 162, 163, 173, 197, 204, 207, 216, 256, 307

Vietnam War *(continued)*
  ad hoc interest groups and, 237
  budget deficit and, 306
  Gulf of Tonkin Resolution and, 48, 209–10, 212
  media and, 247, 254, 268, 271
  purpose of North Vietnamese in, 293
  as undeclared war, 176
  Vietnamization and, 53–54
Villa, Pancho, 9, 12
vital interests, 4–5, 101, 280, 281–82, 299

Walesa, Lech, 75
Wall Street Journal, 266, 313
war(s), 256–57
War of 1812, 9, 10, 11, 12, 13, 36, 49, 208
War Powers Resolution, 96, 176, 197, 204, 206–15
  constitutional ambiguity and, 207–8
  context for passing, 207
  effects of, 212–15
  and executive dominance on matters of war
    and peace, 208–9
  Vietnam experience and, 209–10
Warsaw Pact, 40, 43, 63, 74, 78
Washington, George, 10, 102, 134, 176
Washington Papers, 245
Washington Post, 245, 261, 266
Washington Quarterly, 246
Watergate scandal, 54, 110, 113, 162, 163, 210, 254, 268, 307
Watkins, James, 375
The Wealth of Nations (Smith), 180
Weimar Republic of Germany, 385
Weinberger, Caspar, 59–60, 119, 174, 199, 218–19, 222, 243, 257, 372
Weinberger Doctrine, 257, 298
Wells, Donald T., 346
Wellstone, Paul, 215
Western Europe, 6, 35, 41, 169, 280, 299, 305
West Germany, 40, 52, 75
Westmoreland, William, 268
Weyrich, Paul M., 172
White, John, 137
White Commission, 137
Whitehead, Charles, 222–23
White House Office of Science and Technology, 374, 375
Wildavsky, Aaron, 84, 85, 331, 342
Wilhelm, Kaiser, 14
Wilson, Charles, 45
Wilson, Woodrow
  Fourteen Points and, 336
  human rights and, 336

League of Nations and, 8, 17, 97, 177, 336
  World War I and, 11, 13–14
Wirth, Tim, 149
women's rights, 329, 333, 334–35, 341
Woodward, Bob, 201–2
World Bank, 170, 305
World Court, 336–37
World of Tiers, 84–90
World Policy Journal, 246
World Trade Organization (WTO), 24, 181, 305, 319, 320
World War I, 15, 29, 31
  American involvement in, 10, 11, 13–14
  congressional declaration of war and, 208
  isolationism of United States after, 6, 15, 177
  League of Nations and, 8, 336
  peace treaty ending (Versailles Treaty), 17, 32, 97, 177
  unrestricted submarine warfare and, 13, 14
World War II, 37, 43, 52, 75, 76, 124, 125, 169, 255, 304
  American isolationism after, 19
  American isolationism before, 11, 20, 177
  and atomic attacks on Japan, 36, 38, 107
  changed balance of power following, 29–31
  congressional declaration of war and, 208
  Dwight D. Eisenhower and, 108
  end of, and conduct of foreign policy, 1, 6, 7, 10, 27, 94
  Franklin D. Roosevelt's style and, 106
  "unconditional surrender" of Axis powers and, 15
World Watch, 246
WorldWatch Institute, 246
Wright, Jim, 190–91

Yaneyev, Gennadi, 75
Yeltsin, Boris N., 77, 101, 122, 259, 265, 285
  coup attempt against Gorbachev and, 76, 272
  Marxism abandoned by, 68
Yemen, 362
Yom Kippur War, 306
Yugoslavia, 79
  armed conflict in, 121, 381, 387
  breakup of, 202, 252
  government abuse of citizens in, 4
  OSCE membership suspended, 79

Zaire, 170, 295, 389
zero-zero option, 71–72
Zhironovsky, Vladimir, 385
Zhivkov, Todor, 75
Zimbabwe, 362

Viscoelasticity of Engineering Materials

Viscoelasticity of Engineering Materials

Y. M. Haddad

University of Ottawa
Ottawa, Canada

To the loving memory of my parents

Contents

Preface

I express my full indebtedness to all researchers whose work is referenced in this book. Without their outstanding contributions to knowledge, this book would not have been written.

I convey my thanks to Professor D. R. Axelrad (McGill University), who was the first person to introduce the fascinating subject of rheology to me and to Professor J. T. Pindera (University of Waterloo) for his kind encouragement and stimulating discussions on the subject matter. I am indebted to Dr J. H. Gittus, Editor- in-Chief of *Res Mechanica*, for originally inviting me to write a book on viscoelasticity.

Permission granted to the author for the reproduction of figures and/or data by the following scientific societies, journals and publishers is gratefully acknowledged: Academic Press, American Chemical Society, American Institute of Physics, British Textile Technology Group, Elsevier Applied Science Publishers, Gebrüder Born-traeger, *Helvetica Chimica Acta*, Hermann, International Union of Crystallography, John Wiley & Sons, Pergamon Press, Springer-Verlag Heidelberg, Steinkopff Verlag, *Tappi Journal*, Taylor and Francis Ltd., and the Institute of Physics. In the same context, the author wishes to express his sincere thanks and gratitude to Professors M. F. Ashby (University of Cambridge, United Kingdom), N. Davis (The Pennsylvania State University), H. F. Frost (Thayer School of Engineering), F. A. Leckie (University of Illinois at Urbana-Champaigne), E. H. Lee (Stanford University), J. M. Morrison (AT & T Bell Laboratories), A. K. Mukherjee (University of California, Davis) and Dr H. J. Sutherland (Sandia National Laboratories).

I wish to thank Mrs Denise Champion-Demers for her excellent efforts in the effic-ient execution of the word processing of the manuscript. I would also like to extend my thanks to past and present graduate students, Mrs Ping Yu and Messrs S. Tanary, W. Zhao, S. Iyer and G. Molina for their conscientious assistance during the preparation of the text.

I also wish to express sincere thanks and deep appreciation to Dr Philip Hastings (Senior Editor), the sub editorial staff at Chapman & Hall, to David Norris (Copy Editor) and to Chapman & Hall for the reviewing, editing and the efficient production and distribution of the text.

I am grateful to my wife Dawn and daughter Leila for their understanding, patience and support.

I hope that the work presented in this book will provide guidance to science and engineering students, educators and researchers who are working in the field. Also, it is hoped that the book will be of value to scientists and engineers who are involved in the production and processing of viscoelastic materials and the study of their properties.

Y. M. Haddad
University of Ottawa, Ottawa, Canada

List of symbols

$a(t)$	Amplitude of wave front (time dependent)
$a_T, a_G(T)$	Temperature shift factor
A	Energy per unit mass
A_0	Mean free energy
$\mathbf{A}$	Displacement vector of a particle along the plane of the wave
$^{\alpha\beta}A$	Junction area between two overlapping fibres α and β
c_1, c_2	Magnitude of wave velocity (dilatational, rotational)
$\mathbf{d}(t)$	Interfibre bond displacement
$H(\cdot)$	Heaviside step function
dH	Heat per unit mass
dS	Line element
$D(\cdot)/Dt$	Material derivative
e	Specific internal energy (per unit mass)
$\mathbf{e}_k \ (k = 1, 2, 3)$	Unit vectors associated with an external Cartesian frame of reference
E	Elastic modulus
$E_1(\omega)$	Storage modulus (frequency dependent)
$E_2(\omega)$	Loss modulus (frequency dependent)
$E^*(i\omega)$	Dynamic complex modulus
$\mathbf{E}(t)$	Nonlinear strain measure
$E_E(\varepsilon)$	Equilibrium tangent modulus (strain dependent)
$\check{E}_E(\varepsilon)$	Equilibrium second-order modulus (strain dependent)
$E_I(\varepsilon)$	Instantaneous tangent modulus (strain dependent)
$\check{E}_I(\varepsilon)$	Instantaneous second-order modulus (strain dependent)
$\mathbf{f}(\cdot)$	Constitutive functional
$f(\lambda)$	Retardation spectrum
$\mathbf{F}$	Deformation measure
$F(t)$	Creep (compliance) function
$F_{ijkl}(t)$	Creep tensorial function

$\mathbf{F}_d(t)$	Delayed compliance function
$\mathbf{F}_e(0^+)$	Elastic compliance function
$\mathbf{F}_v(t)$	Viscous compliance function
$F_1(t), F_2(t)$	Creep function (shear, dilatation)
$\mathbf{g}$	Deformation gradient
$\mathbf{g}(T)$	Temperature gradient
$\mathbf{h}$	Heat flux vector
$\mathbf{I}$	Identity matrix
I_1, I_2, I_3	Stress invariants
$\mathrm{II}_1, \mathrm{II}_2, \mathrm{II}_3$	Strain invariants
$\mathbf{J}(t)$	Shear creep compliance (time dependent)
$J_1(\omega)$	Storage compliance (frequency dependent)
$J_2(\omega)$	Loss compliance (frequency dependent)
$J^*(i\omega)$	Dynamic creep compliance
$k = E/E'$	Ratio of elastic moduli E and E'
K	Bulk modulus
$K(t)$	Geometric function (time dependent)
$\mathbf{L}(\cdot)$	Constitutive function
$\mathbf{L}$	Velocity gradient
$\mathbf{n}$	Unit normal vector
$\overset{1}{\mathbf{n}}, \overset{2}{\mathbf{n}}, \overset{3}{\mathbf{n}}$	Unit vectors associated with the stress tensor principal axes
$N(s), N'(s)$	Frequency distribution (creep, relaxation)
$p = d/dt$	Time derivative operator
p, q	Probabilities
$\mathbf{q}$	Heat flux vector
P, Q	Linear differential operators
$\mathbf{P}, \mathbf{Q}$	Nonlinear measures of input and output
$\mathbf{r}(t), \mathbf{R}$	Position vector (deformed, undeformed state)
$\mathbf{R}$	Orthogonal motion indicating rigid rotation
$\mathbf{R}(t), R_{ijkl}(t)$	Stress relaxation function
$R_1(t), R_2(t)$	Stress-relaxation function (shear, dilatation)
R_∞	Equilibrium (relaxed) modulus
$R'(t)$	Time derivative of the relaxation function $R(t)$
$s = 1/\lambda$	Frequency
s	Laplace transform parameter
S	Specific entropy
$S\text{–}S, S_1\text{–}S_1, S_2\text{–}S_2$	Scanning lines
t, τ	Time parameter
T	Absolute temperature
$\mathbf{T}$	Stress traction vector
$\mathbf{u}$	Displacement vector
$\mathbf{u}_I$	Irrotational displacement field

$\mathbf{u}_R$	Rotational displacement field
$\mathbf{U}$	Positive definite symmetric matrix indicating pure stretch
$\mathbf{v}$	Velocity
v_{ij}	Rate of deformation tensor
$V(t)$	Velocity magnitude of a nonlinear wave
$\mathbf{V}$	Positive definite symmetric matrix indicating pure rotation
W	Elastic energy per stress cycle
$\mathbf{x}, \mathbf{X}$	Position vector (deformed, undeformed state)
$\hat{\mathbf{x}}(t)$	Spatial position of a propagating wave at time t
Z_i	Cartesian components of a heat flux vector (per unit area per unit time)
B.	Refers to an intermolecular bond
i.	Refers to a junction area between two microelements
$\cdot$R	Denotes recovery
f.	Refers to a single fibre or a fibre-segment
$(\cdot)^T$	Designates a transpose
$[\cdot]$	Indicates a jump in a function across the trajectory of a wave at a particular instant of time
$\bar{}$	Indicates a transform
$\|\cdot\|$	Denotes a norm
α	Angle of incidence of a dilatational wave; coefficient of linear thermal expansion; propagation constant
α, β	Normalization factors
α, β	Structural microelements
γ	Specific rate (per unit mass) of entropy production
$\gamma_m \ (m = 1, 2, \cdots)$	Exponent factors
Γ	Time rate of entropy production
Γ_1^2, Γ_2^2	Wave operator (dilatational, rotational)
$\Gamma(t)$	Material operator (time dependent)
$\Gamma(\lambda)$	Relaxation spectrum
δ	Phase lag
$\delta(t)$	Depth of penetration (time dependent)
$\Delta = \varepsilon_{kk} = \varepsilon_{11} + \varepsilon_{22} + \varepsilon_{33}$	Dilatation
δ, Δ	Interfibre bond length (deformed, undeformed state)
∇^2	Laplace's operator
$\delta_{ij}, \delta_{\alpha\beta}$	Kronecker delta
$\varepsilon_{ijk}, \varepsilon_{\alpha\beta}$	Alternating tensor
ε_{ij}	Infinitesimal strain tensor
ε_{ij}'	Deviatoric strain tensor
η	Viscosity modulus
θ	Empirical temperature
κ	Morse constant
λ	Relaxation time

$\lambda = \eta/\eta'$	Ratio of viscosity coefficients η and η'
$\hat{\lambda}$	Critical strain gradient
Λ	Rate of dissipation of energy
ν	Poisson's ratio
ξ	Microstress
ξ, ξ'	Reduced time parameters
Ξ	Total energy
Π	Constitutive functional
ρ, ρ_0	Mass density (current, reference configuration)
$\boldsymbol{\sigma}, \sigma_{ij}$	Cauchy stress tensor
σ'_{ij}	Stress deviator
$\bar{\sigma}$	Mean stress
$\sigma_1, \sigma_2, \sigma_3$	Principal components of a stress
σ_I	Instantaneous value of the stress
Σ	Piola–Kirchhoff stress tensor
$\phi_1(\cdot), \phi_2(\cdot), \cdots$	Material functions
χ	Body force
$\psi_1(\cdot), \psi_2(\cdot), \cdots$	Material functions
ψ	Energy per unit mass
$\boldsymbol{\psi}, \boldsymbol{\psi}', \boldsymbol{\psi}''$	Nonlinear material functions
$\psi_{ij}(t)$	Relaxation function (time dependent)
$\varnothing$	Null set

Introduction

With the recent advances in material science and the parallel extensive industrial demands on advanced industrial materials such as high polymers and polymeric base composite systems, the subject of viscoelasticity has gained recently a strong momentum in the realms of engineering techniques and applications.

High polymeric materials are organic substances of high molecular weight, the technical importance of which depends on their particular microstructure (e.g. Leaderman, 1943; Bernal, 1958). This class of materials may include, for example, rubber in its various forms, synthetic rubber-like materials, commercial plastics and natural and synthetic textile fibres. Other examples of a viscoelastic material would include a wide range of inorganic polymeric systems such as silicones and glass resins, constituents of polymeric base systems, natural fibres such as wood and the byproducts of such fibres as, for instance, paper and board, building materials such as concrete, and a large class of biomaterials, among others. As will be demonstrated in this book, these materials are time dependent in response and possess a 'time memory'.

In the mechanics of deformable media, the response behaviour of an elastic solid is dealt with within the realm of the classical theory of elasticity. The most direct description of such response is in accordance with the well-known Hooke's law (Robert Hooke, *De Potentia Restitutiva*, London, 1678). This law forms the basis of the mathematical theory of elasticity (the reader is referred to Love (1944) for an introductory review of the history of the mathematical theory of elasticity). That is, provided that the occurring deformations are small, the stress is considered to be directly proportional to the strain and it is independent of the strain rate. Such a response is termed consequently as 'perfectly elastic' or 'Hookean'.

In a simple uniaxial test, the load–deformation curve of the perfectly elastic solid will follow the same path for both increasing and decreasing load. Thus, the material test specimen will regain its original dimensions instantaneously on removal of the load. Under a constant level of loading, the occurring deformation is constant, i.e. time independent. Further, when such a solid is subjected to a sinusoidally oscillating loading, the deformation will also be found to be sinusoidal and practically in phase with the load. All the energy is stored and recovered in each cycle.

On the other hand, the mechanical response of a viscous fluid is dealt with within the domain of the classical theory of fluid dynamics. In this case, the most direct description of the response is in accordance with Newton's law whereby the stress is considered to be proportional to the occurring rate of strain but independent of the strain itself. This is provided that the rate of strain is small. When a 'Newtonian viscous fluid' is subjected to a sinusoidally oscillating load, the deformation will be found to be 90° out of phase with the load.

The classical theories of linear elasticity and Newtonian fluids, though impressively well structured, do not adequately describe the response behaviour and flow of most real materials. That is, between the above two described responses of the elastic solid and the viscous fluid, a real material may exhibit, even if both strain and strain rate are infinitesimal, the combined response characteristics of these two media. Attempts to characterize the behaviour of such real materials under the action of external loading, consequently, gave rise to the science of rheology within which the phenomenon now labelled 'viscoelasticity' is well defined and intended to convey mechanical behaviour combining response characteristics of both an elastic solid and a viscous fluid. A viscoelastic material is, thus, characterized by a certain level of rigidity of an elastic solid body, but, at the same time, it flows and dissipates energy by frictional losses as a viscous fluid. A few characteristics of a viscoelastic material may be cited as follows.

- When a viscoelastic material is subjected to a constant stress, it does not hold a constant deformation (as it would be the case for a solid material), but it continues to flow with time, i.e. it creeps. Immediately, on removal of the load, the specimen is found to have taken an amount of 'residual' strain the magnitude of which depends on the length of time for which the load is applied and on the level of loading. Following removal of the load, a noticeable reduction in the amount of residual strain gradually takes place with the passage of time. This residual strain may even disappear entirely in the course of time. The latter phenomenon which occurs following the removal of the load is referred to as 'creep recovery'. A specimen of viscoelastic material, tested as mentioned above, eventually regains its original dimensions. Consequently, the creep of such material under load cannot be regarded as a phenomenon of plasticity, as in the case of polycrystalline solids, but rather as a 'delayed elasticity' (Leaderman, 1943). Boltzmann (1874) denoted this property by the term 'elastic aftereffect' (*Nachwirkung* in German). In a simple uniaxial test of a viscoelastic material, a load–deformation loop (hysteresis) is obtained, i.e. the descending load curve corresponds to a larger amount of strain than the ascending load curve. Neither of the two curves is completely linear. The shape of the resulting hysteresis looop is dependent on the magnitude of load, rate of application and removal of the load and temperature.
- Further, when a viscoelastic material is subjected to sinusoidally oscillating stress, the resulting strain, through sinusoidal, is neither exactly in phase with the stress (as it would be the case for a perfectly elastic solid) nor 90° out of phase (as it would be for a perfectly viscous fluid); it is somewhere between. The magnitude

of the strain and the phase angle between the stress and strain are generally frequency and temperature dependent. On loading and unloading a viscoelastic material specimen, some of the energy input is stored and recovered in each cycle and some of it is dissipated as heat.

The particular nature of viscoelastic response considered in the foregoing proves the existence of a property of 'passive resistance' in such materials. This is in contrast to the instantaneous response and reversibility that usually characterize pure elastic behaviour. This passive resistance is of viscous nature and reflects what is usually called the property of 'hereditary response' of the material. That is, the present state of response depends not only on the present state of loading input but also on previous states (Boltzmann, 1874, 1877, 1878). This property is revealed experimentally in different time-dependent phenomena pertaining to the viscoelastic response such as creep, stress relaxation and intrinsic attenuation and dispersion of propagating waves.

The phenomenological theory of viscoelasticity dates from the nineteenth century (Leaderman (1943) and Markovitz (1977) present interesting reviews of the history of viscoelasticity) but, unfortunately, the application of the theory to actual engineering applications is only a development of the last 50 years. This contrasts with the situation of the related field of linear elasticity whereby technological requirements have traditionally stimulated significant research over the last two centuries. Such technological stimulus was lacking for the development of a formal theory of viscoelasticity as engineering design has traditionally made use of materials whose mechanical response behaviour would be adequately described by the laws of classical elasticity. Research in the theory of viscoelasticity has been, however, recently enhanced by the introduction of engineering components that are fabricated from advanced industrial materials such as those mentioned at the beginning of this introduction. A large class of these newly developed materials exhibit, as mentioned earlier, mechanical response behaviour outside the scopes of the more conventional theories of linear elasticity and viscosity. Consequently, a development of the theory of viscoelasticity has become of parallel necessity with the gradual introduction of such new materials.

It is often considered that the response behaviour of a viscoelastic material is a fundamental property of its molecular structure. Hence, the viscoelastic response prediction of polymeric systems (references which focus on polymeric materials include, for instance, Eirich (1956), Staverman and Schwarzl (1956), Ferry (1970) and Doi and Edwards (1986), among others), for instance, has been often considered from the point of view of reaction-rate theory (Tobolosky and Eyring, 1943; Mark and Tobolosky, 1950), that is by treating flow as a bond breakage—bond formation process (e.g. Peters, 1955). Most of the formulations, in this context, however, have referred solely to the deformation of the critical weak bonds in the microstructure by the reasoning that the deformation of the much stronger bonds is likely to be negligible at low stresses. This is, however, an oversimplification of the actual flow process occurring in the real, complex microstructure of viscoelastic material systems such as those mentioned before (e.g. Takehiro and San-Ichiro, 1955; Bernal, 1958). It is well recognized that such materials behave in a manner which depends primarily on the material source, microstructure and previous history, in addition to the current state of loading and environmental conditions. In a large class of viscoelastic materials, such as natural amorphous or semiamorphous types of materials, for example, environmental effects, e.g. moisture content, could enhance the deterioration of the internal microstructure and, hence, the amount of occurring deformation. Furthermore, the energy required to produce a certain deformation may change abruptly at particular temperatures owing to internal transitions in the material (e.g. Kauman, 1966). In the case of polymeric materials, for instance, the level of order (crystallinity), the extent of alignment of the morphological units (orientation) and the degree of polymerization are among the many factors that could influence the viscoelastic response characteristics of such materials. Thus, while in the major part of this book, the continuum mechanics approach is maintained primarily for the characterization of the response behaviour of viscoelastic materials, it is emphasized that such a response is essentially dependent on the effects of a large number of significant microscopic and macroscopic parameters such as those introduced above.

The contents of this book are presented in ten chapters and four appendices. Chapter 1 contains the continuum mechanics background necessary for the presentation of the viscoelasticity theory and pertaining subjects in the subsequent Chapters 2–10. In Chapter 2, the basic formalism of the mechanical response of the linear viscoelastic material is presented. Consequently, in Chapter 2, the formulations are considered entirely within the context of the infinitesimal linearized deformation theory. Here, the ideas set down by L. Boltzmann (1844–1906) and V. Volterra (1860–1940) are taken as fundamental within the context of linear superposition of input histories (Boltzmann, 1874, 1877, 1878; Volterra, 1913; Volterra and Peres, 1936; Leaderman, 1943, 1958). In this chapter, the author confines his attention to the one-dimensional linear theory of isothermal viscoelasticity in the time domain under variable levels of stress or strain inputs. The transition to dynamic viscoelasticity is discussed in Chapter 3 whereby the formulation of Chapter 2 is extended to include the possibility of characterizing the linear viscoelastic behaviour of materials in the frequency domain. In this context, the relationships between the material functions characterizing the viscoelastic response in both the time and frequency domains are considered. In Chapter 4, the formulation of the three-dimensional viscoelastic response behaviour is dealt with whereby the one-dimensional constitutive relations of Chapter 2 are replaced by their corresponding tensorial equivalents. Remarks concerning the thermodynamic restrictions on isothermal linear viscoelasticity are also presented in Chapter 4. Chapter 5 presents the basic formulations of the constitutive relations in thermoviscoelasticity whereby the dependence of the performance of the viscoelastic material on both fixed reference and transient-temperature fields are considered. The fundamental areas considered in Chapter 5 include the thermodynamics of the deformation process, the rheological equations of state and the thermodynamical derivation of the constitutive relations. The treatment of the thermoviscoelastic response of the so-called 'thermorheologically simple materials' and 'thermorheologically complex materials' are dealt with. Various viewpoints concerning constitutive formalism in thermoviscoelasticity as expressed by various authors are presented. In Chapter 6, the more complex subject of nonlinear viscoelasticity is dealt with. Here, one deals primarily with the nonlinear analysis of the deformation process and its effect on the constitutive formalism of the viscoelastic response. In this chapter, illustrations are first given concerning the nonlinear viscoelastic behaviour; then, the characterization of the nonlinear response is dealt with, with the inclusion of the concept of coordinate invariance (the objectivity principle). In this context, the various approaches to the formulation of the governing constitutive equations, as proposed by researchers in the field, are presented. The problem of experimental determination of the pertaining nonlinear viscoelastic material functions in both the one- and the three-dimensional situations is discussed. Chapter 7 deals with a few aspects of the broad subject of numerical analysis in viscoelasticity. In this, the constitutive formalism in linear viscoelasticity is treated to characterize the nonlinear viscoelastic response of materials. This is carried out through an analytical model that includes a differential approximation of the time-dependent behaviour and an optimization procedure. The procedure is illustrated numerically for arbitrary ranges of stress, strain and temperature and a selected extent of time concerning the viscoelastic response.

In Chapter 8, the author deals with the important subject of wave propagation in viscoelastic materials. In recent years, there has been considerable interest in the subject of wave propagation in engineering materials in general, from both theoretical and experimental points of view. Such interest has been motivated primarily by the advancements in testing and measurement techniques. With the recent progress in fields such as electronics and laser optics, stress waves of high frequency can be now produced and detected easily. This has been particularly pronounced in important domains of nondestructive testing such as ultrasonics and acoustic emission. The combination of these two techniques has led further to the newly developed acousto-ultrasonic method (Tanary, 1988; Vary, 1988) as a modern nondestructive tool for the evaluation and prediction of the mechanical properties of engineering materials. The latter technique has been applied recently by Iyer (1993) and Iyer and Haddad (1993) for the characterization and prediction of the viscoelastic behaviour of a class of polymeric materials. Another equally important cause of the ensuing interest in the subject of viscoelastic wave propagation is, as mentioned earlier, the continuous emergence of newly developed industrial viscoelastic materials such as plastics and polymeric composite material systems. In this, the study of the phenomenon of wave motion has been able to identify microstructural problems and to assist in the development of homogeneous and inhomogeneous material systems. Further, any new development within the realm of smart materials and structures (e.g. Yoshiki and Shun-Ichi, 1988; Rogers, 1989; Iyer and Haddad, 1994) is expected to depend on the understanding and utilization of the wide range of mechanical performance of viscoelastic constituents and, hence, on the ability to employ wave propagation as a successful detecting mechanism for a feedback concerning the status of such materials.

In view of the time dependency of the response behaviour in viscoelasticity which is further complicated by the form of the constitutive relations and, hence, the associated boundary conditions, serious attempts to solve viscoelastic boundary value problems have lagged considerably behind those in classical elasticity. It is only in the last few decades that viscoelastic boundary value problems have been actively considered. The classification of boundary value problems in viscoelasticity, their formulations and possible methods of solutions are considered in Chapter 9. The extension of the phenomenological theory of viscoelasticity to include microscopic effects is discussed in Chapter 10. In this chapter, a case study is presented concerning the formulation of the viscoelastic response of a two-dimensional fibrous system with the inclusion of the real microstructure. In this, the material system is regarded as a two-dimensional network of randomly oriented viscoelastic fibres which are bonded together by intermolecular bonds. Thus, the mechanics of the discrete microstructure introduces the relevant field quantities as random variables or functions of such variables and their corresponding distribution functions. The model is presented in an explicit form for a cellulosic system by using available experimental data which permitted the numerical evaluation of the response behaviour of such a system. The analysis is introduced in a general representative form which can be modified for particular applications concerning other classes of structured composite material systems.

Throughout the text, generalized tensorial notations are used. For simplification, however, the presentation has been limited to Cartesian tensors only. The reader is referred to Appendix A for a brief introduction on the subject matter. Appendix B presents the definitions and a summary of the properties of delta and step functions. These functions are used in the connection of presentation of the theory of viscoelasticity in Chapter 2 and throughout the text. The important subjects of Laplace and Fourier transformations are dealt with, respectively, in Appendix C and Appendix D. The two types of transformations are utilized frequently in the book.

In the presentation, vectors and unindexed tensorial quantities in general are indicated by bold. The author has used majuscules to identify the undeformed configuration or state X_I ($I = 1, 2, 3$) and minuscules to designate the corresponding deformed state x_i ($i = 1, 2, 3$). Equations, figures and tables are numbered within the chapter; for example, Fig. 1 of Chapter 2 is identified by 'Fig. 2.1'.

REFERENCES

Bernal, J. D. (1958) Structure arrangements of macromolecules. *Discuss. Faraday Soc.*, **25**, 7–18.
Boltzmann, L. (1874) Zür Theorie der elastichen Nachwirkung, Sitzungsber, Kaiserl. *Akad. Wiss. Wien, Math. Naturwiss. Kl.*, **70**(2), 275–306.
Boltzmann, L. (1877) Zür Theorie der elastischen Nachwirkung. *Akad. Wiss. Wien, Math. Naturwiss. Kl.*, **76**, 815–42.
Boltzmann, L. (1878) Zür Theorie der elastischen, Nachwirkung. *Ann. Phys. Chem., N.F.*, **5**, 430–2.
Doi, M. and Edwards, S. F. (1986) *The Theory of Polymer Dynamics*, Clarendon, Oxford.
Eirich, F. R. (1956) *Rheology Theory and Applications*, Academic Press, New York.
Ferry, J. D. (1970) *Viscoelastic Properties of Polymers*, 2nd edn, Wiley, New York.

Iyer, S. S. (1993) On the characterization of the viscoelastic response of a class of materials using acousto-ultrasonics – a pattern recognition approach. Master's Thesis, University of Ottawa, Canada.

Iyer, S. S. and Haddad, Y. M. (1993) On the characterization of the linear viscoelastic response of a class of materials by acousto-ultrasonics – a pattern recognition approach. CANCOM '93 – 2nd Canadian International Composites Conference and Exhibition (eds W. Wallace, R. Gauvin and S. V. Hoa), Canadian Association for Composite Structures and Materials, Ottawa, pp. 479–89.

Iyer, S. S. and Haddad, Y. M. (1994) Intelligent materials – an overview. *Int. J. Pressure Vessels Piping*, **58**, 335–44.

Kauman, W. G. (1966) On the deformation and setting of the wood cell wall. *Holz Roh- Werkst.*, **24**(11), 551–6.

Leaderman, H. (1943) *Elastic and Creep Properties of Filamentous Materials and Other High Polymers*, Textile Foundation, Washington, DC.

Leaderman, H. (1958) In *Viscoelasticity Phenomena in Amorphous High Polymeric Systems*, Vol. II (ed. F. Eirich), Academic Press, New York, pp. 1–6.

Love, A. E. H. (1944) *A Treatise on the Mathematical Theory of Elasticity*, 4th edn, Dover Publications, New York, pp. 1–31.

Mark, H. and Tobolosky, A. V. (1950) *Physical Chemistry of High Polymeric Materials*, Interscience Publishers, New York.

Markovitz, H. (1977) Boltzmann and the beginnings of linear viscoelasticity. *Trans. Soc. Rheol.*, **21**(3), 381–98.

Peters, L. (1955) A note on nonlinear viscoelasticity. *Textile Res. J.*, **29** (March), 262–5.

Rogers, C. A. (ed.) (1989) *Smart Materials, Structures, and Mathematical Issues*, Selected Papers presented at the US Army Research Office Workshop, Virginia Polytechnic Institute and State University, Blacksburg, VA, September 15–16, 1988, Technomic, Lancaster, PA.

Staverman, A. J. and Schwarzl, F. (1956) Linear Deformation Behaviour of High Polymers, in *Die Physik der Hochpolymeren*, Vol. IV (ed. H. A. Stuart), Springer, Berlin.

Takehiro, S. and San-Ichiro, M. (1955) On the helical configuration of a polymer chain. *J. Chem. Phys.*, **23**(4), 707–11.

Tanary, S. (1988) Characterization of adhesively bonded joints using acousto-ultrasonics. Master's Thesis, University of Ottawa, Ottawa.

Tobolosky, A. and Eyring, H. J. (1943) Mechanical properties of polymeric materials. *J. Chem. Phys.*, **11**, 125–34.

Vary, A. (1988) The acousto-ultrasonic approach, in *Acousto- Ultrasonics: Theory and Applications* (ed. J. C. Duke, Jr), Plenum, New York, pp. 1–21.

Volterra, V. (1913) *Fonctions de Lignes*, Gauthier-Villard, Paris.

Volterra, V. and Peres, J. (1936) *Thérie Générale des Fonctionnelles*, Gauthier-Villard, Paris.

Yoshiki, S. and Shun-Ichi, H. (1988) Development of polymeric shape memory material. *Mitsubishi Tech. Bull.*, no. 184, Mitsubishi Heavy Industries Ltd., New York.

1

Continuum mechanics background

1.1 INTRODUCTION

Continuum mechanics is a branch of general mechanics that deals with the evolution of the mechanical response process in solids and fluids when such media are considered as idealized continua. The emphasis here is on the concept 'continuous medium', whereby the actual microstructure of the medium is disregarded and the medium is pictured as a continuum without gaps or empty spaces. Hence, the configuration of the assumed continuous medium would be described by a continuous mathematical model whose geometrical points are identified with material particles of the actual physical medium. Further, when such a continuum changes its configuration under some boundary conditions, such change is assumed to be continuous, i.e. neighbourhoods evolve into neighbourhoods. Thus, the mathematical functions entering the analysis of, for instance, a deformation process, are assumed to be continuous functions with continuous derivatives. Any creation of new boundary surfaces, such as those developed by internal fracture, would then be seen as extraordinary events that might require alternative formulations outside the realm of continuum mechanics.

A basic concept in continuum mechanics is that of the definition of stress at a point (Cauchy, 1827, 1828). Reference is being made here to a geometric point that has no volume and may be associated with a mathematical limit of an elemental region of the continuum when the volume of such a region shrinks down to zero. This is, in essence, similar to the definition of the derivative in differential calculus and follows immediately from the postulate of continuity of the medium. Through its connection with the definition of the derivative, the concept of the stress at a point makes the powerful methods of calculus available for the analysis of the deformation process or flow in continuous media.

Two other physical postulates are often encountered in continuum mechanics presentations. They are concerned with the following.

1. *Homogeneity*. A medium is homogeneous if it has identical properties at all points. Hence, under this assumption, the medium is uniform and its properties are independent of the position.

2. *Isotropy.* A medium is isotropic with respect to a certain material property if such property has the same value in all directions, i.e. independent of orientation of any reference coordinate system that may be chosen to measure the property. Hence, such a material property remains constant in any plane that passes through a point in the material.

The above-mentioned postulates, together with other basic assumptions and principles of continuum mechanics, are demonstrated during the course of development of the present chapter.

Continuum mechanics theory may be divided into the following three domains of interest.

1. Generalized assumptions and principles that could be applicable to all continuous media.
2. Specialized theories pertaining to an idealized class of media. Such specialized theories are built on the foundations of the generalized assumptions and principles referred to under (1) above.
3. Constitutive equations defining the response behaviour of a particular idealized medium under specified boundary conditions. The boundary conditions may appear in the form of forces and/or displacements and velocities which could arise from contact with other bodies, thermal effects, chemical interactions, electromagnetic fields and other environmental changes. In most cases, however, we are concerned, in continuum mechanics, with media subjected to forces of mechanical origin and thermal influences.

The aim of this chapter is to provide the reader with a concise introduction of the basic assumptions and principles of continuum mechanics with an emphasis on those specifically used in the remainder of the book. Section 1.2 deals with the introduction of a number of general principles of the continuum mechanics theory. Section 1.3 treats the analysis of stress from a continuum mechanics point of view. Section 1.4 considers the kinematics and the measures of strain in a continuous medium. A reader who is not familiar with Cartesian tensor operations is advised to consult Appendix A concurrently with this chapter. The reader is referred to other text-books and references for a comprehensive study of the continuum mechanics theory. Some chosen references are provided at the end of this chapter.

1.2 GENERAL PRINCIPLES

1.2.1 Conservation of mass

From a classical mechanics point of view, mass is assumed to be conserved. Hence, the mass of a material body is considered as a time-independent property. In continuum mechanics, it is further postulated that mass is an absolutely continuous function of volume. Hence, it is assumed that a positive quantity ρ, referred to as density, can be defined at every point in the body by (e.g. Fung, 1965)

$$\rho(x) = \max_{l \to \infty} \frac{\text{mass of } \Omega_l}{\text{volume of } \Omega_l} \tag{1.1}$$

where Ω_l is a suitably chosen infinite sequence of particle sets shrinking down upon the point of the medium. This point is identified by the current position vector x referred to a particular coordinate frame of reference. The counterpoint of the latter, in the undeformed configuration, is given the majuscule symbol $\mathbf{X}$. The mapping between the two positions x and $\mathbf{X}$ is dealt with in section 1.4 where we discuss the deformation kinematics and the measures of strain in a continuous medium.

The conservation of mass is expressed by

$$\int \rho(\mathbf{x}) \, dx_i = \int \rho(\mathbf{X}) \, dX_I \tag{1.2}$$

where the integrals extend over the same sets of particles. Hence,

$$\rho(\mathbf{x}) = \rho(\mathbf{x}) \left| \frac{\partial x_i}{\partial X_I} \right| \quad \text{and} \quad \rho(\mathbf{x}) = \rho(\mathbf{X}) \left| \frac{\partial X_I}{\partial x_i} \right|. \tag{1.3}$$

Equation (1.2) or (1.3) relates, then, the densities of the body for different configurations of the deformation process.

1.2.2 Material derivative of field functions

The derivative of a field function $\phi(x_i, t)$ that is attributable to the motion of a point in a continuum is expressed by the so-called 'mathematical derivative'. The latter is denoted by a dot or, alternatively, by the symbol D/Dt. It can be shown that the material derivative of a field function $\phi(\mathbf{x}, t)$ takes the form

$$\dot{\phi}(\mathbf{x}, t) = \frac{D\phi(x, t)}{Dt}$$

$$= \left(\frac{\partial \phi}{\partial t} \right)_{x = \text{constant}} + v_i \frac{\partial \phi}{\partial x_i} \tag{1.4}$$

where v_i is the velocity associated with the current position x_i. The first term on the right-hand side of (1.4) is due to the time dependence of the function ϕ $(\cdot)$ and is interpreted as the 'local part of the field function'. The second term is contributed by the motion of the particle in the current field of the function ϕ $(\cdot)$ and is referred to as the 'convective' part of $\dot{\phi}(\mathbf{x}, t)$. The field function $\phi(\mathbf{x}, t)$ may take the form of a tensor field of any order.

1.2.3 Continuity of mass (Continuity Equation)

In the derivation of the continuity equations, one of the following two approaches may be taken.

1. One considers a constant mass in a volume that varies with the time.
2. Alternatively, one may consider a constant volume while taking into account the variation in mass between entry and exit.

Consider the second approach. Thus, the rate of mass increase of an arbitrary fixed volume V is equal to the influx of matter through its surface S, i.e.

$$\int_V \frac{\partial \rho}{\partial t}\, dV = -\int_S \rho v_i \mathbf{n}_i\, dS. \tag{1.5}$$

In the above equation, the negative sign accounts for the influx being opposite to the direction of the outward unit normal $\mathbf{n}_i$ and v_i is the velocity of the material entering the control volume. Recalling the three-dimensional form of the divergence theorem of Gauss (e.g. Flügge, 1972), then equation (1.5) is written as

$$\int_V \left[\frac{\partial \rho}{\partial t} + (\rho v_i)_{,i} \right] dV = 0$$

whereby the **continuity of mass equation** is expressed as

$$\frac{\partial \rho}{\partial t} + (\rho v_i)_{,i} = 0. \tag{1.6}$$

An alternative expression may be found by carrying through the indicated partial differentiation in (1.6) to obtain

$$\frac{\partial \rho}{\partial t} + \rho_{,i} v_i + \rho v_{i,i} = 0. \tag{1.7}$$

Employing the derivative operator $D(\cdot)/Dt$ introduced earlier by equation (1.4), then, in terms of this operator, the continuity of mass equation (1.7) is expressed as

$$\frac{D\rho}{Dt} + \rho v_{i,i} = 0. \tag{1.8}$$

1.2.4 Continuity of momentum

Following the approach adopted above in deriving the continuity of mass equation, we consider an arbitrary fixed volume V whereby the total rate of change of linear momentum has two components; one associated with the change of mass within the volume V and the other associated with the influx of the mass through the bounding surface S. Thus,

$$\frac{d}{dt} \int_V \rho v_i\, dV = \int_V \frac{\partial(\rho v_i)}{\partial t}\, dV + \int_S (\rho v_i) v_j \, \mathbf{n}_j\, dS \tag{1.9}$$

which can be written by using the divergence theorem of Gauss as

$$\frac{d}{dt} \int_V \rho v_i \, dV = \int_V \left[\frac{\partial \rho}{\partial t} v_i + \rho \frac{\partial v_i}{\partial t} + (\rho v_i v_j)_{,j} \right] dV$$

$$= \int_V \left[\left(\frac{\partial \rho}{\partial t} + \rho_{,j} v_j + \rho v_{j,j} \right) v_i + \rho \frac{\partial v_i}{\partial t} + \rho v_{i,j} v_j \right] dV. \quad (1.10)$$

In view of the continuity of mass equation (1.7), expression (1.10) reduces to

$$\frac{d}{dt} \int_V \rho v_i \, dV = \int_V \rho \left(\frac{\partial v_i}{\partial t} + v_{i,j} v_j \right) dV \quad (1.11)$$

Expression (1.11) is referred to as the **continuity of momentum equation**.

1.3 ANALYSIS OF STRESS

1.3.1 Body and surface forces

The external forces acting at any time on a free body are classified, from a continuum mechanics point of view, in two categories, namely **body** forces and **surface** forces.

Body forces act on the elements of mass or volume inside the body. Hence, in continuum mechanics, they are expressed as forces per unit mass or forces per unit volume. Examples of body forces are those due to gravity, magnetic effects and inertia. In this book, unless otherwise stated, we regard the body forces acting on a free body as expressed per unit volume. Hence, the term 'volumetric forces' may be used as a reference to these body forces throughout the text.

We shall denote the body force per unit volume acting on an infinitesimal volume element dV of the body by the vector χ. If the resultant of body forces acting on an elemental volume ΔV is designated by $\Delta \mathbf{B}$, then the body force is defined by

$$\chi = \lim_{\Delta V \to 0} \frac{\Delta \mathbf{B}}{\Delta V}. \quad (1.12)$$

In general, the vector χ varies from point to point in the free body at any given instant of time and may also vary with time at any particular point of the body. It can be also dependent on other state variables such as the temperature. The vector sum of all body forces acting on a free body of a finite volume V, at any particular instant of time, is then given by the space integral over this volume. However, in many applications, the body forces are likely to be uniform, e.g. gravity forces or, otherwise, they may be small enough so that they could be assumed to be negligible.

Surface forces are exerted on the bounding surface of the free body. Hence, they are usually expressed per unit area of the surface on which they are acting.

The limit of the surface force per unit area, as the unit area tends to zero, is often referred to as the **stress vector**, or, alternatively, traction vector. It is denoted by the symbol **T**. Accordingly, the force acting on an elemental area dS of the bounding surface is **T** dS and the vector sum of all surface forces acting on a finite region S of this surface is given by the corresponding vector surface integral, that is $\int_S \mathbf{T}\, dS$.

Generally, when applied to a given solid body, the definitions of body and surface forces are taken with reference to the current deformed configuration of the body. However, in many applications of the theory of elasticity, the occurring deformations might be so small that the definitions of such forces could be expressed with reference to the undeformed configuration of the body without a significant error. Alternatively, in applications concerning fluid flow, one may use as a reference a given fixed volume of space, through which different substance or fluid passes at different times. In this context, the concept of the imaginary control surface in a fluid is well recognized in the studies of fluid mechanics (e.g. Malvern, 1969).

1.3.2 Stress vector

We consider, in Fig. 1.1, a continuous free body being acted upon by an externally applied equilibrium force system $\mathbf{F}_1, \mathbf{F}_2, \ldots, \mathbf{F}_N$. Suppose, now, that the body be divided, through a bounding surface S, into two regions R_1 and R_2. If R_1, for example, is to be in equilibrium, forces must be exerted on S by R_2. These forces would be in equilibrium with the externally applied forces on R_1. We consider a point p on S with unit normal **n** surrounded by an elemental surface area ΔS of S. The forces acting on ΔS are statistically equivalent to a force and a couple. At the limit, as ΔS

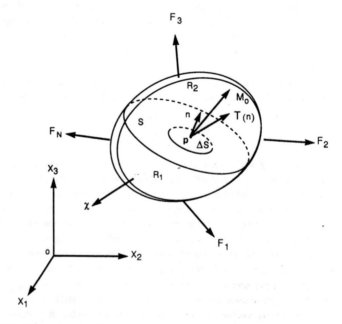

Fig. 1.1 Body and surface forces.

shrinks down to a point, the couple (per unit area) produced, at this point, by the continuous distribution of the internal force may be taken to be zero. This does not, of course, exclude the possibility of the existence of a 'couple stress' whose value may be different from zero. Such couple stress has been proposed in 'higher order' continuum mechanics theories (Malvern, 1969). However, for our purpose, we shall assume, following classical continuum mechanics, that there is no couple stress acting on ΔS and that the action of one body on another across an infinitesimal surface area can be presented solely by the **stress vector**. The latter is defined, at the point p of the elemental surface area ΔS with normal **n** (Fig. 1.1), by

$$\mathbf{T}(\mathbf{n}) = \lim_{\Delta S \to 0} \frac{\Delta \mathbf{F}}{\Delta S}. \tag{1.13}$$

That is, $\mathbf{T}(\mathbf{n})$ is a stress vector function defined on the elemental surface area ΔS and is dependent on the unit normal **n**.

The stress state at any point in a continuum can be determined in terms of the three stress vectors acting on three mutually perpendicular planes intersecting at this point. Hence, the stress vectors acting on planes perpendicular to a rectangular coordinate system embedded at a point in the continuum are considered to be of particular interest. Figure 1.2 shows three such stress vectors acting on the centre points of three faces of a cube surrounding a chosen particular point of interest O. The point O represents, in turn, the centre of the cube and, at the same time, the

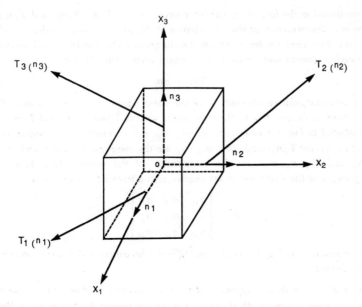

Fig. 1.2 Average traction vectors acting on three planes perpendicular to the rectangular coordinate axes.

origin of the rectangular coordinate system. With reference to Fig. 1.2, let

- $T_1(n_1)$ be the stress vector acting on a plane whose normal n_1, is pointing in the positive x_1 direction,
- $T_2(n_2)$ be the stress vector acting on a plane with normal, n_2, directed in the positive x_2 direction, and
- $T_3(n_3)$ be the stress vector acting on a plane with normal, n_3, in the direction of the positive x_3 axis.

The three stress vectors mentioned above are considered to be the average traction vectors on the corresponding faces of the cube. As the cube shrinks down towards its centre point O, the limit approached by the stress vector on each face is taken, from continuum mechanics point of view, as the stress vector at the point O on a plane perpendicular to one of the coordinate axes. Hence, the three stress vectors may be seen to represent the local stress state at the point O. This approach illustrates a basic concept in continuum mechanics, i.e. the concept of stress at a point, mentioned earlier in the introduction to this chapter. This concept refers to a geometric point in space visualized as a mathematical limit in a manner similar to the definition of the derivative in differential calculus. This approach has been, in fact, a key to the development of continuum mechanics as it immediately makes the powerful methods of calculus available for the study of the deformation and flow in a physical continuum.

1.3.3 Cauchy's stress tensor

As mentioned in the foregoing, the three stress vectors $T_1(n_1)$, $T_2(n_2)$ and $T_3(n_3)$ are taken as a representation of the stress tensor at the particular point under consideration. The stress tensor is denoted by $\boldsymbol{\sigma}$. It is the linear vector function which associates with each argument unit vector n the traction vector $T(n)$. That is,

$$T(n) = n\boldsymbol{\sigma}. \qquad (1.14)$$

The nine rectangular components σ_{ij} of the stress tensor are the three sets of stress components corresponding to the three stress vectors $T_1(n_1)$, $T_2(n_2)$ and $T_3(n_3)$. This is illustrated in Fig. 1.3 where the set $(\sigma_{11}, \sigma_{12}, \sigma_{13})$ constitutes the components of the stress vector $T_1(n_1)$ while $(\sigma_{21}, \sigma_{22}, \sigma_{23})$ are the components of the stress vector $T_2(n_2)$ and $(\sigma_{31}, \sigma_{32}, \sigma_{33})$ are the components of the stress vector $T_3(n_3)$. The components of the stress tensor are displayed in a matrix form as follows:

$$\sigma_{ij} = \begin{bmatrix} \sigma_{11} & \sigma_{12} & \sigma_{13} \\ \sigma_{21} & \sigma_{22} & \sigma_{23} \\ \sigma_{31} & \sigma_{32} & \sigma_{33} \end{bmatrix}.$$

With reference to Fig. 1.3, the following sign convention of the stress components σ_{ij} is adopted.

1. σ_{ij} ($i \neq j$) is the shear component of the stress tensor acting on a face of the cube whose normal is in the ith direction and the component itself is acting in the jth direction.

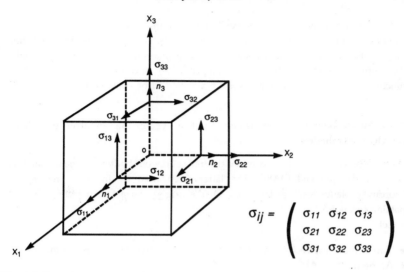

Fig. 1.3 Stress tensor components.

2. $\sigma_{\overline{ii}}$ (no sum over i) is the normal component of the stress tensor. It is acting on a face whose normal is in the ith direction and the component is acting in the same direction. The normal component of stress is positive if drawn outward from the face upon which it acts.

3. If the outward normal **n** to a surface is in the positive direction of the coordinate axis, then the shear component of stress acting on this surface is positive if it is in the positive direction of the associated-with axis. Alternatively, if the outward normal to a surface is in the negative direction of the coordinate axis, then the shear component is positive if it is in the negative direction of the associated-with axis. With reference to Fig. 1.3, positive σ_{23}, for instance, represents an upward-acting stress component on the right-hand side and down-acting component on the left-hand side of the cube. Negative σ_{23}, on the other hand, acts downward on the right-hand side and upward on the left-hand side of the cube. Further, the components on the negative sides of the cube will have senses opposite to those on the positive sides.

When the normal component of stress, $\sigma_{\overline{ii}}$ (no sum over i), is positive it represents a tensile stress but, if it is negative, it is compressive. The algebraic sign of a tangential shear component does not, however, have an intrinsic physical significance. Hence, positive and negative shear components represent the same kind of loading but in different directions.

The state of stress at a particular point in a continuous medium can be specified fully by the second-order tensor σ_{ij} with nine components. However, as will be dealt with later, because of the symmetry property of the stress tensor, only six of the nine components are independent. This is under the assumption that there are no distributed body or surface couples acting on the free body. In general, the components of the stress tensor are functions of the coordinates and time and they may be also dependent on other state variables such as the temperature. Accordingly, they form a second-order tensor field (Appendix A). In continuum mechanics, these functions and their partial derivatives are assumed to be continuous.

1.3.4 Stress boundary conditions: Traction vector on an arbitrary plane, Cauchy's tetrahedron

With reference to Fig. 1.4, we consider the free continuous body to be the tetrahedron or triangular pyramid OABC. The latter is enclosed by the three rectangular coordinate planes through the point O (the origin) and a fourth plane ABC not passing through O.
    Let

- $T(n)$ be the stress vector at a point of the oblique surface ABC whose normal is n,
- ΔS be the area ABC,
- h be the perpendicular distance from the origin O to ΔS,
- $\Delta V = (1/3)h\,\Delta S$ be the elemental volume of the tetrahedron OABC,
- χ_i be the components of the body force vector per unit volume and
- σ_{ij} be the components of the stress tensor.

We apply Newton's second law of motion, that is the sum of forces acting on the tetrahedron is equal to the rate of change of linear momentum. Let v_i denote the

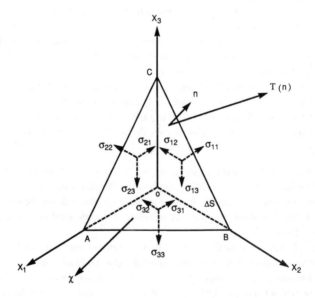

Fig. 1.4 Cauchy's tetrahedron.

components of the velocity vector, then, with reference to Fig. 1.4,

$$\int_{ABC} T_i\, dS - \int_{OAB} \sigma_{3i}\, dS - \int_{OCA} \sigma_{2i}\, dS$$

$$- \int_{OBC} \sigma_{1i}\, dS + \int_{\Delta V} \chi_i\, dV = \frac{d}{dt} \int_{\Delta V} \rho v_i\, dV \quad (1.15)$$

where ρ is the density.

Equation (1.15) can be written with the inclusion of the components of the unit vector **n** as

$$\int_{\Delta S} [T_i - (\sigma_{3i} n_3 + \sigma_{2i} n_2 + \sigma_{1i} n_1)]\, dS + \int_{\Delta V} \chi_i\, dV = \frac{d}{dt} \int_{\Delta V} \rho v_i\, dV$$

or

$$\int_{\Delta S} (T_i - \sigma_{ji} n_j) + \int_{\Delta V} \chi_i\, dV = \frac{d}{dt} \int_{\Delta V} \rho v_i\, dV. \quad (1.16)$$

From both the 'mean value theorem of calculus' and the concept of 'continuity of momentum' (1.11), equation (1.16) can be written in the form

$$(\langle T_i \rangle - \langle \sigma_{ji} n_j \rangle) \Delta S = (\langle \rho \dot{v}_i \rangle - \langle \chi_i \rangle) \Delta V \quad (1.17)$$

where $\langle \cdot \rangle$ indicates the mean value. Taking the limits as both ΔS and ΔV tend to zero, i.e. h also tends to zero, then equation (1.17) is approximated by

$$T_i = \sigma_{ji} n_j \quad (1.18)$$

where σ_{ji} is a second-order Cartesian tensor since both T_i and n_j are components of vectors.

Equation (1.18) establishes the '**stress boundary conditions**' on the free body (tetrahedron) considered and states that for every second-order (symmetric) tensor σ_{ji}, defined at some point in the continuum, there is, associated with each direction (specified by the unit normal **n** at that point), a traction vector **T** given by the form of this equation.

1.3.5 Symmetry of the stress tensor

As dealt with in the foregoing, we consider an arbitrary region of a continuum. This region, Fig. 1.5, is of volume V which is enclosed by a surface S with an outward unit normal **n**. The forces acting on an elemental portion of S are **T** dS while the body forces on an elemental portion of V are $\chi\, dV$.

Applying the principle of conservation of linear momentum to this arbitrary region, then

$$\int_S T_i\, dS + \int_V \chi_i\, dV = \frac{d}{dt} \int_V \rho v_i\, dV. \quad (1.19)$$

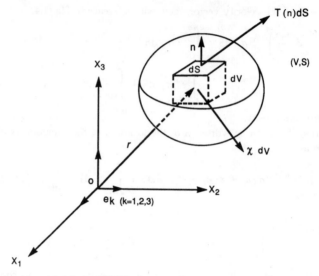

Fig. 1.5 An elemental volume (dV, dS) of a continuous region (V, S).

Thus, in view of (1.18) and the conservation of momentum relation (1.11), equation (1.19) can be written as

$$\int_S \sigma_{ji} n_j \, dS + \int_V \chi_i \, dV = \int_V \rho \dot{v}_i \, dV. \tag{1.20}$$

If we now apply the divergence theorem to the first integral of (1.20), then

$$\int_V (\sigma_{ji,j} + \chi_i - \rho \dot{v}_i) \, dV = 0 \tag{1.21}$$

or

$$\sigma_{ji,j} + \chi_i = \rho \dot{v}_i \tag{1.22}$$

which is known as '**Cauchy's first equation of motion**'.

With reference to Fig. 1.5, one considers the sum of moments of forces about the origin O to be equal to the rate of change of angular momentum;

$$\int_S \boldsymbol{r} \times \mathbf{T} \, dS + \int_V \boldsymbol{r} \times \boldsymbol{\chi} \, dV = \frac{d}{dt} \int_V \boldsymbol{r} \times (\rho \boldsymbol{v}) \, dV$$

or

$$\int_S \varepsilon_{ijk} x_i T_j \boldsymbol{e}_k \, dS + \int_V \varepsilon_{ijk} x_i \chi_j \boldsymbol{e}_k \, dV = \frac{d}{dt} \int_V \rho \varepsilon_{ijk} x_i \dot{x}_j \boldsymbol{e}_k \, dV \tag{1.23}$$

where ε_{ijk} is the alternating tensor and $\mathbf{e}_k$ are the components of the unit vector associated with the coordinate system x_i as shown in Fig. 1.5.

Applying the three-dimensional divergence theorem of Gauss and the boundary conditions (1.18) to the left-hand side of (1.23), the latter equation is expressed as

$$\int_V \mathbf{e}_k\{\varepsilon_{ijk}[(x_i\sigma_{lj})_{,l} + x_i\chi_j]\}\, dV = \mathbf{e}_k \int_V \frac{\partial}{\partial t}\,(\rho\varepsilon_{ijk}x_i\dot{x}_j)\, dV$$

$$+ \mathbf{e}_k \int_S \rho\varepsilon_{ijk}x_i v_j\, v_l n_k\, dS. \qquad (1.24)$$

Equation (1.24) can be written with reference to equations (1.7) and (1.11) as

$$\int_V \mathbf{e}_k\{\varepsilon_{ijk}[(x_i\sigma_{lj})_{,l} + x_i\chi_j]\}\, dV = \mathbf{e}_k\varepsilon_{ijk} \int_V \rho x_i\dot{v}_j\, dV$$

or

$$\mathbf{e}_k\varepsilon_{ijk} \int_V [\sigma_{ij} + x_i(\sigma_{lj,l} + \chi_j - \rho\dot{v}_j)]\, dV = 0. \qquad (1.25)$$

In the above equation, since the expression in parentheses is equal to zero, from Cauchy's first equation of motion (1.22), equation (1.25) becomes

$$\mathbf{e}_k \int_V \varepsilon_{ijk}\sigma_{jk}\, dV = \mathbf{0} \qquad (1.26)$$

which implies that

$$\varepsilon_{ijk}\sigma_{jk} = 0 \qquad (1.27)$$

or, alternatively, in view of the properties of the skew-symmetric tensor ε_{ijk} (Appendix A),

$$\sigma_{ij} = \sigma_{ji}. \qquad (1.28)$$

It is apparent that equation (1.28) expresses the symmetry of the stress tensor. This equation is referred to as 'Cauchy's second law of motion' and it implies the 'conservation of moment of momentum'.

1.3.6 Principal axes of stress, principal planes and principal stresses

Regardless of the state of stress at a given point in a continuum, it is always possible to choose a special set of rectangular axes through this point so that the shear stress components vanish when the stress components are referred to this set of axes. This set of rectangular axes are referred to as **principal axes** or **principal directions**. Thus, on a plane perpendicular to a principal axis, the traction vector is entirely normal.

The principal planes through the point perpendicular to the three principal axes of stress are referred to as the **principal planes of stress**.

The normal stress components on the three principal planes are known as **principal stresses**. The principal stresses are physical quantities whose magnitudes do not depend on the particular coordinate system to which the stress components are referred. Accordingly, they are invariants pertaining to the stress state at the particular point under consideration.

Let **n** define the direction of a principal axis and σ designate the corresponding principal stress; then the stress vector acting on the surface defined by **n** can be expressed, with reference to (1.18), by

$$T_i = \sigma n_i = \sigma_{ji} n_j \tag{1.29}$$

This is with the understanding that

$$n_i = \delta_{ji} n_j \tag{1.30}$$

where δ_{ji} is the Kronecker delta;

$$\delta_{ij} = \begin{cases} 1 & \text{if } i = j, \\ 0 & \text{if } i \neq j. \end{cases}$$

Combining equations (1.29) and (1.30), it follows that

$$(\sigma_{ji} - \sigma\delta_{ji})n_j = 0. \tag{1.31}$$

Expression (1.31) represents three equations to be solved for the components of the unit normal **n**, i.e. n_1, n_2, n_3. In this context, we search a set of nontrivial solutions for which

$$n_1^2 + n_2^2 + n_3^2 = 1. \tag{1.32}$$

Hence, equation (1.31), subject to (1.32), poses an eigenvalue problem. Since the matrix of σ_{ij} is real and symmetric, then there exist three real-valued principal stresses and a set of orthogonal principal axes. The three principal stresses are denoted by σ_1, σ_2, σ_3. The algebraically greatest of the three principal stresses is the algebraically greatest normal stress component acting on any plane through the point. At the same time, the algebraically smallest of the principal stresses is the algebraically smallest normal stress component on any plane through the point. Referring to equation (1.31), this equation has a set of nonvanishing solutions n_1, n_2, n_3 if, and only if, the determinant of its coefficients vanishes, i.e.

$$|\sigma_{ij} - \sigma\delta_{ij}| = 0. \tag{1.33}$$

Equation (1.33) represents a cubic equation in σ. The roots of this equation are the principal stresses σ_1, σ_2 and σ_3. For each value of the principal stress, a unit normal **n** is involved.

Expansion of (1.33) leads to

$$|\sigma_{ij} - \sigma\delta_{ij}| = \begin{vmatrix} \sigma_{11} - \sigma & \sigma_{12} & \sigma_{13} \\ \sigma_{21} & \sigma_{22} - \sigma & \sigma_{23} \\ \sigma_{31} & \sigma_{32} & \sigma_{33} - \sigma \end{vmatrix} \qquad (1.34)$$

$$= -\sigma^3 + I_1\sigma^2 - I_2\sigma + I_3$$

where the coefficients I_1, I_2, I_3 denote, respectively, the following scalar expressions of the stress components:

$$I_1 = \sigma_{11} + \sigma_{22} + \sigma_{33}$$
$$= \sigma_{kk}; \qquad (1.35a)$$

$$I_2 = \begin{vmatrix} \sigma_{22} & \sigma_{23} \\ \sigma_{32} & \sigma_{33} \end{vmatrix} + \begin{vmatrix} \sigma_{11} & \sigma_{13} \\ \sigma_{31} & \sigma_{33} \end{vmatrix} + \begin{vmatrix} \sigma_{11} & \sigma_{12} \\ \sigma_{21} & \sigma_{22} \end{vmatrix}$$
$$= \tfrac{1}{2}(\sigma_{ij}\sigma_{ij} - \sigma_{ii}\sigma_{jj})$$
$$= -(\sigma_{11}\sigma_{22} + \sigma_{22}\sigma_{33} + \sigma_{33}\sigma_{11}) + \sigma_{23}^2 + \sigma_{31}^2 + \sigma_{12}^2; \quad (1.35b)$$

$$I_3 = \begin{vmatrix} \sigma_{11} & \sigma_{12} & \sigma_{13} \\ \sigma_{21} & \sigma_{22} & \sigma_{23} \\ \sigma_{31} & \sigma_{31} & \sigma_{33} \end{vmatrix} = \tfrac{1}{6}\varepsilon_{ijk}\varepsilon_{pqr}\sigma_{ip}\sigma_{jq}\sigma_{kr}. \qquad (1.35c)$$

It is recognized that both equation (1.34) and the coefficients I_1, I_2, I_3 represented by (1.35) do not depend on the choice of the coordinate axes; hence, they are invariants of coordinate transformation. For this reason, the coefficients I_1, I_2, and I_3 of equation (1.34) are conventionally referred to as invariants of the stress tensor.

With reference to equations (1.34) and (1.35), the coefficient I_1 is the first invariant of the stress tensor. It is also referred to as the trace of the stress matrix. That is the sum of the elements on the main diagonal in the matrix of rectangular Cartesian components of σ_{ij}, the three normal stresses; equation (1.35a). The coefficient I_2, the second invariant, is a homogeneous quadratic expression in the stress components. It is the sum of the three minor determinants of the three diagonal elements in the determinant of the stress matrix; equation (1.35b). The third invariant, I_3, is the determinant of the stress matrix and it is a homogeneous cubic expression in the stress components; equation (1.35c).

Further, the invariants I_1, I_2 and I_3 of σ_{ij} can be expressed in terms of the roots of the cubic equation (1.34), i.e. the three principal stresses σ_1, σ_2 and σ_3:

$$I_1 = \sigma_1 + \sigma_2 + \sigma_3;$$
$$I_2 = \sigma_1\sigma_2 + \sigma_2\sigma_3 + \sigma_3\sigma_1; \qquad (1.36)$$
$$I_3 = \sigma_1\sigma_2\sigma_3.$$

We state now an important property of a symmetric second-order tensor:

For a symmetric second-order tensor, the three principal stresses are all real and the three principal planes are mutually orthogonal.

To illustrate the above property, let $\overset{1}{\mathbf{n}}$, $\overset{2}{\mathbf{n}}$, $\overset{3}{\mathbf{n}}$ be unit vectors in the directions of the principal axes, with components $\overset{1}{n_j}$, $\overset{2}{n_j}$, $\overset{3}{n_j}$ ($j = 1, 2, 3$) which are the solutions of equation (1.31) corresponding, respectively, to the principal stresses σ_1, σ_2, σ_3, i.e.

$$(\sigma_{ij} - \sigma_1 \delta_{ij})\overset{1}{n_j} = 0,$$

$$(\sigma_{ij} - \sigma_2 \delta_{ij})\overset{2}{n_j} = 0,$$

$$(\sigma_{ij} - \sigma_3 \delta_{ij})\overset{3}{n_j} = 0,$$

(1.37)

Multiplying the first equation of (1.37) by $\overset{2}{n_i}$ and the second equation of (1.37) by $\overset{1}{n_i}$, summing over i and subtracting the resulting equations, it follows that

$$(\sigma_2 - \sigma_1)\overset{1}{n_i}\overset{2}{n_i} = 0.$$

(1.38)

Assuming tentatively that (1.34) has a complex root and recalling that the coefficients of this equation are real valued, then a complex conjugate root must also exist and the set of roots may be written as

$$\sigma_1 = a + ib, \ \sigma_2 = a - ib \text{ and } \sigma_3$$

where a and b are real numbers and i stands for the imaginary number $\sqrt{-1}$. In this case, equations (1.37) would show that $\overset{1}{n_j}$ and $\overset{2}{n_j}$ are complex conjugate to each other and may be written as

$$\overset{1}{n_i} = \alpha_j + i\beta_j, \ \overset{2}{n_i} = \alpha_j - i\beta_j$$

where α and β are real numbers. Thus,

$$\overset{1}{n_j}\overset{2}{n_j} = (\alpha_j + i\beta_j)(\alpha_j - i\beta_j)$$
$$= \alpha_1^2 + \alpha_2^2 + \alpha_3^2 + \beta_1^2 + \beta_2^2 + \beta_3^2 \neq 0.$$

Hence, with reference to (1.38),

$$\sigma_1 - \sigma_2 = 2ib, \text{ or } b = 0,$$

which means that the original assumption of the existence of complex roots is incorrect and σ_1, σ_2, σ_3 must be all real.

Further, if $\sigma_1 \neq \sigma_2 \neq \sigma_3$, then, recalling equation (1.38),

$$\overset{1}{n_i}\overset{2}{n_i} = 0, \ \overset{2}{n_i}\overset{3}{n_i} = 0 \quad \text{and} \quad \overset{3}{n_i}\overset{1}{n_i} = 0,$$

(1.39)

i.e. the principal stresses are orthogonal to each other.

On the other hand, if $\sigma_1 = \sigma_2 \neq \sigma_3$, one may determine an infinite number of pairs of unit normals $\overset{1}{n_i}$ and $\overset{2}{n_i}$ with $\overset{3}{n_i}$ a vector orthogonal to $\overset{1}{n_i}$ and $\overset{2}{n_i}$.

However, if $\sigma_1 = \sigma_2 = \sigma_3$, then any set of orthogonal axes may be considered as principal axes.

It is evident that, if the reference axes x_1, x_2, x_3 were selected to coincide with the principal axes, then the stress tensor would be expressed as

$$\sigma_{ij} = \begin{bmatrix} \sigma_1 & 0 & 0 \\ 0 & \sigma_2 & 0 \\ 0 & 0 & \sigma_3 \end{bmatrix}. \tag{1.40}$$

1.3.7 Spherical and deviatoric components

The stress tensor σ_{ij} may be expressed as the sum of two parts.

- One tensorial part represents a spherical or hydrostatic state of stress in which each normal stress is equal to $-p$, where p is the mean normal pressure, and all shear stresses are zero:

$$-p = \bar{\sigma} = \tfrac{1}{3}(\sigma_{11} + \sigma_{22} + \sigma_{33}) = \tfrac{1}{3}\sigma_{kk} = \tfrac{1}{3}I_1 \tag{1.41}$$

where $\bar{\sigma}$ is the mean stress and I_1 is the first invariant of σ_{ij} expressed earlier by (1.35a).
- The second part, denoted below by σ'_{ij}, defines the deviator as

$$\sigma'_{ij} = \sigma_{ij} - \bar{\sigma}\delta_{ij}. \tag{1.42}$$

Thus,

$$\sigma_{ij} = \bar{\sigma}\delta_{ij} + \sigma'_{ij}. \tag{1.43}$$

To determine the principal values of the stress deviator, the procedure illustrated in section 1.3.6 for the determination of the principal stresses of the stress tensor may be followed by replacing the determinant equation (1.33) by

$$|\sigma'_{ij} - \sigma'\delta_{ij}| = 0. \tag{1.44}$$

1.3.8 Piola–Kirchhoff stress tensor

As presented earlier, the Cauchy equations of motion (1.22) and (1.28) apply to the current deformed configuration. Here, the Cauchy stress tensor field is a function of the spatial coordinate $\mathbf{x}$ and it was concluded by (1.28) to be a symmetric tensor for the case where there is no couple stress or assigned couples. In the applications of the theory of elasticity, however, it is often assumed that there exists a natural state to which the body would return when it is unloaded. In this case, it is generally preferred that both the stress and the equations of motion be expressed as functions of the material point $\mathbf{X}$ (the reference state) and, hence, to derive the equations of motion in this state. The first and second Piola–Kirchhoff stress tensors (due to Piola in 1833 and Kirchhoff in 1853) are two alternatives for the definition of the stress in the reference state (Truesdell and Toupin, 1960; Malvern, 1969). The two Piola–Kirchhoff tensors are expressed in terms of the force per unit undeformed area.

The first Piola–Kirchhoff stress tensor is the simpler one. However, it has the disadvantage of being antisymmetric. The second Piola–Kirchhoff stress tensor, on the other hand, is symmetric; thus it has often been used in the formulations of the theory of elasticity. In this context, we present below the definition of the second Piola–Kirchhoff tensor.

Second Piola–Kirchhoff stress tensor

The second Piola–Kirchhoff stress tensor Σ gives a force $d\mathbf{P}_0$ on a unit area dS in the undeformed configuration in relation to the actual force $d\mathbf{P}$ on the corresponding elemental area $d\mathbf{s}$ in the deformed configuration according to the following interpretations

$$d\mathbf{P}_0 = \mathbf{g}^{-1}{\cdot}d\mathbf{P} \tag{1.45}$$

where $\mathbf{g} = \mathbf{X}\nabla\mathbf{x}$ is the inverse of the spatial deformation gradient.

The following relation can be proven (Malvern, 1969) between the second Piola–Kirchhoff stress and the Cauchy stress:

$$\Sigma = \frac{\rho_0}{\rho}\,\mathbf{g}^{-1}\cdot\boldsymbol{\sigma}\cdot(\mathbf{g}^{-1})^{\mathsf{T}} \tag{1.46a}$$

or, in indicial notations,

$$\Sigma_{JI} = \frac{\rho_0}{\rho}\,X_{J,l}\sigma_{li}\partial_i X_I \tag{1.46b}$$

which shows that the second Piola–Kirchhoff stress tensor Σ is symmetric.

The inverse relation to (1.46) is

$$\boldsymbol{\sigma} = \frac{\rho}{\rho_0}\,\mathbf{g}\cdot\boldsymbol{\Sigma}\cdot\mathbf{g}^{\mathsf{T}} \tag{1.47a}$$

or,

$$\sigma_{ji} = \frac{\rho}{\rho_0}\,x_{j,J}\,\Sigma_{JI}\,\partial_I X_i. \tag{1.47b}$$

The symmetry of $\boldsymbol{\sigma}$ imposes the following condition on Σ so that the latter can be symmetric

$$\Sigma\,\mathbf{g}^{\mathsf{T}} = \mathbf{g}\,\Sigma^{\mathsf{T}} \tag{1.48}$$

where the superscript T indicates the transpose of the associated matrix. Meantime, the equation of motion corresponding to (1.22) in the reference state is expressed by

$$\nabla\cdot(\Sigma\cdot\mathbf{g}^{\mathsf{T}}) + \rho_0\chi_0 = \rho_0\frac{\partial^2\mathbf{x}}{\partial t^2} \tag{1.49a}$$

or

$$\partial_j(\Sigma_{JI}\, \partial_I x_i) + \rho_0(\chi_0)_i = \rho_0 \frac{\partial^2 x_i}{\partial t^2}. \qquad (1.49b)$$

PROBLEMS

1.1 Briefly discuss the basic postulates and concepts of continuum mechanics leading to the definitions of the stress vector, body force and stress tensor.

1.2 Label the stress tensor components shown.

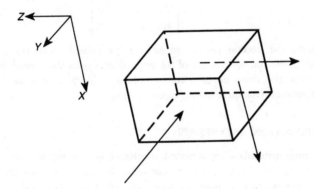

1.3

1. Evaluate the invariants for the stress tensor

$$\sigma_{ij} = \begin{bmatrix} 6 & -3 & 0 \\ -3 & 6 & 0 \\ 0 & 0 & 8 \end{bmatrix}.$$

Determine the principal stress values for this state of stress and show that the diagonal form of the stress tensor yields the same values for the stress invariants.

2. Decompose the stress tensor

$$\sigma_{ij} = \begin{bmatrix} 12 & 4 & 0 \\ 4 & 9 & -2 \\ 0 & -2 & 3 \end{bmatrix}.$$

into its spherical and deviatoric parts and show that the first invariant of the deviator is zero.

3. Determine the principal deviator stress values for the stress tensor

$$\sigma_{ij} = \begin{bmatrix} 10 & -6 & 0 \\ -6 & 10 & 0 \\ 0 & 0 & 1 \end{bmatrix}.$$

1.4 At a point P of a continuous medium, the stress tensor referred to the axes x_i $(i = 1, 2, 3)$ is given by

$$\sigma_{ij} = \begin{bmatrix} 15 & -10 & 0 \\ -10 & 5 & 0 \\ 0 & 0 & 20 \end{bmatrix}$$

If the new axes x_i' are chosen by a rotation about the origin for which the transformation matrix is

$$a_{ij} = \begin{bmatrix} 3/5 & 0 & -4/5 \\ 0 & 1 & 0 \\ 4/5 & 0 & 3/5 \end{bmatrix}$$

determine the traction vectors on each of the primed coordinate planes by projecting the traction vectors of the original axes onto the primed directions. Determine the stress deviator components σ_{ij}'. Verify your result using the transformation relation (consult Appendix A).

1.4 DEFORMATION AND STRAIN

All engineering materials when subjected to external loading may undergo deformation and/or motion. While section 1.3 considers the nature of loads applied to a body, the present section treats the kinematics of deformation and the various measures of strain. Thus, in this section, the relationships between the initial positions of the material points of the continuum and their subsequent positions are considered without taking into consideration the type of material that we are dealing with or the imposed boundary conditions.

1.4.1 Lagrangian and Eulerian descriptions

In studying the motion of a continuous medium, we fix our attention on a single material point with which we associate the geometry of a mathematical Euclidean point and study its path (trajectory). Such trajectory can be established by determining the position vector $\mathbf{p}$ of the point at time t that was initially at position characterized by a position vector $\mathbf{P}$ at time $t = 0$ (Fig. 1.6).

This can be expressed with reference to the Cartesian coordinate system shown in Fig. 1.6 as

$$\mathbf{P} = X_I \mathbf{e}_I, \quad \mathbf{p} = X_i \mathbf{e}_i \tag{1.50}$$

where X_I are the values of the rectangular Cartesian components of the position vector $\mathbf{P}$, i.e. at time $t = 0$ (the initial position) corresponding to a current position coordinates x_i at time t. In (1.50), $\mathbf{e}_I$ and $\mathbf{e}_i$ are the components of the unit base vectors associated with the rectangular Cartesian frames of reference in the undeformed and deformed states, respectively. We have used majuscules to identify

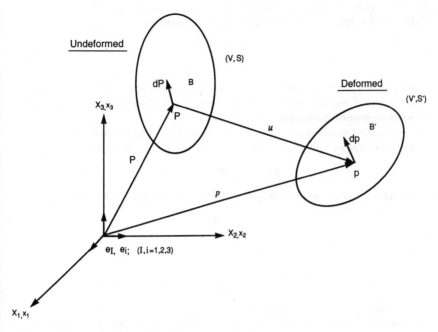

Fig. 1.6 Deformation kinematics of a continuous body.

the undeformed configuration X_I ($I = 1, 2, 3$) and minuscules to designate the deformed configuration x_i ($i = 1, 2, 3$). Hence, the identity of the material point is X_I and its subsequent motion is described by

$$x_i = x_i (X_I, t), \ X_I = X_I (x_i, t). \tag{1.51}$$

The X_I coordinates are known in continuum mechanics by the **material** or **Lagrangian** description while the x_i coordinates are called the **spatial** or **Eulerian** description. Equation (1.51) expresses the evolution of the deformation process in the body as a function of time. From a continuum mechanics point of view, the functions $x_i (X_I, t)$ are single-valued continuous functions whose Jacobian of transformation does not vanish, namely

$$J = |x_{i,I}| = \tfrac{1}{6}\varepsilon_{ILM}\varepsilon_{ilm}x_{i,I}x_{l,L}x_{m,M} \neq 0 \tag{1.52}$$

where ε_{ILM}, ε_{ilm} are the alternating tensors. Equation (1.52) expresses the form of the implicit function theorem of calculus. It is a basic relation for securing the axiom of continuity in continuum mechanics. It points out the fact that the matter is indestructible, i.e. no region of positive, finite volume of matter may be deformed into a zero or an infinite volume. Another axiom secured by this equation is that the matter is impenetrable, that is the motion carries every region into a region, every surface into a surface and every curve into a curve.

With reference to Fig. 1.6, one may also consider a line element d**P** deformed into d**p**. The two line elements are expressed, respectively, by

$$d\mathbf{P} = \mathbf{e}_I \, dX_I = \mathbf{e}_I X_{I,i} \, dx_i,$$
$$d\mathbf{p} = \mathbf{e}_i \, dx_i = \mathbf{e}_i x_{i,I} \, dX_I. \tag{1.53}$$

In equations (1.53), $X_{I,i}$ and $x_{i,I}$ are the deformation gradients referred, respectively, to the spatial and material coordinates. These deformation gradients are the most **'basic or primitive measures of strain'**.

Alternative measures of strain can be expressed from the definition of the square of the line element. Thus, in the undeformed configuration (Fig. 1.6),

$$dS^2 = d\mathbf{P} \cdot d\mathbf{P} = dX_K \, dX_K.$$

The above equation can be written, using the chain rule of partial differentiation, as

$$dS^2 = X_{K,j} X_{K,i} \, dx_j \, dx_i$$
$$= c_{ji} \, dx_j \, dx_i \tag{1.54}$$

where

$$c_{ji} = X_{K,j} X_{K,i}$$

is known as the 'Cauchy deformation tensor'.

Similarly, one may express, with reference to Fig. 1.6, the square of the line element in the deformed configuration as

$$ds^2 = d\mathbf{p} \cdot d\mathbf{p} = dx_k \, dx_k = x_{k,J} x_{k,I} \, dX_J \, dX_I$$
$$= C_{JI} \, dX_J \, dX_I$$

where

$$C_{JI} = x_{k,J} x_{k,I} \tag{1.55}$$

is referred to as the 'Green deformation tensor'.

Both c_{ji} and C_{JI} are symmetric and positive definite. They can be shown to be tensors.

Alternatively, one may consider that the difference between ds^2 and dS^2 to be a measure of strain. Thus,

$$ds^2 - dS^2 = dx_i \, dx_i - dX_L \, dX_L$$
$$= C_{KL} \, dX_K \, dX_L - \delta_{KL} \, dX_K \, dX_L$$
$$= (C_{KL} - \delta_{KL}) \, dX_K \, dX_L$$
$$= 2E_{KL} \, dX_K \, dX_L$$

where relation (1.55) is used and

$$E_{KL} = \tfrac{1}{2}(C_{KL} - \delta_{KL}) \tag{1.56}$$

is the **'material or Lagrangian strain tensor'**.

Similarly,

$$ds^2 - dS^2 = dx_i\, dx_i - dX_L\, dX_L$$
$$= \delta_{ij}\, dx_i\, dx_j - c_{ij}\, dx_i\, dx_j$$
$$= (\delta_{ij} - c_{ij})\, dx_i\, dx_j$$
$$= 2\varepsilon_{ij}\, dx_i\, dx_j$$

where relation (1.54) is used and

$$\varepsilon_{ij} = \tfrac{1}{2}(\delta_{ij} - c_{ij}) \tag{1.57}$$

is the '**spatial or Eulerian strain tensor**'. It can be shown that E_{KL} and ε_{kl} are related

$$E_{KL} = \varepsilon_{kl}\, x_{k,K}\, x_{l,L}$$

and

$$\varepsilon_{kl} = E_{KL}\, X_{K,k}\, X_{L,l}. \tag{1.58}$$

The reader may find it of interest to prove the validity of the two expressions (1.58).

With reference to Fig. 1.6, one may write the following relation:

$$\mathbf{p} = \mathbf{P} + \mathbf{u}$$

or

$$x_i\mathbf{e}_i = X_K\mathbf{e}_K + u_K\mathbf{e}_K$$

and

$$dx_i\, \mathbf{e}_i = dX_K\, \mathbf{e}_K + u_{K,L}\, dX_L\, \mathbf{e}_K$$
$$= (\delta_{KL} + u_{K,L})\, dX_L\, \mathbf{e}_K.$$

Hence

$$dS^2 = dx_i\, dx_i = (\delta_{KL} + u_{K,L})(\delta_{KM} + u_{K,M})\, dX_L\, dX_M.$$

Now, if we choose $ds^2 - dS^2$ as a measure of strain, it can be shown that

$$ds^2 - dS^2 = (u_{M,L} + u_{L,M} + u_{K,L}u_{K,M})\, dX_L\, dX_M$$
$$= 2E_{LM}\, dX_L\, dX_M$$

where

$$E_{LM} = \tfrac{1}{2}(u_{M,L} + u_{L,M} + u_{K,L}u_{K,M}) \tag{1.59}$$

is an alternative expression for the material or Lagrangian strain tensor expressed previously by (1.56).

One may also choose, with reference to Fig. 1.6, the formulation

$$\mathbf{P} = \mathbf{p} - \mathbf{u},$$

i.e.

$$X_I e_I = x_k e_k - u_k e_k$$

and

$$dX_I e_I = dx_k e_k - u_{k,l} \, dx_l \, e_k$$
$$= (\delta_{kl} - u_{k,l}) \, dx_l \, e_k.$$

Thus

$$dS^2 = dX_I \, dX_I = (\delta_{kl} - u_{k,l})(\delta_{km} - u_{k,m}) \, dx_l \, dx_m$$
$$= (\delta_{lm} - u_{m,l} - u_{l,m} + u_{k,l} u_{k,m}) \, dx_l \, dx_m$$

and one can show that

$$ds^2 - dS^2 = (u_{m,l} + u_{l,m} - u_{k,l} u_{k,m}) \, dx_l \, dx_m$$
$$= 2\varepsilon_{lm} \, dx_l \, dx_m$$

where

$$\varepsilon_{lm} = \tfrac{1}{2}(u_{m,l} + u_{l,m} - u_{k,l} u_{k,m}) \qquad (1.60)$$

is another expression for the spatial or Eulerian strain tensor given earlier by equation (1.57). Similar to the stress tensor, both the Lagrangian strain tensor and the Eulerian strain tensor are symmetric tensors; hence, each has only six independent components in a three-dimensional space.

1.4.2 Infinitesimal strain and rotation

We considered in the foregoing the formulations of the three-dimensional nonlinear measures of strain as based only on the implications of assumed continuity. In this section, we introduce some of the simplifying assumptions in the theory of continuum mechanics with the aim of reducing the complexity of mathematics which otherwise would be involved. The definitions of infinitesimal strains and rotations depend upon the following two assumptions:

1. that the occurring deformations u_i (x_k, t) or u_I (X_K, t) are much smaller than the least dimension of the free body under consideration;
2. that the deformation gradient $u_{i,j}$ or $u_{I,J} \ll 1$.

Recall the expression of nonlinear measure of strain given by equation (1.59), that is

$$E_{IJ} = \tfrac{1}{2}(u_{I,J} + u_{J,I} + u_{K,I} u_{K,J}) \qquad (1.61)$$

This expression becomes the infinitesimal or linear Lagrangian (material) strain tensor $\hat{E}_{IJ}$ on requiring the nonlinear term in it to be zero, i.e.

$$u_{K,I} \, u_{K,J} = 0.$$

Accordingly

$$\hat{E}_{IJ} = \tfrac{1}{2}(u_{I,J} + u_{J,I}) = u_{(I,J)} \tag{1.62}$$

is the infinitesimal Lagrangian strain tensor. It is apparent from the above expression that $\hat{E}_{IJ}$ represents the symmetric portion of the tensor $u_{I,J}$. This is indicated in (1.62) by $u_{(I,J)}$ following our notations in Appendix A.

Introducing the Lagrangian infinitesimal rotation tensor

$$\hat{\Omega}_{IJ} = \tfrac{1}{2}(u_{I,J} - u_{J,I}) = u_{[I,J]} \tag{1.63}$$

where $u_{[I,J]}$ is the skew-symmetric portion of $u_{I,J}$. Thus,

$$u_{I,J} = \hat{E}_{IJ} + \hat{\Omega}_{IJ} = u_{(I,J)} + u_{[I,J]}. \tag{1.64}$$

Repeating the same procedure for the infinitesimal or linear Eulerian strain tensor, then, with reference to (1.60),

$$\hat{\varepsilon}_{lm} = \tfrac{1}{2}(u_{l,m} + u_{m,l}) = u_{(l,m)} \tag{1.65}$$

where

$$u_{l,m} = \hat{\varepsilon}_{lm} + \hat{\omega}_{lm} \tag{1.66}$$

and

$$\hat{\omega}_{lm} = \tfrac{1}{2}(u_{l,m} - u_{m,l}) = u_{[l,m]} \tag{1.67}$$

is the infinitesimal Eulerian rotation tensor, which is skew-symmetric (Appendix A).

In three dimensions, it is possible to express a dual vector $\boldsymbol{\omega}$: ω_k in terms of the skew-symmetric tensor $\hat{\omega}_{ij}$. That is

$$\omega_k = \tfrac{1}{2}\varepsilon_{kij}\hat{\omega}_{ij}$$

or

$$\boldsymbol{\omega} = \tfrac{1}{2}\,\text{curl }\mathbf{u} \tag{1.68}$$

where ε_{kij} is the alternating tensor.

At the same time, since $\hat{\omega}_{ij}$ is antisymmetric, it can be shown that (1.68) has a unique inverse, i.e.

$$\hat{\omega}_{ij} = \varepsilon_{ijk}\omega_k. \tag{1.69}$$

Hence, $\hat{\omega}_{ij}$ may be called the dual tensor of a vector ω_k. The latter vector is referred to as the rotation vector of the displacement field u_i.

1.4.3 Equivalence between infinitesimal Lagrangian strain and infinitesimal Eulerian strain

With reference to Fig. 1.6, the deformation vector $\mathbf{u}$ can be expressed as

$$\mathbf{u} = \mathbf{p} - \mathbf{P}$$

which results in the expression

$$u_{i,j} = \delta_{ij} - X_{I,J} \tag{1.70}$$

or, alternatively,

$$u_{I,j} = \delta_{ij} - X_{I,j}. \tag{1.71}$$

Thus, with reference to (1.70) and (1.71), one can write

$$u_{i,j} = u_{I,j} = u_{I,K}X_{K,j}$$

$$= u_{I,K}(\delta_{KJ} - u_{k,j})$$

$$= u_{I,J} - u_{I,J}u_{k,j}$$

which can be approximated, by neglecting the nonlinear term, as

$$u_{i,j} = u_{I,j} = u_{I,J}.$$

That is, within the framework of linear strains expressed by equations (1.62) and (1.65),

$$\hat{\varepsilon}_{kl} = \hat{E}_{KL}. \tag{1.72}$$

At this point, it should be emphasized that both $\hat{\varepsilon}_{kl}$ and $\hat{E}_{KL}$ cannot be considered as strain measures and they are, in fact, only approximations of strain measures within the context of the infinitesimal strain theory. Following (1.72), we shall use in the remaining chapters of the book, the notation ε_{ij} to denote the infinitesimal strain, i.e.

$$\varepsilon_{ij} = \tfrac{1}{2}(u_{i,j} + u_{j,i}) \tag{1.73}$$

unless otherwise mentioned.

1.4.4 Principal strains, principal directions and strain invariants

In section 1.3.6, we considered the treatment of an eigenvalue problem to determine the principal values of stress, principal directions and the three invariants appearing in equation (1.34). This procedure applies to every symmetric second-order tensor. Hence, on following the same analysis, it can be shown that the invariants of the strain tensor are expressed by

$$II_1 = \varepsilon_{11} + \varepsilon_{22} + \varepsilon_{33} = \varepsilon_{kk}, \tag{1.74a}$$

$$II_2 = \tfrac{1}{2}(\varepsilon_{ij}\varepsilon_{ij} - \varepsilon_{ii}\varepsilon_{jj})$$

$$= -(\varepsilon_{11}\varepsilon_{22} + \varepsilon_{22}\varepsilon_{33} + \varepsilon_{33}\varepsilon_{11}) + \varepsilon_{23}^2 + \varepsilon_{31}^2 + \varepsilon_{12}^2 \tag{1.74b}$$

and

$$II_3 = \begin{vmatrix} \varepsilon_{11} & \varepsilon_{12} & \varepsilon_{13} \\ \varepsilon_{21} & \varepsilon_{22} & \varepsilon_{23} \\ \varepsilon_{31} & \varepsilon_{32} & \varepsilon_{33} \end{vmatrix} = \det \varepsilon_{ij}$$

$$= \tfrac{1}{6}\varepsilon_{ijk}\varepsilon_{pqr}\varepsilon_{ip}\varepsilon_{jq}\varepsilon_{kr}.$$

The first strain invariant II_1 has a simple geometrical meaning in the case of infinitesimal strain. It represents the change in volume per unit volume, i.e.

$$II_1 = \Delta V / V = \varepsilon_{kk}. \qquad (1.75)$$

For this reason, ε_{kk} is called the cubical dilatation. If a two-dimensional state (plane strain) is considered, the first invariant represents the change of area per unit area of the surface under strain. In the definition of finite strain, the sum of principal strains does not have such a simple interpretation.

Whereas in our analysis of the stress, section 1.3, we have only dealt with one definition of the stress, we have encountered, here, five different measures of strain. The invariants of the latter are interrelated in terms of algebraic relations of each other. The reader is referred, in this context, to relevant texts in continuum mechanics (as in the list of further reading at the end of this chapter).

1.4.5 Compatibility conditions

We deal now with the problem of determining the displacement components u_i when the strain components are known. Consider, for the simplification of presentation, the expression of linear strain as presented by (1.73), i.e.

$$\varepsilon_{ij} = \tfrac{1}{2}(u_{i,j} + u_{j,i}). \qquad (1.76)$$

The problem is how one would integrate the differential equation (1.76) to determine the components u_i.

Since we have six equations corresponding to the six independent components of ε_{ij} for three unknown functions u_i, the system of equation (1.76) will not have a single-valued solution in general if the functions ε_{ij} were arbitrarily assigned. However, we would expect that a solution for this equation may exist only if the functions ε_{ij} satisfy certain conditions. The conditions of integrability of (1.76) are referred to as the compatibility conditions. The latter are to be satisfied by the strain components and may be determined by eliminating the components u_i from (1.76).

Differentiating (1.76) twice with respect to the coordinates, it follows that

$$\varepsilon_{ij,kl} = \tfrac{1}{2}(u_{i,jkl} + u_{j,ikl}). \qquad (1.77)$$

We interchange subscripts in the above relation, i.e.

$$\varepsilon_{kl,ij} = \tfrac{1}{2}(u_{k,lij} + u_{l,kij}),$$
$$\varepsilon_{jl,ik} = \tfrac{1}{2}(u_{j,lik} + u_{l,jik}), \qquad (1.78)$$
$$\varepsilon_{ik,jl} = \tfrac{1}{2}(u_{i,kjl} + u_{k,ijl}).$$

This leads to the following restriction specifying the compatibility conditions:

$$\varepsilon_{ij,kl} + \varepsilon_{kl,ij} - \varepsilon_{ik,jl} - \varepsilon_{jl,ik} = 0. \qquad (1.79)$$

Equation (1.79) was first obtained by St. Venant in 1860 and is named after him. This equation represents 81 equations of which six only are essential. The remaining equations are repetitions owing to the symmetry of the strain tensor. The six compatibility equations are independent and may be expressed in an uncondensed notation as

$$\frac{\partial^2 \varepsilon_{11}}{\partial x_2^2} + \frac{\partial^2 \varepsilon_{22}}{\partial x_1^2} - 2\frac{\partial^2 \varepsilon_{12}}{\partial x_1 \partial x_2} = 0,$$

$$\frac{\partial^2 \varepsilon_{22}}{\partial x_3^2} + \frac{\partial^2 \varepsilon_{33}}{\partial x_2^2} - 2\frac{\partial^2 \varepsilon_{23}}{\partial x_2 \partial x_3} = 0, \qquad (1.80)$$

$$\frac{\partial^2 \varepsilon_{33}}{\partial x_1^2} + \frac{\partial^2 \varepsilon_{11}}{\partial x_3^2} - 2\frac{\partial^2 \varepsilon_{31}}{\partial x_3 \partial x_1} = 0,$$

and

$$\frac{-\partial^2 \varepsilon_{11}}{\partial x_2 \partial x_3} + \frac{\partial}{\partial x_1}\left(-\frac{\partial \varepsilon_{23}}{\partial x_1} + \frac{\partial \varepsilon_{31}}{\partial x_2} + \frac{\partial \varepsilon_{12}}{\partial x_3}\right) = 0,$$

$$\frac{-\partial^2 \varepsilon_{22}}{\partial x_3 \partial x_1} + \frac{\partial}{\partial x_2}\left(\frac{\partial \varepsilon_{23}}{\partial x_1} - \frac{\partial \varepsilon_{31}}{\partial x_2} + \frac{\partial \varepsilon_{12}}{\partial x_3}\right) = 0,$$

$$\frac{-\partial^2 \varepsilon_{33}}{\partial x_1 \partial x_2} + \frac{\partial}{\partial x_3}\left(\frac{\partial \varepsilon_{23}}{\partial x_1} + \frac{\partial \varepsilon_{31}}{\partial x_2} - \frac{\partial \varepsilon_{12}}{\partial x_3}\right) = 0.$$

In the solution of a boundary value problem, within the realm of continuum mechanics, if the displacement field is unknown and the displacement components u_i are required to be continuous and single-valued functions of the coordinates, the compatibility requirement would then be fulfilled. On the other hand, if the displacements are not explicitly retained as unknowns, the compatibility conditions must then be imposed on the strain field to ensure that there exists a continuous single-valued displacement distribution corresponding to the strain distribution.

PROBLEMS

1.5 The vector $t_i = \varepsilon_{ijk}T_{jk}$ is called a 'dual vector' of the tensor T_{jk}. Show that, if the dual vector vanishes, the tensor is symmetric.

1.6 Show that the strain tensor, using the Eulerian approach, is given by

$$\varepsilon_{jk} = \tfrac{1}{2}(u_{j,k} + u_{k,j} - u_{i,j}u_{i,k}).$$

Compare with the Lagrangian strain tensor and show why no distinction between the two is necessary in the case of small displacement theory.

1.7 Show that the large deformation strain is given by

$$\varepsilon_L = \varepsilon_{ij}\, l_i\, l_j$$

where

$$\varepsilon_L = \frac{ds - dS}{dS}$$

and

$$l_i = \frac{dx_i}{dS}.$$

1.8 The most general form of a linear relationship between the stress and strain components of an elastic isotropic solid is represented by the generalized Hooke's law as follows:

$$\sigma_{ij} = A_{ijkl}\, \varepsilon_{kl}.$$

Prove that the elastic constants are the components of a Cartesian tensor of the fourth order (consult Appendix A).

1.9 Assume that the strain tensor is given as

$$\begin{bmatrix} 2 & 3 & 2 \\ 3 & 2 & 1 \\ 2 & 1 & 2.5 \end{bmatrix}.$$

Determine the principal strains and corresponding principal directions.

1.10 Let a_i be the original direction cosines of an 'undeformed' line element dS in a solid and a_j^* be the final direction cosines of the 'deformed' element ds. Show that

$$a_j^* = \frac{(\delta_{jk} + u_{j,k})a_k}{(1 + \varepsilon_L)^{1/2}}$$

where

$$\varepsilon_L = \frac{ds - dS}{dS}.$$

Show also that the rotation of a line element can be written as

$$\omega_i = \tfrac{1}{2}\, \text{curl}\, u_i = \tfrac{1}{2}\varepsilon_{ijk}(\partial_j u_k - \partial_k u_j).$$

1.11 Find

1. the Green strain tensor C_{KL},
2. the Cauchy strain tensor c_{kl},
3. the Lagrangian strain tensor E_{KL},
4. the Eulerian strain tensor ε_{kl} and
5. the infinitesimal strain tensor

for the following two displacement fields:

• simple extension

$$z_1 = (1 + \varepsilon)\, Z_1, \quad z_2 = Z_2, \quad z_3 = Z_3;$$

● simple shear

$$z_1 = Z_1 + KZ_2, \quad z_2 = Z_2, \quad z_3 = Z_3.$$

1.12 The displacement field of a body is described by

$$u_i = A\,\frac{z_1 z_3}{r^3}, \ u_2 = A\,\frac{z_2 z_3}{r^3}, \ u_3 = A\!\left(\frac{z_3^2}{r^3} + \frac{\lambda + 3\mu}{\lambda + \mu}\frac{1}{r}\right),$$

where $r = (z_i z_i)^{1/2}$ and A, λ and μ are constants.

1. Determine the infinitesimal strains ε_{kl} and rotations ω_{kl}.
2. Sketch the deformed shape of a spherical cavity $r = r_0$.
3. Determine the principal strains.
4. Determine the principal axes.

1.5 CONSTITUTIVE RELATIONS

Different materials of the same geometry may respond differently under identical external effects. Such a difference in response is often attributed to the inherent constitution of the material. Consequently, the response behaviour of a particular material, or of a class of such materials, is described mathematically by so-called 'constitutive relations'. These constitutive equations define the response behaviour of idealized media within a specific range of external effects. Accordingly, they only approximate the response characteristics of real materials. In general terms, constitutive relations establish the connection between the stimuli acting on the material specimen and the evolution of the occurring response. In the majority of situations, the stimuli are the external forces, or the stresses caused by them, and the evolution of the response is expressed by the histories of both the deformation, or the calculated strain, and the temperature. In a continuum mechanics sense, a general form of a constitutive equation may be expressed as (Hunter, 1976)

$$\sigma_{ij} = f_{ij} \text{ (history of deformation, history of temperature)} \qquad (1.81)$$

where σ_{ij} is the stress tensor and f_{ij} are the components of a second-order tensorial response function. In view of the form of the constitutive equation (1.81), continuum mechanics constitutive formulations are deterministic and the science of continuum mechanics itself is a branch of classical deterministic physics.

The constitutive relations of different classes of engineering materials are particular forms of (1.81). For elastic materials, for instance, the stress tensor σ_{ij} is a function of the current strain and temperature. In case of viscoelastic materials, as will be seen in the following chapters, constitutive equations should account for the time history of the deformation process and that of the temperature. Hence, constitutive equations for viscoelastic materials, in general, are of the form of equation (1.81). In this equation, the choice of the independent variables pertaining to f_{ij} is usually guided by the experimental results but, in most situations, this choice is restricted by a number of physical principles. In this context, a properly formulated constitutive equation must satisfy certain invariance principles (Eringen, 1962, 1967; Hunter, 1976) as follows.

1. The constitutive relation is invariant with respect to different stationary coordinate systems. This requirement is readily satisfied by expressing the constitutive law in tensorial form.
2. The constitutive relation is invariant with respect to coordinate systems in an arbitrary relative motion. This condition is usually dealt with within the context of 'material frame indifference' (Hunter, 1976). This is translated into the requirement that the transformation law relating the components of the tensorial function f_{ij} in different coordinate frames in relative motion is exactly the same as the ordinary tensor transformation law.

Conformity of the form of the constitutive relation to the invariance requirements mentioned above together with the assumption of isotropy of the continuous body impose restrictions on the form of (1.81) and lead to explicit forms of constitutive equations for particular materials under specific conditions. The material functions or parameters characterizing the explicit form of the constitutive relation would be then characteristic of the particular material under consideration.

REFERENCES

Cauchy, A. L. (1827) De la pression ou tension dans un corps solide, in *Exercices de Mathématique* (see Love (1944, pp. 8–9)).
Cauchy, A. L. (1828) Sur les équations qui expriment les conditions d'équilibre ou les lois de mouvement intérieur d'un corps solide, in *Exercices de Mathématique* (see Love (1944, pp. 8–9)).
Eringen, A. C. (1962) *Nonlinear Theory of Continuous Media*, McGraw-Hill, New York.
Eringen, A. C. (1967) *Mechanics of Continua*, Wiley, New York.
Flügge, W. (1972) *Tensor Analysis and Continuum Mechanics*, Springer, Berlin.
Fung, Y. C. (1965) *Foundations of Solid Mechanics*, Prentice-Hall, Englewood Cliffs, NJ.
Hunter, S. C. (1976) *Mechanics of Continuous Media*, Ellis Horwood, Chichester.
Malvern, L. E. (1969) *Introduction to the Mechanics of a Continuous Medium*, Prentice-Hall, Englewood Cliffs, NJ.
Truesdell, C. and Toupin, R. A. (1960) The classical field theories, in *Handbuck du Physik*, Vol. III/1 (ed. S. Flügge), Springer, Berlin.

FURTHER READING

Bowen, R. M. (1989). *Introduction to Continuum Mechanics for Engineers*, Plenum, New York.
Chung, T. J. (1988) *Continuum Mechanics*, Prentice-Hall, Englewood Cliffs, NJ.
Coleman, B. D. and Noll, W. (1960) An approximation theorem for functionals with applications in continuum mechanics. *Arch. Ration. Mech. Anal.*, **6**, 355–70.
Davis, J. L. (1987) *Introduction to Dynamics of Continuous Media*, Macmillan, New York.
Fredrick, D. and Chang, T. S. (1965) *Continuum Mechanics*, Allyn and Bacon, Boston, MA.
Green, A. E. and Adkins, J. E. (1960) *Large Elastic Deformations and Nonlinear Continuum Mechanics*, Clarendon, Oxford.

32   *Continuum mechanics background*

Gurtin, M. E. (1981) *An Introduction to Continuum Mechanics*, Academic Press, New York.
Gurtin, M. E. and Williams, W. O. (1967) An axiomatic foundation for continuum thermodynamics. *Arch. Ration. Mech. Anal.*, **26**, 83–117.
Jaunzemis, W. (1967) *Continuum Mechanics*, Macmillan, New York.
Jessop, H. T. (1950) The determination of the principal stress differences at a point in a three-dimensional photoelastic model. *Br. J. Appl. Phys.*, **1**, 184–9.
Lai, W. M., Rubin, D. and Krempl, E. (1978) *Introduction to Continuum Mechanics (SI/Metric Units)*, Pergamon, New York.
Leigh, D. C. (1968) *Nonlinear Continuum Mechanics*, McGraw-Hill, New York.
Love, A. E. H. (1944) *A Treatise on the Mathematical Theory of Elasticity*, 4th edn, Dover Publications, New York.
Mindlin, R. D. and Tiersten, H. F. (1962) Effect of couple-stresses in linear elasticity. *Arch. Ration. Mech. Anal.*, **11**, 415–48.
Noll, W. (1958) A mathematical theory of the mechanical behaviour of continuous media. *Arch. Ration. Mech. Anal.*, **2**, 197–226.
Prager, W. (1961) *Introduction to Mechanics of Continua*, Ginn, Boston, MA.
Sneddon, I. N. and Hill, R. (eds.) (1960–1963) *Progress in Solid Mechanics*, Vol. 1 (1960), Vol. 2 (1961), Vol. 3 (1963), Vol. 4 (1963), North-Holland, Amsterdam.
Sommerfeld, A. (1950) *Mechanics of Deformable Bodies*, Academic Press, New York.
Truesdell, C. (1965a) The nonlinear field theories of mechanics, in *Encyclopedia of Physics*, Vol. III/3 (ed. S. Flügge), Springer, Berlin.
Truesdell, C. (1965b) *The Elements of Continuum Mechanics*, Springer, New York.
Washizu, K. (1958) A note on the condition of compatability. *J. Math. Phys.*, **36**, 306–12.
Williams, .W. O. (1970) Thermodynamics of rigid continua. *Arch. Ration. Mech. Anal.*, **36**, 270–84.

2

Linear viscoelasticity

2.1 INTRODUCTION

As discussed in the introduction of this book, many engineering materials such as polymeric and rubberlike materials, and metals at elevated temperatures, flow when subjected to stress or strain. Such flow is accompanied by the dissipation of energy due to some internal loss mechanism (for example, bond breakage and bond formation reaction, dislocations, formation of substructures in metals). Materials of this type are 'viscoelastic' in response. The description 'viscoelastic' is due to the fact that such materials exhibit both 'elastic' and 'viscous' properties. Figure 2.1 illustrates the differences in strain response of elastic, viscous and viscoelastic specimens when the three specimens are subjected to a constant stress of unit magnitude. The stress is applied at time $t = 0$ to undisturbed specimens and maintained constant for time duration t_1 (Fig. 2.1(a)). As shown in Fig. 2.1(b), the strain–time response of the elastic specimen has the same form as the applied stress. On application of the load, the strain reaches instantaneously a certain level ε_0 and then remains constant. For the viscous fluid (Fig. 2.1(c)) the material flows at a constant rate and the strain response is proportional to the time. For the viscoelastic specimen (Fig. 2.1(d)) there is a relatively rapid increase in the strain response for small values of t immediately after the application of the load. As t increases, the slope of the curve decreases and, as $t \to \infty$, the slope may approach zero or finite value provided that the applied stress maintained is constant.

On removal of the load at time t_1, the strains in the three specimens will recover in the manners shown in Fig. 2.1. The perfectly elastic solid will recover instantaneously on removal of the load (Fig. 2.1(b)), but the viscous fluid will not recover (Fig. 2.1(c)). Meantime, on removal of the load, the viscoelastic specimen will recover immediately its elastic deformation; however, the retarded part of the response will require time for recovery.

Under constant stress, the creep strain in a viscoelastic material may be divided, with reference to Fig. 2.2, into the following three components (e.g. Lethersich, 1950).

1. Instantaneous (immediate) elastic strain $\varepsilon_e(0^+)$. In a polymeric material, for instance, this part of the strain is attributable to bond stretching and bending including the

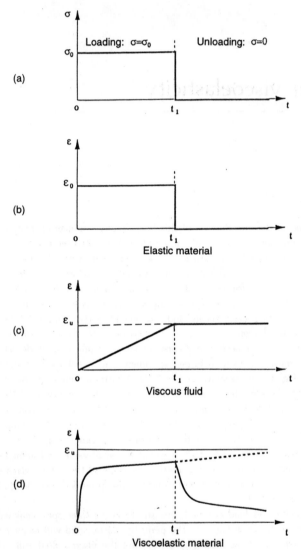

Fig. 2.1 Comparison of strain response for elastic, viscous and viscoelastic material specimens under constant stress of unit magnitude until time t_1.

deformation of weak Van der Waals bonds between the molecular chains. This strain is reversible and disappears on removal of the stress.

2. Delayed elastic strain $\varepsilon_d(t)$. The rate of increase of this part of strain decreases steadily with time. It is also elastic, but, after the removal of the load, it requires

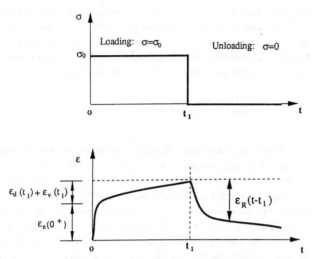

Fig. 2.2 Creep and recovery of a viscoelastic material specimen subjected to a constant stress of unit magnitude until time t_1.

time for complete recovery. It is often called 'primary creep' or 'elastic aftereffect', among other terms. In a polymeric material, the delayed elastic strain is attributable to, for instance, chain uncoiling.
3. Viscous flow $\varepsilon_v(t)$. It is an irreversible component of strain which may or may not increase linearly with time of stress application. In a polymeric substance, it is characteristic of interchain slipping. It is often referred to as 'secondary creep' or 'nonrecoverable strain'.

On unloading the viscoelastic specimen at t_1, the instantaneous elastic response recovers immediately and the delayed elastic response recovers gradually, but the viscous flow remains (e.g. Ward, 1983).

From a phenomenological point of view, two aspects of viscoelastic behaviour are dealt with, i.e. creep response under constant stress and stress-relaxation response under constant strain. As will be dealt with later in this chapter, the correlation between these two aspects of response constitutes an important characteristic of the development of the linear viscoelasticity theory.

2.1.1 Creep response (under constant stress)

In a simple creep experiment, the undisturbed material specimen is subjected initially, at time $t = 0$, to a stress $\sigma_0 = \sigma(0^+)$ which is maintained constant during the experiment; meanwhile, the time-dependent strain $\varepsilon(t)$ is observed. In the linear viscoelastic case, the creep response follows, in general, the pattern discussed above in conjunction with Figs 2.1(d) and 2.2. In this case, the total creep strain can be considered to be the sum of the three separate parts $\varepsilon_e(0^+)$, $\varepsilon_d(t)$, and $\varepsilon_v(t)$ mentioned earlier. Further, the magnitudes of these individual parts of the strain are proportional to the magnitude of the stress input. Accordingly, a creep compliance function $F(t)$, which is a function of time only, may be defined, in the linear viscoelastic case, as

$$F(t) = \frac{\varepsilon(t)}{\sigma(0^+)} = F_e(0^+) + F_d(t) + F_v(t). \tag{2.1}$$

In the above relation, the compliance function $F_v(t)$ which defines the Newtonian flow can be neglected for solid materials with large flow viscosities, e.g. rigid polymers at ordinary temperatures. Linear amorphous polymers, on the other hand, would demonstrate a finite $F_v(t)$ at temperatures above their glass transitions. However, at low temperatures, the viscoelastic behaviour of the latter polymers may be influenced only by the compliances $F_e(t)$ and $F_d(t)$. The same could be valid for the case of high linked polymers and, to a reasonable approximation, in the case of highly crystalline polymers. In general, the separation of the creep compliance $F(t)$, for a particular material at any given temperature, into the compliances $F_e(0^+)$, $F_d(t)$ and $F_v(t)$ may not be an easy task and could involve arbitrary division.

2.1.2 Creep and recovery

With reference to Fig. 2.2, consider the case where the stress σ_0 is applied to an undisturbed specimen at time $t = 0$ and removed at time $t = t_1$. Thus, on the assumption of linear viscoelastic behaviour, the total creep strain $\varepsilon(t)$ at any instant of time $t > t_1$ is given by the superposition of the two individual strains, i.e. $\varepsilon_e = \sigma_0 F(t)$ corresponding to loading the specimen at $t = 0$ and $\varepsilon_R = -\sigma_0 F(t - t_1)$ corresponding to unloading at $t = t_1$. That is,

$$\varepsilon(t) = \sigma_0 F(t) - \sigma_0 F(t - t_1). \tag{2.2}$$

The recovery strain, $\varepsilon_R(t - t_1)$, is defined as the difference between the anticipated creep under the initial stress and the actual measured creep strain. This is shown in Fig. 2.2. Examples of the creep response and creep recovery of a number of engineering materials are shown in Figs 2.3–2.5.

2.1.3 Stress relaxation (under constant strain)

In a simple stress-relaxation experiment, the material specimen is subjected initially to a constant strain $\varepsilon(t) = \varepsilon(0^+)$ and the time-dependent stress response is observed (Fig. 2.6). As shown in the latter figure for a viscoelastic material, the stress-relaxation response is monotonically decreasing with the time. On the assumption of a linear viscoelastic behaviour, a stress-relaxation modulus, which is a function of time only,

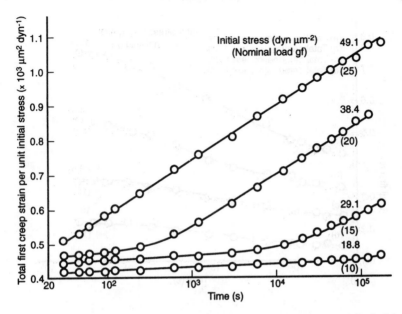

Fig. 2.3 First creep curves reduced in deformation by factors of initial stress. Individual dry summerwood fibres of a longleaf pine pulp after conditioning at 50% RH and 23°C. (Source: Hill, R. L. (1967) The creep behaviour of individual pulp fibres under tensile stress. *Tappi*, **50**(8), 432–40. Reprinted by permission of Tappi.)

is defined as

$$R(t) = \frac{\sigma(t)}{\varepsilon(0^+)}. \tag{2.3}$$

In a stress-relaxation experiment, such as described here, viscous flow affects the limiting value of stress. In the presence of viscous flow, the stress may decay to zero at sufficient long times. On the other hand, if there is no viscous flow, the stress decays to a finite value. This would result in an equilibrium or 'relaxed' modulus $R_\infty = R(\infty)$ at infinite time (e.g. Lockett, 1972; Gittus, 1975). Examples of the stress-relaxation response of a number of materials are given in Figs 2.7–2.9.

The particular nature of the class of viscoelastic materials considered in the above examples proves the existence of a property of 'passive resistance' in such materials. This is in contrast to the instantaneous response and reversibility that usually characterize pure elastic behaviour. This passive resistance is of viscous nature and reflects what is usually called the property of 'hereditary response' of the material. That is, the present state of response depends not only on the present state of loading input but also on previous states. This property is revealed experimentally, in different

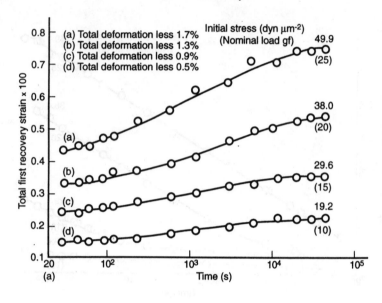

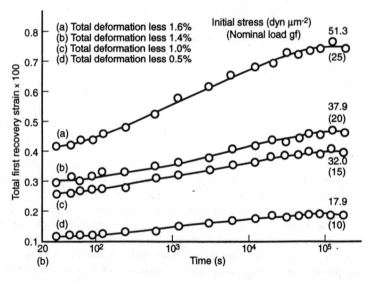

Fig. 2.4 First recovery curves after different time periods of first creep. Individual dry summerwood fibres of a longleaf pine pulp: (a) first recovery after 12 h of first creep; (b) first recovery after 48 h of first creep. (Source: Hill, R. L. (1967) The creep behaviour of individual pulp fibres under tensile stress. *Tappi*, **50**(8), 432–40. Reprinted by permission of Tappi.)

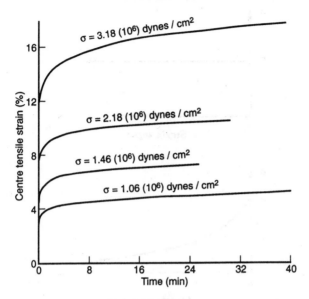

Fig. 2.5 Effect of load on creep of a composite solid propellant at 75°F. (Reprinted with permission from: Blatz, P. J. (1956) Rheology of composite solid propellants. *J. Ind. Eng. Chem.*, **48**(4), 727–9. Copyright (1956) American Chemical Society.)

time-dependent phenomena such as creep, stress relaxation and intrinsic attenuation of propagating waves.

While, in this text, the continuum mechanics approach is maintained primarily for the characterization of the viscoelastic response of materials, it is emphasized that such response is essentially dependent on the effects of a large number of significant microscopic and macroscopic parameters such as those discussed in the introduction of the book and in Chapter 10. Hence, in the present chapter, the presentation is phenomenological and aims at the introduction of the basic formulism of the mechanical response of the linear viscoelastic material. Consequently, the formulations are considered entirely within the context of the infinitesimal linearized deformation theory. Here, as discussed below, the ideas set down by L. Boltzmann (1844–1906) (discussed in Markovitz (1977)) and V. Volterra (1860–1940) are taken as fundamental within the context of linear superposition of input histories (Boltzmann, 1874; Volterra, 1913; Volterra and Peres, 1936; Leaderman, 1943, 1958).

In the present chapter, we confine ourselves to the one-dimensional linear theory of isothermal viscoelasticity under static loading. The transition to the dynamic case is discussed in Chapter 3. Meantime, the generalization to the three-dimensional formulation is dealt with in Chapter 4. The dependence of the viscoelastic performance of engineering materials on the service temperature is treated in Chapter 5. For further studies on the subject of linear viscoelasticity, the reader is referred to the books by

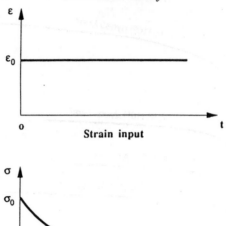

Fig. 2.6 Stress relaxation of a viscoelastic material specimen subjected to constant strain of unit magnitude.

Gross (1953), Eirich (1956, 1957), Bland (1960), Ferry (1961), Christensen (1971), Gittus (1975), Flügge (1975), Tschoegl (1989) and Ward (1983), among others. The technical reviews by Scott-Blair (1949), Lee (1960), Coleman and Noll (1961), Gurtin and Sternberg (1962), Halpin (1968), Leitman and Fisher (1973) and Schapery (1974), among others, must also be mentioned.

2.2 DIFFERENTIAL REPRESENTATION OF LINEAR VISCOELASTIC BEHAVIOUR: MECHANICAL MODELS

The following linear differential relation is often used as a linear viscoelastic constitutive equation connecting the stress to the strain:

$$P\sigma(t) = Q\varepsilon(t) \tag{2.4}$$

where P and Q are linear differential operators with respect to the time t. In a general form, these operators are expressed as

$$P = \sum_{i=0}^{p} a_i \frac{\partial^i}{\partial t^i}$$
$$Q = \sum_{i=0}^{q} b_i \frac{\partial^i}{\partial t^i} \tag{2.5}$$

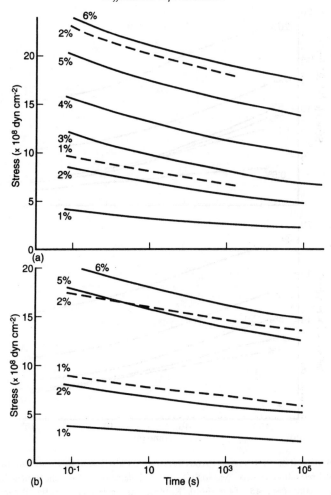

Fig. 2.7 Relaxation of stress in cotton (———) and flax (– – –) at 65% RH and 25°C: (a) first relaxation; (b) fourth relaxation. (Source: Meredith, R. (1954) Relaxation of stress in stretched cellulose fibres. *J. Textile Inst.*, **45**, T438–T460. Reprinted by permission of the British Textile Technology Group.)

where a_i and b_i are material constants. The number of the constants a_i, b_i will depend on the viscoelastic response of the particular material under consideration. By combining (2.4) and (2.5), the former equation is written as

$$a_0 \sigma + a_1 \frac{d\sigma}{dt} + a_2 \frac{d^2\sigma}{dt^2} + \cdots = b_0 \varepsilon + b_1 \frac{d\varepsilon}{dt} + b_2 \frac{d^2\varepsilon}{dt^2} + \cdots. \tag{2.6}$$

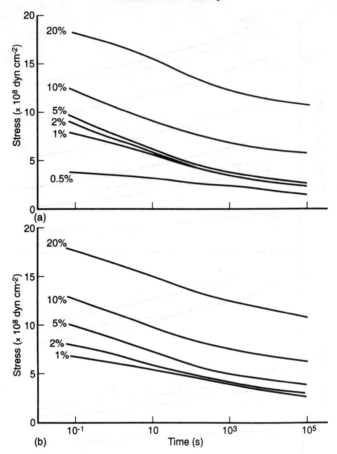

Fig. 2.8 Relaxation of stress in viscous rayon at 65% RH and 20°C: (a) first relaxation; (b) second relaxation. (Source: Meredith, R. (1954) Relaxation of stress in stretched cellulose fibres. *J. Textile Inst.*, **45**, T438–T460. Reprinted by permission of the British Textile Technology Group.)

However, it might be sufficient to represent the viscoelastic response over a limited time scale by considering only one or two terms on each side of (2.6). This would be, then, equivalent to describing the linear viscoelastic behaviour by mechanical models constructed of linear elastic elements, which obey Hooke's law, and viscous dashpots, which obey Newton's law of viscosity. Thus, the viscoelastic behaviour of material, in general, may be investigated by the use of mechanical models which consist of finite networks of springs and dashpots. There are also corresponding electrical models containing resistances and capacitances (or, instead, conductances) which may be used. The invention of mechanical models for the identification of the

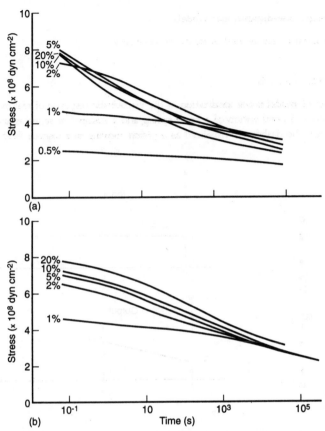

Fig. 2.9 Relaxation of stress in cellulose acetate at 65% RH and 20°C: (a) first relaxation; (b) second relaxation. (Source: Meredith, R. (1954) Relaxation of stress in stretched cellulose fibres. *J. Textile Inst.*, **45**, T438–T460. Reprinted by permission of the British Textile Technology Group.)

viscoelastic responses of materials dates back to the 19th century and coincides with the first introduction of man-made polymers. These models give an indication of the significance of internal parameters of state as represented by the response of the model elements. The presentation below is limited to a number of basic models that are often used. For more information, however, concerning the finite networks of mechanical models for viscoelastic behaviour, the reader is referred, for instance, to Alfrey (1948), Gross (1953), Stuart (1956), Eirich (1956, 1957), Bland (1960), Ferry (1961), Christensen (1971), Flügge (1975) and Gittus (1975).

2.2.1 Single one-dimensional models

Three single mechanical models are dealth with here.

(a) The Maxwell model

The Maxwell model is one idealization of the viscoelastic response of real materials. This model is a combination of a linear spring and a dashpot in series as shown in Fig. 2.10(a). The dashpot is visualized as a piston moving in a viscous fluid. Under

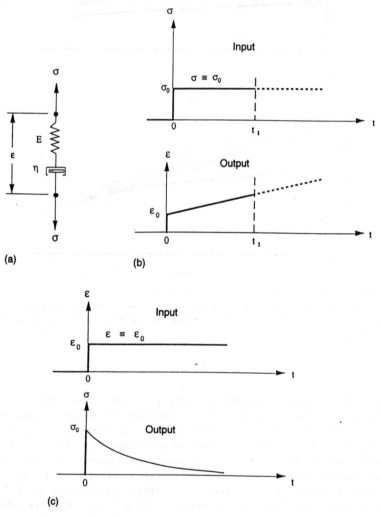

Fig. 2.10 The Maxwell model: (a) the model; (b) creep response; (c) relaxation response.

uniaxial tension, an instantaneous extension of the spring occurs. This is the elastic (Hookean) response of the model. At the same time, the fluid in the dashpot passes slowly through an orifice in the piston resulting in an extension of the overall length of the dashpot. This is a viscous flow which is referred to as the 'time-dependent' response of the Maxwell model. As the spring is in series with the dashpot, the elastic and the viscous strains are additive.

Considering the Maxwell model of Fig. 2.10(a) under uniaxial tension, the following stress–strain relations are obtained: for the spring element 's',

$$\sigma = E\varepsilon_s \tag{2.7}$$

where ε_s is the longitudinal strain displayed by the spring and E is its elastic modulus; for the dashpot

$$\sigma = \eta\dot{\varepsilon}_d \tag{2.8}$$

in which η is the viscosity modulus of the fluid in the dashpot and $\dot{\varepsilon}_d$ is the time rate of the resulting longitudinal strain.

For the spring and dashpot in series (the Maxwell model), the total strain is given by

$$\varepsilon = \varepsilon_s + \varepsilon_d. \tag{2.9}$$

Equation (2.9) can be written, in view of (2.7) and (2.8), in terms of the material properties of the model elements, as

$$\sigma + \lambda\dot{\sigma} = \eta\dot{\varepsilon} \tag{2.10}$$

in which

$$\lambda = \eta/E. \tag{2.11}$$

It is recognized that the response equation (2.10) for the Maxwell model is connected to the differential response relation (2.5) through

$$p = 1, \ a_0 = \frac{1}{\eta}, \ a_1 = \frac{1}{E},$$

$$q = 1, \ b_0 = 0, \ b_1 = 1.$$

In a creep experiment, we apply at $t = 0$ a constant stress $\sigma = \sigma_0$ and we seek the time-dependent creep strain $\varepsilon(t)$. Accordingly, equation (2.10) is a differential equation for ε and has the solution

$$\varepsilon(t) = \frac{\sigma_0}{\eta} t + c \tag{2.12}$$

where c is a constant of integration. The latter can be found subject to the initial condition at $t = 0$, i.e.

$$\varepsilon_0 = \varepsilon(0) = \frac{\sigma_0}{E}, \tag{2.13}$$

which corresponds to the instantaneous elastic response in the spring element. Thus by combining equations (2.12) and (2.13), it follows that

$$c = \varepsilon_0 = \frac{\sigma_0}{E}. \tag{2.14}$$

Utilizing equations (2.12) and (2.14), the creep constitutive equation for the Maxwell model becomes

$$\varepsilon(t) = \frac{\sigma_0}{E}\left(1 + \frac{t}{\lambda}\right) = \sigma_0 F(t), \quad \lambda = \eta/E, \tag{2.15}$$

where $F(t)$ is the creep compliance function or simply the 'creep function' which takes in view of (2.15) for the Maxwell model the form

$$F(t) = E^{-1}(1 + t/\lambda). \tag{2.16}$$

The creep response equation (2.15) is presented in Fig. 2.10(b) for $0 \le t \le t_1$. With reference to this figure, equation (2.15) shows that the instantaneous response at time $t = 0^+$ (i.e. immediately after the application of the load) of the Maxwell model is elastic with a modulus E. The latter is the elastic (or spring) constant. Further, in view of equation (2.15), one can see that the Maxwell model shows a typical properties of a fluid, i.e. its capability of unlimited deformation under finite stress. This is illustrated by the broken lines in Fig. 2.10(b). Such performance would constitute a limiting disadvantage if one attempts to employ the Maxwell model in the prediction of the creep behaviour of real viscoelastic materials. In addition, the Maxwell model cannot demonstrate the time-dependent viscoelastic contraction which occurs in a real viscoelastic material if, during creep, the external stress is removed. Removing the stress from the Maxwell model simply allows an instantaneous elastic strain recovery to occur as a result of the contraction of the spring. There will be no subsequent time-dependent strain recovery as there would be no force acting on the piston to move it back through the fluid of the dashpot when the external stress has been removed (e.g. Gittus, 1975).

On the other hand, if we apply at $t = 0$ a constant strain, i.e. $\varepsilon(t) = 0$ for $t < 0$ and $\varepsilon(t) = \varepsilon_0$ for $t > 0$ which corresponds to a stress-relaxation experiment, then, with reference to equation (2.10), it follows that

$$\sigma + \lambda\dot{\sigma} = 0. \tag{2.17}$$

Integrating this equation with respect to time, one obtains

$$\sigma(t) = \sigma_0 \exp(-t/\lambda) \tag{2.18}$$

whereby the initial condition $\sigma = \sigma_0$ at $t = 0$ has been used. Equation (2.18) indicates that, in a stress-relaxation experiment, the stress decays exponentially with a characteristic time parameter $\lambda = \eta/E$; hence this parameter is referred to as the 'relaxation time' of the Maxwell model at constant strain.

Substituting for σ_0 in (2.18) in terms of the initial strain, this equation may be written in the form

$$\sigma(t) = \varepsilon_0 R(t) \tag{2.19}$$

where $\varepsilon_0 = \varepsilon(0^+)$ and $R(t)$ is referred to as the stress-relaxation modulus or the 'relaxation function'. The latter is expressed in view of equations (2.18) and (2.19) as

$$R(t) = E \exp(-t/\lambda) \tag{2.20}$$

The relaxation response of the Maxwell model is presented in Fig. 2.10(c).

An additional shortcoming of the Maxwell model becomes apparent from examining the form of the relaxation function $R(t)$ (equation (2.20)), which contains only one exponential decay term. This may not suffice for the representation of the stress-relaxation behaviour of real viscoelastic materials. Such real behaviour, as discussed earlier, might not necessarily decay to zero at infinite time as (2.20) suggests.

An alternative procedure for obtaining the constitutive equations for the Maxwell model is by using the Laplace transform (Appendix C). In the relaxation phase, if the strain is applied at time $t = 0^+$ such that the conditions are $\varepsilon(0)$ and $\sigma(0) = 0$ for $t < 0$, then the Laplace transform of (2.10) gives

$$E\, d_t \bar{\varepsilon}(s) = \left(\frac{E}{\eta} + d_t\right)\bar{\sigma}(s) \tag{2.21}$$

where d_t designates the time derivative operator, i.e. $d_t = d/dt$, an overbar $^-$ indicates the Laplace transform of the pertaining variable and s in the Laplace parameter. An operational form corresponding to (2.21) may be written as

$$\bar{\sigma}(s) = d_t \bar{R}(s)\bar{\varepsilon}(s) \tag{2.22}$$

where

$$\bar{R}(s) = \frac{E}{d_t + E/\eta}. \tag{2.23}$$

The inversion of $\bar{R}(s)$ of (2.23) is the relaxation function $R(t)$ given earlier by equation (2.20).

Accordingly, by inverting the Laplace transform (2.23) and using the convolution theorem (see Appendix C), the stress-relaxation equation corresponding to (2.22) can be written as

$$\sigma(t) = \int_0^t R(t - \tau)\, \frac{d}{d\tau}\, \varepsilon(\tau)\, d\tau. \tag{2.24}$$

Similarly, in the creep phase, one may solve equation (2.21) for the strain which would correspond to a constant stress applied to the Maxwell mode at time $t = 0^+$.

Then,

$$\bar{\varepsilon}(s) = d_t \bar{F}(s)\bar{\sigma}(s) \qquad (2.25)$$

in which

$$\bar{F}(s) = E^{-1}\left(\frac{1}{d_t} + \frac{1}{\lambda\, d_t^2}\right) \qquad (2.26)$$

is the Laplace transform of the creep function $F(t)$ expressed earlier by (2.16). Inverting (2.26) and using the convolution theorem, the creep response equation for the Maxwell model is expressed as

$$\varepsilon(t) = E^{-1}\sigma(t) + \eta^{-1}\int_0^t \sigma(\tau)\, d\tau. \qquad (2.27)$$

(b) The Kelvin (Voigt) model

The Kelvin (Voigt) model is built up of a linear spring and a dashpot in parallel (Fig. 2.11(a)).

Because of the parallel arrangement of the spring and the dashpot, this model will exhibit primary (decelerating) creep when first loaded. This is because the spring can only extend as rapidly as the dashpot. Thus, the model cannot by itself exhibit steady-state creep. For the same reason, it also cannot demonstrate steady-state stress relaxation. On the other hand, if, after a period of uniaxial tension, the stress is released, the spring would then attempt to return to its unstressed length, hence exerting compression on the dashpot during the process. The dashpot would, then, slowly retract, under the stress, to its original length permitting the spring to contract.

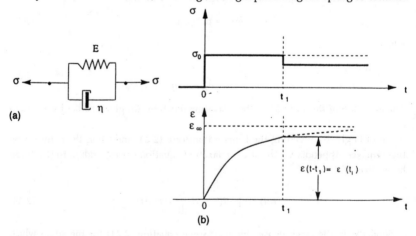

Fig. 2.11 The Kelvin (Voigt) model: (a) the model; (b) creep response (incomplete relaxation of the model is shown for $t > t_1$).

Thus, compressive creep under zero external stress will occur and will eventually, after infinite time, allow all of the prior tensile creep strain to be recovered. Such a property (viscoelastic contraction) can be significant in the creep behaviour of a large class of viscoelastic materials. As one may recall, viscoelastic contraction as described above does not occur in the Maxwell model.

For the spring 's' and dashpot 'd' in parallel arrangement, the Kelvin–Voigt model, the total stress is given by

$$\sigma = \sigma_s + \sigma_d$$
$$= E\varepsilon_s + \eta\dot{\varepsilon}_d. \tag{2.28}$$

This response relation is connected to the differential response equation (2.5) through

$$p = 0, \quad a_0 = 1, \quad q = 1, \quad b_0 = E, \quad b_1 = \eta.$$

In a creep experiment, we let $\sigma = \sigma_0$ for $t \geq 0^+$; thus, equation (2.28) has the solution

$$\varepsilon(t) = \frac{\sigma_0}{E} + C \exp(-t/\lambda), \quad \lambda = \eta/E, \tag{2.29}$$

whereby the constant of integration is given, subject to the initial conditions $\varepsilon_0 = \varepsilon(0) = 0$ at $t = 0$, by $C = -\sigma_0/E$. Hence, the creep constitutive equation (2.29) becomes

$$\varepsilon(t) = \frac{\sigma_0}{E} [1 - \exp(-t/\lambda)] = \sigma_0 F(t) \tag{2.30}$$

where

$$F(t) = E^{-1}[1 - \exp(-t/\lambda)] \tag{2.31}$$

is the creep function for the Kelvin (Voigt) model.

The creep response of the Kelvin model is illustrated in Fig. 2.11(b). As the time t tends to ∞, the strain approaches gradually a final limit. The latter is proportional to the stress, with an asymptotic modulus E_∞, whereby

$$\varepsilon_\infty = \varepsilon(\infty) = \frac{\sigma_0}{E_\infty}. \tag{2.32}$$

Such response behaviour is described as 'delayed elastic' and, hence, the Kelvin–Voigt model does represent the creep behaviour of real materials to a first approximation.

An alternative form of the creep response equation (2.30) for the Kelvin–Voigt model may be obtained by considering the Laplace transformation of (2.28). In this case, provided that, at $t < 0$, both $\sigma = 0$ and $\varepsilon = 0$, the Laplace transformation of (2.28) yields the following relation:

$$\bar{\sigma}(s) = E\bar{\varepsilon}(0) + \eta[d_t\bar{\varepsilon}(s) - \bar{\varepsilon}(0)] \tag{2.33}$$

where $d_t = d/dt$.

Thus, by inverting the Laplace transform (2.33) and using the convolution theorem, the creep response for the Kelvin–Voigt model is obtained as

$$\varepsilon(t) = \eta^{-1} \int_0^t \exp[-(t - \tau)]\sigma(\tau)\, d\tau, \quad t \geq 0. \tag{2.34}$$

On the other hand, during a relaxation experiment, the applied strain is constant, i.e. $\varepsilon(t) = \varepsilon_0 = \varepsilon(0^+)$ for $t \geq 0^+$. In view of the parallel arrangement of the elements of the Kelvin (Voigt) model, it is apparent that the model cannot portray stress relaxation when the external strain is applied at $t = 0^+$ and maintained constant afterwards. As shown in Fig. 2.11(b), when the strain is fixed at $t = t_1$ the stress is immediately relaxed by a certain amount and then remains constant at this value. In other words, the relaxation of the Kelvin model is incomplete.

(c) The three-element model

The three-element model consists of a linear spring in series with a Kelvin–Voigt element (Fig. 2.12(a)). It is sometimes referred to as the **standard linear model**.

With reference to Fig. 2.12(a), the responses of both parts of the model are expressed as

$$\sigma = E\varepsilon_s, \quad \sigma = E'\varepsilon_s' + \eta\dot{\varepsilon}_d \tag{2.35}$$

From equation (2.35), and using the Laplace transformation, the following equation is obtained:

$$(E + E')\sigma + \eta\dot{\sigma} = EE'\varepsilon + E\eta\dot{\varepsilon}. \tag{2.36}$$

In the creep phase, it can be shown that

$$\varepsilon(t) = \frac{\sigma_0}{\zeta_1} \left\{ \lambda[1 - \exp(-t/\lambda)] + \zeta_2 \exp(-t/\lambda)] \right\} \tag{2.37}$$

where

$$\zeta_1 = \frac{E\eta}{E + E'}$$

$$\zeta_2 = \frac{\eta}{E + E'}. \tag{2.38}$$

The creep response of the three-element model is demonstrated in Fig. 2.12(b). The model portrays an instant elasticity with

$$\varepsilon_0 = \varepsilon(0^+) = \frac{\sigma_0 \zeta_2}{\zeta_1} = \frac{\sigma_0}{E} \tag{2.39}$$

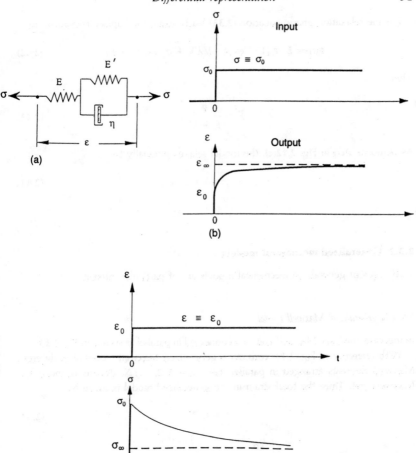

Fig. 2.12 The three-element model (standard linear solid): (a) the model; (b) creep response; (c) relaxation response.

in addition to an asymptotic elastic behaviour given by

$$\varepsilon_\infty = \varepsilon(\infty) = \frac{\sigma_0}{E_\infty} \qquad (2.40)$$

where

$$E_\infty = \frac{EE'}{E + E'}. \qquad (2.41)$$

For the relaxation phase, equation (2.35) leads, using the Laplace transform, to

$$\sigma(t) = E_\infty \varepsilon_0[1 - \exp(-t/\lambda')] + \sigma_0 \exp(-t/\lambda') \qquad (2.42)$$

where

$$\lambda' = \frac{\eta}{E + E'}. \qquad (2.43)$$

As demonstrated in Fig. 2.12(c), the model relaxes gradually to

$$\sigma_\infty = \sigma(\infty) = E_\infty \varepsilon \qquad (2.44)$$

2.2.2 Generalized mechanical models

Two types of generalized mechanical models are of particular interest.

(a) The generalized Maxwell model

In this case, the basic Maxwell units are connected in parallel as shown in Fig. 2.13.

With reference to Fig. 2.13, consider a generalized Maxwell model of N different Maxwell elements arranged in parallel. Let i ($i = 1, 2, \ldots, N$) denote an individual Maxwell unit. Thus, the total strain in the generalized model is given by

$$\varepsilon = \varepsilon_i \qquad (2.45)$$

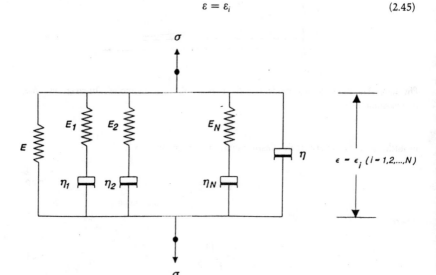

Fig. 2.13 Generalized Maxwell model

and the total stress is

$$\sigma = \sum_{i=1}^{N} \sigma_i. \tag{2.46}$$

This is with the understanding that the stress is not shared equally between all the elements, that is $\sigma_1 \neq \sigma_2 \neq \cdots \neq \sigma_N$. In view of equations (2.10) and (2.45), it can be shown that

$$\dot{\varepsilon}_i(t) = E_i^{-1}(d_t + \lambda_i^{-1})\sigma_i = \dot{\varepsilon}(t) \tag{2.47}$$

and, thus,

$$\sigma(t) = \sum_{i=1}^{N} E_i(d_t + \lambda_i^{-1})^{-1}\dot{\varepsilon}(t) \tag{2.48}$$

where $\lambda_i = \eta_i/E_i$ and $d_t = d/dt$.

Further, with reference to (2.20), it can be shown that the relaxation function of the generalized Maxwell model is given by

$$R(t) = \sum_{i=1}^{N} E_i \exp(-t/\lambda_i). \tag{2.49}$$

(b) The generalized Kelvin (Voigt) model

In Fig. 2.14, a number $i = 1, 2, \ldots, N$ of Kelvin (Voigt) elements are attached in series to form the generalized Kelvin (Voigt) model. In this case, the stress in each

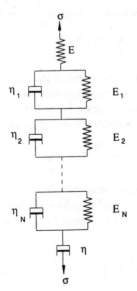

Fig. 2.14 Generalized Kelvin (Voigt) model.

element is the same, i.e. $\sigma_1 = \sigma_2 = \cdots = \sigma_N$. Thus, it can be shown, with reference to (2.28), that

$$\sigma(t) = E_i(1 + d_t\lambda_i)\varepsilon_i(t) \tag{2.50}$$

and

$$\varepsilon(t) = \sigma(t) \sum_{i=1}^{N} E_i^{-1}(1 + d_t\lambda_i)^{-1} \tag{2.51}$$

where, in the above two equations, $\lambda_i = \eta_i/E_i$.

Further, with reference to (2.31), the creep function of the generalized Kelvin (Voigt) model can be written as

$$F(t) = \sum_{i=1}^{N} E_i^{-1} [1 - \exp(-t/\lambda_i)], \quad \lambda_i = \eta_i/E_i. \tag{2.52}$$

2.2.3 Relaxation and retardation spectra

The stress relaxation response of a generalized Maxwell model is expressed, with reference to (2.24), as

$$\sigma(t) = \int_{-\infty}^{t} R(t - \tau)\dot{\varepsilon}(\tau)\,d\tau \tag{2.53}$$

where $R(\cdot)$ is the relaxation function of the model expressed previously by (2.49), i.e.

$$R(t - \tau) = \sum_{i=1}^{N} E_i \exp[-(t - \tau)/\lambda_i], \quad \lambda_i = \eta_i/E_i. \tag{2.54}$$

Now, we consider that the finite number of elements N in the generalized Maxwell model is replaced by an infinite number (spectrum) of elements characterized by a probability density of relaxation times. Let the latter be designated by $\Gamma(\lambda)$. The relaxation function for the spectrum is then expressed in view of (2.54) as

$$R(t) = \int_{0}^{\infty} \Gamma(\lambda) \exp(-t/\lambda)\,d\lambda. \tag{2.55}$$

The function $\Gamma(\lambda)$ which characterizes the infinite number of parallel Maxwell units is nonnegative for $0 \leq \lambda < \infty$ and may have continuous and discontinuous parts.

The relaxation function is often expressed (e.g. Gross, 1947, 1953), as a generalization of (2.55) as follows:

$$R(t) = \int_{0}^{\infty} \beta\Gamma(\lambda) \exp(-t/\lambda)\,d\lambda \tag{2.56}$$

where $\Gamma(\lambda)\,d\lambda$ is the distribution of relaxation times and where β is a normalization factor such that

$$\int_0^\infty \Gamma(\lambda) \, d\lambda = 1, \tag{2.57a}$$

i.e.

$$\beta = R(0). \tag{2.57b}$$

Similarly, for a generalized Kelvin (Voigt) model, the creep function $F(\cdot)$ is identified, for a finite number of Kelvin–Voigt elements arranged in series, by equation (2.52), i.e.

$$F(t - \tau) = \sum_{i=1}^{N} E_i^{-1}\{1 - \exp[-(t - \tau)/\lambda_i]\}, \quad \lambda_i = \eta_i/E_i. \tag{2.58}$$

For an infinite number (spectrum) of Kelvin (Voigt) elements in the generalized model, the creep function may be expressed, in terms of the probability density of retardation times $f(\lambda)$, as

$$F(t) = \int_0^\infty f(\lambda)[1 - \exp(-t/\lambda)] \, d\lambda. \tag{2.59}$$

The creep function $F(t)$ may also be expressed, as a generalization of the expression (2.59), as

$$F(t) = \int_0^\infty \alpha f(\lambda)[1 - \exp(-t/\lambda)] \, d\lambda \tag{2.60}$$

where $f(\lambda) \, d\lambda$ is the distribution function of retardation times and α is a normalization factor. The latter is determined such that

$$\int_0^\infty f(\lambda) \, d\lambda = 1; \tag{2.61a}$$

hence,

$$\alpha = F(\infty). \tag{2.61b}$$

With reference to equations (2.60) and (2.61), the function $f(\lambda)$ is a nondecreasing function for $0 \le \lambda < \infty$ and may have continuous and discontinuous parts.

2.3 PHENOMENOLOGICAL FRAMEWORK OF THE LINEAR VISCOELASTIC THEORY

The assumption that a viscoelastic solid is linear is sufficient to establish explicit single integral expressions connecting responses to inputs without having to specify *a priori* its physical makeups and the physical significance of input and response quantities. If one designates an input stimulus on a viscoelastic specimen by I, then, in view of the hereditary effect, the response at time t, say $\Upsilon(t)$, would be in general a function of the time history of the input $I(t, \tau)$, including its current value $I(t)$. That is,

$$\Upsilon(t) = f[I(t, \tau), \quad I(t)], \quad \tau \le t. \tag{2.62}$$

Let σ represent the one-dimensional Cauchy stress and ε designate the corresponding one-dimensional infinitesimal strain defined at every material point x in a rectangular Cartesian reference frame within the time interval $-\infty < t < \infty$. One seeks the response (constitutive) relationship between σ and ε for the linear viscoelastic model of the material system. Such a linear constitutive relation would be generally consistent with the smallness assumptions of the infinitesimal deformation theory (Chapter 1). In general, the resulting viscoelastic constitutive equation would be a function of both position and time. However, on the assumption that the material specimen is homogeneous, the dependence of the constitutive formulism on position is withheld at present.

If one designates an input stress on the material specimen by $\sigma(t)$, then the resulting strain would be, in general, a function of the history $\sigma(t, \tau)$ and its current value $\sigma(t)$ in the manner expressed by (2.62), i.e.

$$\varepsilon(t) = f[\sigma(t, \tau), \quad \sigma(t)], \quad \tau \le t. \tag{2.63}$$

This equation is again a statement of the concept of the hereditary effect in the viscoelastic material specimen: that is the resulting strain is a function of the history of the stress input and not just its current value. The function $f(\cdot)$ appearing in (2.63) is defined to be linear if, and only if, it satisfies the following two criteria (Schapery, 1974):

1. the criterion of homogeneity (or proportionality), expressed by

$$f[c\sigma(t)] = cf[\sigma(t)] \tag{2.64}$$

   where c is a constant;

2. the criterion of superposition of input histories, i.e.

$$f[\sigma_1(t_1), \sigma_2(t_2), \ldots, \sigma_n(t_n)] = f[\sigma_1(t_1)] + f[\sigma_2(t_2)] + \cdots + f[\sigma_n(t_n)]. \tag{2.65}$$

For a viscoelastic material to be identified as linear viscoelastic, equations (2.64) and (2.65) must be satisfied. In this regard, although the superposition criterion (2.65) is not implied by the homogeneity equation (2.64), it is possible to show that for all practical situations the opposite to this statement is true. Many viscoelastic materials exhibit, to a satisfactory degree of accuracy, the linearity requirements (1) and (2) above. This would be particularly true between certain limiting stress or strain values. For example, the creep curves of a composite solid propellant subjected to different levels of loading are shown in Fig. 2.5 (due to Blatz (1956)) to satisfy these requirements approximately. Linear viscoelastic behaviour is demonstrated in Fig. 2.5 by the fact that at any instant of time the strains are approximately proportional to the stress level (e.g. Lee, 1960). A similar example can be demonstrated for the case of relaxation of stress in stretched cellulose fibres (cotton and flax at 65% RH and 25°C) as shown in Fig. 2.7 (due to Meredith (1954)). Here, linearity is indicated by the fact that at any time t the stresses are approximately proportional to the strain input level. On the other hand, the stress-relaxation response of both viscous rayon (Fig. 2.8) and cellulose acetate (Fig. 2.9) is apparently nonlinear.

In a creep experiment, we consider a viscoelastic material specimen which is subjected to zero stress at time $t < 0$ and a constant stress σ_0 for $t \geq 0^+$. Following expression (2.63), the corresponding strain is given by

$$\varepsilon(t) = f(\sigma_0, t). \tag{2.66}$$

Further, in the case where linearity is assumed, equation (2.66) can be written, with reference to Fig. 2.15, as

$$\varepsilon(t) = F(t)\sigma_0 = F(0)\sigma_0 + [F(t) - F(0)]\sigma_0. \tag{2.67}$$

The first term on the right-hand side of equation (2.67) is the instantaneous strain which occurs on application of the load at time $t = 0$. The second term represents the delayed (retarded) part of strain which is a function of time. The function $F(t)$, introduced earlier, is the creep function. It is a function of time only for the homogeneous material specimen and characterizes the rheological properties of the linear viscoelastic material for the one-dimensional stress–strain situation. For $t < 0$, $F(t) = 0$ and, for $t \geq 0$, $F(t)$ is usually a monotonically increasing function of time. Figure 2.16 demonstrates the function $F(t)$ by comparison with corresponding response functions for elastic and viscous specimens.

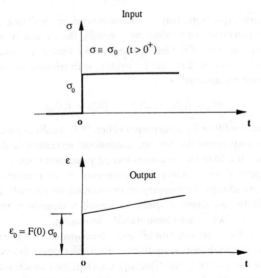

Fig. 2.15 Linear creep response.

Linear viscoelasticity

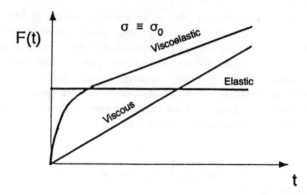

Fig. 2.16 Comparison of the strain response function $F(t)$ for elastic, viscous and viscoelastic material specimens when subjected to a constant unit stress.

Similarly, in a relaxation experiment, if one designates an input strain on the material specimen by $\varepsilon(t)$, then the resulting stress would be, in general, a function of the history of $\varepsilon(t)$, i.e.

$$\sigma(t) = r[\varepsilon(t, \tau), \ \varepsilon(t)]. \tag{2.68}$$

Further, if a constant strain ε_0 is applied to the material specimen at time $t \geq 0$, the resulting stress can be expressed as

$$\sigma(t) = r(\varepsilon_0, t). \tag{2.69}$$

Such a relaxation experiment may be accomplished by applying at time $t = 0$ whatever stress is required to produce very rapidly the amount of strain required, ε_0, and then fixing the ends of the test specimen and recording the variation of stress with time, i.e. $\sigma(t)$. Equation (2.69) can be written, with reference to Fig. 2.17, where linear viscoelasticity is assumed, as

$$\sigma(t) = R(t)\varepsilon_0 = R(0)\varepsilon_0 + [R(t) - R(0)]\varepsilon_0 \tag{2.70}$$

in which the function $R(t)$ is the relaxation function. It is usually a positive decreasing function of time. Experimentally, the one-dimensional relaxation function of a linear viscoelastic material is found to be a monotonically decreasing function of time (Fig. 2.18). This property is not, however, a consequence of compatibility with thermodynamics or of the dissipative property of the viscoelastic material (Day, 1972). In this context, Gurtin and Herrera (1965) presented a dissipative one-dimensional relaxation function which is not monotonically decreasing.

In the study of the linear response of viscoelastic materials, we use the criterion of superposition of input histories, equation (2.65), to determine the output produced by common action of several inputs. This may translate, for a tensile test, for instance, into tensile stresses applied successively with different magnitudes.

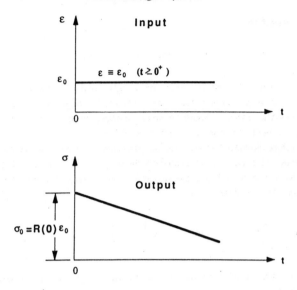

Fig. 2.17 Linear relaxation response.

In a creep experiment, if at $t = 0$ a stress σ_0 is applied suddenly, a creep strain $\varepsilon(t) = F(t)\sigma_0$ is produced whereby $F(t)$ is the creep function. Further, if the input stress σ_0 is maintained unchanged, then the response formula, identified previously by equation (2.67), may be used to describe the strain for the entire range of time considered. This is illustrated in Fig. 2.15. Consider now the case that, at time $t = \tau$, an additional amount of stress $\Delta\sigma_\tau$ is applied. Thus, for $t > \tau$, an additional amount of strain will be produced which will be proportional to $\Delta\sigma_\tau$ via the same creep relationship (2.67) with the time measured from $t = \tau$. Hence, the total strain for

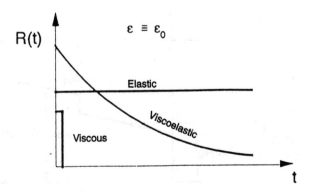

Fig. 2.18 Comparison of the stress response function $R(t)$ for elastic, viscous and viscoelastic material specimens when subjected to a constant unit strain.

$t > \tau$ is expressed by

$$\varepsilon(t) = F(t)\sigma_0 + F(t - \tau)\,\Delta\sigma_\tau. \tag{2.71}$$

As illustrated in Fig. 2.19, the first term on the right-hand side of (2.71) is the original amount of strain at any time t due to the initial value of stress σ_0 and the second term identifies the added amount of strain starting from $t = \tau$ produced by the additional increment of stress $\Delta\sigma_\tau$ applied at that time.

The procedure illustrated above may be generalized to treat cases of discontinuous input histories. This can be accomplished through the use of unit step functions (Appendix B). In this regard, it is always convenient to select the one input as a unit step function $H(t - \tau)$ defined by

$$H(t - \tau) = \begin{cases} 0, & t \leq \tau, \\ 1, & t \geq \tau. \end{cases} \tag{2.72}$$

Thus, in terms of the unit step function, the stimulus $\sigma(t) = 0$ for $t < 0$ and $\sigma(t) = \sigma_0$ for $t \geq 0$ can be written as

$$\sigma(t) = \sigma_0 H(t), \quad -\infty < t < \infty, \tag{2.73}$$

which has the response identified previously by the constitutive equation (2.67). Further, the application of a constant stress σ_τ for a duration of time $t \geq \tau$ can be

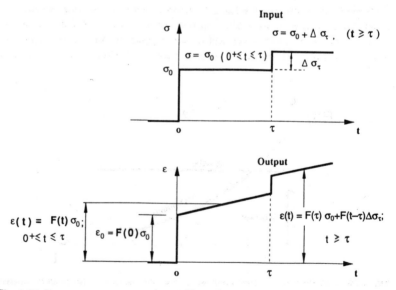

Fig. 2.19 Linear creep response with an additional increment of stress $\Delta\sigma_\tau$ applied at time $t = \tau$.

expressed by employing the unit step function as

$$\sigma(t) = H(t - \tau)\sigma_\tau. \tag{2.74}$$

Hence, the identity

$$\sigma(t) = \int_{-\infty}^{\infty} H(t - \tau) \, d\sigma(\tau) \tag{2.75}$$

can be thought of as a superposition of step functions with $d\sigma(\tau)$ being the height of the step at $t = \tau$ (e.g. Flügge, 1975). Since the linearity assumption guarantees the application of the superposition principle, then, with reference to (2.67), the strain function is a superposition of functions $F(t - \tau) \, d\sigma(\tau)$ with $-\infty < t < \infty$. Hence, the creep response is given by

$$\varepsilon(t) = \int_{-\infty}^{\infty} F(t - \tau) \, d\sigma(\tau) = \int_{-\infty}^{\infty} F(t - \tau)\dot{\sigma}(\tau) \, d\tau. \tag{2.76}$$

The constitutive relations in (2.76) are forms of the 'principle of superposition'. They were introduced as purely empirical laws in the theory of after-effect by Boltzmann (1874). The principle of superposition also appears in the laws of dielectrics (Hopkinson, 1876; Froehlich, 1949) and in the laws of linear electrical networks (Carson, 1926). The integrals in (2.76) were first introduced in pure mathematics where they are called Duhamel's integrals (Duhamel, 1833); Gross (1953) should also be referred to.

For the general case, when a stress σ_0 is applied at time $t = 0$, but that the stress then varies as an arbitrary function of time $\sigma(t)$, the response equation corresponding to (2.76) can be written as

$$\varepsilon(t) = F(t)\sigma_0 + \int_0^t F(t, \tau)\dot{\sigma}(\tau) \, d\tau. \tag{2.77}$$

The creep response equation (2.77) illustrates how the strain at any time t depends on all that has happened before and at present, i.e. on the entire input history. The latter, in the present case of creep, is the stress history $[\sigma(t, \tau), \sigma(t)]$. Hence, the integral in the response equation (2.77) is called the 'hereditary integral' following the introduction by Volterra (1913) of the term 'hereditary law' for functional relations similar to (2.77).

In many applications, the response of a linear viscoelastic material depends only on the time elasped since the application of the load. In this case, equation (2.77) can be written as

$$\varepsilon(t) = F(t)\sigma_0 + \int_0^t F(t - \tau)\dot{\sigma}(\tau) \, d\tau. \tag{2.78}$$

Viscoelastic materials which obey the time differential postulate indicated in (2.78) are referred to as '**non-aging**' or '**time translation invariant**' materials. Equation (2.78) can be further modified to read as

$$\varepsilon(t) = F(0)\sigma(t) + \int_0^t \sigma(\tau) \, \frac{dF(t - \tau)}{d(t - \tau)} \, d\tau. \tag{2.79}$$

While equation (2.78) separates the strains caused by the initial stress σ_0 and by the latter stress increase, equation (2.79) expresses the strain that would occur if the total stress σ were applied at the present time t and the additional strain resulting from the fact that much or all of the stress has been applied earlier and had time to produce creep. Equation (2.79), after some changes, can lead to the following form of the Stieltjes integral:

$$\varepsilon(t) = \int_{-\infty}^{\infty} F(t - \tau) \, d\sigma(\tau). \tag{2.80}$$

This brings us back to the form of equation (2.76).

In the relaxation case, a treatment similar to the above may be carried out based on the concept of the relaxation function $R(t)$ in equation (2.70). In this case, if an input strain $\varepsilon(t) = \varepsilon_0 H(t)$ is maintained in the material, the resulting response may be identified by the constitutive equation (2.70). Further, the application of a constant strain ε_τ for a duration of time $t \geq \tau$ can be expressed as

$$\varepsilon(t) = H(t - \tau)\varepsilon_\tau.$$

Hence, the identity

$$\varepsilon(t) = \int_{-\infty}^{\infty} H(t - \tau) \, d\varepsilon(\tau) \tag{2.81}$$

can be thought of as superposition of step functions with $d\varepsilon(\tau)$ being the height of the step at $t = \tau$. Accordingly, in this case, the stress-relaxation function would be thought of as a superposition of functions $R(t - \tau) \, d\varepsilon(\tau)$ with $-\infty < t < \infty$. Thus, a stress-relaxation response equation corresponding to the creep response equation (2.76) can be written as

$$\sigma(t) = \int_{-\infty}^{\infty} R(t - \tau)\dot{\varepsilon}(\tau) \, d\tau. \tag{2.82}$$

Hence, the stress-relaxation constitutive equation would assume, for a non-aging material, one of the following forms:

$$\sigma(t) = R(t)\varepsilon_0 + \int_0^t R(t - \tau)\dot{\varepsilon}(\tau) \, d\tau.$$

$$= R(0)\varepsilon(t) + \int_0^t \varepsilon(\tau) \, \frac{dR(t - \tau)}{d(t - \tau)} \, d\tau$$

$$= \int_{\tau = -\infty}^{\tau = +\infty} R(t - \tau) \, d\varepsilon(\tau). \tag{2.83}$$

The response equations (2.78) and (2.82) are Boltzmann's formulation (Boltzmann, 1874) of the constitutive equation for a linear viscoelastic material specimen under uniaxial loading. Hence, such material is often referred to as a 'Boltzmann's solid'. Alternatively, as mentioned earlier, it is called a 'linear hereditary material' as it was named about the same time by Volterra (1913).

The creep response relation (2.76) and the corresponding relaxation equation (2.82) are typical aftereffect relations. Also, the creep function $F(t)$ and the relaxation function $R(t)$ are aftereffect functions or memory functions. They are not quite arbitrary functions for thermodynamic reasons. They must be so that for all applied stress functions $\sigma(t)$ and all times t the following inequality holds (König and Meixner, 1958; Meixner, 1965; Axelrad, 1970):

$$\int_{-\infty}^{t} \sigma(\tau)\dot{\varepsilon}(\tau) \, d\tau \geq 0. \tag{2.84}$$

This inequality is referred to as the **'passivity property'**.

2.4 INTERCONVERSION OF CREEP AND RELAXATION DATA

In linear viscoelasticity, the creep function $F(t)$ and the relaxation function $R(t)$ are interrelated and each would permit the construction of the viscoelastic constitutive relation for an arbitrary given behaviour. This is under the condition that the principle of time invariance is applicable; that is the material is influenced only by $\sigma(t)$ and $\varepsilon(t)$ and no other stimuli at any time being present.

Recalling the creep constitutive equation (2.76), namely

$$\varepsilon(t) = \int_{-\infty}^{t} F(t - \tau) \frac{d\sigma(\tau)}{d\tau} \, d\tau,$$

one may consider (e.g. Ward, 1983) a loading programme starting at time $t = 0$ in which the stress would decay exactly as the relaxation function $R(\tau)$. Thus, the corresponding strain would remain constant as in a typical stress-relaxation experiment. That is, if

$$\frac{d\sigma(\tau)}{dt} = \frac{dR(\tau)}{d\tau}$$

then

$$\int_{0}^{t} \frac{dR(\tau)}{dt} F(t - \tau) \, d\tau = \text{constant}. \tag{2.85}$$

For simplicity, one may further normalize the definition of $R(\tau)$ and $F(\tau)$ so that the constant in the above equation becomes unity. Accordingly, one has

$$\int_{0}^{t} \frac{dR(\tau)}{d\tau} F(t - \tau) \, d\tau = 1 \tag{2.86}$$

which is sometimes interpreted to give

$$\int_0^t R(\tau)F(t - \tau) \, d\tau = t. \tag{2.87}$$

On the other hand, for the interconversion of the creep and relaxation time rates, the following relation is sometimes used:

$$m = \frac{d \ln F(t)}{d \ln t} \approx -\frac{d \ln R(t)}{d \ln t} = n \tag{2.88}$$

where m and n are the values of the corresponding shown derivatives.

The accuracy of formula (2.88) is, however, still unknown for a large class of viscoelastic materials (Struik, 1987). According to the latter reference, it is found that

$$0 \leq 1 - R(t)F(t) \leq \tfrac{1}{6}(\pi\mu)^2, \quad \mu \ll 1, \tag{2.89}$$

and

$$\left| \frac{m}{n} - 1 \right| < Bm \quad \text{with} \quad B \approx 1. \tag{2.90}$$

The approximate equality of $F(t)$ and $[R(t)]^{-1}$, corresponding to (2.89), follows from the smallness of the slopes m and n for time $\tau < t$. It was concluded by Struik (1987) that (2.89) can be applied without restriction for the case of glassy polymers whereby m is generally less than 0.05.

Equations (2.88) and (2.90), however, are much less general. They are derived from the assumption that $dF(\tau)/d \ln \tau$ and $-dR(\tau)/dt$ are either increasing with τ for $\tau < t$ or only slowly decreasing. Although for polymers these conditions are always nearly fulfilled, equations (2.88) and (2.90) may fail in some applications even for small values of m and n. In this context, Struik (1987) demonstrated the limitations of the latter two equations for the case of a simple mechanical model consisting of a linear spring in parallel with a Maxwell unit. Struik (1987) concluded that these two equations, (2.88) and (2.90), may be valid only under the condition that the dispersion regions of response of viscoelastic materials are sufficiently broad; however, for dispersions with only a single relaxation time, the two equations (2.88) and (2.90) would fail.

The above condition that the dispersion regions of the material must be sufficiently broad is nearly always fulfilled by glassy polymers. This is illustrated in Struik's paper by two examples concerning PMMAL and CHMA (polycyclohexylmethacrylate).

It is seen from the previous discussion that the creep and relaxation functions of a linear viscoelastic system are mutually connected in a simple manner. This permits the calculation of the distribution function of relaxation times of stress and the distribution function of retardation times of strain, when the relaxation function or the creep function is given. A transformation can be also established for the conversion of one distribution function into another. The reader is referred, in this context, to Gross (1947). Some of the results concerning the above are dealt with in Chapter 3.

PROBLEMS

2.1 Determine the stress–strain relations for the mechanical models shown in the figure below.

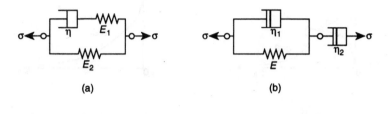

(a)   (b)

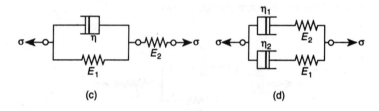

(c)   (d)

2.2 Comment on the use of the Maxwell model for the prediction of the response behaviour of real linear viscoelastic materials.

2.3 Verify the constitutive equations for the three-element model given by (2.37) and (2.42).

2.4 Determine the creep-recovery response of the following mechanical models, if a constant stress of magnitude σ_0 is applied suddenly at time $t = 0$ and maintained afterwards for a duration $t = 2\tau$, when it is completely removed:

 1. the Maxwell model;
 2. the Kelvin–Voigt model;
 3. the standard linear solid.

2.5 Determine, by employing the superposition principle, the response of the Maxwell model and the Kelvin–Voigt model to the stress loadings shown in the figure below.

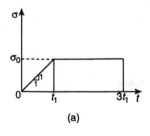

(a)

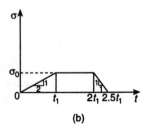

(b)

2.6 Comment on the use of both the Kelvin and three-element models for the prediction of the linear viscoelastic response illustrated in the figure below.

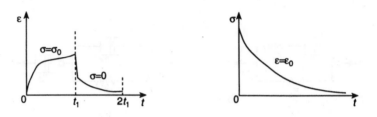

2.7 Determine the creep function $F(t)$ and the relaxation function $R(t)$ for the mechanical models shown in the figure below.

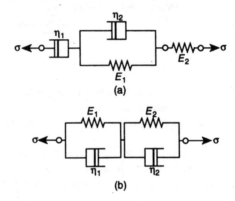

2.8 Use of the superposition principle to determine the creep recovery response of the models shown in the figure below.

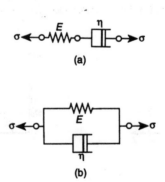

REFERENCES

Alfrey, T. (1948) *Mechanical Behaviour of High Polymers*, Interscience, New York.

Axelrad, D. R. (1970) Mechanical models of relaxation phenomena. *Adv. Mol. Relaxation Processes*, **2**, 41–68.

Bland, D. R. (1960) *The Theory of Linear Viscoelasticity*, Pergamon, New York.

Blatz, P. J. (1956) Rheology of composite solid propellants. *J. Ind. Eng. Chem.*, **48**(4), 727–9.

Boltzmann, L. (1874) Zür Theorie der elastichen Nachwirkung, Sitzungsber, Kaiserlich. *Akad. Wiss. Wien, Math. Naturwiss. Kl.*, **70**(2), 275–306.

Carson, J. R. (1926) *Electrical Circuit Theory and Operational Calculus*, McGraw- Hill, New York.

Christensen, R. M. (1971) *Theory of Viscoelasticity*, Academic Press, New York.

Coleman, B. D. and Noll, W. (1961) Foundations of linear viscoelasticity. *Rev. Mod. Phys.*, **33**, 239–49.

Day, W. A. (1972) *The Thermodynamics of Simple Materials with Fading Memory*, Springer, New York.

Duhamel, J. M. C. (1833) Sur la méthode générale relative au mouvement de la chaleur dans les corps solides plongés dans des milieux dont la température varie avec le temps. *J. Ec. Polytech., Paris*, **14**(22), 20–77.

Eirich, F. R. (1956, 1957) *Rheology Theory and Applications*, Vols 1 and 2, Academic Press, New York.

Ferry, J. D. (1961) *Viscoelasticity Properties of Polymers*, Wiley, New York.

Flügge, W. (1975) *Viscoelasticity*, Springer, New York.

Froehlich, H. (1949) *Theory of Dielectrics*, Clarendon, Oxford.

Gittus, J. (1975) *Creep, Viscoelasticity and Creep Fracture in Solids*, Wiley, New York.

Gross, B. (1947) On creep and relaxation. *J. Appl. Phys.*, **18** (February), 212–21.

Gross, B. (1953) *Mathematical Structure of the Theories of Viscoelasticity*, Hermann, Paris.

Gurtin, M. E. and Herrera, R. I. (1965) On dissipation inequalities and linear viscoelasticity. *Q. Appl. Math.*, **23**, 235–45.

Gurtin, M. E. and Sternberg, E. (1962) On the linear theory of viscoelasticity. *Arch. Ration. Mech. Anal.*, **11**, 291–356.

Halpin, J. C. (1968) Introduction to viscoelasticity, in *Composite Materials Workshop* (eds S. W. Tsai, J. C. Halpin and N. J. Pagano), Technomic, Stamford, CT, pp. 87–152.

Hopkinson, J. (1876) The presidual charge of the Leyden jar. *Philos. Trans. R. Soc. London*, **166**, 489–94.

König, H. and Meixner, J. (1958) Linear Systeme und Lineare Transformationen. *Math. Nachr.*, **19**, 256–322.

Leaderman, H. (1943) *Elastic and Creep Properties of Filamentous and Other High Polymers*, Textile Foundation, Washington, DC.

Leaderman, H. (1958) In *Viscoelasticity Phenomena in Amorphous High Polymeric Systems*, Vol. II (ed. F. Eirich), Academic Press, New York, pp. 1–6.

Lee, E. H. (1960) *Viscoelastic Stress Analysis*, First Symposium on Naval Structural Mechanics, Pergamon, New York, pp. 456–82.

Leitman, M. J. and Fisher, G. M. C. (1973) The linear theory of viscoelasticity, in *Handbuch der Physik*, Vol. VI a/3 (ed. S. Flügge), Springer, Berlin, pp. 1–123.

Lethersich, W. (1950) The rheological properties of dielectric polymers. *Br. J. Appl. Phys.*, **1** (November), 294–301.

Lockett, F. J. (1972) *Nonlinear Viscoelastic Solids*, Academic Press, New York.

Markovitz, H. (1977) Boltzmann and the beginnings of linear viscoelasticity. *Trans. Soc. Rheol.*, **21**(3), 381–98.

Meixner, J. (1965) Linear passive systems, in Proc. Int. Symp. on Statistical Mechanics and Thermodynamics, 1964, North-Holland, Amsterdam, pp. 52–68.

Schapery, R. A. (1974) Viscoelastic behaviour and analysis of composite materials, in *Mechanics of Composite Materials*, Vol. 2 (ed. G. Sendeckj), Academic Press, New York, pp. 86–168.

68   *Linear viscoelasticity*

Scott-Blair, G. W. (1949) *Survey of General and Applied Rheology*, Pitman, London.
Struik, L. C. E. (1987) The accuracy of some formulae for the interconversion of creep and relaxation data. *Rheol. Acta*, **26**, 7–13.
Stuart, H. A. (1956) *Die Physik der Hochpolymeren*, Vol. 4, Springer, Berlin.
Tschoegl, N. W. (1989) *The Phenomenological Theory of Linear Viscoelastic Behaviour, An Introduction*, Springer, New York.
Volterra, V. (1913) *Fonctions de Lignes*, Gauthier-Villard, Paris.
Volterra, V. and Peres, J. (1936) *Théorie Générale des Fonctionelles*, Gauthier-Villard, Paris.
Ward, I. M. (1983) *Mechanical Properties of Solid Polymers*, 2nd edn, Wiley, New York.

FURTHER READING

Aklonis, J. J. (1972) *Introduction to Polymer Viscoelasticity*, Wiley, New York.
Alexander, R. L. (1964) *Limits of Linear Viscoelastic Behaviour of an Asphalt Concrete in Tension and Compression*, Institute of Transportation and Traffic Engineering, University of California, Berkeley, CA.
Andrade, E. N. (1910) The viscous flow in metals and allied phenomena. *Proc. R. Soc. London, Ser. A*, **84**, 1–12.
Alfrey, T. and Doty, P. M. (1945) Methods of specifying the properties of viscoelastic materials. *J. Appl. Phys.*, **16**, 700–13.
Bazant, Z. P. (1975) Theory of creep and shrinkage in concrete structures: a précis of recent developments. *Mech. Today*, **2**, 1–93.
Bernal, J. D. (1958) Structure arrangements of macromolecules. *Discuss. Faraday Soc.*, **25**, 7–18.
Bland, D. R. and Lee, E. H. (1956) On the determination of a viscoelastic model for stress analysis of plastics. *J. Appl. Mech.*, **23**, 416–20.
Berry, D. S. and Hunter, S. C. (1956) The propagation of dynamic stresses in viscoelastic rods. *J. Mech. Phys. Solids*, **4**, 72–95.
Breuer, S. (1969) Lower bounds on work in linear viscoelasticity. *Q. Appl. Math.*, **27**(2), 139–46.
Creus, G. J. (1986) *Viscoelasticity; Basic Theory and Applications to Concrete Structures*, Springer, Berlin.
Findley, W. N. (1944) Creep characteristics of plastics, in Symposium on Plastics, ASTM, pp. 118–34.
Findley, W. N. and Khosla, G. (1955) Application of the superposition principle and theories of mechanical equation of state, strain and time hardening to creep of plastics under changing loads. *J. Appl. Phys.*, **26**(7), 821–32.
Finnie, I. and Heller, W. R. (1959) *Creep of Engineering Materials*, McGraw-Hill, New York.
Glauz, R. D. and Lee, E. H. (1954) Transient wave analysis in linear time-dependent material. *J. Appl. Phys.*, **25**, 947–53.
Haddad, Y. M. (1988) On the theory of the viscoelastic solid. *Res Mech.*, **25**, 225–59.
Hill, R. L. (1967) The creep behaviour of individual pulp fibers under tensile stress. *Tappi*, **50**(8), 432–40.
Hilton, H. H. (1964) Viscoelastic analysis, in *Engineering Design for Plastics* (ed. E. Baer), Reinhold, New York.
Hopkins, I. L. and Hamming, R. W. (1957) On creep and relaxation. *J. Appl. Phys.*, **28**(8), 906–9.
Hunter, S. C. (1960) Viscoelastic waves, in *Progress in Solid Mechanics*, Vol. I (eds I. N. Sneddon and R. Hill), North-Holland, Amsterdam, pp. 1–57.
Kauman, W. G. (1966) On the deformation and setting of the wood cell wall. *Holz Roh Werkst.*, **24**(11), 551–6.
Kolsky, H. (1965) Experimental studies of the mechanical behaviour of linear viscoelastic solids, in Proc. 4th Symposium on Naval Structural Mechanics, Pergamon, London, pp. 381–442.

Lee, E. H. (1956) Special issues on rheology of polymers. *J. Appl. Phys.*, **27**, 665–72.

Lee, E. H. (1960) In *Viscoelasticity: Phenomenological Aspects* (ed. J. T. Bergen), Academic Press, New York, pp. 1–150.

Lee, E. H. (1962) Viscoelasticity, in *Handbook of Engineering Mechanics* (ed. W. Flügge), McGraw-Hill, New York, pp. 53/1–53/22.

Lubliner, J. and Salkman, J. L. (1967) On uniqueness in general linear viscoelasticity. *Q. Appl. Math.*, **25**, 129–38.

Mark, H. and Tobolosky, A. V. (1950) *Physical Chemistry of High Polymeric Materials*, Interscience, New York.

Mazilu, P. (1973) On the constitutive law of Boltzmann–Volterra. *Rev. Roum. Math. Pures Appl.*, **18**, 1067–9.

Meredith, R. (1954) Relaxation of stress in stretched cellulose fibers. *J. Text. Inst.*, **45**, T438–T460.

McHenry, D. (1943) A new aspect of creep in concrete and its application to design. *Proc. ASTM*, **43**, 1064–86.

Odeh, F. and Tadjbakhsh, I. (1965) Uniqueness in the linear theory of viscoelasticity. *Arch. Ration. Mech. Anal.*, **18**, 244–50.

Pipkin, A. C. (1972) *Lectures on Viscoelasticity Theory*, Springer, New York.

Roesler, F. C. and Twyman, W. A. (1955) An iteration method for the determination of relaxation spectra. *Proc. Phys. Soc. B*, **68**(2), 97–105.

Roscoe, R. (1950) Mechanical models for the representation of viscoelastic properties. *Br. J. Appl. Phys.*, **1**, 171–3.

Roy, M. (1966). *Milieux Continus*, Dunod, Paris.

Swindeman, R. W. and Bolling, E. (1989) Relaxation response of A533B Steel from 25 to 600°C, in Proceedings, the 1989 ASME Pressure Vessels and Piping Conference–JSME Cosponsorship, PVP, Vol. 172, Collection and Uses of Relaxation Data in Design, Honolulu, Hawaii, July 23–27, 1989, pp. 21–8.

Tapsell, H. J. and Johnson, A. E. (1940) Creep under combined tension and torsion. *Engineering*, **150**, 24–8.

Tobolosky, A. and Eyring, H. J. (1943) Mechanical properties of polymeric materials. *J. Chem. Phys.*, **11**, 125–34.

Volterra, V. (1909) Sulle equazioni integro diffenziali della teoria dell'elasticita. *Att. Reale Accad. Lincei*, **18**, 295–301.

3

Transition to dynamic viscoelasticity

3.1 INTRODUCTION

In Chapter 2, we introduced the idealized theory of isothermal linear viscoelasticity under the conditions of quasi-static stress or strain. Within the scope of the presented formulations, the linear viscoelastic behaviour of a material may be described by one of the following functions

1. the creep function $F(t)$;
2. the relaxation function $R(t)$;
3. the retardation spectrum $f(\lambda)$;
4. the relaxation spectrum $\Gamma(\lambda)$.

Of the four functions above, the first two can be determined by experiment. That is, the creep function $F(t)$ is determined by a creep experiment and the relaxation function $R(t)$ is determined from a relaxation experiment. The other two functions $f(\lambda)$ and $\Gamma(\lambda)$, however, may be determined by integral transformation. That is, the retardation spectrum $f(\lambda)$ is determined by integral transformation, via equation (2.60), from the creep function $F(t)$ in (1) above. Also, the relaxation spectrum $\Gamma(\lambda)$ is determined by integral transformation, via equation (2.56), from the relaxation function $R(t)$ in (2) above. In view of the interrelation between the functions $F(t)$ and $R(t)$, as discussed in section 2.4, any one of the functions (1)–(4) above may be used to characterize the linear viscoelastic behaviour of the material completely with no other restrictions imposed other than linearity of the response behaviour (Boltzmann's superposition principle) and the constancy of temperature (isothermal) condition.

An alternative approach to the viscoelastic response of the material is to subject the specimen to an alternating stimulus and simultaneously measuring the output. Hence, in the present chapter, we extend the formulation of Chapter 2 to include the possibility of characterizing the linear viscoelastic behaviour of materials under dynamic loading or deformations. This is particularly suitable for gaining information about processes which take place rapidly, e.g. wave propagation. Here, we follow the sequence of development of Chapter 2. First, we present the material functions that characterize the linear viscoelastic material under dynamic conditions. Then, we introduce the interrelations between these functions and their connection to the material functions characterizing the linear viscoelastic response under static input conditions.

3.2 CHARACTERIZATION OF THE LINEAR VISCOELASTIC RESPONSE UNDER DYNAMIC LOADING CONDITIONS

For stresses and strains which are not too large, the linear viscoelastic properties exhibited under dynamic loading are described by a complex modulus $E^*(i\omega)$ which is a function of the frequency of the loading ω. As derived below, a linear relation exists between the stresses and strains in question in the form

$$\sigma(\omega, t) = E^*(i\omega)\varepsilon(\omega, t). \tag{3.1}$$

In the case of periodic loading, both the stress and strain appearing in the above equation are harmonic functions of time and the modulus $E^*(i\omega)$ is given by real and imaginary parts as

$$E^*(i\omega) = E_1(\omega) + iE_2(\omega). \tag{3.2}$$

Because of the effect of delayed elasticity and viscous flow in the viscoelastic material, the stress and strain will be generally out of phase. Thus, $\sigma(t)$ and/or $\varepsilon(t)$ will be complex numbers.

3.2.1 Complex modulus and complex compliance

In the case of linear viscoelastic material subjected to a sinusoidal stress, when equilibrium is reached, both the stress and the strain will vary sinusoidally, but the strain will lag behind the stress, i.e.

$$\varepsilon = \varepsilon_0 \sin(\omega t) \tag{3.3}$$

and

$$\sigma = \sigma_0 \sin(\omega t + \delta) \tag{3.4}$$

where ω is the angular frequency and δ is the phase lag. Expanding equation (3.4),

$$\sigma = \sigma_0 \sin(\omega t) \cos \delta + \sigma_0 \cos(\omega t) \sin \delta. \tag{3.5}$$

We introduce the moduli E_1 and E_2 where

$$E_1 = \frac{\sigma_0}{\varepsilon_0} \cos \delta, \quad E_2 = \frac{\sigma_0}{\varepsilon_0} \sin \delta \tag{3.6a}$$

and

$$\tan \delta = E_2/E_1. \tag{3.6b}$$

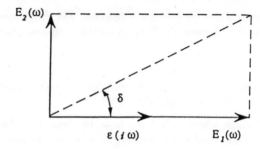

Fig. 3.1 Storage modulus $E_1(\omega)$, loss modulus $E_2(\omega)$ and phase lag δ for a linear viscoelastic material (Gittus, 1975).

Thus, in terms of E_1 and E_2 as expressed in (3.6a), equation (3.5) can be written in the following form:

$$\sigma = \varepsilon_0 E_1 \sin(\omega t) + \varepsilon_0 E_2 \cos(\omega t). \tag{3.7}$$

In other words, the stress–strain relationship (3.7) is defined, in view of (3.6), by the modulus E_1 in phase with the strain and by the modulus E_2 which is 90° out of phase with the strain (Fig. 3.1).

Meantime, if we use a complex representation of the input and output, i.e.

$$\varepsilon = \varepsilon_0 \exp(i\omega t) \tag{3.8}$$

and

$$\sigma = \sigma_0 \exp[i(\omega t + \delta)], \tag{3.9}$$

then

$$\frac{\sigma}{\varepsilon} = E^* = \frac{\sigma_0}{\varepsilon_0} \exp(i\delta)$$

$$= \frac{\sigma_0}{\varepsilon_0} (\cos \delta + i \sin \delta)$$

$$= E_1 + iE_2 \tag{3.10}$$

where equation (3.6a) has been used and E^* is referred to as the 'complex modulus'. In the case of a linear viscoelastic response, however, the amplitude ratio, σ_0/ε_0, and the phase difference remain constant for fixed frequency and are generally independent of the amplitude of excitation (e.g. Lee, 1960). In (3.10), the real part E_1 of the complex modulus, which is in phase with the strain, is often referred to as the 'storage modulus' or, simply, the 'dynamic modulus'. It is associated with the energy stored in the specimen due to the applied strain. The imaginary part E_2 of the complex modulus, which is out of phase with the strain, defines the dissipation of energy. It is often called the 'loss modulus' or 'internal friction modulus'. It forms part of the energy dissipated per cycle. The latter is denoted below by ΔW and is expressed as

$$\Delta W = \int \sigma \, d\varepsilon = \int_0^{2\pi/\omega} \sigma \, \frac{d\varepsilon}{dt} \, dt$$

$$= \omega \varepsilon_0^2 \int_0^{2\pi/\omega} [E_1 \sin(\omega t) \cos(\omega t)$$

$$+ E_2 \cos^2(\omega t)] \, dt$$

$$= \pi E_2 \varepsilon_0^2 \tag{3.11}$$

where equations (3.3) and (3.7) have been used. Typical values of E_1, E_2 and $\tan \delta$ for a polymer would be around 10^{10} dyn cm^{-2}, 10^8 dyn cm^{-2} and 0.01 respectively (Ward, 1983). The angle δ, expressed by (3.6b), is of particular interest. It represents, as mentioned earlier, the phase angle by which the strain lags behind the stress. The tangent of δ is conventionally employed as a measure of 'internal friction' of a linear viscoelastic material. Comparing (3.6b) and (3.10), it follows that

$$\tan \delta = \frac{\text{imaginary part of } E^*}{\text{real part of } E^*} = \frac{E_2}{E_1}.$$

A similar treatment can also be followed to define the 'complex compliance'. The latter is denoted by $J^*(i\omega)$ and it is related to the 'complex modulus' by the relation

$$J^*(i\omega) = \frac{1}{E^*(i\omega)} \quad \text{and} \quad E^*(i\omega) = \frac{1}{J^*(i\omega)}. \tag{3.12}$$

That is, by definition, the complex compliance is the reciprocal of the complex modulus and conversely. As discussed later in this chapter, equation (3.12) allows one to establish correlations between the creep phase and the relaxation phase of viscoelastic behaviour. Thus, the variation of either $E^*(i\omega)$ or $J^*(i\omega)$ as a function of frequency is an alternative form for defining the viscoelastic response of the material.

With reference to (3.12), the complex compliance is decomposed into its real and imaginary parts as

$$J^*(i\omega) = J_1(\omega) + iJ_2(\omega). \tag{3.13}$$

Combining equations (3.10), (3.12) and (3.13), it follows that

$$(E_1 + iE_2)(J_1 + iJ_2) = 1. \tag{3.14}$$

For a meaningful description of the dynamic viscoelastic response of the material, it is necessary to determine the moduli E_1 and E_2 or, alternatively, the compliances J_1 and J_2 in terms of frequency. In this case, we refer back to the basic mechanical models introduced earlier in Chapter 2 (section 2.2).

3.3 MECHANICAL MODELS OF VISCOELASTIC RESPONSE UNDER DYNAMIC LOADING

3.3.1 Maxwell model

We recall equation (2.10), characterizing the response behaviour of the Maxwell model,

$$\sigma + \lambda \frac{d\sigma}{dt} = E\lambda \frac{d\varepsilon}{dt}, \quad \lambda = \eta/E, \tag{3.15}$$

where η and E are the characteristics of the elements of the Maxwell model.
Now, we let

$$\sigma = \sigma_0 \exp(i\omega t) \tag{3.16}$$

which, from equation (3.10), can be also expressed as

$$\sigma = \sigma_0 \exp(i\omega t) = (E_1 + iE_2)\varepsilon. \tag{3.17}$$

Thus, by combining equations (3.15) and (3.17), it follows that

$$E_1 + iE_2 = E \frac{i\omega\lambda}{1 + i\omega\lambda}. \tag{3.18}$$

Equating real and imaginary parts in both sides of (3.18),

$$E_1 = E \frac{\omega^2\lambda^2}{1 + \omega^2\lambda^2}, \quad E_2 = E \frac{\omega\lambda}{1 + \omega^2\lambda^2}, \tag{3.19}$$

and, with reference to (3.6b), the phase lag is expressed, for the Maxwell model, as

$$\tan \delta = \frac{1}{\omega\lambda}. \tag{3.20}$$

Figure 3.2 illustrates schematically the variation with frequency of the moduli E_1 and E_2 and the phase lag for the Maxwell model.

With reference to Fig. 3.2, the following points (Gittus, 1975) may be made.

1. At very small frequency of vibrations (i.e. when ω tends to zero), the energy loss in the Newtonian fluid contained in the dashpot would be extremely small. Hence E_2, which is proportional to the energy loss (equation (3.11)), would also be very small. At low frequencies, only very small displacements will be produced in the Maxwell element. Consequently, the modulus E_1, which is in phase with the displacement (equation (3.7)), would also be very small at low frequencies.
2. At moderate to high frequency (i.e. when ω approaches the reciprocal of the relaxation time λ of the system; ω tends to $1/\lambda$ and $\ln(\lambda\omega)$ tends to zero), the fluid in the dashpot flows relatively rapidly. Thus the viscous force becomes larger and, accordingly, both the energy loss in the system and the modulus E_2 will increase. At the same time, the spring must respond accordingly through large extensions, and hence the modulus E_1 will rise as ω approaches $1/\lambda$.

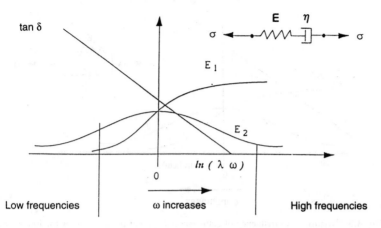

Fig. 3.2 Variation with frequency of moduli E_1, E_2 and phase lag δ for the Maxwell model (Gittus, 1975).

3. At very high frequencies, the spring would support most of the elongation while the dashpot will hardly respond. Accordingly, in view of (3.19), the modulus E_1 will approach its maximum value while the value of the modulus E_2 would approach zero value. Thus, at high frequencies, E_2 is negligible and, in view of (3.10), the value of the complex modulus E^* will be approximately equal to E_1.
4. Following point (3), since $\tan \delta = E_2/E_1$ (equation (3.6b)), $\tan \delta$ decreases monotonically as frequency increases.

3.3.2 Kelvin (Voigt) model

An analytical treatment similar to that carried out above for the Maxwell model leads to the following expressions for the real (storage) compliance J_1 and the imaginary (loss) compliance of a Kelvin model subjected to sinusoidal input. That is,

$$J_1 = \frac{1}{E(1 + \omega^2 \lambda^2)}, \quad J_2 = \frac{\omega\lambda}{E(1 + \omega^2 \lambda^2)} \tag{3.21}$$

and

$$\tan \delta = \omega\lambda. \tag{3.22}$$

The frequency dependence of the compliances J_1 and J_2 and the phase lag for the Kelvin model is illustrated in Fig. 3.3.

1. At very small frequencies of vibration, the viscous drag of the dashpot is small. Accordingly, both the energy loss and loss compliance J_2 are expected to be small.

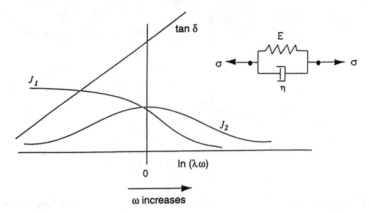

Fig. 3.3 Variation with frequency of compliances J_1, J_2 and phase lag δ for the Kelvin model (Gittus, 1975).

2. At moderate to high frequency (i.e. when ω approaches $1/\lambda$), the dashpot moves more rapidly. Hence the viscous force exerted by the dashpot increases. Thus the applied external force is unable to deform the spring as it counterbalances, at the same time, a large viscous force from the dashpot. Accordingly, the spring elongation and the storage compliance J_1 decrease, while J_2 increases.

3. At very high frequencies, the viscous resistance of the fluid in the dashpot becomes very high, preventing the spring from elongating, and hence J_1 will approach zero. At the same time, the displacement of the dashpot becomes so small that the energy loss per cycle and hence J_2 approach zero.

3.3.3 Three-element model (Standard Linear Solid)

The response of the standard linear solid under static loading is governed by equation (2.36). Solution of this equation for the case of a sinusoidal stimulus follows the same treatment presented earlier for the Maxwell model. This yields, for the moduli E_1 and E_2 and the phase lag δ, the following expressions:

$$E_1 = \frac{E(1 + \omega^2 \lambda \lambda')}{1 + \omega^2 \lambda^2} = \frac{E + \omega^2 \lambda^2 E'}{1 + \omega^2 \lambda^2}; \qquad (3.23)$$

$$E_2 = \frac{E(\lambda' - \lambda)\omega}{1 + \omega^2 \lambda^2} = \frac{(E' - E)\omega \lambda}{1 + \omega^2 \lambda^2}; \qquad (3.24)$$

$$\tan \delta = \frac{(\lambda' - \lambda)\omega}{1 + \omega^2 \lambda \lambda'} = \frac{(E' - E)\omega \lambda}{1 + \omega^2 \lambda^2 E'}; \qquad (3.25)$$

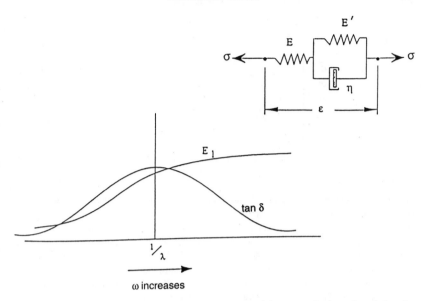

Fig. 3.4 Variation with frequency of the storage modulus E_1 and phase lag δ for the three-element model (Gittus, 1975).

The identification of the parameters appearing in equations (3.23)–(3.25) are presented in conjunction with this model in section 2.2 and shown in Fig. 3.4. In this figure, the variation of moduli and phase lag with frequency is also illustrated. As governed by (3.25), it can be seen in Fig. 3.4 that the phase lag δ goes through a maximum when $\omega^2 = 1/\lambda\lambda'$, instead of varying in a straight line fashion with the frequency, as it does in the case of the Maxwell and Kelvin models. This is, of course, provided that $E = E'$.

As an illustration of the dynamic response of a real viscoelastic material, Fig. 3.5 shows double-logarithmic plots of storage and loss moduli (G' and G'') in shear as functions of circular frequency ω for melts of a standard polystyrene and a binary blend with a low molar mass function (Schausberger, Knoglinger and Janeschitz-Kriegl, 1987).

Figures 3.6 and 3.7, both due to Kolsky (1960), give a comparison between the observed behaviour of four viscoelastic materials, namely polyethylene, polymethyl methacrylate, ebonite and polystyrene, and the predicted behaviour of the two- and three-element mechanical models. The experimental values in the two figures are due to Lethersich (1950) and give the response behaviour of the mentioned materials to time-dependent sinusoidal shear deformation. In Fig. 3.6, it is seen that, whereas the Maxwell and Voigt models are completely inadequate in predicting the variation of tan δ with frequency for real materials, the standard linear solid seems to give a reasonable approximation of the observed behaviour of such materials over at least

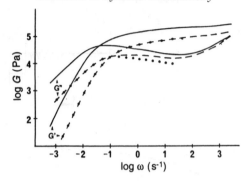

Fig. 3.5 Double-logarithmic plots of storage and loss moduli G' and G'' as functions of circular frequency ω (reference temperature $T_r = 180°C$) for the melts of a standard polystyrene and a binary blend with a low molar mass fraction: measured values for a standard of $M_W = 670$ kg mol^{-1}; $---$, values for a binary mixture of this standard with 35 wt% of a standard with $M_W = 8$ kg mol^{-1}; ●, positions of the full lines after appropriate shifting. (Source: Schausberger, A., Knoglinger, H. and Janeschitz-Kriegl, H. (1987) The role of short chain molecules for the rheology of polystyrene melts. *Rheol. Acta*, **26**, 468–473, Steinkopff Verlag Darmstadt. Reprinted by permission of Steinkopff Verlag Darmstadt.)

one decade of frequency. In Fig. 3.7, the plot of the complex modulus against logarithm of frequency again shows that the predicted behaviour of the two-element model is very inadequate for describing the response of real materials; the standard linear solid seems to be much more suitable, but only over a limited frequency range.

3.4 DYNAMIC VISCOELASTIC BEHAVIOUR

3.4.1 Creep response under alternating stress

Consider a linear viscoelastic solid subjected in the steady state to a sinusoidal stress. This will result, as mentioned earlier, in a sinusoidal strain partly in phase and partly in quadrature with the stress. Thus, using a complex representation of the stress input, the creep response equation can be written as

$$\varepsilon(t) = J^*(i\omega)\sigma(t), \quad \sigma(t) = \sigma_0 \exp(i\omega t). \tag{3.26}$$

In the above equation, $J^*(i\omega)$ is the complex viscoelastic compliance. The latter may be interpreted as the complex strain due to a sinusoidal stress input of unit magnitude. Decomposing the complex compliance into real and imaginary parts, then

$$J^*(i\omega) = J_1(\omega) + iJ_2(\omega), \tag{3.27}$$

where $J_1(\omega)$ is the dynamic storage compliance and $J_2(\omega)$ is the dynamic friction compliance previously introduced in section 3.2.1.

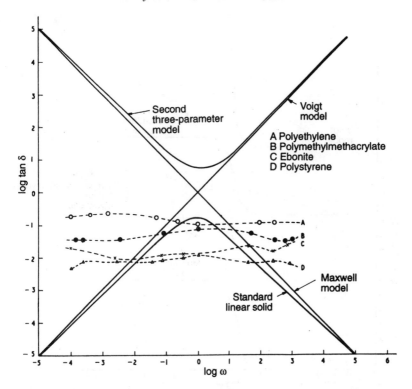

Fig. 3.6 Comparison between response of model solids and measured values of tan δ in shear (Lethersich, 1950). The second three-parameter model is constructed with a dashpot in parallel with a Maxwell model. (Source: Kolsky, H. (1960) Viscoelastic waves, in Int. Symp. on Stress Wave Propagation in Materials (Ed. N. Davids), Interscience Publishers, New York, pp. 59–90. Reprinted with permission.)

Recalling the creep constitutive equation (2.76) in the form of the hereditary integral, one can write

$$\varepsilon(t) = \int_0^\infty F(t - \tau)\, \frac{\mathrm{d}\sigma(\tau)}{\mathrm{d}\tau}\, \mathrm{d}\tau. \tag{3.28}$$

We replace, for convenience, in the above equation the variable $t - \tau$ by ξ; then

$$\varepsilon(t) = \int_0^\infty F(\xi)\, \frac{\mathrm{d}\sigma(t - \xi)}{\mathrm{d}\xi}\, \mathrm{d}\xi. \tag{3.29}$$

Assuming periodic stress input and substituting in the above equation for $\sigma(t) = \sigma_0 \exp(i\omega t)$, then

$$\varepsilon(t) = \int_0^\infty F(\xi) i\omega\sigma_0\, \exp[i\omega(t - \xi)]\, \mathrm{d}\xi \tag{3.30}$$

Transition to dynamic viscoelasticity

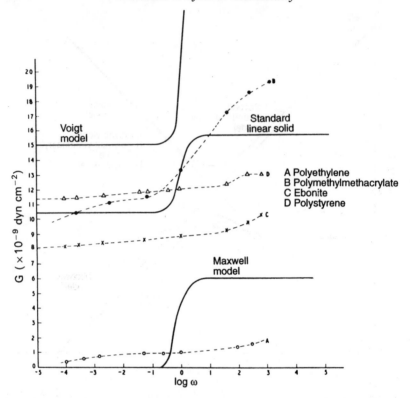

Fig. 3.7 Comparison between response of model solids and measured values of complex modulus in shear (Lethersich, 1950). (Source: Kolsky, H. (1960) Viscoelastic waves, in Int. Symp. on Stress Wave Propagation in Materials (Ed. N. Davids), Interscience Publishers, New York, pp. 59–90. Reprinted with permission.)

which can be written as

$$\varepsilon(t) = i\omega\sigma_0 \exp(i\omega t) \int_0^\infty F(\xi) \exp(-i\omega\xi) \, d\xi. \tag{3.31}$$

On the assumption that the creep function $F(t) = 0$ for $t < 0$, one can replace the lower limit of the integral above by $-\infty$ and write this integral in the following form of Fourier transformation (Appendix D)

$$\bar{F}(\omega) = \int_{-\infty}^\infty F(\tau) \exp(-i\omega\tau) \, d\tau \tag{3.32}$$

where $\bar{F}(\omega)$ is the Fourier transform of the creep function under static stress.

Combining equations (3.31) and (3.32), it follows that

$$\varepsilon(t) = i\omega\sigma_0 \bar{F}(\omega) \exp(i\omega t). \tag{3.33}$$

Equation (3.33) illustrates a basic characteristic concerning the linearity in response; that is, when the stress is periodic, the resulting strain will also be periodic. Hence, if

$$\varepsilon(t) = \varepsilon_0 \exp(i\omega t),$$

then, by comparison with (3.33), it follows that

$$\varepsilon_0 = i\omega\sigma_0 \bar{F}(\omega) \qquad (3.34)$$

or

$$\frac{\varepsilon_0}{\sigma_0} = i\omega\bar{F}(\omega). \qquad (3.35)$$

In the above equation, the ratio ε_0/σ_0 is a complex number which is expressed, in view of (3.10), as

$$\frac{\varepsilon_0}{\sigma_0} = i\omega\bar{F}(\omega) = \frac{\exp(i\delta)}{E^*}. \qquad (3.36)$$

As mentioned in section 3.2, the tangent of δ is often used as a measure of 'internal friction' of a linear viscoelastic material; hence, in view of (3.36), the internal friction can be determined when the Fourier transform of the creep function is known.

3.4.2 Relaxation response under alternating strain

Consider the complex presentation of the alternating strain input. Then the relaxation response equation is expressed in an analogous manner to (3.26) by

$$\sigma(t) = E^*(i\omega)\varepsilon(t), \quad \varepsilon(t) = \varepsilon_0 \exp(i\omega t), \qquad (3.37)$$

where $E^*(i\omega)$ is the complex viscoelastic modulus; this is interpreted as the complex stress resulting from the application of a sinusoidal strain of unit magnitude.

Recalling the stress-relaxation constitutive equation (2.82) in the form of the hereditary integral, one writes

$$\sigma(t) = \int_0^\infty R(t - \tau) \frac{d\varepsilon(\tau)}{d\tau} \, d\tau. \qquad (3.38)$$

Equation (3.38), with a similar procedure to that carried out on the creep constitutive equation (3.28), leads to

$$\frac{\sigma_0}{\varepsilon_0} = i\omega\bar{R}(\omega) = E^* \exp(-i\delta) \qquad (3.39)$$

where equation (3.10) has been used and $\bar{R}(\omega)$ is the Fourier transform of the relaxation function under static strain, i.e.

$$\bar{R}(\omega) = \int_{-\infty}^\infty R(\tau) \exp(-i\omega\tau) \, d\tau. \qquad (3.40)$$

Further, by combining (3.35) and (3.39), a relationship between the Fourier transform of the creep function and that of the relaxation function is expressed as

$$-\omega^2 \bar{F}(\omega)\bar{R}(\omega) = 1,$$ (3.41)

which again is a correlation between the creep and relaxation phases of the viscoelastic response in the linear case.

3.5 RELATIONS BETWEEN MATERIAL FUNCTIONS ASSOCIATED WITH CREEP AND RELAXATION

The material functions characterizing the response behaviour of a linear viscoelastic material are interrelated. That is, one material function is analytically deduced from another. We present below the different relations between the different material functions associated with both creep and stress relaxation of a linear viscoelastic material under static and dynamic loading conditions. For more information, the reader is referred, in this context, to Gross (1947), Alfrey (1948), Leaderman (1954a, b), Schwarzl and Staverman (1952), Fung (1965) and Ferry (1970), among others.

3.5.1 Material functions associated with creep

(a) Complex compliance function and creep function

In order to establish a relationship between the dynamic complex compliance $J^*(i\omega)$ and the creep function $F(\tau)$, pertaining to the static response, we employ the creep constitutive equation (3.28). Substituting $\sigma(t) = \sigma_0 \exp(i\omega t)$ in (3.28), it can be shown that

$$J^*(i\omega) = \int_0^\infty \exp(-i\omega\tau)\, \frac{dF(\tau)}{d\tau}\, d\tau.$$ (3.42)

Decomposing this equation into real and imaginary components gives

$$J_1(\omega) = \int_0^\infty \frac{dF(\tau)}{d\tau} \cos(\omega\tau)\, d\tau$$ (3.43a)

and

$$J_2(\omega) = -\int_0^\infty \frac{dF(\tau)}{d\tau} \sin(\omega\tau)\, d\tau$$ (3.43b)

where $J^*(i\omega) = J_1(\omega) + iJ_2(\omega)$.

It is apparent from equations (3.43) that $J_1(\omega)$ and $J_2(\omega)$ are Fourier transforms of the creep function $F(\tau)$. Thus, by inversion of (3.43a) or (3.43b), the creep function can be determined in terms of the dynamic compliance components. The simultaneous existence of the two relations (3.43a) and (3.43b) implies that a relationship between

$J_1(\omega)$ and $J_2(\omega)$ exists (Gross, 1953). Benbow (1956), for instance, considered the determination of dynamic moduli and internal friction of high polymers from static creep measurements with reference to some measurements made of polythene. This was carried out using an integral transformation as based on a procedure put forward by Roesler and Pearson (1954) and Roesler and Twyman (1955).

(b) Complex compliance function and retardation spectrum

Consider, in view of (2.60), the rate of creep function as

$$\frac{dF(t)}{dt} = \int_0^\infty \frac{\alpha f(\lambda)}{\lambda} \exp(-t/\lambda) \, d\lambda. \tag{3.44}$$

Following Gross (1953), one introduces a creep frequency $s = 1/\lambda$ and a frequency distribution

$$N(s) = \alpha f(1/s)/s^2. \tag{3.45}$$

Hence, $N(s)$ represents also a retardation spectrum. Combining equations (3.44) and (3.45), the former becomes

$$\frac{dF(t)}{dt} = \int_0^\infty s N(s) \exp(-ts) \, ds \tag{3.46}$$

which is a form of a Laplace integral.

Substituting expression (3.46) into (3.42), it can be shown that the complex compliance function can be expressed in terms of the retardation spectrum (the distribution function of retardation times) as

$$J^*(i\omega) = \int_0^\infty \frac{s N(s)}{s + i\omega} \, ds. \tag{3.47}$$

Decomposing the above equation into real and imaginary components, gives

$$J_1(\omega) = \int_0^\infty N(s) \frac{s^2}{s^2 + \omega^2} \, ds \tag{3.48a}$$

and

$$J_2(\omega) = -\int_0^\infty N(s) \frac{\omega s}{s^2 + \omega^2} \, ds. \tag{3.48b}$$

In order to determine the retardation spectrum explicitly from the creep compliance, one substitutes in equation (3.47) $\omega \exp(\pm i\pi)$ for $i\omega$; then, this equation is transformed to (Gross, 1953)

$$J^*[\omega \exp(\pm i\pi)] = \int_0^\infty \frac{s N(s)}{s - \omega} \, ds \mp i\pi\omega N(\omega) \tag{3.49}$$

which results in the determination of the retardation spectrum

$$N(\omega) = \pm \frac{1}{\pi\omega} \text{ Im } J^* \ \omega[\exp(\mp i\pi)] \tag{3.50}$$

or in terms of J_1 and J_2 as

$$N(\omega) = \pm \frac{2}{\pi\omega} \text{ Im } J_1[\exp(\mp i\pi/2)] \tag{3.51a}$$

and

$$N(\omega) = \frac{2}{\pi\omega} \text{ Re } J_2[\exp(\mp i\pi/2)] \tag{3.51b}$$

where $\text{Im}(\cdot)$ and $\text{Re}(\cdot)$ refer, respectively, to imaginary and real parts of the complex variable or function $(\cdot)$. Thus, in terms of the formulations above, one can determine the retardation frequency spectrum from the complex compliance function or from its real and imaginary parts. Approximation formulae for the determination of the retardation spectrum were given by Alfrey and Doty (1945), Schwarzl (1951), Andrews (1952) and Marvin (1952). For a review and evaluation of such approximation formulae, the reader is referred to Leaderman (1954a, b).

3.5.2 Material functions associated with relaxation

(a) Complex modulus function and relaxation function

Substituting the alternating stress input $\sigma = \sigma_0 \exp(i\omega t)$ into the relaxation constitutive equation (3.38), it can be concluded that

$$E^*(i\omega) = i\omega \int_0^\infty \exp(-i\omega\tau)R(\tau) \ \mathrm{d}\tau. \tag{3.52}$$

Further, the complex modulus function, as represented by the above equation, can be decomposed into real and imaginary parts, i.e.

$$E^*(i\omega) = E_1(\omega) + iE_2(\omega)$$

where

$$E_1(\omega) = \omega \int_0^\infty R(\tau) \ \sin(\omega\tau) \ \mathrm{d}\tau \tag{3.53a}$$

and

$$E_2(\omega) = \omega \int_0^\infty R(\tau) \ \cos(\omega\tau) \ \mathrm{d}\tau \tag{3.53b}$$

Equations (3.52) and (3.53) are forms of Fourier integrals. Both equations establish a connection between the dynamic response and the static response in linear viscoelasticity. As shown, these equations permit one to determine the dynamic complex modulus function or its components in terms of the relaxation function in the static case. Conversely, these equations may be inverted to determine the relaxation function explicitly in terms of the dynamic moduli. Considering, for instance, the inversion of (3.53), the relaxation function is expressed as

$$R(t) = \frac{2}{\pi} \int_0^\infty \frac{E_1(\omega)}{\omega} \sin(\omega t) \, d\omega \qquad (3.54a)$$

or, alternatively,

$$R(t) = \frac{2}{\pi} \int_0^\infty \frac{E_2(\omega)}{\omega} \cos(\omega t) \, d\omega. \qquad (3.54b)$$

That is, the relaxation function pertaining to the viscoelastic response under static strain can be determined from dynamic data.

(b) Complex modulus function and relaxation spectrum

Consider the expression (2.56) for the relaxation function, i.e.

$$R(t) = \int_0^\infty \beta \Gamma(\lambda) \exp(-t/\lambda) \, d\lambda. \qquad (3.55)$$

We introduce now a relaxation frequency $s = 1/\lambda$ and a corresponding relaxation frequency spectrum $N'(s) \, ds$ where

$$N'(s) = \beta \Gamma(1/s)/s^2, \quad s = 1/\lambda. \qquad (3.56)$$

Combining (3.55) and (3.56), the relaxation function is expressed in terms of the frequency spectrum as

$$R(t) = \int_0^\infty N'(s) \exp(-ts) \, ds. \qquad (3.57)$$

The integral in this equation is a Laplace transform. Thus, when the relaxation function $R(t)$ is given, the inversion of (3.57) results in the determination of the relaxation frequency spectrum $N'(s)$ (e.g. Gross, 1947, 1953; Macey, 1948; Pol and Bremmer, 1951).

Combining (3.52) and (3.57), it can be shown through an iteration procedure that the complex modulus is

$$E^*(i\omega) = i\omega \int_0^\infty \frac{N'(s)}{s + i\omega} \, ds. \qquad (3.58)$$

Meantime, separating $E^*(i\omega)$ into its real and imaginary parts, the dynamic storage modulus and the dynamic friction modulus are expressed, respectively by

$$E_1(\omega) = \int_0^\infty N'(s) \frac{\omega^2}{\omega^2 + s^2} \, ds \qquad (3.59a)$$

and

$$E_2(\omega) = \int_0^\infty N'(s) \frac{\omega s}{\omega^2 + s^2} \, ds. \qquad (3.59b)$$

Further, by substituting $\omega \exp(\pm i\pi)$ for $i\omega$ in equation (3.58), it can be shown that the latter equation will transform into

$$E^*[\omega \exp(\pm i\pi)] = -\omega \int_0^\infty \frac{N'(s)}{s - \omega} \, ds \pm i\pi\omega N'(\omega). \qquad (3.60)$$

Inversion of equation (3.60) results in the determination of the relaxation spectrum. That is,

$$N'(\omega) = \pm \frac{1}{\pi\omega} \operatorname{Im} E^*[\omega \exp(\pm i\pi)] \qquad (3.61)$$

or, alternatively, in terms of the dynamic moduli E_1 and E_2,

$$N'(\omega) = \pm \frac{2}{\pi\omega} \operatorname{Im} E_1[\exp(\pm i\pi/2)] \qquad (3.62a)$$

and

$$N'(\omega) = \frac{2}{\pi\omega} \operatorname{Re} E_2[\exp(\pm i\pi/2)]. \qquad (3.62b)$$

Thus, one is able to determine the relaxation frequency spectrum from the complex modulus as well as from its real and imaginary components (Roesler and Pearson, 1954; Roesler, 1955; Roesler and Twyman, 1955).

3.5.3 Interrelation between the retardation spectrum and the relaxation spectrum

The retardation and relaxation spectra are time distribution functions of the compliance and the elastic moduli, respectively. As we have discussed in sections 3.5.1(b) and 3.5.2(b), both spectra are determinable from the creep and relaxation data respectively, but with the involvement of the numerical solution of the corresponding integral equations.

As shown earlier, equations (3.12) allow us to establish a correlation between the material functions associated with the creep phase and those pertaining to the relaxation phase of viscoelastic behaviour. In this section, we seek along the same lines a relationship between the retardation spectrum and the relaxation spectrum.

Following Gross (1953), one substitutes $\omega \exp(\pm i\pi)$ for $i\omega$ in (3.12); then

$$E^*[\omega \exp(\pm i\pi)] = 1/J^*[\omega \exp(\pm i\pi)] \tag{3.63a}$$

and

$$J^*[\omega \exp(\pm i\pi)] = 1/E^*[\omega \exp(\pm i\pi)]. \tag{3.63b}$$

Separating into real and imaginary parts and recalling the creep distribution function $f(\lambda)$ and the relaxation distribution function $\Gamma(\lambda)$, it can be shown that (Gross, 1953)

$$\alpha f(\lambda) = \frac{1}{\pi \lambda^2} \frac{\pi \beta \Gamma(\lambda)}{[k(\lambda)]^2 + [\pi \beta \Gamma(\lambda)]^2} \tag{3.64a}$$

and

$$\beta \Gamma(\lambda) = \frac{1}{\pi \lambda^2} \frac{\pi \alpha f(\lambda)}{[K(\lambda)]^2 + [\pi \alpha f(\lambda)]^2} \tag{3.64b}$$

where

$$k(\lambda) = \int_0^\infty \beta \Gamma(u) \frac{u}{\lambda(\lambda - u)} \, du \tag{3.65a}$$

and

$$K(\lambda) = \int_0^\infty \alpha f(u) \frac{du}{\lambda - u}. \tag{3.65b}$$

Relations (3.64) express the interrelations between the distribution functions in creep and relaxation. These relations are of particular interest for the discussion of the variations in the spectra when one shifts from creep to relaxation and vice versa. Figure 3.8 gives schematic illustration of relaxation and retardation spectra (e.g. Gross and Pelzer, 1951). It should be emphasized that equations (3.64a) and (3.64b) are based on the assumption of continuous spectra which might include, as special cases, both line and mixed type spectra (Gross, 1953).

In the theory of viscoelasticity, both the retardation and the relaxation spectra are of interest. This may be due to the fact that either of the two spectra provides an overall reflection of the mechanical properties of the viscoelastic material over the extent of time or frequency considered. Further, there is a general expectation that these spectra could be correlated, in some manner, with the molecular structure of the viscoelastic material.

The interrelations between material functions associated with creep and relaxation, as dealt with in this section, are demonstrated in Fig. 3.9.

As can be recognized from Fig. 3.9, the linear viscoelastic behaviour of material can be determined by one of the functions in the following two groups.

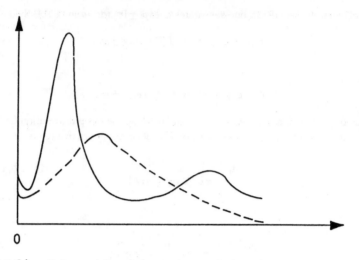

Fig. 3.8 Schematic representation of relaxation (———) and retardation (– – –) spectra (Gross, 1953).

1. Material functions determined by experiment:

    (a) the retardation function $F(t)$;
    (b) the relaxation function $R(t)$;
    (c) the dynamic complex compliance $J^*(i\omega)$;
    (d) the dynamic complex modulus $E^*(i\omega)$.

2. Material functions determined by integral transformation of experimental functions (1):

    (a) the retardation spectrum under static loading, $f(\lambda)$, or the retardation spectrum under dynamic loading, $N(s)$;
    (b) the relaxation spectrum under static loading, $\Gamma(\lambda)$, or the relaxation spectrum under dynamic loading, $N'(s)$.

Both the retardation function $F(t)$ and the relaxation function $R(t)$ in (1) above can be determined directly from an experiment under static loading. That is, $F(t)$ is determined from a creep experiment and $R(t)$ is determined from a relaxation experiment. The complex compliance $J^*(i\omega)$ and the complex modulus $E^*(i\omega)$ may be, however, determined from dynamic oscillation measurements with prescribed stress or strain respectively. On the other hand, in group (2) above, the retardation spectrum $f(\lambda)$ is obtained by integral transformation from the retardation function $F(t)$ and the retardation spectrum $N(s)$ is obtained by integral transformation from the complex compliance $J^*(i\omega)$. Similarly, the relaxation spectrum under static loading $\Gamma(\lambda)$ or that under dynamic loading $N'(s)$ is obtained by integral transformation from the relaxation function $R(t)$ or the complex modulus $E^*(i\omega)$. Thus, any one of the

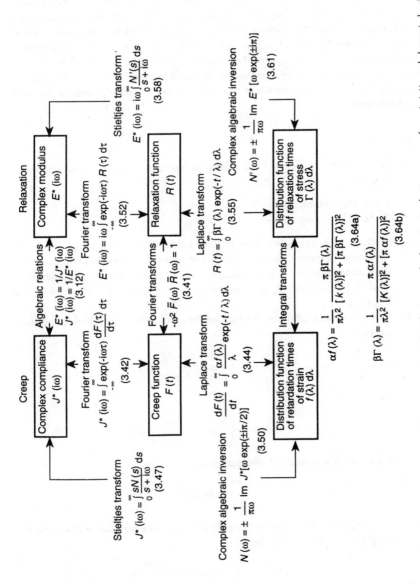

Fig. 3.9 Interrelations between material functions associated with creep and relaxation in the two cases of quasi-static and dynamic loading.

material functions stated above would suffice for the characterization of the linear viscoelastic response behaviour under isothermal conditions. In practice, however, a difficulty arises from the fact that creep and relaxation experiments under static testing conditions cannot be performed in very short times (i.e. instantaneously) and dynamic measurements cannot be easily extended to very long times (Schwarzl and Staverman, 1952). Accordingly, the mathematical transformation formulism mentioned above may not be directly applicable. Thus, approximate methods of transforming operator representation could be required (Lee, 1960). Alternatively, one would be inclined to use the appropriate type of measurement and determine the viscoelastic response of the material by the particular material function pertaining directly to such measurement.

PROBLEMS

3.1 Determine the storage and loss moduli as functions of $\ln(\omega\tau)$ for the following models:

    1. the Maxwell model;
    2. the Kelvin–Voigt model.

    Illustrate, by a sketch, the shape of these functions for each model.

3.2 Determine the energy dissipated per cycle in terms of the loss compliance $J_2(\omega)$.

3.3 For a material with a single relaxation time λ show that E_1 is proportional to $\omega^2\lambda^2/(1 + \omega^2\lambda^2)$ and E_2 is proportional to $\omega\lambda/(1 + \omega^2\lambda^2)$ where ω is the frequency.

3.4 If $\phi(\lambda)$ denotes a spectrum of relaxation times, show that the following relations are valid:

$$E_1(\omega) = \int_0^\infty \phi(\lambda) \frac{\omega^2\lambda^2}{1 + \omega^2\lambda^2}\, d\lambda$$

and

$$E_2(\omega) = \int_0^\infty \phi(\lambda) \frac{\omega\lambda}{1 + \omega^2\lambda^2}\, d\lambda$$

where $\phi(\cdot)$ is a normalized distribution function with

$$\int_0^\infty \phi(\lambda)\, d\lambda = 1.$$

3.5 Prove that the relation between the dynamic complex compliance $J^*(i\omega)$ and the creep function $F(t)$ is given by

$$J^*(i\omega) = \int_0^\infty \exp(-i\omega\tau) \frac{dF(\tau)}{d\tau}\, d\tau.$$

3.6 Derive the expression (3.58) for the complex modulus from expression (3.52).

3.7 Following problem 3.6, derive the expressions for the components of the complex modulus in terms of the relaxation spectrum.

3.8 For a creep frequency $s = 1/\lambda$ and a frequency distribution $N(s) = \alpha f(1/s)/s^2$ where α is a constant, prove that the time derivative of the creep function is given by

$$\frac{dF(t)}{dt} = \int_0^\infty sN(s) \exp(-ts) \, ds.$$

3.9 Following problem 3.8, show that the complex compliance function can be expressed in terms of the distribution function of retardation times $N(s)$ as

$$J^*(i\omega) = \int_0^\infty \frac{sN(s)}{s + i\omega} \, ds.$$

Express the components of the complex compliance function $J_1(\omega)$ and $J_2(\omega)$ for this case.

REFERENCES

Alfrey, T. (1948) *Mechanical Behaviour of High Polymers*, Interscience, New York.
Alfrey, T. and Doty, P. (1945) The methods of specifying the properties of viscoelastic materials. *J. Appl. Phys.*, **16**, 700–13.
Andrews, R. D. (1952) Correlation of dynamic and static measurements on rubber-like materials. *Ind. Eng. Chem.*, **44**, 707–15.
Benbow, J. J. (1956) The determination of dynamic moduli and internal friction of high polymers from creep measurements. *Proc. Phys. Soc. B*, **69**(9), 885–92.
Ferry, J. D. (1970) *Viscoelastic Properties of Polymers*, 2nd edn, Wiley, New York.
Fung, Y. C. (1965) *Foundations of Solid Mechanics*, Prentice-Hall, New York.
Gittus, J. (1975) *Creep, Viscoelasticity and Creep Fracture in Solids*, Wiley, New York.
Gross, B. (1947) On creep and relaxation. *J. Appl. Phys.*, **18**, 212–21.
Gross, B. (1953) *Mathematical Structure of the Theories of Viscoelasticity*, Hermann, Paris.
Gross, B. and Pelzer, H. (1951) On creep and relaxation III. *J. Appl. Phys.*, **22**, 1035–9.
Kolsky, H. (1960) Viscoelastic waves, in Int. Symp. on Stress Wave Propagation in Materials (ed. N. Davids), Interscience, New York, pp. 59–90.
Leaderman, H. (1954a) Approximations in linear viscoelasticity theory: delta function approximation. *J. Appl. Phys.*, **25**, 294–6.
Leaderman, H. (1954b) Rheology of polyisobutylene, IV. Calculation of the retardation time function and dynamic response from creep data, in Proc. 2nd Int. Congr. on Rheology, Butterworth, London, pp. 203–13.
Lee, E. H. (1960) Viscoelastic stress analysis, in 1st Symp. on Naval Structural Mechanics, Pergamon, New York, pp. 456–82.
Lethersich, W. (1950) The rheological properties of dielectric polymers. *Br. J. Appl. Phys.*, **1** (November), 294–301.
Macey, B. (1948) On the application of Laplace pairs to the analysis of relaxation curves. *J. Sci. Instrum.*, **25**, 251–3.
Marvin, R. S. (1952) A new approximate conversion method for relating stress relaxation and dynamic modulus. *Phys. Rev.*, **86**, 644–5.
Pol, B. Van Der and Bremmer, H. (1951) *Operational Calculus*, Cambridge University Press, Cambridge.

Roesler, F. C. (1955) Some applications of Fourier series in the numerical treatment of linear behaviour. *Proc. Phys. Soc. B*, **68**, 89–96.

Roesler, F. C. and Pearson, J. R. A. (1954) Determination of relaxation spectra from damping measurements. *Proc. Phys. Soc. B*, **67**, 338–47.

Roesler, F. C. and Twyman, W. A. (1955) An iteration method for the determination of relaxation spectra. *Proc. Phys. Soc. B*, **68**(2), 97–105.

Schausberger, A., Knoglinger, H. and Janeschitz-Kriegl, H. (1987) The role of short chain molecules for the rheology of polystyrene melts, II. Linear viscoelastic properties. *Rheol. Acta*, **26**, 468–73.

Schwarzl, F. (1951) Näherungsmethoden in der Theorie des viscoelastischen Verhaltens I. *Physica*, **17**, 830–40.

Schwarzl, F. and Staverman, A. J. (1952) Time–temperature dependence of linear viscoelastic behaviour. *J. Appl. Phys.*, **23**(8), 838–43.

Ward, I. M. (1983) *Mechanical Properties of Solid Polymers*, 2nd edn, Wiley, New York.

FURTHER READING

Barker, L. M. and Hollenbach, R. E. (1964) System for measuring the dynamic properties of materials. *Rev. Sci. Instrum.*, **35**(6), 742–6.

Christensen, R. M. (1972) Restrictions upon viscoelastic relaxation functions and complex moduli. *Trans. Soc. Rheol.*, **16**, 603–14.

Davis, J. L. (1987) *Introduction to Dynamics of Continuous Media*, Macmillan, New York.

Day, M. A. (1970) Some results on the least work needed to produce a given strain in a given time in a viscoelastic material and a uniqueness theorem for dynamic viscoelasticity. *Q.J. Mech. Appl. Math.*, **23**, 469–79.

Doi, M. and Edwards, S. F. (1986) *The Theory of Polymer Dynamics*, Clarendon, Oxford.

Edelstein, W. S. and Gurtin, M. E. (1964) Uniqueness theorems in the linear dynamic theory of anisotropic viscoelastic solids. *Arch. Ration. Mech. Anal.*, **17**, 47–60.

Gibson, R. F., Hwang, S. J. and Sheppard, C. H. (1990) Characterization of creep in polymer composites by the use of frequency–time transformations. *J. Compos. Mater.*, **24** (April), 441–53.

Hunter, S. C. (1960) Viscoelastic waves, in *Progress in Solid Mechanics* (eds I. N. Sneddon and R. Hill), North-Holland, Amsterdam, pp. 1–57.

Kolsky, H. (1949) An investigation of the mechanical properties of materials at very high rates of loading. *Proc. Phys. Soc. B*, **62**, 676–700.

Lethersich, W. (1950) The measurement of the coefficient of internal friction of solid rods by a resonance method. *Br. J. Appl. Phys.*, **1**, 18–22.

Magrab, E. B. and Blomquist, D. S. (1971) *The Measurement of Time-varying Phenomena*, Wiley, New York.

Nashif, A. D., Jones, D. I. G. and Henderson, J. P. (1965) *Vibration Damping*, Wiley, New York.

Orbey, N. and Ded, J. M. (1991) Determination of the relaxation system from oscillatory-shear data. *J. Rheol.*, **35**, 1035–49.

Pandit, S. M. (1991) *Model and Spectrum Analysis: Data Dependent Systems in State Space*, Wiley, New York.

Pindera, J. T. and Straka, P. (1974) On physical measures of rheological response of some materials in wide ranges of temperature and spectral frequency. *Rheol. Acta*, **13**, 338–51.

Ricketts, T. E. and Goldsmith, W. (1970) Dynamic properties of rocks and composite structural materials. *Int. J. Rock Mech. Min. Sci.*, **7**, 313–35.

Yu, P. and Haddad, Y. M. (1993) A dynamic system method for the characterization of the rheological response of a class of viscoelastic materials. *Int. J. Pressure Vessels Piping*, in press.

4

Three-dimensional linear viscoelasticity

4.1 INTRODUCTION

In Chapter 2 we introduced the basic formulations concerning the one-dimensional response behaviour of a linear viscoelastic material under static loading. In the present chapter, we extend the presentation to include the generalization of the formulations to the three-dimensional case. The most direct approach in this regard is to replace the one-dimensional constitutive relationships by their corresponding tensorial equivalents.

4.2 THREE-DIMENSIONAL CONSTITUTIVE EQUATIONS

Let $\varepsilon_{ij}(x_i, t)$ denote the strain field defined at every point x_i of the material at time t $(-\infty < t < \infty)$. The latter is derived within the infinitesimal deformation theory from the deformation field $u_i(x_i, t)$ by equation (1.73), i.e.

$$\varepsilon_{ij}(x_i, t) = \tfrac{1}{2}[u_{i,j}(x_i, t) + u_{j,i}(x_i, t)]. \tag{4.1}$$

Consider now the Cauchy stress tensor field $\sigma_{ij}(x_i, t)$ corresponding to $\varepsilon_{ij}(x_i, t)$. For a non-aging viscoelastic material with an arbitrary degree of anisotropy, the hypothesis that the current value of the creep strain depends on the complete stress history is expressed by

$$\varepsilon_{kl}(t) = f_{kl}[\sigma_{ij}(t - \tau), \quad \sigma_{ij}(t)], \quad 0 \le (t, \tau) < \infty, \tag{4.2}$$

where, for notational simplicity, explicit dependence of the stresses, strains and material properties on coordinates x_i is omitted. In equation (4.2), $f_{kl}[\cdot]$ is a linear tensor-valued function which transforms each stress history $\sigma_{ij}(t, \tau)$, $0 \le (t, \tau) < \infty$, into a corresponding strain history $\varepsilon_{kl}(t)$. The functional $f_{kl}[\cdot]$, as seen from equation (4.2), depends also on the current state of the stress $\sigma_{ij}(t)$. In an analogous form to (2.76) the response relation (4.2) above can be written (e.g. Axelrad, 1970) in the following form of the Stieltjes integral:

$$\varepsilon_{kl}(t) = \int_{-\infty}^{\infty} F_{klij}(t - \tau) \frac{\partial \sigma_{ij}(\tau)}{\partial \tau} \, d\tau \tag{4.3}$$

.In this equation, $F_{klij}(\cdot)$ is a fourth-order tensorial function referred to as the 'tensorial creep function'. $F_{klij}(t) = 0$ for $-\infty < t < 0$ and each of its components is of bounded variation in every closed subinterval $-\infty < t < \infty$. The fourth-order tensor components $F_{klij}(t)$ are known as the creep compliances. The creep function $F_{klij}(\cdot)$ is interpreted as the strain response at $t \geq 0$ to a constant unit stress applied at $t = 0$, so that $F_{klij}(t) = 0$ for $t < 0$ and $F_{klij}(0)$ is the instantaneous response at time $t = 0$. It is assumed that $F_{klij}(t)$ and at least its first derivative are continuous for $t \geq 0$, under the understanding that stress and strain histories with discontinuities at $t = 0$ are mathematically permissible (Gurtin and Sternberg, 1962). In the constitutive equation (4.3), it is noticed that the lower limit of the hereditary integral is taken as $-\infty$ which allows for the possibility of input histories prior to the time origin $t = 0$. This could be of benefit in particular engineering applications such as, for example, the study of steady-state vibrational response (Flügge, 1975).

With reference to the constitutive creep equation (4.3), one may also consider the case of discontinuous stress histories. This can be accomplished in equation (4.3), as shown previously in the one-dimensional case (Chapter 2, section 2.3), through the use of unit step functions. Thus, by resolving in equation (4.3) the stress histories $\sigma_{ij}(t)$, which have a step discontinuity at $t = 0$, into a uniformly convergent sequence of continuous functions, the constitutive relation corresponding to (4.3) can be written as

$$\varepsilon_{kl}(t) = F_{klij}(t)\sigma_{ij}(0) + \int_0^t F_{klij}(t - \tau)\, \frac{\partial \sigma_{ij}(\tau)}{\partial \tau}\, \mathrm{d}\tau \tag{4.4}$$

or, alternatively,

$$\varepsilon_{kl}(t) = F_{klij}(0)\sigma_{ij}(t) + \int_0^t \dot{F}_{klij}(\tau)\sigma_{ij}(t - \tau)\, \mathrm{d}\tau \tag{4.5}$$

where the fourth order tensor $F_{klij}(0)$ is usually referred to as the 'instantaneous elastic compliance' of the material. Equations (4.4) and (4.5) can be seen to follow the superposition of input histories principle (Boltzmann's) that the current output is determined by the superposition of the response to the complete spectrum of increments of inputs.

Any discontinuity in the form of a jump in the stress input $\sigma_{ij}(t)$ will contribute a corresponding instantaneous response similar to the first term in equation (4.4). For instance, if $\sigma_{ij}(t)$ experiences another jump, say $\Delta\sigma_{ij}(t_1)$ at time t_1, $0 < t_1 < t$, while $F_{klij}(t)$ and $\partial\sigma_{ij}(t)/\partial t$ are continuous elsewhere, equation (4.4) would take the following form:

$$\varepsilon_{kl}(t) = F_{klij}(t)\sigma_{ij}(0) + F_{klij}(t - t_1)\, \Delta\sigma_{ij}(t_1)H(t - t_1)$$

$$+ \int_0^t F_{klij}(t - \tau)\, \frac{\partial \sigma_{ij}(\tau)}{\partial \tau}\, \mathrm{d}\tau \tag{4.6}$$

where $H(t - t_1)$ is the Heaviside unit step function (Appendix B).

Similarly, in analogous manner to equation (4.2), the relaxation stress can be expressed as a function of the entire strain history in the viscoelastic, non-aging material as

$$\sigma_{ij}(t) = r_{ij}[\varepsilon_{ij}(t - \tau), \quad \varepsilon_{ij}(t)], \quad 0 \le (t, \tau) < \infty. \tag{4.7}$$

Consequently, the stress-relaxation equation can be written, in a corresponding form to equation (4.3), as

$$\sigma_{ij}(t) = \int_{-\infty}^{t} R_{ijkl}(t - \tau) \frac{\partial \varepsilon_{kl}(t - \tau)}{\partial \tau} \, d\tau \tag{4.8}$$

in which $R_{ijkl}(t - \tau)$ is the fourth-order tensorial relaxation function. The components of $R_{ijkl}(t)$ are known as the relaxation moduli.

Further, if the strain is applied to the material specimen at $t = 0$, i.e. if $\varepsilon_{kl}(t) = 0$ for $t < 0$, relation (4.8) can be written, in a similar fashion to equation (4.4), as

$$\sigma_{ij}(t) = R_{ijkl}(t)\varepsilon_{kl}(0) + \int_{0}^{t} R_{ijkl}(t - \tau) \frac{\partial \varepsilon_{kl}(\tau)}{\partial \tau} \, d\tau. \tag{4.9}$$

In the stress-relaxation constitutive relation (4.9), $R_{ijkl}(t, \tau) = 0$ for $-\infty < t < 0$. Both $R_{ijkl}(t, \tau)$ and its first derivative are assumed to be continuous functions of time during $0 \le t < \infty$. An alternative form to (4.9) is the constitutive relaxation relation

$$\sigma_{ij}(t) = R_{ijkl}(0)\varepsilon_{kl}(t) + \int_{0}^{t} \dot{R}_{ijkl}(\tau)\varepsilon_{kl}(t - \tau) \, d\tau \tag{4.10}$$

where the fourth-order tensor $R_{ijkl}(0)$ is the 'instantaneous elastic modulus' of the material, i.e. at time $t = 0$.

Further, it is often assumed (Day, 1972) that

$$\int_{0}^{+\infty} \| \dot{R}_{ijkl}(t) \| \, dt < +\infty, \quad \int_{0}^{+\infty} t \, \| \dot{R}_{ijkl}(t) \| \, dt < +\infty, \tag{4.11}$$

where $\| \cdot \|$ the norm. These assumptions ensure that the 'equilibrium elastic modulus'

$$R_{ijkl}(+\infty) = \lim_{t \to +\infty} R_{ijkl}(t)$$

exists.

Any discontinuity in the form of a jump of the strain history $\varepsilon_{ij}(t)$ will again contribute an immediate discontinuity in the response and, hence, an additional term similar to the first term in equation (4.9). Consider, for instance, that $\varepsilon_{ij}(t)$ has a jump $\Delta\varepsilon_{ij}(t_1)$ at time t_1, $0 < t_1 < t$, while $R_{klij}(t)$ and $\partial\varepsilon_{ij}(t)/\partial t$ are continuous elsewhere; then, equation (4.9) becomes

$$\sigma_{ij}(t) = R_{ijkl}(t)\varepsilon_{kl}(0)$$
$$+ R_{ijkl}(t - t_1) \, \Delta\varepsilon_{kl}(t_1)H(t - t_1)$$
$$+ \int_{0}^{t} R_{ijkl}(t - \tau) \frac{\partial \varepsilon_{kl}(\tau)}{\partial \tau} \, d\tau \tag{4.12}$$

where $H(t - t_1)$ is the Heaviside unit step function.

The constitutive equations (4.3) and (4.8) may also be expressed in the form of a convolution integral which is frequently used in the mathematical branch of abstract algebra. In the creep phase, for instance, consider the two tensorial functions $F_{klij}(t)$ and $\sigma_{kl}(t)$ to be defined in the interval $-\infty < t < \infty$. The convolution of the two functions is established by the convolution product defined in the time range $0 \leq t < \infty$ as follows:

$$F_{ijkl}(t) * d\sigma_{kl}(t) = \int_0^t F_{ijkl}(t - \tau) \frac{d\sigma_{kl}(t)}{d\tau} d\tau$$

$$+ F_{ijkl}(t)\sigma_{kl}(0) \qquad (4.13)$$

which is identical to equation (4.4). The integral in (4.13) is often referred to as a Riemannian or Stietjes' integral and has been used by Gurtin and Sternberg (1962) in their development of the theory of viscoelasticity. An important characteristic of the convolution of functions is the commutativity property. Hence, in view of the latter property, the creep constitutive equation (4.3) can be expressed, with reference to (4.13), as

$$\varepsilon_{ij}(t) = F_{ijkl}(t) * d\sigma_{kl}(t) = \sigma_{kl}(t) * dF_{ijkl}(t) \qquad (4.14)$$

and, in analogous manner, the relaxation constitutive equation (4.8) may be written as

$$\sigma_{ij}(t) = R_{ijkl}(t) * d\varepsilon_{kl}(t) = \varepsilon_{kl}(t) * dR_{ijkl}(t). \qquad (4.15)$$

For other properties concerning the convolution of functions, Appendix C should be referred to.

4.3 CREEP AND RELAXATION FUNCTIONS

With reference to the constitutive equations (4.3) and (4.8), both the creep and relaxation functions, $F_{ijkl}(t)$ and $R_{ijkl}(t)$ respectively, are components of completely symmetric fourth-order tensors. In this context, symmetry of the stress and strain tensors implies that

$$F_{ijkl}(t) = F_{jikl}(t) = F_{ijlk}(t)$$

and

$$R_{ijkl}(t) = R_{jikl}(t) = R_{ijlk}(t) \qquad (4.16)$$

so that at most 36 of the 81 components of $F_{ijkl}(t)$ (or $R_{ijkl}(t)$) are independent. This is in addition to symmetry with respect to an interchange of the first two and last two indices, i.e.

$$F_{ijkl}(t) = F_{klij}(t) \quad \text{and} \quad R_{ijkl}(t) = R_{klij}(t) \qquad (4.17)$$

as considered by Biot (1954) in his study of the thermodynamics of stable, irreversible systems based on the first and second laws of thermodynamics and on Onsager's principle (Fung, 1965; Day, 1971a, 1972). In view of the above, one may consider the creep and relaxation tensors to be completely symmetric (Schapery, 1974). Rogers and Pipkin (1963), however, argued that the symmetry conditions (4.16) cannot be stated in a clear-cut fashion and discussed some additional restrictions imposed by equations (4.16) (Halpin and Pagano, 1968).

A series of tests has been proposed by Hayes and Morland (1969) to determine the possible 36 independent relaxation tensor components of a homogeneous linear anisotropic viscoelastic body. The set of tests comprises 3 simple shear tests and 21 tests of pure compression. Both types of tests employ, essentially, the same testing apparatus.

For each component of the viscoelastic stress–strain relations (4.3) and (4.8) to satisfy the fading memory type of behaviour, it is required that the magnitude of the slope of each component of both the creep and the relaxation function tensors is a continuously decreasing function of time. Thus,

$$\left| \frac{dF_{ijkl}(t)}{dt} \right|_{t=t_2} \leq \left| \frac{dF_{ijkl}(t)}{dt} \right|_{t=t_1}, \quad t_2 \geq t_1 \geq 0, \tag{4.18a}$$

and

$$\left| \frac{dR_{ijkl}(t)}{dt} \right|_{t=t_2} \leq \left| \frac{dR_{ijkl}(t)}{dt} \right|_{t=t_1}, \quad t_2 \geq t_1 \geq 0. \tag{4.18b}$$

This is with the understanding that

$$F_{ijkl}(t) = 0 \quad \text{and} \quad R_{ijkl}(t) = 0 \quad \text{for} \quad -\infty < t < 0. \tag{4.19}$$

The requirement implied by equations (4.18) is often referred to as the 'axiom of nonretroactivity'.

Considering that $F_{ijkl}(0) \neq 0$, $R_{ijkl}(0) \neq 0$ and both are finite, the integrals (4.3) and (4.8) may be inverted to give relations between the two sets of creep and stress-relaxation response functions. One relationship can be written in the form of the following Volterra integral equation:

$$R_{ijkl}(0)F_{klmn}(t) + \int_0^t \frac{\partial R_{ijkl}(t-\tau)}{\partial \tau} F_{ijkl}(\tau) \, d\tau = H(t)\delta_{im}\delta_{jn} \tag{4.20}$$

where $H(t)$ is the Heaviside unit step function and δ_{ij} is the Kronecker delta. On the other hand, applying Laplace transformation to the creep constitutive equation (4.3) and to the stress-relaxation constitutive equation (4.8) with the lower limit of the integral in both equations is taken as zero, it can be shown that

$$[\bar{F}_{ijkl}(s)] = [\bar{R}_{ijkl}(s)]^{-1} \tag{4.21}$$

where s is the Laplace transformation variable.

This equation provides the means for relating the creep tensorial function F_{ijkl} and the relaxation function R_{ijkl} in both the s and the t planes irrespective of the degree of anisotropy. Existence of the inverse tensors of (4.21) is guaranteed by thermodynamics because of the positive–definite and semidefinite characters of these tensors (Schapery, 1974). A similar relation to (4.21) can be shown to be valid for the complex compliances and moduli. This is established by substituting $i\omega$ for s in (4.21), that is

$$[\bar{F}_{ijkl}(i\omega)] = [\bar{R}_{ijkl}(i\omega)]^{-1} \tag{4.22}$$

The corresponding quasi-static approximation to equations (4.21) and (4.22) is

$$F_{ijkl}(t) = [R_{ijkl}(t)]^{-1} \tag{4.23}$$

Equations (4.21)–(4.23) are identical to those for linear elastic media at a particular instant of time or if the time effect is completely eliminated. This is due to the complete symmetry of the tensorial material functions appearing in these equations.

4.4 REDUCTION TO THE ISOTROPIC CASE

In the case of an isotropic medium, the invariance of properties under rotation of the coordinate axes would reduce the constitutive equation of such a medium to two pairs of response operators: one associated with the stress and strain deviators which pertain to pure shear and the other for average hydrostatic compression (dilatation).

For an isotropic viscoelastic material, both the material functions $F_{ijkl}(t)$ and $R_{ijkl}(t)$ are isotropic, i.e. invariant with respect to any rotation of the Cartesian reference coordinates. Consider the creep tensorial function $F_{ijkl}(t)$. The most general isotropic representation of a fourth-order tensor is given by

$$F_{ijkl}(t) = \tfrac{1}{3}[F_2(t) - F_1(t)]\delta_{ij}\delta_{kl}$$
$$+ \tfrac{1}{2}[F_1(t)](\delta_{ik}\delta_{jl} + \delta_{il}\delta_{jk}) \tag{4.24}$$

where F_1, F_2 are scalar functions such that $F_1 = 0$ and $F_2 = 0$ for $-\infty < t < 0$ and δ_{ij} is the Kronecker delta. We recall the definition of the deviatoric stress σ'_{ij} (equation 1.42)), i.e.

$$\sigma'_{ij} = \sigma_{ij} - \tfrac{1}{3}\delta_{ij}\sigma_{kk} \quad \text{with} \quad \sigma'_{ii} = 0. \tag{4.25}$$

Meantime, the deviatoric strain ε'_{ij} is expressed as

$$\varepsilon'_{ij} = \varepsilon_{ij} - \tfrac{1}{3}\delta_{ij}\varepsilon_{kk} \quad \text{with} \quad \varepsilon'_{ii} = 0. \tag{4.26}$$

Accordingly, the constitutive creep equation (4.3) subject to (4.24)–(4.26) reduces to

$$\varepsilon'_{ij}(t) = \int_{-\infty}^{t} F_1(t - \tau) \frac{d\sigma'_{ij}(\tau)}{d\tau} \tag{4.27a}$$

and

$$\varepsilon_{kk}(t) = \int_{-\infty}^{t} F_2(t - \tau) \frac{d\sigma_{kk}(\tau)}{d\tau} \tag{4.27b}$$

where $F_1(t)$ and $F_2(t)$ are the independent creep functions appearing in (4.24). $F_1(t)$ is the creep function in shear and $F_2(t)$ is referred to as the creep function in isotropic compression (dilatation). On the other hand, if (4.24) is substituted in the convolution constitutive relation (4.14), one obtains the following creep response equations for an isotropic material:

$$\varepsilon'_{ij}(t) = \sigma'_{ij}(t) * dF_1(t) = F_1(t) * d\sigma'_{ij}(t); \tag{4.28a}$$

$$\varepsilon_{kk}(t) = \sigma_{kk}(t) * dF_2(t) = F_2(t) * d\sigma_{kk}(t). \tag{4.28b}$$

In a similar manner, the relaxation stress components can be expressed, in the isotropic case, as

$$\sigma'_{ij}(t) = \int_{-\infty}^{t} R_1(t - \tau) \frac{d\varepsilon'_{ij}(\tau)}{d\tau} \, d\tau \tag{4.29a}$$

and

$$\sigma_{kk}(t) = \int_{-\infty}^{t} R_2(t - \tau) \frac{d\varepsilon_{kk}(\tau)}{d\tau} \, d\tau. \tag{4.29b}$$

In the constitutive relations above, $R_1(t)$ and $R_2(t)$ are the independent relaxation functions. $R_1(t)$ is referred to as the relaxation function in shear and $R_2(t)$ is the relaxation function in isotropic compression (dilatation).

Equations (4.29) can be further expressed in a convolution form respectively as

$$\sigma'_{ij}(t) = \varepsilon'_{ij}(t) * dR_1(t) = R_1(t) * d\varepsilon'_{ij}(t) \tag{4.30a}$$

and

$$\sigma_{kk}(t) = \varepsilon_{kk}(t) * dR_2(t) = R_2(t) * d\varepsilon_{kk}(t). \tag{4.30b}$$

The relations between the functions $F_\alpha(t)$ and $R_\alpha(t)$ ($\alpha = 1, 2$) can be obtained (Christensen, 1971), using the Laplace transformation, in the form

$$\lim_{t \to \infty} F_\alpha(t) = \lim_{t \to \infty} [R_\alpha(t)]^{-\infty}, \quad \alpha = 1, 2, \tag{4.31a}$$

and

$$\lim_{t \to \infty} R_\alpha(t) = \lim_{t \to \infty} [F_\alpha(t)]^{-1}, \quad \alpha = 1, 2. \tag{4.31b}$$

For a particular viscoelastic material, the above properties are determined from creep or stress-relaxation experiments (Ferry, 1950; Kolsky, 1967).

4.5 REMARKS ON THE THERMODYNAMIC RESTRICTIONS ON ISOTHERMAL LINEAR VISCOELASTICITY

We present below a few remarks concerning the restrictions imposed by thermodynamics on the formulation of idealized linear viscoelasticity. The reader is referred to the cited references and Chapter 5 of this text for more detailed treatment of the subject matter.

1. Coleman (1964) discussed the thermodynamic restrictions imposed on the relaxation functions in linear viscoelasticity. To this effect, Coleman (1964) advanced, based on the minimal property of free energy, that the difference between the instantaneous and equilibrium elastic moduli, $R(0) - R(+\infty)$, must be positive semidefinite and symmetric. However, it can be argued that, based on the symmetry of the stress and strain tensors, that $R(\infty)$ is symmetric (Day, 1972); thus, Coleman's work (1964) implies that the two moduli $R(0)$ and $R(+\infty)$ are both symmetric and that

$$R(0) \geq R(+\infty) \tag{4.32}$$

2. The relaxation function $R(t)$ is compatible with thermodynamics if the following relation is satisfied (Day, 1972);

$$\int_{-\infty}^{+\infty} \sigma[t, \varepsilon(t)]\dot{\varepsilon}(t) \, dt \geq 0 \tag{4.33}$$

whenever $\varepsilon(t)$ is a closed strain path in the sense that there is a symmetric tensor A and times t_0, t_1 with $\varepsilon(t) = A$ for every $t \leq t_0$ and for every $t \geq t_1$. Relation (4.33) implies that the work done around any closed isothermal strain path starting from equilibrium cannot be negative.

A different restriction, which also has a thermodynamic character (Day, 1972), was proposed by König and Meixner (1958). This restriction implies the requirement

$$\int_{-\infty}^{t_1} \sigma[t, \varepsilon(t)]\dot{\varepsilon}(t) \, dt \geq 0 \tag{4.34}$$

for every time t_1 and for every path starting from the state of zero strain in the sense that $\varepsilon(-\infty) = 0$, i.e. there is a time t_0 such that $\varepsilon(t) = 0$ for every $t \leq t_0$. Relation (4.34) asserts that the relaxation function $R(t)$ is **dissipative**.

3. The following implications of dissipativity for linear viscoelastic materials should be noted (Day, 1972).

(a) Shu and Onat (1965) showed that, if $R(t)$ is dissipative, then the instantaneous elastic modulus $R(0)$ is symmetric. This is in accordance with the implications of Coleman's work (1964) discussed under (1) above.

(b) Gurtin and Herrera (1965) concluded that, if $R(t)$ is dissipative, then, the moduli $R(0)$ and $R(+\infty)$ are both symmetric and positive semidefinite and

$$R(0) \geq \pm R(t) \tag{4.35}$$

for every $t \geq 0$. In addition, relation (4.32) can be rewritten as

$$R(0) \geq R(+\infty) \geq 0 \tag{4.36}$$

and

$$\dot{R}(0) \geq 0. \tag{4.37}$$

(c) Day (1972) established, in addition, the following connections concerning the compatability between dissipative relaxation functions and thermodynamics.

   (i) The relaxation function $\mathbf{R}(t)$ is dissipative if and only if it is compatible with thermodynamics and the equilibrium elastic modulus $\mathbf{R}(\infty)$ is positive semidefinite.

   (ii) The relaxation function $\mathbf{R}(t)$ is compatible with thermodynamics if and only if $\mathbf{R}(t) - \mathbf{R}(+\infty)$ is dissipative and the equilibrium elastic modulus $\mathbf{R}(+\infty)$ is symmetric.

(d) It follows, based on (b) and (c) above, that, if $\mathbf{R}(t)$ is compatible with thermodynamics and in particular if $\mathbf{R}(t)$ is dissipative, then the elastic moduli $\mathbf{R}(0)$ and $\mathbf{R}(+\infty)$ are both symmetric and

$$\mathbf{R}(0) - \mathbf{R}(+\infty) \geq +[\mathbf{R}(t) - \mathbf{R}(+\infty)] \tag{4.38}$$

for every $t \geq 0$. Further, relations (4.32) and (4.34) will hold.

(e) Relation (4.38) reflects, in essence, the connection between the elastic and viscoelastic responses of the material (Day, 1971a, b, 1972):

   (i) A linear elastic material is a linear viscoelastic material whose relaxation function is identically time independent, that is $\mathbf{R}(t) = \mathbf{R}(0)$ for every $t \geq 0$. Thus, the elastic moduli $\mathbf{R}(0)$ and $\mathbf{R}(+\infty)$ coincide. Further, in view of (4.38), if $\mathbf{R}(0) = \mathbf{R}(+\infty)$, then $\mathbf{R}(t) = \mathbf{R}(+\infty) = \mathbf{R}(0)$ for $t \geq 0$. Accordingly, a linear viscoelastic material which is compatible with thermodynamics is elastic if, and only if, its equilibrium and instantaneous elastic moduli coincide.

   (ii) For a linear viscoelastic material which is compatible with thermodynamics and which is not elastic, $\mathbf{R}(0) \neq \mathbf{R}(+\infty)$. The response of such a linear viscoelastic material to rapid changes in strain will be always different from its response at equilibrium.

(f) The positive definiteness of $\mathbf{R}(0)$, relation (4.36), and the negative definiteness of $\dot{\mathbf{R}}(0)$, relation (4.37), together imply the decay of shock and acceleration waves in viscoelastic materials (Coleman, Gurtin and Herrera, 1965; Day, 1972). The subject of wave propagation in viscoelastic materials is dealt with in Chapter 8.

PROBLEMS

4.1 Comment on the symmetry of both the creep function $F_{ijkl}(t)$ and the relaxation function $R_{ijkl}(t)$. What are the implications of such symmetry?

4.2 Comment on the validity of the following two assumptions within the context of linear viscoelasticity (equation (4.11)):

$$\int_0^\infty \| \dot{R}_{ijkl}(t) \| \, dt < +\infty, \qquad \int_0^\infty t \| \dot{R}_{ijkl}(t) \| \, dt < +\infty,$$

where $\| \cdot \|$ indicates the norm and $R_{ijkl}(t)$ is the relaxation tensor.

4.3 Show that, if the assumptions mentioned in problem 4.2 are valid, then the equilibrium elastic modulus

$$R_{ijkl}(+\infty) = \lim_{t \to \infty} R_{ijkl}(t)$$

exists.

4.4 Considering that, if the creep function $F_{ijkl} \neq 0$, the relaxation function $R_{ijkl} \neq 0$ and both are finite, show that the integrals (4.3) and (4.8) may be inverted to give the following relation between the creep and relaxation functions:

$$R_{ijkl}(0)F_{klmn}(t) + \int_0^t \frac{\partial R_{ijkl}(t - \tau)}{\partial \tau} F_{ijkl}(\tau) \, d\tau = H(t)\delta_{im}\delta_{jn}$$

where $H(t)$ is the Heaviside function and δ_{ij} is the Kronecker delta.

4.5 Prove the validity of expressions (4.28) and (4.30).

4.6 Comment on the remarks presented in this chapter concerning the restrictions imposed by thermodynamics on the stress-relaxation function $\mathbf{R}(t)$ in idealized linear viscoelasticity.

REFERENCES

Axelrad, D. R. (1970) Mechanical models of relaxation phenomena. *Adv. Mol. Relaxation Processes*, **2**, 41–68.

Biot, M. A. (1954) Theory of stress–strain relations in anisotropic viscoelasticity and relaxation phenomena. *J. Appl. Phys.*, **25**(11), 1385–91.

Christensen, R. M. (1971) *Theory of Viscoelasticity*, Academic Press, New York.

Coleman, B. D. (1964) On thermodynamics, strain impulses and viscoelasticity. *Arch. Ration. Mech. Anal.*, **17**, 230–54.

Coleman, B. D., Gurtin, M. E. and Herrera, R. I. (1965) *Wave Propagation in Dissipative Materials*, Springer, Berlin.

Day, W. A. (1971a) Time-reversal and the symmetry of the relaxation function of a linear viscoelastic material. *Arch. Ration. Mech. Anal.*, **40**, 155–9.

Day, W. A. (1971b) When is a linear viscoelastic material elastic? *Mathematica*, **18**, 134–37.

Day, W. A. (1972) *Thermodynamics of Simple Materials with Fading Memory*, Springer, New York.

Ferry, J. D. (1950) Mechanical properties of substances of high molecular weight, VI. Dispersion in concentrated polymer solutions and its dependence on temperature and concentration. *J. Am. Chem. Soc.*, **72**, 3746–52.

Flügge, W. (1975) *Viscoelasticity*, Springer, New York.

Fung, Y. C. (1965) *Foundations of Solid Mechanics*, Prentice-Hall, Englewood Cliffs, NJ.

Gurtin, M. E. and Herrera, I. (1965) On dissipation inequalities and linear viscoelasticity. *Q. Appl. Math.*, **23**, 235–45.

Gurtin, M. E. and Sternberg, E. (1962) On the linear theory of viscoelasticity. *Ration. Mech. Anal.*, **11**, 291–356.

Halpin, J. C. and Pagano, N. J. (1968) Observations on linear anisotropic viscoelasticity. *J. Compos. Mater.*, **2**(1), 68–80.

Hayes, M. A. and Morland, L. W. (1969) The response function of an anisotropic linear viscoelastic material. *Trans. Soc. Rheol.*, **13**(2), 231–40.

Kolsky, H. (1967) Experimental studies of the mechanical behaviour of linear viscoelastic solids, in *Proc. 4th Symp. on Naval Structural Mechanics*, April 1965, Pergamon, Oxford, pp. 357–79.

König, H. and Meixner, J. (1958) Linear Systeme und Linear Transformationen. *Math. Nachr.*, **19**, 256–322.

Rogers, T. G. and Pipkin, A. C. (1963) Asymmetric relaxation and compliance matrices in linear viscoelasticity. *J. Appl. Math. Phys.*, **14**, 334–43.

Schapery, R. A. (1974) Viscoelastic behaviour and analysis of composite materials, in *Mechanics of Composite Materials*, Vol. 2 (ed. G. Sendeckj), Academic Press, New York, pp. 86–168.

Shu, L. S. and Onat, E. T. (1965) On anisotropic linear viscoelastic solids, in Proc. 4th Symp. on Naval Structural Mechanics, April 1965, Pergamon, Oxford, pp. 203–215.

FURTHER READING

Bland, D. R. (1960) *The Theory of Linear Viscoelasticity*, Pergamon, Oxford.

Breuer, S. (1969) Lower bounds on work in linear viscoelasticity. *Q. Appl. Math.*, **27**(2), 139–46.

Brown, R. L. and Sidebottom, A. M. (1971) A comparison of creep theories for multiaxial loading of polyethylene. *Trans. Soc. Rheol.*, **15**, 3–23.

Coleman, B. D. and Noll, W. (1960) An approximation theorem for functionals with applications in continuum mechanics. *Arch. Ration. Mech. Anal.*, **5**, 355–81.

Ewing, P. D., Turner, S. and Williams, J. G. (1973) Combined tension–torsion creep of polyethylene with abrupt changes of stress. *J. Strain Anal.*, **8**, 83–9.

Findley, W. N., Reed, R. M. and Stern, P. (1967) Hydrostatic creep of solid plastics. *J. Appl. Mech.*, **34**, 895–904.

Gross, B. (1947) On creep and relaxation. *J. Appl. Phys.*, **18** (February), 213–21.

Gurtin, M. E. and Sternberg, (1963) A reciprocal theorem in the linear theory of viscoelastic solids. *J. Soc. Ind. Appl. Math.*, **11**, 607–13.

Hopkins, I. L. and Hamming, R. W. (1958) On creep and relaxation. *J. Appl. Phys.*, **28**(8), 906–9.

Landel, R. F. and Peng, S. T. J. (1986) Equations of state and constitutive equations. *J. Rheol.*, **30**(4), 741–65.

Leaderman, H. (1954) Approximations in linear viscoelasticity theory: delta function approximations. *J. Appl. Phys.*, **25**(3), 294–6.

Misoulis, E. (1988) A Heuristic Approach to Modeling Viscoelasticity in Polymer Processing, Society of Plastics Engineers, Technical papers, Vol. XXXIV, ANTEC '88, Atlanta, GA, pp. 140–44.

Nolte, K. G. and Findley, W. N. (1974) Approximation of irregular loading by intervals of constant stress rate to predict creep and relaxation of polyurethane by three integral representations. *Trans. Soc. Rheol.*, **18**(1), 123–43.

Nunziato, J. W., Schuler, K. W. and Walsh, E. K. (1972) The bulk response of viscoelastic solids. *Trans. Soc. Rheol.*, **16**(1), 15–32.

Oldroyd, J. G. (1950) On the formulation of rheological equations of state. *Proc. R. Soc. London, Ser. A*, **200**, 523–41.

Onaran, K. and Findley, W. N. (1963) Combined stress creep experiments on viscoelastic material with abrupt changes in state of stress, in Proc. Joint Int. Conf. on Creep, Institution of Mechanical Engineers, London, pp. 285–97.

Tapseh, H. J. and Johnson, A. E. (1963) Creep under combined tension and torsion. *Engineering*, **150**, 24–5.

5

Thermoviscoelasticity

5.1 INTRODUCTION

The viscoelastic response behaviour appropriate to the formulation of the constitutive equations as dealt with in Chapters 2–4 generally exhibits a very strong dependence on the service temperature. The simplest and most direct situation of such dependence occurs when the constitutive equation is to be related or connected with different base temperatures within the context of the isothermal theory. In this, the material functions characterizing the viscoelastic behaviour of the material would be identified in an ambient temperature environment equal to the base temperature at which the constitutive equation is to be applied. On the other hand, when the constitutive equation is to be used in a nonisothermal situation, the identification problem is more involved and must be dealt within the realm of an advanced topic of thermoviscoelasticity. Thus, one generally deals with the following two classifications of the theory of thermoviscoelasticity.

- *Classification I* refers to a thermoviscoelastic treatment which examines the performance of the material as related to a fixed reference temperature T_R. In this treatment, the effects due to infinitesimal temperature variation from T_R would be neglected.
- *Classification II* refers to an advanced thermoviscoelastic theory within which the dependence of the material performance on a transient temperature field is dealt with.

One is generally concerned with the thermomechanical process and its effect on the response behaviour of the viscoelastic medium. For this purpose, the increase of the total energy of the medium is seen to be due to the work done by the external forces as well as the supply of energy (heat) from other sources. In such a study, however, one must differentiate between reversible and irreversible effects. Reversible effects would include cases in which temporary changes are produced in the material. These may include geometrical changes such as expansion and contraction as well as changes in the values of the material parameters or functions characterizing the constitutive equations of the material, but the format of the constitutive equations would essentially remain unchanged. On the other hand, irreversible effects include situations in which permanent changes are occurring in the material. In the case of a viscoelastic medium, such changes may include, for instance, primary bond rupture and weight loss. Polymeric composite materials and their constituents, for instance, are often subject to irreversible changes under a variety of environmental and chemical aging influences. In the latter context, temperature, moisture and water vapour are considered as important factors during the manufacturing process and in service (e.g. Steel, 1965; Fried, 1970; Tsai, 1970; Schapery, 1974). For the purpose of viscoelastic analysis, one simple case is where the response is considered over times that are short compared with the time scale over which changes due to environmental and/or aging effects would occur (Schapery, 1974); otherwise, one must allow for the dependence of the material parameters and functions characterizing the constitutive equations on such changes.

5.2 THERMODYNAMICS OF THE DEFORMATION PROCESS

5.2.1 A thermodynamic process

We consider a solid body B occupying a regular domain of volume V with surface boundary S. A material particle of B is defined in the reference configuration by the position vector $\mathbf{X}$. A thermodynamic process in B is described by the following eight functions of $\mathbf{X}$ and the time parameter t (Coleman, 1963, 1964a, b):

1. the spatial particle position $\mathbf{x} = \mathbf{x}(\mathbf{X}, t)$, which describes the evolution of the deformation process in the medium;
2. the symmetric stress tensor, Cauchy's $\boldsymbol{\sigma} = \boldsymbol{\sigma}(\mathbf{X}, t)$ or Piola–Kirchhoff's $\boldsymbol{\Sigma} = \boldsymbol{\Sigma}(\mathbf{X}, t)$;
3. the body force (per unit mass) $\boldsymbol{\chi} = \boldsymbol{\chi}(\mathbf{X}, t)$, exerted on the body at $\mathbf{X}$ by outside bodies not intersecting B;
4. the specific internal energy (per unit mass) $e = e(\mathbf{X}, t)$;
5. the specific entropy (per unit mass) $S = S(\mathbf{X}, t)$;
6. the local absolute temperature $T = T(\mathbf{X}, t)$, assumed to be positive;
7. the heat flux vector $\mathbf{q} = \mathbf{q}(\mathbf{X}, t)$;
8. the heat supply $r = r(\mathbf{X}, t)$, which is the radiation energy (per unit mass and per unit time) that is absorbed by the body B at $\mathbf{X}$ and supplied by the environment or any other bodies not intersecting with B.

Couple stresses, body couples and other mechanical interactions not included in $\boldsymbol{\sigma}$ or $\boldsymbol{\chi}$ are assumed to be absent or at least negligible. In order for the above set of eight functions to be called a 'thermodynamic process', it must be compatible with both the law of balance of linear momentum and the law of balance of energy. This is with the understanding that the balance of moment of momentum is satisfied by the assumed symmetry of the stress tensor $\boldsymbol{\sigma}$ (Chapter 1, section 1.3.5). In a differential form, the laws of balance of linear momentum and balance of energy can be expressed, respectively, as

$$\operatorname{div} \boldsymbol{\sigma} + \rho\boldsymbol{\chi} = \rho\ddot{\mathbf{x}} \tag{5.1}$$

and

$$\text{tr}(\boldsymbol{\sigma}\mathbf{L}) - \text{div } \mathbf{q} - \rho\dot{e} = -\rho r. \tag{5.2}$$

In the above two equations, ρ is the mass density, $\mathbf{L}$ is the velocity gradient ($\mathbf{L} = \text{grad } \dot{\mathbf{x}}$), 'tr' is the trace operator, a superimposed dot designates the material derivative, i.e. the derivative with respect to the time parameter t keeping the position vector $\mathbf{X}$ fixed, and the operators 'grad' and 'div' refer to spatial derivatives, i.e. the gradient and divergence with respect to the current position vector $\mathbf{x}$ with the time parameter t kept fixed. Thus, to specify a thermodynamic process, it would suffice to prescribe only the six functions $\mathbf{x}$, $\boldsymbol{\sigma}$, e, $\mathbf{q}$, S and T. The remaining functions χ and r are then determined by the two laws (5.1) and (5.2).

The law of balance of energy (5.2) is a form of the first law of thermodynamics. The latter states that the rate at which the total energy of the body increases is balanced by the power of the external forces and the rate at which heat is supplied to the body. In other words, the quantity of heat supplied to the body is measured as the difference between change of the total energy and work done by the external forces (Rivlin, 1975).

Consider that heat enters the body throughout its volume at a rate $\dot{H}$ per unit mass and through its surface at a rate $\dot{h}$ per unit area. Both $\dot{H}$ and $\dot{h}$ are measured in the reference configuration, whereby the superimposed dot indicates differentiation with respect to time. Thus, according to the first law of thermodynamics, the rate of change of the total energy is given by

$$\Xi = \int_V \rho\chi\cdot\dot{\mathbf{x}} \, dV + \int_S \mathbf{F}\cdot\dot{\mathbf{x}} \, dS + \int_V \rho\dot{H} \, dV + \int_S \dot{h} \, dS \tag{5.3}$$

where $\mathbf{F}$ is the force per unit area acting on the body and measured in the reference configuration. Let ψ denote the total energy of the body per unit mass; then, the specific internal energy e is defined by

$$e = \psi - \tfrac{1}{2}\dot{\mathbf{x}}\dot{\mathbf{x}}, \tag{5.4}$$

i.e. e, defined by the equation above, is the total energy per unit mass less the kinetic energy per unit mass.

5.2.2 Restrictions imposed by the Second Law of Thermodynamics

Regarding $\mathbf{q}/T$ to be a vectorial flux of entropy due to heat flow and r/T to be a scalar supply of entropy from radiation, Coleman (1964a, b) defined the time rate of entropy production in a part P of the body B to be

$$\Gamma = \frac{d}{dt}\int_P S \, dm - \int_P \frac{r}{T} \, dm + \int_{\partial P} \frac{1}{T}\mathbf{q}\cdot\mathbf{n} \, ds. \tag{5.5}$$

In (5.5), dm is an element of mass of the body B, $\mathbf{n}$ is the exterior unit normal to the surface ∂P of P and ds is the element of surface area in the current configuration of the body (i.e. at time t). Under an appropriate smoothness (Coleman, 1964a, b), equation (5.5) may be expressed as

$$\Gamma = \int_P \gamma \, dm \tag{5.6}$$

in which

$$\gamma = \dot{S} - \frac{r}{T} + \frac{1}{\rho} \mathrm{div}\left(\frac{\mathbf{q}}{T}\right)$$

$$= \dot{S} - \frac{r}{T} + \frac{1}{\rho T} \mathrm{div}\, \mathbf{q} - \frac{1}{\rho T^2} \mathbf{q} \cdot \mathbf{g}(T) \tag{5.7}$$

is the specific rate of entropy production and where $\mathbf{g}(T)$ is the gradient of the current temperature. In this context, Coleman and Noll (1963) and Coleman (1964a, b) gave the following postulate as a mathematical expression of the second law of thermodynamics.

Postulate 5.1

For every admissible thermodynamic process in a body B, the following 'Clausius–Duhem inequality' must hold for all t and all parts of P of B:

$$\Gamma \geq 0 \tag{5.8}$$

where Γ is the rate of production of entropy in a part P of the body B, equation (5.5).

It is evident that the postulate above places restrictions on the formats of the constitutive equations of materials.

Thermomechanical systems must satisfy the same general conservation laws, concerning mass and momentum, that were introduced earlier in Chapter 1. The law of conservation of energy, however, contains both mechanical and thermal energies. Since the change of thermal energy is related to the change of entropy, a description of the evolution of a thermomechanical system requires a knowledge of the entropy production.

Recalling the conservation of mass principle as expressed by the equation of continuity (1.6), that is

$$\frac{\partial \rho}{\partial t} + \frac{\partial(\rho v_i)}{\partial x_i} = 0, \tag{5.9}$$

the conservation of momentum is expressed by the equation of motion (1.22):

$$\rho \dot{v}_i = \sigma_{ij,j} + \rho \chi_i \quad \text{within} \quad V. \tag{5.10}$$

Meantime, Cauchy's formula (1.18) and (1.28) are respectively

$$T_i = \sigma_{ij} n_j$$

and   (5.11)

$$\sigma_{ij} = \sigma_{ji}.$$

The conservation of energy is given by

$$\rho \dot{e} = \sigma_{ij} v_{i,j} - q_{i,j} \tag{5.12}$$

where the superimposed dot indicates the material derivative defined earlier by (1.4), i.e.

$$(\cdot) = \frac{\partial}{\partial t} + v_j \frac{\partial}{\partial x_j} \qquad (5.13)$$

and v_j are the velocity components.

In order to establish the entropy balance equation, one may assume (Fung, 1965) that the specific entropy S is a function of both the internal energy per unit mass e and the strain ε_{ij} irrespective of the equilibrium of the system. That is,

$$S = S(e, \varepsilon_{ij}). \qquad (5.14)$$

This is in agreement with the expression for the total differential of the specific entropy S as given by Gibb's relation

$$\rho T \, dS = \rho \, de - \sigma_{ij} \, d\varepsilon_{ij}. \qquad (5.15)$$

Thus, along the path of the motion, one may write that

$$\rho T \dot{S} = \rho \dot{e} - \sigma_{ij} v_{ij} \qquad (5.16)$$

where the superimposed dot indicates the material derivative and v_{ij} is the rate of deformation tensor, i.e.

$$v_{ij} = \tfrac{1}{2}(v_{i,j} + v_{j,i}).$$

Combining (5.12) and (5.16), it follows that

$$\rho T \dot{S} = -q_{i,i} \qquad (5.17)$$

which can be equivalently written as

$$\rho \dot{S} = -\frac{q_{i,i}}{T} = -\left(\frac{q_i}{T}\right)_{,i} - q_i \frac{T_{,i}}{T^2}. \qquad (5.18)$$

The first term on the right-hand side of (5.18) is the divergence of the entropy flow and the second term is the entropy production which must be positive as previously discussed (equation (5.8)).

A constitutive law, defining the relationship between the stress tensor σ_{ij} and the strain tensor ε_{ij}, must be further included so that the strain field is uniquely defined. Thus, a sufficient number of differential equations are obtained for which a boundary value problem may be formulated.

5.3 RHEOLOGICAL EQUATIONS OF STATE

Significant research efforts have been undertaken in the last four decades towards the development of a rigorous thermomechanical theory concerning the response behaviour of materials with memory as based on phenomenological considerations. In this context, theories have been presented from different points of view by Biot

(1958, 1973), Coleman and Noll (1963), Coleman (1964a, b), Schapery (1964), Christensen and Naghdi (1967), Crochet and Naghdi (1974), Crochet (1975) and Rivlin (1975), among others. Other work of interest includes that of Coleman and Mizel (1963, 1964), Breuer and Onat (1964), Breuer (1969) and Day (1970) concerning the free energy concept, recoverable work and related work bounds. The reader is also referred to Müller (1967), Meixner (1969) and others for developments in the subject of continuum thermodynamics.

Coleman and Noll (1963) adopted the Clausius–Duhem inequality, as an expression for the second law of thermodynamics, to determine the validity of the constitutive equations of a body of material. In this, their paper demonstrates that the second law of thermodynamics requires the Clausius–Duhem inequality to be satisfied in a process that is compatible with the balance laws of mass, momentum, moment of momentum and energy. This translates into the requirement that the constitutive equations must be compatible with the Clausius–Duhem inequality in order for such constitutive relations to be able to describe the response behaviour of a material under the restrictions imposed by thermodynamics. Following the above approach, Coleman and Mizel (1963) studied heat conduction in rigid bodies and then (Coleman and Mizel, 1964) established the existence of caloric equations of state for materials of the rate type. For applications of the Coleman and Noll (1963) approach to different classes of materials, the reader is referred to the research works by Green and Naghdi (1965), Gurtin (1965), Gurtin and Williams (1966), Wang and Bowen (1966), Coleman and Gurtin (1967a, b), Green and Laws (1967), Laws (1967), Coleman and Mizel (1967, 1968), Owen (1968, 1970) and Coleman and Owen (1970), among others.

As a continuation of the work of Coleman and Noll (1963), Coleman (1964a, b) dealt with the foundations of a thermodynamic theory of materials with memory, from a macroscopic point of view and based on the principles of continuum physics. Again, Coleman takes the Clausius–Duhem inequality to be the expression of the second law of thermodynamics and establishes the restrictions for reducing the constitutive equations to forms compatible with thermodynamics. As the statement of the Clausius–Duhem inequality involves the entropy of the body, one must acquire, in Coleman's approach, the entropy from the beginning to deal with (Day, 1970, 1972).

5.3.1 Simple materials

Neglecting any thermodynamic effect, a substance for which the stress $\boldsymbol{\sigma}(t)$ is determined by the history of a measure of strain is referred to, from a continuum mechanics point of view, as a 'simple material'. The response equation of such material may be written (Coleman, 1964a, b) as

$$\boldsymbol{\sigma}(t) = \overset{\infty}{\underset{\tau=0}{\boldsymbol{\pi}}} \ [\mathbf{F}(t-\tau)]. \tag{5.19}$$

In this equation, $\mathbf{F}(t-\tau)$ is the deformation gradient at time $t-\tau$, $0 \le (t, \tau) < \infty$, and π is a functional mapping the function $F(t - \tau)$ into tensor $\sigma(t)$. π may be considered as a general functional subject to the requirements of material symmetry (Noll, 1958; Coleman and Noll, 1964; Coleman 1964a, b), the principle of material objectivity (Noll, 1958; Coleman, 1964a, b) and the principle of fading memory (Coleman and Noll, 1960, 1961; Coleman, 1964a, b).

In the more general case, i.e. when one includes thermodynamic effects, the stress $\sigma(t)$ would depend on both the deformation gradient history $F(t - \tau)$ as well as the temperature history $T(t - \tau)$. Thus a more generalized form of (5.19) is

$$\sigma(t) = \underset{\tau=0}{\overset{\infty}{\pi}} \; [F(t - \tau), \, T(t - \tau)]. \tag{5.20}$$

One may also assume (Coleman, 1964a, b) that the specific internal energy per unit mass e is determined, similarly to $\sigma(t)$, as illustrated above, by the histories $F(t - \tau)$ and $T(t - \tau)$, i.e.

$$e(t) = \underset{\tau=0}{\overset{\infty}{e}} \; [F(t - \tau), \, T(t - \tau)]. \tag{5.21}$$

On the other hand, the heat flux vector q is dependent on the temperature gradient $g(T)$ during the thermodynamic process. Since, according to (5.20), the stress is assumed to depend on $F(t - \tau)$ and $T(t - \tau)$, it is likely that these histories would influence the dependence of the heat flux q on the temperature gradient $g(T)$. Accordingly, the constitutive equation for the heat flux may be expressed (Coleman, 1964a, b) as

$$q(t) = \underset{\tau=0}{\overset{\infty}{q}} \; [F(t - \tau), \, T(t - \tau), \, g(T)] \tag{5.22}$$

where q is a functional whose arguments are the histories $F(t - \tau)$, $T(t - \tau)$ and the gradient of the current temperature, i.e. $g(T)$.

We recall at this point the 'principle of equipresence' (Truesdell, 1951; Truesdell and Toupin, 1960; Coleman and Mizel, 1964; Coleman and Gurtin, 1967a, b) which, in its present form, reads (Coleman, 1964a, b) as follows.

An independent variable present in one constitutive equation of a material should be assumed to be so present in all, until its presence is shown to be in direct contradiction to the assumed symmetry of the material, the principle of material objectivity, or the laws of thermodynamics.

Thus, the constitutive equations (5.20) and (5.21) should also include in their argument the dependence on the temperature gradient $g(T)$ present in (5.22). Accordingly, one replaces (5.20) and (5.21), respectively, by

$$\sigma(t) = \underset{\tau=0}{\overset{\infty}{\pi}} \; [F(t - \tau), \, T(t - \tau), \, g(T)] \tag{5.23}$$

and

$$e(t) = \underset{\tau=0}{\overset{\infty}{e}} \; [\mathbf{F}(t-\tau),\; T(t-\tau),\; \mathbf{g}(T)]. \tag{5.24}$$

In order to include the restrictions imposed by the Clausius–Duhem inequality on the above-mentioned constitutive relations (5.22)–(5.24), an expression for the specific entropy (per unit mass) is introduced in the form

$$S(t) = \underset{\tau=0}{\overset{\infty}{S}} \; [\mathbf{F}(t-\tau),\; T(t-\tau),\; \mathbf{g}(T)] \tag{5.25}$$

which also satisfies the principle of equipresence.

In Coleman's (1964a, b) theory, it is assumed that the four functionals $\mathbf{q}$, $\boldsymbol{\pi}$, e and S corresponding respectively to equations (5.22)–(5.25) are given at each point $\mathbf{X}$ of the material. These functions, in general, depend on the choice of the reference configuration. However, if there exists a reference configuration that would render these functionals independent of $\mathbf{X}$ for all material points in the body B, then one may consider B to be materially homogeneous.

(a) Admissibility

A thermodynamic process is said to be admissible in B if it is compatible with the constitutive relations (5.22)–(5.25) at each material point $\mathbf{X}$ of B and all times t. In this context, Coleman (1964a, b) showed the following remark to be valid.

Remark   To every choice of the deformation function $\mathbf{x}(\mathbf{X}, t)$ and the temperature distribution $T(\mathbf{x}, t)$, $(\mathbf{x}, \mathbf{X}$ in B; $-\infty < t < \infty)$, there corresponds a unique admissible thermodynamic process in B.

Coleman (1964) also showed that the Clausius–Duhem inequality requires that the temperature gradient $\mathbf{g}(T)$ drops out from relations (5.23)–(5.25). Accordingly, the new set of constitutive equations are expressed as

$$\boldsymbol{\sigma}(t) = \underset{\tau=0}{\overset{\infty}{\boldsymbol{\pi}}} \; [\mathbf{F}(t-\tau),\; T(t-\tau)], \tag{5.26a}$$

$$e(t) = \underset{\tau=0}{\overset{\infty}{e}} \; [\mathbf{F}(t-\tau),\; T(t-\tau)], \tag{5.26b}$$

$$\mathbf{q}(t) = \underset{\tau=0}{\overset{\infty}{\mathbf{q}}} \; [\mathbf{F}(t-\tau),\; T(t-\tau),\; \mathbf{g}(T)] \tag{5.26c}$$

and

$$S(t) = \underset{\tau=0}{\overset{\infty}{S}} \; [\mathbf{F}(t-\tau),\; T(t-\tau)], \tag{5.26d}$$

Equations (5.26b) and (5.26d) may also be used to express a constitutive equation based on the specific Helmholtz free energy. Denoting the latter by A, it is defined by

$$A = e - TS.$$

Since both e and S are given in (5.26b) and (5.26d), respectively, by functionals of $\mathbf{F}(t - \tau)$ and $T(t - \tau)$, it follows that

$$A(t) = \underset{\tau=0}{\overset{\infty}{A}} \ [\mathbf{F}(t - \tau), \ T(t - \tau)], \qquad (5.26e)$$

The reader is referred to Coleman (1964a, b) for theorems and remarks concerning the set of constitutive relations (5.26).

(b) Entropy as an independent variable

Recall the entropy constitutive equation (5.26d). That is,

$$S(t) = \underset{\tau=0}{\overset{\infty}{S}} \ [\mathbf{F}(t - \tau), \ T(t - \tau)].$$

Assume that the above functional transformation is invertible in the sense that there exists a functional $T(t)$ such that

$$T(t) = \underset{\tau=0}{\overset{\infty}{T}} \ [\mathbf{F}(t - \tau), \ S(t - \tau)]. \qquad (5.27)$$

Accordingly, one may rewrite the other constitutive equations (5.26a)–(5.26c) and (5.26e), respectively, as

$$\boldsymbol{\sigma}(t) = \underset{\tau=0}{\overset{\infty}{\hat{\boldsymbol{\pi}}}} \ [\mathbf{F}(t - \tau), \ S(t - \tau)], \qquad (5.28a)$$

$$e(t) = \underset{\tau=0}{\overset{\infty}{\hat{e}}} \ [\mathbf{F}(t - \tau), \ S(t - \tau)], \qquad (5.28b)$$

$$\mathbf{q}(t) = \underset{\tau=0}{\overset{\infty}{\hat{\mathbf{q}}}} \ [\mathbf{F}(t - \tau), \ S(t - \tau), \ \mathbf{g}(T)] \qquad (5.28c)$$

and

$$A(t) = \underset{\tau=0}{\overset{\infty}{\hat{A}}} \ [\mathbf{F}(t - \tau), \ S(t - \tau)]. \qquad \cdot \qquad (5.28d)$$

(c) Internal energy as an independent variable

Consider the constitutive equation for internal energy (5.26b), i.e.

$$e(t) = \underset{\tau=0}{\overset{\infty}{e}} \ [\mathbf{F}(t - \tau), \ T(t - \tau)].$$

Assume now that the above functional transformation is invertible, i.e. there exists a functional $\check{T}(t)$ such that

$$T(t) = \overset{\infty}{\underset{\tau=0}{\check{T}}} \ [\mathbf{F}(t-\tau), e(t-\tau)]. \tag{5.29}$$

Accordingly, one may rewrite the rest of the constitutive equations (5.26), in sequence, as

$$\boldsymbol{\sigma}(t) = \overset{\infty}{\underset{\tau=0}{\check{\boldsymbol{\pi}}}} \ [\mathbf{F}(t-\tau), e(t-\tau)], \tag{5.30a}$$

$$\mathbf{q}(t) = \overset{\infty}{\underset{\tau=0}{\check{\mathbf{q}}}} \ [\mathbf{F}(t-\tau), e(t-\tau), \mathbf{g}(T)] \tag{5.30b}$$

$$S(t) = \overset{\infty}{\underset{\tau=0}{\check{S}}} \ [\mathbf{F}(t-\tau), e(t-\tau)] \tag{5.30c}$$

and

$$A(t) = \overset{\infty}{\underset{\tau=0}{\check{A}}} \ [\mathbf{F}(t-\tau), e(t-\tau)]. \tag{5.30d}$$

Coleman (1964) showed the following remarks to be valid.

Remark In every admissible process

$$\dot{S} \geq \frac{1}{T}\left(\dot{e} - \frac{1}{\rho} \text{ tr } \boldsymbol{\sigma}\mathbf{L}\right) \tag{5.31a}$$

and

$$\dot{S} \geq \frac{1}{T}\left(r - \frac{1}{\rho} \text{ div } \mathbf{q}\right) \tag{5.31b}$$

where $\mathbf{L}$ is the velocity gradient, i.e. $\mathbf{L} = \text{grad } \dot{\mathbf{x}}$.

The inequality in (5.31) above is referred to as '**the principle of positive internal production of entropy**'.

Remark Whenever the strain and internal energy are held constant, the entropy cannot decrease, regardless of the past history.

Remark Whenever the strain and entropy are held constant, the internal energy cannot increase regardless of the past history.

Remark In an admissible thermodynamic process, the material time derivative of the free energy obeys the inequality

$$\dot{A} \leq \frac{1}{\rho} \text{ tr } \boldsymbol{\sigma}\mathbf{L} - S\dot{T}. \tag{5.32}$$

Thus,

$$\text{if } \mathbf{L} = \mathbf{0}, \quad \dot{T} = 0, \quad \text{then} \quad \dot{A} \leq 0, \qquad (5.33)$$

i.e. if, at a given instant of time, material point $\mathbf{X}$ is held at constant strain and temperature (e.g. isothermal stress relaxation), the free energy at $\mathbf{X}$ at that instant cannot increase regardless of the past history.

The significance of Coleman's (1964a, b) work in establishing the restrictions imposed by thermodynamics on the constitutive equations for materials with memory is apparent. However, as pointed out by Rivlin (1975), no prescription was given in Coleman's work for determining the actual form of the constitutive functionals either analytically or by deduction from experiment. Rivlin (1975) criticized Coleman's approach in that entropy cannot be regarded as a 'primitive quantity' since it is not in the same category as the primitive mass, length and time. Rivlin (1975), on the other hand, defined materials with memory as materials for which the Piola–Kirchhoff stress $\mathbf{\Sigma}$ and empirical temperature θ are functions of the histories of the specific internal energy $e(\tau)$ and the deformation gradient tensor $\mathbf{F}(\tau)$, with support $(-\infty, t^+)$, i.e.

$$\mathbf{\Sigma}(t) = \mathbf{\Sigma}[\mathbf{F}(\tau), \quad e(t)], \quad \theta(t) = \theta[\mathbf{F}(\tau), \quad e(\tau)]. \qquad (5.34)$$

Alternatively, one may consider $\mathbf{\Sigma}(t)$ and $e(t)$ as functionals of the histories $\mathbf{F}(\tau)$ and $\theta(\tau)$ with support $(-\infty, t^+)$. That is,

$$\mathbf{\Sigma}(t) = \mathbf{\Sigma}[\mathbf{F}(\tau), \quad \theta(\tau)], \quad e(t) = e[\mathbf{F}(\tau), \quad \theta(\tau)]. \qquad (5.35)$$

The support in (5.34) and (5.35) is taken by Rivlin (1975) to be $(-\infty, t^+)$, rather than $(-\infty, t)$, in order to include the possibility that $\mathbf{\Sigma}$ and θ may depend on the instantaneous values of the time derivatives of $\mathbf{F}(\tau)$ and $e(\tau)$ at the instant t, even though these may change discontinuously at time t.

Rivlin (1975) considered the material to have fading memory if the functionals in (5.34) and (5.35) are such that, for two histories which differ only up to time $t - \tau$, the differences in the functionals decrease to zero as τ increases to infinity. Coleman (1964a, b) considered also a similar assumption for the definition of the 'fading memory' of simple materials, that is the memory of such materials fades in time. Coleman's assumption implies the assertions that deformations and temperatures experienced in the distant past should have less effect on the present values of the entropy, energy, stress and heat flux than deformations and temperatures which occurred in the recent past. In this context, Coleman (1964a, b) introduced an 'influence function' $C(\tau)$, $0 \leq \tau < \infty$, which would characterize the rate at which the memory fades. The influence function $C(\tau)$ is assumed to be positive monotonic decreasing and continuous function for the time parameter τ (Coleman and Noll, 1960, 1961, 1964).

With reference to (5.34), a material is said (Rivlin, 1975) to be perfectly elastic if $\mathbf{\Sigma}$ and θ depend only on the instantaneous values of $\mathbf{F}$ and e. In this case, $\mathbf{\Sigma}$ and θ are ordinary functions of $\mathbf{F}$ and e, i.e.

$$\mathbf{\Sigma} = \mathbf{\Sigma}(\mathbf{F}, e), \quad \theta = \theta(\mathbf{F}, e). \qquad (5.36)$$

Alternatively, Σ and e will be ordinary functions of $\mathbf{F}$ and θ and (5.35) will be replaced by

$$\Sigma = \Sigma(\mathbf{F}, \theta), \quad e = e(\mathbf{F}, \theta). \tag{5.37}$$

Accordingly, in the case of materials with fading memory, if we restrict ourselves to processes carried out quasi-statistically, the constitutive equations (5.34) and (5.35) will ensure the forms of the constitutive equations (5.36) and (5.37), respectively. In other words, materials with fading memory behave as perfectly elastic materials with respect to quasi-static processes.

Rivlin (1975) adopted Carathéodory's principle as a form of the second law of thermodynamics: there are states of a system, differing infinitesimally from a given state, which are unattainable from that state by any adiabatic process whatever. Here, 'state' is used in the sense of 'equilibrium state' and it is postulated that the materials considered can always be taken from any such state to another state by a quasi-static process. As a consequence of the above, Rivlin (1975) asserted the existence of the 'specific entropy' which is a function of the variables used to describe the state and of the absolute temperature which is a function of the empirical temperature. The function through which the specific entropy relates to the state variables depends on the material considered, while the function through which the absolute temperature is associated with the empirical temperature is independent of this material.

As an illustration of the above arguments, Rivlin (1975) considered a body of material with fading memory to be in equilibrium with uniform empirical temperature θ, specific internal energy e and deformation gradient $\mathbf{F}$. The constitutive equations describing the response of such material is assumed to be given by (5.34). Rivlin, then, assumed that the body is taken from a homogeneous equilibrium state by a homothermal quasi-static process to a neighbouring equilibrium state, in which θ, e and $\mathbf{F}$ are changed, respectively, to $\theta + d\theta$, $e + de$ and $\mathbf{F} + d\mathbf{F}$. Thus, letting dH be the amount of heat (per unit mass) which is absorbed by the body in this process, it can be shown, following the first law of thermodynamics, that

$$\rho \, dH = \rho \, de - \text{tr}(\Sigma \cdot d\mathbf{F}). \tag{5.38}$$

In (5.38), ρ is the material density in the fixed reference state with respect to which $\mathbf{F}$ is measured, and de is the increase in specific internal energy in the process.

With (5.34)–(5.37), equation (5.38) yields

$$\rho \, dH = \rho \left(\frac{\partial e}{\partial \theta} \right)_{\mathbf{F}} d\theta + \text{tr}\left[\rho \left(\frac{\partial e}{\partial \mathbf{F}} \right)_{\theta}^{+} - \Sigma \right]\mathbf{F}. \tag{5.39}$$

Based on the Carathéodory principle and on the assumption that the process to be quasi-static, then there must exist values of $d\theta$ and $d\mathbf{F}$ for which $dH \neq 0$ (Rivlin, 1975). In other words, the process must not be adiabatic for the transition between the two neighbouring states to take place. From this fact, Rivlin (1975) asserts, with the support of the work of Wilson (1957) and Kestin (1966), that there exists an integrating factor $1/T(\mathbf{F}, \theta)$ such that $\rho \, dH/T$, from (5.39), is a perfect differential.

Following Rivlin (1975), one may consider unit mass of a material with fading memory to be taken by a quasi-static homothermal process from an equilibrium state A to an equilibrium state B. Let the states A and B be identified, respectively, by the two sets of values $(\theta_A, \mathbf{F}_A, e_A, S_A)$ and $(\theta_B, \mathbf{F}_B, e_B, S_B)$. Let, also, dH denote the heat fed into the body in an infinitesimal step of the process. Since

$$dS = dH/T(\theta) \tag{5.40}$$

and S is a function of θ and $\mathbf{F}$ only, then

$$S_B - S_A = \int_A^B dH/T(\theta) \tag{5.41}$$

where the integration is carried out along the path in the ten-dimensional space $(\theta, \mathbf{F})$ followed by the process.

Consider, now, a body of a material with fading memory to be taken from an equilibrium state A to an equilibrium state B by a process which is not necessarily quasi-static. It can be shown (Rivlin, 1975; Kestin, 1966), by application of Carathéodory's principal, that if dH is the amount of heat (per unit mass) entering the system in an infinitesimal step of the process, at an instant at which the empirical temperature of the system is θ, then

$$\int_A^B \frac{dH}{T(\theta)} \le S_B - S_A. \tag{5.42}$$

In the above relation, the equality sign applies if the process is quasi-static. Formula (5.42) is known as the 'Clausius inequality' or 'Clausius–Planck inequality' whereby the integral is referred to as the 'Clausius integral'.

Recall (5.40), that is

$$dS = \frac{dH}{T(\theta)}$$

where S, the specific entropy, is a function of the instantaneous values of $\mathbf{F}$ and $T(\theta)$. This equation is valid, for example, for an infinitesimal step of a homothermal process, whether quasi-static or not, in a perfectly elastic material.

For a material with fading memory, the path in $(\mathbf{F}, T)$ space which may be followed by the non-quasi-static process could also be followed by a quasi-static process. Accordingly, at each point of an arbitrary homothermal process in a material with fading memory, the Clausius inequality (5.42), i.e.

$$\int_A^B \frac{dH}{T(\theta)} \le S_A - S_B$$

can be replaced by the Clausius–Duhem inequality,

$$\dot{S} \le \dot{H}/T, \tag{5.43}$$

where the dot designates material differentiation with respect to time; thus, $\dot{H}$ denotes the rate at which heat enters the body at the instant considered. There is an essential physical difference between the Clausius and Clausius–Duhem inequalities. This may be illustrated by the following comparison given by Rivlin (1975).

Consider a body of material with fading memory to be taken from an equilibrium state A to an equilibrium state B by quasi-static and non-quasi-static, isothermal, homothermal processes which follow the same paths in (**F**, *T*) space. The Clausius inequality states that less heat is fed into the system in the non-quasi-static process than in the quasi-static process. The Clausius–Duhem inequality asserts, however, that the amount of heat fed into the system, in each infinitesimal step of the non-quasi-static process, is no greater than that for the corresponding step of the quasi-static process. Rivlin (1975), however, showed by an example that the Clausius–Duhem inequality may not be valid for all materials and all processes.

(d) Instantaneous response behaviour

In the case of materials with fading memory, instantaneous changes in the deformation gradient tensor **F** and the empirical temperature θ result in instantaneous changes in the Piola–Kirchhoff stress Σ and in the specific internal energy e which could be followed by further changes in these quantities.

In order to describe the type of behaviour above, Rivlin (1975), following Green, Rivlin and Spencer (1959), made explicit the dependence of Σ and e, at time t, on the instantaneous values of the deformation gradient tensor **F** and of the empirical temperature at time t. Accordingly, the following constitutive equations may be written:

$$\Sigma = \Sigma[\mathbf{F}(\tau), \; \theta(\tau); \; \mathbf{F}, \; \theta)] \tag{5.44}$$

and

$$e = e[\mathbf{F}(\tau), \; \theta(\tau); \; \mathbf{F}, \; \theta] \tag{5.45}$$

indicating that Σ and e are functionals of the histories $\mathbf{F}(\tau)$ and $\theta(\tau)$ with support $(-\infty, t)$ and ordinary functions of **F** and θ.

For materials possessing instantaneous elasticity, for which the constitutive equations (5.44) and (5.45) are valid, Σ and e are functions of **F** and θ only. In this case, we would restrict ourselves to processes for which the histories $\mathbf{F}(\tau)$ and $\theta(\tau)$ are fixed functions of τ, $-\infty < \tau < t$, while only **F** and θ may change.

5.4 THERMODYNAMICAL DERIVATION OF THE CONSTITUTIVE RELATIONS

In their derivation.of the thermodynamic constitutive equation, Christensen and Naghdi (1967) and Christensen (1971) based their work on the balance of energy equation for the infinitesimal theory and the entropy production postulate (Truesdell and Toupin, 1960). The derivation parallels, in essence, the means of deriving the constitutive equation in the linear isothermal case. However, the situation here is more difficult since the free energy not only depends on the strain history but also depends on the temperature history. At this point, a remark should be cited concerning the free energy relationships. In these relationships, the stress and deformation are conjugate variables. One, therefore, has to make a choice as to which will be the independent variable. If the stress is the independent variable, then the appropriate free energy function is the Gibbs free energy. On the other hand, if the strain is taken as the independent variable, then the corresponding free energy function is the Helmholtz free energy. Hence, considering the latter context, the local balance of energy equation for infinitesimal theory is given (Christensen, 1971) by

$$\rho r - \rho(\dot{A} + \dot{T}S + T\dot{S}) + \sigma_{ij}\dot{\varepsilon}_{ij} - Z_{i,i} = 0. \tag{5.46}$$

In equation (5.46), ρ is the mass density, r is the heat supply function per unit mass, $\dot{A}$ is the time derivative of the Helmholtz free energy per unit mass, T is the absolute temperature, S is the entropy per unit mass and Z_i are the Cartesian components of the heat flux vector measured per unit area per unit time. The related local entropy production inequality (Clausius–Duhem) is given by

$$\rho T\dot{S} - \rho r + Z_{i,i} - Z_i(T_{,i}/T) \geq 0. \tag{5.47}$$

With reference to (5.46), it is usually assumed that ε_{ij} and T are continuous in the interval $-\infty < t < \infty$ and that ε_{ij} tends to zero and T tends to T_0 as t tends to $-\infty$. Based on this assumption, the free energy can be expressed (Christensen, 1971) as a polynomial in a set of real, continuous linear functions of ε_{ij} and T as

$$
\begin{aligned}
\rho A = \rho A_0 &+ \int_{-\infty}^{t} D_{ij}(t-\tau)\frac{\partial \varepsilon_{ij}(\tau)}{\partial \tau}\,d\tau - \int_{-\infty}^{t}\beta(t-\tau)\frac{\partial\theta(\tau)}{\partial\tau}\,d\tau \\
&+ \frac{1}{2}\int_{-\infty}^{t}\int_{-\infty}^{t} R_{ijkl}(t-\tau,\,t-s)\frac{\partial\varepsilon_{ij}(\tau)}{\partial\tau}\frac{\partial\varepsilon_{kl}(s)}{\partial s}\,d\tau\,ds \\
&- \int_{-\infty}^{t}\int_{-\infty}^{t}\phi_{ij}(t-\tau,\,t-s)\frac{\partial\varepsilon_{ij}(\tau)}{\partial\tau}\frac{\partial\theta(s)}{\partial s}\,d\tau\,ds \\
&- \frac{1}{2}\int_{-\infty}^{t}\int_{-\infty}^{t} m(t-\tau,\,t-s)\frac{\partial\theta(\tau)}{\partial\tau}\frac{\partial\theta(s)}{\partial s}\,d\tau\,ds
\end{aligned}
\tag{5.48}
$$

where $T = T_0 + \theta$ and A_0 is the mean free energy. In (5.48) the integrating material functions are assumed to be continuous for arguments $\tau_i \geq 0$ and vanish identically for $\tau_i < 0$, i.e.

$$\beta(\tau_1) = 0, \qquad D_{ij}(\tau_1) = 0, \qquad R_{ijkl}(\tau_1, \tau_2) = 0,$$

$$\phi_{ij}(\tau_1, \tau_2) = 0 \qquad m(\tau_1, \tau_2) = 0 \quad \text{for} \quad \tau_1 < 0 \text{ and } \tau_2 < 0. \tag{5.49}$$

For the proposed theory, these integrating functions are necessarily independent of strain and temperature.

Now, if one combines equations (5.46)–(5.48) and, at the same time, carries out the indicated differentiation with respect to time, one obtains (Christensen (1971)

$$
\left[-D_{ij}(0) - \int_{-\infty}^{t} R_{ijkl}(t - \tau, 0) \frac{\partial \varepsilon_{kl}(\tau)}{\partial \tau} \, d\tau \right.
$$

$$
+ \int_{-\infty}^{t} \phi_{ij}(0, t - \tau) \frac{\partial \theta(\tau)}{\partial \tau} \, d\tau + \sigma_{ij} \Bigg] \dot{\varepsilon}_{ij}(t)
$$

$$
+ \left[\beta(0) + \int_{-\infty}^{t} m(t - \tau, 0) \frac{\partial \theta(\tau)}{\partial \tau} \, d\tau \right.
$$

$$
+ \int_{-\infty}^{t} \phi_{ij}(t - \tau, 0) \frac{\partial \varepsilon_{ij}(\tau)}{\partial \tau} \, d\tau - \rho S \Bigg] \dot{\theta}(t)
$$

$$
+ \left[-\int_{-\infty}^{t} \frac{\partial}{\partial t} D_{ij}(t - \tau) \frac{\partial \varepsilon_{ij}(\tau)}{\partial \tau} \, d\tau \right.
$$

$$
+ \int_{-\infty}^{t} \frac{\partial}{\partial t} \beta(t - \tau) \frac{\partial \theta(\tau)}{\partial \tau} \, d\tau + \Lambda - Z_i \frac{\theta_{,i}}{T_0} \Bigg] \geq 0 \qquad (5.50)
$$

where

$$
\Lambda = -\frac{1}{2} \int_{-\infty}^{t} \int_{-\infty}^{t} \frac{\partial}{\partial t} R_{ijkl}(t - \tau, t - s) \frac{\partial \varepsilon_{ij}(\tau)}{\partial \tau} \frac{\partial \varepsilon_{kl}(s)}{\partial s} \, d\tau \, ds
$$

$$
+ \frac{1}{2} \int_{-\infty}^{t} \int_{-\infty}^{t} \frac{\partial}{\partial t} \phi_{ij}(t - \tau, t - s) \frac{\partial \varepsilon_{ij}(\tau)}{\partial \tau} \frac{\partial \theta(s)}{\partial s} \, d\tau \, ds
$$

$$
+ \frac{1}{2} \int_{-\infty}^{t} \int_{-\infty}^{t} \frac{\partial}{\partial t} m(t - \tau, t - s) \frac{\partial \theta(\tau)}{\partial \tau} \frac{\partial \theta(s)}{\partial s} \, d\tau \, ds \qquad (5.51)
$$

and the following symmetry properties are implied:

$$
R_{ijkl}(t - \tau, t - s) = R_{klij}(t - s, t - \tau). \qquad (5.52)
$$

The inequality (5.50) must hold for all arbitrary values of $\dot{\varepsilon}_{ij}(t)$ and $\dot{\theta}(t)$; therefore, it is necessary that the coefficients of $\dot{\varepsilon}_{ij}(t)$ and $\dot{\theta}(t)$ in (5.50) vanish. Hence

$$
\sigma_{ij} = D_{ij}(0) + \int_{-\infty}^{t} R_{ijkl}(t - \tau, 0) \frac{\partial \varepsilon_{kl}(\tau)}{\partial \tau} \, d\tau - \int_{-\infty}^{t} \phi_{ij}(0, t - \tau) \frac{\partial \theta(\tau)}{\partial \tau} \, d\tau \qquad (5.53)
$$

and

$$
\rho S = \beta(0) + \int_{-\infty}^{t} \phi_{ij}(t - \tau, 0) \frac{\partial \varepsilon_{ij}(\tau)}{\partial \tau} \, d\tau + \int_{-\infty}^{t} m(t - \tau, 0) \frac{\partial \theta(\tau)}{\partial \tau} \, d\tau. \qquad (5.54)
$$

Relations (5.53) and (5.54) are the constitutive relations for stress and entropy, respectively. From these it is clear that $D_{ij}(0)$ is the initial stress and that $\beta(0)$ is the initial entropy, ρS_0. The integrating functions $R_{ijkl}(t - \tau, 0)$, $\phi_{ij}(0, t - \tau)$, $\phi_{ij}(t - \tau, 0)$ and $m(t - \tau, 0)$ are appropriate relaxation function norms of the material properties. It is the relaxation function $R_{ijkl}(t, 0)$ in this formulation which corresponds to the relation function $R_{ijkl}(t)$ in the isothermal theory.

5.4.1 Reduction to the isotropic theory

For isotropic materials, ϕ_{ij} must be taken as

$$\phi_{ij}(\tau, s) = \delta_{ij} \, \phi(t, s) \tag{5.55}$$

where δ_{ij} is the Kronecker delta. Using the definitions of deviatoric stress and strain, the free energy for isotropic theory can be expressed (Christensen, 1971) with reference to (5.50) as

$$\rho A = \frac{1}{2} \int_{-\infty}^{t} \int_{-\infty}^{t} G_1(t - \tau, t - s) \frac{\partial \varepsilon'_{ij}(\tau)}{\partial \tau} \frac{\partial \varepsilon'_{ij}(s)}{\partial s} \, d\tau \, ds$$

$$+ \frac{1}{6} \int_{-\infty}^{t} \int_{-\infty}^{t} G_2(t - \tau, t - s) \frac{\partial \varepsilon_{kk}(\tau)}{\partial \tau} \frac{\partial \varepsilon_{jj}(s)}{\partial s} \, d\tau \, ds$$

$$- \int_{-\infty}^{t} \int_{-\infty}^{t} \phi(t - \tau, t - s) \frac{\partial \varepsilon_{kk}(\tau)}{\partial \tau} \frac{\partial \theta(s)}{\partial s} \, d\tau \, ds$$

$$- \frac{1}{2} \int_{-\infty}^{t} \int_{-\infty}^{t} m(t - \tau, t - s) \frac{\partial \theta(\tau)}{\partial \tau} \frac{\partial \theta(s)}{\partial s} \, d\tau \, ds \tag{5.56}$$

where the initial stress and initial entropy effects in (5.50) have been dropped.

Based on the form (5.56) for the free energy, it can be shown that the stress-relaxation equations for isotropic materials are

$$\sigma'_{ij}(t) = \int_{-\infty}^{t} R_1(t - \tau, 0) \frac{\partial \varepsilon'_{ij}(\tau)}{\partial \tau} \, d\tau. \tag{5.57a}$$

and

$$\sigma_{kk}(t) = \int_{-\infty}^{t} R_2(t - \tau, 0) \frac{\partial \varepsilon_{kk}(\tau)}{\partial \tau} \, d\tau - 3 \int_{-\infty}^{t} \phi(0, t - \tau) \frac{\partial \theta(\tau)}{\partial \tau} \, d\tau. \tag{5.57b}$$

If the material functions appearing in the constitutive equations (5.53) and (5.56) are independent of temperature, which in the service life of the material might be true for only small temperature changes, or the temperature is timewise constant, then these constitutive equations will reduce to their counterparts in the isothermal theory. When these two equations do not exist and it is desired to find experimentally the material functions without making any *a priori* assumptions about their tempera-ture dependence, a large number of tests will be needed even for the uniaxial test situation particularly if the temperature varies in a cyclic or a discrete fashion with the time. In this case, one must subject the material specimen to the actual temperature history (Landel and Peng, 1986). The latter approach could prove to be quite impractical. There is, however, experimental evidence (e.g. Schapery, 1974) which implies that viscoelastic characterization for transient temperature applications may be performed by using tests at a set of different constant temperatures. Hence, the phenomenological viscoelastic response description of a large class of polymeric materials and inorganic glasses under nonisothermal conditions is simplified by the adoption of the so-called '**temperature–time equivalence**', also known as the '**thermorheologically simple hypothesis**'.

5.5 THERMORHEOLOGICALLY SIMPLE MATERIALS

Thermorheologically simple materials (TSMs) are a special class of viscoelastic materials whose temperature dependence of mechanical properties is particularly responsive to analytical description. This group of materials generally constitutes the simplest and most realistic viscoelastic constitutive equation for which response under constant temperatures can be used to predict response under transient temperatures. Two temperature states are studied here, i.e. the constant temperature state and the nonconstant temperature one. For detailed description of the temperature dependent properties of thermorheologically simple materials, reference is made to Leaderman (1943), Schwarzl and Staverman (1952), Morland and Lee (1960), Ferry (1970) and Schapery (1974), among others.

5.5.1 Thermorheologically simple materials under constant temperature states

Following Schapery (1974), the uniaxial creep constitutive relation for thermorheologically simple materials can be expressed as

$$\varepsilon(t) = \int_0^t F(\xi - \xi') \frac{d\sigma}{d\xi'} \, d\xi' \tag{5.58}$$

where ε is the uniaxial strain due to stress only, i.e. the total strain less that due to thermal expansion and $F(\xi - \xi')$ is the time- and temperature-dependent creep compliance. In this equation, ξ is called the '**reduced time parameter**' and defined by

$$\xi = \xi(t) = \int_0^t \frac{d\tau}{a_T} \tag{5.59}$$

and equivalently

$$\xi' = \xi(t') = \int_0^{t'} \frac{d\tau}{a_T} \tag{5.60}$$

where $a_T = a_T[T(\tau)]$ is the so-called '**temperature shift factor**'. The latter is dependent on the absolute temperature T within the time interval $\tau = \xi - \xi'$. In the constitutive equation (5.58), it is assumed that $\sigma = \varepsilon = 0$ when $t \leq 0$.

The inverse of (5.58), i.e. the relaxation constitutive equation, can be determined by using Laplace transform with respect to reduced time. In this context, it can be shown that

$$\sigma(t) = \int_0^t R(\xi - \xi') \frac{d\varepsilon}{d\xi'} \, d\xi' \qquad (5.61)$$

in which $R(\xi - \xi')$ is the time- and temperature-dependent relaxation modulus and both the reduced time parameters ξ, ξ' are as expressed previously by (5.59) and (5.60), respectively.

The experimental bases for the constitutive equations (5.58) and (5.61) under constant temperature conditions may be treated by considering isothermal creep and isothermal relaxation tests. That is, for the uniaxial creep test $\sigma(t) = \sigma_0 H(t)$, where σ_0 is the constant stress input and $H(t)$ is the Heaviside step function, the creep constitutive equation (5.58) yields

$$\varepsilon(\xi) = F(\xi)\sigma(t) \qquad (5.62)$$

where ε is the resulting uniaxial strain due to the stress only. Similarly, for the relaxation test $\varepsilon(t) = \varepsilon_0 H(t)$, where ε_0 is the constant strain input, the relaxation constitutive equation (5.61) yields

$$\sigma(\xi) = R(\xi)\varepsilon(t) \qquad (5.63)$$

with the understanding that for both types of isothermal tests

$$\xi = t/a_T. \qquad (5.64)$$

Equation (5.64) indicates that the effect of temperature on the mechanical properties $F(\xi)$ or $R(\xi)$ for a thermorheologically simple material produces only horizontal translations when the property is plotted against log t. Conversely, if it is found that the constant temperature viscoelastic response curves (creep or relaxation) can be superposed so as to form a single curve (master curve) by means of only rigid, horizontal translations then the associated mechanical property (relaxation modulus or creep compliance) would depend only on time and temperature through the one parameter ξ. Such a description is probably a more or less conventional definition of a thermorheologically simple material (Schapery, 1974; Tobolosky and Catsiff, 1956).

An illustration of the time–temperature shift of the stress-relaxation curves at different temperatures to form a master curve associated with a particular reference temperature is given in Fig. 5.1. In Fig. 5.1(a), a series of relaxation moduli curves at different base temperatures are plotted using experimental relaxation data on bisphenol polycarbonate ($M_W = 40\,000$) from Mercier *et al.* (1965). For the purpose of constructing the master curve for these data, the relaxation curve corresponding to a reference temperature $T_R = 141°C$ is assigned as the reference curve. The other curves are then shifted along the logarithmic time scale until they superimpose. The relaxation moduli curves corresponding to temperatures above the reference

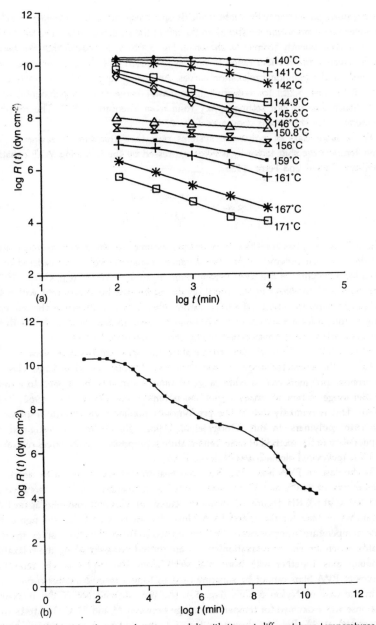

Fig. 5.1 (a) Variation of stress-relaxation moduli with time at different base temperatures for bisphenol polycarbonate ($M_W = 40\,000$); experimental data from Mercier *et al* (1965). (b) Master stress-relaxation curve based on stress-relaxation data presented in (a) with reference temperature $T_R = 141°C$.

temperatures are shifted to the right while those corresponding to temperatures below the reference temperature are shifted to the left of the reference curve. The full master curve is consequently formed as shown in Fig. 5.1(b). It is noticed that the master curve covers a much wider range of time as compared with the original time range covered by the individual relaxation curves. An analogous procedure is followed in Figs. 5.2(a) and 5.2(b) for constructing a master curve using experimental creep compliance data on hot setting epoxy resin from Theocaris (1962). The reference temperature for the data is chosen as $T_R = 25\,°C$.

For a large class of polymeric systems near their transition temperature, the time–temperature shift factor a_T is often expressed by the following WLF equation (Williams, Landel and Ferry, 1955)

$$\log a_T = -\frac{17.44(T - T_g)}{51.6 + T - T_g} \tag{5.65}$$

where T_g is the glass transition temperature, assumed as the reference temperature for the particular polymer under consideration. Equation (5.65) is considered to be valid for a polymer in the temperature range T_g to $T_g + 100\,°C$ (e.g. Gittus, 1975). The numerical constants in this equation are established by experiment within the indicated temperature range. If a temperature other than T_g is chosen as the reference temperature, a form analogous to (5.65) may be used to determine a_T, but with the numerical constants corresponding to the chosen reference temperature.

Although the method of time–temperature superposition has been shown to be useful in the characterization of the rheological properties of a large class of amorphous polymers over a wide range of time, it can only be applied to a much smaller range of time for many crystalline polymers (e.g. Onogi *et al.*, 1962; Ferry, 1970). This is primarily due to the predominant nonlinear viscoelastic response of the latter polymers. In this, Onogi *et al.* (1962), for instance, investigated the applicability of the method of time–temperature superposition to the stress relaxation of PVA (polyvinyl alcohol) and Nylon 6 films.

In the case of PVA films (Fig. 5.3) two heat-treated specimens (with degree of crystallinity of 36.0% and 47.3%) were tested at temperatures varying between 20 and 100°C at 0% RH. Figure 5.3 shows the curves of relaxation modulus against the logarithm of time for the tested PVA films. As can be seen from this figure, the time–temperature superposition cannot be applied to these relaxation curves. In other words, when the shown relaxation curves are shifted vertically along the relaxation modulus axis, together with horizontal shifts along the log t axis, the relaxation curves of PVA films cannot be superimposed to form a smooth master curve.

In the case of Nylon 6 films (Fig. 5.4) the time dependence of the relaxation response was examined for temperature range between 25 and 77°C. The tests were performed at 0% RH. As shown in Fig. 5.4, the curves at temperatures higher than 50°C can be superposed to form a master curve for this temperature range, while those curves corresponding to lower temperatures than 50°C cannot be superposed. According to Onogi *et al.* (1962), the temperature 50°C conforms closely

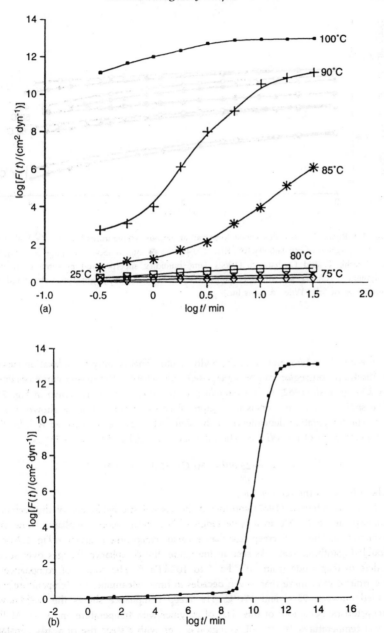

Fig. 5.2 (a) Variation of creep compliance with time at different base temperatures for hot setting epoxy resin (experimental data from Theocaris (1962)). (b) Master creep curve based on creep data presented in (a) with a reference temperature $T_R = 25°C$.

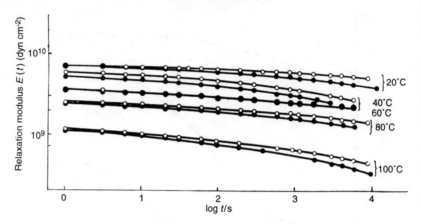

Fig. 5.3 Relaxation modulus versus log(time) at various temperatures for two PVA films of different degrees of crystallinity (0% RH): ○, 47.3%; ●, 36.0%. (Source: Onogi, S., Sasaguri, K., Adachi, T. and Ogihara, S. (1962) Time–humidity superposition in some crystalline polymers. *J. Polymer Sci.*, **58**, 1–17 (John Wiley & Sons Inc. copyright 1962). Reprinted by permission of John Wiley & Sons Inc.)

to the transition temperature of the Nylon 6 film. That is, only the relaxation curves in the transition region can be superposed satisfactorily. The master curve obtained by Onogi *et al.* (1962) with a reference temperature of 50°C is shown in Fig. 5.5. The shift factor log a_T versus the reciprocal absolute temperature is shown in Fig. 5.6. The temperature dependence of the shift factor can be represented well by the following form of the WLF equation (Williams, Landel and Ferry, 1955), i.e.

$$\log a_T = 25.6(\theta - 50°C)/(85.2 + \theta - 50°C)$$

where θ (°C) is the temperature.

Link and Schwarzl (1987) considered the viscoelastic behaviour of the technical polystyrene PS N7000 in a wide range of the shear creep compliance, time and temperature. The shear creep compliance versus creep time is given in Fig. 5.7 on a double-logarithmic scale. As seen in the figure, the compliance changes over seven orders in magnitude from $10^{-8}\,Pa^{-1}$ to $10^{-1}\,Pa^{-1}$. The course of compliance is determined over more than seven decades in time. Meantime, the temperature was varied between 95°C and 170°C. The creep compliance shows the well-known characteristic behaviour of this class of polymer with temperature and time. At the lower temperatures, the transition region is seen with a steep rise of nearly constant slope. At the temperature of 100°C, the beginning of the rubbery plateau may first be seen at longer times. Increasing the temperature further, the rubbery plateau becomes shorter and the viscous contribution would start to dominate even

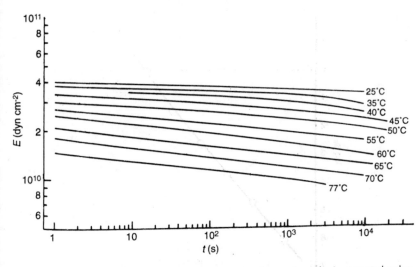

Fig. 5.4 Relaxation modulus versus log(time) at various temperatures for heat-treated nylon 6 film (0% RH). (Source: Onogi, S., Sasaguri, K., Adachi, T. and Ogihara, S. (1962) Time–humidity superposition in some crystalline polymers. *J. Polym. Sci.*, **58**, 1–17 (John Wiley & Sons Inc. copyright 1962). Reprinted by permission of John Wiley & Sons Inc.)

at shorter times. In the flow region, the creep compliance increases with time with a slope which, as seen in the figure, approaches unity on a double-logarithmic scale.

The recoverable creep compliance of polystyrene PS N7000 is shown at the same temperatures in Fig. 5.8 from Link and Schwarzl (1987). As indicated by these authors, two transitions can be seen in the course of the recoverable creep compliance. In addition to the glass–rubber transition, a second pronounced transition becomes

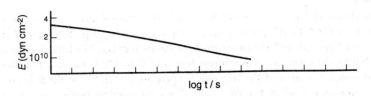

Fig. 5.5 Master relaxation curve for heat-treated nylon 6 film (50°C–77°C) (0% RH) as obtained from relaxation moduli curves of Fig. 5.4. (Source: Onogi, S., Sasaguri, K., Adachi, T. and Ogihara, S. (1962) Time–humidity superposition in some crystalline polymers. *J. Polym. Sci.*, **58**, 1–17 (John Wiley & Sons Inc. copyright 1962). Reprinted by permission of John Wiley & Sons Inc.)

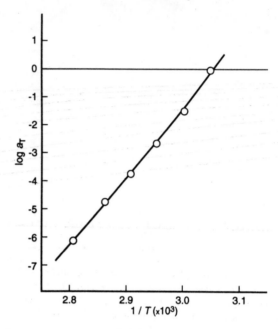

Fig. 5.6 Shift factor a_T against reciprocal of absolute temperature (relaxation moduli data for heat-treated nylon 6 film at 0% RH, Fig. 5.4). (Source: Onogi, S., Sasaguri, K., Adachi, T. and Ogihara, S. (1962) Time–humidity superposition in some crystalline polymers. *J. Polym. Sci.*, **58**, 1–17 (John Wiley & Sons Inc. copyright 1962). Reprinted by permission of John Wiley & Sons Inc.)

evident whereby the recoverable compliance rises from the rubber level of about $5 \times 10^{-6}\,\mathrm{Pa}^{-1}$ up to a long-time-limiting value of $4.7 \times 10^{-4}\,\mathrm{Pa}^{-1}$ which is the steady recoverable compliance. This transition is often referred to as a 'network transition'.

As shown in Fig. 5.9 (Link and Schwarzl, 1987), the reference temperature was chosen as 126.7°C. All the measured compliance curves (Fig. 5.7) were shifted along the time scale with the same time–temperature shift law. The latter was derived by shifting the creep compliance curves from 140°C to 170°C to coincide with the creep compliance curve at the reference temperature of 126.7°C in the flow region at a compliance level of $4 \times 10^{-3}\,\mathrm{Pa}^{-1}$. The corresponding master curve for the recoverable creep compliance is shown in Fig. 5.10 at the same reference temperature of 126.7°C.

Blatz (1956) considered the rheological behaviour of a typical composite solid propellant that is based on a cross-linked polymeric binder. Each of the propellant

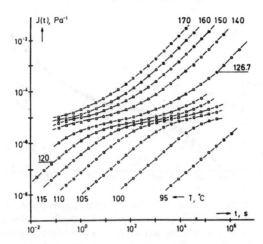

Fig. 5.7 Double-logarithmic plot of the creep compliance versus time for polystyrene (PSN N 7000). (Source: Link, G. and Schwarzl, F. R. (1987) Shear creep and recovery of a technical polystyrene. *Rheol. Acta*, **26**(4), 375–84 (Steinkopff Verlag Darmstadt). Reprinted with permission of Steinkopff Verlag Darmstadt.)

formulations studied includes the following constituents: a linear polymer 'R', a trifunctional cross-linking agent 'X', a low molecular weight plasticizer 'P', an inorganic oxidizer 'F' and a polymeric binder. The latter holds all the above-mentioned constituents except the oxidizer filler 'F'. Figure 5.11 represents the temperature dependence of the creep performance of a propellant of composition (by weight) R–8X–0.6P–60F over a temperature range from −40 to 150°F. The creep

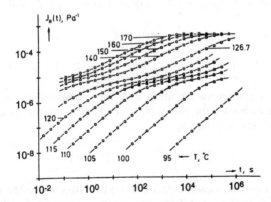

Fig. 5.8 Recoverable creep compliance versus creep time for polystyrene (PSN N 7000). (Source: Link, G. and Schwarzl, F. R. (1987) Shear creep recovery of a technical polystyrene. *Rheol. Acta*, **26**(4), 375–84 (Steinkopff Verlag Darmstadt). Reprinted with permission of Steinkopff Verlag Darmstadt.)

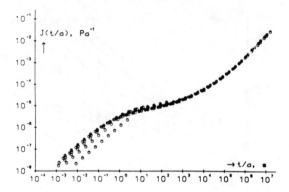

Fig. 5.9 Creep compliance versus reduced time t/a for polystyrene (PSN N 7000); reference temperature, 126.7°C; applied shift function determined in the flow region. (Source: Link, G. and Schwarzl, F. R. (1987) Shear creep and recovery of a technical polystyrene. *Rheol. Acta*, **26**(4), 375–84 (Steinkopff Verlag Darmstadt). Reprinted with permission of Steinkopff Verlag Darmstadt.)

compliance is plotted as a function of temperature on a double-logarithmic scale in Fig. 5.12 for a propellant formulation R–6X–0.6P–60F. The master curve for the creep compliance data of Fig. 5.12 is given in Fig. 5.13. In the latter figure, the master curve is adjusted so that its inflection point is at unity on the reduced time scale (Blatz, 1956).

In the three-dimensional case, the creep equation for the anisotropic thermorheologically simple material is given by (Schapery, 1974).

$$\varepsilon_{ij}(t) = \int_0^t F_{ijkl}(\xi - \xi') \frac{\partial \sigma_{kl}}{\partial t'} \, dt' + \int_0^t \alpha_{ij}(\xi - \xi') \frac{\partial \Delta T}{\partial t'} \, dt'. \tag{5.66}$$

The corresponding stress-relaxation equation is

$$\sigma_{ij}(t) = \int_0^t R_{ijkl}(\xi - \xi') \frac{\partial \varepsilon_{kl}}{\partial t'} \, dt' - \int_0^t \beta_{ij}(\xi - \xi') \frac{\partial \Delta T}{\partial t'} \, dt' \tag{5.67}$$

where the material functions are identical to the corresponding functions in the isothermal case except for the change in argument from physical time to reduced time where the latter is defined by

$$\xi = \xi(t) = \int_0^t \frac{d\tau}{a_T}, \quad \xi' = \xi(t') = \int_0^{t'} \frac{d\tau}{a_T} \tag{5.68}$$

as represented earlier by equations (5.59) and (5.60) respectively. The second-order tensors α_{ij} and β_{ij} in (5.66) and (5.67), respectively, are associated with the thermal expansion characteristics of the thermorheologically simple material and define, respectively, thermal strains in the absence of applied stress and thermal stresses in a completely constrained body.

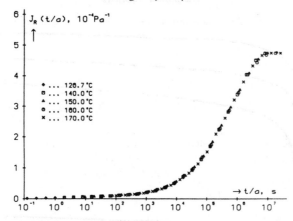

Fig. 5.10 Semilogarithmic plot of the recoverable creep compliance versus reduced creep time t/a for polystyrene at various temperatures (reference temperature, 126.7°C). (Source: Link, G. and Schwarzl, F. R. (1987) Shear creep and recovery of a technical polystyrene. *Rheol. Acta,* **26**(4), 375–84 (Steinkopff Verlag Darmstadt). Reprinted with permission of Steinkopff Verlag Darmstadt.)

The constitutive equations (5.66) and (5.67) may be seen as results of the linear hereditary theory where the input variables (stresses or strains) are combined with the temperature change which is not applied until time $t = 0$ on a non-aging type of material of a reduced time scale ξ. These equations have been derived from thermodynamics theory which predicts complete symmetry of the material functions involved (Schapery, 1974).

5.5.2 Thermorheologically simple materials under nonconstant temperature states

The effects to be studied here are outside the scope of the first-order linear theory. Consequently, a coupled thermoviscoelastic theory which includes the temperature dependence of mechanical properties is necessarily nonlinear. Guided by the work of Crochet and Naghdi (1969), Christensen (1971) presented a nonlinear theory of thermoviscoelasticity which, on the usual linearization of stress and strain, still retains a nonlinear dependence on temperature. Concerning this, Christensen attempted to derive the special results appropriate to the stress–strain constitutive relation without consideration of the other field variables such as energy, entropy, and the heat flux vector which necessarily are involved in the general theory. For this purpose, Christensen extended the uncoupled theory of linear thermoviscoelasticity to account for the temperature dependence of the relevant mechanical properties. The non-constant, nonuniform temperature history is considered to be known.

In Christensen's (1971) work, the starting point is the statement of a general nonlinear function which expresses the dependence of the current value of strain on

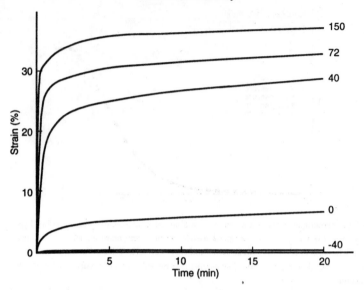

Fig. 5.11 Effect of temperature (°F) on creep of a class of composite solid propellants. (Source: Blatz, P. J. (1956) Rheology of composite solid propellants. *J. Ind. Eng. Chem.*, **48**(4), 727–9 (American Chemical Society). Reprinted with permission of American Chemical Society.)

the histories of stress and temperature, together with their current values. That is,

$$E(t) = \overset{\infty}{\underset{\tau=0}{\Psi}} \ [\Sigma(t-\tau),\ T(t-\tau),\ \Sigma(t),\ T(t)] \tag{5.69}$$

In (5.69), $E(t)$ is the nonlinear strain measure at time t, Σ is the Piola–Kirchhoff stress tensor and T is the absolute temperature.

For the material in a stress-free state, but with nonconstant temperature history, equation (5.69) may be expressed as a separate functional of temperatures only, i.e.

$$E(t)|_{\Sigma} = \overset{\infty}{\underset{\tau=0}{\Psi'}} \ [T(t-\tau),\ T(t)]. \tag{5.70}$$

The functional (5.70) could be restricted (Crochet and Naghdi, 1969, 1979) to express strain at zero stress as a function of current temperature, i.e. (5.70) reduces to

$$\overset{\infty}{\underset{\tau=0}{\Psi'}} \ [T(t-\tau),\ T(\tau)] = \alpha T(t) \tag{5.71}$$

where α is the coefficient of linear thermal expansion. Equation (5.71) may be considered as a special case of the type of behaviour allowed in the infinitesimal theory.

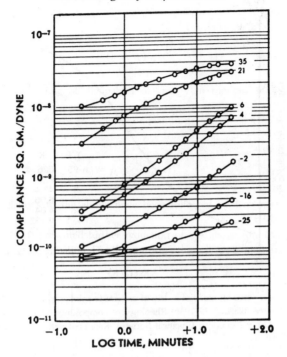

Fig. 5.12 Flexural creep of a class (weighted formulation, R–6X–0.6P–60F) of composite solid propellants as function of temperature. (Source: Blatz, P. J. (1956) Rheology of composite solid propellants. *J. Ind. Eng. Chem.*, **48**(4), 727–9 (American Chemical Society). Reprinted with permission of American Chemical Society.)

Thus, by decomposing $\mathbf{E}(t)$ of (5.69) into two parts such that

$$\overset{\infty}{\underset{\tau=0}{\psi}} [\Sigma(t-\tau), T(t-\tau), \Sigma(t), T(t)] = \overset{\infty}{\underset{\tau=0}{\psi'}} [T(t-\tau), T(t)]$$

$$+ \overset{\infty}{\underset{\tau=0}{\psi''}} [\Sigma(t-\tau), T(t-\tau); \Sigma(t), T(t)] \quad (5.72)$$

where, by adopting (5.70), one must take

$$\overset{\infty}{\underset{\tau=0}{\psi''}} [\mathbf{0}, T(t-\tau), \mathbf{0}, T(t)] = \mathbf{0} \quad (5.73)$$

Thus, using (5.70) and (5.71) in (5.72), gives the form

$$\mathbf{E}(t) - \boldsymbol{\alpha} T(t) = \overset{\infty}{\underset{\tau=0}{\psi''}} [\Sigma(t-\tau), T(t-\tau). \Sigma(t), T(t)] \quad (5.74)$$

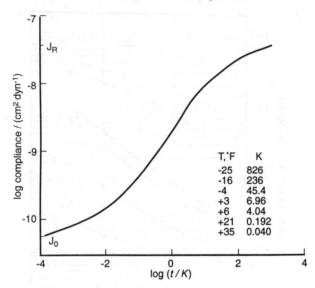

Fig. 5.13 Master curve for creep of a class of composite solid propellants ($-25°$F to $+35°$F) (Fig. 5.12). (Source: Blatz, P. J. (1956) Rheology of composite solid propellants. *J. Ind. Eng. Chem.*, **48**(4), 727–9 (American Chemical Society). Reprinted with permission of American Chemical Society.)

with the understanding from previous definitions that $\mathbf{E}(t)$ is the total strain including both the stress and temperature effects and $\alpha T(t)$ is the thermal strain in the absence of stress.

In a similar manner, on the assumption that the inverse of (5.69) exists, the stress-relaxation equation can be written as

$$\mathbf{\Sigma}(t) = \mathop{\mathbf{Y}}_{\tau=0}^{\infty} [\mathbf{E}(t-\tau),\ T(t-\tau),\ \mathbf{E}(\tau),\ T(t)]. \tag{5.75}$$

Now, if one assumes, following Christensen (1971), that the nonisothermal stress constitutive relation is determined by the corresponding isothermal function with $\mathbf{E}$ replaced by $\mathbf{E} - \boldsymbol{\alpha}$ and with a modified time scale ξ_τ to account for the history of the temperature, the nonisothermal stress relaxation may be expressed as

$$\mathbf{\Sigma}(t) = \mathop{\mathbf{Y}}_{\tau=0}^{\infty} [\mathbf{E}(t-\xi_\tau) - \boldsymbol{\alpha}(t-\xi_\tau),\ \mathbf{E}(t) - \boldsymbol{\alpha}(t)] \tag{5.76}$$

In equation (5.76), the modified time scale ξ_τ is given by

$$\xi_\tau = \mathop{\gamma}_{s=0}^{\infty} [T(t-s),\ \tau] \tag{5.77}$$

where $\overset{\infty}{\underset{s=0}{\gamma}}$ $(\cdot)$ has properties such as

$$\xi_\tau|_{\tau=0} = 0, \tag{5.78a}$$

and

$$\frac{\partial \xi_\tau}{\partial \tau} \geq 0 \tag{5.78b}$$

and

$$\xi_\tau|_{T=T_0} = \tau \tag{5.78c}$$

with the understanding that T_0 designates some constant base temperature.

It has been shown by Christensen (1971) that the appropriate infinitesimal theory form of (5.76) is

$$\sigma_{ij}(t) = R_{ijkl}(0)[\varepsilon_{kl}(t) - \alpha_{kl}(t)]$$

$$+ \int_0^\infty [\varepsilon_{kl}(t - \xi_\tau) - \alpha_{kl}(t - \xi_\tau)] \frac{\partial R_{ijkl}(\tau)\, \mathrm{d}\tau}{\mathrm{d}\tau}. \tag{5.79}$$

In (5.79), the usual infinitesimal theory definitions of stress and strain are taken; however, the general nonlinear dependence on temperature is retained.

5.6 THERMORHEOLOGICALLY COMPLEX MATERIALS

This is the class of viscoelastic materials whose temperature dependence of mechanical properties is not particularly responsive to analytical description through the time–temperature shift phenomenon. Following Schapery (1974), two classifications of such materials are defined, namely TCM-1 and TCM-2.

An example of the class of TCM-1 materials would be a composite material system consisting of two or more TSM phases. The mechanical behaviour of different composite systems belonging to the class TCM-1 has been considered by different researchers under isothermal conditions at different temperatures. In this context, Halpin (1969) dealt with a composite system consisting of two types of elastomers with different glass transition temperatures (-29 and $-75\,°$C). Fesco and Tschoegl (1971) considered the behaviour of two-phase block copolymers at various constant temperatures. The case of TCM-1 under transient temperatures is particularly complicated and further research effort is needed in this area (e.g. Schapery, 1966, 1968, 1969, 1974).

The TCM-2 class of viscoelastic materials is defined (Schapery, 1974) by the following uniaxial constitutive relationship for the cases of constant or transient temperatures

$$\varepsilon(t, T) = F_0(T)\sigma_0 + \int_0^t \Delta F(\xi - \xi') \frac{\mathrm{d}}{\mathrm{d}t'}\left[\frac{\sigma}{a_G(T)}\right] \mathrm{d}t' \tag{5.80}$$

where $F_0(T)$ is the initial value of creep compliance, $a_G(T)$ is a new shift factor for the class of material considered and ξ, ξ' are reduced time parameters introduced earlier by (5.68). Applying (5.80) to an isothermal creep test, the creep compliance $F_T = \varepsilon/\sigma$, is expected to be of the form

$$F_T = F_0(T) + \Delta F(\xi)/a_G(T) \qquad (5.81)$$

where $\xi = t/a_T$. This is with the understanding that, since $F_0(T)$ is the initial compliance, $\Delta F(0) = 0$. However, in order to relate the two shift factors a_T and a_G to experimental data, one writes (5.81) in the following logarithmic form:

$$\log[F_T - F_0(T)] = \log \Delta F(\xi) - \log a_G(T). \qquad (5.82)$$

One also recalls from (5.68) that

$$\log \xi = \log t - \log a_T \qquad (5.83)$$

Equations (5.82) and (5.83) imply that a plot of $\log[F_T - F_0(T)]$ versus $\log t$ at a test temperature T will be identical to that at an arbitrary selected reference temperature T_R, apart from rigid horizontal and vertical translations of $|\log t|$ and $|\log a_T|$ respectively.

A case of particular interest of the constitutive equation (5.80) is when

$$F_0 = F_0(T_R)/a_G(T). \qquad (5.84)$$

In this particular case, the creep compliance (5.81) reduces to

$$F_T = F(\xi)/a_G(T) \qquad (5.85)$$

in which

$$F(\xi) + F_0(T_R)/\Delta F(\xi). \qquad (5.86)$$

On the other hand, assuming as a normalization case that $a_G = a_T = 1$ at T_R, one can write, with reference to (5.81), the following equation:

$$\Delta F(t) = F_T(t, T_R) - F_0(T_R). \qquad (5.87)$$

Meantime, by using (5.87) with the argument t replaced by ξ, it can be shown that the constitutive equation (5.80) becomes

$$\varepsilon(t, T) = \int_0^t F(\xi - \xi') \frac{d}{dt'} \left(\frac{\sigma}{a_G} \right) dt'. \qquad (5.88)$$

The inversion of (5.88) may be expressed as

$$\sigma = a_G \int_0^t R(t - t') \frac{d\varepsilon}{dt} dt'. \qquad (5.89)$$

Accordingly, the relaxation modulus, R_T, for a constant strain input, is

$$R_T = a_G(T)R(\xi). \qquad (5.90)$$

Equations (5.85) and (5.90), within their applicability, indicate that master curves of $F = F(\xi)$ and $R = R(\xi)$ can be plotted by making horizontal ($\log a_T$) and vertical ($\log a_G$) shifts of the experimentally derived creep compliance F_T and relaxation modulus R_T.

For the experimental verification of the constitutive equations (5.80) and (5.88), reference is made to Schapery, Beckwith and Conrad (1973), Schapery (1974) and Watkins (1973). The reader is also referred to McCrum and Pogany (1970) for different procedures by which experimental data can be represented by master curves. At this point, it should be mentioned that the strain response expressed by (5.88) may be converted to total strain by using the procedure presented earlier for the case of thermorheologically simple materials (section 5.5).

For a three-dimensional representation of TCMs, we restrict our analysis, following Schapery (1974), to the isotropic case. For this purpose, two independent material parameters are used. In the creep case, one can use both the uniaxial creep compliance as presented earlier by (5.81), i.e.

$$F_T = F_0(T) + \Delta F(\xi)/a_G(T) \tag{5.91a}$$

together with the shear creep compliance

$$J_T = J_0(T) + \Delta J(\xi)/a_G(T). \tag{5.91b}$$

Thus, with reference to the one-dimensional constitutive creep equation (5.80), the components for the three-dimensional (isotropic) case are

$$\varepsilon_{11}(t, T) = \Gamma_1\sigma_{11} - \left(\frac{J_0}{2} - F_0\right)(\sigma_{22} + \sigma_{33}) + \int_0^t \Delta F(\xi - \xi') \frac{\partial}{\partial t'}\left(\frac{\sigma_{11}}{a_G}\right) dt'$$

$$- \int_0^t \left[\frac{\Delta J(\xi - \xi')}{2} - \Delta F(\xi - \xi')\right] \frac{\partial}{\partial t'}\left(\frac{\sigma_{22} + \sigma_{33}}{a_G}\right) dt' \tag{5.92a}$$

and two additional equations for ε_{22} and ε_{33}. Similarly for the shear components of the strain tensor, one has

$$2\varepsilon_{23}(t, T) = J_0\sigma_{23} + \int_0^t \Delta F(\xi - \xi') \frac{\partial}{\partial t'}\left(\frac{\sigma_{23}}{a_G}\right) dt' \tag{5.92b}$$

and two additional equations for ε_{12} and ε_{13}.

From (5.92), it can be shown that the bulk creep compliance $K_T(t, T) = 3\varepsilon_{ii}/\sigma_{ii}$, where σ_{ii} is constant, is expressed by

$$K_T(t, T) = 3(3F_T - J_T). \tag{5.93}$$

Meantime, the isothermal value of Poisson's ratio is determined at each temperature by

$$v = (J_T/2F_T) - 1. \tag{5.94}$$

The constitutive equations for thermorheologically simple materials can be immediately deduced from (5.92) by setting $a_G = 1$ and assuming that F_1, J_1 and α are constants.

REFERENCES

Biot, M. A. (1958) Linear thermodynamics and the mechanics of solids, in Proc. 3rd US Natl Congr. Appl. Mech., pp. 1–18.

Biot, M. A. (1973) Nonlinear thermoelasticity, irreversible thermodynamics and elastic instability. *Indiana Univ. Math. J.*, **23**, 309–35.

Blatz, P. J. (1956) Rheology of composite solid propellants. *Ind. Eng. Chem.*, **48**(4), 727–9.

Breuer, S. (1969) Lower bounds on work in linear viscoelasticity. *Q. Appl. Math.*, **27**(2), 139–46.

Breuer, S. and Onat, E. T. (1964) On the determination of free energy in linear viscoelastic solids. *Z. Angew. Math. Phys.*, **15**, 184–91.

Christensen, R. M. (1971) *Theory of Viscoelasticity*, Academic Press, New York.

Christensen, R. M. and Naghdi, P. M. (1967) Linear non-isothermal viscoelastic solids. *Acta Mech.*, **3**, 1–12.

Coleman B. D. (1963) The thermodynamics of elastic materials with heat conduction and viscosity. *Arch. Ration. Mech. Anal.*, **13**, 167–78.

Coleman, B. D. (1964a) Thermodynamics of materials with memory. *Arch. Ration. Mech. Anal.*, **17**, 1–46.

Coleman, B. D. (1964b) On thermodynamics, strain impulses, and viscoelasticity. *Arch. Ration. Mech. Anal.*, **17**, 230–54.

Coleman, B. D. and Gurtin, M. E. (1967a) Thermodynamics with internal state variables. *J. Chem. Phys.*, **47**, 597–613.

Coleman, B. D. and Gurtin, M. E. (1967b) Equipresence and constitutive equations for rigid heat conductors. *Z. Angew. Math. Phys.*, **18**, 199–208.

Coleman, B. D. and Mizel, V. J. (1963) Thermodynamics and departures from Fourier's law of heat conduction. *Arch. Ration. Mech. Anal.*, **13**, 245–61.

Coleman, B. D. and Mizel, V. J. (1964) Existence of coloric equations of state in thermodynamics. *J. Chem. Phys.*, **40**, 1116–25.

Coleman, B. D. and Mizel, V. J. (1967) A general theory of dissipation in materials with memory. *Arch. Ration. Mech. Anal.*, **27**, 255–74.

Coleman, B. D. and Mizel, V. J. (1968) On the general theory of fading memory. *Arch. Ration. Mech. Anal.*, **29**, 18–31.

Coleman, B. D. and Noll, W. (1960) An approximation theorem for functionals with applications in continuum mechanics. *Arch. Ration. Mech. Anal.*, **6**, 355–70.

Coleman, B. D. and Noll. W. (1961) Foundations of linear viscoelasticity. *Rev. Mod. Phys.*, **33**, 239–49.

Coleman, B. D. and Noll, W. (1963) The thermodynamics of elastic materials with heat conduction and viscosity. *Arch. Ration. Mech. Anal.*, **13**, 167–78.

Coleman, B. D. and Noll, W. (1964) Simple fluids with fading memory, in Proc. Int. Symp., Second Order Effects, Heifa, 1962, Macmillan, New York, pp. 530–52.

Coleman, B. D. and Owen, D. R. (1970) On the thermodynamics of materials with memory. *Arch. Ration. Mech. Anal.*, **36**, 245–69.

Crochet, M. J. (1975) A non-isothermal theory of viscoelastic materials, in *Theoretical Rheology* (eds J. F. Hutton, J. R. A. Pearson and K. Walters), Applied Science, London, pp. 111–22.

Crochet, M. J. and Naghdi, P. M. (1969) A class of simple solids with fading memory. *Int. J. Eng. Sci.*, **7**, 1173–98.

Crochet, M. J. and Naghdi, P. M. (1974) On a restricted non-isothermal theory of simple materials. *J. Méc.*, **13**, 97–114.

Crochet, M. J. and Naghdi, P. M. (1979) On 'thermo-rheologically simple' solids, in Proc. IUTAM Symp., Thermoelasticity, Springer, New York, pp. 59–86.

Day, W. A. (1970) Reversibility, recoverable work and free energy in linear viscoelasticity. *Q. J. Mech. Appl. Math.*, **23**(1), 1–15.

Day, W. A. (1972) *The Thermodynamics of Simple Materials with Fading Memory*, Springer, New York.

Ferry, J. D. (1970) *Viscoelastic Properties of Polymers*, 2nd edn, Wiley, New York.

Fesco, D. G. and Tschoegl, N. W. (1971) Time–temperature superposition in thermorheologically complex materials. *J. Polym. Sci. C*, **35**, 51–69.

Fried, N. (1970) In *Mechanics of Composite Materials* (eds F. W. Wendt, H. Liebowitz and N. Perrone), Pergamon, Oxford, pp. 813–37.

Fung, Y. C. (1965) *Foundations of Solid Mechanics*, Prentice-Hall, Englewood Cliffs, NJ, pp. 377–446.

Gittus, J. (1975) *Creep, Viscoelasticity and Creep Fracture in Solids*, Wiley, New York.

Green, A. E. and Laws, N. (1967) On the formulation of constitutive equations in thermomechanical theories of continua. *Q. J. Mech. Appl. Math.*, **20**, 265–75.

Green, A. E. and Naghdi, P. M. (1965) A general theory of an elastic–plastic continuum. *Arch. Ration. Mech. Anal.*, **18**, 251–81.

Green, A. E., Rivlin, R. S. and Spencer, A. J. M. (1959) The mechanics of nonlinear materials with memory, Part II. *Arch. Ration. Mech. Anal.*, **3**, 82–90.

Gurtin, M. E. (1965) Thermodynamics and the possibility of spatial interaction in elastic materials. *Arch. Ration. Mech. Anal.*, **19**, 339–52.

Gurtin, M. E. and Williams, W. O. (1966) On the inclusion of the complete symmetry group in unimodular group. *Arch. Ration. Mech. Anal.*, **23**, 163–72.

Halpin, J. C. (1969) Characterization of orthotropic (fiber-reinforced) polymeric solids. Doctoral Dissertation, University of Akron, OH.

Kestin, J. (1966) *A Course in Thermodynamics*, Vol. 1, Blaisdell, Waltham, MA.

Landel, R. F. and Peng, S. T. T. (1986) Equations of state and constitutive equations. *J. Rheol.*, **30**(4), 741–65.

Laws, N. (1967) On the thermodynamics of certain materials with memory. *Int. J. Eng. Sci.*, **5**, 427–34.

Leaderman, H. (1943) *Elastic and Creep Properties of Filamentous Materials and Other Polymers*, Textile Foundation, Washington, DC, pp. 175–85.

Link, G. and Schwarzl, F. R. (1987) Shear creep and recovery of a technical polystyrene. *Rheol. Acta*, **26**, 375–84.

McCrum, N. G. and Pogany, G. A. (1970) Time–temperature superposition in the α-region of an epoxy resin. *J. Macromol. Sci. Phys. B*, **4**(1), 109–25.

Meixner, J. (1969) Processes in simple thermodynamic materials. *Arch. Ration. Mech. Anal.*, **33**, 33–53.

Mercier, J. P., Aklonis, J. J., Litt, M. and Tobolsky, A. V. (1965) Viscoelastic behaviour of the polycarbonate of bisphenol A. *J. Appl. Polym. Sci.*, **9**, 447–59.

Morland, L. W. and Lee, E. H. (1960) Stress analysis for linear viscoelastic materials with temperature variation. *Trans. Soc. Rheol.*, **4**, 233–63.

Müller, I. (1967) On the entropy inequality. *Arch. Ration. Mech. Anal.*, **26**, 118–41.

Noll, W. (1958) A mathematical theory of the mechanical behaviour of continuous media. *Arch. Ration. Mech. Anal.*, **2**, 197–226.

Onogi, S., Sasaguri, K., Adachi, T. and Ogihara, S. (1962) Time–humidity superposition in some crystalline polymers. *J. Polym. Sci.*, **58**, 1–17.

Owen, D. R. (1968) Thermodynamics of materials with elastic range. *Arch. Ration. Mech. Anal.*, **31**, 91–112.

Owen, D. R. (1970) A mechanical theory of materials with elastic range. *Arch. Ration. Mech. Anal.*, **37**, 85–110.

Rivlin, R. S. (1975) The thermodynamics of materials with fading memory, in *Theoretical Rheology* (Eds J. F. Hutton, J. R. A. Pearson and K. Walters), Applied Science, London, pp. 83–103.

Schapery, R. A. (1964) Application of thermodynamics to thermomechanical, fracture, and birefringent phenomena in viscoelastic media. *J. Appl. Phys.*, **35**(5), 1451–65.

Schapery, R. A. (1966) A theory of nonlinear thermoviscoelasticity based on irreversible thermodynamics, in Proc. 5th US Natl Congr. of Appl. Mech., ASME, pp. 511–30.

Schapery, R. A. (1968) On a thermodynamic constitutive theory and its application to various nonlinear materials, in Proc. IUTAM Symp., East Kilbride, pp. 259–85.

Schapery, R. A. (1969) On a thermodynamic constitutive theory and its application to various nonlinear materials, in Proc. IUTAM Symp. on Thermoinelasticity, Springer, Berlin.

Schapery, R. A. (1974) Viscoelastic behaviour and analysis of composite materials, in *Mechanics of Composite Materials*, Vol. 2 (Ed. G. Sandeskj), Academic Press, new York, pp. 86–168.

Schapery, R. A., Beckwith, S. W. and Conrad, N. (1973) Studies on the viscoelastic behaviour of fiber-reinforced plastic. *Mech. Mater. Res. Center Rep. MM 2702-73-3 (AFML-TR-73-179)*, Texas A & M University.

Schwarzl, F. and Staverman, A. J. (1952) Time–temperature dependence of linear viscoelastic behaviour. *J. Appl. Phys.*, **23**(8), 838–43.

Steel, D. J. (1965) The creep and stress-rupture of reinforced plastics. *Trans. J. Plast. Inst.*, **33**, 161–7.

Theocaris, P. S. (1962) Viscoelastic properties of epoxy resins derived from creep and relaxation tests at different temperatures. *Rheol. Acta*, **2**(2), 92–6.

Tobolosky, A. F. and Catsiff, E. (1956) Elastoviscous properties of polyisobutylene (and other amorphous polymers) from stress–relaxation studies, IX. A summary of results. *J. Polym. Sci.*, **19**, 111–21.

Truesdell, C. (1951) A new definition of a fluid. II. The Maxwellian fluid. *J. Math. Pures Appl.*, **30**, 111–58.

Truesdell, C. and Toupin, R. A. (1960) Classical field theories, in *Handbuch der Physik*, Vol. III/1 (Ed. S. Flügge), Springer, Berlin, pp. 226–790.

Tsai, S. W. (1970) In *Mechanics of Composite Materials* (eds F. W. Wendt, H. Liebowitz and N. Peronne), Pergamon, Oxford, pp. 749–67.

Wang, C. C. and Bowen, R. M. (1966) On the thermodynamics of nonlinear materials with quasi-elastic response. *Arch. Ration. Mech. Anal.*, **22**, 79–99.

Watkins, L. A. (1973) Creep of an epoxy resin under transient temperatures. M.S. Thesis, Civil Engineering, Texas A & M. University.

Williams, M. L., Landel, R. F. and Ferry, J. D. (1955) the temperature dependence of relaxation mechanisms in amorphous polymers and other glass-forming liquids. *J. Am. Chem. Soc.*, **77**, 3701–7.

Wilson, A. H. (1957) *Thermodynamics and Statistical Mechanics*, Cambridge University Press, Cambridge.

FURTHER READING

Bataille, J. and Kestin, J. (1979) Irreversible processes and physical interpretation of rational thermodynamics. *J. Non-Equilib. Thermodyn.*, **4**, 229–58.

Biot, M. A. (1954) Theory of stress–strain relationship in anisotropic viscoelasticity and relaxation phenomena. *J. Appl. Phys.*, **25**(11), 1385–91.

Eringen, A. C. (1960) Irreversible thermodynamics and continuum mechanics. *Phys. Rev.*, **117**, 1174–83.

Freeman, J. W. and Voorhees, H. R. (1956) Relaxation properties of steels and super-strength alloys at elevated temperatures. *ASTM, Spec. Tech. 187*, August. (also, *ASTM Publ. DS-114*, August 1961).

Freudenthal, A. M. (1954) Effect of rheological behaviour on thermal stresses. *J. Appl. Phys.*, **25**(9), 1110–7.

Hunter, S. C. (1961) Tentative equations for the propagation of stress, strain and temperature fields in viscoelastic solids. *J. Mech. Phys. Solids*, **9**, 39–51.

Koh, S. L. and Eringen, A. C. (1963) On the foundation of nonlinear thermoviscoelasticity. *Int. J. Eng. Sci.*, **1**, 199–229.

Lee, E. H. (1955) Stress analysis in viscoelastic bodies. *Q. Appl. Math.*, **13**(2), 183–90.

Manjoine, M. J. and Voorhees, H. R. (1982) Compilation of stress–relaxation data for engineering alloys. *ASTM Data Ser. Publ. DS60*.

Pindera, J. T. and Straka, P. (1974) On physical measures of rheological responses of some materials in wide ranges of temperature and spectral frequency. *Rheol. Acta*, **13**, 338–51.

Prager, W. (1956) Thermal stresses in viscoelastic structures. *J. Appl. Math. Phys.*, **7**, 230–8.

Rivlin, R. S. (1972) On the principles of equipresence and unification. *Q. Appl. Math.*, **30**, 227–8.

Wolosewick, R. M. and Gratch, S. (1965) Transient response in a viscoelastic material with temperature-dependent properties and thermomechanical coupling. *J. Appl. Mech.*, **32**(3), 620–2.

6

Transition to nonlinear viscoelasticity

6.1 INTRODUCTION

Material systems are often used under conditions which do not comply with the infinitesimal deformation postulates of the linear theory. The existence of imperfections and discontinuities in the material is particularly cited as a likely source of much of the nonlinearity of the behaviour. In the case of two-phase materials such as particulate and fibre composites, for instance, microstructural damage is often considered to be the most predominant cause of the nonlinear behaviour of such materials. Hence, these materials usually exhibit nonlinearity and strain rate dependent hysteresis over a wide range of temperature and stress or strain rate (e.g. Schapery, 1974).

For a nonlinear viscoelastic material, one or both of criteria (2.64) and (2.65) mentioned in Chapter 2 concerning, respectively, homogeneity and superposition of input histories are not met. However, the memory hypothesis previously introduced in linear viscoelasticity is still valid for the case of the nonlinear theory. This means, for the two theories, that the current value of the output is determined by the complete past history of the input. As we noticed in Chapter 2, this memory hypothesis was the starting point in the development of the linear theory of viscoelasticity and it is also the starting point for the treatment of nonlinear viscoelasticity (e.g. Christensen, 1971).

Linear viscoelastic behaviour of materials has been the subject of extensive studies for over a century, but it is only in the last few decades that researchers have started to pay particular attention to the more complex subject of nonlinear viscoelasticity. This was primarily motivated by the observation of certain nonlinear effects during the course of the study of the performance of a class of viscoelastic materials (Weissenberg, 1948) and, hence, by the failure of the linear theory to predict reasonably the viscoelastic behaviour of such materials. Considerable research efforts characterizing the nonlinear viscoelastic nature of materials have been recorded since then in the literature. A number of nonlinear theories of viscoelasticity have been proposed and many practical problems have been analysed, particularly those pertaining to the steady flow of viscoelastic media. The dynamical aspects of the nonlinear viscoelastic theory have also been dealt with by a number of researchers, but interest in the study of wave propagation in nonlinear viscoelastic materials did not develop until recently (Chapter 8). Further research efforts have also been directed towards incorporating the coupled mechanical and nonmechanical effects in a nonlinear viscoelastic medium (e.g. Christensen, 1971). In this, some results, for instance, have been obtained on the behaviour of heat-conducting viscoelastic materials, but no significant problems have been solved to study other coupled effects. Theorems on the uniqueness of the existence of solutions for initial and boundary value problems in nonlinear viscoelasticity are still at an early stage.

Although the rational approach to nonlinear viscoelasticity may be considered as has been developed, experimental work concerning the validity of the theory is still lagging behind significantly. This is mainly due to the complexity of the experimental programme required to determine the pertaining material functions even in the one-dimensional case (Lockett, 1965, 1972).

6.2 ILLUSTRATIONS OF NONLINEAR VISCOELASTIC PERFORMANCE OF MATERIALS

We provide below some illustrations of the nonlinear behaviour of a class of viscoelastic materials. The examples cited are taken from the work of Ward and Onat (1963), on oriented polypropylene monofilaments. As will be seen from the discussions below, the performance of this class of nonfilaments is nonlinear. For a nonlinear viscoelastic material the following should be noted.

1. Creep compliance is dependent on the level of loading. Let $\varepsilon(\sigma_0, t)$ denote the strain response in a creep experiment performed under the loading

$$\sigma(t) = 0, \quad t < 0; \quad \sigma(t) = \sigma_0 = \text{constant}, \quad t > 0.$$

If the material is linear, the constitutive creep response is expressed by equation (2.67), that is

$$\varepsilon(t) = F(t)\sigma_0 \tag{6.1}$$

where $F(t)$ designates the creep function of the linear material; it is independent of the loading σ_0. On the other hand, for a nonlinear viscoelastic material, the corresponding form of the constitutive relation (6.1) may be written as

$$\varepsilon(\sigma_0, t) = F(\sigma_0, t)\sigma_0 \tag{6.2}$$

where the dependence of the creep function $F(\sigma_0, t)$ on the loading σ_0 is indicated.

Figure 6.1 shows the creep function (compliance) versus time from creep experiments conducted by Ward and Onat (1963) on oriented polypropylene monofilaments under five different load levels. It is seen from the figure that except for short times ($t \approx 10^2$ s) and only for low intensities of loading (67.6 gf and 129.6 gf) the creep compliances do not coincide. This is in contradiction to the response predicted by (6.1), but in agreement with (6.2). This indicates that the

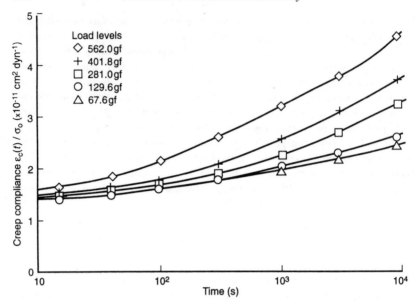

Fig. 6.1 Creep compliance curves of oriented polypropylene under different levels of load. (Reprinted with permission from *J. Mech. Phys. Solids*, **11**, Ward, I. M. and Onat, E. T., Nonlinear mechanical behaviour of oriented polypropylene, copyright (1963), Pergamon Press Ltd.)

material tested is nonlinear in behaviour. To affirm the above characteristics of the nonlinear behaviour of oriented polypropylene monofilaments, Fig. 6.2 (Ward and Onat, 1963) shows the creep compliance against the level of loading for various fixed values of the time t. For a linear material, the creep compliance, as indicated by (6.1), is independent of the loading σ_0 and these curves would be accordingly horizontal. However, in Fig. 6.2, the curves resemble more parabolas, thus indicating the dependence of the creep compliance on the loading level. It is only for small times and low load levels that the tested oriented polypropylene monofilaments may be considered as linear.

2. Recovery compliance is dependent on the level of loading. Denoting by $\varepsilon_R(t, t_1)$ the strain response in a recovery test, then the linear constitutive equation in case of recovery is written in correspondence to (6.1) as

$$\varepsilon_R(t, t_1) = F_R(t - t_1)\sigma_0. \qquad (6.3)$$

In (6.3), $F_R(t - t_1)$ is the linear recovery compliance; it is independent of the loading level. The corresponding recovery equation to (6.3) in the nonlinear case may be expressed as

$$\varepsilon_R(\sigma_0, t, t_1) = F_R(\sigma_0, t - t_1)\sigma_0. \qquad (6.4)$$

indicating that the recovery compliance, in the nonlinear case, is dependent on

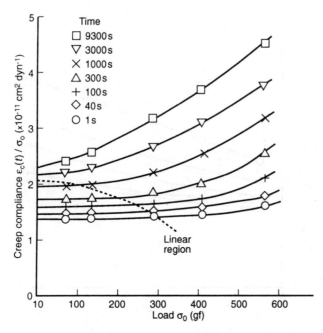

Fig. 6.2 Creep compliance $\varepsilon_c(t)/\sigma_0$ versus load σ_0 for various times (oriented polypropylene monofilaments). (Reprinted with permission from *J. Mech. Phys. Solids*, **11**, Ward, I. M. and Onat, E. T., Nonlinear mechanical behaviour of oriented polypropylene, copyright (1963), Pergamon Press Ltd.)

the level of loading. This is illustrated in Figs. 6.3 and 6.4 (after Ward and Onat, 1963) showing, respectively, the creep compliance versus the time and loading level for oriented polypropylene monofilaments. Thus, the prediction of the linear theory concerning the recovery of the tested oriented polypropylene monofilaments could be contested in view of the observed behaviour of the recovery compliance in Figs. 6.3 and 6.4, similar to what was discussed earlier concerning the creep compliance.

3. With regard to successive creep and recovery, for a nonlinear viscoelastic material, creep and recovery curves do not coincide for a given level of loading. The above remarks concerning the dependence of both the creep and recovery compliances, of a nonlinear material, on the level of loading may be further supported by observing the behaviour of the two compliances at different levels of loading. This is demonstrated in Fig. 6.5, taken from Ward and Onat (1963), concerning the creep and recovery of oriented polypropylene monofilaments. Time on the abscissa of this figure refers, in view of (6.1), to time t for creep curves and, according to (6.3), to time $(t - t_1)$ for recovery curves whereby t_1 is taken as 9.3×10^3 s for the data presented in the figure. According to the linear theory,

Transition to nonlinear viscoelasticity

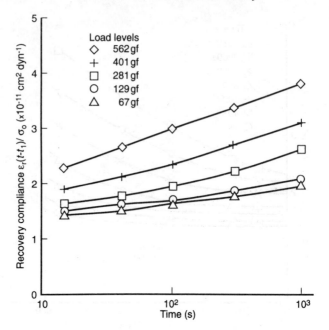

Fig. 6.3 Recovery curves of oriented polypropylene monofilaments for different levels of load (time of loading, 9.3×10^3 s). (Reprinted with permission from *J. Mech. Phys. Solids*, **11**, Ward, I. M. and Onat, E. T., Nonlinear mechanical behaviour of oriented polypropylene, copyright (1963), Pergamon Press Ltd.)

constitutive equations (6.1) and (6.3), creep and recovery curves of Fig. 6.5 would coincide for a given level of loading. As shown in this figure, however, these curves do not coincide for the tested monofilaments, except for low load levels, indicating thereby the nonlinearity of these materials. In Fig. 6.5, it is interesting to observe that the instantaneous recovery, as well as the short time recovery, is larger than the initial creep response and such difference increases with increasing level of loading (Ward and Onat, 1963). For a review of the viscoelastic properties of polymers in general, the reader is referred to Ferry (1960) and Turner (1971, 1973), amongst others.

6.3 OBJECTIVITY PRINCIPLE

In the treatment of a nonlinear theory of viscoelasticity, one must deal with a nonlinear analysis of the deformation process and, hence, nonlinear kinematical quantities need to be introduced. In this context, it is necessary that the particular measures of deformation, or strain quantities, involved in the nonlinear theory have the proper coordinate invariance characteristics. This would also apply to all other

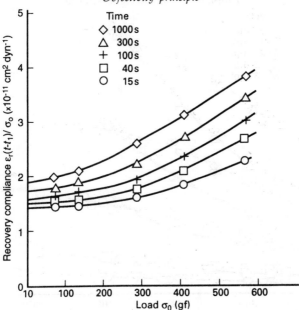

Fig. 6.4 Recovery compliance $\varepsilon_r(t - t_1)/\sigma_0$ against load σ_0 (time of loading 9.3×10^3 s) for various times for oriented polypropylene monofilaments. (Reprinted with permission from *J. Mech. Phys. Solids*, **11**, Ward, I. M. and Onat, E. T., Nonlinear mechanical behaviour of oriented polypropylene, copyright (1963), Pergamon Press Ltd.)

physical quantities and their analysis in the sense that they must be independent of the particular frame of reference with respect to which they are described (e.g. Christensen, 1971). This requirement is often referred to as the principle of objectivity, or material frame indifference (Truesdell and Noll, 1965). This principle is a reflection of the fact that material deformation occurs independently of the observer, i.e. frame independent as we discussed earlier in the introduction to Chapter 1.

As dealt with in Chapters 2 and 4, a viscoelastic material is generally defined as one for which the stress tensor depends on the entire history of the deformation measures involved. A 'simple viscoelastic material', on the other hand, could be characterized (Noll, 1958), by a dependence of the stress tensor σ_{ij} at time t on the deformation gradient $F_{rs}(t - \tau)$ only, describing the motion of the body from time τ up to the time t. Accordingly, a simple material may be defined by the constitutive equation

$$\sigma_{ij}(t) = \pi_{ij}_{\tau = -\infty}^{t} [F_{rs}(t - \tau)] \tag{6.5}$$

where π_{ij} is a particular functional of the deformation gradient tensor function $F_{rs}(t - \tau)$ taken with respect to the configuration at time t where F_{rs} is defined by

$$F_{rs}(t - \tau) = x_{m,r}x_{m,s} \tag{6.6}$$

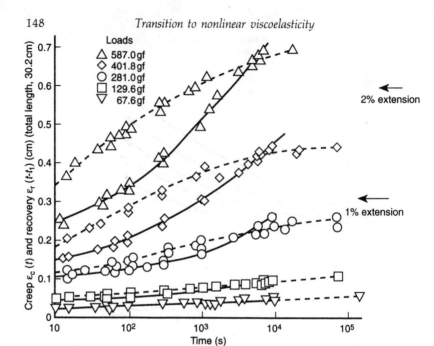

Fig. 6.5 Successive creep (———) and recovery (– – –) of oriented polypropylene conditioned fibres. (Reprinted with permission from *J. Mech. Phys. Solids*, **11**, Ward, I. M. and Onat, E. T., Nonlinear mechanical behaviour of oriented polypropylene, copyright (1963), Pergamon Press Ltd.)

where $x_{m,r}$ is the deformation gradient at time t at the spatial point x_m taken with respect to the configuration at time t.

The deformation gradient tensor **F**, i.e. $F_{rs}(t - \tau)$, appearing in (6.5) may be decomposed (Truesdell and Noll, 1965) as follows (also Lockett, 1972):

$$\mathbf{F} = \mathbf{RU} = \mathbf{VR} \tag{6.7}$$

where **R** is an orthogonal matrix and **U** and **V** designate positive-definite symmetric matrices. In other words, the deformation measure **F** may be regarded, from a physical point of view, as a rigid rotation **R** of the continuous body that is either preceded by a pure stretch **U** or followed by a pure rotation **V**.

A restriction on the form of the functional π of (6.5) follows from the application of the principle of objectivity introduced earlier. Consequently, it can be shown (Truesdell and Noll, 1965) that the functional relation (6.5) may be expressed in the form

$$\sigma_{ij}(t) = F_{rs}(t) \overset{t}{\underset{-\infty}{G_{ij}}} [U_{rs}(t - \tau)] F_{rs}^{T}(t) \tag{6.8}$$

where $\mathbf{F}^T$ is the transpose of **F** and **G** is a new arbitrary functional (Lockett, 1972).

Alternatively, by combining (6.7) and (6.8) it can be shown that

$$\boldsymbol{\sigma}(t) = \mathbf{R}(t) \overset{t}{\underset{-\infty}{\mathbf{H}}} [\boldsymbol{U}(t - \tau)]\mathbf{R}^{\mathsf{T}}(t) \tag{6.9}$$

where again $\mathbf{H}$ is a new arbitrary functional of the stretch tensor $\boldsymbol{U}(t - \tau)$. The constitutive relation (6.9) implies, through the principle of objectivity, that the current stress depends only on the current value of the rotation tensor $\mathbf{R}$, but, meantime, it depends on the entire past history of the stretch $\mathbf{U}$. Expression (6.9) can be simplified further by considering the relation

$$\mathbf{R}^{\mathsf{T}}\mathbf{R} = \mathbf{R}\mathbf{R}^{\mathsf{T}} = \mathbf{I}. \tag{6.10}$$

since $\mathbf{R}$ is an orthogonal matrix and where $\mathbf{I}$ is the identity matrix. Accordingly, the constitutive relation (6.9) may be written in the following form:

$$\boldsymbol{\Sigma}(t) = \mathbf{R}^{\mathsf{T}}\boldsymbol{\sigma}\mathbf{R} = \overset{t}{\underset{-\infty}{\mathbf{H}}} [\mathbf{U}(t - \tau)] \tag{6.11}$$

where $\boldsymbol{\Sigma}$ is the stress matrix evaluated in a coordinate system which is related to the rigid-body-rotation component of the deformation. Equation (6.11) implies, through the principle of objectivity, that a permissible form of the constitutive relation is one in which the stress tensor $\boldsymbol{\Sigma}$ is expressed as an arbitrary functional of the deformation measure $\mathbf{U}$. Accordingly, $\mathbf{U}$ is an 'objective' deformation measure. However, it is not the only objective measure of deformation as any simple function of $\mathbf{U}$ would also be objective. For instance, the right Cauchy–Green strain measure $\mathbf{C}$ and the finite strain measure $\mathbf{E}$ defined, respectively by

$$\mathbf{C} = \mathbf{F}^{\mathsf{T}}\mathbf{F} = \mathbf{U}^{\mathsf{T}}\mathbf{R}^{\mathsf{T}}\mathbf{R}\mathbf{U} = \mathbf{U}^{\mathsf{T}}\mathbf{U} = \mathbf{U}^2 \tag{6.12}$$

and

$$2\mathbf{E} = \mathbf{C} - \mathbf{I} = \mathbf{F}^{\mathsf{T}}\mathbf{F} - \mathbf{I} \tag{6.13}$$

are both objective.

In view of the relations (6.12) and (6.13) between $\mathbf{C}$, $\mathbf{F}$ and $\mathbf{U}$, the following alternative forms of the constitutive equation (6.11) can be expressed

$$\boldsymbol{\Sigma}(t) = \overset{t}{\underset{\tau = -\infty}{\mathbf{f}}} [\mathbf{C}(t - \tau)] \tag{6.14}$$

and

$$\boldsymbol{\Sigma}(t) = \overset{t}{\underset{\tau = -\infty}{\mathbf{J}}} [\mathbf{E}(t - \tau)] \tag{6.15}$$

where $\mathbf{f}$ and $\mathbf{J}$ are constitutive functionals. Their detailed forms need to be established for the particular viscoelastic material under consideration. For an isotropic material, $\mathbf{f}$ and $\mathbf{J}$ are supposed to be isotropic functionals (Lockett, 1972).

Under the conditions that (6.15) is invertible, its corresponding equation in the creep case may be expressed as

$$\mathbf{E}(t) = \underset{\tau = -\infty}{\overset{t}{\mathbf{Y}}} \ [\Sigma(t - \tau)], \tag{6.16}$$

which expresses the current strain as a functional of stress history.

Following Lockett (1965, 1972), it is convenient to consider (6.15) and (6.16) at the same time by utilizing

$$\mathbf{Q}(t) = \underset{\tau = -\infty}{\overset{t}{\mathbf{F}}} \ [\mathbf{P}(t - \tau)] \tag{6.17}$$

where $\mathbf{Q}$ and $\mathbf{P}$ can be interpreted as either

$$\mathbf{Q} = \Sigma = \mathbf{R}^{\mathrm{T}}\boldsymbol{\sigma}\mathbf{R}, \quad \mathbf{P} = \mathbf{E} \tag{6.18}$$

or

$$\mathbf{Q} = \mathbf{E}, \quad \mathbf{P} = \Sigma = \mathbf{R}^{\mathrm{T}}\boldsymbol{\sigma}\mathbf{R} \tag{6.19}$$

6.4 CHARACTERIZATION OF NONLINEAR VISCOELASTIC BEHAVIOUR

The purely mechanical, one-dimensional response of a nonlinear material with memory may be characterized by the following constitutive assumptions (Schuler, Nunziato and Walsh, 1973).

1. At a given material point, the stress at time t is determined by the entire history of the strain. This may be expressed in the following manner:

$$\boldsymbol{\sigma}(t) = \mathbf{L}[\boldsymbol{\varepsilon}(t, \tau)], \quad 0 \leq (\tau, t) < \infty \tag{6.20}$$

where $\mathbf{L}$ is a constitutive functional of strain.

2. The material may exhibit 'fading memory'. This implies (Coleman and Noll, 1960, 1961) that the functional $\mathbf{L}$ in (6.20) has certain smoothness properties. In this context, Schuler, Nunziato and Walsh (1973) defined the norm of strain histories by

$$\| \boldsymbol{\varepsilon}(t, \tau) \| = \| \boldsymbol{\varepsilon}(t - \tau) \| = \left[|\boldsymbol{\varepsilon}(t)|^2 + \int_0^{\infty} h^2(\tau) |\boldsymbol{\varepsilon}(t, \tau)|^2 \, \mathrm{d}t \right]^{1/2} \tag{6.21}$$

where $h(t)$ is a continuous monotonically decreasing, square-integrable function. Thus, the material behaviour would be more influenced by the events occurring in the recent past than those occurring in the distant past. With reference to (6.21), the set of all histories with finite norm forms a Hilbert space. The constitutive functional $\mathbf{L}[\boldsymbol{\varepsilon}(t, \tau)]$, in (6.20), is assumed to be defined in this space and to be twice continuously differentiable with respect to the present value of the strain (Schuler, Nunziato and Walsh, 1973).

Published by Chapman & Hall, 2–6 Boundary Row, London SE1 8HN, UK

Chapman & Hall, 2–6 Boundary Row, London SE1 8HN, UK

Blackie Academic & Professional, Wester Cleddens Road, Bishopbriggs, Glasgow G64 2NZ, UK

Chapman & Hall GmbH, Pappelallee 3, 69469 Weinheim, Germany

Chapman & Hall USA, One Penn Plaza, 41st Floor, New York NY 10119, USA

Chapman & Hall Japan, ITP-Japan, Kyowa Building, 3F, 2-2-1 Hirakawacho, Chiyoda-ku, Tokyo 102, Japan

Chapman & Hall Australia, Thomas Nelson Australia, 102 Dodds Street, South Melbourne, Victoria 3205, Australia

Chapman & Hall India, R. Seshadri, 32 Second Main Road, CIT East, Madras 600 035, India

First edition 1995

© 1995 Chapman & Hall

Typeset in 10/12 Palatino by Techset Composition Ltd., Salisbury, Wilts

Printed and bound in Great Britain by Hartnolls Limited, Boumin, Cornwall

ISBN 0 412 59030 1

A catalogue record for this book is available from the British Library

Library of Congress Catalog Card Number: 94–68787

Printed on permanent acid-free text paper, manufactured in accordance with ANSI/NISO Z39.48-1992 and ANSI/NISO Z39.48-1984 (Permanence of Paper).

Published by Chapman & Hall, 2–6 Boundary Row, London SE1 8HN, UK

Chapman & Hall, 2–6 Boundary Row, London SE1 8HN, UK

Blackie Academic & Professional, Wester Cleddens Road, Bishopbriggs, Glasgow G64 2NZ, UK

Chapman & Hall GmbH, Pappelallee 3, 69469 Weinheim, Germany

Chapman & Hall USA, One Penn Plaza, 41st Floor, New York NY 10119, USA

Chapman & Hall Japan, ITP-Japan, Kyowa Building, 3F, 2-2-1 Hirakawacho, Chiyoda-ku, Tokyo 102, Japan

Chapman & Hall Australia, Thomas Nelson Australia, 102 Dodds Street, South Melbourne, Victoria 3205, Australia

Chapman & Hall India, R. Seshadri, 32 Second Main Road, CIT East, Madras 600 035, India

First edition 1995

© 1995 Chapman & Hall

Typeset in 10/12 Palatino by Techset Composition Ltd., Salisbury, Wilts

Printed and bound in Great Britain by Hartnolls Limited, Bodmin, Cornwall

ISBN 0 412 59030 1

A catalogue record for this book is available from the British Library

Library of Congress Catalog Card Number: 94–68787

♾ Printed on permanent acid-free text paper, manufactured in accordance with ANSI/NISO Z39.48-1992 and ANSI/NISO Z39.48-1984 (Permanence of Paper).

Based on the assumed smoothness of the functional **L**, Coleman and Noll (1961) have shown that the response behaviour of nonlinear material with memory may be approximated in the case of small relative strain histories $\Delta \boldsymbol{\varepsilon}(t, \tau)$ by the linear theory (Chapter 2); also, Coleman, Gurtin and Herrera (1965) should be referred to.

6.5 CONSTITUTIVE EQUATIONS OF NONLINEAR VISCOELASTIC MATERIALS

Based on the thermomechanical theory of materials with memory due to Coleman (1964) (Chapter 5), Christensen (1971) presented a general formulation of the nonlinear viscoelastic response of materials. Although Coleman's approach is not restricted to isothermal conditions, Christensen, for simplification of the presentation, limited his derivation to the isothermal case.

Christensen's derivation of the stress constitutive equation is based on the combination of the local balance of energy expression and the local entropy production. This is, then, joined with the definition of the norm in the collection of past histories within the associated fading memory hypothesis.

As previously discussed in the context of the linear theory (Chapters 2 and 5), the concept of memory in viscoelastic materials provides an expression of the postulate that the current value of a field variable, such as the stress and stored energy, depends not only on the current value of the stimulus but also on the past history of such stimulus. Accordingly, the stress constitutive relation may be expressed through the following functional expression:

$$\sigma_{ij}(t) = f_{ij}[x_{i,L}(t-\tau), \quad x_{j,L}(t)], \quad 0 \le (\tau, t) \le \infty, \tag{6.22}$$

in which σ_{ij} is the Cauchy stress tensor and $x_{i,L}$ is the deformation gradient defined by

$$x_{i,L}(X_K, t) = \frac{\partial x_i(X_K, t)}{\partial X_L}. \tag{6.23}$$

Similarly, the stored energy per unit mass, A, may be expressed as functional of the past history of deformation

$$A(t) = \underset{\tau=0}{\overset{\infty}{\phi}} [E_{KL}(t-\tau), E_{KL}(t)], \quad 0 \le (\tau, t) \le \infty. \tag{6.24}$$

The function (6.24) is assumed to be a continuous function of the nonlinear strain history $E_{KL}(t, \tau)$. Further, both the strain tensor E_{KL} and its first derivative are assumed to be continuous. This is in contrast to the requirements of the linear derivations where only the input histories were needed to be continuous. In view of the objectivity principle, it is necessary that all mathematical descriptions of physical quantities and events be independent of the particular frame of reference employed. Combining the local balance of energy equation and the local entropy production inequality, both under isothermal conditions, one obtains

$$-\rho \dot{A}(t) + \sigma_{ij}(t)d_{ij}(t) \ge 0. \tag{6.25}$$

In equation (6.25), ρ is the mass density and $d_{ij}(t)$ is the deformation rate tensor defined by

$$d_{ij}(t) = v_{i,j}(t) + v_{j,i}(t) \tag{6.26}$$

where

$$v_i(t) = \dot{x}_i(t, X_K). \tag{6.27}$$

To be able to use the stored energy per unit mass, A, from (6.24) in (6.25), it is necessary to obtain its time derivative $\dot{A}$. In order to accomplish this, Christensen (1971) proposed that the nonlinear strain function $E_{KL}(s)$, $s = t - \tau$, constituted a history. In this case, the norm in the collection of histories is defined by

$$\| E \| = \left[\int_0^\infty E_{KL}(t - \tau) E_{KL}(t - \tau) h^2(\tau) \, d\tau \right]^{1/2} \tag{6.28}$$

where $h(\tau)$ is, as mentioned earlier in connection with (6.21), a monotonically decreasing function of the time parameter τ.

The collection of histories with a finite norm, such as (6.28), constitutes a Hilbert space. It is assumed that the stored energy function $\overset{\infty}{\underset{\tau=0}{\phi}} (\cdot)$ (equation (6.24)), is the Fréchet differential in the Hilbert space corresponding to $h(\tau)$. Accordingly, the derivative of the stored energy per unit mass can be defined as

$$\dot{A}(t) = \frac{\partial}{\partial E_{KL}(t)} \overset{\infty}{\underset{\tau=0}{\phi}} [E_{KL}(t - \tau), E_{KL}(t)] \dot{E}_{KL}$$

$$+ \delta \overset{\infty}{\underset{\tau=0}{\phi}} \left[E_{KL}(t - \tau), E_{KL}(t) | \frac{dE_{KL}(t - \tau)}{d\tau} \right], \quad 0 \le (\tau, t) \le \infty. \tag{6.29}$$

This is on the understanding that the strain rate history $\dot{E}_{KL}(t), -\infty \le t \le \infty$, is continuous. Combining (6.25) and (6.29), the former equation can be written as

$$\left\{ \sigma_{ij}(t) - \rho \frac{\partial}{\partial E_{KL}(t)} \overset{\infty}{\underset{\tau=0}{\phi}} [E_{KL}(t - \tau), E_{KL}(t)] x_{i,K}(t) x_{j,K}(t) \right\} d_{ij}(t) \rho \overset{\infty}{\underset{\tau=0}{\Lambda}} (\cdot) \ge 0,$$

$$0 \le (\tau, t) \le \infty, \tag{6.30}$$

where

$$\overset{\infty}{\underset{\tau=0}{\Lambda}} (\cdot) = \delta \overset{\infty}{\underset{\tau=0}{\phi}} \left[E_{KL}(t - \tau), E_{KL}(t) | \frac{dE_{KL}(t - \tau)}{dt} \right], \quad 0 \le (\tau, t) \le \infty. \tag{6.31}$$

is a measure of the rate of dissipation of energy in the viscoelastic material during the deformation process.

In order for (6.30) to be satisfied for a given deformation history, it is necessary that the coefficient of d_{ij} vanishes. This leads to

$$\sigma_{ij}(t) = \rho(t) \frac{\partial}{\partial E_{KL}(t)} \overset{\infty}{\underset{\tau=0}{\phi}} [E_{KL}(t - \tau), E_{KL}(t)] x_{i,K}(t) x_{j,K}(t). \tag{6.32}$$

This leaves (6.30) as

$$\rho(t) \overset{\infty}{\underset{\tau=0}{\Lambda}} (\cdot) \geq 0 \tag{6.33}$$

which states that the rate of dissipation of energy in the viscoelastic material, during deformation, is nonnegative.

Equation (6.33) is the stress constitutive equation in isothermal nonlinear viscoelasticity which can be expressed, with reference to (6.24), as

$$\sigma_{ij} = \rho \, \frac{\partial A}{\partial E_{EL}} \, x_{i,K} x_{j,L}. \tag{6.34}$$

Similar formulations to the above have been followed by Coleman and Mizel (1967).

Christensen (1971) presented further reduction of the above formulation to the case of infinitesimal deformation. For this purpose, the following expression for the free energy was used:

$$\rho_0 A(t) = \frac{1}{2} \int_{-\infty}^{t} \int_{-\infty}^{t} \lambda(2t - \tau - \eta) \, \frac{\partial E_{KK}(\tau)}{\partial \tau} \, d\tau \, d\eta$$

$$+ \int_{-\infty}^{t} \int_{-\infty}^{t} \mu(2t - \tau - \eta) \, \frac{\partial E_{KL}(\tau)}{\partial \tau} \, \frac{\partial E_{KL}(\eta)}{\partial \eta} \, d\tau \, d\eta \tag{6.35}$$

in which ρ_0 is the mass density in the reference configuration and $\lambda(\cdot)$, $\mu(\cdot)$ are time-dependent relaxation functions. Hence, based on equation (6.35) and by employing the general nonlinear stress constitutive equation (6.32), one obtains

$$\sigma_{ij} = \frac{\rho}{\rho_0} \left[\delta_{KL} \int_{-\infty}^{t} \lambda(t - \tau) \, \frac{\partial E_{mm}(\tau)}{\partial \tau} \, d\tau \right.$$

$$\left. + 2 \int_{-\infty}^{t} \mu(t - \tau) \, \frac{\partial E_{KL}(\tau)}{\partial \tau} \right] x_{i,K} x_{j,L} \, d\tau. \tag{6.36}$$

This constitutive expression can be rewritten, within the infinitesimal deformation theory and with the assumption that the mass density is constant, as

$$\sigma_{ij}(t) = \delta_{ij} \int_{-\infty}^{t} \lambda(t - \tau) \, \frac{\partial \varepsilon_{kk}(\tau)}{\partial \tau} \, d\tau + 2 \int_{-\infty}^{t} \mu(t - \tau) \, \frac{\partial \varepsilon_{ij}(\tau)}{\partial \tau} \, d\tau \tag{6.37}$$

in which ε_{ij} is the small strain tensor. Thus, expression (6.37) represents the reduced form of the general nonlinear viscoelastic stress constitutive equation (6.32) within the context of the infinitesimal deformation theory.

Coleman and Noll (1961) derived a special nonlinear theory for solids known as finite linear viscoelasticity. This theory, however, restricts the deformation to be slowly changing in the recent past. In this manner, the current value of stress can be determined by linearly integrating the deformation history with reference to the current configuration. However, in contrast to the infinitesimal theory, the integrating functions in the constitutive integrals are nonlinear functions of the current state of deformation. Green and Rivlin (1957), based on an earlier work by Rivlin and Ericksen (1955), discussed the form of the constitutive equations governing the deformation of a class of materials with memory. It was assumed that the stress in an element of the material depends not only on the deformation gradients in the element at the instant of time considered but also on those of previous instants of time. The limitations imposed on the constitutive formulation by the principle of objectivity (frame indifference) were examined. This was carried out by first considering that the stress depends on the deformation gradients at a number of discrete times up to the instant of measurement. Then, the number of instants of time was considered to increase indefinitely so that the expression for the stress becomes a functional of the deformation gradients. In this analysis, it was found that the form invariance of the constitutive equation under a relation of the physical system leads naturally to a particular form of dependence of the stress on the deformation gradients at the instant of measurement. In this work, Green and Rivlin (1957) assumed that the expression for the stress as a functional of the deformation gradients at times up to and including the instant of measurement is continuous. Green, Rivlin and Spencer (1959) do not, however, make this assumption, but assume that the stress has arbitrary polynomial dependence on the deformation gradients at the instant of measurement, while its functional dependence on the deformation gradients at times preceding the instant of measurement is continuous. Under these assumptions, the limitations imposed by the isotropy of the material in its undeformed state on the form the constitutive relations have been dealt with by these authors.

Green and Rivlin (1960) assumed a constitutive equation in the form of implicit relations between the stress, its time derivatives and gradients of displacement, velocity, acceleration, etc., at a number of instants of time within a specified time interval. In this work, the limitations on the form of the constitutive equation resulting from the requirement that it is unaltered by the imposition on the body of an additional arbitrary rigid rotation, etc., are discussed.

Green and Rivlin (1957, 1960) and Green, Rivlin and Spencer (1959) presented a three-dimensional theory for the nonlinear viscoelastic material based on a multiple integral formulation whereby the output is expressed as a polynomial expansion in linear function of the input histories. In this context, the most general form for an initially isotropic material to third order (Meixner and König, 1958; Lockett, 1965, 1972) is

$$
\mathbf{Q}(t) = \int_{-\infty}^{t} (\mathbf{I}\psi_1 Y_1 + \psi_2 \mathbf{M}_1) \, d\tau_{(1)}
$$

$$
+ \iint_{-\infty}^{t} (\mathbf{I}\psi_3 Y_1 Y_2 + \mathbf{I}\psi_4 Y_{12} + \psi_5 Y_1 \mathbf{M}_2 + \psi_6 \mathbf{M}_1 \mathbf{M}_2) \, d\tau_{(2)}
$$

$$
+ \iiint_{-\infty}^{t} (\mathbf{I}\psi_7 Y_{123} + \mathbf{I}\psi_8 Y_1 Y_{23} + \psi_9 Y_1 Y_2 \mathbf{M}_3
$$

$$
+ \psi_{10} Y_{12} \mathbf{M}_3 + \psi_{11} Y_1 \mathbf{M}_2 \mathbf{M}_3 + \psi_{12} \mathbf{M}_1 \mathbf{M}_2 \mathbf{M}_3) \, d\tau_{(3)} \tag{6.38}
$$

where

$$\mathbf{M}_\alpha = \dot{\mathbf{P}}(\tau_\alpha),$$

$$Y_\alpha = \mathrm{tr}(\mathbf{M}_\alpha),$$

$$Y_{\alpha\beta} = \mathrm{tr}(\mathbf{M}_\alpha \mathbf{M}_\beta), \quad Y_{\alpha b\gamma} = \mathrm{tr}(\mathbf{M}_\alpha \mathbf{M}_\beta \mathbf{M}_\gamma),$$

$$d\tau_{(N)} = d\tau_1 \, d\tau_2 \dots d\tau_N.$$

In the constitutive equation (6.38), matrices $\mathbf{Q}$ and $\mathbf{P}$ represent, interchangeably, nonlinear measures of input and output (stress and strain) and the superposed dot denotes a material time derivative. Material functions ψ_1 and ψ_2 are functions of one variable s_1, $\psi_3, \dots, \psi_6$ are functions of s_1 and s_2 and $\psi_7, \dots, \psi_{12}$ are functions of s_1, s_2 and s_3, where $s_\alpha = t - \tau_\alpha$. These functions characterize the mechanical behaviour of given material. It has been shown by Lockett (1965) that the following symmetries may be assumed without loss of generality:

$$\psi_3, \; \psi_4, \; \psi_6, \; \psi_9, \; \psi_{10} = s(1, \, 2), \; \psi_7, = s(1, \, 2, \, 3),$$

$$\psi_8, \; \psi_{11} = s(2, \, 3) \text{ and } \psi_{12} = s(1, \, 3) \tag{6.39}$$

where $s(i, j)$ denotes symmetry in the ith and jth arguments. A creep response formulation is given by defining $\mathbf{P} = \Sigma$ and $\mathbf{Q} = \mathbf{E}$ and a stress relaxation formulation is given by setting $\mathbf{P} = \mathbf{E}$ and $\mathbf{Q} = \Sigma$ where stress measure Σ and strain $\mathbf{E}$ are defined by

$$\Sigma = \sigma = \begin{cases} \mathbf{R}^\mathsf{T}\sigma\mathbf{R} \\ \mathbf{F}^\mathsf{T}\sigma\mathbf{F} \end{cases}, \quad \mathbf{F} = \mathbf{R}\mathbf{U}, \quad 2\mathbf{E} = \mathbf{U}^2 - \mathbf{I} = \mathbf{F}^\mathsf{T}\mathbf{F} - \mathbf{I}. \tag{6.40}$$

In (6.40), the decomposition of the deformation gradient $\mathbf{F}$ expresses the idea that the deformation may be considered to be a pure stretch $\mathbf{U}$ followed by a rigid rotation $\mathbf{R}$, as discussed previously in section 6.3 (equation (6.7)).

In the general theory, the integral polynomial (6.38) is of infinite order. It is, however, assumed that the terms of the first three orders, written explicitly in (6.38), are the dominant ones. The constitutive equation (6.38) may also be written in terms of the classical strain ε since

$$E = \varepsilon + \tfrac{1}{2}\varepsilon^2. \tag{6.41}$$

This is, of course, with the understanding that the associated material functions will be different in this case.

The one-dimensional constitutive relation corresponding to (6.38) can be written as

$$Q(t) = \int_{-\infty}^{t} \phi_1(t - \tau_1)\dot{P}(\tau_1) \, d\tau_{(1)}$$

$$+ \iint_{-\infty}^{t} \phi_2(t - \tau_1, \, t - \tau_2)\dot{P}(\tau_1)\dot{P}(\tau_2) \, d\tau_{(2)}$$

$$+ \iiint_{-\infty}^{t} \phi_3(t - \tau_1, \, t - \tau_2, \, t - \tau_3)\dot{P}(\tau_1)\dot{P}(\tau_2)\dot{P}(\tau_3) \, d\tau_{(3)} \tag{6.42}$$

where $d\tau_{(n)} = d\tau_1, d\tau_2, \ldots, d\tau_n$ and $\phi_n(\cdot)$, $n = 1, 2, \ldots$, are material functions which can be assumed without loss of generality to be symmetric with respect to their indicated arguments. In the constitutive equation (6.42), $P(t)$ and $Q(t)$ denote, alternatively, stress and strain components in a one-dimensional relation that may be referred to as input and output functions. Thus, if $P(t)$ designates a strain measure, then ϕ_n are stress-relaxation functions of order n for the mode of deformation relevant to the definitions of P and Q. Alternatively, if $P(t)$ denotes stress, then ϕ_n represent creep functions.

The first-order term in (6.42) represents the usual term in the constitutive relation of linear viscoelasticity in which the function $\phi_1(\cdot)$ may be determined from a creep experiment. $\phi_1(\cdot)$ is, then, the response to a homogeneous unit stimulus applied at time $t = 0$.

The set of loading programmes required for the determination of the material functions of the constitutive equation (6.42) is given by Lockett (1965, 1972). For the general three-dimensional case, equation (6.38), Lockett considered the simplification when $P_{ij} = 0$ for $i \neq j$ and it was noted that all of the material functions except ψ_{12} may be determined by experiment. The corresponding set of test programmes required to determine $\psi_1, \ldots, \psi_{11}$ is summarized in Lockett's paper. Lifshitz and Kolsky (1967) have confirmed, however, that these tests are exceedingly difficult to perform accurately. On the other hand, an expression of the form (6.42) was employed by Ward and Onat (1963) to interpret the results of uniaxial experiments for the case of oriented polypropylene. In this context, it was indicated by the latter authors that the experimental results may be described adequately by considering only the first- and third-order terms in the constitutive equation (6.42), and some information was concluded about the material functions involved. Turner (1966), on the other hand, was unable to model creep data conveniently for a polypropylene using the constitutive equation (6.42). Meantime, Gittus (1975) presented an argument that the constitutive equation (6.42) could be invalid for the case of cyclic loading. In this regard, Gittus (1975) shows that, for the same creep load, equation (6.42) can result in creep rate in compression greater than that in tension. Pipkin and Rogers (1968), however, describe the application of the multiple-integral representation of the constitutive equation (6.42), to be effective if the viscoelastic response is weakly nonlinear. Strong nonlinearity would, then, require the inclusion of higher-order multiple integrals.

In order to avoid the enormous number of tests required to determine the material functions in (6.38) and (6.42), as described in Lockett's programme (Lockett, 1965), Pipkin and Rogers (1968) give an integral series representation of the constitutive equation. The first term in this series is a single integral with a nonlinear integrand, and may be determined by a single-step creep or relaxation test. The second term generalizes the exact representation to two-step inputs and so forth. The nth term of the series is obtained by the difference, if any is observed, between the experimental data for n-step tests and the prediction based on $(n - 1)$-step data. The series has the characteristic that it terminates at the nth term whenever the input (stress or strain) is an n-step history. In a study to demonstrate the consistency of the Green–Rivlin (Green and Rivlin, 1957, 1960) representation, Ward and Wolfe (1966) report the results of four different two-stage uniaxial load programmes. An analysis of some of the data presented in their paper could be used to demonstrate the predictive capability of Pipkin and Rogers' one-step extrapolation (Pipkin and Rogers, 1968). Stafford (1969), however, criticizes Pipkin and Rogers' model in that their second function $C_2(\sigma_1, t - t_1, \sigma_2, t - t_2)$ requires the evaluation of a function of four variables which may appear impractical in view of the inability of Lifshitz and Kolsky (1967) to evaluate a function of two variables $K(t_1, t_2)$. Further, Lifshitz and Kolsky's results indicate that the two-step response is a separable function of time and strain. In this context, Stafford (1969) argues that, if such separability were to hold for all step tests, Pipkin and Roger's constitutive equation would reduce to a superposition form. As an alternative simplification of (6.38), Pipkin (1964) developed the following four-function stress-relaxation relation for incompressible materials:

$$\left.\begin{array}{c} \mathbf{R}^T\boldsymbol{\sigma}\mathbf{R} \\ \mathbf{F}^T\boldsymbol{\sigma}\mathbf{R} \end{array}\right\} = \int_{-\infty}^{t} \psi_2 \mathbf{M}_1 \, d\tau_{(1)} + \iint_{-\infty}^{t} \psi_6 \mathbf{M}_1 \mathbf{M}_2 \, d\tau_{(2)}$$

$$+ \iiint_{-\infty}^{t} (\psi_{10} Y_{12} \mathbf{M}_3 + \psi_{12} \mathbf{M}_1 \mathbf{M}_2 \mathbf{M}_3) \, d\tau_{(3)} \qquad (6.43)$$

Lockett and Stafford (1969) have indicated that a similar equation to (6.43) can be derived for the creep case. It has been demonstrated in the latter reference that the resulting formulation can be further reduced to a relationship involving only three material functions. The experimental programmes for evaluating the material functions involved are described by Lockett and Stafford (1969). The number of tests required indicates, however, that such a constitutive relationship may still be too complex for routine practical applications. Stafford (1969) presented a further step toward the simplification of the constitutive equation in nonlinear viscoelasticity. In his paper, Stafford directed particular attention to reducing the evaluation of material functions to simple (one-step) creep or stress-relaxation tests. For this purpose, an isothermal theory of (initially) isotropic materials was primarily considered in the explicit form of a third-order integral polynomial (6.42), taking into consideration the following three simplifications.

1. *Physical linearity.* In this case, Stafford (1969) considers that the material functions would be expressed as a sum of single-argument functions. This approximation produces a response which is linearly dependent on the input history but is nonlinearly dependent on the present value of the input. The application of this approximation to (6.42) yields

$$Q = \int_0^t [\psi_1(t - \tau) + f_2(t - \tau)P(t) + f_3(t - \tau)P^2(t)]\dot{P}(t) \, d\tau. \qquad (6.44)$$

The constitutive equation (6.44) is interpreted by Stafford (1969) to be directly related to the theory of finite viscoelasticity due to Coleman and Noll (1961).

2. *Superposition*. In this type of simplification, Stafford (1969) defines the multiple-argument material function in terms of a single function of one argument. This produces a response in which each term has a linear dependence on the history of an input measure; however, each measure is a nonlinear function of the input. Hence, the resulting constitutive equation is in the form of a convolution integral and may be regarded to be of the Boltzmann superposition type for large deformations. The application of the superposition postulate to (6.42) yields the constitutive equation

$$Q = \int_0^t [\psi_1(t - \tau) + f_2(t - \tau)2P(\tau) + f_3(t - \tau)3P^2(\tau)\dot{P}(\tau)] \, d\tau. \qquad (6.45)$$

Findley and Lai (1966) and Lai and Findley (1968) have also considered a type of nonlinear superposition with equivalent resulting equations.

3. *Product nonlinearity*. Here, in view of the one-step test requirement, Stafford (1969) postulates that the second- and higher-order material functions are separable and may be expressed as the product

$$\psi_i(x_1, x_2, \ldots, x_n) = f_i^{(1)}(x_1) f_i^{(2)}(x_2) \ldots f_i^{(n)}(x_n) \qquad (6.46)$$

where functions $f_i^{(j)}$ are related by the symmetry conditions (6.39). Lai and Findley (1968) and Findley and Onaran (1968) have also proposed forms similar to (6.46).

The application of the postulate of product nonlinearity to (6.42) produces the result

$$Q = \int_0^t \psi_1(t - \tau)\dot{P}(\tau) \, d\tau + \left[\int_0^t f_2^{1/2}(t - \tau)\dot{P}(\tau) \, d\tau\right]^2$$

$$+ \left[\int_0^t f_3^{1/3}(t - \tau)\dot{P}(\tau) \, d\tau\right]^3 \qquad (6.47)$$

where the square and cube roots of f_2 and f_3 are introduced to make the equations identical for one input tests. Thus, for an input $P = P_0 H(t)$,

$$Q = P_0\psi_1(t) + P_0^2 f_2(t) + P_0^3 f_3(t). \qquad (6.48)$$

However, the response of the three equations (6.44), (6.45) and (6.47) to general loads is quite different. Further details concerning the above constitutive equations and the validity of their application can be found in Stafford's (1969) paper. In general, the selection of a constitutive equation must be guided by long-range information such as that obtained from a multi-step test. In this regard, Pipkin and Rogers (1968) observed that multistep inputs constitute a more critical test of the applicability of a constitutive equation. The tests required for two- and three-dimensional equations offer, however, additional complications. In this regard, it has been indicated by Lockett and Stafford (1969) that, when the material functions are completely symmetric, uniaxial tests may be sufficient. Thus, only the superposition form (6.45) can be determined from uniaxial tests, while the linear and product forms, (6.44) and (6.27) respectively, would require biaxial tests (Stafford, 1969).

An alternative approach to the multiple-integral formulation of the constitutive equation is to adopt the reduced-time constitutive equations such as the one developed by Schapery (1966),

$$\varepsilon = g(\sigma) + f(\sigma) \int_0^t D[Z(t) - Z(\tau)] \frac{d}{d\tau}\left[\frac{\sigma}{C(\sigma)}\right] d\tau, \quad Z(t) = \int_0^t \frac{B(\sigma)}{C(\sigma)} d\tau, \quad (6.49)$$

where $D(\cdot)$ is the linear creep compliance. In equation (6.49), the material functions $B(\sigma)$, $C(\sigma)$ and $f(\sigma)$ as well as $g(\sigma)$ and $D(\cdot)$ are determinable from creep and recovery data for several stress levels and times. Here, the evaluation of $B(\sigma)$, for instance, would require only one two-step test, one three-step test, etc., while an integral polynomial theory would require at least n two-step tests, $\frac{1}{2}n^2$ three-step tests, etc. In this regard, Stafford (1969) noted that choosing $B(\sigma)$ to be linear in σ gives excellent results for PVC. However, as indicated in this reference, the reduced-time equations will only follow data in which the functional form of the response is unchanged by additional steps; if it does change, however, one must resort to the more general integral polynomial theories.

6.6 COUPLED EFFECTS IN NONLINEAR VISCOELASTICITY

As we indicated in Chapter 5, in the course of introducing the thermomechanical theory of viscoelasticity, viscoelastic materials are sensitive to thermal variations as well as other environmental effects. Such effects should be coupled with the mechanical effects if a comprehensive constitutive theory were to be developed. Unfortunately, it is only recently that researchers in the field started to incorporate such coupling of effects in the prediction of the response behaviour of nonlinear viscoelastic materials. As we discussed earlier in section 6.3, concerning the objectivity principle, coupled thermomechanical behaviour of nonlinear materials should be treated in the light of the invariance principle of constitutive theory.

Koh and Eringen (1963) proposed a thermomechanical theory of viscoelasticity that includes nonlinear effects. The theory introduces the formalism for the analysis of the response behaviour of nonlinear heat-conducting viscoelastic materials. It postulates a constitutive formulation based essentially on the two sets of equations

$$\boldsymbol{\sigma} = \boldsymbol{\sigma}(\mathbf{c}^{-1}, \mathbf{d}, \mathbf{b})$$

and   (6.50)

$$\mathbf{h} = \mathbf{h}(\mathbf{c}^{-1}, \mathbf{d}, \mathbf{b})$$

where $\boldsymbol{\sigma}$, the stress tensor, is considered a function of the three variables: $\mathbf{c}^{-1}$, the deformation tensor defined by

$$\mathbf{c}^{-1} = C_{kl}^{-1} = x_{k,M} x_{M,l};$$ (6.51)

d, the deformation rate tensor defined by

$$\mathbf{d} = 2d_{kl} = v_{k,l} + v_{l,k};\qquad (6.52)$$

b, the temperature gradient bi-vector defined by

$$\mathbf{b} = b_{kl} = \varepsilon_{klm}\theta_{,m}\qquad (6.53)$$

where θ is the temperature and ε_{klm} is the skew-symmetric alternating tensor. Meantime, the second equation of (6.50) relates the heat flux bi-vector **h** to the same independent variables $\mathbf{c}^{-1}$, **d**, **b**. Accordingly, **h** is defined by

$$\mathbf{h} = h_{kl} = \varepsilon_{klm}q_m.\qquad (6.54)$$

In addition to the above constitutive equations (6.50)–(6.54), the following field equations would be required in the course of the development of the theory:

- continuity equation

$$\dot{\rho} + \rho v_{k,k} = 0;\qquad (6.55)$$

- equations of motion

$$\sigma_{ij,i} + \rho\chi_j = \rho a_j,$$
$$\sigma_{ij} = \sigma_{ji}.\qquad (6.56)$$

In (6.55) and (6.56), v_k are the velocity components, ρ is the density, χ_j are the body forces components and a_j are the components of the acceleration.

Further, the conservation of energy must also be satisfied. The latter principle is expressed by

$$\rho\dot{e} = \sigma_{ij}d_{ji} - q_{j,j} + \rho r\qquad (6.57)$$

where e is the specific internal energy and r is the supply of energy.

With the application of a caloric equation of state, it was concluded by Koh and Eringen (1963) that the principle of conservation of energy (6.57) reduces to a heat conduction equation which for the incompressible case simplifies to

$$\rho K\dot{\theta} = \sigma_{ij}d_{ji} - q_{j,j} + \rho r\qquad (6.58)$$

where K is the specific heat.

The theory of Koh and Eringen (1963) demonstrates the mechanism by which thermomechanical coupling could be introduced to other purely mechanical theories. These authors considered further the modification of their theory to situations involving hygrosteric materials (e.g. Noll, 1955) and to a particular subclass of Rivlin–Ericksen viscoelastic fluids (for instance, Rivlin and Ericksen, 1955).

6.7 EXPERIMENTAL CHARACTERIZATION OF NONLINEAR VISCOELASTIC MATERIALS

6.7.1 One-dimensional nonlinear behaviour

The basis for the experimental work discussed below is the Green–Rivlin multiple integral response relation (6.42),

$$Q(t) = \int_{-\infty}^{t} \phi_1(t - \tau_1)\dot{P}(\tau_1)\, d\tau_{(1)}$$

$$+ \iint_{-\infty}^{t} \phi_2(t - \tau_1, t - \tau_2)\dot{P}(\tau_1)\dot{P}(\tau_2)\, d\tau_{(2)}$$

$$+ \iiint_{-\infty}^{t} \phi_3(t - \tau_1, t - \tau_2, t - \tau_3)\dot{P}(\tau_1)\dot{P}(\tau_2)\dot{P}(\tau_3)\, d\tau_{(3)} \qquad (6.59)$$

The identification of the terms appearing in the above equation is mentioned in section 6.5 where we dealt with this equation. If sufficient data are available to determine the nonlinear material functions ϕ_1, ϕ_2 and ϕ_3, then equation (6.59) can be used to predict the response of the material to other input histories.

The experimental plan that would be required to determine the values of these material functions has been discussed by Ward and Onat (1963), Hadley and Ward (1965), Lockett (1965, 1972) and Lifshitz and Kolsky (1967).

Lockett (1972) dealt comprehensively with the development of an experimental programme to determine the material functions in (6.59) for both creep and stress relaxation. In this context, with reference to (6.59) and depending on whether the input function $P(\tau)$ is a stress or strain, the corresponding experiment is of creep or stress-relaxation type respectively.

Following Lockett (1972), one may consider the simple test

$$P(t) = pH(t), \qquad (6.60)$$

where p is a positive constant input and $H(t)$ is the Heaviside step function. In view of (6.59), the response corresponding to (6.59) is

$$Q(t) = p\phi_1(t) + p^2\phi_2(t, t) + p^3\phi_3(t, t, t). \qquad (6.61)$$

That is, the measured response $Q(t)$ from one experiment alone is insufficient to determine any of the three material functions ϕ_1, ϕ_2 and ϕ_3. However, if the simple test (6.60) is performed for three different values of p, this will provide three output equations, similar to (6.61), for determining $\phi_1(t)$, $\phi_2(t, t)$ and $\phi_3(t, t, t)$. Accordingly, the material function ϕ_1 is known over the time scale of the experiment, but ϕ_2 and ϕ_3 are known only when their arguments are all equal. To establish further values of ϕ_2 and ϕ_3, Lockett (1972) proposed the additional test

$$P(t) = p_1 H(t) + p_2 H(t - k) \tag{6.62}$$

in which p_1, p_2 and k are positive constants. This produces, in view of (6.59), the following response:

$$\begin{aligned}
Q(t) = {}& 2p_1 p_2 \phi_2(t, t - k) \\
& + 3p_1 p_2 [p_1 \phi_3(t, t, t - k) + p_2 \phi_3(t, t - k, t - k)] \\
& + \cdots
\end{aligned} \tag{6.63}$$

with the assumption that ϕ_α are symmetric functions with respect to their arguments. Thus, if three experiments are carried out corresponding to three independent combinations of the parameters p_1 and p_2, then, according to (6.63), the measured responses would allow the determination of the following values of the material functions:

$$\phi_2(t, t - k), \quad \phi_3(t, t, t - k), \quad \phi_3(t, t - k, t - k). \tag{6.64}$$

The number N of the values of k which are required will be determined by the experimental data (on an *ad hoc* basis) during the course of the experiment. Lockett (1972) estimated, however, that N could be of the order of 10 for reasonable characterization.

Similar remarks may apply concerning the value of ϕ_3 obtained from (6.64). In this case, ϕ_3 may be determined along lines in its three-dimensional argument space. The two values of ϕ_3 mentioned in (6.64) lead to the determination of this function when two of its arguments are equal. Accordingly, as a result of $3N$ experiments of the type (6.62), the function ϕ_2 is determined completely and ϕ_3 is established except when its arguments are all unequal. In order to obtain these unknown values of ϕ_3, one may need to apply a triple-step input of the form

$$P(t) = p_1 H(t) + p_2 H(t - k) + p_3 H(t - l) \tag{6.65}$$

where p_1, p_2, p_3, k and l are positive constants. Corresponding to the input (6.65), equation (6.59) gives the following output:

$$Q(t) = 6p_1 p_2 p_3 \phi_3(t, t - k, t - l) + \cdots. \tag{6.66}$$

Accordingly, (6.65) leads to the determination of the material function $\phi_3(t, t - k, t - l)$ and repetition of the experiment for other values of k and l would establish ϕ_3 completely. In this regard, because of symmetry of ϕ_3, one may not wish to repeat the experiment for N values of both k and l. It could be sufficient to consider $0 < k < l$ (both k and l positive). Thus, the total number of experiments of the form (6.66) is $\frac{1}{2}N(N - 1)$.

The complete set of experiments that may be required for the determination of ϕ_α, as discussed above, is given by Lockett (1965, 1972).

6.7.2 Three-dimensional nonlinear behaviour

All of the experiments that are required for three-dimensional characterization of the nonlinear viscoelastic behaviour would generally involve multiple-step inputs and are, in essence, similar to the experiments introduced in the foregoing concerning the one-dimensional behaviour. In the three-dimensional characterization, however, it would be necessary (Lockett, 1965, 1972) to apply different input steps of the input matrix and to measure more than one component of the output matrix.

The basis for the experimental programme here is the Green–Rivlin three-dimensional constitutive relation (6.38). Further to the previous discussion, equation (6.38) is an implicit relation as the matrix P appears in the definitions (6.18) and (6.19) of P and Q. In this, following Lockett (1965, 1972), it would be natural to consider first situations in which $R = I$. Such situations would arise when $P_{ij} = 0$ for $i \neq j$. In the experimental programme of Lockett (1965), introduced briefly below, it is shown that all the material functions $\psi_1, \cdots, \psi_{11}$ can be determined from experiments of this type.

Lockett (1965, 1972) introduced an experimental programme for the determination of the material parameters appearing in the Green and Rivlins' three-dimensional constitutive equation (6.38). In this constitutive equation, terms up to and including those of third order in the input matrix are retained. Since P and Q appearing in (6.38) may be given either of the interpretations (6.18) and (6.19), the experiments referred to below may be of either the creep or the stress-relaxation type. In (6.38), the following material functions are identified:

- ψ_1 and ψ_2 are functions of $t - \tau_1$;
- $\psi_3, \cdots, \psi_6$ are functions of $t - \tau_1$ and $t - \tau_2$;
- $\psi_7, \cdots, \psi_{12}$ are functions of $t - \tau_1$, $t - \tau_2$ and $t - \tau_3$.

That is, an experimental programme would be required to determine

- two functions of a single variable,
- four functions of two variables and
- six functions of three variables.

The set of experimental inputs required to determine the functions $\psi_1, \cdots, \psi_{12}$ is given by Lockett (1965, 1972). The reader is also referred to McGuirt and Lianis (1967).

REFERENCES

Christensen, R. M. (1971) *Theory of Viscoelasticity*, Academic Press, New York.
Coleman, B. D. (1964) Thermodynamics of materials with memory. *Arch. Ration. Mech. Anal.*, **17**, 1–46.
Coleman, B. D. and Mizel, V. (1967) A general theory of dissipation in materials with memory. *Arch. Ration. Mech. Anal.*, **27**, 255–74.
Coleman, B. D. and Noll, W. (1960) An approximation theorem for functionals with applications in continuum mechanics. *Arch. Ration. Mech. Anal.*, **6**, 355–70.

Coleman, B. D. and Noll, W. (1961) Foundations of linear viscoelasticity. *Rev. Mod. Phys.*, **33**, 239–49.

Coleman, B. D., Gurtin, M. E. and Herrera, R. I. (1965) Waves in materials with memory, I. The velocity of one-dimensional shock and acceleration waves. *Arch. Ration. Mech. Anal.*, **19**, 1–19.

Ferry, J. D. (1960) *Viscoelastic Properties of Polymers*, Wiley, New York.

Findley, W. N. and Lai, J. S. Y. (1966) *Brown University Rep. EMRL-27.*

Findley, W. N. and Onaran, K. (1968) Product form of kernel functions for nonlinear viscoelasticity of PVC under constant rate stressing. *Trans. Soc. Rheol.*, **12**(2), 217–42.

Gittus, J. (1975) *Creep, Viscoelasticity and Creep Fracture in Solids*, Wiley, New York.

Green, A. E. and Rivlin, R. S. (1957) The mechanics of non-linear materials with memory, part I. *Arch. Ration. Mech. Anal.*, **1**, 1–21.

Green, A. E. and Rivlin, R. S. (1960) The mechanics of non-linear materials with memory, III. *Arch. Ration. Mech. Anal.*, **4**, 387–404.

Green, A. E., Rivlin, R. S. and Spencer, A. J. M. (1959) The mechanics of non-linear materials with memory, II. *Arch. Ration. Mech. Anal.*, **3**, 82–90.

Hadley, D. W. and Ward, I. M. (1965) Nonlinear creep and recovery behaviour of polypropylene fibres. *J. Mech. Phys. Solids*, **13**, 397–411.

Koh, S. L. and Eringen, A. C. (1963) On the foundations of nonlinear thermoviscoelasticity. *Int. J. Eng. Sci.*, **1**, 199–229.

Lai, J. S. Y. and Findley, W. N. (1968) Stress relaxation of nonlinear viscoelastic material under uniaxial strain. *Trans. Soc. Rheol.*, **12**(2), 259–80.

Lifshitz, J. M. and Kolsky, H. (1967) Nonlinear viscoelastic behaviour of polyethylene. *Int. J. Solid Struct.*, **3**, 383–97.

Lockett, F. J. (1965) Creep and stress-relaxation experiments for non-linear materials. *Int. J. Eng. Sci.*, **3**, 59–75.

Lockett, F. J. (1972) *Nonlinear Viscoelastic Solids*, Academic Press, New York.

Lockett, F. J. and Stafford, R. O. (1969) On special constitutive relations in nonlinear viscoelasticity. *Int. J. Eng. Sci.*, **7**, 917–30.

McGuirt, C. W. and Lianis, G. (1967) Constitutive equations for viscoelastic solids under finite uniaxial and biaxial deformations. *Trans. Soc. Rheol.*, **14**, 117–34.

Meixner, J. and König, H. (1958) Zür Theorie der Linearen dissipativen Systeme. *Rheol. Acta*, **1**(2–3), 190–3.

Noll, W. (1955) On the continuity of the solid and the fluid states. *J. Ration. Mech. Anal.*, **4**, 3–81.

Noll, W. (1958) A mathematical theory of the mechanical behaviour of continuous media. *Arch. Ration. Mech. Anal.*, **2**, 197–226.

Pipkin, A. C. (1964) Small finite deformations of viscoelastic solids. *Rev. Mod. Phys. Solids*, **36**, 1034–41.

Pipkin, A. C. and Rogers, T. G. (1968) A nonlinear integral representation of viscoelastic behaviour. *J. Mech. Phys. Solids*, **16**, 59–72.

Rivlin, R. S. and Ericksen, J. L. (1955) Stress–deformation relations for isotropic materials. *J. Ration. Mech. Anal.*, **4**, 323–425.

Schapery, R. A. (1966) A theory of nonlinear thermoviscoelasticity based on irreversible thermodynamics, in Proc. 5th US Natl. Congr. on Applied Mechanics, pp. 511–30.

Schapery, R. A. (1974) Viscoelastic behaviour and analysis of composite materials, in *Mechanics of Composite Materials*, Vol. 2 (ed. G. Sendickj), Academic Press, New York, Chap. 4, pp. 85–168.

Schuler, K. W., Nunziato, J. W. and Walsh, E. K. (1973) Recent results in non-linear viscoelastic wave propagation. *Int. J. Solid Struct.*, **9**, 1237–81.

Stafford, R. O. (1969) On mathematical forms for the material functions in nonlinear viscoelasticity. *J. Mech. Phys. Solids*, **17**, 339–58.

Truesdell, C. and Noll, W. (1965) The nonlinear field theories of mechanics, in *Encyclopedia of Physics*, Vol. III/3 (ed. S. Flügge), Springer, Berlin.

Turner, S. (1966) The strain response of plastics to complex stress histories. *Polym. Eng. Sci.*, **6**, 306–16.

Turner, S. (1971) Creep studies on plastics, in *Applied Polymer Symposium 17*, Wiley, New York, pp. 25–43.

Turner, S. (1973) *Mechanical Testing of Plastics*, Iliffe, London.

Ward, I. M. and Onat, E. T. (1963) Nonlinear mechanical behaviour of oriented polypropylene. *J. Mech. Phys. Solids*, **11**, 217–29.

Ward, I. M. and Wolfe, J. M. (1966) The nonlinear mechanical behaviour of polypropylene fibres under complex loading programmes. *J. Mech. Phys. Solids*, **14**, 131–40.

Weissenberg, K. (1948) Abnormal substances and abnormal phenomena of flow, in *Proc. Int. Congr. on Rheology*, pp. I-29–I-46.

FURTHER READING

Beham, P. P. and Hutchinson, S. J. (1971) A comparison of constant and complex creep loading programs for several thermoplastics. *Polym. Eng. Sci.*, **11**(4), 335–43.

Bernstein, B., Kearsley, E. A. and Zapas, L. J. (1963) A study of stress relaxation with finite strain. *Trans. Soc. Rheol.*, **7**, 391–410.

Bychawski, Z. and Fox, A. (1967) Generalized creep function and the problem of inversion in the theory of nonlinear viscoelasticity. *Bull. Acad. Pol. Sci.*, **15**, 297–304.

Christensen, R. M. (1968) On obtaining solutions in nonlinear viscoelasticity. *J. Appl. Mech.*, **35**, 129–33.

Distéfano, N. and Todeschini, R. (1973a) Modeling, identification and prediction of a class of nonlinear viscoelastic materials, part I. *Int. J. Solids Struct.*, **9**, 805–18.

Distéfano, N. and Todeschini, R. (1973b) Modeling, identification and prediction of a class of nonlinear viscoelastic materials, part II. *Int. J. Solids Struct.*, **9**, 1431–8.

Drescher, A. and Kwaszczynska, K. (1970) An approximate description of nonlinear viscoelastic materials. *Int. J. Nonlinear Mech.*, **5**, 11–22.

Eringen, A. C. (1962) *Nonlinear Mechanics of Continua*, McGraw-Hill, New York.

Findley, W. N. (1976) *Creep and Relaxation of Nonlinear Viscoelastic Media*, North-Holland, Amsterdam.

Findley, W. N. and Lai, J. S. Y. (1967) A modified superposition principle applied to creep of nonlinear viscoelastic material under abrupt changes in state of combined stress. *Trans. Soc. Rheol.*, **11**(3), 361–80.

Findley, W. N. and Stanely, C. A. (1968) Non-linear combined stress creep experiments on rigid polyurethane foam with application to multiple integral and modified superposition theory. *ASTM J. Mater.*, **3**, 916–49.

Findley, W. N., Lai, J. S. and Onaran, K. (1976) *Creep and Relaxation of Non-linear Viscoelastic Materials*, North-Holland, Amsterdam.

Gottenberg, N. G., Bird, J. O. and Agrawal, G. L. (1969) An experimental study of a nonlinear viscoelastic solid in uniaxial tension. *J. Appl. Mech.*, **36**, 558–64.

Gradowczyk, M. H. (1969) On the accuracy of the Green–Rivlin representation for viscoelastic materials. *Int. J. Solid Struct.*, **5**, 873–7.

Haddad, Y. M. (1987) Un modèle de réponse en viscoelastiticité non-linéaire de matériaux. *Res Mech.*, **20**, 235–53.

Haddad, Y. M. (1988) On the theory of the viscoelastic solid. *Res Mech.*, **25**, 225–59.

Hlavacek, B., Seyer, F. A. and Stanislav, J. (1973) Quantitative analogies between the linear and the nonlinear viscoelastic functions. *Can. J. Chem. Eng.*, **51**, 412–7.

Huang, N. C. and Lee, E. H. (1966) Nonlinear viscoelasticity for short time ranges. *J. Appl. Mech.*, **33**, 313–21.

Lai, J. S. Y. and Findley, W. N. (1968) Prediction of uniaxial stress relaxation from creep of nonlinear viscoelastic material. *Trans. Soc. Rheol.*, **12**(2), 243–57.

Lai, J. S. Y. and Findley, W. N. (1969) Behaviour of nonlinear viscoelastic material under simultaneous stress relaxation in tension and creep in torsion. *J. Appl. Mech.*, **36**, 22–7.

Lockett, F. J. and Turner, S. (1971) Nonlinear creep of plastics. *J. Mech. Phys. Solids*, **19**, 201–14.

Lubliner, J. (1967) Short-time approximation in nonlinear viscoelasticity. *Int. J. Solid Struct.*, **3**, 513–20.

McGuirt, C. W. and Lianis, G. (1969) Experimental investigation of nonlinear, non-isothermal viscoelasticity. *Int. J. Eng. Sci.*, **7**, 579–99.

Molinari, A. (1973) Relation between creep and relaxation in nonlinear viscoelasticity. *C.R. Acad. Sci., Sci. Math.*, **277**, 621–3.

Nakada, O. (1960) Theory of nonlinear responses. *J. Phys. Soc. Jpn*, **15**, 2280–8.

Neis, V. V. and Sackman, J. L. (1967) An experimental study of a nonlinear material with memory. *Trans. Soc. Rheol.*, **11**(3), 307–33.

Ng, T. H. and Williams, H. L. (1986) Stress–strain properties of linear aromatic polyesters in the nonlinear viscoelastic range. *J. Appl. Polym. Sci.*, **32**, 4883–96.

Nolte, K. G. and Findley, W. N. (1970) A linear compressibility assumption for the multiple integral representation of nonlinear creep of polyurethane. *J. Appl. Mech.*, **37**, 441–8.

Nolte, K. G. and Findley, W. N. (1971) Multiple step, nonlinear creep of polyurethane predicted from constant stress creep by three integral representations. *Trans. Soc. Rheol.*, **15**(1), 111–33.

Nolte, K. G. and Findley, W. N. (1974) Approximation of irregular loading by intervals of constant stress rates to predict creep and relaxation of polyurethane by three integral representation. *Trans. Soc. Rheol.*, **18**(1), 123–43.

Onaran, K. and Findley, W. N. (1965) Combined stress–creep experiments on a nonlinear viscoelastic material to determine the kernel functions for a multiple integral representation of creep. *Trans. Soc. Rheol.*, **9**(2), 299–327.

Onaran, K. and Findley, W. N. (1971) Experimental determination of some kernel functions in the multiple integral method for nonlinear creep of polyvinylchloride. *J. Appl. Mech.*, **38**, 30–8.

Peters, L. (1955) A note on nonlinear viscoelasticity. *Textile Res. J.*, **25** (March), 262–5.

Pipkin, A. C. and Rivlin, R. S. (1961) Small deformations superposed on large deformations in materials with fading memory. *Arch. Ration. Mech. Anal.*, **8**, 297–308.

Pipkin, A. C. and Rogers, T. G. (1968) A nonlinear integral representation for viscoelastic behaviour. *J. Mech. Phys. Solids*, **16**, 59–72.

Robotonov, Y. N., Papernik, L. K. and Stepanychey, E. I. (1973). Application of nonlinear theory of heredity to the description of time effects in polymeric materials. *Polym. Mech.*, **7**, 63–73.

Schapery, R. A. (1969) On the characterization of nonlinear viscoelastic materials. *Polym. Eng. Sci.*, **9**(4), 295–310.

Scholtens, B. J. R. and Bodit, H. C. (1986) Nonlinear viscoelastic analysis of uniaxial stress–strain measurements of elastomers at constant stretching rates. *J. Rheol.*, **30**(2), 301–12.

Smart, J. and Williams, J. G. (1972) A comparison of single-integral nonlinear viscoelasticity theories. *J. Mech. Phys. Solids*, **20**, 313–24.

Stouffer, D. C. and Wineman, A. S. (1972) Constitutive representation for nonlinear aging, environmental-dependent viscoelastic materials. *Acta Mech.*, **13**, 31–53.

Ting, E. C. (1971) Approximations in nonlinear viscoelasticity. *Int. J. Eng. Sci.*, **9**, 995–1006.

Turner, S. (1966) The strain response of plastics to complex stress histories. *Polym. Eng. Sci.*, **6**, 306–16.

Yanas, I. V. and Haskell, V. C. (1971) Utility of the Green–Rivlin theory in polymer mechanics. *J. Appl. Phys.*, **42**, 610–13.

Yuan, H. and Lianis, G. (1972) Experimental investigation of nonlinear viscoelasticity in combined finite torsion–tension. *Trans. Soc. Rheol.*, **16**, 615–33.

7

Numerical analysis in viscoelasticity

7.1 INTRODUCTION

As discussed earlier, in Chapters 2 and 4, two functions are significant in the description of the linear viscoelastic behaviour of materials, i.e. the creep function and the relaxation function. Quite generally, they are expressed, in view of Boltzmann's superposition principle, by relations (4.4) and (4.9). Recalling the latter two relations in the same order, one may write that

$$\varepsilon(t) = \mathbf{F}(t)\boldsymbol{\sigma}(0) + \int_0^t \mathbf{F}(t - \tau)\dot{\boldsymbol{\sigma}}(\tau) \, d\tau \qquad (7.1)$$

and

$$\sigma(t) = \mathbf{R}(t)\varepsilon(0) + \int_0^t \mathbf{R}(t - \tau)\dot{\varepsilon}(\tau) \, d\tau \qquad (7.2)$$

where $\varepsilon(t)$ and $\boldsymbol{\sigma}(t)$ are the time-dependent strain and stress tensors, respectively. In (7.1), $\mathbf{F}(t - \tau)$ is the creep function; it is a monotonically increasing function of time. In (7.2), the function $\mathbf{R}(t - \tau)$ is the relaxation function, which is usually a decreasing function of time.

In order to account for a nonlinearity in the viscoelastic response behaviour, Boltzmann's response relations above may be modified, following Distéfano (1970, 1971) and Distéfano and Todeschini (1973a, b), to read for the uniaxial case as follows:

$$\varepsilon(t) = g[\sigma(t), l_1, l_2, \cdots] + \int_0^t h[\sigma(\tau), b_1, b_2, \cdots]F(t - \tau) \, d\tau \qquad (7.3)$$

and

$$\sigma(t) = g_1[\varepsilon(t), k_1, k_2, \cdots] + \int_0^t h_1[\varepsilon(\tau), c_1, c_2, \cdots]R(t - \tau) \, d\tau \qquad (7.4)$$

in which $\varepsilon(t)$ and $\sigma(\tau)$ are the scalar components of strain and stress, respectively, at any time t in the sample subjected to uniaxial loading. In the above relations, the functions $g(\cdot)$ and $g_1(\cdot)$ correspond to the instantaneous elastic response in a parametric form, whereas the functions $h(\cdot)$ and $h_1(\cdot)$ account for the nonlinear hereditary effects and are also given in a parametric form. In both of these relations, unknown constants $l_1, l_2, \cdots, k_1, k_2, \cdots, b_1, b_2, \cdots$ and $c_1, c_2, \cdots$ are involved. The choice of the functions $g(\cdot)$, $g_1(\cdot)$, $h(\cdot)$ and $h_1(\cdot)$ is guided by a qualitative knowledge of the viscoelastic behaviour of the material. The functions $F(\cdot)$ and $R(\cdot)$ are, respectively, the creep and relaxation functions of the material for the uniaxial case. These functions may be assumed (Haddad and Tanary, 1987) to satisfy an Nth-order differential equation with constant coefficients of the following form respectively:

$$a_0 F + a_1 F^{(1)} + a_2 F^{(2)} + \cdots + a_{N-1} F^{(N-1)} + F^{(N)} = 0 \qquad (7.5a)$$

and

$$q_0 R + q_1 R^{(1)} + q_2 R^{(2)} + \cdots + q_{N-1} R^{(N-1)} + R^{(N)} = 0 \qquad (7.5b)$$

where $a_0, a_1, \cdots, a_{N-1}$ and $q_0, q_1, \cdots, q_{N-1}$ are unknown coefficients to be determined.

In the following section, we continue with the identification problem of the creep response. A similar development could, however, be carried out for the characterization of the stress relaxation behaviour of the material as pointed out below in section 7.3.

7.2 CHARACTERIZATION OF THE CREEP RESPONSE

For the simplification of the analysis, we introduce for the instantaneous elastic response a single elastic constant, E, only. Let the constant stress being applied on the material specimen during a creep experiment i be denoted by $\breve{\sigma}_i$ $(i = 1, 2, \cdots, n)$ where n is the number of creep experiments. Hence, the creep response equation (7.3) can be written as

$$\varepsilon_i(t) = E^{-1}\breve{\sigma}_i + h(\breve{\sigma}_i, b_1, b_2, \cdots) \int_0^t F(\tau) \, d\tau \qquad (i = 1, 2, \cdots, n). \qquad (7.6)$$

In order, however, to find the unknown constants $b_1, b_2, \cdots$ and to solve for the creep function $F(\tau)$, it is convenient to adopt differential approximation and minimization procedures as outlined below. In this context, the adopted method will be presented first while an actual numerical evaluation for the nonlinear viscoelastic response of a particular viscoelastic material is shown in section 7.4.1.

7.2.1 Approximate solution of the creep function $F(\tau)$

While equation (7.6) has been shown in a general form for the creep of a nonlinear viscoelastic material, a solution of the kernel $F(\tau)$ can only be given in an approximate form. For this purpose, equation (7.7) will be used which is based on experimental observations of the creep behaviour of a class of materials (for instance, Figs. 2.3–2.5).

Thus, denoting the experimental stress or strain by ' $\check{}$ ', one may express analytically the experimental creep curves as a function of the applied stress and time, for a number of experiments $i = 1, 2, \cdots, n$, in the following manner:

$$\check{\varepsilon}_i(t) = \check{\varepsilon}_i + G_i \theta_i(t, m_{i1}, m_{i2}, \cdots) \qquad (i = 1, 2, \cdots, n) \tag{7.7}$$

in which $\check{\varepsilon}_i = E^{-1}\check{\sigma}_i$ is the instantaneous experimental strain at $t = 0$, G_i are constants and $\theta_i(t, m_{i1}, m_{i2}, \cdots)$ are functions of time. The shape of the experimental creep curves will suggest the forms of the functions $\theta_i(\cdot)$ of (7.7) for the type of material under consideration. In this equation, the constants G_i and $m_{i1}, m_{i2}, \cdots$ are required to be determined, for each creep experiment i, by a fitting procedure.

In order to use the experimentally available data of the creep of the material by means of equation (7.7), it is evident that the coefficients in (7.5a) have to be found by an optimization procedure such that the kernel $\int_0^t F(\tau)$ in (7.6) is approximated by functions $\theta_i(t, m_{i1}, m_{i2}, \cdots)$ in equation (7.7). Hence, one can write

$$F(\tau) \approx \frac{\mathrm{d}}{\mathrm{d}t} \theta_i(t, m_{i1}, m_{i2}, \cdots) \Big]_0^T \tag{7.8}$$

where the time T represents the total time for each creep experiment. Thus, using this approximation, it is convenient for the subsequent analytical development to identify

$$\Gamma_i = \frac{\mathrm{d}}{\mathrm{d}t} \theta_i(t, m_{i1}, m_{i2}, \cdots). \tag{7.9}$$

By substituting the values of Γ_i corresponding to the above equation into (7.5a) and using the method of differential approximation (Bellman, 1970), one requires that the functional

$$\sum_{i=1}^{n} \int_0^T (a_0\Gamma_i + a_1\Gamma_i^{(1)} + a_2\Gamma_i^{(2)} + \cdots + a_{N-1}\Gamma_i^{(N-1)} + \Gamma_i^{(N)})^2 \, \mathrm{d}t \tag{7.10}$$

be a minimum with respect to all possible choices of the coefficients $a_0, a_1, \cdots, a_{N-1}$.

It is evident that the minimization of expression (7.10) with respect to the coefficients a_j $(j = 0, 1, \cdots, N - 1)$, i.e.

$$\sum_{i=0}^{n} \int_0^T \frac{\partial}{\partial a_j} (a_0\Gamma_i + a_1\Gamma_i^{(1)} + a_2\Gamma_i^{(2)} + \cdots + a_{N-1}\Gamma_i^{(N-1)} + \Gamma_i^{(N)})^2 \, \mathrm{d}t = 0$$

$$(i = 1, 2, \cdots, n \text{ and } j = 0, 1, \cdots, N - 1), \tag{7.11}$$

leads to a system of N simultaneous linear algebraic equations in the following manner:

$$\sum_{i=1}^{n} \int_{0}^{T} \Gamma_i (a_0 \Gamma_i^{(1)} + a_2 \Gamma_i^{(2)} + \cdots + a_{N-1} \Gamma_i^{(N-1)} + \Gamma_i^{(N)}) \, dt = 0,$$

$$\sum_{i=1}^{n} \int_{0}^{T} \Gamma_i^{(1)} (a_0 \Gamma_i^{(1)} + a_2 \Gamma_i^{(2)} + \cdots + a_{N-1} \Gamma_i^{(N-1)} + \Gamma_i^{(N)}) \, dt = 0,$$

$$\sum_{i=1}^{n} \int_{0}^{T} \Gamma_i^{(2)} (a_0 \Gamma_i^{(1)} + a_2 \Gamma_i^{(2)} + \cdots + a_{N-1} \Gamma_i^{(N-1)} + \Gamma_i^{(N)}) \, dt = 0, \qquad (7.12)$$

$$\vdots$$

$$\sum_{i=1}^{n} \int_{0}^{T} \Gamma_i^{(N-1)} (a_0 \Gamma_i^{(1)} + a_2 \Gamma_i^{(2)} + \cdots + a_{N-1} \Gamma_i^{(N-1)} + \Gamma_i^{(N)}) \, dt = 0,$$

$$(i = 1, 2, \cdots, n).$$

This can be written in a more compact form as

$$\sum_{i=1}^{n} \int_{0}^{T} \Gamma_i^{(j)} (a_0 \Gamma_i + a_1 \Gamma_i^{(1)} + a_2 \Gamma_i^{(2)} + \cdots + a_{N-1} \Gamma_i^{(N-1)}) \, dt = - \sum_{i=1}^{n} \int_{0}^{T} \Gamma_i^{(j)} \Gamma_i^{(N)} \, dt$$

$$(i = 1, 2, \cdots, n \text{ and } j = 0, 1, 2, \cdots, N - 1). \qquad (7.13)$$

The set of equations (7.13) may be expressed in matrix form as

$$[a_j] \, [x_{jk}] = [x_k]$$

$$(j, k = 0, 1, 2, \cdots, N - 1) \qquad (7.14)$$

where

$$[a_j] = \begin{bmatrix} a_0 \\ a_1 \\ a_2 \\ \vdots \\ a_{N-1} \end{bmatrix}, \qquad (7.15a)$$

$$[x_{jk}] = \begin{bmatrix} \displaystyle\sum_{i=1}^{n} \int_{0}^{T} \Gamma_i \Gamma_i \, dt & \displaystyle\sum_{i=1}^{n} \int_{0}^{T} \Gamma_i \Gamma_i^{(1)} \, dt & \cdots & \displaystyle\sum_{i=1}^{n} \int_{0}^{T} \Gamma_i \Gamma_i^{(N-1)} \, dt \\[2ex] \displaystyle\sum_{i=1}^{n} \int_{0}^{T} \Gamma_i^{(1)} \Gamma_i \, dt & \displaystyle\sum_{i=1}^{n} \int_{0}^{T} \Gamma_i^{(1)} \Gamma_i^{(1)} \, dt & \cdots & \displaystyle\sum_{i=1}^{n} \int_{0}^{T} \Gamma_i^{(1)} \Gamma_i^{(N-1)} \, dt \\[2ex] \displaystyle\sum_{i=1}^{n} \int_{0}^{T} \Gamma_i^{(2)} \Gamma_i \, dt & \displaystyle\sum_{i=1}^{n} \int_{0}^{T} \Gamma_i^{(2)} \Gamma_i^{(1)} \, dt & \cdots & \displaystyle\sum_{i=1}^{n} \int_{0}^{T} \Gamma_i^{(2)} \Gamma_i^{(N-1)} \, dt \\[2ex] \vdots & \vdots & & \vdots \\[2ex] \displaystyle\sum_{i=1}^{n} \int_{0}^{T} \Gamma_i^{(N-1)} \Gamma_i \, dt & \displaystyle\sum_{i=1}^{n} \int_{0}^{T} \Gamma_i^{(N-1)} \Gamma_i^{(1)} \, dt & \cdots & \displaystyle\sum_{i=1}^{n} \int_{0}^{T} \Gamma_i^{(N-1)} \Gamma_i^{(N-1)} \, dt \end{bmatrix}$$

$$(7.15b)$$

and

$$[x_k] = - \begin{bmatrix} \sum\limits_{i=1}^{n} \int_0^T \Gamma_i \Gamma_i^{(N)} \, dt \\[2ex] \sum\limits_{i=1}^{n} \int_0^T \Gamma_i^{(1)} \Gamma_i^{(N)} \, dt \\[2ex] \sum\limits_{i=1}^{n} \int_0^T \Gamma_i^{(2)} \Gamma_i^{(N)} \, dt \\[2ex] \vdots \\[2ex] \sum\limits_{i=1}^{n} \int_0^T \Gamma_i^{(N-1)} \Gamma_i^{(N)} \, dt \end{bmatrix} \qquad (7.15c)$$

In principle, the solution of equation (7.14) can be found by a straightforward matrix inversion method, i.e.

$$[a_j] = [x_{jk}]^{-1} [x_k] \qquad (7.16)$$

where $[x_{jk}]^{-1}$ is the inverse of the matrix $[x_{jk}]$ as given by equation (7.15b) with the understanding that before the inverse exists the determinant of $[x_{jk}]$ must be nonzero.

Having determined the coefficients of the linear differential equation (7.5a), one solution of this equation may be assumed to be of the form $F(\tau) = \exp(A\tau)$. In order that this solution satisfies the linear differential equation (7.5a), identically, one must have the characteristic equation

$$a_0 + a_1 A + a_2 A^2 + \cdots + a_{N-1} A^{N-1} + A^N = 0. \qquad (7.17)$$

This expression yields N roots A_I $(I = 1, 2, \cdots, N)$ which correspond to the N solutions of the original linear differential equation (7.5a). Hence, the general solution can be written as a linear combination of the N solutions in the following form:

$$F(\tau) = \sum_{I=1}^{N} C_I \exp(A_I \tau) \qquad (I = 1, 2, \cdots, N) \qquad (7.18)$$

where C_I $(I = 1, 2, \cdots, N)$ are constants which can be determined by an optimization procedure as outlined below.

Integration of both sides of (7.18) with respect to the time t gives

$$\int_0^t F(\tau) \, d\tau = \sum_{I=1}^{N} D_I[\exp(A_I t) - 1] \qquad (I = 1, 2, \cdots, N) \qquad (7.19)$$

in which

$$D_I = \frac{C_I}{A_I} \qquad (I = 1, 2, \cdots, N).$$

By substituting the value of the integrand corresponding to (7.19) into the analytical expression (7.1), it follows that

$$\varepsilon_i(t) = E^{-1}\breve{\sigma}_i + h(\breve{\sigma}_i, b_1, b_2, \cdots) \sum_{I=1}^{N} D_I[\exp(A_I t) - 1]$$

$$(i = 1, 2, \cdots, n \quad \text{and} \quad I = 1, 2, \cdots, N). \tag{7.20}$$

The identification problem of the nonlinear viscoelastic response of the material can now be formalized in the following manner.

Given n independent experimental functionals $\breve{\varepsilon}_i$ ($i = 1, 2, \cdots, n$), equation (7.7), corresponding to applied stresses $\breve{\sigma}_i$, one wishes to find the constants $b_1, b_2, \cdots$ and D_I ($I = 1, 2, \cdots, N$) in the constitutive equation (7.20) such that the functional

$$\mathrm{II}(b_1, b_2, \cdots; D_I) = \sum_{i=1}^{n} \gamma_i \int_0^T [\varepsilon_i(t) - \breve{\varepsilon}_i(t)]^2 \, dt$$

$$(i = 1, 2, \cdots, n \quad \text{and} \quad I = 1, 2, \cdots, N) \tag{7.21}$$

is minimized. For the purpose of minimizing this functional, a quadratic expression (Mikhlin, 1965) of the difference between the theoretical strain $\breve{\varepsilon}_i(t)$ ($i = 1, 2, \cdots, n$), which is given by (7.20), and the experimental strain $\breve{\varepsilon}_i(t)$ as given by (7.7) is used and where γ_i ($i = 1, 2, \cdots, n$) represent suitable positive weighting factors.

Hence, by substituting for $\varepsilon_i(t)$ and $\breve{\varepsilon}_i(t)$ their corresponding expressions from (7.20) and (7.7), respectively, into (7.21) it follows that

$$\mathrm{II}(b_1, b_2, \cdots; D_I) = \sum_{i=1}^{n} \gamma_i \int_0^T \left\{ h(\breve{\sigma}_i, b_1, b_2, \cdots) \sum_{I=1}^{N} D_I[\exp(A_I t) - 1] \right.$$

$$\left. - G_i\theta_i(t, m_{i1}, m_{i2}, \cdots) \right\}^2 dt$$

$$(i = 1, 2, \cdots, n \quad \text{and} \quad I = 1, 2, \cdots, N). \tag{7.22}$$

The minimization of expression (7.22) can be carried out by using a number of numerical optimization techniques as demonstrated in section 7.4.1.

Once the values of the unknown constants of equation (7.22) have been determined by the above procedure, this expression can be used to represent a 'model equation' for the creep response of a real viscoelastic material.

7.3 CHARACTERIZATION OF THE RELAXATION RESPONSE

We propose in this case an analytical development similar to that followed above for the characterization of the creep response. Let the constant strain being applied on the specimen during a relaxation experiment i be denoted by $\breve{\varepsilon}_i$ ($i = 1, 2, \cdots, n$) where n denotes the number of relaxation experiments. Thus, the stress relaxation equation, analogous to (7.6), is written as

$$\sigma_i(t) = E\breve{\varepsilon}_i + h_1(\breve{\varepsilon}_i, c_1, c_2, \cdots) \int_0^t R(\tau) \, d\tau \tag{7.23}$$

whereby the relaxation function $R(\tau)$ is assumed to satisfy an Nth-order differential equation of the form given by (7.5b), namely

$$q_0 R + q_1 R^{(1)} + q_2 R^{(2)} + \cdots + q_{N-1} R^{(N-1)} + R^{(N)} = 0$$

in which $q_0, q_1, \cdots, q_{N-1}$ are coefficients to be determined.

Further, in a manner corresponding to (7.7), the experimental relaxation curves may be expressed analytically as a function of the applied strain and time for a number of relaxation experiments $i = 1, 2, \cdots, n$ as

$$\check{\sigma}_i(t) = \check{\sigma}_i + g_i \phi_i(t, z_{i1}, z_{i2}, \cdots) \qquad (i = 1, 2, \cdots, n) \qquad (7.24)$$

where $\check{\sigma}_i = E\check{\varepsilon}_i$ is the instantaneous experimental stress at $t = 0$, g_i are constants and $\phi_i(t, z_{i1}, z_{i2}, \cdots)$ are functions of time. The shape of the experimental relaxation curve will suggest the forms of the functions $\phi_i(\cdot)$ for the type of material under consideration. In the above equation, the constants g_i and $z_{i1}, z_{i2}, \cdots$ will be required to be determined for each relaxation experiment i. Meantime, the model response equation in the relaxation phase can be written, with reference to (7.23), in an analogous manner to (7.20), as

$$\sigma_i(t) = E\check{\varepsilon}_i + h_1(\check{\varepsilon}_i, c_1, c_2, \cdots) \sum_{I=1}^{N} \hat{D}_I [\exp(B_I t) - 1]$$

$$(i = 1, 2, \cdots, n \quad \text{and} \quad I = 1, 2, \cdots, N) \qquad (7.25)$$

in which the functions $h_1(\cdot)$ and the constants $\hat{D}_I$ and B_I $(I = 1, 2, \cdots, N)$ are to be identified for the considered range of applied strain and the extent of time covered during the relaxation experiments $i = 1, 2, \cdots, n$.

7.4 NUMERICAL ILLUSTRATION

7.4.1 Creep response

Figure 7.1 illustrates the experimental creep data (Hill, 1967) for a class of wood pulp fibres. In this figure, the first creep strain is presented against the logarithm of time for dry summerwood fibers of a longleaf pine holocellulose pulp after conditioning at 50% RH and 23 °C. Three creep experimental curves are shown, i.e. for initial stress inputs of 29.1, 38.4 and 49.1 dyn μm^{-2}.

Thus, by referring to expression (7.7) and the shape of the creep curves of Fig. 7.1, one may express the experimental creep strain, for the above fibres, as

$$\check{\varepsilon}_i(t) = \check{\varepsilon}_i + G_i t^{m_i} \qquad (i = 1, 2, \cdots, n), \quad n = 3, \qquad (7.26)$$

where $\check{\varepsilon}_i$ is the instantaneous strain at $t = 0$ and G_i and m_i are constants. The values of the parameters G_i and m_i in the above equation can be determined from the corresponding experimental data (Fig. 7.1) by a standard fitting procedure. In this context, the outcome data of each creep experiment can be derived from the

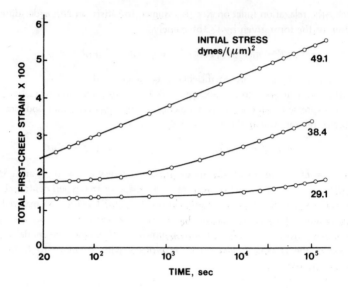

Fig. 7.1 Experimental first creep curves of dry summerwood fibres of a longleaf pine holocellulose pulp after conditioning at 50% RH and 23 °C. (Source: Hill, R. L. (1967) The creep behaviour of individual pulp fibres under tensile stress. *Tappi*, **50**(8), 432–40. Reprinted by permission of Tappi.)

creep curves of Fig. 7.1 and expressed as follows:

$$[t_1, \breve{\varepsilon}_i(t_1)], [t_2, \breve{\varepsilon}_i(t_2)], \cdots, [t_l, \breve{\varepsilon}_i(t_l)], \cdots, [t_\chi, \breve{\varepsilon}_i(t_\chi)]$$

where $t_1 < t_2 < \cdots < t_l < t_\chi$ within the domain of T and the time T represents, as pointed out in section 7.2, the total time for each relaxation experiment.

It is now required to fit for each creep experiment i the parameters G_i and m_i equation (7.26) such that the resulting strain $\breve{\varepsilon}_i(t)$ gives a reasonable representation of the outcome data of the creep experiment i. One fits for each creep experiment i by minimizing a functional

$$Y_i(G_i, m_i) = \sum_{l=1}^{\chi} [\breve{\varepsilon}_i(t_l) - (\breve{\varepsilon}_i + G_i t_l^{m_i})]^2. \tag{7.27}$$

By carrying out the minimization of expression (7.27) for each creep experiment i with respect to all possible choices of the parameter G_i, i.e.

$$\frac{\partial}{\partial G_i} Y_i(G_i, m_i) = \frac{\partial}{\partial G_i} \sum_{l=1}^{\chi} [\breve{\varepsilon}_i(t_l) - (\breve{\varepsilon}_i + G_i t_l^{m_i})]^2$$

$$(l = 1, 2, \cdots, \chi \quad \text{and} \quad i = 1, 2, \cdots, n; \quad n = 3), \tag{7.28}$$

it follows that

$$G_i = \frac{\sum_{l=1}^{\chi} [\check{\varepsilon}_i(t_l) - \check{\varepsilon}_i] t_l^{m_i}}{\sum_{l=1}^{\chi} t_l^{2m_i}}. \tag{7.29}$$

Similarly, by carrying out the minimization of expression (7.27), for each creep experiment i, with respect to all possible choices of the parameter m_i, i.e.

$$\frac{\partial}{\partial m_i} Y_i(G_i, m_i) = \frac{\partial}{\partial m_i} \sum_{l=1}^{\chi} [\check{\varepsilon}_i(t_l) - (\check{\varepsilon}_i + G_i t_l^{m_i})]^2 = 0$$

$$(l = 1, 2, \cdots, \chi \quad \text{and} \quad i = 1, 2, \cdots, n; \quad n = 3), \tag{7.30}$$

one obtains, by combining (7.29) and (7.30), the following relation:

$$\sum_{l=1}^{\chi} [\check{\varepsilon}_i(t_l) - \check{\varepsilon}_i] t_l^{m_i} \ln(t_l) - \frac{\sum_{l=1}^{\chi} [\check{\varepsilon}_i(t_l) - \check{\varepsilon}_i]}{\sum_{l=1}^{\chi} t_l^{2m_i}} t_l^{m_i} \sum_{l=1}^{\chi} t_l^{2m_i} \ln(t) = 0. \tag{7.31}$$

Thus, by using the available experimental data, one can solve numerically equation (7.31) for each experiment i to find the parameter m_i, and then, by substituting the resulting value of m_i into (7.29), the value of the corresponding parameter G_i can be determined.

The secant method (for instance, Jones, Smith and Welford, 1970) has been used in the present work to solve the equation (7.31). The numerical results of the fitting procedure, as applied to the creep curves of Fig. 7.1, are presented in Table 7.1.

(a) Differential approximation of the creep kernel

With the foregoing obtained information from the experimental creep data by means of equation (7.26), it is now possible to proceed using the method of differential approximation indicated in section 7.2 to determine the coefficients of the linear

Table 7.1 Material parameters pertaining to the suggested, experimental creep expression (7.26)

i	$\check{\sigma}_i(\text{dyn } \mu m^{-2})$	$\check{\varepsilon}_i \; (\mu m \; \mu m^{-1})$	$G_i(h^{-m_i})$	m_i
1	29.1	0.012	0.164×10^{-2}	0.192
2	38.4	0.016	0.816×10^{-2}	0.388
3	49.1	0.021	0.205×10^{-2}	0.224

Dry summerwood fibres of longleaf pine holocellulose pulp after conditioning at 50% RH and 23 °C.

differential equation (7.5a). Having determined these coefficients, one may continue to find the roots of the characteristic equation (7.17).

Comparing (7.26) and (7.7), it is evident that, for the present case of wood pulp fibres, the functions $\theta_i(\cdot)$ take the form

$$\theta_i(\cdot) = t^{m_i}. \tag{7.32}$$

Consequently, one can write (7.9) as

$$\Gamma_i = \frac{d}{dt}(t^{m_i}) \tag{7.33}$$

from which the jth derivative required for (7.13) is expressed as

$$\Gamma_i^{(j)} = \frac{d^{j+1}}{dt^{j+1}}(t^{m_i}) = m_i(m_i - 1)(m_i - 2)\cdots(m_i - j)t^{m_i-j-1}$$

$$(j = 0, 1, 2, \cdots, N - 1). \tag{7.34}$$

Hence, by substituting the expression of $\Gamma_i^{(j)}$ corresponding to (7.34) into (7.13) and carrying out the integration of the elements of the matrices $[x_{jk}]$ and $[x_k]$ as indicated in (7.15), then

$$a_j = \begin{bmatrix} a_0 \\ a_1 \\ a_2 \\ \vdots \\ a_{N-1} \end{bmatrix}, \tag{7.35a}$$

and

$$[x_k] = - \begin{bmatrix} \left[\displaystyle\sum_{i=1}^{n} \frac{m_i^2(m_i - 1)(m_i - 2)\cdots(m_i - N)t^{2m_i-N-1}}{2m_i - N - 1}\right]^T 0 \\[4mm] \left[\displaystyle\sum_{i=1}^{n} \frac{m_i^2(m_i - 1)^2(m_i - 2)\cdots(m_i - N)t^{2m_i-N-2}}{2m_i - N - 2}\right]^T 0 \\[4mm] \left[\displaystyle\sum_{i=1}^{n} \frac{m_i^2(m_i - 1)^2(m_i - 2)^2\cdots(m_i - N)t^{2m_i-N-3}}{2m_i - N - 3}\right]^T 0 \\[2mm] \vdots \\[2mm] \left[\displaystyle\sum_{i=1}^{n} \frac{m_i^2(m_i - 1)^2(m_i - 2)^2\cdots(m_i - N + 1)^2(m_i - N)t^{2m_i-2N}}{2m_i - 2N}\right]^T 0 \\[4mm] (k = 0, 1, \cdots, N - 1 \quad \text{and} \quad i = 1, 2, \cdots, n). \end{bmatrix} \tag{7.35c}$$

In (7.35b) and (7.35c) it is apparent that the elements of the matrices $[x_{jk}]$ and $[x_k]$ contain terms such as $t^{2m_i-1}, t^{2m_i-2}, \cdots$, etc. Thus, in view of Table 7.1, since m_i has values ranging from 0.192 to 0.388, we expect the exponent of each of the

$$|x_{jk}| = \begin{vmatrix}
\displaystyle\sum_{i=1}^{n} \frac{m_i^2 t^{2m_i-1}}{2m_i - 1}\Bigg|_0^T & \displaystyle\sum_{i=1}^{n} \frac{m_i^2(m_i-1)t^{2m_i-2}}{2m_i - 2}\Bigg|_0^T & \cdots & \displaystyle\sum_{i=1}^{n} \frac{m_i^2(m_i-1)(m_i-2)\cdots(m_i-N+1)t^{2m_i-N}}{2m_i - N}\Bigg|_0^T \\[3ex]
\displaystyle\sum_{i=1}^{n} \frac{m_i^2(m_i-1)t^{2m_i-2}}{2m_i - 2}\Bigg|_0^T & \displaystyle\sum_{i=1}^{n} \frac{m_i^2(m_i-1)^2 t^{2m_i-3}}{2m_i - 3}\Bigg|_0^T & \cdots & \displaystyle\sum_{i=1}^{n} \frac{m_i^2(m_i-1)^2(m_i-2)\cdots(m_i-N+1)t^{2m_i-N-1}}{2m_i - N - 1}\Bigg|_0^T \\[3ex]
 & & & \displaystyle\sum_{i=1}^{n} \frac{m_i^2(m_i-1)^2(m_i-2)\cdots(m_i-N+1)t^{2m_i-N-2}}{2m_i - N - 2}\Bigg|_0^T \\[3ex]
\vdots & \vdots & \ddots & \vdots \\[2ex]
\displaystyle\sum_{i=1}^{n} \frac{m_i^2(m_i-1)(m_i-2)\cdots(m_i-N+1)t^{2m_i-N}}{2m_i - N}\Bigg|_0^T & \displaystyle\sum_{i=1}^{n} \frac{m_i^2(m_i-1)^2(m_i-2)\cdots(m_i-N+1)t^{2m_i-N-1}}{2m_i - N - 1}\Bigg|_0^T & \cdots & \displaystyle\sum_{i=1}^{n} \frac{m_i^2(m_i-1)^2(m_i-2)\cdots(m_i-N+1)t^{2m_i-2N+1}}{2m_i - 2N + 1}\Bigg|_0^T
\end{vmatrix}$$

$$(j, k = 0, 1, 2, \cdots, N-1 \text{ and } i = 1, 2, \cdots, n)$$

(7.35b)

above terms, i.e. t^{2m_i-1}, t^{2m_i-2}, $\cdots$, etc., to be negative. As a consequence, the singularity of these terms will prevent the use of the lower limit of the integration as zero. In the computational work, this problem has been solved by taking the lower limit of integration greater than zero, namely 0.09 h. A straightforward matrix inversion method (for instance, Jones, Smith and Welford, 1970) has been used to solve (7.14) for the coefficients a_j. The results of the computations are presented in Table 7.2 for $N = 3, 4, 5, \cdots, 8$.

Having determined the coefficients a_j, one continues, as indicated in section 7.2, to find the roots A_I ($I = 1, 2, \cdots, N$) of the characteristic equation (7.17). In this context, the secant method has been employed. The numerical values of the roots A_I are given in Table 7.3.

(b) Minimization of the objective function (7.22)

After we have determined the roots A_1, A_2, $\cdots$, A_N of the characteristic equation (7.17), we continue to determine the values of the unknown constants appearing in the model equation (7.20) where the function $h(\cdot)$ appearing in the latter equation takes, for the present class of wood fibres, the form (Distéfano and Todeschini, 1973a, b; Haddad, 1987).

$$h(\cdot) = \exp(b\breve{\sigma}). \tag{7.36}$$

This involves the minimization of expression (7.22).

Thus, by substituting for $h(\cdot)$ and $\theta_i(\cdot)$ as given by (7.36) and (7.32), respectively, into (7.22), it follows that

$$\text{III}[b, D_I\ (I = 1, 2, \cdots, N)] = \sum_{i=1}^{n=5} \gamma_i \int_0^T \left\{ G_i t^{m_i} - \exp(b\breve{\sigma}) \sum_{l=1}^{N} D_I[1 - \exp(A_I t)] \right\}^2 dt$$

$$(i = 1, 2, \cdots, 5, \quad \text{and} \quad I = 1, 2, \cdots, N). \tag{7.37}$$

The computational analysis for minimizing the objective function (7.37) has been carried out using the steepest descent method (Haddad, 1975), whereby the lower limit of integration is taken as 0.09 h and γ_i assumed to be unity. The values of the parameters b and D_I which minimize (7.37) are shown in Table 7.4 for $N = 3, 4, 5, \cdots, 8$.

In order to test the predictive ability of the model, the predicted values of strain have been computed for each experiment i for $N = 3, 4, \cdots, 8$. This has been carried out by using the model equation (7.20) whereby the function $h(\cdot)$ appearing in this equation is given by equation (7.36). The predicted values of strain have been then compared with the corresponding experimental ones taken from Fig. 7.1 at corresponding stress level and time. The mean square error (MSE) was computed for each experiment i and different values of N through the relation

$$\text{MSE} = \frac{\sum_{l=1}^{\chi} [\varepsilon(t_l) - \breve{\varepsilon}(t_l)]^2}{\chi} \qquad (l = 1, 2, \cdots, \chi). \tag{7.38}$$

Table 7.2 Coefficients a_j ($j = 0, 1, \ldots, N-1$) for $N = 3, 4, \ldots, 8$, equation (7.14)

N	3	4	5	6	7	8
a_0	$0.420\ 050 \times 10^4$	$0.161\ 554 \times 10^6$	$0.791\ 297 \times 10^7$	$0.470\ 653 \times 10^9$	$0.328\ 268 \times 10^{11}$	$0.262\ 029 \times 10^{13}$
a_1	$0.269\ 029 \times 10^4$	$0.157\ 186 \times 10^6$	$0.104\ 922 \times 10^8$	$0.794\ 841 \times 10^9$	$0.676\ 065 \times 10^{11}$	$0.638\ 460 \times 10^{13}$
a_2	$0.129\ 167 \times 10^3$	$0.133\ 574 \times 10^5$	$0.135\ 210 \times 10^7$	$0.141\ 908 \times 10^9$	$0.157\ 559 \times 10^{11}$	$0.186\ 254 \times 10^{13}$
a_3		$0.240\ 356 \times 10^3$	$0.413\ 268 \times 10^5$	$0.642\ 202 \times 10^7$	$0.974\ 957 \times 10^9$	$0.149\ 517 \times 10^{12}$
a_4			$0.385\ 423 \times 10^3$	$0.991\ 915 \times 10^5$	$0.219\ 039 \times 10^8$	$0.453\ 662 \times 10^{10}$
a_5				$0.564\ 305 \times 10^3$	$0.202\ 941 \times 10^6$	$0.603\ 604 \times 10^8$
a_6					$0.776\ 941 \times 10^3$	$0.371\ 908 \times 10^6$
a_7						$0.102\ 323 \times 10^4$

Creep of dry summerwood fibres of longleaf pine holocellulose pulp after conditioning at 50% RH and 23 °C

Table 7.3 Roots A_l ($l = 1, 2, \ldots, N$, $N = 8$) (h^{-1}) of the characteristic equation (7.17)

N	3	4	5	6	7	8
A_1	$-0.760\ 54 \times 10^{-1}$	$-0.169\ 98 \times 10^{-1}$	$-0.174\ 52 \times 10^{-1}$	$-0.181\ 59 \times 10^{-1}$	$-0.192\ 38 \times 10^{-1}$	$-0.204\ 23 \times 10^{-1}$
A_2	$-0.119\ 45 \times 10^{-1}$	$-0.506\ 27 \times 10^{-2}$	$-0.531\ 17 \times 10^{-2}$	$-0.557\ 99 \times 10^{-2}$	$-0.589\ 84 \times 10^{-2}$	$-0.629\ 55 \times 10^{-2}$
A_3	$-0.362\ 55 \times 10^{-1}$	$-0.296\ 65 \times 10^{-2}$	$-0.316\ 80 \times 10^{-2}$	$-0.332\ 85 \times 10^{-2}$	$-0.343\ 48 \times 10^{-2}$	$-0.356\ 62 \times 10^{-2}$
A_4		$-0.481\ 98 \times 10^{-2}$	$-0.500\ 24 \times 10^{-2}$	$-0.512\ 06 \times 10^{-2}$	$-0.517\ 80 \times 10^{-2}$	$-0.524\ 76 \times 10^{-2}$
A_5			$-0.182\ 66 \times 10^{-3}$	$-0.301\ 17 \times 10^{-3}$	$-0.324\ 47 \times 10^{-3}$	$-0.349\ 38 \times 10^{-3}$
A_6				$-0.118\ 53 \times 10^{-3}$	$-0.141\ 94 \times 10^{-3}$	$-0.167\ 21 \times 10^{-3}$
A_7					$-0.234\ 17 \times 10^{-4}$	$-0.487\ 11 \times 10^{-4}$
A_8						$-0.252\ 94 \times 10^{-4}$

Creep of dry summerwood fibres of longleaf pine holocellulose pulp after conditioning at 50% RH and 23 °C

Table 7.4 Parameters D_I ($I = 1, 2, \ldots, N; N = 8$) ($\times 10^8$ dyn μm^{-2}) and b, equation (7.37)

N	3	4	5	6	7	8
D_1	−1.697 959	−1.135 043	−0.843 524	−0.669 838	−0.554 878	−0.473 314
D_2	−23.881 838	−14.475 734	−9.887 900	−7.293 809	−5.676 604	−4.593 259
D_3	−103.587 203	−59.504 077	−39.375 231	−28.263 548	−21.434 256	−16.919 977
D_4		−165.241 146	−104.294 647	−73.314 790	−54.812 592	−42.745 777
D_5			−231.021 697	−155.184 215	−113.886 261	−87.865 797
D_6				−229.578 800	−210.430 911	−159.481 064
D_7					−370.145 498	−268.896 465
D_8						−422.254 346
b	$0.267\ 11 \times 10^{-2}$	$0.119\ 87 \times 10^{-1}$	$0.123\ 08 \times 10^{-1}$	$0.124\ 98 \times 10^{-1}$	$0.125\ 05 \times 10^{-1}$	$0.124\ 97 \times 10^{-1}$

Creep of dry summerwood fibres of longleaf pine holocellulose pulp after conditioning at 50% RH and 23 °C.

Table 7.5 Material parameters characteristic of the suggested experimental relaxation equation (7.39)

i	$\breve{\varepsilon}_i$ (cm cm^{-1})	σ_i ($\times 10^8$ dyn cm^{-2})	$g_i (h^z)$ ($\times 10^8$ dyn cm^{-2})	z_i
1	0.01	4.5	1.919	0.064
2	0.02	9.7	4.285	0.064
3	0.03	13.6	5.682	0.066
4	0.04	17.9	6.908	0.058
5	0.05	22.05	6.906	0.065

Cotton fibres after conditioning at 65% RH and 25 °C.

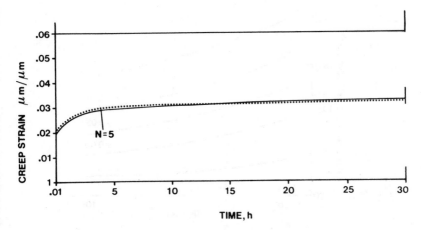

Fig. 7.2 Predictive capability of the proposed model in the case of first creep of pine pulp fibres. (applied stress, 38.4 dyn μm^2): ———, experiment; ⋯⋯, prediction.

It was found that, for the considered fibres, the total MSE reaches a minimum value at $N = 5$. The predictive ability of the model is demonstrated in Fig. 7.2 for a stress level of 38.4 dyn μm^{-2}.

7.4.2 Relaxation response

The experimental curves due to Meredith (1954) showing the relaxation stress, i.e. the stress obtained under constant strain $\check{\varepsilon}_i$ ($i = 1, 2, \cdots, n; \, n = 5$), i indicating a relaxation experiment, against the logarithm of time are presented in Fig. 7.3 for the case of natural cellulose fibres (cotton).

With reference to Fig. 7.3 and expression (7.24), the stress relaxation for the above fibres is expressed in the form

$$\check{\sigma}_i(t) = \check{\sigma}_i - g_i t^{z_i} \qquad (i = 1, 2, \cdots, n) \tag{7.39}$$

where z_i are constants. The values of the parameters g_i and z_i ($i = 1, 2, \cdots, n; \, n = 5$) are given in Table 7.5 for the relaxation experiments presented in Fig. 7.3. In this case, the function $h_1(\cdot)$ of (7.25) is assumed to have the form

$$h_1(\cdot) = \exp(c\check{\varepsilon}_i) \tag{7.40}$$

where c is a constant. Thus, by combining equations (7.25) and (7.40) the former becomes

$$\sigma_i(t) = E\check{\varepsilon}_i + \exp(c\check{\varepsilon}_i) \sum_{I=1}^{N} \hat{D}_I[\exp(B_I t) - 1]$$

$$(i = 1, 2, \cdots, 5 \text{ and } I = 1, 2, \cdots, N). \tag{7.41}$$

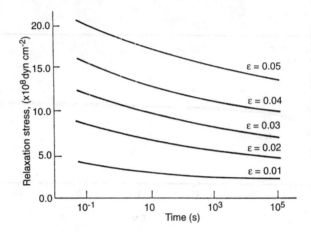

Fig. 7.3 Experimental relaxation curves of natural cellulose fibres (cotton) at 65% RH and 25 °C. (Source: Meredith, R. (1954) Relaxation of stress in stretched cellulose fibers, *J. Textile Inst.*, **45**, T438–T461. Reprinted by permission of British Textile Technology Group.)

With the information obtained from the experimental relaxation data of cotton fibres by means of equation (7.39) as illustrated above, one can proceed, following the analytical scheme introduced earlier, for modelling the creep response, to determine the parameters c, $\hat{D}_I$ and B_I ($I = 1, 2, \cdots, N$) which characterize the relaxation response equation (7.41) (Table 7.6). In this regard, it was found that the total MSE for the number of experiments involved reaches a minimum value at $N = 4$. The predictive ability of the model is demonstrated in Fig. 7.4a for a relaxation strain input of 0.01 cm cm^{-1}.

The numerical values of the parameters characterizing the constitutive equation (7.41), as determined above for cotton fibres, may be used to examine further the predictive ability of the model for a strain level outside the strain range considered in the model. In this context, the experimental relaxation curve corresponding to an applied strain of 0.06 cm cm^{-1} (Meredith, 1954) was used. As shown in Fig. 7.4b, the stress relaxation values predicted by the model comply favourably well with the corresponding experimental ones even at this level of applied strain.

As demonstrated above, a common rheological model was used for the identification of both the creep and relaxation responses of a class of natural fibres by using experimental data from two different fibre sources. This was possible because of the generality introduced in the model in the form of mathematical functions that can be associated with the particular time-dependent performance of the class of fibres under consideration.

Table 7.6 Values of parameters pertaining to the relaxation constitutive equation (7.41)

N	3	4	5	6	7	8
$\hat{D}_l$ ($\times 10^8$ dyn cm^{-2})						
$\hat{D}_1$	64.848 773	$-1.279\ 786$	0.681 772	$-0.191\ 855$	$-1.472\ 124$	$-2.125\ 503$
$\hat{D}_2$	61.622 924	75.680 531	75.206 427	74.943 738	74.828 227	74.793 207
$\hat{D}_3$	85.071 193	99.129 241	98.657 634	98.424 634	98.368 221	98.355 531
$\hat{D}_4$		34.747 69	34.276 117	34.043 117	33.988 159	33.976 572
$\hat{D}_5$			17.350 358	17.350 358	17.295 414	17.283 834
$\hat{D}_6$				20.684 165	20.629 207	20.617 627
$\hat{D}_7$					24.108 952	24.097 379
$\hat{D}_8$						27.570 524
B_l (h^{-1})						
B_1	$-1.099\ 525$	$-0.740\ 515$	$-0.554\ 445$	$-0.443\ 661$	$-0.370\ 971$	$-0.319\ 748$
B_2	$-10.089\ 640$	$-6.308\ 098$	$-4.413\ 529$	$-3.325\ 409$	$-2.640\ 529$	$-2.179\ 361$
B_3	$-38.468\ 035$	$-22.706\ 725$	$-15.347\ 084$	$-11.220\ 736$	$-8.658\ 291$	$-6.953\ 434$
B_4		$-59.359\ 363$	$-38.149\ 942$	$-27.226\ 782$	$-20.638\ 786$	$-16.316\ 638$
B_5			$-81.550\ 000$	$-55.507\ 862$	$-41.212\ 553$	$-32.142\ 377$
B_6				$-104.633\ 550$	$-74.250\ 533$	$-56.795\ 098$
B_7					$-128.372\ 337$	$-94.051\ 185$
B_8						$-152.616\ 160$
c	$-6.492\ 27$	$-7.011\ 54$	-9.5185	$-13.040\ 31$	$-14.585\ 07$	$-14.929\ 95$

Cotton fibres.

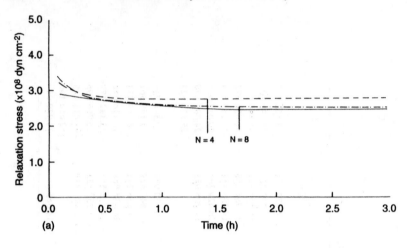

(a)   Time (h)

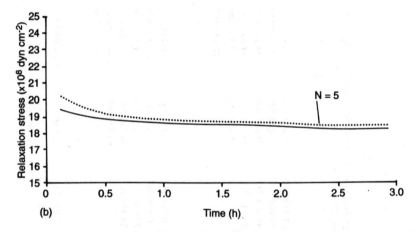

(b)   Time (h)

Fig. 7.4 Testing the predictive ability of the proposed model in the case of relaxation of cotton fibres: (a) applied strain 0.01 cm cm^{-1}; (b) applied strain 0.06 cm cm^{-1}; ——, experiment; – – –, – · –, · · · ·, prediction.

While the above formulation has been illustrated by a procedure applied to the case of single fibres of natural origin, it could be valid for other classes of viscoelastic materials provided that the forms of the experimental curves representing the rheological behaviour of such materials are observed. We demonstrate further below the possibility of application of the above model to the isothermal creep of a class of viscoelastic materials within a specified temperature range.

7.5 IDENTIFICATION OF THE ISOTHERMAL CREEP OF VISCOELASTIC MATERIALS WITHIN A SPECIFIED TEMPERATURE RANGE

In Fig. 7.5, the first creep strain is presented against the logarithm of time for a class of polyester resin (isophthalic polyester) at an applied stress of 4.55 MPa. Three creep experimental curves are shown at constant temperatures of 28.2 °C, 57.2 °C and 76.6 °C.

With reference to the shape of the experimental creep curves of Fig. 7.5, one may use equation (7.26) to express the creep response. The values of the parameters G_i and m_i ($i = 1, 2, \cdots, n; n = 3$) characterizing equation (7.26) for the present case of polyester resin are given in Table 7.7.

Referring to the creep constitutive equation (7.20), the function $h(\cdot)$ appearing in this equation may be assumed, for the case of creep at elevated (constant) temperatures, in a power-law form (e.g. Robotonov, 1969; Gittus, 1975; Haddad and Tanary, 1989) as

$$h(\cdot) = B\breve{\sigma}^k \qquad (7.42)$$

in which k is a constant parameter which takes, usually, the value of 1 for a large number of polymeric materials, whereas B is a temperature-dependent parameter. The latter may be expressed in terms of the activation energy of the associated flow process (Haddad and Tanary, 1989) in the following form:

$$B = B_0 \exp\left(-\frac{U_0}{RT}\right). \qquad (7.43)$$

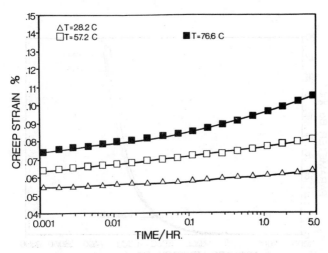

Fig. 7.5 Experimental creep curves of polyester resin (isophthalic polyester) at various base temperatures (applied stress of 4.55 MPa). Experimental data from Jerina *et al.* (1982).

Numerical analysis in viscoelasticity

Table 7.7 Material parameters pertaining to the suggested experimental creep expression (7.26)

i	T_i (°C)	$\breve{\sigma}$ (MPa)	$\breve{\varepsilon}_i$ (%)	$G_i(h^{m_i})$	m_i
1	28.2	4.522	0.0455	$0.149\ 87 \times 10^{-1}$	0.087 06
2	57.2	4.552	0.0455	$0.310\ 82 \times 10^{-1}$	0.079 34
3	76.6	4.552	0.0455	$0.504\ 95 \times 10^{-1}$	0.090 23

Creep of isophthalic polyester resin at different base temperatures.

In the above equation, B_0 is a constant parameter to be determined from the experimental creep data, U_0 is the activation energy, R is the gas constant and T is the creep test temperature. Combining equations (7.20), (7.42) and (7.43), the creep constitutive equation (7.20) can be expressed for the present case as

$$\varepsilon_i(t) = \left\{ E^{-1} + B_0 \exp\left(-\frac{U_0}{RT_i} \right) \sum_{I=1}^{N} D_I[\exp(A_I t) - 1] \right\} \breve{\sigma}_i$$

$$(i = 1, 2, \cdots, n \text{ and } I = 1, 2, \cdots, N). \tag{7.44}$$

In equation (7.44), we first determine the value of the activation energy U_0 that is valid for the considered creep range, i.e. between 28.2 °C and 76.6 °C (Fig. 7.5). This may be done by using the expression for the function $h(\cdot)$ that is given by (7.42). Thus, with reference to (7.42) and (7.43), one can write

$$h_i(\cdot) = B_0 \exp\left(-\frac{U_0}{RT_i} \right) \breve{\sigma}_i = S_i$$

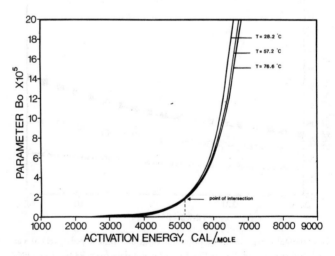

Fig. 7.6 Variation of material parameter B_0 with activation energy.

Table 7.8 Values of parameters pertaining to the creep constitutive equation (7.20) with the inclusion of equation (7.42)

N	3	4	5	6	7	8
D_1	-0.967×10^{-1}	-0.106	-0.104	-0.975×10^{-1}	-0.936×10^{-1}	-0.930×10^{-1}
D_2	-0.581×10^{-1}	-0.100	-0.902×10^{-1}	-0.418×10^{-1}	-0.381×10^{-1}	-0.356×10^{-1}
D_3	-0.581×10^{-1}	-0.101	-0.906×10^{-1}	-0.414×10^{-1}	-0.384×10^{-1}	-0.359×10^{-1}
D_4		-0.101	-0.907×10^{-1}	-0.414×10^{-1}	-0.384×10^{-1}	-0.350×10^{-1}
D_5			-0.907×10^{-1}	-0.415×10^{-1}	-0.385×10^{-1}	-0.360×10^{-1}
D_6				-0.415×10^{-1}	-0.385×10^{-1}	-0.360×10^{-1}
D_7					-0.385×10^{-1}	-0.361×10^{-1}
D_8						-0.360×10^{-1}
A_1	-6.831	-4.177	-2.843	-2.078	-1.592	-1.277
A_2	-75.357	-45.262	-10.282	-21.739	-16.407	-12.855
A_3	-301.811	-174.574	-115.313	-82.173	-61.648	-48.032
A_4		-468.735	-207.088	-208.752	-155.553	-120.675
A_5			-646.302	-435.321	-319.479	-246.079
A_6				-831.174	-584.847	-443.229
A_7					-1021.446	-743.112
A_8						-1215.767
B_0	0.973×10^{-4}	0.506×10^{-4}	0.446×10^{-4}	0.695×10^{-4}	0.658×10^{4}	0.627×10^{-4}

Isophthalic polyester resin.

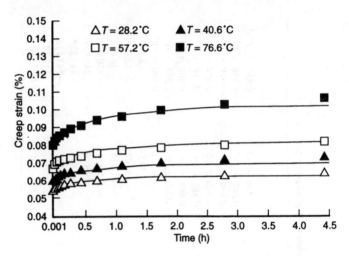

Fig. 7.7 Predictive capability of the proposed model for the creep strain of polyester resin (isophthalic polyester) for a temperature range of 28 °C–76.6 °C (applied stress of 4.55 MPa).

or

$$B_0 = \frac{S_i}{\bar{\sigma}_i} \exp\left(\frac{U_0}{RT_i}\right) \tag{7.45}$$

where the exponent k appearing in (7.42) has been taken as unity and S_i is the numerical value of $h_i(\cdot)$ for each experiment i ($i = 1, 2, \cdots, n$). Thus, the value of U_0 valid for the creep range considered may be defined by the intercept value of the corresponding curves on the B–U_0 graph (Fig. 7.6) that represent the number of experiments ($i = 1, 2, \cdots, n; n = 3$) through the use of equation (7.45).

From Fig. 7.6, it is determined, for the present case, that U_0 has a value of 5.2 kcal mol^{-1}. Having determined the value of U_0, one may proceed to determine the values of the remaining parameters in the creep constitutive equation (7.44), i.e. B_0, D_I and A_I ($I = 1, 2, \cdots, N$). This can be carried out using the differential approximation and minimization procedure outlined earlier in section 7.2. In this context, the values of these parameters for the case of polyester resin are given in Table 7.8 for $N = 3, 4, \cdots, 8$. In this case, the MSE for the total number of creep experiments considered reaches a minimum at $N = 8$. The predictive ability of the model is demonstrated in Fig. 7.7.

REFERENCES

Bellman, R. (1970) *Methods of Nonlinear Analysis*, Vol. 1, Academic Press, New York.
Distéfano, N. (1970) On the identification problem in linear viscoelasticity. *Z. Angew. Math. Mech.*, **50**, 683–90.

Distéfano, N. (1971) System identification problems in hereditary biomechanical processes, in Proc. 5th Asilomar Conf. on Circuits and Systems, Pacific Grove, CA, pp. 248–51.

Distéfano, N. and Todeschini, R. (1973a) Modeling, identification and prediction of a class of nonlinear viscoelastic materials (I). *Int. J. Solids Struct.*, **9**, 805–18.

Distéfano, N. and Todeschini, R. (1973b) Modeling, identification and prediction of a class of nonlinear viscoelastic materials (II). *Int. J. Solids Struct.*, **12**, 1431–8.

Gittus, J. (1975) *Viscoelasticity and Creep Fracture in Solids*, Wiley, New York, pp. 8–12.

Haddad, Y. M. (1975) Response behaviour of a two-dimensional fibrous network. PhD Thesis, McGill University, Montreal, Canada.

Haddad, Y. M. (1987) Un modèle de réponse en viscoelasticité non-linéaire de matériaux. *Res Mech.*, **20**, 235–53.

Haddad, Y. M. and Tanary, S. (1987) Characterization of the rheological response of a class of single fibers. *J. Rheol.*, **31**(7), 515–26.

Haddad, Y. M. and Tanary, S. (1989) On the micromechanical characterization of the creep response of a class of composite systems. *J. Pressure Vessel Technol.*, **3**, 177–82.

Hill, R. L. (1967) The creep behaviour of individual pulp fibres under tensile stress. *Tappi*, **50**(8), 432–40.

Jerina, K. L., Schapery, R. A., Jung, R. W. and Sanders, B. A. (1982) Viscoelastic characterization of a random fibre composite material employing micromechanics, in *ASTM Spec. Tech. Publ. 772* (ed. B. A. Sanders), ASTM, Philadelphia, PA, pp. 225–50.

Jones, M. L., Smith, G. M. and Welford, J. C. (1970) *Applied Numerical Methods for Digital Computation with Fortran*, International Textbook Company, PA.

Meredith, R. (1954) Relaxation of stress in stretched cellulose fibres. *J. Textile Inst.*, **45**, T438–T461.

Mikhlin, S. G. (1965) *The Problems of the Minimum of a Quadratic Functional*, Holden Day, San Francisco.

Robotonov, Y. N. (1969) *Creep Problems in Structural Members*, North-Holland, London, pp. 178–215.

FURTHER READING

Abadie, J. (ed.) (1967) *Nonlinear Programming*, North-Holland, Amsterdam.

Bellman, R. and Kalaba, R. (1965) *Quasilinearization and Nonlinear Boundary-value Problems*, Elsevier, London.

Christensen, R. M. (1968) On obtaining solutions in nonlinear viscoelasticity. *J. Appl. Mech.*, **35**, 129–33.

Distéfano, N. and Pister, K. (1970) On modeling and identification in biophysics with application to the rheology of the red cell membrane, in Proc. 23rd Annu. Conf. on Engineering in Medicine and Biology, p. 110.

Hadley, D. W. and Ward, I. M. (1965) Non-linear creep and recovery behaviour of polypropylene fibres. *J. Mech. Phys. Solids*, **13**, 397.

Hopkins, I. L. and Hamming, R. W. (1957) On creep and relaxation. *J. Appl. Phys.*, **28**(8), 906–9.

Lai, J. S. Y. and Findley, W. H. (1968a) Prediction of uniaxial stress relaxation from creep of nonlinear viscoelastic material. *Trans. Soc. Rheol.*, **12**, 243–57.

Lai, J. S. Y. and Findley, W. N. (1968b) Stress relaxation of nonlinear viscoelastic material under uniaxial strain. *Trans. Soc. Rheol.*, **12**, 259–80.

Lee, E. H. (1955) Stress analysis in viscoelastic bodies. *Q. Appl. Math.*, **13**, 183–90.

Lee, E. H. (1958) Viscoelastic stress analysis, in Proc. 1st Symp. on Naval Structural Mechanics, Pergamon, London, pp. 456–82.

Mitsoulis, E. (1988) A heuristic approach to modeling viscoelasticity in polymer processing, Society of Plastics Engineers Technical Papers, Vol. XXXIV, ANTEC 1988, Atlanta, GA, pp. 140–4.

Numerical analysis in viscoelasticity

Morland, L. W. and Lee, E. H. (1960) Stress analysis for linear viscoelastic materials with temperature variation. *Trans. Soc. Rheol.*, **4**, 233–63.

Pister, K. and Distéfano, N. (1970) On some modelling and identification problems in biomechanics. *J. Biomed. Syst.*, **1**(2), 32–47.

Roesler, F. C. and Twyman, W. A. (1955) An iteration method for the determination of relaxation spectra. *Proc. Phys. Soc. London B*, **68**(2), 97–105.

Schapery, R. A. (1969) On the characterization of nonlinear viscoelastic materials. *Polym. Eng. Sci.*, **9**, 295–310.

Taylor, R. L., Pister, K. and Goureau, G. (1970) Thermomechanical analysis of viscoelastic solids. *Int. J. Numer. Methods Eng.*, **2**, 45–60.

Zakhariev, G., Khadzhikov, L. and Marinov, P. (1971) A rheological model for polymers and glass reinforced plastics. *Polym. Mech.*, **7**, 761–6.

8

Wave propagation

8.1 INTRODUCTION

When a localized disturbance is applied suddenly in a medium, it will soon propagate to other parts of this medium. This simple fact constitutes a general basis for the interesting subject of 'wave propagation'. Well-cited examples of wave propagation in different media include, for instance, the transmission of sound in air, the propagation of seismic disturbances in the earth and the transmission of radio waves. In the particular case when the suddenly applied disturbance is mechanical, e.g. a suddenly applied force, the resulting waves in the medium are due to stress effects and, thus, these waves are referred to as 'stress waves'. Our attention in this chapter is focused on the propagation of stress waves in viscoelastic solid media. In our representation, we consider the solid medium to be a continuum. Hence, the mechanics of wave motion in the medium will be dealt with from a continuous mechanics point of view. The basic concepts of continuum mechanics have been presented in Chapter 1. In such a continuum, the solid medium, the disturbance is generally considered to spread outward in a three-dimensional sense (Graff, 1975). A wavefront is considered to be associated with the outwardly propagating disturbance. Consequently, particles of the medium that are located ahead of the wavefront are assumed to have experienced no motion; meantime, particles that are located behind the front are visualized to have experienced motion and may continue to vibrate for some time.

For a continuum solid, two distinct effects due to a disturbance input may be generally encountered:

1. the solid may transit tensile and compressive stresses and the motion of particles would be generally in the direction of the wave motion;
2. in addition, the solid may transit shear stress, and thus the motion of the particles would be in a direction transverse to the direction of wave motion.

During their motion, waves propagating in a solid may encounter or interact with boundaries of the medium. On striking a boundary, part or whole of an incident wave may be reflected and the mode of propagation of the wave may change.

Although, in this chapter, our main interest is to study the propagation of stress waves in viscoelastic materials, we devote the next section to the consideration of the

motion of elastic waves. This assists as an introductory step to the subject of viscoelastic waves with which we deal in the remainder of the chapter. The comparison
between the strain responses to a pulse of constant stress input, of a specific time
duration, applied to initially undisturbed elastic and viscoelastic material specimens
has been discussed briefly in the introduction to linear viscoelasticity in Chapter 2.

In recent years, there has been considerable interest in the subject of wave
propagation from both theoretical and experimental points of view. Such interest
was motivated primarily by the advancement in testing and measurement techniques.
With the recent progress in fields such as electronics and laser optics (e.g. holographic
interferometry), stress waves of high frequency can be now produced and detected
easily. This has been particularly pronounced in important domains of nondestructive
testing such as ultrasonics and acoustic emission. The combination of these two
techniques has led further to the newly developed acousto-ultrasonic technique as a
modern nondestructive tool for the evaluation and prediction of the mechanical
properties of engineering materials (Vary, 1988; Tanary and Haddad, 1988). Another
equally important cause for the ensuing interest in the subject of wave propagation
is the continuous emerging of newly developed industrial materials such as plastics
and polymeric composite material systems. In this, the study of the phenomenon of
wave motion has been able to identify microstructural problems and to assist in the
development of homogeneous and inhomogeneous material systems. Further, any
new development within the realm of smart materials and structures (Rogers, Barker
and Jaeger, 1988; Tanagi, 1990; Srinivasan and Haddad, 1992) is expected to depend
on the ability to employ wave propagation as a successful detecting mechanism for
a feedback concerning the status of such materials.

For a historical background of the subject of wave propagation, the reader is
referred to Kolsky (1963), Graff (1975) and others. For a review of the common
methods for producing and detecting stress waves in solids, reference is made, for
instance, to the books by Hetenyi (1950), Dove and Adams (1964), Dally and Riley
(1965), Keast (1967), and Magrab and Blomquist (1971). Comprehensive review
articles in this area are due to Hillier (1960), Kolsky (1958, 1960), Worely (1962)
and others. Experimental studies of the dynamic stress–strain relations of materials
under the conditions of shock loading have become significantly important in recent
years. The increased interest in the subject matter has been motivated by the
increasing number of applications and, as well, by the contributions provided by such
studies to a better understanding of the mechanisms of deformation of engineering
materials (for example, Barker and Hollenbach, 1964, 1970 and Frederick, 1965).

8.2 WAVE PROPAGATION IN ELASTIC SOLIDS

8.2.1 Wave propagation in unbounded elastic solids

An unbounded solid is considered to extend indefinitely in the three dimensions of
space so that the complications which might arise from reflections of waves at the
boundaries of the medium might be disregarded.

The equations of motion of a continuum have been derived in Chapter 1 (section 1.3). These equations (1.22) were presented in terms of the stress components acting on a small parallelepiped of the continuum without the inclusion of the response behaviour of the medium. However, in order to employ these equations in the study of wave propagation, one may substitute the stress components by the corresponding components of strain through the use of the constitutive relationships of the particular medium under consideration.

For an isotropic elastic solid, the stress–strain relations can be expressed (e.g. Sokolnikoff, 1956) in component form as

$$\sigma_{11} = \lambda\Delta + 2\mu\varepsilon_{11}, \quad \sigma_{22} = \lambda\Delta + 2\mu\varepsilon_{22}, \quad \varepsilon_{33} = \lambda\Delta + 2\mu\varepsilon_{33},$$

$$\sigma_{23} = \mu\varepsilon_{23}, \quad \sigma_{31} = \mu\varepsilon_{31}, \quad \sigma_{12} = \mu\varepsilon_{12}. \tag{8.1}$$

In the above relations, $\Delta = \varepsilon_{kk} = \varepsilon_{11} + \varepsilon_{22} + \varepsilon_{33}$ is the dilatation which represents the change in volume of unit cube of the solid and λ and μ are Lamé's elastic constants. In the theory of elasticity, four elastic (material) constants are usually used. These are Young's modulus E, Poisson's ratio v, the bulk modulus K and the rigidity (shear) modulus which is Lamé's constant μ. From the definitions of these constants and using equations (8.1) the following relations between the constants, in the case of an isotropic elastic solid, can be determined:

$$E = \frac{\mu(3\lambda + 2\mu)}{\lambda + \mu}, \quad v = \frac{\lambda}{2(\lambda + \mu)}, \quad K = \lambda + \frac{2\mu}{3}. \tag{8.2}$$

Substituting from the constitutive relations (8.1) for the stress components in the equations of motion (1.22), the equation of motion for an isotropic elastic solid, in the absence of body forces, can be written in the x_1 direction in terms of the strain as

$$\rho \frac{\partial^2 u_1}{\partial t^2} = \frac{\partial}{\partial x_1}(\lambda\Delta + 2\mu\varepsilon_{11}) + \frac{\partial}{\partial x_2}(\mu\varepsilon_{12}) + \frac{\partial}{\partial x_3}(\mu\varepsilon_{13}) \tag{8.3}$$

where u_1 is the displacement component in the x_1 direction. Replacing the strain components in (8.3) by the corresponding displacement components from (1.73), it follows that

$$\rho \frac{\partial^2 u_1}{\partial t^2} = (\lambda + \mu) \frac{\partial\Delta}{\partial x_1} + \mu \nabla^2 u_1. \tag{8.4a}$$

∇^2 is Laplace's operator defined by

$$\nabla^2 = \frac{\partial^2}{\partial x_1^2} + \frac{\partial^2}{\partial x_2^2} + \frac{\partial^2}{\partial x_3^2}.$$

Similar relations to (8.4a) can be established for the other two components of the displacement vector, namely

$$\rho \frac{\partial^2 u_2}{\partial t^2} = (\lambda + \mu) \frac{\partial\Delta}{\partial x_2} + \mu \nabla^2 u_2 \tag{8.4b}$$

and

$$\rho \frac{\partial^2 u_3}{\partial t^2} = (\lambda + \mu) \frac{\partial \Delta}{\partial x_3} + \mu \nabla^2 u_3. \qquad (8.4c)$$

Equations (8.4) are the equations of motion, in terms of the displacement, for an isotropic elastic solid in the absence of body forces. These equations may be expressed conveniently in a vector form as

$$\rho \frac{\partial^2 u_2}{\partial t^2} = (\lambda + \mu) \nabla \nabla \cdot \mathbf{u} + \mu \nabla^2 \mathbf{u} \qquad (8.5)$$

which is the form of the well-known Navier equation of motion. The latter is conveniently adopted as the governing equation for the motion of an isotropic, elastic solid. Equation (8.5) corresponds to the propagation of two types of waves through an unbounded isotropic, elastic solid, namely 'dilatational' and 'rotational' waves.

Differentiating (8.4a) with respect to x_1, (8.4b) with respect to x_2 and (8.4c) with respect to x_3 and adding the resulting derivations, one obtains the following 'wave equation' for an unbounded isotropic, elastic medium:

$$\rho \frac{\partial^2 \Delta}{\partial t^2} = (\lambda + 2\mu) \nabla^2 \Delta \qquad (8.6)$$

The above wave equation indicates that the dilatation Δ propagates through the medium with a velocity of magnitude $[(\lambda + 2\mu)/\rho]^{1/2}$. Denoting the latter by c_1, then $c_1 = [(\lambda + 2\mu)/\rho]^{1/2}$.

In view of equations (8.2), the magnitude of the dilatational wave velocity c_1 may be expressed further by

$$c_1 = \left[\frac{(\lambda + 2\mu)}{\rho} \right]^{1/2} = \left[\frac{E(1 - v)}{\rho(1 + v)(1 - 2v)} \right]^{1/2} = \left[\frac{K + 4\mu/3}{\rho} \right]^{1/2}. \qquad (8.7)$$

It is noticed from (8.7) that the velocity c_1 is dependent only on the elastic constants as well as the density of the elastic material. In an operational form, the wave equation (8.6) can be written as

$$\Gamma_1^2 \Delta = 0 \qquad (8.8)$$

where Γ_1^2 is a dilatational wave operator expressed by (Chou, 1968)

$$\Gamma_1^2 = \nabla^2 - \frac{1}{c_1^2} \frac{\partial^2}{\partial t^2} \qquad (8.9)$$

and $\Delta = \nabla \cdot \mathbf{u}$ is the dilatation.

A 'dilatational' wave, corresponding to the wave equation (8.8), is also referred to as 'irrotational' since the propagation of such a wave involves no rotation of an elemental volume of the solid. A dilatational wave is also known as a 'bulk wave' or 'primary (P) wave'.

On the other hand, if we eliminate the dilatation Δ between (8.4b) and (8.4c), that is by differentiating (8.4b) with respect to x_3 and (8.4c) with respect to x_2, and subtracting, then

$$\rho \frac{\partial^2}{\partial t^2}\left(\frac{\partial u_3}{\partial x_2} - \frac{\partial u_2}{\partial x_3}\right) = \mu \nabla^2\left(\frac{\partial u_3}{\partial x_2} - \frac{\partial u_2}{\partial x_3}\right).$$

This equation can be written, in view of (1.69), as

$$\rho \frac{\partial^2 \omega_1}{\partial t^2} = \mu \nabla^2 \omega_1$$

where ω_1 is the rotation about the x_1 axis. Similar relations can be obtained for ω_2 and ω_3 (the rotations about the x_2 and x_3 axes, respectively). Thus, in generalized notation, one can write

$$\rho \frac{\partial^2 \boldsymbol{\omega}}{\partial t^2} = \mu \nabla^2 \boldsymbol{\omega} \tag{8.10}$$

where $\boldsymbol{\omega} = \nabla \times \mathbf{u}/2$ is the rotation vector.

It follows from (8.10) that the rotational wave propagates in an isotropic, elastic solid with a velocity of magnitude $(\mu/\rho)^{1/2}$. We denote the magnitude of the rotational wave velocity by c_2; then

$$c_2 = (\mu/\rho)^{1/2}. \tag{8.11}$$

It is noticed, from the above expression, that the velocity c_2 is dependent only on the elastic constants as well as the density of the elastic material.

Applying the vector operator curl (Appendix A) to (8.5), it can be shown that the vector form of the wave equation (8.10) can be written as

$$\Gamma_2^2 \boldsymbol{\omega} = \mathbf{0} \tag{8.12}$$

where Γ_2^2 is a rotational wave operator of the form (Chou, 1968)

$$\Gamma_2^2 = \nabla^2 - \frac{1}{c_2^2} \frac{\partial^2}{\partial t^2} \tag{8.13}$$

and $\boldsymbol{\omega} = \nabla \times \mathbf{u}$ is the rotation.

A 'rotational' wave is also called an 'equivoluminal' wave since there is no volume change during the propagation of the wave. A rotational wave is also known as a 'distortional' wave or 'secondary (S) wave'.

Equation (8.8), or (8.12), is a necessary, but not a sufficient, condition for the satisfaction of the Navier governing equation of motion (8.5). Thus, for every displacement field that satisfies (8.5), the corresponding Δ and $\boldsymbol{\omega}$ will satisfy (8.8) and (8.12), respectively. On the other hand, a displacement field with a dilatation satisfying (8.8), or a rotation satisfying (8.12), would not be necessarily a solution of the Naviers' governing equation (8.5).

As mentioned previously, the particle motion in a dilatational wave is longitudinal, i.e. along the direction of wave propagation. In case of a rotational wave, the particle motion is transverse, that is perpendicular to the direction of propagation of the wave. Experimentally, one would generally attempt to generate one type of wave with the exclusion of the other. However, it should be emphasized that, in the propagation of dilatational waves in an unbounded solid, the medium would not be simply subjected to pure compression, but to a combination of compression and shear. This is supported by the physical situation and mathematically by the appearance of both the bulk modulus and the shear modulus in the expression of the dilatational velocity (equation (8.7)), as shown for instance in Kolsky (1963) and Tschoegl (1989).

(a) Irrotational and rotational displacement fields

Consider the displacement vector field **u**. In dynamic elasticity, u may be decomposed into an irrotational field, say $\mathbf{u}_{IR}$, associated with a scalar potential ϕ and a rotational field, $\mathbf{u}_R$, associated with a vector potential ψ. Thus, according to the Helmholtz theorem (Morse and Feshbach, 1953), for any displacement field, subject to mild continuity and boundary conditions, one may find at least one set of functions ϕ and ψ such that

$$\mathbf{u} = \nabla\phi + \nabla \times \omega, \quad \nabla \cdot = 0. \tag{8.14}$$

The condition $\nabla \cdot \psi = 0$ is necessary to determine uniquely the three components of the displacement vector u from the four components of ϕ, ψ.

Substituting (8.14) into Navier's equation (8.5) yields

$$c_1^2\nabla\nabla^2\phi + c_2^2\nabla \times (\nabla^2\psi) = (\nabla\phi + \nabla \times \psi)\mathbf{u}. \tag{8.15}$$

Every solution of (8.14), or (8.15), is always a solution of (8.5). Accordingly, equations (8.14) and (8.15) are also governing equations of the induced motion in an isotropic, elastic solid and each constitutes an exact equivalence to (8.5) (Chou, 1968).

A particular class of solutions of (8.15) is

$$\nabla\Gamma_1^2\phi = \mathbf{0}, \quad \nabla \times \Gamma_2^2\psi = \mathbf{0}, \tag{8.16}$$

with a particular solution

$$\Gamma_1^2\phi = 0; \quad \Gamma_2^2\psi = \mathbf{0}. \tag{8.17}$$

This is with the understanding that the class of solutions presented by (8.16) and (8.17) is sufficient, but not necessary, for the satisfaction of (8.5). In equation (8.17), Γ_1^2 and Γ_2^2 are the dilatational and rotational wave operators introduced earlier by equations (8.9) and (8.13), respectively.

(b) An irrotational field

A displacement field, **u**, is referred to as 'irrotational' if

$$\nabla \times \psi = \mathbf{0}, \quad \mathbf{u} = \mathbf{u}_{IR}. \tag{8.18}$$

For an irrotational wave, one has, following equation (8.5)

$$\Gamma_1^2 u_{IR} = 0 \tag{8.19}$$

or, alternatively, according to potential theory,

$$\mathbf{u}_{IR} = \nabla \phi \tag{8.20}$$

where ϕ is a scalar potential function. Equation (8.20) implies that, for an irrotational wave, the rotational vector $\boldsymbol{\omega}$ is equal to zero in magnitude. Following (8.17), then, for an irrotational field

$$\Delta = \nabla^2 \phi \quad \text{and} \quad \frac{\partial \Delta}{\partial x_i} = \nabla^2 u_i \quad (i = 1, 2, 3). \tag{8.21}$$

Accordingly, the scalar potential ϕ is seen to be associated with the dilatational (irrotational) part of the disturbance. Substituting (8.21) into (8.4), one has, for an irrotational field,

$$\rho \frac{\partial^2 u_i}{\partial t^2} = (\lambda + 2\mu) \nabla^2 u_i \quad (i = 1, 2, 3). \tag{8.22}$$

(c) Rotational field

A displacement field, $\mathbf{u}$, is called rotational if

$$\nabla \cdot \mathbf{u} = 0, \quad \mathbf{u} = \mathbf{u}_R. \tag{8.23}$$

For a rotational field, the Navier governing equation (8.5) results in

$$\Gamma_2^2 \mathbf{u} = 0 \tag{8.24}$$

and

$$\boldsymbol{u} = \nabla \times \boldsymbol{\psi}, \tag{8.25}$$

i.e. the vector potential $\boldsymbol{\psi}$ is associated with the rotational part of the disturbance.

The above conditions for a rotational wave translate into, in this case, the dilatation $\Delta = 0$. Hence, the set of equations (8.4) reduces, for a rotational wave, to

$$\rho \frac{\partial^2 u_i}{\partial t^2} = \mu \nabla^2 u_i \quad (i = 1, 2, 3). \tag{8.26}$$

Combining equations (8.14), (8.20) and (8.25), it follows that, in an isotropic, elastic solid, a displacement field $\mathbf{u}$ is decomposed vectorially into an irrotational field $\mathbf{u}_{IR}$ and a rotational one $\mathbf{u}_R$. That is,

$$\boldsymbol{u} = \boldsymbol{u}_{IR} + \boldsymbol{u}_R. \tag{8.27}$$

Further, in view of (8.17), (8.20) and (8.25), it may be concluded that, for every displacement field that satisfies (8.5), there exists a set of functions $\mathbf{u}_{IR}$ and $\mathbf{u}_R$ such that (equations (8.19) and (8.24))

$$\Gamma_1^2 \mathbf{u}_{IR} = 0 \quad \text{and} \quad \Gamma_2^2 \mathbf{u}_R = 0. \tag{8.28}$$

This translates, physically, into the following.

A disturbance in an isotropic, elastic solid would generate two waves, one dilatational, involving no rotation, with velocity c_1 and the other is rotational, involving no volume changes, that propagates at velocity c_2. The ratio of the two speeds may be expressed, with reference to (8.7) and (8.11), as

$$\frac{c_1}{c_2} = \frac{2 - 2v}{1 - 2v}$$

Since $0 \le v \le 1$, then $c_1 > c_2$.

In view of (8.28), these two waves are not coupled within the continuous solid (except perhaps on the boundary where the prescribed boundary conditions must be satisfied).

Table 8.1 summarizes the relationships given in the foregoing, in terms of displacements, while Table 8.2 gives such relationships in terms of potentials. Chou (1968) should also be referred to.

8.2.2 Plane waves in unbounded elastic media

Plane waves are propagating disturbances in two or three dimensions where the motion of every particle in planes perpendicular to the direction of propagation is the same. An example of a propagating (three-dimensional) plane disturbance is given in Fig. 8.1. As shown in the figure, the magnitude of the propagation velocity of the plane is denoted by c while the normal to the plane is designated by $\mathbf{n}$. The position of an arbitrary point P on the plane is indicated by $\mathbf{r}$.

For the plane wave illustrated in Fig. 8.1, the motion of every particle along the plane is defined by

$$\mathbf{u} \cdot \mathbf{r} - ct = \text{constant}. \tag{8.29}$$

Consider now the plane wave

$$\mathbf{u} = \mathbf{A} f(\mathbf{n} \cdot \mathbf{r} - ct) \tag{8.30}$$

where $\mathbf{A}$ is the displacement vector of the particle along the plane of the wave and $f(\cdot)$ indicates an appropriate function of the shown argument. Substituting (8.30) in Navier's governing equation of motion (8.5), it can be shown that

$$(\lambda + \mu)A_j n_j n_i + \mu A_i = \rho c^2 A_i. \tag{8.31}$$

Relation (8.31) represents three homogeneous equations in the amplitude components A_1, A_2, A_3. This leads, on expanding the determinant of coefficients, to

$$(\lambda + 2\mu - \rho c^2)(\mu - \rho c^2)^2 = 0. \tag{8.32}$$

Table 8.1 Wave propagation in an isotropic, elastic (unbounded) solid: Pertaining relations in terms of displacement

---

Displacement field **u**

General governing equation: Navier's

$$\rho \frac{\partial^2 \mathbf{u}}{\partial t^2} = \mu \nabla^2 \mathbf{u} + (\lambda + \mu)\, \nabla \nabla \cdot \mathbf{u}$$

Two propagating waves

Dilatational (irrotational), $(\mathbf{u}_{IR},\, c_1)$

Rotational (distortional), $(\mathbf{u}_R,\, c_2)$

Necessary and sufficient relations for the satisfaction of Navier's governing equation (above)

$$\mathbf{u} = \mathbf{u}_{IR} + \mathbf{u}_R$$

$$\left(\nabla^2 - \frac{1}{c_1^2} \frac{1}{\partial t^2} \right) \mathbf{u}_{IR} = \mathbf{0}$$

$$\left(\nabla^2 - \frac{1}{c_2^2} \frac{1}{\partial t^2} \right) \mathbf{u}_R = \mathbf{0}$$

Necessary but not sufficient relations for the satisfaction of Navier's governing equation

Dilatation Δ:

$$\Delta = \nabla \cdot \mathbf{u}; \quad \left(\nabla^2 - \frac{1}{c_1^2} \frac{\partial^2}{\partial t^2} \right) \Delta = \mathbf{0}$$

Rotation $\boldsymbol{\omega}$:

$$\boldsymbol{\omega} = \nabla \times \mathbf{u}; \quad \left(\nabla^2 - \frac{1}{c_2^2} \frac{\partial^2}{\partial t^2} \right) \boldsymbol{\omega} = \mathbf{0}$$

Sufficient but not necessary relations for the satisfaction of Navier's governing equation

Dilatational (irrotational)

$$\nabla \times \mathbf{u} = \mathbf{0}; \quad \left(\nabla^2 - \frac{1}{c_1^2} \frac{\partial^2}{\partial t^2} \right) \mathbf{u} = \mathbf{0}$$

Rotational (distortional)

$$\nabla \cdot \mathbf{u} = \mathbf{0}; \quad \left(\nabla^2 - \frac{1}{c_2^2} \frac{\partial^2}{\partial t^2} \right) \mathbf{u} = \mathbf{0}$$

where

$$c_1^2 = \frac{\lambda + 2\mu}{\rho} = \frac{E(1-v)}{\rho(1+v)(1-2v)} = \frac{K + \frac{4}{3}\mu}{\rho}$$

$$c_2^2 = \mu/\rho$$

Table 8.2 Wave propagation in an isotropic, elastic (unbounded) solid: Relationships between Navier's equation and other related governing equations in terms of potential

General governing equation: Navier's

$$\rho \frac{\partial^2 \mathbf{u}}{\partial t^2} = \mu \, \nabla^2 \mathbf{u} + (\lambda + \mu) \, \nabla\nabla \cdot \mathbf{u}$$

Displacement field $\mathbf{u}(\phi, \, \boldsymbol{\psi})$

Necessary and sufficient relations for the satisfaction of Navier's governing equation (above)

$$\mathbf{u} = \nabla\phi + \nabla \times \boldsymbol{\psi}; \; \nabla \cdot \boldsymbol{\psi} = 0$$

$$\nabla\left(\nabla^2 - \frac{1}{c_1^2}\frac{\partial^2}{\partial t^2}\right)\phi + \nabla \times \left(\nabla^2 - \frac{1}{c_2^2}\frac{\partial^2}{\partial t^2}\right)\boldsymbol{\psi} = \mathbf{0}$$

$$\left(\nabla^2 - \frac{1}{c_1^2}\frac{\partial^2}{\partial t^2}\right)\phi = 0; \left(\nabla^2 - \frac{1}{c_2^2}\frac{\partial^2}{\partial t^2}\right)\boldsymbol{\psi} = \mathbf{0}$$

Necessary but not sufficient relations for the satisfaction of Navier's governing equation

$$\left(\nabla^2 - \frac{1}{c_1^2}\frac{\partial^2}{\partial t^2}\right)\nabla^2\phi = 0$$

$$\left(\nabla^2 - \frac{1}{c_2^2}\frac{\partial^2}{\partial t^2}\right)\nabla^2\boldsymbol{\psi} = \mathbf{0}$$

where

$$c_1^2 = \frac{\lambda + 2\mu}{\rho} = \frac{E(1 - v)}{\rho(1 + v)(1 - 2v)} = \frac{K + \frac{4}{3}\mu}{\rho}$$

$$c_2^2 = \mu/\rho$$

This equation gives the two roots

$$c_1 = \left(\frac{\lambda + 2\mu}{\rho}\right)^{1/2}$$

and   (8.33)

$$c_2 = (\mu/\rho)^{1/2}$$

which again are, respectively, the magnitudes of the velocities of dilatational and rotational waves. Accordingly, plane waves may propagate at one or the other velocity (i.e. c_1 or c_2) in the isotropic, elastic medium.

8.2.3 Wave propagation in semi-infinite elastic media

When a stress wave encounters a boundary between two media, energy is reflected and transmitted from and across the boundary. On the other hand, if the boundary

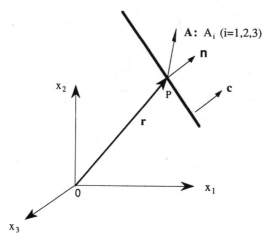

Fig. 8.1 Plane wave motion in an unbounded, elastic medium.

is a free surface, reflection of the waves will be much more pronounced. It is well recognized that a characteristic phenomenon of the elastic wave–boundary interaction in solids is that of mode coonversion. In this, an incident wave, either pressure or shear, on the boundary will be converted into two waves on reflection. Such a mode-conversion phenomenon along with the fact that two types of waves may exist in an elastic solid, as discussed earlier, accounts for the relative complexity of wave propagation in solids in general as compared with equivalent problems in acoustics and electromagnetics (e.g. Graff, 1975).

(a) Governing equations

With reference to Fig. 8.2, we consider, following Graff (1975), plane harmonic waves propagating in the half-space $x_2 \geq 0$. It is assumed that the wave normal n lies in the $x_1 x_2$ plane. This plane will be referred to as the vertical plane while the $x_1 x_3$ plane, the surface of the half-space, will be referred to as the horizontal plane. Recalling the previous discussion concerning the propagation of plane waves in infinite media (section 8.2.2), it is recognized that the particle motion due to dilatation will be in the direction of the wave normal and will, thus, be in the vertical plane only. The transverse particle motion, however, is due to shear and will have components both in the vertical plane and parallel to the horizontal plane. In Fig. 8.2, the normal displacement component is designated by u_n and the transverse components are denoted by u_v and u_3 which are, respectively, in the vertical and horizontal planes. As every particle along the plane of the wave is acquiring the same motion, the motion will be invariant with respect to x_3 if the wave normal is in the vertical plane. In terms of the potentials ϕ and ψ, the governing equations

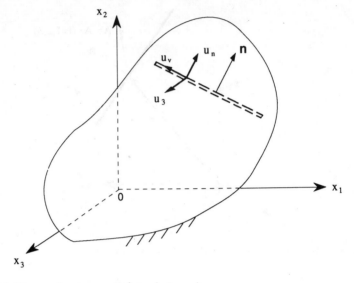

Fig. 8.2 Wave motion in a semi-infinite elastic medium.

can be expressed as

$$u_1 = \frac{\partial \phi}{\partial x_1} + \frac{\partial \psi_3}{\partial x_2},$$

$$u_2 = \frac{\partial \phi}{\partial x_2} - \frac{\partial \psi_3}{\partial x_1},$$

$$u_3 = -\frac{\partial \psi_1}{\partial x_2} + \frac{\partial \psi_2}{\partial x_1},$$

$$\frac{\partial \psi_1}{\partial x_1} + \frac{\partial \psi_2}{\partial x_2} = 0$$

and   (8.34)

$$\nabla^2 \phi = \frac{1}{c_1^2} \frac{\partial^2 \phi}{\partial t^2}, \quad \nabla^2 \psi_i = \frac{1}{c_2^2} \frac{\partial^2 \psi_i}{\partial t^2}$$

where ψ_i ($i = 1, 2, 3$) are the components of the vector function $\boldsymbol{\psi}$. In deriving the above governing equations both the postulate $\boldsymbol{\nabla} \cdot \boldsymbol{\psi} = 0$ and the x_3 independence of all quantities have been used.

Combining the displacement expressions in (8.34) with the stress–displacement constitutive relations for the isotropic elastic solid, the stress components can be established in terms of the potentials ϕ and ψ, i.e.

$$\sigma_{11} = (\lambda + 2\mu)\left(\frac{\partial^2\phi}{\partial x_1^2} + \frac{\partial^2\phi}{\partial x_2^2}\right) - 2\mu\left(\frac{\partial^2\phi}{\partial x_2^2} - \frac{\partial^2\psi_3}{\partial x_1\,\partial x_2}\right),$$

$$\sigma_{22} = (\lambda + 2\mu)\left(\frac{\partial^2\phi}{\partial x_1^2} + \frac{\partial^2\phi}{\partial x_2^2}\right) - 2\mu\left(\frac{\partial^2\phi}{\partial x_1^2} + \frac{\partial^2\psi_3}{\partial x_1\,\partial x_2}\right)$$

$$\sigma_{12} = \mu\left(2\frac{\partial^2\phi}{\partial x_1 \partial x_2} + \frac{\partial^2\psi_3}{\partial x_2^2} - \frac{\partial^2\psi_3}{\partial x_1^2}\right), \tag{8.35}$$

$$\sigma_{23} = \mu\left(-\frac{\partial^2\psi_1}{\partial x_2^2} + \frac{\partial^2\psi_2}{\partial x_1\,\partial x_2}\right) \quad \text{and} \quad \sigma_{13} = 0$$

with boundary conditions

$$\sigma_{22} = \sigma_{21} = \sigma_{23} = 0, \quad x_2 = 0. \tag{8.36}$$

Experimental studies on wave propagation in semi-infinite media may vary considerably in scope. Ultrasonic excitation is often used as an impulsive surface force; meantime, photoelasticity has been conventionally adopted as a recording technique for the patterns of wave motion in elastic materials. Dally, Durelli and Riley (1960), for instance, used small explosive charges of lead azide (PbN_6) to load dynamically a low-modulus urethane rubber plate and the dynamic fringe propagation patterns were recorded by a high-speed camera (Dally, 1968 and Graff, 1975). Dally and Riley (1967) used an embedded polariscope technique to study experimentally the three-dimensional problem of a point load on a half-space using a photo-elastic method (e.g. Pindera, 1986). Riley and Dally (1966) considered the application of the photoelastic recording technique to study the wave motion in layered media.

(b) Surface waves

When the solid has a free surface, 'Rayleigh' surface waves can also exist. These waves were first introduced by Rayleigh (1887) (Lamb (1904) should also be referred to) who showed that their effect decays rapidly with depth and that their velocity is less than that of body waves c_1 and c_2. It is shown by Kolsky (1963) that Rayleigh waves do, in fact, travel with a fraction ξ of the velocity c_2 of distortional waves where ξ is obtained from the equation

$$\xi^6 - 8\xi^4 + (24 - 16b^2)\xi^2 + 16b^2 - 16 = 0. \tag{8.37}$$

In the above equation, b is an elastic constant of the material expressed by

$$b = [(1 - 2v)/(2 - 2v)]^{1/2} \tag{8.38}$$

where v is Poisson's ratio.

In Rayleigh waves, the particle motion is parallel to the direction of wave propagation and it is in a plane perpendicular to the surface containing the waves during travel.

In case of an elastic solid, the velocity of a surface wave is independent of the frequency and depends, similarly to the body waves, on the elastic constants of the material. In other words, there is no dispersion (change of form) of these waves, i.e. a plane surface wave will travel without change in form.

When a dilatational wave is incident on a free surface with an angle α (Fig. 8.3(a)), two waves are generated on reflection: one is a dilatational wave reflected at an angle equal to the angle of incidence α, while the other is a distortional wave reflected at a smaller angle β where $\sin \beta / \sin \alpha = c_2/c_1$.

Similarly, if a distortional wave is incident on a free surface at an angle γ (Fig. 8.3(b)), both distortional and dilatational waves are generally reflected. The distortional wave is reflected at the same angle γ while the dilatational wave is reflected at a generally smaller angle δ where $\sin \gamma / \sin \delta = c_2/c_1$.

Tatel (1954) used a 'model seismogram' approach to study surface wave motion on a half-space. In this, Tatel induced a point impulse on the surface of a large block of steel using a piezo-electric transducer. The vertical components of displacement were detected by a receiving transducer a few centimetres away. Dally and Thau (1967) considered the application of the photoelastic technique to study surface wave propagation (Thau and Dally (1969) should also be referred to). Viktorov (1967) reported a number of studies, using ultrasonics, on the effects of surface defects on Rayleigh waves. Other work in this area is, for instance, due to Goodier, Jahsman

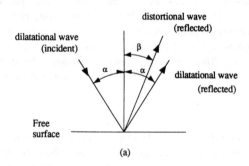

(a)

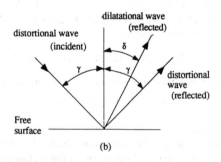

(b)

Fig. 8.3 Reflection of (a) dilatational and (b) distortional waves.

and Ripperger (1959), Dally and Lewis (1968) and Reinhardt and Dally (1970), amongst others.

8.2.4 Wave propagation in bounded elastic solids

A typical representation of a bounded medium is a material specimen of finite dimensions. In the study of the wave propagation in bounded solids, the geometry of the material specimen would be kept simple such that the complex end effects that could be caused by the boundaries are minimized. In rods, a thin rod of uniform circular cross-section is often taken as a simple representation of a bounded medium. In this case, the disturbance would be applied at one end of the rod and propagate along its length whereby the ratio between the dimension of the transverse direction (the radius) and the wave length becomes an important factor in the mode of travel of the propagating wave. The wave equations for rods and plates infinite in length have been known for a long period of time. Chree (1889), among others, developed the results for elastic rods and Rayleigh (1887) and Lamb (1917) established the wave equations for elastic plates. Davies (1948) studied the propagation characteristics of a transient disturbance in rods. Considerable research efforts have been undertaken subsequently whereby particular attention has been given to the determination of the frequency spectra, analysis of transient disturbances and applications concerning wave propagation in plates, rods and shells.

Stress wave propagation in thin rods and bars are conventionally classified in three categories, namely longitudinal, torsional and lateral.

In a **longitudinal** wave, the disturbance may be in the form of a uniaxial force or displacement applied in the direction of the longitudinal axis of the rod. In this case, segments of the rod undergo extension and compression without rotation and with no lateral displacement of the axis of the rod.

If the wavelength is long compared with the lateral dimensions of the rod, longitudinal waves travel with constant velocity given by

$$c_1 = (E/\rho)^{1/2} \tag{8.39}$$

where E is Young's modulus.

When the wavelength is comparable with the lateral dimensions of the rod, the velocity of the longitudinal waves would depend on the wavelength and may approach the velocity of Rayleigh surface waves at very short wavelengths.

A large number of experimental studies on the propagation of longitudinal waves in rods are directed towards the determination of material properties of the rod. In case of elastic solids, the method of mechanical impact is considered to be the most conventional testing method. It is carried out by impacting one solid against the other (Barton, Volterra and Citron, 1958; Ripperger, 1953). Goldsmith, Polivka and Yang (1966), for instance, considered pulse propagation in concrete rods with the aim of evaluating the effects of an inhomogeneous microstructure on wave propagation. Other work of interest on longitudinal waves in elastic rods includes that of Fisher (1954), Becker and Carl (1962) and Lindholm (1964) among others.

The early developments in the subject of wave propagation in plates are due to Rayleigh (1887) and Lamb (1917). The Rayleigh–lamb work is concerned with the propagation of continuous, straight crested waves in plates infinite in length and have traction-free surfaces.

In the case of stress wave propagation in plates and when the wavelength is long compared with the thickness of the plate, the magnitude of the velocity of propagation of a plane longitudinal wave is constant. It is given by

$$c_L = \left[\frac{4\mu(\lambda + \mu)}{(\lambda + 2\mu)\rho}\right]^{1/2} = \left[\frac{E}{\rho(1 - v^2)}\right]^{1/2} \tag{8.40}$$

On the other hand, if the wavelength is short compared with the thickness of the plate, plane longitudinal waves would travel with the velocity of Rayleigh surface waves. Experimental studies of the propagation of elastic waves in plates were carried out, for instance, by Dohrenwend, Drucker and Moore (1944), Press and Oliver (1955) and Medick (1961), among others.

In the case of **torsional** waves, the disturbance may be in the form of a torque or an angular displacement applied at the end of the rod. Here, each transverse section of the rod would rotate in its plane while the axis of the rod encounters no motion.

If the wavelength is long compared with the lateral dimensions of the rod, torsional waves would travel with constant velocity. Its magnitude is given by the following relation for a rod of circular cross-section:

$$c_t = (\mu/\rho)^{1/2} \tag{8.41}$$

where μ is the shear modulus. In view of the definition of the torsional wave propagation mentioned above, it is frequently assumed that such motion is independent of the wavelength.

In **lateral** 'flexural' wave propagation, flexure of portions of the rod occurs whereby segments of the central axis move laterally during wave propagation. In this motion, the velocity of wave propagation depends on the wavelength. For very long wavelengths, the velocity magnitude is given by

$$c_f = 2\pi c_1 k / \Lambda \tag{8.42}$$

where $c_1 = (E/\rho)^{1/2}$ (equation (8.39)), k is the radius of gyration of a cross-section of the rod about its neutral axis and Λ is the wavelength.

The velocity c_f of a flexural wave could also approach that of a Rayleigh surface wave when the wavelength becomes small in comparison with the lateral dimensions of the rod.

In the treatment of propagation of elastic disturbances along a cylindrical bar, it is often assumed in the literature that dispersion will occur only during the travel of flexural pulses, whilst longitudinal and torsional pulses will propagate along the bar without dispersion.

For a review of the phenomenon of wave motion in elastic solids and discussion of problems involved, the reader is further referred to Timoshenko (1921), Prescott

(1942), Hudson (1943), Davies (1948), Kolsky (1954a, b, 1963), Evans *et al.* (1954), Oliver (1957), Hsieh and Kolsky (1958), Graff (1975) and others.

8.3 TRANSITION TO WAVE MOTION IN VISCOELASTIC MATERIALS

8.3.1 Internal friction and dissipation

Real materials are never perfectly elastic. Thus, when a material specimen is subjected to dynamic loading, part of its mechanical energy is converted into heat. The various microstructural mechanisms by which the mechanical energy is converted into heat are conventionally referred to as 'internal friction' (Kolsky, 1963). Because of the complexity of the microstructure, several microscopic and macroscopic dissipative mechanisms exist in the material. The extent of energy loss would generally depend on the input load characteristics and the environmental conditions, as well as the inherent and macroscopic properties of the material specimen.

An internal dissipative mechanism in the case of polycrystalline solids, for instance, is due to the variation in crystallographic orientation of neighbouring grains. This results in nonuniformity of the distribution of local strains when the material specimen is loaded. This is in addition to the nonuniformity of local strains that may be caused by imperfections in the material (e.g. microcracks, fissures, flaws, foreign inclusions and grain boundaries). Consequently, a nonuniform temperature field may exist and thermal currents of varying magnitudes would flow within the crystal lattice. Other microscopic mechanisms could be also responsible for the transfer of energy into heat. One mechanism is due to dislocations, that is the movement of regions of disarray in the crystals (e.g. Orowan, 1934; Polanyi, 1934; Bradfield, 1951). An additional microscopic mechanism is due to the motion of solute atoms in the crystal lattice on the application of external loading (e.g. Gorsky, 1936; Snoek, 1941). A possible microscopic mechanism which attenuates stress waves in polycrystalline solids is 'scattering' (e.g. Kolsky, 1963). This mechanism may occur in a polycrystalline solid when the incident wavelength becomes comparable with the grain size. In this, Mason and McSkimin (1947), for instance, found that when the wavelength is long compared with the grain size, the attenuation is inversely proportional to fourth power of the wavelength (see Rayleigh, 1894).

On the macroscopic level, the following effects of internal friction are particularly important.

(a) Static hysteresis

This is primarily due to the anelastic characteristics of the material. In this case, when a material specimen is taken through a stress cycle, it would show a 'hysteresis loop', that is the stress–strain curve for an increasing stress input does not retrace its earlier downward path, if the material specimen is reloaded in an exact manner reflecting the unloading. The area enclosed by this loop represents mechanical energy which has been dissipated into heat. Although this effect may seem to be insignificant for some materials under static loading, it could be a pronounced factor in the attenuation of stress waves travelling in such materials. In the latter case, each layer of the material is taken through a loading cycle. For sinusoidal oscillations, for example, the number of hysteresis cycles is dependent on the frequency and the latter may be of the order of millions per second.

(b) Viscous loss

Such a loss is particularly noticeable in case of polymers with organic long-chain molecules. The internal forces here are of a viscous nature and imply that the mechanical behaviour of such materials is a function of the rate of strain (e.g. Tobolosky, Powell and Eyring, 1943; Alfrey, 1948; Kolsky, 1963). In the case of viscoelastic materials, it is recognized that stress waves whose periods are close to the relaxation times of the material are severely attenuated when passing through it (Kolsky, 1963). In metallic materials, however, the dissipative mechanism tends to be more related to their macroscopic thermal properties (Zener, 1948).

(c) Stress wave motion effect

In this, the compression and dilatation due to the stress wave motion in the material produces temperature gradients. Thus, the finite thermal conductivity of the solid would be an influential mechanism by which the mechanical energy of waves may dissipate as thermal energy.

8.3.2 Evaluation of internal friction

Internal friction in solids is often defined by the so-called 'specific loss' or, alternatively, 'specific damping' of the specimen. It is denoted by the symbol D and is conventionally expressed by

$$D = \frac{\Delta W}{W}. \qquad (8.43)$$

In the above relation, ΔW is the energy dissipated on subjecting the specimen to a stress cycle and W is the elastic energy stored in the specimen during this cycle (Chapter 3). The magnitude of D depends on the amplitude and the speed of the cycle and other boundary conditions, as well as the past history of the specimen. The reader is referred to Kolsky (1963) for other definitions of internal friction and its measurement.

Mechanical dissipation is particularly pronounced in the case of viscoelastic materials, particularly those of high polymeric origin. In most of these materials, the presence of mechanical dissipation can effectively change the nature of wave motion in them. In addition to the significant mechanical dissipation that can occur in viscoelastic materials, it is well recognized that these materials are 'dispersive'. In view of the latter property, phase velocity of a wave propagating in a viscoelastic material will depend on wave frequency. More specifically, waves of high frequency will propagate in viscoelastic materials with a greater phase velocity than if these waves have a low frequency. Consequently, a mechanical disturbance would continually change in shape during its motion in a viscoelastic medium. Further, the attenuation of high-frequency waves in viscoelastic materials is greater than that of waves of low frequency. In the case of sinusoidal waves, for instance, the above two characteristics of wave motion in a viscoelastic medium would translate into a differential absorption as well as a differential dispersion of the Fourier components of the pulse (Kolsky, 1963).

8.4 VISCOELASTIC WAVE MOTION

As realized in section 8.2, the constitutive equation for a particular material must be combined with the equations of motion in order to solve a specific problem concerning the wave propagation in such material. In contrast to the situation in linear elasticity, the viscoelastic constitutive equation, even in the linear case, is complex by virtue of the existence of integrodifferential terms in this equation and the time dependency of the viscoelastic material functions involved. This added complexity has limited quite significantly the progress in dynamic viscoelasticity in general. Consequently, the majority of problems that have been successfully treated concerning viscoelastic wave phenomena have been limited to simple material representation. A large number of viscoelastic wave propagation problems, within the linear response behaviour of the material, have been attempted by different researchers using a correspondence with an available or deductible solution of an analogous linear elastic problem.

Kolsky (1956, 1960) presented a comprehensive review of the subject of viscoelastic waves in solids from both theoretical and experimental points of view. In his treatment of the subject matter, Kolsky employed the superposition property of solutions in linear viscoelasticity through the application of Fourier analysis. Kolsky (1960) considered, for instance, the motion of a longitudinal disturbance along a thin filament. In this context, the equation of motion along the filament is expressed by

$$\frac{\partial \sigma}{\mathrm{d}x} = \rho\left(\frac{\partial^2 u}{\mathrm{d}t^2}\right) \tag{8.44}$$

where σ is the longitudinal stress, x is the distance along the filament, u is the longitudinal displacement and ρ is the density. For a sinusoidal wave propagating in a linear viscoelastic solid, the stress is related to the strain through a complex modulus representation (Chapter 3):

$$\sigma = (E_1 + iE_2)\varepsilon = (E_1 + iE_2)\frac{\partial u}{\partial x}. \tag{8.45}$$

Combining (8.44) and (8.45), then

$$(E_1 + iE_2) \frac{\partial^2 u}{\partial x^2} = \rho \frac{\partial^2 u}{\partial t^2}. \tag{8.46}$$

The solution of (8.46) for a propagating sinusoidal wave of frequency $\omega/2\pi$, whose displacement at the origin is $u_0 \cos \omega t$, is expressed as

$$u(x) = u_0 \exp(-\alpha t) \cos[\omega(t - x/c)] \tag{8.47}$$

where

$$c = (E^*/\rho)^{1/2} \sec \delta/2, \tag{8.48a}$$

$$\alpha = (\omega/c) \tan \delta/2, \tag{8.48b}$$

$$E^* = E_1^2 + E_2^2 \tag{8.48c}$$

and

$$\tan \delta = E_2/E_1. \tag{8.48d}$$

On the assumption that, for most polymers, $\tan \delta \ll 1$, then $\sec \delta/2 \approx 1$ and $\tan \delta/2 \approx \frac{1}{2} \tan \delta$. Thus, (8.48a) and (8.48b) are, respectively, reduced to

$$c = \left(\frac{E^*}{\rho}\right)^{1/2} \quad \text{and} \quad \alpha = \frac{\omega}{2c} \tan \delta \tag{8.49}$$

where c and α are referred to as 'propagation constants'. Accordingly, if the values of the moduli E_1 and E_2 (or E^* and $\tan \delta$) are known from experiment over a sufficient frequency range, the displacement of the disturbance along the filament may be calculated by (8.47) with the use of (8.49).

From an experimental point of view, two types of disturbance inputs are often considered for the study of wave propagation in materials, i.e. sinusoidal waves and pulse inputs (for example, Hillier, 1949, 1960; Hillier and Kolsky, 1949; Kolsky, 1960).

8.4.1 Sinusoidal inputs

For this type of disturbance input, continuous trains, of small amplitude of vibration, are propagated along filaments of the material. As introduced in the foregoing, if the displacement input on one end of the specimen is $u_0 \cos \omega t$, then the displacement at a distance x along the filament is given by (8.47). Hence, by measuring the amplitude and phase of the vibration at different points along the filament, the propagation constants c and α can be determined from (8.47). Consequently E^* and $\tan \delta$ (or E_1 and E_2) as functions of frequency $\omega/2\pi$ are found from (8.48) or (8.49). Hillier and Kolsky (1949) and Ballon and Smith (1949), for instance, have used this method for the determination of the dynamic properties of viscoelastic materials such as rubber and plastics in the range of 10^2–10^3 cycles s^{-1} (Kolsky (1960) should also be referred to).

For a linear viscoelastic solid, provided that E_1 is not changing too rapidly with frequency, one may write (Ferry and Williams, 1952)

$$\frac{dE_1}{d\omega} \approx \frac{2E_2}{\pi\omega} \qquad (8.50)$$

which can be written in view of (8.48d) as

$$\frac{d(\log E_1)}{d(\log \omega)} \approx \frac{2}{\pi} \tan \delta. \qquad (8.51)$$

For most polymers, at temperatures near their transition from the rubber-like to the glassy-like temperature, $\tan \delta$ varies comparatively little with frequency (e.g. Nashif, Jones and Henderson, 1965). For this case, one may assume that $\tan \delta$ is constant (i.e. independent of frequency). Under the latter assumption, equation (8.51) may be integrated to give

$$E_1 \approx E_1(\omega_0) \exp\left[\frac{2}{\pi} \tan \delta \, \log\left(\frac{\omega}{\omega_0}\right)\right] \qquad (8.52)$$

where $E_1(\omega_0)$ is the value of E_1 at a fixed reference frequency $\omega_0/2\pi$. Further, if one assumes, as mentioned before, that $\tan \delta \ll 1$, one can express the propagation constants α and c, with reference to (8.48) and (8.49), as

$$c \approx \left(\frac{E_1}{\rho}\right)^{1/2} \quad \text{and} \quad \alpha = \frac{\omega}{2c} \tan \delta. \qquad (8.53)$$

Meantime, equation (8.52) is approximated further as

$$E_1 \approx E_1(\omega_0)\left[1 + \frac{2}{\pi} \tan \delta \, \log\left(\frac{\omega}{\omega_0}\right)\right] \qquad (8.54)$$

whereby the exponential term in (8.52) has been expanded asymptotically and the first two terms in the expansion are retained. Accordingly, one writes with reference to (8.53) that

$$c \approx c_0\left[1 + \frac{2 \tan \delta}{\pi} \log\left(\frac{\omega}{\omega_0}\right)\right]^{1/2} \qquad (8.55a)$$

where

$$c_0 = [E_1(\omega_0)/\rho]^{1/2}. \qquad (8.55b)$$

Figure 8.4 (Kolsky, 1960; experimental results after Hillier, 1949) supports a linear relation between c and $\log \omega$ for polyethylene in the frequency range shown.

With reference to (8.49), if $\tan \delta$ is constant, the attenuation constant α would be proportional to ω/c. Further, since the phase velocity c varies comparatively slowly with frequency, over a limited frequency range, equations (8.55), one may expect the attenuation constant α, equation (8.53), to be proportional to the frequency.

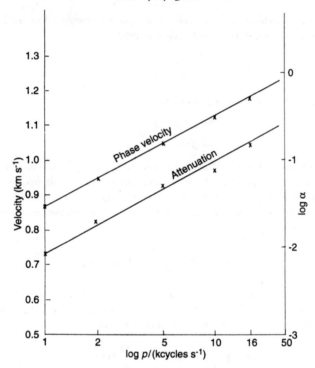

Fig. 8.4 Experimental values of phase velocity c and log α (Hillier, 1949) plotted against log frequency, for polyethylene. (Source: Kolsky, H. (1960) Viscoelastic waves, in Int. Symp. on Stress Wave Propagation in Materials (Ed. N. Davids), Interscience Publishers, New York, pp. 59–90. Reprinted with permission.)

Accordingly, log α should vary linearly with log ω as shown by the graph by Hillier (1949) in Fig. 8.4.

For the study of viscoelastic wave propagation at higher frequencies, pulsed ultrasonic methods are used (for example, Ivey, Mrowea and Guth, 1949; Cunningham and Ivey, 1956). The experimental practice of the technique could vary quite significantly; however, in principle, a finite number of sinusoidal cycles of frequency $\omega/2\pi$ are introduced in one end of the specimen and the resultant wave motion is recorded at a number of points along the length of the specimen. From a measurement of transient time and amplitude ratio, estimates of the phase velocity $c(\omega)$ and the attenuation constant $\alpha(\omega)$ can be made. The ultrasonic technique has the advantage of being relatively simple. It is particularly powerful for investigating the wave propagation properties in elastic materials. In case of viscoelastic materials, however, the technique unfortunately suffers from certain theoretical difficulties of interpretation as pointed out by Kolsky (1960): the time of transit of the pulse depends on the group velocity of the wave packet and, for a dispersive medium, this is, in general, different from the phase velocity c. In the absence of attenuation, these two velocities can be related (Kolsky, 1963); however, in a medium which is dissipative as well as dispersive, the relation between group velocity and phase velocity is not clear yet.

8.4.2 Pulse inputs

Few experimental research efforts have been focused on the study of pulse propagation in viscoelastic materials. In the early work of Hillier (1949) and Hillier and Kolsky (1949) steady-state longitudinal vibrations were induced in prestretched filaments (0.06 cm in diameter) of polythene, neoprene and nylon by means of a transducer element attached to one end of the material specimen. The experimental studies were carried out within low frequency range $< 16 \times 10^3$ cycles s^{-1}. The response of the filament was determined at various points along its length by means of a crystal pick-up. In this, measurements were taken of the variations in the vibration amplitude and the phase. After allowing for the effect of pick-up (Hunter, 1960), the experimental results included both phase velocity and attenuation at a number of frequencies. Kolsky (1956) presented experimental results after Hillier (1949) which show the phase velocity and attenuation in polythene (ICI Alkathene grade 20) against frequency for experiments carried out at 10 °C.

Kolsky (1954a, b, 1956) carried out a number of experiments on the change of the shape of longitudinal stress pulses as they travel along rods of various plastics. These pulses were produced by the detonation of small explosive charges with initial durations of about 2–3 μs. Figure 8.5 shows oscillograph records which were obtained by Kolsky (1960) with rods of polymethyl methacrylate and polyethylene. As noted by Kolsky (1960), with the polyethylene specimen, after two or three reflections, the length of the pulse had become more than twice the length of the specimen, with the result that the movement of the ends of the specimen become continuous. Figure 8.6 (due to Kolsky, 1960) shows the curves of particle velocity with the passage of time for pulses which had propagated in polyethylene rods 30, 60 and 90 cm in length. It can be seen in the figure that the pulses become progressively flatter, but retain an asymmetrical shape.

8.5 VISCOELASTIC WAVE MOTION IN SEMI-INFINITE LINEAR MEDIA

In this section, we deal with the problem of determining the stress distribution in a semi-infinite viscoelastic rod subject to dynamic loading. The problem was examined by Lee and Morrison (1956). In Lee and Morrison's work, the stress and velocity distributions associated with the propagation of an impulsively applied velocity and stress along viscoelastic rods, as presented by different mechanical models, were determined. Morrison (1956) also considered analytically the wave propagation in a viscoelastic rod of the Voigt model type and also studied viscoelastic materials with three-parameter models. In an earlier work, Hillier (1949) (Hillier and Kolsky (1949) should also be referred to) studied the motion of longitudinal sinusoidal waves along a viscoelastic filament assuming a Maxwell solid, a Voigt solid and a three-element

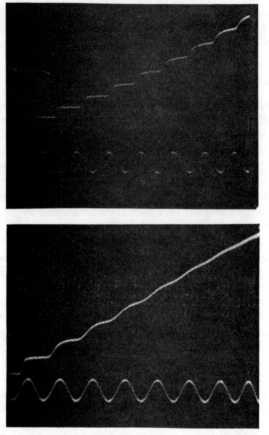

Fig. 8.5 (a) Oscillograph record of displacement at end of polymethyl methacrylate rod 46 cm long and 1.25 cm in diameter when 5 mg charge of lead has been detonated at opposite end. Period of timing wave is 500 μs. (b) Oscillograph record, similar to (a), for polyethylene rod 20 cm long and 1.25 cm in diameter. (Source: Kolsky, H. (1960) Viscoelastic waves, in Int. Symp. on Stress Wave Propagation in Materials (Ed. N. Davids), Interscience Publishers, London, pp. 59–90. Reprinted with permission.)

model representations. Lee and Kanter (1953) considered the stress distribution in a rod of Maxwell material subjected to a mechanical impact. Glauz and Lee (1954), on the other hand, used the method of characteristics to determine the stress in a viscoelastic material made of four-parameter model.

Consider a semi-infinite rod as shown in Fig. 8.7 where $x \geq 0$, with the x coordinate measured along the length of the rod. In this figure, $x(t)$ denotes the position of a section of the rod at time t and $u(x, t)$ is the displacement of this section in the direction of increasing x.

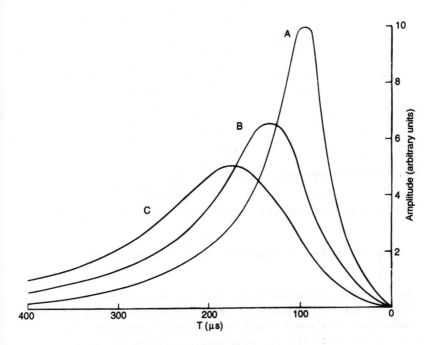

Fig. 8.6 Curves of particle velocity distributions for pulses that have travelled through different lengths of polyethylene rods: curve A, 30 cm; curve B, 60 cm; curve C, 90 cm. (Source: Kolsky, H. (1960) Viscoelastic waves, in Int. Symp. on Stress Wave Propagation in Materials (Ed. N. Davids), Interscience Publishers, London, pp. 59–90. Reprinted with permission.)

Let

- $\sigma(x, t)$ denote the nominal comprehensive stress transmitted across the section x of the rod at time t,
- $\varepsilon(x, t)$ designate the nominal compressive strain corresponding to $\sigma(x, t)$ and
- ρ be the mass density of the material.

The governing equation of motion, in the absence of body forces, in the x direction is

$$\rho \frac{\partial^2 u}{\partial t^2} = -\frac{\partial \sigma}{\partial x}$$

or, in a more compact form,

$$\rho u_{tt} = -\sigma_x \tag{8.56}$$

where a subscript denotes partial differentiation with respect to the corresponding variable.

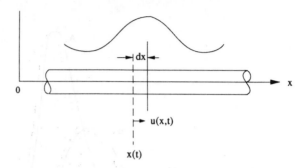

Fig. 8.7 Stress wave propagation in a semi-infinite rod.

The nominal compressive strain $\varepsilon(x, t)$ is written in terms of the displacement u as

$$\varepsilon = -u_x. \tag{8.57}$$

The particle velocity $v(x, t)$ is expressed in terms of the displacement u as

$$v = u_t. \tag{8.58}$$

The semi-infinite rod is considered to be initially unstrained and at rest when, at $t = 0$, the end $x = 0$ is subjected to a mechanical impact (disturbance) with either a constant stress or a constant velocity. In either case, the stress or the velocity at the end $x = 0$ is specified. The governing boundary conditions are

$$\sigma = \sigma_0 H(t) \quad \text{or} \quad v = v_0 H(t), \quad \text{at} \quad x = 0, \tag{8.59}$$

where σ_0 is the applied constant stress, v_0 is the applied constant velocity and $H(t)$ is the Heaviside step function, that is

$$H(t) = \begin{cases} 1 & \text{for } t > 0 \\ 0 & \text{for } t < 0 \end{cases}.$$

In addition to equations (8.56) to (8.59), the constitutive equation for the particular viscoelastic material must be included in the process of determining the stress distribution in the semi-infinite rod. In this section, we consider the representation of the viscoelastic material by different mechanical models; hence, the corresponding constitutive relations are provided accordingly. In this, we follow closely the work of Lee and Morrison (1956). The reader is referred also to Morrison (1956) and Lee and Kanter (1953).

8.5.1 General representation of viscoelastic models

(a) Elastic model: stress–strain law

The stress–strain law is given by

$$\sigma = E\varepsilon \tag{8.60}$$

where E is Young's modulus. Combining equation (8.60) with equations (8.56) to (8.58), then

$$\sigma_{xx} = (\rho/E)\sigma_{tt},$$
$$u_{xx} = (\rho/E)u_{tt},$$
$$\varepsilon_{xx} = (\rho/E)\varepsilon_{tt},$$
$$v_{xx} = (\rho/E)v_{tt}. \tag{8.61}$$

Each of equations (8.61) may be written in the form of the partial differential equation

$$f_{xx} = (\rho/E)f_{tt} \tag{8.62}$$

in which f is an arbitrary variable and whereby equation (8.62) is satisfied by σ, u, ε and v.

(b) Viscous model: stress–strain law

The stress–strain law is given by

$$\sigma = \eta\varepsilon_t \tag{8.63}$$

where η is the viscosity coefficient. Combining (8.63) with equations (8.56) to (8.58), it follows that

$$\sigma_{xx} = (\rho/\eta)\sigma_t,$$
$$u_{xx} = (\rho/\eta)u_t,$$
$$\varepsilon_{xx} = (\rho/\eta)\varepsilon_t,$$
$$v_{xx} = (\rho/\eta)v_t. \tag{8.64}$$

Equations (8.64) lead to the partial differential equation

$$f_{xx} = (\rho/\eta)f_t \tag{8.65}$$

which is satisfied by σ, u, ε and v.

From the above relations for the elastic and viscous models, it is seen that, if we determine the stress solution $\sigma(x, t)$ for the problem in which the end $x = 0$ of the rod is given a constant stress σ_0 at $t = 0$ and this stress is maintained constant afterwards, then we can determine the velocity solution $v(x, t)$ for the alternate problem in which the end of the rod $x = 0$ is given an impulsive constant velocity v_0 which is subsequently maintained, and vice versa. In effect, we have

$$\frac{\sigma(x, t)}{\sigma_0} \equiv \frac{v(x, t)}{v_0}. \tag{8.66a}$$

For convenience, Lee and Morrison (1956) introduced the dimensionless variables

$$\tau = (E/\eta)t \quad \text{and} \quad \xi = \frac{(\rho E)^{1/2}}{\eta} x \tag{8.66b}$$

Wave propagation

so that the partial differential equation (8.62) for the elastic model becomes

$$f_{\xi\xi} = f_{\tau\tau} \tag{8.67}$$

and the partial differential equation (8.65) for the viscous element can be written as

$$f_{\xi\xi} = f_{\tau}. \tag{8.68}$$

The partial differential equations satisfied by f for other mechanical models are given in the appendix of the paper by Lee and Morrison (1956).

The stress solutions for the rod when subjected to a constant applied stress and to a constant applied velocity are to be determined. For convenience, the stress solutions are represented (Lee and Morrison, 1956) by the following dimensionless variables:

$$\Sigma(\xi, \tau) = \frac{\sigma(x, t)}{\sigma_0}$$

for constant applied stress and

$$\Sigma'(\xi, \tau) = \frac{\sigma(x, t)}{(\rho E)^{1/2} v_0}$$

for constant applied velocity.

(c) Elastic models: stress distribution

Combining equations (8.59) and (8.67) and using Laplace transform, the stress distribution for the elastic model is

$$\Sigma(\xi, \tau) = H(t - \xi) \tag{8.69}$$

for constant applied stress and

$$\Sigma'(\xi, \tau) = H(\tau - \xi) \tag{8.70}$$

for constant applied velocity.

Figures 8.8(a) and 8.8(b) show, respectively, schematics of the stress distributions, in the case of an elastic rod subjected to a suddenly applied constant end stress σ_0, against τ for a fixed ξ and against ξ for a fixed τ.

The stress discontinuity in the rod subjected to a sudden dynamic loading travels in the form of a wavefront. Hence, for a fixed ξ, that part of the rod represents the time before the wave front passes. Similarly, for a fixed τ, it contains that part of the bar where the wavefront has not yet reached. In case of the elastic rod, as shown in Fig. 8.8(a), for $\xi = 2\sqrt{2}$, the stress at this section of the elastic rod, when subjected to constant applied stress, is zero as it represents the time before the wavefront passes and, as soon as the wavefront reaches $\tau = \tau_1$, the stress jumps to the value of unity and remains constant afterwards. Similarly for $\xi = 4\sqrt{2}$, as soon as the wavefront reaches $\tau = \tau_2$, the stress jumps to the value of unity and remains

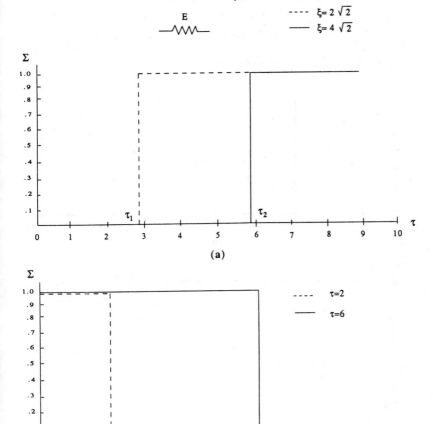

Fig. 8.8 Schematics of stress distributions for an elastic rod under suddenly applied constant end stress σ_0.

subsequently constant. As shown in Fig. 8.8(b), for $\tau = 2$, the stress jumps to the value of unity and remains constant until $\xi = 2$ when the stress instantaneously becomes zero. Similarly for $\tau = 6$, the stress jumps to the value of unity and remains constant until $\xi = 6$ when the stress instantaneously becomes zero.

Similar stress distributions are exhibited by the elastic model in the case of constant end velocity loading as shown in Fig. 8.9.

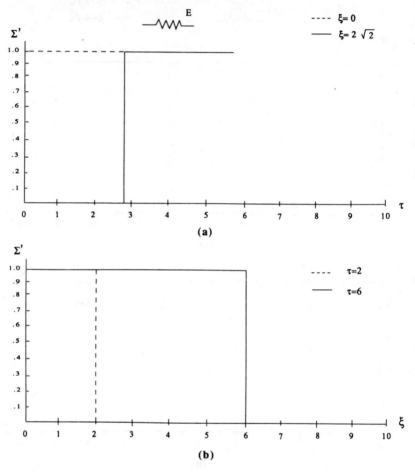

Fig. 8.9 Schematics of stress distributions for an elastic rod under suddenly applied constant end velocity v_0.

(d) Viscous model: stress distribution

Similarly, for the viscous model, the stress distributions are determined from (8.59) and (8.68) as

$$\Sigma(\xi,\ \tau) = Z\left(\frac{\xi}{2\tau^{1/2}}\right) \tag{8.71}$$

for constant applied stress and

$$\Sigma'(\xi,\ \tau) \equiv \frac{\exp(-\xi^2/4\tau)}{(\pi\tau)^{1/2}} \tag{8.72}$$

for constant applied velocity where, in (8.71),

$$Z(z) = (2/\pi^{1/2}) \int_z^\infty \exp(-\mu^2) \, d\mu. \tag{8.73}$$

For a viscous rod under suddenly applied constant end stress, as shown in Fig. 8.10(a), for $\xi = 1$, the stress increases asymptotically as soon as the constant stress loading is applied and continues to increase, ultimately reaching unity. For $\xi = 4$,

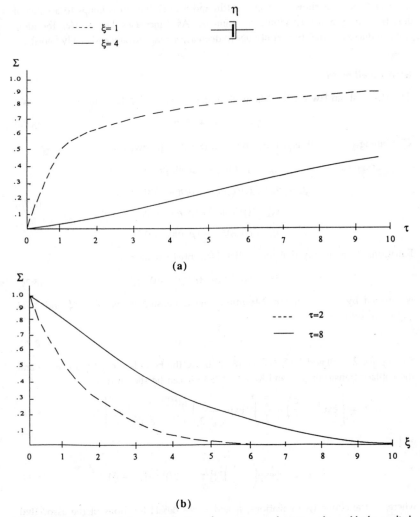

(a)

(b)

Fig. 8.10 Schematics of stress distributions for a viscous element under suddenly applied constant end stress σ_0.

Wave propagation

the stress starts increasing more gradually, but continues to increase asymptotically, ultimately approaching a value less than unity. As shown in Fig. 8.10(b), for $\tau = 2$, the stress continues to decrease rapidly and vanishes. For $\tau = 8$, the stress starts to decrease less rapidly, but ultimately vanishes.

In case of constant applied velocity as shown in Fig. 8.11(a), the stress at the end of the viscous rod, $\xi = 0$, becomes instantaneously infinite as the viscous element resists the deformation due to sudden impact, but it rapidly decreases and may finally vanish. For $\xi = 4$, the stress tends to increase gradually after impact and after some time decreases and may finally vanish.

For a fixed τ, as shown in Figs. 8.11(b) and 8.11(c), the stress jumps to a value of less than unity and then ultimately vanishes. As τ increases, Fig. 8.11(c), the jump value reduces and the stress continues to decrease asymptotically and finally vanishes.

(e) Maxwell model

The stress–strain law for the Maxwell model, in view of (2.15), can be written as

$$\varepsilon_t = (1/E)\sigma_t + (1/\eta)\sigma. \tag{8.74}$$

Combining (8.74) with equations (8.56) to (8.58), it follows that

$$\sigma_{xx} - (\rho/E)\sigma_{tt} - (\rho/\eta)\sigma_t = 0,$$
$$u_{xx} - (\rho/E)u_{tt} - (\rho/\eta)u_t = 0,$$
$$\varepsilon_{xx} - (\rho/E)\varepsilon_{tt} - (\rho/\eta)\varepsilon_t = 0, \tag{8.75}$$
$$v_{xx} - (\rho/E)v_{tt} - (\rho/\eta)v_t = 0.$$

Equations (8.75) signify that the partial differential equation

$$f_{xx} - (\rho/E)f_{tt} - (\rho/\eta)f_t = 0 \tag{8.76}$$

is satisfied by σ, u, ε and v. Meantime, the dimensionless variables ξ and τ, as expressed by (8.66b), satisfy

$$f_{\xi\xi} - f_{\tau\tau} - f_\tau = 0. \tag{8.77}$$

Solving for $\Sigma(\xi, \tau)$ and $\Sigma'(\xi, \tau)$ from (8.77) using the boundary conditions (8.59) and the Laplace transform (Lee and Kanter, 1953), it can be shown that

$$\Sigma(\xi, \tau) = \left[\exp\left(-\frac{\xi}{2}\right) + \frac{\xi}{2} \int_\xi^\tau \exp\left(-\frac{\zeta}{2}\right) \frac{I_1[\frac{1}{2}(\zeta^2 - \xi^2)]}{(\zeta^2 - \xi^2)^{1/2}} \, d\zeta \right] H(\tau - \xi) \tag{8.78}$$

and

$$\Sigma'(\xi, \tau) = \exp\left(-\frac{\tau}{2}\right) I_0[\frac{1}{2}(\tau^2 - \xi^2)^{1/2}] H(\tau - \xi) \tag{8.79}$$

where, in the above two equations, I_1 and I_0 are Bessel functions of the associated arguments. For the evaluation of these functions the reader is referred, for instance,

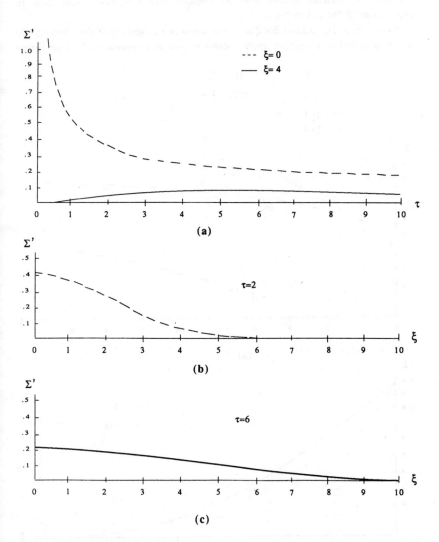

Fig. 8.11 Schematics of stress distributions for a viscous element under suddenly applied constant end velocity v_0.

to Janke and Emde (1945). The stress distributions for the Maxwell model are schematically shown in Fig. 8.12 in the case of constant stress and in Fig. 8.13 in the case of suddenly applied constant velocity with reference, respectively, to expressions (8.78) and (8.79).

As shown in Fig. 8.12(a), for $\xi = 1$, the stress at this section of the Maxwell rod when subjected to a constant applied stress is zero as it represents the time before

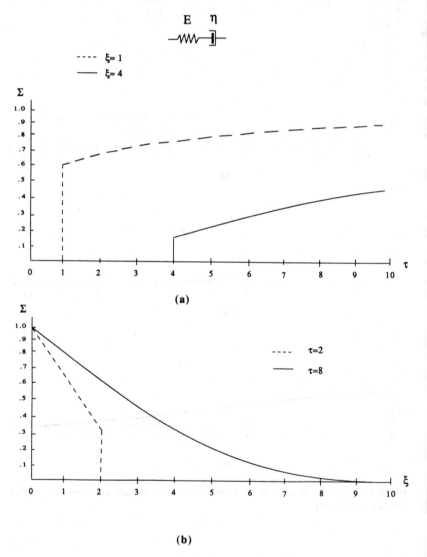

(a)

(b)

Fig. 8.12 Schematics of stress distributions for a Maxwell model under suddenly applied constant end stress σ_0.

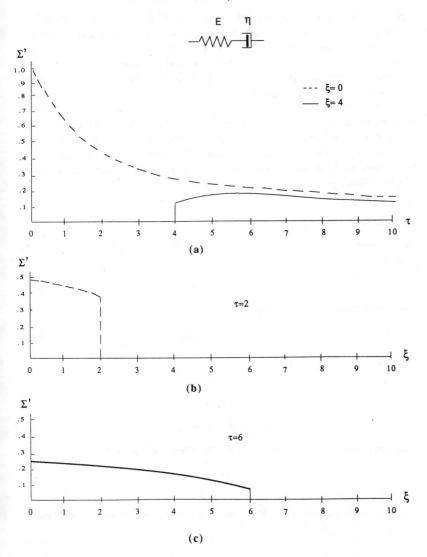

Fig. 8.13 Schematics of stress distributions for a Maxwell model under suddenly applied constant end velocity v_0.

the wavefront passes, but, as soon as the wavefront reaches $\tau = 1$, the stress jumps instantaneously to a value less than unity and continues to increase, ultimately approaching unity. With the increase in ξ, the stress jump reduces drastically, but the stress continues to increase afterwards. For a fixed τ, Fig. 8.12(b), the stress reduces rapidly for lower values of τ, but, as τ increases, the stress decreases more gradually.

In a case of a constant applied end velocity, Fig. 8.13(a), the stress at the end of the rod, $\xi = 0$, jumps instantaneously to the value of unity, but decreases monotonically and becomes eventually zero. At $\xi = 4$, the stress is zero until $\tau = 4$, where the stress jumps to a value much less than unity and continues to increase first and then decreases until ultimately it vanishes. It can be seen that the behaviour of this model is similar to that of a viscous model.

For a fixed τ, Fig. 8.13(b), the stress jumps to a value less than unity immediately following the impact and starts decreasing and vanishes with an instantaneous drop in stress. As time increases, Fig. 8.13(c), the stress jump reduces and the stress decreases more gradually and finally vanishes. This behaviour indicates further that the Maxwell model ultimately behaves like a viscous model for times long compared with the relaxation times.

(f) Voigt (Kelvin) model

The stress–strain law for the Voigt (Kelvin) model is expressed, with reference to (2.28) as

$$\sigma = E\varepsilon + (1/\eta)\varepsilon_t. \tag{8.80}$$

Combining (8.56), (8.57) and (8.80),

$$\rho\sigma_{tt} = E\sigma_{xx} + \eta\sigma_{xxt}. \tag{8.81}$$

Similarly, it can be shown that

$$\begin{aligned}
\rho u_{tt} &= E u_{xx} + \eta u_{xxt}, \\
\rho\varepsilon_{tt} &= E\varepsilon_{xx} + \eta\varepsilon_{xxt}, \\
\rho v_{tt} &= E v_{xx} + \eta v_{xxt}
\end{aligned} \tag{8.82}$$

Equations (8.81) and (8.82) lead to the partial differential equation

$$\rho f_{tt} = E f_{xx} + \eta f_{xxt} \tag{8.83}$$

where the variable f is satisfied by σ, u, ε and v.

Hence, the dimensionless variables τ and ξ, as given by (8.66b), satisfy the relation

$$f_{\tau\tau} = f_{\xi\xi} + f_{\xi\xi\tau}. \tag{8.84}$$

One may solve for the stress distributions using equations (8.59) and (8.84) and the Laplace transform.

The stress distributions for the Voigt (Kelvin) model, as determined by Lee and Morrison (1956), are shown in Figs. 8.14 and 8.15.

Figures 8.14(a) and 8.14(b) show, respectively, the stress distributions, for a constant applied end stress, against τ for a fixed ξ and against ξ for a fixed τ.

As shown in Fig. 8.14(a), for $\xi = 2\sqrt{2}$, the stress commences to increase immediately after loading owing to the stress application and continues to increase

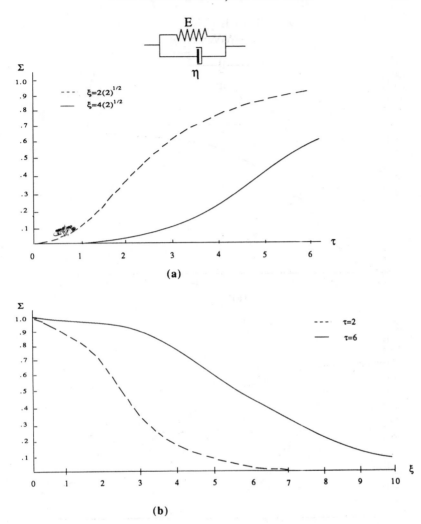

Fig. 8.14 Schematics of stress distributions for a Voigt model under suddenly applied constant end stress σ_0.

asymptotically approaching ultimately the value unity. As ξ increases, the stress commences to increase gradually approaching ultimately the value of unity.

For a fixed τ, at $\tau = 2$, the stress decreases quite rapidly and, as τ increases, the stress decreases more gradually, approaching ultimately the value of zero as shown in Fig. 8.14(b).

In the case of a constant applied end velocity, as shown in Fig. 8.15(a), the stress at the end of the rod, $\xi = 0$, becomes infinite at the moment of the impact owing

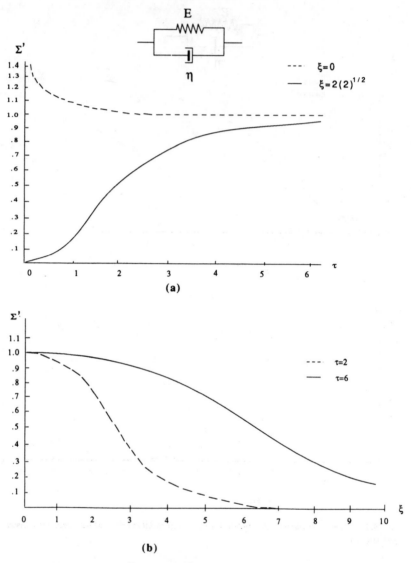

Fig. 8.15 Schematics of stress distributions for a Voigt model under suddenly applied constant end velocity v_0.

to the resistance of the viscous element to deformation but rapidly decreases asymptotically and ultimately reaches the value of unity. At $\xi = 2\sqrt{2}$, the stress commences to increase as soon as the impact takes place and asymptotically approaches the value of unity.

For a fixed τ, as the value of ξ increases, the stress decreases more gradually, approaching ultimately the value of zero as shown in Fig. 8.15(b).

It can be seen from Fig. 8.15 that the Voigt (Kelvin) model behaves ultimately like an elastic model. The spread of the stress distribution in the Voigt (Kelvin) model as compared with the sharp wave front occurring in the case of the elastic model is due to the presence of the viscous element which is in parallel with the elastic element in the Voigt model. However, as the time increases, viscous behaviour tends to die out and the rod behaves as an elastic model. This demonstrates further the fact that Voigt material exhibits a delayed elastic response.

(g) Three-element model (one viscous and two elastic elements)

The model consists of two springs and a dashpot in the configuration shown in Fig. 8.16.

For the model shown in Fig. 8.16, the stress–strain relation is

$$\sigma_t/E' + (1/\eta)\sigma = \varepsilon_t(1 + E/E') + (E/\eta)\varepsilon. \tag{8.85}$$

Combining equations (8.57) and (8.85),

$$\sigma_t/E' + (1/\eta)\sigma = -u_{xt}(1 + E/E') - (E/\eta)u_x. \tag{8.86}$$

Combining further equations (8.56) and (8.86), it can be shown that, after carrying out the appropriate differentiation,

$$\sigma_{tt}/E' + (1/\eta)\sigma_t = -(\sigma_{xx}/\rho)(1 + E/E') - (E/\eta)u_{xt}. \tag{8.87}$$

Differentiating (8.87) with respect to t and combining it with the derivative of (8.56) with respect to x, it follows that

$$\rho\sigma_{ttt}/E' + (\rho/\eta)\sigma_{tt} = \sigma_{xxt}(1 + E/E') + (E/\eta)\sigma_{xx}. \tag{8.88}$$

Equation (8.88) can be written in the following form of the partial differential equation:

$$\rho f_{ttt}/E' + (\rho/\eta)f_{tt} = f_{xxt}(1 + E/E') + (E/\eta)f_{xx} \tag{8.89}$$

which is satisfied by σ. It can also be shown that (8.89) is satisfied by the variables u, ε and v. Hence, the dimensionless variables ξ and τ, as given earlier by (8.66b), will satisfy the partial differential equation

$$kf_{\tau\tau\tau} + f_{\tau\tau} = (1 + k)f_{\xi\xi\tau} + f_{\xi\xi} \tag{8.90}$$

where $k = E/E'$. One may solve for the stress distributions $\Sigma(\xi, \tau)$ and $\Sigma'(\xi, \tau)$ for the three-element model using (8.90) and the boundary conditions (8.59) (Lee and Morrison, 1956). Schematics of stress distributions as determined by Lee and Morrison (1956) are shown, respectively, in Figs. 8.16 and 8.17 for the case when $E = E'$, i.e. when $k = 1$.

It is seen from the schematics of stress distributions (Figs. 8.16 and 8.17) that as the value of τ increases the one-viscous and two-elastic elements model has a stress distribution similar to that of the Voigt (Kelvin) model except for the sharp discontinuity wavefront in case of the three-element model. Such a sharp discontinuity

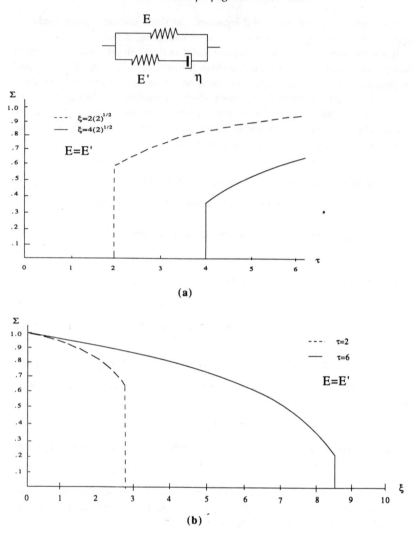

Fig. 8.16 Schematics of stress distributions for a three-element model (one viscous and two elastic elements) under suddenly applied constant end stress σ_0. $E = E'$.

results from the predominance of the two elastic elements. As the value of τ increases, the sharp discontinuity reduces and the stress behaviour of the one-viscous and two-elastic elements model has little or no difference from the stress behaviour of the Voigt model. It is noticed that, for very short times, the dealt-with three-element model behaves more like a Maxwell model than a Voigt (Kelvin) model. This type of

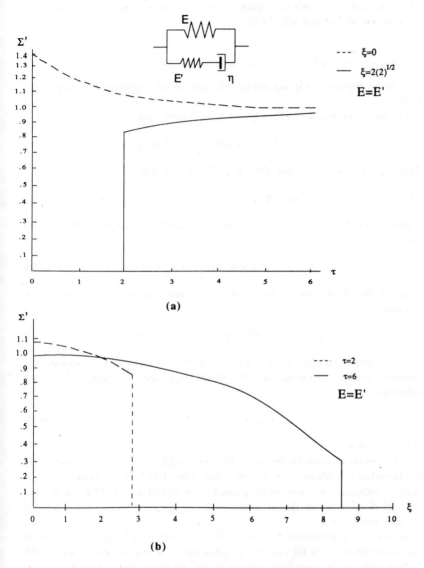

Fig. 8.17 Schematics of stress distributions for a three-element model (one viscous and two elastic elements) under suddenly applied constant end velocity v_0. $E = E'$.

behaviour is seen for both the constant applied end stress (Fig. 8.16) as well as for the constant applied end velocity (Fig. 8.17).

(h) Three-element model (one elastic and two viscous elements)

This model consists of a spring and two dashpots in the configuration shown in Fig. 8.18.

For the model shown in Fig. 8.18, the stress–strain equation is

$$E\varepsilon_t + \eta'\varepsilon_{tt} = (E/\eta)\sigma + (1 + \eta'/\eta)\sigma_t. \tag{8.91}$$

Recalling equations (8.57) and (8.91), it can be shown that

$$-Eu_{xt} - \eta'u_{xtt} = (E/\eta)\sigma_t + (1 + \eta'/\eta)\sigma_t. \tag{8.92}$$

Differentiating (8.56) with respect to x and substituting the resulting differentiation into (8.92),

$$(\rho E/\eta)\sigma_t + \rho(1 + \eta'/\eta)\sigma_{tt} = E\sigma_{xx} + \eta'\sigma_{xxt}. \tag{8.93}$$

It can be also shown that u, ε and v satisfy the same form of the partial differential equation, i.e.

$$(\rho E/\eta)f_t + \rho(1 + \eta'/\eta)f_{tt} = Ef_{xx} + \eta'f_{xxt} \tag{8.94}$$

which is already satisfied by σ in view of (8.93). Accordingly, the dimensionless variables ξ and τ, expressed earlier by (8.66b), will satisfy the partial differential equation

$$f_\tau + (1 + \lambda)f_{\tau\tau} = f_{\xi\xi} + \lambda f_{\xi\xi\tau} \tag{8.95}$$

where $\lambda = \eta/\eta'$.

It is possible to solve for the stress distributions $\Sigma(\xi, \tau)$ and $\Sigma'(\xi, \tau)$ using (8.95), the boundary conditions (8.59) and the Laplace transform. The expressions for the stress distributions are given in the paper by Lee and Morrison (1956). Schematics of stress distributions for the considered model are shown in Figs. 8.18 and 8.19 for the case when $\eta = \eta'$.

In case of the one-elastic and two-viscous elements model, Figs. 8.18 and 8.19, the stress behaviour at the end of the rod is similar to that of the viscous model. Both models exhibit very large stresses at the end of the rods owing to the role played by the viscous element in resisting the sudden deformation caused by the impact. As this deformation is instantaneous, it corresponds to an infinite strain rate which results in an infinite stress to produce it. After a considerable length of time, so that the effects of the sudden impact have delayed, it is seen that the one-elastic and two-viscous elements model behaves like the Maxwell or a viscous model. Thus, the one-elastic and two-viscous elements model can be analysed on the basis of a

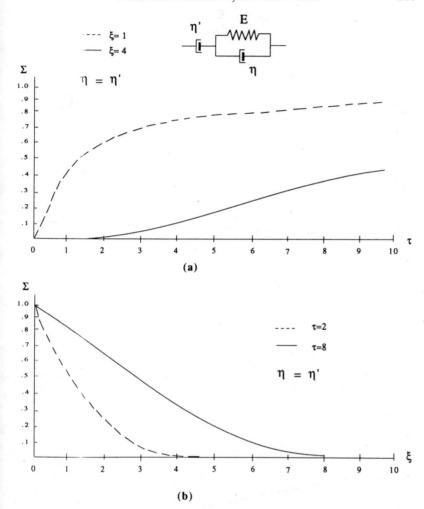

Fig. 8.18 Schematics of stress distributions for a three-element model (one elastic and two viscous elements) under suddenly applied constant end stress σ_0. $\eta = \eta'$.

Maxwell model or a viscous model at large values of τ when the elastic behaviour completely vanishes and the unconstrained viscous element governs the stress distribution. The similarity in stress distributions mentioned above is more pronounced in the case of the constant stress impact than in the case of the constant velocity impact.

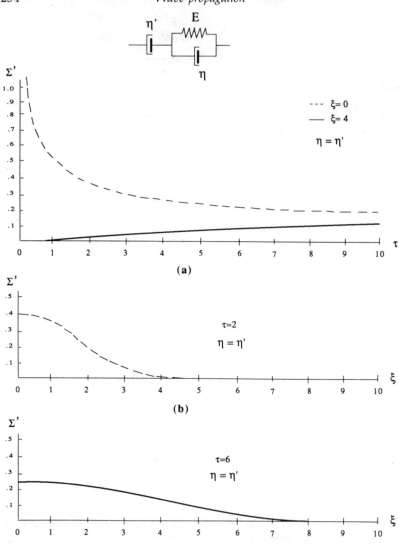

Fig. 8.19 Schematics of stress distributions for a three-element model (one elastic and two viscous elements) under suddenly applied constant end velocity v_0. $\eta = \eta'$.

8.5.2 Comparison of stress distributions for viscoelastic models with ultimate elastic behaviour

This group includes, for example, the elastic element, the Voigt model and the three-element model (one viscous and two elastic elements). We present, in this context, the results obtained by Lee and Morrison (1956).

Figure 8.20 shows comparison of stress distributions for viscoelastic models with ultimate elastic behaviour under constant end stress σ_0. Figure 8.20(a) illustrates the variations in the stress distributions $\Sigma(\xi, \tau)$, where

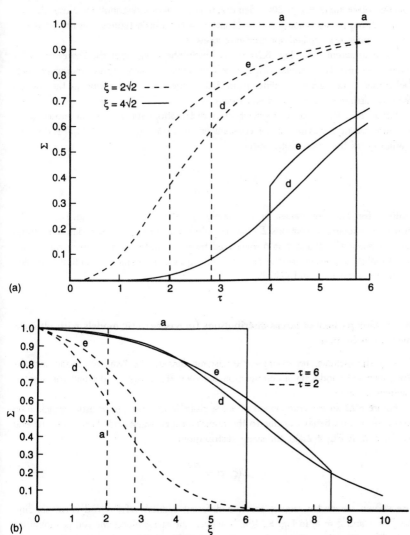

(a)

(b)

Fig. 8.20 Comparison of stress distributions for viscoelastic models with ultimate elastic behaviour (constant end stress σ_0): curves a, elastic element; curves d, Voigt solid; curves e, three-element model (one viscous and two elastic elements, $E = E'$). (Source: Lee, E. H. and Morrison, J. A. (1956) A comparison of the propagation of longitudinal waves in rods of viscoelastic materials. *J. Polym. Sci.*, **19**, 93–110 (Interscience Publishers, Inc., Copyright © 1956). Reprinted by permission of John Wiley & Sons, Inc.)

$$\Sigma(\xi, \tau) = \frac{\sigma(x, t)}{\sigma_0},$$

with τ for two different sections of the rod identified by $\xi = 2\sqrt{2}$ and $\xi = 4\sqrt{2}$. On the other hand, Fig. 8.20(b) demonstrates the stress distributions along the rod at two times corresponding to $\tau = 2$ and $\tau = 6$. In both figures, the impact is due to an impulsively applied constant end stress σ_0.

Most apparent from Fig. 8.20 is that both the Voigt and the three-parameter models exhibit very similar distributions of stress for large times. However, such behaviour would generally differ from that of the elastic rod owing to the viscous flow occurring in the former two models.

Figure 8.21 shows comparison of stress distributions for viscoelastic models with ultimate elastic behaviour under constant end velocity v_0. Figure 8.21(a) shows the variations of the stress distribution

$$\Sigma'(\xi, \tau) = \frac{\sigma(x, t)}{(\rho E)^{1/2} v_0}$$

with τ for different values of ξ, namely $\xi = 0$ and $\xi = 2\sqrt{2}$. In Fig. 8.21(b), however, the stress solutions $\Sigma'(\xi, \tau)$ are plotted against ξ for two different values of τ, namely $\tau = 2$ and $\tau = 6$, measured from the instant $\tau = 0$ when the impact was applied at the end of the rod. In both figures, the impact, as indicated earlier, is due to a constant end velocity v_0.

8.5.3 Comparison of stress distributions for viscoelastic models with ultimate viscous behaviour

This group includes, for example, the viscous element, the Maxwell model and the three-element model (as a combination between the Voigt model and the viscous element in series).

Figure 8.22 shows comparison of stress distributions for viscoelastic models with ultimate viscous behaviour due to the impact of a constant end stress σ_0 at the end of the rod. In Fig. 8.22(a), the stress distributions

$$\Sigma(\xi, \tau) = \frac{\sigma(x, t)}{\sigma_0}$$

are shown versus the time τ for two different sections of the rod corresponding to $\xi = 1$ and $\xi = 4$. In Fig. 8.22(b), however, the stress along the rod is shown for two different times corresponding to $\tau = 2$ and $\tau = 8$. It is seen in these two figures that the stress distributions in the mechanical models dealt with are close to each other at several delay times after the wave front arrival time.

Figure 8.23 shows a comparison of stress distributions for viscoelastic models with ultimate viscous behaviour when the impact is due to a constant end velocity v_0.

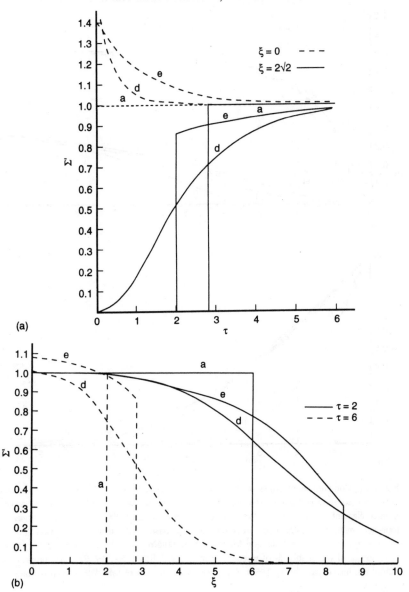

Fig. 8.21 Comparison of stress distributions for viscoelastic models with ultimate elastic behaviour (constant end velocity v_0): curves a, elastic element; curves d, Voigt solid; curves e, three-element model (one viscous and two elastic elements $E = E'$). (Source: Lee, E. H. and Morrison, J. A. (1956) A comparison of the propagation of longitudinal waves in rods of viscoelastic materials. *J. Polym. Sci.*, **19**, 93–110 (Interscience Publishers, Inc., copyright © 1956). Reprinted by permission of John Wiley & Sons, Inc.)

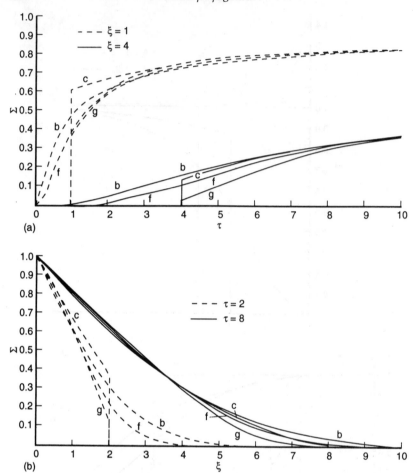

Fig. 8.22 Comparison of stress distributions for viscoelastic models with ultimate viscous behaviour (constant end stress σ_0): curves b, viscous element; curves c, Maxwell model; curves f, three-element model (Voigt model in series with a viscous element, $\eta = \eta'$); curves g, four-element model (Voigt model in series with one elastic and one viscous element, $E = E'$ and $\eta = \eta'$). (Source: Lee, E. H. and Morrison, J. A. (1956) A comparison of the propagation of longitudinal waves in rods of viscoelastic materials. *J. Polym. Sci.*, **19**, 93–110 (Interscience Publishers, Inc., copyright © 1956). Reprinted by permission of John Wiley & Sons, Inc.)

Figure 8.23(a) shows the stress solutions

$$\Sigma'(\xi, \tau) = \frac{\sigma(x, t)}{(\rho E)^{1/2} v_0}$$

against τ for two different values of ξ, namely $\xi = 0$ (i.e. at the end of the rod

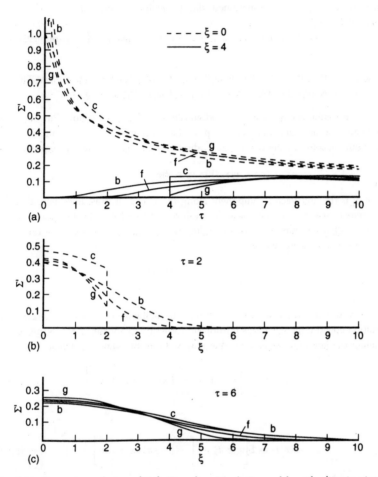

Fig. 8.23 Comparison of stress distributions for viscoelastic models with ultimate viscous behaviour (constant end velocity v_0): curves b, viscous element; curves c, Maxwell model; curves f, three-element model (Voigt model in series with a viscous element, $\eta = \eta'$); curves g, four-element model (Voigt model in series with one elastic and one viscous element, $E = E'$ and $\eta = \eta'$). (Source: Lee, E. H. and Morrison, J. A. (1956) A comparison of the propagation of longitudinal waves in rods of viscoelastic materials. *J. Polym. Sci.*, **19**, 93–110 (Interscience Publishers, Inc., copyright (1956). Reprinted by permission of John Wiley & Sons, Inc.)

$x = 0$) and $\xi = 4$. Meantime, Figs. 8.23(b) and 8.23(c) illustrate the stress distributions along the rod, that is $\Sigma'(\xi, \tau)$ against ξ, for $\tau = 2$ and $\tau = 6$, respectively. The results shown in Fig. 8.23 are, as mentioned, due to an impulsively constant velocity v_0 applied at the end of the rod at $\tau = 0$.

Figures 8.22 and 8.23, introduced above, are due to Lee and Morrison (1956).

8.6 SOLUTION OF THE WAVE EQUATION IN LINEAR VISCOELASTICITY AS BASED ON BOLTZMANN'S SUPERPOSITION PRINCIPLE

Consider a homogeneous, isotropic rod and let x_i ($i = 1, 2, 3$) denote the Cartesian coordinates of any material particle p in the deformed (current) state. For the longitudinal motion of the rod in the x_1 direction, the displacement is expressed as

$$\mathbf{u}(\mathbf{x}, t) = u_1(x_1, t)\mathbf{e}_1 \tag{8.96}$$

where $\mathbf{e}_1$ is the unit vector component along the x_1 axis. It is assumed here that the displacement $\mathbf{u}(\mathbf{x}, t)$ is a continuous function of $\mathbf{x}, t$ for all $\mathbf{x}, t$. In this case, $\varepsilon_{11}(x_1, t)$ and $\sigma_{11}(x_1, t)$ will be the only corresponding nonvanishing components of the strain and stress, respectively, where

$$\varepsilon_{11}(x_1, t) = \frac{\partial u_1(x_1, t)}{\partial x_1} \tag{8.97}$$

and the stress is connected to the strain via Boltzmann's hereditary creep and relaxation constitutive equations introduced earlier by (2.76) and (2.83), respectively. Recalling the latter two equations, one may write in the same order that

$$\varepsilon(x, t) = E^{-1}\left[\sigma(x, t) + \int_0^t F(t - \tau)\sigma(x, \tau)\, d\tau \right] \tag{8.98}$$

and

$$\sigma(x, t) = E\left[\varepsilon(x, t) + \int_0^t R(t - \tau)\varepsilon(x, \tau)\, d\tau \right]. \tag{8.99}$$

Meantime, the equation of motion can be written, in the absence of body forces, in view of (1.22) as

$$\rho\, \frac{\partial^2 u(x, t)}{\partial t^2} = \frac{\partial \sigma(x, t)}{\partial x}. \tag{8.100}$$

Combining now (8.98) and (8.100), the creep wave equation, in the absence of body forces, can be written as

$$\frac{\partial^2 u(x, t)}{\partial x^2} - \frac{1}{c^2}\frac{\partial^2 u(x, t)}{\partial t^2} = \frac{1}{c^2}\int_0^t F(t - \tau)\frac{\partial^2 u(x, t)}{\partial \tau^2} \tag{8.101}$$

where

$$c^2 = E/\rho. \tag{8.102}$$

Further, with reference to (8.99) and (8.100), the relaxation wave equation, in the absence of body forces, is

$$\frac{1}{c^2} \frac{\partial^2 u(x, t)}{\partial t^2} - \frac{\partial^2 u(x, t)}{\partial x^2} = \int_0^t R(t - \tau) \frac{\partial^2 u(x, t)}{\partial x^2} \, d\tau \tag{8.103}$$

with $c^2 = E/\rho$.

The Laplace transforms of the wave equations (8.101) and (8.103) read, respectively, as follows:

$$\frac{d^2}{dx^2} \bar{u}(x, s) = \left(\frac{s}{c}\right)^2 [1 + \bar{F}(s)]\bar{u}(x, s) \tag{8.104}$$

and

$$\frac{d^2}{dx^2} \bar{u}(x, s) = \left(\frac{s}{c}\right)^2 [1 + \bar{R}(s)]^{-1}\bar{u}(x, s). \tag{8.105}$$

Considering, for instance, equation (8.104) corresponding to the creep case, the general transform solution can be written (Graffi, 1982) as

$$\bar{u}(x, s) = A(s) \exp\left\{\frac{xs}{c} [1 + \bar{F}(s)]^{1/2}\right\}$$
$$+ B(s) \exp\left\{-\frac{xs}{c} [1 + \bar{F}(s)]^{1/2}\right\} \tag{8.106}$$

where $A(s)$ and $B(s)$ are functions of the Laplace parameter s. Both $A(s)$ and $B(s)$ are to be determined.

At this point, we shall assume that the rod is semi-infinite in extent and initially undisturbed in the sense that

$$u(x, 0) = \frac{\partial u(x, 0)}{\partial t} = 0. \tag{8.107}$$

The following boundary conditions are further assumed:

$$u(0, t) = u_0(t), \qquad t \geq 0;$$
$$\lim_{x \to \infty} u(x, t) = 0, \qquad t \geq 0. \tag{8.108}$$

In this case, one must impose that $A(s) = 0$ in (8.106) in order to avoid the exponential increase with x of the first term in this equation. Thus, $B(s)$ in (8.106) will assume the value of the Laplace transform of the input $u_0(t)$ and (8.106) becomes

$$\bar{u}(x, s) = \bar{u}_0(s) \exp\left\{-\frac{xs}{c} [1 + \bar{F}(s)]^{1/2}\right\}. \tag{8.109}$$

The inversion of the Laplace transforms in (8.109) leads to (Graffi, 1982)

$$u(x, t) = H(t - x/c) \exp(\alpha x/c) \left[u_0(t - x/c) + \int_0^{t-x/c} F(x, t - \tau - x/c)u_0(\tau) \, d\tau \right]$$

(8.110)

in which $H(\cdot)$ is the Heaviside step function and where the translation and convolution formulae for the Laplace transform (Appendix C) were used. Another representation of the solution (8.110) is due to Mainardi and Turchetti (1975, 1979). Mainardi and Nervosi (1980) have also considered the inclusion of such a presentation in their treatment of transient waves in a viscoelastic rod. A similar treatment may be considered for the relaxation case based on equation (8.105).

8.7 SOLUTION OF THE WAVE PROPAGATION PROBLEM IN A LINEAR VISCOELASTIC SOLID USING THE CORRESPONDENCE PRINCIPLE

In this section, a presentation is given, following Chao and Achenbach (1964), on the utilization of the correspondence principle to solve wave propagation problems in linear viscoelasticity when the solutions of the corresponding elastic problems are known.

The constitutive equations for an isotropic, elastic solid are given in section 8.2 by the set of equations (8.1). With reference to these equations, it is recognized that for an isotropic, elastic solid, two independent constants completely define the stress–strain relations. If the shear modulus μ and the bulk modulus K, for instance, are chosen, the constitutive equations (8.1) can be written in the following tensorial form:

$$\sigma_{ij} = [K - (2/3)\mu]\varepsilon_{kk}\delta_{ij} + 2\mu\varepsilon_{ij}.$$

(8.111)

On the other hand, the constitutive relations for an isotropic, linear viscoelastic material are time dependent. These relations were given for the creep case by (4.27) and for the relaxation case by (4.29). Recalling, for instance, equations (4.27), the following constitutive relations can be written for the creep of an isotropic, viscoelastic solid:

$$2\mu\varepsilon_{ij}'(t) = \sigma_{ij}'(t) + \int_{-\infty}^{t} F_1(t - \tau) \frac{d\sigma_{ij}'(t)}{d\tau} \, d\tau$$

(8.112a)

and

$$2K\varepsilon_{ij}(t) = \sigma_{ij}(t) + \int_{-\infty}^{t} F_2(t - \tau) \frac{d\sigma_{ij}(t)}{d\tau} \, d\tau$$

(8.112b)

in which $F_1(\cdot)$ and $F_2(\cdot)$ are the creep functions governing, respectively, the shear and dilatational behaviours of the medium. The treatment of stress-wave propagation in a viscoelastic solid which obeys the constitutive relations (8.112) leads to complicated mathematical analysis in that the solution of partial integrodifferential equations is involved. Volterra (1931) considered the problem by adopting a functional analysis approach, but it seems that the results of the theory have found, so far, little application in the study of the dynamic behaviour of viscoelastic materials (e.g. Kolsky, 1963).

Chao and Achenbach (1964) discussed the application of the Laplace transform to viscoelastic wave propagation problems using the well-known correspondence principle (Bland, 1960; Schapery, 1974). It was shown by these authors that, under the restricted condition of constant Poisson's ratio, a class of viscoelastic problems may be solved provided that the solution of the corresponding elastic problem is known. Applying the Laplace transform to (8.112a) and (8.112b), with some additional manipulation, yields

$$\bar{\sigma}_{ij} = [\bar{K}(s) - \tfrac{2}{3}\bar{\mu}(s)]\bar{\varepsilon}_{kk}\delta_{ij} + 2\bar{\mu}(s)\varepsilon_{ij} \qquad (8.113a)$$

where

$$\bar{\mu}(s) = \frac{\mu}{1 + s\bar{F}_1(s)} = \mu\beta(s) \qquad (8.113b)$$

and

$$\bar{K}(s) = \frac{K}{1 + s\bar{F}_2(s)} = K\gamma(s) \qquad (8.113c)$$

where s is the Laplace transform parameter.

Meantime, the Laplace transform of the stress equation of motion (1.22), in the absence of body forces, can be written as

$$\bar{\sigma}_{ij,j} = \rho s^2 \bar{u}_i \qquad (8.114)$$

where ρ is the mass density of the material.

Combining (8.113) and (8.114) yields the governing differential equations for the transformed displacements of a viscoelastic medium, that is

$$(\bar{K} + \tfrac{1}{3}\bar{\mu})\bar{u}_{j,ji} + \bar{\mu}u_{i,jj} = \rho s^2 \bar{u}_i. \qquad (8.115)$$

We decompose the displacement vector **u** into dilatational and rotational parts, i.e.

$$\bar{\mathbf{u}} = \bar{\mathbf{v}} + \bar{\boldsymbol{\omega}} \qquad (8.116)$$

where

$$\bar{v}_{i,i} = 0 \quad \text{and} \quad \bar{\omega}_{i,j} = \omega_{j,i}. \qquad (8.117)$$

Accordingly, the transformed equations (8.115) will be satisfied if

$$\bar{v}_{i,jj} = \frac{s^2}{\bar{c}_1^2}\bar{v}_i \qquad (8.118)$$

and

$$\bar{\omega}_{i,jj} = \frac{s^2}{\bar{c}_2^2}\,\bar{\omega}_i \qquad (8.119)$$

where $\bar{c}_1$ and $\bar{c}_2$ are the transformed velocities for the dilatational and rotational waves respectively, i.e.

$$\bar{c}_1^2 = \bar{K}(s) + \tfrac{4}{3}\bar{\mu}(s) \qquad (8.120)$$

and

$$\bar{c}_2^2 = \frac{\bar{\mu}(s)}{\rho}. \qquad (8.121)$$

The same treatment may be applied for the isotropic, elastic medium if the constitutive equation (8.111) is used instead of (8.113a). On the other hand, the analogous equations to (8.118) and (8.119) for the isotropic, elastic body are obtained if $\bar{\mu}(s)$ and $\bar{K}(s)$ in (8.113b) and (8.113c) are replaced by the elastic moduli μ and K respectively. The above treatment was presented by Chao and Achenbach (1964) with the following conclusion: the Laplace transforms of the solutions for a viscoelastic wave propagation problem can be obtained from the Laplace transforms of the solutions for the elastic problem with the same boundary and initial conditions by replacing the shear modulus μ by its Laplace transform $\bar{\mu}(s)$ and the bulk modulus K by its Laplace transform $\bar{K}(s)$.

The above conclusion is, in essence, a form of the well-known **correspondence principle**; that is the problem of obtaining solutions concerning the response behaviour of a linear viscoelastic solid is reduced to a problem of inverting the Laplace transforms of the corresponding elastic solution.

Chao and Achenbach (1964) (Achenbach and Chao (1962) should also be referred to) considered the application of the above approach to the study of the displacement and stress fields inside an infinite, viscoelastic body of a constant Poisson's ratio. In their treatment, the authors assumed the input force to be time dependent and concentrated at one point. Two illustrative examples were subsequently given. In the first example, the displacement components in the radial and the vertical directions on the surface of a viscoelastic half-space loaded suddenly by a vertical force of constant magnitude were evaluated. In the second example, the radial stress for the problem of the expanding spherical cavity in an infinite viscoelastic medium was dealt with.

8.8 NONLINEAR VISCOELASTIC WAVE PROPAGATION

The subject of characterization of the nonlinear viscoelastic response of materials has been dealt with in some detail in Chapter 6. As mentioned in Chapter 6, although considerable research efforts have been made over recent decades towards characterization of the nonlinear viscoelastic nature of materials, interest in the study of wave propagation in such materials did not develop until recently. Most of the studies on wave propagation in nonlinear viscoelastic materials dealt essentially with the one-dimensional motion within the context of the general constitutive theory of materials with fading memory. These studies have considered the propagation of both acceleration and shock waves in viscoelastic media with the objective of establishing the governing conditions for their growth or decay. Such governing conditions implied the existence of steady waves in the dissipative viscoelastic media.

An initial study in the area of nonlinear wave propagation is due to Malvern (1951). Malvern's approach is concerned with the motion of a plastic wave in a ductile material (e.g. a metal with a strain memory effect). As a special case, however, Malvern considered the motion of such a type of wave in a model of a viscoelastic solid. The modes of propagation of acceleration waves in different media have been studied by, among others, Truesdell and Toupin (1960), Thomas (1961), Hill (1962), Varley and Cumberbatch (1965), Coleman, Gurtin and Herrera (1965), Coleman and Gurtin (1965a–c) and Bailey and Chen (1971). Varley (1965) discussed the mode of propagation of an arbitrary acceleration wave as it advances into a finitely strained viscoelastic material which, until the arrival of the front, is undergoing any admissible deformation. The viscoelastic material is seen in Varley's work to be generally inhomogeneous and anisotropic. Coleman, Gurtin and Herrera (1965) and Coleman and Gurtin (1965a–c) dealt comprehensively with the theory of nonlinear viscoelastic wave propagation in a series of research papers. In the first two papers of the series, the authors dealt with the propagation of shock and acceleration fronts in materials with memory resting on the assumption that the stress is a functional of the history of the deformation gradient with the exclusion of any thermal influences. In the subsequent two papers (Parts III and IV of the series), Coleman and Gurtin (1965b, c) have allowed the stress to be affected not only by the history of strain, but also by the history of a thermodynamic variable such as the temperature (Coleman (1964) and Coleman and Gurtin (1966) should also be referred to). An extension of this work to include mild discontinuities was considered by Coleman, Greenberg and Gurtin (1966). The problem of propagation of steady shock waves in nonlinear thermoviscoelastic solids has been also considered, for instance, by Ahrens and Duvall (1966), Greenberg (1967), Chen, Gurtin and Walsh (1970), Schuler and Walsh (1971), Dunwoody (1972), Huilgol (1973) and Nunziato and Walsh (1973). In this, Nunziato and Walsh (1973) expressed the governing equations in terms of material response functions which can be determined from shock wave, thermophysical and bulk response data. The results of the analysis were compared with experimental steady-wave studies concerning the solid polymer polymethyl methacrylate (PMMA). The existence and propagation of steady waves in a class of dissipative materials were considered also by, among others, Greenberg (1968) and Schuler (1970).

On the experimental side, research in the field of shock wave physics has made it possible to produce high amplitude strain waves. Barker and Hollenbach (1970) and Schuler (1970) used a gas gun (Barker and Hollenbach, 1964, 1965) to produce a planar impact between two plates. This has been parallel with the development of advanced recording and measurement techniques such as laser interferometry (Barker and Hollenbach, 1964, 1965, 1970; Barker, 1968). Such experimental efforts were particularly effective in the production of one-dimensional strains of very large amplitude; meantime, they allowed wave motion to be observed with high resolution and accuracy. Chen and Gurtin (1972a, b) discussed the use of experimental results concerning steady shock waves to predict the acceleration wave response of nonlinear viscoelastic materials. Meantime, Nunziato and Sutherland (1973) used acoustic waves for the determination of stress relaxation functions of a class of polymeric materials.

Schuler, Nunziato and Walsh (1973) presented a comprehensive review of some theoretical and experimental developments in the domain of nonlinear viscoelastic wave propagation. Confining their attention to the case of one-dimensional strain, they reviewed theories of shock and acceleration wave propagation in materials with memory and discussed the theoretical predictions with some experimental results for the polymeric solid PMMA. In this, these authors were particularly influenced by the work of Coleman, Gurtin and Herrera (1965), Coleman and Gurtin (1965a–c) and Chen and Gurtin (1970). We follow closely the work of these authors in the following presentation.

8.8.1 Kinematics and balance laws in one-dimensional motion

(a) Kinematics

In the case of one-dimensional motion, we identify the spatial position of a material point (particle) at time t by the coordinate $x(X, t)$. The counterpart of this position coordinate in the reference configuration, R, is $X(x, t)$. It is assumed that the coordinate function $x(X, t)$ is continuous for all X and t. The corresponding displacement function $u(X, t)$ is, thus, a continuous function of X, t for all X and t. Assuming suitable smoothness of the motion (Schuler, Nunziato and Walsh, 1973) the particle velocity is expressed by

$$v(t) = \frac{\partial}{\partial t} u(X, t) = \partial_t u(X, t) \tag{8.122}$$

and the compressive strain is expressed by

$$\varepsilon(t) = -\frac{\partial}{\partial X} u(X, t) = -\partial_x u(X, t). \tag{8.123}$$

A wave propagating in such continuous medium may be seen (Coleman and Gurtin, 1965a–c) as a family of points $\hat{X}(t)$, $-\infty < t < \infty$, where $\hat{X}(t)$ is the material point in the reference configuration R at which the wave front is to be found at time t. Thus, the spatial position of the wave may be expressed by

$$\hat{x}(t) = x[\hat{X}(t), t] \tag{8.124}$$

with $\hat{x}(t)$ designating the spatial position of the wave at time t.

The wave velocity $V(t)$ at time t is defined by

$$V(t) = \frac{d}{dt}\,\hat{x}(t) = \frac{d}{dt}\,x[\hat{X}(t),\,t].$$ (8.125)

The **wave velocity** $V(t)$ is identified with respect to an external fixed frame of reference (i.e. as seen by an external observer at rest).

Meantime, the **wave 'intrinsic' velocity** $U(t)$ is defined as the velocity of propagation of the wave front relative to the material in the reference configuration. It is expressed as

$$U(t) = \frac{d}{dt}\,\hat{X}(t)$$ (8.126)

where $\hat{X}(t)$, as defined earlier, is the coordinate of the material point in the reference configuration R at which the wave front is to be found at time t.

The material trajectory of the wave front is given here the notation $\Omega(t)$. It is defined as the set of ordered pairs $[\hat{X}(t),\,t]$, $-\infty < t < \infty$.

Coleman, Gurtin and Herrera (1965), following the standard notation used earlier by Truesdell and Toupin (1960), advanced that if a function $f(X,\,t)$ has a jump discontinuity at $X = \hat{X}(t)$, one may define the jump in $f(X,\,t)$, labelled below by $[f]$, across the trajectory of the wave $\Omega(t)$ at time t by

$$[f] = \lim_{X \to \hat{X}(t)^-} f(X,\,t) - \lim_{X \to \hat{X}(t)^+} f(X,\,t).$$ (8.127a)

This expression may also be written in the form

$$[f] = f^- - f^+$$ (8.127b)

where, with the wave intrinsic velocity $U(t) > 0$, f^+ and f^- are the limiting values of the function $f(X,\,t)$ immediately ahead and behind the wave front respectively. The associated **condition of compatibility** to (8.127) is expressed (Truesdell and Toupin, 1960) as

$$[\partial_t f] = -U[\partial_x f].$$ (8.128)

In the present section, the function $f : f(X,\,t)$ is used to designate the kinematical function $x(X,\,t)$ or one of its derivatives.

(b) Balance laws

Mass balance

In one-dimensional motion, the mass balance is expressed with reference to (1.3) as

$$\frac{\rho(X,\,t)}{\rho_0} = \frac{1}{1 - \varepsilon(X,\,t)}$$ (8.129)

where $\rho(X, t)$ is the current mass density and ρ_0 is the mass density in the reference configuration of the material specimen.

Balances of linear momentum and energy
With the exclusion of external body forces, heat conduction and external heat supply, the balances of linear momentum and energy are expressed respectively as

$$\frac{\mathrm{d}}{\mathrm{d}t} \int_{x_\alpha}^{x_\beta} \rho_0 v(x, t) \, \mathrm{d}x = \sigma(x_\beta, t) - \sigma(x_\alpha, t) \tag{8.130}$$

and

$$\frac{\mathrm{d}}{\mathrm{d}t} \int_{x_\alpha}^{x_\beta} [\tfrac{1}{2}\rho_0 v^2(x, t) + e(x, t)] \, \mathrm{d}x = \sigma(x_\beta, t)v(x_\beta, t) - \sigma(x_\alpha, t)v(x_\alpha, t) \tag{8.131}$$

where σ is the one-dimensional stress and e is the internal energy per unit volume.

Clausius–Duhem inequality (second law of thermodynamics)

$$\frac{\mathrm{d}}{\mathrm{d}t} \int_{x_\alpha}^{x_\beta} \rho_0 S(x, t) \, \mathrm{d}x \geq 0 \tag{8.132}$$

where S is the specific entropy per unit mass.

8.8.2 Material response functions

Following Schuler, Nunziato and Walsh (1973), we consider a strain jump ε suddenly applied to a material point which has been unstrained for all past times, i.e.

$$\varepsilon(\tau) = \begin{cases} \varepsilon & \tau = 0 \\ 0 & \tau < 0, \tau > 0. \end{cases} \tag{8.133}$$

The instantaneous stress, denoted by σ_1, corresponding to the strain jump (8.133) is expressed in the following functional format

$$\sigma_1(\varepsilon) = F(\varepsilon) \tag{8.134}$$

where F is a constitutive functional defined under the restrictions imposed on such functional as discussed previously in Chapter 6. The constitutive functional $F(\varepsilon)$ is assumed to be twice continuously differentiable, i.e. $\partial_\varepsilon F[\varepsilon(t - \tau)]$ and $\partial_\varepsilon^2 F[\varepsilon(t - \tau)]$ exist where the partial differentiation is with respect to the present value of strain $\varepsilon(t)$.

The stress-relaxation function corresponding to the strain history (8.133) is designated by $R(\varepsilon; \tau)$. Meantime, the **instantaneous tangent modulus** is designated by $E_1(\varepsilon)$ where

$$E_1(\varepsilon) = \frac{\mathrm{d}\sigma_1(\varepsilon)}{\mathrm{d}\varepsilon} = R(\varepsilon; 0). \tag{8.135}$$

Similarly, the **instantaneous second-order modulus** $\check{E}_I$ is defined by

$$\check{E}_I(\varepsilon) = \frac{d^2\sigma_I(\varepsilon)}{d\varepsilon^2}. \tag{8.136}$$

On the other hand, the equilibrium response of the material may be expressed as

$$\sigma_E(\varepsilon) = F(\varepsilon_E). \tag{8.137}$$

From this the **equilibrium tangent modulus** is given as

$$E_E(\varepsilon) = \frac{d\sigma_E(\varepsilon)}{d\varepsilon} = R(\varepsilon; \tau). \tag{8.138}$$

Thus, the **equilibrium second-order modulus** $\check{E}_E(\varepsilon)$ is identified by

$$\check{E}_E(\varepsilon) = \frac{d^2\sigma_E(\varepsilon)}{d\varepsilon^2}. \tag{8.139}$$

Schuler, Nunziato and Walsh (1973) have imposed certain curvature conditions on the constitutive functional $F(\varepsilon)$ of (8.134). They advanced that these conditions would hold valid for most of viscoelastic materials. These conditions may be presented as follows.

For all ε on $(0, 1)$ and all τ on $(0, \infty)$,

1. $\qquad\qquad\qquad\qquad \sigma_I(\varepsilon) > \sigma_E(\varepsilon) > 0,$

$$E_I(\varepsilon) > E_E(\varepsilon) > 0, \tag{8.140a}$$

$$\check{E}_I(\varepsilon) > 0, \quad \check{E}_E(\varepsilon) > 0;$$

2. $\qquad\qquad R[\varepsilon(t - \tau), \tau] > 0, \quad R'[\varepsilon(t - \tau), \tau] \leq 0,$

where $\qquad\qquad R'[\varepsilon(t - \tau), \tau] = \dfrac{\partial}{\partial\tau} R[\varepsilon(t - \tau), t].$ $\qquad$ (8.140b)

The inequalities under (1) imply that the instantaneous and equilibrium stress–strain curves are strictly convex from below and the instantaneous response curve lies everywhere above the equilibrium curve as shown in Fig. 8.24. It is assumed in the latter figure that $\sigma_I(0) = \sigma_E(0) = 0$. Meantime, the inequalities under (2) affirm that, for all strain histories on $(0, 1)$, the stress-relaxation function is positive and a monotonically decreasing function of the elapsed time τ. Gurtin and Herrera (1965) have also discussed inequalities (2) within the context of linear viscoelasticity.

8.8.3 Acceleration waves

The subject of acceleration wave propagation in nonlinear materials with fading time-memory has been considered by, amongst others, Truesdell and Toupin (1960), Varley (1965), Coleman, Gurtin and Herrera (1965), Coleman and Gurtin (1965a–c), Bailey and Chen (1971) and Schuler, Nunziato and Walsh (1973).

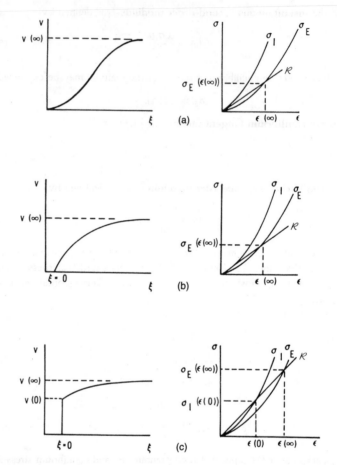

Fig. 8.24 Steady wave solutions (curvature conditions imposed on the instantaneous and equilibrium stress–strain curves). (Reprinted with permission from *Int. J. Solids Struct.*, **9**, Schuler, K. W., Nunziato, J. W. and Walsh, E. K., Recent results in nonlinear viscoelastic wave propagation, copyright (1973), Pergamon Press Ltd.)

Definition Coleman and Gurtin (1965a–c) advanced that if the following two conditions are satisfied, then $\hat{X}(t)$, $-\infty < t < \infty$, is an acceleration wave.

(A-1) $x(X, \tau)$, $\dot{x}(X, \tau)$ and the deformation gradient F are continuous functions of X and τ jointly for all X and τ, while $\ddot{x}(X, \tau)$, $\partial F(X, \tau)/\partial X$, $\dot{F}(X, \tau)$ have jump discontinuities across the wave material trajectory, but are the continuous in X and τ jointly everywhere else.

(A-2) The past history of the deformation gradient, $F_r^t(X_i)$, is a smooth function of X and t with respect to the norm $\|\cdot\|_r$. $F_r^t(X, \cdot)$ is the restriction on the history of the deformation gradient $F(t - \tau)$ to its domain of definition $(0, \infty)$.

The condition (A-2) limits the wildness of the past history for the material with memory.

Coleman and Gurtin (1965a–c) considered, within the general linear theory of simple materials with fading memory, the case when an acceleration wave which since $t = 0$ has been propagating into a region which had been previously at rest in a fixed homogeneous configuration R. For this case, it was remarked by these authors that the hypothesis (A-2) follows from hypothesis (A-1) for all $X > \hat{X}(0)$ and $t > 0$. In other words, whenever the acceleration front is entering a homogeneous medium at rest, the hypothesis (A-1) would generally suffice to ensure that $F_r^t(X, \cdot)$ is a smooth function of X and t with respect to the norm $\|\cdot\|_r$. Thus, following the condition (A-1) above, the compatibility condition (8.128) and taking $f(X, t) = \varepsilon(X, t)$, one can write at $X = \hat{X}(t)$ that

$$[\dot{v}] = U[\dot{\varepsilon}] = U^2[\partial_x \varepsilon]. \tag{8.141}$$

Following (8.127), the stress and the internal energy must also be discontinuous at $X = \hat{X}(t)$. Thus, with reference to (8.130), the balance of linear momentum asserts that

$$[\sigma] = \rho_0 U[v], \quad [\partial_x \sigma] = -\rho_0[\dot{v}]. \tag{8.142}$$

Also, the balance of energy (8.131) implies that

$$-U[e + \tfrac{1}{2}\rho_0 v^2] = [\sigma v], \quad [\dot{e}] = [\sigma \dot{\varepsilon}] \tag{8.143}$$

(Schuler, Nunziato and Walsh, 1973).

The jump in the particle acceleration is conventionally taken as the amplitude of the wave front. Denoting the latter at any instant of time by $a(t)$, then

$$a(t) = [\dot{v}](t). \tag{8.144}$$

Based on purely kinematical considerations, Coleman and Gurtin (1965a–c) affirmed that the amplitude of an acceleration wave obeys the following relationship:

$$2\frac{da}{dt} - \frac{a}{U}\frac{dU}{dE} = [\ddot{x}] - U^2 \frac{\partial \dot{F}}{\partial X} \tag{8.145}$$

where, as introduced earlier, $U = U(t)$ is the intrinsic wave velocity and E_1 is the instantaneous tangent modulus. As an alternate expression to (8.145), Coleman and Gurtin (1965a–c) advanced the following equation for the amplitude of an acceleration wave using condition (A-1) and the balance of momentum equation (8.142):

$$2\frac{da}{dt} = \frac{a}{U}\frac{dU}{dt} + \frac{1}{\rho_0}\left[\frac{\partial^2 \sigma}{\partial t \, \partial X}\right] - U^2\left[\frac{\partial \dot{F}}{\partial X}\right]. \tag{8.146}$$

Meantime, Coleman and Gurtin and Herrera (1965) indicated that the intrinsic velocity U of an acceleration wave satisfies the equation

$$U^2 = R(0)/\rho_0. \tag{8.147}$$

In this equation, $R(0)$ is the instantaneous tangent modulus corresponding to the history $F^{(t)}(\hat{X}(t), \cdot)$, i.e.

$$R(0) = \left. \frac{d\sigma_1(\varepsilon)}{d\varepsilon} \right|_{\varepsilon=0}. \tag{8.148}$$

Thus, equation (8.147) implies that the intrinsic velocity of an acceleration wave $U = U_0$ is a constant given by

$$\rho_0 U_0^2 = R(0). \tag{8.149}$$

Following the above conditions, Schuler, Nunziato and Walsh (1973), following Coleman and Gurtin (1965a–c), affirmed that the amplitude of an acceleration wave is given by

$$\frac{da}{dt} = -\beta a + \frac{\beta}{\gamma} a^2 \tag{8.150}$$

where β and γ are constants given by

$$\beta = -\frac{R'(0)}{2(E_1)_0} = \text{constant}, \quad \gamma = \frac{R'(0)U_0}{(\check{E}_1)_0} = \text{constant} \tag{8.151}$$

and

$$(\check{E}_1)_0 = \left. \frac{d^2\sigma_1(\varepsilon)}{d\varepsilon^2} \right|_{\varepsilon=0}. \tag{8.152}$$

The solution of (8.150) can be written as

$$a(t) = \frac{\gamma}{(\gamma/a(0) - 1) \exp(\beta t) + 1}. \tag{8.153}$$

For a given material, β and γ are constants.

Assuming that the hypothesis of the above theorem holds and supposing that

$$R(0) > 0, \quad R'(0) < 0, \quad (E_1)_0 \neq 0, \tag{8.154}$$

one concludes, with reference to (8.153), following Coleman and Gurtin (1965a–c), the following.

1. If either
   (a) $|a(0)|$ is less than $|\gamma|$, or
   (b) sgn $a(0) = $ sgn $(\check{E}_1)_0$
       then $a(t) \to 0$ monotonically as $t \to \infty$.
2. If $a(0) = \gamma$, then $a(t) = a(0)$.

3. If both

(a) $|a(0)|$ is greater than $|\gamma|$, and
(b) sgn $a(0) = -$ sgn $(\check{E}_1)_0$
    then $|a(t)| \to \infty$ monotonically and in a finite time t_∞ given by

$$t_\infty = -\frac{1}{\beta} \ln\left[1 - \frac{\gamma}{a(0)} \right]. \qquad (8.155a)$$

It is apparent, from the above discussion, that $|\gamma|$ plays the role of the 'critical amplitude' of the input acceleration. The latter may be denoted by a_c which is expressed with reference to equation (8.151) as

$$a_c = |\gamma| = \left| \frac{R'(0)U_0}{(\check{E}_1)_0} \right| = \text{constant}. \qquad (8.155b)$$

Thus (8.155) implies, assuming (8.154), the following.

1. If the amplitude of the input acceleration is sufficiently small ($<$ critical amplitude) or if the amplitude has the same sign as the instantaneous second-order modulus, then an acceleration wave obeying (8.151) is gradually damped out. In this, the internal dissipation of the material is expected to be the governing factor in the mode of wave motion.
2. If, however, the amplitude of the input accleration is greater than the critical amplitude and has its sign opposite to that of the instantaneous second-order modulus, then the wave would achieve an infinite amplitude in a finite time, i.e. a shock wave may be produced. In this, the nonlinearity of the instantaneous stress–strain curve would be the controlling factor (Schuler, Nunziato and Walsh, 1973).

   As noted by Coleman and Gurtin (1965a–c), the presence of internal damping, manifested by a strictly negative value of $R'(0)$, does not always imply that a singular surface moving into a homogeneous region must be damped out.

In the linear theory of simple materials with fading memory, the stress-relaxation function $R(\tau)$, with

$$R'(\tau) = \frac{dR(\tau)}{d\tau},$$

is a material function independent of the strain history $\varepsilon(t - \tau)$. In the physical application of this theory, it is generally expected that (Gurtin and Herrera, 1964)

$$R(0) > 0, \quad R'(0) \le 0.$$

Coleman, Gurtin and Herrera (1965) ruled out, however, the possibility when $R(0) = 0$ or $R'(0) > 0$ in the applicability of relation (8.151). Meantime, Coleman and Gurtin (1965a–c) considered the applicability of (8.151) in the following two cases.

1. $R'(0) = 0$. In this case, it is advanced that the time dependency of the amplitude $a(t)$ of the acceleration wave is expressed as

$$a(t) = \frac{a(0)}{1 + \xi a(0)t}, \quad \xi = \frac{\breve{E}_1}{2UR(0)}, \tag{8.156}$$

where $\breve{E}_1$ is the instantaneous second-order modulus. Two situations may be considered here:

(a) if $\breve{E}_1 \neq 0$, then (8.156) implies, since $\rho_0 > 0$, that, if $a(0)$ has the same sign as $\breve{E}_1$, $|a(t)| \to 0$ monotonically in a finite time;
(b) if $\breve{E}_1 = 0$, then (8.153) would reduce to

$$a(t) = a(0) \exp\left[\frac{R'(0)t}{2R(0)}\right] \tag{8.157}$$

which may be generally valid for a large class of linear viscoelastic materials.

A special class of materials with $R'(0) = 0$ is the class of perfectly elastic materials for which (8.155) is known to be applicable (Thomas, 1957; Green, 1964; Coleman and Gurtin, 1965a–c).

2. $R'(0) < 0$. In this case, it follows from (8.151) that the amplitude of the acceleration wave $a(t) \to 0$ as $t \to \infty$ regardless of the sign of $a(0)$.

8.8.4 Shock waves

The subject of shock wave propagation in nonlinear materials with fading time-memory has been considered by Duvall and Alverson (1963), Coleman and Gurtin (1965a–c), Coleman, Gurtin and Herrera (1965), Chen and Gurtin (1970, 1972a) and Huilgol (1973), amongst others.

Coleman, Gurtin and Herrera (1965) asserted that the following two conditions must be satisfied for the wave $\hat{X}(t)$, $-\infty < t < \infty$, to be called a shock wave in a material with memory.

(S-1) The coordinate function $x(X, t)$ is continuous in both X and t jointly while the deformation gradient $F(X, t) = \partial x(X, t)/\partial X$ and the time derivative of the coordinate $\dot{x}(X, t) = \partial x(X, t)/\partial t$ have jump discontinuities across the wave material trajectory $\Omega(t)$ but are continuous in X and t jointly everywhere else.
(S-2) The past history of the material is not too wild. For this purpose, it is assumed that the past history of the deformation gradient $F_r^t(X, \cdot)$ is a smooth function of X and t with respect to the norm $\|\cdot\|_r$. In this, $F_r^t(X, \cdot)$ is the restriction on the history of the deformation gradient $F(t - \tau)$ to its domain of definition $(0, \infty)$.

Thus, following condition (S-1), the compatibility condition (8.128) together with $f(X, t) = u(X, t)$ affirm that, at $X = \hat{X}(t)$,

$$[v] = -U[\varepsilon] \tag{8.158}$$

where U is the intrinsic velocity of the shock wave. In view of (8.158), either the jump in the particle velocity $[v]$ or the jump in the strain $[\varepsilon]$ may be taken as a measure of the amplitude of the shock. Meantime, equations (8.142) and (8.143) concerning, respectively, the balance of momentum and the balance of energy are also valid for the case of shock waves.

Coleman, Gurtin and Herrera (1965) showed that the intrinsic velocity U of a shock wave satisfies the relation

$$U^2 = \frac{E_I[F]}{\rho_0} \qquad (8.159)$$

where $E_I[F]$ is the instantaneous secant modulus (8.135) corresponding to the history just before the arrival of the shock and a jump of amount $[F]$ where F is the deformation gradient. Consider now the case of a compressive wave propagating into a region at rest and unstrained for all past times (Chen and Gurtin, 1970; Schuler, Nunziato and Walsh, 1973), i.e. for $X > \hat{X}(t)$, $\varepsilon(t - \tau) = 0$, $0 \leq \tau < \infty$ and

$$[\varepsilon] = \varepsilon^- > 0, \quad [\partial_x \varepsilon] = (\partial_x \varepsilon)^-.$$

Thus, the corresponding stress jump is expressed in view of the definition of the instantaneous stress σ_I as

$$[\sigma] = \sigma_I(\varepsilon^-).$$

This implies, in view of (8.158) and (8.159), that the intrinsic velocity can be expressed by

$$U^2 = \frac{\sigma_I(\varepsilon^-)}{\rho_0 \varepsilon^-} = \frac{E_I(\varepsilon^-)}{\rho_0} \qquad (8.160)$$

which, in view of the second inequality of the convexity conditions (8.140a), implies that

$$\frac{\rho_0 U^2}{E_I(\varepsilon^-)} < 1. \qquad (8.161)$$

The inequality (8.161) affirms (Schuler, Nunziato and Walsh, 1973) that the shock velocity is subsonic with respect to the material behind the wave front. From (8.160) it can be seen that the shock velocity depends on the strain amplitude ε^-. Furthermore, one can write with reference to (8.160) that

$$\frac{dU}{dt} = \frac{(1 - \hat{\mu}) E_I(\varepsilon^-)}{2\rho_0 U \varepsilon^-} \frac{d\varepsilon^-}{dt} \qquad (8.162)$$

where

$$\hat{\mu} = \frac{\rho_0 U^2}{E_I(\varepsilon^-)} < 1 \qquad (8.163)$$

given earlier by (8.161).

In view of (8.160), one concludes that the time rate of change of the shock velocity U is proportional to that of the amplitude of the strain behind the front ε^-. Following this and using the assumed characteristics of the deformation gradient F, Chen and Gurtin (1970) derived the following 'shock amplitude equation':

$$\frac{d\varepsilon^-}{dt} = U \frac{1 - \hat{\mu}}{1 + 3\hat{\mu}} [\hat{\lambda} - (\partial_x \varepsilon)^-] \qquad (8.164)$$

where

$$\hat{\lambda} = \frac{R'(\varepsilon^-; 0)\varepsilon^-}{U E_{\mathrm{I}}(\varepsilon^-)(1 - \hat{\mu})}. \qquad (8.165)$$

In (8.165), $R'(\varepsilon^-; 0)$ is the initial slope of the stress-relaxation function corresponding to the jump strain input (8.133). It is evident, in view of (8.140) and (8.165), that $\hat{\lambda} \leq 0$.

Thus, with reference to the shock amplitude expression (8.164), one may conclude that the growth or decay behaviour of the shock wave front would depend on the strain gradient immediately behind the front (Schuler, Nunziato and Walsh, 1973). That is,

1. if $\hat{\lambda} < (\partial_x \varepsilon)^-$, $\dfrac{d\varepsilon^-}{dt} < 0$,

2. if $\hat{\lambda} = (\partial_x \varepsilon)^-$, $\dfrac{d\varepsilon^-}{dt} = 0$, $\qquad (8.166)$

3. if $\hat{\lambda} > (\partial_x \varepsilon)^-$, $\dfrac{d\varepsilon^-}{dt} > 0$,

In view of the above, Schuler, Nunziato and Walsh (1973) referred to $\hat{\lambda}$ as 'the critical strain gradient'. These authors expressed the shock amplitude equation (8.165) in terms of particle velocity as

$$\frac{dv^-}{dt} = \frac{1 - \hat{\mu}^2}{1 + 3\hat{\mu}} [(\dot{v})^- - U^2 |\hat{\lambda}|]. \qquad (8.167)$$

In this equation, $(\dot{v})^-$ is the particle acceleration immediately behind the shock front and $U^2 |\hat{\lambda}|$ is the 'critical acceleration'. It is evident from (8.167) that

1. the front grows if $(\dot{v})^- > U^2 |\hat{\lambda}|$,
2. is steady if $(\dot{v})^- = U^2 |\hat{\lambda}|$, $\qquad (8.168)$
3. decays if $(\dot{v})^- < U^2 |\hat{\lambda}|$.

Further, it can be shown (Chen and Gurtin, 1970) that equation (8.167) reduces for the case of weak shock waves to the following simple expression:

$$\frac{dv^-}{dt} = -\beta v^- \qquad (8.169)$$

where β is a constant given by

$$\beta = -\frac{R'(0;0)}{2(E_l)_0} \qquad (8.170\text{a})$$

in which

$$(E_l)_0 = \frac{d\sigma_l(\varepsilon)}{d\varepsilon}. \qquad (8.170\text{b})$$

The solution of the differential equation (8.169) is

$$v^-(t) = v^-(0)\exp(-\beta t) \qquad (8.171)$$

which asserts that the amplitude of a weak shock wave decays exponentially to zero as $t \to \infty$. Such a response is identical to that predicted by the linear theory of viscoelasticity (e.g. Lee and Kanter, 1953; Chu, 1962; Coleman and Gurtin, 1965a–c; Valanis, 1965).

8.8.5 Thermodynamic influences

(a) Acceleration waves

It is noted by Schuler, Nunziato and Walsh (1973) that thermal effects have no influence on the propagation of acceleration waves in nonconducting materials with memory. Accordingly, on the assumption that a particular material is a thermal nonconductor (which could be reasonable for a large class of polymeric solids), the study of the propagation of acceleration waves in such a material would provide no information about the thermodynamic influence on its mechanical response. Thus, for a thermally nonconducting material, if the relaxtion function and second-order modulus are taken at a fixed entropy, then the velocity of every acceleration wave would satisfy (8.147). Furthermore, the amplitude of an acceleration wave entering a region at rest, unstrained and at uniform temperature, would satisfy (8.153) with the material constants appearing in this equation being given by (8.151) and (8.152).

In the case of conducting materials, however, thermodynamic influences on the propagation of acceleration waves in viscoelastic materials are pronounced. In this, the reader is referred, for instance, to Coleman and Gurtin (1966).

(b) Shock waves

Thermodynamic effects on the propagation of shock waves in nonconducting materials have been considered by Coleman and Gurtin (1966) and Chen and Gurtin (1972b). Meantime, studies on shock wave propagation in materials with memory which conduct heat have been carried out, for instance, by Achenbach, Vogel and Herrmann (1966) and by Dunwoody (1972).

8.9 AN ILLUSTRATIVE EXAMPLE ON THE APPLICATION OF VISCOELASTIC
WAVE PROPAGATION (DETERMINATION OF THE STRESS-RELAXATION
FUNCTION OF A VISCOELASTIC MATERIAL FROM ACOUSTIC DISPERSION
DATA)

We present, in this section, the work of Nunziato and Sutherland (1973) for the
determination of the stress-relaxation function for the solid polymer PMMA using
acoustic dispersion data on this viscoelastic material. This work is based on an earlier
paper by Sutherland and Lingle (1972) concerning the possibility of determining the
phase velocity and attenuation of acoustic waves in polymers over a reasonably wide
range of frequency using the time–temperature superposition concept introduced
earlier in section 5.5. The presented analysis is of interest and offers a possibility of
determining the stress relaxation function for a polymer using acoustic dispersion
data for a reasonably wide range. It was demonstrated by Nunziato and Sutherland
(1973) that the relaxation function for PMMA as determined by the latter method
compares favourably with the relaxation function deduced from experimental observations on steady shock waves in PMMA. This result is shown to be valid for a
time range of 10^{-5}–10^{8} μs.

8.9.1 Acoustical representation of the stress-relaxation function

We consider the linear stress-relaxation constitutive law in the form

$$\sigma(x,\ t) = R(0)\ \frac{\partial u(x,\ t)}{\partial x} + \int_0^\infty R'(\tau)\ \frac{\partial u(x,\ t-\tau)}{\partial x}\ \mathrm{d}\tau \tag{8.172}$$

where σ is the one-dimensional uniaxial stress, $R(\tau)$ is the corresponding stress
relaxation function and $R'(\tau) = \mathrm{d}R(\tau)/\mathrm{d}\tau$. Incorporating the dynamical field equation
for a travelling sinusoidal wave, one has the solution

$$u(X,\ t) = u_0\ \mathrm{Re}(\exp[-(\alpha + i\omega/c)X]\ \exp(i\omega t)) \tag{8.173}$$

where, in general, for viscoelastic materials, the phase velocity $c > 0$ and the
attenuation $\alpha > 0$ are functions of the frequency $\omega > 0$.

The solution (8.173) is admissible if and only if (Hunter, 1960; Nunziato and
Sutherland, 1973)

$$\rho_0 c^2(\omega) = |R(0) + \bar{R}'(\omega)|\ \sec^2[\tfrac{1}{2}\delta(\omega)] \tag{8.174a}$$

and

$$\alpha(\omega) = [\omega/c(\omega)]\ \tan[\tfrac{1}{2}\delta(\omega)] \tag{8.174b}$$

where ρ_0 is the reference density. The phase angle $0 \le \delta \le \pi/2$ is defined by

$$\tan\ \delta(\omega) = \frac{\mathrm{Im}[R(0) + \bar{R}'(\omega)]}{\mathrm{Re}[R(0) + \bar{R}'(\omega)]} \tag{8.175}$$

and $\bar{R}'(\omega)$ is the Fourier transform

$$\bar{R}'(\omega) = \int_0^\infty R'(\tau)\,\exp(i\omega\tau)\,d\tau. \tag{8.176}$$

If the functions $c(\omega)$ and $\alpha(\omega)$ are known, one can then determine the phase angle $\delta(\omega)$ and the stress-relaxation function $R(\tau)$ by using equations (8.174)–(8.176). One possible representation of these functions is

$$\delta(\omega) = 2\tan^{-1}|\alpha(\omega)c(\omega)/\omega| \tag{8.177}$$

$$R(\tau) = \frac{2}{\pi}\int_0^\tau\int_0^\infty \left(\frac{\rho_0 c^2(\omega)}{\sec\delta(\omega)\{[\alpha(\omega)c(\omega)/\omega]^2 - 1\}} - \rho_0 c_\infty^2\right)\cos(\omega\tau)\,d\omega\,d\tau$$

$$+\ \rho_0 c_\infty^2 \tag{8.178}$$

in which c_∞ is the high frequency limit of the phase velocity, i.e.

$$c_\infty = \lim_{\omega\to\infty} c(\omega). \tag{8.179}$$

In deducing (8.178), Nunziato and Sutherland (1973) used the standard cosine inversion of a Fourier transform and noted that

$$R(0) = \rho_0 c_\infty^2. \tag{8.180}$$

8.9.2 Determination of the stress-relaxation function from experimental acoustic data and using the time–temperature shift concept

In the process of determining experimentally the phase velocity and attenuation for PMMA over an extended range of frequency, Nunziato and Sutherland (1973) used, as a first step, the time–temperature superposition technique. The latter is introduced in section 5.5. It is based (Ferry, 1961; Schapery, 1974) primarily on the observation that, below the glass transition temperature of rubber-like material, a temperature change adjusts the time scale of the stress-relaxation function by a factor a_T. That is,

$$R(\tau)|_{T=T_1} = R\left(\frac{\tau}{a_T}\right)\Big|_{T=T_0} \tag{8.181}$$

where $T > 0$ indicates the temperature. Sutherland and Lingle (1972) have employed the relation (8.181) to include the effects of the time–temperature superposition concept on the expressions for the phase velocity and attenuation, namely

$$c(\omega)|_{T=T_1} = c(\omega a_T)|_{T=T_0},$$

$$\alpha(\omega)|_{T=T_1} = a_T\alpha(\omega a_T)|_{T=T_0}. \tag{8.182}$$

Consequently, if the wave propagation velocity and attenuation are experimentally measured as a function of temperature at some frequency, then they can be determined for all frequencies within the frequency range that corresponds to the applicability

Wave propagation

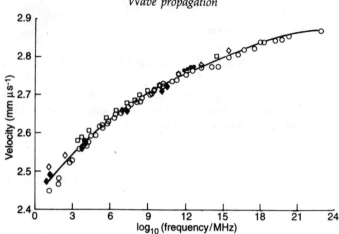

Fig. 8.25 Velocity data for PMMA: ●, Asay, Lamberson and Guenther (1969); □, Lingle (unreferenced data); ◇, Romberger (1970); ◆, Asay *et al.* (unreferenced data); ○, this work. (Source: Sutherland, H. J. and Lingle, R. (1972) An acoustic characterization of polymethyl methacrylate and three epoxy formulations. *J. Appl. Phys.*, **43**(10), 4022–6 (American Institute of Physics). Reprinted with permission.)

of (8.182). Using this technique, Sutherland and Lingle (1972) have determined the values of the functions $c(\omega)$ and $\alpha(\omega)$ for the solid polymer PMMA over 20 decades of frequency. Their results for room temperature are shown in Figs. 8.25 and 8.26 together with similar experimental data due to Asay, Lamberson and Guenther (1969) and Romberger (1970).

To evaluate the stress-relaxation function $R(\tau)$ from the above-mentioned acoustic data, Nunziato and Sutherland (1973) evaluated the integrand

$$F(\omega) = \frac{\rho_0 c^2(\omega)}{\sec \delta(\omega)\{[\alpha(\omega)c(\omega)/\omega]^2 - 1\}} - \rho_0 c_\infty^2 \qquad (8.183)$$

of equation (8.178) pointwise.

Representing the integrand (8.183) with the following series

$$F(\omega) = \sum_{i=1}^{20} f_i \exp\left(-\frac{\omega}{W_i}\right), \qquad (8.184)$$

the equation (8.178) may be integrated to yield

$$R(\tau) = \frac{2}{\pi} \sum_{i=1}^{20} f_i \tan^{-1}(\omega_i \tau) + \rho_0 c_\infty^2 \qquad (8.185)$$

whereby the high frequency limit c_∞ was evaluated by Nunziato and Sutherland (1973), following a method suggested by Walsh (1971), to be 2.87 mm μs^{-1}. The relaxation function $R(\tau)$ (8.185), as determined by Nunziato and Sutherland (1973) using the above procedure is shown in Fig. 8.27 for the solid polymer PMMA.

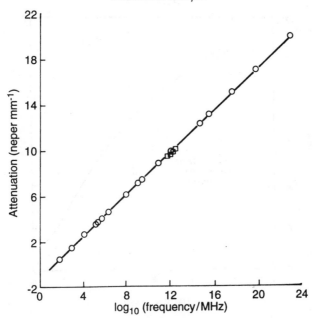

Fig. 8.26 Attenuation data for PMMA: □, Asay, Lamberson and Guenther (1969); ○, this work. (Source: Sutherland, H. J. and Lingle, R. (1972) An acoustic characterization of polymethyl methacrylate and three epoxy formulations. *J. Appl. Phys.*, **43**(10), 4022–6 (American Institute of Physics). Reprinted with permission.)

8.9.3 Determination of the stress-relaxation function from shock wave data

Nunziato and Sutherland (1973) considered plate impact experiments to study the one-dimensional dynamic responses of PMMA. They considered the characteristic time scale for such experiments to be 10^{-2}–1 μs. We denote, over this time scale, the relaxation function by $\hat{R}(\tau)$ where $\hat{R}(0)$ is equivalent to the value of the relaxation function at 10^{-2} μs and $\hat{R}(\infty)$ corresponds to the relaxation function at 1 μs. Using, then, the results (8.173) of the previous subsection, Nunziato and Sutherland (1973) obtained the stress-relaxation function $\hat{R}(\tau)$ shown in Fig. 8.28.

From this figure,

$$\hat{R}(0) = 90.1 \text{ kbar}$$

and   (8.186)

$$\hat{R}(\infty) = 88.0 \text{ kbar}.$$

Meantime, the characteristic relaxation time λ is evaluated by considering the relation

$$\hat{R}(\tau)\big|_{\tau=\lambda} = \frac{R_0 - R_\infty}{e} + R_\infty \qquad (8.187a)$$

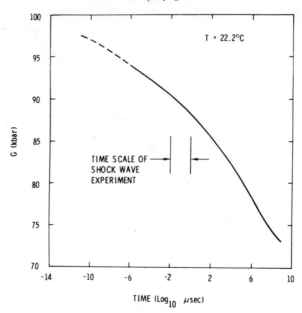

Fig. 8.27 Longitudinal stress relaxation function for PMMA. (Source: Nunziato, J. W. and Sutherland, H. J. (1973) Acoustical determination of stress relaxation functions in polymers. *J. Appl. Phys.*, **44**(1), 184–7 (American Institute of Physics). Reprinted with permission.)

in which e is the Naperian base. From (8.186) and (8.187a), one concludes from Fig. 8.28 that the characteristic relaxation time is

$$\lambda = 0.22 \ \mu s. \tag{8.187b}$$

Schuler (1970) considered the propagation of steady one-dimensional shock waves in PMMA. The relaxation behaviour of PMMA was characterized by a nonlinear constitutive relation of the form

$$\sigma(x, t) = \sigma_E(\varepsilon) + \int_0^\infty R(\varepsilon; \tau) \left[\frac{1 + \varepsilon(t - \tau)}{1 + \varepsilon(t)} - 1 \right] d\tau \tag{8.188}$$

where $\varepsilon = \partial u / \partial x$ is the longitudinal strain, $\sigma_E(\varepsilon)$ is the equilibrium response function and $R(\varepsilon; \tau)$ is the generalized stress-relaxation function. The latter is assumed to have the form

$$R(\varepsilon; \tau) = R(\varepsilon; 0) \exp(-\tau/\lambda). \tag{8.189}$$

Evaluating (8.188) for the strain jump

$$\varepsilon(t - \tau) = \varepsilon, \qquad \tau = 0,$$

$$= 0, \qquad \tau > 0,$$

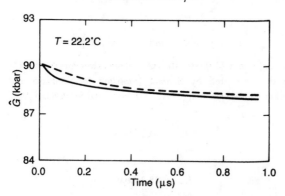

Fig. 8.28 Stress-relaxation function for PMMA appropriate for shock wave experiments: – – –, Schuler (1970, unpublished data); ———, this work. (Source: Nunziato, J. W. and Sutherland, H. J. (1973) Acoustical determination of stress relaxation functions in polymers. *J. Appl. Phys.*, **44**(1), 184–7 (American Institute of Physics). Reprinted with permission.)

it follows from (8.189) that

$$R(\varepsilon; 0) = -(1 + \varepsilon)^2 [\sigma_I(\varepsilon) - \sigma_E(\varepsilon)] / \lambda \varepsilon (2 + \varepsilon). \qquad (8.190)$$

From an analysis of steady waves (e.g. Greenberg, 1968; Schuler, 1970; Schuler, Nunziato and Walsh, 1973), one has

$$\sigma_I(\varepsilon) = \rho_0 U_I^2(\varepsilon) \varepsilon$$

and   (8.191)

$$\sigma_E(\varepsilon) = \rho_0 U_E^2(\varepsilon) \varepsilon$$

where $U_I(\varepsilon)$ and $U_E(\varepsilon)$ are least-square polynomial functions of the steady shock velocity as a function of strain ε at the shock front and at the tail of the wave (Nunziato and Sutherland, 1973). For small strains, the nonlinear constitutive relation (8.188) would reduce to the corresponding constitutive relation in the linear case, equation (8.172), with (Nunziato and Walsh, 1973)

$$\hat{R}(\tau) = \frac{d\sigma_I(0)}{d\varepsilon} + 2 \int_0^\tau R(0; \tau) \, d\tau. \qquad (8.192)$$

Combining, now (8.189) and (8.192), it follows that

$$\frac{d\sigma_I(0)}{d\varepsilon} = \rho_0 U_I^2(0) \qquad (8.193)$$

and consequently

$$\hat{R}(\tau) = (R_0 - R_\infty) \exp(-\tau/\lambda) + R_\infty \qquad (8.194)$$

264   Wave propagation

where

$$R_0 = \rho_0 U_I^2(0) \quad \text{and} \quad R_\infty = \rho_0 U_E^2(\infty).$$

It is noted that $U_I(0)$ and $U_E(0)$ are the zero-strain intercepts of the $U_I(\varepsilon)$ and $U_E(\varepsilon)$ curves. Using data reported by Schuler (reported in Nunziato and Sutherland (1973)) and Barker and Hollenbach (1970), Nunziato and Sutherland (1973) concluded that

$$R_0 = 90.2 \text{ kbars}$$

and   (8.195a)

$$R_\infty = 88.2 \text{ kbars}.$$

Schuler (1970), by fitting the observed steady wave profiles, found that

$$\lambda = 0.25 \ \mu s \qquad (8.195b)$$

which is comparable with the value given earlier by (8.187b). With the above data, the relaxation function (8.194) is given in Fig. 8.28 (after Nunziato and Sutherland, 1973). As demonstrated, there is reasonable agreement with the relaxation function deduced from acoustic dispersion data.

REFERENCES

Achenbach, J. D. and Chao, C. C. (1962) A three-parameter viscoelastic model particularly suited for dynamic problems. *J. Mech. Phys. Solids*, **10**, 245–52.

Achenbach, J. D., Vogel, S. M. and Herrmann, G. (1966) On stress waves in viscoelastic media conducting heat, in *Irreversible Aspects of Continuum Mechanics and Transfer of Physical Characteristics in Moving Fluids* (eds H. Parkus and L. I. Sedov), Springer, Berlin, pp. 1–15.

Ahrens, T. J. and Duvall, G. E. (1966) Stress relaxation behind shock waves in rocks. *J. Geophys. Res.*, **71**, 4349–60.

Alfrey, T., Jr (1948) *Mechanical Behaviour of High Polymers*, Interscience, New York.

Asay, J. R., Lamberson, D. L. and Guenther, A. H. (1969) Pressure and temperature dependence of velocities in polymethyl methacrylate. *J. Appl. Phys.*, **40**, 1768–83.

Bailey, P. and Chen, P. J. (1971) On the local and global behaviour of acceleration waves. *Arch. Ration. Mech. Anal.*, **41**, 121 (addendum: Asymptotic behaviour, *Arch. Ration. Mech. Anal.*, **44**, 212 (1972)).

Ballon, J. W. and Smith, J. C. (1949) Dynamic measurements of polymer physical properties. *J. Appl. Phys.*, **20**, 493–502.

Barker, L. M. (1968) The fine structure of compressive and release wave shapes in aluminium measured by the velocity interferometer technique, in *Behaviour of Dense Media Under High Dynamic Pressures*, Gordon and Breach, London, pp. 483–505.

Barker, L. M. and Hollenbach, R. E. (1964) System for measuring the dynamic properties of materials. *Rev. Sci. Instrum.*, **35**(6), 742–6.

Barker, L. M. and Hollenbach, R. E. (1965) Interferometer technique for measuring the dynamic mechanical properties of materials. *Rev. Sci. Instrum.*, **36**, 1617–20.

Barker, L. M. and Hollenbach, R. E. (1970) Shock wave studies of PMMA, fused silica and sapphire. *J. Appl. Phys.*, **41**, 4208–26.

Barton, C. S., Volterra, E. G. and Citron, S. J. (1958) On elastic impacts of spheres on long rods, in Proc. 3rd US Natl Cong. on Applied Mechanics, pp. 89–94.

Becker, E. C. H. and Carl, H. (1962) Transient-loading technique for mechanical impedance measurement, in *Experimental Techniques in Shock and Vibration* (ed. W. J. Worley), ASME, New York, pp. 1–10.

Bland, D. R. (1960) *The Theory of Linear Viscoelasticity*, Pergamon, New York.

Bradfield, G. (1951) Internal friction of solids. *Nature (London)*, **167**, 1021–3.

Chao, C. and Achenbach, J. D. (1964) A simple viscoelastic analogy for stress waves, in *Stress Waves in Anelastic Solids* (eds. H. Kolsky and W. Prager), IUTAM Symp., Brown University, Providence, RI, April 3–5, 1963, Springer, Berlin, pp. 222–38.

Chen, P. J. and Gurtin, M. E. (1970) On the growth of one-dimensional shock waves in materials with memory. *Arch. Ration. Mech. Anal.*, **36**, 33–46.

Chen, P. J. and Gurtin, M. E. (1972a) On the use of experimental results concerning steady shock waves to predict the acceleration wave response of nonlinear viscoelastic materials. *J. Appl. Mech.*, **39**, 295–6.

Chen, P. J. and Gurtin, M. E. (1972b) Thermodynamic influences on the growth of one-dimensional shock waves in materials with memory. *Z. Angew. Math. Phys.*, **23**, 69–79.

Chen, P. J., Gurtin, M. E. and Walsh, E. K. (1970) Shock amplitude variation in polymethyl methacrylate for fixed values of the strain gradient. *J. Appl. Phys.*, **41**, 3557–8.

Chou, P. C. (1968) Introduction to wave propagation in composite materials, in *Composite Materials Workshop* (eds. S. W. Tsai, J. C. Halpin and N. J. Pagano), Technomic, Stamford, CT, pp. 193–216.

Chree, C. (1889) The equations of an isotropic elastic solid in polar and cylindrical coordinates, their solutions and applications. *Trans. Cambridge Philos. Soc. Math. Phys. Sci.*, **6**, 115–7.

Chu, B. T. (1962) *Stress Waves in Isotropic Viscoelastic Materials*, Division of Engineering, Brown University, Providence, RI.

Coleman, B. D. (1964) Thermodynamics, strain impulses and viscoelasticity. *Arch. Ration. Mech. Anal.*, **17**, 230–54.

Coleman, B. D. and Gurtin, M. E. (1965a) Waves in materials with memory. II. On the growth and decay of one-dimensional acceleration waves. *Arch. Ration. Mech. Anal.*, **19**, 239–65.

Coleman, B. D. and Gurtin, M. E. (1965b) Waves in materials with memory. III. Thermodynamic influences on the growth and decay of acceleration waves. *Arch. Ration. Mech. Anal.*, **19**, 266–98.

Coleman, B. D. and Gurtin, M. E. (1965c) Waves in materials with memory. IV. Thermodynamics and the velocity of general acceleration waves. *Arch. Ration. Mech. Anal.*, **19**(5), 317–38.

Coleman, B. D. and Gurtin, M. E. (1966) Thermodynamics and one-dimensional shock waves in materials with memory. *Proc. R. Soc. London, Ser. A*, **292**, 562–74.

Coleman, B. D., Gurtin, M. E. and Herrera, R. I. (1965) Waves in materials with memory. I. The velocity of one-dimensional shock and acceleration waves. *Arch. Ration. Mech. Anal.*, **19**, 1–19.

Coleman, B. D., Greenberg, J. M. and Gurtin, M. E. (1966) Waves in materials with memory. V. On the amplitude of acceleration waves and mild discontinuities. *Arch. Ration. Mech. Anal.*, **22**, 333–54.

Cunningham, J. R. and Ivey, D. G. (1956) Dynamic properties of various rubbers at high frequencies. *J. Appl. Phys.*, **27**, 967–74.

Dally, J. W. (1968) A dynamic photoelastic study of a doubly loaded half-plane. *Dev. Mech.*, **4**, 649–64.

Dally, J. W. and Lewis, D. (1968) A photoelastic analysis of propagation of Rayleigh waves past a step change in elevation. *Bull. Seismd. Soc. Am.*, **58**, 539–63.

Dally, J. W. and Riley, W. F. (1965) *Experimental Stress Analysis*, McGraw-Hill, New York.

Dally, J. W. and Riley, W. F. (1967) Initial studies in three-dimensional dynamic photoelasticity. *J. Appl. Mech.*, **34**, 405–10.

Dally, J. W. and Thau, S. A. (1967) Observations of stress wave propagation in a half-plane with boundary loading. *Int. J. Solids Struct.*, **3**, 293–307.

Dally, J. W., Durrelli, A. J. and Riley, W. F. (1960) Photoelastic study of stress wave propagation in large plates. *Proc. Soc. Exp. Stress Anal.*, **17**, 33–50.

Davies, R. M. (1948) A critical study of the Hopkinson pressure bar. *Philos. Trans. R. Soc. London, Ser. A*, **240**, 375–457.

Dohrenwend, C. O., Drucker, D. C. and Moore, P. (1944) Transverse impact transients. *Exp. Stress Anal.*, **1**, 1–10.

Dove, R. C. and Adams, P. H. (1964) *Experimental Stress Analysis and Motion Measurement*, Merril, Columbus, OH.

Dunwoody, J. (1972) One-dimensional shock waves in heat conducting materials with memory. I. Thermodynamics. *Arch. Ration. Mech. Anal.*, **47**, 117–48.

Duvall, G. E. and Alverson, R. C. (1963) Fundamental research. *Tech. Summary Rep. 4*, Stanford Research Institute, Menlo Park, CA.

Evans, J. F., Hadley, C. F., Eisler, J. D. and Silverman, D. (1954) A three-dimensional seismic wave model with both electrical and visual observation of waves. *Geophysics*, **19**, 120–36.

Ferry, J. D. (1961) *Viscoelastic Properties of Polymers*, Wiley, New York.

Ferry, J. D. and Williams, M. L. (1952) Second approximation methods for determining the relaxation time spectrum of a viscoelastic material. *J. Colloid Sci.*, **7**, 347–53.

Fisher, H. C. (1954) Stress pulse in bar with neck or swell. *Appl. Sci. Res. A*, **4**, 317–28.

Frederick, J. R. (1965) *Ultrasonic Engineering*, Wiley, New York.

Glauz, R. D. and Lee, E. H. (1954) Transient wave analysis in a linear time-dependent material. *J. Appl. Phys.*, **25**, 947–53.

Goldsmith, W., Polivka, M. and Yang, T. (1966) Dynamic behaviour of concrete. *Exp. Mech.*, **23**, 65–79.

Goodier, J. N., Jahsman, W. E. and Ripperger, E. A. (1959) An experimental surface-wave method for recording force–time curves in elastic impacts. *J. Appl. Mech.*, **26**, 3–7.

Gorsky, W. S. (1936) On the transitions in the CuAu alloy III. On the influence of strain on the equilibrium in the ordered lattice of CuAl. *Phys. Z. Sowjet*, **6**, 77–81.

Graff, K. F. (1975) *Wave Motion in Elastic Solids*, Dover Publications, New York.

Graffi, D. (1982) Mathematical models and waves in linear viscoelasticity, in *Wave Propagation in Viscoelastic Media*, Vol. 52 (ed. F. Mainardi), Pitman, Boston, MA, PR, 1–27.

Green, W. A. (1964) The growth of plane discontinuities propagating into a homogeneously deformed elastic material. *Arch. Ration. Mech. Anal.*, **16**, 79–89.

Greenberg, J. M. (1967) The existence of steady shock waves in nonlinear materials with memory. *Arch. Ration. Mech. Anal.*, **24**, 1–21.

Greenberg, J. M. (1968) Existence of steady waves for a class of nonlinear dissipative materials. *Q. Appl. Math.*, **26**, 27–34.

Gurtin, M. E. and Herrera, I. (1964) A correspondence principle for viscoelastic wave propagation. *Q. Appl. Math.*, **22**, 360–4.

Gurtin, M. E. and Herrera, I. (1965) On dissipation inequalities and linear viscoelasticity. *Q. Appl. Math.*, **23**, 235–45.

Hetenyi, M. (ed.) (1950) *Handbook of Experimental Stress Analysis*, Wiley, New York.

Hill, R. (1962) Acceleration waves in solids. *J. Mech. Phys. Solids*, **10**, 1–16.

Hillier, K. W. (1949) A method of measuring some dynamic elastic constants and its application to the study of high polymers. *Proc. Phys. Soc.*, **52**(2), 701–13.

Hillier, K. W. (1960) A review of the progress in the measurement of dynamic elastic properties, in Int. Symp. on Stress Wave Propagation in Materials (ed. N. Davids), Interscience, London, pp. 183–98.

Hillier, K. W. and Kolsky, H. (1949) An investigation of the dynamic elastic properties of some high polymers. *Proc. Phys. Soc. B*, **62**, 111–21.

Hsieh, D. Y. and Kolsky, H. (1958) An experimental study of pulse propagation in elastic cylinders. *Proc. Phys. Soc.*, **71**, 608–12.

Hudson, G. E. (1943) Dispersion of elastic waves in solid circular cylinders. *Phys. Rev.*, **63**, 46–51.

Huilgol, R. R. (1973) Growth of plane shock waves in materials with memory. *Int. J. Eng. Sci.,* **11**, 75–86.

Hunter, S. C. (1960) Viscoelastic waves, in *Progress in Solid Mechanics,* Vol. I. (eds. I. N. Sneddon and R. Hill), North-Holland, Amsterdam, pp. 1–57.

Ivey, D. G., Mrowea, B. A. and Guth, E. (1949) Propagation of ultrasonic bulk waves in high polymers. *J. Appl. Phys.,* **20**, 486–92.

Janke, E. and Emde, F. (1945) *Tables of Functions,* Dover Publications, New York.

Keast, D. N. (1967) *Measurements in Mechanical Dynamics,* McGraw-Hill, New York.

Kolsky, H. (1954a) Attenuation of short mechanical pulses by high polymers, in Proc. 2nd Int. Congr. on Rheology, Butterworths, London, pp. 79–84.

Kolsky, H. (1954b) The propagation of longitudinal elastic waves along cylindrical bars. *Philos. Mag.,* **45**, 712–26.

Kolsky, H. (1956) The propagation of stress pulses in viscoelastic solids. *Philos. Mag., Ser. 8,* **1**, 693–710.

Kolsky, H. (1958) The propagation of stress waves in viscoelastic solids. *Appl. Mech. Rev.,* **11**, 465–8.

Kolsky, H. (1960) Viscoelastic waves, in Int. Symp. on Stress Wave Propagation in Materials (ed. N. Davids), Interscience, London, pp. 59–90.

Kolsky, H. (1963) *Stress Waves in Solids,* Dover Publications, New York.

Lamb, H. (1904) On the propagation of tremors over the surface of an elastic solid. *Philos. Trans. R. Soc. London, Ser. A,* **203**, 1–42.

Lamb, H. (1917) On waves in an elastic plate. *Proc. R. Soc. London, Ser. A,* **93**, 114–28.

Lee, E. H. and Kanter, I. (1953) Wave propagation in finite rods of viscoelastic materials. *J. Appl. Phys.,* **24**(9), 1115–22.

Lee, E. H. and Morrison, J. A. (1956) A comparison of the propagation of longitudinal waves in rods of viscoelastic materials. *J. Polym. Sci.,* **19**, 93–110.

Lindholm, U. S. (1964) Some experiments with the split Hopkinson pressure bar. *J. Mech. Phys. Solids,* **12**, 317–35.

Magrab, E. B. and Blomquist, D. S. (1971) *The Measurement of Time-Varying Phenomena,* Wiley–Interscience, New York.

Mainardi, F. and Nervosi, R. (1980) Transient-waves in finite viscoelastic rods. *Lett. Nuovo Cim.,* **29**, 443–7.

Mainardi, F. and Turchetti, G. (1975) Wave front expansions for transient viscoelastic waves. *Mech. Res. Commun.,* **2**, 107–12.

Mainardi, F. and Turchetti, G. (1979) Positive constraints and approximation methods in linear viscoelasticity. *Lett. Nuovo Cim.,* **26**, 38–40.

Malvern, L. E. (1951) Plastic wave propagation in a bar of material exhibiting a strain rate effect. *Q. Appl. Math.,* **8**, 405–11.

Mason, W. P. and McSkimin, H. J. (1947) Attenuation and scattering of high frequency sound waves in metals and glasses. *J. Acoust. Soc. Am.,* **19**, 464–73.

Medick, M. A. (1961) On classical plate theory and wave propagation. *J. Appl. Mech.,* **28**, 223–8.

Morrison, J. A. (1956) Wave propagation in rods of Voigt material and viscoelastic materials with three-parameter models. *Q. Appl. Math.,* **14**, 153–169.

Morse, P. and Feshbach, H. (1953) *Methods of Theoretical Physics,* Vols I and II, McGraw-Hill, New York.

Nashif, A. D., Jones, D. I. G. and Henderson, J. P. (1965) *Vibration Damping,* Wiley, New York.

Nunziato, J. W. and Sutherland, H. J. (1973) Acoustical determination of stress relaxation functions in polymers. *J. Appl. Phys.,* **44**(1), 184–7.

Nunziato, J. W. and Walsh, E. K. (1973) Propagation of steady shock waves in nonlinear thermoviscoelastic solids. *J. Mech. Phys. Solids,* **21**, 317–35.

Oliver, J. (1957) Elastic wave dispersion in a cylindrical rod by a wide-band short duration pulse technique. *J. Acoust. Soc. Am.,* **29**, 189–94.

Orowan, E. (1934) Zür Kristall Plastizität. III. Über den Mechanismus des gleitvorganges. Z. Phys., **89**, 634–59.

Pindera, J. T. (1986) New research perspectives opened by isodyne and strain gradient photoelasticity, in Proc. Int. Symp. on Photoelasticity, Tokyo, pp. 193–202.

Polanyi, M. (1934) Über eine Art Gitterstörung, die einen Kristall plastisch machen Könnte. Z. Phys., **89**, 660–4.

Prescott, J. (1942) Elastic waves and vibrations of thin rods. Philos. Mag., **33**, 703–54.

Press, F. and Oliver, J. (1955) Model study of air-coupled surface waves. J. Acoust. Soc. Am., **27**, 45–6.

Rayleigh, J. W. S. (1887) On waves propagated along the plane surface of an elastic solid. Proc. London Math. Soc., **17**, 4–11.

Rayleigh, J. W. S. (1894) Theory of Sound, Dover Publications, New York.

Reinhardt, H. W. and Dally, J. W. (1970) Some characteristics of Rayleigh wave interaction with surface flaws. Mater. Eval., **28**, 213–20.

Riley, W. F. and Dally, J. W. (1966) A photoelastic analysis of stress wave propagation in a layered model. Geophysics, **31**, 881–9.

Ripperger, E. A. (1953) The propagation of pulses in cylindrical bars. An experimental study, in Proc. 1st Midwest Conf. on Solid Mechanics, pp. 29–39.

Rogers, C. A., Barker, D. K. and Jaeger, L. A. (1988) Introduction to smart materials and structures, in Proc. Smart Materials, Structures and Mathematical Issues Workshop, Virginia Polytechnic Institute and State University, Blacksburg, VA, September 15–16, 1992, pp. 17–28.

Romberger, A. B. (1970) MS Thesis, Pennsylvania State University.

Schapery, R. A. (1974) In Viscoelastic Behaviour and Analysis of Composite Materials, Vol. 2 (ed. G. Sendeckj), Academic Press, New York, pp. 86–168.

Schuler, K. W. (1970) Propagation of steady shock waves in polymethyl methacrylate. J. Mech. Phys. Solids, **18**, 277–93.

Schuler, K. W. and Walsh, E. K. (1971) Critical-induced acceleration for shock propagation in polymethyl methacrylate. J. Appl. Mech., **38**, 641–5.

Schuler, K. W., Nunziato, J. W. and Walsh, E. K. (1973) Recent results in nonlinear viscoelastic wave propagation. Int. J. Solid Struct., **91**, 1237–81.

Snoek, J. E. (1941) Effect of small quantities of carbon and nitrogen on the elastic and plastic properties of iron. Physica, **8**, 711–33.

Sokolnikoff, I. S. (1956) Mathematical Theory of Elasticity, 2nd edn, McGraw-Hill, New York.

Srinivasan, S. I. and Haddad, Y. M. (1992) Intelligent materials – an overview. Internal Report, Department of Mechanical Engineering, University of Ottawa, Ottawa.

Sutherland, H. J. and Lingle, R. (1972) An acoustic characterization of polymethyl methacrylate and three epoxy formulations. J. Appl. Phys., **43**(10), 4022–6.

Tanagi, T. (1990) A concept of intelligent material, in US–Japan Workshop on Smart/Intelligent Materials and Systems (eds C. A. Rogers, C. Andrew and A. Masuo), March 19–23, 1990, Honolulu, HI, pp. 3–10.

Tanary, S. and Haddad, Y. M. (1988) Characterization of adhesively bonded joints using acousto-ultrasonics. Final rep. Contract 31946-6-0012/01-ST, Department of Mechanical Engineering, University of Ottawa, Ottawa.

Tatel, H. E. (1954) Note on the nature of a seismogram II. J. Geophys. Res., **59**, 289–94.

Thau, S. A. and Dally, J. W. (1969) Subsurface characteristics of the Rayleigh wave. Int. J. Eng. Sci., **7**, 37–52.

Thomas, T. Y. (1957) The growth and decay of sonic discontinuities in ideal gases. J. Math. Mech., **6**, 455–69.

Thomas, T. Y. (1961) Plastic Flow and Fracture in Solids, Academic Press, New York.

Timoshenko, S. P. (1921) On the correction for shear of the differential equation for transverse vibrations of prismatic bars. Philos. Mag., Ser. 6, **41**, 744–6.

Tobolsky, A., Powell, R. E. and Eyring, H. (1943) The Chemistry of Large Molecules, Interscience, New York.

Truesdell, C. and Toupin, R. A. (1960) The classical field theories, in *Handbuch der Physik*, Vol. III/1 (ed. S. Flügge), Springer, Berlin.

Tschoegl, N. W. (1989) *The Phenomenological Theory of Linear Viscoelastic Behaviour*, Springer, Berlin.

Valanis, K. C. (1965) Propagation and attenuation of waves in linear viscoelastic solids. *J. Math. Phys.*, **44**(3), 227–39.

Vary, A. (1988) The acousto-ultrasonic approach, in *Acousto- Ultrasonics: Theory and Application* (ed. J. C. Duke, Jr), Plenum, New York, pp. 1–21.

Varley, E. (1965) Acceleration fronts in viscoelastic materials. *Arch. Ration. Mech. Anal.*, **19**, 215–25.

Varley, E. and Cumberbatch, E. (1965) Nonlinear theory of wavefront propagation. *J. Inst. Math. Appl.*, **1** (June), 101–12.

Viktorov, I. A. (1967) *Rayleigh and Lamb Waves: Physical Theory and Applications*, Plenum, New York.

Volterra, V. (1931) *Theory of Functionals*, Dover Publications, New York.

Walsh, E. K. (1971) The decay of stress waves in one-dimensional polymer rods. *Trans. Soc. Rheol.*, **15**(2), 345–53.

Worely, W. J. (ed.) (1962) *Experimental Techniques in Shock and Vibration*, ASME, New York.

Zener, C. (1948) *Elasticity and Anelasticity of Metals*, University Press, Chicago, IL.

FURTHER READING

Abbott, B. W. and Cornish, R. H. (1965) A stress wave technique for determining the tensile strength of brittle materials. *Exp. Mech.*, **22**, 148–53.

Achenbach, J. D. and Reddy, D. P. (1967) Note on wave propagation in linearly viscoelastic media. *Z. Angew. Math. Phys.*, **18**, 141–4.

Arenz, R. J. (1964) Uniaxial wave propagation in realistic viscoelastic materials. *J. Appl. Mech.*, **86** (March), 17–21.

Arenz, R. J. (1965) Two-dimensional wave propagation in realistic viscoelastic materials. *J. Appl. Mech.*, **32**(2), 303–14.

Baker, W. E. and Dove, R. C. (1962) Measurements of internal strains in a bar subjected to longitudinal impact. *Exp. Mech.*, **19**, 307–11.

Barberan, J. and Herrera, I. (1966) Uniqueness theorems and speed of propagation of signals in viscoelastic materials. *Arch. Ration. Mech. Anal.*, **23**, 173–90.

Berry, D. S. (1958) A note on stress pulses in viscoelastic rods. *Philos. Mag.*, **8**, 100–2.

Berry, D. S. and Hunter, S. C. (1956) The propagation of dynamic stresses in viscoelastic rods. *J. Mech. Phys. Solids*, **4**, 72–95.

Chu, B. T. (1962) Stress waves in isotropic linear viscoelastic materials (part one). *J. Méc.*, **1**(1), 439–62.

Chu, B. T. (1965) Response of various material media to high velocity loadings. I. Linear elastic and viscoelastic materials. *J. Mech. Phys. Solids*, **13**, 165–87.

Dunwoody, J. (1966) Longitudinal wave propagation in a rate dependent material. *Int. J. Eng. Sci.*, **4**, 277–87.

Dziecielak, R. (1985) The effect of temperature on the propagation of discontinuity waves in a porous medium with a viscoelastic skeleton. *Stud. Geotech. Mech.*, **7**(2), 17–34.

Engelbrecht, J. (1979) One-dimensional deformation waves in nonlinear viscoelastic materials. *Wave Motion*, **1**, 65–74.

Fisher, G. M. C. and Gurtin, M. E. (1965) Wave propagation in the linear theory of viscoelasticity. *Q. Appl. Math.*, **23**, 257–63.

Frydrychowicz, W. and Singh, M. C. (1986) Similarity representation of wave propagation in a nonlinear viscoelastic rod on a group theoretic basis. *Appl. Math. Model.*, **10**(8), 284–93.

Gopalsamy, K. and Aggarwala, B. D. (1972) Propagation of disturbances from randomly moving sources. *Z. Angew. Math. Mech.*, **52**, 31–5.

Graffi, D. (1952) Sulla teoria dei materiali elasticoviscosi. *Atti Accad. Ligure Sci. Lett.*, **9**, 1–10.

Green, W. A. (1960) Dispersion relations for elastic waves in bars, in *Progress in Solid Mechanics*, Vol. I (eds I. N. Sneddon and R. Hill), North-Holland, Amsterdam, Chap. 5.

Harris, C. M. and Crede, E. (1961) *Shock and Vibration Handbook*, Vols I, II and III, McGraw-Hill, New York.

Hatfield, P. (1950) Propagation of low frequency ultrasonic waves in rubbers and rubber-like polymers. *Br. J. Appl. Phys.*, **1**, 252–6.

Hrusa, W. J. and Renardy, M. (1985) On wave propagation in linear viscoelasticity. *Q. Appl. Math.*, **43**(2), 237–53.

Hunter, S. C. (1961) Tentative equations for the propagation of stress, strain and temperature fields in viscoelastic solids. *J. Mech. Phys. Solids*, **9**, 39–51.

Jeffrey, A. (1978) Nonlinear wave propagation. *Z. Angew. Math. Mech.*, **58**, T38–T56.

Jeffrey, A. and Taniuti, T. (1964) *Nonlinear Wave Propagation*, Academic Press, New York.

Knauss, W. G. (1968) Uniaxial wave propagation in a viscoelastic material using measured material properties. *J. Appl. Mech.*, **35**(3), 449–53.

Kolsky, H. (1949) An investigation of the mechanical properties of materials at very high rates of loading. *Proc. Phys. Soc., B*, **62**, 676–700.

Kolsky, H. (1960) Experimental wave-propagation in solids, in *Structural Mechanics* (eds J. N. Goodier and N. Hoff), Pergamon, Oxford, pp. 233–62.

Kolsky, H. (1965) Experimental studies in stress wave propagation, in Proc. Vth US Natl. Congr. on Applied Mechanics, pp. 21–36.

Kolsky, H. and Prager, W. (eds) (1964) *Stress Waves in Anelastic Solids*, IUTAM Symposium, Brown University, Providence, RI, April 3–5, 1963, Springer, Berlin, pp. 1–341.

Langhaar, H. L. (1962) *Energy Methods in Applied Mechanics*, Wiley, New York.

Lifshitz, J. M. and Kolsky, H. (1965) The propagation of spherical divergent stress pulses in linear viscoelastic solids. *J. Mech. Phys. Solids*, **13**, 361–76.

Lindsay, R. B. (1960) *Mechanical Radiation*, McGraw-Hill, New York.

Lockett, F. J. (1962) The reflection and refraction of waves at an interface between viscoelastic materials. *J. Mech. Phys. Solids*, **10**, 53–64.

Love, A. E. H. (1944) *A Treatise on the Mathematical Theory of Elasticity*, Dover Publications, New York.

Mahalanabis, R. K. and Mandal, B. (1986) Propagation of thermomagneto-viscoelastic waves in a half-space of Voigt-type material. *Indian J. Technol.*, **24** (September), 565–7.

Meyer, M. L. (1964) On spherical near fields and far fields in elastic and viscoelastic solids. *J. Mech. Phys. Solids*, **12**, 77–111.

Miklowjiz, J. (1964) Pulse propagation in a viscoelastic solid with geometric dispersion, in *Stress Waves in Anelastic Solids*, Springer, Berlin, pp. 255–76.

Norris, J. M. (1967) Propagation of a stress pulse in a viscoelastic rod. *Exp. Mech.*, **7**(7), 297–301.

Nunziato, J. W. and Walsh, E. K. (1973) Amplitude behaviour of shock waves in a thermoviscoelastic solid. *Int. J. Solids Struct.*, **9**, 1373–83.

Petrof, R. C. and Gratch, S. (1964) Wave propagation in a viscoelastic material with temperature-dependent properties and thermomechanical coupling. *J. Appl. Mech.*, **31**(3), 423–9.

Renardy, M. (1982) Some remarks on the propagation and non-propagation of discontinuities in linearly viscoelastic liquids. *Rheol. Acta*, **21**, 251–4.

Ricker, N. H. (1977) *Transient Waves in Viscoelastic Media*, Elsevier, Amsterdam.

Rubin, J. R. (1954) Propagation of longitudinal deformation waves in a prestressed rod of material exhibiting a strain-rate effect. *J. Appl. Phys.*, **25**, 528–36.

Sackman, J. L. and Kaya, I. (1968) On the propagation of transient pulses in linearly viscoelastic media. *J. Mech. Phys. Solids*, **16**, 349–56.

Sips, R. (1951) Propagation phenomena in elastic viscous media. *J. Polym. Sci.*, **6**, 285–93.

Skalak, R. (1957) Longitudinal impact of a semi-infinite circular elastic bar. *J. Appl. Mech.*, **34**, 59–64.

Stoneley, R. (1924) Elastic waves at the surface of separation of two solids. *Proc. R. Soc. London, Ser. A,* **106**, 416–28.

Sultanov, K. S. (1984) Longitudinal wave propagation in a viscoelastic semispace including an absorbing layer. *J. Appl. Mech. Tech. Phys.,* **25**(5), 790–5.

Timoshenko, S. P. (1928) *Vibration Problems in Engineering,* Van Nostrand, NJ.

Tsai, Y. M. and Kolsky, H. (1968) Surface wave propagation for linear viscoelastic solids. *J. Mech. Phys. Solids,* **16**, 99–109.

Volterra, E. (1955) A one-dimensional theory of wave propagation in elastic rods based on the 'method of internal constraints'. *Ing. Arch.,* **23**, 410.

Watson, G. N. (1960) *A Treatise on the Theory of Bessel Functions,* Cambridge University Press, New York.

Whitham, G. B. (1974) *Linear and Nonlinear Waves,* Wiley, New York.

Zukas, J. A. (1982) Stress waves in solids, in *Impact Dynamics* (eds J. A. Zukas. T. Nicholas, H. F. Swift, L. B. Greszczuk and D. R. Curran), Wiley, New York, Chap. 1, pp. 1–27.

9
Viscoelastic boundary value problem

9.1 INTRODUCTION

In classical elasticity where the response behaviour of the material is time independent, boundary value problems are conventionally classified as static or dynamic in view of the time dependency of the boundary conditions. Static problems of elasticity are often classified into the following two categories (e.g. Fung, 1965; Gakhof, 1966; Fichera, 1972; Gladwell, 1980).

1. Uniform boundary conditions: in this category, either the external loading (stress vector) or, alternatively, the external displacement are specified everywhere on the external boundary.
2. Mixed boundary conditions: here, the external loading is specified over a part of the boundary while the external displacement is specified over the recurring part.

Because of time independency characteristic of the static elastic problem, the boundary conditions as classified by the above two categories are fixed, i.e. they are time invariants. In dynamic problems, however, a set of initial conditions on both the components of the external loading and the displacement must be specified in the volume V and over the surface S of the continuous body.

In view of the time dependency of the response behaviour in viscoelasticity which is further complicated by the form of the constitutive relations and, hence, the associated boundary conditions, serious attempts to solve viscoelastic boundary value problems have lagged considerably behind those in classical elasticity. It is only in the last four decades that viscoelastic boundary value problems have been actively considered. At the beginning, researchers have given attention to the solution of the simpler viscoelastic problems that have analogues in classical elasticity whereby the viscoelastic solution may be expressed directly in terms of the analogous elastic problem. Research efforts have been advanced since then to tackle more difficult viscoelastic boundary value problems with or without correspondence to the theory of elasticity.

9.2 CLASSIFICATION OF BOUNDARY VALUE PROBLEMS IN VISCOELASTICITY

Since the response behaviour of a viscoelastic material is time dependent, it thus follows that no real static viscoelastic problem exists. However, in a large number of cases, it may be admissible (e.g. Hunter, 1967) to neglect the acceleration terms in the equations of motion. In such case, the viscoelastic boundary value problem is referred to as 'quasi-static' or 'quasi-stationary'. As Hunter (1967), for instance, pointed out, the only 'true static' problems in viscoelasticity are those corresponding to the equilibrium limit of complete stress relaxation.

A 'quasi-static' viscoelastic problem is often classified from the point of view of the time dependency of its boundary regions. In this, the following two categories are often dealt with.

1. For quasi-static problems with fixed (time-independent) boundary conditions, the loading history is assumed to be known for all time over a fixed part of the boundary, while the displacement history is specified for the remaining part. This type of problem is generally solvable using a correspondence with an analogous elastic problem, i.e. by employing the correspondence principle (introduced earlier in Chapter 8). This is essentially due to the possibility of obtaining Laplace (or Fourier) transforms of the boundary conditions as illustrated below in Section 9.6 (e.g. Hunter, 1960, 1967; Lee, 1960; Schapery, 1955, 1962, 1974).
2. Quasi-static problems with mixed boundary regions which are time dependent are not generally susceptible to solution by the correspondence principle as it may be impossible to obtain appropriate transforms of the boundary conditions. Examples of such type of problems may include contact problems where the load on the indentor is varying or the indentor is moving into the viscoelastic material specimen with an indentation of varying geometry (for instance, Hunter, 1968; Graham, 1969; Graham and Williams, 1972; Atkinson and Coleman, 1977; Aboudi, 1979; Nachman and Walton, 1978; Sabin, 1987).

Much less research work has been carried out on inertial and dynamic viscoelastic boundary value problems. In this domain, a large portion of the research has concentrated primarily on viscoelastic wave propagation problems that involve only one space variable (Chapter 8). Chao and Achenbach (1964) and Gurtin and Herrera (1964), among others, considered the use of the correspondence principle for the solution of viscoelastic wave propagation problems of this type. In general, however, viscoelastic waves may propagate in three dimensions with different magnitudes of attenuation and dispersion (e.g. Lockett, 1962). In this case, an associated boundary value problem may not be solvable via a dynamic correspondence principle (Hunter, 1967).

Research efforts to solve thermoviscoelastic boundary value problems have often been distracted by the fact that mechanical properties of viscoelastic materials are sensitive to temperature variations. This is complicated further by the heat generated in the viscoelastic material during deformation. The formulation of the governing equations has thus been proven to be difficult. Morland and Lee (1960), for instance, have considered the case of a thermorheologically simple solid (e.g. Schwarzl and Staverman, 1952; Hunter, 1961) in the absence of internally generated heat and thermodynamic coupling effects. Morland and Lee (1960) applied, then, the resulting equations to the quasi-static problem of an incompressible long cylinder subject to radial temperature gradient and internal pressure. Muki and Sternberg (1961) have dealt with the thermal stresses in viscoelastic materials with temperature-dependent properties and considered transient stress problems in plane slabs and spheres subject to temperature variation. Rogers and Lee (1962) have considered the solution of the quasi-static thermoviscoelastic problem of a sphere with an internally ablating cavity. Sternberg and Gurtin (1963, 1964) considered the uniquness of the theory of thermorheologically simple ablating viscoelastic solids.

A classification of boundary value problems in viscoelasticity is presented in Fig. 9.1. For comprehensive studies of the subject matter, the reader is referred further to Read (1950), Lee, Radok and Woodward (1959), Sternberg (1964), Predeleanu (1965), Rogers (1965), Lee (1966) and Golden and Graham (1988), among others.

9.3 FORMULATION OF THE VISCOELASTIC BOUNDARY VALUE PROBLEM

In compliance with the principles of continuum mechanics, the motion of a viscoelastic (continuum) body is generally governed by the laws of conservation of mass and momentum, the stress–strain constitutive relations, the boundary conditions and the

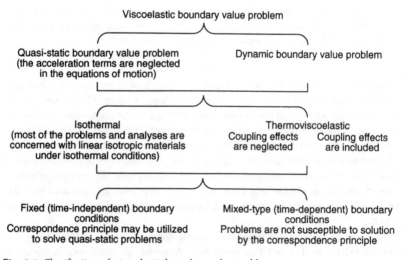

Fig. 9.1 Classification of viscoelastic boundary value problems.

initial conditions. As demonstrated in the remainder of this chapter, the formulation of this set of governing conditions is determined by the type of the boundary value problem considered.

9.4 ISOTHERMAL, LINEAR VISCOELASTIC BOUNDARY VALUE PROBLEM

In this class of boundary value problem, all the geometrical assumptions of infinitesimal elasticity theory are implied. These would usually include the assumptions of small deformations and small strains, the boundary conditions applied to undisturbed surfaces and the neglect of any convective terms in the acceleration. In this class of viscoelastic boundary value problem, only the viscoelastic stress–strain relations would differ from the linear elastic constitutive equations. All other governing conditions would follow directly from linear elasticity with proper inclusion of the time dependency of the pertaining variables. The governing set of conditions for an isothermal, linear viscoelastic boundary value problem are as follows.

9.4.1 Initial conditions

We assume that the body is initially undisturbed. In other words, it is initially stress free and in mechanical equilibrium. Thus, the initial conditions are

$$u_i(t) = 0, \quad \varepsilon_{ij}(t) = 0, \quad \sigma_{ij}(t) = 0, \quad -\infty < t < 0, \tag{9.1}$$

where u_i designate the components of the displacement vector in a rectangular Cartesian coordinate system.

9.4.2 Boundary conditions

The boundary B of the body is considered to be composed of two parts B_σ and B_u. That is,

$$B = B_\sigma + B_u$$

where B_σ denotes the part of the boundary of the body over which the components of the stress $\boldsymbol{\sigma}$ are prescribed and B_u indicates the remaining part of the boundary over which the components of the displacement $\boldsymbol{u}$ are specified. The boundary conditions may be assigned in the form of magnitudes of

- the traction vector components T_i over B_σ such that

$$\sigma_{ij}(\mathbf{x}, t)n_j = T_i(\mathbf{x}, t), \quad \mathbf{x} \text{ on } B_\sigma, \tag{9.2a}$$

where n_j are the components of the outward unit normal to B_σ, or
- the displacement vector components U_i over B_u as

$$u_i(\mathbf{x}, t) = U_i(\mathbf{x}, t), \quad \mathbf{x} \text{ on } B_u. \tag{9.2b}$$

The boundary conditions (9.2) are assumed to be fixed; that is, both the traction vector components T_i and the displacement vector components U_i are considered to be prescribed for all t.

9.4.3 Balance of linear momentum

One of the following two situations may be considered:

- for a quasi-static problem, the equilibrium equation is

$$\sigma_{ij,j} + \chi_i = 0; \tag{9.3}$$

- for a dynamic problem, the equation of motion is

$$\sigma_{ij,j} + \chi_i = \rho \, \frac{\partial^2 u_i}{\partial t^2}. \tag{9.4}$$

In (9.3) and (9.4) χ_i are the body force components per unit volume.

9.4.4 Linear strain–displacement relations

$$\varepsilon_{ij}(t) = \tfrac{1}{2}[u_{i,j}(t) + u_{j,i}(t)] \tag{9.5}$$

in which a comma indicates partial differentiation with respect to the coordinates x_i of the material particle.

9.4.5 Stress–strain relations

General linear constitutive equations for a viscoelastic material with an arbitrary degree of anisotropy may be expressed in the form of Boltzmann superposition integral.

- For the creep case,

$$\varepsilon_{ij}(t) = \int_0^t F_{ijkl}(t - \tau) \, \frac{\partial \sigma_{kl}(\tau)}{\partial \tau} \, d\tau \tag{9.6}$$

where $F_{ijkl}(t - \tau)$ are the components of the creep function.
- For the relaxation case

$$\sigma_{ij}(t) = \int_0^t R_{ijkl}(t - \tau) \, \frac{\partial \varepsilon_{kl}(\tau)}{\partial \tau} \, d\tau \tag{9.7}$$

where $R_{ijkl}(t - \tau)$ are the components of the relaxation function.

As mentioned in section 4.4, the constitutive relation for an isotropic material can be reduced to two pairs of operators, one for the stress–strain deviatoric constitutive relation which covers shear response and one for average hydrostatic tension and dilatation. In this case, a differential operator law in the following form may be used (Lee, 1960):

$$P_1(D)\sigma'_{ij}(t) = Q_1(D)\varepsilon'_{ij}(t)$$
$$P_2(D)\sigma_{kk}(t) = Q_2(D)\varepsilon_{kk}(t)$$

(9.8)

where σ'_{ij}, ε'_{ij} are the stress and strain deviators defined, respectively, by

$$\sigma'_{ij} = \sigma_{ij} - \tfrac{1}{3}\delta_{ij}\sigma_{kk}, \quad \sigma'_{ii} = 0,$$
$$\varepsilon'_{ij} = \varepsilon_{ij} - \tfrac{1}{3}\delta_{ij}\varepsilon_{kk}, \quad \varepsilon'_{ii} = 0.$$

(9.9)

In equation (9.8), P_1, P_2, Q_1 and Q_2 are polynomials of the time derivative operator $D = \partial/\partial t$.

Alternatively, the stress–strain relations (9.8) may be used in either of the following constitutive forms:

- in the creep case,

$$\varepsilon'_{ij} = \sigma'_{ij}(t) * dF_1(t), \quad \varepsilon_{kk}(t) = \sigma_{kk}(t) * dF_2(t)$$

(9.10)

where $F_1(t)$ and $F_2(t)$ are the creep functions in pure shear and pure dilatation, respectively (section 4.4);

- in the relaxation use,

$$\sigma'_{ij}(t) = \varepsilon'_{ij}(t) * dR_1(t), \quad \varepsilon_{kk}(t) = \sigma_{kk}(t) * dR_2(t)$$

(9.11)

where $R_1(t)$ and $R_2(t)$ are the relaxation functions in pure shear and pure dilatation, respectively.

For an isotropic viscoelastic material, an approximate form of the constitutive relation in the relaxation case may be expressed (Hunter, 1967) as

$$\sigma_{ij}(t) = \delta_{ij} \int_0^t \lambda(t-\tau) \frac{\partial \varepsilon_{kk}(\tau)}{\partial \tau}\, d\tau + 2 \int_0^t \mu(t-\tau) \frac{\partial \varepsilon'_{ij}(\tau)}{\partial \tau}\, d\tau$$

(9.12)

where $\lambda(t)$ and $\mu(t)$ are appropriate relaxation functions.

In terms of deviatoric and dilatational components, the isotropic constitutive equations in the relaxation case can be further written as

$$\sigma'_{ij}(t) = 2 \int_0^t \mu(t-\tau) \frac{\partial \varepsilon'_{ij}(\tau)}{\partial \tau}\, d\tau$$

and

(9.13)

$$\sigma_{ii}(t) = 3 \int_0^t k(t-\tau) \frac{\partial \varepsilon_{ij}(\tau)}{\partial \tau}\, d\tau$$

where $\sigma'_{ij}(t)$ and $\varepsilon'_{ij}(t)$ are, respectively, the deviatoric stress and the deviatoric strain components and $\mu(t)$ and $k(t)$ are the relaxation functions in pure shear and pure dilatation, respectively.

In the isothermal linear boundary value problem, the three balance of linear momentum equations (9.3) or (9.4), the six strain–displacement relations (9.5) and the six stress–strain constitutive equations, e.g. (9.13), constitute a set of fifteen field equations for the fifteen dependent variables u_i, ε_{ij} and σ_{ij} under the prescribed boundary conditions $T_i(\mathbf{x}, t)$ and $U_i(\mathbf{x}, t)$, (9.2), and the assumed initial conditions (9.1).

9.5 VISCOELASTIC UNIQUENESS THEOREMS: UNIQUENESS OF SOLUTION

An important question concerning the solution of a boundary value problem in continuum mechanics is whether the formulated problem has a solution and whether the solution is unique or not (Fung, 1965). On physical grounds, this question may be dealt with by reference to the thermodynamics of the problem involved. On mathematical grounds, however, this question must be answered by the theory of partial differential equations. A satisfactory solution to the problem in hand must comply with both the laws of physics and the principles of mathematics. In solving boundary value problems of static equilibrium within classical elasticity, for example, one may proceed in the following sequence: (i) one solves the equations of equilibrium for the stresses σ_{ij}; (ii) the constitutive response equations are then solved for the strains ε_{ij} by using the stress components σ_{ij} obtained from (i). Here, an infinite set of solutions may be found. However, the unique solution would be singled out by employing, for instance, the conditions of compatibility (equation (1.80)).

The existence and uniqueness of solution theorems in classical elasticity have been extended by Gurtin and Sternberg (1962) to the class of linear boundary value problems in viscoelasticity. This was carried out in light of an earlier work by Volterra (1909).

For the most direct case of isothermal, isotropic, linear viscoelastic boundary value problem under a quasi-static condition, Christensen (1971), following Gurtin and Sternberg (1962), presented a uniqueness condition of solution. This condition may be stated, in view of the set of governing equations mentioned in section 9.4, as follows.

Theorem 9.1 Uniqueness theorem

The isotropic, quasi-static, viscoelastic boundary value problem governed by the initial conditions (9.1), the boundary conditions (9.2), the equations of equilibrium (9.3), the strain–displacement relations (9.5) and the stress–strain equations (9.13) possesses a unique solution provided that the initial values of the relaxation functions appearing in the constitutive equations (9.13) satisfy the conditions

$$\mu(0) > 0 \quad \text{and} \quad k(0) > 0. \tag{9.14}$$

For a proof of the uniqueness theorem stated above, the reader is referred to Christensen (1971). Other versions of uniqueness theorems for the above class of boundary value problems are given by Onat and Breuer (1963), Edelstein and Gurtin (1964), Odeh and Tadjbakhsh (1965), Barberan and Herrera (1966) and Lubliner and Sackman (1967), amongst others.

9.6 CORRESPONDENCE PRINCIPLE: THE ELASTIC–VISCOELASTIC ANALOGY

For a large number of technical viscoelastic problems, it is possible to relate mathematically the solution of a linear, viscoelastic boundary value problem to an analogous problem of an elastic body of the same geometry and under the same initial and boundary conditions. This is carried out by transforming the governing equations of the viscoelastic problem to be mathematically equivalent to those governing a corresponding elastic problem. In this, both Laplace and Fourier transforms are often used. Accordingly, one would be able to employ the tools of the theory of elasticity to solve different boundary value problems in linear viscoelasticity.

The above analogy is referred to as the 'correspondence principle'. It implies that elastic analysis procedures may be utilized to derive transformed viscoelastic solutions (for instance, Lee, 1955; Morland and Lee, 1960; Schapery, 1967). Lee (1955) demonstrated the correspondence principle for isotropic media at constant temperature. Meantime, Morland and Lee (1960) considered the application of the correspondence principle for isotropic materials with temperature variations. Biot (1958) argued that the correspondence principle may be also applied to anisotropic materials because of the symmetry of the relaxation modulus tensor, i.e. $R_{ijkl}(t) = R_{klij}(t)$.

9.6.1 Laplace-transformed isothermal, linear viscoelastic boundary value problem

(a) Initial conditions

The body is assumed to be initially undisturbed. Thus, the initial conditions (9.1) will hold.

(b) Boundary conditions

The Laplace-transformed forms of the boundary conditions (9.2a) and (9.2b) are, respectively,

$$\bar{\sigma}_{ij}(\mathbf{x}, s)n_j = \bar{T}_i(\mathbf{x}, s), \quad \mathbf{x} \text{ on } B_\sigma, \tag{9.15a}$$

and

$$\bar{u}_i(\mathbf{x}, s) = \bar{U}_i(\mathbf{x}, s), \quad \mathbf{x} \text{ on } B_u, \tag{9.15b}$$

where s is the Laplace transform variable and the overbar designates the Laplace transform of the variable, i.e.

$$\bar{T}_i(\mathbf{x}, s) = \int_0^\infty T_i(\mathbf{x}, t) \exp(-st) \, dt \tag{9.16a}$$

and

$$\bar{U}_i(\mathbf{x}, s) = \int_0^\infty U_i(\mathbf{x}, t) \exp(-st)\, dt \qquad (9.16b)$$

(Appendix C).

(c) Balance of linear momentum

The quasi-static case is dealt with here. Recalling (9.3), multiplying it by $\exp(-st)$ and integrating over $-\infty < t < \infty$, the Laplace transform of the equilibrium equation is

$$\bar{\sigma}_{ij,j} + \bar{\chi}_i = 0. \qquad (9.17)$$

(d) Linear strain–displacement relations

The Laplace-transformed strain–displacement relation (9.5) is

$$\bar{\varepsilon}_{ij} = \tfrac{1}{2}(\bar{u}_{i,j} + \bar{u}_{j,i}) \qquad (9.18)$$

(e) Stress–strain relations

The constitutive equations (9.6) and (9.7) can be transformed by the rule of convolution integrals (Schapery, 1967) to yield, respectively, the algebraic relations

$$\bar{\varepsilon}_{ij} = \hat{F}_{ijkl}\bar{\sigma}_{kl} \qquad (9.19)$$

and

$$\bar{\sigma}_{ij} = \hat{R}_{ijkl}\bar{\varepsilon}_{kl} \qquad (9.20)$$

where $\hat{F}_{ijkl}$ and $\hat{R}_{ijkl}$ are the s-multiplied (Laplace) transforms of the creep and relaxation functions, respectively, i.e.

$$\hat{F}_{ijkl} = s\bar{F}_{ijkl} \qquad (9.21a)$$

and

$$\hat{R}_{ijkl} = s\bar{R}_{ijkl}. \qquad (9.21b)$$

The quantities $\hat{F}_{ijkl}$ and $\hat{R}_{ijkl}$ are interrelated operational functions, i.e.

$$[\hat{F}_{ijkl}] = [\hat{R}_{ijkl}]^{-1}, \qquad (9.22)$$

and both are completely symmetric. Thus, in view of the thermodynamic theory, the transformed constitutive equations in terms of these operational functions are identical to those of an elastic body with compliances $\hat{F}_{ijkl}$ and moduli $\hat{R}_{ijkl}$ and of the same degree of geometric symmetry (Schapery, 1967).

For the case of an isotropic material, the constitutive equation (9.12) may be used. The Laplace transform of this equation is (Hunter, 1967)

$$\bar{\sigma}_{ij}(s) = \lambda(s)\bar{\varepsilon}_{ii}(s)\delta_{ij} + 2\mu(s)\bar{\varepsilon}'_{ij}(s) \tag{9.23}$$

where $\bar{\sigma}_{ij}$ and $\bar{\varepsilon}'_{ij}$ are the Laplace transforms of σ_{ij} and ε'_{ij}, respectively. In this equation, the transform moduli $\lambda(s)$ and $\mu(s)$ are defined by

$$\lambda(s) = k(s) - \tfrac{2}{3}\mu(s) \tag{9.24}$$

where $k(s)$ is the Laplace transform of the relaxation function in pure dilatation, i.e.

$$k(s) = s \int_0^\infty R_1(t) \exp(-st)\, dt \tag{9.25a}$$

and $\mu(s)$ is the Laplace transform of the relaxation function in pure shear, i.e.

$$\mu(s) = s \int_0^\infty R_2(t) \exp(-st)\, dt. \tag{9.25b}$$

In the general case of nonhomogeneous material, the field quantities $\bar{\sigma}_{ij}$, $\bar{\varepsilon}_{ii}$ and $\bar{\varepsilon}'_{ij}$ of (9.23) are usually functions of both the transform parameter s and the position vector **x**. However, the transform moduli $\lambda(s)$ and $\mu(s)$ are functions of the transform variable s only (Hunter, 1967).

The corresponding format to (9.23) in linear elasticity is the constitutive equation

$$\sigma_{ij} = \lambda\varepsilon_{ii}\delta_{ij} + 2\mu\varepsilon'_{ij} \tag{9.26}$$

where λ and μ are the Lamé constants. Such an analogy reflects the basis of the correspondence principle.

The set of Laplace-transformed relations (9.15), (9.17) and (9.18), together with the transformed constitutive equations (9.19) and (9.20), or alternatively (9.23), constitutes an 'associated' elastic problem corresponding to the original (quasi-static) viscoelastic boundary value problem for the same geometry and subject to surface tractions $\bar{T}_i = \bar{T}_i(\mathbf{x}, s)$, displacements $\bar{U}_i = \bar{U}_i(\mathbf{x}, s)$ and body forces $\bar{\chi}_i = \bar{\chi}_i(\mathbf{x}, s)$. The task then would be to solve this analogous elastic problem (Laplace transformed of the original viscoelastic problem) to determine the transformed components of the stress $\bar{\sigma}_{ij}$ and/or the transformed components of the displacement $\bar{u}_i$ throughout the body. A Laplace inversion procedure would follow afterwards to determine the components of the stress and displacement in the original viscoelastic boundary value problem. The reader is referred, in this context, to Sips (1951), Brull (1953) and Lee (1955, 1960), among others.

Although the presentation above uses the Laplace transform procedure, a similar treatment could be accomplished using Fourier transform (e.g. Read, 1950).

9.6.2 Remarks on the use of the correspondence principle to solve linear viscoelastic boundary value problems

In the course of solving a linear viscoelastic boundary value problem using the correspondence principle, one might consider some simplifications in order to ease the difficulty which might arise in the inversion of the resulting Laplace transforms. For instance (Hunter, 1967), the following could be used.

- In a large number of boundary value problems it may be unnecessary to invert the resulting Laplace transform for all positions on the boundary (i.e. x on B_σ or B_u) if the stress and/or displacement is only required at one particular position.
- In some situations, the integral value of the stress and/or displacement is required to be determined rather than individual values of these variables. In such case, it might be easier if one establishes the relevant integral property before the inversion process.
- The inversion procedure can be simplified significantly if one assumes a constant Poisson's ratio model and particularly if the body forces χ_i are neglected. In this case, if B_σ is considered to be stress free, then, for the same boundary conditions, the resulting displacement field at any given instant of time would be identical to the displacement field of the corresponding elastic problem. A similar example here is when $B_u = 0$ and $B_\sigma = B$, i.e. the traction vector is specified everywhere on the total boundary; then the resulting viscoelastic stress field would be identical with the stress field of the corresponding elastic problem.

9.6.3 Illustrative examples on the use of the correspondence principle to solve linear viscoelastic boundary value problems

Example 9.1 Torsional quasi-static twisting of a linear, viscoelastic cylinder (Hunter, 1967)

This example considers the determination of the time-dependent twisting moment and displacement of a solid cylinder of radius a and length l made of linear viscoelastic material. Let u_r, u_θ, u_z represent the displacement components in cylindrical polar components, θ denote the angle of twist at $z = l$ and M be the twisting moment.

From the theory of elasticity, the displacement field of an elastic solid cylinder under the action of a twisting moment and a stress-free cylindrical surface condition is expressed (e.g. Love, 1944) as

$$u_\theta = \theta rz/l, \quad u_r = u_z = 0. \tag{9.27}$$

For an analogous quasi-static viscoelastic problem with prescribed displacement such as

$$u_\theta = \begin{cases} r_\theta, & z = l, \\ 0, & z = 0, \end{cases}$$

and a stress-free cylindrical surface, the displacement field is given by (9.27) with θ now a time-dependent variable. In this case, the only nonvanishing strain component is

$$\varepsilon_{\theta z} = \tfrac{1}{2}\theta(t)\,\frac{r}{l}. \tag{9.28}$$

The nonvanishing (transformed) stress corresponding to the above strain becomes

$$\bar{\tau}_{\theta z} = \bar{\mu}(s)\bar{\theta}(s)\,\frac{r}{l} \tag{9.29}$$

where $\bar{\mu}(s)$ is the transformed shear modulus.

Thus, the total (transformed) couple required to maintain the (transformed) angle of twist $\bar{\theta}(s)$ can be expressed as

$$\bar{M} = 2\pi \int_0^a \bar{\tau}_{\theta z} r^2 \, dr = \frac{\pi a^4}{2l} \, \bar{\mu}(s)\bar{\theta}(s) \tag{9.30}$$

which may be inverted in either the relaxation form

$$M(t) = \frac{\pi a^4}{2l} \int_0^t \dot{\theta}(t')G(t - t') \, dt' \tag{9.31a}$$

or the creep form

$$\theta(t) = \left(\frac{\pi a^4}{2l}\right)^{-1} \int_0^t \dot{M}(t')G^{-1}(t - t') \, dt' \tag{9.31b}$$

where $G(t - t')$ is the relaxation function of the material in shear.

Equations (9.31) provide a quasi-static linear viscoelastic solution of the presented problem for prescribed $\theta(t)$ or $M(t)$.

Example 9.2 Impact of a flat circular punch on a linear, viscoelastic half-space (Hunter, 1967)

(a) Elastic solution

According to the theory of elasticity, the solution of the problem of the normal indentation of an elastic half-space by a flat-ended rigid-circular punch of radius a gives the pressure distribution (Boussinesq, 1885)

$$p(r) = \begin{cases} \dfrac{4\mu ad}{1 - v}(a^2 - r^2)^{-1/2}, & r < a, \\[2mm] 0 & r > a, \end{cases} \tag{9.32}$$

where d is the depth of the penetration and v is Poisson's ratio of the elastic half-space. Further, the total load is given by

$$F = 2\pi \int_0^a pr \, dr = \frac{8\pi a}{1 - r} \, \mu d. \tag{9.33}$$

(b) Viscoelastic solution

For the linear viscoelastic case, equation (9.33) becomes

$$\bar{F} = \frac{8\pi a}{1 - v} \bar{u}(s)\bar{d}, \quad v = \text{constant},\tag{9.34}$$

where v is Poisson's ratio of the viscoelastic half-space. Accordingly, given $F(t)$ or $d(t)$, equation (9.34), when inverted, gives d or F respectively.

9.6.4 Extension of Example 9.2 to include impact

For the impact problem, the load F is expressed by Newton's second law of motion:

$$F = -m\ddot{d}$$

where m is the mass of the indentor and $\ddot{d}$ is its acceleration. On taking the Laplace transform of the above expression, the (transformed) force is written as

$$\bar{F} = -m(s^2\bar{d} - v)\tag{9.35}$$

where v is the initial impact velocity at the initial conditions $d = 0$ at $t = 0$.
   Solving (9.34) and (9.35) for $\bar{d}$ gives

$$\bar{d} = v\left[s^2 + \frac{8\pi a}{m(1 - v)}\,\mu(s)\right]^{-1}.\tag{9.36}$$

With some physical approximation (Hunter, 1967), the inversion of (9.36) gives

$$d = \frac{v}{\omega}\left(1 + \frac{\tan \delta}{\pi}\right)\exp[-\tfrac{1}{2}(\omega \tan \delta)t]\,\sin(\omega t - \tan \delta)$$

$$+ \frac{v \tan \delta}{2\omega}\exp\left(-\frac{2\omega t}{\pi}\right)\tag{9.37a}$$

where ω is the solution of

$$\frac{\omega(1 - v)}{8\pi a}\,\omega^2 = \mu_1(\omega)\tag{9.37b}$$

where $u_1(\omega)$ is the real part of the complex shear modulus and $\tan \delta = \mu_2(\omega)/\mu_1(\omega)$. For the values of ω where the viscoelasticity is significant, $\mu_2(\omega) \ll \mu_1(\omega)$ and $\tan \delta \ll 1$. Further, the impact terminates at a time given by $\dot{d} = 0$ with solution

$$\omega t = d - \frac{1}{2}\left[1 + \left(\frac{2}{\pi e}\right)^2\right]\tan \delta + O(\tan^2 \delta)$$

when the indentor velocity is $-v(1 - \gamma \tan \delta)$ where

$$\gamma = \tfrac{1}{2}\pi - (1 + e^{-2})/\pi = 1.205.$$

This results in a coefficient of restitution e given by

$$e = 1 - 1.2 \tan \delta \qquad (9.38)$$

Thus, the energy absorbed by the solid is

$$E = 1.2 \, mv^2 \tan \delta \qquad (9.39)$$

(Hunter, 1967).

9.7 SOLUTION OF QUASI-STATIC VISCOELASTIC PROBLEMS IN THE ABSENCE OF THE CORRESPONDENCE PRINCIPLE: MIXED BOUNDARY VALUE PROBLEMS

In section 9.4, the set of conditions governing an isothermal, linear viscoelastic boundary value problem has been introduced. In section 9.6, the correspondence principle was presented to solve a boundary value problem of this type, subject to the condition that B_σ and B_u are independent of time where these are the parts of the boundary upon which stress vector components and displacement components, respectively, are specified. This is necessitated by the requirement that the assumed boundary conditions at a point are time invariant so that the integral transform methods would be applicable. Consequently, an elastic–viscoelastic correspondence principle does not exist when the parts of the boundary B_σ and B_u are functions of time, i.e. when the boundary conditions at the particular point in question may involve with the passage of time both stress and displacement vectors. A representative boundary value problem of the latter type is the time-dependent indentation of a viscoelastic half-space by a curved rigid indentor. In this case, as the indentor is loaded and depression into the viscoelastic half-space is progressing, there are some points on the boundary of the indentation region that, at first, may have traction-free boundary conditions, but later could have displacement followed by stress boundary conditions. In other words, a portion of the boundary is the boundary B_u part of the time and is the boundary B_σ at other times, so that the half-space would conform to the geometry of the indentor in the contact region. Studies concerning this problem were presented, for instance, by Lee and Radok (1960), Hunter (1960), Graham (1965, 1967), Calvit (1967) and Ting (1966, 1968). Other examples of mixed boundary value problems are, for instance, those involving rolling of rigid bodies over a viscoelastic half-space (e.g. Hunter, 1961; Morland, 1962, 1967) and ablation problems in which a phase change could cause the boundaries of a viscoelastic medium to change size and shape. An example of this problem is the case of a spinning rocket's filling burning internally. A similar problem of an internally ablating sphere was considered by Rogers and Lee (1962). Other examples of boundary value problems where integral transform methods are invalid are nonisothermal problems in which the mechanical properties are assumed to be temperature dependent. A number of boundary value problems of the latter types have been solved, but it appears that no systematic methods of solution are available.

Example 9.3 Deformation of a uniform viscoelastic beam by a curved rigid indentor (Christensen, 1971)

The schematics of the problem are shown in Fig. 9.2. As indicated, $P(t)$ is the force applied to the rigid indentor, $a(t)$ is half-length of the contact region (considered a basic unknown of the problem) and $d(t)$ is the displacement (vertical) of the indentor. The indentor is assumed to have a cubic profile expressed by

$$y = d(t) - c|x|^3 \qquad (9.40)$$

where c is a given constant.

In this problem, classical beam theory with simply supported end conditions is assumed. Inertia effects are neglected. Contact is considered to begin at $t = 0$.

Based on the above assumptions, elasticity theory gives

$$EI\frac{d^4w}{dx^4} = q(x) \qquad (9.41)$$

where I is the moment of inertia of the cross-section of the beam, w is the transverse displacement and $q(x)$ is the lateral load.

Meantime, viscoelastic beam theory gives

$$I\int_0^t R(t-\tau)\frac{\partial}{\partial\tau}\left[\frac{\partial^4w(x,\tau)}{\partial x^4}\right]d\tau = q(x,\tau) \qquad (9.42)$$

in which $R(t-\tau)$ is the uniaxial relation function.

- In the contact region, $x < a(t)$, the deflection of the beam must conform to the geometry of the indentor; then, with reference to equation (9.40),

$$w(x,t) = d(t) - cx^3, \quad x < a(t) \quad \text{and} \quad t \geq 0. \qquad (9.43)$$

- Outside the contact region, $x > a(t)$, the lateral load vanishes and equation (9.42) is satisfied by

$$w(x,t) = C_1(t) + C_2(t)x + C_3(t)x^2 + C_4(t)x^3, \quad x > a(t) \quad \text{and} \quad t \geq 0, \qquad (9.44)$$

where $C_1(t)$, $C_2(t)$, $C_3(t)$ and $C_4(t)$ are functions of time required to be determined.

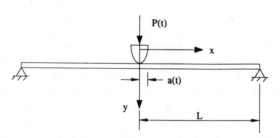

Fig. 9.2 Deformation of a uniform beam by a curved rigid indentor.

Implying the condition that the shear resultants on the ends of the beam balance the applied load $P(t)$ gives, in view of (9.44),

$$12I \int_0^t R(t - \tau) \frac{dC_4(\tau)}{d\tau} \, d\tau = P(t). \tag{9.45}$$

- The end conditions are

$$at - x = L, \quad w = \frac{\partial^2 w}{\partial x^2} = 0$$

which can be specified by (Fig. 9.2)

$$C_1(t) + C_2(t)L + C_3(t)L^2 + C_4(t)L^3 = 0 \tag{9.46}$$

and

$$2C_3(t) + 6C_4(t)L = 0. \tag{9.47}$$

- The continuity conditions at the edge of the contact region $x = a$ imply that w, $\partial w/\partial x$ and $\partial^2 w/\partial x^2$ are continuous. Accordingly, equations (9.43) and (9.44) give

$$C_1(t) + C_2(t)a(t) + C_3(t)a^2 + C_4(t)a^3(t) = d(t) - ca^3(t), \tag{9.48}$$

$$C_2(t) + 2C_3(t)a(t) + 3C_4(t)a^3(t) = -3ca^2(t) \tag{9.49}$$

and

$$2C_3(t) + 6C_4(t)a(t) = -6ca(t). \tag{9.50}$$

Relations (9.45–9.50) give six nonlinear equations.

1. If the load $P(t)$ is considered to be known, then the six equations would be solved for the six unknowns $C_1(t)$, $C_2(t)$, $C_3(t)$, $C_4(t)$, $a(t)$ and $d(t)$.
2. Alternatively, if the displacement of the indentor $d(t)$ is taken to be specified, then the above-mentioned equations can be solved for the unknowns $C_1(t)$, $C_2(t)$, $C_3(t)$, $C_4(t)$, $a(t)$ and $P(t)$.

These two cases are considered separately by Christensen (1971).

Example 9.4 A spherical indentor on a viscoelastic half-space

As a second example of a viscoelastic boundary value problem with mixed-type boundary conditions, the problem of indentation of a viscoelastic half-space by a rigid spherical indentor is considered. Previous studies on this type of problem were carried out, for instance, by Lee and Radok (1960), Hunter (1960) and Graham (1965). The analysis presented below follows that of Hunter (1967) after Graham (1965). Reference is also made to Christensen (1971).

The indentor is considered to be applied at the origin of a rectangular Cartesian coordinate system (x, y, z) and its motion is vertical in the z direction. The shear stresses over the entire boundary of the half-space are assumed to be identically equal to zero. In the contact region, however, the normal component of the displacement of the boundary is considered to conform to the shape of the indentor. Let R be the radius of the indentor, $\delta(t)$ be the depth of penetration, $a(t)$ be the radius of the contact surface, $z = 0$ be the surface of the (viscoelastic) half-space and $r^2 = x^2 + y^2$.

(a) The Problem

This is to determine the stress distribution under the spherical indentor and the relation between the depth of penetration $\delta(t)$ and the radius of the contact surface $a(t)$ subject to the following boundary conditions:

$$\text{at } x = 0 \begin{cases} u_z = \delta(t) - \dfrac{1}{2R}(x^2 + y^2)H(t), & r \leq a(t), & (9.51a) \\[2mm] \sigma_z = 0, & r > a(t), & (9.51b) \\[2mm] \tau_{rz} = 0, & & (9.51c) \end{cases}$$

where $H(t)$ is the Heaviside step function.

(b) Elastic solution

The starting point of Graham's solution is taken as (Hunter, 1967) the Boussinesq formula for the normal surface displacement of an elastic solid subjected to a normal point load P at x', y', i.e.

$$u_z(x, y, 0) = \frac{(1 - v)P}{2\pi\mu} [(x - x')^2 + (y - y')^2]^{-1/2} \qquad (9.52)$$

where μ is the elastic shear modulus.

(c) Viscoelastic solution

Generalizing (9.52) to the case of a viscoelastic half-space subjected to a time variable distributed load $P(x, y, t)$ gives under the assumption of a constant Poisson's ratio (Hunter, 1967)

$$u_z(x, y, 0, t) = \frac{1 - v}{2\pi} G^{-1}(t) * d \iint\limits_{\Omega_m} P(x', y', t')[(x - x')^2 + (y - y')^2]^{-1/2} \, dx' \, dy'$$

$$(9.53)$$

where $G^{-1}(t)$ is the creep function in shear and where the following notation of Gurtin and Sternberg (1962) is used:

$$a * \mathrm{d}\beta = \int_{-\infty}^{t} a(t - t') \, \mathrm{d}\dot{\beta}(t') = \int_{-\infty}^{t} a(t - t')\dot{\beta}(t') \, \mathrm{d}t'.$$

In (9.53) the double (surface) integral is taken over the maximum range Ω_m enclosing all points x', y' for which $P(x', y', t')$ is nonzero for any time t' in the range $-\infty < t' < t$. With reference to equation (9.53), Hunter (1967) considered the following four situations.

1. For given $P(x, y, t)$, equation (9.53) presents the solution for the normal surface displacement and such problems may be considered within the class of the boundary value problems that can be solved by the correspondence principle (section 9.6).
2. For the indentation problem, 'mixed-type boundary conditions' boundary value problem, equation (9.53) may be considered as an integral equation for P subject to the condition that, for $r < a(t)$, the surface displacement u_z is given by (9.51a), while, for $r > a(t)$, P vanishes.
3. For monotonically increasing $a(t)$, Ω_m is time dependent and can be taken as $\Omega(t) = \pi a^2(t)$. In this case, the orders of space and time integration in (9.53) can be changed to give

$$u_z = \frac{1 - \nu}{2\pi} \iint\limits_{\Omega(t)} \mathrm{d}x' \, \mathrm{d}y' [(x - x')^2 + (y - y')^2]^{-1/2} G^{-1} \, \mathrm{d}P \qquad (9.54)$$

in which

$$G^{-1} \, \mathrm{d}P = \eta(x, y, a) \qquad (9.55)$$

where η is the unique solution of the corresponding elastic problem whose solution (Boussinesq, 1885) is given by

$$\eta = \frac{4}{\pi(1 - \nu)R} (a^2 - r^2)^{1/2} \qquad (9.56a)$$

and

$$\eta = 0 \quad \text{for} \quad r > a \qquad (9.56b)$$

so that (9.55) leads to

$$P(x, y, t) = \frac{4}{\pi(1 - \nu)R} \int_0^t G(t - t') \frac{\mathrm{d}}{\mathrm{d}t'} [(a^2(t') - r^2)^{1/2}] \, \mathrm{d}t' \qquad (9.57)$$

in which, for fixed r, the lower limit of the integral may be taken as t'' where t'' is the unique solution of

$$a(t'') = r.$$

Meantime, the total load on the indentor is given by

$$F(t) = 2\pi \int_0^{a(t)} rP(x, y, t)\, dr$$

which can be evaluated by interchanging the order of the space and time integrations (Hunter, 1960, 1967) to give

$$F(t) = \frac{8}{3R(1 - \nu)} \int_0^t G(t - t') \frac{d}{dt'} a^3(t')\, dt'. \tag{9.58}$$

Further, it can be shown that the depth of penetration can be expressed by

$$\delta(t) = a^2(t)/R \tag{9.59}$$

which is the same for the corresponding elastic problem.

4. The radius of the contact surface $a(t)$ increases monotonically to a maximum value at $t = t_m$ and then decreases to zero. In this case, the solution given above is valid for $t \leq t_m$. For $t > t_m$, however, the solution fails because it is no longer permissible to replace Ω_m in (9.53) by $\Omega(t)$. To obtain the solution of (9.53) for $t > t_m$, Hunter (1967) introduced the time function $t_1(t)$ defined by the relations

$$\begin{aligned} &\text{for} \quad t \leq t_m, \quad t_1(t) = t, \\ &\text{for} \quad t \geq t_m, \quad a(t_1) = a(t), \quad t_1 < t_m. \end{aligned} \tag{9.60}$$

In other words, t_1 is the time prior to t for which the radius of the contact circle is equal to the current value.

Further studies concerning the viscoelastic contact problem have been dealt with, for instance, by Calvit (1967) and Ting (1968). Graham (1968) and Ting (1968) have outlined restricted classes of viscoelastic contact problems which may be solved directly using the elastic–viscoelastic correspondence principle.

9.8 THERMOVISCOELASTIC BOUNDARY VALUE PROBLEM

The set of conditions that governs a thermoviscoelastic boundary value problem may be stated as follows.

9.8.1 Initial conditions

Assuming the body is initially undisturbed at a base temperature θ_0, then, the initial conditions are

$$u_i(t) = 0, \quad \varepsilon_{ij}(t) = 0, \quad \sigma_{ij}(t) = 0, \quad \theta(t) = 0, \quad -\infty < t < 0, \tag{9.61}$$

where θ denotes the temperature deviation from the base temperature θ_0.

9.8.2 Boundary conditions

In order to account for the temperature effect, the boundary is visualized (Christensen, 1971) to be composed of two regions, i.e. B_θ is that region of the boundary upon which the temperature is prescribed and $B - B_\theta$ is the complimentary region over which the surface is taken to be perfectly insulated against heat flow. The thermal boundary conditions can then be stated as

$$\theta(\mathbf{x}, t) = \hat\theta(\mathbf{x}, t), \qquad \mathbf{x} \text{ on } B_\theta, \quad t \geq 0 \tag{9.62}$$

and

$$k_{ij}(\mathbf{x}, t)\theta_{,i}n_j = 0 \qquad \mathbf{x} \text{ on } B - B_\theta, \quad t \geq 0. \tag{9.63}$$

where k_{ij} as a second-order tensor accounts for the mechanical properties of the material.

Combining the thermal boundary conditions (9.62) and (9.63) with the traction and displacement boundary conditions stated earlier for the isothermal problem, (9.2), the set of boundary conditions for the thermoviscoelastic problem is written as follows:

$$
\begin{aligned}
\sigma_{ij}(\mathbf{x}, t)n_j &= T_i(\mathbf{x}, t), & \mathbf{x} \text{ on } B_\sigma; \\
u_i(\mathbf{x}, t) &= U_i(\mathbf{x}, t), & \mathbf{x} \text{ on } B_u; \\
\theta(\mathbf{x}, t) &= \hat\theta(\mathbf{x}, t), & \mathbf{x} \text{ on } B_\theta; \\
k_{ij}(\mathbf{x}, t)\theta_{,i}n_j &= 0, & \mathbf{x} \text{ on } B - B_\theta.
\end{aligned}
\tag{9.64}
$$

9.8.3 Balance of linear momentum

The equations of (quasi-static) equilibrium

$$\sigma_{ij,j} + \chi_i = 0 \tag{9.65}$$

or, alternatively, the equations of motion

$$\sigma_{ij,j} + \chi_i = \rho\,\frac{d^2 u_i}{dt^2} \tag{9.66}$$

can be used.

9.8.4 Strain–displacement relations

$$\varepsilon_{ij}(t) = \tfrac{1}{2}[u_{i,j}(t) + u_{j,i}(t)]. \tag{9.67}$$

9.8.5 Stress–strain relations

(a) Anisotropic materials

The relaxation constitutive relation is expressed as

$$\sigma_{ij}(t) = \int_0^t R_{ijkl}(t - \tau) \frac{\partial \varepsilon_{kl}(\tau)}{\partial \tau} \, d\tau - \int_0^t \psi_{ij}(t - \tau) \frac{\partial \theta(\tau)}{\partial \tau} \, d\tau. \tag{9.68a}$$

The creep constitutive relation corresponding to (9.68a) is written as

$$\varepsilon_{ij}(t) = \int_0^t F_{ijkl}(t - \tau) \frac{\partial \sigma_{kl}(\tau)}{\partial \tau} \, d\tau - \int_0^t \alpha_{ij}(t - \tau) \frac{\partial \theta(\tau)}{\partial \tau} \, d\tau. \tag{9.68b}$$

In the case of thermorheologically simple materials, one may employ a stress–strain relation of the form (Schapery, 1964)

$$\sigma_{ij}(t) = \int_0^t R_{ijkl}(\xi - \xi') \frac{\partial \varepsilon_{kl}}{\partial \tau} \, d\tau - \int_0^t \psi_{ij}(\xi - \xi') \frac{\partial \theta(\tau)}{\partial \tau} \, d\tau \tag{9.69a}$$

or, equivalently,

$$\sigma_{ij}(\xi) = \int_0^\xi R_{ijkl}(\xi - \xi') \frac{\partial \varepsilon_{kl}}{\partial \xi'} \, d\xi' - \int_0^\xi \psi_{ij}(\xi - \xi') \frac{\partial \theta(\tau)}{\partial \tau} \, d\tau \tag{9.69b}$$

where ξ, introduced in section 5.5, is the so-called **reduced time** defined by the relation

$$d\xi = dt/a_\theta(\theta). \tag{9.70}$$

Also,

$$\xi = \int_0^t dt/a_\theta(\theta), \quad \xi' = \int_0^\tau dt/a_\theta(\theta), \tag{9.71}$$

where $\tau \leq t$.

The relaxation function $\psi_{ij}(\xi)$ appearing in (9.69) is assumed to have the following exponential series form

$$\psi_{ij}(\xi) = \sum_m \psi_{ij}^{(m)} \exp(-\xi/\gamma_m) + \psi'_{ij} \tag{9.72}$$

where the constants $\psi_{ij}^{(m)}$ and ψ'_{ij} define the thermal stress characteristics of the material before loading (Schapery, 1964, 1967) and γ_m are appropriate exponent factors. Meantime, the relaxation moduli in (9.69) are considered (Schapery, 1964) to be given by

$$R_{ijkl}(\xi) = \sum_m R_{ijkl}^{(m)} \exp(-\xi/\gamma_m) + R'_{ijkl}. \tag{9.73}$$

On the other hand, when the temperature is constant, the relaxation moduli may be taken as

$$R_{ijkl}(t/a_\theta) = \sum_m R_{ijkl}^{(m)} \exp[(-t/\gamma_m)a_\theta] + R_{ijkl} \qquad (9.74)$$

which reflects the effect of constant temperature on relaxation (or creep) behaviour, that is, to simply shift the time scale. Accordingly, a_θ is often referred to as 'time shift factor'.

The creep constitutive equation corresponding to (9.69b) is

$$\varepsilon_{ij}(\xi) = \int_0^\xi F_{ijkl}(\xi - \xi') \frac{\partial \sigma_{kl}}{\partial \xi'} \, d\xi' + \int_0^\xi \alpha_{ij}(\xi - \xi') \frac{\partial \theta}{\partial \xi'} \, d\xi' \qquad (9.75)$$

where the function $\alpha_{ij}(\xi)$ accounts for the strain response in the absence of the stress. It is expressed (Schapery, 1964) by

$$\alpha_{ij}(\xi) = \sum_m \alpha_{ij}^{(m)}[1 - \exp(-\xi/\gamma_m)] + \alpha_{ij} \qquad (9.76)$$

where $\alpha_{ij}^{(m)}$ and α_{ij} define the thermal strain characteristics of the material before loading.

(b) Isotropic materials

The relaxation constitutive relations corresponding to (9.68a) are

$$\sigma'_{ij}(t) = \int_0^t R_1(t - \tau) \frac{\partial \varepsilon'_{ij}(\tau)}{\partial \tau} \, d\tau$$

and $\qquad\qquad\qquad\qquad\qquad\qquad\qquad\qquad\qquad\qquad\qquad\qquad (9.77)$

$$\sigma_{kk}(t) = \int_0^t R_2(t - \tau) \frac{\partial \varepsilon_{kk}(\tau)}{\partial \tau} \, d\tau - 3 \int_0^t \psi(t - \tau) \frac{\partial \theta(\tau)}{\partial \tau} \, d\tau$$

where σ'_{ij} and ε'_{ij} denote, respectively, the deviatoric components of the stress and strain.

The creep constitutive equations corresponding to (9.77) are expressed as

$$\varepsilon'_{ij}(t) = \int_0^t F_1(t - \tau) \frac{\partial \sigma'_{ij}(\tau)}{\partial \tau} \, d\tau$$

and $\qquad\qquad\qquad\qquad\qquad\qquad\qquad\qquad\qquad\qquad\qquad\qquad (9.78)$

$$\varepsilon_{kk}(t) = \int_0^t F_2(t - \tau) \frac{\partial \sigma_{kk}(\tau)}{\partial \tau} - 3 \int_0^t \alpha(t - \tau) \frac{\partial \theta(\tau)}{\partial \tau} \, d\tau.$$

In the case of thermorheologically simple materials, constitutive equations for isotropic materials are expressed (Schapery, 1964) for the relaxation case by

$$\sigma_{ij}(\xi) = 2 \int_0^\xi R(\xi - \xi') \frac{\partial \varepsilon_{ij}}{\partial \xi'} \, d\xi'$$

$$+ \delta_{ij} \int_0^\xi \left[\lambda(\xi - \xi') \frac{\partial \varepsilon}{\partial \xi'} - \psi(\xi - \xi') \frac{\partial \varepsilon}{\partial \xi'} \right] d\xi' \qquad (9.79)$$

where

$$\varepsilon = \varepsilon_{11} + \varepsilon_{22} + \varepsilon_{33}.$$

In (9.79), $R(\xi)$, $\lambda(\xi)$ and $\psi(\xi)$ are relaxation functions which, for thermodynamic reasons (Schapery, 1964), are considered to have the forms

$$R(\xi) = \sum_m R^{(m)} \exp(-\xi/\gamma_m) + R_e,$$

$$\lambda(\xi) = \sum_m \lambda^{(m)} \exp(-\xi/\gamma_m) + \lambda_{\bar{e}}, \qquad (9.80)$$

$$\psi(\xi) = \sum_m \psi^{(m)} \exp(-\xi/\gamma_m) + \psi_e,$$

with constants having the properties

$$\rho_m > 0,$$

$$R^{(m)} \geq 0, R_e \geq 0, \sum_m R(m) + R_e > 0,$$

$$K^{(m)} = \lambda^{(m)} + \tfrac{2}{3} R(m) \geq 0, \qquad (9.81)$$

$$K_e = \lambda_e + \tfrac{2}{3} R_e \geq 0,$$

$$\sum_m K^{(m)} + K_e > 0,$$

where K_e and $K^{(m)}$ define the bulk relaxation modulus

$$K(\xi) = \lambda(\xi) + \tfrac{2}{3} R(\xi) = \sum_m K^{(m)} \exp(-\xi/\gamma_m) + K_e. \qquad (9.82)$$

9.8.6 The heat conduction equation

● For isotropic materials

$$\frac{k_{ij}}{\theta_0} \theta_{,ij} = \frac{\partial}{\partial t} \int_0^t m(t - \tau) \frac{\partial \theta(\tau)}{\partial \tau} \, d\tau + \frac{\partial}{\partial t} \int_0^t \psi_{ij}(t - \tau) \frac{\partial \varepsilon_{ij}(\tau)}{\partial \tau} \, d\tau \qquad (9.83)$$

● and for anisotropic materials

$$\frac{k}{\theta_0} \theta_{,ii} = \frac{\partial}{\partial t} \int_0^t m(t - \tau) \frac{\partial \theta(\tau)}{\partial \tau} \, d\tau + \frac{\partial}{\partial t} \int_0^t \psi(t - \tau) \frac{\partial \varepsilon_{kk}(\tau)}{\partial \tau} \, d\tau \qquad (9.84)$$

where k_{ij} or k, $m(t)$, and $\psi_{ij}(t)$ or $\psi(t)$ are mechanical properties of the material.

In the general anisotropic case, the Laplace-transformed governing equations for the thermoviscoelastic boundary value problem are given by the following.

● The boundary conditions (equations (9.64)) are

$$\bar{\sigma}_{ij} n_j = \bar{T}_i \text{ on } B_\sigma,$$

$$\bar{u}_i = \bar{U}_i \text{ on } B_u,$$

$$\bar{\theta} = \hat{\bar{\theta}} \text{ on } B_\theta \qquad (9.85)$$

and

$$k_{ij} \bar{\theta}_{,i} n_j = 0 \text{ on } B - B_\theta.$$

● For the balance of linear momentum, the equations of quasi-static equilibrium (9.65)

$$\bar{\sigma}_{ij,j} + \bar{\chi}_i = 0 \qquad (9.86)$$

or, alternatively, the equation of motion (9.66)

$$\bar{\sigma}_{ij,j} + \bar{\chi}_i = \rho s^2 \bar{u}_i \qquad (9.87)$$

where s is the Laplace transform variable can be used.

● The strain–displacement relations (9.21) are

$$\bar{\varepsilon}_{ij} = \tfrac{1}{2}(\bar{u}_{i,j} + \bar{u}_{j,i}) \qquad (9.88)$$

● The relaxation constitutive relation (9.68a) is

$$\bar{\sigma}_{ij} = s\bar{R}_{ijkl} \bar{\varepsilon}_{kl} - s\bar{\psi}_{ij} \bar{\theta}. \qquad (9.89)$$

● The heat conduction equation (9.83) is

$$(k_{ij}/\theta_0)\bar{\theta}_{,ij} = s^2 \bar{m}\bar{\theta} + s^2 \bar{\psi}_{ij} \bar{\varepsilon}_{ij}. \qquad (9.90)$$

The viscoelastic boundary value problem governed by the set of equations (9.85)–(9.90) can be solved in the same manner as in the case of coupled thermoelastic problems. Consequently, the complete solution of the viscoelastic boundary value problem under consideration is obtained by inverting the transformed solution. The procedure here is the same as in the case of treating isothermal linear viscoelastic boundary value problems discussed earlier in section 9.4.

In problems where the coupling term involving ε_{ij} in (9.83) and (9.84) can be neglected, mechanical response problems and thermal response problems may be separated. Thus, after obtaining the temperature distribution, either by solving the heat conduction equation or from experimental results, the mechanical response problem would then be governed by (9.61) and (9.64)–(9.68). Integral transform methods could thus provide a useful tool in solving such problems.

REFERENCES

Aboudi, J. (1979) The dynamic indentation and impact of a viscoelastic half-space by an axisymmetric rigid body. *Comput. Math. Appl. Mech. Eng.*, **20**, 135–50.

Atkinson, C. and Coleman, C. J. (1977) On some steady-state moving boundary problems in the linear theory of viscoelasticity. *J. Inst. Math. Appl.*, **20**, 85–106.

Barberan, J. and Herrera, I. (1966) Uniqueness theorems and speed of propagation of signals in viscoelastic materials. *Arch. Ration. Mech. Anal.*, **23**, 173–90.

Biot, M. A. (1958) Linear thermodynamics and the mechanics of solid,s in Proc. 3rd US Natl Congr. on Applied Mechanics, ASME, New York, pp. 1–18.

Boussinesq, M. J. (1885) In Todhunter, I. and Pearson, K. (1960) *A History of Theory of Elasticity and of the Strength of Materials*, Vol. II, Part 2, Dover Publications, New York, pp. 185–357.

Brull, M. A. (1953) A structural theory incorporating the effect of time-dependent elasticity, in Proc. 1st Midwestern Conf. on Solid Mechanics, pp. 141–7.

Calvit, H. H. (1967) Numerical solution of the problem of impact of a rigid sphere onto a linear viscoelastic half-space and comparison with experiment. *Int. J. Solids Struct.*, **3**, 951–66.

Chao, C. and Achenbach, J. D. (1964) Simple viscoelastic analogy for stress waves, in Proc. Stress Waves in Anelastic Solids Symp., Brown University, April 3–5, 1963, Springer, Berlin, pp. 222–38.

Christensen, R. M. (1971) *Theory of Viscoelasticity*, Academic Press, New York.

Edelstein, W. S. and Gurtin, M. E. (1964) Uniqueness theorems in the linear dynamic theory of anisotropic viscoelastic solids. *Arch. Ration. Mech. Anal.*, **17**, 47–60.

Fichera, G. (1972) Boundary value problems of elasticity with unilateral constraints, in *Encyclopedia of Physics*, Vol. VI a/2, Mechanics of Solids II (ed. C. Truesdell), Springer, Berlin, pp. 391–423.

Fung, Y. C. (1965) *Foundations of Solid Mechanics*, Prentice-Hall, Englewood Cliffs, NJ.

Gakhof, F. D. (1966) *Boundary Value Problems*, Pergamon, Oxford.

Gladwell, G. M. L. (1980) *Contact Problems in the Classical Theory of Elasticity*, Sijthoff and Noordhoff, Alphen aan den Riju.

Golden, J. M. and Graham, G. A. C. (1988) *Boundary Value Problems in Linear Viscoelasticity*, Springer, Berlin.

Graham, G. A. C. (1965) The contact problem in the linear theory of viscoelasticity. *Int. J. Eng. Sci.*, **3**, 27–46.

Graham, G. A. C. (1967) The contact problem in the linear theory of viscoelasticity when the time-dependent contact area has any number of maxima and minima. *Int. J. Eng. Sci.*, **5**, 495–514.

Graham, G. A. C. (1968) The correspondence principle of linear viscoelasticity for mixed boundary value problems involving time-dependent boundary regions. *Q. Appl. Math.*, **26**, 167–74.

Graham, G. A. C. (1969) The solution of mixed boundary value problems that involve time-dependent boundary regions, for viscoelastic materials with one relaxation function. *Acta Mech.*, **8**, 188–204.

Graham, G. A. C. and Williams, F. M. (1972) Boundary value problems for time-dependent regions in aging viscoelasticity. *Util. Math.*, **2**, 291–303.

Gurtin, M. E. and Herrera, I. (1964) A correspondence principle for viscoelastic wave propagation. *Q. Appl. Math.*, **22**, 360–4.

Gurtin, M. E. and Sternberg, E. (1962) On the linear theory of viscoelasticity. *Arch. Ration. Mech. Anal.*, **11**(4), 291–356.

Hunter, S. C. (1960) The Hertz problem for a rigid spherical indentor and a viscoelastic half-space. *J. Mech. Phys. Solids*, **8**, 219–34.

Hunter, S. C. (1961) The rolling contact of a rigid cylinder with a viscoelastic half-space. *J. Appl. Mech.*, **28**, 611–7.

Hunter, S. C. (1967) The solution of boundary value problems in linear viscoelasticity, in Proc. 4th 1965 Symp. on Naval Structural Mechanics (eds A. C. Eringen, H. Liebowitz, S. L. Koh and J. M. Crowley), Pergamon, Oxford, pp. 257–95.

Hunter, S. C. (1968) The motion of a rigid sphere embedded in an adhering elastic or viscoelastic medium. *Proc., Edinburgh Math. Soc., Ser. II,* **16** (Part I), 55–69.

Lee, E. H. (1955) Stress analysis in viscoelastic bodies. *Q. Appl. Math.*, **13**, 183–90.

Lee, E. H. (1960) Viscoelastic stress analysis, in 1st Symp. on Naval Structural Mechanics (eds J. N. Goodier and N. J. Hoff), Pergamon, New York, pp. 456–82.

Lee, E. H. (1966) Some recent developments in linear viscoelastic stress analysis, in Proc. 11th Int. Congr. of Applied Mechanics (ed. H. Gortler), Springer, Berlin, pp. 396–402.

Lee, E. H. and Radok, J. R. M. (1960) The contact problem for viscoelastic bodies. *J. Appl. Mech.*, **27**, 438–44.

Lee, E. H., Radok, J. R. M. and Woodward, W. B. (1959) Stress analysis for linear viscoelastic materials. *Trans. Soc. Rheol.*, **3**, 41–59.

Lockett, F. J. (1962) The reflection and refraction of waves at an interface between viscoelastic materials. *J. Mech. Phys. Solids*, **10**, 53–64.

Love, A. E. H. (1944) *A Treatise on the Mathematical Theory of Elasticity*, Cambridge University Press, Cambridge.

Lubliner, J. and Sackman, J. L. (1967) On uniqueness in general linear viscoelasticity. *Q. Appl. Math.*, **25**, 129–38.

Morland, L. W. (1962) A plane problem of rolling contact in linear viscoelasticity theory. *J. Appl. Mech.*, **29**, 345–58.

Morland, L. W. (1967) Exact solution for rolling contact between viscoelastic cylinders. *Q. J. Appl. Math.*, **20**, 73–106.

Morland, L. W. and Lee, E. H. (1960) Stress analysis for linear viscoelastic materials with temperature variation. *Trans. Soc. Rheol.*, **4**, 233–63.

Muki, R. and Sternberg, E. (1961) On transient thermal stresses in viscoelastic materials with temperature dependent properties. *J. Appl. Mech.*, **28**, 193–207.

Nachman, A. and Walton, J. R. (1978) The sliding of a rigid indentor over a power law viscoelastic layer. *J. Appl. Mech.*, **45**, 111–3.

Odeh, F. and Tadjbakhsh, I. (1965) Uniqueness in the linear theory of viscoelasticity. *Arch. Ration. Mech. Anal.*, **18**, 244–50.

Onat, E. T. and Breuer, S. (1963) On uniqueness in linear viscoelasticity, in *Progress in Applied Mechanics*, The Prager Anniversary Volume (ed. D. C. Drucker), Macmillan, New York, pp. 349–53.

Predeleanu, M. (1965) Stress analysis in bodies with time-dependent properties. *Bull. Math. Soc. Sci. Math., Roum.*, **9**, 115–27.

Read, W. T. (1950) Stress analysis for compressible viscoelastic materials. *J. Appl. Phys.*, **21**, 671–4.

Rogers, T. G. (1965) Viscoelastic stress analysis, in Proc. Princeton University, Conf. on Solid Mechanics, Princeton, NJ, pp. 49–74.

Rogers, T. G. and Lee, E. H. (1962) *Brown University Rep. NORD 18594/6*.

Sabin, G. C. W. (1987) The impact of a rigid axisymmetric indentor on a viscoelastic half-space. *Int. J. Eng. Sci.*, **25**, 235–51.

298   *Viscoelastic boundary value problem*

Schapery, R. A. (1955) A method of viscoelastic stress analysis using elastic solutions. *J. Franklin Inst.,* **279**(4), 268–89.

Schapery, R. A. (1962) Approximate method of transform inversion for viscoelastic stress analysis, in Proc. 4th US Natl Congr. on Applied Mechanics, ASME, New York, pp. 1075–85.

Schapery, R. A. (1964) Application of thermodynamics to thermomechanical, fracture, and birefringent phenomena in viscoelastic media. *J. Appl. Phys.,* **35**(5), 1451–65.

Schapery, R. A. (1967) Stress analysis of viscoelastic composite materials. *J. Compos. Mater.,* **1**, 228–66.

Schapery, R. A. (1974) Viscoelastic behaviour and analysis of composite materials, in *Mechanics of Composite Materials,* Vol. 2 (ed. G. P. Sendeckj), Academic Press, New York, pp. 85–168.

Schwarzl, F. and Staverman, A. J. (1952) Time–temperature dependence of linear viscoelastic behaviour. *J. Appl. Phys.,* **23**(8), 838–43.

Sips, R. (1951) General theory of deformation of viscoelastic substances. *J. Polym. Sci.,* **9**, 191–205.

Sternberg, E. (1964) On the analysis of thermal stresses in viscoelastic solids, in *High Temperature Structures and Materials,* Proc. 3rd Symp. on Naval Structural Mechanics (eds A. M. Freudenthal, B. A. Boles and H. Liebowitz), Pergamon, Oxford, pp. 348–82.

Sternberg, E. and Gurtin, M. E. (1963) Uniqueness in the theory of thermorheologically simple ablating viscoelastic solids, in *Progress in Applied Mechanics,* The Prager Anniversary Volume (ed. D. C. Drucker), Macmillan, New York, pp. 373–84.

Sternberg, E. and Gurtin, M. E. (1964) Further study of thermal stresses in viscoelastic materials with temperature dependent properties, in Proc. IUTAM Symp. on Second Order Effects in Elasticity, Plasticity and Fiuid Mechanics, Haifa, pp. 51–76.

Ting, T. C. T. (1966) The contact stresses between a rigid indentor and a viscoelastic half-space. *J. Appl. Mech.,* **33**, 845–54.

Ting, T. C. T. (1968) Contact problems in the linear theory of viscoelasticity. *J. Appl. Mech.,* **35**, 248–54.

Volterra, V. (1909) Sulle equazioni integro-differenziali della teoria dell' elasticita. *Atti Reale Accad. Lincei,* **18**(1), 167; **18**(2), 295.

FURTHER READING

Alblas, J. B. and Kuipers, M. (1970) The contact problem of a rigid cylinder rolling on a thin viscoelastic layer. *Int. J. Eng. Sci.,* **8**, 363–80.

Alfrey, T. (1944) Nonhomogeneous stresses in viscoelastic media. *Q. Appl. Math.,* **2**, 113–9.

Atkinson, C. and Coleman, C. J. (1977) On some steady-state moving boundary problems in the linear theory of viscoelasticity. *J. Inst. Maths. Appl.,* **20**, 85–106.

Battiato, G., Ronca, G. and Varga, C. (1977) Moving loads on a viscoelastic double layer: prediction of recoverable and permanent deformations, in Proc. 4th Int. Conf. on Structural Design of Asphalt Pavements, The University of Michigan, Ann Arbor, MI, pp. 459–60.

Calvit, H. H. (1967) Experiments on rebound of steel spheres from blocks of polymers. *J. Mech. Phys. Solids,* **15**, 141–50.

Comninou, M. (1976) Contact between viscoelastic bodies. *J. Appl. Mech.,* **43**, 630–2.

Edelstein, W. S. (1969a) The cylinder problem in thermoviscoelasticity. *J. Res. Natl. Bur. Stand., Sect. B,* **73**, 31–40.

Edelstein, W. S. (1969b) Ablation and thermal effects in a viscoelastic cylinder. *Acta Mech.,* **8**, 174–82.

Gakhof, F. D. (1966) *Boundary Value Problems,* Pergamon, Oxford.

Gaul, L. (1992) Substructure behaviour of resilient support mounts for single and double stage mounting systems. *Comput. Struct.,* **44**(1/2), 273–8.

Gaul, L., Klein, P. and Kemple, S. (1991) Damping description involving fractional operators. *Mech. Syst. Signal Process.*, **5**(2), 81–2.

Gaul, L., Schanz, M. and Fiedler, C. (1992) Viscoelastic formulations of BEM in time and frequency domain. *Eng. Anal. Bound. Elem.*, **10**, 137–41.

Golden, J. M. and Graham, G. A. C. (1988) *Boundary Value Problems in Linear Viscoelasticity*, Springer, Berlin.

Graham, G. A. C. (1965) On the use of stress functions for solving problems in linear viscoelasticity theory that involve moving boundaries. *Proc. R. Soc. Edinburgh, Sect. A*, **67**, 1–8.

Graham, G. A. C. and Golden, J. M. (1988) The generalized partial correspondence principle in linear viscoelasticity. *Q. Appl. Math.*, **56**(3), 527–38.

Graham, G. A. C. and Sabin, G. C. W. (1973) The correspondence principle of linear viscoelasticity for problems that involve time-dependent regions. *Int. J. Eng. Sci.*, **11**, 123–40.

Graham, G. A. C. and Sabin, G. C. W. (1978) The opening and closing of a growing crack in a linear viscoelastic body that is subject to alternating tensile and compressive loads. *Int. J. Fract.*, **14**, 639–49.

Graham, G. A. C. and Sabin, G. C. W. (1981) Steady-state solutions for a cracked standard linear viscoelastic body. *Mech. Res. Commun.*, **8**, 361–8.

Harvey, R. B. (1975) On the deformation of a viscoelastic cylinder, rolling without slipping. *Q. J. Mech. Appl. Math.*, **28**, 1–24.

Hunter, S. C. (1960) The Hertz problem for a rigid spherical indentor and a viscoelastic half-space. *J. Mech. Phys. Solids*, **8**, 219–34.

Hunter, S. C. (1961) The rolling contact of a rigid cylinder with a viscoelastic half-space. *J. Appl. Mech.*, **28**, 611–7.

Hunter, S. C. (1967) The transient temperature distribution in a semi-infinite viscoelastic rod, subject to longitudinal oscillations. *Int. J. Eng. Sci.*, **5**, 119–43.

Kalker, J. J. (1975) Aspects of contact mechanics, in *The Mechanics of the Contact Between Deformable Media* (eds A. D. de Pater and J. J. Kalker), Delft University Press, pp. 1–25.

Kalker, J. J. (1977) A survey of the mechanics of contact between solid bodies. *Z. Angew. Math. Phys.*, **57**, 13–17.

Koeller, R. C. (1984) Application of fractional calculus to the theory of viscoelasticity. *J. Appl. Mech.*, **51**, 299–307.

Lee, E. H. (1966) Some recent developments in linear viscoelastic stress analysis, in Proc. 11th Congr. of Applied Mechanics (ed. H. Gortler), Springer, Berlin, pp. 396–402.

Lifshitz, J. M. and Kolsky, H. (1964) Some experiments on anelastic rebound. *J. Mech. Phys. Solids*, **12**, 35–43.

Lockett, F. J. (1961) Interpretation of mathematical solutions in viscoelasticity theory illustrated by a dynamic spherical cavity problem. *J. Mech. Phys. Solids*, **9**, 215–29.

Lockett, F. J. and Morland, L. W. (1967) Thermal stresses in a viscoelastic thin-walled tube with temperature-dependent properties. *Int. J. Eng. Sci.*, **5**, 879–98.

Margeston, J. (1971) Rolling contact of a smooth viscoelastic strip between rotating rigid cylinders. *Int. J. Mech. Sci.*, **13**, 207–15.

Margeston, J. (1972) Rolling contact of a rigid cylinder over a smooth elastic or viscoelastic layer. *Acta Mech.*, **13**, 1–9.

McCartney, L. N. (1978) Crack propagation in linear viscoelastic solids: some new results. *Int. J. Fract.*, **14**, 547–54.

Morland, L. W. (1963) Dynamic stress analysis for a viscoelastic half-plane subject to moving surface tractions. *Proc. London Math. Soc.*, **13**, 471–92.

Morland, L. W. (1968) Rolling contact between dissimilar viscoelastic cylinders. *Q. Appl. Math.*, **25**, 363–76.

Pao, Y. H. (1955) Extension of the Hertz theory of impact to the viscoelastic case. *J. Appl. Phys.*, **26**, 1083–8.

Rabotonov, Y. N. (1969) *Creep Problems in Structural Members*, North-Holland, Amsterdam.

Rogers, T. G. (1965) Viscoelastic stress analysis, in Proc. Princeton University Conf. on Solid Mechanics, Princeton, NJ, pp. 49–74.

Sabin, G. C. W. (1975) Some dynamic mixed boundary value problems in linear viscoelasticity. PhD Thesis, University of Windsor, Windsor, Ontario.

Schapery, R. A. (1978) A method for predicting crack growth in nonhomogeneous viscoelastic media. *Int. J. Fract.*, **14**, 293–309.

Schapery, R. A. (1979) On the analysis of crack initiation and growth in nonhomogeneous viscoelastic media, in *Fracture Mechanics*, Proc. Symp. in Applied Mathematics of the AMS and SIAM, Vol. XII (ed. R. Burridge), American Mathematical Society, Providence, RI, pp. 137–52.

Sokolnikoff, I. S. (1956) *Mathematical Theory of Elasticity*, 2nd edn, McGraw-Hill, New York.

Stackgold, I. (1967) *Boundary Value Problems of Mathematical Physics*, Vol. 1, Macmillan, New York.

Ting, T. C. T. (1969) A mixed boundary value problem in viscoelasticity with time-dependent boundary regions, in Proc. 11th Midwestern Mechanics Conf. (eds H. J. Weiss, D. F. Young, W. F. Riley and T. R. Rogge), Iowa University Press, pp. 591–8.

Ting, E. C. (1970) Stress analysis for a nonlinear viscoelastic cylinder with ablating inner surface. *J. Appl. Mech.*, **37**, 44–7.

Willis, J. R. (1967) Crack propagation in viscoelastic media. *J. Mech. Phys. Solids*, **15**, 229–40.

10

Extension of the phenomenological theory of viscoelasticity to include microscopic effects

10.1 INTRODUCTION

A large class of engineering materials have a distinct microstructure and, hence, their response behaviour may be formulated with the inclusion of the effects of such a microstructure. Although most engineering materials may be characterized within this category, the present chaper will consider only one group of such materials, namely randomly structured fibrous systems. The latter may be considered as a good representative of discrete viscoelastic systems. Whilst it might appear that structured viscoelastic materials are significantly different in nature, it is the author's point of view that a general deformation theory could be developed that would be applicable to a large category of such material systems.

It is the main purpose of this chapter to show the development of such a theory within the framework of 'probabilistic micromechanics' (Axelrad, 1970, 1971, 1978, 1984). In this theory, the discrete nature of individual microstructural elements forming the macroscopic material system as well as the interaction effects between these elements are taken, from the onset, into account. Because of the discrete nature of the microstructure, the analysis is based on the concepts of the mathematical theory of probability and statistical micromechanics. Thus, the significant stochastic parameters pertaining to the deformation process are expressed in the formulation of the theory in terms of their statistical distribution functions. Such distribution functions are, in part, experimentally accessible. Although significant research work is still required to be carried out for the development of the probabilistic micro-mechanical approach, it is, by no doubt, a promising approach towards the formulation of the response behaviour of material systems with the inclusion of the real microstructure. For further applications of the latter approach, the reader is referred to Axelrad (1978, 1984), Axelrad and Jaeger (1969a, b), Axelrad, Provan and Basu (1974) and Haddad (1986, 1990).

10.2 STOCHASTIC MICROMECHANICAL APPROACH TO THE RHEOLOGY OF RANDOMLY STRUCTURED MATERIAL SYSTEMS

In the present section, a stochastic microstructural approach to the viscoelastic (rheological) response of randomly structured material systems is developed. This approach recognizes that the microstructure of such a material system consists of randomly arranged microstructural elements which are mutually interacting through a bonding mechanism at particular regions where they cross or are neighbours. Thus, the analysis takes into account the rheological response of individual microelements as well as the effect of interelemental bonding. Because of the inherent randomness of the physical and geometrical characteristics of the microstructure, probabilistic concepts are used. Moreover, the microstructural elements forming the material system possess, in general, time-dependent response characteristics. As a consequence, it is appropriate to consider the significant quantities governing the deformation process as stochastic variables and the deformation process itself is seen in this approach as a stochastic process.

In order to describe the mechanical response of the material system from a microstructural point of view, it is necessary to consider the response of the individual structural elements which on a local scale could differ considerably from an average response if the phenomenological continuum approach was taken. Such local deviations in the response which are usually neglected if one ignores the microstructure are directly related to basic properties of the nonhomogeneous material system. Accordingly, the present analysis begins with a definition of the structural element of the particular material system under consideration and deals with the formulation of its rheological response in a probabilistic sense.

In order to extend the analysis to the practical case of a macroscopic material system, it is necessary to make use of 'intermediate quantities' arising from the consideration of the existence of a statistical ensemble of structural elements within an intermediate domain of the material specimen. Further, it is equally important to find a connection between the microscopic and the macroscopic response formulations. Thus, the analysis aims at the formulation of a set of 'governing response equations' for the structured material system that, in contrast to the classical continuum mechanics formulations, are based on the concepts of statistical theory and probabilistic micromechanics (Axelrad, 1978, 1984; Haddad, 1985). In this context, it has been found useful to employ an operational representation of the various relations. Hence, the notion of a 'material operator' (Axelrad, 1978, 1984) characteristic of the viscoelastic response of an intermediate domain of the material is introduced. This material operator provides the connection between the stress field and the occurring deformations within the intermediate domain under consideration. It contains in its argument those stochastic variables or functions of such variables distinctive of the microstructure within the intermediate domain. In a very reduced and simplified form, such an operator is expressed as

$$\Gamma(t) = \Gamma({}^{t}\Gamma, {}^{j}\Gamma, {}^{\alpha}K, p_1, p_2, \cdots, t) \qquad (10.1)$$

Table 10.1 A comparison between basic concepts of the probabilistic micromechanical approach and the corresponding concepts of classical continuum mechanics

	Classical continuum mechanics	*Probabilistic micromechanics*
Material system	Continuous	Discrete
Local description	Mathematical point	Structural element
Stress and deformation	Continuous	Discontinuous
Analytical approach	• Deterministic	• Stochastic
	• Constitutive theory	• Operational formalism of a structured material system

where ${}^f\Gamma$ and ${}^j\Gamma$ are random material operators expressing the response characteristics of elements of different classes of the microstructure (e.g. a fibre segment and a junction area between two overlapping fibres in a fibrous material system), ${}^\alpha K$ is a function of one or more geometrical parameters, p_1 and p_2 are geometrical probabilities and t is the time parameter. Other variables that may be included in the argument of the material operator $\Gamma(t)$ could include, for instance, the temperature T and relative

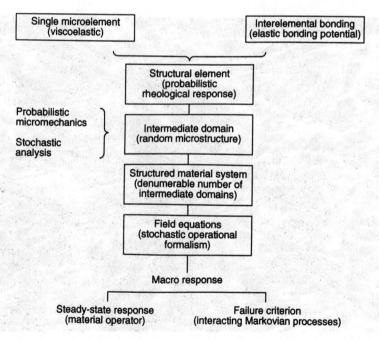

Fig. 10.1 Scope of the stochastic micromechanical approach to the rheological response of a randomly structured (viscoelastic) material system.

humidity ϕ. A comparison between basic concepts of the probabilistic micro-mechanical approach adopted here and the corresponding postulates of the conventional continuum mechanics approach (adopted in the previous chapters of the text) is shown in Table 10.1.

The scope of the stochastic micromechanical approach to the rheological response of a randomly structured material system (of mutually interacting viscoelastic microelements) is demonstrated in Fig. 10.1.

10.3 CASE STUDY: VISCOELASTIC RESPONSE BEHAVIOUR OF A CLASS OF RANDOMLY STRUCTURED FIBROUS SYSTEMS

10.3.1 Theoretical analysis

We consider here the application of the stochastic micromechanical approach, as presented in the previous section, to the rheological behaviour of a class of randomly oriented fibrous systems. In order to illustrate the type of material investigated here, a micrograph ($\times$ 170) of a (cellulosic) fibrous system is shown in Fig. 10.2. It represents a material system of bleached sulphite paper. The microstructure of the system is seen to be heterogeneous showing a random arrangement of single fibres

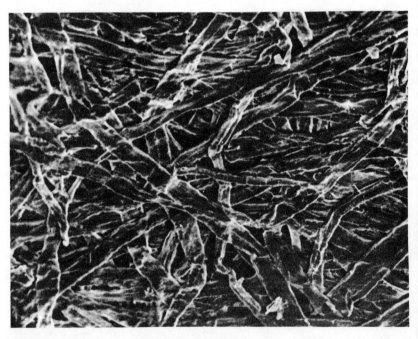

Fig. 10.2 Micrograph ($\times$ 170) of a typical, randomly structured fibrous system; beaten sulphite paper, bleached and dried (Haddad, 1975).

which are bonded together at certain junctions. Fibrous systems such as introduced above have been classified with respect to their response behaviour as viscoelastic materials (Brezinski, 1956; Schulz, 1961).

Traditionally, models that are based on continuum theories have been used for the prediction of the response behaviour of fibrous systems. These models, in general, refer to a homogeneous medium ignoring, thereby, the effect of the microstructure. Several attempts, however, have been made to modify the continuum mechanics approach by allowing for microscopic or 'local' quantities to enter into the analysis, but without removing the main restrictions imposed by continuum physics on such formulations. In this sense, 'modified continuum' models have been proposed by Nissan (1959), Onogi and Sasaguri (1961), Sternstein and Nissan (1962) and Van den Akker (1962), amongst others.

The necessity, however, to develop a new approach to the response of fibrous systems that would be based explicitly on microstructural considerations has been frequently discussed in the literature (e.g. Rance, 1948, 1962; Haddad, 1975). Rance (1948) advanced the argument that the nonrecoverable deformation of a paper sheet, for example, is essentially due to the breakage of interfibre bonding that occurs at an increasing rate leading to the final rupture of the macroscopic specimen. Page, Tydeman and Hunt (1962) verified experimentally that this phenomenon could occur under the effect of elastic tension. Corte (1966) and Nissan (1967) reported, in this regard, that hydrogen bonding is the most effective binding mechanism between two adjacent cellulosic fibres.

On the other hand, the failure of fibre segments during elastic tension of paper samples has been reported by Van den Akker *et al.* (1958). Thus, the opinion has been put forward that the mechanical response of a fibrous network depends on the response characteristics of interfibre bonding as well as those of individual fibres. Experimental investigations by McIntosh and Leopold (1962) supported the last statement. Van den Akker (1970) highlighted further the importance of the statistical approach to the problem of the prediction of the macroscopic response of fibrous systems with the inclusion of the microstructure. In this context, Corte and Kallmes (1962) presented a comprehensive study concerning the statistical geometry of a model of fibrous systems.

(a) Probablistic, micromechanical response

A structural element
A structural element (α) is defined as the smallest part of the medium that represents the mechanical and physical characteristics of the microstructure at the 'micro' level. For the particular material system under consideration (Fig. 10.2), a model of the structural element is introduced that includes the contribution of a single fibre segment between two neighbouring junctions, as well as one-half of each of the junction areas associated with the actual bonding between the overlapping fibres (Fig. 10.3).

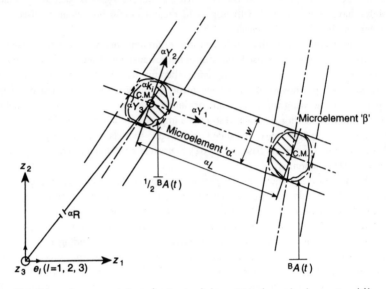

Fig. 10.3 Schematic representation of a structural element (α) of a randomly structured fibrous system.

Throughout the analysis, a superscript (α) to the left of the symbol will refer, in general, to a structural element. However, since a distinction is made between the fibre segment and the two half-junction areas, the quantities referring to such a segment will be denoted by a superscript 'f' while those referring to the bonding interaction within the junction area between two matching fibres are designated by a superscript 'B'.

The kinematics of deformation are considered from the point of view of two coordinate systems, i.e. a local frame of reference $^{\alpha}Y_i$ ($i = 1, 2, 3$) attached to the geometrical centre of the junction between two overlapping fibres and an external coordinate frame Z_i ($I = 1, 2, 3$); Fig. 10.3.

Viscoelastic response of a fibre segment
In view of the fact that we consider, here, the response of 'natural fibres', such as cellulose fibres, which, in most cases, exhibit rheological properties, the viscoelastic response of such fibres will be considered. While, for the simplification of the analysis, the continuum mechanics approach is maintained for the response characterization of the fibre segment, it is understood that the effect of fibre substructural parameters is not considered at this stage of presentation.

Information concerning the microstructure of single fibres of natural cellulose is given by, amongst others, Meredith (1956), Roelofsen (1959), Mark (1967) and Bikales and Segal (1971). Mark (1967) presented a corrolation between the fibril angle in the S_2 layer (the main layer in the single wood pulp fibre) and the tensile strength of the fibre. Schematics of such fibres are shown in Figs. 10.4 and 10.5 after Roelofsen (1959). The importance of synthetic fibres, in particular with respect to papermaking, has been discussed by Battista (1964). The response behaviour of synthetic single fibres has been discussed by Lai and Findley (1968), among others.

We shall consider here, the formulation of the creep behaviour of a single fibre with the inclusion of pertaining experimental data. This is with the understanding that the same approach can be adopted for the relaxation behaviour as we have presented earlier in Chapter 7.

Referring to the creep response equation (7.20), once the values of the unknown constants of this equation have been determined by the procedure mentioned in section 7.2, this equation can be used to represent a 'model equation' for the response behaviour of an actual viscoelastic fibre. For this purpose, an equivalent strain $^f\varepsilon(t)$, in the fibre segment, is assumed which corresponds to the actual strain in such segment that can be determined for the probabilistic theory only from experimental observations, e.g. via a distribution function. Under these circumstances, the model equation (7.20) for the viscoelastic response for the fibre segment can be written as

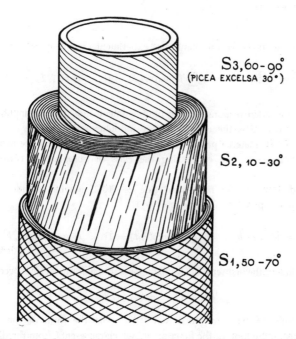

Fig. 10.4 Schema of the orientation of the cellulose microfibrils in the normal three-ply structure. (Source: Roelofsen, P. A. (1959) *The Plant Cell Wall*, © Gebrüder Borntraeger, Berlin-Nikolassee. Reprinted with permission.)

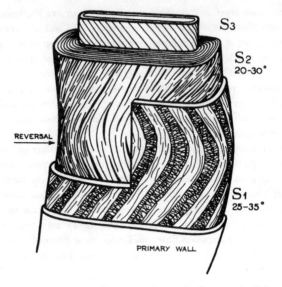

S3

S2
20–30°

REVERSAL

S1
25–35°

PRIMARY WALL

Fig. 10.5 Schema of the structure of the secondary wall of a natural cellulose fibre. (Source: Roelofsen, P. A. (1959) *The Plant Cell Wall,* © Gebrüder Borntraeger, Berlin-Nikolessee. Reprinted with permission.)

follows, where the index for the number of experiment i has been omitted:

$$^f\varepsilon(t) = {}^fE^{-1f}\breve{\xi} + h({}^f\breve{\xi}, b_1, b_2, \cdots) \sum_{I=1}^{N} D_I[\exp(A_I t) - 1] \qquad (I = 1, 2, \cdots, N) \quad (10.2)$$

where $^f\varepsilon(t)$ is the strain response in the fibre segment and $^f\breve{\xi}$ is the input level of the stress. In (10.2), E is the uniaxial elastic modulus and $b_1, b_2, \cdots, D_I$ and A_I ($I = 1, 2, \cdots, N$) are material parameters that can be determined by the inclusion of the experimental creep data concerning the class of fibres under consideration (Chapter 7).

The second term on the right-hand side of (10.2) maybe considered to be represented by an operator $^fL({}^f\breve{\xi}, t)$ where

$$^fL({}^f\breve{\xi}, t)^f\breve{\xi} = h({}^f\breve{\xi}, b_1, b_2, \cdots) \sum_{I=1}^{N} D_I[\exp(A_I t) - 1] \qquad (I = 1, 2, \cdots, N) \quad (10.3)$$

so that, by including the first term of (10.2), the operational form of (10.2) becomes

$$^f\varepsilon(t) = [{}^fE^{-1} + {}^fL({}^f\breve{\xi}, t)]. \tag{10.4}$$

It is noted, with reference to (10.3) and (10.4), that the form of the operator $^fL({}^f\breve{\xi}, t)$ depends on the form of the function $h(\cdot)$ which represents, from the discussion in Chapter 7, the nonlinear behaviour of the fibre material. In the present case of natural cellulose fibres, for instance, the function $h(\cdot)$ may be assumed to have the following simple form:

$$h(\cdot) = \exp(b^f\breve{\xi}) - 1. \tag{10.5}$$

Expanding asymptotically the exponential term in the form of $h(\cdot)$ given by (10.5) and retaining only the first two terms of the resulting expansion, expression (10.3) can be written as

$${}^fL(t){}^f\breve{\xi} = b^f\breve{\xi} \sum_{I=1}^{N} D_I[\exp(A_It) - 1] \qquad (I = 1, 2, \cdots, N) \tag{10.6}$$

whereby the operator ${}^fL(\cdot)$ is now a function of time only.

While the above formulation has been illustrated by a procedure applied to the specific case of cellulosic fibres, it is valid for any other class of viscoelastic fibres provided that the proper material characteristics and the form of experimental curves representing the viscoelastic behaviour of the particular class of material are observed. Hence, in view of the foregoing, a constitutive relation in operational form can be written, in general, as

$${}^f\varepsilon(t) = [{}^fE^{-1} + {}^fL(t)]{}^f\xi(t). \tag{10.7}$$

Further, if one considers, from a system theoretical point of view, that the microstress in the fibre segment is the stimulus and the occurring microstrain is the corresponding response, then equation (10.7) can be written in a more compact operational form as

$${}^f\varepsilon(t) = {}^f\Gamma(t){}^f\xi(t) \tag{10.8}$$

where ${}^f\Gamma(t)$ is a transform operator. This transform operator will be included subsequently as part of another material operator ${}^M\Gamma(t)$ valid for an intermediate domain of the macroscopic material specimen.

The simplification and systematization achieved with the operator formulation is rather important, since, in many cases, it can be used to achieve a response formalism with the inclusion of the microstructure of a material, such as fibrous network, which otherwise cannot be achieved directly (e.g. Axelrad and Basu, 1974).

In view of equations (10.2), (10.5) and (10.6), the expression for the transform operator ${}^f\Gamma(t)$ appearing in (10.8) is written as

$${}^f\Gamma(t) = \left\{ {}^fE^{-1} + b \sum_{I=1}^{N} D_I[\exp(A_It) - 1] \right\} \qquad (I = 1, 2, \cdots, N) \tag{10.9}$$

where the material parameters appearing in the above expression can be determined (as discussed in Chapter 7) with the inclusion of the viscoelastic experimental data concerning the particular fibre material under consideration.

Interfibre bonding

In any mathematical approach to the response behaviour of fibrous systems that would be based explicitly on microstructural considerations, it is of utmost importance to include in the formulation the effect due to bonding between two overlapping fibres. It is readily noticed from Fig. 10.6 showing a micrograph (× 1120) of unbeaten, low yield sulphite network that a junction area between two adjacent fibres shows a distinct discontinuous of fibrils in this area. The fibrils are bonded either partially or wholly as a result of interactions between them at the molecular level.

Corte (1966) and Nissan (1967) dealt comprehensively with the nature of bonding in a cellulosic structure. These authors, among others, claim that hydrogen bonding is the most effective binding mechanism between the fibrils on the surfaces of two adjacent fibres. A hydrogen bond is usually formed by the hydroxyl groups (OH) of the cellulose molecules (e.g. Corte, 1966; Pauling, 1960; Paradowski, 1991). Here, a hydrogen-containing OH group on the surface of a fibre may bond to a corresponding receptor, an oxygen atom on the surface of the matching fibre, forming an intermolecular hydrogen bond, within a junction area between the two fibres. Hemicellulose and portions of lignin molecules, usually encountered in pulp fibres, are also capable of forming this type of bond (Nissan, 1967). Available X-ray data on cellulosic systems indicate that cellulose in natural fibres crystallizes partially or wholly within the fibrils in a manner in which unit cells are formed and which repeat themselves as a common chain. A model of the repeating unit of cellulose (Jacobson, Wunderlich and Lipscomb, 1961) is shown in Fig. 10.7. This, as shown in the figure, is composed of two so-called β-D glucose residues that are linked by an oxygen bridge to adjacent residues and are rotated with respect to one another about a screw axis to form continuous chain segments.

A model (Meyer and Misch, 1937), of the unit cell of cellulose is shown in Fig. 10.8. It has a monoclinic character in which the length of the cellulose repeating unit

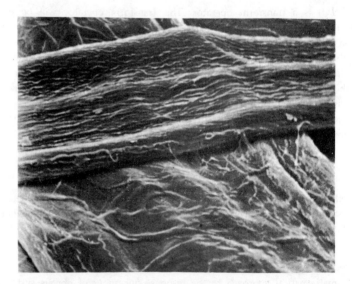

Fig. 10.6 Micrograph (× 1120) of unbeaten low-yield sulphite network (Haddad, 1975).

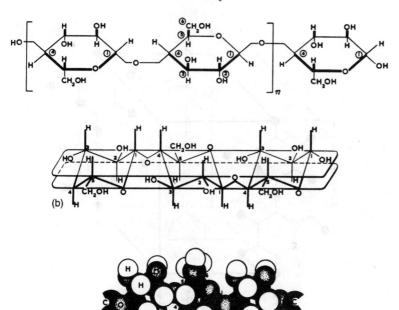

Fig. 10.7 (a) Structural formula of cellulose molecule; (b) three-dimensional structure of cellulose molecule; (c) atom model of cellulose molecule. (Source: Jacobson, R. A., Wunderlich, J. A. and Lipscomb, W. N. (1961) The crystal and molecular structure of cellulose. *Acta Crystallogr.*, **14**, 598–607 (International Union of Crystallography). Reprinted with permission.)

is perpendicular to two other edges which include an angle β. The three edges b, a and c of the unit cell define the crystallographic directions (010), (100) and (001), respectively. Gardener and Blackwell (1974) have shown that the rigid-body least-squares refinement technique (Arnott and Wonacott, 1966) could be used to distinguish between the various possible structures of the cellulosic unit cell, e.g. relative chain polarities and elucidation of the intra- and intermolecular hydrogen bonding. Structural models have been also proposed to describe the way in which the fibrils are built up of molecular chains (e.g. Nissan, 1967; Tonnesen and Ellefsen, 1971; Manley and Inoue, 1965).

In view of the above-indicated Meyer and Misch model of the unit cell, one may define a unit cell area $^{\alpha\beta}\mu$ in the junction as

$$^{\alpha\beta}\mu = b \times a = 10.30 \text{ Å} \times 8.35 \text{ Å}. \qquad (10.10)$$

In order to visualize the notion of matching between two fibres (α, β), it is proposed in the present analysis to follow the geometrical theory of coincidence site lattices

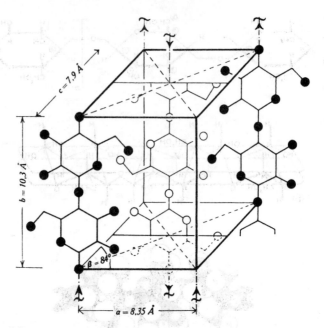

Fig. 10.8 Schematic representation of the unit cell of natural cellulose. (Source: Meyer, K. H. and Misch, L. (1937) Positions des atomes dans le nouveau modèle spatial de la cellulose. *Helv. Chem. Acta*, **20**, 232–44. Reprinted with permission.)

(Bollmann, 1970) in such a manner that the two surfaces of a junction, between two matching fibres, are modelled in terms of two interpenetrating lattices with areas $^{\alpha}A$ and $^{\beta}A$. A three-dimensional picture of the situation, visualized to hold in the present case, is shown in Fig. 10.9. In this figure, each lattice is considered to be formed by cellulosic unit cells in such a manner that the length of the repeating unit it taken in the direction of the appropriate fibre axis. The lattice $^{\alpha\beta}A$ on the surface of one fibre may be assessed by a polarized light technique (Page, Tydeman and Hunt, 1962). The number of unit cells M within $^{\alpha\beta}A$ may be taken as $M = {}^{\alpha\beta}A/{}^{\alpha\beta}\mu$ where $^{\alpha\beta}\mu$ is the unit cell area as defined by equation (10.10).

In Fig. 10.9, a free OH group on the surface of a fibre (α) may bond with a corresponding receptor of the oxygen atoms contained on the surface of the overlapping fibre (β). The lattice area, $^{\alpha\beta}A$, is said to be totally bonded if all its available hydroxyl groups have formed proper interfibre bonds. With reference to Fig. 10.8, for the case of natural cellulose, the number of OH groups on one side of the junction within the unit area $^{\alpha\beta}\mu$ is 6.

It is apparent, however, that not all the hydroxyl groups on the surface of one fibre (α) are free to form a bond with an adjacent fibre (β). This may be attributed to different reasons reviewed previously by Haddad (1975, 1980).

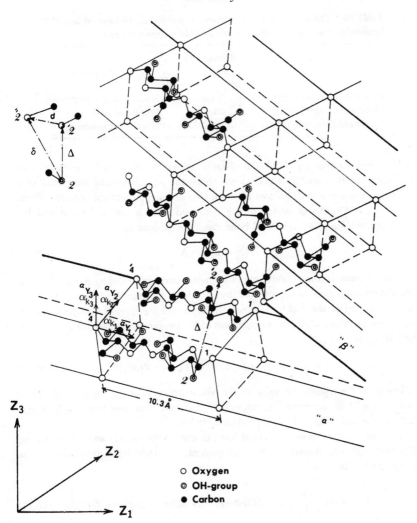

Fig. 10.9 Fibre–fibre interface in a natural cellulosic structure (three-dimensional) (Haddad, 1975).

As a consequence, a restriction on interfibre bonding must be taken into account so that one can assume that only an actual bonded region within the junction area will prevail. This region will, henceforth, be referred to as an 'actual bonded area' ^BA within the 'junction area' $^{\alpha\beta}A$. This actual bonded area can be considered as a percentage of $^{\alpha\beta}A$ in such a way that $^BA = \zeta^{\alpha\beta}A$, where ζ is a bonding ratio, $0 \leq \zeta \leq 1$, accessible only from proper experimental observations. Table 10.2 shows some values of the bonding ratio as proposed by different authors.

Table 10.2 The actual bonded area ^{B}A as compared with the junction area $^{\alpha\beta}A$ between two overlapping fibres. Natural cellulose fibrous systems

Reference	Bonding ratio $(\zeta = {}^{B}A/{}^{\alpha\beta}A)$	Matching fibres
Page and Tydeman (1960)	1.0	Spruce–sulphite pulp finish
Jayme and Hunger (1962)	0.1–0.2	Wood tracheids
Nissan and Sternstein (1964)	0.001–0.008	(Theoretical reasoning)

With reference to Fig. 10.9, the distance vector Δ between, for instance, two matching points 2 and 2' is considered to be the basic kinematic parameter of a hydrogen bond in a junction area between two overlapping natural cellulosic fibres. The counterpart of this vector in the deformed state is denoted by δ and the microdeformation in an individual bond can, thus, be read as

$$\mathbf{d}(t) = \delta(t) - \Delta. \tag{10.11}$$

From classical considerations, one of the usual forms of a binding potential in the one-dimensional case is represented by a 'Morse function' (Morse, 1929). The analytical form of this function, which will represent the three-dimensional case in accordance with the atomistic arrangement of the bonding indicated in Fig. 10.9, can be written as

$$\psi = \psi_0[\exp(-2\kappa|\mathbf{d}(t)|) - 2\exp(-\kappa|\mathbf{d}(t)|)] \tag{10.12}$$

where ψ_0 is the equilibrium value of the Morse potential at the value of $|\mathbf{d}(t)| = 0$ and κ is the Morse constant. The values of ψ_0 and κ are obtainable from spectroscopic data (Corte and Schaschek, 1955; Sokolov, 1959).

Considering the binding potential form of expression (10.12) and differentiating this potential with respect to the displacement, a discrete interaction force in the bond can be obtained.

$$\mathbf{f}(t) = -\frac{\partial\psi}{\partial|\mathbf{d}(t)|}\,\mathbf{k} = 2\kappa\psi_0[\exp(-2\kappa|\mathbf{d}(t)|) - \exp(-\kappa|\mathbf{d}(t)|)]\mathbf{k} \tag{10.13}$$

where $\mathbf{k}$ is a unit base vector associated with the local coordinate frame attached to the centre of mass of the junction (Fig. 10.9; Fig. 10.3 should also be referred to).

Postulating that a bond stress in the continuum sense exists, one may express this stress as

$$^{B}\zeta(t) = \frac{^{\alpha\beta}\mathbf{n}}{^{B}A(t)}\sum_{j=1}^{^{B}N}\mathbf{f}_j(t) \tag{10.14}$$

where $^{\alpha\beta}\mathbf{n}$ is the unit normal to the junction area and $j = 1, 2, \cdots, {}^{B}N$ is the number of interfibre hydrogen bonds in the junction. Combining (10.13) and (10.14), the stress–deformation relation for the interfibre bonding may be written as

$$^B\zeta(t) = \frac{2\kappa\psi_0}{^BA(t)}\,^{\alpha\beta}\mathbf{n} \sum_{j=1}^{^BN} [\exp(-2\kappa|\mathbf{d}_j(t)|) - \exp(-\kappa|\mathbf{d}_j(t)|)]\mathbf{k}. \tag{10.15}$$

In a manner similar to the operational formulation of the response of a single fibre, presented earlier in this section, one may express the bonding response equation (10.15) in an operational form. For this reason, a transform operator $^B\Gamma^{-1}$ for the bonding interaction is introduced such that

$$^B\zeta(t) = {^B\Gamma^{-1}}\ {^B\varepsilon(t)} \tag{10.16a}$$

where $^B\varepsilon(t)$ is the configurational bonding microstrain in the junction area such that

$$^B\varepsilon(t) = {^\alpha\mathbf{V}} \sum_{j=1}^{^BN} \mathbf{d}_j(t)$$

where $^\alpha\mathbf{V}$ is the gradient operator on the bonding displacement expressed, as illustrated in Fig. 10.3, by $^\alpha\mathbf{V} = \partial/\partial^\alpha Y$.

In order, however, to derive from (10.15) the operational form (10.16a), one may expand asymptotically the exponential terms in (10.15) and retain only the first two terms of each resulting series. As a consequence, one may write for the operator $^B\Gamma$ (equation (10.16a)), the following expression:

$$^B\Gamma^{-1} = \frac{-2\kappa^2\psi_0\,^{\alpha\beta}\mathbf{n}kk^{-1}}{^BA(t)}\,^\alpha\mathbf{V}^{-1}. \tag{10.16b}$$

By the inversion of (10.16), the operational response equation for the bonding interaction, corresponding so that for the fibre segment (equation (10.8)), can be written as

$$^B\varepsilon(t) = {^B\Gamma}\ {^B\zeta(t)} \tag{10.17}$$

The adoption of an atomistic approach to the interfibre bonding, as dealt with in the foregoing, is a key point in the present model. This is supported, as indicated earlier, by the fact that the interfibre hydrogen bonding determines primarily the strength of the junction between two matching cellulose fibres.

Probabilistic response of a structural element α
With reference to Fig. 10.10, the following geometrical probabilities are introduced with respect to a scanning line S–S that intersects the surface of a macroscopic specimen:

• p is the probability that the scanning line S–S intersects, at a certain point of the specimen, an individual fibre segment;

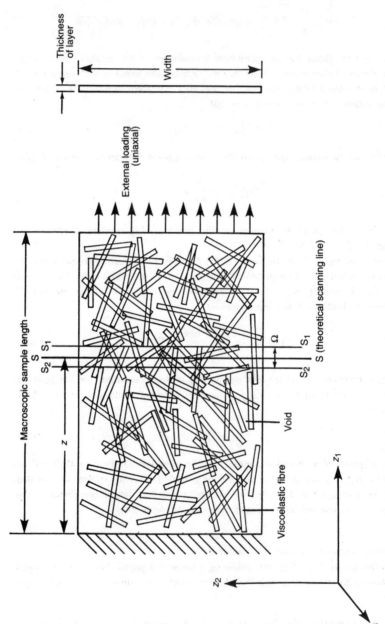

Fig. 10.10 A model of a two-dimensional fibrous network with randomly oriented microstructure.

- q is the probability that S–S intersects, at the same point, a junction between two fibres.

Thus, at the considered point, one may express the microstrain, in a structural element α, in a probabilistic manner as

$$^{\alpha}\varepsilon(t) = p\,{}^{f}\varepsilon(t) + q\,{}^{B}\varepsilon(t) \tag{10.18}$$

where $0 \leq p, q \leq 1$ and $p + q = 1$. In this question, the microstrain $^{B}\varepsilon(t)$ is considered to be totally due to the bonding displacement. That is, the fibre displacement at the point in question is taken to zero. The probability q appearing in (10.18) can be determined in terms of the physical and geometrical characteristics of the fibrous microstructure (Haddad, 1987).

Substituting for the microstrains $^{f}\varepsilon(t)$ and $^{B}\varepsilon(t)$ in (10.18) in terms of the corresponding microstresses from (10.8) and (10.17), respectively, it follows that

$$^{\alpha}\varepsilon(t) = (1 - q)\,{}^{f}\Gamma(t)\,{}^{f}\xi(t) + q\,{}^{B}\Gamma\,{}^{B}\xi(t). \tag{10.19}$$

However, in order to formulate an operational relation that will serve eventually in establishing a response relation for the structural element, it is necessary to employ a relationship between the fibre microstress and the microstress in the junction. This relation may be expressed as (Haddad, 1984),

$$^{B}\xi(t) = {}^{\alpha}K(t)\,{}^{f}\xi(t) \tag{10.20a}$$

where

$$^{\alpha}K(t) = \frac{{}^{f}a}{{}^{B}A(t)}\,[1 - {}^{f}\lambda(t)] \tag{10.20b}$$

where ^{f}a is the fibre cross-sectional area and $^{f}\lambda(t)$ is a time-dependent parameter associated with the equilibrium of the junction between two overlapping fibres α and β. In Haddad (1984), the parameter $^{f}\lambda(t)$ is determined in terms of the orientation of the fibrous elements forming a particular junction.

Now, substituting for $^{B}\xi(t)$ from (10.20a) into (10.19), the latter equation can be written as

$$^{\alpha}\xi(t) = [(1 - q)\,{}^{f}\Gamma(t) + q\,{}^{B}\Gamma\,{}^{\alpha}K(t)]\,{}^{f}\xi(t). \tag{10.21}$$

We introduce the transform operator $^{\alpha f}\Gamma(t)$, associated with the mechanical response of the structural element, such that it corresponds to the expression between square brackets in (10.21), i.e.

$$^{\alpha f}\Gamma(t) = (1 - q)\,{}^{f}\Gamma(t) + q\,{}^{B}\Gamma^{\alpha}K(t). \tag{10.22}$$

Thus, the response equation (10.21) can be written in the following operational form:

$$^{\alpha}\varepsilon(t) = {}^{\alpha f}\Gamma(t)\,{}^{f}\xi(t). \tag{10.23}$$

Further, it is possible, by the inversion of (10.23), to determine the microstress $^f\zeta(t)$ from the microstrain $^a\varepsilon(t)$ as

$$^f\zeta(t) = \,^{\alpha f}\Gamma^{-1}(t)\,\,^\alpha\varepsilon(t). \tag{10.24}$$

In a similar manner, given (10.20), one can express (10.23) as a function of the bonding microstress $^B\zeta(t)$ as

$$^\alpha\varepsilon(t) = \,^{\alpha B}\Gamma(t)\,\,^B\zeta(t) \tag{10.25}$$

where

$$^{\alpha B}\Gamma(t) = \,^{\alpha f}\Gamma(t)\,\,^\alpha K^{-1}(t). \tag{10.26}$$

(b) Transition to the macroscopic response behaviour

Since the fibrous network that occupies a given physical domain is regarded in the present analysis as a discrete medium, a transition from the discrete description to the macroscopic one must be attempted. In this context, the concept of the intermediate domain, or mesodomain (Axelrad, 1978), is employed. The latter is specified by the requirements mentioned by Axelrad (1978, 1984). It is the smallest region of the medium on the boundary of which the macroscopic observables are still valued, but, on the other hand, is large enough to contain a statistical number of structural elements. This permits statistical principles to be introduced in the analysis. It is further postulated that within the macroregion of the system, the mesodomains are denumerable and nonintersecting such that

$$\bigcup_{M=1}^{Q} \,^M V = V$$

and

$$^{M_1}V \cap \,^{M_2}V = \varnothing \qquad (M_1 \neq M_2)$$

where Q designates the total number of mesodomains within a macrovolume V. In the case of a two-dimensional fibrous system under loading in the Z_1 direction, for instance (Fig. 10.10), a mesodomain $\hat{M}$ ($M = 1, 2, \cdots, Q$) may be specified by the region bounded by the two theoretical scanning lines S_1–S_1 and S_2–S_2 which are perpendicular to the direction of loading. The width of this domain is determined, following the above, in relation to the actual dimensions of the structural element α such that, within M, $\alpha = 1, 2, \cdots, \,^M N$, where $^M N$ is very large. In the case of a cellulosic network, such as shown in Fig. 10.2, the width of the mesodomain may be taken of the order of 0.5–2 mm.

Following the concepts of the micromechanical theory of structured media (Axelrad, 1978, 1984), all microscopic field quantities within the intermediate domain are considered to be stochastic functions of primitive random variables. Thus, the components of the microstress, for instance, are seen as stochastic functions $^\alpha\zeta(\mathbf{r}, t)$

that can be regarded as a family of random variables ${}^{\alpha}\xi_t(\mathbf{r})$ within the intermediate domain depending on the time parameter t, or a family of curves ${}^{f}\xi_r(t)$ depending on the structural element position vector ${}^{\alpha}\mathbf{r}$.

Letting ${}^{M}P\{\cdot\}$ denote the probability distribution of a random variable within an intermediate domain M, then, in view of the structural element response equation (10.23), the probability distribution of the microstrain within the intermediate domain may be expressed as

$$ {}^{M}P\{{}^{\alpha}\varepsilon(t)\} = {}^{M}P\{{}^{\alpha f}\Gamma(t)\}\ {}^{M}P\{{}^{f}\xi(t)\}. \tag{10.27} $$

At the same time, with reference to (10.24), one can express the probabilistic distribution of the fibre microstress as

$$ {}^{M}P\{{}^{f}\xi(t)\} = {}^{M}P\{{}^{\alpha f}\Gamma^{-1}(t)\}\ {}^{M}P\{{}^{\alpha}\varepsilon(t)\}. \tag{10.28} $$

Further, following (10.25), the distribution of the bonding microstress becomes

$$ {}^{M}P\{{}^{B}\xi(t)\} = {}^{M}P\{{}^{\alpha B}\Gamma^{-1}(t)\}\ {}^{M}P\{{}^{\alpha}\xi(t)\}. \tag{10.29} $$

In addition, the distribution of the bonding microstress is associated, in view of (10.20), with the distribution of the fibre stress via the relation

$$ {}^{M}P\{{}^{B}\xi(t)\} = {}^{M}P\{{}^{\alpha}K(t)\}\ {}^{M}P\{{}^{f}\xi(t)\}. \tag{10.30} $$

Having established the time evolution of the internal deformation process via equation (10.21), a local failure criterion ${}^{\alpha}S(t)$ of the microstructure, within the intermediate domain, may be conjectured (Haddad, 1986) by setting

$$ {}^{\alpha}S(t) = 1 - \int_{{}^{\alpha}\varepsilon_{maximum}}^{\infty} d{}^{M}P\{{}^{\alpha}\varepsilon(t)\}. \tag{10.31} $$

In this connection, ${}^{\alpha}S(t)$ may be interpreted, in a probabilistic sense, to be associated with the failure of fibrous elements or with the failure of interfibre bonding within the intermediate domain through the relation

$$ {}^{\alpha}S(t) = (1 - q)\ {}^{f}S(t) + q^{B}S(t) \tag{10.32} $$

where the probability q is used.

In (10.32), ${}^{f}S(t)$ and ${}^{B}S(t)$ may be expressed, respectively, in terms of the statistical distributions ${}^{M}P\{{}^{f}\xi(t)\}$ and ${}^{M}P\{{}^{B}\xi(t)\}$ in an analogous manner to (10.31) as

$$ {}^{f}S(t) = 1 - \int_{{}^{f}\varepsilon_{maximum}}^{\infty} d{}^{M}P\{{}^{f}\varepsilon(t)\} \tag{10.33} $$

and

$$ {}^{B}S(t) = 1 - \int_{{}^{B}\varepsilon_{maximum}}^{\infty} d{}^{M}P\{{}^{B}\varepsilon(t)\}. \tag{10.34} $$

This is with the understanding that the two deformation processes ($^t\varepsilon(t)$, $^B\varepsilon(t)$; $t_1 \leq t \leq t_2$) in the intermediate domain are interrelated via equations (10.26) and (10.30). In the context of the above formulations, it may be mentioned that the distribution functions of the significant parameters for the class of material considered can be determined by means of X-ray diffraction techniques, holographic interferometry and electron microscopy (e.g. Axelrad and Kalousek, 1971; Kalousek, 1973).

(c) Extension of the model to include breakage of interfibre bonding

In the present model, a junction area between two adjoining fibres is seen to consist of two regions: a cohesive zone, in which the adjoining fibres act as completely bonded and debonded (free) zone in which interfibre bonding has ceased to exist. The existence of such a free zone could have been initiated by a debonding process due to, for instance, the increase of local stress. From this point of view (Axelrad, 1984), the free zone may initiate an interfibre debonding process towards the cohesive zone. Further, one may assume that the interfibre debonding process occurs in a rather cooperative manner, i.e. bonds can dissociate and reform within the same mechanical state. Thus, it may be visualized that the breakage of interfibre bonds will occur in such a manner that energy is released activating bond formation within the same or neighbouring junction areas. Hence, we consider a process such that the number of interfibre bonds, within the fibrous network, can experience positive as well as negative jumps. Thus, in general, a time-dependent nonhomogeneous birth-and-death model of a process (e.g. Bharucha-Reid, 1960) is seen to be applicable.

If at time t, the material specimen is in the state Σ ($\Sigma = 1, 2, \cdots$) corresponding to a number of existing interfibre bonds $n(t):n_\Sigma$, one considers that both the intensities of positive and negative transitions to be time dependent. The latter are designated, respectively, in the following analysis by $\lambda(t)$ and $\mu(t)$. Accordingly,

1. the probability of transition from the state Σ to $\Sigma + 1$ in the interval $(t, t + \Delta t)$ is $\lambda(t) \Delta t + O(\Delta t)$,
2. the probability of transition from the state Σ to $\Sigma - 1$ in the interval $(t, t + \Delta t)$ is $\mu(t) \Delta t + O(\Delta t)$,
3. the probability of a transition to a state other than a neighbouring state is $O(\Delta t)$,
4. the probability of no change is $1 - [\lambda(t) + \mu(t)] + O(\Delta t)$ and
5. the state $\Sigma = 0$ is an absorbing state corresponding to the breakage of all interfibre bonds within the material specimen.

The above assumptions lead to the relation

$$P_\Sigma(t + \Delta t) = \lambda(t)P_{\Sigma-1}(t) \Delta t + \left\{1 - [\lambda(t) + \mu(t)] \Delta t\right\}P_\Sigma(t)$$
$$+ \mu(t)P_{\Sigma+1}(t)\Delta t + O(\Delta t) \tag{10.35}$$

where P_Σ is the probability that the material system is in the state Σ as defined above. Equation (10.35) leads in the limit to the following differential equation:

$$\frac{dP_\Sigma(t)}{dt} = \lambda(t)P_{\Sigma-1}(t) - [\lambda(t) + \mu(t)]P_\Sigma(t) + \mu(t)P_{\Sigma+1}(t) \tag{10.36a}$$

which holds for $\Sigma = 1, 2, \cdots$. For $\Sigma = 0$, however, one has

$$\frac{dP_0(t)}{dt} = \mu(t)P_1(t). \tag{10.36b}$$

The solution of equations (10.36) can be obtained with the aid of generating functions. Hence,

$$P_\Sigma(t) = [1 - \zeta(t)][1 - Y(t)][Y(t)]^{\Sigma-1}, \quad \Sigma = 1, 2, \cdots, \tag{10.37a}$$

and

$$P_0(t) = \zeta(t) \tag{10.37b}$$

where

$$\zeta(t) = 1 - \frac{\exp[-\gamma(t)]}{\Omega(t)}$$

$$Y(t) = 1 - \frac{1}{\Omega(t)}$$

$$\gamma(t) = \int_0^t [\mu(\tau) - \lambda(t)]\, d\tau$$

and

$$\Omega(t) = \exp[-\gamma(t)]\left\{1 + \int_0^t \mu(t)\,\exp[\gamma(t)]\, d\tau\right\}. \tag{10.37c}$$

The probability of total intergranular bond dissociation is, then, given with reference to (10.37) by

$$P_0(t) = \frac{\int_0^t \mu(t)\,\exp[\gamma(\tau)]\, dt}{1 + \int_0^t \mu(\tau)\,\exp[\gamma(\tau)]\, dt}. \tag{10.38}$$

10.3.2 Numerical illustration

In the present section, the theoretical analysis proposed in the previous section is applied to the case of a natural cellulose fibrous network. The aim here is to incorporate available experimental data concerning the microstructure into the proposed formulation. Hence, in accordance with the introduced model, the internal stress distribution and the response behaviour of an intermediate domain of the material may be predicted. In the context of the application of the theoretical analysis, the following remarks are first made.

1. In practice, the experimental values concerning the response of single fibres, in general, are obtainable, in most cases, from a uniaxial test situation; thus one may only proceed to evaluate numerically the material parameters characterizing the creep behaviour of cellulose fibres for this particular case. Consequently, one may assume, for the purpose of this section, that the microdeformation in the fibre segment as well as the bond deformation in the junction area occur only in the direction of the fibre segment axis, i.e. in the direction of the $^\alpha Y_1$ axis of the local coordinate system.

2. Because of the random orientation of the fibrous elements, these elements may experience tension or compression at different instants of time. Hence, it is necessary to assume that the rheological response of a fibre segment in compression is governed by the same constitutive law in tension. This hypothesis is considered to be valid only for the case of small strain (e.g. Hill, 1967).

3. A review of the literature on the determination of the distribution of orientation of the fibrous elements revealed that no experimental work has been carried out to determine such a distribution for the general three-dimensional case. However, the distribution of orientation of the fibrous elements is accessible for the two-dimensional case (e.g. Kallmes, 1969). Consequently, in the context of the application of the theoretical analysis, one must assume further that

$$^\alpha K_3, \quad ^\alpha k_3 \equiv e_3$$

where $^\alpha K_3$, $^\alpha k_3$ are the local unit vectors (undeformed and deformed states, respectively) that are associated with the local coordinate frame $^\alpha Y_i$ ($i = 1, 2, 3$), attached to the junction area, and e_3 is the unit vector associated with the external frame of reference Z_I ($I = 1, 2, 3$) (Fig. 10.3).

(a) Local response behaviour

Viscoelastic response of a fibre segment
We consider here, as an example, the case of dry summerwood fibres of a longleaf pine holocellulose pulp (conditioned at 50% RH and 23 °C). The numerical evaluation of the creep response of these fibres has been considered in section 7.4.1, where the numerical values of the parameters characterizing the model equation (7.6) or (7.26), with the inclusion of (7.36), were determined for a range of stress input between 29.1 and 49.1 dyn μm^2 and an extent of time up to 10^5 s. These numerical values are given in Tables 7.3 and 7.4 for an order of optimization $N = 3, 4, \cdots, 8$.

Interfibre bonding
The response behaviour of interfibre bonding has been determined for the present case of natural cellulose by using equations (10.16). In this, the numerical values of the parameters characterizing the material operator $^B\Gamma(t)$, equation (10.17) are taken as $\psi_0 = 3.14 \times 10^5$ dyn Å (Corte and Schaschek, 1955) and $\kappa = 2$ Å^{-1} (Sokolov, 1959).

Table 10.3 Geometrical and physical characteristics of a structural element (α) of natural cellulose

Fibre width, w	36 μm
Fibre thickness, *s*	3.6 μm
Fibre cross-sectional area, $^f a = ws$	129.60 μm^2
Actual bonded area of the junction, $^B A$	2000 μm^2
Parameter, $^f \lambda$ (associated with the equilibrium of the junction)	0.50
Probability, *q*	0.30
Bonding equilibrium potential, ψ_0	3.14 $\times$ 10^5 dyn Å
Morse constant, κ	2 Å^{-1}
Rheological response of a fibre segment*	
Order of optimization, *N*	5
Parameter *b*	0.0123 $\times$ 10^8 dyn μm^{-2}
Parameters D_I ($I = 1, 2, \ldots, 5$)	-0.8435×10^8 dyn μm^{-2}
	-9.8879×10^8 dyn μm^{-2}
	-39.3752×10^8 dyn μm^{-2}
	-104.2946×10^8 dyn μm^{-2}
	-231.0216×10^8 dyn μm^{-2}

* Creep of dry symmerwood fibres of longleaf pine holocellulose pulp after conditioning at 50% RH and 23 °C (Table 7.4).

Probabilistic viscoelastic response of a structural element (α)

The response behaviour of a structural element (α) is considered here for the case of natural cellulose. The geometrical and physical characteristics of this element are given in Table 10.3.

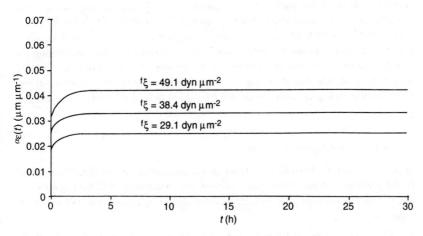

Fig. 10.11 Creep response of a structural element (α), $^f \lambda = 0.50$ and $q = 0.30$; equation (10.23).

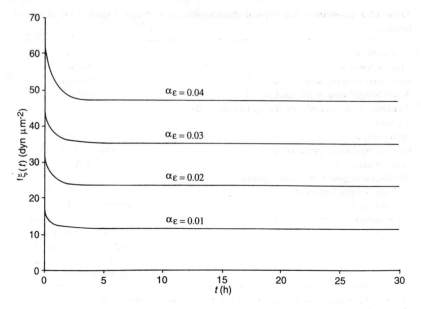

Fig. 10.12 Relaxation response of a structural element (α), $^f\lambda = 0.50$ and $q = 0.30$; equation (10.24).

Proceeding from the information derived earlier in the context of the response behaviour of the fibre segment and that of the interfibre bonding, the numerical values of the material operator $^{\alpha f}\Gamma(t)$, expressed by equation (10.22), for the structural element have been evaluated for different values of the probability q and also for different values of the parameter $^f\lambda$, equations (10.20). The corresponding creep response of the structural element (α), equation (10.23), is illustrated in Fig. 10.11 for stress inputs $^f\zeta = 29.1$, 38.4 and 49.1 dyn μm^2 and for $^f\lambda = 0.50$ and $q = 0.30$. These values of stress inputs are the same values that were used earlier for determining the creep response of the class of individual fibres considered here. Meantime, by using equation (10.24), the relaxation response of the structural element α is shown in Fig. 10.12 corresponding to strain levels of 0.01, 0.02, 0.03 and 0.04 when $^f\lambda = 0.5$ and $q = 0.3$.

Transition to the macroscopic response

In order to give an illustrative example of the application of the theoretical model to the prediction of the rheological response of a (macroscopic) fibrous system, the parameters characterizing the microstructure of such a system are assumed as follows (equation (10.22)).

1. The value of the probability q is assumed to be constant throughout the intermediate domain and is equal to 0.30.

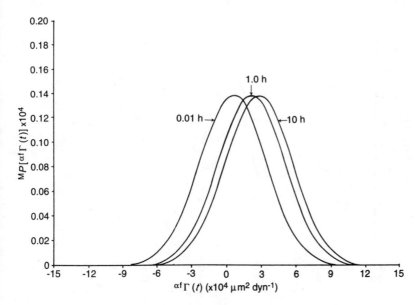

Fig. 10.13 Statistical distribution of the material operator $^{\alpha f}\Gamma(t)$ of a structural element.

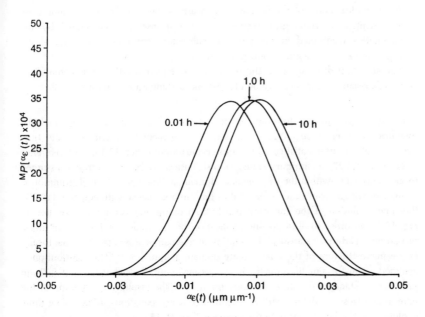

Fig. 10.14 Statistical distribution of microstrain $^{\alpha}\varepsilon(t)$.

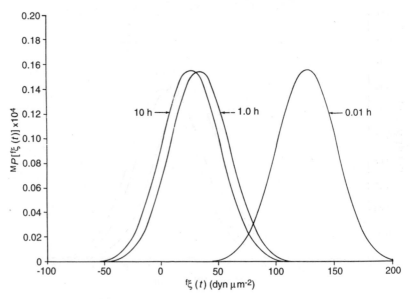

Fig. 10.15 Statistical distribution of microstress $^{\alpha}\zeta(t)$.

2. All individual fibres of the fibrous system are assumed to be of the same class and identical in rheological response. This response is characterized by the parameters mentioned in the previous subsection concerning the viscoelastic response of a fibre segment and given in Table 10.3.
3. The statistical distribution of the parameter $^{f}\lambda$, equation (10.20b), is assumed to be 'Gaussian' with a mean value of 0.50 and a standard deviation of 0.05.

Following the assumptions above, the statistical distribution of the material operator $^{\alpha f}\Gamma(t)$ (equation (10.22)) of a structural element is determined. The time evolution of the latter statistical distribution is illustrated in Fig. 10.13. With reference to equation (10.27), an arbitrary statistical distribution of fibre microstress is assumed to exist internally within the intermediate domain at time $t = 0$. This distribution is 'Gaussian' with a mean value of 38.87 dyn μm^2. In accordance with equation (10.27), the time evolution of the statistical distribution of the microstrain is illustrated in Fig. 10.14. In order to illustrate the application of the model for the case of stress relaxation, an arbitrary statistical distribution of microstrain is assumed to exist locally in the microstructure of the intermediate domain at time $t = 0$. This distribution is assumed again for simplification to be 'Gaussian' with a mean value of 0.007 μm μm^{-1} and a standard deviation of 0.007 μm μm^{-1}. The resulting distribution of the fibre microstress is determined in accordance with equation (10.28). The time evolution of the latter distribution is given in Fig. 10.15.

REFERENCES

Arnott, S. and Wonacott, A. J. (1966) The refinement of the crystal and molecular structures of polymers using X-ray data and stereochemical constraints. *Polymers*, **7**, 157–66.

Axelrad, D. R. (1970) Stochastic analysis of the flow of two-phase media, in Proc. 5th Int. Congr. on Rheology (ed. S. Onagi), University of Tokyo Press, Tokyo, pp. 221–31.

Axelrad, D. R. (1971) Rheology of structured media. *Arch. Mech. Stosow.*, **23**(1), 131–40.

Axelrad, D. R. (1978) *Micromechanics of Solids*, Elsevier, New York.

Axelrad, D. R. (1984) *Foundations of the Probabilistic Mechanics of Discrete Media*, Pergamon, Oxford.

Axelrad, D. R. and Basu, S. (1974) Operational approach to the deformation of structured media, in *Stochastic Problems in Mechanics*, University of Waterloo Press, pp. 61–77.

Axelrad, D. R. and Jaeger, L. G. (1969a) Random theory of deformation in heterogeneous media, in Proc. Southampton 1969 Civil Engineering Materials Conf., Part I (ed. M. Te'eni), Wiley–Interscience, London, p. 571.

Axelrad, D. R. and Jaeger, L. G. (1969b) Local energy fluctuations in yielding in inhomogeneous media, in Proc. Southampton 1969 Civil Engineering Materials Conf., Part I (ed. M. Te'eni), Wiley–Interscience, London, p. 87.

Axelrad, D. R. and Kalousek, J. (1971) Stress holographic interferometry. *Micromechanics Lab. Rep. 71-7*, McGill University, Montreal.

Axelrad, D. R. and Provan, J. W. (1975) Microrheology of crystalline media. *Rheol. Acta*, **12**, 177–82.

Axelrad, D. R., Provan, J. W. and Basu, S. (1974) Analysis of the semi-group property and the constitutive relations of structured solids, in Proc. Conf. on Symmetry, Similarity and Group Theoretic Methods in Mechanics (eds P. G. Glockner and M. C. Singh), University of Calgary.

Bharucha-Reid, A. T. (1960) *Elements of the Theory of Markov Processes and its Applications*, McGraw-Hill, New York.

Battista, O. A. (ed.) (1964) *Synthetic fibers in Papermaking*, Interscience, New York.

Bikales, N. M. and Segal, L. (eds) (1971) *Cellulose and Cellulose Derivatives*, Wiley–Interscience, New York.

Bollmann, W. (1970) *Crystal Defects and Crystalline Interfaces*, Springer, New York.

Brezinski, J. P. (1956) The creep properties of paper. *Tappi*, **39**(2), 116–28.

Corte, H. (1966) Paper and board, in *Composite Materials* (ed. L. Holliday), Elsevier, New York, pp. 475–526.

Corte, H. and Kallmes, O. J. (1962) Statistical geometry of a fibrous network, in *The Formation and Structure of Paper*, Vol. 1 (ed. F. Bolam), Paper and Board Makers' Association, London, pp. 13–52.

Corte, H. and Schaschek, H. (1955) Physical nature of paper strength. *Papier*, **9**, 319–30.

Gardener, K. H. and Blackwell, J. (1974) The hydrogen bonding in native cellulose. *Biochim. Biophys. Acta*, **342**, 232–7.

Haddad, Y. M. (1975) Response behaviour of a two-dimensional fibrous network. PhD Thesis, McGill University, Montreal.

Haddad, Y. M. (1980) A theoretical approach to interfiber bonding of cellulose. *J. Colloid Interface Sci.*, **76**(2), 490–501.

Haddad, Y. M. (1984) A microstructural approach to the rheology of fibrous systems. *J. Colloid Interface Sci.*, **100**(1), 143–65.

Haddad, Y. M. (1985) A stochastic approach to the rheology of randomly structured fibrous networks. *Mater. Sci. Eng.*, **72**, 135–47.

Haddad, Y. M. (1986) A microstructural approach to the mechanical response of composite systems with randomly oriented, short fibres. *J. Mater. Sci.*, **21**, 3767–76.

Haddad, Y. M. (1987) Approche microstructurelle de la rhéologie des systèmes fibreux. I. Analyse théorique. *Res Mec.*, **22**, 243–65.

Haddad, Y. M. (1990) A microstructural approach to the mechanical response of polycrystalline systems: I. Theoretical analysis. *Res. Mec.*, **28**, 177–96.

Hill, R. L. (1967) The creep behaviour of individual pulp fibers under tensile loading. *Tappi*, **50**(8), 432–40.

Jacobson, R. A., Wunderlich, J. A. and Lipscomb, W. N. (1961) The crystal and molecular structure of cellulose. *Acta Crystallogr.*, **14**, 598–607.

Jayme, G. and Hunger, G. (1962) Electron microscope 2- and 3-dimensional classification of fibre bonding, in *The Formation and Structure of Paper*, Transaction of Oxford Symposium (1961), Vol. 1 (ed. F. Bolam), Technical Section of the British Paper and Board Makers' Association, London, pp. 135–70.

Kallmes, O. J. (1969) Technique for determining the fiber orientation distribution throughout the thickness of the sheet. *Tappi*, **52**(3), 482–5.

Kalousek, J. (1973) Experimental investigations of the deformation of structured media. PhD Thesis, McGill University, Montreal.

Lai, J. S. Y. and Findley, W. N. (1968) Stress relaxation of nonlinear viscoelastic materials under uniaxial strain. *Trans. Soc. Rheol.*, **12**, 259–80.

Manley, R. S. J. and Inoue, S. (1965) The fine structure of regenerated cellulose. *J. Polym. Sci. Polym. Lett. B*, **3**(3), 691–5.

Mark, R. E. (1967) *Cell Wall Mechanics of Tracheids*, Yale University Press, London.

McIntosh, D. C. and Leopold, B. (1962) Bonding strength of individual fibres, in transactions of the Oxford Symposium, Vol. 1, British Paper and Board Makers' Association, London, pp. 265–76.

Meredith, R. (ed.) (1956) *Mechanical Properties of Textile Fibres*, North-Holland, Amsterdam.

Meyer, K. H. and Misch, L. (1937) Positions des atoms dans le nouveau modèle spatial de la cellulose. *Helv. Chim. Acta*, **20**, 232–44.

Morse, P. M. (1929) Diatomic molecules according to the wave mechanics. II. Vibrational levels. *Phys. Rev.*, **34**, 57–64.

Nissan, A. H. (1959) The rheological behaviour of hydrogen bonded solids. *Trans. Faraday Soc.*, **55**, 2048–53.

Nissan, A. H. (1967) The significance of hydrogen bonding at the surface of cellulose network structure, in *Surfaces and Coatings Related to Paper and Wood*, Syracuse University Press, Syracuse, NY, pp. 221–65.

Nissan, A. H. and Sternstein, S. S. (1964) Cellulose fibre bonding. *Tappi*, **47**(1), 1–6.

Onogi, S. and Sasaguri, K. (1961) Elasticity of Paper and other fibrous sheets. *Tappi*, **44**(12), 874–80.

Page, D. H. and Tydeman, P. A. (1960) Fibre to fibre bonds. Part 2. A preliminary study of their properties in paper sheets. *Paper Technol.*, **1**(5), 519–30.

Page, D. H., Tydeman, P. A. and Hunt, M. (1962) A study of fibre to fibre bonding by direct observation, in Transactions of the Oxford Symposium, Vol. 1, British Paper and Board Makers' Association, London, pp. 171–93.

Paradowski, R. J. (1991) Pauling develops his theory of the chemical bond, in *Great Events from History II*, Science and Technology Series, Vol. 2 (1910–1931) (ed. F. N. Magill), Salem Press, Pasadena, CA, pp. 926–33.

Pauling, L. (1960) *The Nature of the Chemical Bond and Structure of Molecules and Crystals*, Cornell University Press, Ithaca, NY.

Rance, H. F. (1948) Some new studies in the strength properties of paper, in Proc. Great Britain and Ireland Paper Makers' Association, Vol. 29, pp. 449–76.

Rance, H. F. (1962) Introduction to symposium, in Transactions of the Oxford Symposium, Vol. 1, British Paper and Board Makers' Association, London, pp. 1–11.

Roelofsen, P. A. (1959) Plant cell wall, in *Encyclopedia of Plant Anatomy*, Gebrüder Bointrager, Berlin- Nicolassee.

Schulz, J. H. (1961) The effect of straining during drying on the mechanical and viscoelastic behaviour of paper. *Tappi*, **44**(10), 736–44.

Sokolov, N. D. (1959) On the quantum theory of the hydrogen bonding, in Symp. on Hydrogen Bonding, Ljubljana, 1957 (ed. D. Hadzi and W. H. Thompson), Pergamon, London, pp. 385–92.

Sternstein, S. S. and Nissan, A. H. (1962) A molecular theory of viscoelasticity of a three-dimensional hydrogen bonded network, in Transactions of the Oxford Symposium, Vol. 1, British Paper and Board Makers' Association, London, pp. 319–50.

Tonnesen, B. A. and Ellefsen, O. (1971) Investigations of the structure of cellulose and its derivatives, F. Submicrostructural investigations, in *Cellulose and Cellulose Derivatives*, Vol. V, Part IV (eds N. M. Bikales and L. Segal), Wiley, New York, pp. 265–304.

Van den Akker, J. A. (1962) Some theoretical considerations on the mechanical properties of fibrous structures, in *The Formation and Structure of Paper*, Transactions of the Oxford Symposium (1961), Vol. 1 (ed. F. Bolam), Technical Section, British Paper and Board Makers' Association, London, pp. 205–41.

Van den Akker, J. A. (1970) Structure and tensile characteristics of paper. *Tappi*, 53(3), 388–400.

Van den Akker, J. A., Lathrop, A. L., Voelker, M. H. and Dearth, L. R. (1958) Importance of fibre strength to sheet strength. *Tappi*, 41(8), 416–25.

FURTHER READING

Axelrad, D. R. and Basu, S. (1973) Operational approach to the deformation of structured media, in *Stochastic Problems in Mechanics* (eds S. T. Ariaratnam and H. H. E. Leipholz), Study No. 10, University of Waterloo, pp. 61–77.

Axelrad, D. R. and Basu, S. (1973) Mechanical relaxation of crystalline solids. *Adv. Mol. Relax. Process.*, 6, 185–99.

Axelrad, D. R., Haddad, Y. M. and Atack, D. (1975) Stochastic deformation theory of a two-dimensional fibrous network, in *Proc.* 11th Annual Meet. (ed. G. J. Dvorak), Society of Engineering Science, Duke University, NC, pp. 166–7.

Axelrad, D. R., Basu, S. and Haddad, Y. M. (1976) Microrheology of cellulosic systems, in Proc. 7th Int. Congr. on Rheology, Gothenburg.

Basu, S. (1975) On a general deformation theory of structural solids. PhD Thesis, McGill University, Montreal.

Bernal, J. D. (1958) General introduction: structure arrangements of macromolecules. *Discuss. Faraday Soc.*, 25, 7–18.

Blumenthal, R. C. and Getoor, R. K. (1963) *Markov Processes and Potential Theory*, Academic Press, New York.

Bochner, S. (1942) Stochastic processes. *Ann. Math.*, 48, 1014.

Bourbaki, N. (1951) *Topologie Générale*, Hermann, Paris.

Doob, J. L. (1953) *Stochastic Processes*, Wiley, New York.

Dynkin, E. P. (1965) *Markov Processes*, Vols. 1 and 2, Academic Press, New York.

Ehrenfest, P. and Ehrenfest, T. (1959) *The Conceptual Foundations of the Statistical Approach in Mechanics*, Cornell University Press, Ithaca, NY.

Foguel, S. R. (1969) *The Ergodic Theory of Markov Processes*, Van Nostrand Reinhold, New York.

Gikhman, I. I. and Shorohod, A. V. (1969) *Introduction to the Theory of Random Processes*, Saunders, Philadelphia, PA.

Goffman, C. and Pedrick, G. (1965) *First Course in Functional Analysis*, Prentice-Hall, Englewood Cliffs, NJ.

Högfors, C. (1987) History-dependent systems. *Rheol. Acta*, 26, 317–21.

Hopf, E. (1954) The general temporally discrete Markoff process. *J. Ration. Mech. Anal.*, 3, 12–45.

Jongschaap, R. J. J. (1987) On the derivation of some fundamental expressions for the average stress tensor in systems of interacting particles. *Rheol. Acta*, 26, 328–35.

Kakutani, S. (1940) Ergodic theorems and the Markoff processes with a stable distribution. *Proc. Imp. Acad. Jpn. Tokyo*, **16**, 49–54.

Kampe de Feriet, J. (1962) Statistical mechanics of continuous media, in Proc. 13th Symp. on Applied Mechanics, Hydrodynamic Instability, American Mathematical Society, pp. 165–98.

Kappos, D. A. (1969) *Probability Algebras and Stochastic Spaces*, Academic Press, New York.

Kendall, D. G. (1955) Some analytical properties of continuous stationary Markov transition functions. *Trans. Am. Math. Soc.*, **78**, 529–40.

Khinchine, A. I. (1949) *Mathematical Foundations of Statistical Mechanics*, Dover Publications, New York.

Kolmogorov, A. N. (1956) *Foundations of Probability Theory*, Chelsea, New York.

Moreau, J. J. (1971) Sur l'evolution d'un système elastoviscoplastique. *C.R. Acad. Sci., Ser. A*, **273**, 118–21.

Peterline, A. (1969) Bond rupture in highly oriented crystalline polymers. *J. Polym. Sci. A2*, **7**, 1151–63.

Peters, L. (1955) A note on nonlinear viscoelasticity. *Textile Res. J.*, **25** (March), 262–5.

Pinsker, M. S. (1964) *Information and Information Stability of Random Variables and Processes*, Holden-Day, San Francisco, CA.

Pugachev, V. S. (1965) *Theory of Random Functions*, Addison-Wesley, Reading, MA.

Renyi, A. (1970) *Foundations of Probability*, Holden-Day, San Francisco, CA.

Rosenblatt, M. (1971) *Markov Processes, Structure and Asymptotic Behaviour*, Springer, New York.

Schausberger, A., Knoglinger, H. and Janeschitz-Kriegl, H. (1987) The role of short chain molecules for the rheology of polystyrene melts. II. Linear viscoelastic properties. *Rheol. Acta*, **26**, 468–73.

Shimanouchi, T. and Mizushima, S. (1955) On the helical configuration of a polymer chain. *J. Chem. Phys.*, **23**(4), 707–11.

Simmons, G. F. (1963) *Introduction to Topology and Modern Analysis*, McGraw-Hill, New York.

Sneddon, I. N. (1971) In *Functional Analysis in Continuum Mechanics I* (ed. A. C. Eringen), Academic Press, New York.

Treves, F. (1967) *Locally Convex Spaces and Partial Differential Equations*, Springer, New York.

Van Kampen, N. G. (1962) Fundamental problems in statistical mechanics of irreversible processes, in *Fundamental Problems in Statistical Mechanics* (ed. E. D. G. Cohen), North-Holland, Amsterdam.

Yaglom, A. M. (1962) *Theory of Stationary Random Functions*, Prentice-Hall, New York.

Yosida, K. (1965) *Functional Analysis*, Springer, Berlin.

Appendix A

Introduction to tensors

In continuum mechanics we deal with physical events which are, in general, independent of both the position and the orientation of the observer. That is, if two coordinate systems, fixed at different locations in space and with different relative orientations, are used to observe and, hence, to formulate a physical law governing a particular physical event, the resulting physical law would hold valid in the two coordinate systems and in any coordinate system not moving with respect to the other two systems. In a proper description, such events are represented mathematically by tensorial quantities and the resulting physical laws are expressed in terms of tensorial equations. As a mathematical entity, a tensor has an existence independent of any coordinate system. Specifically, the components of a tensor in one coordinate system would determine the corresponding components of the same tensor in any other coordinate system not moving relative to the first one. Further, the tensorial equations governing specific physical events would be invariant under coordinate transformation. This invariance of tensor equations under coordinate transformation highlights the usefulness of tensor calculus in the study of continuum mechanics. Invariance of the form of a physical law referred to two frames of reference in general motion is, however, more difficult and would require the tools of general relative theory, although in some cases the postulated 'principle of material frame indifference' is used.

In dealing with general coordinate transformations between arbitrary curvilinear coordinate systems, the resulting tensors are conventionally referred to as general tensors. However, when transformation is carried out from one homogeneous coordinate system to another, the tensors are defined as Cartesian tensors. For simplicity, we limit ourselves in this appendix to tensors in three-dimensional Euclidean space.

Tensors may be classified by rank, or order, according to the particular form of the transformation law they obey. Such a classification determines the number of components a given tensor possesses in an N-dimensional space. In this context, a tensorial quantity is conventionally presented using indicial notation. In this notation, letter indices, either subscripts or superscripts, are appended to a general letter or symbol representing the quantity of interest.

A.1 INDICIAL NOTATION

In writing a set of N quantities $a_1, a_2, \cdots, a_N$ the notation a_i $(i = 1, 2, \cdots, N)$ is generally used. In this notation, the subscript i is referred to as the index and it implies that it may take on any integer value from the set $\{1, \cdots, N\}$. The number N is called the range of the index. Hence, the quantity a_i represents any element of the set $\{a_1, a_2, \cdots, a_N\}$ and simultaneously identifies the entire set. In a similar manner, one may use the notation x_i $(i = 1, 2, 3)$ to denote the coordinates of a point in a rectangular Cartesian coordinate system. Further, if we adopt the convention that a Latin index would have automatically the range of 3, then the coordinates of a point in a rectangular Cartesian coordinate system would simply be identified by x_i and it would be understood that x_i: x_1, x_2, x_3. On the other hand, if we are dealing with a two-dimensional space, we may use Greek indices with the understanding that a Greek index has a range of 2, e.g. x_α: x_1, x_2.

A.2 CLASSIFICATION OF TENSORIAL QUANTITIES

In tensorial notation, a system which depends on m indices is conventionally referred to as an mth-order system. As illustrated below, if we denote the range of the index by the letter N, then the number of components in the mth-order tensorial system would be given by N^m. A letter index may occur either once or twice in a given term. When an index appears unrepeated in a term, that index is known as 'free' index. The number and location of the free indices reveal directly the exact tensorial character of the quantity dealt with. For instance, the tensorial order of a given term is equal to the number of free indices appearing in that term. On the other hand, repeated indices are often referred to as 'dummy' indices as they can be replaced by any other letter not appearing as a free index without changing the meaning of the term in which they occur, i.e.

$$a_i b_i = a_j b_j = a_k b_k.$$

- A first-order tensor is denoted by a kernel letter bearing one free index only irrespective of the number of dummy indices that may be present. Examples of a first order tensor are

$$a_i, \quad a^i, \quad a_{ij} b_j, \quad c_{jkk}.$$

In a three-dimensional space, the number of components of a first-order system is 3 while, in a two-dimensional space, the number of components is 2:

$$a_{\alpha\beta} b_\beta = a_{\alpha 1} b_1 + a_{\alpha 2} b_2 = (a_{11} b_1 + a_{12} b_2, \ a_{21} b_1 + a_{22} b_2).$$

- A second-order tensor is identified by two free indices. Thus, a second-order tensor is specified by nine components in any coordinate system in a three-dimensional space, for example

$$a_{ij} = \begin{bmatrix} a_{11} & a_{12} & a_{13} \\ a_{21} & a_{22} & a_{23} \\ a_{31} & a_{32} & a_{33} \end{bmatrix}.$$

Other designations of a second-order system in a three-dimensional space may take the form a_{ij}, a^{ij}, $a^i_{.j}$ where the dot indicates that the j is the second index.

Alternatively, a second-order system in a two-dimensional space would have four components, e.g.

$$a_{\alpha\beta} = \begin{bmatrix} a_{11} & a_{12} \\ a_{21} & a_{22} \end{bmatrix}.$$

- A third-order tensor has three free indices which correspond to either 27 components in a three-dimensional space or 8 components in a two-dimensional space. A third-order system may be constructed through a logical combination of the first-order and second-order tensors. Examples of a third-order tensor are

$$a_{ijk}, \quad a^{ijk}, \quad a^i_{.jk}.$$

- A fourth-order tensor has four free indices which represent 81 components in a three-dimensional space and 16 components in a two-dimensional space. Examples of a fourth-order tensor are

$$a_{ijkm}, \quad a^{ijkm}, \quad a^{ij}_{km}, \quad a^i_{jkm}, \quad a_{\alpha\beta\gamma\delta}, \quad a^{\alpha\beta\gamma\delta}, \quad a^{\alpha\beta}_{\gamma\delta}, \quad a^\alpha_{\beta\gamma\delta}.$$

- A generalized system of the mth order, e.g. $a_{ijkl\cdots m}$, has m indices which concur with 3^m components in a three-dimensional space. Alternatively, in a generalized system of the χth order, e.g. $a_{\alpha\beta\gamma\cdots\chi}$, the number of indices corresponds to 2^χ components in a two-dimensional space.
- A tensorial system with no index, a scalar, is referred to as a zero-order system. It has one component only, for example a zero-order tensor a.

A.3 ADDITION AND MULTIPLICATION OF TENSORIAL SYSTEMS OF THE SAME ORDER AND RANGE

Addition of two systems $a_{ij\cdots k}$ and $b_{ij\cdots k}$ of the same order and magnitude has the following properties.

- Addition is commutative:

$$a_{ij\cdots k} + b_{ij\cdots k} = b_{ij\cdots k} + a_{ij\cdots k}.$$

- Addition is associative:

$$a_{ij\cdots k} + (b_{ij\cdots k} + c_{ij\cdots k}) = (a_{ij\cdots k} + b_{ij\cdots k}) + c_{ij\cdots k}.$$

- There exists a unique system, 0, such that

$$a_{ij\cdots k} + 0 = a_{ij\cdots k}.$$

- To every system $a_{ij\cdots k}$ there corresponds a unique system $-a_{ij\cdots k}$ such that

$$a_{ij\cdots k} + (-a_{ij\cdots k}) = 0.$$

A.4 MULTIPLICATION OF TENSORIAL SYSTEMS OF DIFFERENT ORDER AND OF THE SAME RANGE

An mth-order tensorial system may be multiplied with an nth-order system to produce an $(m + n)$th-order system with the following properties.

- Multiplication is commutative:

$$a_i b_{jk} = b_{jk} a_i.$$

- Multiplication is associative:

$$a_i(b_{jk}\, c_{ls}) = (a_i\, b_{jk})\, c_{ls}.$$

- Multiplication is distributive with respect to addition:

$$a_{ij}(b_k + c_k) = a_{ij}\, b_k + a_{ij}\, c_k.$$

- There exists a unique scalar, 1, called unity such that

$$1 \times a_{ij\cdots k} = a_{ij\cdots k}.$$

A.5 SUMMATION CONVENTION

If x_i is a set of N variables and b_i is a set of N constants, a linear form may be written as

$$\sum_{i=1}^{N} b_i x_i = b_1 x_1 + b_2 x_2 + \cdots + b_N x_N$$

and if b_{ij} is a set of N constants, a quadratic form may be expressed by

$$\sum_{i,j=1}^{N} b_{ij} x_i x_j = b_{11} x_1 x_1 + b_{12} x_1 x_2 + \cdots + b_{1N} x_1 x_N$$

$$+ b_{21} x_2 x_1 + \cdots$$

$$\vdots$$

$$+ b_{N1} x_N x_1 + \cdots + b_{NN} x_N x_N.$$

As shown above, the summation is carried out over repeated indices and, thus, the summation sign could be omitted. Hence, the following convention may be adopted: **the repetition of an index implies the summation over the range of that index in the absence of an explicit statement to the contrary.**

A.6 SYMMETRIC AND SKEW-SYMMETRIC SYSTEMS

A.6.1 Symmetric systems

A tensor is described as **symmetric** if its matrix of rectangular Cartesian components is symmetric. In a system of two or more indices, if the values of the elements do not change by interchanging two indices, the system is said to be symmetric with respect to these two indices. More generally, if the system is symmetric with respect to all indices, the system is referred to as completely symmetric. Examples of symmetric systems are as follows:

- symmetric in i and j,

$$a_{ijk} = a_{jik};$$

- completely symmetric,

$$a_{ij} = a_{ji},$$

$$a_{ijk} = a_{kij} = a_{jki} = a_{kji} = a_{ikj} = a_{jik}.$$

Symmetry is a tensor property in a real sense, i.e. if the matrix of a tensor is symmetric in one Cartesian coordinate system, it would be symmetric in all such systems. However, the product of two symmetric tensors might not be necessarily symmetric.

A.6.2 Skew-symmetric systems

The definitions of skew symmetry in tensors follow those for symmetry except that interchange of a pair of indices would change the sign of the tensor:

- skew symmetric in i and j,

$$b_{ijk} = -b_{jik};$$

- completely skew symmetric,

$$b_{ij} = -b_{ji},$$

$$b_{ijk} = b_{kij} = b_{jki} = -b_{kji} = -b_{ikj} = -b_{jik}.$$

In this situation, the following should be noted.

- If, in a component of a skew-symmetric system, any two indices are not distinct, the value of such a component must be zero. For example, if b_{ijk} is skew symmetric in j and k, then $b_{i11} = -b_{i11} = 0$.
- In the skew-symmetric system $b_{ij} = -b_{ji}$, the diagonal elements b_{11}, b_{22} and b_{33} are all zero.
- If the order of a completely skew-symmetric system is equal to the range of its indices, then the nonvanishing components of the system have only one distinct absolute numerical value. For example, if b_{ijk} is completely skew-symmetric, then the only distinct term is b_{123}.

A.6.3 An important property of all second-order tensors

Any second-order system may be represented as the sum of a symmetric and a skew-symmetric system. For instance, the second-order system a_{ij} may be expressed by

$$a_{ij} = a_{(ij)} + a_{[ij]}$$

in which the first term on the right-hand side is symmetric while the second is skew symmetric. These two terms are expressed respectively by

$$a_{(ij)} = \tfrac{1}{2}(a_{ij} + a_{ji}), \quad \text{symmetric}$$

and

$$a_{[ij]} = \tfrac{1}{2}(a_{ij} - a_{ji}), \quad \text{skew symmetric.}$$

Example A.1

If

$$a_{\alpha\beta} = \begin{bmatrix} \cos\theta & -\sin\theta \\ \sin\theta & \cos\theta \end{bmatrix}$$

then

$$a_{(\alpha\beta)} = \tfrac{1}{2}(a_{\alpha\beta} + a_{\beta\alpha}) = \begin{bmatrix} \cos\theta & 0 \\ 0 & \cos\theta \end{bmatrix}$$

and

$$a_{[\alpha\beta]} = \tfrac{1}{2}(a_{\alpha\beta} - a_{\beta\alpha}) = \begin{bmatrix} 0 & -\sin\theta \\ \sin\theta & 0 \end{bmatrix}$$

thus

$$a_{\alpha\beta} = a_{(\alpha\beta)} + a_{[\alpha\beta]}.$$

A.7 CARTESIAN TENSORS

In a rectangular Cartesian frame of reference, we choose as base vectors the unit vectors $\mathbf{e}_1$, $\mathbf{e}_2$, $\mathbf{e}_3$ parallel to the coordinate axes. Thus, a vector $\mathbf{A}$ in terms of its components A_i is expressed by

$$\mathbf{A} = A_i\,\mathbf{e}_i.$$

We may also consider a transformation of the unit vectors by choosing another rectangular Cartesian system with new unit vectors $\mathbf{e}'_i$ which would be related to the original (unprimed system) by

$$\mathbf{e}'_i = a_{ji}\,\mathbf{e}_j.$$

Thus, $\mathbf{A}$ may be expressed by

$$\mathbf{A} = A_i\,\mathbf{e}_i = A'_i\,\mathbf{e}'_i.$$

Taking dot products of both sides by e'_j and e_j respectively would result into these two equations:

$$A'_j = a_{ij}A_i;$$
$$A_j = a_{ji}A'_i. \tag{A.1}$$

That is, on a transformation of coordinates from one rectangular Cartesian system to another, the components of a vector A would obey the law given by (A.1). Thus, the following definition may be stated.

The components of any first-order system which obeys the law (A.1), on a coordinate transformation, are said to be the components of a Cartesian tensor of first order.

One notes that the first-order Cartesian tensor components are the components of a vector.

Consider now the system

$$A_i B_j = A_{ij}.$$

If A_i and B_j transform as vectors, one has

$$A'_{ij} = A'_i B'_j$$
$$= a_{ki}a_{mj}A_k B_m \tag{A.2}$$
$$= a_{ki}a_{mj}A_{km}.$$

If the components of a second-order system transform according to (A.2) then they are the components of a Cartesian tensor of second order.

In a similar manner, a third-order Cartesian tensor is a third-order system the components of which transform according to

$$A_{ijk} = a_{ip}\, a_{jm}\, a_{kn}\, A'_{pmn}. \tag{A.3}$$

The tensor transformation laws illustrated above may be generalized to Cartesian tensors of any order, i.e.

$$A'_{ijk\cdots} = a_{ip}\, a_{jm}\, a_{kn} \cdots A_{pmn\cdots}.$$

QUIZ

Define the Cartesian tensor of zeroth order.

A.8 SPECIAL TENSORS

The following tensors in rectangular Cartesian systems are used frequently.

A.8.1 The Kronecker delta

This is a second-order tensor defined as

$$\delta_{ij} = \begin{cases} 1 & \text{if } i = j \\ 0 & \text{if } i \neq j \end{cases} = \begin{bmatrix} 1 & 0 & 0 \\ 0 & 1 & 0 \\ 0 & 0 & 1 \end{bmatrix}.$$

Also

$$\delta_{\alpha\beta} = \begin{cases} 1 & \text{if } \alpha = \beta \\ 0 & \text{if } \alpha \neq \beta \end{cases} = \begin{bmatrix} 1 & 0 \\ 0 & 1 \end{bmatrix}.$$

QUIZ

Prove the substitution property of the Kronecker delta:

$$a_i \delta_{ij} = a_j, \quad a_{ij} = a_{ik}\delta_{kj} \quad \text{and} \quad a_\alpha \delta_{\alpha\beta} = a_\beta.$$

A.8.2 The alternating tensor

This exists for any completely skew-symmetric system in which the number of indices is equal to the range of indices. The most important are the second- and third-order alternating tensors defined respectively by

$$\varepsilon_{\alpha\beta} = \begin{cases} +1 & \text{if } \alpha, \beta \text{ is an even permutation of } 1, 2, \\ -1 & \text{if } \alpha, \beta \text{ is an odd permutation of } 1, 2, \\ 0 & \text{if } \alpha, \beta \text{ are indistinct,} \end{cases}$$

i.e.

$$\varepsilon_{\alpha\beta} = \begin{bmatrix} 0 & 1 \\ -1 & 0 \end{bmatrix}$$

and

$$\varepsilon_{ijk} = \begin{cases} +1 & \text{if } i, j, k \text{ is an even permutation of } 1, 2, 3, \\ -1 & \text{if } i, j, k \text{ is an odd permutation of } 1, 2, 3, \\ 0 & \text{if any two of } i, j, k \text{ are indistinct,} \end{cases}$$

i.e.

$$\varepsilon_{ijk} = \begin{bmatrix} 0 & 0 & 0 & 0 & 0 & -1 & 0 & 1 & 0 \\ 0 & 0 & 1 & 0 & 0 & 0 & -1 & 0 & 0 \\ 0 & -1 & 0 & 1 & 0 & 0 & 0 & 0 & 0 \end{bmatrix}$$

QUIZ

Show that the completely skew-symmetric systems $b_{\alpha\beta}$ and b_{ijk} can be written respectively as

$$b_{\alpha\beta} = \varepsilon_{\alpha\beta} \, b_{12} \quad \text{and} \quad b_{ijk} = \varepsilon_{ijk} \, b_{123}.$$

QUIZ

Prove the alternating tensor–Kronecker delta relationship (known as $\varepsilon - \delta$ relation):

$$\varepsilon_{\alpha\beta}\varepsilon_{\gamma\lambda} = \delta_{\alpha\gamma}\delta_{\beta\lambda} - \delta_{\alpha\lambda}\delta_{\beta\gamma}; \quad \varepsilon_{ijk}\varepsilon_{ipm} = \varepsilon_{jki}\varepsilon_{pmi} = \delta_{jp}\delta_{km} - \delta_{jm}\delta_{kp}.$$

A.9 DIVERGENCE AND GRADIENT OPERATIONS

A.9.1 Gradient of a scalar

A time-dependent scalar field $\phi = \phi(X_i, t)$, where X_i represent the components of a position vector, may be partially differentiated with respect to X_i. This partial differentiation is conventionally denoted by a comma, i.e.

$$\frac{\partial \phi}{\partial X_i} = \phi_{,i}$$

and the associated vector is represented by

$$\boldsymbol{\nabla}\phi = \phi_{,i} \, \mathbf{e}_i.$$

The vector field $\boldsymbol{\nabla}\phi$ is referred to as the gradient of the scalar field ϕ. In this context, the symbol $\boldsymbol{\nabla}$ may be regarded to be an operator such that

$$\boldsymbol{\nabla} = _{,i} \, \mathbf{e}_i.$$

A.9.2 Gradient of a vector

For a vector $\mathbf{A} = A_i \, \mathbf{e}_i$ with components A_i being a time-dependent vector field $A_i = A_i(x_i, t)$, the partial derivative of each component with respect to the coordinates is expressed as

$$\frac{\partial A_i}{\partial x_j} = A_{i,j} = \begin{bmatrix} A_{1,1} & A_{1,2} & A_{1,3} \\ A_{2,1} & A_{2,2} & A_{2,3} \\ A_{3,1} & A_{3,2} & A_{3,3} \end{bmatrix}.$$

These nine functions are the components of the gradient of the vector $\mathbf{A}$.

A.9.3 Divergence of a vector

The quantity

$$A_{i,i} = A_{1,1} + A_{2,2} + A_{3,3}$$

is defined as the divergence of the vector **A** and is expressed by

$$\text{div } \mathbf{A} = A_{i,i}.$$

QUIZ

Show that

$$\text{div } \mathbf{A} = \nabla \cdot \mathbf{A} = A_{i,i}.$$

A.9.4 Laplacian operator

Following the definitions of the operations above, one may consider the divergence of the gradient of a scalar:

$$\nabla \cdot \nabla \phi = \phi_{,ii}$$
$$= \nabla^2 \phi.$$

The operator ∇^2 is usually referred to as the Laplacian operator.

A.9.5 Curl of a vector

The vector $\nabla \times \mathbf{A}$ is referred to as the curl of a vector and may be shown to be given by

$$\nabla \times \mathbf{A} = {}_{,i}\mathbf{e}_i \times A_j\mathbf{e}_j$$
$$= A_{j,i}\mathbf{e}_i \times \mathbf{e}_j$$
$$= A_{j,i}\varepsilon_{ijk}\mathbf{e}_k$$
$$= \varepsilon_{ijk}A_{j,i}\mathbf{e}_k$$

A.10 TENSOR FIELDS

If the components of a tensor quantity depend in some manner on the coordinates of a point, for example

$$A_{ij\cdots k} = A_{ij\cdots k}(X_1, X_2, X_3),$$

these components are said to be point functions and the tensor quantity is referred to as tensor field. Further, a tensor field could be time dependent if its components, in addition to being dependent on the coordinates are also time dependent, for instance the time-dependent tensor field

$$A_{ij\cdots k} = A_{ij\cdots k}(x_1, x_2, x_3, t).$$

An important property of tensor fields is that if all components of a tensor field vanish in one coordinate system, they vanish likewise in all coordinate systems which can be obtained by admissible transformations.

In continuum mechanics, one is usually concerned with those tensor fields the components of which, together with all partial derivatives with respect to both the coordinates and time, are continuous functions.

PROBLEMS

A.1 If $a_i = (1, 4, 8)$ and $b_i = (6, -4, -3)$ find the components of $c_i = a_i + b_i$.

A.2

1. If $a_i = (1, 3, 6)$ and

$$b_{ij} = \begin{bmatrix} 1 & 3 & 6 \\ 4 & 0 & 0 \\ 3 & 1 & 2 \end{bmatrix}$$

find the components
   (a) $C_{ijk} = a_i b_{jk}$ and
   (b) C_{iij}.
2. Is $C_{iij} = C_{jii}$?

A.3 Let δ_{ij} denote the Kronecker delta and ε_{ijk} the alternating tensor.

1. Show that
   (a) $\delta_{ij}\,\delta_{ij} = 3$,
   (b) $\varepsilon_{ijk}\,\varepsilon_{jki} = 6$ and
   (c) $\delta_{ij} = \delta_{ik}$
2. If

$$\Delta(u) = \begin{bmatrix} u_{11} & u_{12} & u_{13} \\ u_{21} & u_{22} & u_{23} \\ u_{31} & u_{32} & u_{33} \end{bmatrix}$$

show that

$$\varepsilon_{ijk}\,\Delta(u) = \varepsilon_{pmn}\,u_{ip}\,u_{jm}\,u_{kn}.$$

and

$$6\Delta(u) = \varepsilon_{ijk}\,\varepsilon_{pmn}\,u_{ip}\,u_{jm}\,u_{kn}.$$

3. Using tensor notation, show that

$$\mathbf{A} \times (\mathbf{B} \times \mathbf{C}) = (\mathbf{A} \cdot \mathbf{C})\mathbf{B} - (\mathbf{A} \cdot \mathbf{B})\mathbf{C}$$

where $\mathbf{A}$, $\mathbf{B}$ and $\mathbf{C}$ are vectors.

A.4

1. If a_{ij} is symmetric and b_{ij} is skew symmetric show that $a_{ij}\,b_{ij} = 0$.
2. Furthermore, if d_{ijk} is skew symmetric in the indices i and j, show that

$$a_{ij}\,d_{ijk} = 0.$$

A.5 If $\alpha b_{ij} + \beta b_{ji} = 0$ show that either

1. $\alpha + \beta = 0$ and b_{ij} is symmetric or
2. $\alpha - \beta = 0$ and b_{ij} is skew symmetric.

A.6 Show that $a_{ij}\,\delta_{ik}\,\delta_{jl} = a_{kl}$.
A.7 Prove that $\delta_{ij}\,\delta_{ik}\,\delta_{jk} = 3$.
A.8 Verify that $\varepsilon_{\alpha\beta}\,\varepsilon_{\delta\gamma} = \delta_{\alpha\delta}\,\delta_{\beta\gamma} - \delta_{\alpha\gamma}\,\delta_{\beta\delta}$.
A.9 Show that

1. $\varepsilon_{\alpha\beta}\,\varepsilon_{\gamma\beta} = \varepsilon_{\alpha\gamma}$ and
2. $\varepsilon_{\alpha\beta}\,\varepsilon_{\alpha\beta} = 2$.

A.10

1. Using the indicial notation, prove the following vector identities:
   (a) $\mathbf{V} \times \mathbf{V}\phi = \mathbf{0}$;
   (b) $\mathbf{V}\cdot\mathbf{V} \times \mathbf{a} = 0$.
2. If A_{lm} is a second-order tensor, show that its derivative with respect to x_n, i.e. $\partial A_{lm}/\partial x_n$, is a Cartesian tensor of the third order.
3. For arbitrary tensors $\mathbf{P}$ and $\mathbf{Q}$, both of order unity, show that

$$\mu = (\mathbf{P} \times \mathbf{Q}) \cdot (\mathbf{P} \times \mathbf{Q}) + (\mathbf{P} \cdot \mathbf{Q})^2 = P^2 Q^2.$$

4. If A_{ij} is a symmetric tensor and B_{ij} a skew-symmetric tensor, show that

$$A_{ij}\,B_{ij} = 0.$$

A.11

1. If $b = \det b_{ij}$, verify that $b = \varepsilon_{ijk}\,b_{1i}\,b_{2j}\,b_{3k}$.
2. Show that $\varepsilon_{ijk}\,b_{ri}\,b_{sj}\,b_{tk}$ is skew symmetric in any pair of the indices r, s, t. Hence demonstrate that

$$\varepsilon_{rst}\,\varepsilon_{ijk}\,b_{ri}\,b_{sj}\,b_{tk} = 6b.$$

3. Show that

$$\operatorname{div}\mathbf{T} = \mathbf{V}\cdot\mathbf{T} = T_{i,i}.$$

A.12 Show that

1. $\varepsilon_{ijm}\,\varepsilon_{ijk} = 2\,\delta_{mk}$ and
2. $\varepsilon_{ijm}\,\varepsilon_{ijm} = 6$.

A.13 If

$$a_{ij} = \begin{bmatrix} \frac{1}{2} & -\frac{1}{2} & 0 \\ \frac{1}{2} & \frac{1}{2} & 0 \\ 0 & 0 & 1 \end{bmatrix}$$

and the components of the vector **A** in the unprimed coordinate system are

$$A_i = (1, 2, 3),$$

find A_i'.

A.14 Show that $\varepsilon_{ijk}\, a_j b_k\, c_i = \varepsilon_{ijk}\, a_i b_j c_k$.

A.15 Show, using Cartesian tensor methods, that

1. $\nabla \cdot \nabla \times \mathbf{v} = 0$,
2. $\nabla \times \nabla Q = 0$,
3. $\nabla \cdot (Q\mathbf{v}) = \nabla Q \cdot \mathbf{v} + Q \nabla \cdot \mathbf{v}$,
4. $\nabla \times (Q\mathbf{v}) = \nabla Q \times \mathbf{v} + Q \nabla \times \mathbf{v}$ and
5. $\nabla \cdot (\mathbf{u} \times \mathbf{v}) = \nabla \times (\mathbf{u} \cdot \mathbf{v})$.

FURTHER READING

Aris, R. (1962) *Vectors, Tensors and the Basic Equations of Fluid Mechanics*, Prentice-Hall, Englewood Cliffs, NJ.

Bishop, R. L. and Goldberg, S. I. (1968) *Tensor Analysis and Manifolds*, Dover Publications, New York.

Borg, S. F. (1963) *Matrix–Tensor Methods in Continuum Mechanics*, Van Nostrand, New York.

Brillouin, L. (1946) *Les Tenseurs en Mécanique et en Élasticité*, Dover Publications, New York.

Coburn, N. (1955) *Vector and Tensor Analysis*, Macmillan, New York.

Ericksen, J. L. (1960) Tensor fields, in *Encyclopedia of Physics*, Vol. 3/1 (ed. S. Flügge), Springer, Berlin, pp. 794–859.

Hay, G. E. (1953) *Vector and Tensor Analysis*, Dover Publications, New York.

Jefferys, H. (1931) *Cartesian Tensors*, Cambridge University Press, Cambridge.

Landau, L. and Lifshitz, E. (1951) *The Classical Theory of Fields* (translated from Russian by H. Hammermesh), Addison-Wesley, Reading, MA.

Lass, H. (1950) *Vector and Tensor Analysis*, McGraw-Hill, New York.

Levi-Civita, T. (1927) *The Absolute Differential Calculus* (translated from Italian by M. Long), Blackie, London.

Lichnerowicz, A. (1958) *Eléments de Calcul Tensoriel*, Armand Colin.

McConnell, A. J. (1946) *Applications of the Absolute Differential Calculus*, Blackie, London.

Michal, A. D. (1947) *Matrix and Tensor Calculus with Applications to Mechanics, Elasticity and Aeronautics*, Wiley, New York.

Ricci, G. and Levi-Civita, T. (1901) Methodes du calcul différentiel absolu et leurs applications. *Math. Ann.*, **54**, 125–201.

Sokolnikoff, I. (1964) *Tensor Analysis*, Wiley, New York.

Spain, B. (1953) *Tensor Calculus*, Interscience, New York.

Spiegel, M. R. (1959) *Theory and Problems of Vector Analysis and an Introduction to Tensor Analysis*, Schaum, New York.

Synge, J. and Schild, A. (1949) *Tensor Calculus*, University of Toronto Press, Toronto.

Truesdell, C. A. and Toupin, R. A. (1954) The classical field theories, in *Encyclopedia of Physics*, Vol. 3, Part 1 (ed. F. Flügge), Springer, Berlin.

Wills, A. P. (1938) *Vector Analysis with an Introduction to Tensor Analysis*, Prentice-Hall, Englewood Cliffs, NJ.

Appendix B

Delta and step functions

B.1 THE DELTA FUNCTION $\delta(t)$

The delta function is defined by

$$\delta(t) = \lim_{a \to 0} \delta(t; a) \tag{B.1}$$

where a is a parameter of arbitrary positive value and the function $\delta(t; a)$ is given by

$$\delta(t; a) = \frac{1}{\pi} \int_0^\pi \exp(-apt) \cos(pt) \, dp$$

$$= \frac{a}{\pi(a^2 + t^2)}. \tag{B.2}$$

Thus, by combining (B.1) and (B.2), the delta function may be defined as

$$\delta(t) = \frac{1}{\pi} \lim \frac{a}{a^2 + t^2}$$

$$= \lim_{a \to 0} \frac{1}{\pi} \int_0^\infty \exp(-ap) \cos(pt) \, dp. \tag{B.3}$$

Following the above, it can be shown that the delta function $\delta(t)$ has the properties

$$\delta(t) = \begin{cases} \infty, & t = 0, \\ 0, & t \neq 0, \end{cases} \tag{B.4}$$

and

$$\int_{-\infty}^\infty \delta(t) \, dt = 1. \tag{B.5}$$

The dimension of the delta function is the reciprocal of the dimension of its argument. The delta function is considered as an even function, i.e.

$$\delta(-t) = \delta(t). \tag{B.6}$$

Further, an important property of the delta function is the so-called 'shifting property', that is

$$\int_{-\infty}^{\infty} f(t)\delta(t) \, dt = f(0), \tag{B.7}$$

i.e. the operation of integrating over $f(t)\delta(t)$ shifts the function $f(t)$ to $f(0)$. Equation (B.7) would remain valid if one changed the interval of integration from $-\infty \le t \le \infty$ to $0 \le u \le t$. That is,

$$\int_{0}^{t} f(u)\delta(u) \, du = f(0). \tag{B.8}$$

Further, through a change of variable in (B.5), it follows that

$$\delta(t/c) = c\delta(t) \tag{B.9}$$

with the dimension c/t. The function $c\delta(t)$ appearing in equation (B.9) is often referred to as an impulse of strength c.

The definition of the delta function can be extended to include the argument $(t - t')$. Thus, with reference to (B.4), one can write

$$\delta(t - t') = \begin{cases} \infty, & t = t', \\ 0, & t \ne t', \end{cases} \tag{B.10}$$

with, in view of (B.5),

$$\int_{-\infty}^{\infty} \delta(t - t') \, dt = 1. \tag{B.11}$$

The function $\delta(t - t')$ is kown as the 'shifted' delta function. In view of equation (B.6), the function $\delta(t - t')$ is treated as an even function. That is

$$\delta(t - t') = \delta(t' - t).$$

The shifting property (B.7) can be also applied to $\delta(t - t')$, i.e.

$$\int_{-\infty}^{\infty} f(t)\delta(t - t') \, dt = \int_{-\infty}^{\infty} f(t - t')\delta(t) \, dt = f(t'). \tag{B.12}$$

Further, in analogy to (B.8), one can write

$$\int_{0}^{t} f(u)\delta(t - u) \, du = \int_{0}^{t} f(t - u)\delta(u) \, du = f(t). \tag{B.13}$$

B.2 THE STEP 'HEAVISIDE' FUNCTION $H(t)$

Integrating the function $\delta(t; a)$ of (B.2) leads to a function $H(\infty; a) = 1$ such that

$$H(t; a) = \frac{1}{2} + \frac{1}{\pi} \arctan \frac{t}{a}. \tag{B.14}$$

In (B.14), as the value of the parameter a decreases, the value of the function $H(t; a)$ approaches a straight line at $H(t; a) = 1$ for $0 \leq t \leq \infty$. The resulting function at the limit as $a \to 0$ is known as the 'unit step function' and is given the notation $H(t)$. The latter is often referred to in the literature as the 'Heaviside' unit step function (the name is taken after the British physicist Heaviside (1850–1925).

Combining (B.3) and (B.14), it can be shown that

$$H(t) = \frac{1}{2} + \frac{1}{\pi} \lim_{a \to 0} \int_0^\infty \exp(-ap) \frac{\sin pt}{p} \, dp \tag{B.15}$$

from which it is apparent that

$$\delta(t) = \frac{dH(t)}{dt}, \tag{B.16}$$

i.e. the delta function $\delta(t)$ is the derivative of the unit step function $H(t)$. Thus, the latter is defined as

$$H(t) = \begin{cases} 0, & t < 0, \\ 1, & t > 0. \end{cases} \tag{B.17}$$

For $t = 0$, the unit step function $H(t)$ is undefined unless one distinguishes between $t = 0^-$ and $t = 0^+$ as the last point of negative time and the first point of positive time, respectively (Flügge, 1975).

One can also demonstrate that the Heaviside unit step function $H(t)$ is an odd function of its argument, i.e.

$$H(t) = -H(-t) \tag{B.18}$$

By its definition (B.17), the unit step function $H(t)$ can be used as a restrictive device to limit the values of a given function to its values for a particular range of the argument t.

The definition of the Heaviside function may be extended to include the argument $t - t'$ such that

$$H(t - t') = \begin{cases} 0, & t < t', \\ 1, & t > t'. \end{cases} \tag{B.19}$$

REFERENCE

Flügge, W. (1975) *Viscoelasticity*, Springer, New York.

FURTHER READING

Carslaw, H. S. and Jaeger, J. C. (1941) *Operational Methods in Applied Mathematics,* Oxford University Press, London.

Churchill, R. V. (1958) *Operational Methods,* McGraw-Hill, New York.

Goldman, S. (1949) *Transformation Calculus and Electrical Transients,* Constable, London.

Tschoegl, N. W. (1989) *The Phenomenological Theory of Linear Viscoelastic Behaviour. An Introduction,* Springer, New York.

Appendix C

Laplace transformation

C.1 INTEGRAL TRANSFORMS

In this appendix we introduce briefly the basic concepts and properties concerning the operation of integral transformation of a function $F(t)$ in t space into another function in s space. If we denote the integration operator by I, then the integral transform is expressed by

$$I[F(t)] = \int_a^b \Gamma(t, s)F(t) \, dt = f(s) \tag{C.1}$$

where $\Gamma(t, s)$ denotes some prescribed function of the variable t and a parameter s. The function $f(s)$ is called the integral transform of $F(t)$. The class of function $F(t)$ and the range of the parameter s are to be specified in a manner such that the integral (C.1) exists. Hence, the transformation $I[F(t)]$ applies to all integrable functions whereby the function $f(s)$ may be interpreted as the image of the original function $F(t)$ under this transformation.

In the above example, an inverse transformation exists in the sense that, when the image function $f(s)$ is given, a function $F(t)$ exists which has this image. The inverse transformation of (C.1) is expressed as

$$F(t) = I^{-1}[f(s)]. \tag{C.2}$$

An integral transformation $I[F(t)]$ is described as linear if, for every pair of functions $F_1(t)$ and $F_2(t)$ and for each pair of constants a and b, the following relation is satisfied:

$$I[aF_1(t) + bF_2(t)] = aI[F_1(t)] + bI[F_2(t)]. \tag{C.3}$$

That is, in the case of a linear transformation, the integral transform of a linear combination of two functions is the same linear combination of the transforms of these functions.

Integral transforms have many physical applications. Linear integral transformations are particularly useful in solving problems in differential equations. In this context, with certain kernels $\Gamma(t, s)$, the transformation (C.1) when applied to prescribed linear differential forms in $F(t)$ changes those forms into algebraic

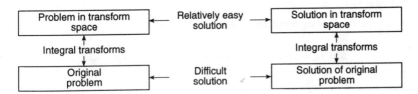

Fig. C.1 Use of integral transforms to solve differential equations.

expressions in $f(s)$ that would involve certain bounding values of the object function $F(t)$. Hence, classes of problems in ordinary differential equations transform into much simpler algebraic problems to solve. Accordingly, if an inverse transformation is possible, the solution of the original problem can be determined (Fig. C.1).

Within the realm of the theory of linear integral transformation, two special classes of integral transforms are of particular importance, i.e. those of the operational mathematics of Laplace and Fourier transformations. We deal in the present appendix with the definition and basic properties of Laplace transforms whilst in Appendix D we introduce those pertaining to Fourier transformation.

C.2 DEFINITION OF LAPLACE TRANSFORM

Laplace transformation is a form of operational mathematics that is of significant importance in the treatment of problems concerning differential equations. Laplace (1749–1827) and Cauchy (1789–1857) were two of the earlier contributors to the development of Laplace transform and the pertaining operational calculus. For a comprehensive review of the subject matter, reference is made to Churchill (1958) and Doetsch (1974), among others.

If a function $F(t)$, defined for all positive values of the variable t, is multiplied by a kernel function $\exp(-st)$ of the variable t and a parameter s and integrated with respect to t, an image function $\bar{f}(s)$ is expressed as

$$\int_0^\infty \exp(-st)F(t)\ dt = \bar{f}(s). \tag{C.4}$$

We note in (C.4) that the integration is carried out over the infinite interval from $t = 0$ to $t = \infty$.

Expression (C.4) is known as the Laplace transformation of the original function $F(t)$ into the image function $\bar{f}(s)$. This transformation is given here the notation $\mathscr{L}[F(t)]$. Hence, with reference to (C.4)

$$\mathscr{L}[F(t)] = \int_0^\infty \exp(-st)F(t)\ dt = \bar{f}(s)$$

The image function $\bar{f}(s)$ is referred to as the Laplace transform of the object function $F(t)$. Although the transform operator may be considered to be real, it generally assumes complex values.

Example C.1

Determine the Laplace transform of $F(t) = 1$ for $t > 0$.

$$\mathscr{L}[F(t)] = \mathscr{L}(1) = \int_0^\infty \exp(-st)\, dt = \left[-\frac{1}{s} \exp(-st) \right]_0^\infty.$$

Thus, for $s > 0$,

$$\mathscr{L}(1) = \frac{1}{s}.$$

Example C.2

Determine the Laplace transform of $F(t) = \exp(bt)$ for $t > 0$, where b is a constant.

$$\mathscr{L}[F(t)] = \mathscr{L}[\exp(bt)] = \int_0^\infty \exp(bt)\exp(-st)\, dt = \left[\frac{1}{b-s} \exp[-(s-b)t] \right]_0^\infty.$$

Thus, for $s > b$,

$$\mathscr{L}[\exp(bt)] = \frac{1}{s-b}.$$

Example C.3

Consider the Laplace transform of the unit step function:

$$H(t_1, t)\begin{cases} = 0 & \text{for } 0 < t < t_1, \\ = 1 & \text{for } t > t_1. \end{cases}$$

$$\mathscr{L}[H(t_1, t)] = \int_t^\infty \exp(-st)\, dt = \left[-\frac{1}{s} \exp(-st) \right]_0^\infty.$$

Thus, for $s > 0$,

$$\mathscr{L}[H(t_1, t)] = \frac{\exp(-t_1 s)}{s}.$$

Example C.4

The Laplace transforms of many other functions can be determined. For instance,

$$\mathscr{L}(t^2) = \frac{2}{s^3},$$

$$\mathscr{L}(\sin at) = \frac{a}{s^2 + a^2}$$

and

$$\mathscr{L}(\cos bt) = \frac{s}{s^2 + b^2}.$$

C.3 EXISTENCE OF LAPLACE TRANSFORMATION

Two conditions need to be satisfied in order for the Laplace transform $\bar{f}(s)$ of $F(t)$ to exist, that is $F(t)$ be sectionally continuous in every finite interval for the variable $t \geq 0$ and $F(t)$ be of exponential order as t tends to ∞. These conditions for the existence of the Laplace transform of a function are sufficient rather than necessary conditions. However, they are convenient for the majority of applications (e.g. Churchill, 1958).

A function $F(t)$ is considered to be sectionally continuous on a finite interval $0 \leq t \leq t_1$ if it is such that the interval $(0, t_1)$ can be subdivided into a finite number of intervals, in each of which $F(t)$ is continuous and has finite limits as t approaches either such limit of the subinterval from inside. The integral of every function of this class over the interval $(0, t_1)$ exists; it is the sum of the integrals of the continuous functions over the subintervals.

An example of a sectionally continuous function is the unit step function $H(\tau, t)$, where

$$H(\tau, t) \begin{cases} = 0 & \text{for } 0 < t < \tau, \\ = 1 & \text{for } t > \tau. \end{cases}$$

It is a sectionally continuous function in the interval $0 \leq t \leq t_1$ for every positive number t_1.

The second condition for the existance of Laplace transform $\bar{f}(s)$ for a function $F(t)$ is that $F(t)$ be of exponential order as the variable t tends to infinity. In other words, $F(t)$ must not grow at a greater rate than that of exponential as $t \to \infty$. This can be expressed as

$$\lim_{t \to \infty} \exp(-\alpha t)F(t) = 0 \qquad (C.5)$$

under the condition that a constant α exists.

An example of a function of exponential order is the function $\exp(2t)$. It is of the order of $\exp(\alpha t)$ as $t \to \infty$ for $\alpha \geq 2$. The unit step function $H(t_1, t)$, mentioned above, as well as the function t^n are also of the order $\exp(\alpha t)$ as $t \to \infty$ for any positive α. On the other hand, the function $\exp(t^2)$ is not of exponential order. It is further emphasized that not every function of s is a transform. The class of functions $\bar{f}(s)$ that are transforms is limited by several conditions concerning the continuity of $\bar{f}(s)$. Under these conditions, $\bar{f}(s)$ is continuous when $s > \alpha$ and $\bar{f}(s)$ vanishes as s tends to infinity (Churchill, 1958).

C.4 TRANSFORMS OF DERIVATIVES

A fundamental property of Laplace transformation is that concerned with the Laplace transformation of derivatives. This property enables us to replace the operation of differentiation of order n by a single algebraic operation on the transform. As a first step, we consider the Laplace transform of the first derivative of the original function $F(t)$. Let $F(t)$ be continuous with a sectionally continuous derivative $F'(t)$ in every finite interval $0 \leq t \leq t_1$. The function $F(t)$ is, further, assumed to be of exponential order as $t \to \infty$. Then,

$$\mathscr{L}[F'(t)] = \int_0^\infty \exp(-st)F'(t)\, dt = \left[\exp(-st)F(t)\right]_0^\infty + s\int_0^\infty \exp(-st)F(t)\, dt$$

$$= [\exp(-st)F(t)]_0^\infty + s\bar{f}(s).$$

Since $F(t)$ is of exponential order $\exp(\alpha t)$ then, for s greater than α, the first derivative on the right-hand side of the above expression becomes $-F(0)$ and accordingly

$$\mathscr{L}[F'(t)] = s\bar{f}(s) - F(0). \tag{C.6}$$

To obtain the transformation of the derivative of the second order, consider $F'(t)$ be continuous and $F''(t)$ be sectionally continuous in each finite interval. Also, let $F(t)$ and $F'(t)$ be of exponential order as t tends to ∞. Thus, for $s > \alpha$, it can be shown that

$$\mathscr{L}[F''(t)] = s^2\bar{f}(s) - sF(0) - F'(0). \tag{C.7}$$

The same procedure above can be applied to obtain the Laplace transformation of the nth derivative of $F(t)$. Let the function $F(t)$ and its first $n-1$ derivatives be continuous. Also, consider $F^n(t)$ to be sectionally continuous in every finite interval $0 \leq t \leq t_1$ and $F(t), F^1(t), \cdots, F^{n-1}(t)$ to be of exponential order $\exp(\alpha t)$ as the variable t tends to ∞. Accordingly, it can be shown, by mathematical induction, that the Laplace transform of the nth derivative of $F(t)$, for $s > \alpha$, is given by

$$\mathscr{L}[F^n(t)] = s^n f(s) - s^{n-1}F^1(0) - \cdots - sF^{n-2}(0) - F^{n-1}(0) \tag{C.8}$$

where

$$F^k(0) = \left.\frac{d^k F(t)}{dt^k}\right|_{t=0} \tag{C.8b}$$

Example C.5

Consider $\mathscr{L}(t)$. The function $F(t) = t$ and its derivative $F'(t) = 1$ are continuous and of exponential order $\exp(\alpha t)$ for any positive α. Hence, with reference to (C.6),

$$\mathscr{L}[F'(t)] = s\mathscr{L}[F(t)] - F(0)$$

$$\mathscr{L}(1) = s\mathscr{L}(t).$$

However, $\mathscr{L}(1) = 1/s$ (Example C.1); then

$$\mathscr{L}(t) = 1/s^2.$$

Example C.6

Determine $\mathscr{L}(\sin at)$. The function $F(t) = \sin(at)$ and its derivatives are all continuous and of exponential order $\exp(\alpha t)$ for $\alpha > 0$. Thus, in view of (C.7),

$$\mathscr{L}[F''(t)] = s^2\mathscr{L}[F(t)] - sF(0) - F'(0) \quad (s > 0).$$

On substitution for $F(t) = \sin(at)$ in the above expression, it follows that

$$-a^2\mathscr{L}(\sin at) = s^2\mathscr{L}(\sin at) - s,$$

i.e.

$$\mathscr{L}(\sin at) = \frac{a}{s^2 + a^2} \quad (s > 0).$$

C.5 INITIAL VALUE THEOREM

If $F(t)$ is Laplace transformable, then the behaviour of $F(t)$ in the neighbourhood of $t = 0$ corresponds to the behaviour of $s\bar{f}(s)$ in the neighbourhood of $s = 0$.

The initial value $F(0)$ of $F(t)$ can be obtained from the transform $f(s)$ through the relation

$$\lim_{t \to 0} F(t) = \lim_{s \to 0} s\bar{f}(s). \tag{C.9}$$

This result is of particular interest as it may be generalized to obtain $F(t)$ for small values of the variable t; if $\bar{f}(s)$ can be expanded in a power series of terms involving $(1/s)^n$, $n \geq 1$, then, in view of the linearity property (C.3), a term-by-term inversion could be applied.

C.6 THE INVERSE TRANSFORM

If

$$\mathscr{L}[F(t)] = \bar{f}(s)$$

then the inverse Laplace transform is

$$F(t) = \mathscr{L}^{-1}[\bar{f}(s)]. \tag{C.10}$$

That is, $F(t)$ is the inverse Laplace transform of $\bar{f}(s)$.

In the strict sense of the concept of uniqueness of functions, the inverse Laplace transform is not unique. A theorem due to Lerch (Carslaw and Jaeger, 1941) concerning the uniqueness of the inverse transform is of interest here. It states that if two functions $F_1(t)$ and $F_2(t)$ have the same Laplace transform $\bar{f}(s)$, then

$$F_2(t) = F_1(t) + \phi(t) \tag{C.11}$$

where $\phi(t)$ is a null function. The latter is expressed by

$$\int_0^{t_1} \phi(t)\, dt = 0 \qquad (C.12)$$

for every positive t_1.

Hence, a given transform function $\bar{f}(s)$ cannot have more than one inverse transform $F(t)$ that is continuous for each positive t. On the other hand, it is possible that a function $\bar{f}(s)$ would not have a continuous inverse transform.

C.7 SHIFTING THEOREM

If the inverse transformation of $\bar{f}(s)$ is $F(t)$, then the inverse transformation of $\exp(-as)\,\bar{f}(s)$ is given by

$$\mathscr{L}^{-1}[\exp(-as)\bar{f}(s)] = F(t-a)H(t-a) \qquad (C.13)$$

where $H(t-a)$ is the unit step function and a is a constant.

C.8 BASIC PROPERTIES OF LAPLACE TRANSFORM

C.8.1 Linearity

An important property of Laplace transform and its inverse is linearity. The latter follows from the definition of the transform. Thus, recalling (C.3)

$$\mathscr{L}[aF_1(t) + bF_2(t)] = a\mathscr{L}[F_1(t)] + b\mathscr{L}[F_2(t)] = a\bar{f}_1(s) + b\bar{f}_2(s) \qquad (C.14)$$

where a and b are constants. That is, the Laplace transform of a linear combination of two functions is the linear combination of the transforms of these functions. It can also be demonstrated that the linearity property can be extended to a linear combination of more than two functions. Such functions again must be sectionally continuous and each be of exponential order for their Laplace transforms to exist.

The linearity property applies also to the inverse of the transform. Thus, the inverse of (C.14) can be written as

$$\mathscr{L}^{-1}[a\bar{f}_1(s) + b\bar{f}_2(s)] = aF_1(t) + bF_2(t) = a\mathscr{L}^{-1}[\bar{f}_1(s)] + b\mathscr{L}^{-1}[\bar{f}_2(s)] \qquad (C.15)$$

C.8.2 Substitution (or shift of origin)

Let the object function $F(t)$, of exponential order $\exp(\alpha t)$, be such that its Laplace integral converges when $s > \alpha$. Recalling the Laplace transform expression (C.4), one may replace the argument of the transform $\bar{f}(s)$ by $s - a$ where a is a constant; then

$$\bar{f}(s-a) = \int_0^\infty \exp[-(s-a)t]F(t)\, dt = \int_0^\infty \exp(-st)\exp(at)F(t)\, dt.$$

Then, for $s - a > \alpha$, one has

$$\bar{f}(s - a) = \mathscr{L}[\exp(at)F(t)]. \tag{C.16}$$

That is, the substitution of $s - a$, where a is a constant, for the parameter s of $\bar{f}(s)$ would translate into multiplying the original function $F(t)$ by the function $\exp(at)$ as expressed in (C.16).

Example C.7

Consider the Laplace transform

$$\mathscr{L}(t^m) = \frac{m!}{s^{m+1}} \qquad (m = 1, 2, \cdots ; s > 0).$$

Replacing the argument s by $s - a$, leads to

$$\frac{m!}{(s - a)^{m+1}} = \mathscr{L}[t^m \exp(at) \cos(bt)] \qquad (s > 0).$$

Example C.8

Consider the following Laplace transform:

$$\mathscr{L}(\cos bt) = \frac{s}{s^2 + b^2} \qquad (s > 0).$$

Replacing the parameter s by $s + a$ gives

$$\frac{s + a}{(s + a)^2 + b^2} = \mathscr{L}[\exp(-at) \cos(bt)] \qquad (s > -a).$$

C.8.3 Change of scale

One may also replace the argument of the object function $F(t)$ from t to at where a is a real positive constant; then

$$\mathscr{L}[F'(at)] = \frac{1}{a}\bar{f}\left(\frac{s}{a}\right). \tag{C.17}$$

C.8.4 Translation

Consider translation of the argument of the object function $F(t)$ from t to $t - \tau$ where both t and τ are variables and $F(t) = 0$ for $t < 0$; then

$$\mathscr{L}[F(t - \tau)] = \exp(-s\tau)\bar{f}(s). \tag{C.18}$$

C.8.5 Differentiation of transforms

It can be shown that

$$\frac{d^n}{ds^n}\bar{f}(s) = \mathscr{L}[(-1)^n t^n F(t)].$$

(C.19)

C.8.6 Integration of transforms

The following property can be proved:

$$\int_0^\infty \bar{f}(s)\, ds = \int_0^\infty \frac{F(t)}{t}\, dt.$$

(C.20)

C.8.7 Transform of integral

Consider the integral

$$\int_0^t F(\tau)\, d\tau.$$

Then

$$\mathscr{L}\left[\int_0^t F(\tau)\, d\tau\right] = \frac{1}{s}\bar{f}(s)$$

and

$$\mathscr{L}\left[\underbrace{\int_0^t d\tau \int_0^t d\tau \cdots \int_0^t F(\tau)\, d\tau}_{n}\right] = \frac{1}{s^n}\bar{f}(s).$$

(C.21)

C.8.8 Transform of convolution integral

Consider two functions $F(t)$ and $G(t)$, both sectionally continuous and of exponential order. The convolution of $F(t)$ and $G(t)$ is defined by

$$\int_0^t F(t)G(t-\tau)\, dt$$

and is conventionally denoted by $F(t) * G(t)$. The following properties of the convolution of functions $F(t)$, $G(t)$ and $J(t)$ defined over $-\infty < t < \infty$ can be verified:

• commutativity,

$$F(t) * G(t) = G(t) * F(t);$$

• associativity,

$$F(t) * [G(t) * J(t)] = [F(t) * G(t)] * J(t) = F(t) * G(t) * J(t);$$

- distributivity,

$$F(t) * [G(t) + J(t)] = F(t) * G(t) + F(t) * J(t);$$

- Titchmarsh theorem,

$$F(t) * G(t) = 0$$

implies that $F(t) = 0$ or $G(t) = 0$.

The Laplace transform of a convolution integral is expressed as

$$\mathscr{L}[F(t) * G(t)] = \bar{f}(s)\bar{g}(s) \tag{C.22}$$

with the property

$$\bar{f}(s)\bar{g}(s) = \bar{g}(s)\bar{f}(s).$$

That is, the Laplace transform of the convolution integral is also commutative.

Some operations for Laplace transformations are given in Table C.1. Meantime, examples of Laplace transforms are shown in Table C.2.

Table C.1 Operations for Laplace transformation

$F(t)$	$\bar{f}(s)$
$F(t)$	$\displaystyle\int_0^\infty \exp(-st)F(t)\,dt$
$aF(t) + bJ(t)$	$a\bar{f}(s) + b\bar{j}(s)$
$F'(t)$	$s\bar{f}(s) - F(+0)$
$\displaystyle\int_0^t F(\tau)\,d\tau$	$\dfrac{1}{s}\bar{f}(s)$
$\displaystyle\int_0^t F(t-\tau)G(\tau)d\tau = f * G$	$\bar{f}(s)\bar{g}(s)$
$tF(t)$	$-\bar{f}'(s)$
$t^n F(t)$	$(-1)^n \bar{f}^{(n)}(s)$
$\exp(at)F(t)$	$\bar{f}(s-a)$
$F(t-a)$, where $F(t) = 0$ for $t < 0$	$\exp(-as)\bar{f}(s)$
$\dfrac{1}{a}F\left(\dfrac{t}{a}\right)$ $(a > 0)$	$\bar{f}(as)$
$F(t)$, where $F(t+a) = F(t)$	$\dfrac{\displaystyle\int_0^a \exp(-st)F(t)\,dt}{1 - \exp(-as)}$
$F(t)$, where $F(t+a) = -F(t)$	$\dfrac{\displaystyle\int_0^a \exp(-st)F(t)\,dt}{1 + \exp(-as)}$

Table C.2 Examples of Laplace transforms

$F(t)$	$\bar{f}(s)$
1	$\dfrac{1}{s}$
t	$\dfrac{1}{s^2}$
$\exp(at)$	$\dfrac{1}{s - a}$
$t^n \;\; (n = 1, 2, \ldots)$	$\dfrac{n!}{s^{n+1}}$
$\dfrac{1}{t^{1/2}}$	$\left(\dfrac{\pi}{s}\right)^{1/2}$
$\exp(at) - \exp(bt) \quad (a > b)$	$\dfrac{a - b}{(s - a)(s - b)}$
$t \exp(at)$	$\dfrac{1}{(s - a)^2}$
$\dfrac{1}{(n - 1)!}\, t^{n-1} \exp(at)$	$\dfrac{1}{(s - a)^n} \quad (n = 1, 2, \ldots)$
$\dfrac{1}{a - b}\,[\exp(at) - \exp(bt)]$	$\dfrac{1}{(s - a)(s - b)}$
$\dfrac{1}{a - b}\,[a \exp(at) - b \exp(bt)]$	$\dfrac{s}{(s - a)(s - b)}$
$\sin at$	$\dfrac{a}{s^2 + a^2}$
$\cos at$	$\dfrac{s}{s^2 + a^2}$
$\dfrac{1}{a}\sin at$	$\dfrac{1}{s^2 + a^2}$
$t^n \exp(at) \quad (n = 1, 2, \ldots)$	$\dfrac{n!}{(s - a)^{n+1}}$
$\exp(-at)\sin bt$	$\dfrac{b}{(s + a)^2 + b^2}$
$\dfrac{1}{a^2}(1 - \cos at)$	$\dfrac{1}{s(s^2 + a^2)}$

Table C.2 *(continued)*

$F(t)$	$\bar{f}(s)$
$\dfrac{1}{a^3}(at - \sin at)$	$\dfrac{1}{s^2(s^2 + a^2)}$
$\dfrac{t}{2a}\sin at$	$\dfrac{s}{(s^2 + a^2)^2}$
$t\cos at$	$\dfrac{s^2 - a^2}{(s^2 + a^2)^2}$
$\dfrac{1}{b}\exp(at)\sin bt$	$\dfrac{1}{(s - a)^2 + b^2}$
$\exp(at)\cos bt$	$\dfrac{s - a}{(s - a)^2 + b^2}$
$\dfrac{1}{a}\sin at - \dfrac{1}{b}\sin bt$	$\dfrac{b^2 - a^2}{(s^2 + a^2)(s^2 + b^2)}$
$\cos at - \cos bt$	$\dfrac{(b^2 - a^2)s}{(s^2 + a^2)(s^2 + b^2)}$
$\dfrac{\cos at - \cos bt}{b^2 - a^2}$	$\dfrac{s}{(s^2 + a^2)(s^2 + b^2)}$ $(a^2 \neq b^2)$
$\dfrac{1}{2a^3}(\sin at - at\cos at)$	$\dfrac{1}{(s^2 + a^2)^2}$
$\dfrac{1}{2a}(\sin at + at\cos at)$	$\dfrac{s^2}{(s^2 + a^2)^2}$
$\sinh at$	$\dfrac{a}{s^2 - a^2}$
$\cosh at$	$\dfrac{s}{s^2 - a^2}$
$(1 + a^2 t^2)\sin at - at\cos at$	$\dfrac{8a^3 s^2}{(s^2 + a^2)^3}$
$\dfrac{1}{2a^3}\sin at \sinh at$	$\dfrac{s}{s^4 + 4a^4}$
$\dfrac{1}{2a^2}(\cosh at - \cos at)$	$\dfrac{s}{s^4 - a^4}$
$\sin at\cosh at - \cos at\sinh at$	$\dfrac{4a^3}{s^4 + 4a^4}$

Table C.2 *(continued)*

$F(t)$	$\bar{f}(s)$
$\dfrac{1}{(\pi t)^{1/2}} \cos 2(at)^{1/2}$	$\dfrac{1}{s^{1/2}} \exp(-a/s)$
$\dfrac{1}{(\pi t)^{1/2}} \cosh 2(at)^{1/2}$	$\dfrac{1}{s^{1/2}} \exp(a/s)$
$\dfrac{1}{t} [\exp(bt) - \exp(at)]$	$\log \dfrac{s - a}{s - b}$
$\dfrac{1}{t} \sin at$	$\arctan \dfrac{a}{s}$
$-\dfrac{(b - c)\exp(at) + (c - a)\exp(bt) + (a - b)\exp(ct)}{(a - b)(b - c)(c - a)}$	$\dfrac{1}{(s - a)(s - b)(s - c)}$
where a, b and c are distinct constants	
$\dfrac{t^n}{n!} \quad (n = 0, 1, 2, \ldots)$	$\dfrac{1}{s^{n+1}}$
$\dfrac{1}{4a^3} (\sin at \cosh at - \cos at \sinh at)$	$\dfrac{1}{s^4 + 4a^4}$
$\cos at \cosh at$	$\dfrac{s^3}{s^4 + 4a^4}$
$\dfrac{1}{2a^3} (\sinh at - \sin at)$	$\dfrac{1}{s^4 - a^4}$
$\dfrac{1}{2a} (\sinh at + \sin at)$	$\dfrac{s^2}{s^4 - a^4}$
$\dfrac{1}{2} (\cosh at + \cos at)$	$\dfrac{s^3}{s^4 - a^4}$

PROBLEMS

C.1 Show the validity of the following transformations, where a, b, and c are constants:

1. $\mathscr{L}(c + bt) = \dfrac{as + b}{s^2};$

2. $\mathscr{L}(\sinh ct) = \dfrac{c}{s^2 - c^2};$

3. $\mathscr{L}[\exp(at)] = \dfrac{1}{s - a};$

4. $\mathscr{L}(t^n) \quad (n = 1, 2, \cdots) = \dfrac{n!}{s^{n+1}};$

5. $\mathscr{L}[\exp(at) - \exp(bt)] \quad (a > b) = \dfrac{a - b}{(s - a)(s - b)};$

6. $\mathscr{L}\left(\dfrac{1}{a} \sin at - \dfrac{1}{b} \sin bt\right) = \dfrac{b^2 - a^2}{(s^2 + a^2)(s^2 + b^2)};$

7. $\mathscr{L}(\cos at - \cos bt) = \dfrac{(b^2 - b^2)s}{(s^2 + a^2)(s^2 + b^2)}.$

C.2 Find the Laplace transform of each of the following functions:

1. $\sin t + 2 \cos t;$
2. $\cos^2 t;$
3. $\sin t \cos t.$

C.3 Find

$$\mathscr{L}^{-1}\left(\frac{s + 1}{s^2 + 2s}\right)$$

and

$$\mathscr{L}^{-1}\left[\frac{a^2}{s(s + a)^2}\right].$$

C.4 Obtain the following inverse transforms where a and b are constants:

$$\mathscr{L}^{-1}\left[\frac{a^2}{s(s^2 + a^2)}\right];$$

$$\mathscr{L}^{-1}\left[\frac{b}{s(s + b)}\right];$$

$$\mathscr{L}^{-1}\left[\frac{b^3}{s(s + b)^3}\right].$$

REFERENCES

Carslaw, H. S. and Jaeger, J. C. (1941) *Operational Methods in Applied Mathematics*, Oxford University Press, London.
Churchill, R. V. (1958) *Operational Mathematics*, McGraw-Hill, New York.
Doetsch, G. (1974) *Introduction to the Theory and Application of the Laplace Transformation*, Springer, Berlin.

FURTHER READING

Abramowitz, M. and Stegun, I. A. (eds) (1965) *Handbook of Mathematical Functions*, Dover Publications, New York.
Cost, T. L. (1964) Approximate Laplace transform inversion in viscoelastic stress analysis. *AIAA* Journal, **2**, 2157–66.
Doetsch, G. (1950, 1955, 1956) *Handbuch der Laplace-Transformation*, Vols 1, 2 and 3, Birkhauser, Basel.
Erdeli, A., Magnus, W., Oberhettinger, F. and Tricomi, F. (1954) *Tables of Integral Transforms*, Vols 1 and 2, McGraw-Hill, New York.
Kreyszig, E. (1972) *Advanced Engineering Mathematics*, 3rd edn, Wiley, New York, pp. 147–87.
Schapery, R. A. (1962) Approximate methods of transform inversion for viscoelastic stress analysis, in Proc. 4th US Natl Congr. of Applied Mechanics, pp. 1075–85.
Tranter, C. J. (1956) *Integral Transforms in Mathematical Physics*, 2nd edn., Methuen, London.
Widder, D. V. (1941) *The Laplace Transform*, Princeton University Press, Princeton, NJ.

Appendix D

Fourier transformation

D.1 DEFINITION OF FOURIER TRANSFORM

Similar to Laplace transformations (Appendix C), Fourier transforms are linear integral transformations with operational properties under which differential functions are converted into algebraic forms involving boundary values.

The Fourier transformation of a sectionally continuous function $F(t)$, defined for all positive values of the variable t, is denoted here by $S[F(t)]$ and expressed by

$$S[F(t)] = \int_{-\infty}^{\infty} \exp(-i\omega t)F(t)\, dt = f(\omega). \tag{D.1}$$

With reference to (D.1), the Fourier transform is based on the kernel function $\exp(-i\omega t)$ and, hence, on this kernel's real and imaginary parts, i.e. $\cos \omega t$ and $\sin \omega t$ where ω is a constant parameter. Since such a kernel's functions are often used to describe the propagation of waves in different media, Fourier transforms are used extensively in such studies for extraction of information from different phases of waves, particularly when phase information is involved.

In equation (D.1), it is understood that $f(\omega)$ is the Fourier transform, or the image, of its object function $F(t)$ and that $F(t)$ is the inverse transform of $f(\omega)$. If t represents the time parameter, for instance, then equation (D.1) and its inverse imply that $F(t)$ can be analysed into an integral sum of harmonic oscillations over a continuous range of frequencies. If $F(t)$ exists only for the range $t > 0$, then a special simplification may be possible in terms of the finite Fourier sine transform $f_s(\omega)$ and the finite Fourier cosine transform $f_c(\omega)$. These forms possess a complete symmetry and could be used in a situation where the variable t represents the time and $F(t)$ implies some stimulus applied to a particular system from zero time onwards. We shall introduce the Fourier sine and cosine transforms later in this appendix.

D.2 RELATIONS BETWEEN FOURIER PAIRS

D.2.1 Linearity

If $f_1(\omega)$ and $f_2(\omega)$ are the Fourier transforms of $F_1(t)$ and $F_2(t)$, respectively, and a and b are two arbitrary constants, then

$$S[aF_1(t) + bF_2(t)] = aS[F_1(t)] + bS[F_2(t)] = af_1(\omega) + bf_2(\omega). \tag{D.2}$$

D.2.2 Scaling

If a is a real constant, then

$$S[F(at)] = \frac{1}{|a|} f\left(\frac{\omega}{a}\right). \tag{D.3}$$

D.2.3 Symmetry

If $F(t)$ is an even function, then its Fourier transform $f(\omega)$ is also even. Also, if the object function $F(t)$ is an odd function, then $f(\omega)$ is also odd.

D.2.4 Shifting

If the function $F(t)$ is shifted by a constant a, then its Fourier spectrum remains the same but its phase angle is adjusted by a linear term $a\omega$:

$$S[F(t \pm a)] = f(\omega) \exp(\pm i\omega t) = A(\omega) \exp\{i[\phi(\omega) \pm a\omega]\}. \tag{D.4}$$

With ω_0 as a real constant, the Fourier integral of $\exp(i\omega t)$ is obtained by shifting $f(\omega)$ by ω_0. That is,

$$S[\exp(i\omega_0 t)F(t)] = f(\omega - \omega_0). \tag{D.5}$$

D.2.5 Differentiation

If $S[F(t)] = f(\omega)$, then

$$S\left[\frac{d^n F(t)}{dt^n}\right] = (i\omega)^n f(\omega) \tag{D.6}$$

and

$$S[(-it)^n F(t)] = \frac{d^n f(\omega)}{d\omega^n}. \tag{D.7}$$

D.3 FINITE FOURIER SINE TRANSFORMS

Consider a function $F(x)$ that is sectionally continuous and defined over the interval between $x = 0$ and $x = \pi$. The Fourier sine transformation of $F(x)$ on that interval is denoted here by $S_n[F(x)]$ and is expressed as

$$S_n[F(x)] = \int_0^\pi F(x) \sin nx \, dx = f_s(n) \qquad (n = 1, 2, \cdots) \qquad \text{(D.8)}$$

where $f_s(n)$ is the finite sine transform. This transformation sets up a correspondence between functions $F(x)$ defined within the interval $0 < x < \pi$ and sequences of numbers $f_s(n)$ $(n = 1, 2, \cdots)$.

For example, the function $F(x) = 1$ has the transform

$$f_s(n) = \int_0^\pi \sin(nx) \, dx = \frac{1 - (-1)^n}{n} \qquad (n = 1, 2, \cdots).$$

Also, the function $F(x)$ $(0 < x < \pi)$ has the transform

$$f_s(n) = \int_0^\pi x \sin(nx) \, dx = \pi \frac{(-1)^{n+1}}{n} \qquad (n = 1, 2, \cdots).$$

In order to obtain an inversion formula for the transformation (D.8), consider both the object function $F(x)$ and its first derivative $F'(x)$ to be sectionally continuous functions. Let, also, $F(x)$ be defined at each point x_0 of discontinuity, $0 < x_0 < \pi$, by its mean value:

$$F(x_0) = \tfrac{1}{2}[F(x_0 + 0) + F(x_0 - 0)] \qquad (0 < x_0 < \pi). \qquad \text{(D.9)}$$

It follows, according to the classical theory of Fourier series, that the Fourier sine series for $F(x)$ converges to the function

$$F(x) = \frac{2}{\pi} \sum_{n=1}^\infty \sin(nx) \int_0^\pi F(\xi) \sin(n\xi) \, d\xi \qquad (0 < x < \pi). \qquad \text{(D.10)}$$

Thus, with reference to (D.8),

$$F(x) = \frac{2}{\pi} \sum_{n=1}^\infty f_s(n) \sin(nx) \qquad (0 < x < \pi) \qquad \text{(D.11)}$$

which is the inversion formula for the Fourier sine transformation (D.8).

In the class of sectionally continuous functions with sectionally continuous derivatives of the first order, there is only one function with a given transform as demonstrated by (D.11). In other words, the inverse transformation is unique. It is apparent that both the transformation $S_n[F(x)]$ and its inverse are linear transformations.

Recalling (D.8), the Fourier sine transform of a function on an interval $0 < x < c$ is expressed in terms of the transform on the standard interval $(0 < x < \pi)$ by the substitution $x' = \pi x/c$ in (D.8), i.e.

$$\int_0^c F(x) \sin\left(\frac{n\pi x}{c}\right) dx = \frac{c}{\pi} \int_0^\pi F\left(\frac{cx'}{\pi}\right) \sin(nx') \, dx' = \frac{c}{\pi} S_n\left[F\left(\frac{cx}{\pi}\right)\right]. \qquad \text{(D.12)}$$

As an example, the function $F(x)$ $(0 < x < c)$ has the sine transform

$$S_n(x)|_c = \frac{c}{\pi} S_n\left(\frac{cx}{\pi}\right) = \frac{c^2}{\pi} \frac{(-1)^{n+1}}{n} \qquad (n = 1, 2, \cdots).$$

An important property of $S_n[F(x)]$ is as follows. If $F(x)$ and $F'(x)$ are continuous and $F''(x)$ is sectionally continuous, then

$$\int_0^\pi F''(x) \sin nx \, dx = [F'(x) \sin nx \,]_0^\pi - n \int_0^\pi F'(x) \cos nx \, dx$$

$$= [-n \cos nx F(x)]_0^\pi - n^2 \int_0^\pi F(x) \sin nx \, dx$$

which can be written as

$$S_n[F''(x)] = -n^2 S_n[F(x)] + n[F(0) - (-1)^n F(\pi)]. \tag{D.13}$$

That is, the finite Fourier sine transformation resolves the differential form $F''(x)$ into a linear algebraic form in the transform $f_s(n)$ and the boundary values $F(0)$ and $F(\pi)$ as expressed by (D.13). Formulae for the transforms of other derivatives $F^{(2n)}(x)$ of even order may be determined in the same manner. This property is employed in the construction of tables of Fourier transforms

Example D.1

Consider $F(x) = x^2$; then, $F''(x) = 2$ and

$$S_n(2) = -n^2 S_n(x^2) - n(-1)^n \pi^2.$$

Also,

$$S_n(2) = 2S_n(1) = 2[1 - (-1)^n]/n.$$

Thus,

$$S_n(x^2) = \frac{\pi^2}{n} (-1)^{n-1} - \frac{2}{n^3} [1 - (-1)^n].$$

D.4 FINITE FOURIER COSINE TRANSFORMS

The finite Fourier cosine transformation of a function $F(x)$, $0 < x < \pi$, is denoted here by $C_n[F(x)]$ and expressed by

$$C_n[F(x)] = \int_0^\pi F(x) \cos nx \, dx = f_c(n) \qquad (n = 0, 1, 2, \cdots) \tag{D.14}$$

where $f_c(n)$ is the resulting finite Fourier cosine transform. Consider both the object function $F(x)$ and its first derivative to be sectionally continuous; also, $F(x)$ is defined, at each point of discontinuity within the interval, by its mean value (D.9). Thus, the inverse transformation $F(x)$ is given by the Fourier cosine series

$$F(x) = \frac{1}{\pi} f_c(0) + \frac{2}{\pi} \sum_{n=1}^{\infty} f_c(n) \cos nx \qquad (0 < x < \pi). \qquad \text{(D.15)}$$

As in the case of the Fourier sine transform, the cosine transform of each sectionally continuous function $F(x)$ exists and it is unique.

In a corresponding manner to the sine transform, the cosine transformation resolves the differential form $F''(x)$ into an algebraic form in $f_c(n)$ and the boundary values $F'(0)$ and $F'(\pi)$, i.e.

$$C_n[F''(x)] = -n^2 f_c(n) - F'(0) - (-1)^n F'(\pi) \qquad (n = 0, 1, 2, \cdots,). \qquad \text{(D.16)}$$

This is again under the condition that $F(x)$ and $F'(x)$ are continuous and $F''(x)$ is sectionally continuous.

D.5 JOINT PROPERTIES OF SINE AND COSINE TRANSFORMS

Under the conditions that $F(x)$ is continuous and $F'(x)$ is sectionally continuous, it can be shown that

$$S_n[F'(x)] = -nC_n[F(x)] \qquad (n = 1, 2, \cdots) \qquad \text{(D.17)}$$

and

$$C_n[F'(x)] = nS_n[F(x)] - F(0) + (-1)^n F(\pi) \qquad (n = 0, 1, 2, \cdots). \qquad \text{(D.18)}$$

Alternative formulations of the joint properties of S_n and C_n are

$$S_n[G(x)] = -nC_n\left[\int_0^x G(x')\, dx'\right] \qquad (n = 1, 2, \cdots) \qquad \text{(D.19)}$$

and

$$C_n\left[G(x) - \frac{1}{\pi} g_c(0)\right] = nS_n\left[\int_0^x G(x')\, dx' - \frac{x}{\pi} g_c(0)\right] \qquad (n = 0, 1, \cdots) \ \text{(D.20)}$$

where $G(x)$ is any sectionally continuous function and $g(n)$ is its Fourier transform.

D.6 FOURIER SINE AND COSINE TRANSFORMS OVER UNBOUNDED INTERVALS

Consider $F(x)$ to be a function defined on a specified unbounded interval, sectionally continuous on each finite subinterval, and that the integral of $F(x)$ over the unbounded interval exists. If k denotes a real parameter, the Fourier sine transformation of $F(x)$ is expressed as

$$S_k[F(x)] = \int_0^\infty F(x) \sin(kx)\, dx = f_s(k) \qquad (x \geq 0, k \geq 0). \qquad \text{(D.21)}$$

At the same time, the Fourier cosine transformation is defined by

$$C_k[F(x)] = \int_0^\infty F(x) \cos kx \, dx = f_c(k) \qquad (x \geq 0, \ k \geq 0). \qquad (D.22)$$

When $F'(x)$ is also sectionally continuous on each finite subinterval $0 \leq x \leq x_1$, then $F(x)$ may be represented by either the Fourier sine or cosine integral formula. That is,

$$F(x) = \frac{2}{\pi} \int_0^\infty f_s(k) \sin kx \, dk = \frac{2}{\pi} S_x[f_s(k)] \qquad (D.23)$$

and

$$F(x) = \frac{2}{\pi} \int_0^\infty f_c(k) \cos kx \, dk = \frac{2}{\pi} C_x[f_c(k)] \qquad (D.24)$$

i.e. the inverse transforms are given by the transforms themselves.

When $F(x)$ is continuous and $F'(x)$ is sectionally continuous and $F(\infty) = 0$, it can be shown that the Fourier sine and cosine transforms are interconnected by the following two relations:

$$S_k[F'(x)] = -kC_k[F(x)]; \qquad (D.25)$$

$$C_k[F'(x)] = kS_k[F(x)] - F(0). \qquad (D.26)$$

Further, when the function $F(x)$ is replaced by its first derivative $F'(x)$, the following relations can be written:

$$S_k[F''(x)] = -k^2 f_s(k) + kF(0) \qquad (D.27)$$

and

$$C_k[F''(x)] = -k^2 f_c(k) - F'(0). \qquad (D.28)$$

In the derivation of (D.27) and (D.28), it is assumed that $F(x)$ and $F'(x)$ are both continuous and integrable, that $F''(x)$ is sectionally continuous and that $F(\infty) = F'(\infty) = 0$. The same procedure can be used for obtaining the transform of $F^{(2n)}(x)$.

PROBLEMS

D.1 Show that

$$S_n^{-1}\left[\frac{1 - (-1)^n}{n^3}\right] = \frac{x}{2}(\pi - x)$$

and

$$S_n^{-1}\left[\frac{1}{n^3}(-1)^{n+1}\right] = \frac{x(\pi^2 - x^2)}{6\pi}.$$

D.2 If $F(x)$ and $F'(x)$ are continuous except that $F'(x)$ has a jump b at $x = c$, where $0 < c < \pi$, and if $F''(x)$ is sectionally continuous, show that

$$S_n[F''(x)] = -n^2 f_s(n) + n[F(0) - (-1)^n F(\pi)] - b \sin nc.$$

D.3 Where a is a constant, prove the following:

1. $f_c(n + a) = C_n[F(x) \cos ax] - S_n[F(x) \sin ax]$;
2. $f_s(n + a) = S_n[F(x) \cos ax] + C_n[F(x) \sin ax]$;
3. $2C_n[F(x) \sin ax] = f_s(n + a) - f_s(n - a)$;
4. $2S_n[F(x) \cos ax] = f_s(n - a) + f_s(n + a)$;

5. $S_r[\exp(ax)] = \dfrac{r}{r^2 + a^2}$.

D.4 Prove the following relations where a is a constant:

1. $2S_r[F(x) \cos ax] = f_s(r + a) + f_s(r - a)$;

2. $C_r[\exp(-ax)] = \dfrac{a}{r^2 + a^2}$;

3. $C_r[\exp(-ax^2)] = \dfrac{1}{2}\left(\dfrac{\pi}{a}\right)^{1/2} \exp\left(-\dfrac{r^2}{4a}\right)$;

4. $C_r\left(\dfrac{a}{x^2 + a^2}\right) = \dfrac{\pi}{2} \exp(-ar)$.

FURTHER READING

Bochner, S. and Chandrasekhoran, L. (1947) *Fourier Transforms*, Princeton University Press, Princeton, NJ.
Churchill, R. V. (1941) *Fourier Series and Boundary Value Problems*, McGraw-Hill, New York.
Churchill, R. V. (1958) *Operational Mathematics*, 2nd edn, McGraw-Hill, New York.
Donoghue, W. F. (1969) *Distributions and Fourier Transforms*, Academic Press, New York.
Paley, R. and Wiener, N. (1934) *Fourier Transforms in the Complex Domain*, American Mathematical Society, Providence, RI.
Sneddon, I. N. (1951) *Fourier Transforms*, McGraw-Hill, New York.
Titchmarch, E. C. (1937) *Introduction to the Theory of Fourier Integrals*, Clarendon, Oxford.
Tranter, C. J. (1956) *Integral Transforms in Mathematical Physics*, 2nd edn, Methuen, London.
Wiener, N. (1933) *The Fourier Integral*, Cambridge University Press, London.

Author index

Author index

Subject index